W9-DIF-814

DEER

and Management

A Wildlife Management Institute Book

Compiled and Edited by

Lowell K. Halls

Illustrated by

Cindy House

Technical Editors

Richard E. McCabe and Laurence R. Jahn

Published by STACKPOLE BOOKS

The *WILDLIFE MANAGEMENT INSTITUTE* is a private, national, nonprofit, scientific and educational organization based in Washington, D.C. The Institute's sole objective, since its founding in 1911, has been to help advance restoration and proper management of North America's natural resources, especially wildlife. As a part of the Institute's program, scientific information generated through research and management experiences is consolidated, published and used to improve understanding and to strengthen decision-making and resource management. *WHITE-TAILED DEER: Ecology and Management* is one of more than 25 wildlife books produced by WMI, including the award-winning *Ducks, Geese and Swans of North America, Big Game of North America, Mule and Black-tailed Deer of North America* and *Elk of North America*. For additional information about the Institute, its programs and publications, write to: Wildlife Management Institute, Suite 725, 1101 Fourteenth Street, N.W., Washington, D.C. 20005.

QL
737
.U55
W445
1984

WHITE-TAILED DEER: Ecology and Management
Copyright © 1984 by the Wildlife Management Institute

Original artwork courtesy of the
Frederick C. Walcott Memorial Fund, North American Wildlife Foundation, Inc.

All rights reserved, including the right to reproduce this book or portions thereof in any form or by any means, electronic or mechanical, including photocopying, recording, or by any information storage and retrieval system, without permission in writing from the Wildlife Management Institute. All inquiries should be addressed to Publications Director, Wildlife Management Institute, Suite 725, 1101 14th Street, N.W., Washington, D.C. 20005.

Published by STACKPOLE BOOKS
Cameron & Kelker Streets
Harrisburg, PA 17105

Printed in the U.S.A.

Library of Congress Cataloging in Publication Data
Main entry under title:

White-tailed deer.

"A Wildlife Management Institute book."
Bibliography: p.
Includes index.
1. White-tailed deer—Ecology. 2. Wildlife management.
3. Mammals—Ecology. I. Halls, Lowell K., 1918–
QL737.U55W445 1984   639.9'797357   84-2626
ISBN 0-8117-0486-6

Photo editing, book design and layout by **Dick McCabe;** *layout assistance and index by* **Ken Sabol**

LONGWOOD COLLEGE LIBRARY
FARMVILLE, VIRGINIA 23901

LONGWOOD
C O L L E G E

LIBRARY

Longwood College
Farmville, Virginia 23909-1897

A center for learning. A window to the world.

PHOTO CREDITS FOR FRONT ENDSHEETS

1   U.S. Fish and Wildlife Service; photo by Robert C. Fields
2   U.S. Forest Service; photo by Freeman Heim
3   Illinois Department of Conservation
4   North Dakota Game and Fish Department
5   Georgia Department of Natural Resources
6   Oklahoma Department of Wildlife Conservation
7   U.S. Bureau of Land Management; photo by James D. Yoakum
8   New Jersey Division of Fish, Game and Wildlife
9   Missouri Department of Conservation; photo by Don Wooldridge
10 Photo by Tom W. Hall
11 Photo by Leonard Lee Rue III
12 Photo by Kenneth J. Forand
13 Photo by Leonard Lee Rue III
14 Kansas Fish and Game Department; photo by Gene Brehm
15 Michigan Department of Natural Resources
16 Oregon Department of Fish and Wildlife
17 U.S. Forest Service; photo by Harold F. Mielenz
18 Michigan Department of Natural Resources
19 U.S. Fish and Wildlife Service; photo by Robert L. Downing
20 Photo by Leonard Lee Rue III

WHITE-TAILED DEER

Ecology and Management

WHITE-TAILED

Ecology

FOREWORD

In 1956, the Wildlife Management Institute released *The Deer of North America*, edited by Walter P. Taylor. This book was destined to serve for the next quarter-century as the definitive text on mule, black-tailed and white-tailed deer. It was followed in 1981 by *Mule and Black-tailed Deer of North America* (edited by Olof C. Wallmo), which is now the principal authoritative reference on those species. With *White-tailed Deer: Ecology and Management*, WMI has come full circle. This new book is expected to be even more informative, attractive and useful than was the Taylor volume in its day—and a worthy companion to the Wallmo edition.

Like the 1956 Taylor classic, *White-tailed Deer: Ecology and Management* pulls together the latest and best information on whitetails. In the nearly three decades since 1956, the science and art of wildlife management have developed greatly. So too have the popularity and value of deer. White-tailed deer are the most studied and generally enjoyed large mammal species in North America and perhaps the world.

These swift, graceful, elusive animals have come to symbolize the elegance, intrigue and intrinsic worth of wildlife and the out-of-doors. Whitetails also reflect the well-being of our natural heritage. Where they abound in North America at stable population levels there remains optimism about man's relationship to his environment, a linkage that is increasingly strained by human population growth and associated activities.

When the study of wildlife emerged as a distinct scientific discipline—50 years before this book was completed—whitetail populations in many parts of North America were seriously depleted, having been previously extirpated from most of their historic range. This no longer is the case. The whitetail's recovery can be attributed directly to the insistence on it by sportsman-conservationists willing to bear the costs; to the gumption and enthusiasm of a dedicated cadre of wildlife biologists, researchers, managers, administrators and conservation law-enforcement officers; and to the whitetail's adaptability to the modifications imposed on its habitats. For these reasons, as Ernest Thompson Seton wrote at the turn of the century, "The Whitetail is the American Deer of the past, and the American Deer of the Future."

Through its encouragement and support of scientific wildlife management, including the publication of such books as this one, the Wildlife Management Institute is pleased to be part of the tradition and momentum to ensure a bright future for white-tailed deer.

Daniel A. Poole, President
Wildlife Management Institute

PREFACE

In man's quest for a better understanding of the world's natural resources it is necessary periodically to take stock of what new information on these resources has accrued, over time, from the widely scattered points at which the natural environment is constantly being observed and experienced. When wild, living resources are the focus of attention, it is essential that available data be updated and synthesized, not merely to improve our knowledge of the subject-matter's dynamic nature and condition, but also to gain insight into how to make wildlife management more compatible with the short- and long-term expectations—equally dynamic—of the dominant force impacting the landscape: mankind itself.

This book is the product of such an effort for the white-tailed deer, the most widely distributed terrestrial big game mammal in North America and perhaps the world. *White-tailed Deer: Ecology and Management* is the culmination of years of intensive research and writing by more than 70 authors who have devoted the greater part of their professional careers to the study and management of this remarkable species and its habitats. Just as important to the completion of this volume have been the contributions of virtually thousands of *other* wildlife biologists, managers, administrators, researchers, educators and communication specialists, who generated most of the information and ideas found on the pages that follow. In part, the intention of this book is to reflect the individual dedication and collective wisdom of these contributors. Also responsible for the accumulation of knowledge contained herein are sportsmen and other conservation enthusiasts, whose appreciation of "wild things and wild places"—and in particular of the white-tailed deer—has supported and encouraged improved scientific research and management. It is the intention of this book to provide these citizens with a reliable, interesting, useful source of information on whitetails and their management.

The book is divided into six major units: Whitetail Biology and Ecology; Whitetail Population Management; Whitetail Populations and Habitats; Whitetail Research and Management Practices; Whitetail Benefits; and Whitetail Management Needs and Opportunities. Within each unit are chapters prepared by recognized authorities in their respective fields of wildlife management. The Whitetail Populations and Habitats unit contains 21 regional chapters that focus on whitetail populations in particular areas. The coverage is worldwide. Because of the generally-accepted concept that the management of white-tailed deer and their habitats should be based on ecological principles, the regional chapters are organized according to ecosystems rather than political boundaries.

The information presented on the pages that follow is as accurate, up-to-date and concise as possible within the scope of a single volume. We, the authors and editors, hope that this publication will serve the best interests of the white-tailed deer, the various habitats the whitetail occupies, and the countless people who in different ways appreciate and benefit from this magnificent animal. We hope the usefulness of this book will last many years. If at the very least *White-tailed Deer: Ecology and Management* serves as a springboard for the continued improvement of scientific whitetail management, our goal will have been achieved.

Lowell K. Halls

ACKNOWLEDGMENTS

The authors and editors of this book wish to express their appreciation to the individuals listed below, each of whom made a significant contribution to one or more parts of this volume. Also, special thanks are given to Bette S. Gutierrez and Lyla B. Baumann for their efficient, thorough and expeditious handling of the many drafts of the book manuscript, and to Carol J. Peddicord, Maureen S. Moore, Dolores A. Taylor, Cathy E. Sabol and Margaret M. McCabe for their conscientious and timely assistance.

G. Abernathy, *North Carolina Wildlife Resources Commission, Raleigh*
D. Adams, *University of Georgia, Athens*
J. Ake, *James Jerome Hill Reference Library, St. Paul, Minnesota*
L. Alexander, *Delaware Division of Fish and Wildlife, Dover*
R. Allen, *National Museum of American Art, Washington, D.C.*
R. Allman, *Davis, West Virginia*
H. Amory, *New Jersey Division of Fish, Game and Wildlife, Trenton*
B. Anderson, *Utah Division of Wildlife Resources, Salt Lake City*
D. Arnold, *Michigan Department of Natural Resources, Lansing*
T. Arnold, *U. S. Forest Service, Roanoke, Virginia*
T. Atkeson, *University of Georgia, Athens*
D. Baerg, *Gorgas Memorial Laboratory, Panama*
J. Baird, *New Brunswick Department of Natural Resources, Fredericton*
T. Baker, *Wyoming Game and Fish Department, Cheyenne*
S. Ball, *Florida Game and Fresh Water Fish Commission, Tallahassee*
C. Banasiak, *University of Maine, Orono*
J. Barber, *Society of American Foresters, Washington, D.C.*
G. Barnes, *North Carolina Wildlife Resources Commission, Raleigh*
I. Bartfield, *National Gallery of Art, Washington, D.C.*
C. Batista, *American Museum of Natural History, New York City*
L. Baumann, *Tracys Landing, Maryland*
R. Bell, *Pennsylvania Game Commission, Harrisburg*
J. Beshears, Jr., *Alabama Department of Conservation and Natural Resources, Montgomery*
R. Blohm, *U. S. Fish and Wildlife Service, Patuxent, Maryland*
T. Blume, *Nebraska Game and Parks Commission, Lincoln*
A. Boer, *New Brunswick Department of Natural Resources, Fredericton*
R. Boetiger, *Maine Department of Inland Fisheries and Wildlife, Augusta*
T. Borg, *South Carolina Wildlife and Marine Resources Department, Columbia*
E. Bossenmaier, *Manitoba Department of Natural Resources, Winnipeg*
W. Branan, *University of Georgia, Athens*
G. Brehm, *Kansas Fish and Game Commission, Pratt*
J. Bright, *The Museum of the City of New York, New York City*
P. Bromley, *Virginia Polytechnic Institute and State University, Blacksburg*
W. Brown, *Wyoming Game and Fish Department, Cheyenne*
E. Bry, *North Dakota Game and Fish Department, Bismarck*
G. Bryanton, *Saskatchewan Department of Tourism and Renewable Resources, Regina*
G. Burgoyne, *Michigan Department of Natural Resources, Lansing*
T. Burke, *U. S. Forest Service, Colville, Washington*
L. Bursie, *Arkansas Game and Fish Commission, Little Rock*
P. F. R. de Leon Campos, *Guatemala*
F. Caron, *Quebec Department of Tourism, Fish and Game, Quebec City*
B. Carroll, *Texas Parks and Wildlife Department, LaGrange*
J. Carter, *Nebraska State Historical Society, Lincoln*
W. Carter, *New Hampshire Fish and Game Department, Concord*
M. Cartwright, *Arkansas Game and Fish Commission, Little Rock*
R. Catlin, *South Dakota Game, Fish and Parks Department, Pierre*
J. Chadwick, *Rhode Island Department of Environmental Management, Providence*
J. Charbonneau, *U. S. Fish and Wildlife Service, Washington, D. C.*
P. Chiles, *Illinois Department of Conservation, Springfield*
A. Christie, *New Zealand Forest Service, Wellington*
A. Clark, *U. S. Fish and Wildlife Service, Cathlamet, Washington*
C. Clark, *Louisiana Department of Wildlife and Fisheries, New Orleans*
R. Colona, *U. S. Forest Service, Roanoke, Virginia*
C. Conley, *Outdoor Life, New York City*
T. Cosby, *Alabama Department of Conservation and Natural Resources, Montgomery*

J. Coykendall, *U. S. Fish and Wildlife Service, Cathlamet, Washington*
J. Crenshaw, *New Mexico Game and Fish Department, Santa Fe*
C. Croken, *Massachusetts Division of Fisheries and Wildlife, Boston*
J. Cromer, *West Virginia Department of Natural Resources, Elkins*
N. Crowe, *British Columbia Ministry of Environment, Victoria*
J. Dabney, *U. S. Forest Service, Roanoke, Virginia*
D. Daughtry, *Arizona Game and Fish Department, Phoenix*
D. Demarchi, *British Columbia Ministry of Environment, Victoria*
R. Demarchi, *British Columbia Fish and Wildlife Branch, Cranbrook*
R. Denney, *The Wildlife Society, Washington, D. C.*
E. De Reus, *Idaho Fish and Game Department, Coeur d'Alene*
M. D. Detweiler, *Stackpole Books, Harrisburg, Pennsylvania*
A. de Vos, *University of Waterloo, Ontario*
N. Dickinson, *New York Department of Environmental Conservation, Delmar*
M. Dieckman, *Belize Audubon Society, Belize*
R. Donohoe, *Ohio Department of Natural Resources, Columbus*
T. Dossett, *North Carolina Wildlife Resources Commission, Raleigh*
G. Doster, *University of Georgia, Athens*
R. Downing, *U. S. Fish and Wildlife Service, Clemson, South Carolina*
G. Duffy, *Oklahoma Department of Wildlife Conservation, Oklahoma City*
D. Dvorak, *Texas Parks and Wildlife Department, Austin*
C. Dyer, *Allen Memorial Art Museum, Oberlin, Ohio*
P. Ebert, *Oregon Department of Fish and Wildlife, Portland*
J. Egan, *Montana Department of Fish, Wildlife and Parks, Helena*
M. Elkins, *Colorado Division of Wildlife, Colorado Springs*
D. Euler, *Ontario Ministry of Natural Resources, New Market*
J. Eve, *Oklahoma Department of Wildlife Conservation, Oklahoma City*
J. Farrar, *Louisiana Department of Wildlife and Fisheries, Baton Rouge*
F. Filion, *Canadian Wildlife Service, Ottawa, Ontario*
J. Firebaugh, *Montana Fish and Game Department, Hamilton*
G. Firth, *New York Department of Environmental Conservation, Albany*
A. Florio, *Delaware Division of Fish and Wildlife, Dover*
K. Forand, *University of Georgia, Athens*
S. Forbes, *Pennsylvania Game Commission, Harrisburg*
W. Freeman, *Montana Department of Fish, Wildlife and Parks, Helena*
M. Frost, *California State College, San Bernadino*
J. Fuller, *South Carolina Wildlife and Marine Resources Department, Columbia*
D. Fulton, *Ann Arbor News, Ann Arbor, Michigan*
P. Galindo, *Gorgas Memorial Laboratory, Panama*
S. Gallizioli, *Arizona Game and Fish Department, Phoenix*
G. Galt, *The Brooklyn Museum, Brooklyn, New York*
J. Garcia, *Unidad de Parques Nacionales y Vida Silvestre, El Salvador*
L. Garland, *Vermont Department of Fish and Game, Barre*
N. Giessman, *Missouri Department of Conservation, Columbia*
J. Gill, *U. S. Forest Service, Amherst, Massachusetts*
T. Godshall, *Pennsylvania Game Commission, Harrisburg*
G. Gookin, *Iowa Conservation Commission, Des Moines*
H. Gore, *Texas Parks and Wildlife Department, Austin*
H. Goulden, *Manitoba Department of Natural Resources, Brandon*
H. Grosch, *New Jersey Division of Fish, Game and Wildlife, Trenton*
S. Guenther, *Washington Department of Game, Spokane*
J. Gunderson, *Indiana State Historical Society, Indianapolis*
C. R. Gutermuth, *Washington, D.C.*
J. Gwynn, *Virginia Commission of Game and Inland Fisheries, Charlottesville*
P. Haas, *American Museum of Natural History, New York City*
E. Hackett, *Mississippi Department of Wildlife Conservation, Jackson*
J. Hagopian, *Alabama Department of Conservation and Natural Resources, Montgomery*
E. Hall, *University of Kansas, Lawrence*
H. Hall, *North Carolina Wildlife Resources Commission, Burlington*
J. Hall, *Vermont Fish and Game Department, Montpelier*
G. Halvorson, *U. S. Fish and Wildlife Service, Albuquerque, New Mexico*
J. Hamilton, *South Carolina Wildlife and Marine Resources Department, Bonneau*
W. Hamrick, *Mississippi Department of Wildlife Conservation, Jackson*
H. Harju, *Wyoming Game and Fish Department, Cheyenne*
D. Harmel, *Texas Parks and Wildlife Department, Hunt*
K. Harmon, *Wildlife Management Institute, Firth, Nebraska*
M. Harrop, *St. Albert, Alberta*

V. Hawley, *Northwest Territories Department of Renewable Resources, Fort Smith*
M. Heff, *Nevada Department of Wildlife, Reno*
T. Hendrickson, *North Dakota Game and Fish Department, Bismarck*
R. Hensler, *U. S. Forest Service, Kalispell, Montana*
R. Hernbrode, *Colorado Division of Wildlife, Denver*
J. Herring, *Louisiana Department of Wildlife and Fisheries, Baton Rouge*
W. Hesselton, *U. S. Fish and Wildlife Service, Newton Corner, Massachusetts*
D. Hewitt, *New Hampshire Fish and Game Department, Concord*
D. Hicks, *Georgia Department of Natural Resources, Atlanta*
C. Hill, *North Carolina Wildlife Resources Commission, Morganton*
K. Hill, *Florida Game and Fresh Water Fish Commission, Tallahassee*
R. Hill, *Friday Harbor, Washington*
R. Hine, *Wisconsin Department of Natural Resources, Madison*
H. Holbrook, *U. S. Forest Service, Atlanta, Georgia*
J. Holman, *Michigan State University, East Lansing*
W. Holsworth, *Bendigo College, Bendigo, Victoria, Australia*
J. Ibarra, *Museo Nacional de Historia Natural, Guatemala*
D. Jenkins, *Michigan Department of Natural Resources, Lansing*
K. Johnson, *Nebraska Game and Parks Commission, Lincoln*
M. Johnson, *U. S. Forest Service, Nacogdoches, Texas*
N. Johnson, *Museum of Fine Arts, Boston, Massachusetts*
R Johnson, *Washington Department of Game, Olympia*
S. Johnson, *University of Georgia, Athens*
D. Jones, *U. S. Forest Service, Washington, D.C.*
J. Jones, Jr., *Texas Tech University, Lubbock*
J. Kaminski, *Michigan State University, East Lansing*
K. Kammermeyer, *Georgia Department of Natural Resources, Gainesville*
P. Karns, *Minnesota Department of Natural Resources, Grand Rapids*
J. Keener, *Wisconsin Department of Natural Resources, Madison*
R. Keil, *Ohio Department of Natural Resources, Columbus*
D. Keith, *Manitoba Department of Natural Resources, Winnipeg*
I. Kent, *Montana Department of Fish, Wildlife and Parks, Helena*
M. Kenworthy, *University of Pennsylvania, Philadelphia*
J. R. King, *Stackpole Books, Harrisburg, Pennsylvania*
J. Kinnear, *Saskatchewan Department of Tourism and Renewable Resources, Regina*
R. Kirkman, *U. S. Forest Service, Rolla, Missouri*
T. Kistner, *Oregon State University, Corvallis*
B. Knudsen, *Manitoba Department of Natural Resources, Winnipeg*
R. Kohl, *Montana State Historical Society, Helena*
E. Komarek, *Tall Timbers Research Inc., Tallahassee, Florida*
P. Krausman, *Auburn University, Auburn, Alabama*
J. Kube, *Illinois Department of Conservation, Petersburg*
R. Kuhn, *Oregon Department of Fish and Wildlife, Portland*
J. Kurz, *Georgia Department of Natural Resources, Atlanta*
D. LaBaugh, *Chateau, Montana*
T. Leege, *Idaho Department of Fish and Game, Coeur d'Alene*
R. Lehman, *Michigan Department of Natural Resources, Lansing*
M. Lennartz, *U. S. Forest Service, Clemson, South Carolina*
W. M. Lentz, *University of Georgia, Athens*
R. Leonard, *Arkansas Game and Fish Commission, Little Rock*
S. Light, *Caesar Kleberg Wildlife Research Institute, Kingsville, Texas*
D. Linde, *South Dakota Department of Game, Fish and Parks, Mobridge*
F. Loomis, *Illinois Department of Conservation, Monmouth*
D. Luce, *James Ford Bell Museum of Natural History, Minneapolis, Minnesota*
J. Ludwig, *Minnesota Department of Natural Resources, Madelia*
W. Macgregor, *British Columbia Ministry of Environment, Victoria*
C. Madson, *Wyoming Game and Fish Department, Cheyenne*
K. McCabe, *South Dakota State University, Brookings*
R. McCown, *University of Iowa, Iowa City*
W. McCracker, *Deere and Company, Moline, Illinois*
J. McDonough, *Massachusetts Division of Fisheries and Wildlife, Westboro*
R. McDowell, *New Jersey Division of Fish, Game and Wildlife, Trenton*
R. McKee, *Michigan Department of Natural Resources, Lansing*
J. McKenzie, *North Dakota Game and Fish Department, Mandan*
G. McNeill, *Idaho Department of Fish and Game, Lewiston*
E. Marchinton, *Bloody Creek Hunt Club, Athens, Georgia*
L. Marcum, *Tennessee Wildlife Resources Agency, Nashville*

D. Marston, *Maine Department of Inland Fisheries and Wildlife, Mechanic Falls*
F. Martinez, *The Miami Herald, Miami, Florida*
C. Martinsen, *Washington Department of Game, Olympia*
A. Mayorga-Law, *Nicaraguan National Parks and Wildlife Service, Managua*
L. G. Medina Padilla, *Ministerio de Agricultura y Cría, Caracas, Venezuela*
T. Meehan, *The Adirondack Museum, Blue Mountain Lake, New York*
C. Melin, *Colorado Division of Wildlife, Denver*
T. Melius, *National Rifle Association, Washington, D. C.*
N. Mendoza, *Departmento de Ecologia y Medio Ambiente, Comayaguela, Honduras*
E. Meslow, *Oregon State University, Corvallis*
E. Michael, *West Virginia University, Morgantown*
H. Michael, *New Mexico Game and Fish Department, Santa Fe*
K. Miers, *New Zealand Forest Service, Wellington*
K. Miller, *University of Georgia, Athens*
R. Miller, *Maryland Wildlife Administration, Annapolis*
Z. Molitor, *University of Texas, Austin*
J. Montgomery, *New Mexico Department of Game and Fish, Santa Fe*
P. Moore, *Oklahoma Department of Wildlife Conservation, Oklahoma City*
W. G. Moore, *South Carolina Wildlife and Marine Resources Department, Columbia*
W. Morison, *U. S. Forest Service, Roanoke, Virginia*
W. Morris, *Walt Disney Productions, Burbank, California*
R. Morsch, *New York City*
H. Mosby, *Virginia Polytechnic Institute and State University, Blacksburg*
D. Musgrove, *Oklahoma Department of Wildlife Conservation, Oklahoma City*
P. Meyer, *Indiana Department of Natural Resources, Indianapolis*
J. Myers, *Wisconsin Department of Natural Resources, Madison*
W. Myers, *Washington Department of Game, Olympia*
M. Naga, *British Columbia Ministry of Environment, Victoria*
D. Nelson, *Alabama Department of Conservation, Forkland*
F. Nesmith, *Kansas Fish and Game Commission, Pratt*
V. Nettles, *Southeastern Cooperative Wildlife Disease Study, Athens, Georgia*
D. Newton, *Virginia Commission of Game and Inland Fisheries, Richmond*
D. Nicholson, *Idaho Fish and Game Department, Boise*
C. Nixon, *Illinois Natural History Survey, Champaign*
J. Norman, *Kansas Fish and Game Commission, Pratt*
J. Norris, *Alexandria, Virginia*
H. Oates, *Texas Parks and Wildlife Department, Austin*
J. Ojasti, *Universidad Central de Venezuela, Caracas*
J. Olson, *Indiana Department of Natural Resources, Bloomington*
P. O'Neil, *U. S. Forest Service, Orono, Maine*
F. Oreamuno, *Ferrocarril Nacional Atlantico, San Jose, Costa Rica*
J. Osborne, *North Carolina Wildlife Resources Commission, Sanford*
J. Osman, *Pennsylvania Game Commission, Harrisburg*
H. Palmer, *Douglasville, Georgia*
L. Parsons, *Washington Department of Game, Olympia*
J. Patterson, *Washington Department of Game, Olympia*
A. Patton, *Nova Scotia Department of Lands and Forests, Kentville*
W. Peabody, *Kansas Fish and Game Commission, Emporia*
C. Peery, *Virginia Commission of Game and Inland Fisheries, Tazewell*
S. Petrie, *Worcester Art Museum, Worcester, Massachusetts*
J. Phelps, *Arizona Game and Fish Department, Phoenix*
J. Phillips, *Kentucky Department of Fish and Wildlife Resources, Frankfort*
E. Plotka, *Marshfield Medical Foundation, Marshfield, Wisconsin*
C. Post, *South Dakota Game, Fish and Parks Department, Pierre*
R. Pratt, *National Geographic Society, Washington, D. C.*
C. Pregler, *Oklahoma Department of Wildlife Conservation, Oklahoma City*
M. Preston, *University of Michigan, Ann Arbor*
T. Prickett, *Louisiana Department of Wildlife and Fisheries, Baton Rouge*
M. Prime, *Nova Scotia Department of Lands and Forests, Halifax*
G. Purvis, *Arkansas Game and Fish Commission, Little Rock*
G. Rasmussen, *New York Department of Environmental Conservation, Albany*
J. Rathert, *Missouri Department of Conservation, Columbia*
J. Raybourne, *Virginia Commission of Game and Inland Fisheries, Richmond*
J. Reagan, *Texas Parks and Wildlife Department, San Marcos*
R. Reagan, *Missouri Department of Conservation, Jefferson City*
W. Reaves, *Texas Parks and Wildlife Department, Austin*
L. Rice, *South Dakota Game, Fish and Parks Department, Rapid City*

B. Rippin, *Alberta Fish and Wildlife Division, St. Paul*
D. Roach, *Ohio Department of Natural Resources, Columbus*
H. Robinette, *Texas Parks and Wildlife Department, Llano*
L. Rogers, *U. S. Forest Service, Ely, Minnesota*
M. Rogers, *Arkansas Game and Fish Commission, Little Rock*
R. Rogers, *Idaho Department of Fish and Game, Coeur d'Alene*
N. Rollison, *U. S. Fish and Wildlife Service, Washington, D. C.*
O. Rosado, *Forestry Department, Belize*
J. Roseberry, *Southern Illinois University, Carbondale*
R. Rossan, *Gorgas Memorial Laboratory, Panama*
W. Ruth, *McKinley, Alaska*
L. Rutske, *Minnesota Department of Natural Resources, St. Paul*
L. Ryel, *Michigan Department of Natural Resources, Lansing*
K. Sabol, *Wildlife Management Institute, Washington, D. C.*
R. Salo, *Michigan Department of Natural Resources, Manistique*
D. Samuel, *West Virginia University, Morgantown*
W. Samuel, *University of Alberta, Edmonton*
W. Santonas, *West Virginia Department of Natural Resources, Morgantown*
F. Satterlee, *Virginia Commission of Game and Inland Fisheries, Richmond*
L. Schaaf, *Kentucky Department of Fish and Wildlife Resources, Frankfort*
C. Scheelhaase, *Saskatchewan Department of Tourism and Renewable Resources, Regina*
T. Schenk, *South Dakota Department of Game, Fish and Parks, Rapid City*
J. Schinz, *Penticton, British Columbia*
R. Schlabach, *Costa Rica*
W. Schoener, *Maine Department of Inland Fisheries and Wildlife, Augusta*
R. Schofield, *Michigan Department of Natural Resources, Lansing*
D. Schultz, *Washington Department of Game, Olympia*
M. Scott, *Vermont Fish and Game Department, Montpelier*
U. Seal, *Veterans Administration, Minneapolis, Minnesota*
C. Segelquist, *U. S. Fish and Wildlife Service, Fort Collins, Colorado*
C. Severinghaus, *New York Department of Environmental Conservation, Voorheesville*
K. Sexson, *Kansas Fish and Game Commission, Emporia*
T. Sharik, *Virginia Polytechnic Institute and State University, Blacksburg*
B. Shattuck, *National Geographic Society, Washington, D. C.*
M. Shaw, *Oklahoma Department of Wildlife Conservation, Oklahoma City*
W. Sheath, *Pennsylvania Game Commission, Harrisburg*
R. Shell, *U. S. Fish and Wildlife Service, Round Oak, Georgia*
N. Sherbert, *Kansas State Historical Society, Topeka*
W. Shope, *Pennsylvania Game Commission, Millerstown*
D. Shroufe, *Indiana Department of Natural Resources, Indianapolis*
R. Simms, *Tennessee Wildlife Resources Agency, Nashville*
J. Skeen, *Oklahoma Department of Wildlife Conservation, Oklahoma City*
T. Smalley, *Minnesota Department of Natural Resources, St. Paul*
D. Smith, *U. S. Fish and Wildlife Service, Washington, D. C.*
D. Smith, *Virginia Polytechnic Institute and State University, Blacksburg*
H. Smith, *Ontario Ministry of Natural Resources, Toronto*
M. Smith, *Ontario Ministry of Natural Resources, Toronto*
R. Smith, *Arizona Game and Fish Department, Phoenix*
N. Snyder, *New Mexico Game and Fish Department, Santa Fe*
L. Sowls, *University of Arizona, Tucson*
M. Spain, *Glenbow Museum, Calgary, Alberta*
J. Spignesi, *Connecticut Department of Environmental Protection, Hartford*
W. Stebbens, *Wadsworth Atheneum, Hartford, Connecticut*
M. Suckney, *New York Department of Environmental Conservation, Albany*
P. Stine, *U. S. Fish and Wildlife Service, Portland, Oregon*
P. Stinson, *Michigan State University, East Lansing*
K. Stockdale, *Tennessee Wildlife Resources Agency, Nashville*
R. Stoll, *Ohio Department of Natural Resources, New Marshfield*
S. Sturmy, *Nova Scotia Department of Lands and Forests, Halifax*
L. Suring, *Oregon State University, Corvallis*
J. Swedberg, *West Millbury, Massachusetts*
J. Sweeney, *Clemson University, Clemson, South Carolina*
P. Swoveland, *Indiana Department of Natural Resources, Indianapolis*
J. Tanck, *Albany, New York*
J. Thiebes, *Oregon Department of Fish and Wildlife, Portland*
G. Thomas, *Illinois Department of Conservation, Springfield*
J. Thomas, *U. S. Forest Service, La Grande, Oregon*

J. Toler, *U. S. Forest Service, Roanoke, Virginia*
T. Townsend, *Ohio State University, Columbus*
M. Traweek, *Texas Parks and Wildlife Department, Kerrville*
W. Trimm, *New York Department of Environmental Conservation, Albany*
R. Umber, *Oklahoma Department of Wildlife Conservation, Oklahoma City*
R. Underwood, *U. S. Forest Service, Roanoke, Virginia*
D. Urbston, *U. S. Forest Service, Hot Springs, Arkansas*
C. Vaughan, *Costa Rica*
J. Victoria, *Connecticut Department of Environmental Protection, Hartford*
B. Villa-R., *Instituto de Biologia, UNAM, Mexico, D. F., Mexico*
J. Vogt, *Michigan Department of Natural Resources, Lansing*
P. Vohs, *U. S. Fish and Wildlife Service, Washington, D.C.*
E. Walker, *Texas Parks and Wildlife Department, Austin*
D. Waller, *Georgia Department of Natural Resources, Atlanta*
M. Walton, *Wildlife Management Institute, Dripping Springs, Texas*
O. Warbach, *Haslett, Michigan*
T. Warren, *Montana Department of Fish, Wildlife, and Parks, Helena*
J. Watson, *U. S. Fish and Wildlife Service, Big Pine Key, Florida*
M. Watson, *Alberta Department of Energy and Natural Resources, Edmonton*
S. Webb, *Florida State Museum, Gainesville*
F. Weddle, *Kamiah, Idaho*
K. Westhouse, *Ontario Ministry of Natural Resources, Toronto*
J. Whelan, *U. S. Fish and Wildlife Service, Blacksburg, Virginia*
C. Whitehead, *Tennessee Wildlife Resources Agency, Nashville*
J. Whittendale, *Delaware Division of Fish and Wildlife, Dover*
A. Wickam, *Wyoming Game and Fish Department, Cheyenne*
J. Wiley, *New Hampshire Fish and Game Department, Concord*
J. Williams, *Clemson University, Clemson, South Carolina*
L. Williamson, *Wildlife Management Institute, Washington, D. C.*
R. Willis, *Kentucky Department of Fish and Wildlife Resources, West Liberty*
D. Wilson, *Texas Parks and Wildlife Department, Austin*
H. Wilson, *Idaho Fish and Game Department, Boise*
E. Wiltse, *Saskatchewan Department of Tourism and Natural Resources, Regina*
C. Winkler, *Texas Parks and Wildlife Department, Austin*
R. Wishner, *Arizona Game and Fish Department, Phoenix*
C. Wolfe, *Nebraska Game and Parks Commission, Lincoln*
R. Wood, *Michigan Department of Natural Resources, Lansing*
D. Wyse, *Oregon State University, Corvallis*
J. Yoakum, *U. S. Bureau of Land Management, Reno, Nevada*
S. Yontz, *Kentucky Department of Fish and Wildlife Resources, Frankfort*
S. Zimmer, *Philmont Scout Ranch, Cimarron, New Mexico*

CONTENTS

TABLES

FIGURES

I. Whitetail Biology and Ecology

Chapter 1

ORIGIN, CLASSIFICATION AND DISTRIBUTION

Rollin H. Baker
Director Emeritus
The Museum
Professor Emeritus
Department of Fisheries and Wildlife
Department of Zoology
Michigan State University
East Lansing, Michigan

ORIGIN OF ARTIODACTYLA

Artiodactyls—even-toed ungulates in which the body weight is supported by the third and fourth metapodials (paraxonic)—had their beginning in the family Dichobunidae during the Eocene Epoch (36–58 million years ago) in both North America and Eurasia (Dawson 1967, Rose 1982) (Figure 1). The origin of hoofed mammals is obscure (Pilgrim 1941*a*), but many paleontologists (Gazin 1955, Matthew 1915, Romer 1966, Simpson 1945) believe that the ancestral even-toed suborder Palaeodonta was derived from the Condylarthra, an early Tertiary Period assemblage of mammals intermediate between insectivores and true ungulates. The earliest recognizable artiodactyls (genus *Diacodexis*) (Figure 2) in the early Eocene already had elongated limb elements for cursorial gait and possessed the distinctive double-pulleyed ankle bone (Guthrie 1968, Schaeffer 1947) (Figure 3). Thus it is very likely that the even-toed ungulates were undergoing development earlier, during the Paleocene Ep-

och. Artiodactyls flourished and diversified throughout the Eocene, and with the decline of the odd-toed ungulates (Perissodactyla) in the Oligocene Epoch, the artiodactyls underwent pronounced adaptive radiation in terrestrial habitats—in the Miocene Epoch (Viret 1961). Many phyletic lines became extinct. Others gave rise to the ancestral stocks of modern artiodactyls (Pilgrim 1941*a*, Simpson 1945, Romer 1966), and continued to overshadow the odd-toed perissodactyls—the horses, tapirs and rhinos.

Modern Artiodactyla (approximately 171 species) include the Suina and the Ruminantia suborders (Figure 4). The Suina contain the pigs, peccaries and hippopotamuses, which have feet with four "functional" toes, separate metapodials usually—instead of coalesced cannon bones, bunodont molar teeth, canine tusks and simple stomachs. The Ruminantia contain the cud-chewers—the modern camelids—as surviving members of the Infraorder Tylopoda, and the tragulids (chevrotains), cervids, giraffids, antilocaprids and bovids of the In-

1

fraorder Pecora. Today's ruminants usually have limbs with two functional toes (Figure 5), metapodials fused as cannon bones, complex selenodont molars, upper incisors reduced or absent, upper canines often lacking but sometimes enlarged in males, and compound stomachs.

AGE DIVISIONS			TIME		
			Duration in millions of years		Beginning millions of years ago
Era			Era		
	Period	Epoch	Period	Epoch	
CENOZOIC	QUATERNARY	Recent Pleistocene	0-1	1	1
		Pliocene	63	12	13
		Miocene		12	25
	TERTIARY	Oligocene	62	11	36
		Eocene		22	58
		Paleocene		5	63
MESOZOIC	CRETACEOUS		72		135
	JURASSIC		46	167	181
	TRIASSIC		49		230
PALEOZOIC	PERMIAN		50		280
	PENNSYLVANIAN		40		320
	MISSISSIPPIAN		25		345
	DEVONIAN		60	370	405
	SILURIAN		20		425
	ORDOVICIAN		75		500
	CAMBRIAN		100		600
PRECAMBRIAN			4000	900	1,500

Figure 1. Geologic time scale. The shaded area represents the known period of existence of artiodactyls, within which modern whitetails evolved, during the Pleistocene. Adapted from Kulp (1961); *see also* Bryant and Maser (1982).

Figure 2. Artistic representation of the "rabbit-sized" *Diacodexis,* the first known member of the Order Artiodactyla, from the early Eocene Epoch. Illustration by Jane Kaminski, after Rose (1982).

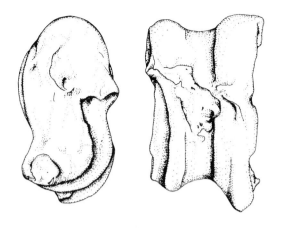

Figure 3. Front (left) and side (right) views, at scale, of the right astragalus of white-tailed deer. This double-pulleyed ankle bone is characteristic of all Artiodactyla. Illustration by Jane Kaminski.

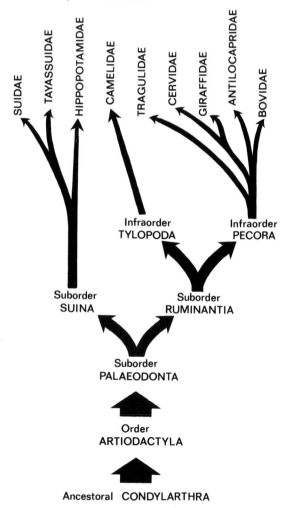

Figure 4. Development and diversification of the modern families of even-toed ungulates.

BEGINNINGS OF CERVIDAE

The earliest pecorans occurred in the Upper Eocene. They have been classified as belonging to Superfamily Traguloidea, the most primitive group of Pecora. Although cervids likely may have had ancestral stock in common with modern representatives of the Family Tragulidae—the chevrotains, *Tragulus* of Asia and *Hyemoschus* of Africa—Webb and Taylor (1980) emphasize that these tragulids are remote from higher ruminants. Nevertheless, early members of this superfamily appear to have been the ancestral stock from which were derived the more advanced cud-chewing families Cervidae, Giraffidae, Antilocapridae and Bovidae (Pearson 1964, Romer 1966, Viret 1961). These families appeared early in the Miocene, with a distinctive developmental hiatus becoming evident between the more primitive deer/giraffe line and the more advanced pronghorn/bovid line. The former became

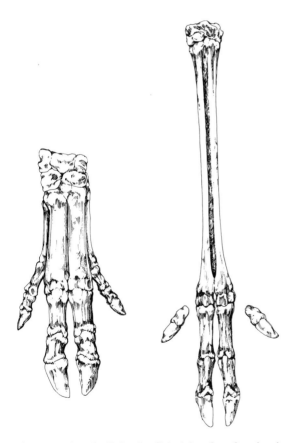

Figure 5. The pig (Suborder Suina) has four functional toes (left); the deer (Suborder Ruminantia) has two (right). Illustration by Patricia Stinson.

chiefly browsing animals, with low-crowned teeth, and generally inhabited forest and/or brush country. The pronghorn/bovid descent, on the other hand, fostered mostly grazing animals, with high-crowned teeth, and lived usually in open areas that were a conspicuous part of the landscape of mid-Tertiary geological times.

Cervids had their origin in the long-extinct pecoran family Palaeomerycidae, which flourished in the Eurasian late Oligocene and Miocene. Representatives of this family, or of Dromomerycidae, a closely related New World counterpart, are known to have existed from the Miocene to the mid-Pliocene of North America (Dawson 1967). This lineage showed progressive development of elongated two-toed limbs, low-crowned teeth adapted for browsing, stout traguloidlike upper canine tusks in primitive forms (persisting in modern cervids, *Cervulus*, *Elaphodus* and *Moschus*) and, in more advanced genera, hornlike structures extending upward at various angles over the orbits. It was the belief of Sir Richard Owen (*see* Scott 1962) that there is an inverse relationship between horns, or antlers, and canine tusks in pecorans, with those species without horns or antlers having long, saberlike upper canines and those species with horns or antlers having reduced (as in *Cervus*) or lost (as in *Odocoileus*, except on rare occasions) upper canines. The modern exceptions are the muntjac, or barking deer (*Cervulus*), and the tufted deer (*Elaphodus*), each of which has both antlers and tusks.

The Eurasian genus *Dremotherium* and the American *Blastomeryx*, despite lacking bony protuberances from the frontal bones, and possessing formidable canine tusks (Matthew 1908) (Figure 6), seem to have been the forerunners of later Miocene palaeomerycids of the genera *Aletomeryx*, *Cranioceras* and *Dromomeryx*. These three fossil forms had hornlike processes (probably not shed as in the case of true antlers) extending upward and over the orbits (Romer 1966) (Figure 6). Apparently lacking the horny coverings typical of the pronghorn/bovid line, the head protuberances of these genera could correspond to the skin-covered outgrowths on the skulls of modern giraffes, or of modern cervids in velvet, or to the basal pedicels of deer antlers (Pilgrim 1941*b*). Of interest is that one of these genera, *Aletomeryx*, had both upper canine tusks and hornlike structures (*see* Gregory 1951). Variation is

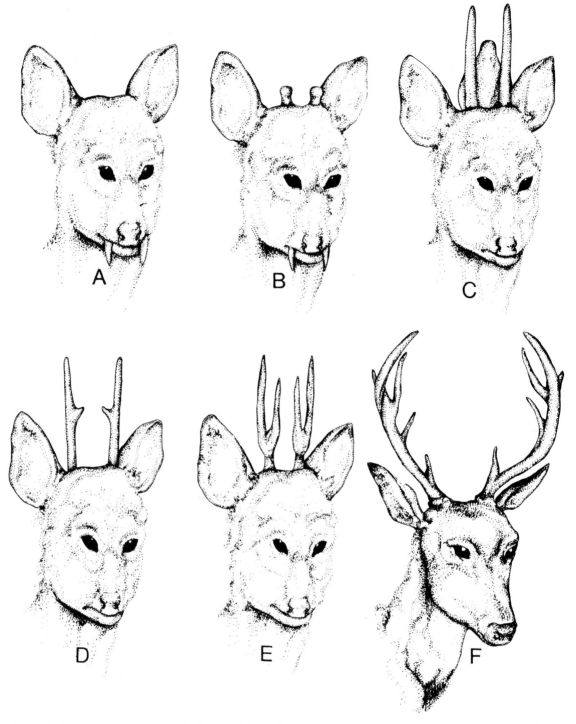

Figure 6. Artistic representations of the heads of late Tertiary (Miocene/Pliocene) and Quarternary (Pleistocene/Recent) cervids, probably in the odocoilein lineage. The tusked *Blastomeryx* (A) of the Miocene lacked bony frontal protuberances; *Aletomeryx* (B) of the Miocene possessed both tusks and knoblike processes; *Cranioceras* (C) of the Miocene/Pliocene was tuskless and had longer head adornments, plus a median "horn" on the occiput; *Lagomeryx* (D) of the Miocene/Pliocene had single-forked structures that were deerlike in appearance but probably not shed; *Dicrocerus* (E) of the Miocene/Pliocene probably had the first true forked antlers; *Odocoileus* (F) of the Pleistocene/Recent represents one of the modern descendants. Drawings by Jane Kaminski, adapted from those in Gregory (1951), Romer (1966) and Scott (1962). Note that the sizes of the older genera are exaggerated.

shown in *Cranioceras,* which bears a median horn extending back from the occiput.

One further step in "antler" development came with the appearance of the genus *Lagomeryx,* a palaeomerycid considered by Romer (1966) as lying at the point of origin of the deer family. This animal had paired, deerlike, vertical, bony spikes with short side branches (Figure 6). Again, these structures probably were not deciduous. In fact, no true intermediates have thus far been found between fossil forms with permanent giraffelike protuberances and the annually shed antlers in modern cervids.

Strange indeed was the course of evolution that developed the "disposable" head adornments of the Cervidae, especially when "permanent" ones, like the bovids', might have served the same functions. The antler growth process requires considerable expenditure of nutrients by the carrier. In fact it seems almost too energy-expensive for the individuals to have endured, despite the fact that antlers grow, then as now, during the vegetative season when foods are usually plentiful. Be that as it may, cervids have diversified successfully and persisted throughout four continents plus northern Africa.

True "antlered" cervids appeared first in the Eurasian Miocene. Persisting however were primitive antlerless and tusked characteristics in at least some forms (continuing in the modern musk deer [*Moschus*]). Because some biologists consider this pecoran as a relict, perhaps it really does not pertain to this discussion—belonging more likely to a distinct family, namely Moschidae (Webb and Taylor 1980). The Old World genera *Dicrocerus* and *Stepanocemas* are perhaps the earliest recognizable members of the Family Cervidae. These deer, whose fossil remains were found in both Miocene and Pliocene beds, were small—muntjaclike in size, and had forked antlers (Figure 6).

From this Pliocene stem stock, specific lines of cervid evolution are obscure, but obviously diversified, appearing first in Eurasia and later in North America. On the latter continent, modern cervids derived as a result of the evolvement of two major groupings. These were the Subfamily Odocoileinae, in which were derived *Odocoileus, Alces, Rangifer,* five neotropical genera, and Old World *Hydropotes* and *Capreolus,* and the Subfamily Cervinae, in which were derived circumboreal *Cervus* and

three Old World genera. In both subfamilies the tendency was toward a gradual increase in body size and antler dimension. These developments culminated in the massive bulk and the huge adornments of the North American "stag-moose" (*Cervalces*) and the Eurasian "Irish elk" (*Megaloceros*). These largest of antlers were thought by some theorists (*see* Lull 1924, Simpson 1951) to be hindrances—perhaps leading to the animals' demise in the wane of the last receding glaciers. However, there is no actual basis for such conclusions (Gould 1974).

The fossil record of the Pleistocene Epoch bears evidence of the presence at that time of all modern genera of New World deer. However, the derivation of these, except perhaps for that of *Cervus* (known from the Eurasian late Pliocene), is obscure. Romer (1966) regarded *Odocoileus* strictly as an American development—with an unknown Asian lineage, and as ancestral to the several distinctive deer genera now found in South America. In the Pleistocene, New World cervids shared both forested and open areas with an impressive array of hoofed associates, including mammoths, mastodons, horses, tapirs, peccaries, camelids, pronghorns and bovids. Only nine cervid genera, one pronghorn, and nine bovid genera—plus a few neotropical tapirs, camelids (llamas and allies), and peccaries—survived the postglacial "ordeals" and inhabit the Western Hemisphere today. The rest of the great assemblage of "Ice Age" ungulates has disappeared, and the reasons why are in dispute (Martin and Wright 1967).

MODERN CERVIDS

Modern members of the deer family are slim, often long-legged and graceful. They have the ability to run, leap and skulk to evade enemies. They possess deciduous antlers, except in the aberrant musk deer and Chinese water-deer (*Hydropotes*). Only males have antlers, except in *Rangifer,* where females are also endowed. Hormones from the testes, the anterior lobe of the pituitary gland, and the thyroid affect antler development. The upper canines are long and tusklike only in three genera (in the Subfamilies Moschinae and Cervulinae), being reduced greatly or absent in all others. The molars are low-crowned (brachyodont) with "half-moon"-shaped cusps (selenodont). The dental formula of deer is: incisors, 0/3; canines, 0/1 or 1/1; premolars, 3/3; molars, 3/3; a total of 32 or 34 teeth. In the skull, the lacrimal and nasal bones are not contiguous. The cannon bone in each limb is formed by the fusion of the two principal metapodials of the third and fourth toes. Lateral toes (remnants of the second and fifth toes) are reduced (*see* Figure 5). The four-chambered ruminating stomach is a prominent feature of the soft anatomy (internal organs) and important in the digestive process. The primitive musk deer is the only cervid with a gall bladder. Tarsal, metatarsal or interdigital glands may be present. Facial glands occur in all genera except the musk deer. Males usually are larger than females. Both sexes may have specific courtship behaviors, and males often maintain harems. The gestation period is five to eight months. Young frequently have spotted coats, but adults rarely do.

Living Cervidae include four subfamilies, 17 genera and approximately 37 species (Ellerman and Morrison-Scott 1951, Cabrera 1961, Koopman 1967).

Family CERVIDAE/Gray 1821:
> Subfamily MOSCHINAE [also arranged as separate Family Moschidae (Webb and Taylor 1980)].
>> Genus *Moschus*/Linnaeus 1758; musk deer (Asian), 1 species
> Subfamily CERVULINAE [=MUNTIACINAE]
>> Genus *Cervulus*/de Blainville 1861 [=*Muntiacus*/Rafinesque 1815]; muntjac (Asian), 4 species
>> Genus *Elaphodus*/Milne-Edwards 1871; tufted deer (Asian), 1 species
> Subfamily CERVINAE
>> Genus *Axis*/H. Smith 1827; chital (Asian), 2 species
>> Genus *Cervus*/Linnaeus 1758; North American elk or wapiti, Eurasian red deer, etc. (Eurasian, North African, North American), approximately 11 species
>> Genus *Elaphurus*/Milne-Edwards 1866; Pere David's deer (formerly Asian, now in parks and zoos), 1 species
>> Genus *Dama*/Frisch 1775 [validity questioned, *see* Ellerman and Morrison-Scott (1951)]; fallow deer (Eurasian), 1 species

> Subfamily ODOCOILEINAE
>> Genus *Alces*/Gray 1821; moose, European elk (Eurasian, North American), 1 species
>> Genus *Ozotoceros*/Ameghino 1891 [=*Blastoceros*/Fitzinger 1860]; swamp deer (South American), 1 species
>> Genus *Blastocerus*/Gray 1850 [=*Edocerus*/Avila-Pires 1957]; Pampas deer (South American); 1 species
>> Genus *Hippocamelus*/Leuckart 1816; huemul (South American), 2 species
>> Genus *Mazama*/Rafinesque 1832; brocket, etc. (Central and South American), 4 species
>> Genus *Odocoileus*/Rafinesque 1832 [=*Dama*/Zimmerman 1780]; mule deer, white-tailed deer (North and South American), 2 species
>> Genus *Pudu*/Gray 1852; pudu (South American), 2 species
>> Genus *Rangifer*/H. Smith 1827; caribou, reindeer (North American, Eurasian), 1 species
>> Genus *Hydropotes*/Swinhoe 1870; Chinese water-deer (Asian), 1 species
>> Genus *Capreolus*/Gray 1821; roe deer (Eurasian), 1 species

The continental distribution of modern cervid genera (Table 1) indicates a high degree of species endemism in Asia (mostly southeastern) and in South America (Figure 7). Genera in the subfamilies Moschinae, Cervulinae and Cervinae are Eurasian in derivation, with only *Cervus* in the Cervinae spreading into the New World in the Pleistocene, presumably by way of the Bering Strait land-bridge that once connected the Soviet Union's Chukchi Peninsula with the Seward Peninsula in Alaska. Genera in the subfamily Odocoileinae, with the exception of *Hydropotes* and *Capreolus*, are typical of the Western Hemisphere. In South America, secondary diversity, probably from *Odocoileus* as stem stock (Hershkovitz 1982, Simpson 1945), resulted in the development of at least 10 cervid genera (5 Recent). *Alces* and *Rangifer*, two northern genera, presumably made their way to Eurasia by traveling across the Bering land-bridge, perhaps meeting east-traveling *Cervus* enroute. Modern mammalogists regard as minor the differences between the pairings: American elk (or "wapiti") and Eurasian red deer; North American moose and Eurasian elk; and caribou and reindeer. Despite their present separation by the Bering Strait, these relatives are considered to belong to the same species—*Cervus elaphus, Alces alces,* and *Rangifer tarandus* respectively.

THE GENUS ODOCOILEUS

As mentioned previously, the ancestral American *Odocoileus* seems to have been the progenitor of the several endemic South American deer. In fact a few authors (*see* Grzimek 1972) have suggested that some of the Neotropical deer—marsh deer (*Ozotocerus*), Pampas deer (*Blastocerus*) and huemal (*Hippoca-*

Table 1. Continental distribution of genera in the Cervidae.

Genera	Asia	Europe	North America	South America
Alces	•	•	•	
Axis	•			
Blastocerus				•
Capreolus	•	•		
Cervulus	•			
Cervus	•	•	•	
Dama	•	•		
Elaphodus	•			
Elaphurus	•			
Hippocamelus				•
Hydropotes	•			
Mazama			•	•
Moschus	•			
Odocoileus			•	•
Ozotoceros				•
Pudu				•
Rangifer	•	•	•	

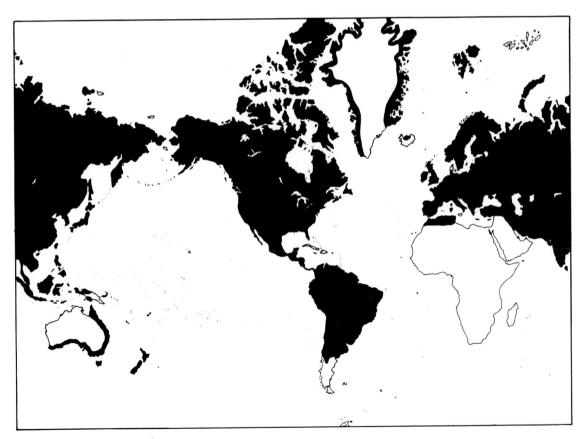

Figure 7. Worldwide distribution of Cervidae (in black), including *Alces, Axis, Blastocerus, Capreolus, Cervus, Dama, Elaphodus, Elaphurus, Hippocamelus, Hydropotes, Mazama, Moschus, Muntiacus, Odocoileus, Ozotoceros, Pudu* and *Rangifer* (Anderson and Jones 1967, Bryant and Maser 1982, Cowan and Holloway 1973, Ellerman and Morrison-Scott 1951, Walker et al. 1975).

melus)—be placed within the genus *Odocoileus*. However, most modern authorities include only white-tailed deer (*O. virginianus*) and mule and black-tailed deer (*O. hemionus*).

Distinctive generic characteristics most commonly used to separate *Odocoileus* from other New World cervids include: from *Rangifer*—the absence of antlers in females, the presence of nonpalmate antlers, and a hairless muzzle; from *Cervus*—the absence of upper canine teeth (except in rare instances), and also of the upper ends of the lateral metacarpals and the vomer dividing the posterior narial cavity; from *Alces*—the presence of nonpalmate antlers, the absence of a dewlap and also of the vomer dividing the posterior narial cavity; from *Pudu*—the presence of large antlers and metatarsal, tarsal and pedal glands, and also the naviculo-cuboid of the tarsus being free from the cuneiform; from *Ozotoceros, Blastocerus, Hippocamelus* and *Mazama*—the presence of metatarsal glands.

The white-tailed deer is distinguished from the mule deer by the shape and configuration of the antlers, the length of the sub-basal snag on the antlers, the lengths of the ears and metatarsal glands, the color of the dorsal tail hairs, and the condition of the lacrimal fossa (Table 2, figures 8 and 9). Distinguishing between the two species is a problem only where their ranges overlap.

NOMENCLATURE

The application of several generic names to white-tailed and mule deer has caused confusion, especially among mammalogists not well oriented to scientific nomenclature. Since the eighteenth century taxonomists have assigned no fewer than 12 generic names to these cervids. Some uniformity was achieved after the turn of the twentieth century, when the name *Odocoileus* came into common use. Nevertheless, nomenclatural work by Hershkovitz (1948) demonstrated conclusively that *Odocoileus*/Rafinesque 1832 was not the earliest valid generic name. Instead, *Dama*/Zimmermann 1780 had precedence. This generic change, according to Hershkovitz, was made in total accord with the Rules of the International Commission on Zoological Nomenclature since, in Opinion 258 (Bulletin of Zoological Nomenclature 1950[4]:549), the Commission declared that the generic names proposed by early-day classifier Frisch were disqualified under the binomial system of classification. This action thus removed *Dama*/Frisch 1775 as a valid taxon for the Old World fallow deer and made *Dama*/Zimmermann 1780 eligible as a generic name. The only difficulty was that Zimmermann had used *Dama* in describing the "Virginia deer" of North America.

Thus, by the law of priority, the older name, *Dama*, correctly replaced the newer one, *Odocoileus* (Hershkovitz 1948). Mammalogists abiding strictly by the Rules began to use *Dama* when referring to white-tailed and mule deer (Hall and Kelson 1959). European scientists were faced with the loss of *Dama* and the prospect of using the next available name, *Platyceros*/Zimmermann 1780, for the fallow deer. Partly because of the furor brought about by these changes in names so long in popular use, the outcome was appealed to the International Commission. In Opinion 581 (Bulletin of Zoological Nomenclature 1960[17]:267–275), the Commission used its plenary powers to make an exception and validated *Dama*/Frisch 1775 as the name for the fallow deer. They rejected *Dama*/Zimmermann 1780—making it a junior homonym—and thereby made *Odocoileus*/Rafinesque 1832 available for the American deer.

Table 2. Characteristics that distinguish white-tailed deer from mule deer.

Characteristic	White-tailed deer	Mule deer
Major beam of antler	Curving forward without dichotomous fork	Growing upward with dichotomous fork
Sub-basal snag of antler	Long	Short
Length of ear	One-half length of head	Three-fourths length of head
Metatarsal gland	Less than 42 millimeters (1.65 inches) long	More than 70 millimeters (2.75 inches) long
Color of tail	Brown above, laterally fringed with white	White or black above, tip black
Lacrimal fossa	Shallow	Deep

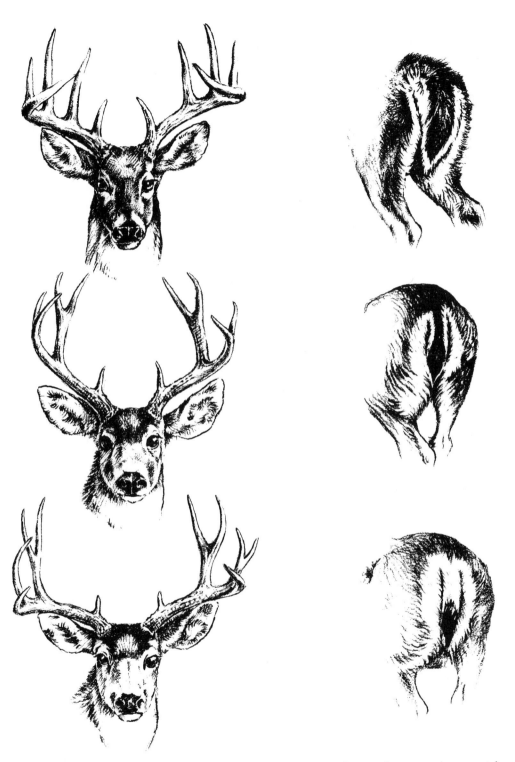

Figure 8. Comparison of antler morphology and facial characteristics of white-tailed deer (top), black-tailed deer (center) and mule deer (bottom) bucks. Illustration by Charles W. Schwartz, from Halls (1978).

Figure 9. Comparative patterns in rump patches and dorsal tail surfaces of white-tailed deer (top), black-tailed deer (center) and mule deer (bottom) bucks. Illustration by Charles W. Schwartz, from Halls (1978).

DISTRIBUTION

The white-tailed deer is extolled widely as the premier big game mammal in most parts of North and Central America, providing millions of people with recreation, food, clothing, footwear, decorations and even utensils. Throughout its extensive range, the ubiquitous whitetail is at home in many north-temperate to tropical environments where ground cover, shrubs and low trees (favored for browse and cover) are floral features of the landscape. Furthermore, when given at least some protection from overkill, the whitetail has fared well in the presence of man and man's hodgepodge of land-use practices, from near-treeline in southern Canada (60 degrees north latitude) to subequatorial South America (15 degrees south latitude) (Figure 10). Habitat manipulations resulting from human encroachment have allowed the species to expand its range in such places as the North American Midwest, where prevention or restriction of periodic burning of open grasslands has allowed the spread of woody vegetation, thereby creating or increasing habitat favorable to deer. Cutting and clearing have set back plant succession in many forested areas, producing edge and brushy growth and, in so doing, increasing carrying capacity for whitetails. Despite man's continual efforts to "tame" the North American landscape, and despite his vigorous pursuit of the whitetail, the deer has persisted and even thrived throughout much of its vast range (*see* Taylor 1956, Trefethen 1970, Whitehead 1972, Figure 11).

Whitetails have been introduced into foreign environments with varying degrees of success. They have fared poorly in the British Isles, whereas introductions in Czechoslovakia, Finland, Yugoslavia and New Zealand have been generally successful. Stocks of white-tailed deer also have been released in Cuba, Curacao and on other Caribbean islands (de Vos et al. 1956).

Whitetails were introduced in the Virgin Islands in 1790 on St. Croix. In 1845, the deer were moved from St. Croix to St. Thomas. Later, some of the deer swam the 5-kilometer (3.1-mile) channel to St. John's Island. As part of a cattle-fever tick-control program there were several unsuccessful attempts to eliminate all wild deer on St. Croix and St. Thomas islands. Following these attempts, whitetails were imported from Texas and the Carolinas. The most recent estimates of whitetail population are 1,000 for St. Croix and 600 for St. Thomas and St. John combined (D. Nellis personal communication:1979).

INTERSPECIFIC RELATIONSHIPS

Today, the white-tailed deer shares most of its vast living space with cervid relatives. The exceptions are in the eastern United States and parts of northern Mexico, where the species enjoys unshared forest-brush-open communities. To the north and northwest moose and elk are neighbors, as are mule deer to the west. From the tropical areas of Mexico southward to northern South America, one or more species of brocket deer share whitetail range, and in montane parts of northwestern South America, the whitetail occupies areas with the huemul. In parts of Colombia, Ecuador and Peru, the pudu perhaps cohabits whitetail range. Although knowledge of habitat resource divisions between—and interactions among—whitetailed deer and most of the aforementioned other deer is rudimentary, it is obvious that these associates have found ways of survival by apportioning local habitat resources.

The geographic relationship between whitetailed deer and mule deer is well-known (Figure 12). Where these two species occupy the same general area, they may be ecologically segregated in their choice of habitats. In the northeastern foothills of the Rocky Mountains, for example, the whitetail follows narrow, wooded river bottoms, while the mule deer lives in adjacent hilly uplands and montane areas (Lechleitner 1969, Turner 1974). In the southwestern United States and northern Mexico, white-tailed deer thrive in pine/oak montane forests while mule deer favor more open, arid terrain at lower elevations (Findley et al. 1975, Leopold 1959). Because the white-tailed deer slowly is expanding its range westward and encroaching on habitats of the mule deer, the latter may be subjected to an ever-increasing possibility of infection by the meningeal worm, *Parelaphostrongylus tenuis* (Anderson 1972, Hibler 1981, *see also* Chapter 7). The adult stage of this roundworm, which lives in the cranial venous sinuses and the subdural space, causes neurologic disease, to which the white-tailed deer is tolerant—but which may lead to paraplegia and death in mule deer and other cervids. A species of terrestrial snail, important as the intermediate host (for the lar-

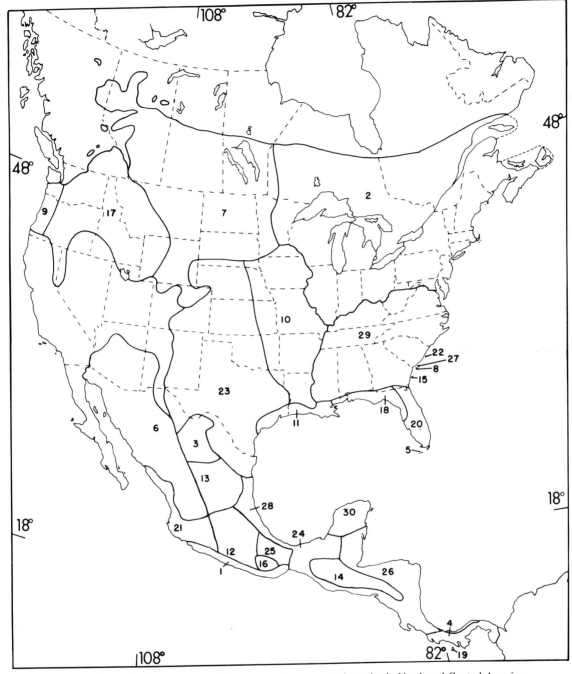

Figure 10. Distribution of white-tailed deer (*Odocoileus virginianus*) subspecies in North and Central America:

1. *O. v. acapulcensis*
2. *O. v. borealis*
3. *O. v. carminis*
4. *O. v. chiriquensis*
5. *O. v. clavium*
6. *O. v. couesi*
7. *O. v. dacotensis*
8. *O. v. hiltonensis*
9. *O. v. leucurus*
10. *O. v. macrourus*

11. *O. v. mcilhennyi*
12. *O. v. mexicanus*
13. *O. v. miquihuanensis*
14. *O. v. nelsoni*
15. *O. v. nigribarbis*
16. *O. v. oaxacensis*
17. *O. v. ochrourus*
18. *O. v. osceola*
19. *O. v. rothschildi*
20. *O. v. seminolus*

21. *O. v. sinaloae*
22. *O. v. taurinsulae*
23. *O. v. texanus*
24. *O. v. thomasi*
25. *O. v. toltecus*
26. *O. v. truei*
27. *O. v. venatorius*
28. *O. v. veraecrucis*
29. *O. v. virginianus*
30. *O. v. yucatanensis*

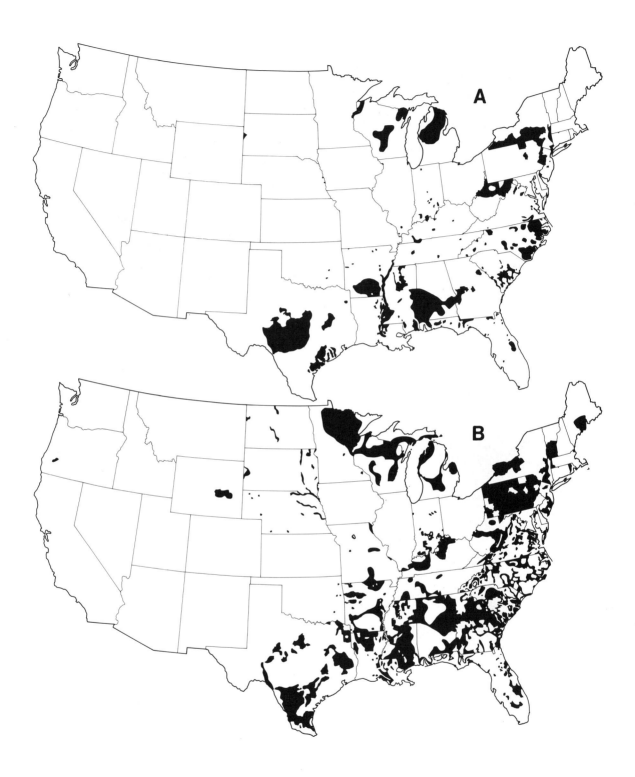

Figure 11. Distribution of white-tailed deer in the United States, 1982 (adapted from Southeastern Cooperative Wildlife Disease Study 1983). Originally prepared from data compiled independently by state fish and wildlife agencies, with additional information provided by the U. S. National Park Service. The dark area in map A represents those lands on

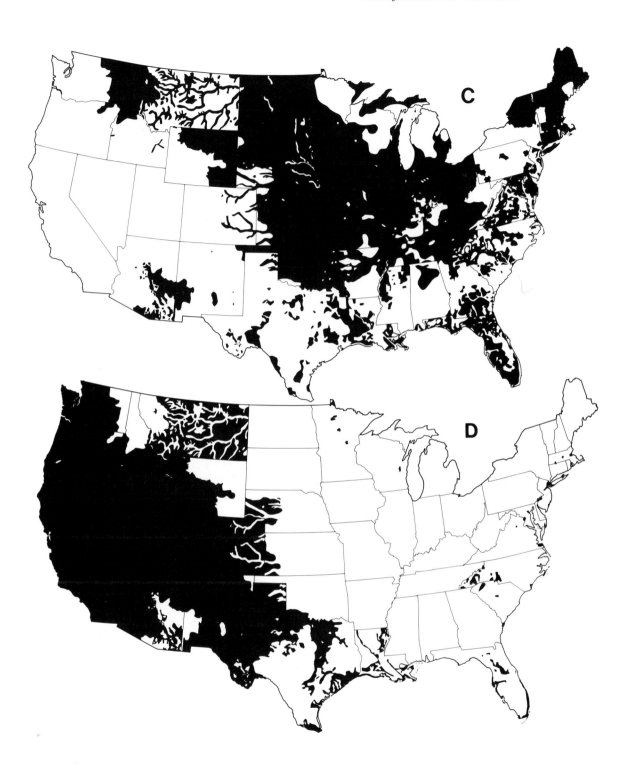

which whitetails exceeded 11.6 deer per square kilometer (30 per square mile); map B shows whitetail densities of 5.8–11.6 deer per square kilometer (15–30 per square mile); map C indicates whitetail numbers at less than 5.8 per square kilometer (15 per square mile); and map D indicates areas where whitetails reportedly were absent or rare.

val stage), is known in Colorado and possibly other western states. This worm could be a major cause of the ecological separation of the two deer. In addition, there is some evidence that where there is actual social contact between the two cervids, the white-tailed deer can be domineering (Severinghaus and Cheatum 1956).

The ranges of white-tailed deer, moose and elk also overlap—mostly near the northern edge of the whitetail's range at the Canadian/United States border, and especially as a result of its

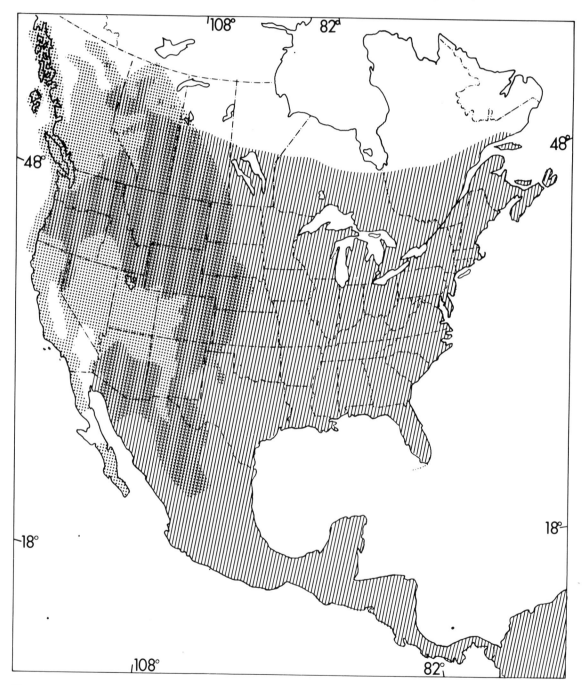

Figure 12. Approximate overlap in the geographic distribution of white-tailed deer (slant design to the right) and mule deer (stippled pattern on the left).

northward movement in historic times. In Minnesota, at least, white-tailed deer and moose may utilize similar plant communities in summer and autumn, but are less apt to resort to the same food sources and living space in other seasons (Irwin 1975). In Michigan, deer and elk appear to coexist in summer along forest edges (Moran 1973). In winter, whitetails prefer to use newly cutover areas and swamp conifers, with yarding often occurring. Elk, on the other hand, range in forested habitats, seemingly without discrimination. There appears to be some variation in habitat preference in the case of both of these species combinations—more so in the cold months and less so in the warm months. One consequence of this coexistence, as mentioned previously in connection with comments about mule deer, is that infestations of the meningeal worm, *Parelaphostrongylus tenuis,* in white-tailed deer produce minor or no symptoms, while in moose and elk serious and often fatal neurological symptoms occur (Anderson 1972, Kistner 1982). The lethal effects of this roundworm on moose and elk could prove a major deterrent to the reestablishment of these cervids in areas now inhabited by northward-moving populations of white-tailed deer, which are infested with this parasite.

In southern latitudes whitetails range from tropical lowlands, approximately at sea level, to mixed forest-brush areas in the Andes of Colombia, Peru, Ecuador and Bolivia—at elevations of from 4,000 to 4,500 meters (13,125–14,765 feet) (Avila Pirés 1975, Borrero 1967, Grimwood 1969, Jungius 1974). In tropical environments at lower elevations, the white-tailed deer thrives best in arid shrub country. In Panama, for example, whitetails frequent the drier Pacific side (Handley 1966, Méndez 1970). Osgood (1914:137) wrote that, in northern South America the white-tailed deer inhabited ". . . lowlands in the arid or semi-arid savannas, regions of light intermittent forest or open grasslands." In these lowland areas the relationship between the whitetail and the resident (and perhaps better adapted) brocket deer is unknown. Needless to say, white-tailed deer and brockets occupy similar space from Mexico southward to the savannas of the Guianas and northeastern Brazil (on the eastern side) and to coastal Peru (on the western side). In humid, montane tropics, these two occur together at elevations as high as 3,200 meters (10,500 feet) in such places as the Amazon-facing slopes of southeastern Peru (Grimwood 1969).

White-tailed deer and populations of the diminutive pudu occur in woody sectors of the Andean paramo of southwestern Colombia, Ecuador and northern Peru, although few descriptive accounts of their associations are available (Grimwood 1969, Hershkovitz 1982). At elevations directly above treeline (3,900–4,100 meters: 12,795–13,450 feet) in northwestern Bolivia, Jungius (1974) found white-tailed deer and the huemul living in close association. Jungius concluded that the two species avoid interaction by using different grazing areas.

GEOGRAPHIC VARIATION

That the white-tailed deer has become well adapted to different environments is shown by the amount of measured geographic variation in this polytypic species. This diversity is reflected in body weight, external dimensions, coat coloration, antler growth and, no doubt, assorted physiological, biochemical and behavioral distinctions yet to be fully understood. Currently, no less than 30 subspecies are recognized in North and Central America (*see* Figure 10), and 8 in South America. Although these named taxa reflect the findings of several generations of mammalogists (earliest name dates from 1784; latest from 1940), it is suspected that a "modern" evaluation of geographic variation in this widespread and plastic species, despite "mixing" resulting from restocking programs, would provide a somewhat similar list. In the last major descriptive study, Goldman and Kellogg (1940) relied primarily on pelage color, external dimensions, cranial details, and antler tine-size and spread. It is possible to evaluate some of these gross characteristics geographically (*see also* chapters 3 and 4).

Color

In general, the white-tailed deer is darker in the humid, forested areas of the eastern United States and relatively paler in the drier, more open brushlands of western and southwestern North America, including much of the Mexican Plateau. Colors may become more reddish (sometimes blackish) in subtropical and tropical environments (Kellog 1956). The presence of a pale (reddish-brown) summer coat contrasting with a more drab (gray or grayish-brown) winter coat characterizes most North and Central American whitetail populations. Brokx (1972a) described like seasonal molts with the same two distinct colors for whitetails in Venezuela. High Andean populations, on the other hand, may retain a grayish pelage year-round, while tropical whitetails may keep the tawny, reddish phase permanently (Hershkovitz 1958). Pelage color of deer from intermediate climatic and altitudinal areas in these tropical latitudes may show a blending of gray and red. In white-tailed deer in northern latitudes and at high altitudes, the pelage is longer and thicker than that of tropical, lowland animals. In the montane tropics, long pelage also is the rule (Behrendt 1960).

Weight

Most authors point to evidence that weight in this species has clinal tendencies, with the heaviest deer—weighing more than 136 kilograms (300 pounds)—living in northern latitudes (northern United States and southern Canada) and the lightest deer—weighing less than 23 kilograms (50 pounds)—living in tropical, insular habitats (Florida Keys and Isla de Coiba in the Gulf of Panama). For example, mature whitetail bucks in different geographic regions have reported-live-weights of 91–137 kilograms (200–300 pounds) in Ontario (Peterson 1966); 110 kilograms (240 pounds) in Wisconsin (Jackson 1961); an average of 93 kilograms (207 pounds) in Kansas (Anderson 1964); 60 kilograms (130 pounds) in Louisiana (Lowery 1974); 37–77 kilograms (81–170 pounds) in Texas (Teer et al. 1965); 36–55 kilograms (80–120 pounds) in Panama (Méndez 1970); 30–50 kilograms (66–110 pounds) in eastern Colombia (R. A. Blouch personal communication:1976); 46 kilograms (101 pounds) in Venezuela (Brokx 1972a); 25–30 kilograms (55–66 pounds) in coastal lowlands of Peru and 44–55 kilograms (99–121 pounds) in Peruvian highlands above 3,500 meters (11,480 feet) (Behrendt 1960). There are, of course, exceptional sizes of adult bucks in all areas. Also, as a rule, mature, nonpregnant does weigh 60 to 75 percent of what adult bucks weigh.

Height and Length

Mature white-tailed bucks of northern latitudes (notably of the subspecies *O. v. borealis*

and *O. v. dacotensis*) are relatively tall, standing approximately 1,020 millimeters (40 inches) at shoulder height. This dimension for Texas white-tailed deer is approximately 914 millimeters (36 inches). In northeastern Brazil, shoulder height of bucks of the subspecies *O. v. cariacou* is about 810 millimeters (32 inches). On Isla Margarita, off the coast of Venezuela, adult bucks of *O. v. margaritae* are approximately 610 millimeters (24 inches) at the shoulder. In Peru, males of the subspecies *O. v. peruvianus* averaged 620 millimeters (25 inches) when from coastal lowlands and 742 millimeters (30 inches) when from highlands above 3,500 meters (11,480 feet) (Behrendt 1960).

Total length (from the tip of nose to the end of the terminal caudal vertebra) also shows a north-south size gradation. In the northeastern United States and southern Canada, adult bucks may be as long as 2,400 millimeters (95 inches). Elsewhere, the approximate lengths for whitetails have been reported as: 1,829 millimeters (72 inches) in Texas; 1,530 millimeters (60 inches) in mountains of the southwestern United States; 1,400 millimeters (55 inches) in Panama; 1,220 millimeters (48 inches) on Isla de Coiba; 1,220–1,480 millimeters (48–58 inches) in eastern Colombia; and 1,570 millimeters (62 inches) in northeastern Venezuela. Data are from R. A. Blouch (personal communication:1976), Kellogg (1956), Méndez (1970) and Osgood (1912).

Antler Size

Although whitetail antler dimensions depend on such factors as age, virility and diet, that latitudinal differences exist in these adornments in the case of healthy, full-prime bucks is well-illustrated by Figure 13.

Metatarsal Gland

This gland, situated on the outer side of each metatarsus, usually presents a darkish, bare aspect, variable in shape. Although smaller than that of the mule deer, the metatarsal of the white-tailed deer reaches a maximum length of about 41 millimeters (1.61 inches). This dimension is attained only in whitetail populations in Canada and the United States, where both the glandular area and the associated circumglandular specialized hair (tufts) are prominent. As demonstrated by Hershkovitz (1958), in white-tailed deer from southern Mexico to

Figure 13. Comparative skull sizes and antler dimensions of adult whitetail bucks of approximately the same age from Venezuela (top) and Michigan (bottom) reflect latitudinal variation.

northern South America the size and major features of metatarsal glands diminish with decreasing latitude, becoming either poorly defined or undeveloped. In Venezuela, for example, Brokx (1972a) found *O. v. gymnotis* lacking the glands completely, but retaining small metatarsal tufts. Although the metatarsal's function has to do with such important matters as sex, age and individual recognition (Müller-Schwarze 1971), the reason for its geographic variation in size is obscure.

One can guess that geographic variations among white-tailed deer could substantially increase in the future. This could happen as a result of the isolating effects of the mosaic distributional patterns to which white-tailed deer are now increasingly being subjected—and surely will continue to be subjected so long as man continues to manipulate the natural environment and, in so doing, set up additional barriers within the habitat-continuum of the species.

Chapter 2

OF SLINGS AND ARROWS:
AN HISTORICAL RETROSPECTION

Richard E. McCabe
Director of Publications
Wildlife Management Institute
Washington, D.C.

Thomas R. McCabe
Assistant Professor
Department of Fisheries
and Wildlife Sciences
South Dakota State University
Brookings, South Dakota

In the annals of wildlife management in North America, there are few success stories as great as that of the white-tailed deer. Some persons contend that the impressive whitetail record is a direct consequence of scientific management. Others point to the animal's innate resilience to altered environments, particularly those of human design. In addition, there are those who consider the recent history of white-tailed deer anything but a success, and are quick to note crop and other property damages and highway accidents that are direct consequences of abundant whitetail populations. These skeptics will argue that the whitetail has received too much investment from the wild-life profession, prompted by the demand for recreational hunting, and that other species and biological problems have been neglected as a result.

These differing perspectives will bear significantly on future attitudes toward the white-tailed deer and its management. No one, however, can deny that the whitetail's modern history has been remarkable. That history—from late pre-Columbian times to the advent and early initiatives of the discipline of wildlife management—is the focus of this chapter.

"To understand fully the culture of a region," proposed Henderson and Harrington (1914:5), "it is necessary to know something of the native animals. . . ." We believe the reciprocal to be equally valid.

This presentation does not purport to be a complete account of the whitetail's historical status and role, even for the brief period under consideration. It is intended to highlight *some* of the important interactions the species has had with the North American landscape and its human inhabitants, particularly the relationship of whitetails and American Indians.

There were tremendous cultural and economic differences among aboriginal groups, both temporally and spatially, within the vast range of the white-tailed deer, and we caution readers against ascribing to all Indians, or even most, the circumstances, industries, social organization and behavior of the tribes documented herein.

Additional whitetail history is presented in the regional chapters of this book.

NEW WORLD WHITETAILS

Range and Habitat

When European vanguards reached the "New World," the white-tailed deer thrived in forest edges, upland glades and riverine woodlands, on the fringes of deserts, and in pockets of montane foothills. The animal's greatest abundance occurred on islands and in coastal wetlands along the eastern seaboard and Gulf region (Trefethen 1970). The whitetail also occupied the timberland belts interspersed with savannahs and prairie between the eastern hardwood forests and the Mississippi River (Bogardus 1874). It inhabited forest and prairie slough edges of the Midwest, and riparian bottomlands of tall- and mixed-grasslands across the Great Plains. Shorelines and river banks in the Northeast and Great Lakes regions supported large numbers of deer as well, although populations in the northern snowbelt experienced marked numerical fluctuation and geographical oscillation as a result of severe winters and also predation, principally by wolves (Bailey 1907, Wood 1910, Shiras 1921, Allen 1929, Young and Goldman 1944, Swift 1946, Richards 1949, Severinghaus and Brown 1956, Silver 1957).

Some writers have concluded that whitetails did not occur extensively in the vast tracts of gentle topography that supported mature, virgin forest (Trefethen 1970, McKeever 1954, *see also* Severinghaus and Brown 1956). Others have reported that deer abounded in climax forests, such as those of central New England (Richards 1949, Hosley 1937). There is a general consensus, however, that white-tailed deer did not regularly or abundantly occupy the treeless western flatlands and deserts, to which they were not well adapted.

Certain meteorological events, such as hurricanes, tornadoes and windstorms, plus insect and disease damage, continually contributed to the rejuvenation of seral stage vegetation and edge, which favor deer. But most influential was fire. Each year within the range of the white-tailed deer, lightning from electrical storms ignited millions of acres of vegetation—greatly more than is burned today (Jenkins and Bartlett 1959). And although wildfires were highly destructive of some native vegetation—occuring, as they did, principally in summer months, when arid conditions and fuel accumulation and flammability are at a peak—they ultimately proved beneficial to many local wildlife populations (*see* Lewis 1977).

Setting back plant succession by fire also was a common practice among most North American Indian tribes (Stewart 1951), although apparently there were great variations in time, place, degree of skill and foresight regarding the utilization of fire both as process and tool. Allen (1970:11) wrote of Indian incendiary practices that, "Wherever plant cover would burn, it was burned repeatedly as part of the cultural way of life." We consider that an overstatement, even though fire was used extensively by Indians for purposes of swidden agriculture, protection against natural fires, insect control, stimulation of certain berry-producing food plants, warfare and defense, hunting, maintenance of travel routes, and rejuvenation of forage and browse vegetation attractive to wildlife (*see* Nuttall 1821, Maxwell 1910, Stewart 1954, Barrett and Arno 1982, McCabe 1982). Each year the aboriginals intentionally fired thousands of square miles in the historic range of whitetails, and in so doing helped to sustain deer populations in many areas

In forested portions of pristine North America, natural fires and those set for a variety of purposes by Indians created open areas and prompted early successional-stage vegetation which were attractive to white-tailed deer and certain other wildlife. On the continent's grasslands, fires also were frequent, but tended to prevent growth and spread of woodland cover required to support high whitetail densities. *Photo from Dengler (1923), after a drawing by Rudolph Friederich Kurz, a Swiss artist who visited the western frontier from 1846 to 1852.*

(Trefethen 1970, *see also* Day 1953, Lay 1957, Prunty 1965).

Distribution

Ernest Thompson Seton (1909[I]:75) presented a map that featured what he termed the ". . . original range" of the white-tailed deer in North and Central America. He based the map and delineated range ". . . on much personal experience and the records of several hundred ancient and modern travellers" (Figure 14). Seton (1909, 1929) described the most favorable parts of the range as comprising 5.2

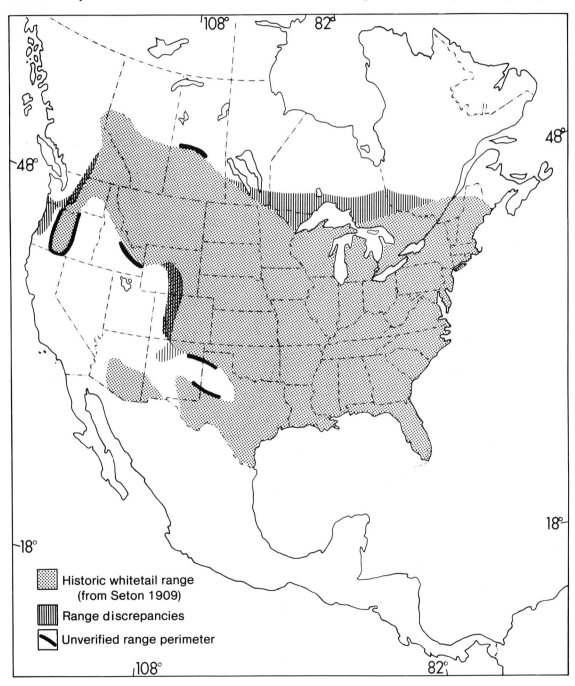

Figure 14. Possible late-prehistoric/early-historic range of white-tailed deer in the United States and Canada.

million square kilometers (2.0 million square miles). As determined by cartographic scaling (R. Pratt personal communication:1983), the full extent of the historic whitetail range in the United States and Canada, shown on Seton's map, closely approximated 7.6 million square kilometers (2.95 million square miles).

By examining historic records, including firsthand accounts of explorers, traders, government surveyors and settlers, plus archeological site investigations and Indian lexicons, we were able to verify most of the historic whitetail range Seton proposed. However there are areas of uncertainty and several discrepancies both within and external to Seton's range perimeter. The external discrepancies represent a somewhat larger total area (Figure 14). Despite problems in precise determination, and in general given the entirely problematic nature of the inquiry, we conclude that 7.8 million square kilometers (3.0 million square miles) is a reasonable estimate of the late-prehistoric/early historic range of the white-tailed deer north of Mexico.

Abundance

The literature is filled with accounts by adventurers who penetrated the American wilderness and appraised the variety and numbers of wildlife. White-tailed deer were mentioned prominently in many of the earliest records. One of the difficulties encountered in documenting early whitetail observations in North America is the fact that the species was known by a variety of names, including Virginia deer, common deer, jumping deer, long-tailed deer, bannertail, flag-tailed deer, fallow deer and roe deer. In exploration and colonial times, for example, "red deer" commonly referred to elk. As late as the 1880s that name was used to characterize whitetails in summer pelage. Also, many firsthand accounts or their translations simply cited "deer," without descriptive detail. For this narrative we excluded references in which conclusive identification was not possible.

Florentine explorer and discoverer of New York, Giovanni da Verrazano, recorded ". . . stags, roes and hares" along the Atlantic coast in 1524 (Lescarbot 1907[I]:54).

From 1539 to 1542, Hernando de Soto's army found venison and whitetail hides extensively used by Indians in what is now Florida, Geor-

gia, South Carolina, southern Tennessee, Alabama, Mississippi, Arkansas and Louisiana (Swanton 1946, Bourne 1904). The same was true of the expeditioners led by Alvar Nuñez Cabeza de Vaca through southern Texas in 1535 (Bandelier 1905). And in the company of Spaniard Francisco Vásquez de Coronado, who led an expedition of conquistadors on a trek through the Southwest from 1540 to 1542, Pedro de Castañeda noted in his journal: "There are large numbers of bears in this providence, and lions, wildcats, deer, and others" (Winship 1896:518). At that time the expedition was in southcentral Arizona, so he may have seen both whitetails and mule deer.

Jacques le Moyne de Morgues, a cartographer and artist with the French Huguenot expedition to Florida under Rene de Laudonniére in 1564, described whitetails as ". . . very plentiful in those regions" (Le Moyne 1875:10).

Jacques Cartier, on his exploration of the St. Lawrence River in 1545, reported, ". . . a great store of Stags Deere, Beares, and other like sorts of beasts . . ." (Hakluyt 1589[III]:231).

In a 1584 report to Sir Walter Raleigh, who was attempting to establish a colony on Roanoke Island, Captain Arthur Barlowe (1589:96) described the site: "This island had many goodly woods, fulle of Deere, Conies [rabbits], Hares, and Fowle, even in the middest of Summer, in incredible abundance." An English mathematician in Raleigh's service in the 1580s, Thomas Hariot (1893:29) nearly echoed Cartier's words of 40 years earlier: "Of. . . Deare, in some places there are great store. . . ." He added that ". . . neere vnto the sea coast they are of the ordinarie bignes as ours in England, & some lesse: but further vp in the countrey where there is better seed they are greater: they differ from ours onley in this, their tailes are longer, and the snags of their hornes looke backward." Reportedly it was this characterization of the whitetails on Roanoke Island and inland Virginia that was the basis for subsequent classification of the species as "Virginia deer" (Seton 1909[I]:73).

Captain John Smith and his company ". . . met diuers Saluages in Conowes, well loaded with the flesh of Bears, Deere and other beasts . . ." (McAtee 1918:5) in June of 1608, in the vicinity of what now is the District of Columbia.

At Plymouth Colony, Puritan leader William Bradford announced that the Massachusetts Bay environment was ". . . but a hideous and desolate wilderness full of wild beasts and wild

In his description of Southern Algonquian Indians inhabiting the coastal area near Roanoke Island, North Carolina, in the late 1500s, Thomas Hariot (1893:57) wrote: "They take muche pleasure in huntinge deer wher of ther is greate store in the contrye, for yt is fruitfull pleasant, and full of Goodly woods." Another member of Sir Walter Raleigh's first colonizing contingent, along with Hariot, was John White. White was the group's artist and, as such, the first English artist in the New World. He later was governor of the ill-fated second "Virginia" settlement (the "Lost Colony") in 1587, but while the first colony's resident artist, he produced a watercolor painting in 1585 of the scene above. That art was copied as an engraving on copper by Flemish goldsmith Theodore de Bry for his publication, *A Briefe and True Report of the New Found Land of Virginia* (1590). *Photo courtesy of the Smithsonian Institution National Anthropological Archives.*

men" (Borland 1975:44). In October of 1621, however, Bradford invited friendly Wampanoag chief Massasoit and 90 of his followers to a three-day thanksgiving feast. When the "wild men" arrived and saw how little food the colonists had for the occasion, they promptly retired to the woods and killed enough deer to feed all of the 140 or so celebrants.

Thomas Morton (1883[14]:20), chronicling the settlement of New England in 1632, noted that: ". . . the most usefull and most beneficiall beast which is bredd in those parts . . . is the Deare. There are in the Country three kindes of Deare of which there are great plenty. . . ."

The first colonists to settle in Maryland in 1634 included Roman Catholic priest Father Andrew White, who observed whitetails so plentiful ". . . that they are rather an annoy-ance than an advantage" (Dozer 1976:22).

Exploring the southern coast of Maine in 1658, Sir Fernando Gorges related that ". . . at our first discovery of those coasts, we found . . . the country plentiful in grain and other fruits besides deer of all sorts . . ." (Allen 1929:253).

In the early 1660s, *coureur de bois* Pierre Radisson (1882:82) provided the first report of ". . . fallow bucks and does" in what now is Wisconsin. Subsequent presettlement (before 1832) visitors to the Great Lakes region—including Jesuit missionary Claude Allouez (1858) in the 1669, trader Pierre Le Sueur (Margry 1886) in the 1690s, soldier John Long (1922) in 1780, soldier Zebulon Pike (Swift 1946) in 1805–1806, and Indian agent, historian and ethnographer Henry Schoolcraft (1855) in 1832—invariably remarked on the abundance of whitetails. For example, on a French military campaign against Fox Indians in the Green Bay (Wisconsin) area in 1728, De Lignery (1868:89) wrote: "Our savages [tribe(s) uncertain] went into the woods, but soon returned bringing with them several roebucks. This species of game is very common at this place, and we [the combined attack force of 400 French soldiers and 1,000 Indians] were enabled to lay in several days provisions of it."

German traveler John Lederer approached the Blue Ridge Mountains west of what now is Culpeper, Virginia, in March 1670, where "Great herds of Red and Fallow Deer I daily saw feeding . . ." (Cumming 1958:17).

Father Jacques Marquette and fur trapper Louis Jolliet, while locating and exploring the upper reaches of the Mississippi River and its major tributaries in 1674, traversed the Illinois/Des Plaines river valleys. Marquette wrote that he had " . . . seen nothing like this river

[the Illinois] for the fertility of the land, its prairies, woods, wild cattle, stag, deer, wildcats, bustards, swans, ducks, parrots, and even beaver" (Cumming et al. 1974:36).

"There is such infinite Herds [of white-tailed deer]," declared Thomas Ashe in 1682, "that the whole country [Carolina] seems but one continued park" (Carroll 1836[2]:72).

From Chautauqua County in New York in 1687, Baron LaHouton corresponded: "I cannot express what quantities of deer and turkeys are to be found in these woods and in the vast meads that lie upon the south side of the lake [Erie]" (Edson and Merrill 1894[I]:40).

From 1690 to 1700, independent fur trapper Samuel York resided in southern Ontario ". . . in the Ottowawas country. . . . There is excellent hunting there for beaver and all sorts of wild beasts as Deer Moose, &c" (O'Callaghan and Fernow 1856–1887[IV]:749).

Christopher Gist, an agent for the Ohio Land

"The Landing of William Penn," painted in oil by Thomas Birch (1770–1851), illustrates a whitetail-hunting Indian's hesitant reception of the Puritan leader's show of friendship upon his arrival in 1682. Unlike many other newcomers to America, Penn treated openly and fairly with the Indians. He also provided a valuable record of the manners and customs of the Delaware Indians, including the remark that males attained esteem among their tribesman ". . . by a good return of [deer] Skins . . ." (Myers 1912:231). *Photo courtesy of the Museum of Fine Arts, Boston.*

Company, explored southwestern Ohio in February 1751 and reported a ''. . . rich, level land, well timbered with large Walnut, Ash, Sugar Trees, Cherry Trees &c, it is well watered with a number of little Streams or Rivulets, and full of beautiful natural Meadows, covered with wild Rye, blue Grass and Clover and abounds with Turkeys, Deer, Elks and most sorts of Game . . .'' (Darlington 1893:57–58).

Ascending the Mississippi River in 1766, surveyor Jonathan Carver (1778:54–55) described the Minnesota/Wisconsin landscape at Lake Pepin: ''The land betwixt the mountains [bluffs], and on their sides, is generally covered with grass with a few groves of trees interspersed, near which large droves of deer and elk are frequently seen feeding.''

Virginian Henry Timberlake, having traversed lands occupied by Cherokee Indians in 1775, remarked on ''. . . an incredible number of . . . deer'' (Burt and Ferguson 1973:75).

Englishman Isaac Weld (1799:463) found on Long Island, New York, ''immense quantities of game and deer . . . amidst the brushwood. . . .''

Frontiersman Daniel Boone remarked to John James Audubon that, in the Green River region of Kentucky not 30 years earlier (in the 1780s), ''. . . you would not have walked out in any direction for more than a mile without shooting a buck . . .'' (Bakeless 1965:403).

Describing the mostly uncharted Midwest in 1785, English naturalist Thomas Pennant wrote of, ''A plain, rich in woods and savannas, swarming with Bisons or buffaloes, Stags, and Virginia Deer . . . from the great lakes of Canada, as low as the gulph of Mexico; and eastward to . . . the Apalachian . . .'' (Matthiessen 1959:72).

U.S. Army Captain Randolph Marcy (1859:238–239) prepared a travelogue of the Southwest for the benefit of prospective pioneers, in which he wrote: ''In passing through Southern Texas in 1846, thousands of deer ['. . . common red deer of the Eastern States . . .'] were met daily, and as astonishing as it may appear, it was no uncommon spectacle to see from one to two hundred in a single herd; the prairies seemed literally alive with them. . . .'' Dodge (1877) reported having seen about 1,000 whitetails in a wintering herd in Texas.

H. M. T. Powell (1931:123) traveled through southern New Mexico and Arizona toward the gold fields of California in 1849, and while in the bottom of Guadalupe Canyon, on the west side of the Guadalupe Mountains, he took note that ''Deer are plentiful here, but very small [undoubtedly in reference to Coues whitetails]; venison plenty in camp.'' Five years later a government party surveying the Gadsden Purchase boundary included Dr. C. B. R. Kennerly, who took notes on the region's flora and fauna. ''The Virginian deer,'' he recorded, ''so common throughout the entire State of Texas, and particularly its southwestern portion, was also observed by us in considerable numbers west of the Rio Grande. Indeed, we believe that few species of animals are so generally spread over the entire continent as this, and at the same time in such great numbers. . . . In the valley of the Santa Cruz river and the adjacent country we found them in such numbers as to influence the belief that a few skillful hunters might have supplied our entire company with fresh meat'' (Davis 1982:82).

The preceding represent *some* of the earliest historical accounts of whitetail abundance; confirming reports by later travelers are equally impressive. However, there also are records of exploration and settlement within portions of the whitetail range that despaired the lack of game, including deer, entirely or seasonally. Notable among these early documentations are those found in Thwaites (1959, 1966, 1969), Coues (1965), Hough (1883), Chittendon (1935) and Wrong (1939). Obviously whitetails were not distributed uniformly throughout the species' total range. And just as certainly their population size varied from year to year, depending on weather conditions, predation and Indian hunting pressure.

Mech (1977b) theorized that whitetail numbers historically were greatest in the territorial overlaps of wolf packs, and these buffer areas may have been reservoirs for the deer. Earlier, Hickerson (1965:43) presented a parallel argument concerning whitetails and Indians: ''Warfare between members of the two tribes [Chippewa and Sioux in Minnesota] had the effect of preventing competing hunters from occupying the best game region intensively enough to deplete the deer supply. . . .''

Additional evidence of the abundance of whitetails in pristine North America comes from early fur trade records. Exportation tallies (Table 3), of which there are many, are simply staggering when one considers how few persons—Indian and white—actually were involved in this unregulated commerce. It should be recognized that the examples in Table 3

Table 3. Records of white-tailed deer hide exportation from some trade centers in the United States and Canada, 1698–1885.

Date	Location	Quantity of hides	Source
1698–1715	Virginia	Averaged approximately 13,755 per year[a]	Crane (1928)
1698–1715	Carolina	Averaged approximately 50,250 per year[a]	Crane (1928)
1715–1735	South Carolina	Averaged approximately 75,000 per year[a]	Crane (1928)
1739–1765	Charleston, South Carolina	Averaged approximately 151,000 per year[a]	Crane (1928)
1753	North Carolina	30,000	Young (1956)
1755–1773	Georgia	90,720 kilograms (100 tons)	Harlow and Jones (1965)
1758	New Jersey	Skins and venison worth 120 pounds sterling	Rhoads (1903)
1763	West Virginia	"Thousands . . . at 18 pence a pound"	Kellogg (1937:473)
1771	Pensacola, Florida and Mobile, Alabama	113,400 kilograms (125 tons)	Harlow and Jones (1965)
1786	Quebec	132,271	Young (1956)
1800	Canada	369,327	Phillips (1961)
1806	Fort William, Ontario	4,971	Coues (1965)
1808	Burlington, Iowa	28,021	Gue (1903)
1815–1830	Santa Fe, New Mexico	68,000 kilograms (75 tons) per year[b]	Chittenden (1935)
1820	Fort Orange and Prairie du Chien, Wisconsin	14,600 kilograms (16.1 tons)	McKenney (1827)
1833	North Dakota[c]	20,000–30,000[b]	Wied (1843)
1835–1836	Green Bay and Milwaukee, Wisconsin	20,966	Schorger (1953)
1844–1853	Texas	75,000[b]	Strecker (1927)
1859	Indiana	1,130[d]	Anonymous (1906)
1870	St. Paul, Minnesota	3,859	Swanson (1940)
1872[e]	Litchfield, Minnesota	5,446 kilgrams (6 tons)	Petraborg and Burcalow (1965)
1877	Iowa	36,300 kilograms (40 tons)	Taylor (1975)
1876–1880	Wyoming	$10,000 worth of whitetail and other big game hides[b,f]	Cook (1923)
1880	Lower peninsula, Michigan	50,000–100,000	Jenkins and Bartlett (1959), Mershon (1923)
1881	Southern Missouri	1,815 kilograms (2 tons) of venison and 680 kilograms (0.75 ton) of buckskins[g]	Robb (1959)
1885	Wisconsin	10,000	Bersing (1966)

[a]Calculated from capacities of hogsheads and chests in which the skins were shipped to England and Germany.
[b]Likely included mule deer hides.
[c]Trading posts of the American Fur Company along the Missouri River, principally in North Dakota and Montana.
[d]Reportedly the harvest of a single trapper.
[e]For the month of December.
[f]The profit of two market hunters.
[g]Marketed by brothers in a single family.

from various parts of the whitetail range do not necessarily represent totals for the entire state or area for the year listed. Furthermore, whitetails were not a preferred or an actively sought trade commodity in the early historical period (Chittendon 1935), except in parts of the Southeast (Franklin 1932, Swanton 1946, Phillips 1961, Hudson 1981) and the Ohio River Valley (Hanna 1911, Goddard 1978). They were harvested first and foremost for food and clothing by both Indians and pioneers. When the commercial trade in deer hides reached its zenith in the 1700s, the best buckskins were sent to England, the next best to Germany and the lightest, least desirable hides were used within the colonies (Crane 1928).

Actual early-historical density estimates of whitetails are few. Morton (1883) wrote of having found 39 whitetails per square kilometer (100 per square mile) during spring in colonial New England. In 1820 Noah Major estimated 22.4 whitetails per square kilometer (58 per square mile) over a 900-square-kilometer (345-square-mile) portion of Indiana (Sandburg 1926). On a 121-hectare (300-acre) park near Baltimore, Maryland, in 1830, ". . . 200 deer may often be seen at a single view" (Young 1956:18). Bersing (1966) suggested a density of 9.7 whitetails per square kilometer (25 per square mile) in parts of Wisconsin prior to initial settlement in the 1830s, and Dahlberg and Guettinger (1956) estimated deer abundance in mature northern hardwood/coniferous forests of the Great Lakes region to have been 3.9–5.8 per square kilometer (10–15 per square mile). Some whitetail hunts by Indians and by settlers accounted for a *minimum* of 19 deer per square kilometer (50 per square mile) (*see* Swanson 1940, Schorger 1953, Thwaites 1959, Bohley 1964).

Seton (1909[I]:78) conjectured that, ". . . in primitive times 10 to the square mile is a safe estimate of white-tailed population" in the 5.2-million-square-kilometer (2-million-square-mile) area—the Mississippi River Valley and eastward—he considered most favorable for the species. Later, Seton (1929[3–1]:244) revised the primitive whitetail density figure to ". . . a very conservative estimate" of 7.7 deer per square kilometer (20 per square mile), for a total of 40 million animals.

Elder (1965:369) wrote: "There is little doubt that deer are much more numerous today than under primeval conditions. Logging, clearing, alternating periods of fire control have vastly increased the area and carrying capacity of modern deer range in much of the United States. The abundance of agricultural crops is another tremendous factor permitting modern deer herds to exceed in size those of the Indian era" (*see also* Matthiessen 1959). We disagree with the assertion that whitetail abundance is greater now than it was "under primeval conditions" or during the "Indian era." As improbable as Seton's various whitetail population-number and density estimates may seem to be by current perceptions and standards, we conclude that they were not unrealistic.

INDIAN SUMMERS

At the time of North America's "discovery" and until about 1800, the Indian population within the assumed range of white-tailed deer was approximately 2.34 million. This is based on density estimates ranging from less than 10 Indians per 100 square kilometers (26 per 100 square miles) to more than 375 per 100 square kilometers (970 per 100 square miles), and averaged at 30 per 100 square kilometers (78 per 100 square miles) (Spinden 1928, Driver and Massey 1957, Driver 1968, Oswalt 1966). The highest concentrations occurred along coastal New York, Massachusetts, Virginia, North Carolina and Georgia. Next highest concentrations were in the Gulf states, the St. Lawrence River region, the forested Midwest and the rest of the eastern seacoast. Least populated were the prairie regions from the Ohio River Valley westward into the Great Plains.

The arrival of Europeans in Canada and the United States, and the concomitant emergence of two critical influences—horses and fur trade—prompted major aboriginal territorial shifts and cultural diffusions during the period in question. There is great irony in the characterization of North America as the "New World" by early immigrants. In reality, it was to them an extension of their homelands. Only for the aboriginal inhabitants—erroneously and forever after called "Indians"—did the continent that was their home, territory and world become "new." The abrupt change was one they were unable to comprehend or prevent. It has been suggested that Amerinds were not so much defeated as simply overwhelmed (DeVoto 1947). Essentially the same can be said for whitetails. It was not coincidental that Indian and whitetail alike succumbed simultaneously to relentless waves of foreigners representing various socioeconomic and political ambitions characterized by the stages of discovery, dominion, sovereignty, nationalization, and finally Manifest Destiny.

Before and even during the colonization of North America, however, the white-tailed deer continued to be a vital element in the subsistence economy and culture of many of the native people.

Subsistence

Even with bison, moose, elk and black bear available in many parts of the whitetail range, deer were the most widespread principal source of meat for Indians (Hodge 1907), followed generally by bison in the West (McHugh 1972, *see also* McCabe 1982) and by beaver, bear,

In 1895, on Key Marco (now Marco Island) off the west coast of southern Florida, archeologist Frank Hamilton Cushing (1896) unearthed a number of exquisite carvings, including the deer-head masquette shown above. The wooden head is 27.3 centimeters (10.75 inches) long, and was thought to have been used in ceremonial rites by the now-extinct Calusa Indians. The carving retains traces of paint, and features individually-carved ears with leather hinges so they could be moved by strings. The eyes were shell inlays, and on the crown at the head were peg holes for the attachment of small antlers. Douglas and d'Harnoncourt (1941:96) wrote: "In delicacy of treatment and degree of realism this deer head is unequalled in Indian art and is the finest surviving creation of the fifteenth century Calusa wood-carving. . . ." *Photo courtesy of the University of Pennsylvania University Museum.*

moose, raccoon, bison, elk, wild turkey, waterfowl, fish, shellfish and other small game in the East (Salwen 1978, Tuck 1978, Ritchie 1969). To be sure, hoe agriculture, wild-plant gathering and fishing were significant in producing food for tribes that also hunted whitetails. But with few exceptions the Indians were meat-eaters (Driver 1969, *see also* Trigger 1978); agricultural crops, native plants and fish supplemented meat in the diet, not *vice versa*. And of the available meats, undoubtedly venison was the most widely available and reliable source of protein (*see* Lawson 1967, Barnwell 1908). Samuel de Champlain (1929[3]:81) wrote in the early 1600s that whitetail hunting by Huron Indians ". . . is considered among them the noblest as it is the most fruitful sport."

The literature is replete with assertions that the whitetail was the most important wildlife species for numerous tribes and cultural groups. Examples include: Snow (1978*a*) for the East

Coast; Witthoft (1953*a*) and Williams (1972) for Upper New England; Allen (1929) for southern New England; Fenton (1978) and Heidenreich (1978) for the St. Lawrence lowlands region; Marston (1912) and Ritzenthaler (1978) for the Upper Midwest; Swanton (1946), Burt and Ferguson (1973), and Maxwell (1978) for the Southeast; Mayhall (1939) and Campbell (1983) for the Gulf Coast; and Opler (1983) for the Southwest (*see also* Morrison 1878), to name a very few. The above authors do not imply that any tribes within the regions mentioned relied exclusively on the whitetail for animal food.

The relative importance of white-tailed deer in the Indian diet also is evidenced by remains found in various middens throughout the East. One example is the Buffalo Village Site in Putnam County, West Virginia (McMichael 1963, Guilday 1971). Located along the Kanawha River, this 1.6-hectare (4-acre) site was occupied—until European contact in the late 1600s—by a long succession of Indians that formed a peripheral group of the Fort Ancient complex (late-Woodland, post-Howellian culture of the central Ohio Valley, 1000–1700 A.D.). They were a fairly sedentary farming and hunting people, whose village contained from 500 to 1,000 persons at any given time. Archeological investigation of site-remains revealed that whitetails comprised 44 percent (746) of the total of individual animals identified. (This total included 24 species of mammals, 30 bird species, 10 reptile species, 1 amphibian species and 13 species of fish.) Next in percentage-of-total after whitetail came wild turkey (11.4 percent), box turtle (8.8 percent), drumfish (6.5 percent) and raccoon (5.5 percent). Second to deer among large mammals was black bear (0.8 percent). In terms of meat yield, whitetails reportedly accounted for 89.2 percent of all animal food, followed by black bear (3.3 percent) and wild turkey (1.9 percent).

Further evidence comes from a great many other archeological investigations in which animal remains were identified (*see* Abbott 1893, Smith 1974). At the Kipp Island Site in New York, for example, whitetail parts represented 33 percent of all identifiable faunal remains (2,255 items) (Guilday and Tanner 1965*a*). Given projected weights of individual animals of 31 identified species, whitetails constituted about 55 percent of the biomass consumed, followed by bullheads (fish) and black bears (15 percent each) and elk (10 percent). Ritchie (1965) indicated that the Kipp Island Site was a sporadically inhabited fishing camp. It is particularly noteworthy, therefore, that even though the inhabitants would be classified principally as fishermen, the vastly greater proportion of their diet while in residence (summer months) appears to have been venison.

Furthermore, at the Mt. Carbon Site in Fayette County, West Virginia (Guilday and Tanner 1965*b*); the Eschelman Site in Lancaster County, Pennsylvania (Guilday et al. 1962); and the Tick Creek Cave Site in Missouri (Parmalee 1965), composite remains of white-tailed deer outnumbered those of black bear by 5 to 1, 5.5 to 1 and 275 to 1 respectively. Whitetail remains outnumbered those of elk at the Mt. Carbon and Eschelman sites 34 to 1 and 8.7 to 1 respectively. Wild turkey, the second most common vertebrate found in eastern Indian refuse collections (Guilday 1971), was outnumbered by deer at those same two sites 7.7 to 1 and 6.25 to 1 respectively. And from a Mohegan site in Connecticut, the archeological record indicates that whitetails constituted 90 percent of the animal meat consumed by Indians at the time of European contact in the 1500s (Salwen 1970, Williams 1972).

When considering the composition and relative abundance of animal remains in middens it should be recognized that most whitetails were taken at some distance from the Indians' villages (often several days' travel) (*see* Feest 1978, Fenton 1978). The usual practice was to butcher the animals on the kill site and haul back only the most edible parts, particularly of the larger mammals. Thus, certain bones and other nondigestible parts were not commonly found in middens. Also, Guilday (1971) made reference to extensive scavenging and removal by camp dogs—commonplace animals in virtually all Indian villages—especially of the larger and presumably meatier bones, such as those necessary to distinguish deer from other fragmentary remains. Thus, in some cases deer may actually be under-represented in midden accumulations.

From the Buffalo Site in West Virginia, researchers examined 345 left-lower jaws of whitetailed deer, separating them into age classes, following Severinghaus (1949*b*). Ages ranged from one week to 10 years or older. The average age at harvest was 3.5 to 4.5 years. Similar results were gained from whitetail age examinations from midden remains at Arnold Research Cave (1000 B.C. to 1000 A.D.), Tick Creek Cave (800 to 1200 A.D.) and the Utz Site (1500 to 1700 A.D.) in Missouri (Elder 1965), the Eschelman Site in Pennsylvania (Guilday et al. 1962), and Conner's Midden in Virginia (McGinnes and Reeves 1958). Also, it was presumed that approximately 60 percent of these whitetails were killed in winter (November to April) (Guilday 1971).

Sexing by frontal bone inspection at the Buffalo Site revealed that at least 43 percent of the whitetails harvested were mature bucks. At the Tick Creek Cave Site, 23 percent of the identified deer (N = 759) were adult males (Parmalee 1965), as were 26 percent (N = 182) at the Eschelman Site (Guilday et al. 1962).

Based on a number of assumptions it is possible to obtain an estimate of the degree of Indian utilization of white-tailed deer for food. As previously discussed, the speculated historic range of whitetails in the United States and Canada was roughly 7.8 million square kilometers (3 million square miles). That range also was the home of approximately 2.34 million Indians. If, on the average, each Indian ate 0.91 kilogram (2 pounds) of animal food each day, of which 25 percent was venison, the total annual consumption of whitetail meat was about 194 million kilograms (427 million pounds). By calculating the food yield at 30.3–42.4 kilograms (66.8–93.6 pounds) per deer—computed from an average live weight of 45.4—63.5 kilograms (100–140 pounds) (*see* Severinghaus 1949*c*) for all ages and both sexes of deer, and accepting edible viscera at 32.5 percent of live weight, meat yield at 48 percent of hog-dressed carcass-weight-minus-bones (Field et al. 1973), and a 1-percent loss due to wastage or damage—we surmise that Indians in Canada and the United States may have harvested 4.6 to 6.4 million whitetails annually.

On the basis of the above information it is possible to estimate the precolonial whitetail population size and density in the United States and Canada. When making such assessments one must take into account a number of deer population characteristics, including the percentage mortality induced by Indians. Because of the impossibility of determining these historic values directly, we must speculate, based on current knowledge, as to what the ramifications would be at various levels of harvest. First, we recognize that Indians harvested deer year round, so their impact on whitetail populations could be considered analogous to that of other major predators. Basic to our conservative estimate of the total white-tailed deer population are several assumptions: (1) the population level was stationary when considered over the entire range of the species; (2) the sex ratio of the population approximated 50:50; and (3) the food resources available to the population allowed for a mean level of reproductive potential. Based on the above assumptions, a minimum population level of 7.1 to 9.9 million (using an average reproductive rate of 1.3 fawns per doe) would have been necessary to allow a consumption rate of 4.6 to 6.4 million deer per year by American Indians. But because wolves, mountain lions, coyotes, bobcats, bears and other nonhunting mortality factors also had an impact on the whitetail population at that time, we can presume that Indians probably were not responsible for more than 50 percent of the annual mortality of deer. At this level of harvest, deer populations would have to have been between 14.2 and 19.7 million—the lower figure approximating the number of white-tailed deer estimated for North America today. If the Indian harvest is considered to have been roughly equivalent to that of modern-day hunters, then Indians would have accounted for up to 30 percent of the annual whitetail mortality. Thus, white-tailed deer populations would have had to have been between 23.6 and 32.8 million—a density of 3.1 to 4.2 deer per square kilometer (7.9–10.9 per square mile) for the total range. These last levels approximate those estimated by Seton (1909, 1929). Although we cannot be certain as to the amount of mortality attributable to Indians, our estimates indicate that the number of whitetails immediately prior to the sixeenth century could have been more than double the current population.

A final assessment of the whitetail's value to aboriginal subsistence was prompted by Rue's (1978:5) remark that "The whitetail was as important to the eastern woodland Indians as the bison was to the Indians of the Plains." We find no evidence to support this generalization and, to the contrary, would argue that although whitetails *supported* Indian tribes in eastern woodlands to varying degrees, the bison *dictated* late-prehistoric/early historic period life on the Plains for virtually *all* the aboriginal inhabitants. Indians of eastern woodlands and other regions that were habitats of white-tailed deer, on the whole, had equal or greater diversity of seasonal food and fiber resources—and certainly more opportu-

nity to utilize them—than did the transient or seminomadic Plains Indians. In our opinion the whitetail was used nearly as *extensively* by whitetail hunters as was the bison by the bison hunters, but not as *intensively*.

A majority of the Indians found on the Great Plains in early historic times had migrated there sometime after 1300 A.D. (Maxwell 1978). Their emergence as a sociological force was largely a result of their acquisition of the horse, about 1500–1650 (Haines 1938). Prior to that time many of the tribes were located in bordering forest regions where shelter and food resources were more accessible, given the Indians' pedestrian mode of travel. It follows, therefore, that many of the relocated Indians of the Plains were familiar with and, to some extent, dependent on whitetails long before they focused subsistence activities on bison. For example, the Sioux word for white-tailed deer is "tahca" or "tahinca" (Riggs 1890:453), meaning "the true meat, the real meat." It is from the generic term "Ta," which originally referred to moose but eventually became the standard prefix in the composition of names for all ruminating animals. Ruth Beebe Hill (personal communication:1983) noted that ". . . 'hca' added to any word gave the word characterization as the 'ultimate.' Translated 'true' and 'real,' *tahca* means only 'the real meat,' the 'true' meat. And that means *the most meat. And that most in meat was the white-tailed deer.* The Dakotah [originally a Woodland tribe east of the Mississippi], the parent stock, provided these early names long before they became a divided people. . . . When the Dakotah named the deer 'real meat,' they were naming their basic meat, the dominant meat. Buffalo covered the country, as we know, but the basic diet was tahca.''

Fabric, Implements and Other Uses

Besides its meat value, the whitetail served primitive economies in numerous ways. Deer-hide clothing—including leggings, shawls, dresses, breechclouts, moccasins, sashes, shirts, robes, skirts, headwear and mittens—was the most universal application. Although fashions differed greatly, deerskin was a common fabric for all whitetail-hunting tribes we were able to identify.

Gramly (1977) hypothesized that sustained yields of whitetail hides were a factor of dissension within the intertribal confederacy of northeastern United States and Ontario. Competition and conflict over the size of hunting territories may actually have determined the distribution of Indian populations. To support his arguments Gramly noted that in winter the wardrobe of seventeenth-century Huron men required hides from six whitetails. Huron women's winter apparel necessitated the hides of eight deer (*see also* Turner 1894, Trigger 1969). Assuming that each set of clothing lasted no longer than two years, the rate of consumption was about 3.45 new hides per Indian per year (the rate is lowered because children needed approximately one-half as much clothing as did adults).

In the seventeenth century there were about 18,000 Hurons, so approximately 62,000 hides were needed per annum. Gramly (1977) estimated that if the carrying capacity of the area was 13.9 whitetails per square kilometer (36 per square mile), and 4.8 deer per square kilometer (12.4 per square mile) could be taken annually on a sustained-yield basis (representing a potential 34-percent harvest rate), then the Hurons needed a hunting territory of about 35,700 square kilometers (13,800 square miles). This amount of area compares favorably (within 5.5 percent) to the estimate of nineteenth-century authorities, who concluded that the minimum requirement for an Indian family of five persons was 24.3 square kilometers (9.4 square miles) (Ellis 1882). The actual Huron territory was about 25,900 square kilometers (10,000 square miles). Consequently, the Hurons needed constant territorial defense and extensive external trade alliances to assure fulfillment of their requirements for deer hides.

In addition to clothing, whitetail hide was widely used in the manufacture of blankets, storage bags, tobacco and pipe pouches, wrist guards, shield covers (or backing), quivers, straps and harnessing. Other uses included mats or rugs (Byrd 1966), snowshoe netting (Bersing 1966), hair-on caps (Day 1978), drumheads (Bersing 1966, Swanton 1946, *see* Goddard 1978), bowstring (Laudonniére 1586, Garcilaso de la Vega 1723, Tyler 1907), thongs (Alvord and Bidgood 1912, Bourne 1904), tepee covering (Rich and Johnson 1949), wrapping for bows (Strachey 1849) and ballgame stick handles (Swanton 1931), glue from scrapings to dilute coloring matter (Swanton 1946), saddle pad (Walker 1978), and a ball for a lacrosse-like game (Burt and Ferguson 1973). Swanton (1946) noted that thongs or cordage were made by placing a knife point in the center of a deer-skin and cutting in a spiral pattern outward. The skin usually was moistened, twisted, and then dried. Garcilaso de la Vega (1723) and others observed that leather bowstrings were made from neck hide. Grinnell (1972[II]:123) related that, "Armlets, in pairs, made of the . . . skin of the shank of a white-tail deer, were sometimes worn [by Cheyenne Indians] in the dance or in medicine-making, or in war, tied about the naked arm."

When Chippewa Indians needed to summon men from different villages for matters of great importance, such as warfare, a messenger was sent bearing a life-size hand ". . . made of buckskin, and lightly filled with moss. There is an opening at the side of the wrist in which tobacco was placed, and the 'hand' is smeared with red paint to represent blood. When sent to warriors a pipe was laid across the palm of the hand, the fingers folded over it, and the whole was wrapped securely in buckskin" (Densmore 1929:133). Men who accepted the tobacco from the hand and smoked the pipe were indicating willingness to accept the summons. In dealings with the United States government, a similar "hand" was placed by Chippewa on the pile of goods given them to seal agreements. It represented the honor of the tribe. *Photo courtesy of the Smithsonian Institution National Anthropological Archives.*

The job of tanning whitetail skins was almost always relegated to women. However, men of several cultural groups in the Southeast—including the Tunica and Choctaw (Nash and Gates 1962)—performed this task (their women reportedly attended only to ''indoor'' work). Part of the mixture used by Indians throughout whitetail range to tan hides was deer brain (boiled) and sometimes deer liver (Lawson 1860, Hodge 1910, Fletcher and La Flesche 1972).

Another widely used by-product of the whitetail was sinew. Adair (1775) and Beverley (1705) testified to the importance and common utilization of whitetail sinew as thread and string. Captain John Smith, at the Jamestown (Virginia) colony in the early 1600s, wrote that ''deare sinews'' were fashioned into thread by women who spun the tendons ''betwixt their hands and thighes. . .'' (Tyler 1907:103, *see also* Lawson 1860). Le Page du Pratz (1758) and Newcomb (1983) recorded bowstrings made

of steeped and twisted sinew, and Swanton (1946) added that the best Creek bowstrings were from deer sinew (twisted squirrel hide reportedly was next best). Swanton also indicated that sinew was used in the construction of fishnets.

Whitetail bones were of enormous utility to Indians. Marrow extracted from leg bones was a favorite food. Among the variety of utensils made from deer bone were awls (ulna), hoes (scapula), digging sticks (leg bones), hide fleshers (foot bones and astragali) and scrapers (leg bones), fishhooks, arrowheads, clubs, arrow straighteners (vertebrae), corn scrapers (jawbone) and cutting tools. Swanton (1946) reported flutes or flageolets made from whitetail tibia (*see also* Bert and Ferguson 1973), and bracelets from ribs. Allen (1929:203) stated that Indians of southern New England ''. . . made coarse needles from small strips of the metapodial bones by deepening the central groove

Arapaho women (left) and Chippewa woman (right) coloring or ''smoking'' fresh deer hides. The method involved forming a scraped hide (or several sewn together) into a rough conical shape. A hole was dug about 46 centimeters (18 inches) in diameter and 15–25 centimeters (6–10 inches) deep, over which a tripod was positioned. The hide then was attached to the frame as shown at left or suspended over it as shown at right, with the lower edge of the hide opened and encircling the hole in which a smoldering fire had been built. Smoke from the fire gradually turned the hide from a white color to golden yellow to greyish-black, depending on individual preference. *Left photo courtesy of the Wyoming State Archives, Museum and Historical Department. Right photo by Frances Densmore; courtesy of the Smithsonian Institution National Anthropological Archives.*

Of skin-dressing by Seminole Indians in Florida, Skinner (1913:72–73) wrote: ". . . the hide is first dried in the sun until it is stiff and hard [left]; it is then thoroughly soaked in water and wrung out by passing it about a tree, tying the ends together, and running a stick through the knot to afford better leverage while wringing. While the skin is still damp it is thrown over the smooth upper end of an inclined log set in the ground, and the hair is scraped off with a beaming tool. While the skin is drying, it is rendered pliable by rubbing it over the edge of a spatula-like stick set up in the ground. Next deer brains are mixed with water until the liquid is thick and soapy, and the skin is then soaked therein. Great pains are taken to saturate the hide thoroughly; it is then wrung, soaked again and again, and dried [right]. Sometimes this ends the process, when the skin is dyed a deep reddish brown by the use of oak-bark and is used without further preparation. Usually however, the leather is finished by smoking." This essentially was the procedure used by Indians throughout North America, although there was a marked difference in finished hide quality from tribe to tribe, depending principally on the amount of attention given to scraping and softening. *Both photos courtesy of the Smithsonian Institution National Anthropological Archives.*

and cutting another parallel to it until a sliver of bone was cut out." Ritchie (1932) mentioned gouges, daggers, pistol-grip awls and notched pendants. Bersing (1966) made reference to "bull roars"—a pierced deer scapula attached to raw buckskin and twirled around to summon chiefs to council. Wetmore (1975) identified decorative beads carved from rib bone. Snow (1978b) presented a primitive form of clothespin, and Tuck (1978) reported spoons—both articles made from unidentified whitetail bone.

Aside from the hide, the anatomical part of a whitetail carcass that was of greatest utility to Indians was antler. Indians throughout the East and Southeast used antler to make arrowheads (Mourt 1963, Wetmore 1975), spear points (Beauchamp 1902) and harpoon points (Wintemberg 1906). Swanton (1946) wrote that, among southeastern Indians, arrowheads made

of antler were commonest, and antler tines sometimes were used as points on clubs used in warfare. Swanton also noted that antler was used for needles, flaking tools, clubs, combs (*see also* Jennings 1978), cutting tools, household utensils (*see also* Skinner 1921)—and that some Florida Indians wore antler parts as hair ornaments. Willoughby (1935) mentioned antler knife handles, clothespins and a prong for opening shellfish. Winters (1969) reported on antler beads. Speck (1909) wrote of a whistle fashioned from whitetail antler. Antler rattles and drumsticks were presented in Rogers (1978). Glue from boiled antlers reportedly was used by Indians in coastal areas of New England (Beverley 1705), the Southeast (Swanton 1946) and Texas (Mayhall 1939).

In reference to the Northern Iroquois, Fenton (1978:317) wrote: ". . . because antlers are the marks of identity for chiefs, a rack is installed with his office; but as deer shed their racks, they are removed from the chief in illness or at death, or for malfeasance in office. Just as the deer rub antlers on brush during rutting season, so the great social dance after the installation of a new chief is called 'rubbing antlers,' when they socialize and diffuse their power.''

The whitetail tongue, heart, liver, buck testicles and fawn venison were preferred food items of many Indians. In the Northeast and probably elsewhere, partially digested contents of the whitetail stomach and intestines sometimes were eaten (Witthoft 1953c, Beverley 1705). Those contents were served—as a thin broth—to people found starving. It reportedly was the only food that would not make them violently ill. Lahontan (1703) also recorded Indians feasting on deer heart as part of a healing ceremony. Whitetail fat was important in food preparation, seasoning and preservation (*see* Densmore 1929), in hide tanning and tallow manufacture, and also as hair oil (Bersing 1966), lubricant, and skin protectant.

In the Southeast, Southwest and High Pla-

teau regions, a number of tribes prepared poison for arrows using whitetail liver. Rattlesnakes were prompted to bite the liver, which then was allowed to putrefy.

The following whitetail carcass by-products were used more locally and/or infrequently. Teeth served as pendants, gaming devices (Culin 1975) and for shelling corn (*see* Callendar 1978c). Hooves were part of armlets (Grinnell 1972), were made into ceremonial ankle rattles (Swanton 1946) and were boiled to make glue (Hoffman 1896). Dewclaws also were made into rattles (Fenton 1978, Fletcher and La Flesche 1972). Tallow was stored in deer stomachs, bladders and large intestines (Densmore 1929, Howley 1915). Laudenniére (1586) referred to bowstrings made from deer gut, and Swanton (1946) wrote that entrails were used to make bowstrings and cordage. Whitetail hair was popular for embroidery (Fenton 1978) and in the making of decorative coronets (Snow 1978b), moccasin insulation (Rue 1978) and roaches (Swanton 1946, Ritzenthaler 1978). Entire deer heads were used for ceremonial masks and as disguises or decoys in hunting.

This remarkable photo of Kiowa Indians, on a reservation in the Oklahoma Territory in 1891, shows a set of whitetail antlers (lower left) hitched to a sulky-like wagon, undoubtedly a child's toy. Other articles that may have been made from whitetail hide include the dresses of the young girls (front right), the moccasins of the woman (far left), the cradle cover next to woman at far left, the leggings of the boy mounted atop the horse, the horse's saddle-blanket and bridle, the shirt of the man standing, his pouch-strap and shield-cover or backing, and the shirt of the youngster at far right. *Photo may have been taken by James Mooney; courtesy of the Joslyn Art Museum.*

Whitetail hoof-rattles 38 centimeters (15 inches) in length worn about the legs during ceremonial dances by Cayuga Indians of eastern Canada. Each hoof is attached to the main strap by a thin leather thong, likely cut from deerskin. *Photo courtesy of the Museum of the American Indian, Heye Foundation.*

A stonehead war club used by an Arapaho Indian. It is decorated with deer hooves, attached by leather thongs beaded at the base. The head itself is attached by a piece of shrunken rawhide pressed in an oval groove. The wrist strop appears to be twisted leather. Except for the hoof-attachment thongs, the other leather parts probably are bison or elk hide, which is thicker, less pliable and more durable than deerskin. *Photo courtesy of the Museum of the American Indian, Heye Foundation.*

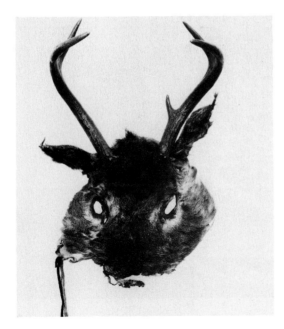

A whitetail mask worn by a Penobscot "clown" in the Trading Dance, a popular and lively gaming ceremony—performed at night—at which spectators bartered with the disguised performer. The Penobscots, an Eastern Abenaki tribe in central Maine, hunted in winter for deer as well as moose, caribou and bear. It is not known if deer-mask disguises were used to stalk or lure whitetails. *Photo courtesy of the Museum of the American Indian, Heye Foundation.*

A deer mask carved of wood, used by Cherokee Indians of North Carolina in the Bugah Dance. This dance was of particular social importance as it was popular for convivial displays of privileged familiarity relationships among relatives (Gilbert 1943). *Photo courtesy of the Museum of the American Indian, Heye Foundation.*

Within many Indian tribes were clans, cults or moieties that were substructures of social and political organization. For the most part these were fraternal societies of men who enjoyed similar social standing and held similar spiritual affiliations. Quite a number of tribes—including the Fox, Seneca, Huron, Mohawk, Onandaga, Sauk, Cayuga, Miami, Omaha and Winnebago—had whitetail groups. The talismanic namesake was a focal point of group and personal power and/or authority, and served as each member's patron.

Similarly, the white-tailed deer was venerated by whole tribes for its supposed mystical powers (based on behavioral traits). Natchez Indians, for example, ate venison so that they might attain the swiftness of whitetails (Maxwell 1978). Grinnell (1972) reported that Cheyenne Indians also believed that whitetails could convey powers of speed and agility. And Apache Indians (Opler 1969), Sioux (R.B. Hill personal communication:1983) and Cheyenne (Grinnell 1972[I]:104) recognized the species as a powerful "helper" in love affairs. Young Cheyenne men who drew on the spiritual aid of whitetails in their romantic quests wore the animal's tail over their shoulder. Opler (1969) explained that drinking the blood of a freshly killed deer was thought by some Apaches to have curative power. Some Wisconsin Indians maintained that dried venison mixed with bear fat also had medicinal value (Bersing 1966).

From children's toys to gambling articles to instruments of warfare to symbols of prestige, the aboriginal use of whitetail parts for practical and ceremonial purposes appears to have been limited only by the American Indians' evolving technology, not their ingenuity.

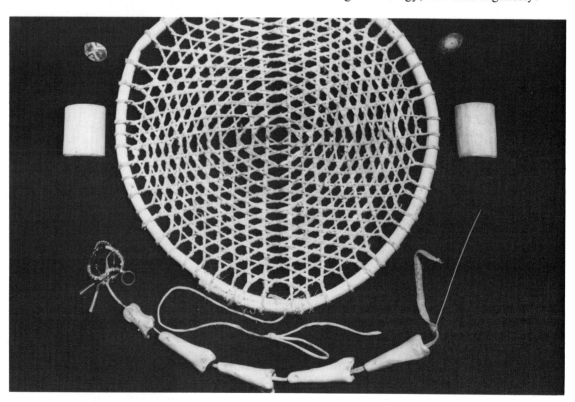

Teton Sioux boys, women and young married men played a "... game with the hoofs of a deer" (Dorsey 1891:344): "They string several deer hoofs together and throw them suddenly upward. They jerk them back again by the cord to which they are attached, and as they fall the player who has a sharp-pointed stick tries to thrust it through the holes of the hoofs, and if he succeeds he counts the number of hoofs through which his stick has gone. A number of small beads of various colors are strung together and attached to the smallest hoof at the end of the string. When a player adds a bead to those on the string he has another chance to try his skill in piercing the hoofs. When one misses the mark he hands the hoofs etc., to the next player. Each one tries to send his stick through more hoofs than did his predecessor. Two sides are chosen by the players. Each player offers articles as stakes for the winners." Walker (1905) described the game as being played with deer foot bones, as shown above. The top article is part of an unassociated Dakota hoop game. *Photo courtesy of the Museum of the American Indian, Heye Foundation.*

A Shoshone (Wyoming) hair roach (left) and a Shawnee (Oklahoma) neck collar both made with deer hair. *Photos courtesy of the Museum of the American Indian, Heye Foundation.*

Hunting

Obtaining white-tailed deer necessitated techniques and skills at which Indians were particularly adept. "In all the territory now occupied by the United States and Northern Mexico at least . . . pursuit of them ['the Common Deer'] was a life study with the Indian" (Caton 1877:380).

Just as the historic Plains Indian hunter is associated with the mounted chase of bison, so is the eastern Woodland Indian traditionally identified with stalking the whitetail. Although such popular images often are accurate, they tend to overemphasize Indian employment of dramatic strategies. Unlike modern hunts, those of yesteryear were events that directly determined the well-being of the hunter and his tribal or blood kin. Stalking required more time and energy than most Indians could afford, and yielded relatively modest returns. While stalking certainly was an important part of the Indians' whitetail-hunting repertoire, it generally was reserved for ritualistic killing, or for times when food was in short supply. We suspect, too, that frequent mention in the literature of Indians stalking whitetails is partly the result of early chroniclers' amazement at the natives' ability to "sneak" up on and kill deer, especially compared to the unpracticed efforts of colonists, who relied more on firepower than stealth. Communal hunting methods, which resulted in kills of large numbers of deer on a single occasion, far outweighed lone hunting in importance to tribal subsistence (*see* Carr 1897). Also, adventure and excitement were much less motivating factors in Indian whitetail hunts than was the pragmatic need for food. Fenton (1978:298) reported that among the Northern Iroquois, "Next to warfare and attending council, hunting enjoyed greatest prestige." Nevertheless, "Hunting was an arduous and time-consuming activity of Indian men, and was not considered a sport in any sense" (Witthoft 1953a:14, *see also* Presnall 1943, Adair 1775, Axtell 1981).

The great majority of whitetail-hunting Indians did not have horses. Securing and transporting animal carcasses in sufficient quantity to sustain a group of Indians generally required community effort. Also, the pedestrian Indians, who occupied the bulk of the historic whitetail range, were semiagriculturists and, consequently, fairly sedentary. Weather, topography, and compact tribal or cultural defensive units further limited the Indians' opportunity to move long distances. Favorable growing conditions, in many areas a rich abundance and variety of nonmigratory wildlife—including most whitetail populations—and well-defended hunting territories obviated extensive village movements. However, particularly in the North, Indian tribes occupied seasonal encampments within territories predicated primarily on proximity to food sources. Spring/summer camps were located in areas

Most whitetail-hunting Indians did not have horses, so traveled on foot or by canoe or dugout. Consequently, many if not most whitetails were taken in communal hunts during seasons when the deer were congregated and in prime condition. However, deer were hunted opportunistically in all seasons by individual hunters. Young deer were sought in summer for their tasty flesh and soft hides. The original oil painting (detail) above is the work of Henry Metzger (1876–1949). *Photo courtesy of the Glenbow Museum.*

where opportunities for fishing, agriculture or other food-harvesting activities were most abundant. Also considered in site selection was protection from fires and insects. Autumn/winter encampments—usually no more than several days' travel from spring/summer camps—tended to be located in relatively secluded areas, initially established near game-concentration areas. Protection from the elements and the accessibility of firewood supplies and fresh water apparently were other important determining factors.

Whitetail hunting was predominantly a male activity (Witthoft 1953*a*, Driver 1969). "The deer is the food of the hunters," wrote Fenton (1978:317), "the man's contribution to the larder, the fulfillment of his marriage contract. . . ." But it was not unusual for women and children to participate in communal drives or surrounds, especially among tribes in northern climates. We found no evidence that women hunted deer without the company of men, and very little evidence that women ever did the actual killing (*see* Jones 1906). As a rule, when women took part in communal hunts they served as drivers, beaters or went along to dress and/or transport the game.

Hunting for white-tailed deer was engaged in year-round, but communal hunting usually took place in autumn, early winter and sometimes in spring. During the summer months subsistence activities centered on villages, where a variety of foods (agricultural products, natural foods, fish and small game) were readily available. Also, during summer the need for hides for clothing was minimal, and whitetail hide quality was relatively poor at this time of year. On the other hand, fawn hides were favored for shirts and the meat of these young animals was a delicacy. We conclude, therefore, that deer were hunted opportunistically during the summer, but apparently with considerably less motivation, organization and effort than in other seasons.

There were good reasons for communal hunting in the spring, even though the deer were in their poorest condition of the year. In some years Indians experienced unusually severe deprivation due to a harsh and/or prolonged winter. And in early spring, vegetable crops and many important forage plants were several months away from being available in quantity. The collective effort of a tribe was then needed to replenish exhausted resources.

Communal hunting in late autumn, as in early spring, did not seriously disrupt the usual division of subsistence labor. During this time the deer were in prime condition. The dormancy of vegetation greatly aided Indians in overland travel to hunting "grounds" and winter camps, and improved visibility not only for locating deer and coordinating large-scale drives, but for maintaining guard against potential aggression from marauding enemies—a persistent and serious threat. Also in autumn, whitetails were congregated to greater extent than in the earlier months because of seasonal herd movements and annual rutting activity. The distraction of mating among whitetails during this period was an advantage to the hunter. Autumn hunting also was essential to northern tribes preparing food and clothing stocks for winter survival.

One of the most widespread and successful hunting methods was the fire drive, and for this procedure the dormancy of vegetation was of critical importance in both spring and autumn. Spring fire drives generally were the safest (a vital consideration for the more sedentary Indians), but autumn fire drives were the most productive (again, because of deer concentrations in that season). In both seasons fires could be set before departure to alternate-season camps and, in addition to the venison harvested, burning served to prepare the area for the group or tribe when it returned later (Nuttall 1821, Maxwell 1910, Lewis 1977).

Winter whitetail hunting was practiced widely. In winter, except in the most southern ranges, food of all kinds was less abundant and subsistence labors other than hunting were minimized. There was time and a need to concentrate on the large land animals, of which whitetail was the predominant species in many areas. Generally such hunts were the enterprise of individuals or small groups, although communal hunts in the North (Heidenreich 1971) and South (Boyce 1978) were tribal affairs. Particularly in the North, where deep snows and cold temperatures were obstacles to drive hunts, snaring, stalking and using snowshoes to "run down" deer were favored techniques. Under these conditions, even with whitetails congregated in deer yards, hunting was energy-expensive work.

It is quite evident from the anthropological literature that, although North American Indians were not especially adaptive to sudden environmental change or social reorganization, they were skilled survivors. Until European trade goods altered Indian subsistence patterns and energies, their labors were rigidly divided for maximum utility and efficiency. Virtually all aspects of their domestic lifestyles were designed to avoid risk to community and personal well-being. Large-scale communal winter hunting for whitetails would not have been in keeping with the resourcefulness that was characteristic of Indians. Weather *and* travel conditions had to be favorable enough so that the energy investment would not be excessive.

Before whitetail hides became an important trade commodity in Indian dealings with whites, the factor that apparently most influenced the number of deer harvested was personal need. Hunting-territory size, whitetail abundance and intertribal trade were important but secondary considerations. There simply was no reason for Indians to kill more deer than were needed for immediate use. Except for quantities of meat converted to pemmican and jerky, venison could not be stored effectively or moved efficiently. Stockpiling hides and other by-products for the sake of material possession was rare (*see* Bishop 1981). Wealth in the modern sense was a practically nonexistent concept. Most Indians were accorded status by character and deed. Further, they tended to view wildlife as their spiritual and/or ecological kin (Witthoft 1953*b*, Tyler 1975, *see also* Hudson 1981). However, it rarely was taboo to kill animals, although in many tribes hunters were advised not to kill without need *and* atonement. A scarcity of animals was viewed not as a biological or ecological phenomenon but rather as a spiritual consequence of a social event or circumstance.

There are few reliable statistics on the number of whitetails killed, but those that exist are convincing testimony to Indians' hunting ability. In a single day, after the season's first snow in November 1794, for example, Iroquois Indians attending the Canandaigua treaty negotiations brought in 100 deer (Fenton 1965, *see also* Morgan 1851). In the early 1600s Samuel de Champlain witnessed 25 Huron men capturing 120 whitetails in 38 days by means of drives to an enclosure (Thwaites 1959[33]:89). Writing of South Carolina in 1682, Samuel Wilson reported that ". . . an Indian hunter hath killed Nine fat Deere in a day all shot by himself . . . and one [Indian] hunter will very well find a Family of Thirty people with as much venison and foul as they can well eat [year round]" (Carroll 1836[2]:28). That same year

Captain Matthews reported that ". . . one hunting Indian has yearly kill'd and brought to his Plantation more than 100, sometimes 200 Deer" (Carroll 1836[2]:72). Captain John Smith described surrounds conducted by Virginia Indians that resulted in a deer kill of ". . . 6, 8, 10, or 15 at a hunting" (Tyler 1907:104). In 1670, Jesuit missionary Peter Raffiex wrote: "More than a thousand deer are killed annually in the neighborhood of Cayuga [west-central New York]" (O'Callaghan 1853[2]:251). The *Marinette* (Wis.) *Star* (1883) recounted the killing of 150 whitetails by three Menominee Indians over a period of a few days. In 1820, at a time when they collectively numbered 5,000, Sauk and Fox Indians harvested no fewer than 28,680 whitetails in northwestern Illinois and northeastern Missouri (Morse 1822, Marston 1912). According to Cabeza de Vaca in Texas in the 1530s a few Indians sometimes killed 200 to 300 deer (Smith 1871). Swanton (1946:321) mentioned a report of a single Indian hunter in the Indian Territory of Oklahoma killing 130 deer ". . . in a single season." And during the severe winter of 1857, in Wisconsin, Menominees on snowshoes and armed with clubs and hatchets killed deer ". . . by hundreds" (Cartwright 1875:239–241). That same year a band of 100 Indians in central Minnesota killed 87 deer and 13 bears before mid-December (*St. Cloud* [Minn.] *Visitor,* December 10, 1857). The next year, 1858, 200 Sioux were said to have taken 1,000 whitetails in Stearns County, Minnesota (*The Weekly Pioneer Press* [St. Paul], December 17, 1858). Moravian missionary David Zeisberger (1910) estimated that in 1768, Delaware Indians from the Goschgosching area in northwestern Pennsylvania killed in excess of 2,000 whitetails.

Estimates vary widely as to how many deer Indian hunters took on the average over any given period of time. Zeisberger (1910) supposed that each Delaware (Munsee) hunter shot 50 to 150 deer each autumn. Missionary J. A. Gilfillan (1896) estimated that Chippewa Indians in northcentral Minnesota took 30 deer per hunter each year. Fenton (1978) figured five whitetails per Iroquois hunter per year to be an unexaggerated estimate. McCauley (1887) ventured that in 1883, at a time when the Seminole Indians in southern Florida numbered fewer than 500, they harvested about 2,500 whitetails each year. From Gramly's (1977) harvest estimates for Huron Indians—correlated with Driver's (1969) "extended family" concept (which allowed for one active hunter per five Indians [20 percent])—the average per-hunter harvest in the 1600s was about 17 white-tails annually. And on the same basis, Sauk and Fox hunters may have taken an average of 28.7 deer each in 1819–1820.

The Indians' need for whitetail venison, hides and other parts undoubtedly differed among tribes, particularly on a regional basis, because of the variable distribution and seasonal abundance of alternative resources. The Huron Indian demand for deer hides, for example, was considerably greater than that of Indians in the Southwest, who needed to wear fewer and smaller articles of clothing. And because of the greater year-round abundance and variety of major food resources in the Southeast, fewer whitetails would have been required by Indi-

ans there than in the Great Lakes/St. Lawrence region.

If, as Driver (1969) and others have concluded, one of every five Indians was an active hunter at least part of the year, and if as previously calculated, their subsistence harvest in the United States and Canada was between 4.6 and 6.4 million deer annually, then the average yearly per-hunter kill was 10 to 14 whitetails.

Some of the techniques used by Indians to hunt white-tailed deer are listed in Table 4. This listing is not complete for all Indians, but it does reveal how common many of the hunting practices were throughout the historic whitetail range (Figure 15). Certain of the methods and implements deserve elaboration and, for this, we borrow mostly from firsthand accounts.

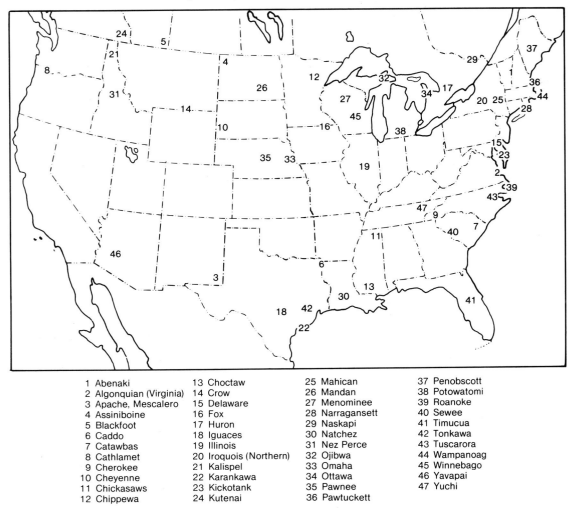

1 Abenaki	13 Choctaw	25 Mahican	37 Penobscott
2 Algonquian (Virginia)	14 Crow	26 Mandan	38 Potowatomi
3 Apache, Mescalero	15 Delaware	27 Menominee	39 Roanoke
4 Assiniboine	16 Fox	28 Narragansett	40 Sewee
5 Blackfoot	17 Huron	29 Naskapi	41 Timucua
6 Caddo	18 Iguaces	30 Natchez	42 Tonkawa
7 Catawbas	19 Illinois	31 Nez Perce	43 Tuscarora
8 Cathlamet	20 Iroquois (Northern)	32 Ojibwa	44 Wampanoag
9 Cherokee	21 Kalispel	33 Omaha	45 Winnebago
10 Cheyenne	22 Karankawa	34 Ottawa	46 Yavapai
11 Chickasaws	23 Kickotank	35 Pawnee	47 Yuchi
12 Chippewa	24 Kutenai	36 Pawtuckett	

Figure 15. Approximate tribal location of some whitetail-hunting Indians in North America between 1500 and 1850 (*see* Table 4).

Table 4. Methods of hunting white-tailed deer by certain North American Indians.[a]

Indian tribe or group	Location[b]	Date	Season(s)	Number of participants[c]	Weapon(s)
Abenaki (Western)	New Hampshire, Vermont	Pre-1830	Autumn		Bow and arrow, knife, spear
Algonquian (Virginia)	Coastal Virginia	1600–1700	Winter	200–300	Bow and arrow, gun
Algonquian (Maryland)	Chesapeake Bay region	1600s	Winter	1	Bow and arrow, spear
				2–3	
Apache (Mescalero)	Southern New Mexico, southwestern Texas			200–300 1 or 2	Spear, bow and arrow
Assiniboine	Western North Dakota	Pre-1870	Winter Summer	1 or several	Bow and arrow
Blackfoot	Southern Alberta	1800s	Winter		Bow and arrow, gun
Caddo	Western Louisiana, southwestern Arkansas				
Catawbas	Eastern South Carolina	Mid-1700s	October	"hundreds"	Gun
Cathlamet	Puget Island, Oregon	Late 1700s		Many	
Cherokee	Southwestern Virginia, western Carolinas, northern Georgia	Mid-1700s	Autumn/early winter	10 or less	Bow and arrow
Cheyenne	". . . near the lakes in the North"; ". . . in timber in the East"	Pre-1700s	Spring Winter	Tribe "whole camp"	Bow and arrow Bow and arrow
	Western South Dakota	1800s			Bow and arrow
Chickasaw	Northern Mississippi	Mid-1700s			
Chippewa	Northern Minnesota, northern Wisconsin	1800s	Autumn, winter	One or a small group	Bow and arrow
Choctaw	Southern Mississippi, southern Louisiana	Late 1700s			
		Mid-1800s		One	Gun
Crow	Eastern Montana, northeastern Wyoming	Pre-1800s 1800s		Group	Bow and arrow, gun
Delaware	Eastern Pennsylvania, New Jersey, eastern Delaware	1600s	Late autumn	100–200	Bow and arrow, gun
Fox	East of Iowa/Missouri watershed	1700s	Late autumn, early spring	". . . small groups . . . parties"	Bow and arrow
Huron	Southcentral Ontario	Early 1600s	Autumn/late winter	25–500	Bow and arrow, spear

Table 4. (continued)

Method(s)	Principal reference(s)
Stalking; still-hunting	Day (1953, 1978)
Fire drive; fire surround; stalking; luring with disguise	Beverley (1705), Le Page du Pratz (1758), Strachey (1849), Spelman (1884), Bassett (1901), Tyler (1907), Clayton (1965), Ewan and Ewan (1970)
Stalking in disguise	Dozer (1976)
Still-hunting at mineral licks Fire drive Stalking	Opler (1969)
Stalking, luring	Kennedy (1961), Curtis (1970)
". . . running down on horseback"; stalking in snow	Thompson (1961:359), Ewers (1980)
Fire surround; stalking in disguise	Mayhall(1939), Swanton (1946)
Stalking; fire drive	Adair (1775), Catesby (1754[2]:XII)
Drive to enclosures and pitfalls; stalking	Strong (1906)
Stalking; fire drives	Adair (1775), Bartram (1794)
Fire surround	Wetmore (1975)
Surround; drive to snowbanks and enclosures; snaring	Grinnell (1972[I]:51)
Stalking; still-hunting; ". . . pens, pitfalls and other traps"	Hoebel (1960), Grinnell (1972[I]:273,277)
Stalking; stalking in disguise	Adair (1775), Romans (1775)
Jacklighting; still-hunting; stalking; luring; baiting	Densmore (1929), Gilfillan (1896)
Fire drive; stalking	Bartram (1794)
Still-hunting; stalking and luring with disguise	Cushman (1899), Swanton (1946)
Drive over cliffs	Lowie (1956)
Stalking in disguise; horseback surround and impounding	Laroque (1910), Lowie (1956)
Fire surround; drive to water	Van der Donck (1841), De Vries (1912), Goddard (1978)
Fire drive; stalking	Forsythe (1911), Tax (1955), Callendar (1978*a*:637), Rogers (1970)
Drive to water, enclosures and traps; snaring; stalking	Champlain (1929[3]:60–61, 81–85), Thwaites (1959[22]:273, [23]:157, [26]:313, [30]:53), Fenton (1978), Heidenreich (1978)

Stalking or Trailing

As a rule, Indians who stalked whitetails in disguise or "decoy" did so using only a partial deerskin (head and cape) (Cushman 1899, Le Moyne 1875, Wetmore 1975, Beverley 1705, Strachey 1953), although some Indians employed entire skins (Le Page du Pratz 1758, Swanton 1911).

John Lawson (1967:29), who traveled extensively through the Carolinas in the first decade of the 1700s, witnessed the expertise with which Indians in disguise stalked whitetails, noting that the practice was not without peril: "In these Habiliments an *Indian* will go as near a Deer as he pleases, the exact Motions and Behaviour of a Deer being so well counterfeited by 'em, that several Times it hath been known for two Hunters to come up with a stalking Head together, and unknown to each other, so that they have kill'd an *Indian* instead of a Deer. . . ."

Observers of Roanoke Indians in early Virginia chronicled the "sneak" method of stalking: "These savages being secretly hidden among high reeds where oftentimes they find the deer asleep and so kill them" (Young 1956:13). John Smith reported in the early 1600s that "When they have shot a Deare by land, they follow him like blood hounds by the blood and straine, and oftentimes so take them" (Tyler 1907:104).

"According to the Chippewa," wrote Densmore (1929:129) of this populous tribe in the Upper Midwest and southern Canada, "it is the habit of a deer to jump, then trot, and then walk in a circle when it is trying to evade a hunter, but a deer never crosses its own path when it has completed the circle. Knowing this, a Chippewa hunter circles outside the circle traveled by the deer, then closes in, and frequently finds the deer tired out and lying down near the place where it began the circle."

Kennedy (1961:118) described Assiniboine hunters in the Dakotas circling in on bedded deer: "It is said that several white-tailed deer could be killed, one at a time in the same bed-ground providing the hunter continued to circle the place after each shot. If there was more than one deer there the rest seemed to become paralyzed. . . ."

"The Seminole [of Florida] always hunt their game on foot," stated McCauley (1887:512). "They can approach a deer to within sixty yards by their method of rapidly nearing him while

Table 4. (continued)

Indian tribe or group	Location[b]	Date	Season(s)	Number of participants[c]	Weapon(s)
Iguaces	Texas	Early 1500s			
Illinois	Southern Wisconsin, northern and western Illinois	Late 1600s	Winter	"individuals or small groups"	
Iroquois (Northern)	Northwestern New York	1500s	Autumn/early winter	Up to about 500	
Kalispel	Northern Idaho			". . . groups"	Bow and arrow, spear
Karankawa	Coastal Texas	Early 1500s			Bow and arrow, spear
Kickotank	Delmarva Peninsula (Virginia)	Mid-1600s			
Kutenai	Southeastern British Columbia, northwestern Montana	1800–1860	Autumn	"Nearly everyone in the village"	
Mahican	Eastern New York	Early 1600s		100+	
Mandan	Southcentral North Dakota	Pre-1870	Summer, winter		
Menominee	Northern Wisconsin	Pre-1880	Autumn, winter	". . . single hunters or small groups"	Bow and arrow, gun, hatchet
Narragansett	Eastern Connecticut	1500s	Autumn/early winter	". . . two or three hundred in a company"	Bow and arrow
Naskapi	Central Quebec	1800s			Bow and arrow, spear
Natchez	Central Louisiana	1700s		". . . a hundred"	Gun
Nez Percé	Central Idaho		Autumn		Bow and arrow
Ojibwa	Southeastern Ontario	1760–1850	Winter	Families or family groups	Bow and arrow, spears
Omaha	Eastern Nebraska		Winter	". . . small party, or . . . a single person" ". . . party of men" and male relatives	

Table 4. (continued)

Method(s)	Principal reference(s)
Running to exhaustion; fire surround	Bandelier (1905)
Stalking; drive to surround	Deliette (1934), Callendar (1978*b*:674)
Stalking on snowshoes; deadfalls; twitch-up snares; fire drive to wing traps; fire surround	Morgan (1851), Cooper (1938), Fenton (1978), Turner (1850), Fleming (1789)
Surround; horseback drive to water	Walker (1978:56)
". . . poisoning . . . at waterholes"; stalking in disguise; "running down . . ."; fire drive	Bandelier (1905), Mayhall (1939:595, 615)
Springpole snaring	Hall (1910)
Drive to enclosure; fire drive	Mullan (1861), Baker (1955), Johnson (1969:71), Walker (1978)
Drive to water; drive to enclosure	De Vries (1857)
Stalking; pitfalls; snaring	Denig (1930), Bowers (1950), Meyer (1977)
Drive along fence; stalking on snowshoes	Foster and Whitney (1850), Marinette *Star* (1883), Phillips *Badger* (1883), Bartlett (1929), Rogers (1970)
Drive; snaring; trapping	Morton (1883), Williams (1936:163)
Snaring	Chamberlain (1906), Turner (1894)
Stalking in disguise; drive; surround	Le Page du Pratz (1758[2]:71), Swanton (1911, 1946)
Fire surround; fire drive to water; horseback drive to water; deadfalls; decoy lures	Walker (1978)
Still-hunting at mineral licks; stalking; stalking on snowshoes; drive to water; snaring; luring; fence drive	Copway (1850), Henry (1901), Jones (1906), Bersing (1966), Rogers (1970)
Stalking; luring; still-hunting	Fletcher and La Flesche (1972[I]:270)
Drive	Fletcher and La Flesche (1972[I]:270)

In a rare photograph documenting an actual Indian hunting technique, a Western Apache is shown wearing a deer-head mask and assuming the posture for stalking. The mask is the head of a mule deer buck, but Western Apaches hunted both mulies and whitetails. With bow and arrows held low and perpendicular to his body, the hunter could approach upwind to well within shooting range of feeding deer. *Photo probably taken in the early 1870s by D. F. Mitchell; courtesy of the Sharlot Hall Museum, Prescott, Arizona.*

Table 4. (continued)

Indian tribe or group	Location[b]	Date	Season(s)	Number of participants[c]	Weapon(s)
Ottawa	Central Michigan, southeastern Ontario	1600s	Winter	"...individual or group"	
Pawnee	Central Nebraska	1860s	Spring		Gun
Pawtucket	Coastal New Hampshire, northeastern Massachusetts	Early 1600s	Autumn/early winter		Bow and arrow
Penobscot	Southcentral Maine	Early 1600s	"...cold months"		Bow and arrow, lance, knife
Potowatomi	Southern Wisconsin, northern Illinois, southern Michigan	1830s	Autumn	Family groups	Gun
Roanoke	Roanoke Island, North Carolina	Late 1500s– early 1600s			
Sewee	Eastern South Carolina	Early 1700s	January		
Timucua	Central Florida	1560s 1600s	January		Bow and arrow Bow and arrow
Tonkawa	Southcentral Texas				Bow and arrow, spear
Tuscarora	Coastal North Carolina		Winter		Bow and arrow, club
Wampanoag	Massachusetts Bay area	1620s			
Winnebago	Central Wisconsin	Mid-1800s	Winter	3–4	Snare, bow and arrow, tomahawk
Yavapai	Central Arizona	1800s		1 or several	Bow and arrow
Yuchi	Eastern Tennessee, western North Carolina	1800s	October/ November	One	

[a]*See* Figure 15.
[b]As identified in the corresponding literature and/or Hodge (1907, 1910).
[c]Most drives and surrounds (except perhaps some in which fire was used) were communal events, usually involving entire tribal, camp or village populations.

Table 4. (continued)

Method(s)	Principal reference(s)
Stalking; fire drive	Feest and Feest (1978:774)
Still-hunting	Weltfish (1977)
Stalking; drive to funnel trap	Wood (1865), Salwen (1978)
Tracking with dogs; stalking in disguise	Snow (1978a:139)
Luring with antler rattles; fire drive	Crane (1878), Bersing (1966), Rogers (1970)
Stalking	Young (1956)
Fire drive	Lawson (1860)
Fire surround	Wenhold (1936)
Still hunting; stalking in disguise	Le Moyne (1875)
Stalking in disguise; fire surround	Mayhall (1939)
Drive to circular trap	Wetmore (1975)
Tip-up snaring; stalking; pitfalls	Marshall (1975)
Tracking; chase in water; fire drive; stalking	Muir (1965), Thompson (1922), Bersing (1966)
Drive to blinds; stalking in disguise	Gifford (1936)
Tracking with dogs; fire drive; luring	Speck (1909), Swanton (1946)

(Opposite page) Charles Livingston Bull (1874–1932) painted this fanciful watercolor/ink scene (detail) entitled, ''Indian Stalking White-tailed Deer.'' The likelihood of an Indian having worn a headdress while hunting, particularly for whitetails, is very remote. Nevertheless, Bull illustrated a common Indian hunting technique. Stalking usually was done by lone hunters or small groups, in autumn and winter, and in proximity to deer feeding sites, mineral licks or watercourses where the animals regularly went to drink. *Photo courtesy of the Glenbow Museum.*

(Below) Timucua Indians observed in Florida by French cartographer/artist Jacques le Moyne de Morges in 1564 ''. . . have a way of hunting deer that we have never seen before. They manage to put on the skins of the largest which have before been taken, in such a manner, with the heads on their own heads, so they can see out through the eyes as through a mask. Thus accoutred, they can approach closer to the deer without frightening them. They take advantage of the time when the animals come to drink at the river, and, having their bows and arrows ready, easily shoot them, as they are very plentiful in those regions'' (Fundaburk 1958:100). The artwork (detail) was Theodore de Bry's (1591) copper engraving, after Le Moyne's painting of same. The latter's watercolor art was the first to represent native life in the United States. *Photo courtesy of the U.S. Library of Congress.*

he is feeding, and standing perfectly still when he raises his head. They say that they are able to discover by certain movements on the part of the deer when the head is about to be lifted. They stand side to the animal. They believe that they can thus deceive the deer, appearing to them as stumps or trees.''

Naturalist John Muir (1965:137) related that in the mid-1800s in central Wisconsin Indians literally ran whitetails down: ''In winter, after the first snow, we frequently saw three or four Indians hunting deer in company, running like hounds on the fresh, exciting tracks. The escape of the deer from these noiseless, tireless hunters was said to be well-nigh impossible; they were followed to the death.'' Muir's boyhood in Wisconsin was not far from the city and county of Waupaca—a descriptive word from the Winnebago language meaning ''stalking place,'' where one went to hunt deer.

Elsewhere in Wisconsin, in the winter of 1841–1842, Unonius (1936) observed an Indian driving four whitetails onto a frozen lake and hamstringing them with a tomahawk—and also participated in a hunt with Indians on snowshoes who were able to overtake and kill deer floundering in deep snow.

Mayhall (1939:615) noted frequent mention in historical accounts of coastal Texas Indians embossing or ''. . . running down deer'' to exhaustion.

Drive

Drives tended to be made along artificial fences of wood or stone or to natural points of isolation such as onto peninsulas or into water, where the animals essentially were ambushed. Morgan (1851) wrote that the Iroquois of northwestern New York constructed brush fence wings in the shape of a V. These wings were 3.2 to 4.8 kilometers (2–3 miles) in length, and deer were driven to the apex, where they were killed (*see also* Fleming 1789). De Vries (1857) described several types of drive hunts for deer by Mohican Indians in eastern New York. One involved 100 or so Indians walking in a line about 100 paces apart and beating sticks on hollow bones. Deer were chased ahead of the line into the Hudson River, where other Indians awaited in canoes to throw snares around the swimming animals' necks and drown or choke them. Whitetails also were driven between the V-shaped wings of a trap approx-

In 1887, Kiowa Indian Silver Horn (Haw Gone) illustrated this scene of still-hunting for whitetails and wild turkey on the southern Plains. It featured an Indian hunter in a sitting position, camouflaged with a blanket or cape, and using a flintlock rifle mounted on the axis of hand-held sticks or rods used for steady aiming. *Photo courtesy of the Smithsonian Institution National Anthropological Archives.*

imately 1.5 kilometers (1 mile) in length. The wing palisades were 2.5 to 2.8 meters (8–9 feet) high, made of split trees. The mouth of the wing-opening was about 2,000 paces wide; the trap end was only 1.6 meter (5 feet) wide. Whitetails reportedly were driven into the narrowing runway by Indians imitating the sound of wolves, and when the deer passed through the trap end, they were snared.

As late as 1880s, Indians in northern Wisconsin drove deer along fences 19.3 and 24.1 kilometers (12 and 15 miles) in length, built of felled trees. The fences were constructed in such a way that the animals could not break out of the narrowing funnel (*Phillips* [Wis.] *Badger* 1883, *Marinette* [Wis.] *Star* 1883). There is a Fence Lake in Vilas County, Wisconsin, and one in Marquette County, both of which may have been named in recognition of their being sites for this hunting technique.

In September 1615, Champlain (1929[3]: 60–61) recorded a Huron drive of whitetails in southcentral Ontario: ". . . four or five hundred savages placed themselves in line in the woods until they reached certain points which jut out into the river; then marching in their order with bow and arrow in their hands, shouting and making a great noise to frighten the animals,

From October 28 to December 4, 1615, the founder of French Canada, Samuel de Champlain (1929[III]:82–85) witnessed an Iroquois deer drive to a V-winged funnel trap in southeastern Ontario: ". . . we went to a spot some ten leagues away where our savages thought there were deer in great numbers. Some twenty-five savages . . . went into the woods near a little grove of firs where they made a triangular enclosure, closed on two sides, open on one. This enclosure was made of great wooden stakes eight or nine feet in height, joined close together, and the length of each side was nearly fifteen hundred paces. At the extremity of this triangle there is a little enclosure, getting narrower the farther it goes, and partly covered with branches, with only one opening five feet wide, about the width of an average gate, by which the deer were to enter. They did so well that in less than ten days their enclosure was ready. . . . When everything was completed, they set out half an hour before daybreak to go into the woods about half a league from their enclosure, keeping about eighty paces apart, each having two sticks which they strike together, walking slowly in that formation until they reach their enclosure. The deer, hearing this noise, flee before them until they reach the enclosure into which the savages force them to enter. Then the latter gradually coming together towards the opening of their triangle, the deer steal along the said palisades until they reach the extremity, whither the savages pursue them hotly with bow and arrow in hand, ready to shoot. And when the savages reach the extremity of their said triangle, they begin to shout and to imitate the cry of wolves, whereof there are many that devour deer. The deer, hearing this terrifying noise, are forced to enter the retreat by the small opening, whither they are very hotly pursued with arrows, and when they have entered, they are easily caught in this retreat, which is so well enclosed and barricaded that they can never get out of it. I assure you one takes a peculiar pleasure in this mode of hunting, which took place every second day, and they did so well that in the thirty-eight days that we were there, they captured one hundred and twenty deer, with which they made good cheer, keeping the fat for the winter and using it as we do butter, and a little of the meat which they carry home for their feasts. They have other devices for catching deer, such as traps wherewith they cause the death of many." Redrawn by Katheryne C. Tabb from Plate V (page 85) in Champlain (1929).

they keep on until they come to the end of the point. In this way all the animals that are between the point and the hunters are compelled to throw themselves into the water, unless they pass through the line at the mercy of the arrows which are shot at them by the hunters. Meanwhile the savages posted in the canoes, ranged . . . along the edge of the shore, easily draw near the stags and other animals, hunted and harried and very terrified.''

On Puget Island in the Columbia River between Washington State and Oregon, ''. . . Indians hunted the deer [Columbian whitetails] in the low marsh lands along the sloughs. In the early times, before they used guns, the bow and arrow were sometimes used, but generally the hunts were elaborate affairs and long lines of skirmishers drove the frightened deer into inclosures or pitfalls; but after the traders came with guns and gunpowder, the same wary tactics and careful stalking were employed in deer hunting as in the pursuit of other wild game'' (Strong 1906:24).

Jones (1906:140) wrote that deer driven to water by Ojibwa in southcentral Canada ''. . . could be overtaken by canoe when swimming, and killed by cutting the throat; a woman could kill a moose or deer by punching an opening between the ribs with a paddle; the hole let in water which caused the animal to weaken and drown.'' Bersing (1966) pointed out that the Ojibwa word for lake was ''Mitchigan,'' literally translating to ''a wooden fence to catch deer near its banks.''

Reporting on Virginia Algonquian Indians, John Smith noted that ''They . . . drive them into some narrowe point of land, when they find that advantage, and so force them into the river, where with their boats they have ambuscades to kill them'' (Tyler 1907:104).

Driving white-tailed deer to rivers or lakes where hunters in boats could easily overtake the swimming animals was common practice among Indians. In this 1836 oil painting by George Catlin, Sioux Indians in canoes are shown in pursuit of a whitetail buck on the Minnesota River. Since Catlin's artistic detail usually corresponded accurately to his observations, it can be assumed that the hunters' use of rifles meant that they had a secure trade outlet or they just happened to come across a swimming deer. Because powder and shot were scarce commodities, Indians generally used other weapons to dispatch deer in such situations, from which the animals had virtually no chance of escaping. *Artwork and photo courtesy of Mrs. Joseph Harrison and the National Museum of American Art.*

When the Mariames of southern Texas traveled to their prickly-pear collecting grounds they passed along the western shore of Copano Bay. "When an offshore breeze was blowing, hunters spread out and drove deer into the bay, keeping them there until they drowned and were beached by onshore winds" (Campbell 1983:31).

Fire Drive

The use of fire to drive white-tailed deer was a popular and widespread practice. However, there is little evidence that it was widely used in conjunction with fences and traps for the obvious reason that the Indians could ill-afford to rebuild continually the extensive and elaborate catchments needed (Schorger 1953, cf. Morgan 1851).

Reporting on deer hunting by Yuchi Indians, Speck (1909:23) wrote that they ". . . do not seem to have used the deer fence so common in many parts of America. They have been known, however, to employ a method of driving game from its shelter to places where hunters were stationed, by means of fire. Grassy prairies were ignited and when the frightened animals fled to water they were secured by the band of hunters who were posted there."

Catesby (1754[2]:XII) reported this technique in use by Siouan Indians of the Southeast: "Their annual custom of fire hunting is usually in October . . . some hundreds of Indians . . . spreading themselves in length through a great extent of country, set the woods on fire, which with the assistance of the wind is driven to some peninsula, or neck of land, into which deers, bears and other animals were drove by the raging fire and smoak, and being hemm'd in are destroyed in great numbers by their guns." Lawson (1860:335–336) added: "When these savages go a hunting, they commonly go out in great numbers, and oftentimes a great many days' journey from home, beginning at the coming in of the winter; that is, when the leaves are fallen from the trees and are becoming dry. Tis then they burn the woods by setting fire to the leaves and withered bent and grass, which they do with a match made of the black-moss that hangs on the trees in Carolina, and is sometimes above six feet long. This when dead, becomes black, though of an ash color before, and will then hold fire as well as the best match we have in Europe. In places where this moss is not found, as towards the mountains, they make lintels of the bark of cypress beaten, which serve as well. Thus they go and fire the woods for many miles, and drive the deer and other game into small necks of land and isthmuses where they kill and destroy what they please. . . ."

On the Illinois/Wisconsin border in autumn 1837, an observer wrote that, ". . . when the prairie grass had become old and dry, smokes were seen rising on the prairies, some days in one direction, others in a different direction. It was ascertained that these fires were started by Indians for hunting purposes. Whenever they [probably Potawatomi] wanted to take a deer, a rifle party would go forward leaving others behind. The rifle party would go to a selected point, when the party behind would start a long line of fires which soon extended for several miles, being driven by the wind, and as the flames approached, the deer would bound along to get away from the fire, and thus rush toward the riflemen and be shot down" (Beloit [Wis.] *Free Press*, January 24, 1878). Original artwork (detail) by George Winter, date unknown but probably from the late 1830s; the engraving was done by C. A. Jewett and Company of Cincinnati, Ohio. *Photo courtesy of the Indiana State Historical Society.*

Fire Surround

Communal fire surrounds by Virginia Indians were termed "fire hunts" by European witnesses who appear to have been awed by the efficiency and brutality of the procedure. Among the first to chronicle the event was Henry Spelman (1884:cvii) in 1609: "Ther maner of their Huntinge is this wher they meett sum 2 or 300 togither and hauinge ther bowes and arrows and euery one with a fier sticke in ther hand they besett a great thikett round about which ye Deare seinge fleeth from ye fier, and the menn comminge in by a litell and litle incloseth ther game in a narrow roome, so as with their Bowes and arrowes they kill them at ther pleasuer takinge ther skinns which is the greatest thinge they desier, and sume flesh for their prouision."

Colonist William Byrd contributed his 1728 observations: "They fired the Dry Leaves in a Ring of the Centre, where they were easily killed. It is really a pitiful Sight to see the Extreme Distress the poor deer are in, when they find themselves Surrounded with this Circle of Fire; they weep and Groan like a Human Creature, yet can't move the compassion of those hard-hearted People, who are about to murder them. This unmerciful Sport is called Fire Hunting, and is much practic'd by the Indians . . ." (Bassett 1901:222).

Other informative documentations of the fire surround by Virginia Algonquians were prepared by Strachey (1849) and Captain John Smith (Tyler 1907).

Turner (1850) wrote of fire-surround hunting of whitetails by the Iroquois Indians of New York in the late 1700s. He described a site near current Groveland, where about 500 Indians ignited a nearly 127-square-kilometer (49-square-mile) area, driving deer and other animals toward the center where hunters were stationed. Another such burning area existed near Masonville, New York.

One would presume that the fire-surround method, aside from its productivity, involved considerable risk to the hunters both from the flames and also from the shooting by fellow participants. The literature confirms the existence of these dangers, but offers only contradiction on the subject of actual injuries. Typical of the divergent conclusions reached are those of Virginia colonists William Byrd and Robert Beverley. Byrd observed that sometimes the Indians, ". . . in the Eagerness of

Most surrounds for hunting whitetails involved the use of fire to encircle the deer, but there was at least one exception. Le Page du Pratz (1758[2]:71–73) detailed a fireless surround by Natchez Indians, performed ". . . expressly to exercise the young men or to give pleasure to the great Sun. . . ." It is quite apparent from du Pratz's description that it was less of a hunt *per se* than a ritualistic practice: ". . . many young men go, who scatter about in their prairies where there are thickets to find a deer. As soon as they have discovered one they approach it in the form of a widely opened crescent. The bottom of the crescent advances until the deer springs up and takes to flight. Seeing a company of men in front, it very often flees toward one of the ends of the crescent or half circle. This point stops it, frightens it, and drives it back toward the other point which is a quarter of a league or thereabouts distant from the first. This second does the same as the first and drives it back." Ultimately, the quarry was run to exhaustion, seized and dispatched. Illustration by du Pratz; *photo courtesy of the Smithsonian Institution National Anthropological Archives.*

their Diversion, are Punish't for their cruelty, and are hurt by one another when they Shoot across at the Deer which are in the Middle" (Bassett 1901:223). Beverley (1705[2]:39), on the other hand, wrote that, ". . . tho' they stand all round quite clouded in Smoak, yet they rarely shoot each other."

Luring

Quite a number of Indians within the white-tail range resorted to calls to attract deer. Some Carolina Algonquians made the sounds of a fawn by sucking on a folded leaf or using a device made of two pieces of willow (Wetmore 1975). Assiniboine Indians of the Dakotas used a deer call made from a hollowed-out piece of thick bark: "A piece of very thin gristle or membrane, pressed and dried, was cut to fit over the entire top. . . . A band of sinew was wrapped around the middle to hold the top parts together and allowed to dry. The device was placed halfway in the mouth . . . and with both hands cupped over it, was blown twice for each call" (Kennedy 1961:118).

Choctaw Indians also used a call, but combined the bleating noise it produced with rubbing stick against shrubbery to simulate a "horning" sound (Cushman 1899). Swanton (1946:310) described another type of deer call made of two pieces of button willow, round in cross section: "The extreme end was covered with a piece of silver in which was a sort of pin with a knob at the end made of cane." The fawn-bleating sound supposedly not only attracted deer, but deer predators and snakes as well.

Speck (1909) reported on a deer call made of a hollow horn with a wooden mouthpiece, which was used with considerable skill by Yuchi hunters.

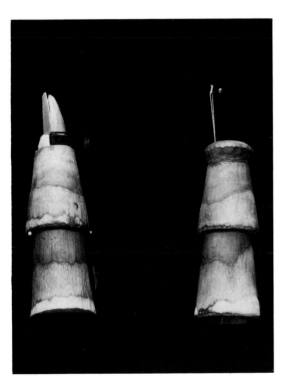 

To lure white-tailed deer within range of bow and arrow, Chippewa hunters used calls that ". . . consisted of two hollow sections, each made of a piece of wood cut in two cones. The two sections fitted together, making a very tight joint. A single-beating reed was in the upper edge of the lower section, the upper section forming the mouthpiece, and the lower section being sufficiently large to permit the free vibration of the reed" (Densmore 1929:129). When blowing into the call, the user cupped his hands over the aperture and opened one hand as the sound was emitted. The tone affected a noise like that of a bleating fawn, and reportedly was very effective at attracting does. The Chippewa deer calls (above left) were collected by Frances Densmore. *Photo courtesy of the Smithsonian Institution National Anthropological Archives.* The wooden deer calls at right were used by Alibamu Indians of Texas. *Photo courtesy of the Museum of the American Indian, Heye Foundation.*

According to Le Page du Pratz (1758), Virginia Algonquians were able to entice deer by making a cry without the aid of an artificial instrument. Fletcher and La Flesche (1972) reported the same for lone Omaha deer hunters.

Potowatomi Indians, reported Bersing (1966), were accustomed to ''rattling up'' deer during the whitetail rutting season by clashing two antlers together to produce the noise of sparring bucks—a technique in use by some hunters today.

Baiting

Chippewa Indians effectively used white cedar slashings to attract deer in winter (*Minneapolis* [Minn.] *Journal,* January 31, 1899). At distances of about 1.6 kilometers (1 mile) apart, groups of up to a dozen trees were cut down. The Indians then returned at night and shot the deer that were feeding on the cedar.

Dogs

Speck (1909) mentioned that Yuchi Indians of the Carolinas used dogs to trail game and hold the quarry at bay until hunters arrived. Other tribes that used dogs in whitetail hunting included the Tonkawas and Karankawas (Mayhall 1939), the Virginia Algonquians (Feest 1978), the Assiniboine (Curtis 1970), the Penobscot (Snow 1978a) and perhaps some Creeks (Swanton 1946). Swanton (1946) thought it entirely improbable that dogs would have been of use to Indians attempting to stalk whitetails—and quite unnecessary in surrounds. Driver (1969:87), Bersing (1966) and others, however, contended that dogs were used extensively in hunting deer and other wildlife, ''. . . probably by the majority of North American tribes. . . .''

Weapons

We were unable to ascertain with satisfaction whether primitive weapons or firearms were used primarily by Amerind whitetail hunters once guns became generally available. Even though Indians across the vast extent of whitetail range acquired guns of different quality, at different times and in different quantity, other investigators, including Goddard (1978), Feest (1978) and Fenton (1978), expressed less uncertainty about the impact of firearms on Indian subsistence and trade. Driver (1969), for

example, cited guns and fur trade as the principal factors of game-animal depletion. Hagen (1961) also implied a direct correlation between Indians obtaining firearms and game disappearance.

It is clear from the literature that some Indians were using firearms to hunt deer by 1630, perhaps earlier. It is not clear however that this practice made primitive weaponry obsolete. Caton (1877:380) wrote that the Indians' ''. . . principal weapon of destruction [in hunting whitetails] was the bow and arrow.'' William Byrd (1928:116), on the other hand, observed in 1728 of the Nottaway Indians in Virginia, to whom guns were readily available: ''Bows and Arrows are grown into disuse except only amongst the Boys.'' However, most other accounts indicate that the Indians tended to use both types of weapons.

At first, the distribution of guns to Indians was prompted by political motivations on the part of the French and British, and by Dutch attempts to undermine the Indian trade alliance with the New Englanders (*see* Trelease 1960). At the time, smoothbore muskets of limited range, questionable accuracy and unreliable function were the only firearms in use. Indians sought these weapons, it seems, not so much for hunting as for intertribal warfare (Bailey 1937, Krech 1981a, Fenton and Tooker 1978). The noise, conspicuousness and enigma of the cumbersome matchlock or wheellock muzzle-loader reportedly afforded the Indians who possessed them a decided psychological boost in dealing with other Indian competitors and enemies (Trigger 1978). But the weapons were apparently of little practical advantage for most hunting.

The guns received by Indians were of poor quality even by the standards of the time. Furthermore, ''. . . their bows and arrows were almost as effective . . . as these firearms had been against . . . encircled animals'' (Camp 1957:539, *see also* Trefethen 1975). The bowman, as George Washington discovered during the French and Indian War, could release half-a-dozen or more arrows to each gunshot by a rifleman (Driver 1969), and the former weapon had a greater killing range (Camp 1957).

No small matter was that of powder and shot, without which the guns were useless. These components were doled out sparingly by the Indians' white allies. Hunting deer for food or hides continued to be primarily an autumn or winter vocation, when it was very difficult for

In his watercolor painting (detail), entitled "Moonlight View on the Mississippi, 75 Miles above St. Louis" (circa 1848), artist Seth Eastman portrayed the popular Indian method of "ambushing" whitetails as they came to drink at dusk. The tribal affiliation of the Indian portrayed was not specified by Eastman, but in 1850 the eastern shore of the Mississippi River "75 miles" above St. Louis was territory of Illinois Indians, perhaps of the Peoria tribe. It appears from the literature and period artwork that lone Indian hunters were not hesitant to use guns instead of primitive weapons to hunt whitetails, at least during mild weather conditions. Although the report of a gunshot would scare away other deer, Indians hunting alone probably were concerned only with killing a single deer, since that likely was all they could carry or transport at a time. *Photo courtesy of the St. Louis Art Museum.*

whites and Indians alike to keep powder dry. Finally, musketry was disadvantageous for communal whitetail hunting because of the noise. A single shot would frighten whitetails away; and since deer hunting then usually was a quantity-harvest mission, the gun was something of a liability in this respect.

By the early 1700s, when the trade impetus had shifted from furbearers to hide animals, at least in the East and Southeast, a significant advance in gun technology had been made. In terms of handling ease and accuracy, the flintlock firearm was a great improvement for both warfare and hunting. This weaponry development may have given an added spur to the trade in whitetail hides. Flintlocks, like predecessor guns, were not readily available to Indians (mostly because whites did not want to lose the firepower edge they held). But the flintlock's improved ballistics elevated warfare to a new lethal dimension. And in this sense, we believe, the bow and arrow became outmoded. The situation created a paradox: Indians needed guns for defense and could obtain them (though still usually only the inferior "trader guns") by bartering deerhides, yet the heightened quest for hides merely compounded intertribal conflict over territorial claims and competition for merchant favor. Just as significantly, the shift of Indian enterprise and subsistence energies in order to acquire guns and other trade goods (Table 5, *see also* Jones 1883, Cumming 1958, Woodward 1965) rendered Amerinds increasingly dependent on whites and vulnerable to white impositions (Brasser 1978, *see also* Morse 1962).

Percussion-discharging and breechloading rifles did not enter the picture until the mid-1800s, by which time the leatherstocking/deerslayer era had all but run its course and populations both of deer and most Indian tribes within the whitetail range were on the decline. Certainly these rifles played a critical role in the market hunting of big game in the 1800s, but with regard to whitetails the most serious damage, or its immutable momentum, likely occurred before the invention of precision firearms.

In our opinion the gun was a formidable factor in the historic relationship of Indians and whitetails not only because it was a hunting weapon, but also because the prospect of its possession—and the corresponding increase in power and defense ability—was a stimulus to the slaughter of deer for hides to be used as currency to purchase more guns. Indeed, the neologism "a buck"—meaning one dollar—originated in the colonial period and reflected the exchange value of a deer hide. The expression "passing the buck" reportedly also was coined from trader parlance of the period (Allen 1929).

Table 5. Barter rates and price schedules for trade goods exchanged with Indians for dressed white-tailed deer hides in parts of the Southeast, 1716 and 1718 (from Crane 1928).

| Trade good | 1716 | | | | 1718 | | | |
| | In Savannah, Georgia | | With Cherokee Indians | | In settlements | | With Creek Indians | |
	Trade good: quantity	Number of deerskins	Trade good: quantity	Number of deeskins	Trade good: quantity	Deerskins (in pounds)	Trade good: quantity	Number of deerskins
Gun	1	30	1	35	1	16	1	25
Pistol	1	20	1	20			1	12
Powder	1 pound	"as you can"			1 pound	1	1 pound	1
Bullets	50	1	30	1	4 pounds	1	40	1
Flints	18	1	12	1	50	1	20	1
Steel	1	1	1	1				
Hatchet	1	2	1	3	1	2		
Cutlass	1	8						
Sword			1	10				
Knife	1	1	1	1	2	1		
Hanger							1	7
Scissors	1	1	1	1				
Axe	1	4	1	5			1	4
Hoe (narrow)	1	2	1	3			1	2
Hoe (broad)	1	4	1	5	1	3	1	4
Kettle (brass)		"as you can"			1 pound	2.5		
Looking glass		"as you can"						
Pipe					24	1		
Rum					1 gallon	4		
Rum (mixed one-third water)	1 bottle	1						
Beads	3 strings	1	2 strings	1	1 pound	3		
Vermillion and red lead					3 pounds mixed 1:2	20		
Strouds	1 yard	6–7	1 yard	7–8	1 yard	4	1 yard	6
Duffel blankets								
White	1	14	1	16	1	8		
Blue or red					2 yards	7	1	6
Striped							1	6
Double-striped cloth					1 yard	3		
Shirt	1	4	1	5	1	3		
Coat								
Broadcloth, laced			1	30				
Strouds, laced							1	20
Half-thick, laced			1	20	1	14	1	14
Double-striped cloth, laced					1	16		'
Strouds, plain							1	18
Half-thick, plain					1	12	1	12
Hat (laced)	1	8			1	3		
Hat (plain)					1	2		
Calico (flowered)					1 yard	4		
Petticoats (calico)	1	12	1	14				
Scarlet caddice	1 yard	1			3 yards	1		
Red girdle	1	2	1	2				

SELLING THE SKY:
TRADE GOODS AND TRADE OFFS

Before the introduction of European mercantile influences, the Amerind and white-tailed deer coexisted in what might be considered "benign symbiosis." Indians subsisted in part on venison and other whitetail by-products, and whitetails benefited to some extent from Indian land-use practices, such as burning and agriculture. Except when disease, certain meteorological events and other decimating factors intervened in localized areas, it likely was a salutary relationship.

As previously mentioned, the Indian perceived himself as having an ecological *and* spiritual bond with wildlife. Some writers have construed this relationship to mean that nature in general was believed by Indians to be controlled by spiritual forces, which the Indians then felt obliged to appease out of fear of retaliation (*see* Presnall 1943, Witthoft 1953*b*, 1967, Speck 1938). Wetmore (1975) reported, for example, that Cherokee hunters who did not apologize to the spirit of a slain deer would suffer from an attack of rheumatism.

That example and much of the literature tend to misinterpret the spiritual Indian/wildlife relationship. As we understand it, the Indian considered the major elements of nature to be embodied forces, and regarded each with awe and reverence (Eastman 1911, Tyler 1975). Nature itself—the life force or spiritual vitality—operated in a self-regulating circular pattern or hoop. Interruption or blockage of circulation by actions against or irreverence toward the elemental forces brought personal, societal or environmental catastrophe, such as disease, famine, flood, etc. Indians believed in the need to maintain contact with the life force, just as animals were able to do by the mysterious wisdom of instinct. By this simplified explanation it can be seen that a Cherokee hunter's prayer (not apology) to the spirit of a slain deer was not offered directly out of fear of retaliation from the animal's embodied force, but rather as a confirmation of the bond between man and animal, and of man's alignment with the circle of life. Basso's (1983) mention of Western Apaches believing that physical or mental illness befell the person who boiled a deer stomach, ate deer tongue or severed the tail of a deer hide reflects the Indian's conscious contact with nature. To treat the deer with perceived disrespect was to lose communion with the animal's spirit and invite blockage in the circulation of nature.

From the animal's standpoint, the Indian reasoned, killing in moderation was a sacrifice of accommodation, and they—the animals—supposedly surrendered themselves voluntarily to needy hunters. Therefore, according to Martin (1978:139), the Amerind considered hunting as ". . . nothing short of a 'holy occupation.'" We know of no reliable evidence that Indians *of the pre-Columbian period* killed deer or other wildlife for reasons considered unnecessary by them, or that they killed animals excessively except very occasionally, when imminent need, limited technology and/or wildlife movements precluded a discriminating harvest—as in the cases of bison (McHugh 1979, cf. Ewers 1980), pronghorn (Frison 1978), elk (McCabe 1982) and caribou (Krech 1981*a*, cf. Hearne 1958). In any case, Martin (1978) emphasized the Indians' compelling metaphysical reasons for not mistreating individual animals, much less overexploiting wildlife populations.

The American Indian's role in nature has received popular acceptance as that of conservationist, even if only passively and before white intrusion (*see* Momaday 1970, Deloria 1970, Jacobs 1972). This characterization also has been advocated in the anthropology literature (MacLeod 1936, Heizer 1955, Fenton 1978) and natural sciences (Marshall 1936, Speck 1938, Ritchie 1955, Elder 1965, Newsom 1969). The notion is not without its skeptics, such as Presnall (1942), Bishop (1981) and Trigger (1976, 1981), and its outright detractors, including Hutchinson (1972). Curiously, Martin (1978) warned against assigning to Amerinds an Old World or Western-type conservation ethic (*see also* Sahlens 1976), but also regarded Indians as too perceptive to have been ignorant of the consequences of overkilling.

The arguments and apparent contradictions would be moot, except that they address a more crucial question: if Indians were "ecological heros," why did they so readily abandon their ecological principles and spiritual values and ultimately dispossess themselves of their successful primitive lifestyles by becoming enthusiastic accomplices in the fur trade? This alteration of values is at the root of the demise of the Amerind as a distinctive cultural entity. Probing it provides insight not only into the historical circumstance of the American Indian, but of the white-tailed deer as well.

"Solemnities at consecrating the skin of a stag to the sun" is the title of this illustration of Timucua Indians in Florida as observed by Jacques le Moyne de Morgues in the 1560s. "Every year, just before spring, Chief Outina's subjects take the skin of the largest stag, with its horns still on, and stuff it with the choicest roots that grow there. On its horns, neck, and body they hang long garlands of the best fruits. Thus decorated, it is carried with music and song to an open, level place and hung on a high tree with its head and breast towards the sunrise. They then pray to the sun that such good things as these offered may grow on their lands. The chief, with his sorcerer, stands near the tree and offers the prayer, while the common people, some distance away, make the responses. After the prayer they salute the sun and depart, leaving the deer's hide on the tree until the next year" (Lorant 1965:105). The artwork is from an engraving by Theodore de Bry (1591) after Le Moyne's drawing. *Photo courtesy of the Smithsonian Institution National Anthropological Archives.*

Of the many theories put forth to explain the Indians' attitude-change toward animals, and the subsequent destruction of whitetails, other wildlife populations, and finally the Indians themselves, four are particularly intriguing.

The first theory holds that Amerinds, because of primitive reasoning, may not have seen the contradiction inherent in their apostasy, or else were indifferent to it (Lévy-Bruhl 1966, Beatty 1964). It is indeed possible that a preliterate people, living day-to-day or season-to-season, could alter or repudiate spiritual relationships if doing so served their empirical best interests: to survive is to be an opportunist by chance or design. This theory however has been criticized as too general, a conjectural rationalization.

Second is a theory proposed by Martin (1978), who suggested that the Indian may have felt that the animals had violated their spiritual pact with him. This pact was to the effect that so long as Indians did not kill carelessly, wantonly or disrespectfully, the animal spirits would not inflict disease. Martin postulated that when Indians began suffering from endemic European diseases, even though they had not violated hunting taboos, they rejected the animal spirits and retaliated. This theory too has been subjected to considerable criticism (*see* Krech 1981*b*), particularly because some of Martin's (1978) ideas regarding primitive life-styles and beliefs did not apply to all Indians.

A more widely accepted theory focuses on economic and political motivations. Bishop

(1981), for example, supposed that Indians joined the fur trade because the goods attainable therefrom could maximize leisure, prestige, generosity and power (*see also* Dailey 1968, Morse 1962). Acknowledging that Indians, like most human beings then and now, were attracted to things new, more and better, Hutchinson (1972) advocated the perspective that they simply were seduced by an innate materialistic impulse (*see also* Rich 1960, Hickerson 1973). Hudson (1981) pointed to the desire of many tribes to align politically with or receive favoritism from traders and the technologically superior society they represented. Intense intertribal hostilities at the time lend credibility to this view. Also, Snow (1981) noted that some Indians recognized their inability to stop overexploitation by competitors, so may have joined in the action out of self-defense. This latter idea coincides with Keating's (1824) explanation of the scarcity of game in parts of the Upper Midwest. He conjectured

A Seminole Indian hunter in the late 1800s, with a whitetail fawn that he may have captured for a pet or which may have imprinted on the hunter after its mother was killed. Note the fresh deer hide on the ground to the Indian's left. Deer hides sold by North American Indians to white traders usually were fully tanned. The traders usually preferred them to hides prepared by whites (Swanson 1940). According to McCauley (1887), Seminoles sometimes marketed dried skins "in the hair." *Photo courtesy of the Smithsonian Institution National Anthropological Archives.*

that Indians turned to indiscriminate hunting because they foresaw the eventual loss of their lands anyway.

Fourth is the idea that Indians in primeval time refrained from overexploiting wildlife only because they lacked the technology to kill and the opportunity to market furs and hides (Farb 1968). This theory is widely disputed from the standpoint that when what Farb (1968:82) termed the ". . . orgy of destruction" got underway, Indians were quite capable of killing animals with primitive weaponry. However, that Indians previously lacked a market that could accommodate their hunting potential and reward their efforts with material benefit is a cogent argument (*see* Brasser 1978).

Whatever the cause(s), the benign symbiosis ended. For countless centuries a venerated kin, the white-tailed deer now was reduced to a commodity, with the North American Indian acting as the white merchant's functionary in a three-century spate of exploitation that left the land nearly barren of certain wildlife and the Indians themselves destitute of subsistence and cultural options. It must be reemphasized that, although "It was the Indian who killed by far the greater number of animals involved in the fur trade . . ." (Cumming et al. 1974:22), the slaughter was inveigled by the white tradesman and underwritten by the European buying public.

In 1832, a force of U.S. Army regulars and militia succeeded in driving the last resisting Indians from the heart of the remaining white-tailed deer range in North America. Led by the aging war chief Mucatamish-kakaekq—better known to history as Black Hawk—the band of about 1,200 Sauk, Fox and Kickapoo Indians looped through northern Illinois and southern Wisconsin in an effort to find sanctuary in their traditional homeland. The maneuver failed, and the Upper Midwest was opened permanently to settlement. Less than a year later came John James Audubon's epitaph to the aeon-old Indian/whitetail relationship . . . and epilogue to Amerind influence on the continent: "For as the Deer, the Caribou, and all other game is killed for the dollar which its skin brings in, the Indian must search in vain over the deserted country for that on which he is accustomed to feed, till, worn out by sorrow, despair, and want, he either goes far from his early haunts to others, which in time will be similarly invaded, or he lies on the rocky seashore and dies" (Graham 1971:17).

PARADISE LOST

In our opinion, white-tailed deer populations historically (1500–1900) went through three distinct stages (Figure 16). The first, from 1500 to the early 1800s, as previously discussed was characterized by massive harvest, primarily at the hands of Indians smitten with trader gee-gaws, metalwares, guns, alcohol, textiles and promises. The period began with a population of perhaps 23 to 34 million whitetails. It ended with a whitetail population of perhaps 35 to 50 percent of its pre-1500 size—but by no means devastated. Habitat modifications of this era probably did not significantly affect deer, in-asmuch as destructive influences seem to have been countered generally by practices that opened the primeval forest. And for the most part settlement was clustered around colonial hubs along the eastern seaboard.

The second stage, from about 1800 to 1865, saw a regrowth of whitetail numbers. Settlement invaded the continental interior, and nearly all Indian influence on the landscape within whitetail range was terminated. The increase was modest (in comparison to the probable pre-Columbian whitetail population) but it was an increase nevertheless. However, it must be recognized that the apparent "boom" of whitetails was observed in new habitats, not necessarily the old, and by persons a generation or more removed from those who had witnessed whitetails in the pristine East. Also, as in the earlier period, land-use practices that altered deer habitat for better or worse on the whole probably offset one another, with the exception that much of the land abandoned in the East and South by westward-bound emigrants was allowed to revert to natural condition and, for a time, was favorable for deer. Therefore, it is this population—some of which was on the biological rebound, some of which was seen for the first time in pristine environs, and some of which was beginning to reestablish in reverting former habitat—that most frequently is regarded as the starting point for historical estimates of the species' abundance.

It is this population that became the target for market and subsistence hunters in the third stage, or exploitation era (1850–1900).

Although more deer were killed in the 300-plus years that constitute the first stage than were killed in the 50-year exploitation era, the latter time-frame represents the period of greatest hunting pressure on wildlife *ever*. With

respect to whitetails, the intensity of harvest was magnified because (1) at the era's outset the deer population was only a fraction of its pre-Columbian size, (2) there were no more wilderness sanctuaries in which whitetails could thrive beyond the reach of hunters, and (3)

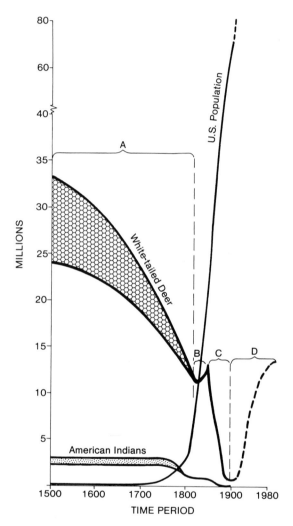

Figure 16. Conceptual diagram of white-tailed deer population status in the United States and Canada, 1500–1980, in relation to the total United States human population and that of American Indians occupying whitetail range, 1500–1900. The whitetail and Indian populations are designated in part by screens to show probable numerical ranges. Letter A indicates the period during which Indians were the principal exploiters of whitetails; B shows the interim period following significant influence of Indians on the species and before intense European contact; C represents the popularly known "era of exploitation"; and D is the modern period of recovery, beginning with enforced protection from overharvest and followed by intensive, scientific management of whitetail populations, habitats and recreational hunting.

positive land-use impacts on habitat were prevented or negated by the continual influx of
people.

As will be elaborated in the following section, we agree that the activities of the exploitation era brought the white-tailed deer to
near-extinction. But we also believe that these
activities figured, collectively, as a "last straw"
rather than an initial or sole cause.

Pilgrim's Progress

By the year 1800, deerskin had lost prominence in the hide trade (Phillips 1961). Immediately before the Revolutionary War, England had secured a monopoly on fur and hide
trade in the colonies and adjacent wilderness.
Spain controlled the trade in Florida, the French
operated out of Canada and Louisiana, and the
Dutch had made some inroads in upper New
England. But most business in deerskins was
done by and for England, which had a considerable demand for leather goods, particularly
inexpensive footwear. While English mer-
chants held sway, nearly all hides, and certainly the best, were shipped from North
America (Crane 1928). Exportation of deer hides
was so extensive that the Court of Connecticut
in 1677 made illegal the ". . . transport out of
this Colony the skinns of bucks and does, which
are so serviceable and vsefull for cloathing"
(Allen 1929:204). When the war ended, however, tanning centers emerged in Philadelphia,
New York City and Boston.

The principal reason for the diminished importance of the deer hide trade was that whitetail populations had been drastically reduced
in the areas of settlement. After 1797 and until
about 1810, foreign markets were inaccessible.
The United States government purchased most
available deerskins for domestic use, but there
were few to be had (Phillips 1961). During that
period in the Northeast and Southeast, the
whitetail was uncommon and viewed as little
more than a curiosity. Though market demand
for deerskins continued, it simply could not be
fulfilled until geographic expansion was feasible.

The trigger for expansion was indepen-
dence. Not only were political and military obstacles (which had hindered movement westward) removed, but economic sanctions also
were lifted. The latter action opened the door
to free enterprise (Cumming et al. 1974), and
the new Americans, enlivened by a spirit of

self-determination, responded enthusiasti-
cally. It had taken nearly 300 years for the
Europeans to push the North American frontier to the Appalachian Mountains. In the next
30 years, from 1780 to 1810—based on a minimum density estimate of at least 0.8 person
per square kilometer (2 per square mile) (Ha-
mond Incorporated 1973)—the settlement area
doubled. By 1850 it had reached the Mississippi River. From a base of slightly more than
1.5 million people in 1776, the United States
population increased nearly 500 percent, to 7.24
million in 1810, and by another 320 percent to
23.19 million in 1850 (U.S. Census Bureau personal communication:1983).

Several factors prompted or contributed to
the press of settlers inland. First, the colonists
were for the most part agronomists (Schmidt
1978a). They cleared, burned and plowed
"stump" and "rock" farms from the New
England uplands, cultivated the thin topsoil
year after year, and rather systematically began to ". . . lose the capacity to exploit agricultural land, woodland and rivers profitably"
(Cumming et al. 1974:22). Marginal farms simply wore out and were abandoned. The invention of the cotton gin sent property seekers
scurrying to previously untrammeled lands of
the South. The Ohio River Valley, the Old
Northwest and beyond offered more and better
agricultural land. Second, transportation improved with the development of railroads and
the construction of canal networks. Time-consuming and laborious overland travel still was
predominant, but the new modes promised access to distant markets with produce and for
supplies. Sustaining the newcomers at each advance was wildlife, primarily deer (*see* Thompson 1853, Caton 1877, DeGarmo and Gill 1958,
Newsom 1969, Schorger 1953).

The whitetail history of the eastern seaboard
was repeated again and again in the Mid-At-
lantic, Midwest and Great Lakes regions, and
the Far South. Annexation of the Louisiana
Territory in 1804 and Florida in 1819 added to
the expansionism momentum and fervor, as
did gold strikes in the West during the mid-
1800s and after the Civil War. Boll weevil in-
vasions that undermined the cotton industry
in much of the South also released waves of
homesteaders.

Clearing for agriculture and commercial logging opened pristine landscapes, giving rise to
the immediate growth of early successional-
stage vegetation that attracted and supported

On the value of white-tailed deer to settlement of North America, William T. Hornaday (1914:86–87) reflected: "To the colonist of the East and the pioneer of the West, the white-tailed deer was an ever present help in time of trouble. Without this omnipresent animal, and the supply of good meat that each white flag represented, the commissariat difficulties of the settlers who won this country . . . would have been many times greater than they were. . . . On every eastern pioneer's monument, the white-tailed should figure. . . ." The original artwork above was painted by C. F. Palmer, entitled "The Pioneer's Home," and produced as a color lithograph by Currier and Ives in 1867. *Photo courtesy of the Harry T. Peters Collection, Museum of the City of New York.*

white-tailed deer (*see* Bartlett 1949). At the van of civilization, mature northern hardwood forests and southern pines fell to an army of lumberjacks. By the 1860s annual lumber production in the United States was in excess of 1.6 billion board feet (Steer 1948). Less than a decade later, more than 1 billion board feet were being cut each year in Wisconsin alone (the second-leading lumber producer behind Michigan), and that total was raised to 3.5 billion before 1890 (Dahlberg and Guettinger 1956).

On grasslands that once had been maintained by natural and Indian-set fires, pioneers followed in the paths of cadastral surveyors, purchased blocks of land for less than $3.50 per hectare ($1.40 per acre), and created a mosaic of cropland and pasture. The result was a diversified habitat for deer, including the growth of palatable woody shrubs and woodlots that were suitable cover.

From about 1800 to 1865 (and even later in some areas), many whitetail populations experienced a temporary rebound, as previously noted. This is confirmed by a number of reliable accounts covering the brief interim between Indian evacuation of—or removal from—traditional homelands and their replacement by loggers, miners, ranchers and farmers (*see* Keating 1824, Jones 1838, McLeod 1846, Agassiz 1850, Wood 1910, Shiras 1921, Foote 1945, Madson 1953). For example, the following appeared in the December 6, 1848 issue of the *Prairie du Chien* (Wis.) *Patriot:* "Since the Indians have left this part of the country, wild game has become plenty. As their principal subsistence has been derived from hunting . . . they have made game of all kinds very scarce. . . . Deer are now found in this vicinity in large numbers.'' Similar sentiments were expressed in *The Minnesota Pioneer* (July 18, 1854): ''Now that the Indians are vamoosed Deer will be more plentiful and killed with less labor than heretofore.''

The recovery continued until settlement growth (Swift 1946, Nixon 1970), expanded agricultural clearing (Oldys 1911, Barnes 1945, Scott 1937), competition with livestock (Trefethen 1970), and overkilling of deer in all seasons forced sharp decline or extirpation altogether. Even during the interim period, the whitetail was used extensively for food and clothing, was perceived as a menace to crop production, and provided a source of income from renewed hide trade and a growing market for venison and other carcass by-products.

As early as 1810, whitetail skins again were appearing regularly on the manifests of fur and hide buyers as trade centers shifted to the forefront of settlement in the South and Midwest, including major depots in New Orleans, St. Louis, Prairie du Chien, Milwaukee, Chicago, and Detroit (Table 6). Philadelphia continued as the hub of the nation's tanning and leather manufacture, which, in 1815, was a 12–20-million-dollar annual industry and ''. . . used all the deerskins available'' (Phillips 1961[II]:161). Deer hides transported from St. Louis and farther north tended to be more valuable than those from the South because they were larger, and southern humidity often caused baled hides to rot in storage or transport.

Deerskins were designated ''wash leather'' or ''oil skins'' depending on individual tanning suitability. Among the clothing uses of deer hide at the time were leatherstockings, hats, caps, gloves, breeches, aprons, waistcoats, doublets, entire suits, coats, belts, shoe uppers and boot linings. Deerskin also was used in window panes in lieu of glass and as rugs, wall covers, snowshoe netting, upholstery fabric, bellows, harnessing, saddles, handbags, book binding and for most leather products requiring a soft and durable hide. Young (1956) described bullwhip ends made of rawhide and buckskin thongs used to splice broken telegraph lines.

In addition to the marketing of hides, there was demand for other whitetail parts. Antler served as chandeliers, umbrella stands, coat and hat racks, gun racks, bootjacks, knife handles, forks, buttons, ornaments, sizing in cloth manufacture, and was used to produce ammonia. Deer hair was used for stuffing in such items as saddles, carriage blankets and furniture. In 1806, 120 kegs of deer tallow weighing 4,536 kilograms (5 tons) were shipped from Green Bay, Wisconsin (Grignon 1857), presumably for the making of candles.

Settlers of each progressive wilderness front brought with them livestock to furnish meat, dairy and poultry staples. Invariably these domestic animals were not brought in sufficient number to sustain the initial farmsteads. Fish and wildlife helped to fill the early larders, with livestock supplementing what could be taken from the land. The same was true at lumber

Table 6. Reported values of white-tailed deer hides marketed in various parts of North America, 1719–1900.

Year	Place	Value	Source
1719	Massachusetts	7 shillings 6 pence per pound for oil-tanned hides 5 shillings per pound for Indian-dressed hides 1 shilling eight pence per pound for hides in the hair	Allen (1929)
1747–1748	South Carolina	17 pence per pound	Crane (1928)
1763	West Virginia	18 pence per pound	Kellogg (1937)
1785	Tennessee	6 shillings per hide	Young (1956)
1786	Quebec	1 shilling 8 pence per hide	Young (1956)
1804	Louisiana	$0.40 per pound	Phillips (1961)
1808	Iowa	$0.26 per hide	Gue (1903)
1814	Michigan	$1.50 per hide	Phillips (1961)
1819	Illinois	$0.50 per hide	Woods (1822)
1832	Wisconsin	$0.27 per hide	Schorger (1953)
1833	Missouri	$0.75 per hide	Rahn (1983)
1850–1870	Minnesota	$0.25–0.30 per pound	Swanson (1940)
1876–1880	Wyoming	$0.20 per pound	Cook (1923)
1881	Missouri	$0.47 per hide	Robb (1959)
1893–1900	Montana	$0.50 per hide	Mussehl and Howell (1971)

and mining camps. Until overland travel routes were established and railroads built, livestock was of secondary importance to pioneer subsistence. There is evidence, too, that once beef was available it was less preferred and valued than venison (Kimball and Kimball 1969). In any case, a continual fresh supply of game was nearly as essential to the first settlers in all regions as it had been to the Indians. And as in colonial days, the most provident source of wild meat was venison, and the most efficient suppliers were Indians (Swanson 1940, Trefethen 1970, *see also* Allen 1929).

With Indians removed, confined or otherwise eliminated, the grangers, miners and sawyers divided their labor between working the land and hunting it. But with the free enterprise system in full swing, even on the frontier job specialization gradually eroded the need for total self-sufficiency. It soon became increas-

ingly common for pioneers to obtain needed food directly from professional hunters or from market places in budding townships.

To a great extent, frontier communities existed with a barter economy, and whitetail hides and venison served as important mediums of exchange (*see* Young 1956, Allen 1929, Williams 1928, Schorger 1953). As settlements grew and manufactured goods became more accessible, currency was exchanged for whitetail products. Records show that the price of venison or "wild mutton" fluctuated very little in the 1800s, except following severe winters. Table 7 shows prices of whitetail venison in various parts of North America from 1638 to 1910. Table 8 focuses on venison prices in Wisconsin during most of what can be considered that state's settlement period. The pricing in both tables may not be an accurate measure of relative abundance of deer or even of venison in

Table 7. Reported values of white-tailed deer venison marketed in various parts of North America, 1638–1910.

Year	Place	Value	Source
1638	Rhode Island	2 pence per pound	Anonymous (1856)
1645–1662	Connecticut	1–2.5 pence per pound	Allen (1929)
1650s	New York	5 guilders per buck	Van der Donck (1841)
1757	New Hampshire	1 shilling 6 pence per pound	Woodbury et al. (1851)
1763	New York	2 pence per pound	De Voe (1862)
1783	Virginia	2 Spanish dollars per hundred-weight	Schoepf (1911)
1819	Illinois	$1.00 per 60–100 pound carcass	Woods (1822)
1830s	Iowa	$1.00 per deer or $0.02–0.03 per pound	Dick (1941)
1831	Illinois	Halfpenny per pound	Burlend (1848)
1833	Missouri	$0.03–0.04 per pound	McKinley (1960)
1838	Illinois	$0.75–1.00 per "ham"	Jones (1838)
1841	West Virginia	$0.03 per pound	Young (1956)
1854	Minnesota	$0.08–0.10 per pound	*The Minnesota Pioneer* (St. Paul), November 7, 1854
1870s	Wisconsin	$0.05–0.06 per pound	Bersing (1966)
1871	Minnesota	$0.04 per pound	*Alexandria* (Minn.) *Post*, November 4, 1871
1874	Illinois	$0.125 per pound	Schorger (1953)
1874	New York	$0.30 per pound	Young (1956)
1878	Missouri	$0.05–0.06 per pound	Rahn (1983)
1880	Michigan	$0.02 per pound	Jenkins and Bartlett (1959)
1880s	Minnesota	$0.10 per pound	Kimball and Kimball (1969)
1881	Missouri	"Hams" at $0.08 per pound	Robb (1959)
1884	New York	$0.25 per pound	Swanson (1940)
1885	Montana	$0.06 per pound	Brown and Felton (1955)
1890	Nebraska	$0.10–0.12 per pound	Nebraska Game and Parks Commission (1979)
1893	Minnesota	$0.08–0.09 per pound	Swanson (1940)
1898	Minnesota	$0.15 per pound[a]	*Minneapolis* (Minn.) *Journal*, January 31, 1899
1910	New York	$0.22–0.25 per pound for whole deer or $0.30–0.35 per pound for a saddle	Oldys (1911)

[a]Resale value after having been purchased from Indians at $0.04 per pound.

the marketplace. However, given inflation over the periods covered, it appears that venison as a commercial product actually decreased in value even as the whitetail populations declined. This likely is explained by the diminishing dependence of citizens on wild animal food. The fairly stable prices over time also indicate a continual supply of venison, but it is incorrect to assume that under such pressure the deer populations were maintained at levels of sustained yield. In fact, market hunters continually were forced farther and farther afield. Blame for local extirpations of deer often was placed on predators, since ". . . there was little evidence or reason to believe that the bounties of the land were limited" (Wildlife Management Institute 1978:420–421). Later voices indicted commercial hunters, even though, according to Swanson (1940), the amount of deer and other game sent to market was small compared with that taken by hungry settlers.

Railroads and Recoils

Whitetail market hunting reached its zenith after the Civil War and with the advent of the widespread availability of repeating rifles. Henderson and Craig (1932:140) characterized this period's onset: "Civilized man, with the arteries of commerce and the development of more luxuriant taste, could easily dispose of his surplus for cash with which to buy the luxuries he craved, and his weapons made it easy for him to obtain a much greater supply of game and furs than he himself could use. Hence the slaughter began."

Table 8. Reported values of white-tailed deer venison marketed in some Wisconsin counties, 1846–1895.

Year	County	Value	Source
1844	Racine	$0.75 per deer	*Racine Advocate,* January 23, 1844
1846–1847	Grant	"Saddles" at $0.02–0.03 per pound	Evans (1910)
1849	Jefferson	$2.00 per 100 pounds	*Watertown Chronicle,* September 5, 1849
1856	Jackson	$0.04 per pound	*Milwaukee Sentinel,* January 16, 1856
1857	Crawford	$3.00–5.00 per 100 pounds	*State Journal* (Madison), January 6, 1857
1860	Outagamie	$0.04 per pound	*Appleton Crescent,* December 1, 1860
1866	Jackson	$0.06–0.08 per pound	*Black River Falls Banner,* December 6, 1866
1868	Adams	"Hams" at $0.06 per pound	*Friendship Press,* December 4, 1868
1868–1869	Eau Claire	$4.00 per deer	Bartlett (1929)
1869	Juneau	$0.05 per pound	*New Lisbon Argus,* November 18, 1869
1873	Adams	"Saddles" at $0.06 per pound	*Friendship Press,* January 3, 1874
1873	Polk	$0.05 per pound	Schorger (1953)
1873	Winnebago	$0.06 per pound	Schorger (1953)
1874	Adams	$0.04–0.05 per pound	*Friendship Press,* December 12, 1874
1874	Polk	$0.07 per pound	*Osceola Press,* January 10, 1874
1877	Eau Claire	$0.18–0.26 per pound	Swift (1946)
1882	Crawford	$0.10 per pound	*Prairie du Chien Courier,* December 12, 1882
1882	Winnebago	$0.125 per pound	*Oshkosh Times,* November 25, 1882
1883	Taylor	$0.05 per pound	*Medford Star and News,* November 17, 1883
1894	Oneida	$0.05–0.06 per pound	*Rhinelander Herald,* October 27, 1894
1895	Wood	$0.08 per pound	Schorger (1953)

The Central Meat Market in Lincoln, Nebraska, sometime before 1879, featured white-tailed and mule deer, elk, pronghorn, geese, ducks, and upland gamebirds for local consumption. Except for whitetails, the other big game represented in the scene were no longer found in the vicinity of Lincoln, so undoubtedly were received from the West via railroad. As much as eastern tanneries and eating establishments clamored for the take of commercial hunters on the fringe of advancing white civilization, so too was game in demand as standard fare for the people who pioneered the new frontiers. Less than a decade after these photos were taken, big game market hunting in most parts of North America came to an end. In some areas such vocation was deemed illegal, but for the most part it simply was no longer profitable. *Photo by E. G. Clements; courtesy of the Nebraska State Historical Society.*

Market hunting grew along the course of—and at the pace of—railroad construction (Kimball and Kimball 1969). The railway system in the United States expanded from 37 kilometers (23 miles) in length in 1830 to 4,535 kilometers (2,818 miles) in 1840, to 14,518 kilometers (9,021 miles) in 1850, to 49,301 kilometers (30,635 miles) in 1860, to 85,155 kilometers (52,914 miles) in 1870, to 150,124 kilometers (93,296 miles) in 1880, to 263,277 kilometers (163,597 miles) in 1890 and to more than 355,000 kilometers (220,000 miles) by 1900 (Figure 17). The addition of 112,650 kilometers (70,000 miles) of rail in the single decade of 1880–1890 was considered ". . . a marvelous achievement unparalleled in the economic history of any other country in the world" (Beach 1911 [XVI]:191). Trains that ran on the labyrinth of tracks across whitetail range were important vehicles, both figuratively and literally, in the species' nearly total demise. By rail, millions of immigrants flooded the continent's interior, and millions of pounds of deer hides and venison were drained out. From Michigan, for example, ". . . of the 70,000 deer killed . . . in 1880, about 50,000 were shipped from the state or destroyed for the hides"

(Mershon 1923:101).

Refrigerator cars came into operation in 1867, on trains first running between Chicago and New York City, with the capability of keeping meat fresh for 10 days in midsummer. Merritt (1904) convincingly argued that market hunt-

Figure 17. Railroads in the United States, 1860, with a combined length of more than 48,280 kilometers (30,000 miles) (from Paulin 1932).

ing was not just the beneficiary of railroad refrigeration, but the actual stimulus for its development.

The principal whitetail venison markets from 1870 to 1900 were Chicago, St. Paul, Boston, Omaha, New York and Philadelphia. In the early 1900s the major markets—conditioned by state and federal laws as well as by supply—were Boston, Chicago, New York and Philadelphia (*see* Oldys 1911). A Philadelphia man wrote of wild-animal food available in St. Paul in 1870: "You can eat grouse three times a day if you please, and the finest flavored of trout and venison are a drug on the market" (Swanson 1940:52–53).

The Christmas 1879 dinner menu for the Maxwell House in Nashville, Tennessee, featured "Saddle of Minnesota Venison, with Red Currant Jelly" among the game served. At the time, whitetails had been nearly eradicated in Tennessee and surrounding states. Importation of venison from depots in St. Paul, Minnesota, via the railroad, gave Nashville diners a chance to taste this "exotic" fare. Market hunting in Minnesota was a thriving industry from the mid-1860s to the early 1890s. Hundreds of tons of venison were shipped annually to eastern markets, and game laws did little to discourage the killing or trade (Swanson 1940). By the mid-1890s, the deer supply had dwindled and, despite continuing demand for venison, market hunting became less lucrative. *Photos courtesy of the Wildlife Management Institute.*

In tandem with stewpot hunting and habitat loss emanating from a prevailing parochial notion that "... civilization and forests were two mutually exclusive propositions" (Leopold 1918:1), unregulated killing had a devastating impact on whitetail populations (*see also* Grinnell and Reynolds 1894, Oldys 1911). While the actual extent of the take in the exploitation era was numerically less than during the 1500–1800 heyday of Indian trade, the rate of kill was considerably more intense. One example, of a great many, is the kill of about 6,000 whitetails by a father and son in Minnesota in 1860. "The profligate attitude of white settlers ... was based upon the assumption that game must all disappear eventually, hence no thought of the future need spoil their pleasure of the day" (Swanson 1940:80). An editorial comment in the *Rousseau County* (Minn.) *Times* (April 10, 1896) reiterated this cavalier point of view: "Great country this for game in and out of season. We have venison ... any time we take the trouble to have it brought in. Nothing like enjoying the good things on the frontier while they last and before civilization makes the game scarce."

The concept that civilization pushed back the American frontier, sweeping wildlife before it, is misleading. Repeatedly, species by species, it became obvious that wildlife, including whitetails, were *not* retreating to habitats "somewhere else"; they simply were being overrun. The decline of wildlife was an unfortunate reality of the time and proved extremely difficult to stem, stop and reverse.

Hunting whitetails for the table or market involved a variety of techniques that were little more refined than those previously used by the Indians. One of the most popular methods was known generally as fire-hunting—another name for the colloquialisms "shining" or "jacklighting" (Huntington 1904, Hornaday 1935, Browning 1972). Still-hunting from blinds or elevated platforms at mineral licks and runways, and baiting with salt or grain, were usual practices in winter, as was stalking, though the latter was done more commonly by sportsmen and subsistence hunters than by market gunners.

Other practices included running with dogs or "hounding" (Goodwin 1859, Swift 1946, Nichols 1923, Shaw and McLaughlin 1951), decoying with tame deer (Benson 1937), shooting from a sleigh in winter while camouflaged in white (Baird 1900, *see also* Park 1877), and

Fire-hunting for whitetails involved the use of pitch-fired torches or lanterns positioned at the bow of a boat. The hunters poled at night along lakeshores or riverbanks until their lights reflected the eyes of a feeding or drinking deer. "If no noise is made the victim will stand and gaze at the light until it is within a few yards, and so give opportunity for the fatal shot. Many are taken in this way in the early autumn ..." (Newhouse 1869:76). *Photo from Gosse (1859).*

pursuing deer in deep snow (*see* Roosevelt et al. 1902, McNeil 1974, Schorger 1953). Caton (1877) gave lengthy descriptions of a number of whitetail-hunting techniques for both woodland and prairie environments in the East and Midwest, including drives, stalking on horseback, decoying with livestock, coursing with greyhounds and chasing in canoes. Murphy (1879) provided similar documentation for the Northwest.

Murphy (1879:190) pointed out that hunters "... in different sections of the country have their own peculiar methods of hunting the Deer. A rifle is ridiculed by the men who hunt in the cane-brakes of Louisiana, and a shotgun is an abomination in the Adirondacks or in the Rocky Mountains. As a rule, along the Atlantic Coast and in the South, hounds are employed in hunting Deer." Seton (1929:285) felt that "The greatest enemy of the whitetail is the buckshot gun; with its unholy confederates, the jacklight and canoe." Hornaday (1931:9–10) laid blame for ". . . about 90 percent of our extirminated game . . ." on the manufacturers of sporting arms and ammunition. Less circumspect was Allen (1929:236), who pointedly wrote: "The main destructive factor was man."

Other devices for hunting whitetails included snares, poison, traps, deadfalls, pitfalls, fire and set-guns (McNeil 1974, Schorger 1953, Shaw and McLaughlin 1951, Jenkins and Bartlet 1959). None was considered sporting, but quantity, not recreation, was the market hunter's objective. Although Newhouse (1869:76–77) supposed leghold traps for deer to be "somewhat barbarous," he condoned and explained their use: "For taking Deer a trap must be a strong one, and the jaws should be spiked, and so shaped and adjusted that when sprung they will remain open about half an inch to prevent breaking the bone. The trap should be placed in the path of the deer where it crosses a stream or enters a lake; and it should be set under water and concealed by some covering. If it is as heavy as it ought to be (say of three or four pounds' weight), it should not be fastened at all or even clogged; as the animal is very active and violent when taken, and will be sure to break loose . . . if his motions are much impeded. If the trap is left loose, the Deer, when caught, will make a few desparate lunges and then lie down; and will seldom be found more than ten or fifteen rods from where he was taken."

Recreational hunting for whitetails appears to have been a logical sequent of subsistence hunting. It began in earnest about 1830 (Reiger 1975), but this does not presume that before that time Nimrods of whatever motivation did not enjoy the hunt. A verse from Edward Johnson's 1648 poem, "Good News from New-England" (Meserole 1968:166), dispels any notion that the pursuit of whitetails was mere drudgery:

"The tripping Deer with length of leaps,
    do burst through frozen snow,
Hunters pursue with bracket shooes,
    at length they weary grow.
Then down the dogs them sudden draw,
    expos'd to hunters pleasure,
Their flesh well welcome, and their
skins, are chiefe of Indian pleasure."

Without restrictions, sportsmen contributed to the overkill of deer, though their actual take prior to 1900 is difficult to quantify.

The literature provides divergent perspectives on the merits of recreational hunting for white-tailed deer in the nineteenth century. Theodore Roosevelt, for one, opined: "To my mind the chase of the whitetail, as it must usually be carried on, offers less attraction than the chase of any other kind of our large game" (Roosevelt et al. 1902:78). Huntington (1904) and Dodge (1877) shared that view. Others, including John D. Caton, George Bird Grinnell and William T. Hornaday, considered the whitetail premier among North America's big game. Their position was cogently summarized by Wolfe (1890:187), who wrote: "The Virginia Deer is the wildest, shyest, shrewdest, and most difficult to hunt, successfully, of all the species of *Cervidae* on this continent. . . ." The argument was (and is) academic.

Sanctions and Sanctimony: The Origin of Conservation

The case for the protection of whitetails began to take form long before the exploitation era of the 1800s. As early as 1646, the decline of whitetails along the Atlantic seaboard prompted the town of Portsmouth, Rhode Island, to order ". . . that there shall be noe shootinge of deere from the first of May till the first of November; and if any shall shoot a deere within that time he shall forfeit five pounds . . ." (Trefethen 1975:39). This ordinance set a precedent that was followed by most of the other colonies. The preamble of the 1698 Connecticut law reflected official concern over whitetails' future: "The killing of deer at unseasonable times of the year hath been found very much to the preiudice of the Colonie, great numbers of them have been hunted and destroyed in deep snowes when they are very poor and big with young, the flesh and skins of very little value, and the increase greatly hindered" (Allen 1929:204). And in 1705 the Rhode Island General Assembly noted that it ". . . hath been informed that great quantities of deer hath been destroyed . . . out of season, either for skins or flesh, which is great destruction of the creatures, without profit, and may prove much to the damage [not only] of this Colony for the future . . . [but] to the whole country, if not prevented" (Anonymous 1856[3]:518).

Matthiessen (1959:57) noted that ". . . the earliest game laws in the colonies were negative in tone, promoting destruction rather than protection." Many such laws related only indirectly to deer. They were in the form of bounties for predators, and although whitetails may have increased as result of local wolf and mountain lion eradications, the effect was only temporary. In any case, predators drew a bounty not so much because of their impact on deer, but because they were a perceived threat to people and a real danger to livestock.

According to Lund (1980:20), initial laws that directly related to whitetails (Table 9) were fashioned ". . . to seek a maximum sustained yield of animals." If this was true, and we doubt it, they were ". . . quite unsuccessful" (Trefethen 1975:40). Seasons closed during the rut or yarding periods were promulgated primarily to ensure that more deer in good condition would be available at other times. Subsequent regulations on deer harvest had little to do with protecting and maintaining whitetail numbers. For example, fire-hunting was banned because of the potential for accidental torching of pastures and settlement dwellings; skinning deer and leaving the carcass in the woods or fields near settlements was prohibited because the carrion attracted wolves; to protect people from gunshots, hunting close to settled areas was forbidden; and devices such as pits, snares and traps were outlawed because of the danger to citizens and livestock.

The early laws to protect deer ". . . were no doubt feebly enforced" (Shaw and McLaughlin 1951:3), partly because they tended to be reactions to temporary shortages of whitetails, such as occurred following severe winters. There were scattered convictions of violators (mostly for hunting out of season) by town-based sheriffs or constables, but most illegal killing took place away from settlements. The first colony to employ persons specifically to enforce game laws was Massachusetts, in 1739, when two "deer reeves" were hired on a commission basis. Even as a forerunner in the enforcement of wildlife regulations, Massachusetts made the appointments more than 40 years after the relevant statute had gone into effect. With few exceptions, the enforcement of deer-hunting and hide-exportation laws in the colonies, territories, states and provinces followed protective legislation by several decades or more (Table 9). Not until 1873 in Maine did a state or province restrict the number of whitetails that could be harvested.

Despite these various attempts to curtail the steady decline of whitetails, inertia was not achieved in most regions until the end of the 1800s, and even later in others. A major problem regarding the wholesale slaughter of deer and other wildlife was legal provincialism. Major differences in hunting regulations existed between neighboring states, so restriction in the traffic of wild meats and wildlife products was almost nonexistent. Not until the federal (U.S.) Lacey Act of 1900—which prohibited interstate traffic in wild game taken in violation of state law—was market hunting and the decimation of wildlife for commercial gain effectively ended (Figure 18).

Although effective legislation and adequate enforcement were outgrowths of an emerging environmental conscience in the late 1800s, the real catalyst for termination of the whitetail overkill, ironically, was deer scarcity. T. S. Palmer of the U.S. Bureau of Biological Survey (antecedent of the U.S. Fish and Wildlife Service) estimated that approximately 300,000 whitetails remained in the United States in 1890

Table 9. Chronology of the initial laws regulating the take of white-tailed deer in the United States and Canada, and the first enforcement by an individual or individuals hired for that purpose.

State or province	Date of first law protecting whitetails	Type of first law[a]	Beginning date of hired enforcement[b]	Source[c]
Rhode Island	1646	Hunting prohibited	Early 1700s	J. Chadwick
New Jersey	1679	Prohibited export of dressed skins of deer killed by Indians	1892	J. E. Applegate
Connecticut	1698	Harvest season set	1866	J. V. Spignesi, Jr.
Massachusetts	1698	Harvest season set	1739	J. McDonough
Virginia	1699	Harvest season set	1916	J. W. Raybourne
New York	1705	Harvest season set	1880	G. P. Rasmussen
Pennsylvania	1721	Harvest season set	1896	T. Godshall
Maryland	1730	Hunting by firelight prohibited	1918	R. L. Miller
North Carolina	1738	Harvest season set	1738	G. L. Barnes

Table 9. (continued)

State or province	Date of first law protecting whitetails	Type of first law[a]	Beginning date of hired enforcement[b]	Source[c]
New Hampshire	1740	Harvest season set	1880	W. Carter
Vermont	1741	Harvest season set	1762	J. Hall
South Carolina	1780	Night hunting prohibited	1878	J. Fuller
Georgia	1790	Night fire-hunting prohibited	1803	D. Waller
Mississippi	1803	Night fire-hunting prohibited	1933	E. J. Hackett
Alabama	1803	Night fire-hunting prohibited within four miles of settlement; no hunting on Sundays	1907	J. Hagopian
Florida	1828	Night fire-hunting prohibited	1897	S. Ball
Maine	1830	Harvest season set	1830	W. T. Shoener
Wisconsin	1851	Harvest season set	1887	F. Haberland
Illinois	1853	Harvest season set	1885	P. Chiles
Iowa	1856	Harvest season set	1896	L. Gladfelter
Ohio	1857	Harvest season set	1886	R. Donohoe
Indiana	1857	Harvest season set	1889	D. Shroufe, P. M. Swoveland
Louisiana	1857	Unknown	1903	T. Prickett, J. Newsom
Minnesota	1858	Harvest season set	1887	L. Rutske
Michigan	1859	Harvest season set	1887	J. Vogt, R. Wood
Delaware	1859	Harvest season set	1912	A. J. Florio
Nebraska	1859	Harvest season set	1901	K. Menzel
Kentucky	1861	Harvest season on does set	1904	H. Barber
Quebec	1868	Harvest season set	1867	F. Potvin, M. Bélanger
Wyoming	1869	Seasonal restriction on sale of venison	1899	W. Brown
British Columbia	1870	Harvest season set	1905	W. MacGregor
Missouri	1874	Harvest season set; sale of venison out of season prohibited	1905	W. Porath
New Brunswick	1875	Harvest season set	Unknown	A. H. Boer
Washington	1875	Harvest season set	1890	W. L. Myers
Manitoba	1876	Harvest season set	1898	E. F. Bossenmaier, B. Knudsen
Colorado	1877	Harvest season set	1877	B. Hernbrode
South Dakota	1881	Prohibited leaving carcass remains on open prairie	1893	C. Post
North Dakota	1881	Prohibited leaving carcass remains on open prairie	1897	J. V. McKenzie
Texas	1881	Harvest season set	1919	C. K. Winkler
Saskatchewan	1883	Harvest season set	1883	J. D. Kinnear
Arizona	1887	Harvest season set	1890s	S. Gallizioli
Nova Scotia	1891	Hunting prohibited	1877	M. H. Prime
Montana	1895	Harvest season set	1901	J. Egan
New Mexico	1895	Harvest season set; prohibited "wanton" killing and killing for hides of protected species; forbade selling hindquarters as well	1895	J. Crenshaw
Idaho	1899	Harvest season set	1899	H. Wilson
Oregon	1899	Harvest season and bag limit set	1899	J. Thiebes
Alberta	1907	Harvest season set	1906	M. Watson
Kansas	1908	Hunting prohibited	1905	K. Sexson
West Virginia	1909	Prohibited sale and shipment; buck-only hunting	1921	J. I. Cromer
Tennessee	1911	Hunting prohibited	1903	L. Marcum
Arkansas	1915	Harvest season set; buck-only hunting	1915	G. Purvis
Oklahoma	1916	Hunting prohibited	1908	J. Skeen
Ontario	1921	Harvest season set	1886	H. Smith, K. Westhouse

[a]In some cases the information provided referred to a colony or a settlement in what is now the state or province in question, or related to a time when the present-day state or province had territorial status or was part of a territory.
[b]Law-enforcement hirees were designated deer reeves, game protectors, game wardens, conservation officers, or by other title.
[c]Respondents to 1983 mail and telephone survey.

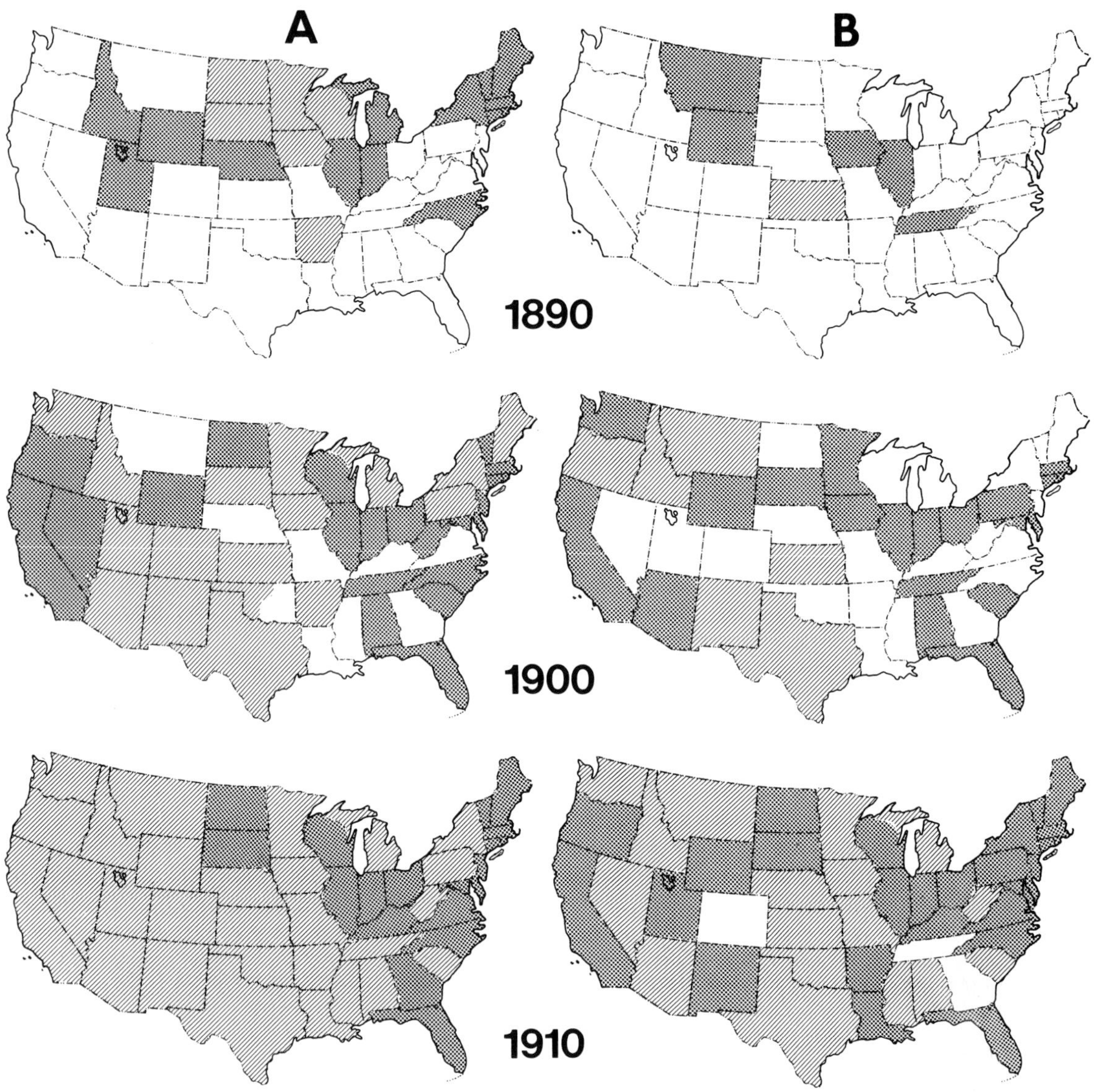

Figure 18. State prohibition of the A. export and B. sale of all game animals (line screen) or certain species (dot screen), 1890–1910 (from Oldys 1911).

(Trefethen 1970). Seton (1909) suggested that the whitetail count for all of North America at the turn of the century was about 500,000, which Trefethen (1975) thought to be a maximum estimate, suggesting that the number may have been as low as 350,000. The species was no longer a regular or featured commodity in the marketplace, primarily because its numbers did not warrant hunter interest and investment. The whitetail rarely was hunted, even for the table, because it was rarely seen. Also, the bison had temporarily supplanted other hides in tanning and fashion industries, and glutted the market; textile manufacture was blossoming with a wealth of immigrant labor; and cattle ranching had achieved the status of big business.

Nevertheless, the laws restricting commercial harvests, and in addition the relatively sudden realization by sportsmen that wildlife was an exhaustible and exhausted resource, helped to give pause to the decline. The history of the white-tailed deer helped to stimulate the concern that was origin of modern wildlife management, initially as a political process of trial and error and eventually a scientific discipline.

Chapter 3

PHYSICAL CHARACTERISTICS

Peggy R. Sauer
Principal Wildlife Biologist
New York Department of Environmental Conservation
Albany, New York

The white-tailed deer. . .its very name evokes an image of a gentle herbivore with graceful movements, beautiful coat, supple legs, alert brown eyes and stately antlers. The whitetail's appearance generates considerable controversy over its management. How, some people ask, can anyone hunt these innocent creatures?

It is difficult to keep perceptions of deer separate from the values, qualities and behavior that people ascribe to themselves. The appealing characteristics of deer actually evolved in response to such factors as imminent predation and seasonal climatic changes. The whitetail's legs, for example, evolved in part as a survival strategy—to be able to run faster and more fluently through a variety of escape covers than can their natural predators. The animal's keen eyesight and acute sense of smell also are mechanisms of survival. Its coat has thermoregulatory qualities as well as serving as camouflage. And the antlers of whitetail bucks evolved as a weapon system and a display mechanism associated with social hierarchy, especially in terms of reproduction. These same adaptive features make the whitetail a challenging adversary when faced with predation by humans.

Pelage

The whitetail fawn's coat coloration of white spots set in a reddish-brown background enables the animal to blend with patterns of sun and shade. Severinghaus and Cheatum (1956) counted the number of white spots on three fawns, and found them to range from 272 to 342. Spot-size averaged between 0.6 and 1.3 centimeters (0.24–0.51 inch) in diameter. Two rows of spots occur along each side of the area of the backbone, extending from the base of the tail to the ears. Spots on the neck essentially are two continuous white lines. The remainder of the pelage spots are restricted to the trunk of the body, occurring at random over the sides and flanks. This spotted coat is lost when the molt occurs in August and September.

During summer, adult white-tailed deer have a thin coat of reddish-brown hair about 1–3.5 millimeters (0.04–0.18 inch) deep on the animal's trunk (Jacobsen 1973). This coat also is shed during August and September. Both fawns and adults replace summer hair with brownish-gray winter hair that is from 5 to 27 millimeters (0.2 to 1.1 inches) deep. Hair depth is a major

73

The distinctive camouflage spot pattern, including two rows of spots dorsally, on whitetail fawns is quite evident on these animals being hand-reared in 1940 by Civilian Conservation Corps workers in North Carolina. *Photo by Clint Davis; courtesy of the U.S. Forest Service.*

Deer have more white hair in their coats than is generally obvious. In addition to the white flag on the raised tail, whitetails have white bellies and white hair under the chin and around the eyes and the muzzle. In a few instances the white hair is extensive enough to produce a piebald or white deer. However these deer are uncommon in wild populations and they seldom survive for any length of time because of their conspicuous coloration.

Studies at the Seneca Army Depot in New York have led to several discoveries concerning the white coat color (Martin and Rasmussen 1981). First, white animals have brown eyes, and their white coats include some brown hairs that give a brown "wash" to the coat. Second, the white color is inherited as a dominant trait. Third, if a deer is heterozygous for coat color, the white predominates. Fourth, true albino deer with pure white coats and pink eyes are rare.

Melanism has been noted in whitetails, but also is rare.

A young whitetail buck beginning to molt following a long winter. This shedding is much more noticeable than the molt of the summer coat. *Photo courtesy of the North Dakota Department of Game and Fish.*

determinant of the thermoregulatory qualities of an animal's coat, and the deeper winter hair helps trap more insulating air than does the summer coat. The winter coat is composed of long guard hairs and short underfur that insulates the deer so well that it may become covered with a layer of snow that does not melt. Winter hair is shed in April, May and June, and is replaced by the reddish-brown summer coat. The growth of two coats of hair each year costs deer energy and protein as part of their cost of living. Based on formulas in Moen (1980) for calculating hair weight, a fawn weighing 36 kilograms (74 pounds) produces a winter coat weighing 802 grams (1.7 pounds), and an adult buck weighing 64 kilograms (140 pounds) produces a winter coat weighing 1,274 grams (2.8 pounds). The metabolic cost of producing the hair would be the amount of protein and energy in the hair plus the overhead required for hair production.

Whitetail bucks in characteristic winter (top) and summer (bottom) pelages. *Top photo by Tom W. Hall. Bottom photo courtesy of the Nebraska Game and Parks Commission.*

Glands

White-tailed deer have four sets of external glands: tarsal glands on the inner surfaces of the hind legs (Figure 19); metatarsal glands on the outer surfaces of the hind legs (Figure 20); interdigital glands between the hooves (Figure 21); and preorbital glands in the corners of the eyes (Figure 22). Each gland secretes a different scent, called a "pheromone," and these scents are part of a communication system that identifies individual animals. Mechanisms for release of glandular secretions are not well understood; both hormonal and sympathetic nervous stimulations may be involved (D. Müller-Schwarze personal communication: 1982).

In black-tailed deer, tarsal scent involves individual recognition, metatarsal scent signals alarm, and preorbital glands are used to mark trees and bushes (Müller-Schwarze 1971). Interdigital glands release liquids that scent trails where the animals walk.

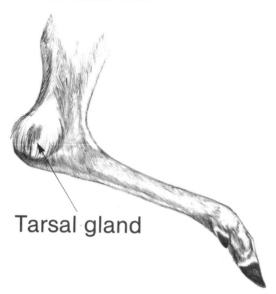

Figure 19. Tarsal glands on the inner surfaces of the hind legs of white-tailed deer produce a scent unique to individual deer, and are involved in rub-urination marking behavior. Illustration by Michael Stickney.

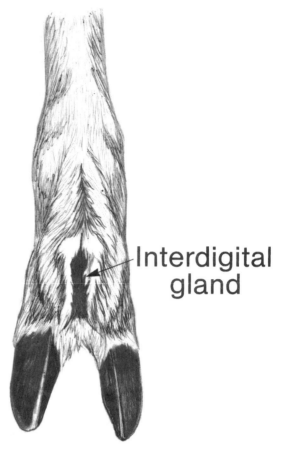

Figure 21. Interdigital glands between the hooves of white-tailed deer scent the deer's trail. Illustration by Michael Stickney.

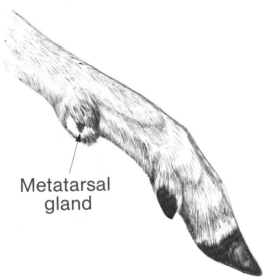

Figure 20. Metatarsal glands of the white-tailed deer are located on outer surfaces of the hind legs. Illustration by Michael Stickney.

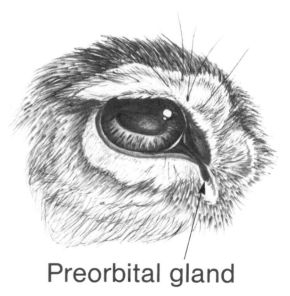

Figure 22. Preorbital glands of white-tailed deer function as tear glands. Illustration by Michael Stickney.

In addition to the pheromones from the glands, deer use urine as a scent. Fawns rub-urinate when they are frightened and older deer do the same in aggressive situations. During this behavior the animals rub the hind legs together while urinating on the tarsal glands.

In white-tailed deer the tarsal glands, inter-digital glands and rub-urination serve the same functions as in blacktails. However, the met-atarsal scent does not produce an alarm re-action (Volkman 1981), and whitetails appar-ently depend more strongly on behavioral clues (such as the raised tail) than on pheromones as alerts to danger. The preorbital glands are reduced in function to tear glands.

Vocalization

Very little of the communication among white-tailed deer is vocal, but they do vocalize more than most people realize, and in a variety of ways (*see* Chapter 6). Adults or fawns may groan in complaint when they are restrained. Fawns may bleat to call their dams, and bucks occasionally bleat when chasing does during the rut (Severinghaus and Cheatum 1956). The deer-sound most commonly heard by people is the familiar snort and foot stamp when the animals are disturbed or frightened.

A whitetail fawn, disturbed from its bedding site beneath rhododendron, bleats to attract its dam's attention. *Photo by E. Shipp; courtesy of the U.S. Forest Service.*

Senses

Whitetails are sensitive to sound and smell. Their large ears are constantly at the alert, and they depend on their acute sense of hearing to monitor the whereabouts and behavior of other animals, including predators. Their sense of smell also helps deer to identify individuals. Individual recognition occurs in large part through scents produced as tarsal phero-mones. Smell attracts whitetails to food. If food smells good, the deer taste it; if it tastes good, they eat it. The senses of smell and taste enable deer to detect differences in palatability of for-age. Smell also attracts whitetail bucks to does in heat.

Food selection by whitetails is predicated to a great extent on smell. Deer usually sniff each morsel before nibbling. *Photo courtesy of the Wisconsin Department of Natural Resources.*

Eyesight plays an important sensory role. Whitetails probably depend strongly on motion, and also depth perception, to locate and identify an object by sight. A combination of monocular vision to each side and binocular vision to the front gives them a wide field of vision (Moen 1982). The structure of the orbit and the size of the retina allow ruminants to see back along their flanks and detect objects behind them (Smythe 1975). Whitetails traditionally have been considered color-blind. Moen (1982) summarized the literature on deer vision. Light-sensitive rods usually are predominant in animals active at night, and color-sensitive cones predominate in animals active during daylight (*see* Cowey 1981). Since white-tailed deer are active both day and night, their perception of color is now open to question.

Gaits

Two classic gaits of the white-tailed deer are trotting and galloping; both are associated with escape behavior. Trotting is performed with the head and tail erect and the tail wagging from side to side. The gallop involves long strides interspersed with graceful leaps. At a gallop, deer can attain speeds of 58 kilometers per hour (36 miles per hour) (Severinghaus and Cheatum 1956). Whitetails are able to bound over formidable obstacles, easily negotiating a 2.1-meter (7-foot) vertical fence from a standing start or a 2.4-meter (8-foot) fence from a running start.

Mature whitetails in good health are able to leap over 2.1-meter (7-foot) obstacles from a standing start, and over fences taller than 2.4 meters (8 feet) approached on the run. When not disturbed, they usually will crawl under or even through a fenceline, but do not hesitate to jump when startled or hurried. *Photo courtesy of the South Carolina Wildlife and Marine Resources Department.*

White-tailed deer have two basic running gaits—trotting and galloping. When trotting, they look straight forward, with head held erect. When galloping, at speeds up to 58 kilometers (36 miles) per hour, they generally take several long strides between each high bound. This gait of whitetails, as opposed to stotting by mule deer in open country, is particularly well-suited for escape in wooded areas. *Top-left photo courtesy of the Oregon Department of Fish and Wildlife. Top-right photo courtesy of the Michigan Department of Natural Resources. Bottom-left photo courtesy of the Montana Department of Fish, Wildlife and Parks. Bottom-right photo courtesy of the Arizona Game and Fish Department.*

The skeleton and musculature of white-tailed deer are particularly adapted for running (figures 23 and 24). Major adaptations of ungulates are described by Hymen (1951). The ilia of the pelvic girdle often are broad and expanded, and the upper leg bone of both the forelimbs and the hind limbs is shortened and included in the body musculature. The first leg joints obvious in deer are the wrist on the foreleg and the ankle on the hind leg. The metacarpals and metatarsals form the long cannon bones, which are the most obvious part of the legs. Deer walk on their toes, which terminate in horny (keratin) hooves about 7.6 centimeters (3 inches) long.

Size

At birth, whitetail fawns weigh 1.8 to 3.6 kilograms (4 to 8 pounds). Adult females weigh approximately 45 kilograms (100 pounds), and adult males weigh approximately 68 kilograms (150 pounds), but actual weights vary according to subspecies, region, habitat-type and quality, age of the animal, and season of the year. Weights over 180 kilograms (397 pounds) are exceptional. Minnesota's heaviest buck on record dressed out at 183 kilograms (402 pounds), or about 232 kilograms (511 pounds) live weight (Erickson et al. 1961). New York State's heaviest documented buck weighed 176

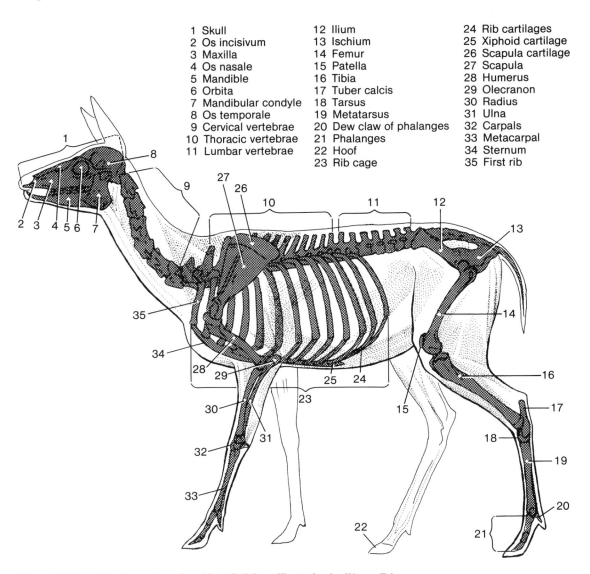

1 Skull
2 Os incisivum
3 Maxilla
4 Os nasale
5 Mandible
6 Orbita
7 Mandibular condyle
8 Os temporale
9 Cervical vertebrae
10 Thoracic vertebrae
11 Lumbar vertebrae
12 Ilium
13 Ischium
14 Femur
15 Patella
16 Tibia
17 Tuber calcis
18 Tarsus
19 Metatarsus
20 Dew claw of phalanges
21 Phalanges
22 Hoof
23 Rib cage
24 Rib cartilages
25 Xiphoid cartilage
26 Scapula cartilage
27 Scapula
28 Humerus
29 Olecranon
30 Radius
31 Ulna
32 Carpals
33 Metacarpal
34 Sternum
35 First rib

Figure 23. The skeletal structure of a white-tailed deer. Illustration by Wayne Trimm.

kilograms (388 pounds) live and 132 kilograms (291 pounds) dressed (Fosburgh 1946). Females attain maximum weight in about four years and males reach peak weight in five to six years.

White-tailed deer are shorter than most people realize. Fawns are about 38 centimeters (15 inches) from the ground at belly level and this measurement for adults is about 51 centimeters (20 inches) (Moen 1980). Shoulder height is about 91 centimeters (36 inches) for adults, with males being slightly taller than females of similar age. Similar shoulder heights have been documented for whitetails from

Florida (91 centimeters:36 inches) (Harlow and Jones 1965) and Texas (81 centimeters:32 inches) (Teer et al. 1965). Hall (1981) listed a range of 66 to 114.3 centimeters (26 to 45 inches) for whitetail shoulder height. Deer appear taller because of their long necks and the antlers on bucks.

Whitetails in the northern part of the country are larger than those in the South. A comparison of dressed carcass weights of yearlings illustrates the magnitude of regional differences (Table 10).

Within each region, comparable age classes will weigh less on poor-quality or overcrowded

1 Arcus zygomaticus
2 Masseter
3 Brachiocephalicus
4 Trapezius
5 Tensor fasciae antebrachii
6 Latissimus dorsi
7 Lumbo-dorsal fascis

8 Serratus ventralis
9 Tensor fasciae externus
10 Gluteus medius
11 Trochanter major
12 Semimembranosus
13 Semitendinosus
14 Biceps femoris
15 Gastrocnemius
16 Deep flexor tendon
17 Tendon of Achilles
18 Lateral extensor
19 Long extensor
20 Superficial flexor tendon
21 Anterior tendon
22 Flexor digitorum (pedislongus)

23 Aponeurosis
24 Obliquus abdominis externus
25 Deep pectoral
26 Serratis ventralis
27 Flexor tendons of metatarsus
28 Tendon of extensor digiti
29 Extensor carpi (ulnaris)
30 Extensor digiti
31 Extensor carpi (radialis)
32 Triceps
33 Deltoid
34 Superficial pectoral (brisket)
35 Shoulder–transverse process muscle
36 Sternocephalicus
37 Sternomandibularis

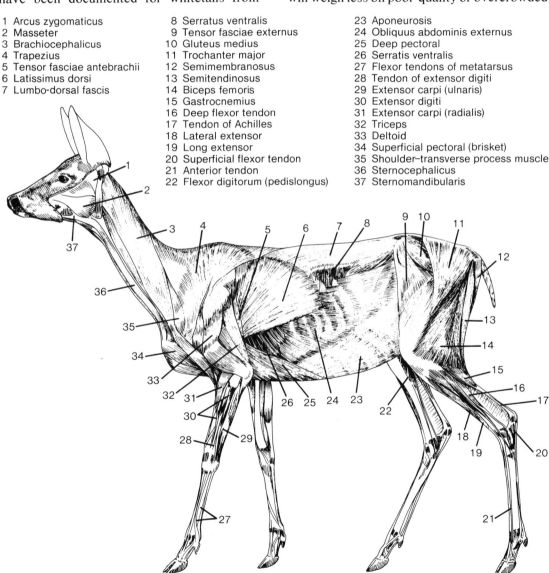

Figure 24. Superficial musculature of a white-tailed deer. Illustration by Robert Pratt and Wayne Trimm.

Table 10. Comparison of dressed carcass weights of yearling white-tailed deer from northern and southern United States.

Location	Males Sample size	Males Weight[a]	Females Sample size	Females Weight[a]	Reference
New Hampshire	701	48.9(107.8)	425	43.4(95.5)	Siegler (1968)
New York					
Adirondacks	166	38.0(83.6)	144	36.0(79.2)	Severinghaus (1955a)
Seneca Army Depot	24	49.9(110)	24	44.0(97)	O'Pezio and Sauer (1974)
Minnesota					
Mud Lake Refuge	NA	57.2(126)	NA	54.5(120)	Erickson et al. (1961)
Tamarac Refuge	NA	55.8(123)	NA	50.4(111)	
Florida					
Statewide total[b]	789	35.0(77.2)	62	21.4(47.2)	Harlow and Jones (1965)
West Virginia					
East region	451	35.9(79)	295	32.7(72)	Gill (1956)
West region	436	47.7(105)	417	41.3(91)	
Texas					
Edwards Plateau	101	25.7(56.7)	36	23.8(52.5)	Teer et al. (1965)
Panhandle	NA	41.9(92.2)			

[a]In kilograms (pounds).
[b]Dressed weights determined from dead weights divided by 1.32—a conversion factor based on the relationship of dead weight to dressed weight (Harlow and Jones 1965).

range than on good range. This difference occurs on northern and southern range. Weight differences within different areas are illustrated by data from New York and Florida (Table 11).

Deer weights also vary seasonally. Winter weight loss has been documented for both bucks and does in the Northeast (Silver et al. 1969, Sauer 1973). Weight loss in bucks begins during the rut, and weight gain begins in spring.

Table 11. Influence of range quality and deer population density on dressed carcass weights of white-tailed deer.

Location and condition of range	Fawns Male Sample size	Fawns Male Weight[a]	Fawns Female Sample size	Fawns Female Weight[a]	Yearlings Male Sample size	Yearlings Male Weight[a]	Yearlings Female Sample size	Yearlings Female Weight[a]
New York								
Adirondacks (poor range)	173	25(55)	173	23(51)	166	38(84)	144	36(79)
Seneca Army Depot[b] (excellent range)	NA	29(63)	NA	25(54)	NA	43(94)	NA	40(88)
Seneca Army Depot[c] (excellent range)	(21)	34(74)	25	30(66)	24	50(110)	24	44(97)
Florida[e]								
Northern flatwoods (good range)					145	35(77)		
Southern flatwoods (good range)					27	32(71)		
Central pine/oak uplands (poor range)								

[a]In kilograms (pounds).
[b]81.2 deer per square kilometer (210 deer per square mile), 1957.
[c]11.6 deer per square kilometer (30 deer per square mile), 1965.
[d]2.5-year-old deer only.
[e]Dressed weight determined from dead weight divided by 1.32—a conversion factor based on the relationship of dead weight to dressed weight (Harlow and Jones 1965).

Biologists measure the leg of a whitetail fawn to ascertain the animal's growth rate. Note (1) how the handler has grasped the fawn and restricted any struggling movements, and (2) the fawn is bleating as they typically do when restrained. *Photo courtesy of the Missouri Department of Conservation.*

Table 11. (continued)

| Adults (2.5 years and older) | | | | |
| Male | | Female | | |
Sample size	Weight[a]	Sample size	Weight[a]	Reference
274	59(130)	514	42(93)	Severinghaus (1955*a*)
14	64(140)[d]	10	47(103)[d]	Hesselton et al. (1965) O'Pezio and Sauer (1974)
154	46(101)	23	33(73)	Harlow and Jones (1965)
47	43(95)			
61	33(73)	124	25(55)	

Weight loss in females and fawns begins in January. Females that successfully carry and nurse fawns usually do not regain weight until summer, after their fawns are weaned. During an average winter, a whitetail can lose 25 to 30 percent of its body weight and still survive. In combination with weight loss, severe winter weather can be a significant cause of mortality. Fawns, being smaller, and least dominant, are particularly vulnerable to starvation in winter. Winter weights at or below which recovery is impossible have been determined for several age classes of white-tailed deer (Table 12).

Weights can be used to predict reproductive rates (Figure 25) and antler size (Table 13). A decrease in any of these three characteristics indicates that a whitetail population may be too large for existing range resources and that young animals are getting less to eat, or less food of nutritious quality, than needed for normal physical development. At New York's Seneca Army Depot, the weights, antler size and reproductive rates of fawns and yearlings increased as population size decreased (Hessel-

Table 12. Estimated winter weights[a] of white-tailed deer, according to sex and age group, in New York, at and below which recovery is impossible (Moen and Severinghaus 1981).

Sex	Age group in years				
	0–1	1–2	2–3	3–4	4–5
Male	22 (48.4)	33 (72.6)	42 (92.4)	49 (107.8)	54 (118.8)
Female	21 (46.2)	30 (66.0)	35 (77.0)	36 (79.2)	38 (83.6)

[a]In kilograms (pounds).

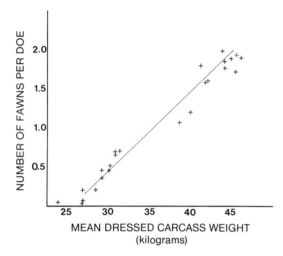

Figure 25. Reproductive rate relative to mean dressed-carcass weight of female white-tailed deer at Seneca Army Depot, New York. Does one year old at parturition are clustered at lower left; does two years old at parturition are clustered at upper right (New York State Department of Environmental Conservation unpublished).

Table 13. Average yearling antler-beam diameters and average dressed carcass weights of white-tailed deer from six regions in New York (Severinghaus and Moen 1983).

Region	Beam diameter		Dressed weight	
	Millimeters	Inches	Kilograms	Pounds
Western region	18.7	0.74	53.8	118.7
Adirondack periphery	17.8	0.70	49.4	109.0
Adirondack central	15.0	0.59	41.3	91.1
Catskill periphery	16.8	0.66	47.8	105.4
Catskill central	16.0	0.63	43.4	95.7
Harriman State Park	11.6	0.46	30.6	67.4

ton et al. 1965). Teer et al. (1965) found a similar relationship between white-tailed deer population density and reproductive rate in Texas.

Antlers

The literal crowning glory of the male white-tailed deer is its antlers. They are composed of true bone that grows from pedicels on the frontal bones (Figure 26). The pedicels form the "buttons" which are the only antler development of most male fawns. A buck's first set of antlers grows during his yearling spring and summer.

Annual antler growth begins in mid-March to April. These beginning dates for antler development have been reported from both northern and southern ranges in the United States. The size of a buck's antlers depends both on age and nutritional intake. The first set of antlers, or rack, can vary from spikes to as many as 10 points (Figure 26). To be counted, a point must be at least 2.54 centimeters (1 inch) long. This length is consistent with Boone and Crockett Club scoring criteria (Nesbitt and Wright 1981).

The growing bone is full of blood vessels and nerves and is covered with hairy skin called

A whitetail buck with a well-developed set of antlers. Note (1) the atypical accessory tines on the animal's right antler, (2) the shreds of velvet on the top tine of that antler, and (3) the damaged point of the right antler that likely occurred during antler growth. *Photo courtesy of the British Columbia Ministry of Environment, Fish and Wildlife Branch.*

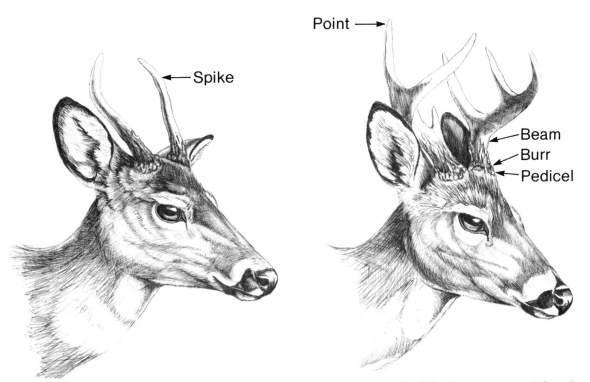

Figure 26. Antler terminology, and variation in antler development of yearling whitetail bucks on poor range (left) and good range (right). Illustrations by Michael Stickney.

"velvet." Injuries occur easily to the soft, sensitive growing bone, and accidents during this stage cause many deformed antlers. Growth continues through August or September on ranges throughout the United States. The bone then hardens and the velvet dries up and sloughs off or is rubbed off. Generally, by late December through early January, the supply of testosterone decreases (Mirarchi et al. 1978). A separation layer forms at the pedicel and the antlers fall off. Occasionally bucks will retain their antlers until spring (Sauer 1973, Zagata and Moen 1974). In March or April, probably under the influence of increasing daylight and increasing prolactin secretion (Mirarchi et al. 1978), the whole process starts over.

The second rack will be bigger than the first, and when nutrition is adequate each successive rack will grow even bigger, until the buck passes his prime (Table 14). On good range in New York State, three-year-old bucks produce an average of eight points—a potential trophy-size rack. On poor range, bucks require an additional year to produce antlers equivalent in size to those of deer of the same age on good range. Many bucks on poor range never develop trophy racks. On extremely overpopu-

lated ranges, food may be so scarce that yearling and two-year-old bucks cannot grow the 8-centimeter (3-inch) antlers which would make them legal quarry, for instance, in New York State. In general, underweight whitetail bucks have relatively small antler-beam diameters (Figure 27).

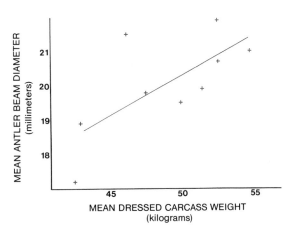

Figure 27. Mean antler-beam diameter relative to mean dressed-carcass weight of yearling whitetail bucks at Seneca Army Depot, New York (New York State Department of Environmental Conservation unpublished).

Table 14. Antler-beam size and number of points in relationship to white-tailed deer age and range in parts of New York and statewide.

	Age						
	1.5 years				2.5 years		
Section	Sample size	Average beam diameter[a]	Sample size	Average number of points[b]	Sample size	Average beam diameter[a]	Sample size
Catskill section	1,321	17(0.67)	1,325	3	473	22(0.87)	476
Adirondack section	233	17(0.67)	234	3	203	22(0.87)	203
Southern Tier section	3,388	19(0.75)	3,383	4	755	25(0.98)	762
Lake Plains section	465	21(0.83)	474	5	94	27(1.06)	96
Statewide[c]	6,213	19(0.75)	6,224	4	1,743	23(0.91)	1,757

[a]The average of the largest and smallest diameter 2.54 centimeters (1 inch) above the burr; measured in millimeters (inches).
[b]The number of points 2.54 centimeters (1 inch) or longer on each set of antlers.
[c]The statewide total is not the sum of the four sections listed, because a few small areas were omitted (*see* New York State Department of Environmental Conservation 1982).

Only rarely will a doe have antlers. These usually are short spikes covered with velvet. Such does generally are fertile, and can carry and raise fawns. The antlers probably are grown in response to abnormally high levels of testosterone.

A captive antlered whitetail doe and her fawn. The antler growth was experimentally induced by injections of testosterone in the spring prior to her autumn conception. *Photo by C. W. Severinghaus.*

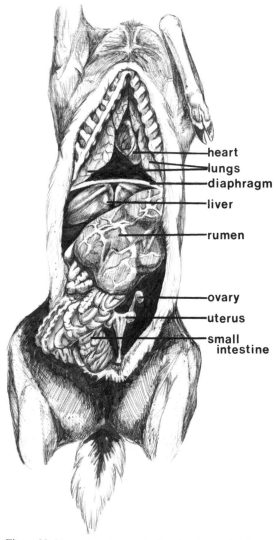

Figure 28. Internal anatomy of a female white-tailed deer. Illustration by Michael Stickney.

Table 14. (continued)

			Age					
2.5 years	3.5 years				4.5 years			
Average number of points[b]	Sample size	Average beam diameter[a]	Sample size	Average number of points[b]	Sample size	Average beam diameter[a]	Sample size	Average number of points[b]
6	98	24(0.94)	97	7	28	26(1.02)	28	7
6	93	28(1.10)	93	8	42	31(1.22)	41	9
7	216	27(1.06)	219	8	19	30(1.18)	20	9
8	36	30(1.18)	37	9	4	38(1.50)	4	10
7	540	27(1.06)	544	8	110	29(1.14)	111	8

INTERNAL ANATOMY

The internal organs of a white-tailed deer are illustrated in figures 28 and 29.

Thorax

The heart is the most obvious organ in the whitetail's thoracic cavity. It lies in a special protective tissue covering, the pericardium, immediately beneath the ribs. The heart is edible and may be removed by cutting through the major blood vessels at the top of the heart and slipping it out of the pericardium.

Directly beneath the heart are the paired, bright-pink lungs. Between the lungs is the windpipe (trachea), reinforced by cartilaginous rings. The diaphragm muscle is attached to the inner rib cage and separates the chest cavity from the abdominal cavity.

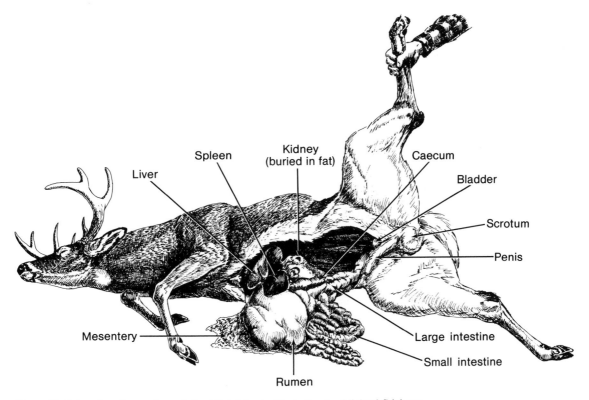

Figure 29. Internal anatomy of an adult whitetail buck. Illustration by Michael Stickney.

Abdomen

The dark red, three-lobed liver is conspicuous on the deer's right side just below the diaphragm. The liver is edible and may be removed by cutting through the blood vessels and connective tissue holding it in place. Deer frequently are infested with liver flukes, and the migration of these flukes through the liver leaves traces of light scar tissue. As long as the liver is well cooked, these parasites present no problems for human consumption.

Most of the abdomen is filled by a four-parted stomach and the intestines. The large paunch lying on top of the intestines is the rumen—a digestive organ unique to ruminants. The rumen is a fermentation tank, in which microorganisms produce volatile fatty acids—a major energy source for ruminants. Anterior to the rumen is the reticulum, and posterior to the rumen are the omasum and abomasum. The reticulum forces liquid into the rumen, suspending smaller food particles which then wash back into the reticulum and on to the omasum (Moen 1973). The omasum functions in water absorption (Short 1964), and the abomasum secretes digestive enzymes, as does the true stomach of nonruminants. Posterior to the rumen are the small and large intestine.

The reproductive organs, kidneys and urinary tract are located in the lower abdominal cavity. The bladder lies inconspicuously under the pelvis in the front part of the cavity. Female reproductive organs lie underneath the bladder. The most conspicuous part of the female tract is the uterus. From November through June, the two horns of the pregnant uterus are distended with fluid and fetuses. Depending on the age of the doe and the quality of the range, the uterus may contain anywhere from one to three fawns, and in rare instances four. The bean-shaped kidneys, which also are edible, lie at the bottom of the exposed abdominal cavity, along each side of the backbone.

Blood Parameters

Blood parameters for white-tailed deer generally are comparable to those for other mammals. Captive fawns achieve adult hematologic values at three to four months of age (Seal et al. 1981). Both nutritional and seasonal effects on blood parameters have been documented.

High versus moderate nutrition levels for two pregnant does over a four-month period produced significant differences in hemoglobin, hematocrit, cholesterol, sialic acid, blood-urea nitrogen and cortisol (Seal et al. 1981). Fawns held on four combinations of protein and energy for 20 weeks showed effects related to both dietary components (Seal et al. 1981). Protein levels affected hemoglobin, red-cell size and blood-urea nitrogen; energy levels affected nonesterified fatty acids, while both protein and energy levels affected red-blood-cell counts and mean corpuscular volume. Other blood parameters affected by these diets included calcium, phosphorus, sodium, chloride, glucose, cholesterol, alkaline phosphatase, serum glutamic pyruvic transaminase, creatinine phosphokinase, cortisol and triiodothyronine.

Seasonal variation in blood parameters is related to the annual cycle of energy expenditure and dietary changes. A 21-month study of penned adult whitetail does documented seasonal variation in blood-urea nitrogen, serum protein and packed-cell volume, with lows during lactation (Seal et al. 1981). Sauer (1973) followed blood parameters related to bone formation for a two-year period in two adult male and two adult female whitetails. Seasonal variation was significant for the following serum parameters: (1) serum inorganic phosphate was low in winter and peaked during summer; (2) alkaline phosphatase was low in winter and peaked in late spring; (3) calcium—significant for females only—was low in spring and peaked in autumn/winter; (4) total protein was low in winter/spring and peaked in summer and early autumn; and (5) protein-bound iodine was low in late summer/autumn, variable in winter, low in late winter/early spring, and peaked in late spring and summer. These changes are consistent with reduced food intake, reduced activity and weight loss in the winter; with increased food intake and energy expenditure in the spring and summer for antler growth, pregnancy and lactation; and with energy storage in the late summer and autumn.

TEETH

Analysis of tooth replacement and wear is the most widely used technique for aging white-tailed deer (Severinghaus 1949*b*). The eruption and replacement of baby teeth follow a predictable schedule. When a fawn is born it has four teeth. As an adult it will have six incisors

and two canines in the lower front, six premolars and six molars in the lower back and
the same in the upper back (Figure 30). Therefore, the permanent dental formula is:

incisors $\frac{0\ 0\ 0}{1\ 2\ 3}$, canines $\frac{0}{1}$, premolars $\frac{0\ 2\ 3\ 4}{0\ 2\ 3\ 4}$,

molars $\frac{1\ 2\ 3}{1\ 2\ 3}$.

Deer normally do not have front teeth on the
upper jaw. The front teeth are separated from
the back teeth by a wide space called a
"diastema."

During the first few weeks after birth, fawns
grow the remaining baby or milk incisors and
all 12 milk premolars. By six months the first
molars have erupted and the second molars
are erupting (Figure 31). The large permanent
first incisors begin to erupt at five to six months
of age, first growing forward and then twisting
upright into proper position. The remaining incisors and canines are replaced by permanent
teeth when the fawns are 9 to 10 months old.
A quick glance at the incisors tells a trained
wildlife biologist or manager whether the animal is a fawn or an adult.

The premolar teeth are replaced during the
second autumn. By the time the deer is 17
months of age, its milk premolars become loose.
By 18 months the permanent teeth underneath
begin to erupt. The three permanent premolars
are fully exposed by 19 months of age and
show virtually no wear. At the same time, the
last molars are erupting.

After all of the whitetail's permanent teeth

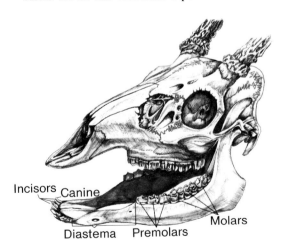

Figure 30. Adult white-tailed deer have 32 teeth—6 incisors and 2 canines in the lower front, 6 premolars and 6
molars each in both the upper and lower back. Illustration
by Michael Stickney.

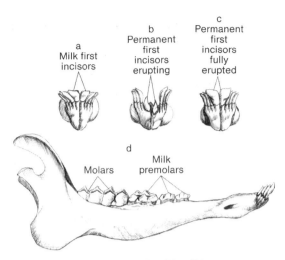

Figure 31. Milk incisors (a) of a whitetail fawn are present
when the deer is five months old; permanent incisors (b)
erupt at five to six months and are fully in place (c) by
six months. By six months, the fawn has three milk premolars and two molars in the back of both the upper and
lower jaws (d). Illustrations by Michael Stickney.

have erupted, further age assignments are made
by the amount of wear on the molars, which
lose about 1 millimeter (0.04 inch) of height
per year. There is a progressive height differential of about 1 millimeter (0.04 inch) between
the three molars on each side of the jaw. This
differential is maintained as the teeth wear
down, and the height above the gum line on
all three molars is used to determine deer age
(Figure 32). By 10.5 years, the teeth are worn
to the gum line. A few whitetails live beyond
10.5 years, and thus cannot be aged by tooth
wear.

The cementum method of aging deer was
developed in the 1960s (Gilbert 1966, Ransom
1966b). Annual layers are formed in the cementum of the tooth root, which is buried in
the gum (Figure 33). In order to examine the
root the extracted tooth has to be softened in
acid, cut in thin sections with a special knife
(microtome), mounted on slides and stained.
Finished slides are then examined under a mi-
croscope and the annual layers counted.

The formation of cementum layers is an internal manifestation. Whitetails are low in blood-
serum protein and phosphate during the late
winter-early spring period, when the cementum layers appear to be formed (Sauer 1973).
These two chemicals are basic in bone and
tooth formation, and the cementum formed
during this period apparently does not calcify
normally, forming winter layers in the teeth.
Thus, a tooth has one layer for each winter it

has been present in the deer. Teeth that erupt during the second summer of the whitetail's life have one less winter layer than those that erupt the first summer. The oldest deer age established by this technique was 20 years—for a doe taken in Orange County, New York.

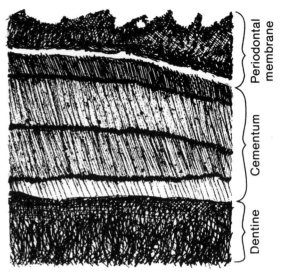

Figure 33. A section of a premolar from a 4.5-year-old whitetail doe shows three broad, light summer layers and two dark winter lines in the cementum.

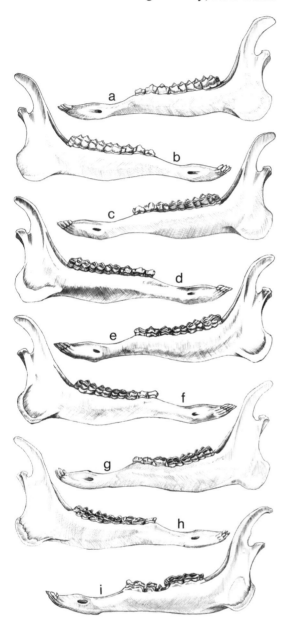

Figure 32. Progressive wear on the molars is used to age white-tailed deer (a) 1 year 7 months, (b) 2.5 years, (c) 3.5 years, (d) 4.5 years, (e) 5.5 years, (f) 6.5 years, (g) 7.5 years, (h) 8.5–9.5 years, and (i) 10.5 years or older. Illustrations by Michael Stickney.

Chapter 4

PHYSIOLOGY AND NUTRITION

Louis J. Verme
Biologist in Charge
Cusino Wildlife Research Station
Michigan Department of Natural Resources
Shingleton, Michigan

Duane E. Ullrey
Professor of Comparative Animal Nutrition
Department of Animal Science
Department of Fisheries and Wildlife
Michigan State University
East Lansing, Michigan

REPRODUCTION

Over most of the whitetail range, does come into estrus (heat) in autumn. These does experience several ovulatory cycles if not successfully mated initially. Onset of breeding activity is governed by photoperiodism, latitude, genetics and nutrition. Reproduction is directly controlled by the endocrine system.

Endocrinology

The whitetail receives external stimuli essential for mating through receptors in the skin and by the organs of sight, smell and hearing. These stimuli are transmitted through the nervous system to the brain; the forebrain funnels messages to the hypothalamus, which regulates the pituitary, or "master" gland. Reproduction depends on hormones produced by the anterior pituitary, namely the follicle stimulating hormone (FSH), luteinizing hormone (LH) and prolactin. Oxytocin, important in parturition and milk release, is secreted by the posterior pituitary.

Follicles in the ovary produce estrogen—the hormone responsible for the doe's mating urge. Another ovarian hormone, progesterone, apparently acts in concert with estrogen to promote optimum heat—the time when a doe will permit copulation. A rise in estrogen greatly increases the secretion of the luteinizing hormone by the pituitary (Figure 34), causing the release of a mature ovum (Plotka et al. 1980).

The corpus luteum, a specialized gland, develops at the site of the ruptured follicle at ovulation. If the shed ovum is not fertilized the corpus luteum degenerates in about three weeks, and the entire cycle recurs at regular intervals until conception takes place, or reproductive activity ceases in late winter (earlier in unthrifty does). Increased secretion of the hormone prostaglandin is believed to cause the demise of the corpus luteum. Production of progesterone by the corpus luteum suppresses estrus during pregnancy. Specialized cells surrounding the embryo secrete a luteinizing-type of hormone that supports development of the corpus luteum, which, together with chorionic hormones released by the placenta, maintains pregnancy. Ovariectomy in deer, by eliminating the main source of progesterone, promptly results in abortion (Plotka et al. 1982).

Serum progesterone increases steadily, from a low level prior to a doe's estrus to a peak during the first two weeks of pregnancy. It exhibits a flat pattern until the final week, then drops sharply after parturition. Estrogen content gradually increases from six weeks prepartum to parturition, then falls drastically. The estrogen/progesterone ratio rises steeply during the final 12 weeks of pregnancy (Plotka et al. 1977*b*).

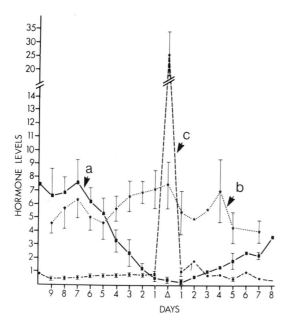

Figure 34. A gradual decline in progesterone (a), an increase in estrogen (b), and a sharp peak in luteinizing hormone (c) are characteristic of estrus onset and ovulation in white-tailed deer (Plotka et al. (1980).

Leydig cells of the testes manufacture testosterone—the substance responsible for a buck's sex drive. Testosterone output depends on a "feedback" control mechanism involving an interaction among the hypothalamus, pituitary and gonads. The luteinizing hormone apparently stimulates testosterone production.

The thyroid gland indirectly influences reproduction by controlling an animal's metabolism. Its hormones, thyroxine and triiodothyronine, are essential for proper fetal development (Seal et al. 1972*b*), and may influence a doe's lactation.

The cortex of the adrenal gland produces substances that play a major role in triggering parturition. Increased levels of steroids are induced by activation of the pituitary-adrenal link in the fetus. This may result in greater secretion of prostaglandin from the uterus. Suppression of progesterone and increased estrogen follows the rise in prostaglandin concentration. These changes cause a marked increase in irritability and contractility of the uterus, thus initiating labor. The adrenals also produce androgens and testosterone precursors, as well as some progesterone. Moreover, the adrenal medulla is the source of adrenaline and noradrenalin, both of which are important in the reaction of deer to hostile confrontation.

Melatonin, a substance secreted by the pineal gland (the "third eye"), influences the release of sex hormones from the pituitary. Many of the seasonal effects of the photoperiod are dependent therefore on an intact pineal, since it presumably serves as a mediator or transducer of photoperiod cues into chemical or endocrine information. Pinealectomy dramatically alters the timing of many seasonal physiological events in deer (Plotka et al. 1979).

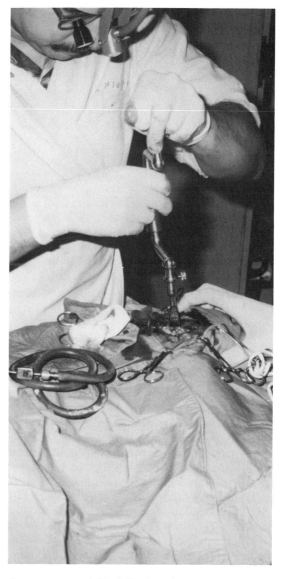

A neurosurgeon deftly drills through the skull of a white-tailed deer to expose the brain in order to remove the pineal gland. This organ—the so-called "third eye" of vertebrates—is a transducer of photic information to the pituitary or "master gland." *Photo by E. Plotka.*

Pinealectomy disrupts the normal seasonal cycles in deer by eliminating the influence of photoperiodism. Following such surgery in March, the yearling whitetail buck (right) failed to shed his winter coat and had just begun to grow antlers in mid-August, whereas the sham-operated buck (left) was in full summer coat with large antlers in velvet. *Photo by Louis J. Verme.*

Photoperiodism

Except near the equator, the rutting season is tied to photoperiodism. A diminishing ratio of daylight to darkness triggers the start of the reproductive cycle. Photoperiodism serves as a time-giver for the inherent (endogenous) rhythm, the so-called "biological clock." Deer shifted from one hemisphere to another adjust their breeding season to the prevailing photoperiod (Marshall 1937).

Since photoperiodism is related to latitude, the rut progresses more or less as a continuum from November in the North to January or February in far southern ranges. Variation within a region possibly is due to genetic differences (Ransom 1966a) or hybridization (Haugen 1959, Adams 1960).

In northern latitudes, antler growth begins in spring, with the increasing length of daylight. Goss (1969a, 1969b) induced four com-plete sets of antlers in one year in Sika deer by subjecting the deer to photoperiods that simulated the natural annual cycle. Bucks exposed to equal periods of daylight and darkness failed to grow new antlers during the three-year duration of the experiment.

Male Reproductive Patterns

Robinson et al. (1965) described a three-phase testicular cycle, in Texas whitetail bucks, consisting of (1) primary development, (2) full production and (3) resting stage. These phases were associated with the onset of antler growth, the shedding of velvet and antler drop, respectively. Relative development of the seminal vesicles lagged slightly behind that of the testes and exhibited a sharper peak. Thus the seminal vesicles more accurately reflected the actual breeding period than did testes size. Mirarchi et al. (1977a) indicated that seasonal fluctuations in testes weight probably are caused by increased and decreased activity of the seminiferous tubules. Numbers of testicular sperm were correlated closely with counts in the epididymus. These results suggest that rising androgen levels may be necessary for sperm formation or maturation. Testosterone might be involved more in initiating than in maintaining spermatogenesis. The follicle-stimulating hormone provides the stimulus for spermatozoan production (Mirarchi et al. 1978).

Lambiase et al. (1972) noted that whitetail sperm production extended from mid-August through March. Number of sperm per ejaculation increased through October, peaked in mid-November, dropped almost in half by mid-December and declined at a slower rate thereafter. Maximum sperm counts were in the billions (3.4×10^9) per ejaculate. Sperm production and testes size are greatest in older males. However, buck fawns are sexually mature and, given the opportunity, can successfully impregnate females.

Testosterone governs the course of antler development. If a buck is castrated while its antlers are in velvet, those antlers are retained, but never harden or lose their velvet. If a buck is castrated after shedding its antlers, the antlers regrow the next year, with the velvet being retained. An animal castrated after the velvet is shed loses its antlers within a week (Wislocki et al. 1947). The pattern of antler casting and regrowth probably involves an interplay between testosterone level and the antler-growth stimulus secreted by the pituitary in response to photoperiodism (Whitehead and McEwan 1973). Mirarchi et al. (1978) believe that prolactin also influences antler regeneration and growth. The role of the growth hormone in this regard still is uncertain.

Testosterone levels are correlated with progressive antler growth and hardening and the shedding of velvet (McMillin et al. 1974). Testosterone concentration and testicular volume begin to increase in August, peaking in October and dropping to low levels from December through July (Figure 35). Peak testosterone output in October implies that this hormone is instrumental in bucks establishing their dominance hierarchy prior to the rut. The superior (dominant) buck probably breeds most of the does within his home range.

Bucks in good physical condition retain their antlers longer than do those in poor vigor (Ozoga and Verme 1982a). Antler development is affected greatly by diet, and its general conformation is dictated by heredity. Antler size in autumn, especially among yearling cervids, may provide a useful index of the animals' earlier (late winter) physical condition (Taber 1958). Experiments in Pennsylvania (French et al. 1955, Cowan and Long 1962) indicated that young bucks had the best antlers and the heaviest body weight when fed a complete ration. Food restriction during winter, however, did not appreciably reduce antler size when the animals received an adequate diet during spring

Increased testosterone output results in shedding of antler velvet, neck swelling and enlarged gonads in whitetail bucks prior to the rut. The alpha male no doubt breeds most of the does in his home area. *Photo courtesy of the South Carolina Wildlife and Marine Resources Department.*

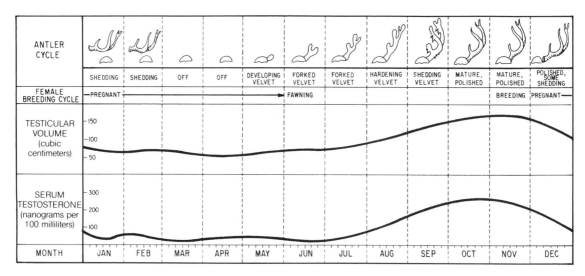

Figure 35. Relationship of antler growth and breeding cycle to testicular size and serum testosterone in white-tailed deer (McMillin et al. 1974).

and early summer. Body growth took precedence over antler formation.

While large antlers are important for successful courtship among adult bucks, a strong body may be more essential to establishing a male's dominance. Antler development, pelage change and antler shedding were delayed when yearling bucks were on a restricted diet for up to 10 weeks beginning in mid-March (Long et al. 1959). These results emphasize the value of proper nutrition when antler growth commences. A delayed, cool spring, for example, could prove detrimental to antler development.

The rut is a very strenuous time for bucks. Physical debilitation at this time could adversely affect subsequent antler development and social rank for bucks past their prime, particularly those on marginal ranges. Perhaps because the breeding season is so taxing, bucks generally have a shorter life-span than do does, even in lightly hunted areas or refuges (Ozoga 1969).

Female Reproductive Patterns

At the onset of estrus the whitetail doe becomes very restless and her nighttime activity increases dramatically (Ozoga and Verme 1975). Increased activity by the doe prior to mating is stimulated by a sharp surge in estrogen production by the ovaries (Plotka et al. 1980). The fact that a doe approaching estrus frequently urinates indicates that the urine and its endocrine products serves a pheromonal function, alerting bucks that she is ready to mate. A doe remains in heat for approximately 24 hours.

When a doe permits copulation, it is termed a "psychological heat." When ovulation occurs, but no distinct sign is manifested, it is called a "physiological heat" or "silent heat." Plotka et al. (1977b) found evidence of ovulation in whitetails 12 to 23 days before they mated. Silent heats are believed to be due to insufficient output of estrogen, although other hormones such as progesterone probably are intricately involved.

Trophy whitetail bucks are the result of good genetic background, a nutritious and mineral-rich food source, and physically mature age. *Photo by Lee Gladfelter.*

An alpha male establishes "scrapes" in an area that he checks periodically during the rut. Pheromones in urine deposited by a visiting doe alert him that she is in estrus. *Photo courtesy of the Minnesota Department of Natural Resources.*

Severinghaus and Cheatum (1956) reported spans of 28 and 29 days between successive heats in two does in New York, whereas Haugen (1959) found a span of 21 days in one case in Alabama. At the Cusino Wildlife Research Station on Michigan's Upper Peninsula, the period between heats for 15 does ranged from 21 to 27 days (L. J. Verme personal data). Plotka et al. (1977a) concluded that estrus cycles recurred in nonpregnant whitetails at intervals of 25 to 30 days from November through early March in Minnesota.

Verme (1965a) showed that poorly nourished whitetail does began breeding several weeks later, and the incidence of twin births was less than that for does on an adequate ration (Figure 36). Yearling does generally achieve estrus later in the rut than do older females. Doe fawns come into estrus after most adults have bred.

The rutting season is typified by intense activity of a relatively short duration. In Upper Michigan, breeding dates for 174 penned does on good nutrition ranged from November 2 to December 21 (Verme 1977). More than 80 percent mated during the last three weeks in November. Cessation of the rut probably is influenced by a combination of photoperiodism, biological-clock activity, hormone levels and nutrition. Except for a few late-breeding does the mating season ends rather abruptly.

The gestation period varies from 187 to 222 days (Haugen 1959, Haugen and Davenport 1950) and differs among subspecies (Adams 1960). In Upper Michigan, the mean gestation period was 199 days for penned does on adequate nutrition, but it was a week or more longer when the mothers were underfed during pregnancy (Verme 1965a). Newborn fawns from the latter group weighed less than those from well-fed does, and thus the gestation period was correlated inversely with fetal biomass. Delayed birth possibly stems from abnormally low levels of fetal adrenal hormones. An extra 5 to 10 days in utero might enhance a stunted fetus' chance of living when born.

Puberty

Doe fawns can attain puberty at six to seven months of age, or when they weigh approximately 36 kilograms (80 pounds) (Moen 1973). However relative physiological state, rather than size, chiefly determines when they become sexually mature (Mueller and Sadleir

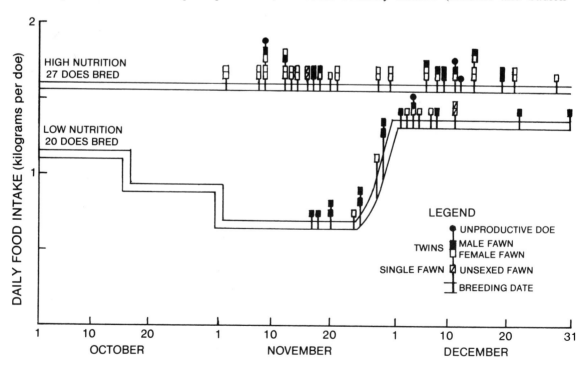

Figure 36. White-tailed does on high nutrition breed earlier and produce more fawns than do does on a low nutritional plane (Verme 1965a).

1979). On ideal range in warm climate, growth and sexual development proceed through autumn; thus, doe fawns can achieve puberty toward the end of the rut. Haugen (1975) reported that 82 percent of 240 doe fawns examined throughout Iowa were fertile; they averaged 41 kilograms (90 pounds) live weight in December, which reflected the superb nutritional levels of the rich farmland habitat. Abler et al. (1976) showed that doe fawns on a high-energy diet had a greater incidence of ovulation and puberty than did fawns on a low-energy diet. Protein level had no effect on serum progestin levels or attainment of fertility. Nutrition evidently affects ovarian development by regulating the rate at which the follicle-stimulating hormone is released by the pituitary. On submarginal range it is not uncommon for yearling (1.5-year-old) does to remain sexually immature.

In northern regions, cold weather causes a fawn's metabolism to shift from a positive to a negative energy balance, and survival takes precedence over reproduction. Even well-fed doe fawns may not breed during this time, because their ovulatory cycle is suppressed by diminishing daylight and increasing cloud cover.

Productivity

The productivity rate (fecundity) of white-tailed deer increases rapidly to its maximum potential in physically prime does (generally three to seven years of age), then gradually declines. Winter malnutrition inhibits the attainment of fertility in young animals and productivity in older does (Morton and Cheatum 1946, Cheatum and Severinghaus 1950). However, Verme (1967) demonstrated that by itself winter malnutrition in doe fawns does not cause a radical setback in their productivity as yearlings, or subsequently, if they receive adequate nutrition the following season.

Winter and summer ranges were of nearly equal importance in regulating the fertility of yearling mule deer does in Utah (Robinette et al. 1955). The condition of the summer range was of greater value in promoting high productivity among older animals. Although the fetal rate of yearlings on poor winter range was greater after a mild winter than after a severe one, it was higher among those yearlings that subsequently occupied good versus poor summer range. Rates of 1.9 and 1.2 fetuses per doe were found in two mule deer populations re-

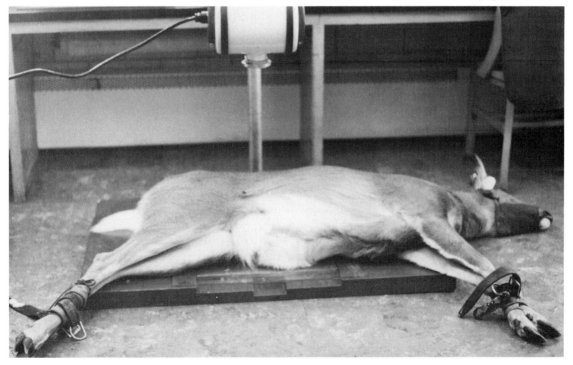

X-raying of does after the third month of pregnancy can ascertain the number of fetuses being carried. The relatively low radiation dosage required for this purpose poses no danger to the mother or her offspring. Complete anesthesia (with pentobarbital sodium) to slow the animal's breathing rate is essential for clear radiograms. *Photo by Louis J. Verme.*

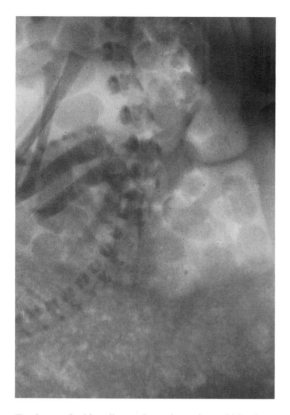

Fetal age of whitetails can be estimated to within about one week, based on relative skeletal size and degree of ossification, using radiograms of known-age specimens as references. This fetus is approximately 135 days old. *Photo by Louis J. Verme.*

siding on summer range of high and low carrying capacity, respectively, following poor nutrition in hard winters (Julander et al. 1961). High-quality summer range was required for optimum reproduction.

The productivity of whitetail does fed a good ration in autumn was nearly twice that of those on a restricted diet (Verme 1965*a, see* Figure 36). Fawning rates almost tripled when does were switched from low to high nutrition in autumn trials (Verme 1967). With adequate diet, the productivity of yearlings jumped from virtually 0 to 1.2 fawns per doe (Table 15).

Does in comparatively poor condition in autumn benefit the most from improved nutrition. However, a short-term dietary improvement may have little effect on reproduction because ovarian activity cannot be effectively altered within the brief interval prior to estrus. Whitetails with access to nutritious forage in autumn generally exhibit high productivity despite winter malnutrition (Ransom 1967, Mansell 1974).

Table 15. Relationship of autumn nutritional plane to whitetail doe productivity (Verme 1967).

Nutritional plane	Fawns per doe			
	Yearling does[a]	Two-year-old does	Prime-age does	All does
Low	0.05	0.50	1.31	0.54
Moderate	0.84	1.40	1.85	1.43
High	1.18	1.53	1.78	1.50

[a]Age at the breeding season.

Lactation stress can modify productivity. Fawning rates of 1.9, 1.7 and 1.6 per doe were found—respectively—among does that had lost twins postnatally, raised one of the set, or successfully nursed twin fawns the summer before breeding (Verme 1967). Ensuing productivity was related to a doe's body weight gain after parturition. A doe whose fawns die at birth is relieved of maternal-care obligations and can recuperate promptly. She is likely to enter the rut early in excellent physical condition and thus have a high ovulation rate. In contrast, a doe nursing fawns is under appreciable strain and is apt to come into estrus at subpar vigor and at a later date.

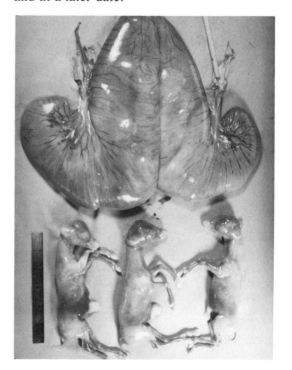

Triplet whitetail fawns are not uncommon if does are in excellent nutritional state when bred. The pointer (upper right) shows ovary location, one on each side of the gravid, bicornate uterus. *Photo by Louis J. Verme.*

Any pronounced change in the proportion of does with or without fawns readily confounds the analysis of a population's reproductive characteristics, since the resulting differences in productivity could cancel each other out. Whitetails on poor winter range in Upper Michigan exhibit a high gross productivity that probably is related to increased fecundity among nonlactating does that suffered natal fawn mortality. A similar pattern was indicated for winter-stressed whitetails in Manitoba (Ransom 1967).

Genetic factors could be responsible for differences in productivity among wild cervid populations (Pimlott 1959, Wegge 1975). For example, in recent years the productivity of Upper Michigan yearling does has increased in the face of progressive winter range deterioration. The most plausible explanation is that the survivors represent a physically superior group that is more prolific than was the original gene pool.

Protein deficiency commonly is considered a limiting factor in deer productivity. On the other hand as little as 7-percent protein intake apparently is sufficient for normal reproduction, as witnessed by a fawning rate of 1.7 per doe in experiments by Murphy and Coates (1966) on captive adult whitetails in Missouri. This rate was only slightly less than that (1.9) of does with a 13-percent protein intake.

Lowered productivity has been reported for animals in crowded laboratory conditions, presumably because the added tension upsets the normal release and interplay of reproductive hormones. However, in a test of this hypothesis on deer, whitetail productivity was not markedly reduced by intense social pressure (Ozoga and Verme 1982a). Well-fed penned deer have reproduced satisfactorily at densities varying from 2.5 per hectare (1.0 per acre) (Verme 1967) to 30 per hectare (12.1 per acre) (Robinette et al. 1973). It would be virtually impossible to find deer densities in the wild where defense mechanisms (pituitary/adrenal/ovarian axis) might react to curtail reproduction.

Conception and Sex Ratio

Ovulation apparently is accomplished between 12 and 14 hours after estrus ends (Verme and Ozoga 1981). The ovum is fertilized as it travels down the Fallopian tube. Implantation of the embryonic blastocyst occurs approximately 30 days after conception—an intermediate time between initial contact and firm attachment to the placenta (Robinette et al. 1955). The mortality rate of ova is related inversely to the number shed (Ransom 1967), but seldom averages more than 5 to 10 percent. Nonfertilization and embryonic mortality rarely can be attributed to nutritional deprivation, since deer ordinarily are in best vitality in autumn.

Prenatal mortality between implantation date and midpregnancy was about 3 percent in mule deer (Robinette et al. 1955). The loss is greater for twins than for single fetuses, and evidently runs higher among the fetuses of poorly nourished does. Hesselton and Jackson (1971) recorded a fetal mortality in whitetails of 0.4 percent for singles, 1.9 percent for twins and 6.4 percent for triplets. Even when acutely malnourished, does rarely abort (Verme 1962). However, disease may cause abortion.

Theoretically, the sex ratio at conception should be even, but at birth, wide variations have been reported, with males usually predominating. The nature and origin of distorted sex ratios remain a controversial subject. Verme (1969) observed that adult does on a low-nutritional plane prior to breeding produced 72 percent males, whereas well-fed mothers produced 43 percent males. Productivity averaged 1.2 versus 1.7 fawns per doe respectively. In feeding trials on goats, diets high in energy produced an excess of female kids, whereas low-energy diets yielded more males (Sachdeva et al. 1973). Variations in protein level did not produce any definite pattern.

Males comprised 42 percent of the fetuses and neonates produced by mule deer living on comparatively good winter range and excellent summer habitat in Utah (Robinette et al. 1957). In contrast, males comprised 65 percent of the fetuses carried by does occupying one of the worst summer ranges. In analyzing the population dynamics of Michigan's George Reserve whitetail population, McCullough (1979) found that more male fawns were conceived in years of high density (and hence a suboptimal nutritional plane) compared with their proportion at lower stocking levels. Verme (1969) postulated that, coupled with a decline in ovulation rate, the tendency for does to produce a heavy surplus of male fawns could accelerate natural population reduction as the range progressively deteriorated. Aside from nutritional factors, does bred late in their estrus cycle produce a preponderance of male fawns (Verme and Ozoga 1981). This could occur where breeding bucks are in short supply. There is good evidence that the sex of progeny varies with maternal age and litter size (Verme 1983).

Prenatal Development

Cell division proceeds rapidly in the embryonic stage, and organ differentiation is apparent approximately 37 days into gestation (Armstrong 1950). At midterm the fetus measures about 200 millimeters (7.9 inches) in forehead/rump length, and weighs about 300 grams (10.6 ounces) (Short 1970). At 180 days a properly nourished fetus may reach 500 millimeters (19.7 inches) in forehead/rump length and exceed 3 kilograms (6.6 pounds) in weight. The reproductive tract averages more than 12 kilograms (26.5 pounds) prior to birth in the case of twins (Verme 1963). Robbins and Moen (1975b) determined that the water content of the fetus decreased during gestation, whereas the amounts of nitrogen, fat, energy and ash increased. Gross energy values of the gravid uterus rose from approximately 43 kilocalories to slightly more than 9,000 kilocalories, and nitrogen levels rose from 1 to 210 grams (0.035 to 7.4 ounces). Shortly before birth, gross energy and nitrogen retention increased curvilinearly and amounted to 280 kilocalories and 6 grams (0.21 ounce), respectively.

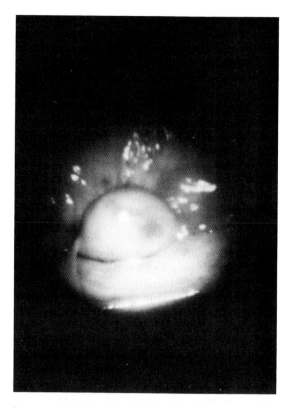

Laparoscopy (below) enables biologists to view a doe's reproductive tract *in situ*, and thus is particularly useful in elucidating the stage of ovarian activity and pregnancy. The ovaries—such as the one above—as observed, are manipulated with a slender probe to look for mature follicles, ovum release sites, incipient corpora lutea, pigmented ''scars,'' etc. *Photos by E. Plotka.*

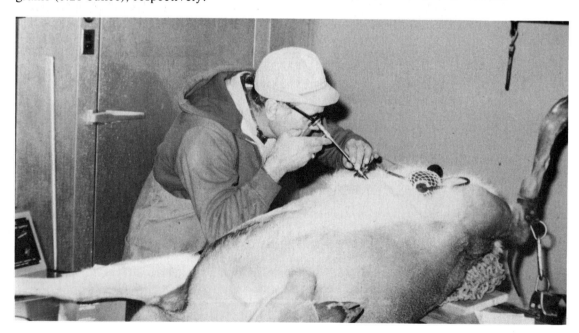

Ullrey et al. (1969, 1970) concluded that the maintenance requirements of pregnant adult does were greater than could be met by consumption of the most nutritious winter browse in northern Michigan. In such an event a doe will catabolize her fat deposits to make up the energy deficit. On a completely inadequate diet she will sacrifice her bone and body tissue to nourish the fetus she is carrying. After a prolonged siege of harsh weather, the physical reserves of a famished mother may be small or nonexistent (Kitts et al. 1956). At this point, fetal growth slows appreciably.

Early nutritive deficiency retards the growth of twins equally. A serious shortage of nutrition beyond midgestation frequently results in physical dimorphism, wherein one littermate receives the bigger share of the limited sustenance that is available. The likely prospects for stunted development in malnourished fetuses preclude an accurate determination of their age by external morphology (Armstrong 1950) or physical measurement (Short 1970).

Mean weight of newborn fawns differed by about 30 percent between the mildest and severest winters in Upper Michigan (Verme 1977). A severe winter definitely was detrimental to fetal development, including the size (and presumably the function) of endocrine glands (Verme 1979). An early spring alleviated maternal stress and favored a resumption of fetal growth, although birth weight was below normal. A difference of a few ounces in natal weight could be crucial to a fawn's survival, and thus, ample nutrition during the final third of gestation is a significant factor in whitetail-population productivity.

Natal Mortality

There is a close relationship between maternal nutrition and neonatal mortality (Verme 1962, 1963). When pregnant does were well fed, fawning loss averaged 7 percent and birth weight averaged 3.5 kilograms (7.7 pounds). At a low plane of nutrition, mortality was 93

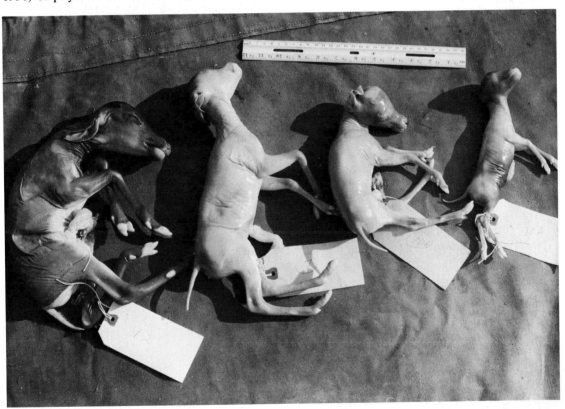

Fetal biomass increases rapidly after mid-gestation. Distinctive changes in external morphology with advancing development provide a rough approximation of age. Body length (forehead-rump) and weight are unreliable criteria for aging fetuses if fetus growth is stunted due to maternal malnutrition. *Photo courtesy of the Florida Game and Fresh Water Fish Commission.*

percent and birth weight averaged 1.9 kilograms (4.2 pounds). Hind-foot length—a good indicator of skeletal development—was 19 percent less for the low diet group. Prenatally dead (mummified fetuses carried to term) and small but fully formed stillbirths occurred more commonly among underfed mothers. Most fawns were born alive but died because they were too weak to stand, they were too small to reach the teats, lactation was delayed or absent, or a mother abandoned or refused to nurse her offspring. Two-year-old does were less successful in rearing their fawns than were older does. Nonetheless, many prime-age mothers in poor vigor lost both members of twins.

Langenau and Lerg (1976) investigated the phenomenon of fawn rejection by malnourished mothers. The death of fawns was attributed to the failure of does to groom their young at birth, fear or aggression toward their young,

failure to eat the afterbirth, and refusal to nurse. The lack of an immediate doe/fawn bond was a critical factor. In the case of twins, both usually were abandoned. Maternal rejection was probably caused by an insufficient pituitary secretion of prolactin, which reaches its highest level in June (Schulte et al. 1981) and is believed to promote the maternal instinct. Crowding in a captive, well-fed whitetail population resulted in high fawn mortality due to maternal territoriality and other behavioral traits at parturition (Ozoga et al. 1982a). First-time mothers lost the most fawns because of their low dominance status in the social hierarchy, and hence their inability to establish or defend a suitable fawning ground.

Murphy and Coates (1966) reported a 42-percent loss of fawns among does in Missouri receiving a 7-percent protein diet; a 27-percent loss among mothers on 10-percent protein intake; and 100-percent fawn survival when does were fed a 13-percent protein diet. Surviving fawns from does on a comparatively high nutritional plane generally averaged heavier in

Fawn mortality is associated with malnutrition in does during pregnancy. Specimen at top died prenatally, became mummified and was dropped at term. Center specimen was stillborn. Although greatly stunted in size, the fawn at bottom was born alive, but died from "nutritive failure" within 48 hours. *Photo by Louis J. Verme.*

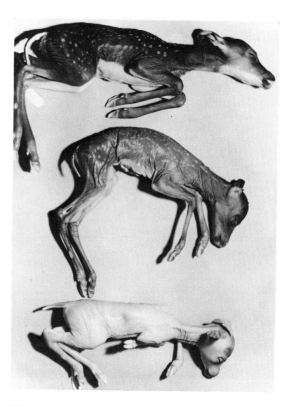

Dimorphism in twins or triplet fetuses of white-tailed deer indicates acute nutritional deprivation during gestation. *Photo by R. Salo.*

birth weight than surviving fawns from mothers on lower protein levels.

Various studies have alluded to the likelihood of serious natal mortality among wild cervids. Ransom (1967) surmised that frequent and severe nutritionally-related natal losses were keeping Manitoba whitetail populations at low densities despite high gross productivity. In red deer, Wegge (1975) estimated that more than 40 percent of the calves died soon after being dropped because the hinds (adult females) were undernourished during pregnancy.

Verme (1977) assessed the annual magnitude of fawn mortality in Upper Michigan in part by examining fetuses in the late stages of gestation. Variations in fetal development and doe physical condition were correlated with indices of winter weather severity (Verme 1968, Verme and Ozoga 1971). Over an eight-year period, fawn mortality ranged from 10 percent of the expected crop following a relatively mild winter to 70 percent after a harsh season. Natal body weights were 3.2 and 2.3 kilograms (7.1 and 5.1 pounds) respectively. The effects of a catastrophic fawning loss would be most noticeable the following year, when the females would have become breeders and the males legal quarry.

FAWN GROWTH

Healthy newborn fawns nurse almost immediately. Intake of colostrum milk during the first 24 to 36 hours provides antibodies that impart a passive resistance to disease until the fawn's immune system begins to function. Hartsook et al. (1975) recorded a gamma-globulin concentration of 27 milligrams per milliliter in the blood of day-old fawns nursed by their mothers, whereas it was absent in fawns not permitted to suckle. During the subsequent three weeks, albumin and beta-globulin concentrations increase in the fawn's blood, while alpha- and gamma-globulin decrease (Youatt et al. 1965).

A whitetail doe thoroughly cleans her newborn fawns of amniotic fluid and membranes, and licks their anal area to stimulate defecation. She promptly eats the afterbirth. Such grooming is important in establishing a mother-infant bond vital to the fawns' survival. *Photo by Leonard Lee Rue III.*

Compared with cow's milk, deer milk is richer in fat, protein, dry solids and energy (Silver 1961). Fat and vitamin A content decline appreciably during early lactation, whereas dry solids and nonfat solids show only minor variation (Table 16). If the milk is not consumed, these constituents become abnormally concentrated in the doe's udder. There is little correlation between a doe's prepartum diet and the composition of her milk (Youatt et al. 1965). If the doe receives insufficient feed to support normal lactation, the milk may be of uniformly high quality, although total yield will diminish.

Table 16. Composition of deer milk at various intervals following birth (Youatt et al. 1965).

Substance assayed	1 day	3 days	7 days	21 days
Vitamin A[a]	67.0	45.0	41.0	27.0
Dry solids[b]	24.7	24.5	24.1	23.2
Fat[b]	10.3	9.9	9.6	8.1
Nonfat solids[b]	14.4	14.7	14.5	15.0

[a]In milligrams per 100 milliliters.
[b]In percentage.

Fawns usually double their birth weight in roughly two weeks and triple it within a month (Verme 1963). On the average, they gain approximately 0.2 kilogram (0.44 pound) per day during this time. Small fawns grow at a faster relative rate than do large fawns. Single fawns gain weight faster than twins do, probably because the former consume more milk per unit of body weight. Milk production of does has not been directly ascertained. Bottle-fed fawns consumed approximately 750 grams (26.5 ounces) of milk per day at a mean body weight of 3 kilograms (6.6 pounds). Daily consumption increased to about 1,000 grams at a weight of 10 kilograms (22 pounds) (Robbins and Moen 1975a). When the milk supply was inadequate, the fawns compensated by increasing their intake of forage. Milk production in black-tailed does peaked at 10 to 37 days in lactation, then gradually declined (Sadleir 1980). The yield averaged around 1 kilogram (2.2 pounds) per day over 60 days. Mean daily digestible energy and protein intake were 247 kilocalories and 11 grams per kilogram of body weight$^{0.75}$, respectively, for fawns up to three months of age (Sadleir 1979).

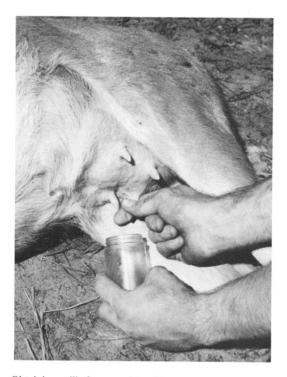

Obtaining milk from a whitetail doe to assess nutritive composition requires injection of the milk-release hormone oxytocin. Deer milk is much richer than cow's milk in content of fat, protein and total solids. *Photo by Louis J. Verme.*

The high nutritive value of its mother's milk enables a newborn whitetail fawn to double its body weight in about two weeks and triple it within a month. *Photo by Louis J. Verme.*

Because of her fawn's high milk demands, a nursing whitetail doe is under appreciable nutritional stress during peak lactation. Even if well-fed, the mother will lose weight until her young are weaned. Milk yield diminishes when a doe is undernourished. *Photo by Leonard Lee Rue III.*

As rapidly growing fawns demand more milk, the mother may lose appreciable body weight and exhibit signs of acute physiological stress, especially if she is underfed (Bahnak et al. 1979). Fortunately, fawns begin grazing when just a few weeks old. They become functional ruminants at roughly two months of age (Short 1964), and hence high-quality forage must be available thereafter if they are to reach their full growth potential. On most summer ranges available forage adequately supplements a doe's milk, but instances of poor growth and starvation of young fawns have been noted (Teer et al. 1965, Cook et al. 1971). On overstocked areas, or where summer drought prematurely cures the forage, serious nutritional problems are apt to arise.

Whitetail fawns begin grazing when just a few weeks old, and high quality forage must be available if they are to reach their full growth potential. Deer are selective feeders, eating only those plants and portions thereof that provide optimum nutrition when forage is plentiful. *Photo courtesy of the New Jersey Division of Fish, Game and Wildlife.*

The stark appearance of this summer range exemplifies horrendous deer overpopulation. Acute malnutrition quite probably caused this whitetail doe to lose her fawn(s) postnatally. *Photo by Leonard Lee Rue III.*

Studies at the Cusino Wildlife Research Station in Michigan have shown that the growth of fawns slowed greatly or came to a halt when the animals received marginal or inadequate nutrition in autumn. When these fawns were sacrificed for examination after a 10-week trial, they were surprisingly fat (Verme and Ozoga 1980b). This indicates that even if food consumption is insufficient for growth, some nutrients still are shunted into fat production. The obligatory tendency to store fat represents an important strategy for survival in winter, when these reserves must be utilized for emergency energy. A deer that is healthy but small will not require as much energy, in absolute terms, to withstand climatic adversity as will one that is healthy and large (Ullrey et al. 1967b). Given an adequate winter diet, lean, small fawns will adjust their foraging strategy to maximize energy conservation (Verme and Ozoga 1980b).

With the advent of cold weather in the northern regions, the nutritional plane of fawns may change drastically when the animals are forced to switch from preferred succulent forage to a low-quality diet of woody browse. Ullrey et al. (1967b) showed that doe fawns receiving 13-percent crude protein gained weight faster in autumn than did those on an 8-percent protein ration. Buck fawns on 20-percent protein gained more weight than did those on lower protein levels. Factors that contribute to high protein reserves and are important to winter survival include selective foraging, delayed nursing and recycling of nonprotein nitrogen (S. H. Smith et al. 1975). Verme and Ozoga (1980a) found that gross energy consumption was more important than dietary protein in promoting growth and lipogenesis of fawns in autumn. As little as a 10-percent reduction in caloric intake stunted their growth.

As a rule, fawns are malnourished in winter, and serious body weight loss may occur. Weight recovery and growth resume in spring. When restored to adequate rations, fawns underfed in winter gain weight faster than do those that were on a high nutritional plane (Verme 1962, Ullrey et al. 1969). This may mean that half-starved deer assimilate their food more efficiently than do well-fed deer, which tend to be wasteful.

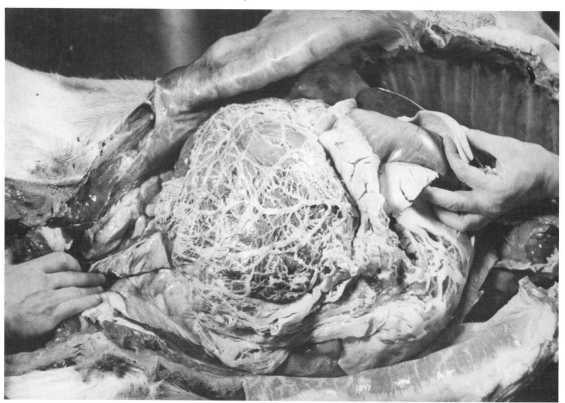

Lipogenesis is an obligatory event in whitetails in autumn, even among malnourished animals. The typically massive accumulation of fat is utilized for energy in winter and often is vital to survival. *Photo by Louis L. Verme.*

PHYSIOLOGICAL INDICES

Many indices have been developed for assessing a deer's physiological state, some of which are used widely.

Fat Reserves

The onset of lipogenesis probably is cued by photoperiodism and subject to endocrine control, being triggered by a decline in prolactin and a rise in adrenocorticotropic hormone, resulting in an increased level of acetyl carboxylase and a decreased recycling of fatty acids in adipose tissue (Verme and Ozoga 1980*b*).

The various body-fat reserves are highly variable, difficult to measure and often are correlated poorly with one another (Ransom 1965, Anderson et al. 1972). Hence, fat indices serve mainly as rough criteria of an animal's health status on a seasonal basis. The fact that deer on an inadequate autumn diet still manage to store appreciable body fat means that one must use caution in equating such reserves with range carrying capacity. Other physical characteristics should also be considered in gauging nutritional status.

The femur (or mandibular) marrow is considered to be the last site of depletion of stored fat, and thus a low femur-marrow fat content indicates serious malnutrition. Assays of dried marrow (Neiland 1970, Verme and Holland 1973) have been used to overcome the imprecision of evaluation of fat levels by visual inspection (Cheatum 1949*a*). Riney (1955) devised a kidney fat index, but it has been questioned because kidney weights vary seasonally (Batcheler and Clarke 1970) and with animal age (Hesselton and Sauer 1973). Monson et al. (1974) recommended using total kidney fat—as opposed to the trimmed portion adopted by Riney (1955)—to provide a more meaningful gauge of physical condition.

Adrenal Gland

An enlargement of the adrenal cortex is believed to reflect social and physiological stress. Christian et al. (1960) found pronounced changes in adrenal size and tissue characteristics during a 60 percent die-off of Sika deer. The changes were thought to be caused by psychological tension in the high population. Welch (1962)

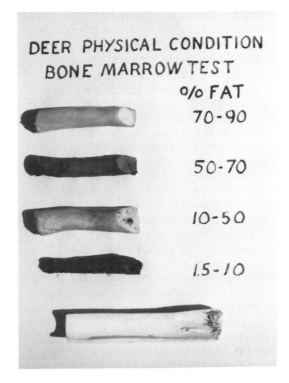

Femur fat analysis provides a useful index to relative nutritional state of deer during winter. However, simple laboratory assays yield more precise data then do visual inspections. *Photo by Louis J. Verme.*

noted larger adrenal glands in whitetails on a densely populated range than in whitetails on a sparsely stocked range. Because the findings often were inconsistent, Welch (1962) and Anderson et al. (1971) concluded that this gland is probably not a reliable index of deer condition. There is increasing evidence that the responses to stress of the adrenal gland in deer (cortisol secretion, for example) differ from those commonly noted in other animals, particularly with regard to population-density effects (Seal et al. 1983).

Thyroid Gland

This gland provides a clue to a deer's current nutritional plane. Hoffman and Robinson (1966) indicated that thyroid activity decreases when temperatures fall and food supplies are scarce or of poor quality. Silver et al. (1969) showed that a decrease in fasting metabolic rate (FMR) coincided with the decline in thyroid weight noted by Hoffman and Robinson (1966).

Seal et al. (1972*b*) reported an appreciable difference between the thyroxine levels of adult does on adequate nutrition in winter and those of adult does on poor nutrition during that season. The data suggest that thyroxine level is influenced by the number of fetuses in utero. Reduced thyroid activity may explain the retarded fetal development and heavy natal mortality observed among malnourished Upper Michigan does following hard winters (Verme 1979).

Autumn feeding trials on fawns showed that triiodothyronine values decreased appreciably with inadequate energy intake, but were not affected by the protein content of the diet (Seal et al. 1978*b*). In contrast, thyroxine levels were not influenced by energy content, but were slightly greater at higher protein levels. The marked decline in heat production and thyroid activity in deer during winter may reflect the triiodothyronine drop that is associated with a decrease in digestible energy intake. The levels of these hormones plummeted when malnourished deer were fasted for a week in late winter, but rose sharply with refeeding (Bahnak et al. 1981).

Thymus Gland

The thymus in deer is large in summer and may be scarcely visible in winter (Browman and Sears 1956, Anderson et al. 1974). It is largest in yearling deer, after which the cyclic oscillations become progressively smaller. The rhythmic fluctuation of the thymus apparently is governed by photoperiodism and tuned by the general endocrine system. Seasonal atrophy of the thymus results secondarily from an excess of adaptive hormones released as a consequence of stress.

Studies by Ozoga and Verme (1978) revealed that the thymic involution of fawns is delayed or minimized in autumn by adequate nutrition, while in spring, thymic enlargement comes earlier for deer on a high dietary plane than for those on a low plane. After seasonal norms are established, variations in thymus-gland weights provide a good indication of current or recent nutritional history (Figure 37), especially during autumn and spring, when other parameters for judging deer-condition are questionable.

Autumn trials on fawns showed wide differences in physical development and organ-size

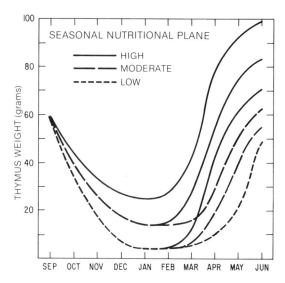

Figure 37. A model for assessment of the recent nutritional history of deer, based on seasonal trends in thymus-gland weight of fawns (Ozoga and Verme 1978).

relative to four combinations of dietary protein-energy intake (Verme and Ozoga 1980*a*). The comparative size of the heart, lungs, liver and kidneys, for example, may be diagnostic of differences in food resources among populations.

Blood Assays

Blood-urea nitrogen appears to be related closely to the protein content of a diet. It was appreciably higher in late winter among well-fed pregnant does than among those on moderate or poor nutrition (Seal et al. 1972*b*). Kirkpatrick et al. (1975) found that whitetail fawns fed high protein diets had substantially greater blood-urea nitrogen levels than did those receiving low protein. Whitetails on high-energy intake had lower blood-urea nitrogen levels than did animals on low-energy intake, probably because of more efficient utilization of protein by rumen microorganisms when digestible energy intake was high.

Blood-urea nitrogen values may become elevated due to tissue catabolism during starvation (Bahnak et al. 1979), and thus an evaluation of energy status also is needed. This can be accomplished by an assessment of nonesterified fatty acids, isoleucine, leucine and perhaps of triiodothyronine (Seal et al. 1978*b*). Because deer can recycle urea as protein intake declines, measurements of blood-urea nitrogen values by themselves are unlikely to designate previous dietary plane.

Ullrey et al. (1967b) noted higher total serum protein in fawns receiving a ration high in crude protein than in those fed less protein. Generally, however, total serum protein is a sensitive indicator of nutritional state only when there is a chronic protein deficiency in the diet (Bahnak et al. 1979).

Because it is elevated by excitement, blood glucose is not a reliable discriminator of nutritional differences. Standardization of handling techniques would prove useful in interpreting glucose variation due to diet alone.

Coblentz (1975) reported that a sharp downward trend in cholesterol content in southern Michigan deer from October through January reflected a progressive decline in the deer's dietary plane. In contrast, no change of cholesterol level in moose was evident between

October and December in northwestern Minnesota (LeResche et al. 1974). A study at Cusino Wildlife Research Station confirmed the autumn decline in cholesterol, but since seasonal change was most pronounced in well-fed deer, factors other than diet evidently were involved.

Although the cellular properties of whole blood are useful for categorizing an animal's physiological status, such data are mainly valuable as support for clinical evidence of any abnormality revealed by serum chemistry. The problem of infection or trauma can be resolved by measuring haptoglobulin levels or by white-cell counts. Franzmann and LeResche (1978) concluded that packed-cell volume and hemoglobin content of blood were among the most diagnostic cellular parameters of physical condition in moose. Seal et al. (1981) summarized the physiologic ramifications of hematology assays on deer.

Blood collection to determine physiological status of captive whitetails used in various experiments is now almost routine, and has application in free-roaming deer populations. Circulating levels of hormones and enzymes in serum can be assayed in parts per billion by means of radioimmunoassay. A catheter inserted into the jugular vein permits serial sampling over a period of many hours. *Photo by Louis J. Verme.*

WINTER ADAPTATIONS

The northern whitetail's ability to cope with extremely harsh winter climate attests to the fact that it is an innately hardy and resourceful animal. The deer undergo certain physiological and behavioral adjustments that contribute greatly to the animals' survival. Along with the deposition of subcutaneous fat, the change to a highly-insulative coat minimizes thermal exchange to the cold environment. Coat molt coincides with a dramatic decrease in heat production, which in turn is associated with reduced thyroid function.

Despite ample feed, deer voluntarily restrict their intake during winter (French et al. 1955). They likewise limit their feeding mainly to the warmer daylight hours (Ozoga and Verme 1970) and are less active overall. To conserve energy further, deer seek the optimum shelter afforded by dense conifer canopy in lowland yards, since this provides the most comfort-able microclimate for bedding (Verme 1965b, Ozoga 1968). By midwinter the deer have in effect geared down to a relatively torpid, almost semihibernating state.

Although these adaptions protect against harsh weather and famine, a prolonged winter spells trouble for deer confined to yards by deep snow. Probably in response to the lengthening photoperiod of late winter, the animals' metabolism shifts back to its higher rate. Thereafter, increased energy demands rapidly sap the deer's scant internal reserves to the point where a whitetail's defense system may collapse suddenly. Grave debilitation and death most commonly result during the winter-spring transition period (Verme and Ozoga 1971). Hence, it is vital that deer get proper nourishment at this time. Even considering the whitetails' physiological adaptations to prolonged cold weather, it is remarkable that most deer are able to survive the winter conditions to which they are exposed.

This emaciated whitetail fawn had mobilized all of its fat reserves by late winter, when a deer's metabolic rate (hence caloric needs) begins to increase. Its search for browse was a case of too little and too late, and death was imminent. *Photo by S. E. Aldous; courtesy of the U.S. Fish and Wildlife Service.*

FOOD CONSUMPTION

White-tailed deer are ruminants with a typical compound stomach (rumen, reticulum, omasum and abomasum). This important adaptive feature permits deer to utilize foods that cannot be digested by man. The energy needs of deer can be met by nutrients consumed in food plus nutrients synthesized by microbial symbionts in the rumen and reticulum. This latter process may be particularly important when only low-quality food is available. However, deer are by no means "super ruminants"—they cannot utilize some woody browse species as well as cattle can (Short and Remmenga 1965, Short et al. 1974, Schoonveld et al. 1974)—and have difficulty surviving on highly lignified foods.

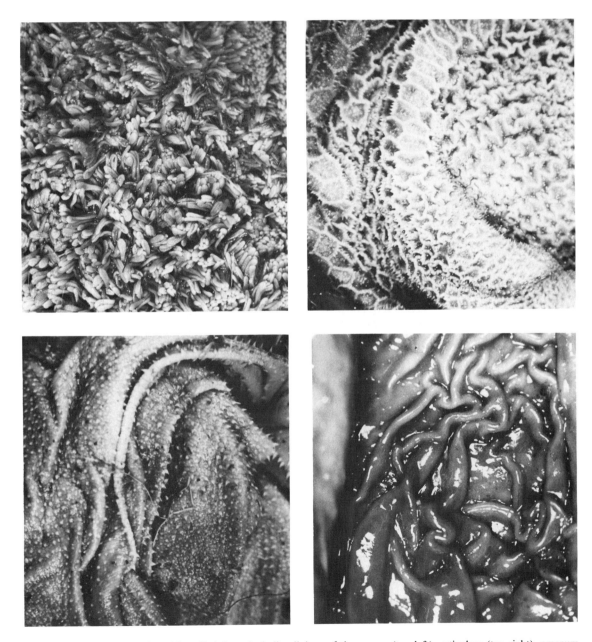

The compound stomach of a white-tailed deer, including linings of the rumen (top left), reticulum (top right), omasum (bottom left) and abomasum (bottom right). *Photos by W. G. Youatt.*

Being a selective feeder that chooses plants and plant parts with considerable discrimination, the whitetail consumes those items that are most likely to meet its nutritional needs. Although purported to be a browser, whitetails consume a variety of foods, including grasses, sedges, fruits, nuts, forbs and mushrooms, as well as portions of shrubs and trees. There is no physiological reason why they cannot be considered true grazers (Nagy et al. 1967), probably turning to browse when herbaceous forage is unavailable.

Palatability

Characteristics that stimulate the selection of certain plants are referred to as "palatability factors" (Heady 1964). They may be chemical or physical, but chemical composition seems to be of major importance, even though the effective constituents are not well defined. Chemoreceptors in the nose and tongue respond to compounds that encourage or discourage consumption of potential foods.

The sense of taste in deer may be different from that in humans, who respond to substances that are sweet or sour, salty or bitter. However, black-tailed deer showed a pronounced preference for water solutions of sucrose and a moderate preference for acetic acid, while sodium chloride or quinine solutions were not preferred over plain water (Crawford and Church 1971). Whether these preferences can be related to natural foods has not been established. An association between essential oil composition and palatability of certain plants has been reported (Oh et al. 1968), and chlorogenic-acid concentrations have been associated with the susceptibility of Douglas-fir clones to browsing by black-tailed deer (Radwan 1972). No obvious preference was found among white-tailed deer for protein-energy supplement blocks treated with extracts of white cedar fronds, cloves, wintergreen or a commercial "attractant," in comparison with that of untreated blocks (Ullrey et al. 1975b).

The sense of smell has not been studied separately from the sense of taste in deer. However, sheep deprived of the smell sense did not eat flowering heads of grasses while normal sheep did (Arnold 1966b). When the sense of touch also was impaired, the consumption of flowering heads was reduced less than by impairment of smell alone. Impairment of taste

alone or touch alone resulted in increased intake of some plants and reduced intake of others.

The importance of sight in deer has not been studied objectively, although fawns tend to mimic the food choices of their mothers—a behavior that depends on sight. Obscured vision in sheep resulted in greater consumption of tall grass and less clover, but sight was most important for space orientation (Arnold 1966a, 1966b).

It is unlikely that deer possess nutritional wisdom, but their survival under a variety of unfavorable circumstances suggests that their food choices generally are beneficial, regardless of the basis for these choices. In any case, survival is not exclusively dependent on the successful acquisition of nutrients, but on avoidance of toxins as well. Black-tailed deer strongly reject poisonous tansy ragwort and have a high tolerance for its toxin (Dean and Winward 1974).

Food availability influences relative preference. During periods of scarcity, any kind of available food, palatable or not, may be consumed out of necessity. This situation prevails regularly in northern climates where winter foods are restricted largely to woody browse.

Previous experience also seems to influence food selection. Young deer raised in captivity on formulated diets frequently prefer food items different from those consumed readily by wild deer. Preferences may be transmitted from one generation to the next through imitations of a doe's food selection by her fawns.

Appetite

Assuming acceptable foods are available, the amount of food consumed per unit of time is a function of appetite. Food intake is physiologically regulated over both the long term and short term, otherwise starvation or obesity would be more common. Hunger and satiety centers have been identified in the hypothalamus, and lesions of these centers may induce undereating or overeating. In monogastrics, blood glucose levels stimulate these centers. In ruminants, very little blood glucose is derived directly from the diet, and volatile fatty acids from microbial fermentation in the rumen-reticulum are major energy sources. Intraruminal infusions of acetate, propionate or butyrate (or mixtures of these acids) depress food intake (Baile and Mayer 1969). However, this effect may not be due to direct action on the hypothalamic appetite-control centers, since intravenous infusion produces less depression in food intake. Perhaps other appetite-control centers exist, or other metabolites are more important in regulating hypothalamic function.

Physical limitations of the digestive tract very likely limit the intake of coarse foods. Foods difficult to digest are retained longer in the rumen-reticulum than are easily digested foods, restricting the amount of food consumed per unit of time. Montgomery and Baumgardt (1965) have shown that in the lower ranges of dietary nutritive value, physical factors such as bulkiness (large volume per unit of mass) may be most important in limiting dry-matter intake, and digestible energy intakes may never reach need. In the upper range, chemostatic or thermostatic mechanisms such as rumen or blood-volatile fatty-acid levels or the body-heat load may regulate intake such that energy consumption corresponds to need, while dry-matter intake declines with increasing nutritive value (Figure 38).

White-tailed deer fawns consume dry matter in conformity with the Figure 38 model, at least in winter (Ammann et al. 1973). When digestible energy density of an artificial diet was increased from 1.9 to 3.5 kilocalories per gram of dry diet, dry-matter intake in grams per kilogram of body weight$^{0.75}$ increased to a dietary-digestible energy density of 2.2 kiloca-

lories per gram, then declined. Dry-matter consumption at a digestible energy density of 2.2 kilocalories per gram was sufficient to meet energy needs for maintenance of body weights in winter in a northern United States environment (Croyle 1969). This digestible-energy density is equivalent to a dry-matter digestibility of about 50 percent. When whitetails are fed diets of less than 50-percent digestibility, physical limitations of the digestive tract will limit dry-matter intake to less than maintenance requirements, and fawns will lose weight. Environmental factors, animal individuality and other characteristics of the food (such as nutrient content) may alter this 50-percent digestibility limit.

When adult white-tailed does were fed northern white cedar fronds with a dry-matter digestibility of 60 percent, dry-matter consumption in a Michigan winter was 0.58 kilogram (1.28 pounds) per day, and the does lost weight (Ullrey et al. 1972). Greater weight loss was experienced when the deer were fed bigtooth aspen shoots with a dry-matter digestibility of 49 percent. Dry-matter intake was only

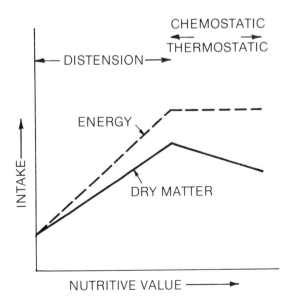

Figure 38. Proposed relationships in the regulation of food intake in ruminants (Montgomery and Baumgardt 1965).

Experiments in the mid-1930s revealed that white cedar is the only species in the northern Lake States region that, by itself, will maintain deer over winter in adequate physical condition. Because of overbrowsing and natural pruning, however, this nutritious food is in short supply now, except from felled trees during logging. *Photo by E. Mikula.*

0.17 kilogram (0.37 pound) per day. Since daily energy intake must balance daily energy loss if weight is to be maintained, any factor that results in very low intakes of food, regardless of digestible-energy density, will be detrimental.

Seasonal factors, and related physiological cycles, also influence dry-matter intake. Young deer fed a pelleted diet with a dry-matter digestibility of 65 percent showed a marked decline in food consumption and weight in midwinter in New Hampshire (Holter et al. 1977) (Figure 39). Food intake by free-roaming adult mule deer in Colorado showed a similar pattern, being greatest in summer; however, food intake by subadults showed little fluctuation (Alldredge et al. 1974). In the South (Short et al. 1969a), captive yearling whitetails increased food consumption from lows in November and December to highs in spring. Food consumption generally decreased during the hot, humid southern summer, but increased slightly in August for bucks and gradually increased from July to October for does. It then fell rapidly to lows in late autumn and early winter. In a northern Michigan winter study, activity and browse consumption by fawns and adult does was high during December-January and in late March (Ozoga and Verme 1970). Activity and food consumption were reduced in the interim. Peaks of activity were noted at four- to six-hour intervals—sunrise, midday, sunset and twice during the night. As winter progressed, nocturnal and early morning movements were reduced, and food consumption was concentrated during the warmer part of the day. Such behavior represents an attempt to maximize energy conservation when food is scarce or of limited nutritive value.

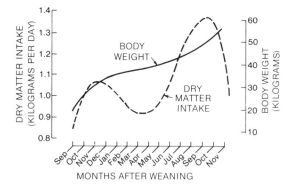

Figure 39. Mean body weight and daily dry matter intake of white-tailed deer from weaning to 18 months of age (Holter et al. 1977).

DIGESTION

At birth, a fawn has a relatively underdeveloped rumen, reticulum and omasum. During nursing, milk flows from the lower end of the esophagus through a reticular groove into the omasum without entering the rumen. From the omasum, milk immediately enters the abomasum and undergoes digestive processes there, as well as in the intestine. These digestive processes are similar to those in monogastrics. The rumen, reticulum and omasum attain adult proportions at about three to four months of age.

The rumen is the largest compartment, and it is here that food, consumed in haste, is stored until regurgitated, remasticated and reswallowed to promote microbial degradation. Digesta in the rumen and reticulum move rather freely from one compartment to another and may account for 7 to 10 percent of body weight in adult deer (Short et al. 1969b). Large volumes of saliva maintain the fluid volume and regulate pH and ionic composition. Protozoa may number 500,000 per gram of rumen-reticulum contents, and bacteria 50 billion per gram of rumen-reticulum contents. The protozoa and bacteria are approximately equal in mass. Some food may pass through the rumen in a few hours, while some remains for days. Even in starvation, the rumen is not empty. Contractions of the rumen-reticulum mix the contents and ultimately result in movement of the smaller, denser particles of the digesta into the omasum and abomasum.

Microorganisms in the rumen-reticulum ferment carbohydrates and produce volatile fatty acids such as acetic, propionic, butyric, valeric, isobutyric and isovaleric, which can be absorbed and used for energy. Of particular benefit is the breakdown of cellulose and hemicellulose, which are found in large quantities in herbaceous materials and which could not be used except for the presence of these microorganisms. They also convert nonprotein nitrogen compounds to amino acids that can be used by the host. These nonprotein compounds may be present in food, but they also are recycled products of nitrogen metabolism, appearing in the saliva and secretions of the rumen wall. B-vitamins and vitamin K also are synthesized by rumen microorganisms. Given sufficient energy, deer can recycle nitrogen in the form of urea, thus allowing rumen microorganisms to synthesize amino acids and protein. The relationship between the two constituents is obscured by the fact that as natural forage declines in protein content, it also declines in energy value, and the animal simply cannot or will not consume enough bulk to obtain the required supply of both.

The products of microbial fermentation, the microorganisms themselves, and those dietary components that escape fermentation undergo further digestion in the abomasum and small intestine. Gases—such as methane and carbon dioxide—which are produced during fermentation, are eliminated largely by belching.

The omasum absorbs water, certain minerals and some products of fermentation.

The abomasum secretes hydrochloric acid, pepsin and rennin. In fawns, the breakdown of proteins to amino acids begins in the abomasum. The splitting of milk fat also begins there, through the action of lipase in the saliva.

Material entering the small intestine is digested by enzymes from the pancreas and the small intestine itself. Pancreatic amylase, lipase and proteases attack starch, lipids and proteins respectively, yielding maltose, monoglycerides, diglycerides, free fatty acids and peptides. Intestinal lactase hydrolyzes milk sugar (lactose) to glucose and galactose, and intestinal maltase hydrolyzes maltose to two molecules of glucose. Sucrase activity is low or nonexistent in ruminants. Intestinal peptidases hydrolyze peptides to amino acids. These endproducts of digestion are absorbed in portions of the small intestine (the duodenum, jejunum and ileum). Items that escape digestion in the small intestine may undergo limited microbial fermentation in the cecum and colon. Some absorption of volatile fatty acids and certain minerals and vitamins occurs in the lower bowel. The indigestible residue is formed into fecal pellets and excreted from the rectum via the anus.

The chemical and physical character of natural foods markedly influences digestion and the supply of nutrients that deer can obtain from such foods. Of particular significance are the concentrations of cell-wall constituents—cellulose, hemicellulose, lignin, cutin, pectin, tannin and silica. An *in vitro* system of estimating the nutritive value of deer foods, which considers these compositional differences, was described by Robbins et al. (1975). Short and Reagor (1970) reported that the cell solubles of deer browse are 98 percent digestible, while lignin-cutin complexes are low in digestibility

(Van Soest 1967). Thus, proportions of the easily digested cell solubles and the more-difficult-to-digest cell-wall fractions directly influence potential nutritive value. Short (1971) and Short et al. (1974) showed that as forages matured, cell-wall constituents increased and digestibility diminished. Forages that were most resistant to microbial digestion in an artificial rumen had higher proportions of lignin in the cell wall than did more-digestible foods.

STARVATION

Deer at the northern limits of their range and in overpopulated wintering areas frequently succumb to starvation. Loss of the rumen function may be involved, although viable bacteria—capable of *in vitro* fiber digestion—have been isolated from starved mule deer in captivity (deCalesta et al. 1974). Malnourished wild mule deer also possessed viable rumen bacteria and had rumen-fluid volatile fatty acid concentrations within a normal range (Dean et al. 1975). However, captive whitetails restricted to difficult-to-digest woody browse lost large amounts of weight, had low rumen volatile fatty acid production, and exhibited biochemical and clinical signs of starvation (Ullrey et al. 1964, 1967a, 1968). Utilization of aspen shoots was markedly improved by both supplemental nitrogen and readily fermentable carbohydrate, suggesting that some winter foods may be so low in available nitrogen and energy that nutrient needs of the rumen-reticulum microorganisms, and thus of the host, are not met (Ullrey et al. 1971). Deer, even fawns, in relatively good physical condition can fast for several weeks without harmful effects (Ozoga and Verme 1970).

Introduction of potentially useful supplements must be gradual. Probably as a consequence of lactic acidosis, rumenitis was diagnosed in nearly 30 percent of white-tailed deer found dead during a severe winter in Saskatchewan (Wobeser and Runge 1975a). A number of the deer were found in or near cattle feedlots, and also in a provincial park where grain-screenings from feed mills had been distributed as deer food. In some of the animals the rumen-reticulum was filled with a large volume of fluid plus wheat or barley. Apparently these readily fermentable foods had been consumed in large quantity and without adequate microbial adaptation. Emergency winter feeding often begins too late and fails to prevent death, despite the presence of food in the animal's digestive tract (Nagy et al. 1967). When conducted properly, however, winter feeding can greatly improve a whitetail population's welfare (Ozoga and Verme 1982*a*).

Supplemental feeding of starving whitetails has been tried in dozens of states, but rarely has it averted disastrous die-offs. This fawn derived scant benefit from visiting a well-used hay pile because it could not digest the coarse stem material. *Photo by K. D. Swan; courtesy of the U.S. Forest Service.*

NUTRIENT REQUIREMENTS

Although not experimentally established in every case, qualitative nutrient requirements of the adult deer probably include water, energy, nitrogen, essential fatty acids (?), calcium, phosphorus, magnesium, sodium, chlorine, potassium, sulfur, iron, copper, iodine, cobalt, manganese, selenium, chromium, fluorine, nickel, silicon, vanadium, tin, arsenic, molybdenum, vitamin A, vitamin D and vitamin E.

In addition, some indigestible fiber must be present in the diet to support normal digestive-tract function. Nursing fawns require the aforementioned nutrients plus vitamin K, thiamin, riboflavin, niacin, pantothenic acid, vitamin B_6, folic acid, biotin and cobalamin. Essential amino acids for the young fawn probably include arginine, histidine, isoleucine, leucine, lysine, methionine, phenylalanine, threonine, tryptophan and valine.

Quantitative nutrient requirements have been established in only a few instances. Water requirements vary with climatic conditions, type of food, physiological state (growth, maintenance, lactation) and amount of activity. In a temperate environment, captive pregnant whitetailed deer typically consume two to three times as much water as dry matter. The amount of

Intense daytime feeding exhibited by these whitetails indicated they were hungry. Artificial feeding only exacerbates a bad situation unless it supplies a balanced ration in adequate amounts to a closely regulated deer population. When competition is severe, the most dominant animals aggressively monopolize the feeders. *Photo courtesy of the North Dakota Game and Fish Department.*

Whitetails need copious amounts of water on hot summer days. Ponds ringed with emergent aquatic plants also supply some useful forage. *Photo courtesy of the Arkansas Game and Fish Commission.*

liquid water consumed is inversely proportional to the concentration of water in food. Snow may be consumed when liquid water is unavailable.

The daily digestible energy requirement for maintenance of pregnant does in a Michigan winter was determined to be 155 to 160 kilocalories per unit of metabolic size (kilograms of body weight$^{0.75}$) (Ullrey et al. 1969, 1970). Croyle (1969) found that male and female fawns required 168 and 155 kilocalories of digestible energy per kilogram of body weight$^{0.75}$, respectively, for maintenance in a temperate environment. Thompson et al. (1973) found that fawns required 199 kilocalories of digestible energy per kilogram of body weight$^{0.75}$ daily for growth during their first summer, and 144 kilocalories of digestible energy per kilogram of body weight$^{0.75}$ for maintenance during their first winter. Free-ranging deer will undoubtedly have higher energy requirements due to

the additional costs of foraging for food. Movement in snow greatly increases energy expenditure, with highest values occuring when deer sink to depths of 25 to 30 centimeters (10–12 inches) or more (Mattfeld 1974). Energy costs of maintaining body temperature are related to heat loss as influenced by exposure to cold and wind, and the insulative properties of subcutaneous fat and body hair. By lying in a curled position underneath evergreens, a deer can minimize heat loss to the immediate environment and the cold winter sky. Energy costs for reproduction are barely discernible from those for maintenance except during the last third of pregnancy and during lactation, when energy requirements are related to milk production.

Protein requirements for growth of fawns after weaning were estimated to be 14 to 22 percent (dry-matter basis), with males having higher requirements than did females (Ullrey et al. 1967*b*). S. H. Smith et al. (1975) proposed that approximately 24 percent protein (dry-matter basis) was required for maximum tissue nitrogen balance by weaned fawns, but as Hegsted (1964) pointed out, an animal may be in nitrogen equilibrium over a wide range of dietary nitrogen intakes. Nitrogen intakes required to maintain or build labile protein reserves are higher than those required to support minimal requirements. Holter et al. (1977, 1979) suggested that about 11 percent protein (dry-matter basis) is adequate for yearling deer. Protein requirements for maintenance of adults may be as low as 6 to 10 percent (dry basis) (French et al. 1956, McEwen et al. 1957). Protein requirements for gestation and antler development are probably intermediate—between those for growth and maintenance, while lactation requirements likely approximate those for growth.

Neither quantitative nor qualitative fatty-acid requirements for deer have been published. An unpublished study (Ullrey et al. 1972) of the effects of low-fat and low-linoleic-acid diets on gestation and lactation in white-tailed deer revealed no deficiency signs, nor any reproductive response to linoleic-acid supplementation.

Calcium requirements (dry-matter basis) to support growth, skeletal development and antler development of weaned fawns are about 0.45 percent (Ullrey et al. 1973). Phosphorus requirements (dry-matter basis) do not exceed 0.28 percent and may be lower (Ullrey et al. 1975*a*).

Other elements that sometimes may be deficient in natural ecosystems (because of the geological origin of the soil and particular climatic conditions) are sodium, cobalt, iodine and selenium. Terrestrial browse species may contain sodium concentrations appreciably lower than those considered necessary for domestic ruminants. White-tailed deer may adapt by using sodium-containing mineral licks (Weeks and Kirpatrick 1976, Weeks 1978). Cobalt deficiencies have been described in domestic ruminants in New York, but white-tailed deer in that region did not seem limited by a shortage of this element (Smith et al. 1963).

Iodine concentrations in deer foods in Michigan range from 0.008 to 3.1 parts per million (dry basis), with the minimum value far below the requirements for domestic livestock species (Watkins 1980). Selective foraging presumably helps deer meet their iodine needs. Watkins (1980) established that a diet containing 0.26 parts per million of iodine (dry basis) is adequate for maintenance and reproduction in captive white-tailed deer.

Selenium-deficient areas are widespread in the United States, with an apparent relationship existing between browse-selenium concentrations and those in the muscle tissue of free-ranging deer (Ullrey et al. 1981). Based on a number of parameters, dietary selenium concentrations of 0.2 parts per million probably are adequate for deer, but freedom from deficiency lesions also is dependent on dietary supplies of vitamin E and the degree of stress to which deer may be exposed (Brady et al. 1978).

Very little research has been conducted on the vitamin requirements of deer. Based on comparisons of liver vitamin-A concentrations in deer with those in domestic ruminants, incipient vitamin-A deficiency was suspected in 2 to 3 percent of vehicle-killed deer at the end of winter in Michigan (Youatt et al. 1976). Vitamin-D requirements presumably are met by exposure to sunlight and conversion of 7-dehydrocholesterol to cholecalciferol (D_3) in the skin, or else by consumption of ultraviolet-irradiated dead-plant material (irradia-

White-tailed deer are attracted to mineral licks that contain sodium and other trace elements. It is not known whether heavy use of salt blocks in summertime represents a physiological need or merely an acquired taste. A nursing doe presumably would rapidly deplete her reserves of sodium, a constituent of milk. *Photo by Leonard Lee Rue III.*

tion resulting in conversion of ergosterol to ergocalciferol [D_2]). Vitamin-E requirements probably do not exceed 45 International Units per kilogram of dry diet when deer consume 0.2 parts per million of selenium and are not excessively stressed (Brady et al. 1978). However, it may be necessary for the diet to contain 80 or more International Units per kilogram to protect against peroxidative lesions in muscle of deer subjected to severe physical exertion. The need for vitamin K and B-vitamins in the diets of fawns before active rumen fermentation begins has not been explored.

Chapter 5

POPULATION GENETICS

Michael H. Smith
Professor of Zoology
Director
Savannah River Ecology Laboratory
University of Georgia
Aiken, South Carolina

Ramone Baccus
Museum of Vertebrate Zoology
University of California
Berkeley, California

Hilburn O. Hillestad
President
Southeastern Wildlife Services, Inc.
Athens, Georgia

Michael N. Manlove
Teaching Assistant
Department of Zoology
University of Florida
Gainesville, Florida

The basic approach to genetic research is through classical breeding studies. Because of the expense of animal maintenance and the length of generation-time, such investigations rarely are undertaken with wild species of large mammals, such as the white-tailed deer. In addition, most traits of interest to wildlife biologists and managers are determined by many genes functioning together, and thus the genetic bases of these traits are not susceptible to simple interpretation.

The modern approach to the genetics of natural populations is through electrophoretic analysis of tissue fluids, a methodology which has been applied to a variety of animal populations (Nevo 1978), including white-tailed deer (Van Tets and Cowan 1966, Manlove et al. 1976, Ramsey et al. 1979). Tissue fluids are examined for differences in the molecular forms of enzymes and general proteins that are essential to the physiological health and functioning of animals. In general, genetically variable proteins can be used as markers to study population processes, such as migration and breeding structure, and as indicators of genetic variability within and between local populations (Berry 1971, Utter et al. 1973, Morgan et al. 1974, Smith et al. 1976, Chesser et al. 1980).

THE ELECTROPHORESIS PROCESS

In electrophoretic techniques, enzymes or other proteins are separated by their electrical charges. Proteins are obtained from body fluids such as blood, or extracted from tissues such as the liver or skeletal muscles. Tissues are ground in a fluid and the solids centrifuged to the bottom of a test tube. The fluid is separated from the solid fraction and usually frozen at a low temperature for later analysis. After thawing, the samples are placed in a gel and subjected to an electric current so that the proteins move varying distances through the gel, depending primarily on their net charge. The gel can consist of various substances, such as hydrolyzed potato starch or acrylamide.

After separation in the gel, the proteins are stained. Most proteins are invisible, but some, such as hemoglobin, can be seen because they are a natural flesh color. Theoretically it is possible to use this approach to examine any protein. In practice, however, metabolic enzymes have been studied more than other forms. Enzymes catalyze critical metabolic reactions, and thus it is possible to add a specific material (substrate) and stain the product of the reaction. To produce energy, for example, sugar is broken down to carbon dioxide and water. Many enzymes are involved in this process, and biochemists have determined the exact sequence of chemical changes that each enzyme affects. By adding a particular substrate, the type of reaction and the specific enzyme involved can be determined and controlled. These enzymes occur in every individual animal, and their absence or severe alteration of structure could result in death or serious disease.

Staining the enzymes involves a series of detailed chemical recipes, but often results in easily interpreted patterns. For example, mannosephosphate isomerase (*MPI*) is controlled by three alleles and has a potential of six phenotypic expressions (Figure 40). Each band is a place where the specific reaction catalyzed by this enzyme has taken place, and is the phenotypic expression of a particular allele. Alleles are the alternate forms of the genes that control the production of specific enzymes. In our example, the three alleles are designated *Mpi*^{64}, *Mpi*^{82} and *Mpi*^{100} on the basis of the relative mobility of the bands they encode (Smith et al. 1973).

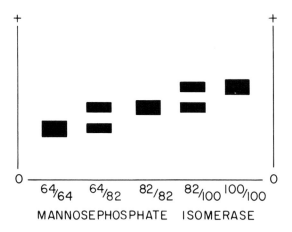

MANNOSEPHOSPHATE ISOMERASE

Figure 40. Banding patterns for a variable protein, mannosephosphate isomerase (*MPI*), with three alleles— *Mpi*^{100}, *Mpi*^{82} or *Mpi*^{64}. *Mpi*^{64} is rare and found only in white-tailed deer from Michigan. The *Mpi*$^{64/64}$ type has not yet been observed in nature. The origin is indicated by 0, and *MPI* moves through the gel toward the anode (+).

Deer have two alleles for each gene locus (diploid); they receive one allele from each parent. If the alleles are the same, the individual is homozygous—for example, *Mpi*^{100}/*Mpi*^{100}—and has one band for mannosephosphate isomerase. If the alleles are different, the individual is heterozygous and has two bands for this enzyme. Other enzymes have different banding patterns depending on their molecular structure. Banding patterns for the white-tailed deer are illustrated in Manlove et al. (1976).

Proteins can be considered individually or as a group. In the latter case it is possible to estimate the level of genetic variability in an individual or population if the proteins chosen for study are a random subset of those available. Three common indices are used to designate variability. $\overline{H}$ is the mean proportion of the population that is heterozygous across a number of loci; *A* is the mean number of alleles per locus; *P* is the percentage of polymorphic loci. $\overline{H}$ and *P* are calculated across loci and also may be used across a series of populations or for a single population. Alleles at a locus occur in a population with a frequency that can vary between zero and one; the sum of the frequencies of all alleles at a locus is one. A locus is defined as polymorphic when it has two or more alleles and when the frequency of occurrence of the common allele at that locus is less than or equal to 0.99. Other criteria—for example, 0.95—for polymorphic loci can be used. A monomorphic locus has little or no allele variation.

GENETIC VARIABILITY

The white-tailed deer is a widely distributed species, occurring throughout much of North, Central and South America (*see* Chapter 1). Generally the larger individuals occur in populations inhabiting northern latitudes, and smaller whitetails—such as the Key deer—live in more tropical climates. Other morphological parameters, such as hair density and color, vary widely among populations.

Genetic differences obviously account for many of the observed phenotypes in deer, but the genetic bases for taxonomic differentiation among subspecies are not known. Six subspecies—northern woodland, Blackbeard Island, Florida coastal, Florida, Texas and Virginia—have been studied electrophoretically at the

A melanistic whitetail fawn. Excessive levels of the melanism pigment are very rarely observed in white-tailed deer; the genetic basis of this phenomenon is unknown. *Photo by C. Graham; courtesy of the Texas Parks and Wildlife Department.*

Savannah River Ecology Laboratory. No significant levels of genetic differentiation, such as fixed alleles, have been detected among these subspecies. Additional studies of more geographically isolated groups may reveal differences however. A significant variable confounding analysis of genetic differentiation of subspecies is the complex stocking histories of many populations. Highly successful stockings have resulted in mixed genetic stocks in many states.

Racial differences among whitetail populations throughout the species' range may have genetic constraints, whereby the races or subspecies are restricted within various physiological/morphological "amplitudes." For example, wildlife biologists and managers traditionally explain size differences in subspecies as functions of nutrition, habitat quality and population density. Until the advent of electrophoresis, there was no tool to examine the other side of the management coin—genetics. In this example, constant high-quality diet may influence deer weights, but a genetically controlled upper-size limit also may operate. The new approach to genetics may yield data to substantiate this hypothesis.

A total of 35 loci have been studied in white-tailed deer. Of these, 27 have more than one allele (Table 17). Most loci (71 percent) in mammals have only one allele (Smith et al. 1978), but white-tailed deer have more than one allele per locus (Table 18).

Levels of genetic variability differ considerably across populations of white-tailed deer (Table 18). Heterozygosity values vary more than the number of alleles per locus and the proportion of polymorphic loci. One population at the swamp on the Savannah River Plant in South Carolina had an $\overline{H}$ value of 0.092.

Table 17. Allele designations for the variable loci, and the molecular structure of the resulting proteins for white-tailed deer from seven southeastern states and Michigan.[a]

Locus[b]	Allele designations	Molecular structure
Acid phosphatase (ACP)	89, 100	Dimer
Adenylate kinase (*AK*)	73, 100	Monomer
Albumin (*ALB*)	100, 104	Monomer
Alcohol dehydrogenase (*ADH*)	−155, −100	Dimer
Asparate amino transferase-1 (AAT-1)	75, 100, 128	Dimer
Asparate amino transferase-2 (AAT-2)	−100, −70	
Esterase-2 (ES-2)	36, 86, 100, 107	Monomer
Esterase-4 (ES-4)	100, 106	Monomer
Glucose-6-phosphate dehydrogenase (GD)	100, 105	Dimer
Glucose dehydrogenase (*GDH*)	88, 100	Hexamere
α-Glycerophosphate dehydrogenase-2 (GPD-2)	83, 100, 112	Dimer
α-Hemoglobin (*HB*)	100, Null	Tetramer
β-Hemoglobin (HB)[c]	95, 100, 105, 110, 115, 120	
Isocitrate dehydrogenase-1 (*ICD*-1)	100, 115	Dimer
Lactate dehydrogenase-1 (LDH-1)	89, 100, 114	Tetramer
Lactate dehydrogenase-2 (LDH-2)	−120, −100	Tetramer
Malate dehydrogenase-1 (MDH-1)	80, 100, 120	Dimer
Malic enzyme-1 (MOD-1)	100, 128	Tetramer
Malic enzyme-2 (MOD-2)	100, 127	Tetramer
Mannosephosphate isomerase (*MPI*)	64, 82, 100	Monomer
Peptidase-1 (PEP)	100, 111	Monomer
6-Phosphogluconate dehydrogenase (*PGD*)	64, 100	Dimer
Phosphoglucomutase-1 (PGM-1)	92, 97, 100	Monomer
Phosphoglucomutase-2 (PGM-2)	87, 100, 104, 133	Monomer
Sorbitol dehydrogenase (*SORDH*)	−340, −100, 240, 330	Tetramer
Tetrazolium oxidase (*TO*) or Superoxide dismutase (SOD)	17, 100	Dimer
Transferrin (TF)	84, 92, 100	Monomer

[a]Monomorphic loci include *ES*-1, *ES*-2, *GPD*-1, *ICD*-2, *MDH*-2, glucose phosphate isomerase (GPI-1, GPI-2) and Plasma Protein B.
[b]Buffer numbers and buffer stain recipes for the various loci are given in Manlove et al. (1976) or are as follows: Buffers: *ADH* Continuous tris citrate (No. 4); *AK* Tris maleate (No. 5); *MPI* Lithium hydroxide (No. 2); *PEP*-1 and *MOD* Tris maleate (No. 5). Stains: *ACP* (Shaw and Prasad 1970); *AK* (Shaw and Prasad 1970); *ADH* (Selander et al. 1971); *MPI* (Nichols et al. 1973); and *PEP*-1 (Shaw and Prasad 1970).
[c]The allele designations correspond to the II (95) through VII (120) types of β chains of Huisman et al. (1968). The IV allele was observed by Harris et al. (1973), and has been arbitrarily designated numerically (105) as being intermediate to the products of the III and V alleles.

Table 18. Levels of genetic variability in representative populations of white-tailed deer collected in 1974 from Georgia and South Carolina.

Location[a]	Heterozygosity $\bar{H}$ (± SE)[b]	Alleles per locus A	Proportion of polymorphic loci P	Number of deer N
Georgia				
Allatoona	0.056 (0.004)	1.47	0.263	96
Clark Hill	0.085 (0.007)	1.37	0.263	46
Fort Gordon	0.056 (0.006)	1.32	0.263	38
South Carolina				
Broad River	0.073 (0.005)	1.58	0.422	53
Savannah River Plant				
Swamp	0.092 (0.004)	1.60	0.450	126
Uplands	0.088 (0.002)	1.65	0.500	316
Waterhorn	0.081 (0.008)	1.50	0.350	32
White Oak	0.065 (0.004)	1.70	0.350	46

[a]Values calculated from 20 loci as follows. For the Savannah River Plant populations: *ALB*; *ES*-2; *GPD*-2; *AAT*-1; α-*HB*; β-*HB*; *ICD*-1; *LDH*-1; *LDH*-2; *MOD*-1; *MDH*-1; *MDH*-2; *PGD*; *PGI*-1; GPI-1; GPI-2; *SORDH*; *TO*; *TRF*. For the other populations: *AP*; *ES*-2; *GDH*; *G*-6-*P*; *AAT*-1; *AAT*-2; *GPD*-2; β-*HB*; *ICD*-1; *ICD*-2; *LDH*-1; *LDH*-2; *MDH*-1; *MDH*-2; GPI-1; GPI-2; *PGM*-2; *SORDH*; *TO*; *TRF*.
[b]Standard error calculated directly from the distribution of individual heterozygosities.

This population resulted from the 1954–1979 expansion of a whitetail population that had persisted after deer were exterminated from most of South Carolina and Georgia (Jenkins and Provost 1964, Urbston 1968). The Fort Gordon population has a low $\overline{H}$ value of 0.056 and was stocked from Pisgah, North Carolina, in 1957, with only 12 deer. The loss of genetic variability by chance processes (genetic drift) should have occurred (Wright 1951). The Allatoona population ($\overline{H}$ = 0.056) was stocked between 1957 and 1959. If high genetic variability is a desirable characteristic, then restocking certain populations with animals from highly heterozygous populations might increase the levels of genetic variability.

White-tailed deer have the highest level of genetic variability of any large grazing mammal species (Smith et al. 1978). Baccus et al. (1983) reported that genetic variability among 10 species of even-toed ungulates did not appear to be correlated with body size within the large mammals. All of the wild mammal species with high heterozygosity have large ranges and occupy a variety of habitats (Nevo 1978). However, some species with low heterozygosities, such as black bear, also share these characteristics (Manlove et al. 1980). It is tempting to speculate that the success of white-tailed deer in North America may be due in part to its high genetic variability.

In general, the loci that contribute most to the genetic variability of the white-tailed deer are those with more than two alleles. Beta-hemoglobin, the most studied locus in deer (Kitchen et al. 1964, 1966, 1967, Huisman et al. 1968, Kitchen 1969, Taylor et al. 1972, Harris et al. 1973, Manlove et al. 1976, 1978, Smith et al. 1976, Taylor and Easley 1977, Ramsey et al. 1979), has six alleles (Table 17). Some of these alleles are associated with sickling of the red blood cells, a phenomenon that has a biochemical mechanism similar in man and white-tailed deer (Houston 1977). The alleles of this locus are ideal for studying changing allele frequencies through space and time (Smith et al. 1976, Manlove et al. 1976), because samples can be taken from live animals. Transferrin has three alleles (Miller et al. 1965, Manlove et al. 1976) (Table 17). Both hemoglobin and transferrin show moderate levels of variability for mammals in general (Selander 1976), so their degree of variation in deer is not surprising.

Loci with four alleles include esterase-2,

phosphoglucomutase-2 and sorbitol dehydrogenase (Table 18). Loci with three alleles include α-glycerophosphate dehydrogenase-2, asparate aminotransferase-1, lactate dehydrogenase-1, mannosephosphate isomerase, malate dehydrogenase and phosphoglucomutase-1. Mannosephosphate isomerase has not been widely studied in other mammals. Other loci with three or more alleles show intermediate to high levels of polymorphism (P = 21–56 percent) but low to high levels of heterozygosity ($\overline{H}$ = 0.01–0.15) across species (Selander 1976). The invariant loci in white-tailed deer are generally invariant in other mammal species as well. The pattern of genetic variability in white-tailed deer is essentially the same as in other mammals.

Albumin, 6-phosphogluconate dehydrogenase and sorbitol dehydrogenase do not fit the usual pattern. Albumin, although having two alleles, was variable in only two specimens from Michigan. Normally it would be expected to be highly variable (Selander 1976). Among the most variable loci in mammals is 6-phosphogluconate dehydrogenase (Selander 1976), but it was variable only in deer from Texas and Michigan, with a low frequency for the second allele. Sorbitol dehydrogenase shows a high percentage of heterozygotes in white-tailed deer (Manlove et al. 1976, Baccus et al. 1977), but rarely is variable in other species. The reason for these deviations from the normal pattern in mammals is not known, but some form of selection is implicated in the case of sorbitol dehydrogenase (Baccus et al. 1977). Selander and Kaufman (1973) predicted that large warm-blooded animals should have low levels of genetic variability. Nevertheless, the white-tailed deer is an exception and has high genetic variability.

Not only do individual deer vary genetically, but their populations also differ in allele frequency through space and time. The white-tailed deer differs morphologically over different parts of the species' range, and was subjected historically to different selective pressures. While these changes are well-known and accepted, allele frequencies were not expected to vary over short distances and time.

The white-tailed deer on the Savannah River Plant area in South Carolina illustrate how genetic differences can occur within a population. This area comprises 77,863 hectares (192,400 acres), but its linear dimensions are such that deer can travel easily across the Plant area in a day. Nevertheless, the whitetails showed significantly different gene frequencies among the several hunting units (Table 19) that were designated arbitrarily several years before the start of the research program and without prior knowledge of the genetics of the deer. Many of the units were similar in allele frequency for sorbitol dehydrogenase-100. However, differences between deer from swamp-unit 29 and those from upland-unit 18 were significant (P> 0.05). When data for the seven most variable loci were tested for spatial differences between allele frequencies, it was clear that a minimum of five genetic units or populations existed on the Savannah River Plant area. This is a minimal estimate, since analysis of the differences among allele frequencies may be confounded by the presence of a part or all of two or more populations in a single unit. The greatest difference in genetics was between deer in the swamp and those in upland units (Table 19).

There were no significant variations in allele frequency for sorbitol dehydrogenase among years, but for beta-hemoglobin, the relative frequency of heterozygotes varied significantly between 1974 and 1976 (Table 19). Other loci also show significant temporal fluctuations. These changes might appear small, but the maximum range of potential variation is 0 to 100 percent. The frequency of beta-hemoglobin for deer in upland-unit 46 changed from 81 to 61 percent, and the occurrence of the heterozygotes changed from 5 to 39 percent during the period 1974–1975. There was no tendency for the populations to deviate from the expected genotypic frequencies for random breeding units. Frequencies for secondary alleles can vary by a factor of 10 between populations located relatively close to one another.

When populations are compared over greater distances and longer time intervals, even larger genetic differences can be expected. For example, the allele frequencies for transferrin varied widely among 25 populations sampled across an eight-state area (Figure 41). The white-tailed deer should be viewed as a series of relatively small populations that vary significantly in allele frequency over relatively small distances (less than 10 kilometers:6.2 miles) and short time periods (less than three years).

Table 19. Percentage occurrence of heterozygotes and common alleles for sorbitol dehydrogenase (*SORDH*$^{-100}$ or SORDH^c) and beta hemoglobin ($\beta - HB$) analyzed in white-tailed deer from 11 hunting units on the Savannah River Plant area in South Carolina.

| | Sorbitol dehydrogenase[a] | | | | | | Beta hemoglobin[b] |
| | Common allele | | | Heterozygotes | | | Common allele |
Unit	1974	1975	1976	1974	1975	1976	1974
Uplands (N = 687)							
15	79	77	77	37	40	25	77
17	76	83	74	24	33	44	68
18	84	80	87	31	41	26	71
20	74	80	74	36	40	32	76
25	80	81	82	32	39	36	72
32	71	69	83	47	50	27	64
42	64	74	79	64	52	27	67
46	72	82	76	45	29	42	81
Mean	75.0	78.3	70.0	39.5	40.5	32.4	72.0
SE	6.12	4.71	4.66	12.39	7.69	7.50	5.71
Swamp (N = 350)							
29	62	69	68	53	34	47	47
44	78	71	75	35	43	43	71
48	77	64	78	46	57	28	66
Mean	72.3	68.0	73.7	44.7	44.7	39.3	61.3
SE	8.96	3.61	5.13	9.07	11.59	10.02	12.66

[a]Significant differences (P > 0.05) were observed between units for the distribution of the common allele, but not for occurrence of heterozygotes. There were no significant differences between years for either variable.
[b]Significant differences (P > 0.05) were observed between years for the occurrence of heterozygotes, but not for the distribution of the common allele. There were no significant differences between units for either variable. Manlove et al. (1976) reported significant differences in allele frequencies between the same units for deer collected in 1974.

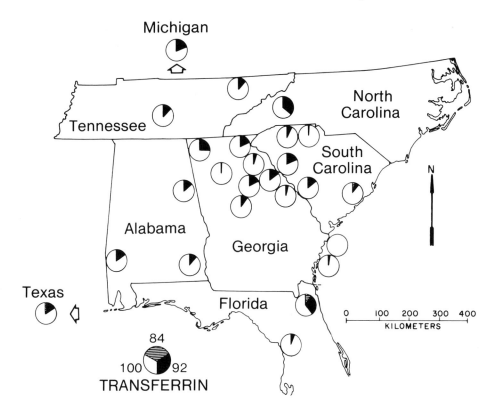

Figure 41. Allele frequencies of transferrin in populations of white-tailed deer in six southeastern states and Michigan and Texas. Frequencies of the three types of transferrin are proportional to the area of the circle occupied (sample size = 1,663; range = 11–442; $\bar{x}$ = 66).

Table 19. (continued)

Beta hemoglobin[b]				
Common allele		Heterozygotes		
1975	1976	1974	1975	1976
68	60	34	30	44
69	63	44	28	44
70	68	28	26	23
66	59	32	28	52
67	59	33	39	58
69	82	36	39	27
63	74	28	18	35
61	73	5	39	33
66.6	67.3	30.0	30.9	39.5
3.16	8.48	11.30	7.61	12.13
71	57	47	59	56
59	65	32	46	42
69	57	18	31	57
66.3	59.7	32.3	45.3	51.7
6.43	4.62	14.50	14.01	8.39

Thus, population differences within a management unit over a period of several years can be due either to genetic or environmental factors.

Genetic differences in time and space are not necessarily significantly related to the functioning of the animals. The genetic changes could be due to chance variations in population structure, and could be essentially neutral in their effect on the quality of the animals (Kimura and Ohta 1971). However, studies on white-tailed deer indicate that biochemical variations are associated with changes in the quality of deer.

Specific variations also may enhance the survival of individuals of certain populations, as reported in sheep by Evans and Whitlock (1964). Sheep from cold environments exhibited high gene frequencies for hemoglobin A, an allelic expression associated with high-oxygen transport and increased survival during low-temperature winter stress. In addition, lower metabolic efficiency associated with reduced oxygen-transport predisposed sheep with low frequencies of hemoglobin A to be more vulnerable to parasitism by *Haemonchus contortus,* an abomasal nematode. This parasite very commonly reaches high levels in southern whitetails, but physiological-genetic studies of its impact have not been undertaken.

On the Savannah River Plant area, does in the swamp with two fetuses had significantly ($p = 0.05$) higher mean heterozygosities ($\overline{H} = 0.107$) than did those with one fetus ($\overline{H} = 0.081$) (Johns et al. 1977). The upland population showed the same trend, but it was not statistically significant ($\overline{H} = 0.094$ versus 0.080). Cothran et al. (1983) analyzed 165 pregnant does and 285 fetuses. Fetal growth was increased significantly by higher fetal and maternal heterozygosity and maternal weight. Maternal weight was associated positively within each age class. Cothran et al. attributed differences in fetal growth-rate associated with heterozygosity to the degree to which the individuals were inbred, and suggested that inbreeding is a result of the subdivision and social structure of deer.

Gonadal development in male fawns on the Savannah River Plant area was correlated positively to increased heterozygosity (Urbston 1976). In another species, the oldfield mouse, both litter size and reproductive rates were correlated positively with heterozygosity (Smith et al. 1975).

Chesser et al. (1982) reported that of 2,455 whitetails studied on the Savannah River Plant, older deer (more than 3.5 years) had significantly higher levels of heterozygotes in beta-hemoglobin than did deer of younger age classes. They suggested that since age is an important determinant of social status in deer, competitive interactions may increase as population age-structure shifts, and that this may be the source of selection differences in heterozygosity. Regardless of whether or not heterozygosity actually causes the quality of animals to vary, it can function as a good index for use in management programs.

Differential selection at various life-history stages would be expected to produce differences in allele frequencies. For example, male fawns had significantly greater numbers of sorbitol-dehydrogenase heterozygotes than did female fawns in the swamp on the Savannah River Plant area (Manlove et al. 1976). Differences among cohorts and between parents and offspring also may occur.

Christiansen and Frydenberg (1973) have provided a model—for testing prenatal and zygotic selection—which is applicable to natural populations. Basically, the allele frequencies of fetuses, mothers, males, and nonbreeding females are compared statistically. Using this approach for sorbitol dehydrogenase, Baccus et al. (1977) found prenatal selection operating in five of seven areas studied in the southeastern United States. Heterozygous females tended to breed later in the season than did homozygous females; there was a deficiency of heterozygous offspring from heterozygous mothers; and there were no deviations from a pattern of random mating. On the Savannah River Plant area there was no overall directional change in allele or heterozygote frequencies across years (Table 19). The genetic differences may have arisen in response to changes in population structure, and they demonstrate the dynamic nature of a population's genetic makeup on a local level.

In summary, genetic characteristics are useful in delineating potential management units. They also cause, or are related to, changes in characteristics of individual deer. The breeding structure of a population can be evaluated using the genetic characteristics of its members. The response of individual whitetails to habitat fluctuations ultimately can be measured in terms of population genetics.

RESEARCH NEEDS

Future research on the genetics of white-tailed deer should attempt to document further the rate at which allele frequencies change through space and time, and to identify the relationship between genetic variability and productivity. It is critical to develop and define, in both a spatial and temporal sense, the genetic characteristics of a deer population. Management units should be based on natural populations if they differ in critical ways that modify the sustainable yield of the resource. Long-term studies are needed to evaluate the importance of genetics to both short- and long-term population fluctuations. Deer populations should be manipulated experimentally to test hypotheses about the cause-and-effect relationships of genetics to population characteristics. For example, different levels of hunting

True albino whitetails (top), with white coats and pink eyes, are exceedingly rare under natural conditions. Albinism is a recessive genetic trait that can increase in frequency by inbreeding within a population. Park or preserve managers frequently select albinos for breeding, thereby increasing the occurrance of such deer, principally for their novelty and corresponding public attraction. Partially white or "piebald" deer (bottom) occur more commonly than albinos, but still at a frequency of less than 1 percent in hunted populations. *Top photo by George Shiras III. Bottom photo by Paige Sawyer; courtesy of the Baruch Institute, Georgetown, South Carolina.*

could affect social structure to varying degrees, and profoundly affect the maintenance of genetic variability in a herd (Ryman et al. 1981).

Additional work on the biochemical genetics of deer would be useful in studying population processes and in increasing the confidence in estimates of genetic variability. Throughout the range of the white-tailed deer, attempts to correlate levels of biochemical variation with appropriate environmental measurements also could be instructive (Bryant 1974), especially in suggesting the physiological mechanism(s) by which these variations affect deer. Studies of enzyme kinetics can be conducted using standard biochemical procedures. The Mendelian inheritance of many of the loci already studied should be checked to verify the interpretation of banding patterns, especially for tetrazolium oxidase and the esterases. The overall goal should be to understand the ways in which environmental and genetic factors interact to produce populations with different characteristics and functional levels.

Chapter 6

BEHAVIOR

R. Larry Marchinton
Associate Professor
School of Forest Resources
University of Georgia
Athens, Georgia

David H. Hirth
Associate Professor
School of Natural Resources
University of Vermont
Burlington, Vermont

Few aspects of white-tailed deer biology are more intriguing than the animal's behavior. Its movements, spatial orientation, adaptations to predators and the activities of man, and its relationships to other whitetails and other animal species represent unique and sometimes complex strategies that permit the whitetail to persist and thrive in a wide variety of habitats.

HOME RANGE

Home range, as used here, is the area traversed on an annual basis by an individual in its normal activities of food gathering, mating and caring for young (Burt 1943). Not included are an animal's temporary excursions away from its normal range. White-tailed deer tend to use the same ranges year after year (McBeath 1941). Instances have been reported in which deer starved to death rather than leave depleted range, even though food was available and accessible in adjacent areas (Severinghaus and Cheatum 1956, Thomas et al. 1964). Deer are not always so inflexible however. Awareness of distant food sources may determine the extent to which they will move away from their normal ranges to meet their needs (Thomas et al. 1964, Byford 1970*a*, Kammermeyer and Marchinton 1976*a*).

There is an element of tradition inherent in deer dispersion (Staines 1974). In Florida, the home range of one doe resembled that of another doe who had died two years previously, even though there was no apparent environ-

mental gradient—such as temperature, moisture or plant community—to which the two ranges conformed (Marchinton and Jeter 1967). A similarity between the ranges of a doe and her fawn suggested to Byford (1970*b*, 1971) that home-range familiarity can be conveyed from generation to generation. R. L. Downing (personal communication:1979) noted more than two-dozen examples of offspring having ranges similar to those of their parents. In two instances, three generations used the same ranges.

Size and Shape

The white-tailed deer's home range must be large enough to provide all the essentials for life and reproduction, yet small enough to permit the animal to gain survival advantage through its familiarity with the area. The whitetail's home range probably is smaller than that of other North American deer species (Seton 1929); seasonally, its radius usually does not greatly exceed 1.6 kilometers (1.0 mile) (Severinghaus and Cheatum 1956). It is apparent, however, that ranges differ in size according to various environmental factors and individual characteristics.

Climate directly affects deer home-range size. In the more northern climates the whitetail home range tends to be larger and less stable than in the South (Severinghaus and Cheatum 1956). In Wisconsin (Dahlberg and Guettinger 1956) and Minnesota (Rongstad and Tester 1969), the deer's home range, including seasonal changes, may be quite long. In South Dakota total range length averaged nearly 19 kilometers (11.8 miles), with one adult buck moving 204 kilometers (126.8 miles) between the winter of 1964 and the autumn of 1965 (Sparrowe and Springer 1970). In milder climates of the southern United States, and on at least one study area in Wisconsin, radio-tracking has shown relatively small home ranges and little seasonal movement (Table 20). Deer rarely moved more than 3.2 kilometers (2.0 miles) from trapping sites during mark-recapture studies in Texas (Thomas et al. 1964, Michael 1965, McMahan 1966, Alexander 1968, Ellisor 1969).

White-tailed deer usually have an elongated home-range pattern, although circular and irregularly shaped ranges have been reported (Marchinton and Jeter 1967). Linearity in an animal's range maximizes available resources while minimizing movement and energy expenditure (*see* Stumpf and Mohr 1962). Uniform habitats with a good "mix" of food, water and cover apparently result in the least range elongation. Hood (1971) found that deer using a single vegetative type, or two very similar types, move out in all directions from a central point, whereas deer that utilize two or more divergent types are more likely to have linear home ranges. On Michigan's Upper Peninsula, seasonal white-tailed deer movements were significantly greater in areas where habitats were less diversified (Verme 1973).

Home ranges of deer living in relatively open habitats often are larger than those of deer in heavily vegetated areas. In Minnesota the average distance moved in coniferous forest was 8.2 kilometers (5.1 miles), with the greatest distance being 35.4 kilometers (22.0 miles)

A radio collar and ear tags allow researchers to locate and identify a whitetail and monitor its movements. A battery-powered collar, such as the one pictured, can be expected to have a one- to two-year life span. Its signal range varies with terrain and density of vegetation. In open country or from an aiplane, a transmitter's range may exceed 8 kilometers (5 miles), but in hilly areas or dense understory vegetation, the signal range may be reduced to less than 1.6 kilometers (1 mile). By fitting the transmitter with a mercury switch, which is sensitive to motion, it is possible to interpret whether the animal is resting, walking or running. Another commonly used feature in transmitters is a mortality detector, which alters the signal when the animal has been motionless for several hours. Although much more expensive than simple ear tags, a radio-telemetry system provides biologists with an ideal method of monitoring movements, home range and habitat utilization 24 hours a day, without having to resight or disturb the deer after its initial capture. *Photo by M. F. Baker.*

Table 20. Average home-range sizes reported for nonmigratory white-tailed deer.

Location	Number of deer	Home range Hectares	Home range Acres	Habitat type	Physiographic province	Source
Florida	4	270	667	Pine/oak uplands	East Gulf Coastal Plain	Bridges (1968)
Alabama	6	81	200	Bottomland hardwood	East Gulf Coastal Plain	Byford (1970b)
Arkansas		520	1,285	Pine/hardwood uplands	Ozark Highlands	Cartwright (1975)
Texas	13	71	176	Mesquite/chaparral	West Gulf Coastal Plain	Hood (1971)
Wisconsin	15	178	440	Tamarack swamp/ agricultural land	Central Lowland, Great Lakes section	Larson et al. (1978)
Louisiana	3	232	573	Longleaf pine/scrub oak	West Gulf Coastal Plain	Lewis (1968)
Florida and Alabama	9	85	210	Several study areas and habitat types included	Coastal Plain, Piedmont, Mountain	Marchinton (1968)
Georgia	4	59	146	Pine/hardwood	Piedmont Upland	Marshall and Whittington (1969)
Florida	5	342	845	Pine/oak uplands	East Gulf Coastal Plain	Smith (1970)
South Carolina	4	171	423	Pine/scrub hardwood	Upper Coastal Plain	Sweeney (1970)

(Carlsen and Farmes 1957). Distances in prairies averaged 15.6 kilometers (9.6 miles), with a maximum of 88.5 kilometers (55.0 miles). In Florida, whitetail home ranges in open portions of a bombing range were much longer than those in wooded areas (Marchinton and Jeter 1967).

Home-range size in mammals often decreases as population density increases (Sanderson 1966). Several researchers have associated small home ranges with high population densities (Marchinton and Jeter 1967, Marshall and Whittington 1969, Ellisor 1969), whereas Dorn (1971) noted that extensive movements of deer probably were due to a very low population density. Bridges (1968) and Smith (1970) both observed threefold increases in home-range size following a die-off in a Florida deer population. Even though there probably is an inverse relationship between home-range size and population density, there is little evidence to indicate whether it is a cause-and-effect relationship.

Adult bucks generally have larger home ranges than do does. The distances between winter yards and kill locations of 20 deer in Minnesota averaged about 3.2 kilometers (2.0 miles) for does and 8.0 kilometers (5.0 miles) for bucks (Olson 1938). The maximum recorded distance of 20.9 kilometers (13 miles) was traveled by a buck. In Minnesota coniferous forests, the distance between captures averaged 10.8 kilometers (6.7 miles) for bucks but only 6.0 kilometers (3.7 miles) for does (Carlsen and Farmes 1957). In the Edwards Plateau of Texas, the average distance from marking to recovery sites was greater for bucks than for does (Thomas et al. 1964). On the Welder Wildlife Refuge, areas used by does varied from 24.3 to 137.6 hectares (60–340 acres), whereas those used by bucks ranged from 97.1 to 356.1 hectares (240–880 acres) (Michael 1965). In Missouri, mean range size was 161.9 hectares (400 acres) for does, and more than 380.4 hectares (940 acres) for bucks (Progulske and Baskett 1958). In Florida, minimum home ranges averaged 622.8 hectares (1,539 acres) for two mature bucks, 245.2 hectares (606 acres) for two does, and 153.0 hectares (378 acres) for a buck fawn (Smith 1970).

Bucks may expand their range during the rut. Marked changes in movement patterns and behavior of bucks in Georgia occurred during the rut, and one buck enlarged his range from 92.3 to 244.0 hectares (228 to 603 acres) (Kam-mermeyer and Marchinton 1976*a*). Coues white-tailed bucks in Arizona left their home area in search of receptive does during the rut (Welch 1960). And in New York, does occupied the same range throughout the spring, summer and autumn, while bucks expanded or shifted their range during autumn (Mattfeld et al. 1977).

Young fawns have small ranges, but as they get older their ranges begin to approximate that of their dams. Yearlings and young adults may move over larger areas than do older adults, at least in localities where extreme seasonal range shifts are common. In Minnesota, 1.5- and 2.5-year-old whitetails moved much longer distances than did mature adults (Carlsen and Farmes 1957). The deer apparently ranged considerable distances during their early years, and gradually diminished their wanderings as they grew older. Inglis et al. (1979), in Texas, noted that home ranges of even sedentary deer gradually shift through time, and lifetime ranges can be substantially larger than are home ranges at any one particular time.

Whitetails often make temporary excursions away from their normal range. When taking these "trips," they usually move rapidly and deliberately. Such exploratory behavior may be a precursor to dispersal (Sweeney 1970, Downing and McGinnes 1976).

DISPERSAL

Dispersal refers to a movement away from the original home range and establishment of a more-or-less permanent new home range. Normally the vacated range includes the individual's birthplace and roughly corresponds to the range of its dam.

Evidence for dispersal among whitetails has been observed at several locations. At the Crab Orchard National Wildlife Refuge in Illinois, dispersal apparently contributed substantially to harvest outside the refuge (Crawford 1962). Later, Hawkins et al. (1971) suggested that the annual dispersal rate from the refuge was about 4 percent for fawns, 7 percent for adult does, 10 percent for adult bucks, 13 percent for yearling does and more than 80 percent for yearling bucks. Social pressures rather than a lack of food were thought to be the main reason for the high dispersal rate of yearling bucks.

At the Berry College Refuge in northern Georgia, 6 of 19 bucks dispersed an average of 4.4 kilometers (2.8 miles) from their previous range at the beginning of the rut (Kammermeyer and Marchinton 1976*b*). Sexual competition among bucks occupying the same habitat probably was the main stimulus for dispersal. Kammermeyer and Marchinton (1976*a*) also suggested that limited removal of deer from a refuge by capture or hunting would reduce dispersal without affecting the animal's long-term population density.

At Radford Arsenal in Virginia, more than 40 percent of the yearling and 2.5-year-old bucks temporarily moved out of their normal ranges during the rut (Downing and McGinnes 1976). These irregular movements were suggestive of dispersal tendencies, and 10 of 19 bucks definitely changed range. Yearlings also were observed outside their normal range during June and July and were obviously alone and on the move, likely due in part to their mothers' antagonism toward them (Downing et al. 1969). Woodson et al. (1980) demonstrated that the does' antagonism alone does not trigger dispersal, however.

Movement patterns of a dispersing yearling

The catalysts for whitetail dispersal from original home range and establishment of a more-or-less permanent new home range usually are social antagonism, sexual competition and intraspecific competition for food. *Photo courtesy of the Minnesota Department of Natural Resources.*

buck were radio-monitored in South Carolina (Sweeney 1970). Around midnight the buck began trotting in a relatively straight line, and by sunrise he was more than 11.3 kilometers (7 miles) from his original range. He remained for six days within an 80.9-hectare (200 acre) area at the new location. For the next 15 days he wandered back and forth along the travel route, entering his original range twice and the temporary range once, but remaining only one day in each. Eventually the buck established a new home range about halfway between his movement extremes.

When deer make annual movements between summer and winter ranges, permanent shifts in home range sometimes are difficult to detect. Sparrowe and Springer (1970) found a yearling whitetail doe in South Dakota that had moved 161 kilometers (100 miles), and they concluded that spring and summer movements by some young deer actually may be dispersal.

Dispersal can influence sex ratios. In unhunted populations where dispersal is apt to be high, females outnumber males because of the emigration tendencies of yearling bucks and the sedentary nature of does. Where barriers to dispersal exist, adult sex ratios are likely to be more even.

Social pressures appear to be the main stimuli for dispersal (Downing et al. 1969, Hawkins et al. 1971, Kammermeyer and Marchinton 1976*b*). When deer are approximately six months old they are driven off by mature bucks courting the does. And when the dam is nearing parturition she will drive off her previous fawns (Downing and McGinnes 1969, Hirth 1977*a*), apparently encouraging some of them to disperse. Bucks are most apt to emigrate when they are approximately 1.5 years old, because of antagonism shown by larger males and competition for breeding privileges. These same pressures may cause 2.5-year-old bucks to disperse. Old whitetails, unable to compete successfully with younger breeding bucks, may be driven away. However this is rare in heavily hunted areas because most white-tailed bucks are harvested before they reach old age.

Habitat characteristics also affect the rate and direction of dispersal. In Finland the spread of white-tailed deer was slowed by extensive forests, bog regions and water courses (Koivisto 1966). The effect that dispersal has on a population depends on the status of the population and on the rate of dispersal (Odum 1971). If a population is "well-stocked" and in balance with limiting factors, moderate immigration or emigration will have little permanent effect, as gains or losses by dispersal will be compensated for by changes in rates of natality and mortality. If a population is well above or below carrying capacity, dispersal may cause a serious imbalance in the population. At the Kerr Management Area in Texas, efforts to control the deer population were unsuccessful until a deer-proof fence was erected to stop ingress of deer from neighboring ranches (Cook 1974, *see* Chapter 25).

It is clear that at certain times during their life many white-tailed deer make dispersal movements that are of significance to the animals' existence. Other factors being equal it appears that emigration increases with population density, and that heaviest dispersal is by yearling bucks during or just prior to the rutting season. Young does may disperse but to a lesser extent than bucks, and this is likely to occur during the fawning period.

SEASONAL MOVEMENTS

Migratory Behavior

Migration between summer and winter ranges is most pronounced where there are marked seasonal differences in weather, such as in northern or mountainous areas (Siglin 1965). Even in Missouri, some deer have distinct summer ranges, which they leave during the winter (Progulske and Baskett 1958). Seasonal shifts in range of as many as 88.5 kilometers (55 miles) are well documented (Table 21). Longer migrations have been reported, particularly in northern Michigan and Wisconsin (Shiras 1935), but Verme (1973) contended that these reports of mass migration of entire populations likely were myth.

Autumn or early-winter migrations largely are responses to cold weather and a sharp drop in temperature (Verme and Ozoga 1971, Hoskinson and Mech 1976). The spring movement back to summer range appears to be a release from a restricted food supply, with the animals moving to newly available spring forage (Severinghaus and Cheatum 1956). Verme (1973) suggested that deer leave winter yards as soon as weather and snowpack conditions permit them to travel freely.

Migrational patterns may vary between sexes and according to weather conditions. In Minnesota, does and juveniles moved directly from winter to summer range while adult bucks tended to wander (Rongstad and Tester 1969). Longest movements are by deer younger than

Table 21. Seasonal migration distances reported for white-tailed deer.

Location	Distance[a]		Source
	Kilometers	Miles	
Northern Michigan	38.6	(Maximum) 24	Bartlett (1950)
	15.6	(Average) 9.7	
Minnesota (Prairie/deciduous biome)	88.5[b]	(Up to) 55	Carlsen and Farmes (1957)
Wisconsin	9.6	(Average) 6	Dahlberg and Guettinger (1956)
North Carolina	9.6	(Up to) 6	Downing et al. (1969)
Maine	9.6[c]	(Average) 6	Gill (1957b)
Northeast Minnesota	10.0–38.1	(Range) 6.2–23.7	Hoskinson and Mech (1976)
Northwest Georgia	7.6	(Up to) 4.7	Kammermeyer and Marchinton (1976a)
Adirondack Mountains, New York	6.2	(Up to) 10	Mattfeld et al. (1977)
Northern Minnesota	6.4–29.0	(Range) 4–18	Morse (1942)
Eastcentral Minnesota	30.6	(Up to) 19	Rongstad and Tester (1969)
Northwest Montana	15.5	(Up to) 25	Schmautz (1949)
Wyoming	16.1	(Less than) 10	Skinner (1929)
South Dakota	23.2	(Average) 14.4	Sparrowe and Springer (1970)
	54.7	(Up to) 34	
Upper Peninsula, Michigan	13.8	(Average) 8.6	Verme (1973)
	51.5	(Up to) 32	

[a]All authors except Hoskinson and Mech (1976) reported distances in miles.
[b]This extreme movement actually may have been dispersal.
[c]Distance estimated.

2.5 years (Carlsen and Farmes 1957). White-tails sometimes leave and return to their winter yard several times before the final move to summer range. If migration starts late, deer move quickly to summer range, and vice versa. In Minnesota, most deer reach their summering areas by early May (Hoskinson and Mech 1976).

Mattfeld et al. (1977) suggested that an individual or a group of deer will occupy almost the same summer range each year, but that winter-range locations are less consistent, possibly because of variations in snow depths and travel conditions.

Minor Seasonal Shifts

Seasonal shifts in centers of activity, which do not involve significant changes in range boundaries, usually are related to food availability. In Alabama, for example, deer temporarily shifted the centers of their activity in response to seasonal food availability, but would not leave well-defined ranges to any great extent to reach a food supply (Byford 1970a).

A different situation was described in South Dakota (Sparrowe and Springer 1970). Deer did not have fixed summer and winter ranges, nor an identifiable year-round range. They used a variable number of subareas—so long as these habitat units furnished basic food and cover requirements. Likewise, some whitetails in Wisconsin did not have a fixed summer or winter range but developed an affinity for a small area and remained in it until habitat conditions deteriorated or other disturbances affected their survival chances (Dahlberg and Guettinger 1956).

Although usually not considered as migration, seasonal movements of deer in the southern United States may be of considerable importance. In the North Carolina mountains, deer moved to green vegetation at lower elevations in early spring (Downing et al. 1969). The Coues white-tailed deer in the Chiricahua Mountains of Arizona also moved seasonally in response to availability of food, water and cover, and also disturbance by hunters (Welch 1960). In the Florida Everglades, deer sometimes follow the receding water southward in unusually dry years and move to the north before rising water in wet periods. Movements in response to flooding are common in extensive southern river swamps (Byford 1970b,

Hood 1971). In northwestern Georgia, deer moved onto a refuge in autumn and returned to their summer ranges in late winter (Kammermeyer and Marchinton 1976b). Habitat conditions, population history and hunting pressure all played roles in this traditional range shift.

YARDING BEHAVIOR

In the northern parts of their range, white-tailed deer frequently congregate during winter in sheltered areas referred to as "deer yards" (Telfer 1967a, Rongstad and Tester 1969, Dahlberg and Guettinger 1956). In the southern Appalachians, although deer do not really yard, there is a tendency for them to concentrate in coves and on hillsides containing mountain-laurel and rhododendron cover (Schilling 1938).

Heavy use of deer yards is associated primarily with cold temperatures rather than snow depth, although the two factors often are related (Ozoga and Gysel 1972). In most years deer enter yards in January and leave in March. However, the timing of their arrival and departure depends on the severity of the winter. In northern Michigan deer may be confined to yards for 12 weeks during mild winters and for 20 weeks during severe winters (Verme and Ozoga 1971).

The function of yarding behavior is to conserve energy—minimize radiant and convective heat loss. However there is reason to believe that yarding evolved as a means of reducing wolf predation during the winter period of increased vulnerability, and that it still functions in this way in places, such as northeastern Minnesota, where there is a viable wolf population (Nelson and Mech 1981). From an energy standpoint yarding is not necessary simply to survive cold temperatures. In Minnesota deer withstand extremely low temperatures while feeding on corn and bedding in open fields with no shelter (Moen 1968b). The high-energy diet of corn apparently provides these deer with enough energy to compensate for metabolic heat loss. Under penned conditions, well-fed fawns in northern Michigan suffered no ill effects from exposure, but the condition of poorly-fed fawns deteriorated rapidly when they were exposed to winter weather (Verme 1965b). In extremely cold weather however, shelter is so important that deer seek it even though food there may be sparse (Verme 1965b).

Wind, deep snow and cold temperatures in many northern areas force white-tailed deer to seek the protection of dense evergreens in swamps, bottomlands, or even on south-facing hillsides. Because food usually is scarce in these "yarding areas," deer frequently starve to death during long or severe winters. *Left photo by Tom Carbone; courtesy of the Maine Department of Inland Fisheries and Wildlife. Right photo by Eugene Sanborn; courtesy of the Wisconsin Department of Natural Resources.*

Northern white cedar is a preferred species in deer yards because it provides excellent protection and high quality food (Gill 1957b, Verme 1965b). In northern Michigan, even-aged stands of mature northern white cedar provided the narrowest thermal range, the highest and most stable relative humidity, the least wind flow, and the firmest snow among six habitats monitored in conifer and hardwood swamps (Ozoga 1968). Other tree species that provide good winter shelter are spruce, hemlock and balsam fir.

In addition to yarding, deer adapt to the rigors of severe midwinter weather by decreasing their mobility and lessening their metabolic rate (Hoffman and Robinson 1966, Silver et al. 1969, Ozoga and Verme 1970). Thus they need and eat less food during midwinter than during other seasons. Deer are less well adapted to withstand early and late winter storms because their metabolic rate is higher at these times—and just before spring their stored energy reserves are apt to be exhausted.

DAILY ACTIVITIES

Daily Movement

Knowledge of daily movement is useful in dispersing food plots on forest regeneration areas, developing census techniques and determining the optimum size of harvest units. One approach to measuring daily movement is to radio-locate telemetry-marked individual deer every 2 hours through complete 24-hour periods, and to calculate the greatest distance between extreme radio locations (DBE) and the sum of distances between sequential locations (MTD) (Marchinton and Jeter 1967, Marchinton 1969). Usually the average extreme locations are less than 1.6 kilometers (1.0 mile) apart (Table 22). However, distances moved by individuals vary greatly according to sex, age, season, habitat, weather and the animal's physical condition. In Minnesota, deer moved 341 to 1,650 meters (0.21–1.02 miles)

Table 22. Average distances traveled by radio-tracked white-tailed deer during 24-hour periods.

Location	Number of deer	Mean DBE[a]		Mean MTD[b]		Source
		Kilometers	Miles	Kilometers	Miles	
Florida	3	1.74	1.08	4.70	2.92	Bridges (1968)
Alabama	6	1.06	0.66	3.11	1.93	Byford (1970a)
Georgia	7	1.06	0.66	2.93	1.82	Kammermeyer (1975)
Florida and Alabama	9	1.09	0.68	2.43	1.51	Marchinton (1968)
Florida	5	1.42	0.88	3.94	2.45	Smith (1970)
South Carolina	2	1.13	0.70	3.38	2.10	Sweeney (1970)
Iowa	9			1.45	0.90	Zagata and Haugen (1973b)

[a]Greatest distance between extreme radio locations.
[b]Sum of distances between sequential locations.

per day during winter and 793 to 3,058 meters (0.49–1.9 miles) per day in the spring (Heezen and Tester 1967). Reduced movement in winter is common (Dahlberg and Guettinger 1956, Hoskinson and Mech 1976), and daily movements covering less than 0.4 hectare (1 acre) have been reported in winter yards (Norberg 1957). Movement decreases as weather severity increases because of the physical difficulty of moving in deep snow and the need to conserve energy (Gill 1957b). Snow depths of about 70 percent of chest heights seriously impede deer movement, but because of their less "weight-load-on-track," females have a movement advantage over males in the snow (Kelsall 1969).

Reduced daily movement is characteristic of malnourished or otherwise weakened deer. Marchinton (1968) reported very limited movement for deer that had suffered trauma or were in poor physical condition. Deer in poor physical condition may extend their movements, however, if this will result in their reaching a substantially better source of food.

The daily movement of malnourished whitetails tends to be reduced, probably because of the animals' weakness and also to minimize energy loss. The deer may extend their movements if conditions permit access to a better food supply. *Left photo courtesy of the Texas Parks and Wildlife Department. Right photo courtesy of the Maine Department of Inland Fisheries and Wildlife.*

Pledger (1975) reported that daily movements of whitetails are greatest in the breeding season and least during late gestation. Another study (Ivey and Causey in press), however, found that does increased activity but actually decreased movement during the rut. Bucks increase their movements at the onset of the rut, and their average daily movements in both summer and autumn are likely to be greater than those of does (Kammermeyer and Marchinton 1977). In Texas, some does moved more during winter, while others traveled farther during summer and autumn (Michael 1965). Does did not alter their movement patterns during the fawning season, although they tended to drop fawns at the periphery of their normal range. The summer season often is thought to be a quiet, lazy time for whitetails (Severinghaus and Cheatum 1956), but increased daily movements during summer have been noted for certain sex, age and social classes (Downing et al. 1969). These "wandering" movements probably are related to dispersals.

Deer tend to use one portion of their range during the night and another during the day. In Pennsylvania, deer moved from the woods into open fields one or more hours before sunset in winter and during the hour of sunset in summer (Montgomery 1963). They moved back to the woods just before dawn. Elsewhere, movement patterns similar to these are common. Daily movement undoubtedly is dependent on the interspersion of cover, food and water, and human activity.

Bedding

Bedding patterns by white-tailed deer vary from place to place as well as among individuals. Deer beds were distributed widely over home ranges in New York (Townsend and Smith 1933) and in Louisiana (Lewis 1968). In Florida and Alabama, deer usually bedded in a "core area" at one end of their range during the day, whereas night beds were near a feeding area at the other end of the range (Marchinton and Jeter 1967). Deer in hilly terrain often bed at higher elevations during the day and move into lower areas for feeding and bedding at night (Montgomery 1963, Marchinton and Jeter 1967). At Eglin Air Force Base in Florida, deer normally bedded in woods during the day and in open areas at night. Occasionally they remained bedded in the open until midmorning (Jeter and Marchinton 1967, Bridges 1968, Smith 1970). In Texas deer did not rest in open sites during daylight hours (McMahan 1966). In Iowa they bedded in ungrazed timber with a dense understory in preference to overgrazed, open timber stands (Zagata and Haugen 1973*a*).

During severe winter weather, whitetails usually bed in sites that offer the best shelter (Cook and Hamilton 1942, Severinghaus and Cheatum 1956). However, cover is less important when deer have an abundant supply of high-energy food (Moen 1968*b*). When temperatures are moderate, beds may be in the open with little or no shelter. Deer try to avoid areas where temperatures are high and insects annoying.

Some deer in winter yards repeatedly use the same beds (Severinghaus and Cheatum 1956), but apparently there are individual differences in this tendency. Marchinton (1968) observed a doe bedding 17 times, but never in exactly the same place during the summer. On the other hand a yearling buck, who was observed bedded more than 50 times, repeatedly returned to previously used beds. On some occasions he walked several hundred yards from his feeding area to lie down in a preferred spot.

Whitetails generally remain bedded for less than two hours at a time, and most of that time is spent ruminating or grooming. Occasionally a deer will rest its head flat on the ground or curl up by tucking its nose into its flanks with its eyes closed, but these apparent interludes of sleep seldom last more than a few minutes and even then the animal is easily aroused. *Photo courtesy of the South Carolina Wildlife and Marine Resources Department.*

Feeding Patterns

Deer spend more time feeding than in carrying on any other activity (Michael 1970). When traveling to and from feeding areas whitetails often move in single file at a fairly steady walk along well-established trails, occasionally stopping to take a few bites of food. Once in the feeding area they usually separate and move about, rarely stopping long enough to consume a food source completely.

The lead deer or the lead group usually determines the direction of travel (Michael 1970). It may be a yearling or an adult, a male or a female. An adult doe customarily assumes leadership in small groups of three to five. Individual deer do not maintain any particular place within the group. Leadership is most evident when one or two adult does are grouped with yearlings and fawns. When groups of bucks feed and bed together, it is difficult to identify a leader.

Use of Water

White-tailed deer are strong swimmers and will readily cross sizable streams within their home range. Bodies of water often are used to escape predators or to throw hounds off the deer's trail (Sweeney et al. 1971). In areas where biting flies and mosquitos are abundant, deer sometimes partially submerge themselves during a portion of the day in order to escape the painful bites.

Deer are particularly cautious and alert when drinking, and may spend several minutes waiting and listening before taking a drink (Severinghaus and Cheatum 1956). Michael (1968a) observed that single does and does with fawns were more cautious than bucks or groups of does prior to entering tank areas. Deer have been observed, however, drinking and playing in water without showing unusual wariness. Their actions when drinking apparently are more a function of experience with predators—and

Several whitetail family groups traveling together in single file. The lead doe shows the greatest alertness. When the feeding area is reached, the deer will spread out. Large groups such as this may consist of an older doe and two or more generations of her offspring. *Photo by Harold F. Mielenz; courtesy of the U.S. Forest Service.*

Whitetails are good swimmers and have been observed crossing rivers, lakes and even swimming several miles to offshore islands on the coast. They often take to water to escape predators and noxious insects. *Photo by Len Rue, Jr.*

of where the water source is located—than a special behavior pattern.

Water consumption by adult deer depends on temperature, the animal's physical condition and the kind of food available. On air-dry feed in spring and autumn, a 45.4-kilogram (100-pound) deer drank approximately 1.42 liters (1.5 quarts) of water per day, but 0.71 liter (0.75 quart) or less when succulent browse was available (Nichol 1936).

Although Leopold (1933) concluded that the white-tailed deer requires drinking water, more recent research indicates that they use surface water when it is readily available but often can survive without it for extended periods where rainfall, humidity and plant succulence are relatively high (Marchinton 1968). In Arizona, when water becomes scarce in June, whitetails (especially pregnant does) move closer to permanent water, but disperse when summer rains start. Most deer drink during the twilight hours, but pregnant does will drink throughout the day (Welch 1960). In south Texas, Michael

(1968a) found that deer drank any water available, but drank more often in hot seasons than in cold weather. Peaks of drinking activity during summer were at 7 a.m., 11 a.m., 4 p.m. and 6 p.m. Pregnant does drank frequently, although some deer obtained water primarily from vegetation. Immediately after rain, deer drank at ditches or temporary pools in preference to waterholes.

Most white-tailed deer in the eastern United States have surface water within their home ranges, but where this is not the case they often are able to survive on water in vegetation, temporary rain puddles, and dew (Tyson 1952, Strode 1954, Downing and McGinnes 1976). Even in a dry Florida sandhill habitat, a doe did not use waterholes during 15 days of radio-tracking, and other deer did not depart significantly from their normal ranges to obtain water (Marchinton 1968). White-tailed deer in New York were able to meet their water requirements during winter by eating snow (Maynard et al. 1935).

Whitetails drink water if it is available, particularly during summer. But under some conditions they can survive without open water, apparently by obtaining sufficient moisture from other sources, such as succulent plant tissues and dew. Whitetails are particularly alert when drinking, and pause frequently in the process. *Left photo by Leonard Lee Rue III. Right photo by Leland J. Prater; courtesy of the U.S. Forest Service.*

CIRCADIAN RHYTHMS

White-tailed deer tend to be most active around dawn and dusk (Figure 42), but they are capable of much cycle flexibility. The times of peak activity for individual animals differ, sometimes in response to environmental variables or human activities, at other times inexplicably.

Relationships between weather phenomena and deer activity are highly variable. Hawkins and Klimstra (1970*b*) reported that trapping success was better on cool, dry days when barometric pressure was high (cf. Barick 1952). Others have observed a negative correlation between deer activity and barometric pressure (Semeyn 1963, Cartwright 1975). Thomas (1966) concluded that a change in barometric pressure resulted in reduced activity, and that greatest activity occurred at moderate pressures.

Deer are likely to be most active at low relative humidities (Tibbs 1967, Hawkins and Klimstra 1970*b*, Cartwright 1975). The effect of rainfall on whitetail activity is not as conclusive. In northern areas, rain appeared to depress deer activity (Tibbs 1967, Hawkins and Klimstra 1970*b*). In Texas, light rains increased the summer activity of deer and heavy rains depressed it (Thomas 1966, Michael 1970).

Cloud cover was correlated negatively with deer movements in some cases (Barick 1952, Kammermeyer and Marchinton 1977), but was determined to be unrelated in others (Carbaugh et al. 1975). Marchinton (1964) observed greater activity during the summer on overcast days in Florida than on clear days.

At low velocities, wind has little effect on whitetails, but at higher velocities it reduces the animals' movement and causes them to seek shelter (Thomas 1966, Howard 1969, Michael 1970). Zagata and Haugen (1974) found that deer movement into Iowa cropfields (largely standing corn) at dusk increased as wind velocity increased, and that wind direction affected movement in the morning but not in the evening. Semeyn (1963) concluded that the effect of wind velocity on deer activity is related to temperature.

Studies done under moderate or warm

weather conditions show that deer activity increases when temperatures drop (Hawkins and Klimstra 1970*b*, Cartwright 1975, Kammermeyer and Marchinton 1977). Behrend (1966), however, observed that activity tends to increase with rising temperatures during cold, New York winters. Considering all seasons together, Carbaugh et al. (1975) found no discernible relationship between temperature and the number of deer seen along an interstate highway in Pennsylvania.

The combined interaction of temperature, precipitation, relative humidity, cloud cover and wind probably affects deer activity more than does any single meteorological factor (Progulske and Duerre 1964). The interaction is complex and often confusing, however. It is evident that deer adjust their activity rhythms to maintain physical comfort and, at least in cold weather, to minimize energy consumption and loss. In very warm temperature regimes, deer are likely to be most active during the cooler portions of a 24-hour period. But in both the northern (Ozoga and Gysel 1972) and southern (Michael 1970) United States, deer activity was greatest during the warmer daylight hours of winter. In northern Michigan,

Semeyn (1963) also noted that at extremely low temperatures (about −29 degrees Celsius: −20 degrees Fahrenheit), deer became active to keep warm. As the temperature moderated, activity diminished and normal bedding and loitering took place, but with a further increase in temperature deer activity increased again. Under severe winter conditions whitetail activity increases heat production if high quality foods are available. In situations where nutritional levels are low, the best energy-conservation strategy may be for deer to remain inactive in sheltered areas. This has been reported for some deer yards in northern latitudes.

Michael (1970) reported that the activity of white-tailed deer in south Texas decreased when summer temperatures were above-average. When daylight was longest, the deer fed earlier in the morning and later in the evening. During long summer days the periods of daylight activity came around 6 a.m., noon and 6 p.m. The noon feeding activity may have occurred because of the increased length of time between the major morning and evening feeding periods.

Deer generally are inactive during violent weather such as high wind, heavy rain and

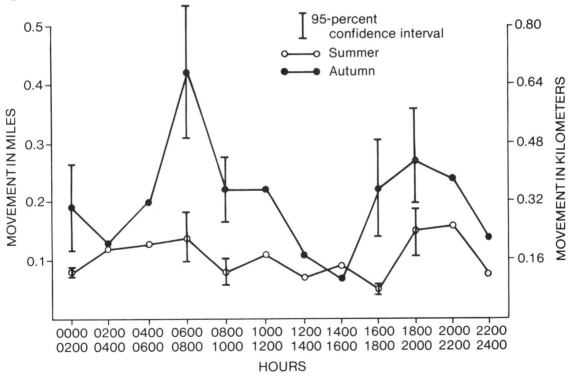

Figure 42. Peaks in whitetail activity occur about dawn and dusk during summer and autumn, but are most noticeable in autumn (from Kammermeyer and Marchinton 1977).

snowstorms. In the case of snowstorms, white-tails may remain inactive for one to three days following a storm (Severinghaus and Cheatum 1956).

Whitetails often increase their feeding activities prior to bad weather (Ruff 1938, Barick 1952, Semeyn 1963, Marchinton 1964, Behrend 1966). In the mountains of North Carolina, Barick (1952) was able to increase trapping success greatly by setting deer traps when the barometer was falling, with a forecast of rain or snow within 24 hours. On one area he caught 68 deer in four nights by trapping ahead of storm fronts, compared with only 65 deer captured in a 10-week period the previous year.

There is still some question as to how deer respond to lunar cycles. Several researchers found no consistent relationship between deer activity and moon phases (Harlow and Oliver 1967, Michael 1970, Zagata and Haugen 1974, Carbaugh et al. 1975). Thomas (1966) concluded that the greatest nocturnal activity occurred during nights with moderate light intensity, somewhere between very bright and very dark nights. However, Barick (1952) indicated that deer activity was greatest on bright moonlit nights. Likewise, Kammermeyer (1975) observed more deer feeding in fields on bright moonlit nights, and his radio-tracking data indicated greater deer movement during both daylight and dark hours when the moon was in the light phase.

Because of their behavioral flexibility deer apparently can adjust their periods of activity to provide asynchrony with the activities of man (Montgomery 1963, Marchinton 1964, Kammermeyer 1975), with predators (Jackson et al. 1972), and with other disturbing influences such as insects. Habitat characteristics are a factor in these adjustments since good cover allows activity to be undetected.

In summarizing activity rhythms, several generalizations can be made. White-tailed deer tend to be most active at dawn and dusk, yet are quite capable of varying the times when they are active to include or exclude any portion of the day or night. Some contradiction exists in the literature concerning the effect of environmental variables on activity, but these differences often can be explained or even predicted in terms of their survival value. In other words, deer apparently adjust their active periods to some extent to avoid dangerous or annoying situations, maintain physical comfort, and optimize energy conservation.

SOCIAL GROUPINGS

In most areas, the whitetail is an animal of the forest and its edge, where the deer occur in small social groups. However, in some western parts of their range and some agricultural areas, whitetails occupy open habitats, where they frequently occur in larger social units. In general, they form two basic types of social groups: (1) doe (or family) groups, which include adult does and their fawns; and (2) buck groups, which include adult bucks and perhaps yearlings. Usually there is little or no contact between adult does and adult bucks except during the autumn breeding season. Where large social groups occur, family groups and buck groups may feed together.

Doe (or Family) Groups

In woodland areas does tend to be intolerant of other adult does. Thus, doe groups usually represent a single family. In the month prior to the birth of her fawns an adult doe will forcibly and repeatedly drive away her fawns of the previous year. At this point, fawns can be considered yearlings.

New family groups form as the current year's fawns become old enough to travel with their mothers. During summer, the family group consists of a single doe and her fawn(s). By autumn, does become less protective of their young and will once again tolerate their offspring of the previous year. While female yearlings often rejoin the family group at this time (Hawkins and Klimstra 1970a), it is unusual for male yearlings to do so (Hirth 1977a). During autumn and winter, therefore, family groups commonly include an adult doe, a yearling doe, and the adult's fawns of the year.

Buck Groups

Whitetail bucks are more social than does. In woodland habitat, groups of two or three adult bucks often travel together in all months, except during the rut. In more open habitat, groups of three to five bucks frequently occur. These buck groups are not permanent associations; membership is constantly shifting (Hirth 1973). Very little overt interaction takes place between members of buck groups, although smaller bucks sometimes can be seen

This whitetail fawn is old enough to travel with its mother, thus forming a new family group. The transition from remaining hidden most of the day to staying with their mothers full time occurs gradually between about four and eight weeks of age. After fawns are traveling with their mothers, a doe's female offspring from previous years may join the group. *Photo courtesy of the Texas Parks and Wildlife Department.*

During much of the year, whitetail bucks prefer the company of other males and, except in the rut, tend to occupy areas different than those used by does. This "bachelor group" will split up shortly before the autumn rut, to begin courting does. *Photo courtesy of the Arkansas Game and Fish Commission.*

stepping out of the way of larger dominant bucks. Two bucks may pause briefly to groom each other.

In late spring and early summer, when male and female yearlings are driven out of family groups, they often try to associate with buck groups. These yearlings may be tolerated by members of a buck group, but often they are driven away for no apparent reason. Even when tolerated, the yearlings stay close together and remain apart from older members of the group. Perhaps because of their partial exclusion from buck groups during the summer, male and female yearlings frequently are seen associating in exclusive yearling groups. By early autumn, yearling does are no longer seen in buck groups, and aggression toward yearling bucks by members of buck groups diminishes.

Mixed Groups

Mixed groups of adult does and adult bucks occur occasionally, but social contact between sexes usually occurs only during the autumn breeding season. During feeding periods in open habitats, whitetails commonly form large groups, including does and bucks. These temporary groups normally break up at the end of morning and evening feeding periods, and the subgroups return to cover for bedding. Large social groups probably are a protective adaptation against predators (Hamilton 1971, Estes 1974, Hirth 1977a).

Mixed groups represent a distinctive social experience for deer in open habitat. Fawns join these large feeding groups with their mothers as soon as they are strong enough to travel. Social bonds between these fawns and their mothers are not as strong as among fawns and does in woodland populations. Does with newborn fawns may feed in larger doe groups or mixed groups, but they will leave at intervals to visit their young. Yearlings remain with the mixed groups when their mothers leave to tend new fawns.

Aggregations

An aggregation is a gathering of deer forced together by restricted distribution of resources. A familiar example is the deer yard, where large groups assemble in a favorable site for protection against the weather, not because of social affinity. Aggregations often are seen during the winter. As snow melts in spring, large groups may form where the ground is clear and new green growth appears, often on south-facing hillsides or slopes.

SOCIAL HIERARCHY

The actions of an individual deer are linked closely to its position in a social hierarchy. Most encounters within groups are aggressive interactions in which a high-ranking animal dominates a subordinate member. Occasionally a subordinate is driven from the group entirely. More often it simply is forced to move away from the aggressor. Subordinate members learn to avoid dominant members, and thus aggressive interactions are minimized and both groups save energy and avoid risk of in-jury. Mutual grooming is the only type of frequently seen interaction that is not aggressive. It occurs in family and buck groups. Subordinates may be the primary initiators of grooming (Hirth 1977a), but otherwise its significance in terms of social rank is not known.

Whitetail aggregations occur when deer are forced together by limited distribution of available resources, usually food. *Photo courtesy of the North Dakota Game and Fish Department.*

Grooming is a common behavioral interaction within social groups, especially does and their offspring. One study found that members of a family group spent 1.3 percent of their time grooming each other (Sawyer 1981). Bouts of social grooming last from a few seconds to several minutes. Most social grooming as well as self-grooming occurs just prior to bedding, after rising from a bed, and while loafing. In family groups, grooming usually is directed toward the neck, head, ears or thighs. *Left photo by Bill Cross; courtesy of the Maine Department of Inland Fisheries and Wildlife. Right photo by Tom W. Hall.*

In addition to physical avoidance, subordinates also shun direct eye contact with dominants (Thomas et al. 1965). When deer are bedded, group members face in the same direction or away from each other, but they never face toward each other.

When bedding, whitetails in groups tend to position themselves so that direct eye contact is avoided. This has social implications in that direct eye contact is an aggressive behavior, but it also has advantages in terms of detection of any approaching danger. *Photo by Kenneth J. Forand; courtesy of the University of Georgia School of Forest Resources.*

A smaller whitetail (right) averts his eyes from a large buck in a gesture of subordination. Such eye aversion is particularly evident in feeding and bedding situations. *Photo by Ken Gray; courtesy of the Maine Department of Game and Inland Fisheries.*

Aggressive intentions are expressed by stereotypical postures, which signal the intent of the dominant deer. The lowest level of aggression is a direct stare coupled with dropping the ears back along the neck (Thomas et al. 1965). Many encounters begin and end with this signal. The next (more-aggressive) postures have been termed "head-high" and "head-low" threats (Hirth 1977*a*), and seem to be of equal value in foretelling subsequent displays of aggression. A head-low threat indicates a readiness to chase, while the head-high posture signals a readiness to rear at the subordinate.

Chasing normally is accompanied by striking (kicking or "slapping" with a foreleg) at the opponent's flank. This maneuver frequently is used by does to drive reluctant yearlings away at parturition time. Rearing involves flailing at the opponent with both forelegs (Thomas et al. 1965, Michael 1968*b*) and is not seen as often as chasing.

When deer of equal rank fail to back off in the face of each other's threat postures, they both may rear and flail at each other for as long as five seconds. Aggressive behavior of does is identical to that of bucks during most of the year. Bucks, however, use hardened, polished antlers in threat postures during the rut, which will be discussed later in this chapter.

Social rank in whitetails is based primarily on size and age (Townsend 1973). Larger bucks almost invariably dominate smaller bucks. Incidences of large but faint-hearted bucks are rare (Hirth 1973). Size differences among adult

Even whitetail fawns may use the "foreleg kick." This six-month-old male also is exhibiting the "head-high" aggressive posture. The foreleg kick is an aggressive behavioral pattern that serves to force a subordinate deer away from a choice feeding or bedding location or just away from the dominant "kicker." *Photo by Leonard Lee Rue III.*

A large doe has risen on her hind legs, signaling intention to "flail" if the subject of her aggression (partially hidden by the doe in the foreground) does not move. This is a more aggressive form of behavior than the foreleg kick, and typically is the most intense form of agonistic encounter seen between does. Flailing is performed by dominant does toward subordinate, usually younger does. The conflict pictured here appears to have been mainly over food. *Photo by Lynn L. Rogers.*

does are less than those among bucks. Thus, for does, age is a better predictor of rank than is weight (Townsend 1973). Adult bucks dominate does, although there may be little contact between them. Yearling bucks usually (but not always) dominate yearling does. Adult does dominate yearling does. When the rut begins, yearling bucks become more aggressive and are no longer dominated by does (Townsend 1973).

Dominance and leadership are entirely different things. The presence of a stable dominance hierarchy does not imply that the dominant member of a group also is the leader. In a single family group, the adult doe clearly is the leader. However, leadership is not apparent in buck groups, multifamily groups or mixed groups. A doe and her fawns may wander away from a multifamily group or a mixed group with no other members appearing to notice.

RUTTING BEHAVIOR

The rut consists of several phases extending over three or four months, starting with sparring activity among bucks and ending after breeding (Figure 43). In much of North America, rutting begins in September and terminates by January. Photoperiodism probably is the factor most responsible for triggering rutting behavior. In northern areas, local variations in the breeding season seem to be minimal, but in many southern areas significant variations occur within a single state. In Florida (Loveless 1959), Mississippi (Noble 1974), and south

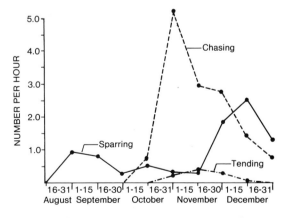

Figure 43. Sequence of sparring, chasing and tending acts by white-tailed deer at the Welder Wildlife Refuge in southern Texas (Hirth 1977a).

Texas (White 1973*b*), onset of the rut and occurrence of actual breeding vary by as much as two months at distances of only about 161 kilometers (100 miles). Where seasonal conditions show little variation, such as southern Florida and Venezuela, breeding may occur in all months of the year (Loveless and Ligas 1959, Brokx 1972*c*).

The degree of synchrony in estrus periods probably is greater in northern whitetail populations because of a shorter growing season. Most fawns are born over a two-week period in southern Michigan (Hirth 1973), a three-week period in western Virginia (McGinnes and Downing 1977), a four-week period in central and southern Texas (Teer et al. 1965, White 1973*b*) and apparently a period of at least six months in Suriname, South America (Branan and Marchinton in press). In North America, the start of the rutting season is signaled by bucks' loss of antler velvet, which is coincident with an increase in serum androgen levels (Mirarchi et al. 1977*b*). Loss of antler velvet occurs first in older animals and gradually thereafter in younger ones (Hirth 1977*b*).

Sparring

Sparring appears among bucks as soon as velvet is removed from antlers. At this time, bucks are in buck groups (Teer et al. 1965) and show no interest in does. Sparring matches represent low-level aggressive encounters and are distinct from antler fights that may occur later when competition for breeding takes place. The function of sparring seems to be the establishment of a well-defined rank-order or hierarchy among males prior to the breeding period (Townsend 1973). A sparring match often begins when one buck lowers his antlers toward another buck feeding nearby. The second buck usually accepts the challenge and engages his antlers with those of the initiator. In what can best be described as a pushing contest, the smaller of the two animals often is shoved backwards and withdraws, clearly the loser. These pushing contests enable each buck to assess his own strength against that of the other males (Hirth 1977*a*). Frequently both bucks will stop sparring simultaneously and resume feeding side-by-side, with no obvious winner or loser having emerged. Small bucks often challenge larger bucks only to be forced into hasty retreat. On other occasions larger bucks will tolerate the challenges of small bucks, often standing still while yearlings push at them with all their strength. These contests vary in duration from a few seconds to several minutes. The most vigorous sparring takes place between males of similar size, and it is here that the outcome is in greatest doubt.

Sparring patterns vary among bucks of different ages. In all but the smallest bucks, sparring has ceased by the time actual breeding takes place. Bucks in the yearling and two- and three-year classes are more active than are older bucks, probably because the younger animals are less certain about their position in the hierarchy. Older bucks, by contrast, are well-established in their dominance positions. The significance of antlers is that in a given area their size closely reflects body size and physical condition, which means that antlers can serve as visual indicators of position in the hierarchy (Geist 1966).

Courtship

Courtship or chasing of does begins four to six weeks after the onset of sparring (*see* Figure 43). Buck groups break up, and mature bucks start to travel alone and chase does. This change in behavior may be triggered by an increased level of male hormone production (Robinson et al. 1965), a change in scent of does approaching estrus, or perhaps a combination of the two.

Bucks trailing does at distances of 50 meters (164 feet) or more frequently trot along with their noses to the ground obviously following the does' scent. The does do not allow bucks to approach at close range. Long-distance pursuit such as this may cover 500 meters (1,640 feet) or more before bucks lose interest and leave. On other occasions, bucks make short dashes in pursuit of does. A doe runs hard to prevent a buck from catching up, and frequently leaves her fawns trotting far behind. In the early stages of courtship, bucks usually abandon chases after 200 meters (656 feet) or more, perhaps to seek more-receptive females.

At closer range, a buck follows a doe in a courtship posture with his neck extended and lowered and his chin slightly elevated (Brown and Hirth 1979). While being pursued a doe may pause to urinate, and the buck frequently stops to sniff the urine, apparently testing the doe's stage of estrus. After scenting the urine

A subordinate whitetail buck (top) grooms the forehead of a dominant as a prelude to nonaggressive sparring. The two animals begin to spar (bottom), with the dominant buck merely offering resistance to the smaller deer's test of strength. Such sparring activity occurs frequently after velvet is shed but before bucks start chasing does. Young bucks spar much more often than large, older bucks. *Photos by Kenneth J. Forand; courtesy of the University of Georgia School of Forest Resources.*

As the rut progresses, young whitetail bucks may continue to spar among themselves, while the older, dominant individuals turn their attention to does. *Photo by Len Rue, Jr.*

the buck will often perform a lip-curl, or "flehmen" (Dagg and Taub 1970, Geist 1971, 1981, Hirth 1977*a*). This display consists of extending the neck and chin to a 45-degree angle and curling back the upper lip for about five seconds. Ironically, many does escape while their pursuers stop to lip-curl.

During courtship, tolerance among bucks disappears, and the male hierarchy becomes quite evident. All breeding-age bucks participate in courtship chases, but the largest buck follows closest behind the doe. Smaller bucks, if present, follow the dominant buck and doe at a respectful distance and will quickly turn away if the larger buck looks at them. If a larger buck joins a chase in progress, smaller bucks defer to him and drop back from the doe.

Masturbation is autoerotic behavior that has been observed in subordinate whitetail bucks after they were driven away from a doe by a dominant male (Marchinton and Moore 1971). *Photo by Leonard Lee Rue III.*

A whitetail buck displaying lip-curl (or flehmen) behavior. Bucks usually lip-curl after smelling urine from a doe during the breeding season. The real function of the lip-curl is not known, but it is widespread in ungulates. *Photo by Jim Rathert; courtesy of the Missouri Department of Conservation.*

During the courtship phase, aggressive signals between bucks start with a direct stare and laid-back ears. Most subordinates will then turn away, indicating submissiveness. If this fails to happen, the dominant buck may bristle his hair, lower his antlers, and advance slowly and deliberately in a stiff-legged walk toward his adversary. Most aggressive encounters end at this point, with the smaller buck turning away. Antler threats are met by an adversary only when bucks are closely matched. Even then, one may suddenly turn away.

Instances where neither buck will accept a subordinate role are rare. Threatening bucks may charge at each other from distances of 1 to 2 meters (3.3–6.6 feet), or they may circle briefly before suddenly coming together (Thomas et al. 1965). Both bucks push hard, sometimes throwing up clumps of turf behind them, until one is driven back and forced to retreat. The victor may chase his adversary a short distance, but returns quickly to the doe. Charges seem to be aimed at the opponent's antlers, and usually no attempt is made to gore the opponent's body, even if he stumbles and falls (Michael 1968*b*, Hirth 1977*a*).

Doe groups do not change during the rut. In woodland areas the majority of doe groups

Fights among equally large dominant bucks are uncommon events, but when they occur, they are intense bouts of shoving and neck twisting. Antler fights such as these usually do not last more than 15–30 seconds before one buck is driven back and forced to retreat. *Top photo by Don LaBaugh. Center photo by Leonard Lee Rue III. Bottom photo by Wilbert N. Savage.*

contain only one adult doe. Therefore, courtship involves a single pair. In more open habitat, doe groups frequently contain two or more family units, and one buck may try to dominate a doe group containing as many as 10 does. Large doe groups occasionally attract more than one buck, in which case the dominant buck simultaneously tries to court does and keep subdominant bucks away. Individual family units frequently move in or out of large doe groups, and bucks may follow a doe close to estrus if she moves away from the doe group. Control of doe groups changes as dominant bucks leave the group in pursuit of does or as larger bucks arrive and drive away the formerly dominant males. The antler-threat posture normally is sufficient to make a smaller buck relinquish control of a doe group. Subdominant bucks are kept well beyond the perimeter of the doe group by dominant bucks, but yearling and small two-year-old bucks are tolerated in the group among the does. Clearly the subdominant bucks are perceived as competitors, but the much smaller bucks are not.

It is not uncommon for combating whitetails with locked antlers to perish from exhaustion and the inability to eat or drink. In this instance, one buck is still alive. Note how extensively vegetation in the vicinity has been knocked down. Serious dominance fights that result in permanently locked antlers are likely to be disputes between bucks of similar size and usually the largest animals in an area. *Photo courtesy of the Wisconsin Department of Natural Resources.*

These whitetail bucks apparently died of injuries, exhaustion or both while in combat. Dominance fights resulting in the death of both participants, but not involving locked antlers, are extremely rare. *Photo courtesy of the Missouri Department of Conservation.*

Tending and Copulation

The actual estrus period—when a doe is willing to stand for copulation—lasts perhaps only 24 hours (Haugen 1959, Michael 1966, Moore and Marchinton 1974). Does no longer run from courting bucks, and single pairs isolate themselves. The buck tends the doe by standing behind her, occasionally testing her readiness to copulate by nosing her rump, and feeds and beds in unison with her for several hours (Hirth 1977*a*, Brown and Hirth 1979). The doe eventually is ready to stand for copulation. Intromission occurs as a single hard thrust by the buck that frequently knocks the doe out from under him (Haugen 1959, Warren et al. 1978). After copulation the buck remains with the doe and drives other bucks away for at least several hours and perhaps as many as 24 hours. This defense is only of the doe, wherever she goes, and not of a specific piece of ground or territory. A single pair may mate several times while the doe is in estrus (Haugen 1959, Moore and Marchinton 1974). Does that do not become pregnant at their first estrus will come into estrus again 28 days later.

Although all bucks participate in courtship, only dominant bucks are involved with tending and copulation in populations of normal age structure. Younger bucks are capable of breeding, but they may not have an opportunity to breed until they are 3.5 to 4.5 years of age. Then they may mate with several does at each succeeding rut. Where the age structure among bucks is greatly reduced, breeding is accomplished by yearlings and two-year-olds.

Signpost Communication and Related Behavior

At least two distinct types of visual and olfactory signposts are displayed by bucks during courtship and breeding periods (Moore and Marchinton 1974). "Buck rubs" are stems of shrubs or saplings debarked by bucks rubbing them with their antlers and head (Figure 44A). The forehead skin contains glands that become more active during the breeding season and leave scent on the objects rubbed (Atkeson and Marchinton 1982*b*). Occasionally a buck will break a sapling when rubbing escalates into vigorous thrashing. Rubbing is most intense during and shortly after velvet removal, but continues throughout the rut (Kile and Marchinton 1977) (Figure 45). Rubs can function in communication between the sexes as does sometimes sniff, lick or even "mark" buck rubs with their foreheads.

Early in the rutting season, whitetail bucks tend to thrash saplings vigorously, often breaking them. Rubs made later in the rut have greater visibility and may serve more of a signpost function since they characteristically are left standing but with the bark removed. Bucks very deliberately rub their glandular foreheads on debarked saplings. This leaves a scent that may allow other deer to identify the metabolic condition and perhaps the individual identity of the buck that made the rub. However, other bucks and occasionally even does may rub over a scent mark left by an earlier buck. *Photo by Leonard Lee Rue III*.

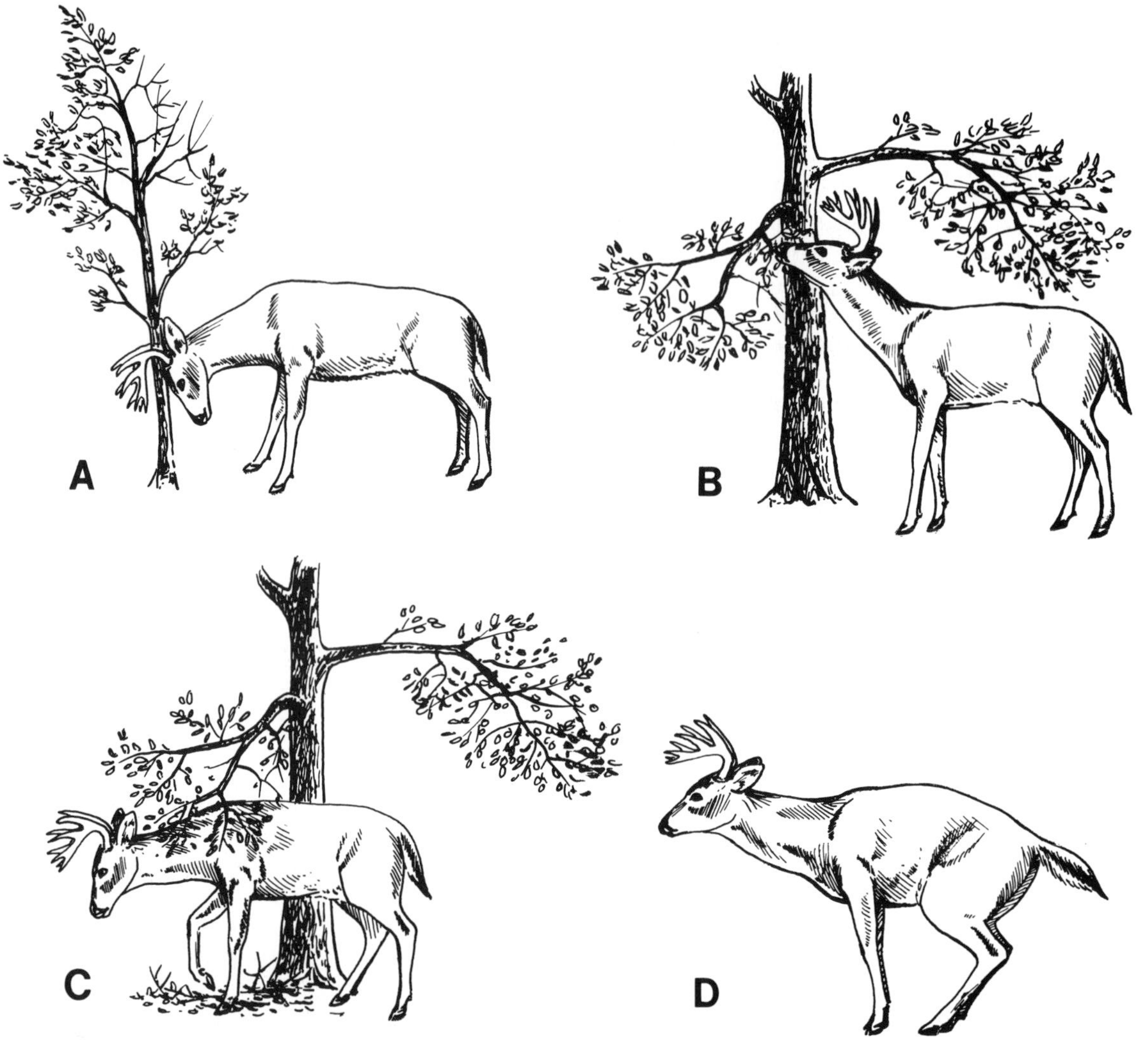

Figure 44. Postures assumed by whitetails during scent-marking activities: (A) rubbing, (B) marking branch, (C) pawing under marked branch and (D) urination on tarsal glands (Moore and Marchinton 1974).

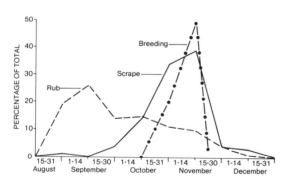

Figure 45. Frequency of rubbing, scraping and breeding activity by whitetail bucks during the rut (Kile and Marchinton 1977).

A "buck scrape" usually consists of a broken twig or branch 1 to 2 meters (3.3–6.6 feet) above the ground with a depression pawed in the soil directly beneath it. In making a scrape a buck first reaches up into a tree or bush, sometimes standing on his hindlegs, and mouthes and pulls the end of a branch down, frequently breaking it (Figure 44B). The buck then releases the branch, allowing it to spring back across his forehead. Following this he paws and scrapes free of litter a shallow depression beneath the branch, into which he generally urinates (Figure 44C).

Scrapes appear primarily during courtship and breeding periods (Figure 45), and clearly function as signposts. Whitetail bucks may return to scrapes and "freshen" them or make other scrapes nearby. Does are thought to visit scrapes and also leave an olfactory message, but clear scientific documentation of this is not yet available (Sawyer 1981). A buck locating the scent of a doe at or near a scrape, however, often trails her at a fast walk with his nose near the ground, making a characteristic grunting sound (Moore and Marchinton 1974).

Both marking routines also serve as threat displays. Threatening bucks sometimes pause to thrash a bush before facing each other again.

Buck "marking" a rubbed sapling with his forehead glands. Scent left on rubs persists for several days, and the visible evidence of a rub will last at least through the rutting season. Saplings selected for rubbing generally range from 1 to 10 centimeters (0.4–4 inches) in diameter, with certain aromatic species apparently being preferred. Nielson et al. (1982) showed that damage to young trees by rubbing bucks can cause substantial economic loss in tree nurseries. *Photo by Irene Vandermolen.*

During a rubbing episode, whitetail bucks frequently stop to sniff and lick the rubbed area. Bucks and does also may smell rubs made by another buck. Note the distinctively sexually dimorphic pelage of the forehead gland of this buck (*see* Atkeson and Marchinton 1982*b*). Some observers are able to identify bucks at a great distance by the presence of this "patch." *Photo by R. Larry Marchinton; courtesy of the University of Georgia School of Forest Resources.*

A mature 5.5-year-old whitetail buck "marking" a twig with his mouth (left) prior to pawing a scrape during the rut. He also may push his glandular forehead against the twig, thus creating a signpost. The twig commonly is broken or twisted and may hang down toward the scrape site. The buck then paws away leaves, grass and other debris (right) before urinating on the bare soil. *Photos by Kenneth J. Forand; courtesy of the University of Georgia School of Forest Resources.*

Whitetail buck following a doe's scent trail in the breeding season. His behavior tends to be quite stereotyped as he moves along the doe's trail: tail up, nose to the ground, uttering a protracted grunt. Note the darkly stained tarsal gland on the inside of his hind leg. *Photo by Leonard Lee Rue III.*

Similarly, a buck may assert his dominance by making a scrape in the presence of a subordinate buck (Hirth 1977a). Despite the prevalence of signposts, whitetail bucks usually are not thought to be territorial (Thomas et al. 1965, Smith 1976, Coblentz 1977), even though they become intolerant of one another during the rut. Studies in Texas (Brown 1974) and Michigan (Hirth 1977a) showed that home ranges of bucks continued to overlap during the rut with no evidence of area defense. However, working in Georgia, Moore and Marchinton (1974) found that whitetail scrapes were associated with "areas of dominance," and suggested that the expression of dominance or submission in bucks is influenced by where the interaction occurs. This also may be true for whitetail does. Also, Ozoga et al. (1982a) reported does defending fawning sites against other deer. And there is evidence that whitetail does or family groups, under certain circumstances, will defend feeding territories (Marchinton and Atkeson in press), as it has been suggested that mule deer do (Miller 1974). Geist (1981:211) used the term "facultative territoriality" to describe this behavior in mule and blacktail does, since it occurred only under certain circumstances—high and uniform resource availability. Although both whitetail bucks and does sometimes show evidence of facultative territoriality, their behavior is better characterized by its plasticity than by such labels. The social organization observed in a population, regardless of how it is termed, represents local adaptation to local conditions (Marchinton and Atkeson in press).

The social importance of rubs and scrapes, then, apparently depends on characteristics of the habitat and on the density, sex and age structure of the deer population. In populations with a high percentage of does and a young age-structure among bucks (typical of many heavily hunted populations), the communicative role of rubs and scrapes may be less significant. In open habitat direct visual cues have relatively greater importance than signpost communication. The function of rubbing and scraping in white-tailed deer social behavior is not fully understood. This is highlighted by the recent discovery that does also make scrapes on occasion, and that this behavior among does is not limited to the breeding season (Sawyer et al. 1982).

A behavioral pattern often associated with rubbing and scraping involves the buck urinating on his tarsal glands while rubbing them together (Figure 44D). This is referred to as "urine marking," "scenting" or "rub-urination," and produces a strong, far-reaching odor that may intimidate other bucks, as it has been suggested is the case for mule deer (Linsdale and Tomich 1953). Urine marking probably serves to attract does, but undoubtedly also has other social functions. During any season bucks, does and even fawns may routinely rub-urinate once or twice a day in response to threats—or sometimes for no apparent reason.

Geist (1981) found that black-tailed deer sniffed or licked others' hocks frequently. He concluded that this licking may have been to remove tarsal scent, especially when the tarsals of fawns were licked, or when a deer licked its own tarsals. Large male black-tailed deer rarely lick their tarsals, which also is true of whitetails. Tarsal glands of dominant whitetail bucks become heavily stained during the rut, and the stain sometimes extends down the leg all the way to the hoof (Atkeson and Marchinton 1982a). The smell becomes very pronounced at this time, and even a human can detect it at a considerable distance.

Whitetail buck rub-urinating on his tarsal glands during the rut. The odor of rub-urinating bucks has been detected at distances greater than 100 meters (110 yards). Although rub-urination seems to be most important as a form of olfactory communication by bucks during the rut, it also is performed by does and even fawns throughout the year in alarm situations. *Photo by Leonard Lee Rue III.*

White-tailed deer have several other olfactory or scent-producing glands on their body. These include interdigital glands located between the toes on each foot, preorbital glands found just below the eyes, metatarsal glands on the outside of each hind leg, and possibly nasal glands, found just inside the nose (Atkeson et al. unpublished, *see* Chapter 3). The precise social function of these glands remains largely a mystery, but their presence further emphasizes the significance of scent communication in deer behavior.

GESTATION AND PARTURITION

The behavior of does apparently is little affected by pregnancy until the approach of labor. Some authors (Seton 1929, Downing and McGinnes 1969, White et al. 1972) have suggested that does isolate themselves and seek out a secluded spot to give birth, but others (Severinghaus and Cheatum 1956, Michael 1964) feel that does make no particular effort to choose a special site to fawn. In observations of penned whited-tailed deer, pacing was the only noticeable change in behavior prior to parturition (Halford and Alldredge 1975, Townsend and Bailey 1975).

The birth process in whitetails proceeds quickly and may occur with the doe in a prostrate or standing position. In one of the two births observed by Michael (1964), 28 minutes elapsed from the time the doe laid down until her fawn was born and completely licked clean. A second fawn was born and cleaned off in 24 minutes. In another study, labor lasted 115 minutes and 133 minutes for two penned whitetail does prior to birth of the first fawns (Townsend and Bailey 1975). The mean interval between first birth to second birth was 24 minutes.

Following birth, does immediately remove fetal membranes from fawns starting at the nose and working posteriorly until the fawn is clean and dry. Fawns usually attempt to stand 20 to 30 minutes after birth and sometimes earlier (Haugen and Speake 1957, Michael 1964, Townsend and Bailey 1975, Rue 1978).

Nursing begins soon after the fawn has learned to stand, about 35 minutes after birth. Both fawns and does may stand or lie down during initial nursing sessions. As they nurse, fawns wag their tails vigorously and their mothers respond by licking the fawn's anogenital area almost constantly. This licking, which may continue for two or three weeks after the birth of fawns (Hirth 1973), stimulates urination and defecation, and may prevent constipation. By consuming these metabolic by-products, a doe may allow her fawn to be better concealed from predators.

Does also invariably consume fetal membranes and afterbirth. It has been suggested that some nutritional benefit may accrue to the doe as a result of this behavior (Hafez 1968), but its greatest benefit undoubtedly is in removal of material that could attract predators to the birth site (Fraser 1968).

Birthing of a white-tailed deer. Opposite top left: the doe has selected a dry and isolated site and lain down as her labor contractions increase in intensity and frequency. Opposite top right: straining to give birth, the doe thrashes about. If she has not dilated sufficiently to allow the fawn's passage, she may rise and walk about before returning to the same spot at the onset of intensified contractions. Opposite center left: the doe strains as the fawn's feet emerge from her dilated vagina. Opposite center right: the fawn's head comes out between its forelegs—the normal emergence position. Opposite bottom left: the fawn is born partially covered by the placental sac, which the doe will eat as she immediately begins grooming her offspring. Opposite bottom right: after a few minutes, the fawn crawls forward along the doe's belly and is groomed continuously. Top left: within about 10 minutes, the newborn fawn will begin to nurse as its dam continues her thorough cleaning ministrations. Top right: within 15 minutes or so, the fawn begins attempts to rise. Bottom left: usually the initial efforts of a newborn to stand fail because of its own weakness and awkwardness, and the mother's attentions compound its unsteadiness. Bottom right: with the fawn cleaned and standing on wobbly legs at approximately 20 minutes, its birth process—which began with the doe's labor several hours earlier—is complete. A doe's first labor usually is more difficult and prolonged than are subsequent deliveries, including of twins or triplets. *Photos by Leonard Lee Rue III.*

MATERNAL BEHAVIOR

Mother/young behavior for the first month of a fawn's life is oriented toward the fawn's survival. Does greatly reduce the size of their home ranges at parturition and vigorously exclude other deer from the area immediately surrounding their fawn(s) for the first month postpartum (Ozoga et al. 1982). Dominant does may return to the same site each year to bear their fawns. One study of radio-marked deer showed yearling and two-year-old daughters of a matriarch doe establishing fawning sites adjacent to that of their mother (Ozoga et al. 1982a). Although sibling fawns are born at the same site, they are separated soon after birth and are maintained at separate locations for three to six weeks (Downing and McGinnes 1969, White et al. 1972, Jackson et al. 1972, Hirth 1973). By this age they are able to elude most predators.

For the first few days after birth, fawns nurse two or three times a day during daylight (Jackson et al. 1972), and usually bed again in less than half an hour. Newborn fawns nurse as long as they want, but by their second week, does initiate weaning by terminating the second and third daily nursing sessions. By the time the fawns are a month old, almost all nursing is terminated by the doe, and the rate of attempted nursings declines rapidly. Fawns start to ruminate at about two weeks and are "essentially dependent" on rumination by five weeks (Short 1964). Fawns nurse occasionally during their first autumn, but by 10 weeks they seem to be functionally weaned.

Does are intolerant of nursing attempts by fawns other than their own. However, fawns have been observed to nurse a strange doe when the doe's own fawn(s) also were nursing (Hirth 1973). Does normally kick strange fawns away when they try to nurse.

A whitetail doe grooms its nursing fawn. This position is most common, but fawns also will nurse from between the doe's hind legs. Does begin to wean fawns by about four weeks of age by stepping away while the fawn is nursing; by 10 weeks, fawns make only occasional attempts to nurse. Does normally are very intolerant of nursing by fawns that are not their own, but occasionally a strange fawn may sneak in briefly while a doe's own fawns are nursing. *Photo by Tom W. Hall.*

Fawn Location

At all ages, fawns appear to choose their own bedding sites. Fawns only one or two days old often are observed to nurse and then walk approximately 10 meters (33 feet) into brush to bed by themselves while their mothers feed and pay little or no attention to them (Hirth 1973). This behavior obviously disassociates the scent of the doe from the fawn's bedding site. By their second week, fawns remain active with their mothers for 10 to 15 minutes after nursing and may nurse a second time before bedding. Young fawns normally make no attempt to follow their mothers after nursing, but Rue (1962) watched a doe push her fawn back with her forehead repeatedly and force it to lie down with her forefoot.

Does visit their fawns three or four times a day during their first two weeks, gradually increasing the number of visits over the month that follows (Jackson et al. 1972). A doe returns to the general vicinity where she left her fawn at its last nursing period. Usually the fawn is standing and waiting, and frequently runs 10 to 30 meters (33–98 feet) to meet the approaching doe. Infrequently a fawn will run to a doe other than its mother, returning to its bed after being rejected. A doe searches for her fawn(s) with her neck outstretched and her ears forward (Downing and McGinnes 1969, White et al. 1972), and probably depends heavily on olfactory cues to locate and identify her young. Occasionally does call with "a soft plaintive mew" while searching for fawns (White et al. 1972:898).

Whitetail fawns are "hiders" (as opposed to "followers"), meaning that young fawns remain hidden for most of the day rather than travel with their mothers. It is during this time that people find fawns and mistakenly think that they have been abandoned. If such fawns are approached they become very quiet, so much so that their breathing and heart rates are reduced sharply (Jacobsen 1979). Until they are better able to run, their survival from predators may hinge on remaining undetected. *Photo by Richard Simms; courtesy of the Tennessee Wildlife Resources Agency.*

Play

After fawns finish nursing they timidly explore the environment around them. By their second week they exhibit playfulness (Hirth 1973). A fawn may run 10 to 20 meters (33–66 feet) from its mother, pause briefly and then dash back, often bucking and dodging back and forth as it runs. This play-running sequence may be repeated several times, leaving the fawn panting beside its mother. The doe is always present when playing occurs.

Because fawns are isolated for their first three or four weeks, early play is solitary and continues to be so even when sibling pairs are together. In larger family groups, play by one fawn may stimulate play in other fawns, but frequently no interaction between playing fawns is evident—each runs in a circle out from its mother and pays no attention to other fawns. In fawns a month or more old the playful runs occur in a 50- to 100-meter (164–328-foot) radius about the dam. Interactive play occurs throughout the summer, especially in older fawns, which can be seen chasing each other in apparent games of tag or bouts of bucking. By autumn, incidents of playing have become increasingly uncommon; by winter, play has virtually ceased.

Whitetail fawns more than a week or two old are surprisingly agile and likely to flee when disturbed, rather than remain immobile. Researchers attempting to place tags on fawns have found that healthy ones a few days old generally can outrun a man, and those more than two weeks old are faster than dogs trained to help capture them. *Photo by Tom W. Hall.*

Whitetail does rearing and flailing at one another. At left, the does are playing. Romping and splashing in shallow water sometimes induces bouts of play even among young adults. At right, the behavior probably is a hostile interaction stemming from competition for food. Playfulness among whitetails during winter stress periods is uncommon. Flail fights generally are of short duration, with the smaller or less aggressive doe moving away. *Left photo by Lynn L. Rogers. Right photo by Eugene Sanborn; courtesy of the Wisconsin Department of Natural Resources.*

Fawn Movements

In their first week or two, whitetail fawns are quite sedentary, although they may not bed in the same spot more than once (Jackson et al. 1972, Ozoga et al. 1982a). Occasionally a doe will lead her very young fawn(s) as far as 200 to 300 meters (656–984 feet) in response to a specific disturbance. As fawns get older, their periods of activity become longer, they become progressively more mobile, and siblings begin to appear together. After fawns are two months old their activity cycle corresponds closely to that of the dam (Jackson et al. 1972, Hirth 1973). By autumn, a doe is accompanied constantly by her offspring.

Fawn Adoption

Whitetail does rarely adopt fawns, but there are a few reports in the literature of fawn adoption. In New York, two penned does that had lost fawns rejected new fawns, but two other does at the same facility that had also lost fawns accepted orphan fawns readily (Severinghaus 1949a). Fawn adoption in free-ranging does has been reported by Palmer (1951) and McGinnes and Downing (1970). However, Hirth (1977a) never observed does to be tolerant of strange fawns. It seems probable that most fawns orphaned or lost before being weaned are not adopted by other does, and die.

VOCAL COMMUNICATION

Anecdotal observations of deer vocalizations have been recorded since the earliest writings on this species (*see* Seton 1929, Severinghaus and Cheatum 1956, Faatz 1976), but only recently have systematic studies been undertaken (Richardson 1981, Atkeson 1983). Through the use of sonographic analysis these studies show that deer possess a varied vocabulary.

Thirteen sounds have been recognized, with only one—the footstomp—being nonvocal. The footstomp is a "thumping" sound made during alarm situations (Hirth 1973) by sharply striking a forefoot on the ground. The snort, a sound which augments the footstomp, is familiar to most hunters. It is made by a violent expulsion of air through the nostrils with the mouth closed, producing sound by vibration through the nasal passages. Snorts often are given in a long series when deer perceive danger but do not feel directly threatened, and are more likely to be given by family groups than by buck groups (Hirth and McCullough 1977). The bawl is an intensive call given only when a deer is being physically traumatized or restrained. It is a voiced sound of moderate tonality and its pitch generally varies with the age of the animal. Investigating the possibility that does might recognize their fawns by these distress calls, Richardson (1981) found that a high proportion of his subjects could identify their young sonographically.

Three calls are associated with agonistic situations. A low guttural grunt is made by both sexes throughout the year, usually being coupled with postural threats. It is a brief, voiced sound of low tonality, pitch and intensity, and can be produced with the mouth closed or open. It might be given, for instance, by an old doe while exhibiting a head-high threat as she displaces a younger animal from a food source. In more intense encounters involving either sex, one to four snorts may be added to the basic grunt. These snorts are brief, atonal, unvoiced fricative sounds caused by air expelled through open nostrils. Atkeson (1983) heard this type of snort most frequently from bucks during the sparring and breeding seasons. A typical encounter begins when a small buck encroaches on a larger, dominant buck, who then gives the antler threat and a grunt-snort response as he takes a few steps toward the subordinate. The most intensely agonistic vocalization consists of the grunt-snort plus a drawn-out wheezing inhalation through pinched nostrils. This moderately intense sound has some tonality because of its whistling quality. This grunt-snort-wheeze sequence is given by dominant bucks during the breeding season (Atkeson 1983).

Bucks actively courting does make a drawn-out grunt that sounds like an unoiled hinge, or a branch swaying in the wind. It is a voiced sound of moderate intensity and pitch, low tonality and considerably longer duration than the other grunts of deer. When making this sound the buck often is on the trail of a doe and moving at a rapid pace with his nose right to the ground.

In doe/fawn interactions, several calls have been discerned. The mother makes a low grunt to call her fawn as she searches for it to initiate a nursing bout. This is a voiced call of moderate pitch, low tonality and short duration.

A whitetail doe (left) with fawn (probably less than one week old) stamps her foot in alarm at the approach of a photographer. She remains between the intruder and her fawn and begins to snort repeatedly. In a crouch, the fawn moves quickly to tall grass for concealment. As the alarm intensifies (right) with the photographer remaining nearby, so do the dam's stamping and snorting. These actions and noises may not only be signals of danger to her fawn and other deer in the vicinity, but along with a head-high threat posture, may cause a potential predator to expose itself and serve as a warning to the intruder. Had the fawn been concealed initially, the doe might have attempted to lure the intruder away, perhaps by moving away from the area and feigning injury. *Photos courtesy of the Arizona Game and Fish Department.*

The fawn might answer with a mew; a sound of high pitch, moderate tonality and low intensity. If the fawn is anxious or just too-long separated from its mother or caretaker its calls become more insistent bleats. Bleats are care-solicitation calls of moderate pitch and tonality and variable intensity. When the fawn succeeds in finding its mother it gives a nursing whine as it suckles. This is a voiced sound of high pitch and tonality, low intensity, and brief duration, made repeatedly as the fawn nurses.

Another vocalization is the contact call (Sawyer 1981)—a voiced bleat of moderate pitch, intensity and tonality. Four deer in a group of free-ranging but tame deer in Sawyer's study all made this call when they became separated from one another.

The results of these recent studies show that deer are not the silent animals that many have assumed. Rather, they make a variety of calls, and it is probable that the ones now identified are only part of their vocal repertoire.

INTERSPECIFIC BEHAVIOR

Other Ungulates

The mule deer is the wild ungulate most frequently encountered by whitetails. The ranges of these two species overlap in 18 western states and provinces as far east as South Dakota and Kansas (*see* Chapter 1). Direct contact between mule deer and white-tailed deer is minimized because whitetails tend to occupy timbered or brushy habitat, whereas mule deer are more inclined toward open habitat. In areas of overlap in Alberta, the two species had little behavioral impact on each other, showing avoidance only at distances under 50 meters (164 feet) (Krämer 1972). Dominance was divided evenly in interspecific encounters and apparently was based on size. In Arizona, whitetails and mule deer ignored each other in 50 percent of encounters within 50 meters (164 feet), but mule deer, which were much larger than whitetails, were dominant in all instances (Anthony and Smith 1977). In the Big Bend area of Texas, the normal pattern of deer behavior is to ignore members of different species (Krausman 1976). It appears that any competitive exclusion between species is not based on behavioral interaction.

Whitetails react to the presence of domestic cattle with complete indifference or mild avoidance (Michael 1967, Krämer 1973, Hirth 1973). Likewise, cattle pay little or no attention to white-tailed deer. Michael (1967) reported some competition for shaded bedding sites, but otherwise cattle had little behavioral impact on deer.

Predators

Despite the wolf's reputation as an efficient predator, observations of wolves hunting whitetails and examination of the age distribution of wolf-killed deer indicate that most deer escape attacks by wolves (*see* Chapter 8). During winter, wolves are most successful at killing deer older than five years of age (Pimlott et al. 1969, Mech 1970, Mech and Frenzel 1971*a*), but fawns are taken frequently in summer (Thompson 1952). Mech and Frenzel (1971*a*) observed wolves chasing deer 14 times and witnessed only one successful hunt. When deer had a headstart of about 100 meters (328 feet), they apparently escaped, and wolves gave up the chase within 400 meters (1,312 feet). Fawns were no more vulnerable than yearlings during the winter. Deer's normal response to wolves is to run rather than to hold their ground as moose frequently do.

The coyote and bobcat usually are associated with whitetails as scavengers more than as actual predators (Knowlton 1964, Niebauer and Rongstad 1977). Although coyotes and bobcats kill few whitetails more than one or two months old (Ozoga and Harger 1966, Cook et al. 1971), the deer are always alert to them. The deer's normal response to a coyote is to stare, with neck and ears erect, and to move away if necessary (Michael 1967, Hirth 1973). The deer will continue to watch the coyote intently until it has passed from sight. Does frequently chase coyotes from the vicinity of fawns during the summer, and in some instances strike coyotes with their forefeet.

Bobcats kill very few young fawns compared with the number taken by coyotes (Cook et al. 1971), but surprisingly, deer are more alarmed by bobcats than they are by coyotes. Whitetails (does in particular) stare at passing bobcats and frequently follow them until they are at least 100 meters (328 feet) beyond where the deer have been feeding (Michael 1967, Hirth 1973). Deer stamp their forefeet and snort repeatedly, alerting other deer in the vicinity to a bobcat's presence. This reaction may be the result of the bobcat's ambush style of hunting, in contrast to the coyote's chase style.

Domestic Dogs

Hunting hounds, free-ranging pets and feral dogs probably have more contact with white-tailed deer than any of the wild carnivore species. Contrary to many popular articles (*see* Neil et al. 1975), domestic dogs usually are ineffective as deer predators (Progulske and Baskett 1958, Marchinton et al. 1971, Perry and Giles 1971, Scott and Causey 1973). Although dogs often chase deer, they normally have no detrimental effect (Sweeney et al. 1971, Gavitt et al. 1975, Gipson and Sealander 1977) unless deep snows or other environmental hazards are contributing factors.

Sweeney et al. (1971) reported several kinds of behavior by deer in their escape from hunting hounds. Sometimes the hounds did not detect deer that remained quietly bedded in thick cover and did not bolt even when the dogs approached. When chased by dogs, deer (par-

When moderately alarmed, white-tailed deer (left) often raise their tails, exposing white underside and rump, and bound away. Piloerection of the tail and rump exaggerates the signal. This behavior alerts other deer within sight and apparently serves to maintain visual contact among deer as they run through cover. When badly frightened, as by the sudden appearance of a human a few meters away, whitetails (right) are more likely to bolt off at top speed without signaling (Hirth and McCullough 1977). *Left photo by Ernest Alfstad; courtesy of the U.S. Fish and Wildlife Service. Right photo by George Shiras III; courtesy of the Wildlife Management Institute.*

ticularly bucks) often ran a relatively straight course, using speed and endurance to elude and lose the hounds. In other instances whitetails ran a circuitous zigzag pattern, frequently crossing their own trail and confusing the pursuing dogs. After mingling with other deer the pursued animal would separate suddenly from the group, causing the hounds to switch trails. Pursued deer also ran or swam through water when it was accessible. Barkalow and Keller (1950) observed an unspotted fawn escape pursuing hounds by submerging itself in water under a ditch bank with only its eyes and nose above the surface.

Gipson and Sealander (1977) found that deer being chased by dogs would often run along roads for considerable distances and then turn off them at right angles. This tactic generally resulted in at least a temporary loss of the trail by the pursuing hounds.

White-tailed deer caught by dogs are likely to be sick, injured or otherwise debilitated (Corbett et al. 1972). Exceptions to this may occur in winter, when deep snow has a frozen crust that will support a dog's weight but not that of a deer (Hosley 1956, Brazda 1957, Lowry and McArthur 1978). Under those conditions, free-ranging dogs can cause considerable direct mortality. Dogs also may be more effective at running down deer in rugged mountainous terrain than in coastal plain areas (Corbett et al. 1972).

Besides using waterways to escape from pursuing predators (*see* Chapter 8), whitetails sometimes use windswept frozen lakes, rivers and streams for winter travel. Even when a deer is not being pursued in winter, its footing on ice can be very precarious. Pelvic and limb ligament and muscle damage is likely if the animal slips and falls. Such accidents are not uncommon. In many cases, a whitetail's legs will splay out as it falls, and unable to rise the deer will freeze, starve or become victim to predators. *Photo courtesy of the New Brunswick Department of Natural Resources.*

White-tailed deer are very adept at negotiating fences, either by leaping over or crawling under. Considering the number of times whitetails cross fences in most areas, accidents are quite rare. But when they do occur it generally is because ground conditions are poor, especially when there is deep snow cover. *Top-left photo by Phillip K. White; courtesy of the U.S. Fish and Wildlife Service. Center-left photo by Leonard Lee Rue III. Bottom-left photo courtesy of the North Dakota Game and Fish Department. Top-right photo by Clarence Benkert; courtesy of the Wisconsin Department of Natural Resources. Center-right photo by Larry Kruckenberg; courtesy of the North Dakota Game and Fish Department. Bottom-right photo by Frank Haberland; courtesy of the Wisconsin Department of Natural Resources.*

Whitetails readily leave their home range when chased by dogs, but usually return within a matter of hours, or at most a few days, with no apparent long-term disruption of their behavioral patterns (Sweeney et al. 1971, Corbett et al. 1972, Gavitt et al. 1975, Gipson and Sealander 1977). Recently stocked deer without well-established home ranges may be an exception, and dog harassment probably reduces the success of some restocking programs (Perry and Giles 1971).

Interaction with Human Activity

Activities such as timber cutting, drilling for oil and gas, hiking and canoeing have little effect on whitetails. Deer in the north woods learn to associate the sound of a chainsaw with fresh browse in the winter, and deer often move into or return to areas being cut as soon as the cutting crews leave in the afternoon (Ozoga 1972, Lavigne 1976). In brushlands of southern Texas, deer feed preferentially in newly mowed areas surrounding oil or gas wells and along pipelines.

The influence on white-tailed deer of off-road vehicles (ORV's), such as light motorcycles and snowmobiles, has been viewed with some concern. Dorrance et al. (1975) reported that fewer whitetails were seen along snowmobile trails during heavy-use periods, but the deer returned to the vicinity of the trails less than 24 hours after snowmobile traffic ceased. In Maine, the combination of newly-made snowmobile trails and the sound of a chainsaw attracted deer to new feeding areas (Lavigne 1976). The noise made by off-road vehicles warns the deer of approaching trail bikes and snowmobiles. A study in Wisconsin showed that deer were more frightened by the silent approach of cross-country skiers than by snowmobiles (O. J. Rongstad personal communication:1977).

The potential for serious impact on deer by off-road vehicles is greatest in the North, in winter, and when deer exist on a tight energy budget (Moen 1968*a*). Snowmobilers may follow deer for long distances with no intention to harm, but mindless of or without regard to the drain being imposed on a deer's energy reserves. The use of snowmobiles in deer yards and their vicinities should be carefully controlled whenever possible.

Hunting is the primary form of disturbance during autumn (*see* Chapter 7). In one study, Behrend and Lubeck (1968) reported that antlered bucks on a hunted area had twice the flight distance—53 meters (58 yards) versus 27 meters (30 yards)—as did bucks on a non-hunted refuge. In addition, deer on the hunted area were more likely to run than walk and more likely to snort in response to disturbance than were deer on the refuge. Deer that survive several hunting seasons are likely to be more elusive than younger animals. In New York, young bucks were more vulnerable early in a hunting season than later that season (Maguire and Severinghaus 1954). Whitetails usually are considered to be more wary and difficult to hunt than their close relative, the mule deer, where the two species are sympatric. In fact, white-tailed deer are able to survive intensive hunting pressure as well as any big game species on the North American continent and quite possibly in the world.

Even though hunting and related disturbances affect whitetails' movement patterns (Tester and Heezen 1965, Robinette 1966, Downing et al. 1969), one hunter per 4 hectares (9.9 acres) did not cause deer to leave their normal range in Georgia (Marshall and Whittington 1969). In other areas, however, disturbances by hunters and hunter densities may be factors in annual range shifts (Zagata and Haugen 1973, Kammermeyer and Marchinton 1976*a*).

Chapter 7

POPULATION INFLUENCES

George H. Matschke
Wildlife Research Biologist
U.S. Fish and Wildlife Service
Denver, Colorado

Kathleen A. Fagerstone
Wildlife Research Biologist
U.S. Fish and Wildlife Service
Denver, Colorado

Richard F. Harlow
Research Wildlife Biologist
U.S. Forest Service
Clemson, South Carolina

Frank A. Hayes
Director
Southeastern Cooperative Wildlife
Disease Study
Athens, Georgia

Victor F. Nettles
Research Associate
Southeastern Cooperative Wildlife
Disease Study
Athens, Georgia

Warren Parker
Wildlife Biologist
U.S. Fish and Wildlife Service
Asheville, North Carolina

Daniel O. Trainer
Dean
College of Natural Resources
University of Wisconsin
Stevens Point, Wisconsin

White-tailed deer have an average lifespan of eight years (Flower 1931), but most do not live beyond four to five years of age. Although hunter harvest is the major cause of mortality in hunted whitetail populations, many other interrelated forces constantly depress deer survival. This chapter discusses constraints, other than nutrition (*see* Chapter 4) and predation (*see* Chapter 8), that determine how long deer will live. To a large extent, the factors are capable of being subjected to management by man.

HUNTING

Buck-only Versus Either-sex Hunting

Newly stocked whitetail ranges of the 1940s and 1950s required protection to ensure population welfare, and this included the need for a buck law. Once established, however, whitetail populations expanded into every nook and cranny of available habitat. To control these expanding populations, either-sex or antlerless hunts became essential.

Even though regulated either-sex harvests repeatedly have proven successful in maintaining white-tailed deer populations and their habitats, many hunters, nonhunters, and all too often state fish and wildlife commissioners are against killing does. The roots of this attitude are based mostly on the regulation requirements of the 1940s and 1950s, when deer were being restored to much of their original range. When populations were reestablished, however, wildlife administrators found it difficult to convince the public that does could and should be legally harvested.

Most or all of a whitetail population's annual recruitment must be removed to maintain the population at or just below the habitat carrying capacity. Since annual recruitment in a healthy population will average 30 to 40 percent, mature animals must be displaced or harvested at approximately the same rate to keep the population in balance with its habitat. But such a harvest is difficult to obtain with buck-only hunting. Despite longer seasons (46 days) and multiple bag limits (two whitetails of either sex) between 1958 and 1960, the annual whitetail harvest in the Llano Basin of Texas averaged only 14 percent of the population (Teer et al.

1965, *see* Chapter 12). In 1961 the limit was increased to three deer, including one antlerless deer, and approximately 20 percent of the population was harvested. For all of Texas, hunters are unable to harvest sufficient numbers of deer; consequently, thousands of whitetails die annually from disease and starvation.

Buck-only hunting alters the age and size structure of a whitetail population. Under heavy harvesting, bucks of more than 3.5 years of age may be eliminated, and an abnormally high number of does will lead inevitably to a higher percentage of smaller-antlered, younger bucks than would otherwise exist. Fawns are harvested only accidentally with buck-only hunting.

Many hunters will pass up fawns under either-sex hunting, and yearlings are harvested heavily early in the season. Lewis and Safley (1967*a*) indicated that male yearlings and fawns were more vulnerable to hunting than were bucks older than 3.5 years. The old bucks tend to seek out thickets and quickly alter normal habits to avoid hunters.

Two important factors interact to limit harvest, even when hunting pressure on both sexes is heavy. The first factor is unequal hunter

Even before the turn of the century, total protection of does from harvest was advocated as a panacea that would spur the recovery of depleted whitetail populations. Such protection worked as a means of rebuilding some deer populations, but not in terms of maintaining them at favorable management levels. Whitetail numbers eventually exceeded habitat carrying-capacity in many areas, especially in the snowbelt region. Despite massive winter die-offs of overpopulated deer in various parts of the United States from the 1930s through the 1950s, sportsmen in particular found it difficult to accept that the traditional buck-only harvest was not appropriate at all times and in all places. Such resistance persists in some states, in spite of biological evidence to the contrary. *Photo by Gardiner Bump.*

distribution. Poor access will virtually ensure hunter concentration along roads and well-defined trails. Only a relatively small number of hunters will leave the roads and trails to go any great distance (White 1968b). Whitetails tend to move away from areas of intense hunting and, by doing so, frequently escape detection by the majority of hunters. The second factor is severe weather. Unusually low temperatures, ice, snow and rain often limit or preclude hunter participation, and almost invariably limit the harvest.

Antlered deer are driven by powerful reproductive urges at a time of year that coincides with most hunting seasons. During the rut, bucks are very active and sometimes leave their home ranges in search of estrus does. During this brief but intense period, they sometimes ignore normal caution (White 1968b) and increase their vulnerability to shooting. Buck harvest can be increased or decreased to some extent by setting the hunting season to coincide with or avoid the rut, respectively.

As white-tailed deer populations become increasingly large and competition for food increases, does respond with lowered fertility or fecundity or both (Payne 1970). However, by the time this inverse relationship becomes operable, habitat may have deteriorated, adversely affecting the animals' health. Even though the range may recover, the price paid in the loss of deer likely will be high for the interim years. In most cases, problems of dramatic fluctuations of deer numbers can be avoided if both sexes are harvested—if not equally, then at least subject to proscribed limits consistent with the management objective for the management unit in question.

Quality Versus Quantity Hunting

Nelson (1969:88) proposed that "quality" hunting be defined as ". . . the chance to bag a trophy head, freedom from other hunters, and better-than-average hunter success ratios." Cheatum et al. (1969:124) elaborated, suggesting that quality hunting includes ". . . reasonable solitude, primitive surroundings, rugged exercise, suspense, excitement, and a chance to pit the skill of the hunter against the innate cunning of the prey, resulting in a hunt to remember with satisfaction whether or not a full legal bag is taken."

Some people demand a quality hunting experience. They are unwilling to tolerate heavy hunter densities and travel long distances to enjoy remote conditions. Unfortunately, areas possessing many of the attributes desired by hunters of such disposition may not have "quality" deer. As pointed out by Lang (1971:9), ". . . many of our poorer quality deer are found in our 'big woods' country where deer populations are usually high." Generally the more remote, semiwilderness areas do not lend themselves to a good hunter distribution and adequate harvest, primarily due to fewer miles of trails and roads for hunter access. As stated by Hendee et al. (1978:299), "The geographical distribution of wilderness use is very uneven—there are many people in a few places and only a few are in many others." Because of this, whitetail populations are apt to exceed carrying capacity, resulting in animals of smaller-than-normal body size with poor antler development.

As human-population pressures increase, wildlife managers have an increasingly difficult task in attempting to maintain quality hunting opportunities. Many state wildlife management areas, private lands and national wildlife refuges that permit deer hunting teem with deer hunters during the opening day of deer-hunting season. For the more accessible areas, state wildlife agencies are forced to set hunter and harvest quotas and manipulate season openings and lengths to protect deer populations from overharvest. Despite their remarkable reproductive capability and wariness, white-tailed deer populations can be adversely affected by insufficiently regulated hunting pressure.

Setting aside special "wilderness" areas and restricting the number of hunters by a permit system can allow for quality hunting experience near large human population centers. In some areas a series of short, two- to three-day, either-sex seasons with maximum hunter participation would make possible harvest levels compatible with the whitetail population's welfare and maintain or reinstitute "quality" aspects of the hunting experience. This management emphasis has been used for a number of years by the Tennessee Wildlife Resources Agency on the Tellico Wildlife Management Area.

Some hunters are more concerned with "quantity" hunting and are satisfied with harvesting any kind of deer. To these individuals, trophy-class animals are desirable but not essential, because they feel that any deer bagged is a trophy (Nelson 1969).

The overriding factor in quality versus quantity hunting is the tolerance of hunters to each other. Many hunters find nothing wrong with "rubbing elbows" in the woods, while others will not hunt under such circumstances. Hunters who are crowded tend to take "chance" shots at fleeing deer, or other high-risk shots that are apt only to cripple the animal and endanger other people. With buck-only hunting, high hunter-densities generally result in some mortality of adult and yearling females and yearling (antlerless) bucks.

Whether for quality or quantity, management of whitetail populations often is not consistent from state to state, province to province, or even from one region to the next in the same state or from one area to another in the same county. In some cases harvest regulations are derived from a bio-political base. When this happens, biological realities all too often are discarded and hunt regulations are developed that reflect local opinions or customs. Under such circumstances deer-population welfare and, ultimately, hunter success are likely to decline.

Hunting Methods

Traditionally, white-tailed deer have been hunted primarily with rifles and shotguns (*see* Chapter 44). But since the 1960s, archery hunting has become popular and has led to the enactment of special archery seasons that usually are liberal in length and generally precede the gun season. Bow-hunter success usually is substantially less than 19 percent, but may be as high as 25 percent (one deer harvested per four hunter-days) on exceptional areas where deer populations are high. An example is the Harris Neck National Wildlife Refuge, Georgia, where 123 man-days of bow hunting in 1982 resulted in the harvest of 30 deer.

Some states allow group or party hunting on wildlife management areas. On specific dates specified numbers of hunters are assigned designated areas in which to still-hunt or drive hunt. Certain days may be set aside for the use of dogs. Although relatively rare today, the "party permit" system is steeped in tradition, especially in the South.

The "quota" system is another type of man-

Factors of particular importance to adequate harvests of white-tailed deer are seasonable weather and sufficient access to huntable lands by a reasonable number of hunters. "Reasonable" in context refers to (1) enough hunters to cull the deer population to the desired management level, yet (2) not so many that loss of opportunity for achievement of the myriad satisfactions discourages hunter participation. *Photo by Daniel O. Todd; courtesy of the U. S. Forest Service.*

aged deer hunt. Quotas may be placed on the number of hunters allowed in an area or on the number of deer that may be harvested. In the first case, hunters usually are chosen at random from among applicants by computer drawings, and those chosen are assigned and restricted to specific areas or units. This harvest-management method assures a degree of hunt-quality by providing for better hunter distribution than might otherwise be possible. A harvest quota, on the other hand, is appropriate when a predetermined number of deer (usually does) needs to be harvested. After the appropriate number of does has been taken the hunting regulations may be altered (such as from either-sex to bucks-only) for the remainder of the season, or the hunt may be terminated altogether in that management unit. Such a system has worked well in Louisiana for a number of years.

Hunting Versus No Hunting

In recent decades there has been an increase in public concern over the ethical, moral, legal and biological validity of recreational hunting. During the 1970s there reportedly was a significant increase in the proportion of people in New Jersey who disapproved of deer hunting (Applegate 1975, *see also* Chapter 42). This trend is likely to continue, especially in states with large urban populations. Peterle (1967:376) stated that hunting ". . . will continue to represent a shrinking proportion of those people who seek recreation outdoors. The figures already available indicate not only a proportional decrease in hunting but a decrease significantly correlated with population growth." This trend is not surprising since sport hunting is based on cultural values rural in origin (Hendee 1969).

TRAUMA

Traumatic injuries are a major mortality factor in white-tailed deer populations. Legal hunting, poaching, predation, and highway accidents accounted for 98 percent of the white-tailed deer deaths in North Carolina in 1968 (Barick 1969). On Crab Orchard National Wildlife Refuge in Illinois, 86 percent of tagged whitetails succumbed to traumatic injuries via hunting, collisions with automobiles, predation by dogs, poaching, or miscellaneous accidents during the period 1962–1968 (Hawkins et al. 1970). In Missouri, trauma accounted for 72 percent of the nonhunting whitetail mortality between 1950 and 1958 (Murphy 1959). In West Virginia, 91 percent of the deer found dead had died from injuries (Ward 1948). Crippling from hunting-season wounds and poaching accounted for 1 and 13 percent of the deaths, respectively.

Crippling loss refers to deer shot by legal hunters but not retrieved, with death occurring a short period after wounding. Nettles et al. (1977) compiled crippling-loss estimates, which varied from "negligible" to 175 percent of legal harvests (Table 23). Downing (1972) showed

Table 23. Crippling loss of white-tailed deer, in percentage of legal harvest (Nettles et al. 1977).

Time period	Location	Crippling loss	Source
1940	Utah	42[a]	Costley (1948)
1940	Utah	25[b]	Costley (1948)
1972	Wisconsin	7[b]	Creed and Kubisiak (1973)
1956–1957	Wisconsin	175[a]	DeBoer (1957)
1957–1958	Wisconsin	44[c]	DeBoer (1958)
1965–1966	Kentucky	19[b]	Dechert (1968)
1959–1969	Georgia	19[b]	Downing (1972)
1974	Illinois	20[b]	Hardin and Roseberry (1975)
1967–1968	Ontario	5[b]	Holsworth (1973)
1951–1953	Minnesota	Negligible[b]	Krefting et al. (1955)
1939	Utah	18[b]	Robinette (1947)
1966	Illinois	33[b]	Roseberry et al. (1969)
1937	Wisconsin	29[a]	Sanders (1939)
1954–1960	Michigan	10–15[b]	Van Etten et al. (1965)
1955	Michigan	79[b]	Whitlock and Eberhardt (1956)

[a]Bucks only.
[b]Either-sex.
[c]One antlerless permit for each party of four hunters.

a crippling loss of 50 percent for archery, 26 percent for buckshot and 7 percent for shotgun slugs in a large enclosure in southern Georgia. In other studies, bowhunting accounted for a 10-percent crippling loss in Wisconsin (De-Boer 1958) and an 8.9-percent "wounding" incidence in Vermont (Garland 1972).

In contrast to mortal wounding, nonmortal wounds are observed much less often. Of the deer examined at checking stations on the Crab Orchard National Wildlife Refuge, only 3 percent had been wounded previously (Roseberry et al. 1969). Dechert (1968) observed few deer with old wounds in the hunter harvest at Fort Knox, Kentucky, and concluded that mortality due to crippling was 95 to 100 percent. After hunting seasons in Utah and Nevada, 0.5 to 1.3 percent of the mule deer were lame (Robinette 1947).

Burgin (1964) rated highway mortality as the "second deadliest deerslayer" in New York; roadkills were responsible for 17 percent of the annual mortality as compared with 46 percent by hunting. Deer/vehicle collisions in Wisconsin in 1967 equalled 18 percent of the total hunter harvest of that year (McCaffery 1973a), 19 percent of the 1969 harvest in Pennsylvania (U.S. Department of Interior 1970, Bellis and Graves 1971), and 33 percent of the 1963 harvest in Ohio (Nixon 1965a). Highway losses of deer are most pronounced in autumn and then in spring (Bellis and Graves 1971, Puglisi et al. 1974). In southern Michigan, 92 percent of the deer reported to have been struck by automobiles died of the traumatic injuries sustained (Allen and McCullough 1976).

Miscellaneous whitetail accidents such as falls, drowning, collisions with or entanglements in fences, and interlocked antlers of bucks during fighting occasionally occur, but are not known to cause significant losses.

Necropsy records in the southeastern United States indicated that the frequency of chronic debilitation of white-tailed deer due to injuries was low (Nettles et al. 1977). Previous injury was evident in 7.6 percent of the deer examined. There was no significant relationship between prior injury and the animals' sex, physical condition, or time of collection in relation to hunting season. However, the prevalence of injuries increased with age for both sexes of deer. Thirty percent of the injuries were related to gunshot or arrow wounds, but the cause of the remaining 70 percent was not determined. Most traumatic injuries due to gun-shot or vehicle-collision are apparently fatal, and those that are not result in very little chronic debilitation in the few deer that survive.

DISEASE

Many diseases affect white-tailed deer (Karstad 1964, 1969, Davidson et al. 1981). And although morbidity and mortality are the more obvious results, the effects of disease on whitetail behavior, reproductive success and susceptibility to other mortality factors are equally important. The presence and significance of diseases must be recognized as essential elements in deer management programs. The common causative agents of infectious deer diseases are viruses, bacteria and protozoa.

Viral Diseases

Epizootic hemorrhagic disease (EHD). This infectious, highly fatal disease is characterized by extensive hemorrhages in the host. Best-known and most spectacular among white-tailed deer diseases, EHD was first reported in 1955 in New Jersey, in which instance approximately 700 deer succumbed (Shope et al. 1955). Since then, outbreaks of varying magnitudes have occurred throughout North America (Trainer and Karstad 1970). In 1976, an epizootic hemorrhagic disease outbreak killed thousands of whitetails in Nebraska, Wyoming, Kansas and the Dakotas, as well as 4,000 antelope in Wyoming. Also in 1976, more than 1,000 deer died of the disease in New Jersey. Although white-tailed deer are the major targets, mule deer and pronghorn occasionally are affected. For example, a 1962 outbreak of epizootic hemorrhagic disease in Alberta caused the deaths of 440 whitetails, 18 mule deer and 13 pronghorn (Chalmers et al. 1964).

The relationship between the epizootic hemorrhagic and bluetongue viruses is uncertain. The diseases they produce, including epidemiology, signs and pathology, are very similar. Some researchers consider epizootic hemorrhagic disease and bluetongue to be distinct diseases caused by two different viruses (Hoff and Trainer 1978). Others consider them to be the same disease caused by different serotypes of the same virus (Hoff and Trainer 1981). In this review, both are considered as one malady.

With the exception of deer/vehicle collisons, accidental deaths are not known to be a significant cause of mortality in most whitetail populations. Whitetails are not accident-prone animals, but are susceptible to mishap during periods of stress (such as chase by predators), severe weather (such as deep snow and/or icy conditions) and unusual events (such as flooding or wildfire). *Top-left photo by Wilbert N. Savage. Top-right photo courtesy of the U.S. Forest Service. Bottom-left photo courtesy of the U.S. National Archives. Bottom-right photo courtesy of the North Dakota Game and Fish Department.*

Epizootic hemorrhagic disease usually occurs in late summer and early autumn. The major mode of transmission is through arthropod vectors, such as blood-sucking gnats (*Culicoides* spp.). Outbreaks usually result in large numbers of deer dying in a limited geographical area. However, in 1971, scattered outbreaks occurred throughout the entire southeastern United States (Prestwood et al. 1974).

Characteristic of EHD is its sudden onset. An infected deer initially loses its fear of man, then loses its appetite, grows progressively weaker, salivates excessively, and has elevated temperature (58 degrees Celsius:136 degrees Fahrenheit) and rapid heartbeat along with labored breathing. The animal finally becomes comatose.

Lesions of epizootic hemorrhagic disease are characterized by extensive hemorrhaging of many tissues and organs. Externally, the mucosa of the orbital and oral regions are hemorrhagic, and the feces, urine and saliva often are blood-tinged. No organ appears to be exempt from hemorrhage, but those involved most regularly are the heart, liver, spleen, lungs and intestinal tract. There usually is an increase in the amount of body fluids, which often are blood-tinged. Extensive hemorrhaging results from dysfunction of the blood-clotting mechanism, accompanied by degenerative changes in the blood-vessel walls.

Skin tumors. The most conspicuous disease of deer is skin tumors, often referred to as warts, papillomas, fibromas or fibrosarcomas. Skin tumors occur wherever deer live and can be found on almost any part of the body. Tumor causative agents can be transmitted by insects, contaminated vegetation or direct contact with other deer. The deer-tumor virus is specific to its host, and thus there are no human health threats. Pathogenesis and pathology of skin tumors in deer are presented by Cosgrove et al. (1981).

Arboviruses. Some of the better known arboviruses are eastern viral encephalitis, western viral encephalitis, St. Louis viral encephalitis, California viral encephalitis and vesicular stomatitis. They are carried and multiply within the bodies of arthropods, and infect vertebrate animals, including man.

Many of the more than 300 known arboviruses infect white-tailed deer, but the infections usually are subclinical and, except for vesicular stomatitis, have little documented impact on deer populations (Seymour and Yuill 1981). Deer have been studied as possible vectors and reservoirs (Trainer and Hanson 1969), and are useful as monitors of arbovirus activity (Bigler and McLean 1973).

Foot-and-mouth disease. In 1924, foot-and-mouth disease—an exotic disease in the United States—was introduced in cattle and swine in California. Deer became infected and a slaughter program was implemented in the Stanislaus National Forest, where more than 22,000 deer were killed. Of these, 2,214 had active or healed lesions of the disease. The deer slaughter, accompanied by an infected livestock elimination program, effectively eradicated the disease from the United States. However, if it should reoccur, the disease would have widespread implications for whitetail management.

Clinical lesions and signs of foot-and-mouth disease in deer resemble those in cattle. Included are stomatitis, blisters on the oral region and on the feet, and lameness (Hedger 1981).

Miscellaneous. Rabies, pseudorabies, malignant catarrhal fever, infectious bovine rhinotracheitis, parainfluenza and bovine virus diarrhea/mucosal disease have been reported in

Epizootic hemorrhagic disease (EHD) is an infectious, highly fatal, viral disease that can devastate local populations of white-tailed deer. There presently is no effective treatment. *Photo by Tim Hergenrader; courtesy of the North Carolina Wildlife Resources Commission.*

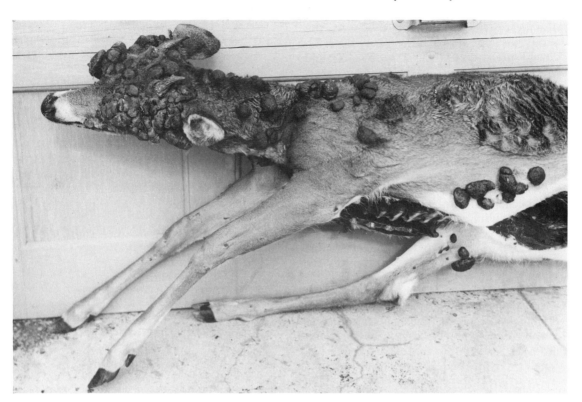

Skin tumors on whitetails are fairly common, but they have little detrimental effect on the general health of deer except in extreme instances when massive tumors impair normal functions, such as eating, sight or mobility. Under normal conditions, virus-caused tumors regress with time. *Photo by E. L. Cheatum.*

deer. They can be important to individual animals (Davidson et al. 1981) and their potential for epigrostis exists, but to date they have not been effective in regulating or influencing deer populations.

Bacterial and Protozoan Disease

Anthrax. Anthrax is an acute, infectious, febrile disease caused by *Bacillus anthracis*. Only a few parts of the world are free of anthrax (Choquette 1970), and it has caused significant die-offs of white-tailed deer in virtually all states in the United States and also in Canada (Van Ness 1981).

With respect to wildlife, anthrax is usually a soil-borne infection. Soil and water become contaminated by discharges or carcasses of diseased animals. Susceptible animals then contract the organism by feeding or drinking in these contaminated environments. Scavengers and predators also transmit the infection, as do blood-sucking insects. The latter, however, play a minor role.

Deer infected by anthrax appear dull and apathetic, lose coordination, stagger and become stiff-legged. Bloody discharges from the nostrils and anus are common signs, and the animals usually die within 48 hours of contracting the disease. Dead animals bloat rapidly. Common necropsy findings include dark, unclotted blood, enlarged black spleen (approximately three times normal size), diffuse hemorrhages, and blood-stained bladder and intestinal-tract contents.

Whenever anthrax is suspected, the discoverer should notify a health laboratory. No attempt should be made to move or examine the animal closely except by a qualified pathologist, inasmuch as humans are highly susceptible to this disease.

Anthrax is an excellent example of wildlife disease that has been controlled by the use of sanitary measures and vaccination. In the Wood Buffalo National Park of Canada, anthrax killed more than 1,000 bison in 1962, 1963, 1964 and 1967 (Choquette and Broughten 1981). During the outbreaks, 4,000 to 5,000 bison annually were rounded up by helicopters, branded and vaccinated.

Listeriosis. *Listeria monocytogenes* affects the central nervous system. The resulting brain damage often causes "circling" by deer and other wild ruminants, hence the common name—circling disease (Dijkstra 1981). Presumably listeriosis is contracted by deer from sheep. Ectoparasites and other arthropods are suspected vectors. The organism also has been isolated in normal deer. Therefore, the real significance of listeriosis is undetermined.

Foot rot. Necrobacillosis, or foot rot, is caused by *Spherophorus necrophorus*. Epizootics are apt to occur during dry weather in late summer and early autumn, when deer crowd around waterholes or crowd in feeding areas (Wobeser et al. 1975). Fawns are more susceptible than mature deer. The organism persists in soil for long periods of time and has been detected in pastures one year after the pastures were used by infected animals.

Infected animals exhibit high fever, go off feed, develop ulcerated lesions in the mouth and on the feet, and salivate excessively. Even after lesions on the feet have healed, a deer will limp or sometimes run on three feet. Oral abscesses result in a so-called "bottle-jawed" appearance of deer.

Brucellosis. Brucellosis, a common disease of domestic livestock, is caused by *Brucella abortus*. Although rare or nonexistent in white-tailed deer (Witter 1981), it is found in other wild ruminants, such as bison, elk, moose and caribou, in which animals it causes reproductive problems and mortality.

Tuberculosis. Tuberculosis is caused by the acid-fast bacterium *Mycobacterium tuberculosis*. It is detected most often in captive deer and those that are crowded or closely associated with man or livestock (Towar et al. 1965). The possibility of deer serving as reservoirs for tuberculosis in humans emphasizes the need for constant surveillance of diseases in captive and free-ranging wild animals, especially whitetails because of their prevalence and wide distribution.

Actinomycosis. This infectious disease, often called "lumpy jaw," is caused by the anaerobic bacterium *Actinomyces bovis*. It is widespread in nature and is inoculated into the oral region of deer with contaminated feed, such as poor-quality hay. Infection usually is established in the mandible, and abscesses cause obvious swellings that alter the animal's feeding habits. Bone is destroyed and replaced by granular material. The organism may spread

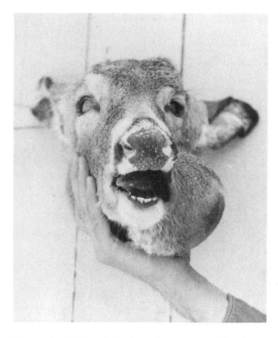

"Lumpy jaw" is an infectious disease caused by the anaerobic bacterium *Actinomyces bovis*. Whitetails usually contract the disease by consuming contaminated grain; death results if bacteria infect the animal's brain. *Photo by R. Hine.*

to other parts of the animal and cause direct mortality if the brain is infected. Lesions are common in aged and artificially fed deer.

Salmonellosis. Bacteria of the genus *Salmonella* affect a wide range of wildlife, including whitetails, causing serious and often fatal infections, particularly in newborn animals. The causative organism is acquired by ingestion, and then spreads via the bloodstream. Bacteria are transmitted through the feces to other hosts. In Texas this disease caused a high mortality in newborn fawns and was responsible for keeping a deer population in a stable condition (Robinson 1981).

Anaplasmosis. Anaplasmosis, from the non-contagious rickettsial parasite *Anaplasma marginale,* is an important infectious disease of livestock, but it is not considered a problem for deer, although it is known to occur commonly in many wild ruminants, including the white-tailed deer (Kuttler 1981). This disease is usually transmitted mechanically, by biting insects, and deer provide a source for arthropod transmission to other deer and livestock. Serologic tests for anaplasmosis are unreliable, and the specific role of deer in the natural history of anaplasmosis is not documented completely.

Theileriasis. This disease, caused by the hemoprotozoan organism *Theileria cervi* and transmitted by ticks, is widespread in southwestern states. In Texas more than 57 percent of the white-tailed deer carry this parasite. Infectious rates are highest where deer density is high and nutritional level low. Clinical disease and mortality usually occur in deer that have experienced environmental stress, such as may be caused by severe weather and food shortage (Kingston 1981).

Sarcocystis. This common protozoan is found in the striated muscle of a wide variety of wild mammals and birds. Most adult deer are infested with sarcocytes, but alone, the sarcocytes do not cause any overt sign of illness (Kingston 1981).

Miscellaneous. Diseases that are important to humans and livestock and which have been detected in deer but whose population-significance for deer remains undetermined include tularemia (*Franciscella tularensis*), pasteurellosis (*Pasteurella multocida*), pseudotuberculosis (*Pasteurella pseudotuberculosis* and *Yersinia enterocolitica*), erysipelas (*Erysipelothrix rhusiopathiae*), leptospirosis (*Leptospira serotypes*), Rocky Mountain spotted fever (*Rickettsia rickettsi*), Q fever (*Coxiella burneti*), blackleg (*Clostridium chauvoei*), malignant edema (*Clostridium septicum*) and Johne's disease (*Mycobacterium paratuberculosis*). Excellent summaries of the current status of knowledge regarding these maladies are provided by Davidson et al. (1981) and Davis et al. (1970).

PARASITES

Under most present-day circumstances, with natural predation on white-tailed deer virtually nil except in a few localities (*see* Chapter 8) and the screwworm essentially eradicated from the United States, it is increasingly unrealistic to contemplate scientific management of deer without taking into account the parasite fauna that cohabit environments in which the host lives. The Walker and Becklund (1970) checklist of the internal and external parasites of deer in the United States and Canada provides an excellent starting point.

Although the total parasite fauna of white-tailed deer includes the protozoa, helminths and arthropods, only the helminths produce significant accounts of disease. A checklist of 35 helminth parasites of white-tailed deer in the southeastern United States is presented in Table 24. This list essentially includes most of the trematodes, cestodes and nematodes reported from deer in North America. Also included are *Dicrocoelium dendriticum*, described from white-tailed deer in New York (Mapes and Baker 1950), and *Haemonchus similis*—from deer in Florida (Dikmans and Lucker 1935). *Cysticerus krabbei, C. lyncis, Echinococcus granulosus, Skrjabinema parva, Ostertagia circumcincta, Oesophagostomum columbianum, Chabertia ovina, Dictyocaulus filaria, Protostrongylus coburni* and *P. rufescens* have been recovered from white-tailed deer in other regions of the United States and Canada (Walker and Becklund 1970).

Meticulous dissection is imperative for adequate parasitologic examination of deer carcasses. The most pathogenic forms of nematodes often are microscopic or near-microscopic and thus are often easily overlooked, whereas the larger, most spectacular-appearing helminths frequently are inconsequential to the host or to the general health of the deer population.

Poor health of deer and mortality associated with parasitic worms usually are accompanied by overpopulation and subsequent malnutrition. Several nematodes that are capable primary pathogens include the adult and larval forms of meningeal worms *Parelaphostrongylus tenuis* (Prestwood 1970), muscle worms *P. andersoni* (Prestwood 1972), cattle lungworms *Dictyocaulus viviparus* (Prestwood et al. 1971), and large stomach worms *Haemonchus contortus* (Prestwood and Kellogg 1971).

The presence of parasites in white-tailed deer is now being used as an aid in management. For example, stomach worms in particular are host-density dependent; the number of individual species and the total number of species encountered vary with deer density. This knowledge about abomasal parasites (Prestwood et al. 1973) is used as indicators of habitat carrying capacity and the nutritional status and feeding habits of white-tailed deer (Eve and Kellogg 1977).

White-tailed deer are normal hosts for the meningeal worm *Parelaphostrongylus tenuis* and the large American fluke *Fascioloides magna*. Meningeal worms have been associated with fatal neurological disease in sheep (Kennedy et al. 1952, Nielsen and Aftosmis 1964, Anderson and Strelive 1966), and the large

Table 24. Checklist of helminth parasites in white-tailed deer of the southeastern United States.

Location in host	Helminth parasite	
	Scientific name	Common name
Subcutaneous	*Onchocerca cervipedis*	Footworm
Musculature	*Parelaphostrongylus andersoni*	Muscleworm
Brain	*P. tenuis*	Meningeal worm
Circulatory	*Heterobilharzia americana*	Blood fluke
	Elaeophora schneideri	Arterial worm
Lungs	*Dictyocaulus viviparus*	Large lungworm
	Protostrongylus alpenae	Deer lungworm
Abdominal cavity	*Cysticercus tenuicollis*	Bladder worm
	Setaria yehi	Abdominal worm
Liver	*Fascioloides magna*	Liver fluke
Esophagus, tongue	*Gongylonema pulchrum*	Gullet worm
Rumen	*G. verrucosum*	Gullet worm
	Paramphistomum liorchis	Rumen fluke
Abomasum	*Haemonchus contortus*	Large stomach worm
	Ostertagia dikmansi	Medium stomach worm
	O. mossi	Medium stomach worm
	O. ostertagi	Medium stomach worm
	Skrjabinagia sp.	Medium stomach worm
	S. odocoilei	Medium stomach worm
	Trichostrongylus askivali	Small stomach worm
	T. axei	Small stomach worm
	T. dosteri	Small stomach worm
	Obeliscoides cuniculi	Rabbit stomach worm
Small intestine	*Moniezia benedeni*	Sheep tapeworm
	M. expansa	Sheep tapeworm
	Thysanosoma actinioides	Fringed tapeworm
	Capillaria bovis	Capillary worm
	Cooperia punctata	Cooper's worm
	Monodontus louisianensis	Deer hookworm
	Nematodirus odocoilei	Thread-neck worm
	Strongyloides sp.	Threadworm
	Trichostrongylus longispicularis	Small intestinal worm
Cecum	*Trichuris* sp.	Whipworm
Large intestine	*Eucyathostomum webbi*	Colon worm
	Oesophagostomum venulosum	Nodular worm

Liver flukes positioned on the inside of the right hind leg of an autopsied whitetail (left). The deer showed no evidence of malnutrition, and the cause of death was determined to be liver-fluke infestation. Approximately 75 flukes were in the lobes of the deer's liver, and those displayed above came from about one-fifth of that organ. Right: deer-liver lesions caused by *Fascioloides magna*. *Left photo by Harold Jordahl; courtesy of the Wisconsin Department of Natural Resources. Right photo by Ian McTaggert Cowan.*

American fluke causes a fatal liver condition in sheep and significant liver condemnation in cattle (Soulsby 1968, Pursglove et al. 1977). Although white-tailed deer host other species of helminths that are transmittable to sheep or cattle, they have not been shown to be significant reservoirs (Prestwood et al. 1973, 1975, Pursglove et al. 1976, Hayes and Prestwood 1969).

Blood flukes and hydatid tapeworms are the only helminths of white-tailed deer that have implications for human health. The blood fluke, however, is far more prevalent in raccoons than in white-tailed deer (Byrd et al. 1967). The presence of hydatid cysts, caused by hydatid tapeworms (*Echinococcus granulosis*), serves only as an indicator that dogs or related wild canidae are definitive hosts in the area (Soulsby 1968). There are no helminth parasites of white-tailed deer that render the deer meat unsafe for handling or human consumption.

As deer populations increase and habitat dwindles, the significance of parasitism as a regulatory mechanism for deer populations becomes increasingly apparent. Although there will be localized die-offs, deer will continue to thrive regardless of the presence of indigenous parasitic protozoa, helminths or arthropods.

The major disease threat to the white-tailed deer of North America is in the form of infectious agents from foreign shores (Hayes 1981). The most significant parasites of white-tailed deer today are helminths, but protozoa and arthropods may soon replace the worms as a matter of importance and concern. East Coast Fever and "Nagana," for example, may be capable of infecting deer from coast to coast. Either of these diseases could be established on this continent, thus ". . . creating a problem of enormous economic significance" (Mare 1976:72) with a devastating impact on deer management and the livestock industry.

POLLUTANTS

Radionuclides

Radioactive contamination usually comes from the manufacture and processing of nuclear fuel, reactor operation, disposal of radioactive wastes and fallout from nuclear explosions. By far, fallout is the major source of contamination (Comar 1965). Columbian black-tailed deer (Book et al. 1972), Rocky Mountain

mule deer (Whicker et al. 1968) and white-tailed deer (Jenkins and Fendley 1968) have been shown to accumulate radionuclides from fallout. The effect on deer of a radionuclide is determined by its half-life, the extent to which it enters parts of plants eaten by deer, its retention in body tissues, and the sensitivity of those tissues. Iodine-131, strontium-90 and cesium-137 present the greatest hazard to wildlife because they are readily assimilated into body tissues. Because deer tend to accumulate detectable concentrations of radionuclides, they can be sensitive indicators of these chemicals in the environment.

Iodine-131. Because iodine-131 has an eight-day half-life it is likely to produce the greatest radiation exposure immediately after a nuclear detonation (Comar 1965). Most of it is ingested by the deer as fallout that has reached the surface of plants. That which reaches the soil normally decays before it can be absorbed into growing plants.

Deer can accumulate significant amounts of iodine-131 in the thyroid gland—up to 10,000 times the amount normally present in the diet (Whicker et al. 1966). Thyroid doses received during the 1962–1963 nuclear tests conducted by Russia, France and the United States were 20 rads in Colorado mule deer, 2.5 rads in New York and Maryland white-tailed deer, and 0.8 rad in Alaskan reindeer (Hanson et al. 1963). Thyroid doses received by Colorado mule deer after the 1964–1965 Chinese nuclear tests ranged from 12 to 254 millirads (Whicker et al. 1966).

In studies of sheep, Marks and Bustad (1963) found that histological damage became apparent only after the animals received a dose of 30,000 millirads of iodine-131 per week for five years. Whicker et al. (1966) reported that, if deer thyroids have similar sensitivities, iodine-131 fallout levels would have to increase 2,700 times over the 1964–1965 levels (12 to 254 millirads) and be maintained for several years before histological damage would occur.

Studies by Whicker et al. (1966) and Dahl et al. (1967) showed that young deer contained higher concentrations of iodine-131 than did old deer, apparently because thyroid function was related closely to growth and metabolism. Fetal thyroids had very high iodine-131 concentrations, which increased exponentially with fetal age. Near-term fetuses had concentrations 10 times that of the dam.

Strontium-90. Strontium-90 has a half-life of about 28 years. Deer ingest it through forage contaminated by direct fallout deposition or absorption from the soil. Strontium-90 behaves much like calcium in biological systems; major accumulation occurs during bone formation and in younger age classes of deer. During antler development, strontium-90 can be translocated from the skeleton to the antler (Schultz 1965).

Levels of strontium-90 concentration in animals usually are closely associated with levels of fallout from nuclear tests. However, strontium-90 levels can become extremely high through biomagnification as well. In the lower Coastal Plains of the southeastern United States, the concentration in deer was 12,000 picocuries per kilogram net weight (Jenkins and Fendley 1971). This concentration was three times as high as those measured in surrounding areas that had received the same amount of fallout.

So far as is known, strontium-90 does not occur in concentrations sufficient to affect the reproduction or mortality of deer.

Cesium-137. Cesium-137 has a half-life of 30 years and is chemically similar to potassium. It is ingested by deer feeding on vegetation contaminated by direct fallout deposition. Skeletal muscle normally accumulates the highest concentration. Although stored in animal soft tissue, cesium-137 has a rapid turnover time of one or two months. Concentrations vary, therefore, with seasonal and annual fallout rates from nuclear tests (U.S. Energy Research and Development Administration 1976). Concentrations also vary with differences in individual diet, amount of forage consumed, elevation and climate (Whicker et al. 1965, Book et al. 1972). Highest concentrations occur in deer during the winter months, apparently because of differences between winter and summer diets. Concentrations on the upper Coastal Plain in South Carolina, for instance, were three times as high in winter, when deer fed on lichens and perennial plants, than in summer, when deer fed on annual plants (Rabon 1968).

In Florida, deer muscle averaged 45,000 picocuries per kilogram of cesium-137–12 times greater than found in other southeastern states (Jenkins and Fendley 1971). The average level in deer food was 5,850 picocuries per kilogram, but the average level in deer tissue was 28,000. Thus there was a concentration factor of almost 5 from the producer to the consumer. Lichens apparently were the only food with enough cesium-137 to produce these high con-

centrations in deer tissue, although Johnson and Nayfield (1970) found consumption of mushrooms could also produce high concentrations. Cesium-137 levels in mushrooms averaged 11,000 picocuries per kilogram net weight and were as high as 29,000. Levels in surrounding vegetation averaged only 143 picocuries per kilogram.

Pesticide Residues

Hydrocarbon insecticides, such as DDT and dieldrin, can accumulate in animal tissues, particularly in body fat. Weight loss of deer subsequent to dosage accumulation may cause a release of the pesticide held in the body fat and induce mortality. Deer gradually rid themselves of these pesticides once they have been removed from the diet (Walker et al. 1965). Pesticides are unlikely to be fatal to deer at low levels (Barrier et al. 1970), but sublethal doses may impair reproduction, reduce resistance to disease or stress, and alter behavior (Stickel 1968).

DDT residues found in the body fat of deer have in some instances been measured at levels in excess of 7 parts per million, the allowable limit established by the U.S. Food and Drug Administration for domestic livestock. One or two months after a forested area was sprayed with 1.12 kilograms per hectare (1 pound per acre) of DDT, the fat of 25 mule deer contained an average of 8.86 parts per million of DDT. Eleven to 12 months later, the fat averaged 0.17 part per million (Pillmore and Finley 1963). There were no immediate gross effects on the deer.

In Montana, DDT residues of up to 24 parts per million were found in the body fat of mule deer one month after a spraying, and 19 parts per million were found after two months (Pillmore 1961). Apparently, deer accumulated residues during the first 30 days and did not continue accumulation during the second 30 days. One year later residues were being eliminated from the fat. Pillmore and Finley (1963) reported that 500 parts per million of DDT were acutely toxic to mule deer when administered as a single intrarumen dose. But when fed 15.2 grams (0.54 ounce) of DDT over a period of 67 days, these deer showed no visible symptoms of poisoning.

Pillmore (1961) and Finley and Pillmore (1963) found that DDT was converted to DDD in animal tissues, and stored in the adrenals where it caused atrophy of the adrenal cortex. Because the adrenal cortex is important in an animal's resistance to stress, pesticides may influence deer survival during times of stress. Research on this relationship is needed.

The toxicity of dieldrin is much greater than that of DDT in mammals (O'Brien 1967), but residues of dieldrin are quite low in deer. In a laboratory test in which does ingested 25 parts per million of dieldrin daily, their reproductive rate dropped from 1.8 fawns per doe the first season to 1.1 fawns per doe the second season (Korschgen and Murphy 1967). Fawns from these does had a lower birth weight, grew less rapidly and showed higher mortality than did fawns from does fed 0 or 5 parts per million of dieldrin daily. The most common causes of fawn mortality were white-muscle disease and malnutrition. Residue tests of fawns born dead indicated that dieldrin crossed the placenta to the fetus.

Barber and Nagy (1971) tested 18 pesticides for inhibitory activity toward mule deer rumen bacteria and found three that lowered the bacterial growth rate: (1) Mema RM, containing mercury; (2) Bordeaux mixture, containing copper; and (3) 2,4-D, a synthetic auxin herbicide. Chlorinated organic insecticides and the organophosphates were inhibitory only at concentrations much higher than those likely to be found in rumen of deer eating treated foliage. Schwartz and Nagy (1974) investigated the effects of Mema RM, Bordeaux mixture, toxaphene, DDT, dieldrin and Sevin on digestion of alfalfa hay by deer-rumen microorganisms. All of the pesticides caused a significant decrease in the digestion of dry matter at 1,000 parts per million; Bordeaux mixture caused a significant decrease at 100 parts per million. However, for most of the compounds to reach a concentration of 1,000 parts per million in the rumen, intake would have to be well over LD_{50} (Schwartz and Nagy 1974).

Insecticides sprayed on agricultural crops and orchards may be ingested by deer, but at levels well below the permissible limits established by the U.S. Food and Drug Administration for domestic livestock (Greenwood et al. 1967, Jewell 1966, Barrier et al. 1970).

Snowmobile Activity

Snowmobiles can have both adverse and beneficial effects on white-tailed deer. Adverse effects include predation by dogs traveling on snowmobile trails (Doherty 1971) and harassment of deer by snowmobiles (Wettersten 1971, Heath 1974, Shoesmith and Koonz 1977). A less-obvious adverse effect of snowmobiles is the disruption of normal home-range and other activity patterns (Kopischke 1972, Dorrance et al. 1975). The extent to which snowmobiles adversely affect deer movements and activity usually is proportional to the degree of snowmobile use. In southern Minnesota, deer were unaffected by light snowmobile use (as evaluated by the number of snowmobile tracks in an area). But on areas with heavy snowmobile traffic, deer became scarce (Kopischke 1972). When vegetative cover was available in areas of heavy use, deer sought thick cover and remained motionless even when snowmobiles came within 30.5 meters (100 feet). Dorrance et al. (1975) found a significant negative correlation between the number of snowmobiles and the number of deer along a trail. Light snowmobile traffic caused displacement of whitetails from areas adjacent to trails, but the deer returned to their original areas less than 24 hours after the traffic ceased. Home-range size, movement, and distance from deer to the nearest trail increased with increasing snowmobile activity. Researchers have demonstrated that white-tailed deer can be very sensitive to disturbance, to the extent of moving their home ranges to completely different locations (Kopischke 1972, Hood and Inglis 1974, Dorrance et al. 1975). Forced movement caused by snowmobile activity could be detrimental to the whitetail's energy budget and possibly increase mortality during severe winters. White-tailed deer behavior is adapted to enhance the conservation of energy in the winter and any disturbance that alters the deer's activity patterns can potentially depress productivity (Moen 1978).

There is some evidence, however, that deer grow accustomed to snowmobile use (Young and Boyce 1971, Bollinger et al. 1973, Richens and Lavigne 1978). Judicious use of snowmobiles may even be beneficial by creating trails in deer wintering areas to improve deer mobility and feeding conditions. In some instances, snowmobile trails could reduce the energy expenditure of moving deer and improve overwinter deer survival (Doan 1970, Richens and Lavigne 1978). Snowmobile trails also could be used to induce deer movement to better feeding areas or to unexploited sites in a winter area (Richens and Lavigne 1978).

Persistent snowmobile traffic in a critical wintering area can force whitetails to other locations that may not provide sufficient food or cover for the season's duration. On the other hand, light and patterned snowmobile use in or near wintering areas can provide deer with relatively unstressful avenues of travel to additional food supplies. *Photo by Tom Carbone; courtesy of the Maine Department of Inland Fisheries and Wildlife.*

REPRODUCTIVE INHIBITORS

In areas where hunting is prohibited, such as national parks, and where deer have increased beyond the carrying capacity of their habitat, there often is a need to limit reproduction. Several techniques have been tried: (1) oral feeding of estrogen or progestin compounds to does before or during the breeding season to inhibit ovulation, prevent implantation or terminate pregnancy; (2) insertion of estrogen or progestin compounds beneath the skin with Silastaic[R] tube-type implants to prevent ovulation in the female or sperm production in the male; (3) injections of an estrogen intramuscularly into pregnant does to stimulate abortion; and (4) insertion of mechanical contraceptive devices into the vagina to prevent intromission and ejaculation by the male or to prevent sperm survival.

Reproductive inhibitors are not yet registered with the U.S. Environmental Protection Agency for controlling big game populations, and their future status is uncertain.

Oral Treatments

Harder and Peterle (1974) tested diethylstilbestrol (DES), a synthetic estrogen compound, at a concentration of 4.4 grams per kilogram (0.07 ounce per pound) of shelled corn and molasses. When fed *ad libitum* before and during the breeding season to a free-ranging but enclosed herd, this ration did not reduce significantly the number of fetuses per doe. Significant reduction occurred in the fetal rate when tablets containing 25 milligrams of diethylstilbestrol were inserted into apple quarters and fed to does. However, this treatment did not reduce fetal numbers sufficiently to represent a practical method of population control.

Microencapsulated diethylstilbestrol (17-percent modified gelatin: 83-percent diethylstilbestrol) was formulated and prepared at a concentration of 1,000 milligrams per 908 grams of a 16-percent protein dairy ration (Matschke 1977a). When does were fed this formulation every 17 days postcoitum, pregnancy was interrupted after the first feeding in four out of five does, in two out of four does after the second feeding, and in none after the third feeding.

Roughton (1979) tested melengestrol acetate (MGA), a progestin, on penned deer of both sexes. When fed an estimated daily oral dosage of 0.6 to 1.0 milligram before and during the breeding season, 1 of 18 treated does became pregnant. When fed to the does at two- and three-day intervals, melengestrol acetate did not significantly affect the number of pregnancies or the date of conception (Matschke and Roughton personal files). In additional tests, Matschke (1977*b*) fed progestins to does at different levels and frequencies and concluded that melengestrol acetate was effective only when fed daily.

Subcutaneous Implants

Pregnancies were reduced significantly when silastic tube-type implants containing 0, 50, 100 or 150 milligrams of melengestrol acetate or 75 milligrams of diethylstilbestrol were inserted under the foreleg of does (Bell and Peterle 1975). Pregnancies also were reduced when silastic tube-type implants containing 75 milligrams of diethylstilbestrol or 150 milligrams of synthetic progestin, coded as DRC-6246, were inserted in the base of the ear in deer (Matschke 1977*c*). The computed life of the implants was 12 months for diethylstilbestrol and 52 months for DRC-6246. Ovulation was suppressed in all treated deer.

Silastic implants containing 75 milligrams of diethylstilbestrol were implanted into male deer before the breeding season (Matschke 1976). During the breeding season, the diethylstilbestrol effects were measured on the testes, seminal vesicles, Cowpers glands and prostrates. Testes weights were significantly less than those of control animals. Spermatogenesis in the treated animals ranged from almost complete cessation to limited sperm production. Secretory cells were affected in the seminal vesicles and Cowpers and prostrate glands. Antler growth also was suppressed.

An implant containing 150 milligrams of synthetic progestin was placed into free-ranging female deer (Matschke 1980). For the next three breeding seasons, does were examined for pregnancy. Ovulation was suppressed for two breeding seasons, but by the third season the

progestin had been depleted. That infertility can be induced for no longer than two breeding seasons at a time makes this implant impractical for managing free-ranging deer populations, because of the costs of capturing and handling the deer. Nevertheless, these implants may have application in confined populations, where periodic retreatment is possible.

Intramuscular Injections

Harder and Peterle (1974) reduced pregnancy rates among free-ranging does by stimulating abortion with intramuscular injections of 250 milligrams of diethylstilbestrol. As pregnancy progressed, it became more difficult to terminate.

Mechanical Devices

Intravaginal mechanical devices, either a homemade or a commercial device (ABCD[R]), did not effectively reduce conception among does in tests conducted by Matschke (1976).

WEATHER AND HABITAT FACTORS

Weather

Weather influences the movement, productivity and mortality rate of white-tailed deer by affecting the growth and seasonal availability of food and by placing an energy stress on animals. The effects vary among climatic regions and seasons.

Snowbelt regions. In the North, snow occasionally causes high deer mortality (B. W. Day 1964). In Ontario, deer mobility dropped sharply when snow depths increased to 25 to 35 centimeters (9.8 to 13.7 inches) (Hepburn 1959). Hosley (1956) indicated snow depths of about 50 centimeters (19.7 inches) or more made travel difficult for white-tailed deer. Although Kelsall (1969) noted that 40 centimeters (15.7 inches) of snow was a critical depth, he suggested that 24 centimeters (9.4 inches) of snow was sufficient to initiate movement of deer to lower ranges.

Verme (1968) observed that hard crusts allowed deer to roam freely, but weak crusts broke repeatedly, causing injury and excessive tiring. Energy resources are drained when deer are forced to traverse on snow (Wallmo and Gill 1971), and the energy output required for deer to feed in deep snow often exceeds that supplied by the food eaten (Kelsall 1969). In northern Lower Michigan, Ozoga and Gysel (1972) found that deer increased their use of protective cover during periods of low temperature even when snow was not deep.

In the central Adirondack Mountains, whitetails tended to avoid north-facing slopes and hardwood types that had low cover value (Webb 1948). Protection from cold was more important than availability of food in the animals' selection of cover. For example, spruce flats and swamp types were utilized heavily even though little food was available. On Michigan's upper peninsula, white-tailed deer selected areas of heavy conifers that provided food and protection from storms in preference to open hardwood stands with few or no conifers (Bart-

lett 1950). During severe midwinter weather in northern New York, deer moved from a clear-cut area where food was plentiful to an uncut area because of the shelter it provided (Krull 1964).

Cook and Hamilton (1942) noticed that during winter, deer in central New York tended to concentrate in areas that, along with other desirable attributes, were protected from wind. Severinghaus and Seamans watched 30 deer in Vermont move from a slope that was being swept by a cold west wind to another slope that was protected from this wind (*see* Severinghaus and Cheatum 1956). Based on studies of deer trapping success on Crab Orchard National Wildlife Refuge near Carbondale, Illinois, it appeared that deer capture may be enhanced by trapping on relatively cold, dry days with a high barometric pressure (Hawkins and Klimstra 1970*b, see also* Chapter 39).

A severe browse line is evidence of an unusually severe and/or prolonged winter, an insufficient harvest the previous hunting season, a high overwintering mortality and poor condition of survivors. *Photo courtesy of the Maine Department of Inland Fisheries and Wildlife.*

Southern and southeastern United States. For short periods, snow may decrease deer movement in the southern Appalachian Mountains by concentrating the animals in sheltered coves and hollows located at lower altitudes (Ruff 1938, Schilling 1938). Both Ruff (1938) and Downing et al. (1969) noticed that deer in the high mountains of North Carolina would move during late March and early April to lower altitudes when early green growth was available as food. As the green-up advanced into higher altitudes, the deer again followed it upward.

Rainfall mainly affects the quality and quantity of vegetation. In Texas, asymptotic levels of deer numbers were related to mean annual precipitation and its influence on vegetative growth (Teer et al. 1965). Studying the activity patterns of whitetails in southern Texas, Michael (1970) noticed that high winds caused deer to seek shelter. He reported that activity patterns over a two-year period indicated that:
1. the two main peaks of feeding were 6 a.m. and 6 p.m.;
2. deer were more active throughout the day in winter than in summer;
3. deer were not adversely affected by temperatures over 37.8 degrees Celsius (100 degrees Fahrenheit) or by temperatures below 0 degrees Celsius (32 degrees Fahrenheit);
4. high winds caused deer to take shelter; and
5. inclement weather was associated with a decrease in feeding.

Movements of 10 white-tailed deer fawns were monitored on the Welder Refuge in southern Texas during 1967 and 1968 (Samuel and Glazener 1970). Seven fawns born in lowland areas traveled to upland areas immediately before or during Hurricane Beulah in September 1967; three moved more than 1,140 meters (1,250 yards). This observed behavior was in contrast to reduced travel—400 meters (440 yards)—by three fawns born in the uplands. Short et al. (1969a) considered the scarcity and small size of deer in some southern upland forests to be the result of low-quality diet and climatic stress.

During a trapping program in the mountains of North Carolina, Barick (1952) found that most deer were caught during periods of low or falling barometric pressure. This tended to support observations that deer feed more heavily just before low-pressure storms.

Localized flooding disrupts deer movements and may cause death. In northeastern Louisiana, which lies entirely within the Mississippi River Delta, many deer drowned as a result of spring flooding (Brunett 1959). Other whitetails migrated to nearby upland areas but returned to bottomlands when floodwater receded. During high water in the Florida Everglades, deer moved to high ground where they were forced to consume low-quality foods, and as a result many died of malnutrition and starvation (Loveless 1959b, *see* Chapter 42).

Food Production and Availability

The quantity, availability, variety and palatability of foods exert regulatory pressure on whitetail population levels regardless of geographic location. When food is scarce, as in overbrowsed winter deer yards or large forested areas covered by dense canopies, deer may starve or become so weakened that reproduction declines. Deer die-offs and population decreases due to food scarcity have been reported in Vermont (Foote 1945, Seamans 1946, B. W. Day 1964, Marsh 1976), Wisconsin (Swift 1946), Michigan (Bartlett 1950), Ontario (Bartlett 1955), New York (Severinghaus 1956), Texas (Hahn and Taylor 1950), Florida (Loveless 1959b)— and in popular magazine articles by Allen (1956), Crichton (1956) and East (1963).

Starvation can occur in regions south of the snowbelt. When forage was depleted on experimental areas in the Edwards Plateau of central Texas, followed by several days of continuously cold weather, 116 white-tailed deer died (Hahn and Taylor 1950). During a critical winter period in the Florida Everglades, approximately 30 percent of the deer population was lost to starvation and associated diseases (Loveless 1959b).

Habitat Changes and Losses

Several examples illustrate the extent to which habitat is being lost to other land uses, thus placing a continuing restriction on whitetail populations. In New Jersey, 116 square kilometers (44.8 square miles), or approximately 9.1 percent of the deer range, was lost to developments from 1958 to 1972 (Burke et al. 1973). Carroll (1961) predicted that Pennsylvania would lose 300,000 hectares (741,300 acres:2,059 square miles) of forest land from 1961 to 1975. In Louisiana, approximately 400,000 hectares (988,400 acres:2,746 square

Urban and suburban expansion in response to human population growth eliminates virtually hundreds of square miles of whitetail habitat annually in North America. Combined with the exurbanization trend of recent decades, unplanned residential and commercial developments have a number of indirect adverse influences on whitetails and their management, including placing a greater productivity burden on remaining farmland and fostering increased intolerance of deer damage and/or hunting. *Photo by Hugo Bryan; courtesy of the U. S. Soil Conservation Service.*

miles) of bottomland hardwood forests were cleared for agricultural production between 1962 and 1967 (Newsom 1969). Some of these lands supported 25 deer per square kilometer (65 deer per square mile). In Florida, urban and highway development and agriculture reduced forest land by 506,000 hectares (1,250,326 acres:3,473 square miles) from 1947 to 1957 (Harlow 1959). In Texas the demand is for agricultural lands to produce more food and fiber, and deer often are the losers (Teer 1963).

Competition with Other Land Uses

As long as whitetail population levels are low, there is little direct competition with other land uses. In some areas, crop depredation is a sure sign of too many deer (*see* Chapter 38). In other areas it can indicate that the crops are the preferred food of a few deer. Deer may damage row crops, such as soybeans, as well as citrus orchards and natural forest reproduction. In Pennsylvania, studies showed that where deer populations were in balance with the range, only 5 to 10 percent of the stems were browsed heavily. However, in areas with heavy populations of deer, 25 to 75 percent of the stems were browsed heavily, making it difficult to practice good forestry (Farrand 1961). Buck-only hunting and closing private lands to hunting often lead to excessive deer populations and subsequent habitat deterioration.

Cattle compete with deer seasonally for certain kinds of food (Lay 1957*b*), and continued heavy woodland use by cattle may force whitetails to abandon habitats where this occurs. Although improved pastures may attract deer, competition between livestock and deer generally is minimal on such areas. During winter months, hogs compete with deer for mast, especially acorns. However, through persistent rooting of the forest floor hogs can open up areas that will produce the lush forage sought by whitetails in the spring.

Some livestock owners fear parasite transmission from deer to cattle and sheep. This is rarely a serious problem however, except when deer populations are high. Deer evidently are the host species for the giant liver fluke (*Fascioloides magna*), which will critically affect cattle and sheep, and the meningeal worm (*Pneumostrongylus tenuis*), which affects sheep but not cattle (Davidson et al. 1981).

Chapter 8

PREDATORS AND PREDATION

L. David Mech
Wildlife Research Biologist
U.S. Fish and Wildlife Service
Patuxent Wildlife Research Center
Laurel, Maryland

The effect of predation on white-tailed deer populations has been difficult to measure. Nevertheless, most public champions of the whitetail long ago concluded that every deer killed by a predator was wasted and certainly resulted in one less deer for the hunter. Such thinking was part of the public's general attitude that predators were significant competitors with humans—an attitude that persists (Nelson 1971, Turner and Caron 1973).

Perhaps it is the whitetail's big brown eyes, its portrayal as "Bambi," or its secretive and nonaggressive demeanor that causes people to be upset when they learn of a deer's demise to a predator. Many people automatically agree with the wildlife laws of several states that allow the open shooting of domestic dogs chasing deer, for example, despite little evidence that dogs actually harm deer populations. It was similar thinking that fostered the use of bounties (Nelson 1971) on predators and helped eradicate the wolf from Wisconsin (Keener 1970) and most of Michigan (Douglass 1970).

This common "wisdom"—most prevalent in the past among woodsmen and other frontier dwellers, but also given serious expression in government predator control programs—fails to consider the concepts of compensatory mortality and compensatory reproduction (Errington 1967, Mech 1970). If a predator kills a whitetail that was starving to death anyway, does the predator actually have an ill effect on the population? If predation increases the productivity or survival of the remaining members of a deer population, is it really harmful?

As the discipline of wildlife management began exerting its influence (Leopold 1933), the effect of predators was examined in more detail by scientists. Results were mixed. However, the public was fascinated by the findings of several studies that seemed to indicate that predation really did not harm prey populations (Allen 1954). Nature was kept in balance by predators, the public believed. When carnivores killed whitetails, they were helping to prevent the deer from overpopulating. A backlash against predator control developed.

The truth about predation is still being sorted out by wildlife biologists, for predator-prey systems are extremely diverse. There really is no reason to believe that the relationships that characterize one predator-prey system must hold true for all (Mech 1970), or even for the same system under different conditions (Mech 1966, cf. Peterson and Page 1983). Two facts becoming clearer, however, are that (1) predator/prey ratios in any system may vary considerably and (2) the predator/prey ratio is crucial in determining the degree to which predators may limit prey (Mech 1970, Connolly 1978, Keith 1983).

Furthermore, other factors, such as weather and human hunting harvest, may greatly influence prey density and thereby alter predator/prey ratios, thus changing the effect of the predators. A dramatic instance of weather-triggered wolf limitation of white-tailed deer came to light in northeastern Minnesota in the early 1970s (Mech and Karns 1977). This case, plus similar events in other predator-prey sys-

In the late 1920s, N. H. Kent, a trapper and prospector for the Flin Flon Mining Company of northern Manitoba, allegedly photographed this scene of wolves bringing down a white-tailed deer. Kent reportedly was running his trapline along a chain of lakes when he heard the wolves running the deer. The chase brought the animals out onto a small, frozen, snow-covered lake right in front of the trapper, who claimed that he was able to take the photograph from the concealment of a bush. The photo was sent by George E. Purvis of the Canadian Department of Interior (Ottawa) to *Forest and Stream* magazine, in which it was published in the March 1929 issue, under the title "The Kill." Five months later, the photo ran in *Rod and Gun*, captioned as "A Wilderness Tragedy in Northern Canada." Biologists who have analyzed the photo recently are not convinced of its authenticity, and believe that it may have been staged using frozen and/or mounted animals. Note, for example, that the deer is standing on the snow surface, but the wolves have sunk in. In any case, the photograph appeared in print at a time when a lack of understanding of ecological relationships caused an aroused public to view the situation not as a biological happenstance, but rather as an indictment of predators in general and wolves in particular. *Photo courtesy of the U.S. National Archives.*

tems (Peterson and Page 1983, Gasaway et al. 1983) have begun to swing the pendulum of thinking in wildlife biology back toward its original position. Hopefully, the pendulum will not reach the other extreme again, for that position is clearly unwarranted. Just as hopefully, the general public will be able to follow the swing and realize that refinements are as necessary in wildlife management as in any other science.

THE WHITETAIL AS PREY

White-tailed deer are preyed upon by a wide variety of carnivores—a situation easily deduced from many of the species' characteristics. The extensive distribution of whitetails,

for example, brings them in contact with both northern and southern carnivores. In the eastern half of its historic range, the whitetail was the only plentiful large herbivore, at least since about 1880, when elk had been extirpated there (Boyd 1978, Bryant and Maser 1982). Even a density of perhaps 4 deer per square kilometer (11 per square mile) and an annual turnover of 30 percent would have provided sufficient biomass to help support many predators. The polygamous nature of the whitetail allows the species to lose a large proportion of its total male members without significant damage to its biotic potential. Also, the disparate size of newborn fawns and mature bucks exposes deer to predation from carnivores of many sizes.

In the northern part of its range, the whitetail's need to contend with snow and low temperatures adds significantly to its vulnerability. Hindered mobility in deep snow (46 centimeters [18 inches] or more), reduced food intake, increased exposure to cold (and resulting weight loss) each winter may kill some individuals outright or, under less extreme conditions, greatly dispose them to predation (Figure 46). In addition, since fawns are *in utero* throughout this energetically stressful period, those born following severe winters have a low viability (Verme 1962, 1973, 1977). During the autumn and early winter rut, bucks also are in poor condition, having exhausted themselves in searching for estrus does and in fighting competitors. They then enter the winter at a disadvantage and have little chance to improve until early summer.

Therefore, it is not surprising that under some conditions just about every type of meat-eater in the deer's range feeds on deer, including foxes, coyotes, domestic dogs, bobcats, bears, mountain lions, wolves, wolverines, golden eagles, bald eagles and even ravens (*see* Hosley 1956, Hunter and Yeager 1956, Cowan 1956, Connolly 1981). To these the fisher and lynx almost certainly can be added, at least as incidental predators on fawns.

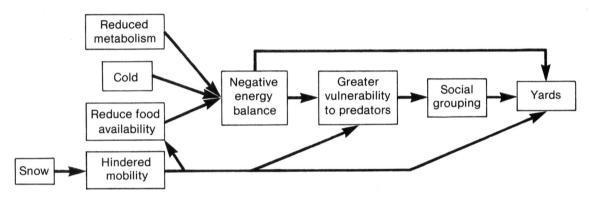

Figure 46. Conceptual model of factors influencing winter yarding by white-tailed deer in northern Minnesota (from Nelson and Mech 1981).

Scavengers such as eagles, ravens and jays often benefit considerably from deer killed by various predators. During winter, in fact, such kills probably form the bulk of the diet of scavengers. *Photo by J. E. Swedberg.*

For several of the deer-eating carnivores, venison forms only a small part of their total diet, although it may be important to some at certain times of the year (Ozoga et al. 1982*b*). To such carnivores, including foxes and fishers, a fawn may represent a bonanza compared with their usual smaller fare. At the other extreme, even a large buck may constitute a small meal for any single member of a large pack of wolves. In between are other carnivores, especially coyotes and bobcats, that depend to varying degrees on venison as a source of overall diet. Furthermore all deer predators also will feed on deer as carrion resulting from starvation, hunting, accidents, roadkills, drowning or other causes. Thus the whitetail is an important food source for many carnivores.

The importance of carnivores to whitetail numbers, however, is highly variable. Only the dog, bobcat, coyote, bear, mountain lion and wolf conceivably could kill enough deer to influence a whitetail population to any significant degree. Of these larger carnivores, only some mountain lions and wolves depend strictly on deer.

Domestic Dogs

The effects of domestic dogs on white-tailed deer populations are widely disputed. High deer losses have been attributed to uncontrolled dogs in the Southeast (Bowers 1953, Ward 1954, Giles 1960, Morrison 1968). In Pennsylvania, dogs kill an estimated 500 to 1,000 deer annually (Forbes et al. 1971). In Tennessee, more than 50 percent of 26 released whitetails were lost either directly or indirectly because of dogs. Nichols and Whitehead (in press) concluded that dog harassment could significantly affect the success or failure of deer restoration in Tennessee. Dogs are most perilous to young fawns, pregnant does immediately prior to fawning, and undernourished whitetails. In Arkansas, heavy parasitism increased the vulnerability of deer to dogs (Segelquist et al. 1969).

In contrast, several studies indicated that dogs are not a serious menace to deer. Trained deer hounds caught or killed radio-equipped deer in only a few instances involving debilitated deer in mountainous terrain (Marchinton et al. 1971, Corbett et al. 1972, Sweeney et al.

A white-tailed deer that starved to death and its carcass, fed on by foxes. One of the problems in assessing the effects of predation on deer populations is the fact that, whereas deer succumbing to old age, disease, malnutrition or accidental death may lie undisturbed for hours or days, predator-killed carcasses are devoured, hidden, scattered or scavenged and soon vanish, making discovery and mortality identification very difficult (Robinson 1952, Knowles 1976). *Photo courtesy of the New York Department of Environmental Conservation.*

The domestic dog is the most widespread deer predator at present. Dogs of most breeds, whether feral or pets, will chase and attempt to kill deer. Dogs usually eat very little of their kills. Their effects on whitetail populations vary. In the South, for example, dogs often seem to be ineffective deer predators. However in the North, during late winter, when deer are weak or snow hinders their movement, dogs frequently kill many in yards or concentration areas. *Photo by Bob Harrington; courtesy of the Michigan Department of Natural Resources.*

1971). Deliberate dog harassment of deer in Missouri (Progulske and Baskett 1958) and Virginia (Gavitt et al. 1975) did not result in capture or mortality. Radio-telemetry studies of feral dogs in Alabama indicated that deer were not a prey species (Scott and Causey 1973). Further evidence of the variable impact of dogs on whitetails is indicated by discussions in the regional chapters of this book.

Bobcats

It is well established that bobcats kill deer, including adults, especially in winter (Newsom 1930, Marston 1942, Smith 1945, Dill 1947). However, the consensus of biologists studying bobcat predation on deer is that such predation usually is not intensive enough to affect deer numbers seriously (Hosley 1956, Connolly 1978). One experiment that included killing 188 coyotes and 120 bobcats showed at least a temporary increase in the number of whitetail fawns in the removal area compared with a nonremoval area (Beasom 1974). However, the relative effects of removal of bobcats versus coyotes were not sorted out, and the period for which the difference in number of fawns persisted between the two areas was not measured.

Because the bobcat's main prey usually consists of rabbits, hares, and other small mammals and birds, these cats rarely affect deer populations significantly. Their deer-killing habits, however, have been well-documented (Marston 1942). They tend to hunt deer at night, generally by stalking and catching them in their beds. A bobcat will jump on a deer's back and bite the prey's throat, puncturing the windpipe. Of 34 whitetails found killed by bobcats one winter in Maine, 1 was a fawn, 8 were yearlings and 25 were at least two years old (Marston 1942); 20 were bucks. *Photo by H. P. Wagner; courtesy of the U.S. Forest Service.*

Coyotes

Although coyotes in most areas feed on a wide variety of items, deer usually is included during at least some seasons. Furthermore, in areas such as Texas, coyotes apparently kill many fawns during summer. Studies employing removal of coyotes or radio-telemetry of whitetail fawns have indicated that coyotes caused up to 80 percent of fawn mortality and that fawn/doe ratios ran up to 40 percent higher in areas where coyotes, and in some cases coyotes and bobcats, were removed (Cook et al. 1971, Beasom 1974, Daniel 1976). Similar studies involving mule and black-tailed deer fawns and coyotes produced similar results (Brown 1961, McMichael 1970, Trainer 1975, Ebert 1976, Robinette et al. 1977). Some of these investigations have assessed only the short-term effects of coyotes on fawn cohorts. Because large numbers of fawns die of many causes (Verme 1962, 1963, 1977), coyote predation on fawns could be largely compensatory (Errington 1967). However, at least some studies have demonstrated coyote-removal effects lasting as long as a year (Beasom 1974, Austin et al. 1977).

Because of the extreme variability in coyote/deer ratios throughout the overlapping range of these species, as well as over time, the effect of coyote predation must vary considerably. The great diversity of—and fluctuation in abundance of—coyote foods compounds this variation in its effect on deer numbers. These factors preclude any strong generalizations except that, apparently under certain circumstances, coyotes can influence deer numbers.

Moreover, the possible additive effect of coyote predation on deer populations also must be considered. Thus, even though coyote density may not be high enough in a particular area by itself to affect deer numbers seriously, when added to the noncompensatory mortality caused by bears, bobcats, domestic dogs, weather, accidents, drowning, etc., coyote predation may have a significant impact.

A wildlife biologist examines the remains of a whitetail doe killed by coyotes near Meridian, Texas. Usually when a deer carcass is found, biologists attempt to determine the cause of death to learn how various mortality factors influence a deer population. Deer killed by coyotes frequently have canine tooth-puncture wounds at the junction of the head and neck and in the nasopharyngeal region (Connolly 1981). Nielson (1975) and Bowns (1976) showed that coyotes usually kill deer by collapsing the trachea, causing suffocation. Under most circumstances, healthy adult whitetails can elude or outrun coyotes. *Photo by Guy E. Connolly; courtesy of the U. S. Fish and Wildlife Service.*

Bears

There are a few records of black bears killing whitetails (Peterson 1940, Ozoga and Verme 1982*b*, L. L. Rogers personal communication:1983), but no studies have determined how important such predation is to deer numbers. Analysis of thousands of black bear scats in Tennessee and Minnesota produced very little evidence of whitetail remains (M. Pelton personal communication:1983, L. L. Rogers personal communication:1983). However, under some conditions black bears have caused losses as high as 68 percent of elk calves in an area (Schlegel 1976) and 34 percent of young moose calves (Franzmann et al. 1980). Ballard et al. (1981) reported a kill of 43 percent of the moose calves in another area by brown bears. Thus it is apparent that bears can be significant predators of ungulates, especially calves and fawns. It is not unreasonable then to suggest that, because black bears and whitetails are sympatric throughout much of their ranges, the black bear might be an important predator on deer fawns under some conditions.

Mountain Lions

Although there is little information about mountain lion predation on white-tailed deer, the ranges of thriving populations of the two species overlap in the western United States and southwestern Canada.

In Idaho, mountain lions annually consumed, on the average, an amount of mule deer and elk equal to 13 to 20 deer each from 1964 through 1968 (Hornocker 1970). Depending on the relative densities of mountain lions and deer, and the amount of buffering by other prey species in an area, lion predation could exert a significant effect on whitetails. This seems especially possible if mountain lions preyed very heavily on fawns in summer, as coyotes sometimes do. In the Idaho study, lion/deer ratios varied from 1:135 to 1:201, yet deer still increased, indicating that lions were not limiting deer numbers at those ratios.

Mountain lions frequently cover a partly eaten deer carcass with leaves and other debris, and return to feed again later. This behavior also has been reported for bobcats (Connolly 1981). Lions may consume 9.1–13.6 kilograms (20–30 pounds) during the first day of feeding after a deer kill; their daily consumptive average is approximately 1.8–2.7 kilograms (4–6 pounds). Between feedings, a lion will spend a great deal of time resting and sleeping in the immediate vicinity of a carcass (Hornocker 1970). *Photo by Leonard Lee Rue III.*

Mountain lions usually ambush the deer they kill, and dispatch prey by biting the throat or the nape of the neck (Robinette et al. 1959). A study in Idaho indicated that a lion would kill an amount of prey equal to 13–20 deer per year (Hornocker 1970). *Photo by Leonard Lee Rue III.*

Wolves

Along with the mountain lion, the wolf was the other primary predator on deer throughout the deer's historic range. Even today wolves and whitetails share range in northern Wisconsin, Michigan, Minnesota and much of southern Canada. Because the exact historic densities of these animals will be unknown forever (*see* Chapter 2), the degree to which wolves affected deer numbers must remain uncertain. However, in much of the eastern United States whitetails would have been the wolf's main prey, just as they are today in the remaining overlap of wolf and deer ranges (Mech 1970).

Wolves kill whitetails year round, and they constitute the primary natural mortality factor on deer populations in coterminus range (Stenlund 1955, Pimlott et al. 1969, Hoskinson and Mech 1976, Mech and Karns 1977, Nelson and Mech 1981, Fritts and Mech 1981). Thus it would seem that the wolf is in an excellent position to affect deer populations. In actuality, however, the degree to which wolves limit whitetail populations still is not clear. Perhaps this is because of the extreme influence that humans have had on both species.

Currently the most accurate generalization one can make about wolf/deer interaction is that it is highly variable. Under most conditions today, wolves do not seem to be able to limit a deer population seriously. But in some circumstances they can actually exterminate local whitetail populations (Mech and Karns 1977, Huot et al. 1978). One must know the precise nature of wolf predation and deer defenses to be able to understand each varying situation.

For a rough approximation of the constraints on wolf/deer relations, it is useful to look at some general population figures. Maximum wolf populations in deer areas usually reach densities of about one wolf per 26 square kilometers (10 square miles) (Pimlott 1967, Mech 1970, 1973). The highest natural wolf density known was one wolf per 11 square kilometers (4.2 square miles), and this population crashed soon after reaching that density (Peterson and Page 1983). Wolves tend to consume an average biomass amounting to about 20 adult-sized deer per wolf per year (Mech and Frenzel 1971a, Kolenosky 1972). But considering that they also eat other prey, such as beaver and moose, a more realistic average annual kill rate is 15 adult deer per wolf (Mech 1971).

To supply this number of deer each year in a 26-square-kilometer (10-square-mile) area, a density of about 1.16 adult deer per square kilometer (3.0 per square mile) would be necessary, assuming an even sex ratio and a mean productivity of about 1.0 fawn per doe. This also means that wolves, at a density of 1 per 26 square kilometers (10 square miles), could consume enough deer to limit the population if the deer density were less than about 1.16 adults per square kilometer (3.0 per square mile). With a lower density of wolves, a higher density of deer, or both, deer numbers would not be expected to be limited by the wolves unless other deer mortality factors became important. Wolf densities generally are much lower than one per 26 square kilometers (10 square miles), and deer densities—even in the northern part of their range, where wolves still are found—usually are higher than 1.16 adults per square kilometer (3.0 per square mile). Thus one can readily see why wolves rarely seem to limit deer numbers (Pimlott 1967, Mech 1970, 1971).

Those figures, however, obscure the limiting effect wolves possibly could have on whitetails by preying heavily on fawns. If wolves ate nothing but fawns during the summer, especially during the fawns' first month—when many would be required to support a wolf (perhaps up to 15), they easily could control a deer population, even at higher densities than 1.16 adult deer per square kilometer (3.0 per square mile).

Furthermore it is reasonable to ask why a full-time deer predator such as the wolf cannot necessarily limit deer numbers when a part-time predator, such as the coyote, can. The answer is that coyotes, which weigh about half what wolves weigh, can achieve densities perhaps five times as high as the usual wolf densities. Also, coyote numbers can be subsidized by a multitude of alternate types of prey, whereas the wolf depends much more exclusively on deer, especially in winter when there are few alternative food sources. Thus, if the wolf overexploits its primary food supply, its own population must decline (Mech 1977a, Mech and Karns 1977), which tends to relieve pressure on deer numbers.

The forementioned high deer/wolf ratio may explain why wolves kill the classes of deer they do. It appears that in summer wolves prey mostly on fawns, and in winter they kill primarily fawns and deer more than five years of age (Pimlott et al. 1969, Mech and Frenzel 1971a, Mech and Karns 1977, Fritts and Mech

1981). They also tend to take a disproportionate number of deer that have some sort of abnormality (Mech and Frenzel 1971*a*), and winter fawns that have low fat supplies (Seal et al. 1978*a*). In addition they often tend to prey disproportionately on adult bucks (Pimlott et al. 1969, Mech and Frenzel 1971*a*, Kolenosky 1972, Mech and Karns 1977). Perhaps the fact that a high proportion of bucks more than five years of age are afflicted with arthritis of the hind "knee" joint contributes to the vulnerability of this class (Wobeser and Runge 1975).

Watching wolves hunting deer it is easy to see how they end up killing certain classes that probably have relatively low survivability (Mech 1966, 1970, Rutter and Pimlott 1968, Pimlott et al. 1969, Mech and Frenzel 1971*a*, Mech and Korb 1978). Wolves are hunting whenever they travel. When they sense a deer they try to move closer to it without spooking it. However, most deer are quite alert. As soon as they detect approaching wolves, they flee. The wolves then make a half-hearted chase or are left far behind. Most chases last only a few minutes in time and less than about 1,100 meters (1,200 yards) in distance, although a most unusual pursuit lasted more than two hours and covered at least 20.8 kilometers (12.9 miles) (Mech and Korb 1978).

Examination of the remains of wolf-killed deer has indicated that wolves generally kill fawns, deer more than five years old, or those with a physical anomaly, such as arthritis, dental abnormalities, broken limbs or low blood fat. *Photo by L. David Mech.*

Antipredator Adaptations and Strategies

It appears that deer depend considerably on their alertness to allow them to detect threats and flee before a predator can get close enough to catch them. Even if a whitetail does not sense a predator until it is close, the deer's fleetness—56 kilometers-per-hour (35 miles-per-hour) (Cheatum and Severinghaus 1956)— usually enables it to outdistance wolves quickly.

Deep snow hinders deer. But it also hinders wolves, often more so, because wolves run at a shallower angle and thus meet more resistance than do deer, which tend to spring up out of the snow. On the other hand, wolves gain about twice as much support from snow as do deer (Foromozov 1946, Kelsall 1969, Mech and Frenzel 1971*a*). Sometimes in the early winter or late spring a crust develops that is thick enough to support wolves but too thin to support deer, and this gives the former a temporary advantage (Mech and Frenzel 1971*a*) However, these conditions are rare. More often, if the crust is thick enough to hold a running wolf it will also be strong enough to support a running deer and, thus, of no particular advantage to either.

During summer, a deer closely pursued by wolves often will head for open water, where it will try to swim away (Pimlott et al. 1969, Mech 1970). Pursuing wolves may try to swim after it. However if the water is too deep to allow the wolves a foothold on the bottom, they usually are ineffective in trying to attack the deer—although there is at least one record of a swimming wolf killing a swimming deer in freezing water (Nelson and Mech 1984). There is some indication that deer living on islands, peninsulas and along lakeshores have a higher survivability than those that do not (Hoskinson and Mech 1976).

During winter as well, deer being chased by wolves will head for bodies of water, most of which usually are frozen. Sometimes, however, an escaping deer plunges through thin ice, particularly atop rapids in rivers. The wolves may keep the deer in the icy water until it succumbs, then drag it out. Other times they may continue to harass the deer for hours on end by swimming out to it or by trying to intercept it if it tries to leave the water (Pimlott et al. 1969). In an unusual case in northeastern Minnesota, one of my research associates found a standing deer frozen into the ice of a shallow lake. Wolves had been feeding on the erect carcass. An explanation may be that the wolves had chased the deer into the shallows while the lake was still open, or held only thin ice, and then kept it out there alive while the water froze, locking the deer into it.

Deer pursued by wolves may not distinguish ice from open water, for they will run out onto ice even though their chances of eluding wolves there are very poor. On snow-covered ice, wolves apparently can run faster—or at least have greater mobility—than deer do, for a high proportion of wolf-killed deer fall victim on the ice (Mech and Frenzel 1971*a*).

Also, deer may run to ice only as a last resort, when capture by wolves is imminent. In summer the tactic of moving to bodies of water normally allows deer to escape; in winter, whether the water is frozen or not, it usually seals their fate.

Several other behavioral adaptations help white-tailed deer to contend with predation, including skulking by fawns, protective behavior by does, solitary living by does during summer and herding in winter. Because fawns are so vulnerable during their first weeks of life, most deer predators—including wolves (Nelson and Mech 1981, Fritts and Mech 1981)—tend to concentrate their efforts on the

very young. Thus it seems highly adaptive for a fawn to freeze in place when left by its dam. Fawns' speckled coats usually blend well with the forest floor so that unless they move they are not easily seen. Furthermore, fawns less than a week old seem to be scentless, and dogs have been observed passing right by them (Severinghaus and Cheatum 1956) and even jumping over them without detecting them (W. Darby personal communication:1983). In addition, a doe—which usually remains near her fawn during its first few weeks—shows complex distraction behavior (Severinghaus and Cheatum 1956) that tends to lead predators away from the vulnerable fawn. In the Adirondack Mountains of New York State I once observed a partial albino fawn hiding motionless while the doe assumed a display much like the "broken wing" act of some birds, trying to lure me toward her and away from her fawn.

Presumably whitetail does are also quite protective of their fawns if a predator tries to attack. One reported observation suggesting this involved aerial observation of a black bear carrying a fawn in its mouth; a doe was following the bear, apparently unwilling to give up her fawn (L. L. Rogers personal communication:1983). Furthermore I once watched

In winter, wolves often kill white-tailed deer on frozen lakes, to which the deer run as a last resort. A pack of five wolves can easily consume a deer in a day. They usually eat all of its flesh and viscera, leaving only the rumen contents, large bones and some of the hide, but if hard-pressed for food they will devour even the bones and hide. When deer are plentiful or easier to catch, these predators may leave the head and lower legs intact, eating only the larger muscle masses and viscera. After the wolves have finished the carcass, they immediately begin to hunt again. Scavengers—such as ravens, which follow wolf packs as they hunt—then take over and pick up any bits of food the wolves have left. Meanwhile, the wolves may hunt for many more days before finding another deer they can catch and kill. *Photo by L. David Mech.*

from an airplane as a whitetail defended itself very aggressively against a lone female wolf, suggesting that does might defend their fawns just as vigorously.

The following is an edited excerpt from my field notes of 5 January 1971, concerning the aforementioned incident: "Then the deer stopped, and the wolf caught up to within about 25 feet. Suddenly the deer rushed the wolf and hit her with both front feet. This bowled over the wolf. The wolf arose again immediately, and the deer charged again and chased the wolf about 25 feet. Three times the deer charged the wolf. When charging, twice the deer jumped right over the wolf and kicked its hind feet back upon landing with its front. Then the deer and wolf reached a stand-off with each circling around and moving slowly and cautiously. Finally at 10:54 a.m., the wolf curled up and rested while the deer stood facing her about 25 feet away. We continued circling until 11:28 and each animal remained in the same position. At 12:10 p.m., when we returned, they were still in the same position. We left again right away. At 3:55 p.m. we returned and found both animals gone. There was no sign of a kill."

Rutter and Pimlott (1968) found tracks recording an incident in which a single wolf brought a whitetail to bay three times. Each time the deer was able to stand off the wolf.

A whitetail's hooves are sharp and can inflict extensive damage on a wolf that does not manage to stay clear of them. A rabid member of a wolfpack in Algonquin Park, Ontario, was killed by a deer and sustained the following damage: ". . . the lower left canine tooth was broken, the left cheek was slit open and part of the facial bones crushed" (Frijlink 1977:136).

As a whitetail fawn grows, it becomes increasingly agile and fleet, and by three weeks of age is almost impossible for a human to catch (Severinghaus and Cheatum 1956). No doubt coyotes, mountain lions and wolves have little trouble catching fawns, but these carnivores must first find them. Whitetail does with young fawns tend to restrict their movements considerably, space themselves out and become solitary (Nelson and Mech 1981, Ozoga et al. 1982b). This behavior reduces the chance of fawns being discovered by scanning and wandering predators and helps ensure that if a predator locates one deer it does not necessarily find them all (Nelson and Mech 1981). Considering the vulnerability of fawns in their

first several weeks it is highly adaptive of whitetails to force carnivores to spend most of their time searching, thus minimizing the amount of time they have for killing.

The opposite strategy is adaptive in winter, however. By that time surviving fawns are much less vulnerable, yet the population as a whole tends toward a negative energy balance (Moen 1968a, Silver et al. 1969, Seal et al. 1972). Although no particular age class is supervulnerable, as the summer fawns were, the vulnerability of all deer is increased. Under these conditions there is safety in numbers because of (1) greater mobility in deep snow, (2) increased vigilance, (3) improved ability to confuse attackers, (4) exposure of more-vulnerable older individuals (hence improved survival chances for younger members), (5) greater ratio of deer to predators (thus decreasing relative risk to each individual deer), and (6) increased time for feeding and ruminating because of decreased vigilance time (Nelson and Mech 1981). To gain these advantages by herding, however, some whitetails must travel to concentration areas or winter yards in northern latitudes, which may require autumn migrations of 40 kilometers (25 miles) or more (Hoskinson and Mech 1976, Nelson and Mech 1981).

Despite all the adaptive features of deer biology and behavior, whitetail populations in the northern part of the species' range may succumb to combinations of extreme adverse conditions, including wolf predation. Where this has been documented, a series of record-breaking severe winters combined with a high wolf density and relatively poor deer habitat proved too much for local whitetail populations (Huot et al. 1978). In northeastern Minnesota, for example, deer were decimated in an area of about 3,108 square kilometers (1,200 square miles) of their poorest habitat from 1968 to 1974 (Mech and Karns 1977). Even in this extreme case, however, it is notable that along the periphery of the depletion zone, deer populations survived while the wolf population continued to decline (Nelson and Mech 1981). In early 1983, whitetails still survive there at continued low but relatively stable numbers (Nelson and Mech unpublished). Most of the deer that survived the decline inhabited buffer zones between wolf-pack territories (Mech 1977b, Nelson and Mech 1981). In such zones wolves from adjacent packs tend to minimize their hunting, probably to avoid contact with their neighbors—contact that usually leads to altercations and mortality (Mech 1977*a*). Presumably, as the wolf population continues to decline, whitetails surviving in these reservoirs eventually will repopulate the area, probably whenever a series of mild winters prevails.

Conclusion

Although many carnivores prey upon whitetailed deer, including some for which deer is their primary prey, whitetails persist and thrive almost everywhere throughout their historic range and even beyond (Halls 1978). Today, extirpation of deer by its natural predators, while possible for relatively short periods and local areas, is the great exception. Control by predators no doubt holds some whitetail populations below the carrying capacity of their habitats. Nevertheless, the white-tailed deer can continue to prevail as a species because it is superbly adapted for contending with all its natural predators.

If, however, whitetail hunting becomes more intensive and attempts are made to maximize hunter harvest in some areas, increasing pressure probably will develop for controlling deer predators in those areas. Currently, wolves are controlled around important deer yards in Ontario, and wolves, dogs and coyotes are removed from the vicinity of such yards in Quebec (Connolly 1978).

Nevertheless, because of the complex nature of deer/predator relations, the wildlife biologist or manager must thoroughly analyze any particular deer population for which predator control is being considered. A logical scheme for determining when or where control should be applied is shown in Figure 47.

Even if an appropriate analysis results in an indication that predators should be controlled, an important philosophical consideration also must be confronted. In some regions, an increasing proportion of the public is questioning who has the greater right to a prey animal, a natural predator or a human hunter. Fortunately whitetails are common enough over large regions so that there should be vast areas where deer can be managed intensively for hunters and other areas where predators can be allowed to prey on deer without control.

In fact, such whitetail predators as bobcats, coyotes, mountain lions and wolves may have so much commercial and/or aesthetic value that they can compete with the value of deer. Bobcats usually are not abundant in most deer areas,

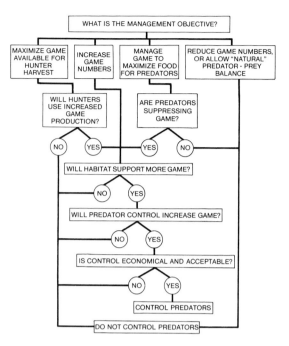

Figure 47. Proposed logic for the use of predator control in ungulate management (from Connolly 1978).

and wolves are considered by the U.S. Fish and Wildlife Service to be threatened in Minnesota and endangered elsewhere in the contiguous 48 United States. Thus, there is reason to minimize or eliminate control of these species in designated sanctuaries, or in areas they may be colonizing, even if that means fewer deer for awhile.

A more palatable approach to improving whitetail populations without predator control—in northern areas at least—might be to compensate for severe weather by artificially feeding deer during later winter (Nelson and Mech 1981). This would be a viable option only if the deer were in extremely low numbers or if hunting pressure in a particular area was so intense that each deer was at a premium. Artificial feeding could improve the deer's condition during late winter and presumably minimize their vulnerability to predators. As the population rebuilt, artificial feeding could be terminated gradually.

Through the millennia, white-tailed deer have never been without the threat and influence of predation. Not only have they survived, but they even extended their northern distribution. The species' future, therefore, seems well-assured despite the multitude of predators—man included—that contribute to the annual harvest of its numbers.

II. Whitetail Population Management

Chapter 9

POPULATION DYNAMICS AND ANALYSIS

Don W. Hayne
Technical Director (Retired)
Southeastern Cooperative Fish and Game Statistics Project
North Carolina State University
Raleigh, North Carolina

Population dynamics include all the elements of change by which a particular population exists. Even when maintaining a relatively constant level, a population changes continuously—animals grow old and are replaced by younger members.

This chapter addresses three elements of population dynamics: mortality, reproduction and movement—and three types of population description that reflect population dynamics: population size, sex ratio and age distribution. It also addresses the combining of rates of mortality and reproduction, as well as the use of models.

Practical suggestions for interpreting deer population data are presented here with as few assumptions as possible. For a description of some refined methods of population analysis and their difficulties, the reader is referred to Eberhardt (1969) and Caughley (1977). Ordinarily the refined methods require many assumptions, demand much detailed information, and are more suitable for research than for applied management.

As used here, the terms "herd" and "population" are synonymous and refer to an interacting group of animals living on a specific area. In some way these animals are more similar to each other than to members of any other population. It is impossible to set up a more precise definition of a population because its characteristics change regionally and sometimes locally, as described in Chapter 6.

This account is focused mainly on the dynamics of the female portion of a white-tailed deer population—a common procedure in the study of any vertebrate population whose members are polygamous and do not select permanent mates. It is much easier to analyze the female portion and then calculate what happens to males than it is to consider both sexes simultaneously. It is assumed that there are enough males to service every available female. If the number of males falls below some critical level, the dynamics of the population's female segment is affected. From a management standpoint, until such a level is reached, the number of males need not be recognized as a factor in population dynamics, important though this number may be to hunters.

At birth, each whitetail joins a "cohort"— a group of animals of like age and sex. A cohort is the basic unit of population dynamics. As time passes a cohort is subject to mortality only, never gaining members, until finally it is eroded completely. At any given time a population is composed of a number of cohorts— one for each sex and year of birth still represented.

ELEMENTS OF POPULATION DYNAMICS

Mortality

If mortality remains out of approximate balance with reproduction for long, the number of deer will either decrease or increase. Because the mortality rate can be manipulated by varying hunting pressure, the regulation of hunting has been a principal tool for managing whitetail population size. Wildlife biologists and managers must understand how mortality functions in order to recognize the status and potential of a deer population, to set management policy for it, and to be able to explain this policy to the public. For the white-tailed deer, however, it is difficult to measure with regularity any mortality except the number of deer harvested legally.

Mortality sometimes is recorded as numbers dying, but usually it is computed as a proportion or percentage: the number of deer dying during the year divided by the total number beginning the year (multiplied by 100 and expressed as a percentage). It is more convenient in calculations to use survival rate (the complement of mortality rate): the number of deer surviving a given year divided by the number that began that year. Mortality usually is divided into two types: (1) hunting—deaths due directly to the action of legal hunting and including crippling losses; and (2) natural—deaths from all other reasons, some of which are man-caused, such as illegal and highway kills.

There are a number of methods for measuring mortality.

1. Determining survival rate by close and direct monitoring of a single cohort. Cause of death and the animal's age must be known, and this rarely is possible for North American deer populations.
2. Inferring survival rate from a series of recoveries of marked animals. This method requires large-scale tagging of animals for several years, which is costly. The rate of survival must be estimated by statistical procedures based on several important assumptions (Otis et al. 1978).
3. Ascertaining the age at death for a reliable sample of each cohort in a deer population. In principle, this requires information on all causes of death for the entire life of a cohort of deer, and provides an estimate of past mortality only after the entire cohort has died. In practice, through use of radio transmitters (*see* Cook et al. 1971), marked animals provide age-specific information on mortality. With sufficient assumptions, the successive numbers of deer harvested year after year from the same cohort can yield estimates of mortality rates (Downing 1980).
4. Determining the age distribution of a population and making certain assumptions about its history. This method was described by Eberhardt (1969) as the use of "kill-curves." Basically it was used by Severinghaus (1969) to estimate minimum population and by Lang and Wood (1976) to calculate population reduction rate.

A life table summarizes information on mortality by systematically presenting data on the survival of a single cohort. Dealing with mortality, it could just as well be called a "death table." Life tables are used here in a partial form to illustrate the history of cohorts of unhunted whitetail females and heavily hunted males (Table 25), and to follow the reproductive history of this female cohort.

When two or more kinds of mortality act on a population, they "compete" for each animal. To calculate total mortality, one must know how the mortalities combine. The simplest logical model for combining competing risks of death is to assume that the mortalities are statistically independent. In this case, mortalities become "additive"—the term referring to addition of the logarithmic forms as instantaneous rates of mortality. To calculate a combined rate of mortality, assuming the individual rates are additive, one multiplies together the survival rates that would apply if each mor-

Table 25. Survival series (l_x) for cohorts of a white-tailed deer population.[a]

Age in years (x)	Number of surviving females[b] (l_x)	Number of surviving males[c] (l_x)
0 (birth)	1000	1000
1	580	580
2	406	162
3	284	45
4	199	13
5	139	4
6	97	1
7	68	
8	48	
9	33	
10	23	
11	16	
12	11	
13	8	
14	6	
15	4	
16	3	
17	2	
18	1	
19	1	
20	1	

[a]Data from Table 22.1 of Eberhardt (1969), modified.
[b]Information on female survival is from the "northeast area" of Michigan's Lower Peninsula, with annual survival rates of fawns 0.58 and adults 0.70.
[c]Data for males added, with survival rates of fawns 0.58 and adults 0.28.

tality were acting in the absence of all other mortality. This estimates survival to the combined effect of the two or more mortality factors.

For example, in Table 25 the data assume that both female and male fawns experience a survival of 0.58 during the first year. Thereafter both sexes of the adult segment of the population are considered subject to natural mortality, as characterized by a survival rate of 0.70. In addition, however, adult males were under heavy hunting pressure, which further reduced their annual survival rate to 0.28. If the two kinds of mortality were additive, then the survival rate to this hunting pressure alone would be 0.40 (0.28 ÷ 0.70 = 0.40). If this hunting pressure were doubled—and still additive—the adult male survival rate would be reduced to 0.11 (0.70 × 0.40 × 0.40 = 0.11).

The alternative to additive mortality would be "compensatory mortality," which often has been postulated in wildlife management (for example, *see* Dasmann 1964). Mortalities are compensatory when the combined effect of two or more factors is less than expected under the additive hypothesis. Mortality would be com-

pletely compensatory where the added influence of hunting produced no change in mortality above that due to natural causes. Mortality would be partially compensatory where hunting caused additional mortality but less than expected if additive. Traditional discussions of compensatory hunting mortality have stressed carrying capacity and the role of predation, disease and behavior in excess populations, but have not provided an explicit model of how mortalities may be expected to combine. Therefore whitetail population managers, who often must speculate on the effects of increased hunting pressure, have little choice but to assume, first, that mortalities are additive, and then to modify these conclusions on the basis that mortalities may be compensatory.

Reproduction

Reproduction adds animals to a whitetail population. In the long run, and subject to the effects of movement, these additions must balance mortality in order for the population to persist. In the short term the wildlife biologist or manager is more likely to discover whether or not reproduction and mortality are in approximate balance by learning whether or not the population size is changing, rather than by trying to measure reproduction and mortality rates.

Rate of reproduction can be measured two ways. The first is by making embryo counts in dead does, either those collected or those available through roadkill or other accidents. The carcass then can be aged, embryos sexed, and rates of reproduction calculated for each age-class of females as female fawns per doe. These age-specific reproductive rates vary and reflect the quality of the does' habitat (Eberhardt 1969, Haugen 1975). They may be combined with data on age distribution to calculate the crude rate of reproduction (female fawns per adult doe) for the deer population at a point in time (Table 26). Such age-specific reproductive rates also may be used with cohort survival information to calculate the per-generation rate of increase (Table 27).

The second method of appraising reproduction is based on field observation of the fawn/doe ratio, and assumes that the ratio can be determined reliably. Its application seems to be successful in the western parts of the country, but results may be suspect where vegetation is dense (Eberhardt 1969).

Table 26. Calculation of crude reproductive rate for the white-tailed deer population shown in Table 25.[a]

Age in years[b]	Number of does	Age-specific reproductive rate[c] (m_x)	Number of female fawns produced
0.5	155	0.05	8
1.5	83	0.50	42
2.5	63	0.66	42
3.5+	178	0.72	128
Total	479		220

$$\text{Crude reproductive rate} = \frac{220}{479 - 155} = \frac{220}{324} = 0.68^{d}$$

[a]Data from tables 22.1 and 22.3 of Eberhardt (1969), modified.
[b]At harvest.
[c]Female fawns produced per doe at next birth date, specific for age class.
[d]Ratio of female fawns to adult females calculated on the basis of total fawn production and does 1.5 years and older. Note that observed fawn-doe ratio (155/324 = 0.48) is less than calculated rate.

Table 27. Calculation of per-generation rate of increase (R_0) for the female segment of white-tailed deer population shown in Table 25.[a]

Age[b] (x)	Number of surviving females (l_x)	Age-specific reproductive rate[c](m_x)	Product $(l_x m_x)$
0	1000	0	0
1	580	0.05	29
2	406	0.50	203
3	284	0.66	187
4+[d]	660	0.72	475
Total			894

$$\text{Per-generation rate of increase} = R_0 = \frac{894}{1000} = 0.89$$

[a]Data from Table 22.1 of Eberhardt (1969) modified.
[b]As of birth date; fawns, age 0, are just born.
[c]As of birth date (for example, female fawns of previous year becoming one year old bear 0.05 female fawns, on average).
[d]Survivors four years of age and older summed (*see* Table 25) with reproductive rates averaged.

Movement

The convenient assumption often is made that the effect of deer movements into and out of a population can be ignored because these movements are balanced. The practical manager has little choice but to accept this assumption. Deer movements can be followed using visible markers and radio tags, and studies have shown that movement may cover considerable distances and that deer swim miles to reach islands (Verme 1973, Schemnitz 1975, Kammermeyer and Marchinton 1976b). But whether such whitetail movements into and out of a population are balanced remains to be documented.

DESCRIPTIVE CHARACTERISTICS

Population Size

Estimates of whitetail population size interest the public and appeal to the media. Often, however, the importance of knowing the population size is overestimated as a tool for deer management. It is more important to know the relative abundance of deer—whether the population is increasing or decreasing, and whether it is above, below or nearly in balance with the carrying capacity of the environment.

On the other hand, one must know the number of deer in a given habitat to be able to calculate the potential consumption of food resources, though any serious effort to calculate this drain would require age-specific information on energy needs of the deer (Moen 1973).

Many methods have been derived for estimating the size of animal populations (Overton and Davis 1969, Otis et al. 1978). As applied to deer populations these methods usually are expensive and difficult to use. One may use either a direct count or an indirect method.

A direct count of an entire deer population rarely is possible, though Overton and Davis (1969) mentioned cases in which total counts were made from records of tracks of migrating deer, or where all deer were exterminated on an area. A drive count of a sample area is a direct count; some deer may be missed, but results may be stated as a minimum number. Drive counts are costly in terms of manpower, but may be justifiable as education of the public, especially if volunteer help is used.

Indirect methods require the measurement of certain ratios and their statistical interpretation based on important and sometimes doubtful assumptions. These methods may be classified under four headings.

Although the number of whitetails in a given population is interesting and useful information, it is less important than knowledge of the population's relative abundance, over time and in relationship to the carrying capacity of its habitat. *Photo courtesy of the Nebraska Game and Parks Commission.*

1. *Mark and recapture.* With this technique, deer are trapped, tagged and released. Estimates are made by one of a number of methods (*see* Otis et al. 1978), including use of the Lincoln Index, based on the ratio of marked to unmarked deer harvested by hunters. Because of the high costs of trapping, this method usually is impractical for routine use in management.

2. *Change in antlered-antlerless deer ratio.* This ratio is determined by field observation before and after the hunting season. Population size can be determined from the change in the ratio and the numbers of antlered and antlerless deer removed by hunters, provided these quantities have been measured accurately.

3. *Change in hunter success.* This method assumes that (a) vulnerability of deer to hunting remains constant throughout the season and (b) hunter success is proportional to the num-

ber of deer surviving. Not only does this method require the careful measurement of hunter success, but there is doubt that vulnerability of deer to hunting remains constant throughout the season.

4. *Reconstruction of deer population status from harvest data.* This method assumes that the only deaths are from hunting, and that a mortality rate can be estimated from the age structure of harvested deer. Results are termed "minimum population estimates," because failure to account for unrecorded deaths reduces the estimated total. Mortality rate has been estimated two ways.

First, Severinghaus (1969) and Lang and Wood (1976) derived a mortality rate for males from a ratio of numbers in the age classes of bucks, in modification of the kill-curve method of Eberhardt (1969), which assumes equal recruitment and constant survival. They then estimated the female segment by use of ratios. Second, a survival rate is derived by comparison of older age classes in the harvest of two successive years (Downing 1980). This assumes that the age samples are equal (or known) fractions of the total harvest each year; the method is used for both sexes.

A practical advantage of the reconstruction method is that the basic data (age distributions and harvest) may be available at low cost because they are gathered for other purposes. If an approximate figure is useful, even though known to be questionable, then this technique is attractive.

The assumption that harvest remains proportional to population—as used in interpreting change in hunter success and in deer population reconstruction methods based on harvested deer—has been used by wildlife managers for a long time. This assumption is expressed in the common belief that when hunting "quality" (deer killed per hunter-day) declines, there must be fewer animals. Deer killed per hunter-day is a widely used and fairly reliable index, although it is influenced by hunter skill, removal of the most vulnerable deer first, conditioning and learning by the deer, and fluctuating weather conditions (Holsworth 1973, Roseberry and Klimstra 1974). The number of deer killed on highways also has been used as an index to population size, and has the advantage that it provides data in well-traveled regions not hunted (McCaffery 1973).

Sex Ratio

Except that the adult sex ratio of a whitetail population indicates whether mortality has been higher for one sex than for the other, it is not a very useful management tool. Hunters often observe that does outnumber bucks and complain about it. But this is the unavoidable result of heavy buck-only hunting.

The overall sex ratio of a deer population is a weighted average of the sex ratios of combined age classes. In any age class, this ratio reflects the ratio at birth (which is approximately but not exactly equal) and the differential survival rates since birth. When bucks are more heavily hunted than does, there are fewer bucks than does in the hunted age classes because the sexes started with about the same numbers at birth and a higher proportion of bucks have been removed (*see* Table 25).

Age Distribution

A cautious interpretation of age distribution in a whitetail population can provide a wildlife biologist or manager with insight to the relative survival rate. If a graph of the frequency of age classes in the harvest shows rapidly decreasing numbers for each successively older age class, with the highest numbers in the youngest age classes, then low survival (high mortality) may be suspected. The opposite pattern (a "flatter" graph) suggests a higher rate of survival. However, these conclusions may be in error if rates of mortality or of reproduction are changing.

Such a graph often will under-represent the frequency of fawns and yearlings in the harvest. That this is under-representation and not a deficiency in year-classes can be confirmed by examining data from the same population for two successive years. In the first year, for example, the relative frequency of 1.5-year-olds in the harvest may exceed only slightly or even be less than that for 2.5-year-olds. In the second year, the now-2.5-year-olds will exceed the next older age class by a considerable margin.

Age distributions of the male and the female segments of a population reveal the relative number of survivors from a succession of cohorts. Each cohort is represented in the age distribution in proportion to its relative abundance at the time it entered the population as fawns and the cumulative relative mortality to which it was subjected thereafter. Thus, each age distribution reflects mostly ancient history, and tells very little about current survival except when a constant survival rate and equal recruitment can be assumed. Only under these special and unusual conditions can the true age distribution be used to estimate survival rate by the method of kill curves (Eberhardt 1969). A further problem is that the age distribution in the harvest will accurately reflect true age distribution of the population only if hunting takes the same proportion of each cohort.

COMBINING MORTALITY AND REPRODUCTION

In determining whether a given deer population actually is increasing or decreasing, the wildlife biologist or manager probably can get better information from continued biological observation of index values reflecting condition of the habitat and population than from mathematically combining measurements of population mortality and reproduction. If mortality and reproductive rates are seriously out of balance, the manager soon will recognize that the deer population is increasing or decreasing. If mortality and reproduction are only slightly out of balance, the biologist or manager cannot afford to measure that slight imbalance with useful precision. However, he often must defend management policy, debate the uses of available information and calculate the effect of changing regulations. Three ways of combining information are suggested for such practical purposes.

To determine whether data indicate an increasing or decreasing population, one may calculate either the per-generation rate of increase (R_0) or the intrinsic rate of natural increase (r). The term "increase" includes the idea of decrease, which is measured as value less than 1.0 with the per-generation rate, or as a negative value with the intrinsic rate. One also may compare the crude rate of reproduction of the population for successive years, although this comparison does not indicate whether the population is increasing or decreasing, but only whether fawn production is changing.

The per-generation rate of increase describes the entire reproductive history for a single cohort of females from their birth until the last member dies. Calculation requires sound information on survival and reproduction. In theory, calculation should be based on observed year-by-year rates of mortality and reproduction for a single cohort, but in practice the per-generation rate of increase must be calculated from available information on these rates. Table 27 illustrates the calculation for the population represented by survival of females in Table 25, with information added on reproductive rates. The method consists of calculating for its entire history the year-by-year production of fawns expected of the cohort and then comparing this total with the number of fawns that began the cohort. In Table 27, 894 female fawns would be produced by the cohort that began as 1,000, thus indicating that this cohort was not replacing itself. Therefore, the population must decrease, assuming unchanged rates of mortality and reproduction.

The intrinsic rate of natural increase is a purely hypothetical value—a tool for the specialist rather than for the manager. Its general nature is described here because this is the only rate that measures the potential for increase inherent in a particular combination of age-specific rates of mortality and reproduction. The intrinsic rate of natural increase allows standardized comparison of populations with differing patterns of mortality and reproduction. But calculation of this rate (not illustrated here) requires, first, good age-specific information on mortality and reproduction, and second, an assumption that the stated age-specific rates will continue until the population has reached the stable age distribution that theory indicates would result. Under this hypothetical condition the population would be changing at the intrinsic rate. Common sense indicates that indefinite continuation of constant mortality and reproductive rates would be biologically impossible except when mortality and reproduction balance exactly. But the intrinsic rate uses the idea of rates remaining constant indefinitely to derive a numerical value standardized for the changing age structure; the complexity of the idea illustrates the difficulty of the problem. Eberhardt (1969) explained the method and demonstrated the calculation with data from white-tailed deer populations, although he did not use the term "intrinsic rate." The use and calculation of this rate was discussed by Caughley (1977:110), who called it the "survival-fecundity rate of increase."

A current crude rate of reproduction (*see* Table 26) reveals the ratio of female fawns produced per doe. This rate is calculated entirely from measured values, assuming only that the data on age-specific rates of reproduction and age structure represent the population and that mortality is the same for all ages for the period from hunting season (when age distribution can be determined) to the time of fawn birth. This fawn/doe ratio has no direct value in interpretation of change in population size, but may be used to compare differences in fawn production among populations. The ratio should be calculated as: numerator—the total number of female fawns expected to be produced; denominator—the number of does 1.5 years and older (even where fawns are carrying young). This ratio will be less biased by the under-representation of fawns than will be a hunter-collected sample of does and fawns (as illustrated in Table 26), and the same ratio can be used regardless of any reproduction by fawns in the first year.

MODELS

A model is simply someone's idea of how events occur. For example, if a hunter says that the more deer there are, the better the hunting will be, he is using a model. Although a model need not be any more mathematical than the hunter's statement, scientific models increasingly are mathematical, large-scale, and require the use of computers.

When working with models one tries to answer questions about what would happen if certain processes and certain values were assumed. For example, the model used for Table 25 specifies that the annual survival rate of a cohort of females is 0.58 their first year and 0.70 thereafter. The table lists the numbers of females surviving; these are easy to calculate by hand for this simple model. In similar models, and more complex models, computers and simulation programs are helpful and usually necessary to handle large amounts of arithmetic and make repeated runs to explore the consequences of changing conditions and assumptions. Thus, a computer makes speculation possible. But what comes out depends on what went in. A computer adds no new knowledge, although it can help the user develop insight and perspective (*see also* Chapter 10).

Models are built on assumptions. Models of whitetail population dynamics must make simplified assumptions to remain practical. Current computer models have problems with what assumptions to make about population self-limitation and how rates of natural mortality and reproduction may change with decreases or increases in hunting mortality. The attempt to use a model usually points up a lack of fundamental biological information.

Computer models can be stimulating to learning and helpful in research. However they also can do harm, by lending undeserved authority to results based on questionable methods or assumptions, especially if this leads the biologist or manager to disregard his field-judgment, experience and training.

SUMMARY

There is no simple and easy method of using knowledge of population dynamics with data available on a given whitetail population to manage that population. The wildlife biologist or manager must weigh all information and consider how reliable each item may be, how good were the methods used to gather the information, what the harvest success has been, what the physical status of the deer and the habitat are, and whether these conditions have changed or remained constant since the information was gathered. Then he must make his decisions in light of his objectives for the particular population.

Chapter 10

LESSONS FROM THE GEORGE RESERVE, MICHIGAN

Dale R. McCullough
Professor of Wildlife Biology and Management
Department of Forestry and Resource Management
University of California
Berkeley, California

The George Reserve in southern Michigan has been yielding information on white-tailed deer for more than 50 years. Biologists at the University of Michigan have been studying the deer population there since 1928, when whitetails were introduced by Colonel Edwin S. George, a Detroit industrialist who established the area as a personal estate. I began intensive studies of the population in 1966 and, with the support of the National Science Foundation, these studies have continued to the present.

The George Reserve is a 464-hectare (1,146-acre) area enclosed by a 3.5-meter (11.5-foot) deer-proof fence. It is located in Livingston County, about 7.7 kilometers (3 miles) west of Pinckney, Michigan. It is in a glaciated area where one of the most recent southward advances of the ice shield terminated.

The soils are young and poor in fertility, consisting in the uplands of mainly sands and gravels. It should be kept in mind that productivity of the George Reserve deer population is not the result of superior soils; most soils in the lower Great Lakes and Upper Midwest region are far more fertile that those of the George Reserve. What the Reserve has is diversity, due to recent glaciation. The topography is rough and broken, with rolling uplands, steep-sided eskers and kettle-hole sinks.

The varied topography supports a complex mosaic of vegetation, with five major types and a number of minor ones being recognized (Figure 48). Of the major types, oak/hickory hardwood forest on the uplands predominates (47 percent), while open grasslands, created by the clearing of forests by man in the late 1800s, are second (26 percent). Tamarack swamps are the most common lowland type (about 16 percent), while freshwater marshes cover 8 percent and leatherleaf bogs about 2 percent. The remainder (1 percent) is made up of assorted minor types and open water. For a more complete description of the area and its vegetation, *see* McCullough (1979).

After completing the fence in 1928, Colonel George introduced six whitetails—two bucks and four does (presumed to be pregnant)—from Grand Island in Lake Superior. George then gave the Reserve to the University of Michigan in 1930. The deer population increased rapidly and, by 1933, a minimum of 160 deer were accounted for in a drive count (Hickie 1937, O'Roke and Hamerstrom 1948). Because it is known that drive counts in the early years were low, a revised estimate of more than 220 deer appears more likely (McCullough 1979).

Severe damage to vegetation was being caused by this number of deer. And although the Reserve was managed by the university as a natural area for research, it was apparent that the whitetail population would have to be controlled. Hunting was begun in 1933 and continued thereafter to control the population at desired levels.

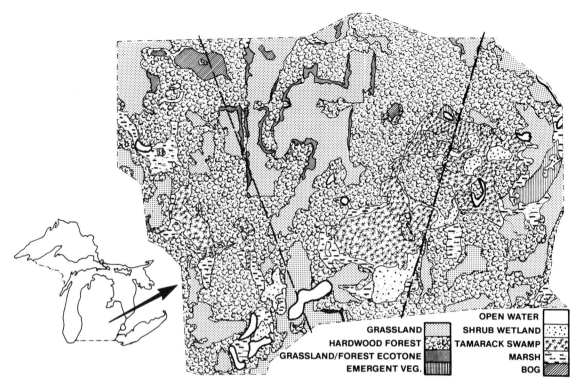

Figure 48. Vegetation of the 464-hectare (1,146-acre) George Reserve in southcentral Michigan (after Roller 1971).

Since 1966, the population size has been altered purposely, in an attempt to determine experimentally the role of density on population dynamics. The population was reduced gradually to about 10 animals in 1975 and then protected from shooting and allowed to increase again, until 212 animals were present in 1980. Since then, the population has been held to 130 animals by shooting.

SEASONAL HABITS

Deer on the Reserve have social systems similar to those of whitetail populations elsewhere in the region (Hirth 1977a). Small groups predominate due to heavy concealment cover. Individuals have home ranges that overlap and usually extend over parts of the major vegetation types (Queal 1962). Deer use all of the vegetational types on the Reserve, shifting about as resources become available and the animals' physiological needs change.

Based on the mean for five years of pellet-group counts, measurements of habitat-use by plant phenological seasons show distinct patterns (McCullough 1982a) that relate primarily to food habits (Figure 49). However, there is substantial variation in use from year to year depending on the acorn crop size, amount of snowfall and other environmental variables. Deer are quite discriminatory, selecting the best food available in any given season.

In early spring, grasses predominate in the whitetail diet, and use of openland habitats is prevalent. As forbs become more available in late spring and early summer, they replace grasses in the diet. As most forbs begin to dry in late summer, the deer switch to green leafy browse and spend much of their time in the wetland types, particularly tamarack swamps (Figure 49). The swamps also are the coolest type when temperatures are highest in July and August. Acorns become available in autumn most years, and use of hardwood forests increases rapidly as acorns become predominant in the diet. If the acorn crop fails, autumn use of hardwood forests is low, as the deer seek out other seeds and fruits, including sumac, hawthorn, lespedesa, apples, grape and chokeberry. These foods are taken in minimal amounts if acorns are available.

In most years acorns disappear by late November. But particularly in years of heavy crops

Oblique aerial view of the central part of the George Reserve. The image area corresponds to the area between the dash lines on Figure 48. Note the rough terrain and interspersion of vegetational types. *Photo by James W. Wheeler; courtesy of The University of Michigan Press, Ann Arbor.*

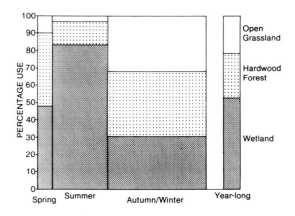

Figure 49. Habitat use of white-tailed deer on the George Reserve by season and yearlong, as indicated by pellet-group counts over five years, 1966–1972 (McCullough 1982a). Yearlong result is weighted by length of seasons. Wetlands include tamarack swamps, leatherleaf bogs and marshes.

they will predominate in the diet into January, and the whitetails will paw through more than 0.3 meter (1 foot) of snow to obtain them. When acorns are gone, deer shift back to grass, which undergoes an autumn flush due to increased rainfall after the drier period in August and September. Grass remains green next to the ground throughout the winter, and deer feed on this material as well as on some green rosettes of forbs at ground level. Browse is used to fill out the winter diet.

These food habits hold as long as snow cover is not present. However, with a snow cover of 7.5 centimeters (3 inches), the deer abandon herbaceous diets and shift almost entirely to evergreen woody browse (Coblentz 1970), primarily redcedar, ground juniper and, to a much lesser extent, leatherleaf. Hardwood forest stands and tamarack swamps are used as thermal cover for bedding, and deer come into the openlands at night to obtain the two species of juniper, of which redcedar is by far the pre-

Redcedar is the most important deer food in winter on the George Reserve when snow depth reaches 7.5 centimeters (3 inches). Whitetail browsing pressure results in a distinct highline on this species. *Photo by Dale R. McCullough.*

ferred. Deer trails after snows form a network connecting the scattered individual redcedar trees, which show a pronounced hedged appearance. Under the coldest conditions, with subzero temperatures and strong winds, deer are restricted to dense tangles of brush in the tamarack swamps.

Does with young occur in social groups separate from male social groups except during the rut (Hirth 1977*a*, Newhouse 1973, McCullough 1982*a*). There also is some evidence that does with young occupy geographic areas separate from those occupied by males (McCullough 1979).

Rutting behavior is shown by bucks from October through December (Hirth 1977*a*), with conception in yearling and adult does occurring in late October and early November (McCullough 1979). Conception of female fawns—which reach sexual maturity at about seven months of age under the good food conditions prevailing at low population densities—occurs in early December (McCullough 1979). Fawns are born in June and July and are hidden in hardwood forest or on the forest-tamarack swamp edge for the first few weeks of life, until they are able to follow their mothers.

MODELS FOR MANAGEMENT

A model is nothing more than a miniature conceptualization of a real-world system (*see* Chapter 9). Models are necessary because the real world is big and complex, and cannot possibly be completely understood. Even after intensive research, many answers elude investigators. The scale over which the typical wildlife agency must operate, and the budget available to do so, are such that only a few statistics can be gathered about the status of a given deer population. Nevertheless, the agency must set regulations for all of the deer population units under its jurisdiction. Models are ways of coping with this problem. But they are always deficient to some extent because, of necessity, they are simplified.

Modern models, because they are invariably mathematical, often are incomprehensible and have created an aura of mystery. Practicing professionals have tended to react to models in one of three ways. First, and most common, is simple bewilderment—not knowing what to think. Second is defensive rejection—considering models as witchcraft or the nasty tricks of mathemagicians. Third is to consider them akin to religion, something to believe in—a miracle that will make the impossible task possible.

Models are tools, nothing more. They differ from religions in that one does not have to die to find out if they are right. They differ from beliefs in that one does not have to accept them in total. Before applying a model to the whole, a separate part can be tested. By themselves, models do nothing. In the hands of a good craftsman, they can produce useful information. Models do not eliminate work; but they can make it easier. On the other hand if a model is misused, as with any decision-making aid it can be dangerous. More than one agency wound has been self-inflicted, and it is inevitable that some nasty gashes will be received from the use of an inadequate model or the misuse of an adequate one.

The first wildlife population models were word models, and they began with Aldo Leopold's *Game Management* (1933). Unfortunately, the wildlife profession accepted this work as a literal description of the real world rather than a word model for how one man thought the real world worked. The genius of Leopold is attested to by the degree to which his wisdom served the wildlife profession so well for so long. It detracts not at all from his genius to observe that, while it served adequately for 30 years, it is inadequate today. However, while Leopold's science has become dated, his philosophy promises to live forever.

Mathematical models have been developed because the symbolic manipulations possible are so powerful and words usually are inadequate to express complex relationships. The computer aided in this development because of its computational power, but a computer simply is a rapid calculator. It is the program that is important, and the computer should receive neither the credit nor the blame for what the programmer does.

There are two different approaches to predictive modeling for white-tailed deer population management. These can be classified broadly as "accounting" models and "black box" models. Accounting models keep track of population size and composition through elaborate bookkeeping of births and deaths. Best known of this kind of model in deer management is ONEPOP (Walters and Gross 1972, Gross et al. 1973) and its offshoots (Bartholow 1981), but there are many other examples (*see* Medin and Anderson 1979, F. M. Anderson et al. 1974).

Accounting models have substantial heuristic value. One can play "what if" games (Pojar 1977, Williams 1981) by changing parameters to test population responses to changes in birth rates or by shifting mortality rates between sex and age classes. But these models have drawbacks as tools for practical management, the most significant of which is their great requirement for data. One needs information on population size, age and sex composition, and birth and death rates by age class. Indeed, if all these data are available, one hardly needs a model.

A second drawback of accounting models is that the rates for sex and age groups are not synchronized within the model. Thus, changes in one parameter are not simultaneously compensated for by changes in other parameters. While some linkages are possible, the programming necessary to integrate the array of categories and variables in the model is overwhelming (Pospahala 1969).

Black box models, on the other hand, assume that a deer population is a far more effective integrator of variables than the population's researchers are. Black box models assume that natural selection over millions of years has shaped responses to perturbations by hunting, habitat change, predation, etc., to the best solution the population is capable of attaining. Thus, a few high-order variables are all that need to be measured, since they represent the population's integration of the total complex of lower-order variables.

Models for whitetail management are useful as practical tools only to the extent that they incorporate the important integrating variables of vegetation/deer/predator systems. One of the failings of the wildlife profession is an erroneous belief that an understanding of the population will somehow emerge from increasingly detailed measurements of plant species composition and pounds of browse, or better estimates of birth and death rates and population size. Having point estimates of these parameters is of some value. But they do not address the fundamental problem—how do changes in each parameter vary in relation to changes in all of the other variables? Deer population response to changes in density integrates all of those variables into numbers of deer with a precision that researchers will never achieve, and that is the bottom line.

Similarly, it is argued whether predators regulate, or deer self-regulate, or hunting is necessary to regulate, without any agreement on what is being argued. What is meant by regulating—holding between limits? Or at a stable point? And if the latter, at what point? I carrying capacity or K carrying capacity (*see* Carrying Capacity)? or somewhere in between? And how does one establish that regulation has occurred? Does any outcome (other than total extinction) mean that regulation has occurred? If not, by what criteria do we determine whether regulation has or has not occurred? If we are to progress it is imperative that our questions be framed the right way. Asking the wrong questions or stating questions in a fuzzy manner diverts attention from real informational needs.

What is important to know is the shape of the productivity curve and the point on it where the population stands. The population density response is independent of the causes of mortality. It makes no difference whatsoever to the survivors in the residual population whether the individuals no longer present fell to bullet, fang, radiator grill or the vagaries of time. If the population's position on the productivity curve is known, the outcome of a higher or lower human hunting harvest can be predicted, and harvests can be changed carefully and incrementally to test those predictions. Model and practice cross-check and reinforce each other. Conversely, current hunting regulations can be fixed and tested to assess how other mortality factors relate to hunter harvest. For example, it can be hypothesized that predators are having an impact on a deer population sufficient to lower the hunting harvest. Thus, if predators are reduced by increasing investment in predator control, the return (deer in the hunter take) can be measured. If the hunting harvest increases as predicted, the cost of the predator-control program can be weighed against the benefit of more deer in the bag. If hunter harvest does not increase, there certainly is no value in predator control for deer management. This is much more useful than knowing exactly how many deer a given predator was killing.

I propose that it is time for management to abandon the quest for the absolute estimate, which is difficult or impossible to obtain and of limited use if known. It is time to concentrate on functional relations that are amenable to discovery through manipulation of controllable variables, such as hunting.

The empirical models I propose in the following discussion are based on this approach. These models are of the black box type known as "stock-recruitment" models. They have been used by fisheries biologists for many years (*see* Ricker 1954, 1975, Beverton and Holt 1957). However, the models presented here are modified somewhat, being derived empirically through data fitting rather than through predetermined mathematical formulations.

RATE OF POPULATION INCREASE

After the introduction of six adult whitetails in the George Reserve in 1928, the population grew to an estimated 222 deer in seven years (McCullough 1979). This is an instantaneous growth rate of 0.516. This population-growth phenomenon was repeated in 1975, when the population was reduced to 10 (primarily fawns) by heavy harvesting and then protected. In 1980, six seasons later, the population was 212 (McCullough 1982*b*). The instantaneous growth rate for this period was 0.509. If the different starting numbers are corrected for, the results of the two periods with deer of different ages

are virtually identical. However, for an opposing view, *see* Van Ballenberge (1983); for a response to that view, *see* McCullough (1983).

It should be noted that although these rates of population growth are among the highest recorded for white-tailed deer, they do not equal the unimpeded rate. With no mortality, and maximum reproductive rate, the population after six years would be 303 for a starting population of 6. For a starting population of 10 it would obviously be still higher. Thus, the rate of growth was actually declining as population increased in a density-dependent fashion (*see* Recruitment Rate, *see also* McCullough 1983).

These growth rates are significant for several reasons. First, they illustrate the capacity of a white-tailed deer population to increase rapidly, even in an environment that inherently is not very fertile, so long as intraspecific competition for resources is minimal. At low densities most does reproduce as fawns, and twins (and even triplets) in fawns have been recorded (Haugen 1975, McCullough 1979). Yearlings commonly have twins, while triplets occur frequently in older females.

Second, the growth rates illustrate that density-dependent effects are subtle but measurable if census methods are reliable. The fact that density effects were present in both growth-rate experiments before high density (indeed before I carrying capacity) was achieved means there is considerable fine-tuning of population-growth response to the quality and quantity of resources available. That the initial introduction was made with adult animals—and that growth would be lowered by the addition of young animals, with their lower reproductive rates—could be put forward as an explanation for the decline in population-growth rate in the years following the experiment's inception. However this explanation was eliminated in the repetition of the experiment, in which an attempt was made to remove all yearlings and adults, leaving primarily fawns. Density-dependence effects, then, are the only reasonable explanation.

That resource availability rather than density *per se* was responsible for the declining population growth rate is demonstrated by a comparison of population densities at different resource states. Impacts on the vegetation were observed—heavy browsing on redcedar being particularly obvious (Hickie 1937, O'Roke and Hamerstrom 1948, Chase and Jenkins 1962)—following the initial increase, and recruitment rates declined in response to vegetation damage. High recruitment rates before vegetation damage and low rates after damage were obtained at the same population size (*see* Figure 51). If density *per se,* rather than resources, had been the cause of the growth-rate decline, the recruitment rate should have been equal at the same density. Recovery of the vegetation occurred during subsequent periods of low deer density. This point will be covered further later in the chapter. Although some changes in major vegetational types have occurred—particularly expansion of the hardwood forest ecotones into the openlands (Roller 1974)—the basic capacity of the area to support deer has not been altered appreciably.

Third, these population growth experiments show that social behavior factors, such as purported social regulation (Wynne-Edwards 1962) or "immature" behavior patterns (Bubenik 1971, 1982), do not play a significant role in white-tailed deer. The first increase began with animals that were two years old or older, and the second began primarily with fawns. The outcome was virtually the same.

Fourth, these experiments reply to the criticism of Smith (1981) about genetic factors being ignored, particularly the effects of inbreeding depression. The George Reserve whitetail population has passed through two genetic bottlenecks and, no doubt, has suffered loss of heterozygosity. That there have been some genetic effects seems likely. For example, George Reserve bucks have an exceptional number of points and other antler characteristics that suggest the influence of the "founder effect" (McCullough 1982c). Because a few individuals establish the population, the genes contributed are limited, and particular characteristics of these initial members are strongly represented in the subsequent population.

However, the George Reserve deer population has had the highest sustained growth recorded for white-tailed deer—not once, but twice. At least 70 percent of fawn does have achieved sexual maturity and recruited young to the population; twins by fawn does have been recorded. Buck fawns commonly exceed 45 kilograms (100 pounds) by autumn; yearling bucks have eight-point antlers; and trophy heads are produced by four years of age (McCullough 1982c). These are the effects of reduced density. And if there was "deleterious" inbreeding, it was overshadowed completely by compensatory processes.

This is not to deny the potential of genetic problems associated with small populations, but rather to question the assumption that they are inevitable, or that they are more important than maintaining the population within the environment's resources—even if that means maintaining a small population.

RECRUITMENT RATE AND PRODUCTIVITY

The dynamics of any population can be described by reproduction, mortality, immigration and emigration over time. Because of the deer-proof fence on the George Reserve, movements as a population variable can be ignored. Gross reproduction was estimated by embryo rates. Although abortion and resorption do occur in deer, they are relatively infrequent and no case of either has been observed on the George Reserve. Furthermore, corpora luteal counts have been virtually equal to embryo counts in the same sample of does (McCullough 1979).

Net reproduction was measured as recruitment. Recruitment is a useful concept in population studies since it is measured at an age when the young are at some threshold of practical importance. In this case, recruitment age was considered to be six months of age—the autumn of the first year, when fawns were large enough to be included in the harvest. The value of recruitment as a concept is that it integrates births and early mortality when death is most probable—each of which is exceedingly difficult to measure in practice—into one measure after survivorship begins to approach that of older animals.

Recruitment rate is the number of recruits per individual in the population producing the recruits. The population producing the recruits will be referred to as the "residual population"—that remaining after hunting and other mortality factors have had their effect. This population was referred to as the "posthunt population" by McCullough (1979). However, because it includes cases where hunting is not present, the term "residual population" is more appropriate.

It is useful to divide mortality occurring after recruitment age into two categories. "Chronic mortality" includes those deaths that are routine and inevitable. They include deaths due to the combined effects of old age, typical parasite loads, nonvirulent diseases, malnutrition,

A deer-proof fence around the George Reserve has made the site a valuable outdoor "laboratory" for study of white-tailed deer populations. *Photo by Doug Fulton.*

debilitating accidents and similar causes. Because they are chronic does not mean that they are density independent. In fact, most are density dependent. The other form is "traumatic mortality," and it includes deaths due to direct intervention of outside forces such as hunting, predators, vehicle collisions and virulent diseases that kill by gross physical damage. These deaths have the characteristic of cutting the lives of individual deer short of what they would have been had only chronic-mortality factors been operating.

Thus, total mortality is comprised of three kinds: prerecruitment, chronic and traumatic. This division is useful because a major source of traumatic mortality, hunting, is under the control of wildlife managers through regulations established for deer management units. Thus, it is necessary to determine how increasing or decreasing hunting-harvest influences traumatic mortality due to other variables, and how total traumatic mortality influences prerecruitment and chronic mortality. The pivotal question is whether hunting mortality is ad-

ditive (that is, in addition to other mortality) or substitutive (that is, compensated for by decreases in other mortality). If it is additive, then the wildlife biologist or resource manager is dealing with an inflexible biological system with little resilience (very prone to overexploitation). Hunting is liable to be, so to speak, the straw that breaks the camel's back, and very conservative approaches are required. If, on the other hand, hunting mortality is compensated for by a reduction in other mortality, then the biologist or manager is dealing with a resilient biological system that is tolerant of exploitation—one in which hunting can be used as a driving variable to milk the proverbial camel for all it is worth.

Net recruitment rate—called "population change" in McCullough (1979)—is defined as the number of recruits minus mortality of animals of recruitment age and older divided by the residual population (Figure 50a). Productivity is the number of fawns born minus the combined mortality of all three kinds at a given residual population size.

The productivity curve of the George Reserve whitetail population is shown in Figure 50b. Maximum sustainable yield is the largest value on the curve (49), and it is obtained at a residual population of 99. It occurs at the inflection point on the net recruitment rate curve, where a linear relationship at lower residual population becomes curvilinear (Figure 50a). It also is at the inflection point of an S-shaped population growth curve, where the increasing curve bends into a decreasing curve (Figure 50d).

CARRYING CAPACITY

Carrying capacity, K, is that residual population at which productivity declines to zero.

K carrying capacity is defined further as the maximum number of animals an environment will support on a sustained basis (that is, without destruction of the vegetation). Indeed, there will be substantial impact, and K is the residual population size causing the maximum defoliation the vegetation is capable of sustaining. Whitetail populations clearly are capable of exceeding K and causing damage to vegetation, as discussed later (*see* Time Lags).

In McCullough (1979), the residual population yielding maximum sustainable yield is referred to as I carrying capacity ("I" for inflection point) to distinguish it from K carrying capacity. There has been considerable confusion in the wildlife literature, and carrying capacity has frequently been defined as that population yielding maximum sustainable yield.

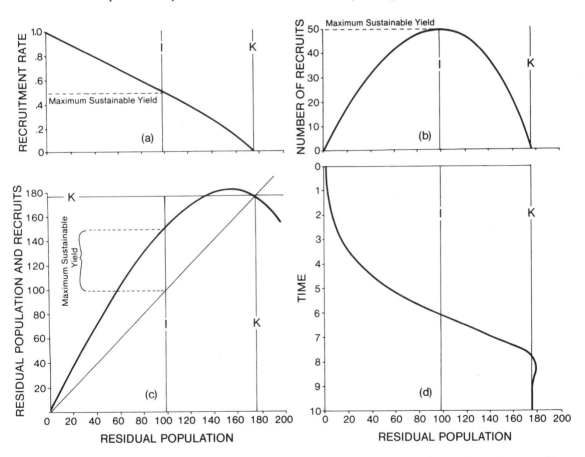

Figure 50. Graphic representation of equilibrium (without time lags) population dynamics for the George Reserve white-tailed deer population in Michigan, showing equivalent values of I and K carrying capacity, based on data gathered from 1952 to 1971: (a) recruitment rate on residual population size; (b) net recruitment or productivity curve; (c) stock-recruitment curve; and (d) population-growth curve over time. K = maximum residual population (density) at which productivity (number of recruits) declines to zero—this is carrying capacity of an area, and represents the maximum number of deer the area will support on a sustained basis without destruction of habitat. I = residual population yielding maximum sustainable yield.

Much of the confusion apparently arose from thinking of the balance of population size and vegetation as representing a given point, when in actuality it is an array of points in a continuum of residual populations from zero to K that represents the functional relationship between the dynamics of deer and the dynamics of vegetation.

In ecology, carrying capacity has been the term applied to K, and this is the correct usage. Referring to residual population yielding maximum sustainable yield as "carrying capacity" clearly is a misnomer. But because of past confusion in the wildlife literature, it seems less confusing at this stage to retain the term and refer to it as I carrying capacity. Curiously, the residual population that yields maximum sustainable yield has not been given a label, for maximum sustainable yield refers to the yield, not the residual population giving the yield. Thus, "I" is an appropriate label for this important residual population on the productivity curve, just as "K" refers to the maximum-equilibrium residual population.

Optimum sustained yield is the yield that a population can sustain that maximizes human benefits in a given case. Because the benefits to be achieved (that is, defining what should be optimized) are derived subjectively, optimum sustained yield depends on the goals of the management program.

IMPACT OF EXPLOITATION

Illustration of the impact on a whitetail population at various levels of exploitation can be made most easily in the simplest case. Thus, no variation from the mean values is assumed, and the productivity curve in Figure 50b is treated as a deterministic model. It can be assumed further that hunting is the only form of traumatic mortality operating on the population, which was true of the George Reserve deer population.

The first point to be made is that with the exception of maximum sustainable yield, which has a single intercept point on the productivity curve at a residual population 99, all smaller values of Y have two intercept points. Thus, a harvest of 30 animals yields a balance point of 38 and 150 residual population, and the same yield can be obtained from two residual populations. This is true of all harvests less than maximum sustainable yield, including zero harvest that is stable at extinction and at K. This phenomenon explains why wildlife populations occasionally are observed to go from a low and stable level to a very much higher and stable level. The reverse of high-to-low also occurs. These are a result of the prevailing mortality rate being temporarily increased or decreased and the population either growing or declining to the opposite balance point where

Recent glaciation created the George Reserve's broken topography and sandy and gravelly soils of low fertility. Oak/hickory forests contribute woody browse and mast crops to the deer diet. *Photo by Dale R. McCullough.*

a resumed mortality rate will stabilize it once again (McCullough in press).

This dual balance-point relationship holds promise for management because it means that a given yield can be obtained from a high or low residual population. If the wildlife biologist or resource manager wants to minimize crop damage or deer/vehicle collisions, the lower residual population can be favored. If the desire is to maintain a higher residual population to satisfy protectionists, or so hunters will not worry about the population being over-exploited, the high balance point can be favored. This case is treated more fully in McCullough (in press).

However, the next point to be made is that the balance point on the left arm of the productivity parabola (Figure 50b) is highly unstable, while the one on the right arm is highly stable. Therefore, management for the high residual population is forgiving of errors because the population responses are compensatory. At the low population, population responses are destabilizing.

For example, if a fixed harvest of 30 whitetails is being taken at the lower residual population balance point, and 31 are killed accidentally, the residual population will be reduced and an offsetting harvest the following year will be necessary to bring the population to the original residual population. The same is true of a harvest that is accidentally too low, such as 20. Because the higher residual population will recruit additional individuals, a greater correcting harvest will be required to establish the original balance point.

Conversely, on the right arm of the parabola, errors are self-correcting. If too many deer are killed, the reduced residual population has increased recruitment, which tends to force the population back toward the original balance point. If too few are killed, the increased residual population has a lower recruitment, and the population tends to decline back to the original balance point. Therefore, the right arm of the parabola is a highly stable region since the density-dependent population responses tend to correct for errors in management.

Residual populations giving maximum sustainable yield behave like residual populations on the left arm if maximum sustainable yield is exceeded, and like those on the right arm if underharvested. Thus, maximum sustainable yield is unstable in the face of harvests too high, and stable for harvests too low. The rules for deciding how a population will respond can be stated as follows:

1. If a fixed harvest exceeds maximum sustainable yield, continuing the fixed harvest will lead to population extinction no matter what the residual population.
2. If the residual population is on the left arm of the parabola or at the residual population level that yields maximum sustainable yield, a fixed removal equal to recruitment will stabilize the population at that residual.
3. If the residual population is on the left arm of the parabola, and the fixed harvest exceeds the recruitment, the population will be driven to extinction. If the recruitment exceeds the harvest, the residual population will grow to the balance point on the right arm of the parabola for that fixed harvest.
4. If the residual population is on the right arm of the parabola and if the harvest exceeds the recruitment at that residual population, but is less than maximum sustainable yield (*see* rule 1.), the residual population will decline to the balance point for that fixed harvest on the right arm of the parabola. If the harvest is less than the recruitment, the residual population will grow to the balance point nearer to K.

RELATIONSHIP OF PRODUCTIVITY TO RESIDUAL POPULATION

The relationship of productivity to residual population is best illustrated by a stock recruitment graph (Figure 50c), where the productivity curve represents net recruitment. If human hunting is the sole form of traumatic mortality, the entire productivity needs to be removed to stabilize the residual population at a given value.

From Figure 50c it can be seen that moderate harvests from a white-tailed deer population can result in prehunt populations greater than K and posthunt (residual) populations less than K. At the residual population yielding maximum sustainable yield (that is, I carrying capacity), both the prehunt and the posthunt populations are less than K. This illustrates an important point that has been overlooked by wildlife biologists and resource managers: management for maximum sustainable yield results in fewer deer in the field. This point has resulted in much failure of communication among biologists, hunters and others. Biologists and managers emphasize the high and sustainable harvest that is being supported, while hunters worry about the number of deer and other signs of deer seen in the field while hunting (McCullough 1979). Failure to appreciate that hunting harvests approaching maximum sustainable yield inevitably reduce the deer population has caused loss of credence among hunters, who see that there are fewer deer in the field and therefore assume that antlerless seasons have resulted in overexploitation of the population. Furthermore, because a higher harvest is being taken from a lower population, the average effort of the hunter per deer harvested goes up, which further convinces the hunter that the population is not what it was before antlerless hunting began.

INADEQUACY OF THE HARVESTABLE SURPLUS CONCEPT

The preceding discussion illustrates the deficiency of harvestable surplus as a management strategy. Leopold (1933) defined harvestable surplus as those animals above the replacement population. The replacement population would be equivalent to the residual population, and harvestable surplus equivalent to the recruitment in this context. Because recruitment tends to balance the harvest at any sustainable residual population, the harvestable surplus is a characteristic of the management program practices. Thus, if a white-tailed deer population is lightly harvested, the surplus will be small in the following year because the excess above the replacement population will be small. Because a small surplus suggests that a small harvest should be taken, the concept logically suggests that what has been done in the past should be continued in the future. If a heavy harvest has been taken, recruitment will be high, indicating a high surplus.

Thus, the harvestable surplus concept leads to the conclusion that the right program is being followed, no matter what the program. The productivity-curve approach given here indicates what the potential surplus might be if the population were forced to its maximum productivity (maximum sustainable yield). It also

Deer harvests on the George Reserve between 1953 and 1969 were conducted by drivers pushing deer past shooters on stands. Here a harvest crew takes a break in Camburn Laboratory under a mounted trophy buck taken in the early years. Bucks taken recently, when the population has been low density, exceed this trophy in size and antler quality. *Photo by Doug Fulton.*

indicates removals that exceed maximum sustainable yield and cannot be sustained, as well as the residual population associated with any sustainable harvest.

DETERMINISTIC POPULATION GROWTH

White-tailed deer population growth without destructive vegetative overshoots can be projected using the previous functional relationship between residual population and productivity. Because of the whitetail's high reproductive rate, population growth has a tendency to overshoot K slightly and dampen out to K even without destruction to vegetation (McCullough 1979, in press). Population growth without destruction of vegetation (Figure 50d) shows a substantial difference from the growth rates beginning from very low populations covered in the earlier section, "Rate of Population Increase."

TIME LAGS

There are two types of time lag: those that occur within the constraints of the mean equilibrium values of the productivity curve, and those due to lags in the deer/vegetation system that result in departure from equilibrium conditions (that is, lowering of K by vegetation damage).

The first type, those that follow the mean productivity curve, include lags due to shifts in size of harvest, and temporary nondestructive overshoots of K. Lags due to shifts in harvest occur because the density-dependent response is not instantaneous. For example, if one were stabilizing the residual population on the left arm of the productivity curve with a given harvest and then lowering the harvest, it would take some time for the residual population to grow to the right arm of the parabola and come to equilibrium on that arm with the new harvest.

Nondestructive overshoots (Figure 50d) occur because the mean recruitment curve of the stock-recruitment graph exceeds the horizontal line through K (Figure 50c). Illustrations of population growth curves giving temporary overshoots are shown in McCullough (in press), and seasonal overshoots can be produced by managing for residual populations (138–175) where the recruitment curve is above the horizontal line in Figure 50c.

Destructive overshoots occur where "accumulations" of resources allow population growth that exceeds the equilibrium values. This occurred on the George Reserve following the initial whitetail population increase, which deviated from the mean value at the inflection point of the mean productivity curve (McCullough 1979, in press). Therefore, the critical departure of destructive overshoot occurs not when K is exceeded, but rather when the population growth rate exceeds the mean equilibrium value at I carrying capacity. This departure is shown with reference to recruitment rate in interval B of Figure 51. Note that the same departure was recorded in the experimental increase of the population conducted in recent years, one purpose of which was to study the phenomenon of destructive overshoot.

The harvests imposed in the initial overshoot were too conservative to prevent vegetation destruction, and recruitment rates below the mean values persisted in the following years (interval C of Figure 51). This lowered capacity shows that deer were responding to resources and not to density *per se,* for if the latter were responsible, recruitment should have been the same at the same density. After the residual population on the Reserve was lowered below 80 animals, vegetation recovery occurred, and the recruitment rates returned to the mean value (interval D of Figure 51). Subsequent increases in the residual population (interval E of Figure 51) and decreases in the population as a whole (interval F of Figure 51) followed the mean equilibrium values.

As noted earlier, the recent increase followed the original increase (intervals A and B of Figure 51). The overshoot experiment I currently am conducting is to show that vegetation destruction is not inevitable given the departure of population growth from the mean equilibrium curve at I carrying capacity. Thus, while the initial growth was curbed too slowly, I am trying to show that if sufficient control is exerted to allow time for the population to use up the accumulation of resources remaining from the period of extremely low population, the recruitment rate will decline to the mean equilibrium value without damage to the vegetation and lowering of K. That is, interval B in Figure 51 can be brought down to the equilibrium curve and maintained there without continuing in interval C. That is being done by holding the residual population to 130 animals,

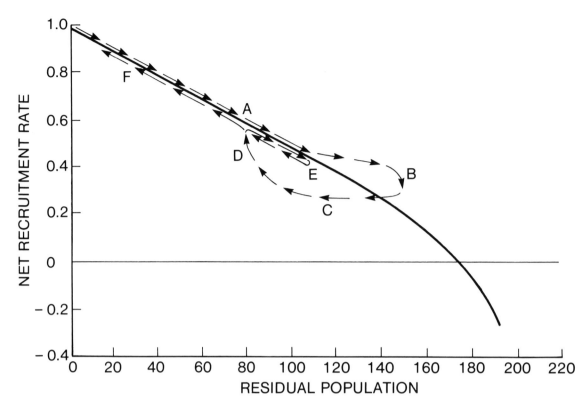

Figure 51. Observed recruitment rates (smoothed) compared with equilibrium rate for white-tailed deer of the George Reserve in Michigan over time, showing time lag. Time intervals are: (A) initial population growth rate following introduction and experimental population growth (1928–1931, 1975–1980); (B) initial population overshoot (1932–1935, 1981–1982); (C) decline in growth rate due to vegetation damage (1936–1946); (D) recovery rate due to population reduction and vegetation recovery; (E) subsequent population increase with observed rate and equilibrium rate comparable (1947–1967); and (F) recent population with observed rate comparable to equilibrium rate (1968–1974).

which is below equilibrium K of 176. However, the recruitment plus the residual population exceeds K on a seasonal basis. This is particularly true early in the overshoot (212 animals in 1980), but the tendency declines as the accumulation of resources is used up. Thus, the first removal required to reduce the population to a residual of 130 was 82 animals. And the hypothesis is that, within the next few years, the required harvest will decline to an average of 44—the equilibrium harvest for a residual population of 130.

STOCHASTIC BEHAVIOR

With the behavior of the whitetail population outlined according to a deterministic model, the model can be complicated to approximate more nearly the conditions of the real world. One of the major problems confronting the wildlife biologist or resource manager is the year-to-year variation in habitat quality due to variable amounts of precipitation, severity of winter, presence or absence of an acorn crop, etc. These variables are beyond managerial control, but whitetail management programs must take them into account. If the environmental stochasticity is small relative to density-dependent responses of the population, management based on empirical models can be followed. This is the case on the George Reserve. If the environmental stochasticity is great relative to the density-dependent response of the environment, an *ad hoc* strategy will be required. That is, the biologist or manager will not be able to develop predictive models based on the density-dependent response of the population and follow a more-or-less consistent management plan. Instead, management decisions will have to be made on a year-by-year basis in response to the environmental factors of the particular year. This does not mean that the deer population does not behave in a density-dependent fashion, or that the conceptual model presented here cannot be used as a general guide to show how the population will respond after an environmental deviation, such as a hard winter, has had its effect. It is just that if extreme conditions occur too frequently, the environmental variation will overshadow the density-dependent response. By analogy to radio communication, what the investigator is dealing with is a signal-to-noise ratio. If the signal-to-noise ratio is high, the signal can be managed, given the level of the noise. If the signal is weak relative to the noise, then response is possible only when the signal is clear, because the noise masks the signal much of the time.

Fortunately, most white-tailed deer populations occur in relatively benign environments and respond well to density-dependent management. However, in the extreme northern and desert fringes of whitetail range, environments can be extreme, and management may well have to be *ad hoc*—or at least require more *ad hoc* interventions than in a density-dependent scheme. Elsewhere I have discussed frequency distributions of good and bad years, and their likely impact on management programs (McCullough 1979, in press).

Stochasticity on the George Reserve can be assigned variance in the regression equation that describes the relationship of recruitment rate to residual population. The confidence bounds on the productivity curve (Figure 50b) are shown in Figure 52, where it can be seen that variation is small at low residual populations but increases rapidly at high residual populations. Good or poor years have a greater impact on high populations of deer.

By analogy, at low deer density the signal (density-dependent effect) is so strong that it greatly exceeds the noise, while at high density the noise has a greater masking effect on the signal. At high densities, most adult whitetail does attempt to reproduce (McCullough 1979), and the potential number of recruits is very high. If a good year occurs, a large number of recruits may be added. Conversely, a poor year may virtually eliminate recruitment in that year, and because the population is on the margin of maintenance costs, many individuals in the residual population will drop below the maintenance level and die of malnutrition. In management terms, this means that populations subject to little hunting that are close to K will show greatest fluctuation, while harvests re-

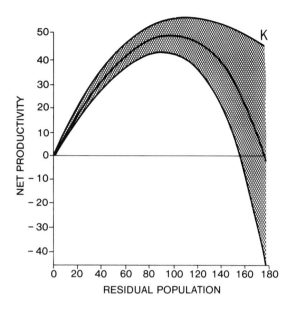

Figure 52. Net productivity of the George Reserve whitetailed deer population in Michigan, based on data from 1952 to 1971, with a 95-percent confidence limit.

ducing the population to lower residual sizes will result in greater stability.

The instabilities previously discussed regarding the left arm of the parabola are intensified by stochasticity (however, *see* Functional Refugia). Because balance at any given residual population on this arm requires exact removal of the number of recruits added, the precision required of management is unrealistic, given that recruitment will vary somewhat even though it is minor compared with that on the right arm (Figure 52).

Because maximum sustainable yield management has instability characteristics similar to those associated with the left arm of the parabola and leads to overexploitation, it is susceptible to excessive removals. However, errors of underharvest are corrected for by density-dependent responses characteristic of the right arm of the parabola. If the mean maximum sustainable yield (49 for the George Reserve deer population) is removed as a fixed harvest over time, extinction of the population is inevitable, because the mean harvest sooner or later will exceed the actual recruitment and move the residual population to the left arm of the productivity parabola. If a disproportionately large recruitment does not occur in the following year, extinction will result.

This characteristic of the population explains why populations overexploited by man show sustaining capability and then apparently collapse suddenly. On the right side of the productivity parabola, the incremental change to removals of maximum sustainable yield, or slightly greater than maximum sustainable yield, are gradual. But once the residual population is reduced to values on the left of maximum sustainable yield, the same fixed harvest that resulted in gradual change in residual populations on the right arm results in rapid extinction.

Simulations of fixed harvests on the George Reserve whitetail population showed that the likelihood of extinction increased as maximum sustainable yield was approached (Figure 53). At maximum sustainable yield, 16 of 20 simulations of 100 years lead to extinction while, with a harvest of 50 (slightly exceeding maximum sustainable yield), all 20 lead to extinction within 100 years. A fixed harvest of 46 was the highest harvest that did not lead to extinction in 20 simulations of 100 years.

If the harvest cannot be controlled and also varies stochastically, probabilities of extinction become even higher. Applying stochastic variation to the harvest in the George Reserve model based on variance in harvest for deer hunting in legal seasons in Michigan with constant regulations (McCullough 1979) resulted in 43 being the highest harvest that did not lead to any extinctions in 20 simulations of 100 years (Figure 53). Harvests of maximum sustainable

yields led to extinction within 100 years for all 20 simulations.

Environmental variation can lead to overshoot of K and vegetation damage in unhunted populations as well as in those whitetail populations hunted very conservatively. Thus, particularly good years may increase the residual population above K. Population adjustments to K accomplished through failure in recruitment have relatively little damaging effect on vegetation even if K is temporarily exceeded, because the young do not live long and are present during the better season of the year. However, adjustments to stochastic overshoots are accomplished by increased mortality of recruited animals. Because these whitetails are larger and have greater reserves, they can persist longer and put correspondingly larger defoliation pressure on the vegetation. Also, several good years in a row can result in relatively great overshoot and destabilize the natural tendencies toward equilibrium between residual population and K. For further treatment of these time lags, *see* McCullough (1979, in press).

NATURAL PREDATORS

Selectivity of natural predators, as previously mentioned, was reviewed for white-tailed deer by McCullough (1979) (*see also* Chapter 8). There is strong evidence that predators take the young, old and unfit. This is not to say that healthy deer are not killed sometimes. In fact they are, and review of wolf predation on deer showed clear evidence that success in taking a greater proportion of prime deer is related to lower deer density (that is, wolves can kill healthier deer by greater effort). However, on the basis of age-class frequency, young, old and unfit are overrepresented in wolf-kill samples. And because large predators have higher reproductive potential than do deer, a vulnerability variable has to be present to account for the long coexistence of prey and predators.

Because human hunting, by reducing whitetail density, increases deer body growth and size, improves health and lowers the age distribution of the population (McCullough 1979), it decreases the overall vulnerability of the deer population to natural predation. Even young deer are less vulnerable because good health of both fawns and does results in rapid growth rates by fawns and alertness on the part of

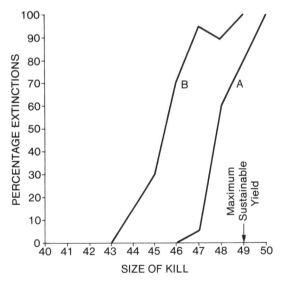

Figure 53. Population extinction rates from simulations of Michigan's George Reserve white-tailed deer model with stochastic recruitment (A) and stochastic recruitment and harvest (B). Percentage of extinctions is based on the percentage of 20 runs that went to extinction within 100 years.

Openlands on the George Reserve contribute high-quality forage to the spring and summer whitetail diet, and also during winter when snow does not cover basal rosettes of forbs and new sprigs of grass that remain green at ground level. *Photo by Doug Fulton.*

mothers. Therefore, heavy hunting by humans results in fewer deer in the population and lowered vulnerability. These changes cannot help but reduce vulnerability to predators and, thus, while hunting by humans and natural predation almost certainly are not entirely substitutive, they are substitutive to some considerable extent. As the proportion of the deer population taken by human hunters is increased, the proportion taken by natural predators should decrease.

The wildlife biologist or manager almost never is in a position to determine the kill of deer by natural predation. It is difficult even in research. However, in managing whitetails the objective should be to derive the empirical relationship between productivity and density. If derived in a management unit where natural predators are present, the empirical productivity curve will reflect the harvest available to hunters with the predator take removed. If human hunting is highly substitutable for nat-

ural predation, the slope of the right arm of the productivity curve derived will be steep and, because human hunting is coming at the expense of natural predators, those predators will have to switch to alternative prey, emigrate or decline in population. If human hunting is less substitutable for natural predation, the slope of the productivity curve will be shallow, and hunter harvests will be reduced because of the greater additivity of human and predator take. In either case, managing for maximum sustainable yield of hunter harvest on the basis of such an empirical model will manage the deer population for maximum sustainable yield since the take of natural predators already is included in the empirical results. This is the approach I am taking in a current set of experiments on Columbian blacktailed deer at the Hopland Field Station in California, where coyotes and other natural predators take an unknown (and perhaps undeterminable) number of deer.

FUNCTIONAL REFUGIA

An exception to the general rule that the left arm of the productivity curve is unstable is the presence of functional refugia. These may be in the form of an actual designated refuge where hunting is not allowed, an impenetrable vegetation type, a large roadless area or legal restrictions on hunting methods and equipment. The functional refuge sets a constraint on the lower limit to which a population can be reduced (Figure 54). In any event, if the variable under consideration is constrained by a refuge, it may set limitations on what can be accomplished by management. By the same token, a refuge may prevent deer population extinction in the face of large errors in management. Thus, if an unhuntable vegetational type sets a limit on a legal harvest with a one-buck season, increasing the limit to two bucks is not likely to result in any appreciable increase in the kill. Also, because hunters vary in ability (Holsworth 1973), the one-deer bag limit is a refuge effect in itself because good hunters are removed from the hunter population and poor hunters retained as the season progresses.

The Crab Orchard National Wildlife Refuge in Illinois (Hawkins and Klimstra 1970*a*) and Berry College Refuge in Georgia (Kammermeyer and Marchinton 1976*b*) are examples of legal refuges, and the tamarack swamp on the George Reserve is an unhuntable type. In a similar example, Van Etten et al. (1965) reported that it took six hunters 124 hours of hunting even to see a buck in a 2.6-square-kilometer (1-square-mile) enclosure in northern Michigan with seven bucks present. In contrast, Creed and Kubisiak (1973) reported

a harvest of all deer in a Wisconsin enclosure approximately 4,050 hectares (10,000 acres) where escape cover was poor and hunter density high. Swenson (1982) found that mule deer in forested areas were far less vulnerable than those in prairie areas. Northern states, such as Minnesota, Wisconsin, Michigan and Maine, and the eastern Canadian provinces have large roadless areas where obtaining harvests of white-tailed deer is difficult or impossible. Restrictions include prohibition of night spotlighting, baiting, use of dogs, etc. Most refugia are not absolute, but apply to one or a few forms of protection for deer. Thus, a legal refuge may prevent hunter harvest, but natural predation and poaching may continue. And a refugium based on vegetation may prevent a human hunter from ever getting a shot, but legalizing the use of dogs may overcome the effect of the refuge. Peterson (1969) reviewed hunter behavior as it relates to the deer harvest.

GOAL SETTING

Any program of white-tailed deer mangement must start with the definition of what the program is intended to achieve. Who is the audience served? What are ramifications of the program on the deer resource and the satisfactions of the user group or groups? What are the criteria by which the program can be judged as successful or unsuccessful? Will these criteria be acceptable to the user group or groups? What dissatisfactions will be accepted as the cost of allocating the deer resource among user groups? Often, the programs of wildlife biologists and managers have been good in practice; it is the in-depth explanations of deer-population characteristics that have needed firmer foundations.

The frequently heard justification of managers that they managed deer for "the carrying capacity" of the range was a bit of self-delusion, often dressed up by the euphemism "scientific management." While most people can agree that programs resulting in vegetation destruction are self-defeating in the long run, there is a great deal more arbitrariness about impacts on vegetation below K. It is necessary to distinguish defoliation impact from impact so great that it cannot be sustained. Even one deer has some impact, and the impact shows a functional relationship similar to the productivity curve, in that impact increases up to the max-

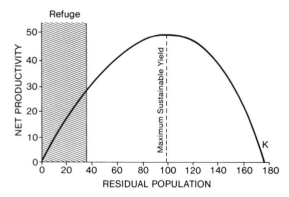

Figure 54. Productivity curve for white-tailed deer on the George Reserve in Michigan, showing the effect of a hypothetical functional refuge.

imum sustainable which, by definition, occurs at K. Some of the least fruitful arguments among big game biologists have revolved about which point estimate of vegetation impact was "correct," when all up to K are arbitrary and can be evaluated only by reference to a predetermined program goal and set of specific objectives. It must be recognized that any point on the residual population axis of Figure 50b from zero to K is a sustainable point (given sufficient skill on the part of the manager), and no scientific method will determine which point is any better than any other. The perception of a given point being best by the manager was a reflection of an unrecognized *a priori* assumption of what was best. It is time to abandon this bit of circular logic.

The goal of a deer management program is arbitrary, not scientific, which may be upsetting news to some wildlife biologists and other resource managers as well as citizens. Science does not make the decision. People do. And the views of various interest groups have to be considered because they cannot be ruled out on scientific grounds. Protectionist groups have recognized intuitively that decisions by biologists and managers may have been biased toward hunter interests, as the overall goal of maintaining sustainable harvests has been pursued (*see* Favre and Olsen 1982). While the protectionists still have a way to go and are diverted by their own shibboleths, they clearly are influencing the goals and objectives used in managing deer populations.

Once the goal has been established for a given management unit, then science—in the form of productivity curves (or some comparable model)—can be used to develop a program to achieve the goal and its associated objectives for the deer population.

There are four major biological goals. First, one wants to avoid extinction of the deer population. Second, one can decide to minimize the residual population to reduce negative impacts of the population. Thus, one might want to reduce the frequency of deer/vehicle collisions, or deer damage to agricultural crops, orchards or forest reproduction. Third, one can decide to maximize the sustainable yield (harvest). And fourth, one can maximize the size of the residual population in the field. Therefore, establishing the optimum sustainable yield is dependent on management program goals, and may range from very low to very high residual populations and sustained yields.

Under circumstances of crop or forest damage, deer/vehicle collisions, etc., it may be desirable to maintain whitetail populations at very low levels, well below I carrying capacity. If a functional refuge is present, more liberal seasons or bag limits, beyond a certain point, are not likely to have an effect. If the degree of control over the deer population is accomplished by the residual population maintained by a refuge, then the management system is easily implemented. If a greater harvest is required, some other hunting methods (depending on the nature of the refuge) may have to be legalized, such as the use of dogs, or hunting at later hours when deer venture out from the refuge. In some cases it may be difficult to motivate hunters to put forth the extra effort required to achieve the desired degree of control.

If one wants to maintain a high residual population for tourists, nature study groups, etc., but also wants some hunting, buck-only hunting is a good strategy. Most sportsmen approve of such programs and find them philosophically satisfying, even though probability of success in taking deer is relatively low, and probability of overshoot of K and vegetation damage is high.

Maximizing the harvest usually would involve manipulating residual populations to just to the right of maximum sustainable yield (Figure 50b) where stability of the population responses is high. Seasons with antlerless hunting will need to be liberal, and the hunter effort per deer taken will need to be high. Deer populations managed in this way are less affected by environmental variations, except, perhaps, in the most extreme years. They respond rapidly to adjustments in management and are most easily modeled for functional relationships. They yield the greatest harvest and, therefore, the highest harvest success rate for hunters. Because residual populations are low, deer damage problems usually are moderate to low or infrequent.

In addition to biological goals, there are social goals. One can manage for deer-hunter satisfaction that may or may not be achieved by management for maximum sustainable yield. One can manage for landowner satisfaction, or for protectionist-group satisfaction. Just as a given program cannot simultaneously achieve all biological goals, it is unlikely that all social goals can be achieved simultaneously. The tough problems confronting wildlife management agencies are the decisions about who gets what—a statement that will come as no surprise. Nevertheless, progress is being made. An important step has been to recognize that landowners and operators accommodate deer on their properties. Thus, more states are realigning deer-hunting regulations to give landowners and/or operators first preference for hunting opportunities in designated management units.

Once decisions have been made, implementation of a new program should be made in

Annual drives, in which a line of people moves across the area, have been conducted on the George Reserve since 1933 to determine whitetail population size. *Photo by Doug Fulton.*

increments. In the first place it should be verified that the direction taken was correct, and conforms to predictions. Second, there is considerable inertia in large public programs, and deviations from past practice cause skepticism among the users. Leadership consists not just of "being out in front," but also in having public backing. Getting too far out in front results in loss of touch with the public. New programs should be geared to a pace the public will follow. Some agencies still are suffering from continuing weak support caused by the attempt to solve a chronic deer overpopulation problem with a massive antlerless kill in the 1950s and 1960s. Changing the reactive attitudes of citizens established two to three decades ago requires a well-founded informational/educational effort based on a fundamentally sound deer management program.

REGULATING THE SEX AND AGE OF THE KILL

Buck-only Versus Any-age-or-sex Hunting

Setting seasons restricted to bucks only is the surest way to minimize the harvest short of no season at all. While there may be good reasons for minimizing the harvest, it is unfortunate that this management approach is applied supposedly in the interest of large harvests. Surely few professions have been cursed by such an intuitively appealing practice—one that is immensely popular with the constituents involved and that works in the diametrically opposite manner from what is intended. It is ironic that those opposing hunting are most incensed by trophy hunting—the hunter's quest for large and inedible antlers—a practice that assures that the fewest deer will die from gunshots.

The failing of buck-only hunting for yielding bucks, much less total deer, can be seen in Figure 55, where the potential harvest curve on residual population size, as shown for the George Reserve deer population, is separated by sex. Sex-ratio variation due to population density, with males predominating at high density (Verme 1965a, McCullough 1979), is included, but the results are approximately the same for a 50:50 ratio.

Because does are spared under buck-only hunting, the residual population grows toward

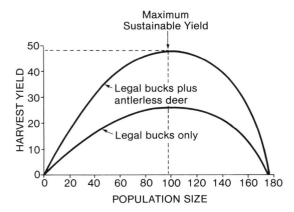

Figure 55. Relationship of white-tailed deer harvests of only bucks to any deer on the George Reserve in Michigan, based on data from 1952–1972.

K. This results in reduction of all recruitment, including recruitment of bucks (Figure 55). Since the harvest is dependent on recruitment, a harvest of only bucks assures a low recruitment of bucks to be harvested.

Maximum sustainable yield of bucks is obtained by the same management as is total maximum sustainable yield, namely by taking harvests of both sexes to reduce the residual population to near I carrying capacity (with due regard to the instability of this point as discussed earlier). Model simulations on the 464-hectare (1,146-acre) George Reserve deer population of buck-only hunting give a buck yield of 2.9 to 6.8 (depending on which model was used), while buck yield at maximum sustainable yield was 26. Furthermore, no antlerless deer take is present in bucks-only hunting, while 23 antlerless deer are taken when the deer population is managed for maximum sustainable yield.

This illustrates a very important point in deer management. Once the residual population has reached or exceeded I carrying capacity, there is no advantage to being selective for sex and age in hunting. To state it another way, the population is quite insensitive to unbalanced sex and age composition. Results from the George Reserve clearly show that most hunters used in earlier years to take the harvest were selective for bucks even when instructed to shoot all deer randomly. This resulted in bucks being taken out of proportion to their presence in the population, but the inevitability of achieving the desired size of harvest required that females be taken. When I assumed the job of doing the harvesting, I selected strictly

for the first clear target. Because of their behavioral vulnerability, yearling bucks were killed in greater poroportion than their prevalence in the population. Most of the other sex and age classes were taken nearly in proportion to their occurrence in the population (McCullough 1979). Despite the different approaches and selectivities of the two harvest systems, the functional outcome was the same.

The constraint of the productivity curve on sex-selective harvest can be illustrated by a further simulation of the George Reserve deer population. Considering a system of harvest that begins with the population being managed for maximum sustainable yield, but then switches to bucks only, with every buck greater than yearling age harvested (Figure 56), the kill of bucks inevitably declines. When it bottoms out, the management system is changed, and all bucks older than yearling age are taken, but does are taken to bring the kill to maximum sustainable yield. Inevitably the size of the buck kill increases until the initial state of maximum sustainable yield is achieved.

Is there evidence that the deer-population response in management units elsewhere shows the same behavior? Yes, virtually universally. As wildlife biologists throughout white-tailed deer range will note, buck-only hunting invariably results in: (1) high residual populations predominantly of females; (2) low overall recruitment rates; and (3) legal bucks comprising 10 percent or less of the population.

These conditions hold for the black-tailed deer at the 2,024-hectare (5,000-acre) Hopland Field Station in California, where only bucks are taken in legal hunts. Given the relation-

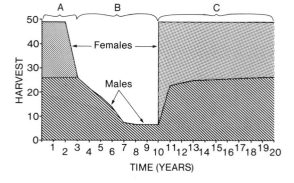

Figure 56. Simulations of multiple sustainable yield harvesting of white-tailed deer on the George Reserve in Michigan (A), switching to buck-only (yearling and older bucks) (B), and then harvesting again at multiple sustainable yield by taking bucks only and completing the harvest with antlerless deer (C).

ships outlined previously, it follows that increased harvests of does should be followed by increased harvests of bucks. By reanalyzing the data of Connolly and Longhurst (1975), who collected various numbers of does for other study purposes that had nothing to do with buck production, I got the relationship shown in Figure 57. There was a highly significant correlation between the number of does taken and the number of bucks taken three years later when recruits of the subsequent residual population first reached legal size with forked-horn antlers. This relationship was strong, despite the fact that the doe harvest varied greatly between years and did not follow a pattern of consistent change. An experiment with incremental increases in doe harvest is one I have begun, and there is every reason to believe that the correlation between doe removal and antlerless harvest will be much higher without the "noise" due to highly variable doe harvest.

Though Figure 57's equation has the best fit (highest r^2), it is not a good predictor of a productivity curve; extreme values on the x-axis distort (project to infinity) the shape. If the extreme points on both ends are eliminated, an exponential equation $Y = 3.35e^{-0.03x}$ ($r^2 = 0.81$) gives the best fit. It can be modified by elimination of the righthand tail resulting from this equation, to project a George Reserve-like "productivity curve" of legal buck harvest dependent on doe removal (Figure 58), which hypothesises a maximum sustainable yield of about 47 legal bucks and 44 does.

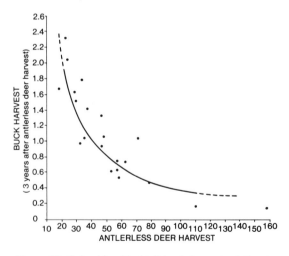

Figure 57. Columbian blacktail buck harvest relative to antlerless harvest three years earlier at California's Hopland Field Station, 1951 to 1974 (from Connolly and Longhurst 1975). $Y = ax^b = 46.79x^{-1.04}$, $r^2 = 0.88$.

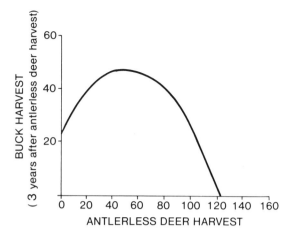

Figure 58. Predicted buck harvest in relation to antlerless harvest of black-tailed deer at Hopland Field Station in California, as derived from Figure 57.

As an aside, it should be noted that on Hopland Field Station, deer density was a far more important variable in controlling productivity than all other variables combined, including coyotes and other natural predators, poaching, drought and variable acorn crops (oaks are abundant on the area). While Hopland Field Station does not represent the extreme in environmental variation that deer face in North America, it certainly is not a benignly stable area. Its Mediterranean climate—mild, wet winters and dry, hot summers—and its vegetation of annual grassland, oak savanna and chaparral certainly present a stark contrast to the George Reserve. That two different species of deer in two very different environments respond similarly to density suggests that these lessons about deer management probably are not endemic to the George Reserve.

Trophy Buck Production

Another irony in the buck-only story is the widely held belief that this scheme of management is the route to production of trophy bucks. While it is true that some trophy bucks are obtained under buck-only hunting, they are relatively few and require a long time to grow to trophy size (McCullough 1979). Management for maximum sustainable yield will produce the greatest number of bucks; and because of rapid growth rate under such management, bucks will reach a large size in a short time.

Trophy bucks are considered those with large, heavy antlers bearing at least four points on either antler (eight-pointers by eastern count, which includes both antlers). Because antler weight (grams) of George Reserve whitetails is correlated highly with body weight (kilograms) according to the formula $Y = -1695.5 + 28.8 \times (r^2 = 0.57)$ (McCullough 1982c), the management system that produces the largest body size will also produce the largest antlers. Similarly, the number of antler points is related significantly both to antler weight ($Y = 15.7 + 89.15X$, $r^2 = 0.71$) and body weight ($Y = -6.08 + 0.17 \times r^2 = 0.45$). Thus, comparison of maximum sustainable yield management with buck-only management, according to survivorship curves for the George Reserve bucks (McCullough 1979) and assuming selectivity in both systems for the largest bucks and growth rates, shows that management for maximum sustainable yield would yield 26 bucks, of which 12 would be eight-pointers or larger, 10 six-pointers, and 4 three-pointers. Buck-only hunting, by the most liberal calculation, would give 6.8 bucks with eight-point antlers. Note that mean number of points per buck taken is less with management for maximum sustainable yield (weighted $\bar{x} = 6.5$ points), as previously reported for mule deer from Texas (Brownlee 1975). However, absolute numbers by antler-size class as well as averages must be compared under the two systems of management. Declining averages do not show that trophy production and maximum sustainable yield are incompatible, as concluded by Connolly (1981), although the generally lower growth potential of mule deer (McCullough in press) may make the difference less pronounced as compared with that of white-tailed deer.

These conclusions are supported by results from the George Reserve as population size has varied over time (Table 28, Figure 59). Reserve caretaker Lawrence Camburn weighed deer in 1941 and 1942 when the population was about 126. Mean weight of yearling and older bucks was 66.4 kilograms (146.6 pounds). Between 1958 and 1971, the population size averaged 67 whitetails, and yearling and older bucks averaged 71.3 kilograms (157.5 pounds). When the whitetail population was reduced to 10 between 1971 and 1975, the average buck weight rose to 75.9 kilograms (167.6 pounds). Following rapid increase in the whitetail population with protection (*see* Rate of Population Increase), when harvesting was resumed in 1980–1981, average buck weight was 77.6 kil-

ograms (171.4 pounds). Because of the high whitetail densities, weight of bucks harvested the following season (1981–1982) declined to 71.2 kilograms (157.3 pounds). Weight ranges in yearling and adult bucks showed the same patterns as the means (Table 28), as did the

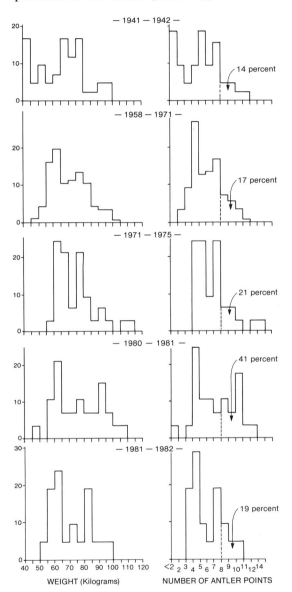

Figure 59. Frequency histograms of fresh kill weights and numbers of antler points of yearling and older white-tailed deer bucks for different periods and population densities on the George Reserve. Population size and buck harvest for periods are as given in Table 28. Because the number of antler points was not recorded for all periods, all results are based on weight according to the equation $Y = -6.08 + 0.17X$ (McCullough 1982c). Less than two antler points—<2—refers to spike antlers averaging less than 15 centimeters (6 inches) in length.

Table 28. Relationship of size and status of the white-tailed deer population to fresh-kill weight of yearling and older bucks on the George Reserve, Michigan.

Years	Mean posthunt population size	Number killed	Mean weight		Standard deviation		Range
			Kilograms	Pounds	Kilograms	Pounds	Kilograms
1941–1942	126[a]	44	66.4	146.4	16.5	36.4	40.3–100.5
1958–1971	67[b]	141	71.3	157.2	11.8	26.0	47.5–101.4
1971–1975	33[c]	35	75.9	167.3	13.5	29.8	59.3–113.6
1980–1981	130[d]	29	77.6	171.1	16.6	36.6	46.2–109.1
1981–1982	± 130[e]	21	71.2	157.0	13.0	28.7	53.4– 98.2

[a]Estimated from corrected drive count (McCullough 1979).
[b]Estimated from reconstructed population (McCullough 1979).
[c]Estimated from drive count. Population reduced from an estimated 60 in 1971–1972 to 10 in 1974–1975.
[d]Estimated from drive count (*see* Rate of Population Increase and Time Lags).
[e]Approximate population size. The most severe winter on record prevented a successful drive count in 1982.

weights of yearling bucks (Figure 59). The first peak in the weight histograms in Figure 59 are predominantly yearlings, and it can be seen from Figure 59 that yearlings in 1941–1942 weighed 40 to 50 kilograms (88–110 pounds). This rose to 55–65 kilograms (121–143 pounds) in the period 1958–1971, to 60–70 kilograms (132–154 pounds) in the period 1971–1975, and fell back to 50–60 kilograms (110–132 pounds) in the periods 1980–1981 and 1981–1982. Note that yearlings during the latter two periods were produced under high densities, while largest bucks harvested in 1980–1981 were born early in the increase experiment, and achieved their growth at low population density. Antlers of yearling animals show the same pattern (Figure 59).

Record bucks were produced not at high densities, which have the oldest individuals, but rather at the lowest densities (1971–1975). The largest buck ever taken (113.6 kilograms [251 pounds]) and the next largest (110.4 kilograms [224 pounds]) were taken in 1971, when total buck harvest was 37. The largest buck of 44 taken in 1941–1942 was 100.5 kilograms (222 pounds). The highest proportion of bucks weighing more than 90.5 kilograms (200 pounds) was obtained at lowest densities, in the period 1971–1975, reflecting low density during the population-growth experiment (1980–1981 harvest) (Table 28). This occurred despite these periods of heavy harvest having the youngest age structure in both the population and the kill. The record buck was five years old and the next largest was three years old. No buck taken in 1971–1975 or 1980–1981 exceeded five years of age and most were yearlings, two- and three-year-olds.

Antler size showed the same relationship, with the greatest proportion of eight-point or better racks obtained in 1971–1975 and 1980–1981 (Figure 59). Furthermore, under heavy exploitation yearling bucks obtain antlers that are much larger than the simple spikes typically associated with this age class. Thus,

The number and trophy quality of George Reserve bucks are determined by the size of the antlerless harvest and its impact on total deer density. *Photo by Doug Fulton.*

Table 28. (continued)

Range		Number of deer more than 90.5 kilograms (200 pounds)	Percentage of deer more than 90.5 kilograms (200 pounds)
Pounds			
88.8–221.6		4	9.1
104.7–223.5		11	7.8
130.7–250.4		5	14.3
101.9–240.5		8	27.6
117.7–216.5		2	9.5

on the George Reserve, when residual populations were well below I carrying capacity (McCullough 1982*c*), eight-point yearlings were common, although the beams of the antlers were substantially lighter than those of older age classes. Because there is a genetic component involved in antler conformation (Harmel 1980), as well as a nutritional component, there may be justification for removing spike-antlered bucks in heavy exploitation programs, since the genetically superior yearlings will have large antlers. And of course the true trophy-rack bucks are those that escape heavy exploitation to become venerable six- to eight-year-olds. Because of great flexibility in the age-sex structure of deer, any workable system to protect bucks until they are older will pay off in trophy antler production under heavy exploitation.

In conclusion, management for maximum sustainable yield has substantial advantage over buck-only harvests in terms of the number of quality bucks produced. There may be considerable public-relations value in billing management for buck-only hunting as trophy management, but a tacit rule of propagandizing is ''don't believe it yourself.''

RELATIONSHIP OF REGULATIONS TO HARVEST

It is necessary to establish the relationship between regulations and harvest. Does issuance of additional antlerless permits result in the desired increase in harvest? And what is the ratio of permits to harvest? Does the larger hunter population encouraged by antlerless hunting result in an increase in the buck harvest because most hunters will take a buck given the opportunity? Freddy (1982) reported that the number of antlerless animals taken

from a Colorado mule-deer population was correlated with the number of either-sex permits issued, but that antlered-deer harvest was not predictable.

Regression analysis of the whitetail harvest in Michigan (Department of Natural Resources harvest records) that I did for the period 1958–1974—when firearms regulations were fairly consistent—showed variable patterns for the three management regions (Table 29). The size of antlerless harvest was related closely to the number of antlerless hunters in all three regions and, therefore, the number of antlerless hunters to achieve a desired antlerless harvest can be predicted: Region I $\hat{Y} = 1108.6 + 0.223X$; Region II $\hat{Y} = 2074.4 + 0.283X$; and Region III $\hat{Y} = 513.8 + 0.169X$.

However, the relationship of buck harvest to number of buck hunters was correlated significantly only for Region III. In the other two regions buck harvest was correlated more closely to number of antlerless-deer hunters than to number of buck hunters—but not significantly. Probably the major effect was due to the influence of numbers of antlerless-deer permits on the total number of hunters afield, since antlerless permit holders could take a buck instead. In Region I, each antlerless-deer hunter increased the total number of hunters by 0.27 hunter. For example, 5,000 antlerless-deer hunters resulted in 1,350 additional deer hunters in the field. By the same token, each

Table 29. Influence of number of antlerless-deer hunting permits on the white-tailed deer harvest by management region in Michigan: P = probability; r^2 = coefficient of determination.

Region		Buck hunters	Antlerless-deer hunters	Total hunters
Region I[a]				
Buck kill	r^2	0.005	0.178	0.136
	P	0.392	0.247	0.073
Antlerless kill	r^2	0.739	0.804	0.550
	P	<0.001	<0.001	<0.001
Region II[b]				
Buck kill	r^2	0.027	0.184	0.183
	P	0.263	0.176	0.043
Antlerless kill	r^2	0.428	0.799	0.168
	P	0.002	<0.001	0.051
Region III[c]				
Buck kill	r^2	0.827	0.827	0.824
	P	<0.001	<0.001	<0.001
Antlerless kill	r^2	0.484	0.761	0.537
	P	0.009	<0.001	0.005

[a]Upper Peninsula.
[b]Upper part of Lower Peninsula.
[c]Lower part of Lower Peninsula.

antlerless-deer hunter decreased the number of buck hunters by 0.73, which suggests that approximately 73 percent of the hunters who hunted in buck-only seasons obtained antlerless permits when whey were available. Since the time these data were assembled, antlerless hunting in Region I has been curtailed by political intervention.

In Region II, antlerless-deer permits had an even stronger influence on the total hunting population. Each antlerless-deer hunter increased the total number of hunters by 0.55, while 45 percent of the buck-only hunters obtained antlerless-deer permits. This greater effect of numbers of antlerless-deer hunters on total hunters afield resulted in the buck harvest correlated significantly to total hunters afield (Table 29).

In Region III, the total number of hunters increased rapidly during the period covered by the data because of the expanding deer population in southern Michigan. Nevertheless, about 83 percent of the increase was attributable to the number of antlerless-deer hunters, while only 17 percent was due to growth in the number of buck-only hunters. Both buck harvest and antlerless harvest were quite predictable.

While this analysis is cursory, it shows the general approach of analyzing the influence of hunting regulations on hunter numbers and deer harvest by developing predictive tools. Other information on both deer and hunter demography clearly is necessary to interpret results. Hunter dynamics and deer-harvest results are not the same for Region I in the Upper Peninsula of Michigan—a remote and poorly roaded area with a low human population and a stagnant deer population—as for the Lower Peninsula. Similarly, within the Lower Peninsula, the more remote Region II—with its long tradition as a good deer area—is different from the heavily populated, easily accessible Region III with its expanding deer population.

MODELING BUCK HARVEST BY MANIPULATION OF DOE HARVEST

The historic dominance of buck-only hunting means that it may be possible to model populations on the basis of manipulation of doe harvest in order to influence buck harvest, as presently is being done at the Hopland Field Station in California. This assumes that density-dependent responses are present, and are not overshadowed by environmental variation. It makes no assumptions about other mortality factors, except that they behave in some rational fashion. Only the harvests of bucks and does need to be obtained with reasonable precision, and a relative value (or index) will work as well as an absolute value so long as the requirement of precision is met. The total deer population does not need to be known.

In Figure 58, the relationship for Hopland Field Station is presented on the basis of currently available data and suggests that, in the absence of doe harvests, the mean number of bucks taken will be 23. The maximum sustainable yield for bucks and does occurs at the same point, and Figure 58 suggests this should occur at a harvest of 44 does and 47 bucks.

The approach I propose to take is to make the doe harvest under a collecting permit. Examination of reproductive tracts will yield an embryo rate to suggest the reproductive effort. Over time, the kill of does will be incrementally increased. The embryo rate, individual weights, antler size and total buck-kill should increase as doe harvest increases. These data will be the basis of a refined model, probably with lower variance because the harvest of does is incremental and not fluctuating wildly from year to year as in the data presented in Figure 57.

As the buck harvest begins to plateau, maximum sustainable yield is approached. For management purposes, one probably would elect to stop at this point, given that maximum sustainable yield is an unstable point on the left arm of the productivity parabola. On Hopland Field Station, it probably will be desirable to overexploit to verify that maximum sustainable yield has been exceeded (thereby reducing the residual population to the left arm of the productivity parabola temporarily), then decrease the harvest to allow recovery, and once again increase to as near to maximum sustainable yield as seems feasible, given the variance in the new model derived.

Elsewhere (McCullough in press), I have estimated that for mule deer the residual population yielding maximum sustainable yield is about 63 percent of K and will represent 27 percent of the prehunt population, the other 73 percent being the residual population. These values give crude expectations of a residual population (I carrying capacity) of 337 yielding a maximum sustainable yield of 91. Estimated population at K would be 535. These values are slightly below the range of population estimates made by Longhurst, as cited by Connolly (1970), on the basis of mark and recapture, change in ratios and pellet-count methods, although there was great disparity among methods used.

The difference between embryo rates (expected) and harvest rates of individuals born in the same year (observed) will indicate mortality due to factors other than hunting, and serve as a cross-check of total deer-population estimates.

Although the objective is to establish the functional relationship between doe and buck harvests, estimation of absolute values of population size inevitably results from the cross-referencing that becomes possible with data accumulation. These estimates cost little and promise to be at least as reliable as those presently used, which are notoriously difficult and expensive to obtain and lack the cross-checking for consistency that typifies an empirical modeling approach.

STOCK RECRUITMENT MODELS

This approach to empirical modeling has been proposed previously (McCullough 1979). Figure 50c is a stock recruitment model. It is based on the tendency of recruitment to come to an average balance with the harvest. It requires that the harvest be determined and be broken down by new recruits versus older animals. The estimate of recruitment rate is based on dividing the recruits by the older animals taken in the same time-specific hunting-harvest sample. It will work well only if hunting is not selective for sex and age, but will be approximate if the antlerless harvest is relatively liberal. It further requires an estimate of total population, which can be derived from the harvest data (McCullough 1979) or a reasonable reliable index of total population (McCullough 1978).

The approach works best with populations that have been hunted quite conservatively, so that the beginning harvest is small relative to maximum sustainable yield. Therefore, the harvest can be increased incrementally by gradually liberalizing regulations. For further description of the method, *see* McCullough (1979).

MANAGING FOR HUNTER SATISFACTION

Traditionally, whitetails have been managed for deer in the bag, so long as the removal was sustainable, under the assumption that the higher the number and percentage of hunters successful, the greater the hunter satisfaction. However, sociological studies in the 1970s showed that hunter satisfaction was much more complex, and not closely correlated with size of the harvest. This discovery led to the suggestion that the goal of deer management should not be based on yield of deer, but rather on the yield of hunter satisfaction (Hendee 1974).

In principle, this goal is laudable, since the endproduct of recreational hunting is satisfying recreation. In practice it has been difficult to implement. Motivations for hunting are complex and varied, and the sources of satisfaction are equally diverse (Hendee 1972, 1974, Hendee and Schoenfeld 1973, Schole 1973, *see* Chapter 42). Hunters enjoy planning the hunt and build up considerable anticipation of the experience. They enjoy getting away from the routines of home and job and other complexities of modern life. They enjoy being out of doors, close to nature, and living the simple life of hunting cabins or tents, campfires and stoves, sleeping bags, and not shaving. They enjoy camaraderie—to discuss hunts past, present and future. Finally they enjoy the hunt itself, with the potential if not actual ending with the harvesting, dressing, and hauling out of a deer, and the attendant bragging rights.

The wildlife biologist or manager embarking on a program with the goal of hunter satisfaction is confronted with the fact that few of the sources of satisfaction are dependent on the deer-management program. Most are dependent on field experiences of the individual hunter. The wildlife biologist or manager cannot control the satisfaction of the hunter getting away from the home, change in life style, or selection of companions. The program of management can control only a few variables involving the hunt itself. Recent studies at Hopland Field Station in California showed that only 28 percent of total satisfaction was attributable to variables under control of the wildlife manager (McCullough and Carmen 1982). Thus, the manager should not be deluded about the extent to which he can influence hunter satisfaction. However, it is clear that those elements of hunter satisfaction associated with variables that are under control should be incorporated in planning and decision making.

The controllable variables are essentially as follows:

1. Control of hunter density by regulation of number of permits, assignment to hunting units and timing of hunting (that is, weekdays versus weekends, early versus later parts of the hunting season, etc.);
2. Control of size of the deer harvest by length of season, bag limits, and designation of sex and age of legal deer;
3. Control of residual population by regulation of size of the hunt; and
4. Control of harvest success rate through control of hunter density and harvest size.

The response of hunters to hunter densities has been one of the more labile satisfaction variables. It varies tremendously from place to place. Hunters in Maryland were satisfied with extremely high hunter densities (up to 35 per square kilometer: 91 per square mile) (Kennedy 1974), while densities in the West with mule deer hunting are quite low (0.4–8.9 per square kilometer: 1.0–23.1 per square mile) (Miller et al. 1977). It is necessary to keep in mind that hunters are not a uniform population, and several things seem to influence their response to hunter density. People who go hunting for solitude are less likely to want encounters with others than are those who enjoy companionship. Hunters who employ a strategy to hunt are likely to be annoyed by encounters with other hunters who upset that strategy; those who trust to luck probably are not bothered (or are less so) by encounters. It is significant that in the high-density whitetail hunting in Maryland, many hunters thought there were not enough hunters to keep the deer moving (Kennedy 1974). This variable probably is most important in heavy cover where deer are difficult to stalk, and where hunters are relatively unskilled.

A hunter-density experiment on the Sandhill Recreation Area in Wisconsin was particularly instructive on this point. While many hunters objected to frequent encounters with other hunters, some hunters did not, because the high hunter density resulted in moving deer and a higher probability of harvesting a deer (Heberlein et al. 1982). Although frequent encounters lowered hunter satisfaction, the positive aspects of increased harvest caused a disproportionate increase in satisfaction in that subset of hunters, so that net satisfaction was greater in the most densely used hunting areas.

Reaction of hunters to hunter density is highly conditioned by past history and also by their expectations (Heberlein et al. 1982). Hunters accustomed to high hunter densities find them less objectionable than do those who have not accepted such densities. And it is important to recognize that hunters have practiced selection in their choices of where to hunt. Hunters wanting few encounters select places with lower hunter densities (often with either more rugged hunting conditions or lower deer density or both), while those who do not find encounters with other hunters objectionable hunt in high-density areas.

Although further work is needed, these patterns suggest that hunter-density satisfactions are influenced by human demographic patterns. Higher densities are acceptable in habitats with heavy cover that conceal both deer and hunters, and among relatively unskilled hunters who depend on chance to see deer, which improves as other hunters inadvertently serve as "bird dogs." Hunters who employ skill, whether stalking or selecting carefully considered stands, are less likely to want encounters with other hunters. And, related to the aforementioned hunter characteristics, hunters who place great emphasis on harvesting a deer are more likely to consider high hunter-density acceptable than are those who emphasize quality of the pursuit. It seems likely that the latter are attracted to wilderness hunting, and to bow or muzzleloader seasons if firearm hunting is crowded.

The relationship of size of the deer harvest, percentage of hunter harvest success and size of the residual population is a complex interlinkage of variables. Earlier assumptions that hunters were motivated primarily by taking home a deer were brought up short by resistance to antlerless seasons and adherence to the buck-only philosophy. Hunting traditionally has been a conservative activity, and a majority of hunters have been older, less educated and more rural than the population at large (Hendee and Schoenfeld 1973, Schole 1973). Most studies of hunter satisfaction show that perceptions of the deer population being large and hunting harvest posing no threat to it are the major elements of hunter satisfaction (Langenau et al. 1981, McCullough and Carmen 1982). In a study of hunters at Hopland Field Station, perception of the populaton size being large accounted for nearly all of the satisfaction accounted for (20 of 28 percent), while harvesting a deer accounted for most of the rest. Harvesting a deer remains an important variable for hunter satisfaction in most cases (Schole 1973, Stankey et al. 1973, Gilbert 1977, Langenau et al. 1981), and the possibility of harvesting a deer surely must be present even where expectations of success are not high (Potter et al. 1973, Kennedy 1974).

Management for maximum sustainable yield increases the deer harvest and, assuming hunter density is unchanged, the hunter success ratio. However, as pointed out earlier, this is accompanied by reduced residual populations (Figure 50c). Therefore, if hunters use perception of the size of the deer population as their major reference point for satisfaction, management for increased harvest invariably will result in lower satisfaction. And this probably explains much of the tremendous resistance to antlerless seasons encountered by agencies over the years. Information and educational programs have met with a notable lack of success, and hunter attitudes appear to be formed by peer-group association rather than by information disseminated by management agencies (Shaw 1975). Indeed, there frequently is mistrust and antagonism, and some hunters have charged that wildlife agencies have tried to wipe out the deer population—a belief no less firmly held for being illogical. As a result, high-yield deer-harvest programs in many cases have been constrained by political and social pressure.

A better understanding of the interrelationship of deer productivity, harvest yield and residual deer population may result in better communication among management agencies and hunters. And, as demography of hunters changes, it is likely that hunter attitudes may change as well. The diverse attitudes of hunters toward hunter density demonstrate that hunters are a variable group. And as the hunter population becomes more urban and better educated, shifts are virtually inevitable. After all, Maryland, at one time, was wilderness. Information probably will become more important relative to traditional belief in shaping public attitudes. When probabilities of getting a deer— any deer—get too low, attitudes are likely to change about high-yield management.

I suspect that the backwoods buckhunter is a dying breed. Although they will survive longer in the rural western states, they are doomed by "progress." I further suspect that much of the opposition to antlerless-deer hunting had little to do with the facts under dispute—that biologists in state capitals presumed to know how to manage *their* deer, and general resistance to remote authority may have been the fly in the ointment. The old buckhunters will have modern imitators, but like urban cowboys they will pale by comparison and are not liable to carry the influence the originals did.

The nature and sources of hunter satisfaction are bound to remain labile so long as society and demographic characteristics change. Wildlife management agencies just now are establishing what it is that hunters want (*see* Heberlein and Laybourne 1978), and still have not begun to determine what the vast majority of the population that does not hunt wants from the deer resource. Societal attitudes about wildlife are complex (Kellert 1978, 1979, 1980). These attitudes change over time, and the job is not done when they have been first assessed. A continuing monitoring program is necessary, to update information. Science can assess the deer population, its habitat resource, and also the attitudes and desires of the segments of society to be served. But the real challenge to management is the art of blending the biological properties of the deer population with human uses to optimize or maximize sustained benefits to society.

IS HUNTING NECESSARY?

To many wildlife biologists and resource managers, it is an article of faith that deer populations need to be hunted. That a hunting harvest is sustainable is not the same as being necessary. Certainly, the damage to vegetation that results in lowering K and the productivity curve of a given management unit is a good argument in favor of hunting. Indeed, the George Reserve deer population is a classic case. This research area is managed as a natural area for research, and the deer population is harvested only because of the destruction of vegetation that resulted when it was not controlled. Deer are the only animals (or plants) on the Reserve that are artificially controlled.

However, it does not follow that all deer populations should be or need to be hunted. First, environments that are stable can sustain equilibrium relationships between residual populations and K. Most wildlife biologists and managers can point to situations where deer populations have not been hunted yet do not fluctuate greatly or cause damage to vegetation. Certainly deer reach overpopulation status in some park situations, but the surprising thing is how many parks containing deer populations have no problem.

Second, in extremely fluctuating environments, hunting is not necessary because environmental variation regularly results in the population being below K. The very characteristics that make *ad hoc* management for hunting necessary in such environments make it unnecessary to hunt at all.

Third, hunting in moderately fluctuating environments is not necessary if a good complement of effective natural predators is present. The selectivity of natural predators (more correctly stated as the vulnerability of the prey) is a more exact way to retain equilibrium values of residual populations. Hunting can accomplish the same end, but because of its lack of selectivity, a higher kill is required than for natural predation to achieve the same end. Stated another way, natural predators are better at reducing chronic mortality than are human hunters, because the former remove the vulnerable individuals most likely to succumb to chronic mortality factors. Thus, there is very high substitutability of predator kills for chronic mortality, while for human hunting, chronic mortality is somewhat more additive, although still substitutable to a considerable extent (McCullough 1979).

As professionals, wildlife biologists and managers must distinguish between cases where hunting is necessary and where it is not. It is possible to recognize the legitimate interests and necessary roles of human hunters without becoming apologists or advocates for the recreation. Bias toward hunting in situations where hunting is not necessary can only result in loss of credibility. Professional integrity demands that no side of a controversy be given favor on biological grounds that cannot be justified by the biology of the case under review. If hunters are favored because they pay the costs of management through license fees and special taxes, let that be the justification, and not an indefensible position that hunting is necessary in cases where it is not.

MANAGING FOR NONHUNTER SATISFACTION

Hunters and antihunters appear to be at such opposite philosophical poles that resolution of the conflict between them seems unlikely (Kellert 1978, McCullough 1979). If so, programs that satisfy one group, even to a small degree, are not likely to satisfy the other. It seems to be the unavoidable lot of the agencies that manage deer to suffer the anger of some segments of society in order to satisfy the desires of some other segment.

However, the protectionist philosophy is young and naive, and hopefully will mature with age. It contains a belief in the benevolence of nature that is fostered by being removed, indeed isolated, from nature. A majority of its advocates are urban-born and reared, and thus insulated from the processes of life and death. Nature is what they see in parks or zoos, which is rather reminiscent of Bambi, and their knowledge of wildlife comes from the public media, books and movies. Even their knowledge of domestic animals comes from the little farm or the petting zoo where the fact that these animals grow up to be slaughtered is never mentioned. Their beefsteak comes in a styrofoam tray covered with cellophane. The fact that some calf was bred, born, raised, fattened and then slaughtered to satisfy their wants probably never crossed their minds, or was quickly blotted out if it did. Their thoughts run more to sound nutrition and quality of life—the backyard barbecue with its good food, drink and friends. These people are not in the white cedar swamps in late February or early March when the deer reap the devastating rewards of the protection afforded them. But then, neither are most hunters, many of whom also have some rather quaint beliefs about deer populations.

When deer are starving in the cedar swamps and elsewhere, protectionists want to feed or move them. It often seems that whether such deer live or die is less important than getting the problem out of sight. It is as if doing something, no matter how absurd, will absolve these people of the guilt of their benevolence turning out to be less benevolent than they had expected from their "model" of how deer populations work. This is understandable. Most people mentally blot out things they know to exist that are unpleasant—war, the poor, teenage runaways, organized crime or whatever. Nor do people like to be confronted and forced to face unpleasant realities, particularly if they are in contradiction to philosophical beliefs.

Whether protectionists and antihunters will evolve more realistic views with time remains

The University of Michigan, owner of the George Reserve, holds a Game Breeder's license from the State, and all meat and hides harvested are sold, with the proceeds going to the George Reserve research fund. *Photo by Doug Fulton.*

to be seen. But I am sure they will not if the wildlife profession writes them off as a bunch of bleeding hearts. Certainly the buck-law syndrome of hunters was not overcome by categorizing them as beer-guzzling yahoos with a compulsion to shoot up signs—a characterization that, unfortunately, was appropriate in a discouraging number of cases. Nevertheless, the hunters were right about the decline in deer population that accompanies the liberalization of antlerless seasons, and there was a bit of truth too in the hunter's characterization of wildlife biologists and managers as people brainwashed in universities and who did not know what was going on in the woods.

DEER MANAGEMENT AND PROFESSIONALISM

Many of my colleagues in wildlife management believe that they should have a free hand in managing wildlife—a position I find a little uncomfortable. After all, we are public servants, and if we are not satisfying the public interests with our deer management programs, just what is it we are managing deer populations for? I agree that the public often does not realize the consequences of what they want, but I see it as the job of our profession to give the public not only what it asks for but more—an accurate prediction of the consequences. A medical doctor's job is to make an accurate diagnosis of the illness of a patient and give a reliable prognosis of various treatments. It is the patient's decision what to do about it. It does not reflect on the doctor's professionalism if a patient decides to die of cancer rather than undergo chemotherapy or an operation.

This is the role I advocate for the wildlife profession. Many things have been said about professionalism, but I believe they all are for naught until the profession develops sound diagnostic skills and predictive capabilities about various actions that might be taken. When that is achieved, wildlife management will be rec-ognized as a scientific discipline by the public and other professionals. In the absence of such capability, no amount of signing of codes of ethics, supporting lobbying efforts or organizing memberships is going to gain wildlife management the respect and stature its participants aspire to.

The art of asking the right questions and framing testable hypotheses must be advanced to improve the mangement of white-tailed deer and other wildlife populations. Solid empirical studies (equivalent to clinical tests) are needed to prove that the wildlife biologists' and managers' prescriptions and remedies work.

Chapter 11

HARVEST MANAGEMENT: THE WISCONSIN EXPERIENCE

William A. Creed
Group Leader
Forest Wildlife Research
Wisconsin Department of
Natural Resources
Rhinelander, Wisconsin

Frank Haberland
Big Game Management
Specialist
Wisconsin Department of
Natural Resources
Madison, Wisconsin

Bruce E. Kohn
Project Leader
Forest Wildlife Research
Wisconsin Department of
Natural Resources
Rhinelander, Wisconsin

Keith R. McCaffery
Project Leader
Forest Wildlife Research
Wisconsin Department of
Natural Resources
Rhinelander, Wisconsin

Details of white-tailed deer population management policy, survey design and harvest regulation may vary from state to state and province to province, but the basic ingredients of a management program are similar. All states and provinces must identify objectives, measure populations and establish regulations. This chapter describes how one state in the Midwest, Wisconsin, goes about the annual business of regulating its white-tailed deer resource. It is a synthesis and update of Creed and Haberland (1980).

The evolution of Wisconsin's whitetail program reveals a history of trial-and-error experimentation to find a system that could provide for both resource management and public acceptance. The first major initiative was a one-buck-per-season law in 1915 and 1916. This harvest regulation was followed by traditional any-deer hunting seasons from 1917 through 1919, although fawns were protected in 1918.

The one-buck law returned for the 1920–1924 seasons. And from 1925 through 1935, closed seasons alternated with buck-only seasons. Annual buck-only seasons were held during the 1936–1942 period. The 1943 season was split, with four days of buck-only hunting followed by four days of antlerless-deer hunting. This stimulated considerable negative public response and a return to buck-only seasons from 1944 through 1948. The 1949, 1950 and 1951 whitetail hunting seasons were for antlerless or either-sex deer and, again, adverse public reaction forced a return to buck-only hunting. The concept of limiting antlerless-deer harvests was introduced with the party-permit system in 1957 and continued through 1960, until public dissatisfaction once more required buck-only seasons in 1961 and 1962.

Starvation of white-tailed deer in Wisconsin first was reported in 1930 and, from 1934 through 1954, a massive state-financed winter feeding

Successful whitetail hunting party after three-day hunt near Phillips, Wisconsin, in 1880, 35 years before the state placed effective regulations on deer harvests. *Photo by S. A. Johnson; courtesy of the Minnesota Historical Society.*

program was conducted. The inability of this program to prevent widespread whitetail starvation prompted various attempts to manage deer populations with some type of antlerless-deer harvest. Each of the approaches to deer population management was successful in some areas of the state, but there was an inability to direct harvest pressure to all those parts of the state where it was needed. Hunters were able to bag antlerless deer in unlimited numbers almost anywhere in the state where that type of harvest system was in effect. As a result, the most popular hunting areas often were overharvested, while other areas continued to carry excessive deer numbers. Despite very high hunter-success rates (about 50 percent) during the uncontrolled antlerless or either-sex deer-hunting seasons, a fear of overshooting caused hunters to rebel, and wildlife managers sought a system that could provide both harvest control and relatively long-term stability of deer population and harvest.

Gun deer-hunting seasons traditionally (since 1955) have been nine days long, starting the Saturday before Thanksgiving, with shorter either-sex seasons in some southern and western counties. Adult bucks—with 7.6-centi-

Winter starvation of white-tailed deer in Wisconsin was locally severe in the 1930s. It continues to be a problem in some years, particularly in northern parts of the state. *Photo by Staber W. Reese; courtesy of the Wisconsin Department of Natural Resources.*

meter (3-inch) spikes or larger antlers—are legal statewide, with a regulated take (by quota) of antlerless deer prescribed in units that are not in the either-sex zones. Longer (16-day) seasons occasionally have been allowed in the northern forest range and may be permitted in the future depending on hunter demand (Figure 60). Adult bucks are lightly harvested (less than 30 percent annual hunting mortality) in most of the northern forest range which provides the longer hunt option. Bucks in the central forest and agricultural regions are closely harvested (more than 60 percent annual hunting mortality), and shorter than nine-day seasons may be in order there to reduce the buck harvest and late-season shooting of illegal deer.

Archery deer-hunting seasons began in Wisconsin in 1934 and have been for either sex of whitetails since 1946. Since 1956, bow-hunting seasons have been about 83 days long, commencing the third Saturday of September and continuing until December 31, with a 17-day closure beginning 5 days before the gun deer-hunting season. Archers have a separate license entitling them to an extra deer whether or not they are successful with their gun deer-hunting license. Long seasons have been possible because archery harvests historically have been a negligible mortality factor. In recent years (since 1980), archery harvests have increased, and now exceed 5 percent of the estimated autumn whitetail population in some eastcentral management units.

The variable-quota system of white-tailed deer management has been in operation continuously since 1963. The mechanism used to harvest the antlerless-deer quota over most of those years was called a "party permit," because it required the formation of a group or "party" of at least four hunters to submit a valid application. The permit entitled the party to harvest one deer of any age or sex in addition to the one deer allowed on each hunter's regular license. In practice it was an antlerless-deer permit, because only about 3 percent of the whitetails harvested under the permit were antlered bucks.

In 1980 the party permit became a "hunter's-choice" permit issued to individual hunters. It authorized the use of a hunter's regular

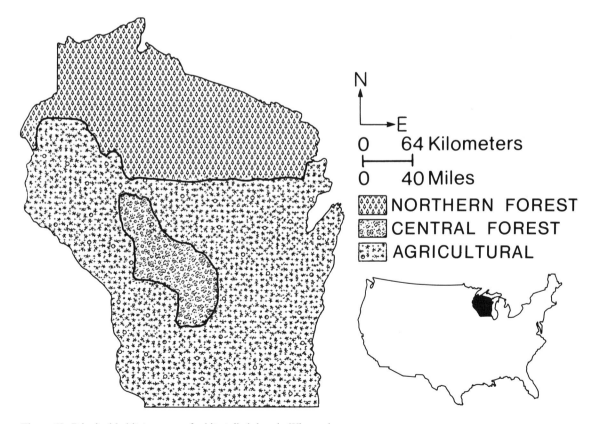

Figure 60. Principal habitat ranges of white-tailed deer in Wisconsin.

deer-hunting license and tag for one deer of any age or sex in a specified unit. The change was made primarily to improve the individual-hunter success rate by distributing the gun harvest of deer among a maximum number of hunters. The "one hunter/one deer" aspect of the hunter's-choice permit is believed to improve hunter ethics by discouraging gang hunting. It also has proven to be simpler to apply for, and easier for the Wisconsin Department of Natural Resources to administer, than was the party permit. The hunter's-choice permit has shown a lower antlerless-deer success rate (56 percent) and a higher buck harvest rate (9 percent) than was evident with the party permit (70 and 3 percent, respectively), but these differences are simple to adjust for and have had negligible effect on the permit system.

WHITETAIL POPULATION MANAGEMENT POLICY AND GOALS

The Wisconsin Department of Natural Resources is governed by the Natural Resources Board, which consists of seven members appointed by the Governor for staggered six-year terms. An important function of the Board is the establishment of policy for guiding the Department's programs. The Wisconsin deer-management policy (Wis. Admin. Code, Sec. NR 1.15(2)(a):11) states, in part, that ". . . regulations shall be designed to maintain a deer herd in balance with its range and at population levels reasonably compatible with agricultural and forest management objectives in each deer management unit." White-tailed deer management units are areas of similar habitat bounded by major roads. Currently there are 96 such units, averaging about 1,500 square kilometers (580 square miles) in size (Figure 61).

Net deer range in each unit was measured by dot counting on black and white aerial photographs (McCaffery 1973*b*). U.S. Agricultural Stabilization and Conservation Service photography was used for most of the state. Photo coverage is reflown at about 10-year intervals and deer-range remeasurements are planned for a similar time interval. Dot grids were constructed for four scales of photography ranging in representative fractions from 1:20,000 to 1:7,920. Sampling intensity was about 1.5 dots per square kilometer (4 per square mile) sampled. Each dot was circumscribed with a ring corresponding to a 100-meter (330-foot) radius.

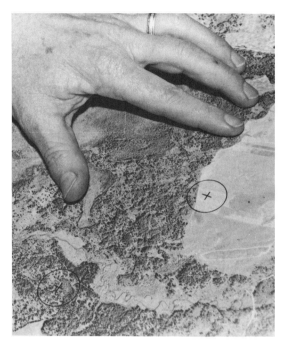

Whitetail range area in Wisconsin is measured by using an acetate grid overlay on aerial photographs. Dots (crosses) falling on permanent cover (as below the investigator's thumb) are recorded as deer range, as are dots on agricultural fields within 100 meters (330 feet) of permanent cover (as below the index finger). Depending on the scale of photography, grids have 14 to 25 sample points. *Photo courtesy of the Wisconsin Department of Natural Resources.*

An investigator uses a transect to tally vegetational composition in a forest opening in Wisconsin. Since the mid-1960s, habitat inventories in the Great Lakes states increasingly have focused on measurement of nonwinter sources of food for whitetails. *Photo courtesy of the Wisconsin Department of Natural Resources.*

In the counts, dots falling on water, improved roads, farmyards, buildings, large fields, etc., were not tallied as representing deer range. Dots falling on permanent cover (woodland, brush, marsh land, goldenrod, tall herbaceous plants, etc.) or farm fields within 100 meters (330 feet) of cover were tallied as representing deer range. Isolated patches of cover less than 4 hectares (10 acres) were excluded. Though centrally coordinated, the survey was conducted by regional wildlife managers familiar with whitetail habits and habitats in their localities (counties). Some discretion was exercised by each of these surveyors. The proportion of dots falling on deer range was applied against gross area measurements obtained by using a planimeter on county highway maps to calculate the percentage of deer range.

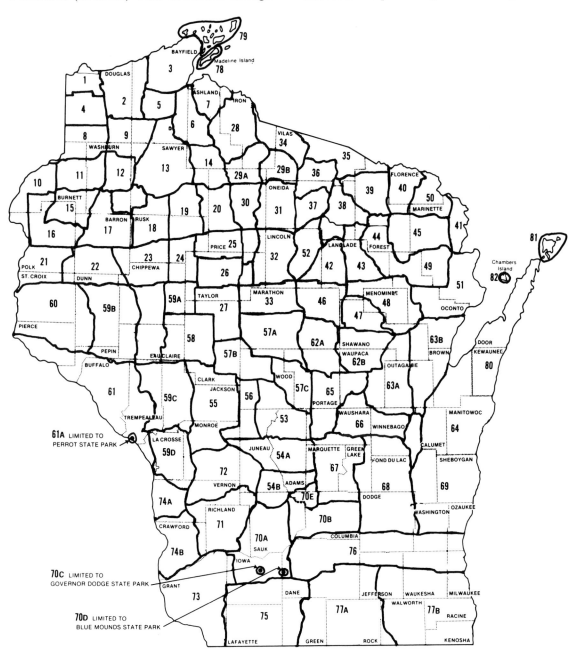

Figure 61. Wisconsin's 96 white-tailed deer management units.

Overwinter whitetail population goals in individual management units range from 2 to 12 deer per square kilometer of range (approximately 5–30 deer per square mile), and total 575,000 deer statewide. Whitetail population goals in the forested deer range are based on long-term average carrying capacity as determined by unit population responses to past winters of varying severity. Population goals in the agricultural range reflect an estimate of hunter demand balanced against an assessment of human tolerance of deer numbers, particularly as relates to severity of crop damage and frequency of deer/vehicle collisions.

An overwinter population level of 575,000 whitetails in Wisconsin is capable of providing an autumn population in excess of 800,000 deer, which permits an annual gun harvest of up to 150,000 or more animals depending on the effects of winter severity.

Wisconsin is primarily known as a dairy state with corn, hay and oats as the principal crops, but a wide variety of special crops such as commercial vegetables and fruits also are grown. Some farming occurs in every county, but "agricultural deer range" refers to most of the southern two-thirds of the state, where at least

Deer/vehicle collisions in Wisconsin result in loss of more than 20,000 whitetails each year. Their costs in terms of property damage and personal injury are equally staggering. *Photo by Dean Tvedt; courtesy of the Wisconsin Department of Natural Resources.*

White-tailed deer in southern Wisconsin commonly forage in agricultural fields. The result is high productivity of deer, but crop damage—a severe and expensive problem in parts of the state—is a negative factor. Most compensation claims have been for deer damage to corn, although damages to commercial vegetable and orchard crops account for the greatest dollar cost. *Photo by Staber W. Reese; courtesy of the Wisconsin Department of Natural Resources.*

50 percent of the land is devoted to agricultural crops (*see* Figure 60).

Wisconsin has had an agricultural deer-damage compensation program since 1931. The distribution and magnitude of that program from 1978 through 1980 are shown in Figure 62. Damage claims reflect both whitetail population size and agricultural land use. The greatest number of claims were for damage to corn, while the greatest dollar value of claims involved commercial vegetables and orchards.

Figure 62 also shows the distribution of road-killed whitetails for 1978 through 1980. It too indicates concentration of whitetails in central Wisconsin, but roadkill figures also reflect the extent of highway systems and traffic volume.

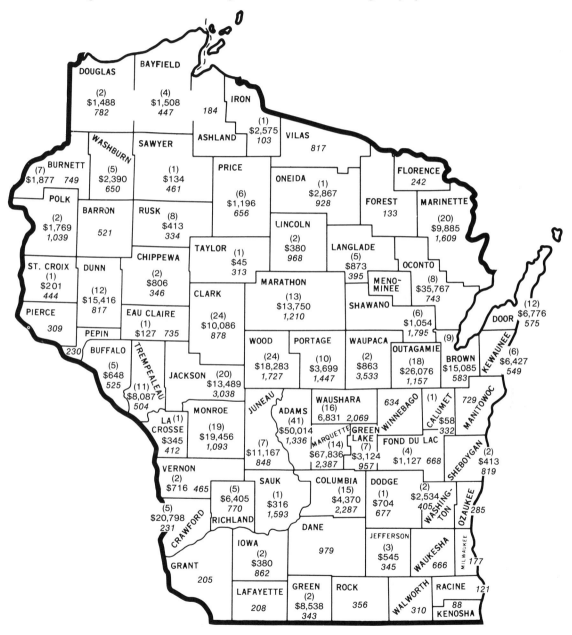

Figure 62. Extent and distribution in Wisconsin of claims for crop damage caused by white-tailed deer, and known road-killed and other seized (illegally killed) whitetails, 1978 through 1980. The number in parenthesis represents the number of claims by county for crop damage caused by deer; the dollar expresion is the amount paid for claims; and the number in italics shows road-killed and other seized deer.

Management policy prescribes annual hunting seasons to maintain deer population goal levels. It allows the use of buck (7.6 centimeter:3 inch-or-greater antler), either-sex, or buck and antlerless-deer-permit harvest strategies. Buck-only seasons occasionally are used to allow population increases where deer numbers are below goal levels because of the effects of severe winters or continuous either-sex harvest seasons. Either-sex seasons regularly apply in the intensive agricultural areas of southern Wisconsin. Buck hunting combined with antlerless-deer quotas for specific management units is the system applied over most of the state.

Since 1963, Wisconsin white-tailed deer hunters have enjoyed an average annual gun harvest of more than 111,000 deer, ranging from a low of about 71,000 in 1971 to a high of nearly 167,000 in 1981 (Table 30). These totals include an annual average of almost 68,000 bucks and more than 43,000 antlerless deer.

In 1934, Wisconsin became the first state in the nation to establish an archery deer-hunting season. Since that time, bow-hunter numbers and harvests have increased steadily and at a faster rate than that of gun hunters and harvests (Table 30). As discussed previously, bow hunters have a separate license and season (approximately 85 days) and may take one deer of either sex in addition to the deer available to them from the gun license and season. In 1981, nearly 174,000 archers bagged more than 29,000 deer in Wisconsin.

WHITETAIL POPULATION INVENTORIES

Wisconsin has had compulsory registration of harvested deer since 1953, and also a long period of stable season-structure (season start and length, basic buck-plus-quota hunting). This stability has greatly facilitated interpretation of survey results indicating deer and hunter demographics.

Management-unit whitetail populations are monitored through a variety of surveys adapted to specific range types and harvest problems. The primary inventory methods have included registered harvest trends, sex-age-kill population estimates and, in northern units, pellet-group surveys and trail counts.

Deer Registration

Wisconsin's deer-registration system requires hunters to present their deer to official registration stations for inspection and tagging. These stations—including gasoline stations, stores, Department of Natural Resources' offices, sheriff's offices and similar public places—total about 450 and are well-dispersed state-

Table 30. Wisconsin white-tailed deer harvest and hunters, 1964 through 1981.

Year	Gun season				Archery season			
	Antlered bucks	Antler-less	Total harvest	Licensed hunters	Antlered bucks	Antler-less	Total harvest	Licensed hunters[a]
1964	65,052	28,393	93,445	386,519	711	2,453	3,164	
1965	60,994	37,750	98,744	405,023	1,134	3,861	4,995	63,964
1966	67,362	42,700	110,062	432,111	1,357	4,629	5,986	85,144
1967	71,302	57,295	128,597	470,782	1,714	5,878	7,592	101,573
1968	62,521	57,465	119,986	503,190	1,924	5,010	6,934	114,975
1969	52,655	45,353	98,008	506,526	1,576	4,411	5,987	106,699
1970	50,308	22,536	72,844	501,799	1,775	4,745	6,520	101,573
1971	48,994	21,841	70,835	509,447	1,696	4,826	6,522	100,206
1972	49,416	25,411	74,827	517,724	1,956	5,131	7,087	98,720
1973	57,364	24,741	82,105	514,626	2,594	5,862	8,456	105,875
1974	67,313	33,092	100,405	556,815	3,390	9,124	12,514	119,960
1975	73,373	44,005	117,378	582,113	4,439	9,149	13,588	133,775
1976	69,510	52,999	122,509	589,590	4,775	8,861	13,636	133,318
1977	82,762	49,148	131,910	617,109	5,993	10,797	16,790	146,760
1978	87,397	63,448	150,845	644,594	6,472	11,641	18,113	157,838
1979	76,550	49,020	125,570	617,109	6,203	9,815	16,018	144,511
1980	81,041	58,583	139,624	618,333	8,950	12,004	20,954	155,386
1981	99,034	67,639	166,673	629,034	11,867	17,216	29,083	173,874

[a]Separate archer's license not required until 1965.

wide. Initially, cooperators were paid $0.10 per deer registered or $10 per season, whichever was greater. In 1979 this was increased to $0.20 or $20. Registration data include breakdowns by sex, age (fawn or adult), license type, and county and management unit of harvest.

Registration is the cornerstone of Wisconsin's white-tailed deer population management program. It has convinced most doubters about the reliability of deer harvest figures. More importantly, registered buck harvest trends have supplied one of the most dependable measures of deer population change. Harvests are pinned down to much smaller land units than would be possible with all but the most elaborate questionnaire schemes. Furthermore, high-volume registration stations facilitate gathering of detailed age-sex data and other biological information. Trained agers examine from

Each year, 12,000–16,000 harvested Wisconsin whitetails are examined at more than 400 check stations to determine individual age and population age structure. *Photo by Dean Tvedt; courtesy of the Wisconsin Department of Natural Resources.*

12,000 to 16,000 deer per year at about 70 sample stations statewide.

Sex-Age-Kill

Used in Wisconsin since the early 1960s (Creed 1964), the sex-age-kill method for calculating whitetail densities has become increasingly important in the statewide management picture. It currently serves as the primary index to deer populations over most of the state.

Wisconsin's version of the sex-age-kill method was modified after Eberhardt (1960)—the prime difference being the use of a 20-percent nonharvest adjustment for calculating populations of adult bucks. Also, the Severinghaus and Maguire (1955) procedure for estimating adult sex ratios was incorporated. Fawn recruitment estimates are obtained from routine July–September observations by Department of Natural Resources' field personnel. Steps in the analyses are:

1. *Adult buck populations.* Minimum numbers of adult bucks (1.5 years and older) for a previous year are determined by totaling the subsequent legal harvest of adults living (shown by age structure) in that previous year. To correct for nonharvest mortality, an 80-percent final recovery rate is assumed. This nonharvest adjustment is somewhat speculative, since this factor obviously must vary from year to year and also by area. Comparisons of pellet survey and sex-age-kill results show that this adjustment should be *at least* 20 percent and, in years with heavy winter mortality, could be much higher. Because of the lack of adequate annual data, the nonharvest adjustment is used as a constant, recognizing that it has certain limitations.

2. *Adult sex ratios.* Adult sex ratios are computed by procedures described by Severinghaus and Maguire (1955). The calculation involves dividing the proportion of yearling bucks by the proportion of yearling does, after first correcting the yearling buck proportion according to the buck/doe ratio derived from shot samples of fawns.

3. *Fawn/doe ratios (net recruitment).* Fawn/doe ratios are obtained from observed numbers of fawns and adult does annually reported by Department of Natural Resources' field personnel during July, August and September. In any-deer hunting season zones, fawn/doe ratios in the legal kill are substituted for observed summer ratios.

4. *Buck-to-total-population expansion factors*. Expansion factors (E.F.) are recomputed annually for each of 13 zones accordingly:

$$E.F. = 1.00 + (B/D) + (B/D)F$$

where

B = corrected yearling buck proportion, which is determined from the proportion of yearling bucks in the adult-buck harvest divided by male/female fawns aged;

D = proportion of yearling does; and

F = fawn/doe ratio from summer observations.

Zone expansion factors are updated annually and used to calculate whitetail populations for all units with adequate age samples. Annual expansion factors are used where samples are adequate (200 bucks aged, 200 does aged and 200 doe/fawn observations), and long-term factors are used where samples are small. These expansion factors then are converted to buck-kill-to-total-population factors and applied regionally to obtain approximate population estimates for units where aging information is not available.

Deer Management Unit 54A, which lies in the southcentral portion of Wisconsin and has 1,103 square kilometers (431 square miles) of deer range, is used here as an example. The following numbers of deer were added to the buck harvest in 1978 (1,901) to estimate the adult buck population in Unit 54A that year:

1. In 1979, 22.1 percent of the bucks harvested (1,597) were 2.5-years-old or older—therefore, 353 of these were adults in 1978;
2. In 1980, 6.6 percent of the harvest of bucks (1,755) were 3.5-years-old or older—therefore, 116 of these were adults in 1978;
3. In 1981, 0.5 percent of the bucks harvested (2,705) were 4.5-years-old or older—therefore, 14 of these were adults in 1978;
4. Adding up all the bucks that were alive in 1978 results in an estimate of 1,901 + 353 + 116 + 14 = 2,384 adult bucks *known* to have been alive in 1978; and then
5. The number of adult bucks is divided by 0.8 to correct for mortalities other than gun harvest—therefore, 2,384 ÷ 0.8 = 2,980 = total number of adult bucks alive in Unit 54A in 1978.

After the total number of adult bucks alive in a given year has been determined, the buck harvest rate is calculated for that year. In the Unit 54A example, hunters registered 1,901 of the estimated 2,980 adult bucks alive in Unit 54A in 1978. The buck-harvest rate for that unit in that year was 1,901 ÷ 2,980 = 63.8 percent.

Wisconsin Department of Natural Resources personnel routinely observe and record the fawn/doe ratio from July through September to obtain an index of whitetail productivity trends. *Photo by Keith R. McCaffery; courtesy of the Wisconsin Department of Natural Resources.*

Previous buck harvest rates can be used to estimate more recent buck populations that have large numbers of adult bucks still at large and remaining to be accounted for in future seasons. Basically, an average buck harvest rate is calculated from the last three years for which figures are available and then divided into the legal harvests of the most recent years. The calculations for the Unit 54A example were:

1. The buck harvest rates were 62.9 percent, 62.7 percent and 63.8 percent in 1976, 1977 and 1978 respectively, for an average buck harvest rate of 63.1 percent during this period.
2. Hunters registered 1,597 bucks in the unit in 1979—assuming this harvest represented 63.1 percent of the bucks available there were $1,597 \div 0.631 = 2,531$ adult bucks alive that year; and
3. Using similar calculations, the unit's buck population was $1,755 \div 0.631 = 2,781$ in 1980, and $2,150 \div 0.631 = 3,407$ in 1981.

These estimates are valid only if there were no significant differences in buck harvest between the 1976–1978 and 1979–1981 periods. Also, these calculations must be reworked annually to provide updated buck harvest-rate estimates. Each additional year of age and harvest records permits more accurate appraisal of whitetail populations of some previous year.

Unit 54A lies in Summer Deer Observation Zone "L" (Central Forest Units). In 1978, 661 (84.4 percent) of the 783 bucks and 97 (35.0 percent) of the 277 does aged in Zone L were yearlings. If there were equal survival and numbers of male and female fawns, the adult sex ratio could be calculated simply by dividing the yearling doe percentage into the yearling buck percentage. However, since there are more male fawns than female fawns (Zone L sex ratio = 117 males:100 females), the yearling buck percentage must be corrected by the primary sex ratio. Thus the corrected yearling buck percentage is 84.4 percent $\div$ 117 = 72.1 percent, and the adult sex ratio (B/D) = 72.1 percent $\div$ 35.0 percent = 2.1 does per buck.

The 1978 summer observations in Zone L showed a ratio of 0.96 fawns per doe. The fawn segment of the population was calculated as (B/D)(F) = 2.1 (0.96) = 2.0. Adding these values according to the formula, the expansion factor = 1.0 + 2.1 + 2.0 = 5.1

Since the Zone L whitetail population was 5.1 times as great as the Unit 54A buck population in 1978, the Unit 54A deer population would have been $2,980 \times 5.1 = 15,198$, or 13.8 deer per square kilometer (35 per square mile) of deer range in the unit.

The calculated expansion factors for Zone L were 5.8, 5.3 and 4.3 in 1979, 1980, and 1981 respectively. The Unit 54A whitetail populations for these years can then be calculated as follows:

Year	Buck population	Expansion x factor =	Total population =	Whitetails per square kilometer (square mile)
1979	2,531	5.8	14,680	13.3(34)
1980	2,781	5.3	14,740	13.4(34)
1981	3,407	4.3	14,650	13.3(34)

The sex-age-kill method provides one of the best available indices to deer populations, especially in more heavily hunted units. Wisconsin is fortunate to have the deer registration system and aging data necessary to use this method.

Pellet Surveys

Deer pellet surveys (*see* Eberhardt and Van Etten 1956, Olson et al. 1955) formed the basic technique for whitetail population inventory for Wisconsin's northern forest range from 1955 through 1978. They also provided the initial background for establishment of unit population goals in 1962.

Application of the method involved sampling 11 or 12 deer management units per year on a three-year rotation. Estimates of whitetail density per unit area of deer range were then computed for individual management units and also projected for the entire northern forest range—about 38,500 square kilometers (14,835 square miles) of deer habitat.

This type of survey samples deer range for deer pellet groups deposited over an approximate six-month period, from leaf-fall into May (Thompson 1978). The survey commences following snow-melt and is completed before green-up. The basic sampling layout—called a "course"—consists of a linear array of five plots spaced 80 meters (4 chains:264 feet) apart. Three strata of deer range types are delineated within each management unit and each stratum is sampled separately. These range strata are designed as: "yard"—the range that usually gets the heaviest use over winter; "intermediate"—range consisting of a 0.8-kilometer (0.5-mile) band surrounding yarding areas; and "open"—the remainder of the deer range.

Allocation of 100 courses among these three range strata is made according to the percentage-composition of type, and usually with an additional weighting in the ratio of approximately 2.0:1.5:1.0 for the three strata respectively. This weighting feature, on the average, improves the statistical efficiency of the survey by about 20 percent since yard and intermediate ranges usually show greater variation among courses than do open ranges. Naturally this artificial weighting is removed when unit totals are computed. Its only purpose is to help narrow the 95-percent confidence limits on the density estimate.

In Wisconsin, courses in each stratum were randomized with starting points located along available roads, trails or water access routes. Each plot was 81 square meters (872 square feet) in size, with each course of five plots encompassing 0.04 hectare (0.1 acre). This was the area searched for deer pellet groups and snowshoe hare droppings that had accumulated on top of leaf litter from the preceding autumn. Plot data were summed to give course totals.

Leaf-fall dates were determined by local wildlife managers. The conversion rate used for the pellet-group average was 12.7 groups per deer per day.

The course averages for pellet groups were determined for each range stratum, and these averages were combined after weighting for the percentage of each range stratum in the management unit. An adjustment was deducted for deer harvested from the units during the hunting season. At the same time, a stratum-weighted estimate of the sampling variation was computed and expressed as a 95-percent confidence limit—this estimate was the range within which one would expect that 19 to 20 repeats of the survey would fall, assuming that no bias errors were present.

A dead-deer search was made by an observer scanning a 20-meter (1-chain:66-foot) strip as he proceeded on the course. The return trip was offset and, thus, covered a 20-meter (1-chain:66-foot) strip 800 meters (0.5 mile) in total length, or 1.6 hectares (4 acres) per completed course. Cause of death was ascertained where possible. In the final computation, correction for stratum weighting was made.

Snowshoe hare pellet occurrence (only presence, not numbers) was noted for each plot, and the overall frequency, as a percentage, was transformed to a density index. An adjustment was made for stratum weighting.

The main value of the pellet-group survey was to establish modern deer-density "bench marks." Prior to 1955, whitetail-density estimates in Wisconsin came primarily from deer-drive censuses (Swift 1946). Reliability of pellet surveys on a unit basis was highly variable, but when projected to the entire northern forest range the survey correlated closely (r = 0.83, P<0.01) with subsequent buck harvests (McCaffery 1976*a*) and even better with buck harvests of the previous autumn (r = 0.92, n = 15).

Pellet counts lost favor in Wisconsin during the late 1970s, primarily because of increased costs, but also because other methods—especially sex-age-kill estimates and trail counts—produced similar information. Hence, pellet counts were discontinued following the spring survey in 1978.

Trail Counts

Trail counts (McCaffery 1976*b*) now substitute in part for pellet-group surveys. Similar coverage can be achieved for about one-fourth the cost (3–4 man-days per unit) of pellet surveys (12–15-man-days per unit) and the precision is somewhat better (±15–20 percent, P = 0.05). Fifty randomized 0.4-kilometer (0.25-mile) line-transects are used to sample each unit. Transects begin at a roadside and run into the woods. Deer trails (paths in ground vegetation or forest litter caused by repeated use by whitetails) intersecting the transect are tallied at 80-meter (4-chain:246-foot) intervals along the transect. Forest overstory also is recorded at these intervals to permit evaluations of deer use of habitat. Surveys are conducted in late autumn or early spring and indicate autumn whitetail densities and distribution. Trail counts are not as yet considered fully operational in Wisconsin because training of field personnel is still underway. However, results to date look quite promising (*see also* McCaffery 1979, Kubisiak 1982).

SUPPLEMENTAL SURVEYS

A continued search for more accurate, less expensive and less time consuming inventory methods has led to the development of a number of surveys that play important roles in assessing the current status of Wisconsin white-tailed deer populations and harvests.

Hunter Pressure Poll

A sample of 10,000 buyers of white-tailed deer hunting licenses is used, with a questionnaire mailed to determine where and when they hunted. Response rates generally are about 50 percent. Expansion of figures from replies produces estimates of hunter density for management units by day and for the season.

Confidence limits are broad for lightly hunted northern management units where hunter density may be as low as 1.5 hunters per square kilometer (4 per square mile), but are acceptable (±10–20 percent) for those units where hunting pressure is high enough (4 hunters per square kilometer: 10 per square mile) to be a significant factor regulating deer abundance.

Data from the poll are used as perspective in interpreting whitetail harvest rates, defining areas of potential hunter/landowner conflict, providing wildlife biologists and managers with information on hunter distribution, and showing trends in hunter density. Confidence in this supplemental survey method has been strengthened by a remarkable consistency of estimated hunter densities within units over time.

Dead Deer Surveys

Dead deer searches associated with the pellet survey, as previously discussed, involved one-man transects that were 20 meters (1 chain:66 feet) wide and 800 meters (40 chains:0.5 mile) long at each of 100 pellet-transects (courses) per unit. Despite stratification for three range types (yards, intermediate and open) and running 1,100 to 1,200 transects per year, precision of the mean estimate for northern Wisconsin following severe winters was about ±50 percent (P=0.05). A replacement dead-deer survey was prepared in anticipation of terminating pellet-group counts. This survey involved 80 search plots of 16 hectares (40 acres) each, scattered throughout northern Wisconsin with stratification similar to that of the pellet-group surveys (McCaffery 1978). This dead-deer check required about 100 man-days and has been used only once. The dead-deer estimate was 57,000 ±80 percent (Thompson 1979).

Although imprecise estimates have been obtained by the two dead-deer surveys, the general magnitude of losses has corresponded well to a winter-severity index based on snow depths and temperature (Kohn 1975).

Wisconsin Department of Natural Resources field crews conduct cross-country transect surveys to assess winter losses of white-tailed deer. *Photos courtesy of the Wisconsin Department of Natural Resources.*

Analysis of Winter Severity

In view of the high cost of field checks and the limited utility of dead-deer survey results, Wisconsin now relies heavily on the winter-severity index as a predictor of winter impact on subsequent whitetail population and harvest trends. It uses U.S. Department of Commerce weather records to determine the relative severity of each winter. This is done by adding together the number of days with 46 centimeters (18 inches) or more of snow on the ground and the number of days with minimum temperature of −18 degrees Celsius (0 degree Fahrenheit) or below between December 1 and April 30. Records are taken from 12 stations (Figure 63), and the average for all the stations is used as a winter-severity index for the entire northern forest range.

Snow depths at the 12 weather stations often are much less than in the woods. Therefore, the data provide a relative index to winter severity rather than an actual expression of conditions experienced by deer.

Winter-severity index values for the northern forest have ranged between 37 and 118 since 1960 (Table 31). The number of days with 46 centimeters (18 inches) or more of snow on the ground has varied much more—0 to 75 days—than has the number of days with low temperatures of −18 degrees Celsius (0 degrees Fahrenheit) or less—32 to 58 days. Therefore, the range in the winter-severity index reflects snow depths more than temperature extremes.

Earlier analyses showed that the winter-severity index made possible reasonable predictions of winter deer losses and subsequent fawn production (Kohn 1975). Winter losses amounted to about 5 percent of the whitetail population in "mild" winters, 10 to 15 percent

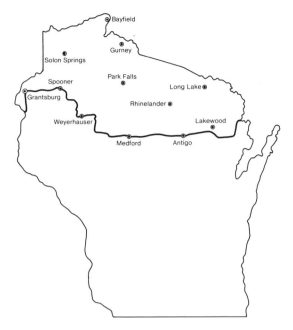

Figure 63. U. S. Department of Commerce weather stations used to calculate winter severity index values for Wisconsin's northern forest range.

in "moderate" winters, and more than 20 percent in "severe" winters. And severe winters decreased subsequently observed fawn/doe ratios by about 25 percent.

More recent analyses have shown a strong inverse relationship between the winter-severity index and the buck harvest of the subsequent hunting season in the northern forest range (Figure 64). Generally the buck harvest increases 20 to 30 percent when the index is less than 60, remains relatively stable (±10 percent) when the index is between 60 and 100, and decreases 20 to 25 percent when the index exceeds 100. However, this relationship did not hold true when the antlerless-deer/buck ratio in the previous year's harvest exceeded 0.60

Table 31. Winter severity index calculations for northern Wisconsin, 1960 through 1982.

Index calculations	1960	1961	1962	1963	1964	1965	1966	1967	1968	1969	1970	1971	1972	1973	1974	1975
Days with 46 centimeters (18 inches) of snow cover on the ground	15	3	47	9	8	36	2	57	0	75	30	70	62	5	11	42
Days below −18 degrees Celsius (0 degrees Fahrenheit)	32	36	42	51	37	56	37	42	38	42	44	47	52	35	41	34
Winter severity index[a]	47	39	89	60	45	92	39	99	38	117	74	117	114	40	52	76

[a]A winter is considered "mild" if its index value is less than 50, "moderate" if between 50 and 80, and "severe" if over 80.

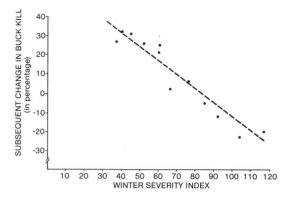

Figure 64. Relationship between winter severity index and subsequent-hunting-season buck harvest in Wisconsin's northern forest range. Y = 60.51 − 0.73x; r = −0.96.

after a severe winter. When that occurred, the buck harvest the next year fell below expectations.

Wisconsin now uses the winter-severity index to predict buck harvests in the northern forest range and to determine numbers of antlerless deer to be harvested.

ANNUAL REVIEW OF WHITETAIL POPULATION STATUS

Each whitetail hunting season in Wisconsin begins a reappraisal of deer population levels. Buck harvests especially are examined closely, because harvest rates are relatively consistent for a given management unit and, thus, buck-harvest trends approximate population changes. Percentages of yearlings in age samples are studied to determine recruitment. Upturn or stability in yearling percentages generally indicates satisfactory recruitment, while downturn reflects population losses subsequent to the previous hunting season. Preliminary deer-harvest estimates are available soon after the

hunting season ends, and computer-summarized data are available by mid-February.

Creed et al. (1979) calculated expansion factors, relating long-term average buck harvest to total population. These factors are quickly and easily used by field biologists and managers to estimate whitetail population levels (Figure 65). Final estimates are computed by the normal sex-age-harvest method in early March. By this time, biologists and managers are able to update the management-unit histories of harvest, population and hunting pressure (Figure 66).

By reviewing and updating management-unit histories, biologists and managers can quickly determine the status of current whitetail population levels relative to long-range goals, and also assess whether past harvests were consistent with these goals. They are then able to weigh antlerless-deer harvest rates relative to trends in the buck harvest, and adjust harvest recommendations accordingly.

Table 31. (*continued*)

1976	1977	1978	1979	1980	1981	1982
44	6	8	61	1	1	50
41	54	58	57	42	36	54
85	60	66	118	43	37	104

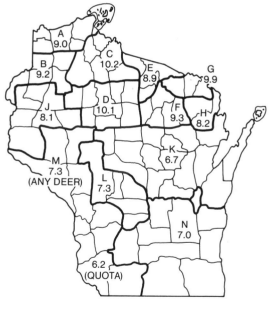

Figure 65. Summer deer observation zones and expansion factors used to estimate Wisconsin's white-tailed deer population. Internal lines show deer management units. To obtain minimum winter whitetail density for any of zones A–H and minimum autumn density for any of zones J–N, multiply the buck harvest per square mile for a given zone by the appropriate factor shown (from Creed et al. 1979).

HARVEST RECOMMENDATIONS

In the initial years of variable-quota management—the early and mid-1960s—it was common to harvest from 15 to 25 percent of the estimated autumn whitetail population, with heaviest harvests in central and southern units and with buck harvests usually exceeding the take of antlerless deer. These harvest rates often failed to halt deer population growth when recruitment was good, but occasionally were excessive in years immediately following severe winters.

Procedures for setting antlerless-deer harvest quotas were improved after a long accumulation of harvest histories for individual management units. It was found that most whitetail populations will sustain an antlerless-deer harvest of from 70 to 80 percent of the buck harvest. In effect this means a proportionately heavier antlerless-deer harvest in the central and southern units, where both buck-harvest rates and recruitment are higher than

they are in units farther north. Antlerless-deer harvest recommendations now are based primarily on three considerations:
1. The status of the management-unit deer population in relation to established population goals (at the goal, higher, or lower), as determined by inventories previously described;
2. The past effect on the management-unit deer population of varying antlerless-deer harvest levels—gained from experience since 1963 with the variable-quota system; and
3. The estimated impact of the previous winter's severity on deer survival and subsequent fawn recruitment.

The upcoming buck harvest is estimated in each management unit by applying the harvest/winter-severity relationship shown in Figure 64 to the previous year's harvest. Antlerless-deer quotas are then related to this estimated buck harvest, with the recommended proportion of antlerless deer taken per buck, as shown in Table 32.

Deer Management Unit History
Form 2300-74

Department of Natural Resources

Management Unit or County
54A

Gross Area **620** Sq. Mi.

Deer Range **431** Sq. Mi.

Population Goal [a.]
Deer/Sq. Mi. **25**

Total Deer **10,775**

	19**72**	19**73**	19**74**	19**75**	19**76**	19**77**	19**78**	19**79**	19**80**	19**81**
Spring Population Estimate										
Fall Population Estimate	26.0	29.8[b]	32.8[c]	29.8	27.6	33.8	35.3	34.1	34.2	34.0
Buck Kill	1400	1572	1624	1601	1550	1815	1901	1597	1755	2150
Antlerless or Quota Kill	801	1016	1311	1288	1254	1096	1594	867	928	1757
Total Harvest	2201	2588	2935	2889	2804	2911	3495	2464	2683	3907
Deer Quota Recommended	800	1200	1400[d]	1300	1300	1150	1600	850	700	1700
Deer Quota Approved	800	1000	1200	1300	1300	1150	1600	850	700	1700
Permits Issued	1200	1500	1850	1900	1875	1675	2400	1300	1775	3275
Yearling Buck Harvest Percent		77.2	82.1	74.0	71.6	79.7	83.0	77.9	85.5	84.8
Hunters/Sq. Mi. Opening Day	27	25	34	24	27		27	29	31	30

Remarks: a - Overwinter
b - Extrapolated by wildlife manager
c - Extrapolated from Zone 1
d - First recommended map 8

Figure 66. Sample history of a white-tailed deer management unit (Unit 54A) in Wisconsin, 1971 through 1981.

Table 32. Recommended antlerless-deer/buck ratios in the Wisconsin white-tailed deer harvest according to deer population status and winter severity.

Population status in relation to goals	Antlerless-deer/buck ratio according to winter severity index[a]		
	Less than 80	80–100	100 +
20 percent or more above	1.25	1.0	0.5–0.7
Within 20 percent	1.0	0.5–0.7[b]	0.25–0.5[b]
20 percent or more below	0.0–0.25[c]	0.0	0.0

[a]*See* Figure 64.
[b]Dependent on whether the deer population is on the low or high side of goals.
[c]Dependent on the expected buck harvest and the minimum number of antlerless-deer permits issued in any unit.

PROCESSING RECOMMENDATIONS

Field wildlife biologists and managers submit whitetail harvest-quota recommendations to their respective district headquarters. A consolidated recommendation from each of the six district offices is then submitted each March to the Department of Natural Resources' Bureau of Wildlife Management in the central office. The Bureau resolves any differences between districts, reviews recommendations with the Forest Wildlife Research Group and prepares a statewide deer quota proposal. The statewide proposal is then returned to the field managers and made available to members of the Wisconsin Conservation Congress prior to official public hearings held yearly in April.

The Wisconsin Conservation Congress is an important organization in the rulemaking process for all hunting and fishing regulations. It is an official citizens' advisory body to the Natural Resources Board. Three regular and two alternate delegates from each county are elected to staggered three-year terms by the citizens attending the public hearings. Wildlife managers are instructed to meet with their local Conservation Congress members to explain the deer-harvest quota recommendations.

Wisconsin law requires public hearings on proposed administrative rules (regulations). A public hearing on fish and wildlife regulations is held in each county on the fourth Monday in April. Citizens in attendance vote on the proposals, including deer-harvest quotas, and these votes and other public testimony become part of the official hearing record. Wildlife managers are present at many of these hearings to explain and answer questions about the DNR or the Natural Resources Board.

The Conservation Congress conducts a statewide meeting in late May or early June. Approximately 300 delegates discuss and vote on the Department of Natural Resources' proposals, to develop recommendations for presentation to the Natural Resources Board.

Then, at its June meeting, the Natural Resources Board acts on quota recommendations for the upcoming white-tailed deer hunting season. These recommendations, from the Department of Natural Resources and the Conservation Congress and the public-hearing results, are presented to the Board for a decision. From early March until the Department of Natural Resources' final recommendations to the Natural Resources Board in June, wildlife managers have evaluated the effects of the past winter on the white-tailed deer in individual management units, and have had the opportunity to submit revisions of their original quota recommendations.

Following the Natural Resources Board's decision, the resulting rules are submitted to the state legislature for review. After a 30-day review period, if no objections are raised by the legislature the rules are published and become the regulations for the hunting season that year. During the history of this procedure the legislature has never rejected the deer-harvest quotas put forth by the Natural Resources Board. The time period and procedures in effect for public review and response to proposed quotas have been successful in minimizing unnecessary legislative involvement in the regulations process.

THE FUTURE

The major problem now facing deer management in Wisconsin is the growth—both in number and distribution—of gun hunters for white-tailed deer. The impact of 630,000 whitetail hunters (gun) during the maximum nine-day deer-hunting season, even in a state the size of Wisconsin (145,439 square kilometers: 56,154 square miles), is the creation of a highly competitive atmosphere over much of central and southern Wisconsin. This situation has resulted from two trends: first, a 62.7-percent increase in the number of gun hunters for white-tailed deer in Wisconsin from 1964 through 1981, including a 23.5-percent increase for 1971–1982 (*see* Table 30); and second, the steady diminishment of the state's outdoor recreational space and wildlife habitat (*see* McCabe 1976), due to urban sprawl, exurbanization, posting, roadway construction and other human developments. The competition for deer-hunting opportunities is likely to increase further, particularly near human population centers in the southern and central parts of the sate.

Excessive hunter concentrations tend to foster poor hunter behavior and a bad image of the recreation and its participants to nonhunters. Wisconsin's white-tailed deer management policy listed another objective as ". . . achieving and maintaining opportunities for a quality deer hunting experience while still allowing to the extent possible, freedom of choice by hunters. Regulations should provide incentives or disincentives to encourage better distribution of hunting pressure. If hunter numbers continue to increase, control of hunting pressure may become necessary" (Wis. Admin. Code, Sec. NR 1.15(2)(b):11).

Efforts to achieve this objective have met with little success. In line with the policy of allowing freedom of choice and avoiding the politically unpalatable step of limiting license sales, proposals to improve the distribution of gun hunters of white-tailed deer over time and area were developed by an *ad hoc* committee of wildlife professionals and tested for public reaction. This was done through a series of public hearings in 1976 and again in 1979. The proposals would offer a number of choices but limit hunting activities to the choice selected. Examples include:

1. *Hunter's-choice zones.* A deer hunter would select a management unit or area (combination of units) and be limited to hunting in that zone. This would reduce concentrations closer to urban areas later in the season by preventing hunters who go north for the opening weekend from returning to hunt near the cities.

2. *Hunter's-choice days.* A hunter would choose a short hunt early in the season or a longer hunt later and be limited to that selected hunting period. This would tend to spread hunter concentrations and highway traffic over time according to individual preferences for a hunting experience. Hopefully, no more than half the hunters would choose an early short season, thereby improving hunt quality and assuring legal animals for the later hunters.

3. *Longer northern season.* Extending the whitetail hunting season in the northern part of the state would be an incentive for hunters to go north, particularly so if combined with an earlier opening date (*see* proposal 4). Such

a season would be of greatest benefit to northern residents, besides serving to reduce hunter concentrations in the southern and central management units. Many hunters from the southern part of the state likely would complete their hunts early, leaving the rest of the season and many legal deer to local hunters.

4. *Earlier opening date.* Improved buck hunting can be expected from a season opening earlier in November, due to greater rutting activity. This is particularly important in the northern part of the state, where there are too few hunters to move deer, and especially with split seasons, when there would be even fewer hunters out on a given day. An earlier season opening could add to the wilderness aspect of the hunt, and increase reliance on the natural movements of deer during the rut.

5. *Midweek opening.* Starting the season on a weekday rather than a weekend would be a means of reducing opening-day concentrations in some areas and spreading hunters over time. Hunters forced by vocational circumstances to accept weekend openings would be attracted elsewhere, thereby relieving congestion in management units with midweek openings.

6. *Half-day hunting in any-deer zones.* This would discourage the influx of hunters from outside a unit or area where half-day hunting was in effect, and afford local residents—particularly landowners—improved hunting opportunity. Such a system also would preserve either-sex hunting, thus reducing illegal waste and avoiding the use of variable-quota permits, which attract outside hunters.

7. *Hunter's-choice permit.* A hunter's-choice permit would improve success for more individual hunters by eliminating the "bonus deer" feature of the party permit. It also could help reduce hunter concentrations by discouraging group hunting, which the party permit fosters.

The sole survivor of public opinion was the hunter's-choice permit, the effectiveness of which in improving hunter distribution has not yet been determined.

Studies of Wisconsin deer-hunter attitudes indicated a strong adherence to tradition and resistance to change (Heberlein and Laybourne 1978). Learned from the experience of testing new ideas is that change is more acceptable if made in small steps over time.

Wildlife biologists, managers and administrators in Wisconsin continue to seek methods to improve hunter distribution in the quest for quality white-tailed deer hunting.

Chapter 12

LESSONS FROM THE LLANO BASIN, TEXAS

James G. Teer
Director
Welder Wildlife Foundation
Sinton, Texas

Wildlife is a major natural resource in Texas (*see* Chapter 25). It is a form of wealth in a state known for abundances, and is measurable in economic, recreational, cultural and social currencies. The quantity and quality of it have brought it to the marketplace where it can and does compete with other forms of land use. It is integrated into the more than 69.2 million hectares (171 million acres) of extensively managed rangelands and forests, or about 71 percent of the area of the state. It is complementary to primary uses of the land and it is paying its way.

Recreational and cultural values are measured in hundreds of thousands of man-days of pleasure for hunters, fishermen, campers, hikers, birders and all other nature enthusiasts who enjoy the beauty and wonder of the natural world. The natural world has a heritage and historical value, not measurable in dollar expression, which has shaped the minds and mores of Texans, especially those who control the land. It was worth more than $108,000,000 to landowners engaged in commercial hunting programs in 1971 (Berger 1974), and many believe this to be a conservative estimate because lease prices today are two to three times what they were in the early 1970s. Undoubtedly the business and industry surrounding hunting is many times larger today than it was in the past. And it reaches into urban life more and more these days because 80 percent of Texans live in metropolitan areas, and these urbanites search for ways to get back to the land.

This case study is an account of the ecology and management of a particularly important deer population in central Texas—the Llano Basin deer population of the Central Mineral Region. Ecological and management studies were begun there in 1954, and these studies, and population-monitoring surveys, have continued to date. The major portion of this chapter comes from Wildlife Monograph No. 15, "Ecology and Management of White-tailed Deer in the Llano Basin of Texas" (Teer et al. 1965).

LLANO BASIN

The Llano Basin of Texas has a total area of approximately 379,200 hectares (937,000 acres) and is a part of the Central Mineral Region. All of Llano County and parts of nine other central Texas counties are included in the Central Mineral Region (Sellards et al. 1932) (Figure 67), the total area of which is approximately 809,400 hectares (2,000,000 acres). About 90 percent of the land area of the Llano Basin lies in Llano, Mason and Gillespie counties.

The Central Mineral Region is a shallow, irregularly shaped basin with a rolling floor studded with "mountains" 122–183 meters (400–600 feet) high and surrounded by the eroded and dissected but higher escarpments

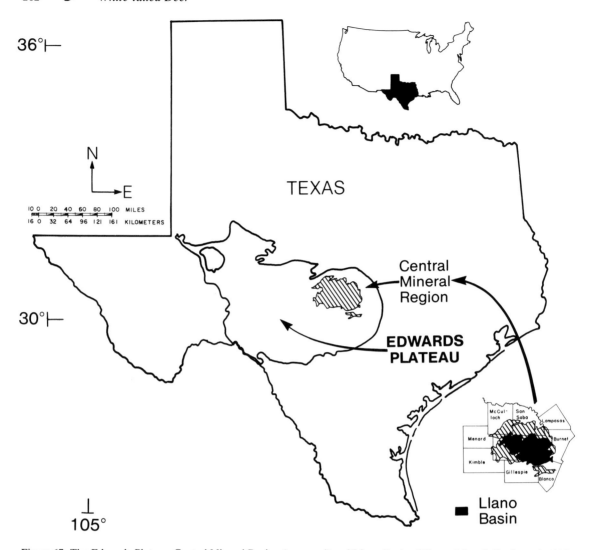

Figure 67. The Edwards Plateau, Central Mineral Region (screened) and Llano Basin of Texas (after Sellards et al. 1932).

of the Edwards Plateau. The Central Mineral Region's most characteristic topographic feature is the Llano Basin, a shallow depression within the more extensive basin. The interior basin is the eroded remains of the Llano Uplift, where granite, sandstone, gneiss, schist and other igneous intrusions and metamorphosed rocks of Precambrian and Prepaleozoic ages are exposed (Paige 1912, Sellards et al. 1932, Plummer 1943). Most soils in the Llano Basin were derived from granite, sandstone, schists and mixtures of these (Carter 1931). The climate of central Texas is both maritime and continental, and the vegetation is a part of the southernmost extension of the Great Plains grassland (Fenneman 1931).

All of the Llano Basin is privately-owned ranches that average approximately 405 hectares (1,000 acres), but most of the area is rough, stony and cannot be farmed. Beef cattle are the principal grazing animals. Most ranchers stock cows for production of calves. Sheep normally pastured from October through May for production of mutton and angora goats kept throughout the year for the production of mohair are stocked with cattle on the same range. However, there are fewer sheep and goats than in areas of comparable size on the Edwards Plateau.

Livestock stocking-rates average about one animal unit per 5.7 hectares (14 acres). Most ranges are overgrazed at this rate. When deer are added to the stocking rates of domestic livestock, many ranches have more than one

Hills and rocks of Precambrian age characterize the landscape of the Llano Basin of the Central Mineral Region. The low line of hills in the extreme background is part of the scarp of the Edwards Plateau. *Photo courtesy of the Texas Parks and Wildlife Department.*

animal unit per 4 hectares (10 acres), which results in serious overuse of range vegetation on many ranches, since carrying capacity of most range sites is about 7.3 to 8.1 hectares (18–20 acres) per animal unit. In years of drought, die-offs of deer due to starvation are common and extensive (Hahn 1945, Taylor and Hahn 1947).

WHITETAIL POPULATION

Census Technique and Sampling Effort

The Hahn (1949) deer cruise-census technique—an adaptation of King's method of censusing ruffed grouse (Leopold 1933)—was used to census the deer population. Center lines of transects were marked permanently by blazing trees and establishing small rock cairns where there were no trees. Blazes and cairns were painted yellow to help the observer stay on

line. All transects were 3.2 kilometers (2 miles) long, but width of the sampled strip in each transect varied because of differences in topography and vegetative density. Census of the population was conducted each year in September, October and the first week of November. Two counts per transect were made in most years.

Fifty-three transects were used to census approximately 212,470 hectares (525,000 acres) of deer range in those parts of Llano, Gillespie and Mason counties in the Llano Basin from 1954 through 1961 (Figure 68). After 1961, census data relate only to Llano County, but densities of deer for 1962 through 1981 are representative of those in other areas of the Basin.

Censusing played an important role in the population study, so particular care was taken in evaluating the technique. While the number of transects used probably was too small to obtain the precision of estimate that such a study deserves, census results surely were representative of changes in the deer population

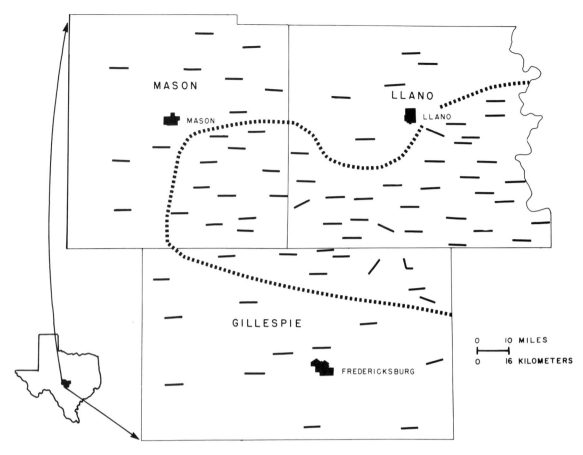

Figure 68. Distribution of transects used to census white-tailed deer in Gillespie, Llano and Mason counties of Texas. The area enclosed by the broken line is the densely populated rangeland in the Llano Basin.

Field observation is part of seasonal censusing of white-tailed deer in the Llano Basin. *Photo by John Suhrstedt; courtesy of the Texas Parks and Wildlife Department.*

and reasonably accurate in estimating population levels.

The population density averaged 35.8 whitetails per 100 hectares (14.5 per 100 acres) from 1954 through 1981 (Table 33). Within this 28-

Table 33. Population densities of white-tailed deer in the Llano Basin of Texas, 1954 through 1981.[a]

Year	Number of transects	Whitetails per 100 hectares (100 acres)
1954	49	44.2 (17.9)
1955	49	21.0 (8.5)
1956	48	29.4 (11.9)
1957	52	22.7 (9.2)
1958	53	33.9 (13.7)
1959	44	43.2 (17.5)
1960	47	44.2 (17.9)
1961	53	46.7 (18.9)
1962	35	35.8 (14.5)
1963	35	65.0 (26.3)
1964	35	52.6 (21.3)
1965	38	50.4 (20.4)
1966	38	56.1 (22.7)
1967	23	41.3 (16.7)
1968	23	32.6 (13.2)
1969	23	32.1 (13.0)
1970	23	33.4 (13.5)
1971	23	32.6 (13.2)
1972	17	32.6 (13.2)
1973	8	43.2 (17.5)
1974	11	34.3 (13.9)
1975	24	29.4 (11.9)
1976	12	26.7 (10.8)
1977		24.7 (10.0)
1978		25.9 (10.5)
1979		27.7 (11.2)
1980		18.5 (7.5)
1981		19.0 (7.7)
Average		35.8 (14.5)

[a]Whitetail population densities from 1954 to 1961 are for about 212,470 hectares (525,000 acres) of deer range in Llano, Mason and Gillespie counties. Densities for 1962–1981 are for 131,530 hectares (325,000 acres) in Llano County, but these densities are considered to be representative or equivalent to those for the Llano Basin population in the three counties.

year period, fluctuations in numbers of deer from year to year have ranged from almost 0 (stability) to near 100 percent. Trends in deer numbers have included a long series of increases (1954 through 1966), followed by a leveling-off at lower densities (1967 through 1981). Within these trends there have been some dramatic losses and gains in population size, such as described by Marburger and Thomas (1965). To be sure, some of the perturbations and fluctuations have not been detected by the cruise census, and there have been some errors in the estimates. Nonetheless, the important feature of these data is that the population has not fluctuated any more dramatically than its rates of increase would permit (*see* Lack 1954).

Densely populated range includes the southern half of Llano County south of the Llano River (127,854 hectares: 315,900 acres), the southeastern quarter of Mason County south of the Llano River and east of Shep Creek (60,540 hectares: 149,600 acres), and the part of the Llano Basin that extends into the northern part of Gillespie County (24,080 hectares: 59,500 acres) (Figure 68). This block of rangeland is devoted primarily to ranching, and has had dense populations of whitetails for many years. Investigators working in the Central Mineral Region reported high population levels in the Basin as early as 1938 (Table 34).

Whitetail population densities in large areas of the United States and Canada apparently do not approach those in the Llano Basin (Table 35). I believe that the Basin has the highest density of white-tailed deer of any area of similar size in North America.

Relatively wide fluctuations around a mean are characteristic of white-tailed deer populations. These fluctuations reflect changes in rates of productivity and mortality. Hahn (1945) and Taylor and Hahn (1947) reported the Llano Basin population to be subject to rather wide

Table 34. Estimates of white-tailed deer densities in the densely populated range in the Llano Basin of Texas, 1938–1961.

Year	Size of study area		Whitetails per 100 hectares (100 acres)	Source
	Hectares	Acres		
1938	77,440	191,350	44.5 (18.0)	Sanders (1941)
1942	485	1,200	80.3 (32.5)	Hahn (1945)
1946	260	640	29.4–169.0 (11.9–68.4)[a]	Taylor and Hahn (1947)
1947	23,880	59,000	61.8 (25.0)	Hahn (1949)
1948	260	640	81.5 (33.0)	Whisenhunt (1949)
1961	212,470	525,000	46.7 (18.9)[b]	Present study

[a]Thought by Taylor and Hahn (1947) to represent "concentrations" of deer on particular sections.
[b]The highest density from 1954 to 1961 occurred in 1961.

Table 35. Estimates of white-tailed deer density in parts of the United States and Canada.

State or province	Location	Years estimated	Census techniques	Whitetails per 100 hectares (100 acres)	Source
Florida	Everglades	1956	Aerial	2.2 (0.9)	Loveless (1959*b*)
Michigan	Lower Peninsula	1938	Drives	16.3 (6.6)	Bartlett (1939)
Minnesota	Northern forest zone	1936–1960	Drives, harvest data, aerial	4.9–7.7 (2.0–3.1)	Erickson et al. (1961)
Oklahoma	Southeastern zone	1940	Transects	0.5 (0.2)	Krefting and Fletcher (1941)
Pennsylvania	Centre County	1938	Pellet group	16.6 (6.7)	Bennet et al. (1940)
Wisconsin	Northern forest zone	1935–1941	Drives	17.3 (7.0)	Swift (1946)
Ontario	Rondeau Provincial Park	1951	Drives	6.9 (2.8)	Bartlett (1958)
Saskatchewan	Aspen parklands	1955	Not reported	3.2 (1.3)	Symington and Benson (1957)
Texas	Llano Basin	1954–1981	Hahn cruise census	35.8 (14.5)	Present study

Whitetail population density in the 3,790-square kilometer (1,465-square mile) Llano Basin of Texas from 1954 through 1981 averaged 35.8 deer per square kilometer (92.8 per square mile), for an approximate average annual count of 135,780. This apparently represents, for an area of such size, the highest concentration of whitetails anywhere. However it has been estimated that habitat carrying capacity was exceeded by roughly 200 percent, creating a precarious situation for the deer and extensive habitat destruction for wildlife and other potential land users. *Photo by Art Cowert; courtesy of the U.S. Soil Conservation Service.*

fluctuations in response to environmental conditions—mainly grazing pressures of domestic livestock and weather patterns.

Fluctuations in whitetail numbers occur seasonally and often trending through several years. Weather patterns—especially the amount and distribution of rainfall over time—trigger events in the ranch country that affect deer numbers and welfare. Seasonal fluctuations occur as an annual cycle of numbers; whitetails reach their highest densities shortly after the fawning season. Attrition due to hunting and natural mortality, occurring especially in winter months, may reduce the population as much as 20 to 35 percent by late winter. Wet and dry periods—either condition often lasting for several years—change carrying capacities of the rangeland for both livestock and deer. Ranchers increase their stocking rates of domestic livestock to accommodate the increased forage, and competition between livestock and whitetails becomes more direct and severe when livestock stocking-rates are heavy. Conversely, when droughts occur ranchers often sell off their livestock, but most strive to maintain their base herds by feeding them supplements during the worst times. Deer and remaining livestock are then reduced to eating the same forages because the drought reduces the amount and kinds of forage available to all herbivores, domestic and wild.

The carrying capacity of Llano Basin rangeland is not a fixed number; it varies with perturbations induced by man and nature. As a rule of thumb, however, I adopted the figure of 17.3 whitetails per 100 hectares (7 per 100 acres) as a working value for the carrying capacity of the Basin ranges. Densities of deer in the Basin for most years of the study exceeded that value. Management efforts during the past three decades have been directed at reducing whitetail density to prevent losses and to improve the quality of the deer population.

Factors Affecting Distribution and Density

Illegal hunting. Two extensive areas within the Llano Basin had widely different population levels prior to the 1960s. Range vegetation and soils were essentially the same. Land-use practices in terms of kinds of domestic livestock and rates of stocking were similar. The difference seemed to be the attitude toward deer of the landowners in the low-density area. Crop depredations by whitetails on small farms, es-

pecially in northeastern Mason and northwestern Llano counties, probably were responsible for the landowners' attitudes. These small farms—much more numerous prior to 1950—were interspersed among relatively large ranches. Farmers killed deer to protect their crops, which primarily included peanuts, small grains and hay. Many ranchers in the area permitted the public free access to hunt by any method at all times of the year because of problems presented by the deer to farmers. Only a few ranchers in this area leased their pastures for hunting privileges. Whisenhunt (1949) concluded from a study of deer populations on two ranches—one in the densely populated whitetail range of southern Mason County and the other in the low-density area in northeastern Mason County—that yearlong illegal hunting in the latter area was an important factor contributing to differences in deer densities.

That these low-density areas north of the Llano River could support larger numbers of deer is attested to by the fact that a few ranches did have deer populations whose densities exceeded by several times the average density in the area. The Fitzsimmons Land and Cattle Company, the Luke Moss Pecan Creek Ranch and the Larkin Renick Ranch were examples of ranches having dense populations of whitetails within the low-density range in early years of the study.

The Fitzsimmons Land and Cattle Company, a 11,330-hectare (28,000-acre) ranch, had so few deer in the 1930s that hunting was not rewarding. Employees of the ranch stated that weeks often passed between sightings of deer. In the early 1940s, a warden was hired by the ranch to patrol its pastures, and illegal hunting presumably was decreased by these efforts. By 1947 the whitetail population had increased to a level the owners deemed adequate to hunt. Hunting rights were leased to a group of hunters, and 125 fork-horned bucks were harvested on 9,715 hectares (24,000 acres) of the ranch that year. The harvest increased each year after 1947. To control the population, antlerless deer were included in the harvest in 1954, and anysex seasons were in effect through 1961. Results of a census conducted on 3 transects on the ranch indicated that the population fluctuated between 24.7 and 34.6 deer per 100 hectares (10–14 per 100 acres) from 1954 through 1961.

Similar instances of whitetail population buildup following protection from illegal hunting were noted on other ranches in the Llano Basin. Economics of the hunting-lease system seemed to have been the motivating factor.

Since the early 1960s, the deer population in sparsely populated areas of the Basin has increased in density to levels that rival those of historically heavily populated ranges in the southern half of Llano County. This increase in density has been brought about through the commercial hunting system. Ranchowners now protect whitetails on their properties because the deer have market value.

Livestock.   Numbers of domestic livestock and white-tailed deer in the Llano Basin were compared with those in selected counties of the Edwards Plateau to determine the influence of livestock on deer population levels.

The southern, eastern and western boundaries of the densely populated range agree reasonably well with the geological boundary separating the Llano Basin and the rest of the Edwards Plateau. Transition zones of soils and vegetation are especially narrow on the south-

ern boundary where the escarpment of the Edwards Plateau breaks downward sharply to meet the floor of the Llano Basin. Soils change within a few hundred yards, from primarily calcareous—black clays and loams—to granitic and sandstone origins. Associated with changes in soils are changes in plant composition. Texas oak, shinoak, juniper and other trees and shrubs become important elements of vegetation in the limestone soils on the Edwards Plateau, whereas post oak, blackjack oak, hickory, whitebrush and other browse plants decrease or fade out completely. Live oak, shinoak and Texas oak are preferred deer foods wherever they occur (Hahn 1945, Whisenhunt 1949, McMahan 1961). Other browse and mast species, such as juniper and Lacey oak, also are abundant in limestone soils and important in the deer diet. Because of the dominance and abundance of these species on limestone soils, the Edwards Plateau has more browse than does the Llano Basin and, therefore, is a better winter deer range.

Live oak is an important food and cover plant for white-tailed deer on the Edwards Plateau. *Photo courtesy of the Texas Parks and Wildlife Department.*

Rainfall. Population densities of white-tailed deer in the Llano Basin and on Edwards Plateau were distributed on an east-west gradient that corresponded to the distributional pattern of mean annual precipitation. A decrease in precipitation occurs from east to west with the isohyets oriented in a north-south direction. Annual precipitation decreases from more than 81.3 centimeters (32 inches) to less than 30.5 centimeters (12 inches) in a distance of approximately 645 kilometers (400 miles) (Figure 69). In the vicinity of the Balcones Escarpment, which forms the southern and eastern boundaries of the Edwards Plateau, the mean annual precipitation changes for a short distance at the rate of 0.4 centimeter per kilometer (0.25 inch per mile) (U.S. Weather Bureau 1961).

While censuses of the population showed that whitetails occurred throughout the Plateau, densities in the Basin and the eastern part of the Plateau decreased from about 25 to 37 deer per 100 hectares (10–15 per 100 acres) to less than 5 deer per 100 hectares (2 per 100 acres) in the western part. On the Stockton Plateau, which lies west of the Pecos River and has been designated as the extreme western extension of the Edwards Plateau (B.C. Tharp personal communication:1962), whitetailed deer are sparsely distributed and occur on some of the same ranges inhabited by desert mule deer.

The Edwards Plateau is geologically of a single origin, but it is not a single, continuous ecological type. The habitat, as it relates to grazing and browsing ungulates, is quite diverse. The primary difference between eastern and western ranges on the Plateau is manifested in kinds and volumes of forage. Carter (1931) divided the Plateau into three belts in which climate, soils and vegetation are differ-ent. These belts comprise cross-sections of north-south soil/climate divisions of continental scope. Rainfall is the factor underlying the differences. Although there are no lines sharply separating the divisions, the eastern belt lies within the humid region, the central is in the subhumid, and the western belt occurs in the semiarid region. Vegetation in the eastern belt, of which the eastern portion of the Plateau and the entire Llano Basin are part, is relatively dense compared to that of the central and western belts. Trees reach heights of 9.1 to 12.2 meters (30–40 feet) on the uplands and even greater heights in valley lowlands and along streams. Ground vegetation ordinarily is dense, forming almost complete coverage on most range sites. The vegetation becomes sparser and of a lesser height with decreasing rainfall. In the extreme western part of the Plateau, the vegetation tends toward a low-growing semi-desert scrub. Lecheguilla, sotol, various yucca species and other plants of arid western Texas occur on ranges occupied by white-tailed deer.

Lack (1954) postulated that populations of many animals, while fluctuating rather irregularly, do so in very narrow limits and that this relative stability is controlled by density-dependent factors. With deer, interaction of populations with their food supply is the ecological mechanism that determines population densities and range carrying capacities (Leopold 1943, Leopold et al. 1947).

For the Llano Basin and Edwards Plateau whitetail populations, I believe that precipitation is the chief factor regulating range carrying capacity, and that deer population densities fluctuate about the carrying capacity in response to interaction of populations with their food supply. The whitetail populations in the Basin and on the Plateau are relatively stable at particular locations. On the extreme western part of the Plateau, populations rise and fall around a density of approximately 15 deer per 100 hectares (6 per 100 acres), while populations in the Basin fluctuate around a density more than double that.

Whitetail population densities in the Basin also were related to mean annual precipitation of the preceding year (Figure 70). This relationship was close during years of severe drought (1953–1956), but loosened after precipitation increased to average or above-average amounts. Population densities were reduced drastically during the drought, and remained low until 1958. Significantly, in the

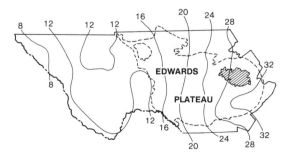

Figure 69. Isohyets of precipitation in the Llano Basin (screened) and Edwards Plateau of Texas (after U.S. Weather Bureau 1960).

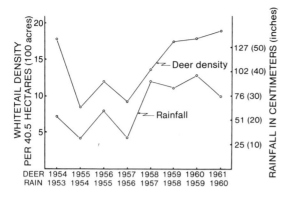

Figure 70. Relationship of population levels of white-tailed deer in the Llano Basin of Texas to annual precipitation of the preceding year.

year following the first year that precipitation approached the long-term average, the population increased. After the drought ended in 1957 the population began to increase without interruption despite minor fluctuations in annual precipitation. However, at no time during the above-average period did rainfall drop below the long-term average, and rainfall patterns in the previous two decades (1960s and 1970s) generally have been average or above.

The relationship of population densities to precipitation of the preceding year was established partially by the whitetail population's breeding cycle. Physical condition of deer during the autumn rut influences reproductive rates, but increment gain to the population does not occur until the following year.

A delay in range vegetation's response to and recovery from changes in precipitation seems to be a chief reason for the lag in deer-number fluctuations. Thomas and Young (1954) found a close correlation (r = 0.637) between rainfall of the previous year and the density of several species of range plants on the western Edwards Plateau. Most species showed a one-year lag, but others were two years behind in responding to years of high or low rainfall (*see also* Nelson 1934, Craddock and Forsling 1938, Clawson 1950).

REPRODUCTION AND PRODUCTIVITY

Studies of reproduction and productivity of the Llano Basin whitetail population were made by examining 2,719 uteri and 2,469 pairs of ovaries of does shot by hunters in the years 1957–1961, and by conducting counts of sex and age composition in conjunction with the annual censuses. These studies were made to determine: (1) the reproductive performance of age classes; (2) changes in reproductive performance in response to changes in density of deer and associated ecological factors; and (3) the gross (potential) and net (realized) productivity of the population.

A jawbone (either the left or right ramus of the mandible) was collected from each deer from which a reproductive tract was collected, and was labeled in the same way. After the hunting season the deer were aged, and counts of corpora albicantia, embryos and fetuses were made from the collection of reproductive tracts by using the technique described by Cheatum (1949*b*).

Reproductive Performance of Age Classes

The method used here to estimate reproductive performance differs somewhat from that of Cheatum (1949*b*), who showed that either corpora albicantia or corpora lutea could be used to calculate ovulation incidence. However, when Cheatum used corpora lutea, the assumption was made that all does had completed the breeding cycle. Collections from the Llano Basin population were made during the rutting season, and all does had not had an opportunity to breed. I used corpora lutea to determine ovulation incidence, and therefore ovulation rates first were calculated for does that had ovulated before they were collected. This figure then was multiplied by the conception rate to obtain ovulation incidence for the entire age class. Ovulation incidence multiplied by the fertilization frequency (the number of ova fertilized, as obtained from corpora lutea and embryo content) gives an estimate of reproductive performance.

Fawns. Reproductive tracts of 160 fawns were collected in the Llano Basin from 1957 to 1961. None of the fawns was pregnant. Five tracts (3 percent) had a single corpus luteum in the ovaries (Table 38).

An examination of 520 sets of ovaries collected from yearlings 16 to 20 months of age showed that most fawns were collected before they had reached sexual maturity and commenced breeding activity. Eighty-five (16 percent) yearlings had corpora albicantia in their ovaries. If 3 percent of the fawns had ovulated prior to collection in November and December, and 16 percent ultimately ovulated, then 81 percent (13 ÷ 16) of the estrus cycles (and perhaps pregnancies) occurred after the tracts

Table 38. Reproductive performance of age classes of white-tailed deer does harvested in the Llano Basin of Texas, 1957 through 1961.

Age class	Number of deer that had ovulated	Number of corpora lutea	Ovulation rate (A)	Fertilization rate (B)	Conception rate (C)	Embryos per doe (A − B − C)
Fawns	5	5	1.00	[a]	0.16	0.14
Yearlings	268	336	1.25 ± 0.06	0.88	0.68	0.75
Adults						
2.5	187	276	1.48 ± 0.08	0.84	0.77	0.96
3.5	265	393	1.48 ± 0.08	0.86	0.81	1.03
4.5	165	259	1.57 ± 0.08	0.94	0.78	1.15
5.5	157	239	1.52 ± 0.08	0.83	0.86	1.08
6.5	131	208	1.59 ± 0.10	0.85	0.82	1.11
7.5	64	97	1.52 ± 0.14	0.88	0.88[b]	1.18
8.5+	101	155	1.53 ± 0.12	0.96	0.88	1.29
Total[c]	1,070	1,627				
Average			1.52 ± 0.03	0.88	0.81	1.08

[a]The fertilization rate of fawns was not determined because none of the fawns was pregnant. Therefore, the average fertilization rate of all age classes was used to calculate reproductive performance of fawns.
[b]The conception rate of does 8.5 years old and older was used to calculate reproductive performance of 7.5-year-old does.
[c]Only adults.

were collected.

Evidence gathered at checking stations indicated that some fawns conceived. Hunters were questioned to determine the percentage of harvested yearlings whose mammary glands contained milk. Many responses were not considered reliable because some hunters were reluctant to report that their deer had been nursing fawns. When asked about the development and milk content of mammary glands removed from field-dressed deer, some hunters simply did not know. However, a number of yearlings obviously were lactating because mammary-gland fragments still attached to the deer contained milk. Lactating yearlings could be impregnated only as fawns.

Two fawns collected on 3 March 1959 at the Camp Bullis Military Reservation in Bexas County were pregnant. Two yearlings collected in September 1959 in Sutton County were lactating. These were the only records of conception by fawns obtained without the aid of hunters' reports, and all occurred outside the Basin.

Yearlings. Yearlings were not as productive as older does. Of 520 sets of ovaries of yearlings, 268 (52 percent) had ovulated at a rate of 1.25 ± 0.06 ova per doe (Table 38), of which 88 percent were fertilized. Counts of the number of 2.5-year-old does with corpora albicantia showed that only 68 percent of the yearlings conceived. Reproductive performance of yearlings was 0.75 fawn per doe—a rate about two-thirds that of older does. The average number of embryos per doe in 49 pregnancies was 1.32 (Table 39).

Table 39. Numbers of embryos in 525 pregnancies of white-tailed deer does harvested in the Llano Basin of Texas, 1957 through 1961.

Year	Yearlings			Adults			
	Conceptions of		Embryos per doe	Conceptions of			Embryos per doe
	Singles	Twins		Singles	Twins	Triplets	
1957	2	3	1.60	16	62	1	1.81
1958	2	3	1.60	54	54		1.50
1959	13	10	1.43	50	60	1	1.57
1960	10		1.00	55	35		1.39
1961	6		1.00	59	27	2	1.35
Total	33	16		234	238	4	
Average			1.32				1.52

Adults. Inspection of the confidence intervals showed that ovulation rates for age classes of adults were not significantly different (P = 0.05), but that the ovulation rate for yearlings was significantly different from that for all adult ages (Table 38).

Sample sizes might have biased the overall estimate. The largest samples of reproductive tracts were collected in Llano County in 1958 and 1959. Ovulation rates were tested for differences between age classes for each of these two years using Duncan's multiple-range test (*see* Steel and Torrie 1960).

In 1958 there were no differences among rates for any age classes of adult does, but significant differences were found among ovulation rates for all age classes of adults and yearlings (P = 0.05).

Some age classes of adult does produced significantly different numbers of oocytes than did others in 1959. However, there was no consistent trend of increase or decrease in the rates. There were significant differences between the ovulation rate for 7.5-year-old does and those for four other age classes of adults. The ovulation rate for 7.5-year-old does was 1.27 in 1959, based on 11 sets of ovaries. This rate was far below that for the same age class in other years. I feel that sampling error or variation was involved in the difference. The only other significant difference in ovulation rates for adult does occurred between those for the 4.5-year and 5.5-year age classes. The ovulation rate for yearlings was significantly different from those for four of the seven age classes of adults.

Frequencies of fertilization and conception rates among adult does also were uniform. A chi-square test of the relationship of embryos to corpora lutea of pregnancy revealed no significant differences in fertilization frequencies for all does older than fawns (x^2 = 1.35; at P = 0.05, with 10 df, x^2 = 18.31).

The close similarities in fertilization frequencies, conception rates and ovulation incidences in adults permitted the combining of adult age classes into a single group.

The overall reproductive performance of adults averaged 1.08 embryos per doe (Table 38), and pregnant does averaged 1.52 embryos (Table 39). If the estimate of embryos per pregnant doe is corrected for nonfertile animals by multiplying 1.52 by 0.81 (the conception rate), an estimate of 1.23 embryos per doe is obtained. The difference of 0.15 embryo per doe

(1.23 − 1.08) probably is due to several potential sources of error: (1) errors in identifying and interpreting ovarian structures; (2) monozygotic twins and polyovular follicles resulting in multiple conceptions that tend to increase estimates of fertilization frequencies; and (3) sampling error.

Errors in interpretation and sampling could not be detected easily. The other possible source of error—that caused by two or more embryos resulting from a single oocyte in one follicle (corpora lutea of pregnancy after conception)—was assessed by finding the number of pregnant deer having more embryos than corpora lutea. Presumably such cases represented embryos developing from polyovular follicles and identical twinning from one oocyte. Thirteen (2.5 percent) of 525 pregnant deer had fewer corpora lutea than embryos. All except one pregnancy had embryos too small to sex, and the incidence of monozygotic twins could not be determined. Such a small number of cases of identical twinning and polyovular follicles could reduce the estimate obtained from ovarian material by not more than 0.03 embryo per doe. Overlooking or misinterpreting 12 to 15 corpora lutea in a sample of similar size would accomplish the same result.

Whitetail Density and Reproductive Performance Relationships

The reproductive performance of whitetails decreased each year from 1957 to 1960 (Table 40). Performance in 1960 by fawns, yearlings and adults was 33, 45 and 60 percent, respectively, of that in 1957. Reduction was accomplished by decreases in ovulation (Figure 71) and conception (Figure 72), and was reflected in estimates of embryos per doe.

An inverse relationship between ovulation incidence and density of deer was found for the Llano Basin population. As the population level increased, ovulation incidence decreased. The slopes of the regression equations for adult and yearling does were practically the same (0.056 versus 0.058). This suggests that responses of yearlings and adults to population-level changes were similar.

An additional check of the relationship between ovulation and density was made. Ovulation rates were determined for each year of the study from reproductive tracts of adults collected on ranches whose deer population

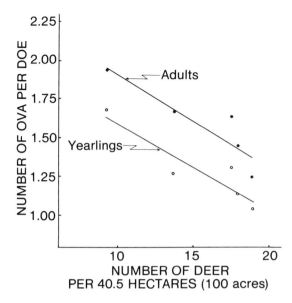

Figure 71. Regression of ovulation rates of yearling and adult whitetail does on deer density in the Llano Basin of Texas, 1957–1961. $\hat{Y}$ = 2.48 − 0.058x (adults); $\hat{Y}$ = 2.15 − 0.056x (yearlings).

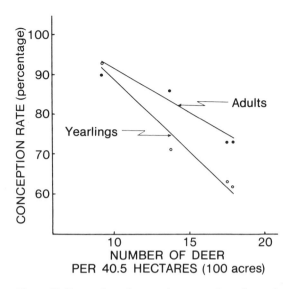

Figure 72. Regression of conception rates of yearling and adult does on density of deer in the Llano Basin of Texas, 1957 through 1960. $\hat{Y}$ = 1.12 − 0.021x (adults); $\hat{Y}$ = 1.23 − 0.035x (yearlings).

Table 40. Reproductive performance of white-tailed deer does in the Llano Basin of Texas, 1957 through 1961.

Age and year	Number of deer with corpora lutea (A)	Number of corpora lutea (B)	Ovulation rate (B ÷ A)	Fertilization rate[a]	Number of deer examined for corpora albicantia (C)	Number of deer with corpora albicantia (D)	Conception rate[b] (D ÷ C)	Embyros per deer
Fawns								
1957			1.00[c]	0.88[d]	77	28	0.36	0.32
1958	4	4	1.00	0.88	222	28	0.13	0.11
1959			1.00	0.88	95	11	0.12	0.11
1960	1	1	1.00	0.88	113	14	0.12	0.11
1961			1.00	0.88				
Yearlings								
1957	13	22	1.69 ± 0.37	0.88	40	37	0.93	1.38
1958	67	85	1.27 ± 0.10	0.88	70	50	0.71	0.79
1959	103	135	1.31 ± 0.10	0.88	73	46	0.63	0.73
1960	48	55	1.14 ± 0.10	0.88	94	58	0.62	0.62
1961	37	39	1.05 ± 0.08					
Adults								
1957	109	212	1.94 ± 0.10	0.88	288	260	0.90	1.54
1958	320	536	1.67 ± 0.10	0.88	361	312	0.86	1.26
1959	314	515	1.64 ± 0.12	0.88	256	186	0.73	1.05
1960	239	347	1.45 ± 0.10	0.88	349	255	0.73	0.93
1961	269	337	1.25 ± 0.06	0.88				

[a]Fertilization rates for age classes and for years were not significantly different and, therefore, the average for all years was used in the calculations.
[b]Conception rates for each year were determined from corpora albicantia in ovaries collected the following year. Data from ovaries collected in 1962 were not available; thus, reproductive performance (embyros per doe) could not be determined for 1961.
[c]Only five fawns had ovulated five ova. A rate of 1.00 ovum per doe was used for fawns in all years.
[d]No fawns were pregnant when collected, and fertilization rates could not be determined for this age class. The average for all ages was used in the calculations.

densities were: (1) less than 24.7 deer per 100 hectares (10 per 100 acres); (2) 24.7–49.4 deer per 100 hectares (10–20 per 100 acres); and (3) more than 49.4 deer per 100 hectares (20 per 100 acres) (Table 41). Each estimate of ovulation in a particular year for a particular density class was considered to be independent of estimates of ovulation in other years for that density class. Only reproductive tracts from ranches on which there were transects, and therefore population estimates, were used in the analysis.

A highly significant correlation between ovulation incidences and deer density was found (r = 0.83; at P − 0.01, with 9 df, r = 0.74). In all cases, despite small samples for some density classes in some years, ovulation decreased as density increased. Slopes of the regression lines suggest that yearlings were more responsive to density increases than were adults.

Estimates of embryos per doe, although partly disposed by ovulation, are not entirely dependent on ovulation because some oocytes are not fertilized. Further losses occur in embryonic life. These losses are included in fertilization frequencies. Thus, estimates of embryos per doe reflect ovulation and loss of oocytes and embryos from the time of ovulation to the stage of gestation at which the deer were harvested. Embryos per pregnant adult doe decreased from 1.81 to 1.35 between 1957 and 1960, and remained at 1.00 in 1961.

Ovulation and breeding occurred later in the rutting season as population levels increased. This delay was shown by the percentages of yearlings and adults that had ovulated by the same date in each successive breeding season from 1957 through 1961 (Table 42). Except in 1960, when ovulation occurred earlier than in 1959, the percentage of deer that had ovulated

Table 41. Ovulation rates of adult whitetail does harvested on ranches with different deer population densities in the Llano Basin of Texas.

Year	Less than 24.7 deer per 100 hectares (10 per 100 acres)		24.7–49.4 deer per 100 hectares (10–20 per 100 acres)		More than 49.4 deer per 100 hectares (20 per 100 acres)	
	Number of tracts	Ovulation rate[a]	Number of tracts	Ovulation rate[a]	Number of tracts	Ovulation rate[a]
1957	52	2.05 ± 0.14	49	1.92 ± 0.11	6	1.50 ± 0.71
1958	14	1.86 ± 0.32	155	1.79 ± 0.09	122	1.52 ± 0.10
1959			108	1.58 ± 0.12	91	1.42 ± 0.11
1960			87	1.49 ± 0.11	91	1.30 ± 0.10
Total	66		399		310	
Average		2.02		1.69		1.43

[a]Confidence interval for ovulation rate = $t_{.05} \cdot s_{\bar{x}}$.

Table 42. Percentages of white-tailed deer does that had ovulated before being collected for three consecutive two-week periods in the antlerless-deer hunting seasons of 1957 through 1961 in the Llano Basin of Texas.

Age and year	November 16–30		December 1–15		December 16–31	
	Number of deer examined	Percentage that had ovulated	Number of deer examined	Percentage that had ovulated	Number of deer examined	Percentage that had ovulated
Yearlings						
1957			13	100		
1958			76	88		
1959	80	36	74	53	68	52
1960	41	17	30	73	23	83
1961	21	10	27	19	65	46
Adults						
1957			109	100		
1958			322	97		
1959	141	63	155	73	134	83
1960	132	48	77	86	118	91
1961	58	50	135	50	247	72

decreased progressively in each breeding season from 1957 through 1961.

Of several hypotheses that might help explain the relationship between density and reproduction, two seem most applicable to the Llano Basin population. First, deer density reached a level at which crowding resulted in competition for living requirements and this competition produced a physiologically and perhaps psychologically stressed population unable to reproduce at maximum or high rates.

If crowding and competition played any part in governing or restricting breeding, observations of irritability in the animals might have been expected. While there was no initial intent to study and measure whitetail behavioral patterns in relation to population density, several thousand deer were observed on many ranches with different population densities. Behavior that could be considered aberrant was not observed at any time, nor was any unusual irritability of deer seen either in small or large groups. On the contrary, large aggregations of deer were the rule on most ranches where densities were high. These large aggregations appeared to be completely socially compatible. Therefore, I dismissed this hypothesis as a cause of reproductive declines.

The second hypothesis was that deer densities increased to a level at which the food supply was inadequate to meet the nutritional demands of high reproductive rates. This hypothesis seemed more plausible for the Llano Basin population. A number of investigators have reported regional differences in productivity and inverse relationships between deer reproductive performance and range forage supply (*see* Morton and Cheatum 1946, Dunkeson and Murphy 1953, Robinette and Gashwiler 1950, Robinette et al. 1955, Short 1981, Julander et al. 1961, Taber 1953, Cheatum and Severinghaus 1950, Mautz 1978, Anderson 1981).

In the Llano Basin, evidence pointed strongly to the range forage crop as determinant of reproductive performance of the Basin's whitetail population. The range was in poor condition during the drought years that began in the Llano Basin in 1950 and by the end of 1956 had come to be regarded as one of the most serious, prolonged droughts on record. Except for 1952, rainfall was below the long-term average each year from 1950 through 1956. Much of the vegetation, including woody species, died. During the worst of the drought, vegetation failed to become green except after a few scattered thundershowers during the growing season. In 1954 and 1956, rainfall was less than half of the average, and many ranchers had little more than prickly pear and tasajillo in their pastures to feed livestock. Most ranchers reduced their livestock, burned spines from the aforementioned cacti, and fed cottonseed cake, molasses and other supplements to maintain their herds. When the drought ended in early 1957, ranges began to recover and ranchers began to replace the livestock they had sold.

Whitetails foraging in a mesquite flat during the drought years of the mid-1950s. The deer were in very poor condition during this period, and malnutrition and related complications were the primary causes of mortality. *Photo courtesy of the Texas Parks and Wildlife Department.*

While numerical inventories of vegetation were not made, the trend in vegetative composition and succession after 1957 was strikingly apparent. Annual forbs responded most conspicuously during the first year, followed by annual grasses and perennial plants in succeeding years. Forbs were extremely abundant in 1957 and 1958. Bobwhite quail, normally present in very low densities on most range sites in the Basin, increased to a density of at least 2.5 quail per hectare (1 per acre) in 1958 and 1959, presumably as a consequence of improved food and cover conditions afforded by the upsurge of forbs.

The stocking of domestic livestock on Basin rangeland increased approximately 19 percent between 1957 and 1961 (Table 43). The rates were excessive in all years. Range management technicians of the U.S. Soil Conservation Service recommended stocking of about 12.4 animal units per 100 hectares (5 per 100 acres) on most ranges in the Basin. According to this standard, ranges in the Basin were overstocked with livestock six of nine years from 1953 through 1961. In the three years when stocking was less than the recommended rate, grazing pressure was excessive because range forage was in short supply due to drought. When whitetails are included in the estimates, range utilization was extremely high, especially in 1961, when deer and livestock numbers were double the recommended rate.

Productivity and Rates of Increase of the Llano Basin Whitetail Population

Pimlott's (1959) definitions of productivity, gross productivity and net productivity are used here because they appear to be most applicable in interpreting data from the Basin whitetail population. Pimlott's expressions reflect Leopold's (1933) definition of productivity, which embodies a connotation of yield or harvestable surplus.

Either fawns or yearlings ordinarily are used as units of productivity in ungulate populations. I chose fawns as the age class of increment for three reasons. First, it seemed desirable to use as the unit of productivity and increment the youngest age class available for harvest. Hunting regulations allowed the taking of any deer, and fawns were harvested along with other sex and age classes. Second, measurements of productivity and annual increment using fawns accruing to the breeding population seem more realistic and probably are more precise than those that use yearlings, which have experienced hunting mortality as fawns. If reliable estimates of hunting and natural mortality are available, expressions of productivity in terms of accruing yearlings are useful measurements, particularly in ungulate populations from which only antlered males are harvested. And third, the timing of the census during which sex and age counts were taken was particularly suited to the use of fawns as the unit of productivity. The census was begun after most neonatal mortality had occurred and ended within 10 days of the hunting season. The importance of the period of the census cannot be overemphasized because mortality of newborn fawns was extremely high in some years, principally from myiasis of screwworm flies. Fawns are especially vulnerable at birth because their unhealed, moist navels provide ready sites for such infestations. Counts earlier in the season miss a great part of this mortality, and those made as near to the hunting season

Table 43. Stocking rates of livestock and numbers of white-tailed deer in the Llano Basin of Texas, 1953 through 1961.

Year	Number of ranches in sample	Ranchland size		Animal units of livestock per 100 hectares (100 acres)	Animal units of deer per 100 hectares (100 acres)[a]	Total animal units of ungulates per 100 hectares (100 acres)
		Hectares	Acres			
1953	14	16,606	41,034	12.4 (5.0)		
1954	18	19,724	48,738	11.9 (4.8)	7.2 (2.9)	19.0 (7.7)
1955	18	19,724	48,738	12.6 (5.1)	3.5 (1.4)	16.1 (6.5)
1956	18	19,724	48,738	12.4 (5.0)	4.9 (2.0)	17.3 (7.0)
1957	18	19,724	48,738	13.8 (5.6)	3.7 (1.5)	17.5 (7.1)
1958	22	18,610	45,984	15.3 (6.2)	5.7 (2.3)	21.0 (8.5)
1959	22	18,610	45,984	15.6 (6.3)	7.2 (2.9)	22.7 (9.2)
1960	22	18,610	45,984	16.8 (6.8)	7.4 (3.0)	24.2 (9.8)
1961	22	18,610	45,984	16.8 (6.8)	7.9 (3.2)	24.7 (10.0)

[a]Whitetail numbers were derived from census, with the numbers converted to animal units by using six deer as an animal-unit equivalent.

as possible more accurately reflect the increment available for removal by hunting.

Gross productivity. The producing segments of the population consisted of fawns, yearlings and adult does. And since each of these groups produced at different rates, the relative production by each had to be determined. A combination of census and kill data was used to establish the percentages of fawn females, yearling females and adult females in the population.

The percentage of doe fawns in the female segment of the herd was determined by assuming that half the fawns observed were females and then finding the relationship of doe fawns to other does:

$$\text{Doe fawns (f)} = \frac{F_d}{F_d + (Y_d + A_d)} \cdot 100,$$

where f = number of doe fawns in 100 females;
$\quad F_d$ = number of doe fawns observed in census; and
$(Y_d + A_d)$ = number of yearling does and adult does in census.

Yearling does and adult does could not be separated from the field because they were almost identical in weight and stature. The ratio of yearling does to adult does was determined from the kill of females one year of age and older. This ratio then was used to establish the percentage of yearling females in the segment of the herd:

$$\text{Yearling does (y)} = \frac{Y_k}{Y_k + A_k} \cdot (100 - F),$$

where Y = number of yearling females in 100 females;
$\quad Y_k$ = number of yearling does in the kill; and
$\quad A_k$ = number of adult does in the kill.

The percentage of adult does in the female segment of the population then was obtained by subtraction:

Adult does (a) = 100 − (f + y),
where (a) = number of adult does in 100 females.

The number of males per 100 females was established from the autumn census, by assuming that half of the fawns were males and adding this number to the number of antlered bucks observed in the census:

Males: 100 females (b)

$$= \frac{F_b + A_b}{(Y_c + A_c) + F_d} \cdot 100,$$

where b = number of males per 100 females;
$\quad F_b$ = number of buck fawns observed in census; and
$\quad A_b$ = number of antlered bucks observed in census.

Estimates of the number of doe fawns, yearling does, adult does and males were summed and then reduced to numbers of each sex and age class in 100 members of the population.

Assumptions presupposed by these determinations were that (1) all members of the population were equally observable in the autumn census, (2) hunters did not selectively harvest yearling or adult does, and (3) yearling does and adult does were equally vulnerable to hunting.

Gross productivity and rates of increase declined from 1957 through 1960 (Table 44). While decreases in ovulation, conception and number of embryos per doe, as previously discussed, were arithmetically responsible for declines in gross productivity from year to year, shifts in sex and age composition of the population also were involved. Generally, the percentage of producing females decreased as the annual increment put larger numbers of bucks in the population. In addition, age composition of the female segment shifted to higher percentages of fawns and yearlings, both of which produced at lower rates than did adults.

Net productivity. Net productivity of the Llano Basin whitetail population from 1953 through 1961 is presented in Table 45. The estimates are percentages of fawns in the population in early autumn relative to the population prior to the hunting season. Net productivity ranged from 12 to 44 percent and averaged 30 percent.

Comparisons with other whitetail populations indicated that net productivity of the Llano Basin population was lower than normally achieved. For Michigan's enclosed George Reserve deer population between 1928 and 1947, O'Roke and Hamerstrom (1948) recorded that annual increases ranged from 12 to 104 percent and averaged 43.8 percent. Between 1942 and 1961, net productivity averaged 39 percent, and removals—largely by simulated hunting—also were sustained at 39 percent (Chase and Jenkins 1962).

Table 44. Sex and age composition, gross productivity and rates of increase of the white-tailed deer population in the Llano Basin of Texas, 1957 through 1960.

Population characteristics and elements of productivity	1957	1958	1959	1960	1957–1960
Census and kill data used to determine age composition of females					
Yearling and adult does[a] observed in census ($Y_d + A_d$)	784	785	803	944	3,316
Doe fawns[b] observed in census (F_d)	107	385	333	296	1,121
Buck fawns observed in census (F_b)	108	386	333	297	1,124
Antlered bucks observed in census (B_a)	133	198	283	389	1,003
Yearling does in kill (Y_k)	13	77	222	95	407
Adult does in kill (A_k)	50	289	375	304	1.018
Age composition of females[c]					
Fawns	12	21	29	26	25
Yearlings	18	17	26	18	19
Adults	70	62	45	58	56
Bucks (all ages) per 100 does	27	49	54	56	48
Sex and age composition of 100 deer					
Doe fawns (f)	10	14	19	15	17
Yearling does (y)	14	11	17	12	13
Adult does (a)	55	42	29	37	38
Bucks (b)	21	33	35	36	32
Reproductive rate[d]					
Fawns	0.32	0.11	0.11	0.11	0.16
Yearlings	1.38	0.79	0.73	0.63	0.88
Adults	1.54	1.26	1.05	0.93	1.20
Rate of increase[c]					
Fawns	3.2	1.5	2.1	1.6	2.7
Yearlings	19.3	8.7	12.4	7.6	11.4
Adults	84.7	52.9	30.5	34.4	45.6
Total	107.2	63.1	45.0	43.6	59.7
Gross productivity[c]	52	39	31	30	37

[a]Yearling and adult does could not be separated visually in the field. Kill data were used to determine the percentage of these age groups in the female segment of the population.
[b]Buck and doe fawns could not be separated visually in the field. The sex ratio of fawns was assumed to be 50:50, and the total number of fawns observed was divided between the two sexes.
[c]In percentage.
[d]Number of embryos per doe.

Table 45. Net productivity[a] of the white-tailed deer population in the Llano Basin of Texas, 1953 through 1961.

Year	Number of deer classified	Percentage of fawns
1953	580	43 ± 4.0
1954	1,910	27 ± 2.0
1955	1,210	12 ± 2.0
1956	1,286	34 ± 2.5
1957	1,132	19 ± 2.0
1958	1,754	44 ± 2.5
1959	1,752	38 ± 2.5
1960	1,926	31 ± 2.0
1961	2,367	25 ± 1.5
Total	13,916	
Average		30 ± 0.2

[a]Confidence limits = $\bar{x} \pm t_{.05} \cdot s_{\bar{x}}$.

Percentage increases of fawning-season populations over pre-fawning-season populations—compiled by Severinghaus and Cheatum (1956) as part of life tables—were: 76.8 in western New York; 60.8 in Massachusetts; 55.0 in Ohio; 68.6 in Wisconsin; and 64.3 in Pennsylvania. Apparently, net productivity of the Llano Basin population was approximately half that reported for representative whitetail populations in other states.

MORTALITY AND YIELD

Natural Mortality

The extent of natural mortality occurring annually and beginning in mid-November was determined indirectly by finding the difference in the autumn (prehunting season) population sizes for successive years, subtracting hunting mortality and adding the annual increment to the difference (Table 46). The validity of estimates

Table 46. Estimates of natural mortality of white-tailed deer on 141,645 hectares (350,000 acres) of densely populated rangeland in southern Llano County, Texas, 1954 through 1961.

Year	Prehunting season population[a]	Autumn harvest[b]	Spring increment[c]	Natural mortality[d]	Percentage of prehunting season population lost
1954	62,650	4,235	16,915	32,235	52
1955	29,750	5,670	3,570		
1956	41,650	3,815	14,161	11,753	28
1957	32,200	2,800	6,118	2,548	8
1958	47,950	5,705	21,098	4,270	9
1959	61,250	9,415	23,275	8,426	14
1960	62,650	10,640	19,241	2,433	4
1961	66,150	13,125	16,573		
Total	404,250	55,405	120,951	61,665	
Average					16

[a]Established from annual censuses conducted in September, October and November. This prehunting-season population estimates the standing crop.
[b]*See* Table 47.
[c]Established from estimated net productivity.
[d]Determined empirically from differences in prehunting-season population in successive years from which hunting mortality had been subtracted and to which the increment of fawns had been added.

of total natural mortality obviously is related to the precision of population estimates used in the calculations. Some of these, especially estimates of population densities, were characterized by rather large errors. Thus, these estimates are rough approximations at best.

In general, the estimates showed high natural mortality during years of drought and food shortage, and lower mortality after a drought and food shortage. In 1954 and 1956, when rainfall was less than half the average and ranges were in poor condition, losses mounted to 52 and 28 percent of the population, respectively.

Starvation was the primary cause of mortality during the drought. Many dead and dying (emaciated) deer were observed in drought years. In 1954 and 1956, hunters were reluctant to shoot emaciated deer, and total harvests in those years were influenced accordingly. Many deer brought to check stations were considered unfit for the table. Three deer that died during the first week of February 1956 were autopsied by pathologists at Texas A&M University and reportedly died from malnutrition.

After 1957, mortality from causes other than hunting was not as great as during the drought,

During the drought years of the 1950s, many starved or starving whitetails were observed in the Llano Basin. Hunters understandably were reluctant to harvest emaciated deer, but their unwillingness to do so merely compounded the deer population's problem by not removing enough of the excess animals. *Photo by James G. Teer.*

probably because of improved range conditions, reduced screwworm fly infestations, and increased hunter harvests. Highest losses occurring after the drought ended were in 1959, when 14 percent of the population apparently was lost. Most of this mortality occurred in summer and early autumn. About 10 to 15 percent of the deer observed were in poor physical condition. Three emaciated deer were collected and autopsied at the Texas Agricultural Experiment Station at Sonora, Texas. The causes of emaciation were (1) heavy parasitism by stomach worms and hair worms, and (2) malnutrition.

Prenatal and Neonatal Mortality

Mortality of white-tailed deer in the Llano Basin was estimated for all stages of life beginning with ova produced by does. Four hundred eighty-two deer produced 815 oocytes of which 719 resulted in implanted embryos. These data suggest that mortality of oocytes was about 12 percent. Losses of implanted embryos also occurred, but these losses were very small. A sample of 525 does pregnant with 787 embryos had 10 embryos (about 1 percent) that were poorly developed or being resorbed. There was no way that I could estimate losses of embryos through abortion; however, there was no evidence in the uteri examined to suggest that this was even a minor loss. In total, *in utero* losses amounted to about 13 percent of the potential production (12 percent loss of oocytes plus 1 percent loss of embryos).

Neonatal mortality, on the other hand, was considerable in some years. Surveys for dead deer, conducted in early August each year from 1957 through 1960, using transects from the autumn census of live deer as sample plots, indicated that many fawns died soon after birth. The plots were standardized for the survey of dead deer at 80.5 by 3,219 meters (88 by 3,520 yards), giving a sample area of 25.9 hectares (64 acres). Dead fawns were found in the plots in all years except 1959 (Table 47), and from 1957 to 1959, fawn losses loosely paralleled those indicated by differences in gross and net productivity (Table 48). In four of the five years, when differences in gross productivity and net productivity were large, densities of dead fawns in the plots were correspondingly large. The converse also was true. These estimates were minimal because many fawns were represented by only a few pieces of bones and skin

Table 47. Differences between gross and net productivity of white-tailed deer in rangeland densely populated with deer in southern Llano County, 1957–1961.

| Year | Deer per 100 hectares (100 acres) | | | |
	Prefawning population in spring	Gross productivity (A)	Net productivity (B)	Loss of fawns (A − B)
1957	26.7 (10.8)	13.1 (5.3)	5.2 (2.1)	7.9 (3.2)
1958	20.8 (8.4)	10.9 (4.4)	9.1 (3.7)	1.7 (0.7)
1959	29.9 (12.1)	11.6 (4.7)	11.4 (4.6)	0.2 (0.1)
1960	36.6 (14.8)	11.4 (4.6)	11.4 (4.6)	0.0 (0.0)
1961	36.8 (14.9)	11.1 (4.5)	9.1 (3.7)	2.0 (0.8)
Average	30.1 (12.2)	11.6 (4.7)	9.1 (3.7)	2.5 (1.0)

after scavengers had destroyed the carcasses. Many surely were missed in the surveys.

Causes of death were not always determined because few fawns were found soon after death. Circumstantial evidence suggests that the very low net productivity in 1955 and 1957 was due to myiasis caused by screwworm flies. In these two years, ranchers had very heavy infestations of screwworms in their livestock. Some ranchers reported that the navel of every newborn calf was infested within a few hours of birth. Scratches, cuts, abrasions, wounds from tick and other insect bites, and even moist, irritated skin in the groin region that had been wetted by dew were predisposing sites for infestations. Whitetails were affected equally in these years. Large numbers of fawns were observed with screwworms in their navels. Screwworms were also observed in birth wounds of does, in ears where ticks had caused an issue of blood or serum, and at the base of the buck's antlers.

Weather factors were favorable for over-

Table 48. Mortality of white-tailed deer fawns occurring within approximately two months of birth on rangeland densely populated with deer in southern Llano County, 1957–1961.

Year	Number of plots	Hectares (acres) in sample	Number of dead fawns	Density of dead fawns per 100 hectares (acres)
1957	18	466 (1,152)	22	4.74 (1.92)
1958	14	363 (896)	3	0.84 (0.34)
1959	14	363 (896)	0	
1960	14	363 (896)	7	1.93 (0.78)
1961	8	207 (512)	9	4.32 (1.75)
Total	68	1,761 (4,352)	41	
Average				2.32 (0.94)

wintering of screwworm flies and subsequent buildup of high populations in the late springs and summers of 1955 and 1957. When the flies overwinter, increases in the number of infestations occur. Migration of flies from Mexico and southern Texas reestablishes flies when they do not overwinter, and losses or infestations often are not as large because the fawning season precedes fly buildup.

Hunting

A summary of hunter harvest of whitetails from 1954 through 1961 on 141,645 hectares (350,000 acres) of range in the Llano Basin is presented in Table 49. Because it was not broken out for the various density areas of the Basin after 1961, the harvest of deer is combined for all areas in Llano County (Table 50).

Predation does not play a significant role in limiting whitetails in the Llano Basin or elsewhere on the Edwards Plateau. The only major potential predators are coyotes and bobcats, but coyotes are effectively excluded from the area by the activities of livestock owners—principally sheep and goat ranchers. Bobcat predation on whitetail fawns is negligible. *Photo by J. J. McEntire; courtesy of the U.S. Soil Conservation Service.*

Table 49. Estimates of hunter harvest of white-tailed deer on 141,645 hectares (350,000 acres) of rangeland densely populated with deer in southern Llano County, Texas, 1954 through 1961.

Year	Autumn prehunting-season population per 100 hectares (100 acres)[a]	Fawn increment, in fawns per 100 hectares (100 acres) of autumn prehunting-season[b] population	Fork-horned buck harvest per 100 hectares (100 acres)[c]	Antlerless-deer harvest per 100 hectares (100 acres)[d]	Total harvest per 100 hectares (100 acres)	Total harvest	Percentage of increment removed by hunters	Percentage of autumn prehunting-season population removed by hunters
1954	44.2 (17.9)	11.9 (4.8)	1.7 (0.7)	1.2 (0.5)	3.0 (1.2)	4,235	25	7
1955	21.0 (8.5)	2.5 (1.0)	3.0 (1.2)	1.0 (0.4)	4.0 (1.6)	5,670	160	19
1956	29.4 (11.9)	9.9 (4.0)	2.0 (0.8)	0.7 (0.3)	2.7 (1.1)	3,815	28	9
1957	22.7 (9.2)	4.4 (1.8)	1.5 (0.6)	0.5 (0.2)	2.0 (0.8)	2,800	44	9
1958	33.9 (13.7)	14.8 (6.0)	2.7 (1.1)	1.2 (0.5)	4.0 (1.6)	5,705	27	12
1959	43.2 (17.5)	16.3 (6.6)	3.5 (1.4)	3.2 (1.3)	6.7 (2.7)	9,415	41	15
1960	44.2 (17.9)	13.6 (5.5)	3.7 (1.5)	4.0 (1.6)	7.7 (3.1)	10,644	56	17
1961	46.7 (18.9)	11.6 (4.7)	4.2 (1.7)	5.2 (2.1)	9.4 (3.8)	13,130	81	20
Average	35.6 (14.4)	10.6 (4.3)	2.7 (1.1)	2.2 (0.9)	4.9 (2.0)	6,927	47	14

[a]Determined from annual censuses conducted in September, October and November. This prehunting-population figure estimates the standing crop.
[b]Determined from estimates of net productivity.
[c]Determined from shooting-preserve record books and includes crippling losses, assumed to be 15 percent of the registered kill.
[d]Determined from records at check stations.

Table 50. Hunter harvest of white-tailed deer in Llano County, Texas, 1962 through 1981.[a]

Year	Bucks	Antlerless does	Total
1962	3,829	1,502	5,331
1963	6,248	5,460	11,708
1964	6,453	6,124	12,577
1965	9,309	6,105	15,414
1966	9,417	9,090	18,507
1967	8,662	8,987	17,649
1968	9,464	6,700	16,164
1969	8,736	5,579	14,315
1970	7,375	5,390	12,765
1971	6,925	6,548	13,473
1972	8,230	6,157	14,387
1973	12,124	7,914	20,038
1974	8,389	6,821	15,210
1975	10,298	5,129	15,427
1976	8,787	6,639	15,426
1977	9,627	5,001	14,628
1978	8,915	5,026	13,941
1979	9,973	5,912	15,885
1980	5,273	3,065	8,338
1981	7,935	3,719	11,654
Total	165,969	116,868	282,837

[a]Estimates for 1962 through 1972 were made from shooting-preserve records and for 1973 through 1981 from a survey of hunters selected from a frame of licenseholders.

In the 28-year period commencing in 1954 and ending in 1981, 325,117 deer of both sexes were harvested.

Estimates of the harvest and hunting effort from a sampling frame of hunting-license holders were made for the years 1973 through 1981 (Boydston and Harwell 1982) (Table 51). These surveys showed that, despite increased kills through rather intensive effort and high success rates, the Llano Basin whitetail population has been underharvested through the three-decade period 1950–1980.

Population and harvest data in Table 49 show conclusively that whitetails were underharvested even at lowest population density. Population yield averaged less than 50 percent of the annual increment and was less than the annual increment in every year except 1955. Despite increased harvests when population densities were extremely high, the kill averaged only 14 percent and never exceeded 20 percent of prehunting-season population. This trend in harvest rates has continued to the present. The kill of bucks registered in shooting-preserve records was adjusted to correct for deer not reported in the books. Comparison of shooting-preserve records with tabulations of kill obtained by interviews with landowners indicated that about 10 percent of the average ranch's kill was not entered in the record books (Walker et al. 1955). Therefore, reported kill was increased by 10 percent.

The kill of bucks also was adjusted to include crippled, unretrieved deer. In 1955, kill on the 8,763-acre Mark A. Moss Bar O Ranch was 698 deer of both sexes. During and immediately after the season, ranch employees searched the pastures on horseback for unretrieved deer and found 71. These 71 animals suggest a crippling loss of about 12 percent. Reports of hunters on the Max Otto Ranch suggested about the same loss. However, in adjusting kill data from the Basin, 15 percent was used as the crippling loss because surely not all unretrieved animals on the two ranches were found.

Prior to 1953, bucks having at least one forked antler were the only legal deer. The bag limit per hunter for the season was two such bucks, and the season ran from 16 November through 31 December. The first provision for taking

Table 51. White-tailed deer hunting effort and harvest rates for Llano County, Texas, 1973 through 1981.[a]

Year	Number of hunters	Number of hunter days	Total kill	Percentage of hunter success	Kills per hunter	Hunter days per hunter	Kills per 100 hectares (100 acres)
1973	20,821	80,225	20,038	63	0.96	3,85	8.6 (3.5)
1974	19,598	86,213	15,210	51	0.78	4.40	6.7 (2.7)
1975	20,374	73,785	15,427	54	0.76	3.62	6.7 (2.7)
1976	19,560	73,806	15,426	60	0.79	3.77	6.4 (2.6)
1977	19,025	83,761	14,628	61	0.77	4.40	6.2 (2.5)
1978	17,684	68,951	13,941	61	0.79	3.90	5.7 (2.3)
1979	16,884	66,705	15,885	71	0.94	3.95	6.7 (2.7)
1980	14,606	71,092	8,338	47	0.57	4.87	3.5 (1.4)
1981	14,730	59,868	11,654	66	0.79	4.06	4.9 (2.0)

[a]Adapted from Boydston and Harwell (1982).

Although whitetails in the Llano Basin are hunted from vehicles on private roads or from blinds, still-hunting from stands in natural cover is most common. From 1973 through 1981, hunter success in the Basin was 0.85 deer per hunter, and about 60 percent of all hunters killed at least one whitetail. *Photo courtesy of the Texas Parks and Wildlife Department.*

Antlerless-deer hunters unload their harvest at the Mark A. Moss Bar O Ranch in 1955. The harvest rate for hunters on this ranch was 19.8 whitetails per square kilometer (51.2 per square mile). *Photo courtesy of the Texas Parks and Wildlife Department.*

antlerless deer in any area in Texas was made in 1953 for two small areas in the Llano Basin in Mason and Gillespie counties. Length of the season for taking antlerless deer was set at 15 days, and an antlerless deer was defined as one without hardened antlers protruding through the skin. The bag limit was kept at two deer per hunter, which could be two bucks or two antlerless deer or one of each.

As the whitetail population continued to increase from the low densities of the drought years, the need for increased harvest became even more apparent. Hunting-season length for taking antlerless deer was increased from 15 to 46 days in 1958—the dates coinciding with those of the regular buck season. Further liberalization of regulations was effected by making spikehorn bucks legal in 1960, but the season bag limit per hunter was kept at two deer. In 1961 the bag limit was increased to three, one of which had to be an antlerless deer. Thus, the history of regulations providing for harvest of deer is one of increasing liberalization, reflecting the ongoing attempt to reduce deer population densities to minimize competition with domestic livestock and prevent losses of deer from starvation.

Socioeconomic Factors Affecting Harvest

By 1961, virtually all whitetail range in the densely populated portions of the Llano Basin was leased to hunters. The few ranchers who did not lease had too few deer to attract paying guests, or their ranches were too small for leasing arrangements, or they chose to retain all hunting rights for themselves and their families and friends. The number of shooting preserves in other parts of the Basin increased as the deer population increased (Table 52).

Even though fish and nonmigratory game are property of the State, landowners have complete legal control of access to game in their pastures. The trespass law is rigid and vigorously enforced by civil and conservation law-enforcement officers. In addition, landowners are empowered to file trespass cases. Many large ranches employ "pasture riders" to patrol their ranches and prevent illegal hunting of deer. Groups of ranchers in sportsmen's clubs and associations contribute funds toward the employment of "deputy rangers" who patrol property for club members. The trespass law provides for large fines, jail sentences for second and subsequent offenders, confiscation of firearms and other hunting equipment, and loss of hunting licenses. County and justice courts handle trespass violations. If the trespass law was not responsible for the origin and development of the commercialized system of harvesting deer, it most certainly encouraged it. In effect, if not by legal definition, the Texas trespass law has transferred the control—though not the ownership—of game to landowners.

Access rights to harvest deer are valuable to ranchers in the Llano Basin. There is not sufficient information to compare income from the sale (lease) of hunting-access rights and income derived from the production and sale

Table 52. Numbers and combined size of shooting preserves in Llano County, Texas, 1953 through 1961.[a]

	Shooting preserves in 101,175 hectares (250,000 acres) of low density range north of the Llano River			Shooting preserves in 141,645 hectares (350,000 acres) of high density range south of the Llano River			Total		
		Size			Size			Size	
Year	Number	Hectares	Acres	Number	Hectares	Acres	Number	Hectares	Acres
1953	13	6,954	17,183	91	64,913	160,399	104	71,867	177,582
1954	8	5,006	12,370	139	104,124	257,286	147	109,130	269,656
1955	8	5,141	12,703	107	81,568	201,553	115	86,746	214,346
1956	15	6,613	16,341	107	92,569	228,735	122	99,182	245,076
1957	9	2,426	5,995	137	115,891	286,364	146	118,318	292,359
1958	10	2,396	5,920	147	96,786	239,156	157	99,182	245,076
1959	23	12,773	31,561	151	113,961	281,595	174	126,734	313,156
1960	47	25,246	62,381	184	136,823	338,084	231	162,068	400,465
1961	79	36,920	91,228	221	137,979	340,942	300	174,899	432,170

[a]The figures are minimal estimates, because some records were not available.

of livestock, but unquestionably the lease of access rights is the ranchers' second most-important source of income and represents a substantial sum.

Some ranchers in the densely populated whitetail rangeland in southern Llano County provided data on income from leasing of hunting rights from 1957 through 1961 (Table 53). The data show that: (1) income increased from $1.95 to $3.01 per hectare ($0.79 to $1.22 per acre) and averaged $2.59 per hectare ($1.05 per acre); (2) the price received for fork-horned bucks (average of $51.47 per deer) decreased as the number harvested increased; (3) the ratio of does to bucks in the harvest increased, averaging approximately 50:50 for the period; and (4) ranchers harvested more deer as the whitetail population density increased.

Prices for season leases and day hunting in the Llano Basin have increased more than threefold since intensive studies of the deer population made in the late 1950s and early 1960s. There are no definitive data from surveys or studies to document these trends. Berger (1974) reported that hunters paid Texas landowners $108,000,000 for leases in 1971. Henson et al. (1977) indicated that hunting leases in some areas of Texas brought up to $24.70 per hectare ($10 per acre). W.I. Morrill and R. Whitson (personal communication:1980) surveyed a sample of hunters who had purchased hunting licenses in 1977, and reported that 45 percent of the respondents had paid a fee for hunting in the 1977–1978 season, and the average season lease amounted to $224 per person. Leases in the Llano Basin average $7.40 to $9.90 per hectare ($3–$4 per acre), with some going as high as $14.83 per hectare ($6 per acre).

Lease arrangements with the ranchers interviewed in the 1950s were typical of arrangements ordinarily made in the Basin. All ranchers in the sample leased their pastures for buck hunting to a group of hunters for most of the six-week season. Some ranchers retained part of their property for hunting by their own families or made arrangements to hunt when the leaseholders were not in the pastures. Most ranchers permitted their "buck hunters" to substitute an antlerless deer for a buck, or they permitted friends and family members of the leaseholders to harvest antlerless deer. Other ranchers, especially those who could not persuade their buck hunters to take antlerless deer, leased by the day to other hunters who took antlerless deer only.

Season leases usually were made at the rate of 2.5 hunters per 100 hectares (1 hunter per 100 acres) in the 1950s. Prices ranged from $50 to $200 per man. Additional charges usually were made for the harvest of antlerless deer. When arrangements were made by the day with "doe hunters," a flat fee of approximately $15 per antlerless deer was charged. This price ranged from $10 to $25, but ranchers who asked more than $15 soon learned that hunters would not pay that much, and they could not find enough hunters to remove as many deer as the ranchers wished. Throughout the nine years, prices for taking antlerless whitetails held at about $15 per deer.

Chambers of commerce at the county seats in the Basin operated a listing service for ranchers. Ranchers needing hunters to harvest antlerless deer supplied the chamber of commerce office with the number of hunters needed, open dates and prices. Some ranchers advertised both in local newspapers and in those of

Table 53. Harvests and economic returns from white-tailed deer hunting on a sample of ranches in rangeland densely populated with deer in southern Llano County, Texas, 1957 through 1961.

Year	Number	Size Hectares	Acres	Bucks	Does	Harvest per 100 hectares (100 acres)	Does to bucks in harvest	Total income[a]	Income from all does	Income per buck	Income per hectare (acre)
1957	9	7,686	18,993	183	79	3.5 (1.4)	0.43	$ 15,065	$ 1,185	$75.85	$1.95 ($0.79)
1958	25	19,109	47,217	633	231	4.4 (1.8)	0.36	43,055	3,465	62.54	2.25 (0.91)
1959	25	19,109	47,217	841	776	8.4 (3.4)	0.92	48,785	11,640	44.17	2.55 (1.03)
1960	25	19,109	47,217	747	827	8.2 (3.3)	1.11	54,040	12,405	55.74	2.82 (1.14)
1961	25	19,109	47,217	788	1,224	10.6 (4.3)	1.55	57,395	18,360	49.54	3.01 (1.22)
Total	109	84,122	207,861	3,192	3,137			$218,340	$45,870		
Average						7.4 (3.0)	0.98			$51.47	$2.59 ($1.05)

[a]Total income derived from does determined by using $15 as the average cost per doe.

the state's large cities. At least one rancher successfully used radio and television media in Houston to solicit hunters for his ranch. Usually, ranchers wanting hunters were able to find them. The kill of antlerless deer was not limited by a lack of people wanting to hunt.

The commercialized harvest system undoubtedly contributed to inadequate numbers of deer being removed from the ranges in Llano Basin. Ranchers were extremely conservative in estimates of numbers of deer needed to be

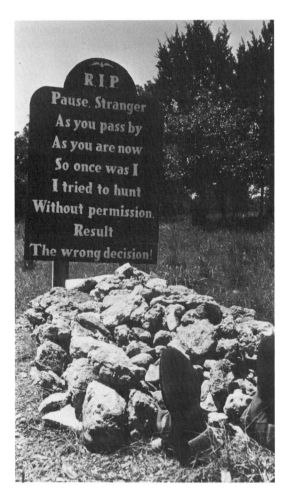

Landowner resolve—in addition to a rigid law and its rigorous enforcement—is an effective deterrent to trespassing in Texas. On one hand it reduces hunting violations and unethical conduct which tend to cast recreational hunting in a bad public light. On the other hand it has fostered commercialized hunting through leasing of hunting privileges that, although lucrative to landowners, encourages excessively high white-tailed deer productivity in some areas and prevents biologically adequate harvests. *Photo by Leroy Williamson; courtesy of the Texas Parks and Wildlife Department.*

removed. They were influenced in this regard by the conservatism of their season leaseholders. With the bag limit set at two deer per hunter per season, rates of harvest could hardly exceed 4.9–7.4 whitetails per 100 hectares (2–3 per 100 acres) at hunting pressures prevalent under most leasing arrangements. The only practical method to increase the legal harvest was to increase the number of hunters. This was done by many ranchers in their buck harvest programs and also in their leasing by day to hunters wanting to harvest antlerless deer. However, even at increased hunting intensities, the harvest was still inadequate. And despite an increase in the bag limit to three deer per hunter per season in 1961, the harvest was insufficient. Unquestionably, hunting pressures were much lower than would have been possible had the range been open to all who desired to hunt.

MANAGEMENT

In discussing or recommending management of white-tailed deer in the Llano Basin, socioeconomic factors and consequences are at least as important as biological considerations. Indeed, solutions to biological problems are largely contingent on solutions to socioeconomic problems.

Three socioeconomic factors must be considered in the management of the Basin whitetail population: (1) the economic value of deer to landowners; (2) protection of the range resource; and (3) demand for hunting opportunity by sportsmen. Clearly, the three are interrelated. Thus, management will be discussed from the landowner's point of view because they control the deer range and, therefore, the deer population. Also, the landowners' interest in deer, while partly aesthetic, is related primarily to the deer population's economic value. And not least of all, the present system of management, whereby deer are "produced," "owned" and "sold," offers the highest probability for sustaining the population and the greatest potential for providing the optimum amount of hunting recreation. Unless drastic change occurs in traditions and current laws governing private ownership of property, any other approach to management would be unrealistic.

I am not unaware of the downgrading in quality of hunting that the commercialized system promises for many sportsmen (*see* Teer and Forrest 1968). In this important respect, the commercialized "game-cropping" system lessens the aesthetic and cultural values of hunting that Leopold (1949) described.

Ranchers have a choice with respect to use of rangeland forage for the production of protein and fiber. At present, because deer have considerable economic value, part of the forage crop is given over to production of deer. If there were no market for deer, forage could be diverted to production of conventional livestock. In short, while ranchers have the usual reasons for wanting deer, they are governed in their choice of forage-utilization programs by the strength of prevailing markets. It is not inconceivable that, without compensation for deer, the whitetail population could be extirpated from most ranges in the Basin.

Control of rangeland and deer by Llano Basin landowners is practically absolute. Regulations for taking deer affect the consumers (sportsmen) much more directly than they do the producers (ranchers). Bag and possession limits, season lengths, and means and methods of taking deer regulate the conduct and harvest by sportsmen. Total harvests of fork-horned bucks and, to a certain extent, harvest of other sex and age groups, are regulated by ranchers.

The overriding necessity in management of the Basin deer population is the reduction of deer density by hunting. At densities prevailing from 1953 to 1961, the whitetail population consisted of small animals, productivity was much below potential, and natural mortality was extremely high and even exceeded the harvest by several times in most years. These three characteristics are symptomatic of underharvested white-tailed deer populations. Solutions obviously are related to increasing the nutritional level of the population.

In the Llano Basin, where ranges generally are overstocked with livestock that competes with whitetails for food, increasing the nutritional level of the deer population is a complex problem. It is not simply one of producing enough forage to sustain large numbers of deer. Rather, it is one of producing forage for deer on ranges already overused by livestock. And the three principal kinds of livestock—cattle, sheep and goats—are extremely efficient harvesters of range forage. They are efficient competitors with deer because their individual and collective grazing and browsing habits include all but the most unpalatable species of range plants.

Confounding the problem of overuse of range forage by livestock and deer is the dynamic nature of the carrying capacity of rangeland in the Basin. Changes in carrying capacity occur rapidly and frequently, and often are independent of the density of grazing herbivores. Studies showed that 56 percent of a long series of years were characterized by below-average total rainfall, and 25 percent had rainfall less than 75 percent of the long-term average (*see* Thomas and Hildreth 1957). Five serious droughts of at least seven years' duration have occurred in the Basin since 1893. Drought apparently is a frequent cause of downward trends in the carrying capacity of rangelands in the Llano Basin. Also, the great majority of ranchers in the Basin stock cows for production of calves that usually are sold and shipped to the Midwest and West for stocker and feedlot purposes. This stocking system requires that a base herd of mother cows be maintained yearlong on the range. Replacements to the base herd are made as needed.

"Mother cow" systems are not conducive to the flexibility needed to adjust stocking rates to frequent changes in the Basin's carrying capacity. When carrying capacity is lowered by drought or exceeded through overuse of range forage by overstocking, most ranchers are reluctant to dispose of their base herds, and they resort to supplemental feeding. Continued heavy use of already depleted forage eventually impoverishes the range. Conversely, in years of high rainfall ranchers often increase their rates of stocking to utilize the additional forage simply by buying additional mother cows or by holding a larger number of replacements. These animal-husbandry and range-use practices create a near impasse to increasing nutritional levels of the deer population.

Reducing deer density and stocking rates of domestic livestock is the solution. Such reductions in the long run will make for greater stability in range vegetation, and larger economic returns from both deer and livestock will be the important result. The large whitetailed deer population now in the Basin is extremely wasteful of forage. Low rates of population increase are predisposed by high densities, and most of the production is not harvested. Reduction of the whitetail population to half its average density of the period 1953–1961 still would result in production and increments larger than the harvests at present rates of exploitation. Moderate stocking rates of livestock well within the long-term carrying capacity of the range will protect the range and yield greater returns.

The alternative to reducing deer and livestock numbers or to the present system of heavy forage cropping portends the great possibility of eventually producing a "goat economy" not unlike that of the Mediterranean areas. Past overuse has changed the native vegetation in the Basin from a savannahlike grassland to a brush-covered community much less productive than the original range. Under such a regimen of grazing and browsing herbivores, further range deterioration is inevitable.

III. Whitetail Populations and Habitats

Chapter 13

SOUTHEASTERN CANADA

Jean Huot
Professor
Department of Biology
Université Laval
Ste-Foy, Québec

François Potvin
Deer Biologist
Ministère du Loisir, de
la Chasse et de la Pêche
Orsainville, Québec

Michel Bélanger
Big Game Biologist
Ministère du Loisir, de
la Chasse et de la Pêche
Orsainville, Québec

ENVIRONMENT

In southeastern Canada, white-tailed deer range covers the southern part of Quebec including Anticosti Island, and all of New Brunswick and Nova Scotia including Cape Breton Island (Figure 73). It extends from the Quebec-Ontario border in the west to the eastern tip of Cape Breton Island. The northern limits are the edge of the boreal forest in Quebec and the Gulf of St. Lawrence. This range encompasses a surface area of some 280,000 square kilometers (108,100 square miles). In the western part, the climate is typically continental, whereas the eastern portion of the range is influenced by the Atlantic Ocean and the Gulf of St. Lawrence.

Physiography and Soils

Southeastern Canada includes three physiographic regions: the Canadian Shield; the Great Lakes-St. Lawrence Lowlands; and the Appalachian Uplands. The three regions were covered by the last continental glaciation, which retreated approximately 10,000 to 12,000 years ago.

The Canadian Shield makes up most of Quebec north of the St. Lawrence River. It is made of precambrian granitic rock covered with glacial till. It is a rather rugged area of low hills and numerous lakes and rivers. The region's cool climate retards the decomposition of ground litter, and excess precipitation leaches the bases and colloids of soil into deeper horizons. Podzolic soils resulting from this process are of little value for sustained agriculture.

The St. Lawrence Lowlands occurs on both sides of the St. Lawrence River west of Quebec City and on Anticosti Island. It is underlain by sedimentary rocks forming very low relief, covered with clay, fine sand and gravel. Most of the area is covered by brown forest soils showing very little evidence of podzolization. In the lowlands, clay will produce gley soils. Organic material is well decomposed and these soils have the highest agriculture-potential in Quebec, despite poor drainage in some areas.

The Appalachian Uplands include the hilly parts of New Brunswick, Nova Scotia and that portion of Quebec south of the St. Lawrence River. The landscape includes some mountains, forested valleys and small rivers. Some uplands southwest of Gaspé, in southeastern Quebec, reach 1,300 meters (4,265 feet) above sea level. There are no elevations higher than 1,000 meters (3,280 feet) above sea level in New Brunswick or Nova Scotia. Glaciation left a blanket of coarse rocky material over a bedrock composed mainly of shales, limestones and sandstones in the lowlands. Soils of the highlands are very rocky and, in some places, the bedrock has only a thin covering. These soils are classified as infertile podzols or even regosols. This is the case of the large plateaus bordering the St. Lawrence Lowlands and extending into New Brunswick as well as the southern half of Nova Scotia and most of Cape Breton Island. Agriculture is restricted

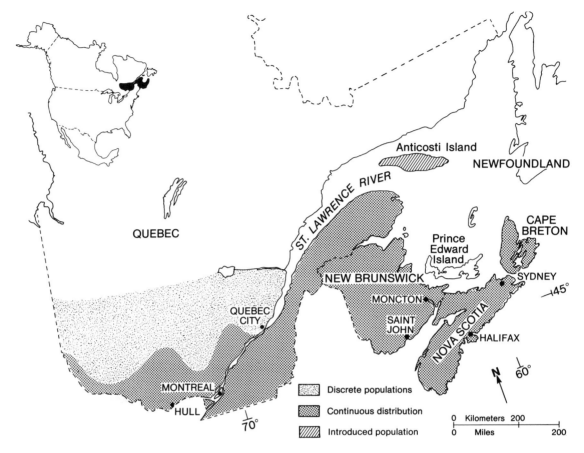

Figure 73. Distribution of white-tailed deer in southeastern Canada.

to the coastal lands and the valleys tributary to the Bay of Fundy. Most of the central and eastern lowlands of New Brunswick are swampy.

As a general rule, in the Appalachian Uplands production of vegetation is related closely to drainage in the lowlands and, consequently, the high-potential soils are scattered and usually intensively used for agriculture. In the forested valleys, calcarous parent material may result in locally high forest production and good whitetail habitat.

Climate and Weather

Winter snow depths (March 31) average 5 centimeters (2 inches) or less in southern New Brunswick and Nova Scotia, and then increase to 50 centimeters (20 inches) or more farther north and westward. Over a large portion of the whitetail range in Quebec, including Anticosti Island, the ground may be covered with 60 to 70 centimeters (26.4–27.6 inches) of snow

as late as early April. In the coastal area of Nova Scotia, the average maximum temperature in January is 0 degrees Celsius (32 degrees Fahrenheit), but it drops markedly inland to −7.5 degrees Celsius (18.5 degrees Fahrenheit) or less in the Appalachian Uplands. Annual precipitation is moderate and usually spread equally throughout the year. Totals range from 90 to 100 centimeters (36–40 inches) in Quebec and New Brunswick, but increase eastward to more than 140 centimeters (55 inches) on the Atlantic shores of Nova Scotia. The maritime influence favors deer survival in winter, in contrast to the harsh inland climates of other parts of southeastern Canada.

Vegetation

Forests occupy approximately 80 percent of the land area in southeastern Canada. Rowe (1972) divided them into the Great Lakes-St. Lawrence, Acadian, and Boreal Forest regions (Figure 74). The number of growing days ranges

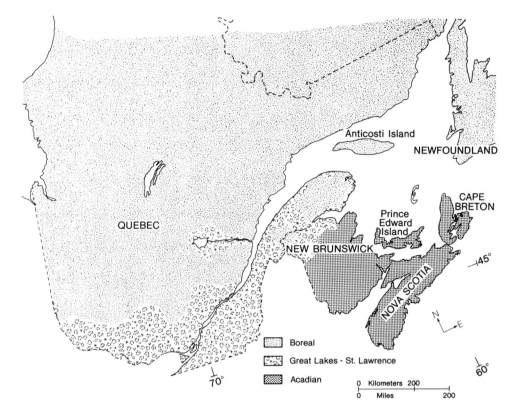

Figure 74. Forest regions of southeastern Canada (Rowe 1972).

from less than 150 on Anticosti Island to more than 200 in the southern half of Nova Scotia.

The Great Lakes-St. Lawrence Region covers most of southern Quebec and Ontario and extends into northern New Brunswick. It in- cludes elements of boreal and deciduous forest, and is characterized by eastern white pine, red pine, eastern hemlock and yellow birch. Deciduous forests are dominated mainly by sugar maple, northern red oak and basswood,

Mixed forest stands along lakes and rivers are among the best winter habitats for white-tailed deer in Quebec. The visible browse line on cedar is a good indication of the past use of this forest by wintering deer. *Photo by Jean Huot.*

which become less abundant in the northeastern part of the region. Balsam fir, white and black spruce, paper birch, and trembling aspen are important species in the northern section close to the boreal forest. Northern white cedar is present throughout the region, but usually is concentrated in poorly drained depressions.

The Acadian Forest Region extends over Nova Scotia and New Brunswick, and is characterized by red spruce, balsam fir, yellow birch and sugar maple. Other species are black spruce, red oak, red maple, paper birch, gray birch, trembling aspen and balsam poplar. Northern white cedar is rare except in New Brunswick (Rowe 1972). Large areas of open peat bogs occur within forests dominated by black spruce, especially in the eastern part of New Brunswick.

Mountain maple, striped maple, beaked hazel, hobblebush and various species of dogwood are the common shrubs of both the Great Lakes-St. Lawrence and Acadian regions.

The Boreal Forest Region covers the northern edge of the whitetail range in Quebec. Only small, scattered white-tailed deer populations inhabit this region, except on Anticosti Island where introduced whitetails inhabit a typical boreal forest. The principal trees of this region are white and black spruces and balsam fir. Tamarack is distributed sparsely in open bogs that cover large areas of Anticosti Island. Small sections of boreal forest are present in the highlands southwest of Gaspé, but white-tailed deer occur mainly in valleys occupied by intrusions of the Great Lakes-St. Lawrence Forest Region.

Land Use

Sixty-five percent of the land in southeastern Canada is privately owned. Urbanization is limited. Forty percent of the population lives in the metropolitan Montreal area. Smaller urban centers such as Quebec, Halifax, Saint John, Moncton and Sidney account for another 14 percent of the population. Most of the land is forested or used for agriculture. The intensity of farming is greatest along the St. Lawrence River close to Montreal, where more than 90 percent of the land is in agriculture. Elsewhere, farms are scattered in the lowlands. Most of the best white-tailed deer range is associated with a patchy pattern of small-scale agriculture.

WHITETAIL POPULATIONS

History

White-tailed deer were present along the upper St. Lawrence River and in Nova Scotia long before French exploration. As shown in archeological sites, whitetails were abundant in Nova Scotia until 500 A.D., but decreased in the following centuries. Historical records indicate that deer were very scarce in Nova Scotia during the 1500s and 1600s (Benson and Dodds 1977). In Quebec, the early explorers reported white-tailed deer and elk along the St. Lawrence River in the oak/hickory forests west of Montreal, but eastward, deer were scarce (Boucher 1663).

In the mid-1800s, whitetails from New Brunswick extended their range into northern Nova Scotia, and some were introduced to the southwestern part of the province (Dodds 1963). In Quebec, whitetails were abundant along the Outaouais River near Hull in the late 1880s (Lett 1884), and they were first reported in the Gaspé area in the 1800s (Duguay 1949). They probably were abundant in the late 1800s along the south shore of the St. Lawrence River east of Quebec City, as 150 to 200 animals were captured in two winters and introduced to Anticosti Island. In all these newly invaded areas, whitetails increased rapidly, and 30 to 40 years later they were generally abundant. Evidence of high populations was shown by heavy winter mortality in 1935 in Nova Scotia (Benson and Dodds 1977) and in 1933 on Anticosti Island.

There is no evidence that white-tailed deer ever were present on Prince Edward Island before colonization. The few individual deer introduced in the 1950s apparently were killed shortly after their release, and at the present time there are no free-living whitetails on the Island. Despite the presence of favorable habitat, it does not appear desirable to establish deer on the Island due to the risk of conflicts with agricultural production (D. Guignion personal communication:1982).

In the second half of the nineteenth century there began a northward and eastward extension of deer into previously unoccupied range. This still was occurring as far north as Temiscamingue, Quebec, in the 1950s. The expansion of the whitetail population and occupied range coincided with above-average winter temperatures from the late 1800s through the 1950s (Hare and Thomas 1974). Winter temperatures were especially warm in the late 1950s, concurrent with a general exploitation of forests that progressed from the main urban centers along the coast and the St. Lawrence River toward the interior of the land.

The peak of logging for large timber in the region, and especially in Nova Scotia, was reached during the nineteenth century when building wooden ships was an important industry. This was followed by sawmilling in the last quarter of the 1800s.

In addition to logging activity, fires of all sizes and patterns opened the mature forests. The newly opened forests offered better habitat for deer than ever before in most of southeastern Canada. In the 1920s, the pulp industry created a demand for small trees. The most productive forests were located mainly at the northern fringe of the Great Lakes-St. Lawrence Forest Region east of Hull, north of Montreal and along the south shore of the St. Lawrence. The Acadian Forest Region in central New Brunswick and western Nova Scotia also was very productive of trees for pulp.

Along with development of the silviculture industry, new areas were opened to agriculture in southern Quebec and in New Brunswick and Nova Scotia. Most of the whitetail range was created by small-scale farming near settlements and towns. Many marginal farmsteads were abandoned in the early 1900s, while new areas were opened to agriculture. Browse conditions were improved greatly in farm woodlots by the annual cutting of maple and birch for firewood and by the exploitation of cedar stands for shingles and fence posts. These events and practices created dynamic changes in forest structure and produced interspersions of food and shelter attractive to white-tailed deer.

Farmers continued to overcut forest stands and abandon their farms through the 1960s. In the maritime provinces, there was a 34-percent decrease in total area of improved lands between 1941 and 1961 (Putnam and Putnam 1970). In Quebec, the number of small farms decreased 61 percent between 1951 and 1966 (Chatillon 1976). At the same time the size of farms increased markedly, logging for pulpwood became more mechanized, the size of cuttings increased, and smaller trees were harvested. In many local areas, conifers—mainly spruce and fir—were overharvested, while deciduous second-growth species such as trembling aspen and paper birch were underharvested. On the farm woodlots in Quebec, the annual overharvesting of conifers was close to 25 percent, while deciduous trees were cut at 40 percent of their annual rate of increase (Lussier 1970).

Recent Deer Population Trends

During this century, peaks in white-tailed deer populations of the region have occurred at different times in different areas, but were especially evident in the 1940s and early 1950s. Between the late 1950s and mid-1970s, whitetail populations declined in most areas of southeastern Canada, but a recovery followed in the late 1970s and early 1980s. Associated changes in deer harvest in the three provinces are shown in Figure 75. The harvest on Anticosti Island, which averaged between 2,000 and 3,000 deer annually between 1965 and 1980, is not included in the figure.

After the first legal hunting season in Nova Scotia in 1916 (Dodds 1963), the whitetail harvest in that province increased slowly until the late 1930s, when the bag limit changed first from one buck to one deer of any age or sex, and later to two deer. Thereafter the harvest increased rapidly and, in most areas, the highest kill was recorded in the mid-1950s. The severe winters of 1951–1952, 1955–1956 and 1960–1961 greatly reduced the overall whitetail population (Benson and Dodds 1977), and the harvest declined sharply. The bag limit was reduced locally to one deer in 1961 when it became evident that legal hunting was the main limiting factor. The annual harvest stabilized at about 20,000 deer, or approximately 0.4 deer per square kilometer (1 per square mile), in the 1960s and early 1970s, but started to increase again in the late 1970s. On the assumption that about 20 percent of the autumn whitetail population was harvested (Dodds 1963), the total October deer population in the mid-1950s averaged 7–8 deer per square kilometer (18–21 per square mile) or more in high-density counties.

On Cape Breton Island, the whitetail population probably peaked at 5–6 deer per square kilometer (13–15 per square mile). Based on a harvest of 0.4 deer per square kilometer (1 per square mile), the October white-tailed deer population has dropped to about 2 deer per square kilometer (5.2 per square mile) in the recent years.

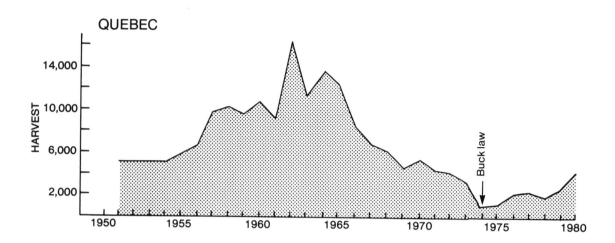

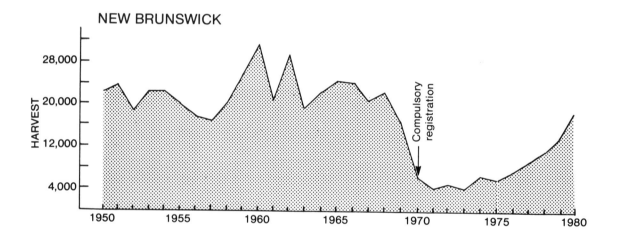

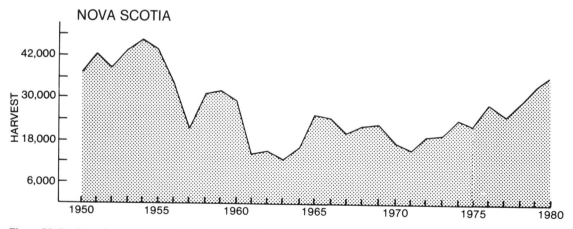

Figure 75. Registered deer harvest in southeastern Canada, 1950–1980 (in part from Potvin et al. 1977).

Although whitetails in southeastern Canada do not reach density levels encountered in regions with milder winter weather conditions, bucks exceeding 91 kilograms (200 pounds) dressed weight are not uncommon. *Photo courtesy of the New Brunswick Department of Natural Resources.*

In New Brunswick, the harvest of whitetails between 1950 and 1960 averaged 22,000 per year, or 0.3 deer per square kilometer (0.8 per square mile). The peak years were 1960 and 1962, when 31,000 and 29,469 deer, respectively, were harvested.

In Quebec, deer populations increased in the late 1950s. On the mainland, a record kill of 16,000 whitetails (0.2 deer per square kilometer: 0.5 per square mile) was attained in 1962).

Overharvesting in the 1960s has been suggested as the triggering factor in the deer decline in these northern areas, especially in the accessible areas close to Montreal (Pimlott et al. 1968). Severe winters in the 1970s prompted a further decline in most parts of Quebec and New Brunswick. The impact of winter was most severe in habitats where conifers had been logged intensively (Huot 1973, Crête 1976, Potvin et al. 1977).

It now appears that, under the present regime of farming in areas of heavy snowfall and cold temperatures, and in the absence of adequate cover following large-scale clearcut-

tings, whitetail populations cannot be restored and maintained to previous levels (Benson and Dodds 1977, Huot 1977, Potvin et al. 1977). This is especially evident along the southern shore of the St. Lawrence River and in the northern portion of the whitetail's range.

HABITAT AND FOOD

During winter, white-tailed deer of southeastern Canada concentrate in areas offering good sheltering cover. Stands of mature conifers are especially important when snow is deep (Telfer 1967b, Huot 1972, Drolet 1976). Mixed stands opened by partial cuttings usually offer the best combination of food and cover (Huot 1972, Drolet 1976). Hemlock is the best cover species, followed by white spruce, red spruce and balsam fir. Red spruce is particularly important in New Brunswick and Nova Scotia. Except in Nova Scotia, northern white cedar is present in most yards, but in dense stands it is less attractive than in good mixed stands (Huot 1972).

Over much of southeastern Canada deer feed primarily on browse in winter. The most important species in Quebec and Nova Scotia are beaked hazel, mountain maple, honeysuckle, sugar maple, red maple, striped maple, yellow birch, balsam fir and paper birch. Species of low nutritional value, such as balsam fir and paper birch or even alder and beech, are occasionally browsed in Nova Scotia. Preferred species such as northern white cedar usually

Even with relatively low whitetail densities in southeastern Canada, northern white cedar can be overbrowsed by deer in winter. Pure white cedar stands do not offer much alternative forage. *Photo courtesy of the New Brunswick Department of Natural Resources.*

are not available within the yards, and ground hemlock has been virtually eliminated by deer in Nova Scotia (Dodds 1963).

In Nova Scotia, overbrowsing can be a problem when whitetail densities exceed 6 per square kilometer (15 per square mile) as happened in some areas in the 1940s and 1950s. Deer winter ranges seldom are overused in most of Quebec and New Brunswick. Occasional severe winters usually reduce deer populations to a level that prevents chronic overbrowsing. Mortality occurs mainly when deer are restricted for long periods in closed stands where food is scarce and low in quality. The poorest winter ranges are found on Anticosti Island and Cape Breton. On Anticosti Island, balsam fir comprises 80 percent or more of the deer winter diet when snow depth reaches 25 centimeters (10 inches). Arboreal lichens, seaweed and white spruce are used frequently (Huot 1982).

Summer distribution of white-tailed deer in southeastern Canada is associated with forest types (Drolet 1976). Whitetails consistently select habitats that contain mixed stands, openings and clearcuts. Good management of summer range should be aimed at producing a mosaic of dense and open-mixed stands, well-interspersed with small (50–75-hectare: 125–185-acre) clearcuts. However, within the Boreal and Acadian Forest regions, adjacent clearcuts over a period of five years frequently cover 5 square kilometers (2 square miles) or more.

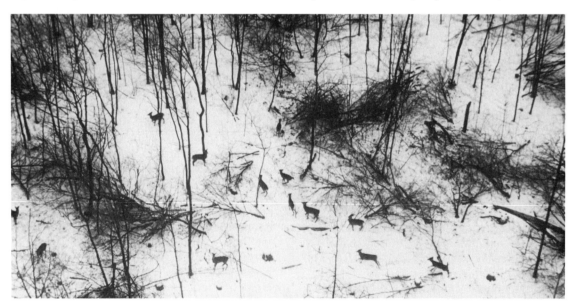

Early winter cutting of hardwood near deer yards in southeastern Canada is beneficial for wintering whitetail populations. *Photo by A. B. Stephenson.*

Most of the white-tailed deer studies in southeastern Canada have been concerned with winter food and cover conditions. Thus, relatively little is known about the animals' needs and preferences during the spring and autumn seasons. Also, very little information is available on how the condition of summer ranges influences the physical status and survival of deer in winter, as well as the subsequent reproductive performance of does and fawn survival following stressful winters. Recent studies on Anticosti Island indicate that body reserves could supply one-third of the energy needs of a fawn during winter and 20 to 25 percent for an adult doe (Huot 1982).

REPRODUCTIVE RATES

Reproductive rates of white-tailed deer vary regionally and little is known about the productivity of the northern populations. The number of fawns per female (all ages) is highest—1.36 embryos per doe—in the western part of the Nova Scotia mainland, and lowest in Cape Breton—1.14 embryos per doe (Dodds 1963). In the north Montreal area, approximately 1.37 fawns are produced per adult female (≥ 1.5 years). If fawns are included in this assessment, the rate of reproduction drops to one fawn per doe (Stephenson 1973). The reproductive rate is lowest on Anticosti Island, where female fawns and 60 percent of the yearlings do not breed. The ovulation rate of adult females (≥ 1.5 years) is 0.8.

LIMITING FACTORS

Hunting

In most parts of southeastern Canada, whitetail population size and hunting success were lower in the 1970s than they were during the 1950s and 1960s. Hunting apparently was the main cause of the deer decline in Quebec during the 1960s. Severe winters from the mid-1960s to the mid-1970s limited whitetails in Quebec and New Brunswick. In Nova Scotia and on Anticosti Island, severe winters reduced the deer populations on overused ranges in the 1950s and early 1960s.

In the lower St. Lawrence region, mortality is related closely to winter severity (Potvin et al. 1981). When snow depth is less than 50 centimeters (20 inches), deer mortality ranges from 20 to 25 percent of the autumn population. In a severe winter, such as 1974–1975 or 1976–1977, the mortality rate may reach 40 percent. Fawns accounted for 44 percent of the dead deer found, and females accounted for 45 percent. More than 50 percent of the fawns died during these winters. In areas where neither timber wolf nor coyote was found, starvation was responsible for most deaths.

Under these conditions, hunting usually accounts for less than 50 percent of whitetail mortality. In the lower St. Lawrence region during the early 1970s, hunters killed 15 percent of the autumn population, but when only bucks were killed, starting in 1974, the exploitation rate decreased to 6 percent. However, in areas where the climate is relatively mild and accessibility is good, hunter harvest may exceed 20 percent. The hunting zones close to Montreal offer examples of places where hunting was the primary limiting factor, under the liberal conditions of the 1950s and early 1960s.

Predation

The timber wolf and the coyote, two major predators of white-tailed deer in southeastern Canada, currently are restricted to only a part of the deer range. Wolves reportedly usually select the weakest animals, but after deer populations have been reduced by hunting or severe winters, wolves may kill prime-age animals in winter (Huot et al. 1978). The wolf is present only on the northern shore of the St. Lawrence, and apparently has become a limiting factor for whitetail populations living at the northern limit of deer range following the initial stages of decline (Huot et al. 1978). The coyote invaded the southern part of Quebec in the 1940s and spread eastward. Its distribution now covers most of the deer range in Quebec and New Brunswick. Coyotes kill some whitetails in winter yards, but little is known about the extent of this impact. Predation is likely to be most severe where deer populations are low and concentrated in small wintering areas where habitat has been reduced by intensive agriculture. Coyote control is undertaken mainly to protect farm animals and reduce deer losses in southern Quebec. Neither wolves nor coyotes are present on Anticosti Island.

The bobcat is distributed over southern Quebec, all of New Brunswick and Nova Scotia with the exception of Cape Breton. It is known to prey on white-tailed deer, but its impact has not been assessed.

The domestic dog is a nuisance in many deer yards, particularly those near human habitations. However, its effect on deer populations is unknown.

Predator control has been practiced for many years in Quebec, but a recent study has shown that it has been mostly inefficient in reducing the effects of predation (Banville 1981). A bounty system was prevalent from 1905 to 1971, with a short interruption between 1962 and 1967. However, before the mid-1960s, the objective was mainly to reduce predation on farm animals. Only in 1965 was a control program set up in relation to deer. At that time, poison (strychnine) was commonly used to control wolves and coyotes. In 1972 this practice was officially banned by the Minister of Tourism, Fish and Game after a comprehensive predator-control program had been initiated. Professional trappers and conservation officers, usually under the supervision of regional biologists, currently remove predators using traps and snares. Due to a lack of rigid control over the trapping activities it appears that in many cases the removal is haphazard and inefficient.

Predation by timber wolves has contributed to the decline of whitetails north of Montreal. Within three or four days, these carcass pieces are the only remnants of an average-size deer killed by wolves. *Photo by Jean Huot.*

MANAGEMENT

For many years, white-tailed deer management has been limited primarily to periodic further restrictions on hunting. In recent decades however, some efforts are being made to maintain and improve habitats. In Quebec, where deer populations have declined, the hunting season has been curtailed sharply. Only bucks have been harvested since 1974, but this restriction is being revised to allow the harvest of does in areas where deer are increasing. Quebec uses the buck law to reduce hunting pressure. The department responsible for fish and wildlife management (Ministère du Loisir de la Chasse et de la Pêche) and the department responsible for lands and forests (Ministère de l'Energie et des Ressources) have agreed on a program to protect winter habitat on public lands. Special prescriptions apply to timber cuttings in conifer stands. Timber cutting is restricted in conifer stands used by deer as cover. In cedar swamps and deer yards, logging is limited to 20-meter (66-foot) strips covering one third of the stand. In a limited number of yards, hardwoods are cut selectively to improve the deer food supply. The Ministère de l'Energie et des Ressources encourages better management of private forest lands by grouping the owners on a voluntary basis and signing 15-year agreements with them to improve the forest by selective cuttings and reforestation.

In New Brunswick, hunting pressure is moderate to light in most areas. The hunting season varies from five days in eastern New Brunswick to almost a month in the western part. Deer of any sex or age can be harvested. Hunting success increased from about 8 percent in the mid-1970s to about 20 percent in the early 1980s. Land managers emphasize the multiple use of forests, which includes prescriptions to create or improve whitetail winter habitats in conjunction with commercial timber harvest. It is recommended that individual openings do not exceed 4 hectares (10 acres) and that they be separated by uncut areas at least equal in size to the cut area. In winter habitat, which comprises only 4 percent of the forested land of New Brunswick, the cutting cycle should be short (four to five years), and at least 50 percent of the area should be maintained in suitable shelter stands.

Deer of either sex can be harvested in Nova Scotia. Hunting success exceeded 45 percent in 1980 (Patton 1982). Winters were mild in the late 1970s and the whitetail population has since been recovering rapidly. Densities are reaching a point where there is a growing concern about the potential damage on agricultural crops, especially blueberry production.

Various forest-cutting patterns or methods have been tried experimentally in conifer stands of southeastern Canada in an attempt to accommodate timber industry needs and retain traditional whitetail winter yards. The top scene shows strip-cutting in a deer wintering area; the strips are approximately 61 meters (200 feet) wide. The bottom scene features patch-cutting in a wintering area; the patches range in size from 2 to 10 hectares (5–25 acres). *Photos courtesy of the New Brunswick Department of Natural Resources.*

THE FUTURE

It is difficult to predict the future of white-tailed deer in southeastern Canada. High deer densities of the past likely will not be restored and maintained in the foreseeable future, nor will it be possible to reproduce the favorable habitats that accompanied the early developments of logging and agriculture. Wildlife biologists and managers have a better knowledge of whitetail population status and an improved understanding of the habitat requirements of deer, but they must accept the fact that range conditions have changed. It would be unrealistic to attempt to reproduce good habitat on extensive areas through expensive management efforts. However, priority should be given to the protection of the existing deer yards. Elsewhere, the potential of the land for deer production could be improved if commercial exploitations were conducted on a sustained-yield basis. In areas where hunting has been an important mortality factor and where winter mortality still is high despite no overuse of the range, it appears that the best approach is to allow a low-level harvest, and maintain and improve winter habitat. This is the case in Quebec, where the harvest strategy is to adjust hunting regulations annually, according to the severity of winters. However, where the climate is milder, such as in Nova Scotia, liberal regulations can be maintained, and the main concern is detecting the first signs of overpopulation.

Chapter 14

NORTHEASTERN HARDWOOD AND SPRUCE/FIR FORESTS

George F. Mattfeld
Environmental Management Specialist
New York Department of Environmental Conservation
Albany, New York

ENVIRONMENT

The Northeastern Hardwood and Spruce/Fir Forests region occurs over nearly 204,000 square kilometers (78,800 square miles) of the New England and Middle Atlantic states and extends nearly as far south as Cleveland, Ohio (Küchler 1964) (Figure 76). Generally excluding coastal areas of the Atlantic Ocean and Great Lakes, this region approximates the size of Washington State and includes all of Vermont, nearly all of Maine and New Hampshire, most of New York, the northern one-fourth of Pennsylvania, and portions of western Connecticut, western Massachusetts, northern New Jersey and northeastern Ohio. The region constitutes 2.5 percent of the United States land area, but has approximately 23 percent of the nation's human population (Lull 1968). Despite current land-use pressures and the land abuses of the past, more than 70 percent of these humid forestlands still, or once again, are forested.

Physiography

Near the end of the Paleozoic era, 230 million years ago, a portion of this region was cataclysmically folded upward over the course of 160 million years to form parts of the Appalachian Mountain range. In the subsequent 70 million years these mountains have been rounded by the elements, including three gla-cial periods, the last of which receded only about 12,000 years ago (Milne and Milne 1962). Except for small portions of the Allegheny Plateau and Mountains in northern Pennsylvania, the entire region has been glaciated. Upraised plains and plateaus at elevations of 120 to more than 610 meters (395 to 2,000+ feet) are dominated by mountain groups from 600 to 1,800 meters (1,970–5,900 feet) high in the White, Green, Adirondack, Catskill and Taconic mountain areas. The topography is extremely variable, and features glacial valleys with lakes, ponds and bogs numbering in the thousands (Fenneman 1938).

Soils

Extremely variable and well-mixed soils of the region were developed from glacial till derived from granite, gneiss, schist, slate and shale in most of New England and the Adirondacks, and from shale, limestone or sandstone in the remainder of New York and Pennsylvania. Podzolic soils, usually acidic and weak in lime and phosphorous, are typical. They vary in texture from rough-gravely loams to moderately fine-textured clay loams. They generally are well-drained, although some portions of the region (southern New York and northern Pennsylvania) are poorly drained, with a fragipan at depths of 30 to 75 centimeters (12–30 inches) (U.S. Department of Agriculture 1957, Cline 1961).

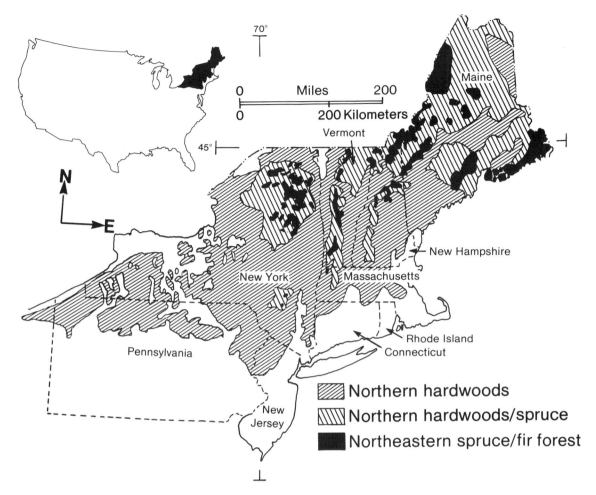

Figure 76. The Northeastern Hardwood and Spruce/Fir Forests region (from Küchler 1966).

Climate and Vegetation

Climate, soils, topography, previous land use and current vegetation (Banasiak 1964, Silver 1968a, Lull 1968) are interrelated closely in the region. An inflowing westerly continental air circulation deemphasizes periodic coastal influences. Mountains and elevated plateaus induce a near-arctic climate that is more variable than that of similar latitudes farther inland. Summers are cool to semitropical, and mean annual precipitation is 93 to 134 centimeters (36.6–52.8 inches), 30 to 40 percent of which is in the form of snow.

Two predominant climax forests are the spruce/fir and northern hardwood types. The former is composed of red, white and black spruce in association with balsam fir (Society of American Foresters 1967). This boreal forest type is found on the cool-climate, acidic, organic, podzol soils of northern and central Maine, and extends southward into mountainous sectors of New Hampshire, Vermont and New York. Northern white cedar is found in poorly drained areas and white pine intrudes on sandy soils. The prevailing climatic conditions for the spruce/fir forest include a frost-free season of only 90 to 120 days. Winters are cold, with a mean daily temperature high in January of from −7 to 1 degrees Celsius (19.4–34 degrees Fahrenheit), and a mean daily low of from −17.8 to −3 degrees (Celsius (0–26.5 degrees Fahrenheit). Summers are cool, with a mean daily high in July of from 21 to 27 degrees Celsius (70–81 degrees Fahrenheit) and a mean daily low of from 1.2 to 4.5 degrees Celsius (34–40 degrees Fahrenheit).

Up to certain elevations on mountainsides and high plateaus, better sites and more moderate climatic conditions favor the northern hardwood association. Beech, yellow birch and sugar maple are the dominant species. Sandy sites and abandoned fields or burns tend to support white pine and oaks, predominantly northern red oak. Hemlock and red spruce are highly shade-tolerant and commonly extend into the canopy or occur as part of the understory in the northern hardwood type.

Infertile or cold sites have a spruce/fir climax and swampy land may be occupied by northern white cedar or black spruce. On many lowland sites a mixture of hemlock, spruce, balsam fir and yellow birch—underlain by witch-hobble, striped maple and honeysuckle—is found. In this mixture the overstory intercepts snow and the understory provides winter browse. Growing seasons of the northern hardwood forest type—120 to 150 days—are somewhat longer than those of the spruce/fir forest. Temperature is slightly less extreme, with a mean daily high in January of from -4 to -2 degrees Celsius (24.7–28.3 degrees Fahrenheit) and a mean daily low of from -8.5 to -5.5 degrees Celsius (16.7–22 degrees Fahrenheit). July mean daily highs are from 23.5 to 29 degrees Celsius (74.3–84.2 degrees Fahrenheit), and mean daily lows are from 11 to 16 degrees Celsius (51.8–60.8 degrees Fahrenheit).

A third association in the region is the white pine/hemlock/hardwood forest type, located in the St. Lawrence and Champlain drainages of New York and the coastal-influenced portions of New Hampshire, Vermont, Massachusetts, northwestern New Jersey and southwestern Maine. The frost-free season lasts 120 to 180 days. Soils are more productive and temperatures more moderate, so growing conditions are improved. Hemlock typically occurs on moist-cool sites. Beech/birch and maple and northern red oak types provide the major hardwood components, with gradually more important additions of red maple and less tolerant species, notably white ash and black cherry. Poorly drained sites tend to be occupied by hardwoods including red maple, black ash and elms. White pine is the typical species of old fields, pastures, agricultural burns and former Indian village sites.

Land Use and Vegetation

Current distribution of the three cover types is highly dependent on past and present land uses. Much of the Northeastern Hardwood and Spruce/Fir Forests region clearly reflects the three centuries of settlement. Occupation of land by people and their farmsteads peaked between 1850 and 1880. Agricultural practices were exploitive, and when the farmers moved west, the idled fields reverted to early stages of forest succession.

White pine, found on areas disturbed in precolonial times, was the first tree species to be removed by early logging along the Atlantic coast and major river drainages. Subsequently, prime coniferous trunks (pine and the spruce) were removed selectively from the hardwood and spruce/fir regions and floated to mills. Finally, pulpwood operations replaced lumber production and gave rise to even-aged, township-scale forest management in the spruce/fir forests.

In hardwood areas, the advent of trucking and mechanized logging made possible repetitive harvesting of the denser woods. In more accessible areas, these woods already had been used heavily for fuelwood. Reverting farmlands also were subjected to fuelwood cutting and periodic high grading. The pattern resulted in broad areas of heavily cut or poor quality old-field pine and hardwood stands interspersed with settlements and dairy farms. The habitat condition, although highly productive of deer in the short run, tends to make management economically difficult or impossible due to the poor quality and small size of the growing forest stands.

Climate and Whitetail Habitat

Two aspects of the region's climate/vegetation/soil system are especially important to white-tailed deer. In much of the northern and mountainous parts of the region, temperature and precipitation interact to form snowpacks 36 to 51 centimeters (14–20 inches) or more in depth. These snowpacks usually last from early or mid-December until early April, and vary in depth and duration depending on latitude, elevation or temperature, and evaporative influences of large lakes. Whitetails are forced to concentrate during this period in yards where coniferous tree canopies intercept up to 50 percent of the snowfall. The lengthy duration (often 100 days and more) of deep-snow accumulations, associated with burial and depletion of available food supplies, can result in widespread starvation of deer (Severinghaus 1947, Hepburn 1959, Mattfeld 1974).

Deep snow means less food and more energy cost to get it for this young whitetail in Maine. It will be forced to stay in the "yard," where evergreen trees will intercept snow and make what reaches the ground easier to traverse when frozen. Other deer will help to maintain trails between feeding spots. With luck and sufficient fat reserve, the fawn crop will survive. *Photo by Tom Carbone; courtesy of the Maine Department of Inland Fisheries and Wildlife.*

In the more southern or moderate parts of the region, generally more populated by people, winter conditions are not as severe. Winter deer range is not used as consistently and can be more difficult to identify (Banasiak 1964). During periods when snow supports domestic dogs but not weakened deer, direct loss of deer can be a significant resource management concern.

WHITETAIL POPULATIONS

The hardwood and spruce/fir forests of the Northeast are inhabited by about 1 million white-tailed deer, whose recovery from near extirpation annually benefits nearly 2 million hunters. Countless other persons enjoy observing and photographing deer. The white-

tail's beauty, speed, elusiveness and adaptability to the land as it is reshaped by humans, all reinforce the species' popularity in the region. These benefits, as well as easily recognizable impacts on agricultural crops, forest regeneration and highway safety, have ensured deer a central position in the wildlife management programs of the region.

In the past 300 years, the region's whitetail population has been characterized by marked numerical fluctuations. Local fluctuations occur over a variety of time periods—some less than 20 years' duration. The whitetail often has been called a "creature of disturbance" and, in the Northeast, it certainly has come by the title honestly.

History

The history of deer in the Northeastern Hardwood and Spruce/Fir Forests region is largely a product of the economies and land-use practices of the region's human inhabitants, beginning with the native Indians (*see* Foote 1945, Shaw and McLaughlin 1951, Severinghaus and Brown 1956, Silver 1957, 1968, Banasiak 1961, Stanton 1963).

Whitetail densities in the disturbed forests of the region during immediate precolonial time may have been 3.8–5.8 per square kilometer (10–15 per square mile), paralleling estimates for similar forests in Wisconsin (Dahlberg and Guettinger 1956). The tree species composition of the virgin forests suggests that deer probably did not drastically exceed the 5.4–5.8 per square kilometer (14–15 per square mile) density proven necessary to allow regeneration of northern hardwoods in cut stands of New York's Adirondack Mountains (Behrend et al. 1970). In contrast, Cooperrider (1974) estimated the unharvested or undisturbed northern hardwood forest to have a carrying capacity of one deer per square kilometer (2.6 per square mile)—a level similar to Dasmann's (1971) estimates for mature West Coast coniferous forests. Whitetail populations probably were higher in the less severe climatic zones and in areas where the habitat was repeatedly disturbed by Indians (*see* Chapter 2). Historically, the predominantly spruce/fir portions of the region were moose and wolf range, with relatively few deer.

Historical accounts from the early 1600s through the 1700s indicate considerable forest clearing for agriculture by European settlers in parts of the region. Coupled with selective logging and possibly influenced by reduction of predators, the clearing allowed the region's whitetail populations to increase. However, with intensive farming in the southern and non-mountainous parts of the region, and with the unregulated shooting of whitetails for food, hides and market, the deer declined near the denser human settlements. Hunting regulations (usually prohibiting hunting during part of the year) and localized enforcement by "deer reeves" came about in response to obviously diminishing deer populations. The actions generally were too late or inadequate to halt the decline.

Until the 1800s, the mountainous and northern portions of the region remained essentially unsettled. Much of the landscape was primeval forest. A shaded forest floor, predation, and deer populations that exceeded habitat carrying capacity during periodically harsh winters combined to create poor deer range with limited deer densities.

As early as 1820, the future of deer in the region was associated with farm abandonment for western agricultural land, industrial employment and a gold rush. By the period 1820–1850, whitetails were extirpated from most of the region. Half of New Hampshire's forests had been cleared. By 1860, more than 50 percent of each southern New Hampshire county had been converted to improved farmland. Vermont was only 35 percent wooded by 1880, and 75 percent of New York was cleared. In each of the latter cases, the forested areas remaining were nearly all mountainous and, with poor soil and harsh climate, were unsuitable for farming. In Maine, 2.6 million hectares (6.5 million acres)—more than 30 percent of the total land area—had been cleared. Dairy cattle and sheep grazed the remnant woodlots. Wolves

Resistance in recent decades to harvest of antlerless white-tailed deer in the Northern Hardwood and Spruce/Fir Forests region stems from long-standing traditional beliefs that taking does limits herd productivity or is unsportsmanlike. Despite historic experience and scientific evidence to the contrary, favorable public attitudes toward managed harvests of both sexes of deer have emerged slowly in some states. Original 1855 artwork, entitled "Deer Shooting on the Shattagee" (northern New York) by L. Maurer; reproduced as a lithograph by N. Currier for Currier & Ives, Publishers. *Photo courtesy of the Museum of the City of New York.*

and mountain lions probably were eliminated from the region by 1820, but any predatory influence on deer was replaced and soon exceeded by the rapidly growing human population. In the 1870s and 1880s, for the region as a whole, whitetails were scarce. For a time, the short growing seasons, thin soils, and steep slopes of the mountainous and northern parts of the region became the new frontier of land use and the habitat of an exiled deer resource.

Inland Maine, the White Mountains of New Hampshire's Coos, Grafton and Carroll counties, the Green Mountain ridge and Essex County in Vermont, the Adirondacks and Catskills of New York, the Berkshires of Massachusetts, and portions of the Allegheny and Pocono Mountains of Pennsylvania all saw deer habitats and populations fluctuate in response to logging, postlogging fire, scattered subsistence farming, predator eradication, improved transportation and market hunting in the early 1800s. The familiar pattern involves a deer population increase following logging and fire, loss of some logged coniferous winter range, and then exploitation exceeding the improved habitats' carrying capacity *or* periodic starvation of deer populations depressing and exceeding the carrying capacity of their habitat.

The post-Civil War period was a period of dramatic change, leading to more stable land use and the recovery of deer populations. Whitetail populations in the Adirondacks and southern Maine, for example, did not expand to an appreciable extent until the 1890s and early 1900s, respectively. Killing deer was prohibited, although not prevented—due to a lack of effective or consistent conservation law enforcement—until about 1900. Sanctuaries and refuges for deer were tried, with a notable lack of success.

The period of protection from about 1865 to 1920 began with the hope of prolonging the deer demise in remote habitats. Simultaneously, farmland abandonment intensified and sheep grazing declined. The deer, their habitat and whitetail hunting profited from these changes.

From 1890 to 1920, effective hunting regulations were developed throughout the region. Bag limits gradually were reduced to one deer per season. The use of dogs and snares, float hunting, and nighttime jacklighting were prohibited. The export and/or sale of venison was curtailed. Counties in the Catskills and southern Maine were closed to deer hunting. Vermont reopened a one-month bucks-only season. Maine also used that approach for two years in two counties before joining New Hampshire and Massachusetts in setting up either-sex harvest regulations. Pennsylvania established a bucks-only season in 1907, and New York followed suit in 1912. Regulatory management, modern-day habitat patterns, and a recreational hunting tradition were all in place by about 1915.

After 1920, the southern portions of the states in the Northeastern Hardwood and Spruce/Fir Forests region began to reemerge as range capable of accommodating intensive whitetail cropping. This region's managed deer populations were able to rebound quickly after periodic climatic setbacks. Successful whitetail population management tailored to agricultural damage situations may have been the key to public acceptance of variable liberal harvest regulations instead of strict protection. In the 160 or more years since the beginning of land abandonment in the region, these southern ranges have become 50 to 80 percent forested or reforested and, in many cases, ideal for deer. Northern ranges within the region have shifted to largescale logging and pulpwood production. Large tracts of land have been purchased to provide the timber industry with sustained yields of trees. Despite the more favorable habitat conditions for deer, periodically severe winters with prolonged deep snow force deer to concentrate. These "yarding" conditions continue as a major constraint to deer populations.

Destruction of winter range carrying capacity by intensive pulpwood logging, and positive responses of underharvested deer herds to hardwood cutting, fire or hurricane disturbance have produced some whitetail populations with "boom or bust" histories. In parts of the region, northern New York and Vermont, the buck-only harvest tradition is clung to tenaciously, making the deer population unstable and their management nearly impossible.

Population Characteristics

Sex ratio. The proportion of males and females added to a healthy whitetail population through births consistently favors males. Severinghaus and Cheatum (1956) reported whitetail embryo collections from 11 states with a ratio of 117 males per 100 females; Shaw and McLaughlin (1951) reported 118:100 in Massachusetts; and

Colonization, pioneering and settlement of the Northeastern Hardwood and Spruce/Fir Forests region placed considerable stress on whitetail populations and their habitats. Subsistence use and hide trade contributed to the near-extirpation of the species. The take of a single animal in the late-1800s was an uncommon event (top). With enforced hunting regulations (including either-sex harvests) and habitat change (primarily land abandonment), the whitetail population recovered to a level of abundance in the late 1930s and 1940s (bottom). Through sound management, whitetails continue to be a popular and valued feature of the region's landscapes. *Photos courtesy of the New York Department of Environmental Conservation.*

White (1968*a*) reported 113:100 for New Hampshire. The sex ratio at birth and its range of variability are not known. Prenatal mortality (Verme 1962, Murphy and Coates 1966, Hesselton and Jackson 1973), neonatal mortality (O'Pezio 1978) and summer (postnatal) mortality (Banasiak 1964) occur at significant levels. Their cumulative effect has resulted in pre-hunting-season fawn sex ratios of 114:100 (White 1968*a*) and 112:100 (Banasiak 1964)—estimated from harvested fawns in New Hampshire and Maine, respectively. A ratio of 106:100 was reported from a summary of 18 hunting-season evaluations in 10 eastern and mid-western states during the 1940–1960 period (Clarke and Severinghaus 1979).

Immigration and emigration. An experimental whitetail population-reduction program in New York by Behrend et al. (1970), coupled with telemetry studies by Mattfeld et al. (1977), revealed: no net movement response to a 50-percent reduction in deer density from 10.8 whitetails per square kilometer (28 per square mile) to 5.4 per square kilometer (14 per square mile); no net movement associated with hunting pressures peaking at 9 hunters per square kilometer (25 per square mile); and a characteristically fixed pattern of seasonal range occupation by deer. The latter consistently appeared to be conditioned more by social relationships among deer than by foraging opportunities in habitats relieved of deer pressure. Winter logging was the only habitat influence affecting whitetail distribution. Shifts in range were nearly always temporary. The forage provided by downed tree tops and/or the energy-savings effect of deer traveling on skid trails through deep snows probably accounted for the response.

Most bucks and a few 1–2.5-year-old does dispersed. They changed their spring-summer-autumn range and usually their winter range as well. However, no *net* effect from these dispersal movements was detected, even though the whitetail population reduction portion of the study site was only 2,023 hectares (5,000 acres) and surrounded by areas closed to hunting or hunted very lightly. There is no evidence that year-to-year immigration or emigration of deer significantly affects whitetail population structure at the scale of physiographic, ecological or political management units in the Northeast. Whitetail range and population expansion certainly have occurred on longer time frames.

Nutrition and reproduction. Reproductive potentials and performance of whitetails have been studied throughout the region with corpora lutea and embryo counts. Unfortunately these studies sometimes have been used to compare the potential replacement rate of deer in subregional units or habitats without compensating for the prior history of the deer population sampled or its status relative to carrying capacity at the time of the study.

In general, if there is plenty to eat for many deer or if fewer whitetails are sharing limited forage, similar reproductive performance can be expected throughout the region. Limits to the forage base due to lower basic productivity or excessive numbers of deer are expressed in a familiar sequence. First, fawns do not grow fast enough to achieve physiological maturity for reproduction. Reproductive ability is associated with a dressed carcass weight of 29 kilograms (65–70 pounds) or more (Hesselton and Sauer 1973). Failure of fawns to mature may be conditioned by limitations on winter and spring range. These can result in a doe body-mass deficit too large for the summer range to replace while simultaneously supporting lactation (Moen and Severinghaus 1981, Severinghaus 1980). Successful reproduction by females bred as fawns varies from 0 to 50 percent; more than one fawn per doe of this age class is rare.

On overpopulated or otherwise poor (including historically deer-damaged) range, 20 percent or more of the yearling does will not be pregnant, and reproductive rates—based on embryo counts—may be less than 0.89 per doe (Hesselton and Jackson 1974). The ability of this class to contribute to population growth or replenishment depends on the size of the fawn crop and the number that *survive* to be yearlings. Yearling frequency often is used to estimate the realized increment of deer to the population. Reproduction by yearlings is critical in a population where 35 percent of the breeding does are of this age class.

Poorly nourished fawns are ill-prepared to withstand winter weight loss, yet they must compete with more dominant older deer for forage (Ozoga 1972). Spring and summer forage may be inadequate to provide prompt recovery and resumption of growth and development. Yearling does subjected to these stresses as fawns may fail to ovulate or conceive, will have fewer embryos, and their fetuses may experience a higher rate of prenatal mortality. In contrast, whitetail populations at carrying capacity have yearling reproductive rates of 1.7 or 1.8 embryos, and rates of 2.00 may occur. In these cases, virtually all yearling does become pregnant.

Adult whitetail does 2.5 years of age and older generally have pregnancy rates of 85 to 96 percent and reproductive rates of 1.3–2.05 fawns (embryos) per doe. Rates of 1.8–1.9 are associated with carrying capacity, as denoted by other physical condition attributes. The typical adult doe must recover from a winter weight loss *and* the lactation drain of a single fawn or twins, prepare herself for the coming winter, maintain her fetuses during winter and spring, and again support lactation. Verme

(1967, 1969) indicated that on northern ranges, reproductive performance of adult does depends especially on the timing of snowmelt and green-up in spring and, on poor or overpopulated ranges, rearing fawns may decrease the probability of successfully carrying fawns the next year.

The physical condition of deer harvested in autumn and early winter has been used to rank the range potential of subregional habitats, as well as to estimate whitetail population status relative to habitat carrying capacity or maximum turnover rate on specific management units. The latter is appropriate; the former has been attempted but often confounded by the latter. Unfortunately, "good" physical condition of deer does not indicate clearly whether a whitetail population could be significantly higher. For example, in western New York, whitetail populations were held in check at a level associated with a buck harvest of 0.4 to 1.2 per square kilometer (1–3 per square mile) to protect agricultural crops. Populations in the St. Lawrence plain area of northern New York exhibit chronic lack of growth and are subjected to buck-only harvests of less than 0.2 per square kilometer (0.5 per square mile). The St. Lawrence populations contain deer with physical conditions similar to those of whitetails in western New York.

Nutrition and physiology. Weight of whitetails clearly is related to winter survival potential on ranges with varying climatic extremes (*see* Moen and Severinghaus 1981, Robbins et al. 1974*a*), since it represents a margin of fat reserve for such conditions. Weight also is related to reproductive performance, which is conditioned by nutritional status of does. Mean round weights (early winter) of 39.5 kilograms (87 pounds) and 57.7 kilograms (127 pounds) were recorded for female fawns and yearlings, respectively, at carrying capacity in the Seneca Army Depot of New York. Comparable weights for male whitetails were 41.8 kilograms (92 pounds) and 67.2 kilograms (148 pounds). In a chronic starvation area, weights of 32.7 kilograms (72 pounds) and 52.7 kilograms (116 pounds) were obtained for female fawns and yearlings, respectively. Comparable weights for males were 35.4 kilograms (78 pounds) and 55.4 kilograms (122 pounds).

Deer are able to maintain themselves as long as the digestible energy of their food exceeds 2.17 kilocalories per dry gram (Ammann et al. 1973) and the essential plant oils that inhibit rumen bacteria are below a level that inhibits choice and consumption of vegetation (*see* Longhurst et al. 1968, Nagy et al. 1964). These basic foraging and digestive constraints, together with an annual cycle of demand for protein and other nutrients (Robbins et al. 1974*b*) and the effect of dominance on competition for available food (Ozoga 1972), help explain some of the patterns and exceptions observed in forage use by whitetails in the region.

Most early evaluations of deer foraging focused on woody browse. Woody browse preference scales and browsing intensity on selected index species have been used to provide a crude estimate of whitetail population status relative to carrying capacity (Doig 1968) and to map the extent of deer winter range (Dickinson 1978). Winter always has been considered critical for deer in the region, and woody browse essentially is the only forage present in many winter habitats.

Studies—most notably those using tame deer on natural sites—have shown substantial seasonal use of herbaceous plants by whitetails (Sauer et al. 1969, Healy 1971, Gill and Wallmo 1973, Watts 1964, Pekins 1981). They also have revealed significant shifts in species comprising the deer diet and constant change in selective feeding sequence. Some investigators, notably Tierson et al. (1966), have documented a gradual shift in species composition of northern hardwood communities used by deer.

These observations suggest that, as each season progresses, individual plants and species undergo chemical compositional changes sometimes affected by site, which can result in shifts of forage use by whitetails *from one day to the next.* Each day brings a new selection opportunity conditioned by plant development of each species, rain and sun, and the withdrawal of yesterday's food. Thus, without specifying time and area or deer population history, citing a "preferred" food may have little meaning. Healy's (1971) direct observations of foraging deer showed that 67 percent of deer foraging was on herbaceous plants in early spring (mid-March to mid-May) and 10.0 percent on woody browse. By late spring (mid-May to early July), the leaves of woody plants constituted 46.3 percent of the deer diet, and herbaceous plants had dropped to 16.7 percent. Use of agricultural crops in this period is common and can be a serious problem.

As summer progresses and herbaceous groundcover plants are "hardened off" or already eaten, it is relatively easy to account for the disappearing new growth of sugar maple, yellow birch, white ash or black cherry. They apparently are most vulnerable in August and September (Wiersma 1968), when deer populations are at their peak. In agricultural areas, truck gardens can be damaged.

The persistent green leaves of raspberry and blackberry become important in autumn. A whitetail's need for rich, digestible food to convert to fat in preparation for winter helps explain why acorns, beechnuts, and other mast or fruit (including agricultural varieties) are frequent autumn foods. Whitetail preference for apple clearly is at odds with orchardists' trend toward dwarf species and fruit harvest mechanization. Electric fencing using high-tensile steel is gaining popularity as a deterrent to crop damage by deer, and the search continues for practical, inexpensive repellents.

In winter, the nutritional value of clumped witch-hobble takes on new meaning, especially when the clumps are near enough to conifers that intercept snow and condition it rel-

ative to foraging costs. In such situations the cost of using such clumps is less than the cost of travel by deer to collect more uniformly distributed browse of lower digestibility (Mattfeld 1974). In some areas striped maple, or even worse alder, may be all that is available above deep snow. Whitetails in forested areas are not hesitant to dig for evergreen-woods fern, acorns, other mast and dead leaves. Cornfields, orchards and vineyards are frequented in agricultural areas.

Northern white cedar, perhaps the ideal deer support species because of its high digestibility and effectiveness as winter shelter, is virtually nowhere to be found as a regenerating species, except possibly in parts of Maine (C. Banasiak personal communication:1983). Ground hemlock, once a conspicuous groundcover shrub in the region, essentially is gone, having been eliminated through decades of selective browsing by hungry whitetails.

Putting the knowledge of forage value together with the cycle of deer requirements to appraise carrying capacity is possible at var-

Northern white cedar is a valuable winter food for whitetails in the region. The sleek deer shown above, however, will soon be thin because of the limited amount of accessible understory plants and an established browse line on the cedar. Furthermore, browsing by whitetails sharing such a winter yard will prevent regeneration of vegetation that provides nutrition and cover. *Photo by Irene Vandermolen.*

ious levels of precision, as illustrated by Cooperrider and Behrend (1980), Wallmo et al. (1977), and Whelan (1975). Although such appraisals are probably not practical as a routine management approach for each range in the Northeastern Hardwood and Spruce/Fir Forests region, they help to identify the workings of a system that has dramatic effects on the environment of deer. They can be the key to solving management problems that do not respond to normal prescriptions.

Antler development. Antler growth of yearling whitetail bucks has been used throughout the Northeastern Hardwood and Spruce/Fir Forests region as an indicator of deer population status. Yearling bucks in managed herds on productive range typically produce four- and six-point racks, and eight-point antler sets are not uncommon. In contrast, yearlings in poor habitat or on overpopulated range rarely have more than spike antlers. In these populations it is not unusual for more than half the yearling bucks to have sublegal racks (less than 7.6 centimeters: 3 inches long), and many 2.5-year-old bucks retain spike antlers.

Yearling antler-beam diameter has proven to be a better measure of whitetail physiological status than number of antler points. Mean beam diameters of 15 to 16 millimeters (0.59–0.63 inch) or less generally are associated with chronic starvation of populations exceeding habitat carrying capacity. Beam diameters in the 19–22-millimeter (0.75–0.87-inch) range usually are associated with whitetails at carrying capacity. Antler-beam changes are most useful when observed within a range or management unit over some period of time. Changes are checked with other parameters of deer population condition, particularly fawn reproduction and yearling frequency, as well as documented deer winter-loss patterns relative to winter conditions.

It is important to remember that as a whitetail population is maintained at carrying capacity for a time and forage recovers, the carrying capacity of the habitat may increase. Maintaining the proper deer population, therefore, means allowing harvest and population to increase at proportionate rates, assuming population growth is not in conflict with other

A whitetail population within carrying capacity of its habitat in the Northeastern Hardwood and Spruce/Fir Forests region is reflected by heavier, larger-antlered bucks in greater abundance and at younger ages than in populations exceeding carrying capacity. Such a population experiences rapid turnover and provides optimum values to hunters and other recreational users of deer. *Photo by Bill Cross; courtesy of the Maine Department of Inland Fisheries and Wildlife.*

resource interests, such as agricultural or forestry investments. The various physiological indices, such as antler development, are important biological signals. If they reveal whitetail population imbalance with habitat carrying capacity in intensively managed units of the region, management must respond immediately to avoid rapid growth by these volatile populations that cause damage, depress carrying capacity, and result in direct loss of deer or in reduced potential. In the areas with more severe climatic conditions, but under management and full utilization, these signals are especially important, since deer overpopulation can seriously affect the carrying capacity of winter yards for extended periods. The indices are somewhat more difficult to use, however, because winter severity varies from year to year.

Influences on Population Growth

White-tailed deer productivity concerns in the Northeastern Hardwood and Spruce/Fir Forests region are not limited to reproduction rates and population gains. As elsewhere, mortality due to winter starvation, predation, accidents, crippling loss, illegal kill and disease represents population loss. If it is heavier in does than in bucks, such mortality is particularly important. By holding whitetail populations at carrying capacity, winter starvation was reduced from 25 percent of the posthunt population (virtually equal to the entire fawn crop) to 1 percent at the Seneca Army Depot in New York (Hesselton et al. 1965). Such a complete conversion of mortality to harvest yield would not be consistently possible in parts of the region with relatively severe climatic conditions, since it would mean managing for the very worst winter carrying capacity. In Maine, 27 percent of the annual mortality was estimated as winter all-cause mortality—the majority being starvation loss (Banasiak 1964). Winter loss and fawn loss may equal legal kill in northern New Hampshire (Silver 1968*b*).

Crippling loss typically is reduced in areas of intensive hunting pressure. It has accounted for 6 percent of the annual mortality in Maine (Banasiak 1964) and 7 percent of the known accidental and illegal kill in New Hampshire (Silver 1968*b*).

Illegal kill was estimated at 11 percent of the annual mortality in Maine (Banasiak 1964) and

9.7 percent of the known "other" mortality in New Hampshire (Silver 1968*b*). However, Severinghaus and Eabry (1973) showed that, in Adirondack areas of New York that did not have antlerless-deer harvests, "unaccounted for" mortality was 66 percent of the estimated total. The authors could account for 64 percent of the mortality where there were antlerless-deer harvests. Estimates of illegal kill equalling legal kill have been provided by studies such as those using covert sampling methods (Vilkitis 1971). Dickinson (1982) showed that whitetail population performance in response to legal harvest manipulations will not easily reveal such illegal losses if the latter occur randomly with regard to sex and age.

Banasiak (1964) showed that failure to realize reproductive rates indicated by embryo counts can be nearly equal to the harvest in some of the region's whitetail populations. The reproductive potential of a deer population that turns over rapidly exceeds 0.8, but that rate cannot be achieved without realizing full reproductive potential.

Verme (1962) and Murphy and Coates (1966) demonstrated fawn mortality of 0 to 90 percent in trials with penned deer. Low rates of embryo loss are typical, although a 9-percent loss of fetuses at mid-gestation, followed by 8 percent during the final gestation stages, was reported. Embryo counts by Hesselton and Jackson (1974) revealed very low rates of evidence of loss. Nonetheless, O'Pezio (1978) summarized the typical 30-percent loss of fawns reported from embryo counts and deer population reconstruction in northern states. O'Pezio recorded a 50-percent loss of the fawn reproductive potential, 22 percent of the yearling potential and 18 percent of the adult potential. The overall loss was 22 percent. All losses apparently occurred during the prenatal or neonatal period, since virtually no mortality occurred after observation of family groups during their first two weeks postparturition.

Evidence of lactation in autumn has been used with reproductive potential from corpora lutea counts to estimate fawn survival. Yearlings had a lactation rate of 16.6 percent, and 2.5-year-old does had a rate of 68.5 percent. Does 3.5 years of age and older had a rate of 77.8 percent. Estimated fawn survival approximated the fawn/doe ratio estimated from the harvest (Banasiak 1964).

Body weight is an excellent barometer of whitetail condition, because it is the *net* result of all nutrient/energy exchanges between a deer and its habitat. In the Northeastern Hardwood and Spruce/Fir Forests region, those exchanges are influenced most by the (1) number of deer sharing the basic production of habitats, (2) annual cycle of energy and nutrient availability, (3) effect of snow on the cost of collection of food as well as time spent using body reserves during periods of food shortage, and (4) direct effects of temperature, wind and radiation on the cost of maintaining body temperature. Survival or recovery to reproductive status is a function of the body-mass development rate, depletion rate and the time spent in each phase. Since recruitment of one year's fawns to the next autumn's breeding population and the yield or harvest component is most important, this annual cycle is critical to the management of deer in the region.

Severinghaus (1980) and Moen and Severinghaus (1981) have summarized observations of whitetail weights in autumn and weights of dead deer found in winter for three ranges in New York. Two of the ranges—the Adirondacks and Catskills—are mountainous and forested with some differences in climatic severity. The third range—the Central-Southern Tier—has less severe winter conditions, and a strong agricultural influence. The weight cycle of deer in the three ranges was expressed mathematically, and minimum survival weights were predicted. Females—the most critical for herd-production management—are used here as examples. In all three ranges, females in winter habitat had predicted minimum survival weights of 21 kilograms (46.3 pounds) for fawns, 30 kilograms (66 pounds) for yearlings, and 35–38 kilograms (77–83.6 pounds) for 2.5–4.5-year-olds. Under more stressful nonwinter habitat conditions, fawns were predicted to have a minimum survival weight about 4.2 kilograms (9.35 pounds) higher, or about 25.2 kilograms (55.5 pounds).

Maximum predicted autumn weights (influenced by the downside of the body-mass cycle in the previous winter) were 32.7 kilograms (72 pounds), 31.3 kilograms (69 pounds) and 43.1 kilograms (95 pounds) for the Adirondack, Catskill and Central-Southern Tier ranges, respectively.

Whitetails in the Central-Southern Tier range had a higher probability of survival because (1) the habitat—generally not stressed by overpopulation—provided for a greater body-mass reserve, (2) more of the reserve was energy-rich fat, (3) the rate of weight loss per day was relatively less, (4) the period of winter restriction was relatively short, and (5) the forage base often was more nutritious. In most winters, more deer in this range could survive per unit of range even if areas with little energy-conservation potential have to be utilized.

During most winters, fawn survival outside of winter range is not possible in the Adirondacks and Catskills. On winter ranges shared by an overabundance of deer, many fawns die, since the margin between maximum autumn weight and death weight is quickly depleted. Too many whitetails on poor spring, summer and autumn range also reduce the probability of achieving safe autumn weights, and slow the maturation of fawns and even yearling deer in some cases. This results in late breeding, late fawn drop and fawns that do not have time to reach a safe autumn weight.

Some sense of the regional differences in probability of deer loss can be gained by converting and comparing these estimates of predicted minimum weights to autumn dressed weights of deer in the region. In Maine, for example, dressed weights of whitetails analyzed for the period 1954–1957 suggest that female fawns in the farm woodland zones and some fawns of both sexes in the forested zones were in peril each year (Banasiak 1964, 1976). Statewide averages in 1976 were less critical. Integration of pooled statewide weight samples can be misleading, but fawns appeared to be relatively safe in Massachusetts and southern New York excluding the mountainous Catskills areas. Some deer in northern New York and the Catskill Mountains will be lost every year. Until recently, Pennsylvania used yearling weight on a six-point scale to help formulate deer population carrying capacity and harvest quotas (Lang and Wood 1976). Whitetails in the worst class, with a dressed weight of 40.9 kilograms (90 pounds) or less, probably were in peril even in the more moderate climatic conditions. At present, overwinter whitetail population densities have been targeted for each county based on acreages of seedling/sapling, pole-stage and saw timber forests or noncommercial forest stands. Autumn weights of yearling bucks in three areas of Vermont, and most weights reported throughout the region, suggest losses would only be significant in the most severe winters. The autumn weights are close enough to an estimated safe dressed weight (about 43 kilograms:95 pounds). However, it is apparent that some yearlings are in peril most years.

Deer reported lost in collisions with vehicles equalled 18 percent of the reported legal harvest (11 percent of the estimated total harvest) in Pennsylvania in 1977 (Godshall 1978) and 53.9 percent of the total known mortality other than legal harvest in New Hampshire between 1945 and 1962. Losses due to a variety of accidents and some diseases generally are considered unavoidable through practical management. The number of whitetails killed in response to crop depredation is insignificant and expected to remain so.

Domestic dogs, coyotes, bobcats and black bear are predators of deer in the Northeastern Hardwood and Spruce/Fir Forests region. It has yet to be determined whether coyotes, bobcats and black bears could have an impact on fawn survival in these habitats. Deer populations typically are below the levels able to sustain significant coyote predation in the West. No population level effect due to predation has been demonstrated, and only losses to domestic dogs are considered significant in a management sense. New Hampshire reported that loss of whitetails to dogs accounted for 13.4 percent of the reported kills between 1945 and 1962, and ranked only behind legal hunting and winter starvation. Predators accounted for about 1.1 percent of the total known mortality of deer, excluding legal harvest (Silver 1968b). Less than 50 reported kills in Vermont each year are attributed to coyotes and bobcats, while more than 400 are attributed to domestic dogs. Shaw and McLaughlin (1951) converted this type of information to estimates of population mortality, and reported that dog predation in Massachusetts accounted for 1 percent of the annual whitetail mortality.

The occurrence of a variety of parasites has been noted in deer of the region. High rates of incidence of some parasites have been reported. For example, more than 75 percent of an Adirondack deer population were hosting liver flukes (Behrend et al. 1973). Lungworms and bot fly larvae also are commonly encountered.

The brain worm, *Parelaphostrongylus tenuis*, has received the most attention. Its high incidence in whitetails in Maine and New York (Behrend and Witter 1968, Behrend 1970) is associated with potentials to infect, debilitate and kill moose in parts of those states. Stratified winter habitat for moose and deer has been shown to reduce the potential for moose infection (Telfer 1967b). Lack of such stratification has been cited as ensuring high infection rates if moose return to northern New York (Severinghaus and Jackson 1970). In recent years, moose populations have expanded into New York and parts of Vermont and New Hampshire. The infection rate of these moose with *P. tenuis* and any effect on population establishment have not been determined, but they remain a source of concern.

Major disease concerns of the region have been pneumonia associated with winter stress, the possibility of a brucellosis epidemic affecting deer and livestock, and outbreaks of epizootic hemorrhagic disease in northwestern New Jersey in 1955 and 1975. McConnell et al. (1976) provided evidence that approximately 1,000 whitetails died in a 1975 outbreak of epizootic hemorrhagic disease in an area of approximately 389 square kilometers (150 square miles) in New Jersey. Analysis of whitetail harvest figures indicated a loss of 12 to 28 percent in two management zones, but almost half of that loss occurred in two units, totalling 73.6 square kilometers (28.4 square miles). Methods to control outbreaks of this disease are not known, and its lack of identified associations with ecological factors other than deer density offer little hope for delineating areas with high potentials for outbreak.

Diseases affecting man, such as dermatophilosis—a fungilike organism causing pustules on the skin of persons coming in contact with infected deer—or salmonella, cause some localized alarm each year. However they have not been significant problems on a local or regionwide scale. Rabies is known in deer but considered rare, and no cases of transmittal to humans could be found for the region.

Population Estimates

When people ask how many deer there are, usually they are inquiring about population size during the summer/autumn peak of abundance. This peak population is observed by vacationers, sought by hunters, and is a source of concern for farmers and foresters. An average of 1.0 to 1.5 million probably is a reasonable estimate for the Northeastern Hardwood and Spruce/Fir Forests region. That estimated range of abundance allows for climatic fluctuations, variations in land-use within the region, and differences in deer populations among management units due to the variety of harvest and census procedures used to generate numerical estimates. But a regionwide or even statewide deer population estimate has little utility. For modern management, whitetail populations must be assessed and managed on the basis of habitat potential in management units or areas (combinations of units).

In some cases, whitetail populations have been estimated for particular areas using such techniques as deer drives and life tables. At the intensively studied Seneca Army Depot in New York, where 4.5 square kilometers (11.7 square miles) of fenced old-field shrub communities are interspersed with woodlots and hedgerows typical of New York's Finger Lake region, minimal annual whitetail populations were reconstructed from sex and age data from all deer harvested on the area. Managed hunts were conducted from 1957 to 1962. At the 1957 peak population there was an average of 83 deer per square kilometer (215 per square mile). A carrying capacity population—13.8 deer per square kilometer (36 per square mile) in summer and 8.1 per square kilometer (21 per square mile) in winter—was achieved by 1962 (Hes-

selton et al. 1965). With little loss to other mortality, such a population yields 1.9 to 2.7 bucks per square kilometer (5–7 per square mile) each year.

In comparison, on a 60-square-kilometer (23-square-mile) managed forest in the Adirondack Mountains of New York, The Archer and Anna Huntington Wildlife Forest Station, Behrend et al. (1970) used drives, with track count weighting factors for deer distribution in major forest types, to estimate whitetail population size. The drives indicated a pre-harvest population density of 10 deer per square kilometer (26 per square mile) in 1966. On the basis of available forage, Cooperrider (1974) estimated the carrying capacity of the uncut portions of this area to be 1 deer per square kilometer (2.6 per square mile).

In the surrounding heavily forested region, about half of which was in uncut preserve status and half was under private forest management by paper companies, the whitetail density was increasing and was believed to average near 5.8 deer per square kilometer (15 per square mile). An antlerless-quota harvest system was being applied to utilize more of the growing population, but because of few roads and lim-

When an area that is chronically overpopulated with whitetails is finally subjected to management, three benefits result: a healthier deer population; enhanced venison- and recreational-yields; and improved human knowledge of the resource. The sex, age and weight of these hunter-harvested whitetails at the Seneca Army Depot in New York provided base data to track the progress of a successful management program that protected habitat potentials and provided an optimum sustained yield of deer. *Photo by Nick Drahos; courtesy of the New York Department of Environmental Conservation.*

ited hunter access, the increased harvests were not preventing population growth. The buck harvest peaked at more than 12,041, or 0.32 whitetail per square kilometer (0.82 per square mile) of deer range for the entire 14-county area in northern New York in 1968 (Severing-haus 1972).

Between 1966 and 1968, deer drives and counts confirmed that quota harvests on the Huntington Forest (achieved with intensive hunting pressure and adequate road access as previously noted) had reduced deer density to the target of 5.4 whitetails per square kilometer (14 per square mile).

Three severe winters—1968–1969, 1969–1970 and 1970–1971—virtually eliminated the annual fawn increment and killed enough adults on the damaged winter range to reduce the 14-county area's buck kill by 60 percent to 4,298, or 0.11 per square kilometer (0.29 per square mile). After 1970, no hunting was needed to hold the Huntington Forest density below 5.4 deer per square kilometer (14 per square mile). The Forest's depleted habitat, particularly the winter range used by deer, apparently could not even support half the peak whitetail population during and following the severe winter periods, when substantial numbers of deer starved. Roadside observations indicated densities probably dipped to about 1.2 to 1.9 deer per square kilometer (3–5 per square mile) (Sage et al. 1983).

During the same years—1968–1971—buck harvest in the two forested counties adjacent to the Huntington Forest declined from 0.42 per square kilometer (1.09 per square mile) of deer range to 0.12 per square kilometer (0.32 per square mile) (Hamilton County) and from 0.22 per square kilometer (0.56 per square mile) to 0.12 per square kilometer (0.31 per square mile) (Essex County). Immediately to the north, in agrarian Clinton County, the buck harvest declined from 0.10 per square kilometer (0.26 per square mile) to 0.04 per square kilometer (0.10 per square mile) of deer range. About 64 kilometers (40 miles) from Hamilton County, in the dairy farming countryside of Otsego County, with the deer population under control, the buck harvest in 1968 was 1.23 per square kilometer (3.19 per square mile). By 1970 the harvest had only dropped 35 percent to 0.81 per square kilometer (2.10 per square mile).

In the forested portions of the Northeastern Hardwood and Spruce/Fir Forests region, un-regulated whitetail populations change tree species composition of regenerating forests by preventing growth of preferred species in logged stands (Jordan 1967, Marquis 1981, Tierson et al. 1966, Webb et al. 1956). In the longer run, these unmanaged whitetail populations create their own instability. Within a few years, as previously described, range depleted by populations exceeding 5 to 6 deer per square kilometer (15 per square mile) may carry only 1 to 1.5 per square kilometer (3–4 per square mile) during the 1 or 2 severe winters that occur out of every 14. The impact may be greater, depending on forage quality on the whitetail's home range, the amount of available winter range and the nutritional value of its forage.

Pure climax forest stands or areas of mature spruce/fir in parts of New York, Vermont, New Hampshire and particularly northern Maine have a carrying capacity for deer close to 0. Their value as winter shelter for whitetails depends on their extent and proximity to more varied and productive habitats with some forage.

HARVEST MANAGEMENT

Optimum meat production, maximum trophy availability and enhanced viewing opportunities are kinds of yield best obtained with specific but different whitetail population structures. However, throughout the Northeastern Hardwood and Spruce/Fir Forests region, the dominant goal has been a sustained opportunity for optimum recreational hunting. Biologists and resource managers have tried to protect whitetail habitats from the excesses of both people and the deer themselves, while providing a relatively stable annual hunting harvest and protecting other land-use interests.

The structure of all whitetail populations is the product of input (reproduction and immigration) versus output (mortality and emigration). Seasonal movements, immigration or emigration presently do not condition harvest outcome or sex and age composition. Except for brief periods during some years and certain primitive weapon seasons, deer hunting seasons in the region avoid winter-concentrated deer.

Because the basic ability of land to support white-tailed deer is variable in the region, different scales of habitat homogeneity have been applied, and the trend has been toward more and smaller management units. New York has

Forest management can benefit or devastate white-tailed deer populations. Heavy timber harvest in a critical winter habitat strains the deer that use the area, as well as the whitetails whose winter range becomes the next alternative for the displaced deer. With consideration for deer habitat needs incorporated, prescribed management of softwood, hardwood, or mixed forest stands maintains winter cover and enhances carrying capacity through forage production. *Photo by Tom Carbone; courtesy of the Maine Department of Inland Fisheries and Wildlife.*

62 such units, Maine has 8, Vermont has 3 to 12, and Pennsylvania's 66 counties serve as individual deer management units. New Hampshire recognizes four to five ecological areas, but like Maine, uses north and south zones for either-sex deer-hunting seasons. Massachusetts has 14 ecological deer management zones (J. McDonough personal communication:1983).

For 70 or 80 years, wildlife management agencies for all states of the region have collected deer harvest data. Mandatory registration or checking of bagged deer has been traditional in Maine, Vermont, Massachusetts, and more recently New Jersey. New York, New Hampshire, Pennsylvania and Connecticut have used mail reports. The relationship between these harvest data and the actual "population" has been a topic of sustained professional interest and some debate. Consistently appropriate decisions routinely are based on "changes" in harvest level, population structure or physical condition of the deer.

Anticipated Yields of Deer

Comparing the status of whitetail management in the Northeastern Hardwood and Spruce/Fir Forests region to that of other regions of whitetail range in North America requires an appreciation of the varied capabilities of habitat in the Northeast to sustain deer. Despite limitations in comparing information from different states, a general picture of carrying capacity can be devised using the most recent series of low deer population levels experienced throughout the region. These followed the aforementioned three successive severe winters (1968–1971), and are reflected by the estimated low buck harvests for 1971 and 1972. The picture is clouded by differences in the intensity of management and different management goals or achievements in particular areas.

In Maine (C. Banasiak personal communication:1983), with either-sex deer hunting and a northern and southern zone structure, harvests in the forest and farmland areas of the northern zone fell to 0.05–0.07 deer per square kilometer (0.14–0.17 per square mile). In the western and eastern forest border areas a low of 0.13 deer per square kilometer (0.34 per square mile) occurred. In the central forest area and southern farm woodlands, the whitetail harvests dipped to 0.25 and 0.35 deer per square kilometer (0.66 and 0.91 per square mile), respectively. Overall, the buck harvest for Maine in 1972 was 0.17 per square kilometer (0.44 per square mile), and the total harvest was 0.36 whitetail per square kilometer (0.94 per square mile).

New Hampshire (with a season structure similar to that of Maine) saw the harvest in Coos County in the north fall to 0.19 whitetail buck per square kilometer (0.5 per square mile). In the forest and farmland of Carroll and Grafton counties, the harvest dropped to 0.27 buck per square kilometer (0.7 per square mile). And in the central and western counties, it declined to 0.12 buck per square kilometer (0.3 per square mile), and to 0.08 per square kilometer (0.2 per square mile) in the more urban southeastern counties.

Lows in Vermont, with a buck-only season, were more difficult to group, but buck harvests of 0.15, 0.23, 0.27 and 0.46 per square kilometer (0.4, 0.6, 0.7 and 1.2 per square mile) were experienced in the northeastern counties. Harvests in the Upper Lake Champlain Valley counties fell to 0.12–0.23 bucks per square kilometer (0.3–0.6 per square mile). And in the central and southern counties, the harvest fell to levels of 0.35–0.42 bucks per square kilometer (0.9–1.1 per square mile).

In 1967, Massachusetts switched from an either-sex hunting season to antlered-buck and antlerless quota-system harvest management. The statewide deer harvest is achieved nearly entirely in the western forested portion of the state. In the early 1970s, buck harvests fell to 0.15 deer per square kilometer (0.3 per square mile), perhaps influenced to some degree by previous overharvesting.

Portions of New York's northern forested areas, with poor hunter access, were subject to a buck and antlerless quota system during the 1960s, but whitetail populations still were rising when the stressful winter sequence of 1968–1971 began. The harvest in these areas fell to 0.12–0.15 buck per square kilometer (0.3–0.4 per square mile) of deer range. The more accessible, managed forest areas adjacent to the Adirondacks were restricted to buck-only hunting, and harvests declined to 0.08–0.23 bucks per square kilometer (0.2–0.6 per square mile). Buck harvests in the Ontario/St. Lawrence and Lake Champlain Valley areas decreased to 0–0.08 deer per square kilometer (0–0.2 per square mile).

The harvest under buck and antlerless-deer quota systems in well-managed areas of the southern zone fell to a variety of levels in central and western management units, ranging from 0.5 to 1.35 bucks per square kilometer (1.3–3.5 per square mile) of deer range. In the Catskill region, harvest lows of 0.5–0.93 antlered whitetails per square kilometer (1.3–2.4 per square mile) were typical.

In Pennsylvania, with buck-only and two days of permit quota antlerless-deer hunting, low buck harvests of 0.90–1.03 per square kilometer (2.33–2.66 per square mile) were estimated for 12 northern counties.

These declines in 1971–1972 whitetail harvests represent 30 to 50 percent reductions from pre-1968 levels. Declines appeared to be less pronounced and recoveries more rapid in intensively managed units throughout the region. A deer population size per square mile may be crudely approximated by multiplying buck kill per square mile by a factor of 6 to 15, depending on hunting system, hunting pressure and whitetail population structure for the area in question.

Recent Deer Harvests

In Maine, about 200,000 hunters—15 percent of whom were nonresidents—harvested from 26,000 to 38,000 deer a year during the 1978–1982 period.

Maine's northern either-sex firearm season lasts nearly all November, and a southern season lasts about 19 days between the second and last weeks of November. Archery season takes place throughout most of October in the northern zone and ends with the beginning of the firearm season. In the southern zone, the archery season runs from the beginning of October to the opening of the firearm season. Sunday hunting is prohibited. A compulsory registration of bagged deer has been in effect since 1919. The 72,500 square kilometers (28,000 square miles) of whitetail range estimated for the state yields between 0.36 and 0.52 deer per square kilometer (0.93–1.36 per square mile).

In New Hampshire, 70,000 to 80,000 hunters—20 to 25 percent of whom are nonresidents—take between 4,700 and 11,500 deer each year. A consistent either-sex season, with a compulsory mail report and a north/south split (November 1–30 in the north and December 1–21 in the south), is supplemented with archery and muzzleloader seasons. An antlerless quota system now occurs in specific zones of the state. Approximately 97 percent of the state, or 22,670 square kilometers (8,750 square miles), is considered to be whitetail range, and its annual yield to recreational hunters is 0.19 to 0.52 deer per square kilometer (0.5–1.34 per square mile).

Vermont has 20,464 square kilometers (7,901 square miles) of deer range that attracts from 130,000 to 150,000 whitetail hunters each year, 40 to 45 percent of whom are nonresidents. The annual 16-day buck-only (7.6-centimeter:3-inch antler minimum) season begins 12 days before Thanksgiving. Since 1953, the annual yield has been 7,500 to 17,000 whitetails. An either-sex archery season, beginning in mid-October and lasting 16 days, has involved as many as 28,000 deer hunters and yielded up to 1,606 deer. A muzzleloader season is provided. Antlerless seasons, with permits issued to parties of hunters and a landowner-preference system, have been held when sportsmen and political support has been achieved. Antlerless seasons have not been frequent or consistent enough to demonstrate modern deer management benefits. In 1969, 10,657 permittees took 6,964 antlerless deer (Garland 1977). Buck harvests in the state yield about 0.39 to 0.83 deer per square kilometer (1.0–2.15 per square mile). Controlled antlerless harvests would result in more stable populations and a considerably higher average annual yield. At a statewide deer population density of 5.8 whitetails per square kilometer (15 per square mile), the allowable harvest could be 1.5 to 1.9 deer per square kilometer (4–5 per square mile) or 31,000 to 39,500 total, perhaps higher.

Since 1967, an antlerless-deer permit system has been used in Massachusetts with an antlered-buck firearm season of six days' duration in early December. An either-sex archery season occurs for two weeks in mid-November. Between 65,000 and 80,000 deer hunters participate each year, and the total harvest has reached 5,000 (the targeted level being 4,000–5,000). An antlerless harvest not to exceed 38 percent of the herd's female segment is desired. Most of Massachusetts deer range and deer hunting occurs in the Berkshires and the northern parts of the state adjacent to Vermont and New Hampshire. The buck harvest was 0.53 per square kilometer (1.36 per square mile) in 1981, and the total deer harvest often will exceed 0.77 per square kilometer (2.0 per square mile) under current management (J. McDonough personal communication:1983).

In New York, 700,000 to 800,000 hunters pursue white-tailed deer each year. Under a deer management system, with permits issued to parties of one to four individuals and a landowner preference, deer of either sex may be taken in addition to an antlered deer (antlers 7.6 centimeters:3 inches or more) in designated southern-zone management units. This system was initiated in the mid-to-late-1960s in parts of the northern zone, which contains about 40 percent of the state's deer range. Authority for using the antlerless-permit system was lost when killing does was blamed for the drastic decline of deer seen throughout the Northeast and elsewhere following the severe winters of 1968–1971.

The regular firearm season in the southern zone lasts for more than three weeks, beginning in mid-November. It is preceded by an either-sex archery season beginning in mid-October, and followed by five more days of either-sex archery hunting in December. A seven-day buck-only muzzleloader period completes the deer-hunting season.

Presently in New York's northern zone, a buck-only firearm season from late October through early December is preceded by a one-month either-sex archery season beginning in late September and overlapping with a seven-day, either-sex muzzleloader season taking place just before the opening of the regular firearms season.

A license stub mail-reporting program and a system of deer-check stations establish a reporting percentage and allow a harvest calculation. Until management can be applied statewide, a total annual harvest of between 100,000 and 120,000 whitetails is desirable. The 82,587 square kilometers (31,887 square miles) of deer range in New York—a 1964 estimate for 1959 conditions (Severinghaus and Sauer 1969)—should consistently yield 1.2 to 1.4 whitetails per square kilometer (3–3.5 per square mile), with explicit consideration for agriculture.

Parts of the northern one-third of Pennsylvania are within the Northeastern Hardwood and Spruce/Fir Forests region. Statewide, Pennsylvania has about 1,100,000 deer hunters, and the annual reported deer harvest is 100,000 to 150,000. Between 57 and 60 percent of the total take is reported (W. Shope personal communication:1983). Counties serve as deer management units. Each normally has a two-day antlerless-deer season (with a quota of permits) that follows a two-week buck-only season in early December. An either-sex archery season of up to 40 days during parts of September, October, December and January and an either-sex muzzleloader season also are provided. Mail reporting with check stations allows a calculation of the adult buck harvest. Deer age, weight and antler data were used previously to characterize the whitetail population status in each county. Deer sex and age, county of harvest, and hunter license number are now recorded for approximately 20,000 harvested deer of either sex each year. Reported harvests are adjusted to total harvests and used with age data to estimate pop-

A chance encounter with a prime whitetail buck in autumn is a rewarding experience in any region. In the Northeastern Hardwood and Spruce/Fir Forests region such encounters can and do occur because of a concerted effort by the represented states to ensure sustained wildlife resources and related recreational opportunities for all citizens. *Photo by Bill Cross; courtesy of the Maine Department of Inland Fisheries and Wildlife.*

ulations. Antlerless-deer quotas are established as a function of computed population levels, the desired overwintering population for each county, and hunter-success rate for the previous three years. Overwinter populations for each county are established from forest inventory data and desired deer densities of 15.4 deer per square kilometer (40 per square mile) for seedling/sapling acreage, 3.8 deer per square kilometer (10 per square mile) for pole-stage forest, and 7.7 deer per square kilometer (20 per square mile) for saw timber and noncommercial forest stands (W. Shope personal communication:1983).

Twelve counties (more or less the southern extremity of the Northeastern Hardwood and Spruce/Fir Forests region) account for about 30 percent of Pennsylvania's annual reported deer harvest. If the deer-range portion of these counties is similar to the 67-percent average estimated in New York, it then has provided an estimated yield of 2.75 to 4.5 deer per square kilometer (6.67–11.67 per square mile).

Effects of Deer Harvest Systems

A comparison of the sex and age structure of a whitetail population before and after a hunting season, and after winter losses are subtracted, can illustrate the influence of the three basic harvest systems used in the Northeastern Hardwood and Spruce/Fir Forests region.

Due to climatic and associated deer population variations in the region and a lack of public understanding and trust, hunting in Vermont and the northern zones of New York has been restricted to buck-only seasons in most years. Under this season type, the proportion of adult does increases in the population. Individual reproductive performance of does declines, along with the physical condition of both sexes, and each fawn crop maintains or worsens the situation. The forage used by the overabundant and protected does reduces the rate of fawn survival and, thereby, the annual increment to the harvestable population segment. Degraded habitat and associated deer physical condition means fewer yearling bucks will have legal antlers and thus will be excluded from the potential harvest yield. Deer population statistics from Vermont illustrate the sex and age structure of a whitetail population subjected to buck-only harvests (Table 54). Information on the female segment of the

Table 54. Representative sex and age structure of a white-tailed deer population subject to buck-only harvest in Vermont or northern New York.

Population segment	Number	Proportion in age class (percentage)[a]				
		Fawn	1.5 years	2.5 years	3.5 years	4.5 + years
Prehunting season						
Male	69	60	18	14	5	2
Female	139	29	10	12	14	35
Total	208					
Yield	17 (bucks)					
Posthunting season						
Male	52	78	10	8	3	1
Female	139	29	10	12	14	35
Total	191					
Postwinter						
Male	31	62	16	12	6	4
Female	119	16	12	14	17	41
Total	150					
Overwinter loss	41					

[a]Values adjusted to compensate for rounding and total 100 percent.

population was estimated from data on deer killed by autos and from periodic antlerless harvests (Day 1968, Garland 1977). It assumes: (1) male and female harvest is an unbiased sample of the population age structure; (2) approximately 17 percent of the yearling bucks do not bear legal antlers; (3) the sex ratio of adult whitetails killed by deer/vehicle collisions in early autumn is about 30 bucks:100 does; (4) the fawn/doe ratio is 80:100; (5) 60 percent of the adult buck population is harvested; 50 percent of fawns of both sexes die over winter; and (6) for the sake of simplicity, no adults are lost over winter. (In fact, the total turnover of females typically is 25 percent each year. Such a loss would prevent the population

growth seen under the above assumptions.)

A structure can be similarly illustrated—for a whitetail population in Maine or New Hampshire—that is regulated by the second basic type of harvest system, an either-sex hunting season (Table 55). In this case, season timing leads to a harvest favoring males (Banasiak 1964, 1977, White 1968a). A 20-percent total harvest mortality and a 0.95-fawn/doe ratio are reasonably typical. Other than an assumed 50-percent winter mortality of fawns, non-harvest mortality was not portrayed.

Data from a whitetail population at carrying capacity in New York (Hesselton and Sauer 1973) provide the basis for two final examples of management with a buck season and an ant-

Table 55. Representative sex and age structure of a white-tailed deer population subject to either-sex harvest in Maine or New Hampshire.

Population segment	Number	Proportion in age class (percentage)[a]				
		Fawn	1.5 years	2.5 years	3.5 years	4.5 + years
Prehunting season						
Male	108	28	26	19	9	18
Female	100	28	24	15	9	24
Total	208					
Yield	41 (18 antlered bucks, 16 does, 7 fawns)					
Posthunting season						
Male	83	29	25	19	10	17
Female	84	27	24	15	10	24
Total	168					
Postwinter						
Male	71	17	30	22	11	20
Female	72	15	28	18	11	28
Total	143					
Overwinter loss	24					

[a]Values adjusted to compensate for rounding and total 100 percent.

Table 56. Representative sex and age structure of a white-tailed deer population subject to buck-only harvest plus an antlerless-deer quota system, but with no overwinter losses, in New York.

Population segment	Number	Proportion in age class (percentage)[a]				
		Fawn	1.5 years	2.5 years	3.5 years	4.5+ years
Prehunting season						
Male	90	51	38	8	2	1
Female	118	35	31	16	7	11
Total	208					
Yield	87 (35 bucks, 32 does, 20 fawns)[b]					
Posthunting season						
Male	44	80	16	3	1	0
Female	77	42	19	14	6	19
Total	121					

[a]Values adjusted to compensate for rounding and total 100 percent.
[b]Commonly, other forms of mortality remove a percentage of the population each year, reducing the allowable yield.

lerless quota (tables 56 and 57). The reciprocal relationship between the sex ratio of the fawn crop in autumn and the ratio of adult bucks to adult does in an allowable harvest or composite annual mortality (Dickinson 1982) is shown.

For illustrative purposes Table 57 assumes that a similarly managed whitetail population encounters a severe winter loss *anticipated* by the resource manager. Its autumn, prehunting-season structure approximates full production and the population experiences no mortality other than hunter harvest and overwinter kill. A reduction of the harvest to maintain stable numbers of deer, despite an "anticipated"

winter loss of 50 percent of the fawn crop (accompanied by depressed reproductive ability), has an obvious effect. Protecting adult deer (1.5 years of age and older) to stabilize yield depresses the allowable yield by 42 percent and shifts the age structure of both males and females to older age classes. Accounting for differential seasonal mortality of adult deer, particularly sex-ratio differences, would require further reduction of the total yield. It also should be noted that this condition requires that the winter range support 158 deer instead of 121.

The difference between the deer populations

Table 57. Representative sex and age structure of a white-tailed deer population subject to buck-only harvest plus an antlerless-deer quota system, in a year of significant overwinter starvation.

Population segment	Number	Proportion in age class (percentage)[a]				
		Fawn	1.5 years	2.5 years	3.5 years	4.5+ years
Prehunting season						
Male	90	51	38	8	2	1
Female	118	35	31	16	7	11
Total	208					
Yield	50 (20 bucks, 18 does, 12 fawns)					
Posthunting season						
Male	64	63	30	6	1	0
Female	94	37	29	16	6	12
Total	158					
Postwinter						
Male	44	45	45	9	1	0
Female	77	23	36	20	8	13
Total	121					
Overwinter loss	37 (fawns)					
Reproduction[b]	87	(0)	(31)	(56)		
Prehunting season						
Male	90	51	22	22	4	8
Female	118	35	15	23	13	14
Total	208					

[a]Values adjusted to compensate for rounding and total 100 percent.
[b]Number contributed by age class due to reproduction of: 0 fawns per 1-year-old female fawn; 1.1 fawns per 2-year-old doe; and 1.8 fawns per 3-year-old and older doe.

reflected in Table 56 and Table 57 shows why biologists and resource managers seek to eliminate winter mortality and keep all age classes of the female segment as productive as possible. More deer are available, particularly more antlered deer, and less demand is placed on the winter habitat per unit of yield. Note that the loss of 37 harvestable deer is precisely the difference between 121 wintering deer (Table 57) and 158 wintering deer (Table 56) in this somewhat simplistic example. A more precise way to deal with such a habitat limitation would be to include a population-structure-and-yield adjustment to take advantage of the different energy demands of small (young) versus large (older) deer (Moen 1973).

At present, management attention in the region is focused on maintaining deer harvest levels that (1) sustain optimum whitetail populations within the carrying capacity of the region's divergent habitat types, (2) do not exceed landowner tolerance limits and (3) provide for optimum hunting and viewer/appreciative recreational uses of deer. Well-nourished, productive whitetail populations are the objective, inasmuch as such populations do not deplete their habitats and thereby do not gradually lower their own carrying capacity.

It is difficult to justify habitat management or attempts to convert other mortality to yield when deer population control has not been achieved in all areas. However, some attempts have been made, notably: cooperative management of winter habitat by woodland companies in New Hampshire, Maine, Vermont and New York; legal protection of deer winter habitat in Maine and Vermont; active winter-habitat management in New Hampshire; a conservation law enforcement program stressing public participation in Pennsylvania; and a deer trap-and-translocate effort in part of northern New York, with intensified law enforcement to overcome the suspected limiting factor—illegal killing of deer.

Socioeconomic Considerations

Values of deer usually offset the costs of deer. With proper whitetail population management, most values can be obtained with minimal or tolerable costs. Many values of whitetails and deer-related recreation are not measured in dollars. However, minimal economic values have been estimated on the premise that deer hunters, viewers and photographers "buy" their recreation by spending money for goods and services required for their recreation. Approximations for the Northeastern Hardwood and Spruce/Fir Forests region can be derived from a 1980 national survey by the U.S. Fish and Wildlife Service (1982). About $239 million was spent in 1980 in the region to hunt deer and $188 million was spent for trips to view or photograph whitetails. On a per-unit area basis, that approximates a minimum of $12 to $13 per hectare ($4.85–$5.25 per acre) per year for the entire region. The value per unit of deer range would be significantly higher. In New York, for example, it would be about $18.50 per hectare ($7.50 per acre).

Feeding together in summer are the coming autumn's whitetail-harvest potential and the next year's reproductive base. If they are members of a managed whitetail population that is in balance with forage supply during *each* critical season, both deer will recover from the rigors of the previous winter, grow, and fatten for the harvest or the coming winter. *Photo courtesy of the Maine Department of Inland Fisheries and Wildlife.*

The cost of human life and property damage due to deer/vehicle collisions is nearly impossible to estimate on a per-acre basis for the entire region. However, some sense of the magnitude of these losses can be gained. Reported highway mortality and hunting harvest figures indicate that, for every five or six deer harvested in Pennsylvania, at least one is killed on the highway.

In areas of more moderate climate, better soils and relatively gentle topography in the Northeastern Hardwood and Spruce/Fir Forests region, whitetail populations often cause significant agricultural damage long before they show physiological evidence of overpopulation. These populations have greater ability to withstand the rigors of winter due to the habitat's substantial diversity and relatively high productivity. Their proximity to human populations also tends to result in relatively high hunting pressure, and managed harvests can prevent population eruption. Populations of from 5 to 17 whitetails per square kilometer (15–45 per square mile) may be sustained, depending on landowner tolerance of agricultural and forestry impacts. Deer populations of from 4.6 to 5.8 per square kilometer (12–15 per square mile) in many situations—with a corresponding buck harvest of from 0.38 to 0.77 per square kilometer (1–2 per square mile)—can be tolerated even by the most sensitive fruit-growing landowners (Brown et al. 1978). In a dairy-farming community, populations 2 to 3 times as large may be tolerable to farmers (Decker et al. 1981).

The impact of whitetail populations on woodlot forestry in agricultural areas is not well documented. However, impacts of high deer populations on Alleghany hardwood forests were estimated as $32+ per hectare ($13+ per acre) annually (Marquis 1981), and agricultural damage in Potter County, Pennsylvania, has been reported at $142,000 (Carroll 1961). Deer in the Adirondacks can contribute to the conversion of a $100–200-per-thousand-board-feet stand of beech/birch/maple to a $35-per-thousand-board-feet, or less, two-story beech monoculture (Tierson et al. 1966, Behrend et al. 1970). However, Pennsylvania deer enclosure studies in northern hardwood plots have *not* shown similar results even at much higher densities (21 deer per square kilometer [55 per square mile] to 82 deer per square kilometer [213 per square mile]). Silvicultural procedures and the condition of regeneration prior to clearcutting have been suggested as contributing factors in a management question more complex than sometimes appreciated (W. Shope personal communication:1983). Climate, soil potentials, coppice growth, and the seasonal availability of whitetail forage alternatives to the commercially desired species probably are part of the regional puzzle. Obtaining benefits from deer and timber is the challenge in each situation. Where spruce and fir are the desired forest products, and fir is more susceptible to windthrow or spruce budworm loss, whitetail browsing on hardwoods and fir may be beneficial.

An autumn whitetail population of 5.8 deer per square kilometer (15 per square mile) has been discussed as a "safe" level for forest regeneration and "typical" agricultural areas of the region. It also is a population level that, under intensive management, might be compatible with winter range resources and conditions for most of the region. Although some portions of the region do not appear to be capable of sustaining such populations, much of the region's pasture land has a higher tolerance and support capacity for deer. Under even-aged management, northern hardwood stands may only require such protection for 5 to 10 years of an 80–100-year rotation. In some areas, deer may not affect regeneration significantly. Such a population level probably is conservative. Nevertheless, at current harvest success rates, such a population could support 3 to 5 million whitetail hunters. Conversely, the 1.4 million persons who now hunt deer in the region would have to harvest one whitetail for every 2 to 3 hunters—a very significant improvement in harvest success rate. Furthermore, there is no reason to suspect that nonhunting benefits would be reduced. Such a whitetail population could generate up to $32+ per hectare ($13+ per acre) per year due to increased hunter and sustained nonhunting benefits *without* incurring costs of $32 per hectare ($13 per acre) or more. Thus, the total value of management would be about $64.25 per hectare ($26 per acre) annually.

Such values do not accrue evenly. Some areas have limited recreational access. The New England states experience nonresident recreationist expenditures nearly equal to resident expenditures, while in New York and Pennsylvania, nonresidents account for only 10 and 19 percent, respectively. Achieving the right mix of land uses and corresponding levels of deer productivity is not a simple land-management problem.

MANAGEMENT OF DEER WINTERING HABITATS

In the Northeastern Hardwood and Spruce/ Fir Forests region, there is no single management formula to protect or enhance winter habitats. Such habitats include south-facing pastures in southern New York, steep west- and north-facing hemlock slopes in Vermont, hemlock/fir/spruce/yellow birch/red maple forests in the Adirondacks, white cedar swamps in New Hampshire, strip-harvested spruce/fir flats in Maine and pure hardwood slopes on the Appalachian Plateau. The boundaries of occupied winter range units are expanded or contracted by snowfall and temperature fluctuations that condition snowpacks and impede or expand deer movement patterns. Starvation during the previous winter or a particularly heavy autumn harvest can reduce the number and distribution of whitetails on a given winter range.

Despite great concern over the limiting effect of winter on whitetails and the usually limited amount of winter range in most of the region, direct habitat management to increase such range has not been a frequent undertaking. The principal management emphasis to date has been habitat protection; first, through deer population control, second, through cooperation with timber companies and, finally, by statutory restriction of habitat modification. The characteristics of deer wintering range—at least the traditional conifer yarding habitat (Gill 1957*b*)—have become well enough known that their presence can be predicted from forest inventory data (Weber et al. 1981). Production of new yards has not been attempted to any great extent, probably because the current deer resource is not fully utilized and social aspects of deer yarding behavior in traditional sites might preclude deer use of new but unlocated wintering habitats. Trying to produce a softwood shelter area, of conifer tree species other than spruce, adjacent to an existing and used wintering area is considered futile.

Programs to protect and improve existing deer wintering habitat have been developing in the region since the 1950s. The New Hampshire program of cooperative agreements with timber companies has produced demonstrably more stable local deer populations (Wiley et

Trails used heavily by wintering whitetails confined by 51 centimeters (20 inches) or more of accumulated snow may be essential in parts of the Northeastern Hardwood and Spruce/Fir Forests region from late December to early April. Ideally, travel on such trails will cost a deer no more energy than is gained by food resources to which the trail network leads. *Photo by John Hall; courtesy of the Vermont Fish and Game Department.*

al. 1978). Biologists and timber company foresters prepare management and specific cutting plans to protect, enhance and, if possible, regenerate wintering habitats for deer. Hardwood-stand management is integrated with proximate winter habitat to produce a stable browse supply. Tree-cutting schedules emphasize leaving 60 percent of existing and potential upper age and size classes, protecting core shelter areas, and regenerating softwood sites through marked-wood partial cutting or all-age management.

Maine's cooperative program shifted to a regulatory process with establishment of a Land Use Regulatory Commission in 1971. Winter range units were identified and established through formal hearings. Permits are required for timber harvesting in zoned winter range areas, and state wildlife biologists guide the cutting plans. The biologists and forest managers attempt to maintain approximately 50 percent of the softwood shelter portion of yarding areas at heights of 10.7 meters (35 feet) or more and with a crown closure of 70 percent or more. Ideally, the remainder of the concen-

To permit deer movement to nearby browse-producing stands, areas where conifers intercept snow must be maintained in the forest management plans for spruce/fir forests of the region. *Photo by Tom Carbone; courtesy of the Maine Department of Inland Fisheries and Wildlife.*

tration area is managed for a replacement sequence of seedlings, saplings and pole-size trees on a 15-year cutting cycle. Where clearcutting is used, openings are limited to 2 hectares (5 acres) or strips not exceeding 2 chains (40.2 meters:132 feet) in width. Even-age stand composition is broken with lighter cuts at shorter intervals, and integrated with management of adjoining stands, particularly as the latter contribute to hardwood browse production (Marston 1977).

In Vermont and New York, maps showing the locations of deer wintering areas have been distributed as a reference to help avoid conflicts as individuals, corporations or agencies contemplate development, roadway construction, utility corridors, etc. Under Vermont's land-use and development law, Act 250, most development plans are subject to review and require permits. Winter deer habitat value has been upheld in Act 250 hearings. However, most success in maintaining deer wintering areas has come about through cooperative planning to avoid or mitigate development impacts. Only state and local governmental agencies or publicly funded projects in New York are subject to impact review. Although materials identifying and describing wintering areas are requested routinely to modify proposed developments so as to avoid or minimize adverse impacts on deer winter habitats, outright prevention of development has not yet occurred on a significant scale.

THE FUTURE

In the foreseeable future, white-tailed deer management in the Northeastern Hardwood and Spruce/Fir Forests region likely will increase its focus on human dimensions—specifically, people's expectations, demands for and conflicts with whitetails as a significant biological, aesthetic and recreational resource. There seems now to be enough expertise to manage the region's deer populations and habitats successfully, at least to the extent that financial constraints and biopolitical pressures permit. However, the human population in this region will intensify its requirements for uses of and products from the land. Additional investments, knowledge and management skill will be necessary to retain and enhance key habitats and keep the whitetail populations productive and at optimal size. Increased public understanding of the values of white-tailed deer and appreciation for the role of scientifically-based management will be needed to provide the support and wherewithal for what inevitably will be intensified management.

Chapter 15

APPALACHIAN MOUNTAINS

Paul A. Shrauder
Staff Officer
Range, Timber and Wildlife
U.S. Forest Service
Jefferson National Forest
Roanoke, Virginia

The white-tailed deer is one of the most studied and intensively managed game animals in the Appalachian Mountains region. Its values as an aesthetic, ecological and recreational resource are virtually incalculable. But it can be said with a strong degree of certainty that the whitetail is the region's most popular wildlife species.

The region itself contains three distinct physiographic provinces and three major forest types overlapping parts of 12 states. Even excluding the geopolitical boundaries, the region is so diverse—in terms of geography, vegetation, meteorological influences and land use—that it is difficult to analyze and discuss the whitetail as a singular, regional biological entity. When the political components are added—including differing deer management goals, objectives and practices—the task of characterizing the region's whitetail population(s) is nearly prohibitive.

Nevertheless, this chapter examines the white-tailed deer of the entire Appalachian Mountains region. Generalizations are made when possible—based on information from throughout the region—and supported by site-specific examples.

ENVIRONMENT

Physiography

The Appalachian Mountains region is an irregularly shaped mountainous area of approximately 480,000 square kilometers (185,330 square miles) extending about 1,450 kilometers (900 miles) from southern New York to northern Alabama (Weeks et al. 1968). It consists of three physiographic areas—the Blue Ridge, Valley and Ridge, and the Appalachian Plateaus—and includes parts of New York, Pennsylvania, Maryland, Virginia, Kentucky, Tennessee, Ohio, North Carolina, South Carolina, Georgia and Alabama, and all of West Virginia (Figure 77). It forms a transitional zone between the northeastern and central hardwood regions to the north and west and the coastal

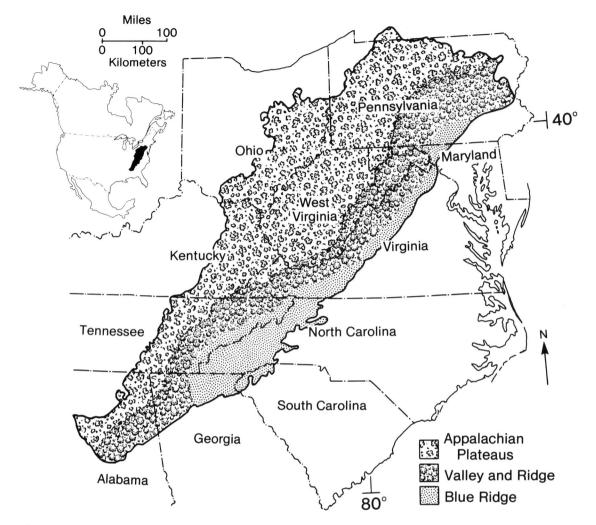

Figure 77. The Appalachian Mountains region. It includes three geographical areas in parts of 12 states (modified from Fenneman 1938).

plain, southern pine and southern bottomland hardwood regions to the east, south and west (Barrett 1962).

Elevations range from 305 meters (1,000 feet) in Alabama to more than 1,800 meters (5,900 feet) in the Great Smokies. Relief varies from 150 to 750 meters (492–2,460 feet) and slopes from 15 to 45 degrees or more.

Vegetation

The three major forest types (Figure 78) are: (1) mixed mesophytic forest occupying the unglaciated Appalachian Plateau from northern Alabama to northwestern Pennsylvania (*see also* Chapter 16); (2) Appalachian oak forest centered in the Blue Ridge and Valley and Ridge

provinces; and (3) northern hardwood forest, extending from central New York to central Pennsylvania, with outliers reaching into the high Allegheny Mountains of West Virginia.

A fourth type, identified by Küchler (1966) as the oak/hickory/pine forest, occurs in two significant portions of the region, both principally within the Valley and Ridge province. The northernmost portion extends southward from southcentral Pennsylvania to westcentral Virginia. The pine component is predominantly yellow pine. The other portion is at the southernmost part of the region, and loblolly pine is the primary pine species represented. Although pines in both portions are particularly important to whitetails—primarily as cover plants—in the region, the forest type is not considered here as major, since pines represent less than about 20 percent of the forested area. The forest type is recognized, then, as an intergrade among the three major forest types of the region.

Mixed mesophytic forest. Existing vegetation is substantially different from that of presettlement times. A considerable amount of the land has been converted to crop or forage production and to urban and industrial development. Land remaining in forests has been cut repeatedly (often selectively), burned, and in many cases grazed. Most forests contain an overstory of trees less than 100 years old and of poor form. The lands usually are understocked and even-aged, but some are two-aged

as a result of high-grading (selective logging of designated species and ages). Since white settlement and loss of the American chestnut there has been a reduction in uneven-aged mixed mesophytic forest communities and an increase in even-aged mixed oak and oak/hickory communities (Braun 1950). This change implies a greater degree of lignification in understory vegetation and greater mast production. Exceptions to these two trends occur on protected mesic sites, especially cove positions, where the well-developed mixed mesophytic forests were replaced by nearly pure stands of yellow poplar.

Initial harvesting of virgin upland forests from the mid-1800s to the 1920s consisted of con-

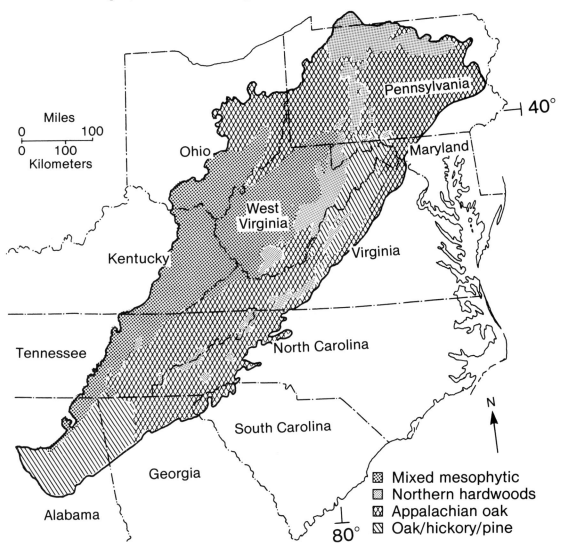

Figure 78. Forest types of the Appalachian Mountains region (from Küchler 1966).

tinuous clearcuts of entire mountains, often encompassing thousands of acres and usually followed by fire. Since then, high-grading of second-growth stands probably has occurred at least once, and in many cases two or three times. Many of the present second-growth forest stands are being clearcut. However, the harvest unit is relatively small (10–30 hectares: 25–74 acres), and is separated in space by an area of equal size or larger.

The intensity of forest tree removal for lumber and pulp also has changed greatly from that of the original cuts. In the virgin forests, only the highest quality material was removed and as much as 40 to 50 percent or more of the above-ground phytomass was left on site to decay in place. Today, in areas where there are both sawtimber and fiber markets, harvest removal may include all trees down to an 8–10-centimeter (3.1–3.9-inch) diameter and represent 90-percent of the above-ground phytomass.

At higher elevations, the former old-growth northern hardwood stands now contain a much larger proportion of birch, pin cherry and red maple (Braun 1950). Extensive pure stands of eastern white pine have been largely eliminated. Many former areas of old-growth red spruce appear to have been altered so radically by cutting and burning as to preclude the reintroduction of spruce (Core 1966). Thickets of aspen, pin cherry and hawthorn prevail in some areas. Occasionally a dense cover of herbaceous perennials and ferns will form a meadow community, while other areas have the appearance of heath barrens.

Secondary forests more closely reflect topographic and edaphic variation in the landscape than did presettlement forests (Braun 1950). Accordingly, current differences in vegetation between south- and north-facing slopes and between limestone/ and sandstone/shale-derived soils are perhaps greater than in the past. This increased sensitivity to site, coupled with increased cutting and clearing, leads to the conclusion that present-day landscapes offer a greater diversity of plant communities

Whitetail buck in typical pine (yellow/loblolly) forest type in the Appalachian Mountains region. All pine species in the region are gradually decreasing. *Photo courtesy of the Georgia Department of Natural Resources.*

Whitetail doe in typical stand of mixed mesophytic forest of the Appalachian Mountains region. *Photo courtesy of the U.S. Forest Service.*

than did presettlement landscapes. This is due to lesser amounts of settlement clearing and catastrophic modification (fire, disease and ice storms) than have occurred in more recent times.

Studies in West Virginia illustrate how cultural practices have changed the vegetational complex in the mixed mesophytic forest (Core 1966). About one-fourth of the vascular plant species now growing wild in that state were introduced. The bulk of these species are forbs and grasses that form a substantial acreage of early successional stage communities. They include active and recently abandoned cropland, recently cutover or burned-over forest land, pasture, roadsides, suburban lands and industrial wastelands, particularly surface-mine spoils. Introduced shrubs, such as multiflora rose, also are important vegetational components, especially on abandoned farmlands.

Appalachian oak forest. Before loss of American chestnut as a significant species, the forest type was recognized as oak/chestnut (Braun 1950). Chestnuts still occur sporadically throughout the region, but are eliminated by blight after reaching a diameter of about 15 to 20 centimeters (6–8 inches).

In contrast to the mixed mesophytic forest, the existing vegetation in Appalachian oak forests appears to be little modified relative to presettlement times, except for the elimination of the American chestnut and reduction of yellow pine types. In the more xerophytic and less productive landscapes of this forest type, cultivation has been confined largely to major valleys underlain by limestone, and to heads of coves and flat-topped ridges (Robison 1960). Since their clearing, which began in the early to mid-1800s, most of these lands have remained in cultivation or been taken over by urban expansion. The xerophytic and relatively nonproductive slopes adjacent to the lowlands have remained forested for the most part, although subject to repeated cutting and burning. Timber harvesting in the Appalachian oak forests was spread over a relatively long period and occurred in less extensive units than did harvests of the mixed mesophytic forest. The overall landscape pattern tends to appear as large blocks of nonforested land alternating with equally large blocks of forested land, with a relatively little transition from nonforest to forest.

Northern hardwood forest. Most of the present forests originated from large-scale clearcutting near the turn of the present century and contrast dramatically with old-growth presettlement forests (Marquis 1975). In poorly drained areas, tree regeneration has been completely or severely restricted, giving rise to "savannahs" or "orchards" with a few scattered trees—mostly black cherry, sugar maple, red maple and aspen (Horsley 1977a, 1977b). Such areas exhibit a dense cover of ferns, grasses and forbs. Better drained upland sites are occupied by stands of black cherry, red and sugar maple, and white ash. Understory vegetation is spotty, with patches of herbaceous ground cover and scattered tree regeneration. The limited regeneration appears to be related to a number of factors, including fire, overbrowsing by white-tailed deer and rabbits, frost, and competition with herbaceous vegetation (Horsley 1977a, 1977b).

White-tailed deer in the northern hardwood forest type of the Appalachian Mountains region. *Photo by Stanley E. Forbes.*

Land Use and Soils

Following the Civil War, the region's timber resources were exploited and, in many areas, mountains were denuded. This had a detrimental impact on soil-related site qualities, and delayed timber and wildlife production for future generations (U.S. Forest Service 1970). Agriculture was inhibited because the mountainous terrain was difficult to cultivate and soils were thin, stony and easily eroded.

Pasture and cropland account for about 30 percent of the land use in the region (Davies 1968). The largest block of farming land is concentrated in the Hagerstown and Shenandoah valleys of the Valley and Ridge province (Austin 1965). This is due to the low relief and rich soils that occur over limestone (Davies 1968). Lands devoted to hay and feed grains generally are restricted to small fields along valleys and lower slopes. Ownership is mostly in small private holdings; about 65 percent of the land is forested and used mainly for recreation and timber production. Some of the larger tracts are controlled by federal and state governments, and others are owned by coal mining and timber companies.

In the Blue Ridge province, soils are derived mainly from metamorphic and igneous rock (Davies 1968). They are generally several feet thick and have better inherent fertility than do soils derived from the sandstone and shales of the other provinces (G. Hawkins personal communication:1980).

The Valley and Ridge province is characterized by long ridges separated by deep valleys. Soils on the narrow ridges and steep side slopes are generally shallow to only a few feet thick and low in inherent fertility. The small coves and toe slopes usually have deep colluvial soils. Valley soils are derived from shale and limestone and are relatively fertile. Alluvial soils occur along the major streams and rivers. The stream systems tend to be angular and commonly are referred to as having a trellis pattern (Davies 1968).

Soils in the Appalachian Plateau are similar to those in the Valley and Ridge province. However, in contrast to the trellislike stream pattern of the Valley and Ridge, the mountains of the Appalachian Plateau are incised with wandering stream courses that give way to a dendritic stream pattern. Water seeps and springs are more common in the Appalachian provinces than in the region's other provinces.

Climate and Weather

Generally, the Appalachian climate can be termed as moderate (U.S. Soil Conservation Service 1968). In winter and into early summer, arctic air moves down into central portions of the country and then eastward. During this period, afternoon convection storms are common in the south, whereas the frontal storm dominates in the north (Van der Leeden and Troise 1974).

Annual precipitation ranges from 89 centimeters (35 inches) in the north to more than 140 centimeters (55 inches) in the south. The average is approximately 109 centimeters (43 inches). The highest recorded annual precipitation exceeds 203 centimeters (80 inches) in western North Carolina.

Average annual temperatures range from 10 degrees Celsius (50 degrees Fahrenheit) in the northern end of the mountains to 18 degrees Celsius (65 degrees Fahrenheit) in the southern mountains. Despite the region's relatively close proximity to the Atlantic Ocean and the Gulf of Mexico, the temperature is not modified by these water bodies because of the region's easterly movement of the air masses.

WHITETAIL POPULATIONS

History

Each state, acting independently, has experienced the rise and fall and rise again of whitetail populations in the Appalachian Mountains (Severinghaus and Brown 1956). During the early 1900s, the white-tailed deer nearly was extirpated from the entire region. The states almost simultaneously recognized the need for regulating whitetail hunting, and an aroused public supported efforts to salvage, rebuild and maintain the deer population. These efforts first involved protection from harvest, then restocking followed by habitat improvements, and finally, management through research and regulated harvests. Following extensive forest clearcutting in the Southeast during the 1920s, whitetail populations increased dramatically due to the emergence of more favorable habitat and the deer's own adaptability. However, as population densities increased, both deer and their habitat deteriorated, and it soon was obvious that an overabundance of deer was more of a problem

Early 1900s clearcut in mixed mesophytic forest in Jackson County, Kentucky. The area shown (a northwest exposure) now supports a yellow poplar/white oak/northern red oak stand that is favorable white-tailed deer habitat. However, at the time of intensive forest cutting in this area and throughout much of the Appalachian Mountains region, whitetails—unable to withstand the combined effects of extensive habitat loss and unregulated deer harvests—were nearly extirpated. With the emergence of second-growth forest and enforced game laws, whitetail populations in much of the region experienced a dramatic increase during the 1920s. *Top photo courtesy of Bruce Slover. Bottom photo courtesy of the Pennsylvania Game Commission.*

than too few. It also became apparent that hunting only bucks did not curtail a growing deer population and doe hunting eventually became an accepted practice. Finally, wildlife managers realized that "people management" was a necessary prerequisite for proper deer management.

The modern history of whitetails in Virginia probably is typical for deer populations throughout the Appalachian region. With deer populations on the decline in the 1700s and 1800s, Virginia—in 1849—was the first state with seasonal restrictions on deer hunting west of the Blue Ridge Mountains. Nevertheless, by 1900 the whitetail populations in the mountains of Virginia had been nearly eradicated. Very few deer population increases were noted (less than 700 deer were harvested statewide each year) until the extensive clearcut operations of the 1920s. Since then, whitetails have increased to more than 411,000 animals statewide (Peery and Coggin 1978), and the annual deer harvest now exceeds 60,000.

Today, throughout the Appalachian Mountains region, the whitetail probably attracts more interest and attention from sportsmen and wildlife officials than does any other game species.

Population Characteristics

There are no reliable data from which to calculate white-tailed deer populations in the Appalachian region. Most states estimate deer numbers statewide, but do not delineate the populations by region or area. Whitetail populations vary within the Appalachian Mountains region. In general, however, the deer populations in the Appalachian Mountains are smaller than those of the Piedmont and coastal plains. At present, whitetail populations generally are increasing in all three regions, and either-sex hunting seasons are needed to keep deer from exceeding habitat carrying capacity.

The pattern of deer hunting regulations throughout most of the region tends to be on the conservative side. Selective antlered-deer hunting predominates and has resulted in a population with a high proportion of does (Hergenrader and Wooten 1978).

Generally, deer populations in the Appalachian region are in healthy condition. With few exceptions, yearling bucks attain 45-kilogram (100-pound) hog-dressed body weight by No-

vember. The state wildlife agencies have used information on body weight, antler development and reproductive rates to educate deer hunters to the need for harvesting antlerless deer and thus keeping populations within the range carrying capacity.

Productivity

Throughout most of the Appalachian Mountains region, the white-tailed deer breeding season begins in early October and continues to the middle of January. It usually peaks the latter part of November, but generally a little later in the more southern states. In the mountains of Alabama, for example, the peak breeding dates ranged from December 1 through February 5 (Davis 1979).

According to most research in the Appalachian Mountains region, the majority of does breed first at 1.5 years of age (*see* Forbes et al. 1979). Only 10 percent or less of the fawns breed, depending to a large extent on their age and condition. The first time a female is bred she usually produces a single fawn, but at the second birth twins are quite common. Although rare, triplets—and an occasional quadruplet—have been recorded in areas of excellent habitat condition in Pennsylvania (Forbes et al. 1979). When undernourished, adult does frequently carry only single fetuses, generally female. On portions of the deer range where competition for food is great, twin fawns frequently are both female. On the other hand, male offspring predominate in first-time births to females on a high nutritional level, whether the births are single or multiple. This varies throughout the region according to soil fertility and its influence on available food and other habitat factors.

On the average, adult does produce 1.5 fawns per year when and where the Appalachian habitat is not overcrowded and the nutritional level is adequate.

Food and Feeding Habits

White-tailed deer move slowly while browsing on twigs and leaves. Usually they do not feed long on one plant, but pick and select as they move, often choosing between plants of the same species growing side by side. They also graze and utilize herbaceous plants, depending on the availability of the plants, time of year and soil type. Winter months are the most critical for food.

Harlow and Hooper (1972) analyzed the deer diet in the southern Appalachians by examining the rumen content of 298 deer. Food consumed in greatest abundance during the spring included green deciduous leaves and succulent stems of woody plants and green herbaceous stems and leaves. Yellow poplar fruit and green leaves, acorns, apples, and leaves of sourwood, honeysuckle, blueberry, blackberry, and legumes were the dominant items. The most abundant summer foods were green leaves of red maple, oak, sourwood, flowering dogwood and honeysuckle, leaves and stems of legumes, fruits of chinaberry, and fungi. Oak mast was the most abundant food item in autumn. Also, fruits of apple, persimmon and grape and green leaves of rhododendron and honeysuckle frequently were eaten. The most abundant evergreen forbs were galax and wintergreen. Other important food items included grasses, sedges and fungi. Major foods in the winter included dried leaves of deciduous woody plants, green herbaceous stems and leaves, grasses, sedges, and mushrooms. Hardened woody stems occurred frequently but in small amounts. Individual items included rhododendron, dry leaves of oak and green leaves of mountain laurel, honeysuckle and galax. Although rhododendron leaves frequently were found in autumn and winter samples, their presence in the diet indicated a shortage of palatable food.

SPECIAL PROBLEMS AND CONSTRAINTS

Limiting Factors

Severe winter weather—such as ice storms and deep and persistent snows—is considered a significant limiting factor only in the northern portion of the Appalachian Mountains (Forbes et al. 1979, Drake et al.1978, R. Miller personal communication:1980). However, the quantity and quality of available food is a significant factor throughout the region, particularly during winter.

Honeysuckle is an important year-round food of white-tailed deer in the Appalachian Mountains region. *Photo by Stanley E. Forbes.*

An alert 2.5-year-old whitetail buck interrupted while feeding in a dense stand of rhododendron. *Photo by E. E. Ripper; courtesy of the U.S. Forest Service.*

Whitetail does in hemlock/northern hardwood forest. Severe winter weather can be a significant limiting factor for deer in the northern part of the Appalachian Mountains region. Deep and prolonged snow cover can severely limit winter food availability or accessibility in the region, particularly in the more mountainous areas. *Photo courtesy of the Pennsylvania Game Commission.*

In several cases, areas of low soil fertility and accompanying low-quality forage scattered throughout the Appalachian Mountains region are responsible for decreased range-carrying capacities for deer and lowered natality weights, growth rate and size, and antler development (Cromer 1967, C. M. Smith 1974, DeGarmo and Gill 1958, Kubota and Swanson 1958, Severinghaus et al. 1950, Cheatum and Severinghaus 1950, Nixon 1965*b*, Coffman 1968, R. Miller personal communication:1980, W. G. Moore personal communication:1980, P. Shatley personal communication:1980).

Limited food supplies in conjunction with severe winter weather were a significant limiting factor in the northern Appalachians (Drake et al. 1978), and were responsible for low carrying capacities in the mountains of South Carolina (P. Shatley personal communication:1980).

Throughout the Appalachian Mountains region the most serious predators of the whitetail, other than man, are free-ranging dogs, especially where there are low populations of deer and in recently-stocked areas (Perry and Giles 1971, Peery and Coggin 1978, M. Smith 1974, Cromer 1966, Forbes et al. 1979).

Poaching is considered a general limiting factor, especially in areas with a low deer population (M. Smith 1974, Cromer 1967), as are automobiles in areas with both high deer and human populations (Forbes et al. 1979, Cromer 1967).

Predation of whitetails by dogs and illegal hunting are not serious in most parts of the Appalachian Mountains. Predation, however, can be a problem in newly stocked areas, and both predation and poaching can be limiting factors where deer populations are low. *Left photo courtesy of the North Carolina Wildlife Resources Commission. Right photo by Ted Borg; courtesy of the South Carolina Wildlife and Marine Resources Department.*

Disease and parasite infestations are serious only where deer populations are high, as in parts of Pennsylvania and Virginia, and in areas where habitat has been depleted to such an extent that the animals are in poor physical condition, as in parts of West Virginia (*see* Forbes et al. 1979, Peery and Coggin 1978).

Competition

Whitetail competition with other mammals for food is minimal in the Appalachian Mountains region. However, overpopulations of deer and subsequent overbrowsing often destroy the habitat of rabbits, hares, grouse and numerous small mammals that depend on a bushy understory for food and cover (Forbes et al. 1979).

Conflicts

Conflicts between deer and other land users are a major problem in many areas of the Appalachians. In many farmland localities, deer damage to agricultural crops has generated serious concern.

In the northern portion of the region, after a harvest cut, browsing by deer often retards or eliminates the growth of new forest stands important for timber production (Jordan 1967,

Marquis and Grisez 1978, Forbes et al. 1979, Drake and Forbes 1971). In the southern portion, deer seldom cause serious damage to young forest stands, probably due to the greater number of stems per acre, the longer growing season, and lower deer populations (Moore and Johnson 1967). Browsing damage may be severe, however, when fertilized seedlings are planted in regeneration areas, even where the deer population is relatively low (Davis 1979).

Deer damage to truck farms, small grains, and fruit orchards is common throughout most of the region, and quite serious in some areas. Young fruit trees are especially susceptible. If not damaged by browsing, they often are killed by bucks rubbing their antlers during the rut (Peery and Coggin 1968, Forbes et al. 1979, DeGarmo and Gill 1958, P. Shatley personal communication:1980). Some states, such as Virginia, appraise deer damage and compensate landowners.

Control of agricultural crop and timber damages often involves some type of deer repellant or expensive deer-proof fencing (DeGarmo and Gill 1958, Forbes et al. 1979). But the principal method of reducing whitetail damage is by regulated hunter harvest of deer, with relatively liberal harvests in areas or management units where damages are most severe and persistent.

Twenty-one-year-old conifer plantation damaged by intensive whitetail browsing in Elk County, Pennsylvania. White spruce was severely retarded and red pine completely eliminated by deer. *Photo by Stanley E. Forbes.*

Repellents are applied to conifer seedlings prior to planting, for protection against whitetail browsing damage. Where deer damage in the Appalachian Mountains region is extensive, fencing exclosures also are used. The cost of such measures is justified in most instances by minimization of damage payments and maintenance of whitetail numbers at a level consistent with public demand. *Photo by Stanley E. Forbes.*

MANAGEMENT

Hunter Harvest

Practically all of the Appalachian Mountains region now supports huntable populations of white-tailed deer. In fact, the deer harvests have increased substantially throughout the region in recent decades.

Hunting regulations generally are set by the state wildlife agencies. Rifle and/or shotgun seasons, during which whitetails are harvested most, range from a minimum of three days to more than two months. Bag limits range from one deer per season to one buck per day for a 70-day season in Alabama. Bag limits tend to be more liberal in the southern states of the region. Antlerless or either-sex hunting seasons, some by permit only, are held in most of the states.

The setting of seasons and other regulations often is influenced by political pressures sometimes contrary to biological recommendations. Hunter opposition to doe harvests is an example of a continuing argument that sometimes is resolved contrary to the biological best interests of the deer population. However, doe harvests are beginning to be understood by hunters, the public, and decision makers as a necessary means in certain areas and for certain periods of time to regulate and manage a whitetail population effectively and productively.

Special archery and primitive-weapons hunting seasons are becoming increasingly popular. In most states they are confined to particular management units and do not coincide with the gun season(s). In all states, these special seasons account for only a small percentage of the harvest.

The annual harvest in New York is calculated from the number of hunters who report having bagged deer, with compensation then made for the number who do not report their kill. To obtain as reliable a harvest count as possible, a number of the states require deer hunters to tag the animals they bag and present the animals at a check station. Except for Pennsylvania and Alabama, all other states represented in the region monitor hunter harvests of whitetails by means of check stations. South Carolina additionally conducts surveys of hunting clubs, and Georgia also uses a mail-in reporting format. Pennsylvania uses the mail-in system and spot checks of locker plants and

Although archery and primitive weapon hunting for whitetails are growing rapidly in popularity in the Appalachian Mountains region, they account for only a small percentage of the annual deer harvest. The author is shown with a large nine-point buck bagged with a .50-caliber Thompson-Center Hawkins muzzleloader on the Jefferson National Forest, Virginia (*see* Cochran 1978). *Photo by Bill Cochran; courtesy of the Roanoke (Va.) Times and World-News.*

other processing facilities. Alabama, at present, does not have a set procedure for harvest registration or inventory.

Throughout much of the Appalachian Mountains region and particularly in the northern portions, deer hunting is an important annual social event. Many permanent camps have existed for decades, hosting a number of generations of hunters from the same family or friendship groups. However, the camp tradition is changing. Today, given greater mobility, and with increased pressure for space by a growing number of hunters, a majority of whitetail hunters are inclined to drive from home early in the morning and return home when the day's hunt is concluded. Nevertheless, deer hunting still is a major outdoor recreation in the region and, in most states, is an important stimulus of local economies (Forbes et al. 1979, Peery and Coggin 1978, Severinghaus 1974).

Whitetail hunting in the Appalachian Mountains region is an increasingly popular recreation. The deer population and hunter harvest also have grown in proportion to that popularity. Although the region is not known for producing many Boone and Crockett trophy bucks, there are whitetails with excellent racks and harvest rates are high. Furthermore, hunters have a variety of wilderness and semiwilderness conditions from which to choose. *Left photo courtesy of the Pennsylvania Game Commission. Right photo courtesy of the Kentucky Department of Fish and Wildlife Resources.*

Current Practices, Policies and Philosophies

Although white-tailed deer management philosophies are strikingly similar from state to state throughout the Appalachian Mountains region, management practices and policies vary according to economics, politics and public opinion. For example, all states agree that deer should be harvested in numbers sufficient to hold the populations at or below the capacity of the range (Madson 1961), but emphasis on doe harvest to meet this objective differs markedly from state to state. Virginia, for example, recommends that does constitute 30 to 40 percent of the total harvest when the intent is to hold the population at a stable level (Hayne and Gwynn 1976). Doe harvest by special permit following the rifle season is successfully used by Pennsylvania. Antlerless-deer hunting

seasons are concurrent with the buck season in Maryland, Virginia and other states, although the buck season will vary in length depending on the desired harvest level. Either-sex hunting seasons of longer duration are employed where whitetail numbers are in need of reduction. Buck-only harvest regulations are desirable only when the management intent is to expand a white-tailed deer population or its range. Buck-only hunting, however, will not control a growing deer population (Moore and Bevill 1978).

Similar goals and objectives are shared by most wildlife agencies in the Appalachian Mountains region. The following set of objectives expressed by the Pennsylvania Game Commission (Lang 1968) have been echoed by other states of the region (*see* Severinghaus and Darrow 1976, Gwynn 1965).

Whitetail population build-ups in parts of the Appalachian Mountains region, particularly where hunter harvests are prohibited (as in some state parks) and when weather conditions do not permit adequate harvests, can result in extensive damage to vegetation and ultimately to the deer. *Photo by Bluford W. Muir; courtesy of the U.S. Forest Service.*

1. Maintain the maximum breeding stock on all suitable areas consistent with other land uses, and harvest all surplus animals through public hunting;
2. Maintain the best possible range conditions in conformance with other land uses and interests;
3. Annually establish hunting regulations that will produce a stable harvest with a carry-over of a maximum breeding stock in keeping with existing food supplies, and provide maximum hunting opportunities to the maximum number of hunters;
4. Conduct a year-round deer research program;
5. Maintain an active public information program on the mechanics of deer management.

On national forest land within the region, the objective is to manage habitat so that wildlife (including deer) will be maintained at levels consistent with the requirements for other products and services of the land, and in accordance with wildlife's recreational and related public uses and values. Supplementing this objective, the U.S. Forest Service manages land to meet the habitat requirements of wildlife species and populations (Strode and Cloward 1969). The management specifics are described in the white-tailed deer section of the Wildlife Habitat Management Handbook (U.S. Forest Service 1971).

OUTLOOK

The future of whitetails and deer hunting in the Appalachian Mountains region looks bright. State wildlife agencies are aware of their responsibilities to the people—particularly those who bear the costs of producing deer and those who share in the benefits of the whitetail populations. Programs involving doe harvests and habitat have been established to monitor and manage changes in the deer populations and habitats. Landowner incentive programs may be started to help develop habitat, maintain lands open to recreational hunting, and provide adequate harvests of deer (Allen and Cromer 1977). A continuing search is being made for better ways to assure optimum utilization of the deer populations and to increase the productivity of their habitats.

Chapter 16

EASTERN MIXED FOREST

Harold L. Barber
Chief Forest Wildlife Biologist
Kentucky Department of Fish and Wildlife Resources
West Liberty, Kentucky

ENVIRONMENT

The Eastern Mixed Forest region occupies approximately 11 million hectares (27 million acres), extending from southwestern Pennsylvania through West Virginia, Ohio, Kentucky, Virginia, Tennessee and northeastern Georgia (Figure 79). The region includes the western portion of the Appalachian Highlands and lies mainly within the Appalachian Plateau province (Fenneman 1938, Küchler 1966).

The topography is characterized mainly by steep-sloped ridges and valleys, although gently sloping sites are present on the uplands and in the valley floors. Elevations range from about 180 meters (600 feet) in the river valleys to 1,370 meters (5,000 feet) in the mountains.

Podzolic soils predominate. The main associations are Shelocta/Wellston/Zanesville, Steinsburg/Shelocta and Vandalia/Upshur. Local exceptions to these general classifications are common, however, with the primary example being alluvial soils along stream banks and on river terraces. Parent materials are derived mainly from sedimentary rocks, primarily sandstone, limestone and shale. Soil moisture and fertility vary greatly, with relatively moist and fertile soils predominating in valleys and coves, on lower northeast-facing slopes and below limestone outcroppings. Relatively dry and infertile soils predominate on ridgetops and southwest-facing slopes.

The climate is temperate, with moderately cold winters and warm humid summers. Temperatures average about 2 degrees Celsius (35 degrees Fahrenheit) during January and about 24 degrees Celsius (75 degrees Fahrenheit) during July, although a low of -34 degrees Celsius (-30 degrees Fahrenheit) and a high of 41 degrees Celsius (105 degrees Fahrenheit) have been recorded. Average annual precipitation is about 127 centimeters (50 inches), and is relatively uniform throughout the year. The average annual snowfall varies from 102 centimeters (40 inches) in the north to 13 centimeters (5 inches) in the south, and remains on the ground an average of 60 days a year in the north to 5 days in the south. The growing season averages 150 days in the north and on the higher elevations, and 180 days in the south (U.S. Department of Agriculture 1941).

The region was entirely forested prior to settlement, primarily in mixed mesophytic hardwoods. Approximately 80 percent remains forested. Cleared lands occur mainly in stream valleys, where the acreage devoted to agriculture is about evenly divided between grasslands and cultivated row crops. About 94 percent of the land is under private ownership, although the region includes parts or all of five national forests and a number of state forests and parks (Austin 1965). Many of the private lands are owned by part-time farmers and are relatively small, the average farm unit being about 37 hectares (92 acres). A number of coal and timber companies own large tracts of 2,800 hectares (7,000 acres) or more.

As the term "mesophytic" implies, most of the plants in the region are intermediate in their need for soil moisture. Since the site conditions are highly variable and frequently interspersed, the vegetative types overlap and

Figure 79. The Eastern Mixed Mesophytic Hardwood Forest region.

produce a profusion of plant species within a small area (Braun 1950). For example, I have identified 54 species of native trees, shrubs and vines on a 0.4-hectare (1.0-acre) plot consisting partly of woodland and partly of old field, and containing both north- and south-facing slopes. The dominant species typically found on north- and east-facing slopes and in coves are sugar maple, basswood, American beech, yellow poplar, eastern hemlock and northern red oak. Tree species typically found on south- and west-facing slopes and on ridgetops include chestnut oak, scarlet oak, white oak and pignut hickory. Common understory species are flowering dogwood, mountain laurel, rosebay rhododendron, cat greenbrier, highbush blueberry, Japanese honeysuckle and strawberry bush.

WHITETAIL POPULATIONS

History

Explorers and settlers who first crossed the Appalachian Mountains were lured on by glowing accounts of fertile lands and abundant wildlife. One hunting expedition, consisting of 14 men, passed through the Cumberland Gap into present-day Kentucky in autumn of 1771 and reported seeing thousands of buffalo, elk and white-tailed deer, with wild turkeys scattered among them (Caruso 1959:69). One day, when only three of the men were present in camp, they were attacked by Indians and all of their peltry taken. A member of the expedition carved a terse epilogue in the trunk of

Isolated parts of the Eastern Mixed Forest region were not settled until after the Civil War. In these mountainous areas—such as the Canaan Valley in West Virginia, shown above in the 1880s—white-tailed deer were plentiful (Allman 1976) and ". . . very valuable to the early residents" (R. C. Allman personal communication to R. E. McCabe:1983). Intensive logging and hunter harvests reduced the deer populations and, in some areas, such as the Canaan Valley, few if any whitetails were seen between 1900 and the 1930s. *Photo courtesy of Richard M. Harr, Porter J. Brown and Ruth Cooper Allman.*

a barkless poplar tree: "2300 Deer Skin Lost—Ruination by God."

Throughout the settlement period of the late 1700s and early 1800s, white-tailed deer played an important part in the lives of frontier families. Deerskins were used for clothing, and deer meat often meant the difference between starvation and plenty. The demand soon led to overhunting. Within a single generation of men, the deer became scarce, and by the mid-1800s they had been extirpated from nearly all parts of the region (DeGarmo and Gill 1958).

Deer restoration in the region began in the 1930s due to several factors. Human populations had begun to shift from coves and hollows to industrialized cities, and portions of the region experienced a 23-percent decline in human population between 1940 and 1960. About 65 percent of the cultivated land was abandoned during the same period, leaving many small clearings in close proximity to deer cover and mast-producing woodlands. The land-use changes vastly improved deer habitat. Also, deer poaching was greatly reduced with the

Restocking of depleted, former whitetail ranges in various states of the Eastern Mixed Forest region was begun in earnest in the mid-1930s. *Photo courtesy of the U.S. National Archives.*

reduction in human inhabitants. And the Pittman-Robertson Federal Aid to Wildlife Restoration Act was passed in 1937, which provided funds for management.

Deer stocking got underway as early as 1936 in West Virginia and has continued in portions of other states of the region. Kentucky alone has stocked about 2,600 whitetails in counties that lie within the mixed mesophytic forest.

Deer Populations

As a result of favorable habitat, efficient trapping and translocating, and upgraded law enforcement, deer populations have increased dramatically. Deer numbers on some refuges and management areas increased from 0 to 10 per square kilometer (0 to 26 per square mile) in a 10-year period after stocking began. The Beaver Creek Refuge, located on national forest land in Kentucky, and the Shawnee State Forest in southeastern Ohio were among the areas where such increases occurred. Autumn populations of at least 12 deer per square kilometer (31 per square mile) were achieved on a few areas that had exceptionally good habitat and efficient protection from illegal hunting. On lands without special protection, deer increases have been slower. In southeastern Ohio, the whitetail population has varied from less than 1 to 5 per square kilometer (2.6–13 per square mile) (R. J. Stoll personal communication:1978). Eastern Tennessee has supported an average autumn population of about 6 deer per square kilometer (15.5 per square mile) for the last decade (C. Whitehead personal communication:1978). Populations of 5 to 8 whitetails per square kilometer (13–21 per square mile) have built up in parts of eastern Kentucky, while in other parts, deer stockings have failed mainly because of illegal hunting.

Population Structure

Examinations of highway mortalities of whitetailed deer in Kentucky during the 10-year period from 1971 through 1980 revealed a sex ratio of 82 (males):100 (females). In West Virginia, male fawns slightly outnumbered females at birth, and males comprised 51 percent of the prehunting-season fawn population (Allen and Cromer 1977). In Ohio, sex ratios prior to hunting seasons have been 1:1 for fawns, but 0.8:1.0 for whitetails in the yearling age group or older (R. J. Stoll personal communication:1978). Studies in both Ohio and West Virginia indicated that the predominance of does among deer 1.5 years old or older was due mainly to buck-only hunting seasons (Stoll 1978, Allen and Cromer 1977).

Ascertained from hunting seasons in West Virginia from 1965 through 1976, legally harvested adult does averaged 3.5 years of age, and bucks were just over 1.5 years old. The age composition of a typical male deer population prior to hunting season was 39 percent fawns, 36 percent yearlings, and 25 percent adult bucks 2.5 years of age and older (Allen and Cromer 1977).

Productivity

When plenty of good quality food is available, some doe fawns breed at six to seven months of age and usually produce one fawn. All 1.5-year-old does are sexually mature, but usually produce fewer fawns than do older does. A doe usually gives birth to two fawns in her third year. Data collected at deer check stations in Ohio revealed that 77 percent of the fawn does, 99 pecent of the yearlings, and 100 percent of the does 2.5 years and older had ovulated. The mean number of fetuses per doe was 1.29 for fawns, 1.87 for yearlings and 2.04 for older deer (Nixon 1971). In Tennessee, the number of fawns produced per doe among all age groups varied from year to year, with a low of 1.04, a high of 1.84 and a long-term average of 1.27 (C. Whitehead personal communication:1978).

Harvests

Hunting regulations vary annually among and within states of the region. Either-sex hunting seasons were held on most of Kentucky's restocked deer range five years after the date of stocking, but since 1967, seasons have been buck-only in all of the mesophytic forest counties. In West Virginia, buck-only seasons have prevailed since 1968. Beginning in 1974, however, a limited number of antlerless deer permits were issued in West Virginia counties where the whitetail population exceeded desired levels (Allen and Cromer 1977). In both Ohio and Tennessee, a limited number of antlerless permits are issued in selected counties (R. J. Stoll personal communication:1978, C. Whitehead personal communication:1978). In Tennessee, the number of antlerless permits issued is predetermined mainly by browse and mast surveys.

The portion of the deer population that is legally havested is unknown over much of the region. C. Whitehead (personal communication:1978) estimated that 26 percent of the total hunting season population was legally harvested in eastern Tennessee, where hunts were mainly for bucks only. Antlered bucks were estimated as comprising about 30 percent of the prehunting-season deer population, and thus the Tennessee harvest represents a rather high harvest ratio of legal deer. Since the whitetail population has remained fairly stable for the last decade, the total annual deer removal from all causes combined—legal, illegal and accidental—evidently was equal to the annual increment brought on by the fawn crop. R. J. Stoll (personal communication:1978) esti-

mated that 45 to 55 percent of the bucks 1.5 years or older were legally harvested during buck-only seasons in Ohio. In West Virginia, the 1975 deer harvest represented about 16 percent of the estimated total deer population (Allen and Cromer 1977). In eastern Kentucky, however, not more than 15 percent of the whitetail population was legally harvested during buck-only seasons.

FOOD AND FEEDING HABITS

DeGarmo and Gill (1958) reported that 138 species of plants were eaten by deer in West Virginia. Barber (1962) found that 29 generic groups contributed significant amounts to the deer browse diet in Kentucky. Preference ratings for those plants are shown in Table 58.

Table 58. White-tailed deer browse preference from 14 areas in Kentucky.[a]

Browse species[b]	Preference rating[c]
Strawberry bush	2
Greenbrier	3
Common trumpetcreeper	3
Grape	6
Black locust	6
Redcedar	7
Sumac	8
Rose	8
Blackberry	9
Viburnum	9
Sourwood	10
Blueberry	10
Maple	10
Dogwood	12
Serviceberry	12
Eastern hophornbeam	12
Buckthorn	13
Cherry	13
Common sassafras	13
Elm	13
Ash	13
Poison-ivy	14
Coralberry	14
Redbud	15
Blackgum	15
Hickory	15
Oak	15
Pine	18
Common spicebush	20

[a]Each survey area involved 100 plots, each 40.5 square meters (435.6 square feet).
[b]All plant genera listed were utilized by deer in three or more of the areas surveyed. They are listed in order of their use, as indicated by the percentage of the available twigs—ground level to 1.83 meters (6 feet)—that had been browsed. No attempt was made to identify leafless late-winter shrubby growth; thus the category "Oak," for example, represents about 12 species.
[c]Rating scale from 1 (high) to 20 (low).

The Eastern Mixed Forest region is approximately 80-percent forest and supports large and stable whitetail populations. Consequently, deer hunting is a popular recreation and important to local economies. In Kentucky in recent years, bow hunting has accounted for about 12 percent of the legal deer harvest. *Photo courtesy of the Kentucky Department of Fish and Wildlife.*

Pines normally are not a preferred browse food of white-tailed deer in eastern mixed forests, but old-field stands of Virginia pine or white pine are a preferred habitat type during persistent snow and cold weather. Japanese honeysuckle and greenbrier are important whitetail foods that often occur in young stands of pine. *Photo by Ron Keil; courtesy of the Ohio Department of Natural Resources.*

In heavily forested portions of the Eastern Mixed Forest region, woody twigs probably make up less than 10 percent of the food consumed by deer (Stiteler and Shaw 1966). The amount of browse eaten by whitetails varies according to the severity of the winter weather. Browse has been utilized heavily in Kentucky only when other foods were scarce or covered for several weeks by deep snows. Browse was not eaten in great quantity in southeastern Ohio (Nixon et al. 1970). In mixed oak stands in Pennsylvania, whitetails preferred dry leaves over woody browse (Watts 1964). Shaw and Ripley (1965) placed the browse topic in a proper perspective with their statement that, although woody browse comprises a small part of a whitetail's year-round diet, it is an important part because of its availability during winter.

When available, foods such as acorns, other mast and fruits, leaves, herbs, clovers, grasses, or cultivated crops are preferred foods of the white-tailed deer. A close correlation was found between acorn production trends and deer condition trends in Kentucky (H. L. Barber 1971). Antler size of bucks increased following winters when a good acorn crop was present, but decreased in the years following poor acorn crops. Reproductive success of yearling does also was related to acorn availability.

SPECIAL PROBLEMS AND CONSTRAINTS

The mixed mesophytic forest provides a favorable environment for white-tailed deer. The terrain furnishes sheltered coves where deer are protected from winter winds and snowstorms. During relatively cold winter weather and extended periods of snow cover, the deer tend to congregate in evergreen cover and especially in dense old stands of Virginia pine and Japanese honeysuckle. Winter yarding does not occur, however, and cold weather is seldom if ever a limiting factor. Also, because the forest supports an abundance and great variety of vegetation, whitetail populations in the region rarely are restricted by a lack of available food (Barber 1962, Braun 1950).

Undiagnosed die-offs of white-tailed deer occurred in portions of the region, particularly in eastern Kentucky and Tennessee in 1954, 1955 and 1971. In retrospect, either bluetongue virus or epizootic hemorrhagic disease virus is believed to have been the cause (Hayes and Prestwood 1969, Southeastern Cooperative Wildlife Disease Study 1980). Bluetongue virus was isolated from deer in Georgia, Kentucky and Tennessee in 1971, and epizootic hemorrhagic disease was identified from deer in Kentucky and West Virginia. Domestic cattle can be asymptomatic carriers of either disease, although bluetongue is not always benign in cattle, and the presence of either disease among deer probably reflects an infection in nearby cattle (Southeastern Cooperative Wildlife Disease Study 1980).

The region's whitetails also are host to a number of internal and external parasites. Parasitic infestations can become a limiting factor where deer densities are high, but rarely are a problem where the whitetail numbers are in proper balance with seasonal habitats. While the optimum population level varies with the quality of the deer range, one deer per 6–10

Winters can be harsh periods for whitetails in mixed mesophytic forests. When deep snows persist for extended periods of time, whitetail foods such as acorns, other seeds and fruits, leaves, and grasses become scarce or inaccessible. Woody browse then becomes the deer diet staple. *Photo by J. E. Osman; courtesy of the Pennsylvania Game Commission.*

hectares (15–25 acres) appears to be about the maximum desirable level throughout most of the region.

Free-ranging domestic dogs are abundant throughout most of the region and are a cause of nonhunting deer mortality, but they are mainly a nuisance factor and have little effect on established whitetail populations (Perry and Giles 1971). Dogs may have a serious impact in areas of low deer population or in recently stocked areas, but once the deer population reaches an optimum level, harassment by dogs has little effect (Allen and Cromer 1977).

During the deer restoration period of the 1950s and 1960s in Kentucky, numerous instances were recorded of a whitetail population having built up in a given county or management area after restocking, only to be decimated severely when the area was opened to either-sex deer hunting. The dog problem remained fairly constant throughout the period of population buildup and decline.

Poaching is a continual problem. Many whitetails are killed illegally during closed seasons, and many antlerless deer are killed by hunters during buck-only seasons. The actual loss to poaching is an unknown factor, since such incidents usually are unreported.

Deer tag recoveries in Kentucky during a 20-year period, 1960 through 1979, indicated that the total whitetail loss to all illegal and accidental causes combined was double the removal by legal harvests. In West Virginia, illegal killing ranks next to deer/vehicle collisions as the largest known cause of nonhunting mortality (Allen and Cromer 1977).

On military reservations and wildlife management areas that have special security measures, whitetail population levels and sustained deer harvests have been much higher than on adjoining privately-owned land providing similar habitats. In most cases the major limiting factor on the uncontrolled lands appeared to be the illegal kill.

Collisions with vehicles, drownings, falls from cliffs and fence entanglements contribute to the nonhunting deer mortality. Deer/vehicle collisions are a growing problem in some areas, but they probably have little effect on the total deer population. In Kentucky, 10,781 instances of known deer mortality from causes other than legal or illegal hunting were recorded from 1960 through 1980. Highway vehicle collisions accounted for 81 percent of that total, dog predation represented 4 percent, and all other causes combined, including unknown causes, constituted 15 percent. A questionnaire survey of wildlife management areas in 11 southeastern states indicated that 73 percent of the known miscellaneous whitetail mortalities, exclusive of poaching and predation, were caused by cars with 12 percent caused by fences, 5 percent by trains, 3 percent by diseases or parasites, 2 percent by falls from cliffs, 1 percent by drowning and 3 percent by unknown causes (Barick 1969). The total deer removal by such causes represented an estimated 6 percent of the annual increment.

A whitetail doe shot and abandoned during a buck-only hunting season. In portions of the Eastern Mixed Forest region, the total deer removal from all illegal shooting and accidental causes exceeds the number of deer legally harvested. *Photo courtesy of the Pennsylvania Game Commission.*

A trophy whitetail buck in typical Eastern Mixed Forest habitat. Even though dormant and leafless during winter months, the vegetation provides favorable concealment cover. *Photo by Joni H. Norris.*

MANAGEMENT

Habitat management in the Eastern Mixed Forest region usually has focused on the effects of forest cutting for lumber and pulp on whitetail food production and the animals' distribution. DeGarmo and Gill (1958) reported that clear-cuttings supply an abundance of forage for up to 10 years. Thereafter, browse plants grow out of reach of whitetails and form dense thickets that the deer are reluctant to enter. DeGarmo and Gill recommended partial forest cuttings at intervals of 10 to 15 years to increase forage yields. Goodrum (1969) stated that adequate amounts of browse and other forage are produced for a period of only three to five years after cutting, and Harlow et al. (1966) stated that the use of cutover areas by deer decreased markedly after the first year. These various findings can be summarized and reconciled by noting that woody browse declines rather quickly in quality with the passing of time, although it may appear to be adequate in quantity. The best management approach during timber harvests is to cut as lightly as possible, in order to cut again as soon as feasible.

In cases where mast-producing oaks and other types of deer food are removed, forest cuttings may detract from habitat values. Lay (1965*b*) concluded that a range with a large variety of hardwoods of fruit-producing size provides more deer food than one offering little food except browse.

Ideally, in hardwood forests, at least 50 percent of the acreage should consist of mature mast trees with the remaining percentage containing an interspersion of evergreens, shrubs and vines, and openings with herbaceous and young-growth woody vegetation. Wildlife biologists and managers can best manipulate the habitat toward these goals by forest harvests to yield commercial timber products.

Wildlife clearings and supplemental agricultural plantings may increase habitat potential, but they afford only temporary improvement, are costly to establish and maintain, and are not widespread enough to influence critical land areas (Harlow et al. 1966). Prescribed burns are more cost-efficient and often can accomplish comparable results.

Whitetail habitat carrying capacity varies widely within the region. Limited areas con-

Understory in some mixed mesophytic forests is relatively barren. Nevertheless, the region supports a variety of food and cover vegetation, particularly along forest edges and in openings. Both deer shown above are ear-tagged, as part of a mark/recapture program in the Monongahela National Forest of West Virginia, to obtain information on whitetail movements and mortality. *Photos by B. W. Muir; courtesy of the U.S. Forest Service.*

tain too many deer, whereas others are understocked. Thus, each state within the region should be subdivided into management units to permit intensive management of deer harvests to ensure sustained deer population consistent with landowner tolerances for crop depredations and citizen acceptance of vehicle/deer accident risks.

White-tailed deer populations are expected to increase over much of the Eastern Mixed Forest region during the next several decades. The extent of this increase, and the benefits to be derived from hunting, will depend to a large extent on intensive regulation of the harvest. Among the greatest needs is to reduce the illegal deer kill.

Chapter 17

PIEDMONT PLATEAU

Richard W. Whittington
Wildlife Biologist
Georgia Game and Fish Division
Fort Valley, Georgia

ENVIRONMENT

The Piedmont Plateau encompasses about 163,000 square kilometers (63,240 square miles), and includes the midsections of Maryland, Virginia, North Carolina, South Carolina, Georgia and Alabama (Figure 80). Although the Piedmont contains few extensively forested areas, it has about 96,200 square kilometers (37,140 square miles) of woodlands that are prime white-tailed deer habitat.

Physiographic Features

The topography of the northern portion of the Piedmont Plateau ranges from gently rolling to rough and deeply dissected (Winters 1957). Soils are generally acidic and low in organic matter, phosphorous and nitrogen, and underlain by crystalline rock. Cecil sandy loam is the representative topsoil and the subsoil is red clay. The southern portion is hilly with steep slopes, with a history of severe erosion (Pearson and Ensminger 1957). Soils were developed from igneous rocks and range in texture from Cecil sandy loams to clay loam subsoils. The inherent mineral nutrient level of these soils is high, but the nitrogen level is low.

Elevations in the Piedmont vary from 90 meters (295 feet) above sea level in the east to 450 meters (1,475 feet) in the west (Fenneman 1938). Streams are numerous and the stream valleys are narrow.

Climate

Kincer (1941) characterized the climate as mild winters and hot summers, with freezing temperatures in winter rarely persisting for more than 48 hours. Mountain ranges in the west provide partial protection from cold fronts moving in a southeasterly direction. Snowfall averages range from 45 centimeters (18 inches) annually in the north to 10 centimeters (4 inches) in the south. Rare accumulations of snow do not create a problem with winter stress in deer. From north to south the mean temperature ranges are 0 to 10 degrees Celsius (32–50 degrees Fahrenheit) in January and 25 to 27 degrees Celsius (77–81 degrees Fahrenheit) in July. Annual rainfall averages 111 to 134 centimeters (44–53 inches), and the growing season is 187 to 225 days.

Vegetation

The natural climax forest in much of the Piedmont is the oak/hickory association (Oosting 1956). The mixed pine/hardwood is more

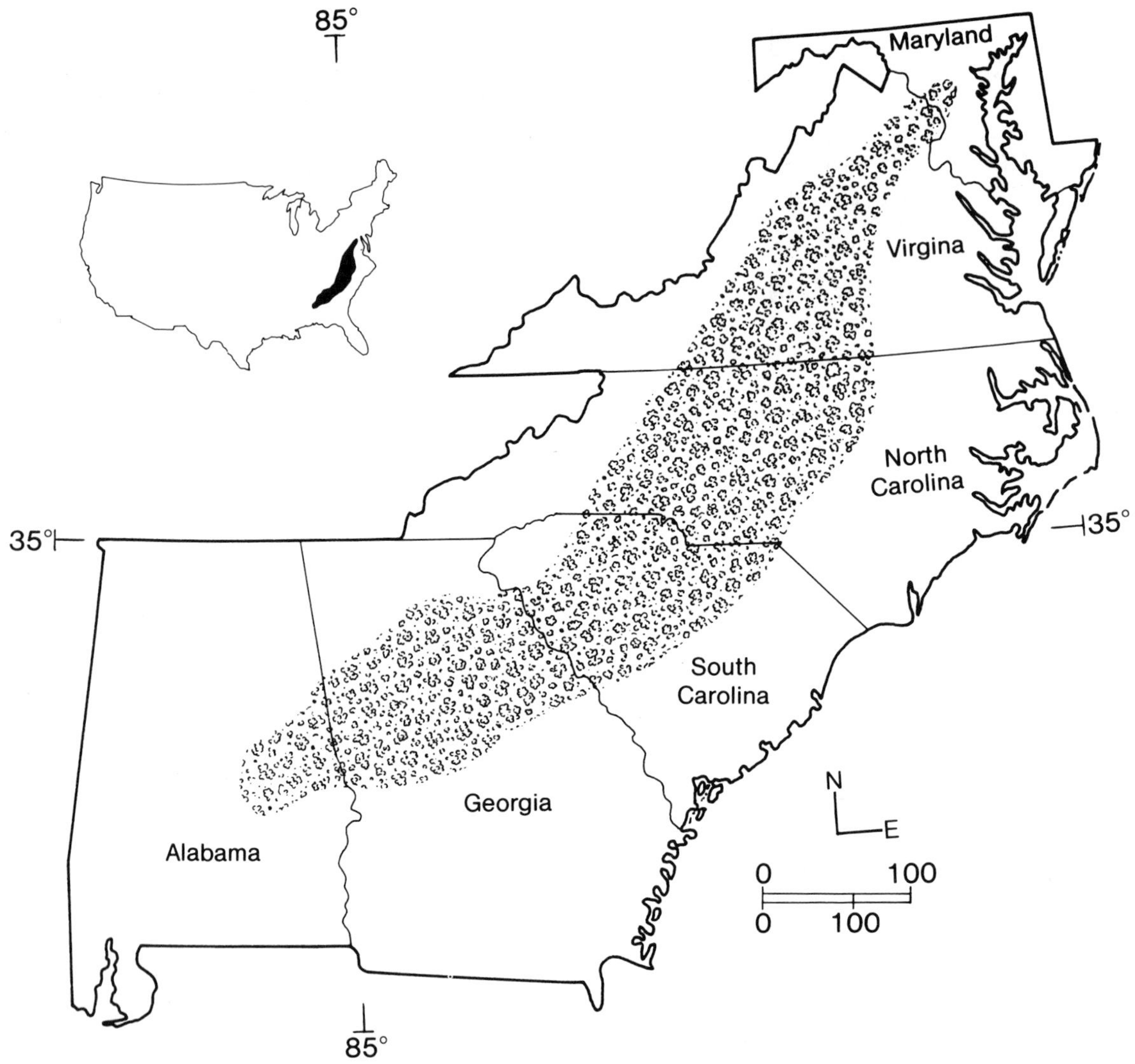

Figure 80. The Piedmont Plateau.

common in the south.

In the early 1800s, nearly all of the Piedmont was cleared for farming. A few years of growing cotton, tobacco and corn resulted in extensive erosion and depletion of soil nutrients (Winters 1957). As soils were depleted and croplands subsequently abandoned, these lands reverted to forest. Simultaneously, virgin forests were cut to provide farmlands. The disaster of the cotton boll weevil in 1921 and the 1930s depression saw farms abandoned on a large scale.

Land abandonment played a major role in forming the present vegetational patterns. Old-field succession usually begins with horse-weed, followed by aster and bluestems. At about five years, pine, common persimmon and sweetgum dominate the upland sites (Oosting 1956). Later, the old fields usually support sub-climax stands of loblolly and shortleaf pines in the south and east, and Virginia pine in the west. Predominant species in lowlands are sweetgum, yellow poplar, American sycamore, red maple, ashes, elms and hackberry.

Dominants of the remaining oak/hickory climax forest are white oak, northern red oak, black oak, post oak, blackjack oak and hickory. Typical subordinate species are sourwood, flowering dogwood, blackgum and sweetgum.

Principal forest habitat associations in the Piedmont are oak/hickory in the north (left) and mixed pine/hardwood in the south (right). *Left photo by Abbie Lowe; courtesy of the U.S. National Park Service. Right photo by Robert W. Neelands; courtesy of the U.S. Forest Service.*

HISTORY

Early historical writings describe the forests of the Piedmont as wild country with vast forests, detached groves of trees, chains of hills with bare summits and many old Indian fields along the rivers (Bartram 1928). Testimony to the abundance of white-tailed deer is found in reports of trade in deerskins by settlers. For example, 30,000 deerskins were shipped from North Carolina in 1753, and 600,000 were exported from Georgia between 1755 and 1773 (Young 1956, *see* Chapter 2). Whitetails were killed year-round for hides and meat, in great part as commercial enterprise.

With continued exploitation, whitetail populations declined rapidly. In an attempt to curtail the overharvest, state legislatures enacted game laws in the 1700s and 1800s, with deer being prominently mentioned. However, the laws were loosely enforced and proved ineffective in controlling the largely commercial slaughter.

Whitetails probably disappeared from the Piedmont in the late 1800s. The extirpation was hastened by the loss of habitat to agriculture, as well as night hunting and the use of dogs. Deer were noticeably absent from the Piedmont for several decades following the exploitation period. By 1920, remnant whitetail populations in the southeastern states were restricted largely to rugged terrain in the mountains and hardwood swamps in the coastal plain (Allen 1965, Jenkins 1953).

Interest in deer was renewed in the late 1930s when newly organized state wildlife agencies recognized the need for restoration programs. Two major historical events at the national level were significant. The U.S. Forest Service purchased extensive forest holdings that provided valuable deer habitat in various stages of reforestation. Later, the Federal Aid in Wildlife Restoration Act of 1937 provided funds for wildlife restoration.

Wildlife management areas were established and stocked with deer. These areas served as

Killing whitetails for the hide markets in Europe greatly reduced Piedmont deer populations in the 1700s and 1800s. Unrestricted and unregulated night hunting and "dogging" in the late 1800s and early 1900s, along with habitat loss, hastened the species' near extirpation in the region. Hunting whitetails with dogs still is permitted in some states, but under strict regulation. *Photo courtesy of the U.S. Forest Service.*

refuges from which deer spread to adjacent suitable habitat or were trapped and moved to other strategic locations. Initial restockings were made in Alabama in 1939, followed by Virginia in 1942, Georgia in 1944, North Carolina in 1945, Maryland in 1948 and South Carolina in 1952 (Blackard 1971, Patterson 1949). By 1966, whitetail populations had become established over a sizeable portion of the Piedmont. Although restocking played a major role in the restoration, other factors such as improvement of deer habitat through changing land use, public interest in deer hunting and better law enforcement also contributed to the success (Allen 1965).

Native whitetails of the Southeast as well as deer from Texas, Wisconsin, Ohio and Pennsylvania were restocked in the Piedmont. South Carolina was the only state that did not import subspecies of the whitetail (Blackard 1971). The primary consideration in restocking was economic; intentional alteration of genetic composition of the population was not a factor. Whitetails were trapped, purchased or traded from any available source. As shown by subsequent success, the imported subspecies were quite adaptable to Piedmont habitats.

WHITETAIL POPULATIONS

In 1971, the Southeastern Cooperative Wildlife Disease Study group compiled data from state wildlife agencies, which estimated that whitetail populations were below or equal to environmental capacity in approximately 80 percent of the Piedmont, above the range carrying capacity in about 3 percent of the region, and rare or absent in about 17 percent of the region (Figure 81). In 1980, huntable populations of deer were present in all counties except those with large metropolitan areas. Whitetail populations were equal to the environmental capacity in more than 50 percent of the Piedmont in 1980 (Figure 81).

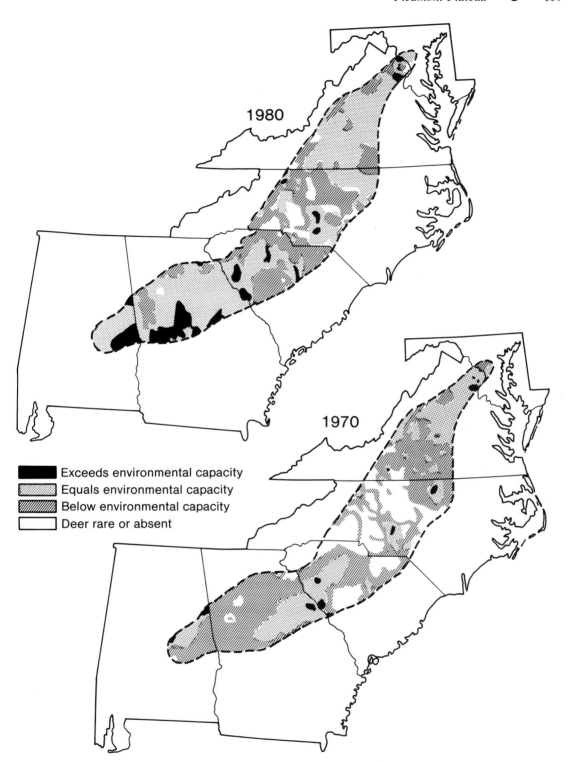

Figure 81. White-tailed deer populations in the Piedmont Plateau, 1970 and 1980, relative to environmental carrying capacity (from maps prepared by the Southeastern Cooperative Wildlife Disease Study, through cooperative agreements 12-16-5-1057 and 12-16-5-2230 between the U.S. Fish and Wildlife Service and the USDA Veterinary Services, Animal and Plant Health Inspection Service).

The following examples indicate, by state, the present-day whitetail populations on the Piedmont Plateau.

D. Nelson (personal communication:1983) provided data on the Alabama Piedmont that indicated that whitetails average 7.7 per square kilometer (20 per square mile) on private and industrial lands and 9.7 per square kilometer (25 per square mile) on wildlife management areas. The population trends are stable, but deer density exceeds environmental capacity on managed lands. Both body and antler size of Piedmont deer reportedly are smaller than for other physiographic regions in Alabama.

Georgia's highest deer population densities—approximately 15.4 per square kilometer (40 per square mile)—were reached around 1972 in the state's eastern and central counties. Since then the populations have declined moderately and now are stable. The northern and western counties have increasing trends and have not yet reached carrying capacity. Historically, wildlife management areas had the highest whitetail densities, with an estimated peak of 30.9 deer per square kilometer (80 per square mile) at the Clark Hill area in 1965. This same population was estimated by the Lincoln Index Method at 26.3 whitetails per square kilometer (68 per square mile) in 1969 (Whittington 1970). Wildlife management area populations currently average 10 deer per square kilometer (25 per square mile). An exceptional managed population of 15.8 deer per square kilometer (41 per square mile) occurred at Piedmont National Wildlife Refuge in 1982 (R. Shell personal communication:1983).

Deer size in Georgia has been exceptional, with Piedmont whitetails generally larger than deer elsewhere in the state. Field-dressed weights of 145 kilograms (320 pounds) and 138 kilograms (304 pounds) were confirmed in Upson County in 1967 and Oglethorpe County in 1968, respectively. State-record antlers in Georgia, using the Boone and Crockett measurement system, were taken in the Piedmont. A typical rack taken from Paulding County in 1962 scored 184 points. In 1973, a nontypical rack taken in Monroe County scored 240⅝ points. Georgia currently has 11 Piedmont deer in the Boone and Crockett records listing.

In South Carolina, the Enoree section of the central Piedmont supported 19 to 27 whitetails per square kilometer (50–70 per square mile) in 1977 (D. Urbston personal communication:1977). Data provided by W. Moore (per-

A trophy whitetail buck harvested in Georgia's Cedar Creek Wildlife Management Area in the Piedmont Plateau. As a rule, Piedmont whitetails in Georgia are larger than deer elsewhere in the state. *Photo by Richard W. Whittington.*

sonal communication:1983) show present deer densities are moderate to high over most of the Piedmont, but a few counties still are sparsely populated. Populations average 7.7 to 9.7 whitetails per square kilometer (20–25 per square mile) and are considered stable. Wildlife management areas are very much intermixed with private lands, and differences in deer population densities are indistinguishable. Animal size is reported to be stable, and Piedmont deer have larger bodies and antlers than do other whitetails in South Carolina. Reproduction by doe fawns was measured at 17 percent, and the overall reproductive success was 1.78 fawns per adult doe in the late 1970s.

The North Carolina Piedmont whitetail population averages 9.7 deer per square kilometer (25 per square mile), which equals the carrying capacity on private lands (J. Osborne personal communication:1983). The Butner and Uwharrie Game Lands average 7.7 deer per square kilometer (20 per square mile), which is slightly below carrying capacity. Piedmont whitetails are larger than other North Carolina deer.

Virginia deer biologists estimate that Piedmont whitetail populations average 12 deer per square kilometer (31 per square mile) (J. Gwynn personal communication:1983). Fort Pickett and Quantico military installations currently support 13.5 and 15.4 deer per square kilometer (35 and 40 per square mile), respectively. Carrying capacity of Virginia Piedmont habitat does not exceed 15.4 deer per square kilometer (40 per square mile). A very good reproductive rate was calculated at 1.7 fawns per adult doe on managed lands in 1983.

Food and Feeding Habits

Plant groups utilized throughout the Piedmont by white-tailed deer are shown in Table 59. Japanese honeysuckle is reported to be the most important food during every season. Fruits of greenbrier, blueberry, sumac, grape, honeylocust and blackberry are seasonally important. When available, acorns are whitetails' first choice. Some species of mushrooms are consumed readily. They were particularly abundant in rumens of deer from the Forks Game Management Area in South Carolina and the Choccolocco Wildlife Management Area in Alabama (Kirkpatrick et al. 1969).

Table 59. Percentages of plants consumed in different seasons by white-tailed deer in the Piedmont of the southeastern United States (Harlow and Hooper 1972).

| Season | Number of deer sampled | Fruits | Woody plants | | | | Herbaceous plants | | | |
| | | | Leaves | | Twigs and buds | | | | | |
			Green	Dry	Succulent	Hardened	Forbs	Grasses and sedges	Fungi	Other
Spring	32	1.5	39.7	0.5	7.4	0.1	49.9	0.5	0.5	
Summer	31	20.3	36.8	1.2	5.4	5.9	6.0	8.0	15.6	0.8
Autumn	192	32.7	34.3	7.1	9.7	2.9	0.7	4.0	8.6	
Winter	46	10.1	29.0	10.9	0.5	4.7	7.6	32.3	4.9	

Grasses, forbs and twigs are important components of seasonal diets of white-tailed deer in the Piedmont Plateau, although less so than green leaves, acorns and other fruits. *Left photo courtesy of the South Carolina Wildlife and Marine Resources Department. Right photo courtesy of the U.S. Forest Service.*

Harvest

Still-hunting from stands and stalking are the most prevalent methods of hunting whitetails in Maryland, North Carolina, South Carolina, Georgia and Alabama. Hunting with dogs is the most popular method on private lands in the Virginia Piedmont. All states allow harvest of both sexes, and either-sex harvest seasons range from 2 to 10 days in certain areas. Virtually all wildlife management areas have a systematic doe harvest to control deer numbers.

According to D. Nelson (personal communication:1983), Alabama wildlife management area harvests average 0.85 buck per square kilometer (2.2 per square mile) and 0.66 doe per square kilometer (1.7 per square mile). Does comprise about 40 percent of the deer harvest on managed lands. The percentage of three-year-old and older bucks on both managed and private lands is low. The Alabama management strategy provides a long buck season (74 days) on private lands and one week on managed lands. These seasons are followed by two days of doe hunting.

In Georgia, buck seasons are 50 days, with doe seasons ranging from 1 to 7 days. The buck harvest in 1982 was 0.85 per square kilometer (2.2 per square mile) for private lands and 1.43 per square kilometer (3.7 per square mile) for managed lands. Yearling bucks comprised 68 percent of the antlered buck harvest on private lands, while 17 percent of the bucks were three years old or older. Managed lands had 55 percent yearling bucks and 10 percent older bucks in the harvest. Does made up 16 percent of the harvest on private lands and 56 percent on managed lands. The Piedmont National Wildlife Refuge sustained average yields of 2.2 bucks per square kilometer (5.7 per square mile) and 2.1 does per square kilometer (5.4 per square mile) from 1977 to 1982 (R. Shell personal communication:1983).

In a group of seven lower Piedmont counties in Georgia, the percentage of yearling does in the adult doe harvest increased from 50 percent in 1979 to 68 percent in 1982. This doe age structure closely resembles that of bucks in the same area. The population is approaching a one-to-one sex ratio, but at a lower density level than is desired.

South Carolina's harvest is practically uniform over private and managed lands (W. Moore personal communication:1983). Buck harvests, recorded at mandatory check stations, are 0.71 per square kilometer (1.84 per square mile), and doe harvests are 0.3 per square kilometer (0.78 per square mile). The harvest of does has stabilized at 30 percent of the total harvest. Buck hunting is allowed for 80 days, and does are legal game for a 6–8-day season annually. Three-year-old and older bucks declined in the harvest, from 13 percent to 9 percent in the six-year period 1977–1982.

North Carolina's deer harvest data are collected through cooperator agents throughout the 36-day buck season and the 2 to 10 days of either-sex hunting. J. Osborne (personal communication:1983) indicated harvest rates of 0.31 buck per square kilometer (0.8 per square mile) on private lands and 0.71 per square kilometer (1.83 per square mile) on managed lands. Doe harvests comprise approximately 20 percent of the total harvest.

Mandatory check stations account for whitetail harvest totals in Virginia. J. Gwynn (personal communication:1983) calculated buck harvests at 0.69 per square kilometer (1.8 per square mile) on private lands and 1.66 per square kilometer (4.3 per square mile) on managed lands. Doe harvests are 29 percent of the total harvest on private lands and 40 percent on managed lands. Hunting seasons range from 12 to 50 days for bucks and 1 to 6 days for does.

Whitetail harvest rates for state-operated wildlife management areas in Alabama, Georgia and Virginia during the 1978–1982 seasons are presented in Table 60.

SPECIAL PROBLEMS

Diseases and Parasites

Epizootic hemorrhagic disease is the most serious disease of white-tailed deer in the Piedmont Plateau region. Cases first were documented from the Piedmont in Georgia and North Carolina in the late summer and autumn of 1971 (Prestwood et al. 1974). Since then, substantial losses have been recorded in local areas of the lower Piedmont. W. Moore (personal communication:1983) reported that epizootic hemorrhagic disease has been present in South Carolina in recent decades, but has not reduced deer populations to any noticeable extent. Georgia's lower Piedmont had scattered losses in 1980 that damaged small areas. Losses from epizootic hemorrhagic disease usually are

Table 60. White-tailed deer harvest[a] on wildlife management areas in Alabama, Georgia and Virginia, 1978–1982.

Area	1978	1979	1980	1981	1982
Alabama[b]					
Choccolocco	1.2 (3.1)	1.6 (4.1)	1.5 (4.0)	2.0 (5.2)	1.4 (3.7)
Coosa	1.0 (2.7)	1.3 (3.3)	1.4 (3.5)	1.2 (3.1)	1.7 (4.5)
Georgia					
Clark Hill	2.5 (6.5)	5.0 (12.9)	3.8 (9.9)	2.1 (5.4)	2.0 (5.2)
Cedar Creek	2.2 (5.7)	2.4 (6.3)	1.9 (4.9)	1.5 (3.9)	1.9 (5.0)
Central Georgia	3.6 (9.3)	3.9 (10.1)	2.1 (5.5)	2.0 (5.3)	1.9 (4.8)
Virginia[c]					
Quantico	3.2 (8.2)	3.5 (9.1)	3.5 (9.1)	2.9 (7.5)	3.2 (8.2)

[a]Per square kilometer (square mile).
[b]D. Nelson (personal communication:1983).
[c]J. Gwynn (personal communication:1983).

confined to areas with high deer population densities, and are not likely to be a limiting factor in well-managed deer populations.

Few if any of the common internal parasites kill large numbers of whitetails on the Piedmont Plateau, and they do not constitute a limiting factor to well-managed populations. Ectoparasites have not caused a problem with fawn mortality (V. Nettles personal communication:1983).

Predation

Predator/prey relationships are worthy of mention here although the Piedmont Plateau lacks a natural predator capable of taking adult deer with any frequency. Bobcats, feral dogs and an increasing coyote population are responsible for some whitetail losses, but established deer populations are not limited by these predators. Predator control is difficult to justify economically, but should not be ruled out during restoration efforts when a small nucleus of deer could be especially vulnerable in the new environment.

Competition

Whitetails in the Piedmont do not compete for cover with other wild species to any appreciable degree, although they and the other species occasionally search for the same foods. In some instances, rabbits may consume low-growing deer foods, but the overall effect usually is insignificant. Rodents, other small mammals, birds and feral hogs compete directly with deer for food in localized areas, especially during winter. Cattle in the Piedmont, however, usually are confined to improved pastures.

Frequently, whitetails damage fruit orchards and agricultural crops such as soybeans, watermelons, peanuts and various vegetables. Commercial forests are likely to be damaged where deer populations are exceptionally high. For example, in Georgia, deer severely damaged planted loblolly pine seedlings that had been grown in a nursery. Taste and scent repellents and noise-making devices are being used widely to repel whitetails, but they frequently have only short-term effectiveness because deer become accustomed to their repeated use.

White-tailed deer in a Virginia apple orchard. Throughout the Piedmont Plateau, build-ups of deer populations can result in extensive local damage to agricultural and nursery crops. *Photo by W. S. Boardman; courtesy of the U.S. National Park Service.*

Deer and deer hunting may conflict with small game hunting since the seasons overlap in the entire Piedmont. Deer may distract hunting dogs used for other game species, such as small mammals and birds. Also, concentrations of deer hunters can preclude any other recreational uses of the land, but for only a few days out of the total year, and in seasons (late autumn or early winter) when other recreational activities are minimal.

MANAGEMENT

Habitat Management

The objective of habitat management is to provide adequate supplies of a variety of palatable deer foods during all seasons. Cover seldom is a critical factor in the Piedmont except where whitetails are subjected to harassment by night hunting, shooting from roads and persistent chasing by free-running dogs.

Several opportunities are available to the land manager to maintain or improve habitat for white-tailed deer in the Piedmont without seriously detracting from other land uses such as forest production for timber. These opportunities include prescribed burning, improved food plantings, forest thinnings, prescribed cutting units, and forest regeneration practices.

Prescribed burning in predominantly pine forests has been used to maintain permanent openings, reduce browse species to sprouts, prepare seedbeds, increase soil nutrients and reduce wildfire hazard. The merits of prescribed fire are pointed out by Cushwa and Brender (1966), who found significantly more plants in burned plots than in unburned plots. In many instances, prescribed fire is the only economically feasible method that can be applied to large acreage. Except when and where control of undesirable hardwoods is needed, fire should be excluded from the hardwood forest types. Palmer and Devet (1966) described prescribed burning techniques that can be used as a guide in the Piedmont.

Improved food plantings have a place in white-tailed deer management even though they may be difficult to justify economically in the short term. They can provide high-quality food during critical seasons and in areas during the later stages of timber growth where native foods are scarce or nutritionally deficient. Food plots attract deer, thus they may increase hunter

success substantially, especially in areas and during periods of low hunter density.

During the successional stages of both pine and hardwood stands, the understory layer can simply grow out of reach of deer. Thinning of mature stands with closed canopies and the associated site disturbance are effective methods of starting a new layer of vegetation. Since shading frequently controls the abundance of understory vegetation, thinning trees to a basal area of 6.75 square meters per hectare (27 square feet per acre) will allow adequate sunlight penetration to release the understory.

Even-aged forest management is practiced widely in the Piedmont. When stands are clear-cut and regenerated, the area produces a lush new growth that temporarily improves range quality. But the stand usually provides considerably less deer food during the middle and later stages of a 20-year rotation. And when the cutting units are large—more than 24 hectares (60 acres)—there may be a scarcity of food within the deer's home range. On the other hand, when the even-aged stands are smaller than 24 hectares (60 acres), and well-dispersed and diversified in species composition, they can provide excellent whitetail habitat throughout the forest rotation. The value of a cutting unit also is influenced by the unit's shape. Long, irregularly shaped units are preferred over square or round units.

A modified even-aged forest management plan is used at the Piedmont National Wildlife Refuge to sustain high deer densities within carrying capacity. The plan is based on an 80-year rotation with an 8-year cutting cycle. In a typical forest compartment during an 8-year cycle, 85 percent of the area is commercially thinned, 10 percent is regenerated and 5 percent is retained in wildlife openings. Approximately 20 percent of the stands are retained in hardwoods, and harvested stands are regenerated by the shelterwood method. At the end of the 80-year rotation, each compartment contains 10 different age classes of trees for timber production. This system for managing forest harvest and regeneration is an excellent example of blending timber yields with wildlife habitat needs. It requires broader application.

Population Management

Although controversial, either-sex deer hunting is used widely throughout the Pied-

Forage for whitetails is sparse (left) in dense pole-size loblolly pine plantations in the Georgia Piedmont. Cutting trees in small units (right) can establish several age classes of pines within a small area and provide whitetails with adequate cover and an abundance and variety of food. *Left photo by Richard W. Whittington. Right photo by W. H. Bryant.*

mont Plateau. In Virginia, whitetail populations are controlled by manipulating the percentage of does in the legal harvest (Gwynn 1976). Where deer ranges are at carrying capacity and the objective is to maintain a stable population, either-sex hunting seasons are regulated so that does constitute 30 to 40 percent of the total harvest. Where whitetails exceed carrying capacity and the objective is to reduce deer populations, the harvest of does is increased to 40 or 50 percent. South Carolina maintains population levels within carrying capacity by allowing a long buck-only hunting season, followed by liberal either-sex hunting and a bag limit of five deer per season (W. Moore personal communication:1983).

Bag limits vary among states, but there is some consistency in regard to season length. The usual magnitude of the buck kill is of little consequence in controlling a whitetail population, provided that either-sex harvest is regulated. Either-sex seasons mixed in, or at the end of, long buck-only seasons seem to provide maximum recreational opportunities and an effective deer harvest.

Whitetail population management necessarily involves manipulation of hunter numbers and distribution within and among deer management units. With the exception of opening day, heaviest hunting pressure is on weekends and holidays. Hunting seasons may be timed

to take advantage of these days to increase or decrease hunter densities, depending on the extent of harvest desired. Setting quotas is yet another method of regulating hunter numbers to achieve a desired harvest. In North Carolina, both low and high hunter densities harvested more deer than did intermediate numbers. In Uwharrie, North Carolina, 40 percent of the deer were killed within 90 meters (295 feet) of a road or trail, and 81 percent were killed within 180 meters (590 feet) of access roads (James et al. 1964). A regular pattern of access roads has helped produce a more uniform deer kill and higher hunter success at Piedmont National Wildlife Refuge in Georgia (R. Shell personal communication:1983).

Land ownership patterns and leasing practices also affect whitetails harvests. In some instances, only a few hunters have access to large tracts of privately owned lands. In other cases, small groups of hunters lease extensive forest holdings and set conservative hunting policies for themselves. Under these conditions, deer usually are underharvested. In retrospect, the harvest can be quite satisfactory with intermediate numbers of hunters, but exceed safe limits with high hunter densities. Examples of this were found in hunting-club survey data collected following Georgia's 1982 deer-hunting season. In Heard County, the hunter density of 12 clubs responding was 4.2

A good system of all-weather access roads at Piedmont National Wildlife Refuge in Georgia contributes to uniform hunter distribution and a sufficiently high harvest rate of whitetails. Although much of the Piedmont Plateau has a roadway network to accommodate a reasonable spatial distribution of deer hunters, whitetail populations in some parts of the region are underharvested because large tracts of privately owned land are leased by a relatively small number of hunters. *Photo by W. H. Bryant.*

hunters per square kilometer (11 per square mile) on leased land. The kill was 3.1 deer per square kilometer (8 per square mile)—within safe limits. A few miles away in Meriwether County, hunter density of 17 clubs was 8.1 hunters per square kilometer (21 per square mile). The resulting kill was in excess of safe harvest limits at 5.4 deer per square kilometer (14 per square mile).

Efforts by wildlife biologists and managers to distribute hunters evenly over private and industrial forest leases may be futile. The lessor's price and the hunter's ability to pay largely will determine hunter density. When facing lease-fee increases during the last few years, many clubs have recruited new members to offset the costs. As a result, hunter density is increasing over much of the Piedmont. Hunters should self-impose limits on their numbers to about 5 per square kilometer (13 per square mile).

OUTLOOK

Whether white-tailed deer will continue to thrive in the Piedmont depends on many factors, such as public acceptance of doe hunting,

habitat alteration, economic values of deer hunting and good habitat management practices. The future of good hunting rests (1) with the various wildlife agencies through their consistent regulation of the harvest and (2) with forest owners who make lands available to hunters.

Conservative hunting regulations that stockpile deer are ineffective and invariably counterproductive. Yet, because some sportsmen still oppose doe harvesting, carrying capacity of range may be exceeded and the habitat damaged. Unless the modern concept of an either-sex harvest is promulgated and accepted, it may take a drastic reduction in animal quality to convince the public of the need for deer population control.

White-tailed deer habitat continually is being lost to agricultural interests, and this may become even more serious, since little farmland in the region is abandoned or allowed to revert to forest. Even-aged forest management has altered habitat over much of the Piedmont Plateau and will continue to be a major factor in the carrying capacity of pine forests. However, foresters and wildlife managers have an excellent opportunity to plan forest regeneration and cutting treatments that favor browse production.

Economic returns from deer, such as from hunting leases, help boost the earnings of a multiple-use forest to a profitable level. The increasing awareness of this potential source of additional income may encourage landowners to include the needs of white-tailed deer in forest managment plans. This is best accomplished by breaking the forest into individual management units where deer habitat within timber stands may be managed more intensively.

Lease hunting probably will increase until much of the opportunity to hunt whitetails in the Piedmont is available only to those who form clubs and negotiate with forest owners for hunting lands. However, some industrial forest owners likely will diversify their hunting programs to include fee hunting, lease hunting and free hunting with unlimited access. State and federal wildlife agencies will continue to make lands available to hunters and scientifically manage them for optimal whitetail-hunting opportunity.

Chapter 18

COASTAL PLAIN

John D. Newsom
Assistant Secretary
Office of Wildlife
Louisiana Department of Wildlife and Fisheries
Baton Rouge, Louisiana

ENVIRONMENT

The Atlantic-Gulf Coastal Plain is a variable-width belt of land extending about 3,000 kilometers (1,865 miles) from New York to the Rio Grande River in Texas, and inland from the Gulf of Mexico along the Mississippi River for about 1,000 kilometers (620 miles) to Cape Girardeau, Missouri, and southern Illinois (Figure 82). It encompasses approximately 124 million hectares (306.4 million acres) of land area. Because of vast differences in soils, vegetation, climate and physiography, it is divided into two regions—the Middle Atlantic Coastal Plain and the South Atlantic-Gulf Coastal Plain (Griffin et al. 1968).

Physiography

Long stretches of sandy beaches, tidewater marshes, flat plains, wide estuaries, peninsulas and swamps—near the ocean, and gently-rolling to steep hills—inland—characterize the Middle Atlantic Coastal Plain. Elevations range from sea level along the many tidal streams and bays to about 90 meters (295 feet) in inland Maryland.

The South Atlantic-Gulf Coastal Plain land surface is more diverse. Near the coast the surface is flat, while the more mature inner edge is dissected, hilly and deeply eroded. Estuaries, deltas in various stages of development, barrier beaches, vast coastal marshes and freshwater swamps mark the seaward edge.

Subsidence and beach erosion are common in the more mature portions near the coast. The typical belted Coastal Plain, evident in Alabama, gives way to the alluvial plain of the lower Mississippi River valley and tributaries, where large expanses of land are flooded annually unless protected by artificial levees. Elevations range from sea level to about 240 meters (790 feet) in Georgia, 120 meters (395 feet) near Cape Girardeau, Missouri, and 300 meters (985 feet) at the Rio Grande River on the inner edge of the Plain (Fenneman 1938).

Vegetation

In the Coastal Plain, there are five forest and grassland types of major importance: coastal marshes; longleaf/slash pine; shortleaf pine/oak; loblolly pine/hardwood; and bottomland hardwood (Society of American Foresters 1967).

Coastal marshes. Coastal marshes generally are subdivided into freshwater, intermediate, brackish and saline. Typical plants of the freshwater marsh are maidencane, pennywort, common waterhyacinth, pickerelweed, bulltongue arrowhead, alligatorweed and hornwort. In intermediate marshes, the most common plants are marshhay cordgrass, deer pea, California bulrush, Walter's Millet, sawgrass and common reed. Olney bulrush, saltmarsh bulrush, dwarf spikesedge and widgeongrass dominate the brackish marsh. Dominant plants of salt marshes are smooth cordgrass, needlegrass, maritima saltwort, black-mangrove and seashore saltgrass (Chabreck 1970).

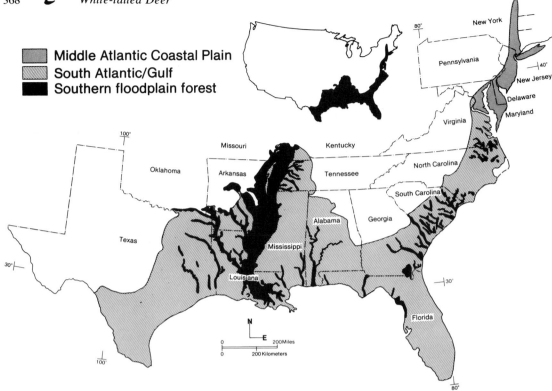

Figure 82. The Coastal Plain.

As they did historically, coastal wetlands support large and healthy white-tailed deer populations. *Photo courtesy of the Maryland Wildlife Administration.*

Because of the abundance and variety of plants, cover is seldom a limiting factor. White-tailed deer generally are limited to higher elevations in coastal marsh natural ridges, dredge spoil deposits and canal banks. Thus, the total amount of occupied habitat usually is small and the deer populations are low. Available food resources, such as alligatorweed and deer pea, usually are capable of supporting existing whitetail populations. Salt marshes support low populations primarily because of a lack of available deer food.

Longleaf/slash pine. In relatively dry areas, the dominant pines are associated with water oak, laurel oak, post oak and blackjack oak. On wetter sites, the association is with loblolly pine and blackgum. Common understory plants are yaupon, southern waxmyrtle, inkberry, tall gallberry, sawpalmetto, blueberries and poison-oak. In this forest type, modern forestry practices tend to eliminate hardwood species that compete with the pines; as a result, the deer carrying capacity is low.

Shortleaf pine/oak. Common species of oaks are white, scarlet, blackjack, black, post and southern red. On some sites, hickories, black-gum, sweetgum, Virginia pine and pitch pine occur. Common understory plants are parsley hawthorn, American beautyberry, common witchhazel, flowering dogwood, blueberries, greenbriers and rusty blackhaw viburnum. Because of a wide variety of desirable species in the overstory and understory, this forest type has a higher carrying capacity for whitetails than does the coastal marsh or longleaf/slash pine type.

Loblolly pine/hardwood. Hardwoods such as sweetbay, redbay, blackgum, red maple, post and southern red oaks are associated with the dominant pines. Predominant understory species are yaupon, greenbriers, tall gallberry, blackberries, swamp cyrilla and dahoon. Deer carrying capacity here closely approximates that of the shortleaf pine/oak forest type.

Bottomland hardwoods. Several forest types and numerous dominant species are included in various associations. Usually, eastern cottonwood, American sycamore, black willow and sandbar willow invade the newly accreted portions of river bottoms adjacent to main streams and on natural levees. Sweetgum, sugarberry, pecan, American elm, willow oak, Nuttal oak, cherrybark oak, swamp chestnut oak and green ash occur on the higher elevations. Overcup oak and water hickory are dominant in lower,

This lush understory of shrubs and forbs provides excellent upland habitat for Coastal Plain whitetails. The condition of this habitat is indicative of a well-managed deer population. *Photo courtesy of the U.S. Forest Service.*

wetter sites. Important understory species are blackberries, dwarf palmetto, deciduous holly, roughleaf dogwood, poison-ivy, peppervine, swamp fetterbush, supplejack, willow, Japanese honeysuckle, Virginia sweetspire, swamp privet, boxelder and reproduction of the dominant tree species in the association. The wide variety of high-quality food-producing species makes bottomland hardwoods the most productive forest type for white-tailed deer in the Coastal Plain.

The baldcypress/water tupelo type occurs within the bottomland hardwood zone and is relatively unimportant to deer because it is inundated for long periods of the year and produces relatively small quantities of desirable deer food. Common understory species are common buttonbush, swamp privet and Virginia sweetspire (Society of American Foresters 1967, Halls and Ripley 1961).

Soils

Most Coastal Plain soils are low in fertility and require fertilizers to produce agriculture crops commercially (U.S. Department of Agriculture 1957). However, the Mississippi Delta and other river deltas, which have derived from alluvial and loessial deposits, are sufficiently fertile to produce agricultural crops without the addition of large quantities of fertilizers.

Climate

Temperatures range from a yearly mean of about 20 degrees Celsius (69 degrees Fahrenheit) in Florida to about 10 degrees Celsius (50 degrees Fahrenheit) in Maryland. They range from 0 to 37 degrees Celsius (32–100 degrees Fahrenheit) in southern Florida to −20 to 37 degrees Celsius (6–100 degrees Fahrenheit) in Maryland. Average annual rainfall ranges from a high of about 152 centimeters (60 inches) in Louisiana to 40 centimeters (15.8 inches) in south Texas. Length of the growing season ranges from about 300 days in south Florida and Texas to 185 days in Maryland (U.S. Department of Agriculture 1941).

Land Use

Of the land devoted to agriculture (about 55 percent of the total land), 33 percent is intensively cultivated for row crops, such as corn, cotton, soybeans, rice, sugarcane and peanuts, and 67 percent is used as livestock pasture, most of which is unimproved.

Forests comprise about 45 percent of the total land area. Approximately 75 percent of the forested land is owned by private nonindustry, 18 percent by private industry, and 9 percent by state and federal governments. The private nonindustrial forests rarely are managed from the standpoint of timber and wildlife (Sternitzke and Christopher 1972, U.S. Department of Agriculture 1975).

WHITETAIL POPULATIONS

History

At the time of initial settlement of the Coastal Plain by Europeans, white-tailed deer were widespread and fairly abundant (Hariot 1893, Le Page du Pratz 1975, Bartram 1928, *see* Chapter 2). With human expansion that occurred in the 1600s and 1700s, deer were heav-

Periodic flooding along major river systems of the Coastal Plain often causes whitetails to be stranded on small elevated mounds for extended periods of time (*see* Chapter 42). In areas of high deer populations, excessive mortality can occur as a result, but this is infrequent. The most important impact on whitetails involves reduced reproductive rates and generally diminished physical condition. Flooding does not cause permanent displacement of deer even though they may move several miles. *A Wildlife Management Institute photo.*

ily utilized for food and clothing by settlers (Young 1956, Harlow and Jones 1965, Strecker 1927). Continued and intense exploitation of deer resulted in their decline at the beginning of the eighteenth century. This overall decline continued until an historical low was reached about 1920. Whitetail populations remained at low levels until after World War II, when restoration efforts were initiated by federal and state wildlife agencies. Trapping and translocation programs, improved habitat conditions, and conservation law enforcement brought quick results and deer populations increased dramatically. By 1969, the estimated population of whitetails in Coastal Plain states was 1.7 million, with an annual harvest of 266,000 (Newsom 1969). During the next few years, the deer population more than doubled in number and, in 1975, the estimated population was 4.3 million, with a harvest of 557,000. Whitetail populations and harvests for 1975, including portions of states not in the Coastal Plains, are shown in Table 61 (Wilcox 1975).

Table 61. Estimated white-tailed deer autumn population and harvest in Coastal Plain states, 1975 (from Wilcox 1975).

State	Prehunt population	Harvest	Percentage of prehunt population harvested
Alabama	1,000,000	120,727	12.1
Arkansas	425,000	33,322	7.8
Delaware	7,500	1,272	17.0
Florida	550,000	55,000	10.0
Georgia	350,000	57,000	16.5
Louisiana	375,000	76,769	20.5
Maryland	63,000	9,737	15.5
Mississippi	410,000	37,000	9.0
New Jersey	75,000	12,688	16.9
North Carolina	500,000	53,000	10.6
South Carolina	215,000	46,000	21.4
Tennessee	150,000	14,490	9.7
Texas	3,100,000	348,000	11.2
Virginia	356,880	63,443	17.8
Total	7,577,380	929,341	12.3

The deer hunting camp is traditional in Coastal Plain states; the most significant changes over the years have been vast improvements in weapons and equipment. The double-barrelled shotgun and buckshot, for example, gradually are being replaced by modern scope-sighted big game rifles, and the use of dogs for hunting deer is becoming less popular. With the phenomenal increases in whitetail populations in many parts of the Coastal Plain in recent decades, season lengths and bag limits have been liberalized substantially. *Left photo by Paul S. Carter; courtesy of the U.S. Forest Service. Right photo by Daniel O. Todd; courtesy of the U.S. Forest Service.*

Population Structure and Productivity

Data on white-tailed deer population structure are limited. Noble (1974) found an *in utero* buck-doe ratio of 1:1.37 in Mississippi. Strode (1954) observed the ratio to be 1:3.85 in northern Florida, and Adams (1960) reported it as 1:3 on overpopulated range in Alabama. In most states, buck-doe ratios reflected in the harvest are not representative of the true population ratio, due to the disproportionate amount of hunting pressure placed on bucks. It is likely that deer populations subjected to longer periods of buck-only hunting are composed primarily of does. Thomas and Marburger (1965) reported a reduction in the fawn-doe ratio of 1:1.1 to 1:5 in one year for an overpopulated deer population in the Edwards Plateau, Texas; and Noble (1974) indicated the low reproductive rate of Mississippi whitetails (fawn-doe ratio of 1:1.42) was due to a general statewide overpopulation. On an overpopulated range in Alabama, the number of adult does carrying a single fetus increased in comparison with the number of does carrying two fetuses (Adams 1960). The indication was that this was caused by range deterioration that resulted in nutritional deficiencies of the deer.

Failure of some hunters and wildlife agency administrators to accept the philosophy of either-sex deer hunting undoubtedly has led to unbalanced sex ratios, lowered reproductive rates, and generally unthrifty deer populations in many areas of the Coastal Plain.

Food and Feeding Habits

The diet of Coastal Plain whitetails is extremely varied. Murphy and Noble (1973) reported 81 species of plants utilized by deer in the bottomland hardwood area of Louisiana; Lay (1965*b*) identified 69 plant species utilized by deer in East Texas; and Harlow (1961) found 193 different deer food items in Florida.

Feeding habits of white-tailed deer of the Coastal Plain change seasonally (Halls 1970, Lay 1969, Short 1971, 1975). Fruits of such species as oaks, dwarf palmetto, American beautyberry, hawthorns and common persimmon are important during autumn and early winter when they are available. In late winter and early spring, grasses and winter rosettes of many composites are locally important. During spring and summer, tender shoots,

Japanese honeysuckle is a preferred whitetail food plant whenever it occurs in the Coastal Plain. Overbrowsing, as shown here, is quite common in heavily populated bottomland hardwoods, especially where other green vegetation is in short supply during winter. The condition of these plants may indicate need for deer population reduction. *Photo by Joe L. Herring; courtesy of the Louisiana Department of Wildlife and Fisheries.*

leaves and twigs of trees, shrubs and vines, and many broad-leaved herbaceous plants constitute the major portion of deer diets.

Some of the woody plant species preferred by Coastal whitetails are listed in Table 62.

SPECIAL PROBLEMS

Climate and Weather

The usually warm, humid climate is conducive to a high incidence of disease and parasite entities that can be detrimental to deer. On the positive side, high rainfall and hot temperatures produce an abundance of vegetation that is available to deer during spring, summer and early autumn. Winter weather in the Coastal Plain generally is not considered to be a limiting factor for whitetails.

Table 62. Common browse species and their parts preferred by white-tailed deer in the Coastal Plain.

Browse species	Frequency of use	Plant parts utilized	Season of greatest utilization
Red maple	Intermediate	Leaves, twigs	Spring, Summer
Rattan (supplejack)	Common	Leaves, twigs	Spring, Summer
American beautyberry	Common	Leaves, fruit	Spring, Summer, Autumn
Common trumpetcreeper	Common	Leaves, twigs	Spring, Summer, Autumn
Fringetree	Common	Leaves, twigs	Spring, Summer
Swamp cyrilla	Intermediate	Leaves, twigs	Spring
Common persimmon	Common	Fruit	Autumn
Strawberry bush	Common	Leaves, twigs	Year round
Carolina jessamine	Intermediate	Leaves, twigs	Year round
Smooth hydrangea	Intermediate	Leaves, twigs	Year round
Deciduous holly	Common	Leaves, twigs	Spring, Summer
Yaupon	Intermediate	Leaves, twigs, fruit	Autumn, Winter
Virginia sweetspire	Common	Leaves, twigs	Year round
Japanese honeysuckle	Common	Leaves, twigs	Year round
Sweetbay	Intermediate	Leaves	Year round
Red mulberry	Common	Leaves	Spring, Summer
Blackgum	Common	Leaves, fruit	Spring, Summer
Redbay	Intermediate	Leaves	Year round
Buffalo-nut	Common	Leaves, twigs, fruit	Spring, Summer
Oak			
White	Common	Fruit	Autumn, Winter
Laurel	Common	Leaves, fruit	Spring, Autumn, Winter
Water	Common	Leaves, fruit	Spring, Autumn, Winter
Willow	Common	Leaves, fruit	Spring, Autumn, Winter
Poison-ivy	Common	Leaves	Spring, Summer
Blackberry	Common	Leaves, fruit	Year round
Dewberry	Common	Leaves, fruit	Year round
Black willow	Common	Leaves, stems	Year round
Sandbar willow	Common	Leaves, stems	Year round
American elder	Common	Leaves	Year round
Common sassafras	Common	Leaves	Spring, Summer
Saw greenbrier	Common	Leaves, shoots	Year round
Cat greenbrier	Common	Leaves, shoots	Year round
Laurel greenbrier	Common	Leaves, shoots	Year round
Common greenbrier	Common	Leaves, shoots	Year round
Lanceleaf greenbrier	Common	Leaves, shoots	Year round
Mapleleaf viburnum	Intermediate	Leaves, twigs, fruit	Spring, Summer, Autumn
Arrowwood viburnum	Common	Leaves, twigs, fruit	Spring, Summer, Autumn
Summer grape	Common	Leaves, twigs, fruit	Spring

Food Quality and Quantity

Whitetail diets in upland forests of the Coastal Plain are deficient in protein and minerals, and probably account for the small size and relatively low density of the deer populations (Short et al. 1969*a*). Quantity of forage produced in some of the various forest types is best illustrated by estimated carrying capacity figures developed by the Mississippi Game and Fish Commission (1972); bottomland hardwood, one deer per 4 to 6 hectares (10–15 acres); mixed pine/hardwood, one deer per 8 to 16 hectares (20–40 acres); upland hardwoods, one deer per 10 to 18 hectares (25–45 acres); loblolly/shortleaf pine, one deer per 12 to 20 hectares (30–50 acres); and longleaf/slash pine,

one deer per 24 to 32 hectares (60–80 acres). All available data indicate that highest quality deer foods are produced in bottomland hardwoods, and lowest quality foods occur in homogenous loblolly and slash pine forests.

Predation

During the present century, feral dogs have become a significant predator of white-tailed deer in the Coastal Plain (Barick 1969, Gipson and Sealander 1974, Hardister 1965, Morrison 1967). Some investigators imply that dogs are not a serious predator (Gavitt 1973, Scott and Causey 1973), whereas others claim that dogs can eliminate marginal deer populations and prevent establishment of deer in new range (Barick 1969). Feral dogs may take a number of deer each year, but the overall impact is greatest on sparsely populated ranges.

The coyote recently has expanded its range to all states in the Coastal Plain. Being an opportunist, it usually takes the most easily obtainable food materials. In areas of high deer density and high coyote populations, some coyotes feed almost exclusively on fawns during peak fawning periods (Hall and Newsom 1978). At the Welder Wildlife Foundation Refuge in Texas (Cook et al. 1971) and in western Oklahoma (Garner et al. 1978), coyotes limited deer populations by taking fawns within the first few weeks of life. It is conceivable that coyotes may become sufficiently numerous in portions of the Coastal Plain to exert a limiting influence on local white-tailed deer populations by taking substantial numbers of fawns.

Although the bobcat preys on fawns and occasionally on larger deer, it is not an important predator of whitetails in the Coastal Plain. The mountain lion population in the Coastal Plain currently is limited to possibly two dozen animals in Florida and an occasional animal in Texas. Although black bear are more numerous in the region, reports of the species preying on whitetails are not available.

Disease and Parasites

The most prevalent and potentially dangerous deer diseases in the Coastal Plain are anthrax, salmonellosis, leptospirosis, epizootic hemorrhagic disease and bluetongue (Trainer 1964, Ferris and Verts 1964, Wilhelm and Trainer 1966, Hoff et al. 1974, Kellogg et al. 1970, Cook et al. 1965). The bluetongue/epizootic hemorrhagic disease complex is endemic, and outbreaks have reduced deer populations in Tennessee, Texas and Arkansas (*see* Fox and Pelton 1974, Hoff et al. 1974, Karstad 1962, Prestwood et al. 1974, Stair et al. 1968, Pledger 1977). Anthrax also is endemic and has great potential for becoming epizootic, particularly in flooded river bottoms (Hayes and Prestwood 1969, Kellogg et al. 1970). The region's warm-moist climate provides ideal conditions for perpetuation of certain disease entities harmful to whitetails.

In all likelihood, every whitetail older than six months harbors several species of parasites. At least 30 species of helminth parasites

are carried by deer in the Coastal Plain (Hayes and Prestwood 1969). Their overall effects depend mainly on the physical condition of deer and the severity of infestation. Some of the most common and potentially troublesome parasites are lungworms, stomach worms, hookworms and large American flukes. Endoparasitic infestations usually are associated with high deer densities, and are secondary to the primary problem of overpopulation and deteriorating range conditions. Screwworm infestations are potentially dangerous to deer, particularly in Texas and Louisiana. Ticks, primarily the lone star tick, may cause excessive mortality in deer fawns (Logan 1973). Fawn mortality measured 64 percent during one year of study.

Competition

The white-tailed deer cohabits range with a large number of wild and domestic animals, some of which compete directly for food. Free-ranging cattle, sheep and goats compete for available browse; squirrels, raccoons, wild turkeys and various kinds of songbirds vie for mast. Locally, feral hogs also utilize large

Whitetails in parts of the Coastal Plain compete with wild turkeys for mast, but such competition is not believed to be limiting for either species. *Photo by Roy Morsch.*

Readily available sources of freshwater are extremely important components of whitetail habitat in the Coastal Plain. Restricted availability may cause excessive exposure to poaching and other debilitating factors, such as parasitism and disease. *Top-left photo courtesy of the Arkansas Game and Fish Commission. Top-right photo by Clint Davis; courtesy of the U. S. Forest Service. Bottom photo by Daniel O. Todd; courtesy of the U.S. Forest Service.*

amounts of mast. Intraspecific competition with livestock for food does not influence white-tailed deer populations except where ranges are overstocked with livestock (McMahan 1964, McMahan and Ramsey 1965). Livestock/deer relationships have not been documented ade-

quately on forested land in the Coastal Plain. However, recent studies in Texas have demonstrated that exotic game species pose a serious threat to whitetail populations from the standpoint of competition for the available food resource (Baccus et al. 1983).

Land Use

Even though the white-tailed deer competes successfully with most other animals, it fares poorly with some changing land-use practices. Conversion of bottomland hardwood forests to agriculture is eliminating some of the most productive deer habitat in the Coastal Plain. In Louisiana, approximately 500,000 hectares (1.2 million acres) of bottomland hardwood habitat were converted to agricultural production, primarily soybeans, between 1962 and 1974 (Corty and Main 1974). This trend likely will continue until virtually all bottomland hardwoods, except batture lands, are converted to agriculture. With the decrease in natural habitat, Coastal Plain whitetails are forced into agricultural areas where they damage crops. Consequently, unknown but reportedly large numbers of deer are killed during spring and summer by farmers in an attempt to limit crop depredations.

Forest management practices in the Coastal Plain have undergone major changes in recent years. Selective cutting and long rotations of southern pines are being replaced rapidly by short rotations, even-aged monoculture and clear-cut harvesting. This system, coupled with hardwood removal in older pine stands, likely will cause a further reduction of suitable deer habitat. It has been demonstrated repeatedly that intensively managed southern pine forests produce lower yields of deer foods than do mixed pine/hardwood forests (Blair 1967, 1969, Goodrum 1969, Reid and Goodrum 1958, Rhodes 1952).

Deer damage young planted pine seedlings infrequently (Robinette 1973), but this likely will increase as the overall habitat base shrinks and whitetails resort to less palatable forage.

MANAGEMENT

Deer hunting regulations in Coastal Plain states are quite liberal. The open season in South Carolina runs from August 15 to January 1. In Alabama and Mississippi, each licensed hunter is allowed one deer per day during the open season of up to 60 days in length. Other Coastal Plain states have somewhat shorter seasons and lower bag limits, ranging from a 6-day season with a season limit of one deer to a 54-day, six-deer season. Most Coastal Plain states have a tagging system, but few require mandatory validation. Hunting with dogs is allowed in all or parts of most states. Either-sex deer hunting is authorized in all states, generally on a limited or area-of-need basis. Doe harvests still are regarded by some administrators of state wildlife agencies (not wildlife biologists) as a necessary evil for deer population reduction rather than as a practical tool of management. Traditional deer hunting customs continue to influence harvest regulations. There is need for whitetail management based on a unit system within states based on habitat, deer population size and harvest pressure, and within which the deer resource can be managed more intensively.

Whitetail population management is hampered seriously by buck-only hunting, particularly on privately owned lands leased to hunting clubs. Even though state agencies may authorize the harvest of either-sex deer, some hunting clubs are reluctant to take antlerless whitetails. Some clubs do not shoot spike bucks in the mistaken belief that they are providing for a future population of large-antlered bucks. In reality, by not harvesting does and young bucks, these clubs are compounding the problem of whitetail overpopulation by perpetuating small antlers, small body size and reduced reproductive rates. Moreover they are increasing the potential for disease and parasite problems. Archaic attitudes about the complete protection of does from harvest are becoming less prevalent each year, but they persist and remain serious problems, particularly in the deep South. Nowhere are these problems statewide.

Many years of selective harvest of large-antlered bucks likely will reduce the genetic potential for superior antler development. It is not unusual to see yearling bucks of near normal body size without visible antlers. Yearlings with antlers of 2.5 to 5.0 centimeters (1–2 inches) are common. Inferior antler development is attributable mainly to overcrowding and nutritional deficiencies, but genetics also play a significant role.

Although it is not economically feasible to determine exact deer numbers in the Coastal Plain, wildlife management agencies can utilize certain techniques to evaluate whitetail population conditions and to estimate relative population levels. Information about annual harvest, buck/doe ratios, fawn/doe ratios, antler development, body size, and the seasonal quality and quantity of preferred browse species can be used to regulate deer populations, provided the manager or biologist has administrative and public support. With the option of an either-sex deer hunting season in deer management units, hunting regulations can be adjusted to provide a whitetail harvest that will help to maintain a healthy deer population.

In the Coastal Plain there are a number of options for deer management ranging from maximum or optimum productivity to trophy buck prodcution. All require close surveillance of the deer population's condition on a management unit by unit basis. Maximum productivity requires the harvest of both sexes and all ages of deer, and an annual kill of approximately 35 percent of the population (Wilson and McMaster 1974). Management for optimum productivity is virtually mandatory on publicly owned areas where conflicting land uses require that the deer population not exceed habitat carrying capacity. Management of a deer population for trophy bucks can be accomplished best on privately owned lands where a substantial portion of the income is derived from the sale of trophy hunting per-

mits. This is occurring to a limited extent in parts of Georgia and Texas, and is growing in popularity. Trophy production requires knowledge of range carrying capacity and deer population level, and stringent control over the harvest. The trophy potential is highest when deer populations are maintained somewhat below carrying capacity. The buck-doe ratio should be 1:2 or less. The annual harvest should consist of approximately equal numbers of both sexes. The buck kill should be directed at inferior yearlings with small body size (less than 45 kilograms:100 pounds) and poorly developed antlers and at older trophy-size bucks. Young bucks with large body size (57–64 kilograms:125–140 pounds) and well-developed branched antlers of four to eight points should be retained (Brothers and Ray 1975).

To some extent, deer habitat is being improved on publicly owned or operated wildlife management areas by the planting of hardwoods, browse and herbaceous perennials. The plantings undoubtedly have some effect on deer condition and distribution, but the overall impact on population productivity is unknown.

A whitetail doe feeds on forbs produced as a result of brush removal, root plowing and seeding in Texas. Habitat management of this type—the transformation of dense, relatively unproductive brushland into productive range—has caused substantial increases in whitetail populations in many parts of the Coastal Plain. *Photo by Jack Megason; courtesy of the U. S. Soil Conservation Service.*

A camera-point study of a Coastal Plain loblolly pine site subjected to prescribed burning: (opposite top) experimental area before the last of a series of burns; (opposite bottom) same area shortly after the last prescribed burn; (above) same area eight years after prescribed burn, demonstrating the powerful influence of fire on the composition and structure of vegetation. When used by experienced wildlife managers, fire can develop or maintain floral diversity on nearly any landscape. It is important that the factors of fire intensity and size of burn be considered, as well as the timing of such events and the types of wildlife to be benefitted. *Photos by Roy Komarek; courtesy of the Tall Timbers Research Station.*

Habitat needs of white-tailed deer frequently are ignored in southern pine forests managed solely, or almost solely, for timber. However, in recent years, wildlife managers have co-operated with private and public foresters to enhance deer habitat on forested lands managed for timber production. As a result, many private and public forest managers have adjusted their practices so as to maintain hardwood stands in stream bottoms, and have tailored the size, shape and distribution of clearcut harvests to obtain maximum wildlife use.

Deer disease and parasite surveillance on public areas is a routine part of white-tailed deer management programs through state wildlife agencies and the Southeastern Cooperative Wildlife Disease Study. Some states provide this service on privately owned areas.

Leasing of large acreages of deer range to hunting clubs frequently leads to overpopulations of deer, habitat deterioration, deer disease and parasitism outbreaks. The most ef-

fective and consistent management of whitetails in the Coastal Plain—to minimize such problems as crop depredations and deer/vehicle accidents, and to maximize the species' recreational, aesthetic and economic benefits—is regulated harvests. Although sometimes constrained by biopolitical circumstances, biologists and managers continue to press for harvests that maintain whitetail populations balanced between optimal habitat carrying capacity and landowner tolerance.

In Mississippi, about 90 percent of the annual legal harvest of whitetails occurs on privately owned land. In an effort to facilitate collection of information sufficient to manage deer populations in the state, the Mississippi Deer Management Program was instituted in 1977 (Guynn et al. 1983). The program objectives were to: (1) develop a system for collection, analysis and reporting of harvest data; (2) involve sportsmen in the management process; (3) reduce deer density and crop depredation where needed; and (4) increase the quality of harvested deer. In the program's first four years, 1977 through 1981, the results were most favorable. Landowner/sportsman participation in data collection was enthusiastic and, reportedly, increased understanding of deer biology and receptivity to management recommendations. Deer harvest and antlerless harvest have increased dramatically each year the program has been in effect. The program also has stimulated landowner and sportsman interest in trophy management and improved habitat management for whitetails on private lands. The educational and public-relations aspects of the program were seen as significant gains. A similar program was initiated on a statewide basis in Louisiana in 1981, with similar results reported.

OUTLOOK

The perpetuation of white-tailed deer as a valuable natural resource in the Coastal Plain depends on a continuing and close working relationship among wildlife biologists, forest managers, other resource managers and the public. In this region, most whitetails are produced on privately owned forested lands. Therefore, forest management guidelines and practices must be implemented that will economically and practicably enable landowners to maintain or produce habitat for white-tailed deer.

In view of the present and predicted demands for deer hunting, wildlife management must be directed toward optimum productivity of whitetail populations. This can be accomplished only by adequate harvest of both sexes of deer.

In the future, white-tailed deer will be produced primarily in upland forest habitats because much of the highly fertile river-bottom forests will be converted to agricultural cropland. Overall, deer likely will decline in numbers, but continue to be a valuable recreational resource for the foreseeable future.

Chapter 19

FLORIDA KEYS

James W. Hardin
Associate Professor of Wildlife
College of Natural Resources
University of Wisconsin
Stevens Point, Wisconsin

Willard D. Klimstra
Distinguished Professor of Zoology
Director
Cooperative Wildlife Research Laboratory
Southern Illinois University
Carbondale, Illinois

Nova J. Silvy
Associate Professor
Department of Wildlife
and Fisheries Science
Texas A & M University
College Station, Texas

ENVIRONMENT

Key deer, smallest of the North American white-tailed deer, occupy islands south of Miami, Florida, from Little Pine Key to Sugarloaf Key (Figure 83). Big Pine Key, the historic center of the population, is 3.3 kilometers (2.0 miles) wide and 13.3 kilometers (8.3 miles) long, and includes about 2,400 hectares (6,000 acres) of land. The maximum elevation is 3 meters (10 feet). The distance from Big Pine to adjacent islands ranges from 0.1 to 6.4 kilometers (0.06–4.0 miles). These islands range in size from about 8 to 1,200 hectares (20–2,965 acres), and show evidence of Key deer activity.

The Florida Keys have two types of surface rock, as a result of two Pleistocene age formations (Hoffmeister and Multer 1968). Most of the lower Keys are composed of exposed oölitic Miami Limestone. This formation has a laminated crust broken into plates in many places by tree roots. Key Largo Limestone, an elevated coral-reef rock, comprises most of the upper Keys (Hoffmeister and Multer 1968). Much of Big Pine Key is oölitic in nature; only the southeast point is Key Largo Limestone. Soils vary from a blue-gray marl to a black peaty muck (Dickson 1955). From 61 to 76 centimeters (24–30 inches) of humus-rich soils oc-cur in older hammocks and buttonwood parks, while pinewoods have little or no soil.

Vegetation of the Florida Keys is of West Indian origin (Stern and Brizicky 1957). Plants with high salt tolerance, such as red mangrove, occur at the fringe of islands and in low-lying areas. Plants with low salt tolerance, such as hammock and pineland vegetation, occur only at higher elevations. Much of the vegetation on Big Pine and adjacent islands reflects the heavy influence of fires, farming and land clearing by early residents. In the absence of fire, plant succession is from pinelands to hammocks.

Dickson (1955) recognized nine plant communities on Big Pine Key: pineland; hammock; southeast point hammock; regrowth burned pineland; land previously cultivated; grass prairie; transition zones; open scrub-type mangrove/prairie; and beach dune communities. Yaw (1966) considered only mangrove thicket, open scrub, button-mangrove park, open-mixed hardwood, hammock and pinewoods. Silvy (1975) combined the open scrub and button-mangrove park, but recognized open developed areas as an additional type. Dense red mangrove thickets that fringed many islands have been replaced by residential developments following canal dredging which yielded marl for filling these low areas.

Figure 83. Islands of the Florida Keys within the range of Key deer.

Stands of white indigo berry and saffron plum are excellent sources of food for Key deer. They are extensively utilized on Big Pine Key where these plants invaded areas when agricultural practices ceased in the late 1930s and early 1940s. *Photo courtesy of the Southern Illinois Cooperative Wildlife Research Laboratory.*

Stands of slash pine are limited to a few Keys; the largest of such acreage occurs on Big Pine Key. These stands are important because they afford Key deer a variety of useful plant foods. Also, their many depressions with palmetto provide shelter for fawns, and the extensive and widely-dispersed silver and Key thatch palms serve as both food and cover. The highest populations of Key deer are associated with Keys with pine stands that, when subject to controlled burns, yield significant increases in high-quality deer foods. *Photo courtesy of the Southern Illinois University Cooperative Wildlife Research Laboratory.*

The mean maximum temperature is 27.8 degrees Celsius (82 degrees Fahrenheit). Mean monthly highs range from 24.1 to 31.5 degrees Celsius (75.4–88.7 degrees Fahrenheit) and lows from 18.4 to 25.6 degrees Celsius (65.1–78.1 degrees Fahrenheit). Annual rainfall varies among the islands, but is approximately 102 centimeters (40 inches) at Key West (Dickson 1955). The monthly average from December to March is 4.47 centimeters (1.76 inches).

Land use varies from intensive commercial and residential development along U.S. Highway 1 (Big Pine, Little Torch, Ramrod, West Summerland, Cudjoe and Sugarloaf), to moderate development on Keys with secondary country roads (No Name, Middle Torch and Big Torch), to little or no development on remote islands accessible only by water (Little Pine and Johnson). Approximately 424 hectares (1,050 acres) or 17.6 percent of Big Pine Key were in housing subdivisions in 1969, with 96 kilometers (60 miles) of roads, 27 kilometers (17 miles) of firelanes, more than 160 kilometers (100 miles) of mosquito ditches, and 29 kilometers (18 miles) of canals (Klimstra et al. 1974). During the period 1968–1973, 46 hectares (114 acres) of land were cleared annually, in contrast to 32 hectares (80 acres) each year during the period 1979–1982. Similar rates of development occurred on several other islands within the Key deer range.

Clearings in subdivisions and along roadways have increased diversity, created areas of abundant browse adjacent to cover and temporarily increased localized carrying capacity for the deer. However, completion of developments generally results in a sudden loss of habitat. The accompanying increase in human activity and traffic can be presumed to increase the risk of deer accidents on highways—a continuing major source of mortality, as is an increase in poaching and losses to predation by dogs.

WHITETAIL POPULATION

Earliest mention of the Key deer is found in the memoirs of d'Escalante Fontaneda (1575), a Spaniard who was held captive by Indians. Later references suggest that deer were abundant as far as Key West, and were used as food by residents and crews from passing ships (Romans 1775, Mathews 1908, Maynard 1987, de Pourtales 1877).

Unfortunately, the published record provides little reliable information on population levels and distribution of this deer in the lower Keys. However, one can presume that where there were mature forested lands—which seemingly was the case for much of the Keys except the marl prairie, scrub mangrove and mangrove border portions of at least the larger land masses—carrying capacity for deer probably was low, especially so for such a diminutive animal. Storms, in particular hurricanes, probably released segments of this dominating vegetation, creating successional stages that improved food availability. With the development of human populations in the mid- to late-1800s (and associated farming activities), clearing and harvest of the wooded areas surely enhanced habitat, and the response was an increase in deer numbers. This evolved people/deer setting surely resulted in Key deer being viewed as a pest, and also encouraged expanded use of it for food. The intensity of this interaction probably began in the late 1800s and the very early 1900s, reaching annihilation levels by the early 1930s. The banning of hunting in 1939 by the Florida legislature was ineffective, as there was little if any effort at enforcement. Hunting continued, with dogs used and Keys burned to drive deer into the open for easy harvesting. Although various factors—especially the 1934 Ding Darling cartoon captioned "The Last of the 'Toy' Deer of the Florida Keys"—contributed to this ban on hunting, residents of the Keys resisted or ignored all efforts to relieve the plight of the Key deer. Hence, by the 1950s it was suggested that the population was as low as 25 deer, but this likely was a poor if not highly erroneous estimation. Official action occurred around 1950, when an effort was made to introduce legislation to establish a Key Deer National Wildlife Refuge. Also during that year a protection plan was developed by the Boone and Crockett Club. And in 1951, Jack C. Watson, who had devoted nearly 25 years of his life to the deer, was employed and endowed with both state and federal enforcement authority. That same year Florida established a Federal Aid Project and hired John Dickson to study the Key deer. These initial actions, largely from private interests and groups encouraged by C. R. "Pink" Gutermuth, yielded the foundation and dollars for land acquisition, leasing, and legislation to establish protection of the Key deer and its shrinking habitat.

THE LAST OF THE "TOY" DEER OF THE FLORIDA KEYS

Shortly after assuming office as chief of the U.S. Bureau of Biological Survey (predecessor of the U.S. Fish and Wildlife Service), cartoonist and conservationist Jay N. "Ding" Darling made an extensive search of the nation's wetlands with an eye toward establishing refuges, principally for the benefit of waterfowl. Cruising in a commercial fishing launch past mangrove thickets of the Florida Keys in 1934, Darling observed an uninhabited islet charred and still smouldering from the effects of a recent fire. He learned that the devastation was caused by Cuban fishermen who frequently visited the Keys to obtain meat. They commonly set fire to island vegetation to drive deer into the water where the animals were shot or clubbed. Stunned and horrified at the callous lawlessness of the activity and the wanton destruction that resulted, Ding then and there drew a caricature of the incident. Entitled "The Last of the 'Toy' Deer of the Florida Keys," the cartoon ". . . played an important part in whipping up support for a bill calling for a federal Key deer refuge" (Lendt 1979:130, *see also* Trefethen 1975). *Photo courtesy of the Jay N. Darling Collection, Special Collections Department, University of Iowa Libraries.*

In 1957 a 2,400-hectare (5,930-acre) Key deer refuge was established, including parcels of land on islands between Cudjoe and Little Pine Key, through efforts of the Boone and Crockett Club, Wildlife Management Institute, North American Wildlife Foundation and U.S. Fish and Wildlife Service. The Key deer was placed on the federal list of endangered species on March 11, 1967. However, Florida identifies it as threatened (Hendry et al. 1982).

In 1974 there were an estimated 200 to 250 deer on Big Pine Key and evidence of 100 to 150 deer on 22 other islands (Klimstra et al.

1974). Although there is some consensus to the effect that population stability occurs at these levels, our appraisal of 1982 suggests that a decline has occurred. However, in the absence of current research data, such a decline cannot be documented.

A study made from 1968 to 1973 revealed an apparent increase in the adult component of the population and a decrease in fawns, suggesting a low rate of increment (Hardin 1974). Male fetuses outnumbered females 1.75:1.00, and newborn male fawns outnumbered females 2:1. Older fawns were captured at a rate of 2.7 males to 1.0 female. The continuation of such statistics in the population must be presumed to be biologically negative.

The body size (weight and height) of Key deer is extremely variable, suggesting a genetic impact that yields subpopulations in the evolution of island inhabitants. The maxima in Key deer measurements show a very limited overlap with those of deer of the Florida Everglades; generally, Key deer measurements tend to be less. Barbour and Allen (1922) believed the Key deer to be a legitimate subspecies and the smallest white-tailed deer in the United States. Dickson (1955) shared this opinion, and our findings yield considerable data that strongly support the morphological distinctiveness of the race *clavium* in contrast to *osceola* and *virginianus* of the Florida mainland.

At birth Key deer fawns weigh 1 to 2 kilograms (2.2–4.5 pounds), with a mean of 1.7 kilograms (3.8 pounds). Males attain 40.3 percent of average maximum total weight during the first 12 months; in the same period, females attain 33.3 percent of average maximum total weight. The average weight of males is 19.1 kilograms (42.5 pounds) at one year, 26.9 kilograms (59.7 pounds) at two years and 35.9 kilograms (79.8 pounds) for all three years or older. Does show average weights of 16.7 kilograms (37.0 pounds) at one year, 24.7 kilograms (54.9 pounds) at two years and 28.4 kilograms (63.2 pounds) for all three years or older; maximum weight is reached at four to five years, whereas bucks continue weight gain until impacted by old age problems. Height at the shoulder for animals more than two years ranged from 43.18 to 82.55 centimeters (17–32.5 inches)—with a mean of 62.54 centimeters (26.98 inches)—for bucks, and 31.75 to 74.95 centimeters (12.5–29.5 inches)—with a mean of 64.87 centimeters (25.54 inches)—for does.

Based on weights of animals, fat deposits, and the absence of parasites and diseases, it appeared that Key deer were in good condition. However, they had a low rate of reproduction. Based on examination of 35 carcasses of does two years old or older, 31 were reproductively active, 19 had single fawns, 7 had twins and 5 were lactating, indicating at least 1 fawn. Only three two-year-old does bred as yearlings. Our studies during September 1969 through December 1972 suggested that 71 percent of 117 marked does of reproductive age had fawns. The data indicate a 20-percent mortality between preparturition and four to six months of age.

The physical stature of Key deer is distinctively small, but maxima overlap those of whitetails of the Florida Everglades. Generally, legs of Key deer are shorter, and the body and head are "blockier." Adult shoulder height averages 68 centimeters (26.8 inches), with a range of 32 to 83 centimeters (12.6–32.7 inches). *Photo courtesy of the Southern Illinois University Cooperative Wildlife Research Laboratory.*

There is substantial mortality of Key deer even though there is no legal hunting, nor any natural terrestrial predators. It is thought that the rate of loss from year to year probably is quite variable, fluctuating sharply in response to drought, violent storms, seasonal patterns of human activity and deer behavior. From 1968 through 1973, 304 deaths were recorded on 10 different islands. A computer simulation using mortality and natality data gathered during that period suggested a net increase of 8 percent in the population per year, as expected if the level was 50 animals in 1949 and had increased to 350 by mid-1970s (Silvy 1975). From 1968 through 1980, highway mortalities show annual variation from 36 to 74 and have totalled 627 animals, with 85 to 90 percent occurring on Big Pine Key. During the period 1968–1973, traffic losses represented 76 percent of all recorded mortality. Since that time, however, there have been very significant increases in the free-running dog population and the probability of poaching.

Drought may have contributed to mortality by causing deer to shift to areas where they were more vulnerable to automobiles. Six skeletons were found near dry waterholes on outer islands during the severe drought of 1970 and 1971. Others may have drowned while swimming between Keys in the shark-infested channels, many of which have hazardous currents.

Big Pine Key has more than 161 kilometers (100 miles) of ditches connecting basins of standing water to the saltwater of Florida Bay, and these are a major cause of fawn mortality. From 1970 to 1973, 6 of 33 marked newborn fawns and 5 unmarked fawns drowned in these ditches. Many of the ditches flush daily with the tides, and fawns falling into them cannot escape and are likely to be carried into the Bay.

Key deer utilize a wide variety of plants and habitat types. Virtually no plant species is immune to deer use at one time or another. Red mangrove, black mangrove, apes-earring, Indian mulberry, Florida silverpalm, brittle thatch palm and pencilflower are some of the most heavily eaten species (Dooley 1974). New growth of browse and herbaceous species are heavily grazed after fire; grazing declines sharply six to nine months after fire.

The availability of early succession plants for limited periods and the movements and feeding of deer are influenced by land-use activities such as mosquito ditching, clearing, roadway and right-of-way management, subdivision development and fire trails.

The greatest cause of recorded mortality among Key deer is collision with vehicles on U.S. Highway 1 and state roads on several Keys (*See* Figure 83). Annual losses vary considerably and do not appear to mirror speculated deer population levels or traffic patterns. *Photo courtesy of the Southern Illinois University Cooperative Wildlife Research Laboratory.*

Mortality of Key deer fawns drowning in mosquito ditches on Big Pine Key—which has more than 161 kilometers (100 miles) of such ditches—is believed to be significant when fawns are less than two to three weeks old. At this age, the fawns cannot jump the 35–40-centimeter (14–16-inch) wide, steep-sided, water-filled ditches, and once having fallen in, are unable to escape. The same is true for an occasional adult. *Photos courtesy of the Southern Illinois University Cooperative Wildlife Research Laboratory.*

The several types of palms on Big Pine and Little Pine Keys provide an important source of food for Key deer; flower stalks, fruits and new frond shoots are heavily used. Such a food source as provided by silver and Key thatch palms becomes unavailable as the palms increase in height; only the palmetto remains continuously available. *Photo courtesy of the Southern Illinois University Cooperative Wildlife Research Laboratory.*

Red, white and black mangroves constitute major portions of deer habitat in the Florida Keys and, in some cases, cover entire islands. They are valuable sources of food and cover for Key deer. Fruits of white and black mangroves are especially important food of the deer, as are leaves, fruit and flowers of red mangroves; their nutritional levels are roughly equivalent to that of alfalfa. *Photo courtesy of the Southern Illinois University Cooperative Wildlife Research Laboratory.*

SPECIAL PROBLEMS AND CONSTRAINTS

Availability of fresh water for drinking does not appear to be a primary limiting factor for deer on Big Pine Key, but it may limit year-round utilization of the outer Keys. After an extremely dry winter in 1971, two deer skeletons on Howe Key and one on Big Johnson Key were found near dry or saline waterholes, indicating that the deer were victims of drought. During this same period, a radio-tagged doe with a fawn on Porpoise Key—an island lacking fresh water—made daily trips to Big Pine Key where she watered and fed. Immediately after the rains, she remained on Porpoise Key. On Big Pine Key, many deer shifted to areas having fresh water during the drought. Even where water is available, it may exceed the 1.5 percent salt-tolerance level that appears to be critical for livestock (Pierce 1957, 1959, Weeth and Haverland 1961).

The phenomenon of Key deer swimming between islands has been recorded on many occasions and is believed to be important in the distribution of deer among the lower Florida Keys. This adult doe was captured swimming between Big Pine and Porpoise Keys. She was radio-collared and subsequently recorded as swimming a roundtrip every 24 hours to accommodate a fawn on Porpoise Key, while feeding and probably obtaining fresh water on Big Pine Key. *Photo courtesy of the Southern Illinois University Cooperative Wildlife Research Laboratory.*

In certain areas, browse and selected plant species are "pressured," but there is no evidence that current food quantity and quality are limiting factors. The mean energy value of 25 plants important in the diet of Key deer was 4,534 calories per gram (Klimstra et al. 1974). This is equivalent in energy to various commercial animal feeds.

As previously indicated, there are no native terrestrial predators of the Key deer. Dogs and alligators have been seen feeding on deer, but this probably represents scavenging. However, there has been a significant increase in recent years of free-roaming dogs, and kills of deer by dogs are being reported.

There is no evidence of disease-related mortality, although some deer have fibromas growing on their skin. Key deer are relatively free of ectoparasites except ticks, mosquitoes and deer flies. At times, deer will move to open areas or to shallow water in mangroves in order to escape mosquitoes. Three genera of nematodes, one trematode and a protozoan have been recorded in fecal samples of Key deer, but there was no indication that these intestinal parasites produced pathogenic effects (Schulte et al. 1976).

There is little adverse interaction between Key deer and other native fauna, except perhaps the raccoon, which may compete for fruits and water.

As a result of policy of the U.S. Fish and Wildlife Service concerning endangered species, the Florida Key Deer Recovery Plan was developed and approved in 1980 (Klimstra et al. 1980). Only limited segments of recommendations are being implemented due to budgetary constraints. Emphasized in the Recovery Plan are matters that reflect administration, land acquisition, management, monitoring, education and experimentation in research. It was noted that, administratively, there should be enforced prohibitions to protect habitat and the deer population; inviolate areas need be designated and appropriately identified; and there should be control of visitor access and reduced speed limits and posting of warning signs. Land acquisition is of urgency so as to secure quality habitat before further development occurs and to consolidate public holdings to reduce people-related problems. The management objectives included the employment of an experienced biologist who could continuously examine and interpret monitoring data and adjust management as required.

Also, it was strongly recommended that deer be removed and translocated selectively, especially when and where problems occur, to restock appropriate, currently unpopulated Keys; to clean out, develop and maintain freshwater basins; to develop and maintain fire trails; to prescribe burn to ensure continuity of the pine/palm habitats; and to fill mosquito ditches on lands under jurisdiction of the Key Deer National Wildlife Refuge. To accommodate continuity of important biological data gathering, a monitoring program was recommended. It would include regular road censuses, continued routine inspection of outer islands for evidence of deer utilization, continuous monitoring of freshwater supplies, autopsy of all mortalities, development of vegetational exclosures and evaluation of deer impact on important food supplies, continuation of marking animals to develop and maintain a cohort of marked known-aged animals, and monitoring the patterns of highway crossing by deer. An educational program was recommended to develop and provide informational materials to residents and tourists, to build and staff a visitors' center, and to hire an information specialist who could provide advice and expertise.

Because the Key deer has been researched for such a short period of time and because of rather distinctive problems associated with this insular subspecies, it is appropriate that there be continuing experimentation and research in an effort to respond better to requirements for the protection of this unique animal and its habitat. Suggestions include fencing around the Port Pine Heights subdivision in an effort to restrict people/deer interactions, manipulating the habitat of the Little Pine Key complex to ensure its capability to support possibly the last really isolated population, and conducting a variety of additional studies on the natural history and population dynamics of the Key deer population. Since this deer is a product of evolution in an island setting, and because it probably still is not completely genetically isolated from those animals on the mainland from which it originated, every effort must be made to ensure its integrity. It is likely that only those deer semi-isolated on outlying Keys may still be subjected to the pressures of natural selection characteristic of the Keys. This process must be optimized, and under no circumstances must Key deer maintained in zoological gardens be considered as a reserve for restocking Key deer ranges either now or in the future.

OUTLOOK

The greatest obstacle to Key deer is human use of land for residential and commercial enterprises. And since the number of tourists and the resident human population are likely to increase, the deer and their habitat undoubtedly will decrease except in specific areas set aside for them. Also, the negative impact of increased dog harassment and probable kills and human feeding of the deer cannot be overemphasized.

Key deer have been a food source, an oddity of nature and a tourist attraction. In the past, most residents strongly supported the creation and maintenance of a refuge to protect the deer. But in recent years, attitudes have changed. Many now view the deer as a nuisance because they feed on cultivated and ornamental plants,

Damage by Key deer feeding on shrubbery and citrus trees in backyards is extensive on Big Pine Key and requires either complete fencing of yards or isolation of selected shrubs with cylinders of wire for protection. *Photo courtesy of the Southern Illinois University Cooperative Wildlife Research Laboratory.*

Since 1976, an increasing problem for Key deer is people befriending the deer on Big Pine and No Name Keys. Besides tourists offering food to the wildlife, some permanent residents have enticed large numbers of deer to front and backyards by providing feed. Recent Florida legislation to make feeding deer a misdemeanor may aid in reducing this problem. *Photos courtesy of the Southern Illinois University Cooperative Wildlife Research Laboratory.*

cause property loss as a result of collisions with vehicles and present a hazard to human life on heavily traveled roadways. As Key deer become associated more closely with people due to expanded development, there will be decreasing interest in saving the deer. Also, the public tends to resist restrictions on private land or access areas to accommodate deer.

There is no room for complacency regarding this diminutive subspecies of white-tailed deer. Its future clearly is threatened by human ac-

tivity. Management steps must be taken to (1) provide optimum habitat on refuge lands, (2) acquire quality Keys (such as No Name), (3) continue study of Key deer population levels, mortality and habitat utilization, and (4) accommodate the deer more appropriately on private land. Without question, there must be concern that the predicted increase in competition for land use (Smith et al. 1970) likely will reduce the Key deer population, possibly to its precarious status of the 1950s.

Chapter 20

NORTHERN GREAT LAKES STATES AND ONTARIO FORESTS

Ralph I. Blouch
Wildlife Research Supervisor (Retired)
Michigan Department of Natural Resources
Lansing, Michigan

ENVIRONMENT

In the northern Great Lakes states and Ontario, there is a natural division of white-tailed deer habitat between forest and farmland. The line of demarcation tends to be irregular and discontinuous, but is generally a north-south separation that conforms rather closely to the southern edge of the coniferous/northern hardwood biome. This chapter deals with the forest range that extends north to the limits of the whitetail's distribution, east to the Ottawa River and west to the tallgrass prairies (Figure 84). The range covers about 363,000 square kilometers (140,000 square miles). Two-thirds of it is divided about equally across northern portions of Minnesota, Wisconsin and Michigan, and one-third extends into Ontario.

Physiography and Soils

This region is glaciated, varying from flat to rolling and hilly, with a few low mountains. Precambrian bedrock is exposed in the north, but glacial deposits predominate south of the Canadian shield. Moraines, outwash and till plains, kames, eskers, and alluvial lake beds have produced a wide variety of soils, principally podzols, ranging from arid deep sands to heavy clay and loam. Many basins and low areas have filled with peat and muck. Lakes and ponds of all shapes and sizes dominate much of the landscape.

Climate and Weather

Winters in the Northern Great Lakes States and Ontario Forests region typically are long and cold with continuous snow cover; summers are short and warm. In areas closest to the Great Lakes, temperatures are relatively moderate, growing seasons longer and, in some places, snowfall much greater than in the inland areas. Average annual temperature ranges from 3 to 7 degrees Celsius (37–45 degrees Fahrenheit). Average monthly means in winter vary across the region from −7 to −18 degrees Celsius (0–20 degrees Fahrenheit), and in summer from 16 to 21 degrees Celsius (69–70 degrees Fahrenheit). The growing season generally ranges from 80 to 135 days.

Average annual precipitation is 64 to 81 centimeters (25–32 inches), and annual snowfall ranges from 127 to 508 centimeters (50–200 inches). Snow usually begins to accumulate in November and lasts through April. In most areas, snow depths of 30 centimeters (12 inches) or more are present for at least 90 days. Snow accumulations of 91 to 122 centimeters (36–48 inches) are not unusual near Lake Superior, especially along the southern shore.

Vegetation

The Northern Great Lakes States and Ontario Forests region is a transitional vegetation zone containing a mixture of conifer and hard-

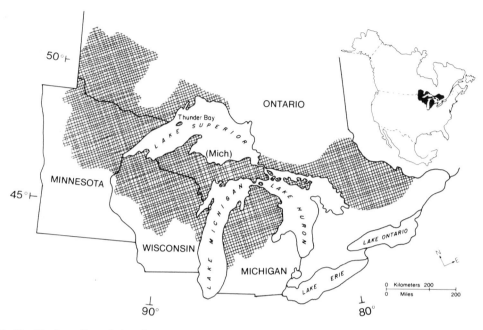

Figure 84. The Northern Great Lakes States and Ontario Forests region.

wood types. Boreal spruce/fir forests blend southward into pines and northern hardwoods, which are outriders from the austral broadleaf forests of the southern zones.

From the mid-1800s to the early 1900s, axe and saw brought down the forests of pine, hemlock, northern hardwoods and swamp conifers. Trees were converted to lumber to fulfill the needs of the growing midcontinent. Most large stands of eastern white pine and red pine were obliterated. Then came vast and uncontrolled fires, burning off the slash and undergrowth and often consuming the rich forest floor including humus from the topsoil. By the 1920s and 1930s, large-scale efforts by public agencies brought fire control and protection, and an era of recovery began. Second-growth forest gradually spread over the region. Attempts at farming held some areas open for a time, but most agricultural enterprises failed; those that persist are marginal.

The land now is predominately forested with both broadleaf and needleleaf species. Trembling and bigtooth aspens occupy 26 percent of the commercial forest land (Brinkman and Roe 1975). Truly a phoenix rising from the ashes, aspen resprouts or reseeds immediately after burning, and often completely replaces other plant types that were burned off. Aspen occurs in pure stands or in a variety of mixtures (Graham et al. 1963). Usual associates are paper

birch, jack pine, red maple, balsam fir and northern red oak. Aspen is logged extensively for pulpwood and also is very important for deer and ruffed grouse and their management.

Several other major forest types reflect the region's different soil and moisture regimes. The heavier and more fertile soils usually are occupied by northern hardwoods such as sugar maple, yellow birch, American beech and eastern hemlock. Jack pine, often in pure stands, typically grows on very poor and arid sands. Oak types—mainly northern red oak but including northern pin, white, and bur oaks—are common on moderately poor and dry soils in the southern part of the range. The spruce/fir type—black and white spruce and balsam fir—is prevalent in moist northern areas. Conifer swamps occupy scattered lowlands that often are former lake basins or stream floodplains. They support tamarack/spruce bog forests or northern white cedar/balsam fir swamps, and occur throughout most of the region. Eastern white pine and red pine commonly are scattered through all forest types.

Shrubs in the forest understory include blueberry, beaked hazel, American hazel, sweetfern, blackberries and witchhazel. Upland brush areas support shrubs or shrubby trees such as hawthorn, serviceberry, willow, pin cherry and mountain maple. Shrubs of lowland edges often include red-osier dogwood, gray dogwood,

Typical whitetail habitats in the Northern Great Lakes States and Ontario Forests region. Driving backroads looking for deer is a favorite pastime throughout this region. *Left photo by Robert Harrington; courtesy of the Michigan Department of Natural Resources. Right photo by Freeman Haim; courtesy of the U.S. Forest Service.*

speckled alder and several of the viburnums. Sphagnum bogs occupy many basins and usually are blanketed with ericaceous shrubs such as leatherleaf, downy andromeda, Labrador-tea ledum, blueberries, willows and bog birch.

Wintergreen, Canada mayflower and bunchberry dogwood are typical of low, groundcover plants in much of the forest. Bracken fern grows almost everywhere on poorer upland soils.

Open grassy areas are scattered through the region's forest types, mainly on poorer soils. They usually are stabilized by sod grasses and may include bracken fern, sweetfern, blueberry, other low or scattered shrubs, and a variety of herbs (Levy 1970).

Land Use

Land use in the region is predominately forest-oriented, because the climate and soils present formidable obstacles to most kinds of agriculture. Early cultivation attempts on poor soils quickly failed and the land reverted to forest. On better soils, particularly in southern parts of the region, marginal and subsistence farming has persisted. Crops mainly are hay, small grains and pasturage grasses. In some areas corn, potatoes, small fruits and truck crops are grown with fair success. Farmlands generally are scattered and irregular in distribution, and do not exceed 25 percent of the region.

Mining occupies a very small portion of the region's landscape. Large-scale operations produce iron, copper and nickel in Minnesota, Michigan and Ontario. Some of the largest cities are centered in mining localities.

On approximately 75 percent of the forested area, commercial forest management for timber production and recreation overshadow all other uses, usually are compatible and concurrent, and seldom are mutually exclusive. Publicly owned lands, which include some 30 to 40 percent of the total region, are managed for a variety of benefits, including sawtimber, pulpwood, hunting, fishing, camping and other outdoor recreational activities. Private ownership ranges from small individual holdings to large industry-owned tracts. Forest products are the primary income producer, with tourism and seasonal recreation also economically important. The latter use includes summer and weekend homes, vacation resorts, campgrounds, hunting clubs, and winter sports developments. Much of the private land is open to public access, especially the larger holdings in the more remote and undeveloped areas.

WHITETAIL POPULATIONS

Brief History

Historically, the Northern Great Lakes States and Ontario Forests region was marginal white-tailed deer range. Long winters, deep snow and virgin timber with little undergrowth all worked against the deer. Before 1880, estimated densities in northern Wisconsin were 4 whitetails per square kilometer (10 per square mile) as opposed to densities of 8 to 19 deer per square kilometer (20–50 per square mile) in the southern part of the state (Dahlberg and Guettinger 1956). The former low-density figure probably held for the rest of the region as well.

In the nineteenth century, the white-tailed deer/range relationship drastically reversed—deer became common in the north and less abundant in the southern part of the region. As lumbermen advanced and cleared land in the north, they created openings and brushy second growth; whitetails consequently thrived. Commercial hunting for meat and hides became commonplace. In 1880, for example, more than 100,000 deer carcasses were shipped to market by railroad in Michigan (Bartlett 1950, *see* Chapter 2).

Wildfires repeatedly burned vast areas of the cutover land. Their devastation, combined with unregulated hunting, reduced deer numbers to low levels by the early 1900s. Movements by state wildlife agencies to regulate hunting and control forest fires were supported by newly formed sportsmen's groups and, by the 1920s, whitetail populations again were on the upswing (Peterson 1979). Great expanses of cutover and burned land regenerated to new forests that provided suitable habitat for whitetails, and the deer increased throughout the region during the 1930s and 1940s. In many localities of Michigan and Wisconsin, deer densities probably exceeded 19 per square kilometer (50 per square mile) (Bartlett 1950, Swift 1946). In Minnesota and Ontario, whitetail density was lower, with maximum densities probably about 8 to 12 per square kilometer (20–30 per square mile). In recent years, as second-growth forest matures and provides less food and cover, there has been a general downward trend in deer numbers.

Turn-of-the-century white-tailed deer hunting party in Ontario. The Northern Great Lakes States and Ontario Forests region then was extremely popular with recreational and market hunters alike. *Photo courtesy of the Public Archives of Canada, #PA 67301.*

Regardless of habitat conditions, whitetail numbers fluctuate from year to year in response to alternating periods of mild and severe winters. At the region's northern limit of whitetail ranges, a greater-than-normal snow accumulation causes starvation, die-offs, and lowered productivity. The deer populations decrease dramatically following two or three successive winters of unusually severe conditions. Conversely, with two or more successive mild winters, populations increase and the deer are apt to overbrowse their winter range. These periodic fluctuations tend to be most pronounced in the middle and northern portions of the region. A good example of this phenomenon is shown in Figure 85, which illustrates hunter harvests of whitetail bucks in northern and southern parts of Michigan over a 32-year period—the northern part being the forested region.

Population Size and Structure

In the mid-1970s, autumn population densities of white-tailed deer were approximately 1.2 to 6.0 deer per square kilometer (3–15 per square mile) in the northern parts of the region, and 6 to 17 per square kilometer (15–45 per square mile) in the middle and southern parts.

There are two types of sex/age structure in the deer population of the forest region, primarily because of two basic kinds of hunting seasons. Until recently, either-sex deer hunting seasons have been the rule in Minnesota and Ontario. In these parts of the region, hunters usually took the first deer that came along, thereby maintaining fairly even ratios of bucks, does and fawns—approximately 40:30:30. With new regulations now in effect, however, there may be a shifting of whitetail population composition toward less-balanced ratios.

In northern Michigan and northern Wisconsin, hunters can take one adult buck, but limited numbers of does and fawns are harvested under special permits in designated areas. Buck harvests are substantial, and older-age bucks are few. Northern Wisconsin's autumn whitetail population composition typically is 20 to 25 percent adult bucks, 40 to 45 percent adult does and 30 to 40 percent fawns. In Michigan, the ratio is approximately 15:50:35.

Condition

In northern Michigan, average dressed weights of yearling bucks harvested in autumn ranged from 43 kilograms (95 pounds) on poor range after severe winters to 53 kilograms (117 pounds) on good range following moderate winters (Ryel and Youatt 1972). In the same areas, the average beam-diameter of yearlings' antlers varied from 15.8 to 20.2 millimeters

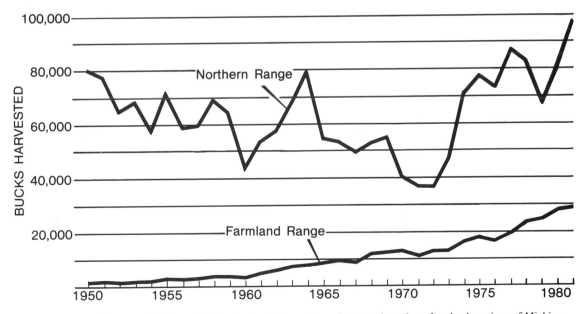

Figure 85. Hunter harvests of white-tailed deer bucks in the northern forest and southern farmland portions of Michigan, 1950–1981.

(0.6–0.8 inch), and the average number of antler points ranged from 2.6 to 4.3 (Burgoyne 1976).

Productivity

The reproductive rate of Northern Great Lakes States and Ontario Forests region whitetails is lower than that found on ranges immediately southward. In northern Michigan, from 1950 to 1981, the *in utero* rate averaged 1.67 embryos per adult doe, whereas the average rate was 1.92 in the southern farmland range (Youatt et al. 1975, Friedrich and Burgoyne 1981). Feeding experiments with penned deer showed that *in utero* losses on the northern range vary from 10 to 75 percent (Verme 1962, 1967, 1974), depending on severity of winter and nutritional level of does. In Michigan's northern ranges, the actual number of fawns added to the spring population may vary from 40 to 150 per 100 does. In the southern farmland range, natal fawn losses are relatively light and average fawn production appears to be at least 170 per 100 does.

In a Minnesota study, the average autumn ratio of fawns to does was 113:100 in the north and 127:100 in the south—considered to be a direct reflection of regional differences in food supply and winter severity (Erickson et al. 1961). Wisconsin fawn/doe ratios vary from 70:100 in the north to 160:100 in the south (Dahlberg and Guettinger 1956).

Harvest

Deer hunters in all of Michigan, Minnesota, Wisconsin and Ontario presently number more than 2 million, and they annually harvest 300,000 to 500,000 deer (Figure 86). In these states and province, the northern forest range is the most popular area in which to hunt whitetails. Thus, approximately two-thirds of the total deer harvest comes from this range, in which bucks comprise about 75 percent of the total harvest. The antlerless portion of the harvest differs from year to year depending on the current size and reproductive rate of the deer population and the resulting hunting regulations established in the various designated deer man-

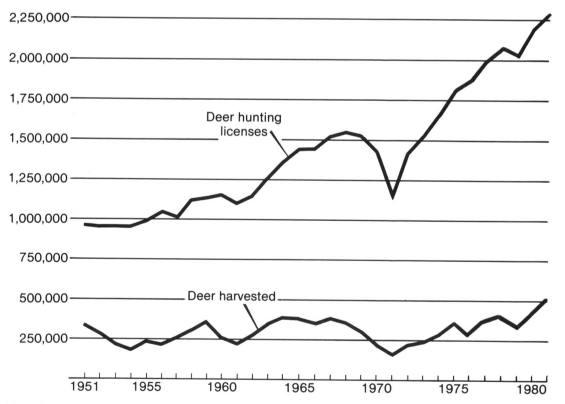

Figure 86. Number of white-tailed deer hunting licenses sold and total deer kill in Michigan, Minnesota, Wisconsin and Ontario, 1951–1981.

agement units. Antlerless deer quotas are reduced or increased as deer numbers and productivity fluctuate in response to changes in winter severity. In buck-only hunting areas, yearlings may vary from 50 to 75 percent of the total harvest following shifts in reproductive rate.

Hunting pressure varies from 0.4 to 1.9 deer hunters per square kilometer (1–5 per square mile) on poor and remote range up to 9.7 to 19.3 per square kilometer (25–50 per square mile) on good, accessible range. As many as 38.6 hunters per square kilometer (100 per square mile) have been reported on small areas of unusually popular and productive range (Ruch 1965). On lightly hunted ranges, the harvest rate is less than 0.4 deer per square kilometer (1 per square mile), and approximately 3.8 whitetails per square kilometer (10 per square mile) on heavily hunted ranges.

Opening day success greatly influences the total season harvest of white-tailed deer in the region. If the weather that day is particularly bad, hunter success will be poor and will likely remain so for the remainder of the season.

Many whitetail hunters in the Northern Great Lakes States and Ontario Forests region are "sandwich hunters," driving out for the day and "tailgating" their meals. *Photo by Robert Harrington; courtesy of the Michigan Department of Natural Resources.*

Present-day deer hunting camps in the region often combine tents and house-trailers . . . time-out for a quick card game on an unusually warm, snow-free November afternoon. *Photo by Robert Harrington; courtesy of the Michigan Department of Natural Resources.*

Although most whitetails are harvested with firearms in November, all three states and Ontario have special bow and arrow seasons that start four to six weeks before the gun season and, with the exception of Ontario, extend into December. The region's total of 400,000 bow hunters kill about 60,000 deer annually—a harvest success rate of 15 percent. In Michigan alone, 200,000 bow hunters take about 30,000 deer annually.

In the past decade, deer hunting with muzzle-loading firearms has gained considerable popularity in Michigan and Ontario. Michigan has a 10-day buck-only season in early December for black powder enthusiasts. Ontario has designated an area where big game hunting is limited to primitive weapons, including bow and arrow and muzzle-loading guns. Minnesota began a special muzzle-loading season in 1977. Wisconsin has a few state parks open to muzzleloaders only. In all, perhaps 30,000 muzzleloader hunters take about 5,000 deer.

Food and Feeding Habits

Browse is the primary source of food for whitetails in the Northern Great Lakes States and Ontario Forests region, mainly because it is the only food available for nearly half the year. Northern white cedar, red maple, hemlock, American mountain-ash and alternate leaf dogwood are high-preference winter foods for whitetails. Second-level preference species include eastern white pine, yellow birch, mountain maple, serviceberry and jack pine. Next are aspen, northern red oak, beaked hazel, paper birch, balsam fir and red pine. Speckled alder, black and white spruce, and tamarack are last resort foods of the region's white-tailed deer. On the other hand, acorns are highly preferred in autumn and winter, as are beechnuts and such fruits as black cherries and hawthorns. Fruit and mast crop production is inconsistent from year to year. Periods of abundance often are followed by several years of scarcity or failure.

After snow melts in early spring, deer spend most of their feeding time seeking herbaceous vegetation (Healy 1971). The most common plants eaten are grasses, sedges, basal rosettes of perennial forbs such as sheep sorrel, and fiddleheads of bracken fern (McNeill 1971). Grassy openings in forests are especially important at this time of year (McCaffery and Creed 1969).

White-tailed deer in the Northern Great Lakes States and Ontario Forests region seek grassy openings for grazing, especially during spring and autumn. *Photo by Robert Harrington; courtesy of the Michigan Department of Natural Resources.*

In winter, deep snow often forces whitetails in the region to feed on low-preference browse, such as balsam fir. Deer can starve to death with stomachs full of poor food plants. *Photo courtesy of the Michigan Department of Natural Resources.*

Succulent new growth of browse is the principal diet component of the region's whitetails in late spring and early summer. In newly cut forest stands, aspen root suckers, stump sprouts of oak and red maple, and seedlings of many kinds are eaten readily. From midsummer to early autumn, whitetails feed on a wide variety of herbs, shrubs and tree foliage. Aspen leaves are especially preferred (McCaffery et al. 1974b, Bauer 1977). In years of good production, serviceberries, raspberries, blackberries, cherries and hawthorns are eaten in quantity. In autumn, leaves and herbs become less attractive, but early autumn rains usually stimulate grasses in edges and openings, and grazing increases accordingly. In years of good mast crops, acorns and beechnuts are preferred whitetail foods in early autumn and into winter. With the coming of frosts, the deer turn to woody browse. When snow arrives, they complete the shift. On the George Reserve in southern Michigan 7.6 centimeters (3 inches) of snow on the ground dramatically changed the herbaceous portion of whitetail diets from 63 percent to 0 (Coblentz 1970).

SPECIAL PROBLEMS AND CONSTRAINTS

Limiting Factors

Climate. In the Northern Great Lakes States and Ontario Forests region, snow depth and low temperatures combine to limit the northward range of the whitetail. Snow restricts deer movement and covers nourishing food; cold temperature and wind tap the animals' energy reserves. The whitetails' built-in response to these stresses is to concentrate (yard) in heavy coniferous cover, which blocks snow and reduces wind and radiation heat loss. Northern white cedar swamps provide the most attractive cover and often are heavily occupied. Dense stands of hemlock, jack pine and other upland conifers, such as balsam fir, are likely wintering yards where cedar or mixed conifer swamps are lacking.

Whitetails may travel considerable distances to reach suitable yarding areas. In northern parts of Michigan (Verme 1973), Minnesota (Rongstad and Tester 1969) and Wisconsin (Dahlberg and Guettinger 1956), the average distance from summer range to winter yards is 10 to 16 kilometers (6–10 miles), and may be as great as 32 to 48 kilometers (20–30 miles).

Movement to winter yards usually starts in December and may be triggered more by cold weather than by snow depth (Ozoga and Gysel 1972). Once yarded, the deer may remain concentrated or, depending on both temperature and snow conditions, move in and out of the yards. In southern parts of the region, deer yards are loosely defined and winter range usually includes a rather wide fringe of summer range around a core of true winter habitat.

Snow restricts whitetail movements when it reaches depths of from 36 to 43 centimeters (14–17 inches) (Kelsall 1969). Thus, snow is a serious obstacle to deer in more northern parts of the region where it usually stays light and uncompacted, and often accumulates to depths of 60 to 90 centimeters (24–36 inches) and, in places, as much as 122 centimeters (48 inches). Southward, snow depths rarely exceed 30 to 60 centimeters (12–24 inches), and fluctuating temperatures often help to compact or crust snow to the extent that deer can move over it into surrounding areas.

Wildlife management agencies in Michigan and Minnesota use an electrical device to determine air chill and a snow-depth-compaction-

Movement by white-tailed deer to wintering yards in the Northern Great Lakes States and Ontario Forests region usually begins in December, when triggered by cold weather and accumulating snowfall. *Photo by Earl Gingles; courtesy of the Wisconsin Department of Natural Resources.*

Soft, uncrusted, deep snow severely restricts white-tailed deer movements and covers up much of their food. Deer in the region tend to concentrate (yard) in evergreen swamps when snow depth exceeds 46 centimeters (18.1 inches). *Photo courtesy of the Michigan Department of Natural Resources.*

Whitetails in a cedar swamp deer yard. The dense evergreen canopy of this forest type—a mixture of northern white cedar, balsam fir and black spruce—provides a good shelter from the relentless elements of a northern winter, but good food is nonexistent. *Photo by Robert Harrington; courtesy of the Michigan Department of Natural Resources.*

Dense stands of jack pine in the Northern Great Lakes States and Ontario Forests region are likely winter yarding areas where cedar or mixed conifer swamps are not accessible to whitetails. Jack pine is a secondary winter food source for the deer. *Photo by J. W. Trygg; courtesy of the U. S. Forest Service.*

measuring instrument at numerous fixed stations throughout the northern deer range (Verme 1968). Weekly measurements provide a severity index for each station. At winter's end, a seasonal index is derived by adding the weekly values. These then are averaged to produce a statewide winter severity index that can be compared with conditions in previous years. A similar index of temperature and snow cover is derived from official weather-station records in Wisconsin. The three states incorporate their index values in the procedures used to make deer harvest recommendations and set hunting regulations each year.

Food quality and quantity. ʹDeficiencies in the quantity and quality of food in deer yards are caused by severe weather, dense forest stands and high concentrations of deer. Northern white cedar swamps provide high quality food when foliage is within reach of deer, but many swamps are barren of foliage to a height of at least 1.8 meter (6 feet). Foliage is available only in blowdowns or scattered brushy edges. In Minnesota, where northern white cedar is uncommon, balsam fir provides protection from wind chill and excessive heat radiation. However balsam is a low-quality browse, and its dense growth shades out better understory food plants.

In mild winters, deer move out from the yards and seek food in surrounding areas, but in severe winters, the animals remain tightly yarded and are limited to a starvation diet. Whitetails are able to survive two or three months of severe midwinter weather (Verme and Ozoga 1971), and if the spring breakup comes in March or earlier, most deer survive. However, if cold and snow persist into April, many of the weakest deer die, and the fetal fawn crop is devastated. In the early 1950s, when the region's deer populations probably were at a peak, Michigan, Minnesota and Wisconsin each experienced die-offs of 20,000 to 50,000 whitetails. In Michigan, losses of this magnitude also occurred in four winters during the seven-year period 1956–1962 (Ryel and Bennett 1971). During the severe winter of 1958–1959, 40 percent of a whitetail population died on the lands of a hunting club covering 10,878 hectares (42 square miles), and 38 percent of another population died on hunting club lands of 7,252 hectares (28 square miles) (Blouch 1961). Fawns constituted 69 and 84 percent of starved deer on the two areas, respectively. In Wisconsin, after the long hard winter of 1964–1965, whitetail starvation losses were estimated to be 49,000.

Besides direct losses from winter starvation, there usually is a decided drop in neonatal survival the following spring. In Michigan's Upper Peninsula, when more than 15,000 deer died following a severe winter in 1971, it was likely that 100,000 fawns—75 percent of the potential fawn crop—failed to survive at birth (Verme 1974, Ryel and Bennett 1971).

Over time, natural plant succession can result in deficiencies in quantity and quality of deer food on spring, summer and autumn ranges (Verme 1967, 1969, 1974). Forest openings may become stocked with trees that shade out ground cover. On better upland soils, forest stands change in composition to more shade-tolerant species. For example, aspen—the region's leading deer-producing forest type (Byelich et al. 1972)—is converted, in many cases, to maple, pine and balsam fir types that are poor producers of deer forage. This deterioration of food quality in summer range may limit the size and distribution of a whitetail population in much the same manner as poor winter range. However, many summer range deficiencies are more amenable to management measures than are those of winter habitat. Aspen can be regenerated quickly and maintained by clearcutting. Openings can be retained and improved by mechanical or chemical treatment or prescribed burning.

Predators, diseases and parasites.   Predators in the Northern Great Lakes States and Ontario Forests region usually do not affect whitetail populations seriously. Mountain lions are absent from the region. The ranges of deer and gray wolf overlap in Ontario and northern Minnesota. There, where deer densities are 3.1 to 5.8 per square kilometer (8–15 per square mile) and wolf-to-deer ratios are at least 1:100, predation can be a major mortality factor (Pimlott et al. 1969, Mech and Frenzel 1971*b*, Kolenosky 1972). Wolves occur in a few remote areas of Wisconsin and Michigan, but their numbers are few and their effect on deer is negligible.

Coyotes and bobcats prey on whitetails to some extent in yards when the deer are handicapped by deep crusted snow and weakened by starvation (Ozoga and Harger 1966, Petraborg and Gunvalson 1962). Newborn fawns are vulnerable to coyotes and bobcats, but the extent of such mortality is unknown.

In areas where people live nearby, whitetails frequently are harassed and sometimes killed by domestic dogs. The problem is most serious in northern range when crusted snow favors the dogs. In both Michigan and Wisconsin losses due to dogs may exceed the take of all wild predators; dogs annually kill around 5,000 deer in Michigan.

During a winter of prolonged cold temperature and deep soft snow in the Northern Great Lakes States and Ontario Forests region many of the weakest and smallest deer in a whitetail population starve to death. Fawns, in particular, with greater energy needs and smaller body size, cannot compete effectively for available food. *Photo courtesy of the Michigan Department of Natural Resources.*

Dog harassment can be a serious hazard to wintering deer in the Northern Great Lakes States and Ontario Forests region. This free-running pet has cornered a young whitetail after a chase and could easily kill it. *Photo by Robert Harrington; courtesy of the Michigan Department of Natural Resources.*

Diseases, except epizootic hemorrhagic disease, seldom pose a serious health problem for the region's white-tailed deer populations. During 1955, about 50 dead or dying animals were infected with epizootic hemorrhagic disease in 11 or more counties of northern Michigan (Fay et al. 1956). Although unrecorded, whitetail mortality from this cause likely was much higher, considering the extent of area involved. The virus occurred again in 1975 on a limited scale.

Several parasites are common but well-tolerated by deer. In the northern forested range, the frequent occurrence of giant liver fluke in livers of harvested whitetails can alarm hunters unnecessarily. Nose bots infest a high proportion of adult deer, but they seldom are seen by hunters because they occur deep in nasal passages or the upper throat. Meningeal worms also appear to have a high incidence in the region's deer. Stomach worms (nematodes) are common but usually not in heavy infestations. Biting lice are frequently encountered ectoparasites.

Interspecific competition. Other wild and domestic animals do not compete seriously with whitetails in the Northern Great Lakes States and Ontario Forests region. Moose and deer generally winter in different habitats and they do not prefer the same food plants in other seasons. In some areas, snowshoe hares possibly could compete with deer for northern white cedar and other important winter browse species, but the deer invariably are dominant in this respect and ultimately affect hare populations by reducing both food and cover (Bookhout 1965).

Deer feed on livestock pastures to some extent in spring and autumn, but the impact on deer of grazing by livestock, and vice versa, is of negligible significance. In fact, livestock grazing in some areas serves to maintain open areas and forest edge to the benefit of whitetails and other wildlife.

Land use. Commercial timber operations frequently favor deer. Pulpwood logging predominates in the region. Clearcutting of shade-intolerant tree types on relatively short rotations produces areas of second-growth vegetation that benefit whitetails, especially where cutting units are intermixed in a variety of age classes.

White-tailed deer and livestock may pasture together in farmed areas of the region, but curiosity usually is their only interaction. *Photo by Robert Harrington; courtesy of the Michigan Department of Natural Resources.*

On the other hand, selective logging of northern hardwoods for sawtimber is not good deer-habitat management. Although browse production increases for a short period immediately following selective logging, the stands are locked into long rotations that do not produce attractive whitetail habitat for many years. Hardwood stands extensively logged 20 to 40 years ago are low in deer carrying capacity, and there will be little chance to improve them for another 40 to 60 years. Reforestation plantings of red pine for sawtimber also result in lean decades for deer, often obliterating the open areas so essential to good whitetail habitat in the region.

At extremely high population levels, whitetailed deer damage regenerating forest stands managed for timber production. Even so, resprouting or stem regrowth usually restores stands to adequate levels for hardwood cuttings. In stands of swamp conifers or pines and sometimes northern hardwoods, deer browsing alters the species composition. For example, when cedar swamps are logged, deer consume the cedar seedlings and convert regrowth to a balsam fir/black spruce type. Also, when deer are abundant, they virtually eliminate yellow birch and hemlock from northern hardwoods after cutting, and convert the type to sugar maple (Graham 1954). Eastern white pine restocking usually is futile when and where deer populations are at high levels.

Aerial view of a commercial aspen-cutting operation. This is a clearcut, using a new method involving mechanized harvesting and chipping entire trees on the site. Chips are hauled to a mill in large trailer trucks. The aspen will regenerate by rapid sprout growth and become excellent deer habitat. *Photo by Robert Harrington; courtesy of the Michigan Department of Natural Resources.*

Whitetails of the region are benefitted by clearcuts of shade-intolerant trees on relatively short rotations, particularly where cutting units are intermixed in a variety of age classes. *Photo by Dean Tvedt; courtesy of the Wisconsin Department of Natural Resources.*

In limited areas of the northern range, deer damage specialty crops such as cherries, strawberries, and occasionally corn, potatoes and truck crops. Usually landowners tolerate the damage with few complaints because they like to see and hunt deer. However, tolerance can be exceeded when local concentrations of deer eat and otherwise damage more than farmers can afford to overlook. From 1978 through 1980 Wisconsin indemnified more than 420 farmers' claims of damage totalling in excess of $400,000 (*see* Chapter 11). In Michigan, shooting permits are given to farmers in response to verified damage complaints. The number of such permits issued each year varies from 300 to 500, reflecting not only whitetail population levels but also economic conditions.

Regulation of Hunting

A persisting problem in white-tailed deer management of the region is the issue of either-sex harvest. For nearly two decades, resistance to hunting does as well as bucks prevented adequate harvests in Michigan and Wisconsin, caused serious damage to large areas of northern deer range, and permitted unnecessary deer starvation losses.

The either-sex harvest issue first arose in the mid-1930s. Overbrowsed winter ranges and winter die-offs provided ample evidence that whitetails exceeded the carrying capacity of their habitats. Biologists and wildlife managers repeatedly recommended antlerless-deer harvests, but sportsmen opposed them vociferously. After long and hard political debates, the legislatures authorized limited antlerless seasons in the 1940s. However, not until the periods 1949–1951, in Wisconsin, and 1952–1954, in Michigan, did legislators authorize either-sex deer hunting on a scale large enough to reduce the overabundant populations.

When finally approved, the decision to hold antlerless deer harvests shocked most of the public. Local newspapers carried such headlines as "Deer Slaughter" and "Are there any deer left?" Letter campaigns, petitions and other forms of protest deluged state officials. But deer were not exterminated, and it soon was apparent that whitetail populations had been reduced to reasonable levels, at least in some areas.

Public reaction resulted in brief moratoriums on antlerless hunting in the mid-1950s, but within a few years both Michigan and Wisconsin had again authorized special antlerless-deer hunting seasons, requiring permits issued on a quota basis for delineated deer management units. The two states' wildlife management agencies now use these seasons to achieve desired harvest levels with a fairly high degree of precision. Nevertheless, some people still exert pressure to reduce quotas or block antlerless seasons on particular management units and areas. Although deer hunters are becoming increasingly aware of the need for whitetail population control through harvesting does and fawns, disapproval of it still is widespread (Moncrief 1970, Ryel 1976, 1980). A feeling has long prevailed that shooting anything but antlered bucks is not good sportsmanship.

Illegal killing of white-tailed deer in the region is a significant mortality factor, but it is difficult to measure. Not only do illegal kills cheat responsible sportsmen and other citizens, but they also leave a gap in the balance sheet of annual deer population gains and losses. Wounding losses, illegal kills (intentional or mistaken) during hunting seasons, and deliberate out-of-season poaching taken together may exceed the total legal harvest. In order to regulate whitetail populations properly, wildlife managers must recognize these losses and adjust for them accordingly, even though the exact numbers are unknown. Harvest regulations also require adjustment for the factor of land ownership. While public land predominates in the region, private ownership—particularly large blocks of club lands—may require different antlerless-deer quotas or other special consideration to assure desired harvest levels. Michigan gives first preference to landowners within management units when issuing hunter's-choice permits.

Biopolitical and Socioeconomic Considerations

Wise use and enjoyment of the white-tailed deer resource involves many interrelated factors. For example, whitetails have a biological impact on habitat. At low intensities, their browsing may stimulate sprout growth of preferred food plants or halt successional changes toward tolerant forest types. At high densities, deer may eliminate preferred foods and cause rapid conversion from desirable to undesirable forest types; thus, their habitat is degraded and the value of future timber crops reduced.

Deer/vehicle accidents represent a serious social and economic cost. In Michigan, 20,000 deer/vehicle accidents were reported in 1981.

Michigan averaged about 17,000 such accidents over the six-year period 1976–1981. About half of these occurred on roadways through the northern forest range. Wisconsin's records were similar for the same period. Property damage costs are high. Statewide in Michigan in 1980, they totaled $15.6 million—an average of $825 for the year's total of 18,932 accidents. Human injuries and fatalities occur all too frequently. Again, in 1980 in Michigan, deer/vehicle collisions cost three human lives and resulted in injury to 991 persons—at a monetary cost of $6.5 million. Since these accidents are related closely to deer densities, whitetail populations must be kept to a tolerable level—a point that must be decided by public acceptance.

Clearcutting of forests also is an item of great concern to wildlife managers. To citizens, clearcuts may be aesthetically offensive, but to wildlife managers they are the most practical and productive method of regenerating deer foods. Generally, deer hunters tolerate higher cutting levels than do tourists and other recreationists (Langenau and Jamsen 1975, Langenau et al. 1975). Extensive clearcutting, with little variety among forest types, causes the recreationist to go elsewhere, to the detriment of local businesses.

Forest clearcutting in the Northern Great Lakes States and Ontario Forests region is very important to maintenance of healthy and productive whitetail populations. However, extensive cutting can be offensive to non-deer-hunting tourists and recreationists, who also exert a major economic influence on the region. This dichotomy has been tempered by carefully planned and managed harvests of both deer and timber resources. *Photo by Lynn L. Rogers.*

These and other factors, such as crop damage, must be weighed in setting white-tailed deer population goals. Wisconsin has a statewide winter population goal of 575,000 deer, and a carefully worked out system of individual deer management units designed to sustain that level through controlled harvests and habitat improvements (*see* Chapter 11). Michigan, with a winter population of 550,000 deer in 1970, established a statewide autumn population goal of 1,000,000 whitetails, to be achieved by 1980. The goal was reached in 6 years instead of 10, largely because of several mild winters in the northern range. License fees were increased $1.50 to help expand the state's habitat improvement program. In this case, benefits exceeded costs by a healthy margin (Hansen 1977), harvests have increased and the whitetail population continues to hold at slightly more than 1 million deer.

MANAGEMENT

Current Practices, Policies and Philosophies

In the Northern Great Lakes States and Ontario Forests region, each state and provincial wildlife agency regulates deer hunting and tries to maintain a desired whitetail population through its own particular framework of harvest regulations. None has broad enough authority to permit a harvest wholly responsive to management needs, and deer population control frequently is not as flexible and precise as agency biologists and managers would like it to be.

In the past, the region's three states and one province differed rather widely in their whitetail hunting regulations. In recent decades, however, evolutionary changes toward managed harvests have been taking place throughout the region. At present, all four governments have developed essentially similar systems. Basic deer licenses for taking antlered bucks are sold to all buyers. Antlerless or hunter's-choice permits are then issued for specific management areas on a variable quota basis. When applicants exceed established quotas, lottery-type drawings decide who gets permits. Buck-only and/or either-sex harvests are carried out concurrently on the management units where increases or decreases in deer populations are desired. The logic and fairness of this plan seem to appeal to most people, and

the old "doe hunting" controversies seem to be fading away.

All three states and Ontario have special bow and arrow deer-hunting seasons in which whitetails of either sex can be taken. Such hunting is growing in popularity, and although archery hunting-harvest success is lower than that of gun hunting, it is improving each year. In 1981, Wisconsin bow and arrow deer hunters numbered an all-time high of 174,000 participants and killed 29,000 deer, for a success rate of 16.7 percent. During the same year, the state's 629,000 gun hunters took 167,000 whitetails—a 26.6 percent success rate.

Until recently, white-tailed deer habitat management in the Northern Great Lakes States and Ontario Forests region was largely a by-product of logging. Pulpwood harvesting in aspen types benefits deer significantly, but annual cutting is not keeping up with yearly growth (Brinkman and Roe 1975). When unharvested for decades, aspen stands important for deer and ruffed grouse convert to more shade-tolerant but less desirable types, such as white pine, balsam fir and northern hardwoods. In poorly stocked stands, or scattered in other types, aspen is not economically harvestable and will die out without regenerating. In many cases, commercial clearcutting does not remove all standing trees, and the shade of those left standing prevents optimum renewal of the aspen type.

In order to amplify habitat improvement effects of commercial logging, state wildlife agencies in Michigan, Minnesota and Wisconsin have been applying special management techniques for deer on public lands. Tree-cutting bulldozers and handcutting crews are used to clearcut nonmerchantable stands and to remove residual trees following commercial operations. Occasionally, prescribed burning and herbicides supplement or enhance the cuttings.

During severe winters in Michigan and Wisconsin, white cedar trees are cut in deer yards to provide browse for starving deer. This usually hastens conversion of the cut areas to balsam fir and speckled alder, and is done only in emergencies.

In the 1970s, Michigan, Minnesota and Wisconsin incorporated the concept of forest openings as part of their white-tailed deer habitat management programs. Plans call for maintenance of existing openings and creation of new ones. McCaffery and Creed (1969) recommended that 3 to 5 percent of Wisconsin's

As an emergency measure during severe winters, northern white cedar trees are cut in wintering yards in the Northern Great Lakes States and Ontario Forests region to provide food for hungry white-tailed deer. *Photo by Robert Harrington; courtesy of the Michigan Department of Natural Resources.*

commercial forest area be designated as permanent openings, withdrawn from reforestation, and occasionally treated with herbicides or fire to prevent invasion of shrubs and trees (McCaffery et al. 1974). Clearings are seeded with oats, clover and bluegrass in Wisconsin, and often with rye in Michigan. In both states, cost factors tend to hold actual acreage of openings nearer to 1 percent of the total area managed.

Until recently, forest openings and all other habitat improvements have not significantly affected the total deer range. Prior to 1971, the area treated for deer habitat management in Michigan averaged about 2,428 hectares (6,000 acres) per year, or about 5 percent of the area cut commercially in the state's northern forests. Habitat work in the other Great Lakes states was on a similar scale. The challenge was to design a habitat maintenance and management program that benefited deer and also was economically sound.

In 1971, Michigan raised the cost of a deer hunting license from $5.00 to $7.50, and earmarked $1.50 of revenues received from license sales for deer habitat improvement. The stepped-up program generates close to $1 million annually—enough to treat approximately 6,500 hectares (16,000 acres) of forest land in the state per year. Habitat work is focused on zones of the state's northern range that produce a major portion of the deer harvest. Management goals aim for at least 35 percent of the upland areas to be maintained in aspen and 15 percent in openings. Tree-cutting rates and distribution will be regulated for a 10-year period to leave 25 percent of upland forest types in the 1- to 10-year age class. Michigan plans to improve the habitat on 81,000 hectares (200,000 acres) over a 10-year period in order to sustain an autumn population of 1 million whitetails.

While the overriding concern in managing whitetails in this region is keeping the deer within the limits of their food supply, their ten-

A noncommercial stand of aspen in Gladwin County, Michigan, is cleared to improve habitat for white-tailed deer. *Photo by C. Allison; courtesy of the Michigan Department of Natural Resources.*

dency to overpopulate often requires reining in for other important reasons. Both agricultural damage and highway hazard can reach nonacceptable proportions. The management tool of choice for these problems of abundance is public hunting—the orderly harvesting of antlerless deer along with adult bucks. Wildlife agencies, therefore, annually design their hunter's-choice areas and permit quotas to assure adequate harvests in localities with high deer/vehicle accident records and a high incidence of crop or forest damage, as well as in areas of deer-food shortage or winter starvation. Michigan, in fact, is required by law to base any antlerless-deer hunting regulation on one or another of these three justifications.

Efforts to mitigate agricultural damage by using payments or shooting permits are costly, difficult to administer and opposed by sportsmen.

Various approaches to control or reduction of illegal killing of deer are never entirely successful, but may have some merit. Wisconsin is trying a system of assessing violators with very high fines, as much as $1,800. Michigan and Minnesota are promoting campaigns to encourage the public to report and provide information about poaching on toll-free telephone lines. The degree of success of such efforts is hard to measure, and the efforts' true effectiveness probably is that of stimulating greater public awareness.

OUTLOOK

Whitetail numbers in the region are declining as second-growth forests mature and shrink in carrying capacity. In order to stabilize the populations at acceptable levels, money must be spent to restore and maintain the habitat. Funding sources other than hunting licenses should be sought, since many people besides hunters use, enjoy and benefit from an abundant whitetail population.

The region's state and provincial wildlife agencies will need to improve techniques and procedures to assess the amount and carrying capacity of whitetail habitats, and the size and seasonal distribution of whitetail populations. As implied earlier, the greatest need is for habitat, population and harvest management on a deer management unit basis. In conjunction with regional or state/province overviews, management by units holds the greatest promise for maintaining whitetail populations at desirable levels.

Consistent with biological parameters of deer management in the region are sociological considerations. Because these considerations actually dictate the goals and priorities of management and determine the framework within which management takes place, the agencies must be in a position to respond efficiently and effectively to shifts, however subtle, in public demand. This "balancing act," also best accommodated on a management unit basis, is essential because of the ever-changing and sometimes diametric status of the resources in question and public sentiment.

Assuming (1) public attitudes continue to encourage sound, scientific and progressive management of white-tailed deer, and (2) wildlife agencies gain the resources, manpower and expertise necessary to advance management capabilities, there is no reason not to expect productive and healthy populations of whitetails on a continuing basis in the Northern Great Lakes States and Ontario Forests region.

Chapter 21

MIDWEST OAK/HICKORY FOREST

Oliver Torgerson
Wildlife Research Superintendent
Missouri Department of Conservation
Columbia, Missouri

Wayne R. Porath
Wildlife Research Supervisor
Missouri Department of Conservation
Columbia, Missouri

ENVIRONMENT

The oak/hickory forest community is distributed widely throughout the deciduous forests of eastern North America. It represents the western limit of the deciduous forest, where reduced precipitation causes the forest to grade into savannah or prairie vegetative communities. It also forms the southern limit of the upland hardwood forest, where irregular and indefinite boundaries occur. Unlike most other forest regions, the oak/hickory extends over land of very dissimilar geologic and climatic history. Its center of distribution is in the Ozark and Ouachita mountains (Braun 1964).

Location and Size

The Midwest Oak/Hickory Forest region stretches from southwest Ohio to northeast Oklahoma, and from extreme northern Alabama and Mississippi into Iowa and Nebraska (Figure 87). It also is found in southern Michigan and eastern Texas. The heart of this region is in northern Arkansas, Missouri, southern Illinois, Kentucky and Tennessee. Fingers of oak/hickory forest reach north and west along the Mississippi and Missouri rivers and their tributaries. In all, 16 states have representative stands of oak/hickory forest (Küchler 1966).

This chapter deals with areas where the oak/hickory forest occurs on unglaciated land, and includes the Cross Timbers section of Oklahoma. The area contains approximately 411,482 square kilometers (158,830 square miles) of land. It features five national forests of 19,425 square kilometers (7,500 square miles) and several thousand hectares of other public forests.

Physiography

Much of the region is divided into the Interior Highlands and the Interior Low Plateau province (Figure 87). Interior Highlands include the Ozark, Boston and Ouachita mountains of Missouri, Arkansas and Oklahoma, respectively. The Interior Low Plateau includes the Highland Rim section of Kentucky and Middle Tennessee, the Bluegrass section of Kentucky, the Nashville Basin of Tennessee, and the Shawnee section of southern Illinois and Indiana and northwestern Kentucky (Fenneman 1938). This unglaciated land is underlain by ancient sedimentary rock which was uplifted and shaped by the forces of nature and time into mountains, ridges, hills, valleys and plateaus. Topography varies dramatically, and can be classed from rolling and hilly to moderately rugged. Elevations range from 7.6 meters (25 feet) along the Mississippi River to 610 meters (2,000 feet) in the Ouachita Mountains. The landscape is heavily dissected and well-drained.

411

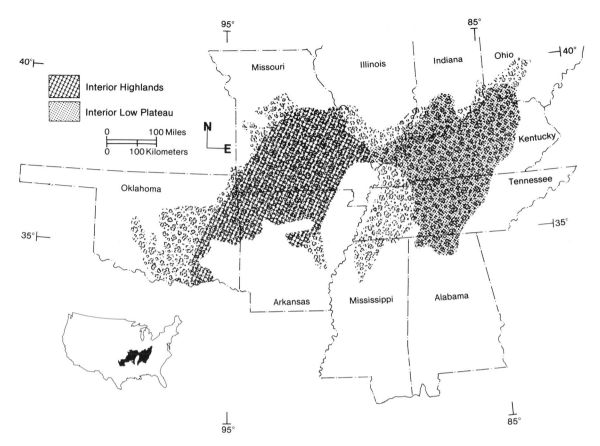

Figure 87. The Midwest Oak/Hickory Forest region.

Vegetation

Man has eliminated millions of hectares of oak/hickory forest and vastly altered the forest and prairie ecosystems—sometimes to the benefit of deer, many times to their detriment. *Interior Highlands.* Oaks are the dominant trees, hickories are generally abundant, and the forest is interrupted locally by prairie. In some places, shortleaf pine is codominant with oak, and the two species may combine to form an oak/pine forest. Cedar glades, an edaphic climax plant community, are a distinctive feature of the Ozark Mountains (Braun 1964).

Post oak and blackjack oak usually dominate the dry ridges and south-facing slopes. Black oak, black hickory, winged elm and common persimmon are other common trees.

On the relatively moist, northerly slopes, white oak generally is the most abundant oak species. Black oak, northern red oak, southern red oak, bitter pecan, shagbark hickory and sugar maple are common associates.

Prevailing understory trees throughout the uplands are dogwood, redbud, eastern hophornbeam and serviceberry. Sumacs and blueberries occur frequently.

Interior Low Plateau. The forests of the Interior Low Plateau have been classified as western mesophytic rather than oak/hickory (Braun 1964). They constitute a mosaic of different vegetative types that form ecotones or transitions between the oak/hickory forests of the Interior Highlands and the more luxuriant forests of the Appalachians. Oak/hickory communities interspersed with prairie represent the western portion. Yellow poplar, beech and sugar maple mix with oaks and hickories to form intermediate forest types eastward. Shortleaf and Virginia pine combine with oaks to the south, similar to pine/oak communities of the Interior Highlands. Cedar glades of the Nashville Basin are a distinctive vegetative community.

Black, white, southern red, chinkapin and chestnut are the most prevalent oak species. Shagbark and pignut are common hickories. Post oak, blackjack oak and black hickory oc-

The Interior Highlands of the Midwest Oak/Hickory Forest region are dissected by many rivers and streams that create diverse landscapes. Some forests are relatively unbroken while others include agricultural fields along riverways. *Photo by Don Wooldridge; courtesy of the Missouri Department of Conservation.*

Cedar glades within the Interior Highlands are edaphic climax plant communities that generally occur on infertile, droughty soils. Whitetails found in this habitat type and in the Cross Timbers section generally are smaller and less productive than are deer from other portions of the Midwest Oak/Hickory Forest region. *Photo by Don Wooldridge; courtesy of the Missouri Department of Conservation.*

cur less frequently. On rich, moist sites, sugar maple, red maple, yellow poplar, beech, basswood, blackgum and buckeye become codominant with oaks and hickories. In general, the trees are taller and form a denser canopy than those of the Interior Highland. Understory trees and shrubs vary according to the dominant tree species. For instance, along the loess hills near major rivers, beech, tuliptree, red oak, hickories, cucumber tree, sugar maple and basswood are dominant overstory trees, while understory vegetation includes reproduction of canopy species plus dogwood, redbud, mulberry, devil's walking stick, pawpaw, blue beech and hophornbeam. Common shrubs are hydrangea, strawberry bush, bladdernut, elderberry and spice bush. In contrast, within parts of central Tennessee, limestone hills rise above the plateau and drier types of forests occur. Oaks and hickories are prominent overstory trees, and red cedar/prairie communities may

form bands around the hills. Xerophytic and understory or invader species include redbud, persimmon and dogwood. Shrubs such as aromatic sumac, dwarf hackberry, Carolina buckthorn and southern buckthorn may be interspersed with the cedars.

Cross Timbers section. The Cross Timbers section represents an ecotone between the oak/hickory forest and grasslands of the West. Forests are an oak/savannah or oak/hickory savannah type. Numerous prairie plants also are present, including sunflowers, goldenrods, sedges, big and little bluestem, sideoats grama, switchgrass, Indiangrass, leadplant, compass plant and gayfeather. Dominant tree species are post oak and blackjack oak, with black hickory comingling southward on better soil types. The trees usually are small and scrubby with broad, low crowns, and understory is sparse and low in species diversity. Common small trees or shrubs include farkleberry,

Because of relatively greater rainfall and higher soil fertility, trees in typical oak/pine communities of the Interior Low Plateau are taller than those in the Interior Highlands. *Photo by Don Wooldridge; courtesy of the Missouri Department of Conservation.*

A typical forest in Cross Timbers landscape includes small, scrubby oaks and hickories with sparse understory, and is dissected by savannahs and fingers of prairie. *Photo by Robert E. Rolley; courtesy of the Oklahoma Cooperative Wildlife Research Unit.*

southern black haw, dwarf sumac, hawthorn, deciduous holly, yaupon, coralberry and sand plum (Duck and Fletcher 1945, Shelford 1963).

Soils

Oak/hickory forest soils are formed from limestone, sandstone and shale bedrock. Red and yellow podzolic soils are typical of the Interior Highlands and Cross Timbers section. They are strongly leached, acid in reaction, and low in organic matter and inherent fertility. Their generally high rock content reduces water-holding capacity, and clay hardpans frequently interfere with water movement and root penetration.

Gray-brown podzolic soils are characteristic of the Interior Low Plateau. They generally are fertile, slightly acid and have a moderate organic-matter content. These soils do not have a hardpan. Consequently, they have a higher water-holding capacity and are silviculturally superior to the red and yellow podzolic soils (Wilde 1958, Winters 1957).

Climate and Weather

The Midwest Oak/Hickory Forest region has a temperate climate. The frost-free season is from April to October, providing a growing season of 170 to 220 days. Late frosts sometimes reduce acorn and hickory nut production. Winters are brisk, but not severe. Snowfall usually occurs each winter, but seldom exceeds 15 centimeters (6 inches) in depth or lasts longer than two or three weeks. Ice and freezing rain occur almost as frequently as snow. Annual precipitation occurs primarily in spring and autumn, and ranges from 89 to 127 centimeters (35–50 inches). Late summer droughts frequently occur in western portions of the forest. Average January temperature varies between −4 and 3 degrees Celsius (24–38 degrees Fahrenheit), while July temperature averages 24 to 27 degrees Celsius (76–80 degrees Fahrenheit). Temperature extremes include winter lows of − 40 degrees Celsius (− 40 degrees Fahrenheit) in northern portions of the region to summer highs of 48 degrees Celsius (118 degrees Fahrenheit) in its southern reaches (U.S. Department of Agriculture 1941).

Land Use

Because of its topography, soils and climate, the region is well-suited to timber and wildlife production. The forested, scenic character has made tourism and recreation a major industry. Although sparsely populated at present, the Ozarks rapidly are becoming a major retirement center.

Much of the better sites in the Interior Low Plateau and the alluvial soils of river and stream bottomlands have been converted from forest to row crop agriculture. In Missouri, Arkansas and Oklahoma, extensive areas of upland forests—approximately 1 percent per year—were transformed in the 1960s and early 1970s by aerial spray and bulldozer to pastures for beef production.

The forest products industry is well-developed. Lumbering, charcoal production and wood novelty manufacturing contribute to the region's economy.

Mining for coal, lead, iron, zinc and clay is locally important.

WHITETAIL POPULATIONS

History, Population Density and Status

Historically, deer populations in the Midwest Oak/Hickory Forest region have experienced great fluctuations. Whitetails increased with early settlement, when small-scale clearing and agriculture improved habitat. During the early 1800s, deer were quite abundant (Bennitt and Nagel 1937, Pietsch 1954). Extensive logging, overgrazing by domestic livestock and annual burning during the late 1800s and early 1900s depleted much of the region's whitetail habitat. This, coupled with uncontrolled market hunting, led to almost total extirpation of white-tailed deer by the early 1900s.

A one-day "bag" of wildlife at a hunting camp in the Midwest Oak/Hickory Forest region about 1910. Wildlife in the region declined dramatically during the late 1800s and early 1900s, due to overhunting and habitat destruction. Harvest laws, including seasons and limits, did not exist or were poorly enforced until people realized that wildlife numbers were finite and entire species were threatened by indiscriminate harvests. *Photo courtesy of the Missouri Department of Conservation.*

Deer recovery began in the 1930s, as a result of closed seasons, strict law enforcement and restocking. Initially, some of the whitetails for restocking came from Michigan, Wisconsin, Pennsylvania and North Carolina, but the most successful restockings were with native deer taken from refuges and game farms. Public support was a vital factor in the success of the restoration efforts.

Whitetail recovery in the Midwest Oak/Hickory Forest region began in the 1930s, as a result of closed seasons, strict law enforcement and restocking efforts. Deer were trapped on refuges and game farms and translocated to areas of suitable habitat. *Photo courtesy of the Missouri Department of Conservation.*

As deer populations were restored, hunting was resumed, but with enforced regulations. State fish and wildlife agencies quickly recognized the need to keep whitetail populations in balance with the food supply. Hunting was the only practical means of deer population control, since most natural predators of deer had been exterminated. At first, hunting seasons were limited to certain counties and to antlered bucks. Later, they were extended statewide and included either-sex harvests.

Today, whitetails can be found in nearly every section of the region. Deer densities vary from only an occasional deer to heavy populations of 39 to 78 per square kilometer (101–202 per square mile) (Murphy 1962, Dechert 1968, Logan 1973). In general, carrying capacity ranges from 2 to 10 deer per square kilometer (5.2–25.9 per square mile) or more (Murphy and Crawford 1970, Donaldson et al. 1951). In most cases, whitetail populations are within habitat carrying capacity and appear to be stationary or slowly increasing at present.

Population Structure

The structure of current whitetail populations of the region apparently differs considerably from those of the past. Elder (1965) attempted to reconstruct the age distribution of deer from five early populations by examining mandibles recovered from Indian middens in Missouri. As much as 20 to 26 percent of the deer mandibles identified represented whitetails 6.5 years and older. Today, whitetails 6.5 years or older seldom make up 2 percent of the harvest (Giessman 1982). However, harvest age structure does not necessarily represent the population age structure.

Modern whitetail populations are comparatively young-aged (Table 63), because legal and illegal hunting and other man-related causes of mortality have reduced the average life expectancy of deer—1.5 years for bucks, 2.7 years

Table 63. Age structure of whitetails taken in any-deer seasons in parts of the Midwest Oak/Hickory Forest region.

State	Year	Sample size	Percentage of deer by age class		
			0.5 years	1.5 years	2.5+ years
Illinois	1981	6,982	32	37	31
Kentucky	1981	1,300	11	58	29
Missouri	1979–1981	3,998	17	46	36
Oklahoma	1981	1,500	11	48	41
Tennessee	1981	743	31	41	28

for does. The buck/doe ratio usually is high (prehunting season average is 42:58; posthunting season average is 33:67) because of more liberal seasons on antlered males. In some areas, only antlered bucks are hunted legally.

Body Weight and Antler Size

Whitetails generally are smaller in western portions of the Midwest Oak/Hickory Forest region, and largest where agricultural crops add significant amounts of nutrients to their diet. Live weights of bucks and does of various age classes are shown in Table 64.

Antler-beam diameter for yearling males, on the average, is 19.1 millimeters (0.75 inch). Each antler has 2.1 points and 24 percent of bucks are spikes (Table 65). At prime (usually 4.5 to 7.5 years of age), healthy bucks can produce Boone and Crockett trophy "racks."

Productivity

The extent to which does in the oak/hickory forest region breed successfully and raise fawns to weaning varies widely, depending on population and habitat conditions. Nutrition is the

The world-record nontypical white-tailed deer antlers, with a Boone and Crockett score of 333-7/8, were on a buck found dead by a deer hunter in November 1981 in an agricultural area of St. Louis County, Missouri. The deer was 5.5-years-old, and its live weight was 113.4 kilograms (250 pounds). Trophy-size whitetails are produced throughout the Midwest Oak/Hickory Forest region, but are most common where agricultural crops are a significant diet component. *Photo by Andy Cassimatis; courtesy of the Missouri Department of Conservation.*

Table 64. Live weight of whitetails of various age and sex classes in parts of the Midwest Oak/Hickory Forest region.

State	Year	Live weight in kilograms/pounds (sample size)					
		Male			Female		
		0.5 years	1.5 years	2.5 + years	0.5 years	1.5 years	2.5 + years
Arkansas	1981–1982	30/66.1 (35)	51/112.4 (202)	61/134.5 (32)	26/57.3 (35)	45/99.2 (26)	47/103.6 (39)
Illinois	1978–1982	33/72.8 (140)	60/132.3 (437)	77/169.8 (195)	29/63.9 (154)	49/108.0 (201)[a]	54/119.0 (415)[a]
Kentucky	1981		70/154.3 (800)			56/123.5 (200)	
Missouri	1977	33/72.8 (244)	57/126.7 (973)	72/158.7 (510)	29/63.9 (263)	48/105.8 (177)	52/114.6 (368)
Tennessee	1981	27/59.5 (496)	54/119.0 (3,266)	66/145.5 (943)	25/55.1 (401)	40/88.2 (362)	46/101.4 (493)
Mean		30/66.1 (915)	57/126.7 (5,678)	69/152.1 (1,680)	27/59.5 (853)	47/103.6 (966)	50/110.2 (1,315)

[a]Estimated.

Table 65. Antler characteristics of 1.5-year-old whitetail bucks in parts of the Midwest Oak/Hickory Forest region.

State	Year	Sample Size	Number of points per antler	Beam diameter		Percentage of spike bucks
				Millimeters	Inches	
Arkansas	1982–1983	122	2.1	19.6	0.77	33
Illinois	1966	391	2.0	21.6	0.85	16
Kentucky	1981	800		21.8	0.86	11
Missouri	1977	944	2.1	19.6	0.77	17
Oklahoma	1981	800	2.5			17
Tennessee	1981	3,355	2.0	18.0	0.71	31
Mean			2.1	19.1	0.75	24

A spike buck in the Oklahoma section of the Ouachita National Forest. Whitetails generally are smaller in western portions of the Midwest Oak/Hickory Forest region, and largest where agricultural crops add significant amounts of nutrients to their diet. A higher percentage of spike bucks occurs when and where deer have an inadequate diet. *Photo by Daniel O. Todd; courtesy of the U. S. Forest Service.*

major factor controlling reproductive performance in white-tailed deer (Harder 1980). The number of fawns per doe averages 0.33 for one-year olds, 1.66 for two-year olds and 1.87 for does three years and older (Table 66). The percentage of fawns that breed has a significant influence on population growth rate (Slobodkin 1961). About 39 percent of the fawns breed, but the rate ranges from 24 to 51 percent.

Pregnancy or birth rates, however, do not necessarily reflect recruitment. Based on fetus counts in a northern Arkansas enclosure, 67

fawns should have been born, but only 32 were counted (Segelquist et al. 1973). Nutritional stress on pregnant does can result in malnourished fawns, which may accentuate fawn starvation or predator mortality (Knowlton 1976, Verme 1977).

Food and Feeding Habits

Deer food availability varies widely among soil types, timber stand conditions and land uses. In national forests in Missouri, yields of

Table 66. Reproductive rates of whitetails in parts of the Midwest Oak/Hickory Forest region.

State	Year	Number of fawns per doe of specified age (sample size)[a]			Percentage of pregnant does at specified age		
		1 year old	2 years old	3 years old	Fawn	1.5 years old	2.5 + years old
Arkansas	1971	1.66 (24)[b]			97 (31)[b]		
Illinois	1966	0.41 (160)	1.68 (110)	1.88 (278)	41 (160)	96 (110)	98 (278)
Kentucky	1981				51 (200)		
Missouri	1981–1982	0.38 (40)	1.63 (30)	1.69 (35)	32 (40)	90 (30)	91 (35)
Tennessee	1975–1982	0.25 (175)	1.65 (318)	1.87 (685)	24 (175)	95 (318)	97 (685)
Mean[c]		0.33 (375)	1.66 (458)	1.87 (998)	39 (570)	95 (458)	97 (998)

[a]Adjusted from *corpora lutea* and *in utero* fetus counts.
[b]Data from these age classes were pooled.
[c]Excludes Arkansas data.

preferred deer forage ranged from 31 to 69 kilograms of air-dry forage per hectare (28–62 pounds per acre) in summer, and from 27 to 37 kilograms of air-dry forage per hectare (24–33 pounds per acre) in winter. Yields usually were higher when pine or eastern redcedar were present because of their relatively open canopies (Murphy and Crawford 1970). In a northern Arkansas enclosure, oven-dry yields of preferred deer forage averaged 78 and 3 kilograms per hectare (70 and 3 pounds per acre) in summer and winter, respectively. Acorn yields ranged from 224 kilograms per hectare (200 pounds per acre) in good years to practically none in poor years (Segelquist et al. 1973).

When available, acorns are the most preferred whitetail food in autumn and winter (Lindzey 1950), and may comprise 50 percent or more of the animal's diet (Korschgen 1962). Competition for acorns is high since acorns are preferred by many other kinds of forest animals and are eaten by insects as well. Fruits of beech, coralberry, sumac, grapes, persimmon and honeylocust also are preferred by deer in autumn and winter (Korschgen 1962).

Preferred browse in Tennessee includes blackgum, honeysuckle, greenbrier, straw-

Whitetail doe feeding on eastern redcedar, a preferred winter food in the Midwest Oak/Hickory Forest region. This cedar tree shows severe overbrowsing caused by deer overpopulation. Such overpopulation usually is the product of severe winter, underharvest or both. *Photo courtesy of the Missouri Department of Conservation.*

berry bush and sumac. Perennial plants that remain green during winter—such as aster, goldenrod, panicum, pussytoes, sedge rosettes and the foliage of eastern redcedar—may be used heavily (Dunkeson 1955, Korschgen 1962, Segelquist et al. 1973). Considerable amounts of deciduous browse twigs and dead leaves are eaten when preferred foods are scarce (Segelquist et al. 1973). Where available, corn, soybeans, winter wheat and sorghum add significantly to the deer's diet (Korschgen 1962).

Although many kinds of plants are eaten by whitetails in spring and summer, only 26 are considered principal foods in the Missouri Ozarks (Korschgen et al. 1980). Grapes are very important. Other preferred species include elm, sumac, wild lettuce, fungi, blackberry, cinquefoil, common pokeberry, persimmon, flowering spurge, rusty blackhaw viburnum, rose and greenbrier. Agricultural plants, such as red clover, Korean lespedeza, soybeans, corn and sorghum, also are used heavily.

SPECIAL PROBLEMS

Limiting Factors

Weather. Weather usually is not a limiting factor for white-tailed deer in the Midwest Oak/Hickory Forest region. Winters are relatively mild and snow rarely is deep enough to hinder deer movement. However, late spring frosts and summer droughts may reduce mast production.

Food quality. Seasonally, whitetails in the region are likely to have difficulty meeting their nutritional requirements. Protein is deficient in winter, and phosphorus in several preferred foods is deficient year-round (Murphy and Coats 1966, Torgerson and Pfander 1971, Segelquist et al. 1972). Summer foods are 1.5 times more digestible than winter foods (Snider and Asplund 1974), and cellulose is more than 4 times more digestible in summer than in winter (Torgerson and Pfander 1971). However, it is dangerous to judge forage quality by a single factor. A forage may be low in digestibility but contribute significantly to the diet by providing easily available cell solubles. Principal component analysis has demonstrated the importance of forage variety in meeting the nutritional needs of white-tailed deer (Vangilder et al. 1982).

Winters generally are mild in the Midwest Oak/Hickory Forest region, and snow seldom is deep enough to hinder whitetail movements to adequate food supplies. However, harsh winters during the years of acorn crop failure can adversely affect the production of healthy fawns, especially on overpopulated range. *Photo by Charles W. Schwartz; courtesy of the Missouri Department of Conservation.*

Adequate summer and autumn nutrition may be critical to winter survival and successful production of healthy fawns the following spring (Julander et al. 1961, Nordan et al. 1968). Usually, whitetails build up sufficient fat reserves during late summer and autumn to carry them through the winter. But when acorns are scarce, the deer are apt to suffer a negative energy balance during winter. Even when winter foods are plentiful, deer may voluntarily decrease consumption and lose weight (Long et al. 1965, Torgerson and Porath 1976). Deer apparently have adapted through evolutionary time to poor quality and quantity of winter foods, and depend on fat reserves to supply much of their winter energy needs.

Predation. In the past, mountain lions and red and gray wolves were significant predators of deer in the region (Schwartz and Schwartz 1981). Today, wolves have been extirpated from the region, and mountain lions occur only in very limited numbers in northern Arkansas and possibly Missouri and Oklahoma. Whitetails usually do not comprise a significant part of bobcat and coyote diets (Korschgen 1957*a*, 1957*b*), although both were major mortality factors on fawns in a northern Arkansas enclosure (Rogers and Cartwright 1977). Deer was the third most common bobcat food listed in a Tennessee study, but most of the deer meat

consumed by bobcats likely was carrion (Buttrey 1974).

Dogs are considered a serious predator of deer in several states (Madson 1961, Murphy 1970*b*, Donaldson et al. 1951), but actual predation by dogs may be less serious to the whitetails' well-being than is year-round harassment (Progulske and Baskett 1958, Lindzey 1950). The harassment impact of dogs is greatest in areas of low deer population or newly stocked habitat (Perry and Giles 1971). Energy expenditure due to harassment in winter months can be a potentially significant factor affecting deer survival (Moen 1976). Most studies using radio-equipped deer and dogs have indicated that dog predation occurs only on old or weakened deer and that harassment only temporarily disrupts normal behavior patterns (Corbett et al. 1972, Gavitt et al. 1975, Sweeney et al. 1971). However, dog harassment on the Cumberland plateau caused translocated whitetails to abandon the vicinity of the release site (Anderson 1979), and more than 50 percent of the deer in a simulated restoration in northeastern Tennessee were lost because of harassment by free-running dogs (Nichols and Whitehead 1978). Dogs also prey on fawns. Approximately 8 percent (8 of 96) of the fawns radio-tagged in a fawn mortality study in the Missouri Ozarks were killed by dogs (Dalton 1984).

Dogs are considered by many to be a serious predator of white-tailed deer in the Midwest Oak/Hickory Forest region, but their actual predation influence may be less serious than is their year-round harassment of whitetails, especially in areas of low deer population or newly stocked habitat. *Photo courtesy of the Missouri Department of Conservation.*

Diseases and parasites. A variety of parasites affect white-tailed deer in the Midwest Oak/Hickory Forest region. Meningeal worms, in combination with winter food scarcity, limited deer numbers in a northern Arkansas enclosure (Segelquist et al. 1973). Severe brain and lung lesions caused by meningeal worm infections were observed in whitetails on overpopulated refuges in eastern Oklahoma (Eve 1975). Blood loss and gross infection resulting from lone star ticks caused mortality of young fawns in an overpopulated deer refuge in eastern Oklahoma, with survival increasing when acorn yields were high. In good acorn years, the improved nutritional plane of whitetail does apparently allows the production of relatively healthy fawns that are more mobile and, therefore, less susceptible to tick infestation (Logan 1973). The number of abomasal roundworm parasites has been found to be associated closely with relative deer density (Eve and Kellogg 1977). High abomasal par-

asite counts were observed in deer collected from overpopulated refuges in eastern Oklahoma (Eve 1975). Stomach worms are found in deer throughout the oak/hickory forest, but except for the large stomach worm, they pose little threat to the health of deer (Davidson et al. 1980, Prestwood and Pursglove 1981).

Several diseases affect whitetails in the region; epizootic hemorrhagic disease is the most serious. Extensive die-offs were recorded during late summer in the mid-1950s (Madson 1961, Karstad 1962, Murphy 1970*b*), and several states in the Midwest Oak/Hickory Forest region diagnosed the disease during the early and mid-1970s and in 1980 (Prestwood et al. 1974, Brannian et al. 1983, Southeastern Cooperative Wildlife Disease Study 1981). Diseases such as leptospirosis, anthrax, anaplasmosis and brucellosis, which are common to domestic cattle, have spread to deer. However, with the exception of anthrax, they have little effect on whitetails (Kellogg et al. 1970). Extensive studies have shown deer to be unimportant in the spread of these diseases (Robb 1959, Roth 1962, Calhoun and Loomis 1974, Carlile and Lowry 1975, Maas et al. 1981, Jones et al. 1983).

In general, deer of the Midwest Oak/Hickory Forest region are healthy, and epizootic hemorrhagic disease poses the only serious threat at present.

Other mortality. Legal hunting and poaching currently are the major causes of white-tailed deer mortality in the region. Although reliable data are not available, most states in the region consider poaching to be a major drain on their deer resources (Lindzey 1950, Donaldson et al. 1951, Pietsch 1954, Murphy 1970*b*). In some cases, poaching may exceed the legal harvest (Bennitt and Nagel 1937). Also, deer are killed illegally during the hunting season. Deer hunters in Missouri consider poaching to be the greatest threat to whitetail management in the state (Porath et al. 1980). Studies show that Missouri deer poaching is a year-round activity, but is heaviest during autumn and winter months. Violations are most numerous on weekend evenings between 8:00 p.m. and midnight, and most violators are less than 40 years of age and are blue-collar workers. Meat and recreation are the primary reasons for closed-season poaching. Violators selected a poaching area based on availability of deer more than on any other factor (Glover 1982). Some states have instituted incentive programs to encourage citizens to provide information on poaching activity. Incentives include a toll-free telephone number monitored 24 hours a day, guaranteed anonymity, and financial reward if the information provided leads to an arrest and/or conviction.

Deer/vehicle collisions annually kill thousands of whitetails. This deer mortality ranges from 1 to 10 percent of the legal harvest in the oak/hickory forest states. Deer-crossing signs, reflective mirrors, improved visibility along roadways, public education and increased legal harvest are techniques used to reduce collisions. Reduced highway speed limits in 1973 decreased deer/vehicle accidents by approximately 10 percent in Missouri's oak/hickory forest (Porath and Torgerson 1975).

Trains and fence entanglements are minor sources of deer mortality. And fawns sometimes are killed by mowers during spring haying operations.

Competition

Other animals. At one time, domestic livestock competed heavily with wildlife for food, and may have contributed to the decline of whitetails in the Midwest Oak/Hickory Forest region in the late 1800s and early 1900s. For example, a 1935 "game drive" census by the U.S. Forest Service of 51.8 square kilometers (20 square miles) of Ozark forest produced an estimate of 14 deer, 378 cattle, 111 sheep, 141 goats and 482 hogs, as well as 89 dogs and 14 house cats (Bennitt and Nagel 1937). Widespread annual burning and open range grazing were common through the 1940s and into the 1960s, and reduced food available to whitetails. Today, these practices are much reduced; farmers and ranchers rely primarily on improved pastures for livestock grazing.

Whitetails in the region probably do not compete with other wildlife for forage, but they compete directly with other animals for acorns. High deer populations may be a limiting factor to wild turkey and squirrels (Latham 1943, Lewis 1967).

Other land uses. Large-scale clearing for agriculture, highway construction, urban sprawl, stream channelization, reservoir construction, mining and certain forest management practices cause long-term or permanent loss of wildlife habitat and represent the most serious problem facing white-tailed deer today. On the other hand, the purchase of recreational prop-

The once-common practice of annual spring burning has been largely discontinued in the Midwest Oak/Hickory Forest region. Fires were set to control snakes, chiggers and ticks, and to increase grass growth, but indiscriminate burning was detrimental to wildlife and forest management. *Photo by Don Wooldridge; courtesy of the Missouri Department of Conservation.*

"Open range" was eliminated in much of the Midwest Oak/Hickory Forest region in the 1960s and helped reduce livestock competition with deer and other wildlife. It also improved highway safety. *Photo by Don Wooldridge; courtesy of the Missouri Department of Conservation.*

These wintering whitetails in good condition in oak/hickory forest habitat were attracted to corn left for wild turkeys at a trapping site. Note the cannon protruding from snow between the two center deer. It was used in a research project to propel a hidden net over baited turkeys. Both whitetails and wild turkeys from oak/hickory forest habitats in Missouri have served as a reservoir for restocking and introductions of the species in other states. *Photo by John B. Lewis; courtesy of the Missouri Department of Conservation.*

erty, improved forest management techniques and certain farming practices can serve to maintain and improve deer habitat. In extensive, unbroken blocks of forest, small-scale clearing for pasture will improve deer habitat, especially where legumes are planted. Whitetails flourish where cropland and forest are interspersed. However, extensive damage may be caused to crops, vineyards, orchards, nurseries and gardens if deer numbers are not controlled carefully.

Forest management practices for timber production largely determine carrying capacity for deer of oak/hickory forests. Even-aged management will sustain adequate forage and mast as well as timber products, if regeneration, pole, sawlog and old-growth stands are well-interspersed within the 2.6-square kilometer (1-square mile) home range of deer. Much of the oak/hickory forests consist of dense second-growth pole and sawlog trees, but with thinning and balancing of age and size classes of trees, these stands can produce much more deer food. Large-scale conversion of oak/hickory to pure pine stands reduces deer habitat quality by eliminating oak mast. Whitetails do not restrict regeneration of oaks and hickories if their numbers are controlled (Sander 1977).

MANAGEMENT

Regulation of Hunting

White-tailed deer hunting seasons serve to maintain deer populations in balance with the carrying capacity of their habitats, and provide a maximum amount of the type of hunting opportunities desired. Biological harvest goals and public hunting objectives frequently differ from deer population to deer population. It is necessary, therefore, to manage the deer and regulate their harvests on a unit by unit basis throughout most of the Midwest Oak/Hickory Forest region. Critical to management in all units, particularly with respect to harvest, is knowledge of the deer population—its size, sex and age characteristics, annual recruitment, and the quality, quantity and distribution of its seasonal habitat. Browse surveys, crop depredation reports, computer-simulation models, highway mortality, aerial surveys, parasite investigations, and ovary or fetus counts are some of the techniques used to assess deer population status. Harvest data from prior hunting seasons are evaluated to project potential hunting pressure and harvest during the upcoming season. All information is re-

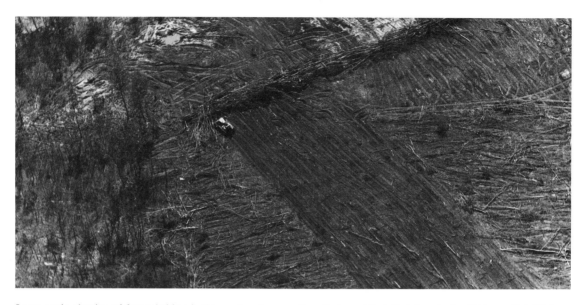

Large-scale clearing of forest habitat is the most serious problem facing white-tailed deer in the Midwest Oak/Hickory Forest region. Clearing for agriculture, highway construction, urban sprawl, mining, reservoir construction and stream channelization can cause long-term or permanent loss of habitat for deer and other wildlife of the region. *Photo by Don Wooldridge; courtesy of the Missouri Department of Conservation.*

viewed to determine unit-specific harvest regulations in concert with public desire.

In most states of the region, whitetail numbers are controlled by a combination of liberal hunting seasons on antlered bucks, special and/or extended seasons, and restricted any-deer seasons or quota permits for antlerless deer. Firearm hunts normally occur in November and December, and range in length from 6 to 35 days (Table 67). Bag limits range from 2 deer per season in Kentucky, Illinois and Missouri to 12 in Tennessee (gun and bow combined). Use of dogs and buckshot are illegal except in Arkansas, and rifles are legal except in Illinois. In all states, hunters are required to register their deer at check stations.

The most common form of whitetail hunting is from tree or ground stands. Stalking and organized drives are preferred methods by many whitetail hunters. In Arkansas, dogs commonly are used to chase deer past standing hunters. Generally, hunters tend to be non-selective for age and sex during any-deer seasons, but will choose an antlered or the largest deer when two or more animals are seen at the same time.

In 1981, more than 105,000 whitetails were harvested by 665,000 hunters in the Midwest Oak/Hickory Forest region. Hunter success rates ranged from 7 to 27 percent, and averaged 16 percent (Table 67).

Biological, Social, Economic and Political Interactions

Hunting is the most effective and efficient means of keeping deer numbers in balance with their food supplies, but many individuals and organizations strongly oppose recreational hunting and exert considerable social and political pressure to curtail it. The problem of how to appease the hunting and antihunting publics and yet maintain proper balance between whitetails and their habitat is complicated further in some areas by opposition to either-sex harvests. Misunderstanding often has led to vigorous argument for buck-only seasons, despite biological evidence that either-sex harvests in designated areas are necessary for sustained whitetail productivity. And since deer harvest regulations and other resource policies ultimately are decided by elected state officials—who understandably are politically sensitive to public wish and expression—biological considerations and recommendations sometimes are overruled. Biopolitical constraints will continue to generate and prolong resource management issues in the Midwest Oak/Hickory Forest region just as in other regions.

Economics largely dictate land use in the region. Most of the land (95 percent) is in private ownership. And since deer add little to

Table 67. White-tailed deer hunting seasons and harvests from portions of states in the Midwest Oak/Hickory Forest region, 1981.

State	Number of licensed hunters	Number of deer harvested	Percentage of harvest success	Season dates	Type of weapon	Type of season
Arkansas[a]	106,001	14,657	14	10/1–2/15	Longbow	Any-deer; no dogs
				10/18–10/26	Muzzleloader, longbow	Any-deer; no dogs
				11/10–11/22	Rifle, shotgun, muzzleloader, longbow, crossbow, handgun	Buck-only; dogs legal
				11/28–11/29	Same as above	Any-deer; no dogs
				12/8–12/13	Same as above	Buck-only; dogs legal
				12/26–1/1	Muzzleloader, longbow	Any-deer; no dogs
Illinois	29,122	7,790	27	11/20–11/22 12/11–12/13	Shotgun, muzzleloader	Any-deer; quotas on residents
Kentucky	128,000	22,183	17	11/6–11/15	Rifle, shotgun, muzzleloader, handgun, longbow, crossbow	Primarily buck-only; one day any-deer in 21 counties
Missouri	161,566	27,225[b]	14[c]	11/14–11/22	Rifle, shotgun, muzzleloader, longbow, crossbow, handgun	Buck-only; quota for any-deer permits
Oklahoma	90,000	6,120	7	11/21–11/29	Rifle, shotgun, muzzleloader, handgun	Buck-only; quota for any-deer permits
				12/5–12/13	Muzzleloader	Buck-only
Tennessee[d]	150,000	27,400	18	9/26–10/31	Longbow	Any-deer
				11/7–11/8	Rifle, shotgun, muzzleloader, longbow, handgun	Any-deer; juvenile hunters only
				11/21–12/6	Same as above	Buck-only
				12/12–12/18	Muzzleloader	Buck-only
				12/19–1/1	Rifle, shotgun, muzzleloader, longbow, handgun	Buck-only
				1/8–1/10	Same as above	Any-deer; by quotas

[a]1980–1981 data; includes archery-season harvest.
[b]Includes 5,244 deer taken by unlicensed farmers.
[c]Percentage excludes farmer-kill.
[d]1981–1982 data; includes archery-season harvest.

economic returns of individual landowners and operators, the animals receive small consideration in overall land resource management plans. The degree to which landowners improve habitats and grant hunters access to private lands will depend largely on their personal interests as well as whether they receive incentive payments for those activities. It is not common practice for landowners to charge for hunting in the Midwest Oak/Hickory Forest region, and they receive very little of the money expended by hunters for recreation (Porath et al. 1980). But a trend toward fee-assessment is developing.

Hunters must have written permission to enter private property in Kentucky and some Tennessee counties. The statewide Kentucky trespass law has not reduced landowner complaints (J. Phillips personal communication:1983), but the Tennessee county laws significantly reduced hunter trespass and hunting in general (L. C. Marcum personal commu-

nication:1983). Deer hunter trespass generally is a problem throughout the region. Land posting has not affected most states' ability to obtain adequate harvests of white-tailed deer.

Current Practices, Policies and Philosophies

Harvest by hunting will continue to be the main method for managing white-tailed deer populations in the Midwest Oak/Hickory Forest region. State wildlife agencies are applying regulations and guidelines more precisely in managing deer hunting because hunter numbers continue to grow and deer habitat continues to shrink. Penalties for mismanagement can be great. Recovery from overharvest may take years. Conversely, underharvest can reduce productivity and fawn survival, and even cause starvation or disease die-offs in extreme cases.

Efforts of state wildlife agencies to regulate deer harvest by habitat type or management unit, as opposed to political boundaries, have been encouraging. The framework of such units permits intensive management that is vital to whitetail populations and the diverse interests of the public in that resource (Figure 88).

Public lands comprise about 5 percent of the Midwest Oak/Hickory Forest region. They are hunted heavily for deer, and in some cases, overhunted (Murphy 1962). Well-distributed, small refuges of 202 to 405 hectares (500–1,000 acres) in size may be worthy of trial to maintain optimum sustained yields of whitetails on heavily hunted public lands.

The plan developed by Mark Twain National Forest and the Missouri Department of Conservation is a good example of how forest management practices can be organized to improve timber production and habitat for wildlife. According to the plan, 40 percent of the forest is in mast-producing condition, 20 percent in forage and 10 percent in old-growth timber. These habitat objectives will be achieved when the age- and size-class distribution of trees are balanced within each forest management compartment of approximately 405 hectares (1,000 acres) each (Evans 1974). The plan has been funded by Congress and serves as a model forest-wildlife management procedure throughout the Midwest Oak/Hickory Forest region and the United States. The plan currently is being revised to improve its applicability to various land types.

Figure 88. White-tailed deer management units in Missouri.

Recommendations

1. Retain existing oak/hickory forests and avoid their conversion to other land uses.
2. Provide landowners with incentives to manage their lands to the benefit of wildlife.
3. When and where needed, adopt regulations (such as extended, special and split whitetail hunting seasons) and harvest quotas to distribute hunter pressure.
4. Adjust regulations for antlerless whitetails to achieve appropriate doe harvest levels.
5. Reduce poaching by improved conservation law enforcement and public education.
6. Expand research to provide additional information on: effects of land use on deer populations; impact of free-running dogs on deer; causes and levels of fawn mortality; enhancement of preferred and nutritious deer food plants; forest management techniques that enhance timber production and wildlife; deer inventory techniques; and effects of diseases and parasites on deer health and productivity.
7. Better inform the public on: the need to maintain and manage existing habitats; the importance of either-sex harvests to control deer populations in certain management units (areas); and safe, ethical and responsible hunter behavior.
8. Base whitetail population, habitat and harvest management recommendations on sound ecological principles rather than political expediency.

OUTLOOK

The Midwest Oak/Hickory Forest region's potential to produce white-tailed deer is likely to increase in the immediate future, especially on public lands. Control of indiscriminant burning and grazing already has improved forest understory conditions, and the maturation of second-growth trees has increased mast production. In some cases, forest management plans now consider the needs of deer and other wildlife. In the long run, however, the rise or decline in whitetail productivity and recreational hunting will depend primarily on the availability of suitable habitat and its proper management.

Chapter 22

MIDWEST AGRICULTURAL REGION

H. Lee Gladfelter
Wildlife Research Biologist
Iowa Conservation Commission
Boone, Iowa

The Midwest agricultural region extends from the beech/maple forests of Ohio westward to the native tallgrass prairies of eastern North and South Dakota, Nebraska and Kansas, and from the oak/hickory and maple/basswood forests of southern Michigan, Wisconsin and Minnesota southward to the interspersion of bluestem prairie and oak/hickory forests of northern Missouri and southern Illinois (Küchler 1966). This region covers approximately 880,600 square kilometers (340,000 square miles) of land area (Figure 89).

ENVIRONMENT

Pleistocene glaciation caused leveling of much of the landscape, leaving relatively flat to gently rolling topography beneficial to eventual farming. Parent soil materials are geologically young, high in available nutrients, and rich in organic matter, with very little leaching to impair natural fertility (Buckman and Brady 1960). Native prairie has been converted to cropland which comprises about 75 percent of the land area (Den Uyl 1962). Major crops include corn, soybeans, alfalfa, oats, winter wheat, sorghum and barley.

Temperature extremes usually are of short duration, but severe winter wind chill factors can add greatly to animal stress. Annual precipitation ranges from 64 to 152 centimeters (25–60 inches) and increases from west to east (Den Uyl 1962). Whitetails rarely are impeded by snow, and most of their preferred food is available throughout winter.

Forests cover 1 to 35 percent of the Midwest agricultural region, with a range of 2 to 18 per-cent in most states (Huemoeller et al. 1976). Forest areas are limited mainly to stream bottoms or areas too steep for agriculture. Oak/hickory is the most extensive forest type and is dispersed in narrow bands throughout the cropland (Braun 1950). The elm/ash/maple forests commonly are found in bottomland areas. The maple/basswood and beech/maple forests also are found in the region. These major forest types do not have definite boundaries and frequently are interspersed in the same area.

LAND USE

Agriculture is the primary land use in the region, and recent changes have affected the amount of white-tailed deer habitat present. Between 1950 and 1969, cropland increased 16 percent, with a corresponding decrease in forest and pasture (Huemoeller et al. 1976). Future economic pressures are likely to continue this conversion. Also, dam construction has inundated large tracts of deer habitat and reduced seasonal flooding, making cultivation possible where forests once grew (Crawford 1970). It is apparent that whitetails in the region have adapted well to limited forest resources, but they probably are affected more severely by forest loss than are whitetails in other regions of the country.

Another land use that affects deer habitat is livestock grazing, which reduces browse, may eliminate natural forest regeneration, and usually reduces carrying capacity. The amount of forest land sustaining grazing varies from 15 percent in Michigan to 80 percent in Iowa (Murphy 1970a).

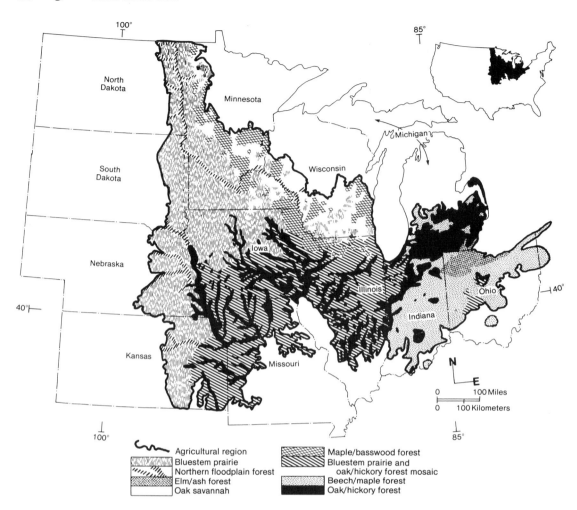

Figure 89. The Midwest agricultural region and its major vegetative communities (from Küchler 1966).

Intensive farming throughout much of the Midwest agricultural region provides an abundant source of food for white-tailed deer, but limits the amount and diversity of woodland habitat except in riparian systems and the driftless area. *Left photo by O. V. Gordon. Right photo courtesy of the U.S. Soil Conservation Service.*

White-tailed deer have adapted well to farming practices in the Midwest agricultural region and generally benefit from them. The most serious competition whitetails face from livestock in the region are browse reduction, elimination of forest regeneration and conversion by farmers of woodland to pasture. *Photo courtesy of the Michigan Department of Natural Resources.*

Other competing land uses include highways, airports, railroads, urban developments and mining. These account for 4 to 9 percent of the land area in the Midwest region (Huemoeller et al. 1976). Many states have large deposits of coal within 30 meters (100 feet) of the surface and, if mined, could severely damage existing habitat. Land and vegetative reclamation following coal extraction would be essential to reestablish suitable deer habitat.

WHITETAIL POPULATIONS

History

When settlers first arrived, whitetails were abundant in native forests of the Midwest region (Cook 1945). At first, clearing for lumber and agriculture in the mid-1800s benefited deer by creating new openings and producing early successional habitat. As clearing continued, however, habitat declined and so did deer numbers. The whitetail decline was accelerated by market hunting and a number of severe winters in the 1880s and 1890s.

By 1900, deer nearly were extirpated in most states of the region. Legislatures reacted by closing or restricting hunting seasons and establishing funds to hire agents to enforce new conservation laws. The whitetail population began increasing rapidly during the 1930s and 1940s due to protection from overharvest, restocking, immigration from surrounding areas,

Whitetails were a vital source of food for early settlers of the Midwest agricultural region. Intensive land clearing and hunting in all seasons led to the near extirpation of the species from the region by about 1900. *Photo courtesy of the State Historical Society of Missouri.*

effective wildlife law enforcement and habitat improvement following abandonment of farm fields.

In the 1940s and 1950s, increased crop damage from growing deer populations forced states to reopen or liberalize hunting seasons to keep populations within tolerable limits. Hunting pressure caused dispersal of whitetails into suitable habitat and reduced the large concentration causing damage. Current management goals are to maintain whitetails at population levels compatible with agricultural interests, since carrying capacity may be more dependent on landowner tolerance for economic loss than on habitat quantity and quality.

Population Density

Statewide whitetail densities range from 0.4 to 6.0 deer per square kilometer (1–15 per square mile) of land area, and from 2 to 31 deer per square kilometer (5–80 per square mile) of forest habitat. Biological carrying capacity is high, since agricultural crops are an abundant food source for whitetails and the forests provide necessary cover. Highest deer densities are found in refuges, where hunting is restricted and crops are readily available. The total number of white-tailed deer in the Midwest agricultural region is difficult to estimate, but populations in most areas seem to be increasing.

Age Structure

Age structure usually is determined from biological data collected at check stations or from tooth samples returned by hunters. Two methods of assigning age to harvested animals are tooth replacement and wear (*see* Severinghaus 1949) and incisor cementum annuli counts (*see* Low and Cowan 1963, Gilbert 1966, Lockard 1972). One problem with these techniques is aging errors. The rate and direction of errors may vary between age classes, techniques used and geographic regions (Roseberry 1980). Another problem is that the harvest sample may not accurately represent the wild population because of differences in age class vulnerability, hunter selectivity or restrictive harvest requirements. Standardization of technique, use of trained observers to estimate age, and improved understanding of possible sources of bias will help overcome these inherent problems.

Even though whitetail densities in the Midwest agricultural region are 0.4–6.0 deer per square kilometer (1–15 per square mile), including a density range of 2–31 deer per square kilometer (5–80 per square mile) in forested areas, serious crop damage by deer is not a widespread problem. In general, farmers and other landowners in the region place high aesthetic and recreational value on white-tailed deer and are quite tolerant of nominal crop damage. Where tree nurseries and fruit crops are involved, landowner tolerance levels are lower. *Photo by Walter Wettschreck; courtesy of the Minnesota Department of Natural Resources.*

High mortality rates, mainly from legal harvest and illegal kills, have created a very young age structure. In states with either-sex hunting regulations, about 40 percent of the harvest is fawns, 25 to 30 percent is yearlings, 25 to 30 percent is 2.5- to 4.5-year-olds and 4 to 6 percent is represented by whitetails older than 4.5 years (Nixon 1970). However, a number of states have buck-only and limited either-sex harvest regulations that provide a degree of protection for does and fawns, but place intense pressure on bucks, especially yearlings. In these states, only 2 to 25 percent of the harvest is fawns, 35 to 60 percent is yearlings, 20 to 30 percent is 2.5- to 4.5-year-olds and only 1 to 3 percent is deer older than 4.5 years. Average life expectancy at birth is less than two years, but whitetails that survive their first year are expected to live another two or three years.

Condition

Generally, the region's whitetails are in excellent condition, due to nutritious foods provided by agricultural crops. Bucks reach maximum weight after 4.5 years, while does reach maximum weight at 2.5 to 3.5 years of age. Autumn live weights for bucks in Iowa average 45 kilograms (100 pounds) for fawns, 74 kilograms (164 pounds) for yearlings, 88 kilograms (195 pounds) for 2.5-year-olds, and 103 kilograms (227 pounds) for bucks 4.5 years and older (Kline 1965). Live weights for Iowa does average 41 kilograms (91 pounds) for fawns, 62 kilograms (137 pounds) for yearlings, and 68 kilograms (150 pounds) for does 2.5 years and older.

Another indication of good body condition is that most yearling bucks have branched antlers while mature bucks (3.5 years and older) carry a large rack. The Midwest region accounts for 8 of the top 20 typical whitetail racks in the Boone and Crockett Club records (Nesbitt and Wright 1981), and 18 of the top 20 in Pope and Young records (Helgeland 1981).

Productivity

Whitetail recruitment rates in the region are high because 50 percent of fawn does and 95 percent of adult does breed successfully (Table 68). High fawn pregnancy rates probably are a consequence of a nutritious food supply, which allows the deer to reach critical body weight during their first breeding season (Hesselton and Sauer 1973, Harder 1980). The best example of this is the 65 to 70 percent fawn pregnancy rate in states where farm crops are readily available.

Table 68. Reproductive performance of white-tailed deer in the Midwest agricultural region.

State	Sample size	Number of embryos per doe			Percentage of does pregnant			Year of study	Source
		Fawns	Yearlings	2.5 + years old	Fawns	Yearlings	2.5 + years old		
Illinois	271	0.68	1.74	2.10	70	100	100	1979–1981	F. Loomis (personal communication:1982)
Indiana	172	1.00	1.53	1.94	20	100	100	1971	Stormer (1972)
Iowa	260	0.95	1.87	1.74	69	96	93	1978–1979	H. Gladfelter (personal files)
Kansas	400	0.78	1.87	1.96	65	96	98	1975–1981	K. Sexson (personal communication:1982)
Michigan	2,352	0.63	1.86	1.95	51	96	96	1952–1982	Friedrich and Hill (1982)
Minnesota	1,716	0.54	1.51	1.89	48	92	97	1978–1982	J. Ludwig (personal communication:1982)
Missouri	140	0.38	1.25	1.46	29	68	84	1981–1982	Giessman (1982)
Nebraska	663	0.68	1.74	1.95	61	94	99	1961–1973	Menzel and Havel (1974)
North Dakota	200	0.60	1.75	2.26	50	100	100	1954–1982	J. McKenzie (personal communication:1982)
Ohio	237	0.74	1.86	1.80	60	97	98	1982	R. Stoll (personal communication:1982)
South Dakota	335	0.78	1.56	1.92	62	87	98	1976–1980	L. Rice (personal communication:1982)
Wisconsin	181	0.33	1.38	1.91	31	89	97	1982	K. McCaffery (personal communication:1983)
Mean		0.67	1.66	1.91	51	93	97		

Edge created by the interspersion of hardwood forest and tallgrass prairies is excellent whitetail habitat in the Midwest agricultural region, which is gaining considerable recognition for its production of trophy whitetails. *Photo by Lee Gladfelter; courtesy of the Iowa Conservation Commission.*

Fawn does produce an average of 0.7 embryos, 1.5-year-olds produce 1.7 embryos; and does 2.5 years and older average 1.9 embryos (Table 68). If only pregnant animals are considered, fawns produce an average of 1.3 embryos each, while older does average 1.9. Based on embryo counts and a population that has a 50:50 sex ratio and consists of 40 percent fawns, the theoretical annual rate of increase is about 70 percent. However, this high potential may be reduced by a 2 to 4 percent fetus mortality rate (Roseberry and Klimstra 1970, Woolf and Harder 1979) and 30 to 35 percent mortality during the first three months of life (Bryan 1980).

Peak breeding for adult does occurs between November 5 and 20, and from December 1 to 20 for fawn does (Nixon 1971, Haugen 1975). Later fawn breeding reflects the time necessary for fawns to reach sexual maturity. The peak fawning period is late May and early June for adult does and late June to early July for yearling does.

Whitetails in the Midwest agricultural region are very productive. Most adult does produce two fawns annually. *Photo by James Scheffler; courtesy of the Iowa Conservation Commission.*

Harvest

Hunter success and harvest data are collected from field check stations or postseason mail questionnaires. Hunter numbers and whitetail harvests have increased rapidly since the mid-1960s. Firearms harvest in the Midwest region increased from 145,000 deer in 1966 to 200,000 in 1976. By 1978, harvest had increased to 225,000 and continued to climb to around 300,000 in 1981. This rapid increase in harvest from 1978 to 1981 probably was due to more hunters, more liberal seasons and a growing deer population. In addition, about 50,000 deer were harvested by archers in the Midwest region in 1981.

Hunter success in 1981 varied greatly among states, mainly due to differences in weapon types, season length, season timing, whitetail population density, and hunting regulations (Table 69). In 1981, about 1.2 million hunters participated in whitetail deer hunting in the

Table 69. Statistics for firearm hunting of white-tailed deer in the Midwest agricultural region, 1981.

State[a]	Number of licenses issued	Number of deer harvested	Percentage success	Season length (days)	Type of weapon[b]	Type of license issue
Illinois	77,665	20,908	27	6	S,M	Either-sex
Indiana	113,020	13,650	12	9, 15	S,M	Buck-only; limited either-sex
Iowa	83,598	21,578	26	4, 7	S,M	Buck-only; 20 percent either-sex
Kansas	9,537	4,788	50	9	R,S,M	Buck-only; 43 percent either-sex; 3 percent antlerless
Michigan	225,430	45,330	20	7, 16	S,M	Buck-only; 37 percent antlerless
Minnesota	140,530	45,361	32	1–9	R,S,M	Buck-only; 32 percent antlerless
Missouri	101,950	22,922	22	9	R,S,M,H	Buck-only; 13 percent either-sex
Nebraska	8,292	4,864	59	9	R,H,M	Buck-only; 30 percent either-sex
North Dakota	3,371	1,875	56	10	R,S,M	Buck-only; 34 percent antlerless
Ohio	57,000	5,966	10	5	S,M	Buck-only; limited antlerless; one day either-sex
South Dakota	11,258	8,700	77	9	R	Buck-only; 75 percent either-sex
Wisconsin	346,500	100,900	29	2–9	R,S,M	Buck-only; either-sex

[a]Includes only the portion of the state located in the Midwest agricultural region.
[b]R = rifle, S = shotgun, M = muzzleloader and H = handgun.

A number of states in the Midwest agricultural area—including Iowa, Illinois, Indiana and Ohio (in 1982)—do not permit the use of breechloading rifles for white-tailed deer hunting. The principal objective of permitting shotguns only during firearm-hunting season (exclusive of primitive firearms) is public safety. In the relatively open agricultural region, and where livestock and farm buildings, machinery, etc., are in close proximity and fairly exposed, the decision has been made to restrict or limit the use of modern rifles and projectiles that may carry considerable distance. *Photo courtesy of the Iowa Conservation Commission.*

region. Deer harvest and hunter interest should continue to increase in response to a healthy and growing deer population.

Other Mortality

In addition to legal harvest, several other factors contribute to whitetail mortality in the Midwest agricultural region. Poaching loss may approach the magnitude of legal harvest in some states. Increased enforcement efforts, hunter check stations, public awareness programs and hotline numbers for reporting violations are being utilized in an attempt to control this loss.

The coyote is the whitetail's major natural predator, but the extent of its impact is not known. Fawn mortality studies in Texas, Oklahoma and Arkansas found that coyotes were the primary nonhunter cause of death, but studies in Missouri indicated that other factors mainly were responsible (Porath 1980). Free-ranging dogs are an increasing problem because they harass and sometimes kill deer.

Another important factor is deer/vehicle accidents, which account for a 3 to 5 percent annual loss in the population. Extensive highway systems intersect good deer habitat in the region and are responsible for high accident rates. Reflective devices, warning signs, barrier fences and bypasses have been used in an attempt to reduce the problem, but have not been very successful, due to driver disregard, high cost and system ineffectiveness. New reflective devices are being studied and show some promise in reducing deer/vehicle accident rates. Reflector systems are expensive, but may be justified by reduction in human injury, property damage and deer loss.

Epizootic hemorrhagic disease outbreaks in the Midwest agricultural region were first reported in 1955 in Michigan, where 112 deer were confirmed dead and many others were thought to have perished (Fay et al. 1956). Severe loss from epizootic hemorrhagic disease also was reported in South Dakota in 1956 (Karstad 1962). More recently, an outbreak was reported in 1976 in the Missouri River basin of Nebraska, South Dakota, Iowa and Missouri. A loss of 30 to 40 percent was estimated for the deer population in Nebraska during this outbreak (Menzel and Havel 1977). Less severe outbreaks occurred in Missouri in 1980 and in Nebraska in 1981. Occurrence of epizootic hemorrhagic disease in deer appears to be related to biting flies and gnats, and climatic conditions favorable to this vector can lead to serious problems (Thomas 1981).

Although predation by dogs on white-tailed deer in the Midwest agricultural region is a problem only in local areas, it remains a concern of wildlife managers and biologists because of the potential impact on deer populations in limited habitat. The sprawl of urban and suburban areas and roadways onto agricultural lands not only diminishes habitat, but increases the number and improves the outreach of marauding dogs. *Photo by Leo Foulk; courtesy of the Wisconsin Department of Natural Resources.*

Deer/vehicle collisions represent the third greatest cause of mortality in the Midwest agricultural region, ranking behind legal harvests and illegal kills. Highway losses of whitetails in the region are a particular problem in forested areas. *Photo by Lee Gladfelter; courtesy of the Iowa Conservation Commission.*

Food Habits

Agricultural crops, especially corn and soybeans, make up the major portion of the whitetail diet in the Midwest region (Korschgen 1962, Mustard and Wright 1964, Watt et al. 1967, Nixon et al. 1970). In Iowa, for example, crops made up 78 percent by weight, 56 percent by volume and 89 percent by occurrence of whitetail stomach samples analyzed (Mustard and Wright 1964). Included in the samples were corn (40 percent), soybeans (13 percent), alfalfa (3 percent), other grains (less than 1 percent), woody foods (21 percent), forbs (18 percent) and grasses (about 1 percent). Grain residues left in fields after crop harvest are utilized heavily by deer from September to April.

SPECIAL PROBLEMS

Limiting Factors

Continuing loss of forest habitat is one of the main limiting factors for deer in the Midwest agricultural region. Clearing for pasture and agriculture has accelerated because of increasing land value, larger field size, and the trend toward fewer and larger farms. Since the mid-1960s, loss of forest land has ranged from 15 percent in Kansas to 50 percent along the Missouri River in Nebraska, and continues at an annual rate of 1 to 3 percent.

As previously indicated, high hunting and poaching losses are other major limiting factors. Legal harvests are carefully regulated to provide measurable results. However, illegal loss cannot be measured effectively and is difficult to control. Without good estimates of poaching loss, management strategies to obtain proper legal harvest levels are handicapped. Several methods of estimating illegal loss have been developed, but the validity of these estimates has not yet been established (Beattie et al. 1980).

Crop Damage

Farmers frequently complain about crop damage because it can seriously reduce their profit. Whitetails in the region feed on agricultural crops during the entire crop-growing season, but mainly depend on waste grain left after fields have been harvested. However, damage during the growing season can be severe in areas of—or adjacent to—high deer densities. On a refuge in Illinois, 39 percent of the soybean crop was damaged during the first three weeks of growth when plants were most palatable (Klimstra and Thomas 1964). Alfalfa also can be affected by heavy whitetail browsing, which may reduce production potential by 17 to 22 percent (Palmer et al. 1982). Deer damage to orchards, nursery stock and vegetable crops also occurs.

Whitetails are attracted to soybean fields in the region, and feed there most heavily from August to October. *Photo by Lee Gladfelter; courtesy of the Iowa Conservation Commission.*

In Missouri, most crop damage complaints came from areas where food habit studies indicated that crops composed more than 50 percent of the whitetail diet (Korschgen 1962). Reimbursement to landowners for crop damage is uncommon, but state wildlife agencies do provide technical assistance on repellents, fencing, lure crops and scare devices. In extreme cases, landowners may be allowed to kill depredating deer.

Reducing whitetail densities with legal hunting seasons is the most effective form of deer population control. Since 98 percent of the Midwest agricultural region is in private ownership (Jenkins 1970), landowners directly control access to most hunting areas. Whether hunters can get permission to hunt is determined largely by the number of deer seen by farmers and the incidence of crop damage (Queal 1968). In addition, most wildlife agencies provide landowners with special hunting privileges. These may include a free hunting license, an either-sex license in areas with buck-only harvest restrictions, or extra licenses to distribute to other hunters. The success of these control programs is dependent on deer densities, hunter access, landowner cooperation and liberal hunting season regulations.

MANAGEMENT

Current Policies and Philosophies

The main objective of white-tailed deer management in the Midwest agricultural region is to allow a maximum amount and variety of quality recreational opportunity while keeping the deer population within economic tolerance limits of landowners. This philosophy has resulted in harvest rates of up to 32 percent of the autumn whitetail population (Nixon 1970), which is sufficient to sustain a young, productive and healthy deer population in the region.

Wildlife agencies also are concerned with economic aspects of deer management, from the standpoint of their own needs as well as benefits to local economies. For example, hunting license sales are a major source of agency funding, and hunter expenditures for food, gas, lodging and equipment are of economic importance to many businesses and communities. A national survey found that big game hunters spent an average of $236 per season on their sport (U.S. Fish and Wildlife Ser-

vice 1982). In the Midwest agricultural region, that would mean an average annual expenditure for deer hunting of around $300 million. In addition, the dollar and nutritional values of venison from the harvest are significant.

Habitat Management

On public land, of which there is very little in the region, habitat management efforts are continuing. Whitetails are benefiting from the identification of management objectives and long-term evaluation of goals. Establishing 0.4 to 1.2-hectare (1–3-acre) food plots and eliminating grazing from forest areas increase habitat carrying capacity for deer. Traditional whitetail wintering areas are being identified and purchased to protect them from further development. Fawning habitat and other critical cover needs also are being provided. Small openings are being created in large forest blocks to stimulate browse and herbaceous growth, and shrubs are being planted along forest and field borders to create a wider and more desirable edge.

On the other hand, management on private land is more difficult because landowners seldom have funds available for wildlife habitat improvement. Some landowners are more concerned about too many deer than too few. However, technical assistance for habitat management on private land is available through state and federal wildlife agencies.

Survey Methods

The ability of wildlife agencies to predict whitetail population size or trends accurately is critical to the formulation of proper management goals, hunting regulations and public relations programs. Many survey methods currently are in use in the Midwest agricultural region (Gladfelter 1980). Deer mortality from highway accidents indicates population trends after adjustments are made for traffic volume. Sex and age ratio data collected at check stations are compared with previous years and used to estimate population size. Another trend indicator is the change in buck harvest or hunter effort per deer harvested. Other techniques include spring spotlight surveys, roadside counts, autumn doe/fawn ratios, winter aerial surveys, population estimates by landowners or wildlife law enforcement personnel, and changes in reported crop damage complaints. A method gaining rapidly in popularity is population-modeling, which utilizes sex and age data, productivity, and harvest rates and other mortality factors to estimate whitetail population trends and predict effects of various hunting season alternatives.

A young whitetail fawn is fitted with a neck-collar radio transmitter that will help the study of deer movements, feeding and bedding patterns, and mortality rates. *Photo courtesy of the Illinois Department of Conservation.*

All trend surveys are based on major assumptions that may bias results (Gladfelter 1980). Utilizing more than one survey allows comparisons that enhance the probability of obtaining a useful measure of whitetail population trends. However, there remains a need for more reliable and economical techniques to indicate deer population changes in delineated management units.

Hunting Seasons

Hunting season modification is the most important white-tailed deer management tool. Hunter numbers have increased dramatically in recent decades, and whitetails are particularly vulnerable in the limited-cover habitat of the Midwest agricultural region. A partial buck-only season has been used by some states to keep recruitment at a high level. Often, a limited number of either-sex or antlerless-deer hunting licenses are issued to remove surplus deer and increase hunter success rates in designated areas. Also, season length and method of take are regulated in specific management units to control harvest. Some states have reduced hunter pressure by using split seasons or allowing hunters to choose a hunting period.

Recommendations for hunting seasons usually begin at the field level. Resource managers consider the biological aspects of the deer population and the prevailing habitat conditions. Population maintenance and harvest goals then are presented to the next higher level of agency personnel, where sociological and political factors are considered. Often, hearings are held to provide public input on hunting season recommendations. In some states, final approval is made by the agency director or commission. In other states, however, regulations have to be reviewed, authorized and promulgated by the state legislature and/or governor. At any level, adjustment can be made to the initial, biologically oriented recommendations provided by the resource manager. Invariably, hunting seasons, fees and regulations are a compromise between what's best for the resource and public demand for recreation and population control.

Current Research

Research projects are necessary to provide a better data base for maintaining and managing whitetail populations. Trend indicators

Bucks comprise a large percentage of annual whitetail harvests in the Midwest agricultural region, principally because of hunting regulations designed to afford protection for does and fawns. Such protection—generally regulated on the basis of management units—helps assure whitetail population productivity and keep a balance between public demand for and landowner tolerance of deer. *Photo courtesy of the Michigan Department of Natural Resources.*

such as the aerial survey, spring spotlight count, and doe/fawn ratio are being evaluated for accuracy and standardization of survey technique. Studies on animal behavior and biology include investigations of productivity, disease and habitat preference. For use in computing and simulating whitetail population dynamics, several states are conducting projects on the causes and extent of fawn mortality. Landowner attitudes about deer and deer hunting as well as hunter attitudes are being evaluated and documented. Research projects designed to evaluate temporary and permanent refuges include the study of deer movement and behavior in response to refuge implementation, optimum refuge size, harvest potential, dispersal distances and food plot requirements. Several projects are being conducted to evaluate reflectors as a method of reducing deer/vehicle accident rates. Equal distribution

of harvest between hunter groups, feasibility of check stations, and the impact of deer depredation are other current research topics. The last major study area is population modeling, which is being evaluated for validity, accuracy of input variables, effects of harvest alternatives and usefulness in predicting trophy animal production.

Several important areas will require additional research effort. A more reliable trend indicator must be devised for the specific habitat and whitetail-density conditions in the Midwest agricultural region. Continued improvement in scientific management of the resource will depend on research findings in this area. Reliable estimates of poaching loss are necessary but difficult to obtain because of legal and moral implications. Research objectives should include ways of estimating poaching loss and how it relates to economic trends, deer population density, geographic region and violator background. Once poaching is better understood, more effective law enforcement techniques can be developed to reduce loss, and management goals can be altered to adjust for this major mortality factor. Whitetails living in marginal habitat should be studied to determine their needs and how they have adapted to the agricultural interests of man. The future for white-tailed deer in the Midwest agricultural region may depend on management of marginal habitat and the development of alternative overhead winter cover to replace declining forest habitat.

OUTLOOK

Perpetuation of a stable-to-increasing whitetail population in the Midwest agricultural region hinges on several factors. First and foremost is the need to maintain and enhance forest habitat. The purchase of forest tracts by public agencies is needed, but money for such acquisition is limited. In 1976, Missouri passed a constitutional amendment to add one-eighth of 1 percent to the annual sales tax for use in conservation programs. Similar tax programs in other states could raise more than $10 million annually. Other possible sources of income are special hunting or habitat stamps, and fines levied on conservation-law violations. These funds could be earmarked for habitat purchase or long-term leasing of forest lands for management and public hunting. The current rate of decline in forest habitat should start to level off as it becomes less economical

to clear land. Increasing demands for firewood will intensify interest in forests, but this could be beneficial if woodlands consequently are preserved and managed properly.

Many states encourage the protection and management of forest land through property-tax incentives. Examples include the woodland tax law and forest crop law in Wisconsin, which reduce property tax for following sound forest management practices and prohibiting grazing. Another example is Iowa's "slough bill," which provides total property-tax exemption for forest areas and other types of wildlife habitat. To qualify, forest tracts must be larger than 0.8 hectare (2 acres) and have at least 494 trees per hectare (200 per acre). Livestock must be excluded, but limited harvest of wood products is allowed. Also, most states offer technical advice and assistance to landowners who want to manage their forest land economically and in the best interest of deer and other wildlife.

One method of dealing with diminishing habitat may be the establishment of permanent deer refuges on public land. Several research projects are underway to evaluate this concept. Whitetails can utilize standing corn, brush, tall weeds or cattails during most of the year, but usually rely on forests for wintering habitat, especially during severe winters. Refuges would serve as a nucleus for high winter densities from which deer could disperse 16 to 32 kilometers (10–20 miles) into areas where they could be hunted. The dispersal of whitetails from a refuge area has been well-documented in the Midwest agricultural region (Sparrowe

Management for whitetails on public hunting areas and refuges in the Midwest agricultural region includes leaving strips of standing corn as a winter food source for deer. *Photo by Jim Zohrer; courtesy of the Iowa Conservation Commission.*

and Springer 1970, Hawkins *et al.* 1971, Zagata 1972, Torgerson and Porath 1977). Winter food plots would be necessary to maintain high whitetail densities and provide a buffer against crop depredation on surrounding private land. Funds for purchase of such refuge areas could come from the sources previously mentioned.

The outlook for white-tailed deer in the Midwest agricultural region is optimistic. Deer populations are increasing because of favorable landowner attitudes and progressive management, research and enforcement programs. Forest habitat is declining, yet the whitetail population flourishes.

Chapter 23

NORTHERN PLAINS

Lyle E. Petersen
Regional Supervisor (Former)
Game and Fish Division
South Dakota Department of Game, Fish and Parks
Rapid City, South Dakota

ENVIRONMENT

The range of white-tailed deer in the Northern Plains region includes the prairie grasslands of southcentral Canada, Montana, North Dakota, northeastern Wyoming, northern Nebraska and South Dakota, plus the Black Hills of South Dakota and Wyoming (Figure 90). Habitats are characterized by shortgrass, mixed-grass and tallgrass prairies, and the landscape varies from flat, undulating prairie to steep-sided badland formations. Elevations on the Plains vary from 200 meters (655 feet) in Alberta to about 1,000 meters (3,280 feet) above sea level in southwestern South Dakota. The Black Hills are a marked contrast to the surrounding prairie, with Harney Peak in South Dakota rising to an elevation of 2,207 meters (7,242 feet).

Plains

The most important white-tailed deer habitat on the Northern Plains consists of draws, swales and lowlands that receive added moisture by virtue of their position relative to the surrounding area. The main tree species are green ash, American elm, boxelder and, to a lesser extent, hackberry and cottonwood. In the Badlands of North Dakota and South Dakota and in the Missouri River Breaks of Montana, the hardwood type is replaced primarily by Rocky Mountain juniper. Juniper draws are used more heavily by mule deer than by whitetails in the Dakotas. In Montana, these draws are not regarded as white-tailed deer habitat (E.O. Allen personal communication:1977). Shrub communities are associated with more mesic sites in the hardwood draws. Rubber rabbitbrush, silver buffaloberry and western snowberry are common in North Dakota (J.V. McKenzie personal communication:1977). Silver buffaloberry occurs in limited quantity in South Dakota along with serviceberry, common chokecherry, common snowberry, currant and rose. The shrub communities are used as year-round cover and food by whitetails.

River floodplains are perhaps the second most important habitat type. Cottonwood is the main tree species. Ash, boxelder, cottonwood and willow are prevalent along rivers in Montana (Allen 1971); cottonwood, buckthorn and other shrubs are common along streams on the plains of Alberta (Soper 1964). Shrub species in river floodplains are essentially the same as those in hardwood draws. Where heavily grazed by livestock, the floodplains have a relatively low carrying capacity for deer.

Although marshes and sloughs occupy a relatively small portion of the Northern Plains, they serve as cover and feeding areas for whitetails throughout much of the eastcentral Dakotas. Along with planted windbreaks, they often are the only cover available to deer in intensively farmed areas, particularly in the eastcentral Dakotas. Dominant species are cattail, willow and sedges.

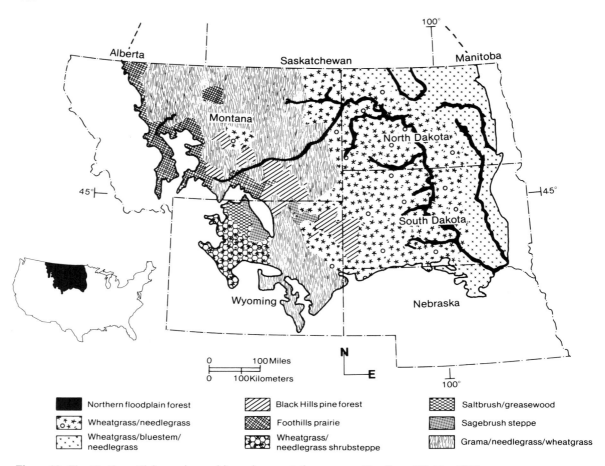

Figure 90. The Northern Plains region and its major vegetative communities (from Küchler 1966).

Whitetails feeding on forbs and grasses in a windswept field in river floodplain habitat—important winter cover for deer—in the Northern Plains. *Photo courtesy of the Manitoba Department of Natural Resources.*

Wetlands are an important habitat type for white-tailed deer in the open landscape and intensively farmed portions of the Northern Plains region. *Photo by Ed Bry; courtesy of the North Dakota Game and Fish Department.*

Ridgetops and the upper south-facing slopes of drainageways often are devoid of trees and shrubs, and thus are only lightly used by deer for cover. In the Badlands, Rocky Mountain juniper and ponderosa pine dominate mesic sites. North-facing slopes usually support stands of common chokecherry, common snowberry, sagebrush, rabbitbrush and skunkbush sumac.

Gently rolling upland is perhaps the habitat type least used by white-tailed deer in the region. Vegetational types range from shortgrass prairie to tallgrass prairie to vast areas of predominantly sagebrush. Intensively farmed areas in eastern and northern portions of the region support whitetails in significant numbers wherever there is ample winter cover.

Black Hills

The Black Hills are an isolated extension of the Rocky Mountains on the westcentral border of South Dakota and the northeastern border of Wyoming. They extend approximately 190 kilometers (118 miles) in a north-south direction and 95 kilometers (59 miles) east to west. Topography varies from extremely rugged mountainous terrain to broad grass-covered valleys.

Ponderosa pine is the dominant tree species. White spruce occurs as a codominant at high elevations along drainages (Froiland 1962). Trembling aspen stands containing limited amounts of birch are found primarily at the higher elevations in the northern and central Hills. Bur oak is present in small stands at lower elevations in the northern Hills. American elm, green ash and boxelder occur in limited stands, principally along watercourses.

Climate and Weather

Average annual precipitation ranges are from 25 to 38 centimeters (10–15 inches) in the northwest and from 45 to 58 centimeters (18–23 inches) in the southeast (Austin 1965). Periodic droughts are common and, according to the Rapid City, South Dakota Weather Bureau (personal communication:1983), appear to follow a 20-year cycle. The region's growing season is longest in the southern portion and of shorter duration in the north. In general, it extends from May into September. Northern South Dakota has an annual average of 130 days without killing frost (Westin et al. 1959).

Winters can range from very mild, with little or no snow and thawing daily temperatures, to severe, with complete snow cover and sub-zero temperatures for a month or more at a time. Snow cover is of short duration in southwestern South Dakota during most winters, whereas it may be continuous throughout the winter in northern portions of the region. The average annual temperature is 8 to 10 degrees Celsius (46–50 degrees Fahrenheit) in the southeastern part of the region and 4 to 6 degrees Celsius (39–43 degrees Fahrenheit) in the northwest (Austin 1965). Temperature extremes range from approximately 43 degrees Celsius (110 degrees Fahrenheit) to less than −32 degrees Celsius (−26 degrees Fahrenheit).

Whitetails can persist in the Northern Plains region, despite periodically severe winter weather, so long as they have adequate shelter and can reach palatable food. Note the dense coat of this doe. *Photo courtesy of the Wyoming Game and Fish Department.*

Land Use

Land use of the Northern Plains is highly variable. Eastern portions of the Dakotas and southern Canada are intensively farmed for wheat and other small grains. Dryland farming and ranching are common throughout the central part of the region, with ranching more predominant to the west. Deep-well irrigation systems are becoming more prevelant. Coal and uranium mining and oil and gas development also are important land uses in the region.

WHITETAIL POPULATIONS

History

During their celebrated expedition across lands of the Louisiana Purchase, 1804–1806,

Lewis and Clark reported white-tailed deer along the Missouri River Breaks from the North Dakota border to foothills of the Rocky Mountains in central Montana (Allen 1971).

The Homestead Acts, transcontinental railways and the cessation of Indian hostilities in the 1860s and 1870s opened a floodgate of settlement on the Plains. At the time, wildlife abounded. In the beginning it served as a vital source of food and fiber for the multitude of immigrants, but the advance of civilization was too relentless to be mindful of the exploitation it wrought, particularly in terms of big game. Subsistence killing of animals to support growing legions of homesteaders, miners, soldiers, railroad crews and passing pioneers was compounded by market hunting and the take of "sportsmen." It was a profitable but devastating episode that ended abruptly in the 1880s. By then, the region's big game—including bison, pronghorn, elk, and mule and white-tailed deer—was all but eradicated.

In 1875, Richard Irving Dodge reported that "red deer" (whitetails) were more numerous than any other animal in the Black Hills, and that "blacktails" (mule deer) also were abundant (Hipschman 1959). By 1900, however, both species were nearly eliminated from the Black Hills and from surrounding areas as well. In eastern Montana, the white-tailed deer disappeared from much of its historic range prior to 1941. At the time, large numbers of whitetails persisted in the Missouri River Breaks of northcentral Montana. In southern Alberta, white-tailed deer had declined drastically by 1890, mainly as a result of a series of severe winters (Webb et al. 1967).

With the enactment of wildlife laws (principally hunting regulations) and the initiation of translocation programs in the early 1900s, whitetails started to return to former ranges. By the mid-1940s, most of the former white-tailed deer range of the Northern Plains was reinhabited. Ironically, by the 1950s the deer had increased to the point that starvation and range overuse were major problems in the Black Hills of South Dakota. In 1953, a two-deer, either-sex hunting season was set to bring this population into line with available forage. A total of 26,693 permits were issued, resulting in a harvest of 42,663 deer. The management objective was met, but the harvest was not popular with the general public. Consequently, the two-deer-per-hunter legal bag limit was not continued.

Late-1800s residents of Montana pose beneath a wall of mounted big game heads, mostly trophy whitetails. At the time, most big game populations had been seriously depleted, and hunting emphasis shifted from a subsistence labor to a recreational endeavor. Such displays, when photographed and shown in the East, attracted wealthy sportsmen to the Northern Plains. *Photo courtesy of the Montana Historical Society.*

Population Characteristics

Recent whitetail densities in the region are: North Dakota—1 per square kilometer (2.6 per square mile) in intensively farmed and short-grass prairie areas to 10 per square kilometer (26 per square mile) in mixed-grass prairie areas (J. V. McKenzie personal communication: 1977); northeastern Wyoming—10 to 12 per square kilometer (26–31 per square mile) (J. J. Nemick personal communication:1977); Alberta—1 to 3 per square kilometer (2.6–7.8 per square mile), with infrequent densities of up to 20 deer per square kilometer (51.8 per square mile) (Webb et al. 1967). Overall, the whitetail densities throughout the Northern Plains are fairly consistent with those reported in North Dakota and Alberta.

Whitetail productivity in the region is high. In eastern South Dakota, for example, approximately 70 percent of the doe fawns conceived and 33 percent carried two fetuses (L. Rice personal communication:1977).

White-tailed deer harvest levels have been fairly high throughout the Northern Plains. In North Dakota, 25 to 40 percent of the population has been removed annually over a period of several years without hampering the population's productivity (J. V. McKenzie personal communication:1977). In Wyoming, 25 to 35 percent of the whitetail population normally is harvested through an either-sex harvest season (J. J. Nemick personal communication:1977). Similar harvest levels have been the rule in eastcentral South Dakota. The harvest was reduced in the mid-1970s in the Black Hills when whitetail numbers declined from undetermined causes. Buck-only seasons were reinstated in 1975 to stem the decline. As a result, only 4,500 bucks were harvested in 1976, in contrast to 8,790 bucks and 6,210 does taken in 1968. Total annual harvest of white-tailed deer west of the Missouri River in South Dakota is approximately 8,000 to 10,000 animals, roughly half of which are harvested in the Black Hills.

Outside the Black Hills and west of the Missouri River in South Dakota, white-tailed deer comprise approximately 40 percent of the total whitetail/mule deer population, but the percentage of whitetails in the harvest is proportionately much less. In an effort to increase the proportion of whitetails in the total deer harvest, South Dakota designed the season to include only mule deer bucks, but either sex of whitetails. The system first was adopted on a one-county basis in 1959, but has since become a standard management practice in South Dakota, and is used to some extent in Montana and North Dakota.

Allen (1971) reported that white-tailed deer consistently comprised at least 20 to 25 percent of the total annual harvest of approximately 22,000 deer (including mule deer) taken annually in Montana. During the 1970s, however, the percentage rose to 35 to 40 percent, due to a decline in the number and harvest of mule deer (E. O. Allen personal communication:1977).

In Wyoming, 11,681 white-tailed deer were harvested in 1975 and 8,921 in 1976. Approximately 45 percent were antlerless. Because of crop depredations, Wyoming attempted to reduce its whitetail population by issuing approximately 1,600 second licenses in both 1975 and 1976 that were valid for only antlerless deer (J. J. Nemick personal communication: 1977).

Food Habits

Foods of white-tailed deer are quite similar throughout the Northern Plains. In Montana, preferred browse species include common chokecherry, serviceberry, skunkbush sumac, common snowberry and dogwood. Rose, rabbitbrush, greasewood, buffaloberry and various species of sagebrush are eaten to a lesser extent (Allen 1971). Common chokecherry, serviceberry and common snowberry are preferred in the South Dakota prairies, as are bearberry and snowberry in the northern Black Hills (Schneeweis et al. 1972). The most important autumn foods in the southern Black Hills are bearberry, grasses, creeping mahonia, common snowberry and forbs (Schenck

et al. 1972). Agricultural crops such as alfalfa and winter wheat attract whitetails in spring.

SPECIAL PROBLEMS

Landowner tolerance is the most critical aspect of white-tailed deer management on the Northern Plains, and it becomes increasingly significant as pastures and forested areas are converted to croplands. In fact, harvest management in the region is based to a large degree on the number of deer that landowners will tolerate, rather than range carrying capacity. Whitetail depredations on alfalfa and winter wheat in spring and on stacked alfalfa hay in winter can be very costly to landowners in certain localities. South Dakota assists these landowners by furnishing them with material to fence haystacks and by using aircraft to herd deer into noncrop areas. Wyoming makes depredation payments to landowners, but this is expensive. Special deer hunting seasons are held in delineated local areas of Montana to control depredation problems. Montana considers these seasons to be the most effective way of reducing the negative aspects of depredation (N. Martin personal communication: 1983).

Land use in the Northern Plains, such as coal and uranium mining, is expected to continue to have direct impacts on the habitat base for deer. Human population increases associated with these activities and attendant subdivision in rural areas pose problems for wildlife managers in terms of poaching, harassment of whitetails by dogs, and general habitat loss or degradation.

Except on northern ranges, weather normally is not a limiting factor for white-tailed deer. Extended severe winter storms occasionally exact a heavy toll from whitetail populations where habitat is marginal. During the winter of 1978–1979, for example, snow began to accumulate in November and remained on the ground until spring. An undetermined but large number of whitetails were lost because of the deep and crusted snow in Montana and the Dakotas.

Predators, primarily coyotes, kill an undetermined number of whitetails, particularly in the Black Hills. Also, the coyote is an alternate host for *Sarcocystis hemionilatrantis*. This parasitic protozoa can kill mule deer fawns (Hudkins and Kistner 1977), and thus may be

Landowner tolerance of crop depredations by whitetails is a primary consideration in managing deer population levels throughout most of the Northern Plains. *Photo by Tyler Hendrickson; courtesy of the North Dakota Game and Fish Department.*

a factor in whitetail productivity. The parasite quite likely is spread across the deer range in South Dakota (E. J. Hugghins personal communication: 1977), but its distribution elsewhere in the region is unknown.

Epizootic hemorrhagic disease annually affects whitetails throughout the region, particularly in areas where deer are underharvested, such as the section southwest of the Missouri River in North Dakota (J. V. McKenzie personal communication:1977). In South Dakota, this disease was detected in 37 of 63 counties (Richardson and Petersen 1974). An estimated 60 percent of the whitetails west of the Missouri River were lost to epizootic hemorrhagic disease in 1952 (Richardson and Petersen 1974).

Other whitetail diseases are of little consequence in the region. During 1957 and 1966 in South Dakota, a total of 103 deer were tested for brucellosis and found to be negative; only 3 of 104 tested were positive for *Leptospira pomona;* 4 of 79 tested were positive for *Leptospira icterohaemorrhagiae;* and all 79 tested were negative for *Leptospira canicola* (Richardson and Petersen 1974).

Both papilloma and lumpy jaw have been observed in South Dakota, but their incidence is low (Richardson and Petersen 1974).

Visceral samples were collected from hunter-killed deer in South Dakota during the 1966 hunting season to determine parasite incidence. Roundworms were found in 2.7 percent of 84 whitetails sampled and 13.3 percent of 30 mule deer. Flatworms were found in 6 percent of the sample of 84 whitetails and in 16.7 percent of the 30 mule deer (Boddiker and Hugghins 1969).

Management of whitetails and mule deer has long been a controversial subject throughout the Northern Plains. Charges of "money hungry" and "overharvest" often are directed at wildlife agencies when deer populations are reduced to fit habitat conditions or landowner tolerance. Invariably the number of whitetails that would satisfy deer hunters would not be acceptable to many landowners, especially farmers and ranchers. The art and science of deer management by wildlife agencies in this region involves a continual attempt to provide a deer population size that is a reasonable balance between the expectations and demands of the various publics the agencies serve. The fulcrum in such determinations is the best interest and well-being of the deer population or populations in question.

Also, sale of nonresident deer hunting licenses is a sensitive issue. There is an understandable sense of "territorialism" among many resident hunters, who resent the intrusion and increased competition from "outsiders." Some residents tend to feel that a large population of deer in their state or province, whether it resulted by chance, enlightened and progressive management, or a combination of factors, is a by-product of their own investments (taxes, habitat maintenance, etc.). Understandably they

Harvest by regulated recreational hunting is the most effective, practical and desirable means of managing whitetail population size and distribution in the region. *Photo courtesy of the North Dakota Game and Fish Department.*

are reluctant to some extent to share equally in the rewards by providing access and recreational opportunities to nonresidents. The result has been increasingly expensive license fees for nonresident hunters of white-tailed deer and other big game. In addition, wildlife agencies—as in Wyoming—give landowners and operators first opportunity for licenses when quotas are used to limit the deer harvest in management units. In Wyoming, $5.00 from the license fee paid by a nonresident successful in bagging a deer on a landowner's property is paid to the landowner by the state wildlife agency upon receipt of the appropriate part of the license signed by both the successful hunter and the landowner. This system of sharing state license income with landowners has been well-received by farmers and ranchers. Each state and province in the region has its own system of landowner assistance.

Regardless of problems generated by whitetails, these deer are a valuable natural, recreational and economic resource. For example, in 1973, 4,590 nonresident deer hunters in South Dakota each spent an average of $141 in addition to license fees—a total of $647,024. At the same time, 53,162 resident hunters each spent $29 in addition to license fees—more than $1.5 million (Volk and Montgomery 1974).

MANAGEMENT

In agricultural areas of the Northern Plains region, whitetail populations seldom exceed available food and cover before reaching the threshold of landowner tolerance. During years of ample moisture and good crops, deer are tolerated more than in years when hay and other crops are scarce. Permanent deer-proof stackyards frequently are constructed where deer depredation on hay in winter is a problem.

Management of white-tailed deer on public lands, where hunter access is unrestricted, usually is more flexible than on private land. Through interagency cooperation, key wintering areas can be identified and management systems developed to enhance the use of these areas by deer. Some of the areas are fenced to exclude livestock, particularly during the summer when livestock grazing is most destructive to deer habitat. Rest-rotation grazing systems, where certain pastures are protected from livestock grazing for part or all of a year, are used to favor certain shrub species. On the Black Hills National Forest, forest cuttings for timber on deer winter range are designed to improve forage conditions for deer by removing more trees than would be cut under normal circumstances. However, much heavier cuts of trees are needed to create a significant impact on understory food production. Prescribed burning may be the habitat management tool of the future on public lands in this region. To date, the limited use of controlled fire has been directed primarily at fuel reduction.

In order to determine annual use and trend for key browse species on deer winter range, South Dakota has established linear transects in the Blacks Hills (Richardson and Petersen 1974). In general, 40 to 60 percent removal of the annual leader growth on most browse species appears to be acceptable.

Questionnaires, hunter report cards included with hunting permits, and check stations are used commonly to ascertain harvest success rates and the sex/age ratios of harvested whitetails. Age data obtained by microscopic inspection of sectioned incisors have been used to establish permit quotas in South Dakota. The current trend is toward limited permits for designated deer species and deer of specified sex in delineated management units throughout the Northern Plains region.

Chapter 24

CENTRAL AND SOUTHERN PLAINS

Karl E. Menzel
Big Game Specialist
Nebraska Game and Parks Commission
Bassett, Nebraska

ENVIRONMENT

The Central and Southern Plains region encompasses about 650,000 square kilometers (251,000 square miles) between the 31st and 43rd parallels and the 97th and 105th meridians (Figure 91). Maximum dimensions are about 1,500 kilometers (930 miles) north to south and 725 kilometers (450 miles) east to west.

Average temperatures in the region vary from −7 to 7 degrees Celsius (19–45 degrees Fahrenheit) in January and from 18 to 28 degrees Celsius (64–84 degrees Fahrenheit) in July. The average growing season is 120 to 220 days. Mean annual precipitation ranges from 28 to 85 centimeters (11–33 inches), and generally decreases from southeast to northwest; about 70 percent occurs from April through September (U.S. Department of Agriculture 1941). Prolonged snow cover, even in the northern parts, is not an annual occurrence.

The region's topography essentially is low or moderate in relief, consisting of a series of plains (Wedel 1957). The climate favors herbaceous vegetation and low shrubs rather than trees.

Native vegetation is predominantly grassland. Shortgrasses, such as the gramas and buffalograss, dominate in the west; midgrasses and tallgrasses, such as bluestems and western wheatgrass, prevail in the east. A large variety of forbs are interspersed with grasses, rushes and sedges.

Much of the native vegetation has been replaced by cultivated crops. Winter wheat is the most widely planted crop, but corn, milo, barley, oats and alfalfa also are important. Sprinkler irrigation, particularly for corn, has increased substantially since the early 1970s.

Native woody vegetation is confined mainly to stream courses. Dominant trees in the Texas Panhandle are cottonwoods. Shrubs include Chickasaw plum, skunkbush sumac, netleaf hackberry, shin oak and sagebrush. In western Oklahoma, the dominant trees are cottonwoods, post oak and blackjack oak. Primary trees in western Kansas include cottonwoods, American elm, hackberry, willows, red mulberry, boxelder and various oaks. Shrubs include sumacs, western snowberry, coralberry, American plum, common chokecherry, gooseberry, tamarisk and sand sagebrush.

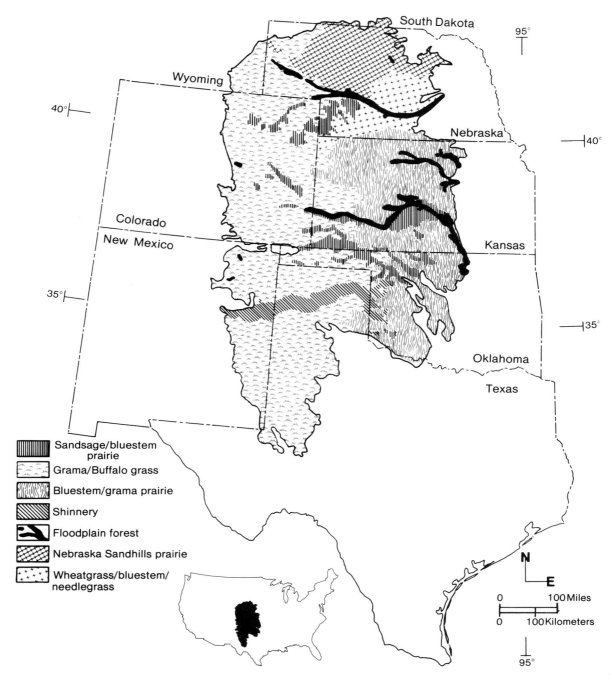

Figure 91. The Central and Southern Plains region and its major vegetational communities (from Küchler 1966).

Conifers are less important than broad-leaved trees. Eastern redcedar is fairly well distributed in the east, and Rocky Mountain juniper occurs farther west. Ponderosa pine is the dominant tree along parts of the Niobrara River and some of its major tributaries and in the Wildcat Hills and Pine Ridge escarpments of Nebraska.

Stream courses are the primary habitat of whitetails in the region. The quality and quantity of these habitats—which vary in width from several meters to about 2 kilometers (1.2

Whitetails in the Central and Southern Plains region utilize dense herbaceous cover, such as native warm-season tallgrasses—including switchgrass, big bluestem and Indian grass. *Photo by Ron Spomer; courtesy of the Kansas Fish and Game Commission.*

White-tailed deer habitat on the Central and Southern Plains often is restricted to a narrow belt along stream courses. *Photo by Carl Wolfe; courtesy of the Nebraska Game and Parks Commission.*

Agricultural crops comprise a substantial portion of the white-tailed deer diet in the Central and Southern Plains region. Cornfields provide good cover during summer and early autumn, allowing whitetails to move considerable distances from natural cover sources. *Photo by Gene Brehm; courtesy of the Kansas Fish and Game Commission.*

miles)—normally are the limiting factors for whitetails. When crops, such as standing corn, provide sufficient cover, deer may move several kilometers out from the stream courses.

Afforested areas, such as shelterbelts and larger tree plantings or claims, are used to some extent by whitetails, depending on the distance of these areas from stream courses. Small windbreaks adjacent to farm dwellings normally do not benefit deer, but larger tree plantings associated with farmsteads may be used for fawn-rearing or winter cover.

Marshy areas are of local significance, but their suitability for deer often is reduced or eliminated by livestock. The Nebraska Sandhills contain approximately 9,000 permanent and periodic wetlands, many of which provide good cover. Some of the wetlands most attractive to deer are on the Valentine National Wildlife Refuge in the Nebraska Sandhills, where grazing and mowing are less intense than on private land. In 1981, this 28,000-hectare (69,200-acre) area had a legal harvest of 59 white-tailed deer and 18 mule deer. Minimum postseason populations were 130 whitetails and 52 mule deer, for densities of 0.46 and 0.19 per square kilometer (1.20 and 0.48 per square mile), respectively.

About 95 percent of the land area in the Central and Southern Plains region is privately owned. Nearly all is farmed, grazed or mowed, or subject to a combination of these uses. Deer are considered incidental products.

WHITETAIL POPULATIONS

Early records are vague about white-tailed deer on the Plains, in part because early chroniclers did not always distinguish between whitetails and mule deer. However, unregulated hunting apparently resulted in the extirpation of whitetails in Kansas and Nebraska (*see* Jones 1964) by the early 1900s and in Colorado (Lechleitner 1969) by the 1920s, while remnant populations remained in Oklahoma and Texas. Whitetails were observed again in the late 1930s to early 1940s in Kansas and Nebraska, but not until the 1950s in Colorado (Armstrong 1972). This return was due to immigration, since the only translocation of whitetails in the region was to Colorado in the 1960s.

Hay land or moderately grazed range with scattered woodlots or tree plantings provide suitable cover for whitetails of the Central and Southern Plains. *Photo courtesy of the Oklahoma Department of Wildlife Conservation.*

A successful hunting expedition in the Cherokee Strip of Oklahoma and southern Kansas in the 1880s. The bag included wild turkeys, a coyote and two whitetails—a doe and a large buck. *Photo courtesy of The Kansas State Historical Society.*

White-tailed deer currently are present over most of the region, but have a limited distribution in the western one-third of the Central and Southern Plains. East of the 100th meridian, they are more abundant than mule deer, and are the predominant species on parts of some stream courses, to nearly the 104th meridian. They also have increased in relative abundance in parts of the range. In northern Nebraska, for example, from 1962 to 1968 the line of whitetail dominance shifted westward from about the 98th to the 100th meridian.

In 1981, about 15,500 whitetails were harvested on the Central and Southern Plains; 11,500 (74 percent) were antlered. This was a harvest of approximately 0.02 whitetail bucks per square kilometer (0.05 per square mile)—a low density overall. About 9,900 antlered mule deer were taken in the same area. Compared with the 1975 harvest, the 1981 harvest of whitetail bucks increased 110 percent, while that of mule deer bucks was nearly unchanged (2 percent increase).

Harvested white-tailed deer normally are in good-to-excellent condition. Average field-dressed weights of yearling bucks were 56 kilograms (123 pounds) in Kansas and 49 to 59 kilograms (108–130 pounds) in Nebraska.

Although populations may be high in local areas, large portions of the Southern and Central Plains are devoid of whitetails or have only occasional transients. Deer move back and forth between local cover areas and surrounding pastures or cropland, so it is difficult to delineate their home ranges. Expressions of whitetail densities, therefore, frequently are meaningless in the prairie environment.

Productivity of whitetails is high in areas adjacent to farms. In Nebraska, for 1961 through 1973, embryos averaged 0.68 per female fawn, 1.74 per female yearling, and 1.95 per adult (2.5 years and older) doe. In Kansas, the averages were 0.78, 1.87 and 1.96, respectively. With little cropland in the northern Sandhills of Nebraska, the indicated pregnancy rate of whitetail fawns was 28 percent, compared with 63 percent for fawns in the rest of the state.

Fawn survival apparently is low in the Plains states. Losses to predators (primarily coyotes), and to human-induced hazards such as mowing and fences, are greater than would occur in a forest environment. Pre-hunting season buck-doe-fawn ratios on selected areas in 1975 were 68:100:46 in Colorado, 37:100:41 in Kansas, 36:100:106 in Nebraska and 27:100:42

in Oklahoma. For 1982, the ratio in Nebraska was 26:100:94. The ratios indicate that fawn survival is substantially higher in Nebraska than in the other three states.

FOOD AND FEEDING HABITS

Quantitative food habits data for whitetails are limited to results from one study in the Texas Panhandle, in which 29 stomachs were examined (Jackson 1961). Panhandle grape, shin oak, common persimmon, eastern cottonwood, western soapberry and Chickasaw plum were the most prevalent species. Grasses constituted 9 percent, forbs 6 percent and milo 13 percent of the diet.

Mohler et al. (1951) found that western snowberry constituted 21 percent, rose 12 percent and sunflower 10 percent of the native species eaten by mule deer on the Bessey Division of the Nebraska National Forest. In the Pine Ridge, corn, wheat, and alfalfa comprised 41 percent of the deer's diet. Western snowberry comprised 13 percent and ponderosa pine 18 percent of the native foods. In the North Platte Valley, farm crops contributed 51 percent of the diet, western snowberry 13 percent and cottonwood 6 percent. Although these Nebraska studies were all on mule deer, the results are indicative of whitetail diets in the same area (*see* Hill and Harris 1943).

Farm crops probably constitute 40 to 50 percent of the annual diet of white-tailed deer in most parts of Kansas and Nebraska. Where crops are adjacent to suitable cover, signs of browse use are relatively scarce.

MANAGEMENT

White-tailed deer seldom are affected adversely by snow conditions in the region. In early 1969 and 1979, when average snow depths were about 61 centimeters (24 inches) for three months in northern Nebraska, deer movements were partially restricted and crop depredations were severe, but no mortality to starvation was known.

Whitetails are more vulnerable to hunter harvest on the Plains than in areas with more cover. Colorado, Kansas, Nebraska and South Dakota limit the numbers of hunters within deer management units and areas, in order to restrict the deer harvest, distribute hunters and

Winter wheat is particularly attractive to whitetails when other succulent vegetation is unavailable in the Central and Southern Plains region. *Photo by Gene Brehm; courtesy of the Kansas Fish and Game Commission.*

maintain the whitetail populations within tolerance limits of private landowners.

Whitetail numbers in the region are controlled mainly by harvests. Modified buck-only seasons are based primarily on relative hunter success and sex and age composition of the deer population. The 1981 harvest included 26 percent nonantlered deer, less than normally are removed in stable populations.

Quantity and quality of cover are major limiting factors in the Southern and Central Plains region. Conversion of native vegetation to farm crops, removal of trees adjacent to watercourses, elimination of shelterbelts, and grazing and mechanical damage from livestock reduce or destroy suitable deer habitat. In a 103,800-square kilometer (50,490-square mile) area within the region, forested land declined by 14 percent—from 2,330 square kilometers (900 square miles) to 2,000 square kilometers (770 square miles)—between 1955 and 1977 (Shasby and Jennings 1977). Irrigation and increased land values also have contributed to the destruction of woody cover.

Biological carrying capacity of white-tailed deer habitat likely will not be reached over much of the Southern and Central Plains because of landowner intolerance to crop damage by deer. This sometimes receives as much consideration in setting harvest regulations as do deer population levels.

Narrow stringers of willow and/or cottonwood (in which the whitetail buck above was harvested) may be associated with intermittent streams. If ungrazed or fenced to exclude livestock, such areas provide good herbaceous and woody cover for deer. Generally, the lack of continuous cover on the Plains makes deer more vulnerable to hunter harvest than is the case in forested areas of other regions. By the same token, the relative sparsity of cover makes it that much more difficult to approach deer. *Photo by Ron Spomer; courtesy of the Kansas Fish and Game Commission.*

Accidental mortality of white-tailed deer is not a limiting factor in the Central and Southern Plains region, but it is not unusual. At left, a drowned whitetail buck is pulled from a steep-sided irrigation canal. At right, a buck is unable to regain footing atop thin ice that it fell through. Even more common are fence entanglements. Losses in the region from human-induced hazards are greater than in forest environments. *Left photo courtesy of the Nebraska Game and Parks Commission. Right photo by Gene Brehm; courtesy of the Kansas Fish and Game Commission.*

Removal of woody cover for agricultural purposes is a major threat to whitetails in the Central and Southern Plains region. In Nebraska, for example, forested land declined by 14 percent between 1955 and 1977. *Photo by Carl Wolfe; courtesy of the Nebraska Game and Parks Commission.*

The restriction or elimination of livestock grazing is the primary tool of habitat management on public lands. Development of food plots and waterholes improves the distribution of deer and helps reduce deer damage on private lands. Because public lands in the Plains states represent only a limited acreage, they are of local significance only.

In the absence of substantial direct economic returns, private landowners are little interested in habitat management. Some charge hunter-access fees, but the possibilities of acceptable leases are lessened by the transient nature of whitetails in this region. Recoveries of 26 of 97 whitetails tagged in the Nebraska Sandhills between 1965 and 1971 (May to October) showed movements of 11 to 221 kilometers (7–137 miles), with an average distance of 61 ± 12 kilometers (38 ± 7.5 miles) from place of tagging to kill site. All but two of these recoveries were deer tagged at about 11 to 16 months of age. From 1971 to 1977, 82 whitetails were tagged in the winter on the South Republican Wildlife Area (Bonny Reservoir) in Colorado, and 20 were recovered. All of eight does tagged as adults were taken on the Area. Of those tagged as fawns, and males tagged as adults, eight deer moved from 24 to 234 kilometers (15–145 miles), with an average of 128 kilometers (79 miles).

Wintering whitetails in a fenced pasture featuring sand bluestem and little bluestem grasses. The trees in the background are ponderosa pine with some redcedar. Important wildlife management practices in the Central and Southern Plains are regulation of livestock grazing, fencing-off of cover habitat and rest-rotation. *Photo courtesy of the Nebraska Game and Parks Commission.*

In the absence of substantial direct economic return to the landowner, it is impractical to expect and difficult to obtain habitat management for deer on private lands. The best hope is to try to maintain what currently exists. One line of attack is the curtailment of subsidies for stream channelization and impoundments, which normally are destructive to critical habitat. Given adequate funding, landowners could be paid to maintain or improve potentially suitable habitat. Reduction or elimination of grazing, in areas capable of growing woody species or other vegetation of substantial height, would be more beneficial in improving habitat than would all other practices combined.

Chapter 25

TEXAS

Robert L. Cook
Leader (Former)
Statewide White-tailed Deer Program
Texas Parks and Wildlife Department
Kerrville, Texas

ENVIRONMENT

This region includes all of Texas except the High Plains, that portion of the Rolling Plains along the Canadian River in the Panhandle, and the Pineywoods. It includes 52.6 million hectares (130.1 million acres) in eight ecological zones (Figure 92) (Gould 1962); 23.9 million hectares (59.1 million acres) are classified as Texas white-tailed deer habitat (Table 70). The Carmen mountain whitetail occurs in isolated parts of the Trans-Pecos area.

Gulf Prairies and Marshes

The coastal prairie is a nearly level, slowly drained plain dissected by streams flowing into the Gulf of Mexico. Elevation is less than 46 meters (150 feet). The marsh area occurs as low, wet, narrow belts adjacent to the coast. Average rainfall varies from less than 51 centimeters (20 inches) in the west to about 127 centimeters (50 inches) in the east. The growing season is more than 300 days, characterized by warm temperatures and relatively high humidity. Soils are acidic sands, sandy loams and clay loams. Most of the region is grazed by cattle. Prairie rangelands are interspersed with farms. Climax vegetation largely is tallgrass prairie or post oak savannah, and much of the area has been invaded by trees and brush, such as honey mesquite, oaks, prickly pear and several acacias.

Post Oak Savannah

This region is gently rolling to hilly with elevations of 91 to 244 meters (300–800 feet).

Annual rainfall is 89 to 114 centimeters (35–45 inches). Soils are light-colored acidic sandy loams or sands on uplands, and light-brown to dark-gray acidic sandy loams and clays in bottomlands. Climax grasses include little bluestem and other tall bunchgrasses. The overstory primarily is post oak and blackjack oak. Brush and weedy species are numerous.

Blackland Prairies

Elevations in the Blackland prairies are 91 to 244 meters (300–800 feet). Topography is gently rolling to nearly level, with rapid surface drainage. Annual precipitation varies from 76 centimeters (30 inches) on the west to slightly more than 102 centimeters (40 inches) on the east. Soils are fairly uniform, dark-colored, calcareous clays interspersed with some gray acidic sandy loams. This region is classed as a true prairie; bluestem is the climax dominant. Honey mesquite has invaded some hardland sites, and post oak and blackjack oak have increased on medium to light textured soils. Most of the region is in agricultural crops, mainly small grains and cotton.

Cross Timbers and Prairies

Most of this region is rolling to hilly and deeply dissected, with rapid surface drainage. Elevations range from 152 to 686 meters (500–2,250 feet). Average annual rainfall is 63 to 102 centimeters (25–40 inches). Soils vary from dark-colored calcareous clays over limestone to acidic sandy or sandy loam. Much of the better soils are cultivated or in improved pastures. Brush species such as post oak and

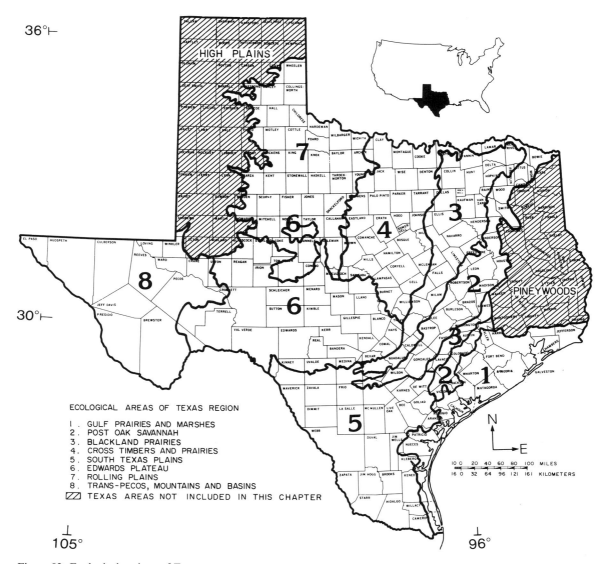

Figure 92. Ecological regions of Texas.

blackjack oak have invaded the prairie, along with weedy annual and perennial grasses. The East and West Cross Timbers range from open savannah to dense brush.

South Texas Plains

The topography is level to rolling, and the land is dissected by streams flowing into the Gulf. Elevations range from sea level to about 305 meters (1,000 feet). Average annual precipitation is 41 to 89 centimeters (16–35 inches), increasing from west to east. Soils range from

clays to sandy loams, and vary from calcareous to slightly acid. Most of the region is dominated by a dense brush canopy composed of mesquite, cacti, whitebrush, condalia and a variety of acacias.

Edwards Plateau

The "Hill Country" is a rolling to rough area in westcentral Texas. It includes the Central Mineral Basin of Mason and Llano counties. The area is bounded on the east and south by the distinct Balcones Escarpment, but blends

Whitetails in the Gulf prairies and coastal marshes area, which has poor drainage and is subject to heavy rains and periodic flooding. *Left photo by Luther C. Goldman; courtesy of the U.S. Fish and Wildlife Service. Right photo courtesy of the Texas Parks and Wildlife Department.*

into other areas on the north and west. Elevations range up to 914 meters (3,000 feet). Average annual precipitation varies from about 36 centimeters (14 inches) in the west to more than 84 centimeters (33 inches) in the east. Soils are shallow and rocky, underlain by limestone and caliche. This area is predominantly rangeland and often is heavily stocked with combinations of cattle, sheep and goats. Whitetailed deer are abundant. Climax grasses include several species of bluestem, switchgrass, Texas needlegrass and curlymesquite. The predominant brush overstory includes a variety of oaks, honey mesquite and Ashe juniper.

Rolling Plains

The Rolling Plains are gently rolling to moderately rough. Elevation is 244 to 914 meters (800–3,000 feet). Annual rainfall ranges from about 56 centimeters (22 inches) in the west to almost 76 centimeters (30 inches) in the east. Soils vary from coarse sands to tight clays or red-bed clays and shales. Approximately two-thirds of the area is rangeland, and the primary class of livestock is cattle. The original prairie vegetation included tallgrasses and midgrasses. Honey mesquite and various oaks are common invaders on all soils.

Trans-Pecos, Mountains and Basins

This region of diverse habitat and vegetation varies from arid desert valleys and plateaus to wooded mountain slopes. Elevation is about 762 meters (2,500 feet) to more than 2,590 meters (8,500 feet). Average annual rainfall over most of the area is less than 30 centimeters (12 inches). Typical range sites are stony hills, clay flats, sands, salty-saline soils, gypsum flats, deep upland, rough and stony mountains, gravelly outwash, and badlands. Most land remains in large ranches, typically featuring cattle or sheep, some mixed cattle and sheep, and some Angora goats. The most important vegetative types are creosotebush/tarbush desert shrub, grama grassland, yucca and juniper savannahs, pinyon pine and oak forest, and a limited amount of ponderosa pine forest.

Alerted whitetails congregated on a site recently chained for brush control in the transition zone between the Edwards Plateau and the South Texas Plains. *Photo by W.G. Lindley; courtesy of the U.S. Soil Conservation Service.*

WHITETAIL POPULATIONS

Brief History

Indiscriminate slaughter by commercial meat and hide hunters and ignorance of the deer's habitat requirements caused the near extirpation of white-tailed deer in Texas near the end of the nineteenth century.

Public concern prompted a series of protective measures by the legislature near the turn of the century. A five-month closed season was enacted in 1881. A bag limit of six bucks per season was established in 1903, but was reduced to three bucks in 1907. Hunting licenses were first issued in 1909, with 5,000 being sold that year. In 1919, six game wardens were hired to patrol the entire state (Texas Parks and Wildlife Department 1972).

Whitetails increased in numbers and distribution during the 1930s and 1940s (Sanders 1941, Hahn 1945). The increase resulted from several factors: protection from illegal and commercial exploitation; exclusion of fire; invasion of woody plant species into grasslands; deer restocking; and interest and cooperation shown by hunters, landowners and the general public (Teer et al. 1965, Buechner 1944). By 1941, deer populations were too high; ranges were depleted and die-offs were imminent (Teer 1963, Carroll 1957).

During the late 1950s and 1960s, white-tailed deer populations reached their highest levels and extended their ranges into almost all suitable habitat throughout the state. Recently, whitetail numbers have declined substantially in portions of the Post Oak Savannah and the Cross Timbers due to habitat degradation and livestock overgrazing.

Population Size and Density

White-tailed deer now occur in all counties of the area represented by this chapter, with the possible exception of El Paso and Hudspeth.

In autumn of 1980, the whitetail population was approximately 2.5 million (*see* Table 70). The Edwards Plateau was the most populated area with an estimated 15 deer per square kilometer (40 per square mile) (*see* Chapter 12). It supported more than 1.3 million deer, or about 53 percent of the state's whitetail population. Mason, Llano and Gillespie counties of the Edwards Plateau's Central Mineral Basin had more than 25 deer per square kilometer (65 per square mile). The South Texas Plains or "Brush Country" was second in deer numbers with 446,436 deer. Areas with an average density of at least 1.2 deer per square kilometer (3.2 per square mile) are shown in Figure 93. Whitetails are scarce in approximately 40 counties.

Table 70. Range, size and density of white-tailed deer in eight ecological regions of Texas, 1980.

Region	Land area		Deer range		Number of deer	Deer density per square kilometer (square mile)
	Hectares	Acres	Hectares	Acres		
Gulf Prairies and Marshes	4,047,000	10,000,137	670,818	1,657,523	130,000	19.31(50.00)
Post Oak Savannah	2,772,195	6,850,094	3,187,959	7,877,129	337,748	10.61(27.47)
Blackland Prairies	5,099,220	12,600,172	244,747	604,746	7,725	3.16 (8.17)
Cross Timbers and Prairies	6,191,910	15,300,209	2,439,451	6,027,639	204,686	8.41(21.77)
South Texas Plains	8,478,465	20,950,287	6,727,548	16,623,099	446,436	6.64(17.20)
Edwards Plateau	10,299,615	25,450,348	8,665,895	21,412,561	1,341,461	15.44(40.00)
Rolling Plains	8,498,700	21,000,287	1,285,391	3,176,073	51,813	4.03(10.44)
Trans-Pecos	7,264,365	17,950,245	709,179	1,752,310	24,365	3.44 (8.90)
Total	52,651,470	130,101,779	23,930,988	59,131,080	2,544,234	
Average						10.63(27.54)

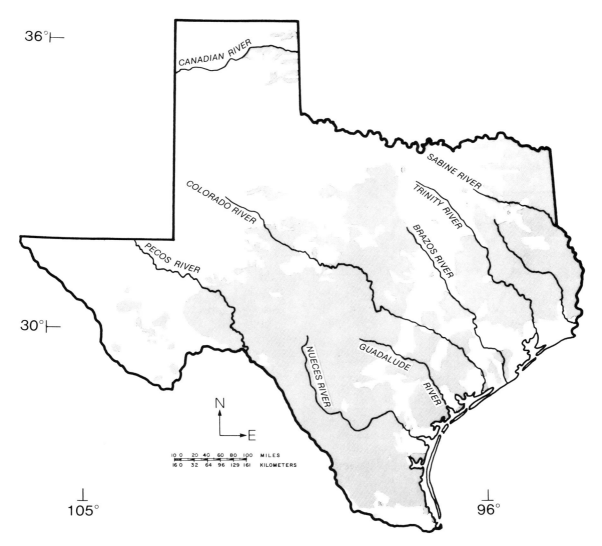

Figure 93. Distribution of white-tailed deer in Texas, 1976. Screened area represents deer densities of 1.2 deer per square kilometer (3.2 per square mile) or more.

Most whitetail populations in Texas contain approximately one buck per three or four does (Table 71). Most sportsmen and landowners prefer a ratio of about one buck per two does, but one buck per seven or eight does may be adequate for reproduction purposes. Bucks in the 1.5- to 3.5-year age classes constitute 60 to 90 percent of the total buck harvest (Table 72). This indicates moderate to heavy hunting pressure. Although hunting pressure does not threaten the deer populations, it limits the harvest of mature bucks through rapid turnover of the populations in the Post Oak Savannah and the Cross Timbers regions.

In the South Texas Plains—known for trophy bucks—hunting pressure is light to moderate, and one-third of the harvested bucks are 4.5 years or older.

In general, the white-tailed deer population in Texas reflects moderate to heavy hunting pressure on bucks but only light pressure on does. The state's whitetail population has a reasonably even sex ratio. This is due to deer die-offs from malnutrition, and also because sex ratios of fawns at birth are almost equal, thereby maintaining relatively even sex ratios in the adult population despite disproportionately heavy hunting pressure on bucks.

Body Weight and Antler Size

In 1980, the average field-dressed weight of a 4.5-year-old whitetail buck harvested in the South Texas Plains region was 51 kilograms (112 pounds) (Table 73). Deer in this region generally are the largest whitetails in Texas.

Whitetails in the Post Oak Savannah area are subject to fairly heavy hunting pressure, but their populations are not limited by hunting. Loss of habitat has reduced the deer population severely in this area of Texas since about 1960. *Photo courtesy of the Texas Parks and Wildlife Department.*

Table 71. White-tailed deer population composition in Texas by ecological region, 1980.

Region	Percentage in population			Number of does per buck
	Bucks	Does	Fawns	
Gulf Prairies and Marshes	17	57	26	3.3
Post Oak Savannah	12	64	24	5.3
Cross Timbers and Prairies	14	54	32	3.8
South Texas Plains	21	66	13	3.2
Edwards Plateau	16	62	22	3.7
Trans-Pecos	16	65	19	4.2

Table 72. Percentage of white-tailed bucks, by age class, harvested in Texas during the 1980–1981 hunting season.

Region	Sample size	Percentage of bucks in each age class (years)								
		0.5	1.5	2.5	3.5	4.5	5.5	6.5	7.5	8.5 +
Gulf Prairies and Marshes	118	2.5	44.1	28.0	18.6	2.5	2.5	0.9	0.9	0.0
Post Oak Savannah	426	1.6	63.6	21.1	9.9	3.1	0.7	0.0	0.0	0.0
Cross Timbers and Prairies	203	2.5	60.6	17.7	13.8	3.0	1.0	0.5	1.0	0.0
Edwards Plateau	997	1.2	20.4	34.4	27.8	11.2	3.9	0.8	0.3	0.0
South Texas Plains	636	0.2	20.1	17.8	28.8	16.0	9.6	6.3	0.9	0.3

Table 73. Average field-dressed weight in kilograms (pounds) of white-tailed bucks harvested in Texas during the 1980–1981 hunting season.

Region	Sample size	Weight of bucks in each age class (years)								
		0.5	1.5	2.5	3.5	4.5	5.5	6.5	7.5	8.5+
Gulf Prairies and Marshes	118	16(36)	30(66)	33(73)	40(89)	54(119)	46(102)	51(112)	49(109)	
Post Oak Savannah	426	19(42)	33(72)	38(84)	42(94)	50(110)	53(117)			
Cross Timbers and Prairies	203	23(50)	32(70)	36(80)	40(89)	44(97)	53(118)	60(134)	52(116)	
Edwards Plateau	997	20(44)	28(62)	31(68)	35(77)	38(84)	41(90)	41(90)	41(90)	
South Texas Plains	636	23(50)	31(68)	37(83)	44(97)	51(112)	55(121)	56(125)	55(122)	54(120)

This is a reflection of the region's relatively high quality food and the animals' medium-to-low population density. In contrast, field-dressed 4.5-year-old bucks weighed an average of only 38 kilograms (84 pounds) in the Edwards Plateau, an area of exceptionally high deer density and a 30 to 40 year history of livestock overgrazing.

A mature whitetail buck during the rut in the thick brush country of the South Texas Plains area. Mesquite trees and other varieties of brush provide suitable deer cover and forage in this area, which generally produces the biggest Texas whitetails. *Photo courtesy of the Texas Parks and Wildlife Department.*

Antler characteristics from harvested whitetail bucks in various ecological regions of Texas show the same phenotypical relationships (Table 74) (Sanders 1941, Hahn 1945, Teer 1963, Teer et al. 1965, Cook 1974, Thomas and Marburger 1965). Weight and antler measurements of white-tailed deer in Texas decline as their populations increase in density and as competition for preferred forage intensifies. Whitetail weights and antler size also are affected adversely by lack of rainfall, poor soil quality and inadequate supplies of quality forage.

Productivity

In general, the recruitment rate of white-tailed deer in Texas has been less than 50 percent of the animals' potential, because of poor range conditions, malnutrition and predation, which lead to high postnatal fawn mortality. Most whitetail does first breed successfully at 1.5 years of age and give birth to a single fawn the next summer. Usually, mature does give birth to twin fawns each year under good range conditions. Bucks breed for the first time when 1.5 years old.

In the Post Oak Savannah, the whitetail breeding season peaks between November 8 and 21. Most does 1.5 years of age and older breed and conceive successfully. The reproductive rate varies from 1.14 to 1.65 fawns per doe. Fawn mortality is fairly high during the summer; annual autumn fawn/doe ratios average approximately 40:100. Predation by coyotes substantially reduces fawn numbers in heavily grazed areas with reduced cover (Carroll and Brown 1977).

On the Edwards Plateau, the breeding season peaks in mid-November, and most fawns

Table 74. Average antler characteristics of white-tailed deer bucks harvested in Texas during the 1980–1981 hunting season.

| | | Age class (years) | | | | | | | | |
| | | 1.5 | | | 2.5 | | | 3.5 | | |
Region	Antler characteristic	Sample size	Millimeters (Inches)	Number	Sample size	Millimeters (Inches)	Number	Sample size	Millimeters (Inches)	Number
Gulf Prairies and Marshes	Beam circumference	52	54(2.1)		33	67(2.6)		22	79(3.1)	
	Spread		153(6.0)			219(8.6)			299(11.8)	
	Points[a]			3.7			6.6			7.6
Post Oak Savannah	Beam circumference	271	59(2.3)		90	72(2.8)		42	82(3.2)	
	Spread		191(7.5)			273(10.7)			300(11.8)	
	Points[a]			4.8			6.5			7.5
Cross Timbers and Plains	Beam circumference	123	52(2.0)		36	64(2.5)		28	73(2.9)	
	Spread		178(7.0)			244(9.6)			302(11.9)	
	Points[a]			3.9			5.6			7.3
Edwards Plateau	Beam circumference	203	46(1.8)		343	59(2.3)		277	67(2.6)	
	Spread		145(5.7)			215(8.5)			251(9.9)	
	Points[a]			3.0			4.9			6.0
South Texas Plains	Beam circumference	128	50(2.0)		113	64(2.5)		183	78(3.1)	
	Spread		143(5.6)			228(9.0)			299(11.8)	
	Points[a]			3.1			5.3			7.1

[a]Number on both antlers.

Triplet whitetail fawns are a rarity in Texas. The norm is twin fawns produced by does on good range. *Photo courtesy of the Texas Parks and Wildlife Department.*

Table 74. (continued)

	4.5			5.5			6.5			7.5			8.5+	
Sample size	Millimeters (Inches)	Number	Sample size	Millimeters (Inches)	Number	Sample size	Millimeters (Inches)	Number	Sample size	Millimeters (Inches)	Number	Sample size	Millimeters (Inches)	Number
3	95(3.7)		3	95(3.7)		1	118(4.6)		1	120(4.7)				
	349(13.7)	9.3		341(13.4)	10.3		414(16.3)	12.0		307(12.1)	9.0			
13	95(3.7)		3	114(4.5)										
	356(14.0)	8.5		428(16.9)	9.7									
6	85(3.3)		2	102(4.0)		1	100(3.9)		2	134(5.3)				
	356(14.0)	7.8		372(14.6)	10.0		312(12.3)	9.0		428(16.8)	10.5			
112	76(3.0)		39	81(3.2)		8	81(3.2)		3	83(3.3)				
	290(11.4)	7.2		330(13.0)	8.0		324(12.8)	8.0		318(12.5)	7.7	2	115(4.5)	
102	90(3.5)		61	100(3.9)		40	103(4.1)		6	107(4.2)				
	354(13.9)	8.4		388(15.3)	9.0		420(16.5)	9.0		451(17.8)	9.8		478(18.8)	13.0

are born the last two weeks of June. The reproductive rate of whitetails in this region averages 1.1 fawns per adult doe and 0.8 fawn per yearling doe (Hahn 1945, Hahn and Taylor 1950, Sanders 1941, Teer et al. 1965, *see also* Chapter 12). The autumn crop averages about 44 fawns per 100 does on poor to fair ranges, and 86 fawns per 100 does where range conditions are good and grazing by livestock is moderate.

The breeding season in the South Texas Plains region extends from November to February, and peaks between December 15 to January 3 (Illige 1951, Barron and Harwell 1973, Harwell and Barron 1975). The whitetail birth rate averages 1.3 to 1.6 fawns per doe. Predation on fawns by coyotes and bobcats reduces production dramatically (Beasom 1974, Cook et al. 1971, Jackson et al. 1972, Michael 1965, Samuel and Glazener 1970); the autumn crop averages approximately 42 fawns per 100 does.

The Cross Timbers region averages about 50 fawns per 100 does during autumn. Fawn production and survival are believed to be similar in the Trans-Pecos, Rolling Plains and Edwards Plateau regions, based on a comparison of census data.

Harvest

In 1980, the total estimated white-tailed harvest in these eight ecological regions of Texas was 233,772 deer—167,127 bucks and 66,595 does (Table 75)—or approximately 9 percent of the population.

The low harvest of antlerless deer is attributable to several factors: (1) practically all land in Texas is privately owned, operated and controlled, and landowners or operators tend to restrict the number of hunters on their properties; (2) under the Uniform Wildlife Regulatory Act the landowner is issued antlerless permits where there is a surplus of deer, but in fact he rarely allows hunters to harvest more than 30 to 40 percent of the surplus antlerless deer; (3) most hunters kill antlerless deer only if they cannot kill a buck or after they have killed their bucks; and (4) county commissioners' courts in 30 counties have the authority to reject the Texas Parks and Wildlife Commission's proposed regulations, and have resisted attempts to liberalize antlerless deer hunting.

Hunting pressure is highest in the Cross Timbers and prairies, Gulf prairies and marshes,

Table 75. Harvest of white-tailed deer in various regions of Texas during the 1980–1981 hunting season.

Region	Number of deer in September			Estimated total harvest			Number of deer per square kilometer (square mile)		Percentage of September population harvested
	Bucks[a]	Antlerless[a]	Total[b]	Bucks	Antlerless	Total	September population[b]	Harvested	
Gulf Prairies and Marshes	22,100	107,900	130,000	6,671	1,606	8,277	19.31 (50.00)	1.24 (3.20)	6
Post Oak Savannah	40,530	297,218	337,748	25,814	3,688	29,502	10.61 (27.47)	0.92 (2.39)	9
Blackland Prairies			7,725	394	0	349	3.16 (8.17)	0.16 (0.42)	5
Cross Timbers and Prairies	28,656	176,030	204,686	13,042	5,241	18,283	8.41 (21.77)	0.75 (1.94)	9
South Texas Plains	93,794	352,642	446,436	40,276	10,512	50,788	6.64 (17.20)	0.76 (1.96)	11
Edwards Plateau	214,634	1,126,827	1,341,461	76,727	43,739	120,466	15.44 (40.00)	1.39 (3.60)	9
Rolling Plains			51,813	3,280	631	3,911	4.03 (10.44)	0.30 (0.78)	8
Trans-Pecos	3,898	20,467	24,365	923	1,169	2,092	3.44 (8.90)	0.29 (0.76)	9
Total			2,544,234	167,127	66,595	233,668			
Average							10.63 (27.54)	0.98 (2.53)	9

[a]Computed from Table 71.
[b]From Table 70.

Whitetail hunters scan brushy hill country of the Edwards Plateau. Harvest success in Texas is highest in this ecological area. *Photo courtesy of the Texas Parks and Wildlife Department.*

and Post Oak Savannah. This is due to these areas' proximity to major metropolitan centers. However, harvest success is highest in the Edwards Plateau (Table 76).

Food and Feeding Habits

White-tailed deer in Texas prefer mast (acorns, nuts, fruit), the fresh green growth of woody plants, and forbs.

Deer in the Central Mineral Basin of the Edwards Plateau spent 62 percent of their feeding time consuming forbs and grasses, 7 percent for browse, and 31 percent for mast (Whisenhunt 1949). Rumens contained 42 percent mast, 24 percent browse, and 23 percent forbs and grasses.

In the Edwards Plateau, 74 species of herbaceous plants, 7 shrubs and 13 trees were utilized by whitetails (Hahn 1945). Oak leaves and acorns constituted 38 percent of the diet. Hackberry, Spanish oak, scrub oak, blackjack oak, post oak and live oak were preferred by deer, in that order (May 1959). Whitetails on the Kerr Wildlife Area—representative of the Edwards Plateau—preferred forbs, but shifted to browse when forbs were unavailable (McMahan 1964). Deer in the Edwards Plateau may change home range temporarily depending on the availability of preferred foods such as oak, common persimmon and honey mesquite mast, especially in areas overgrazed by livestock (Hahn 1945, McMahan 1966, Merrill et al. 1957, Reardon and Merrill 1976, Teer et

al. 1965, Thomas et al. 1964). They preferred fertilized plants to unfertilized (Shult 1975).

Browse is the main source of whitetail food in the Post Oak Savannah. In one food habit study, deer stomachs contained 92 percent browse during autumn and winter, 70 percent grasses and sedges in late winter and early spring, and 67 percent browse in late spring and summer. At the Engeling Wildlife Area, in the Post Oak Savannah, browse constituted 85 percent, forbs 3 percent, grasses 11 percent and mushrooms 1 percent of the whitetail diet during autumn (Veteto et al. 1971). The annual diet consisted of 60 percent browse, 19 percent grasses, 11 percent legumes and forbs, and 10 percent sedges, mushrooms, lichens and fruits. The more important plant foods were blackberry, yaupon, elm, greenbrier and low panicum grasses.

Woody plants and forbs most important to white-tailed deer in the Rolling Plains are broomweed, redberry juniper, scrub oak, fourwing saltbush, nailwort and catclaw acacia. Plains prickly pear accounted for more than 50 percent of the yearly diet of deer in northcentral Texas (Horejsi 1973).

Browse constitutes the major portion of deer diet in the South Texas Plains, but forbs rank relatively high (Davis 1951, Davis 1952, McMahan and Inglis 1974). Arnold (1976) reported that the whitetail diet consisted of 21 percent cacti, 33 percent browse, 27 percent forbs and 8 percent grass. Everitt and Drawe (1974) found that forbs comprised 37 percent of the deer's spring diet, browse 33 percent,

Table 76. Hunting pressure and harvest success in various regions of Texas during the 1980–1981 white-tailed deer hunting season.

Region	Number of hunters	Number of hunter-days	Number of hunters per square kilometer (square mile)	Number of hunter-days per square kilometer (square mile)	Percentage of harvest success	Number of deer kills per hunter	Number of hunter-days per hunter	Number of hunter-days per deer kill
Gulf Prairies and Marshes	21,689	146,784	3.2 (8.3)	21.9 (56.7)	35	0.44	6.7	18
Post Oak Savannah	104,119	649,259	3.3 (8.5)	20.4 (52.8)	30	0.33	6.2	22
Blackland Prairies	3,397	20,817	1.4 (3.6)	8.5 (22.0)	14	0.15	6.1	60
Cross Timbers and Prairies	54,770	352,690	2.2 (5.8)	14.4 (37.4)	31	0.38	6.4	19
South Texas Plains	99,605	629,970	1.5 (3.8)	9.4 (24.3)	48	0.57	6.3	12
Edwards Plateau	173,940	996,311	2.0 (5.2)	11.5 (29.8)	55	0.76	5.7	8
Rolling Plains	13,360	63,780	1.0 (2.7)	4.9 (12.9)	33	0.34	4.8	16
Trans-Pecos	3,709	15,316	0.5 (1.4)	2.2 (5.6)	41	0.64	4.1	7
Total	474,589	2,874,927						
Average			2.0 (5.1)	12.0 (31.1)			6.1	12

cacti 18 percent and grass 3 percent. Davis and Winkler (1968), Drawe (1968) and Chamrad and Box (1968) stressed the importance of forbs, browse and cacti.

Cattle and deer compete for browse and green shoots during the winter months at the Aransas National Wildlife Refuge on the Gulf prairies (Halloran 1943). Deer on the refuge rely mainly on acorns during autumn and winter. They eat browse sparingly, even though it is abundant (White 1973*b*).

Food habit studies have not been conducted in the Cross Timbers, Blackland prairies, and Trans-Pecos regions. However, general observations indicate that whitetails in the regions rely heavily on green forbs and grasses in spring and early summer, and consume large quantities of browse throughout the year.

SPECIAL PROBLEMS

Food Quality and Quantity

Quality and quantity of forage in Texas varies widely and often is seasonally inadequate for optimal growth, reproduction and survival of white-tailed deer. Several die-offs have occurred as a result of malnutrition corresponding to extremes in weather, competition with livestock, overpopulated ranges, disease outbreaks and parasite infestations (Hahn 1945, Sanders 1941, Thomas and Marburger 1965, Marburger and Thomas 1965, Taylor and Hahn 1947). The most severe die-offs have occurred in the heavily grazed Edwards Plateau. Seasonal fluctuations in nutrient level are smallest and calcium/phosphorus ratios best on ranges of the South Texas Plains, and die-offs are rare (Weishuhn et al. 1972). The relatively high nutritional level contributes to the large body size and antlers of whitetails in this region. However, following a two-year drought in 1979 and 1980, a 27-percent decline in deer numbers was recorded in South Texas during the 1980 autumn census by the Texas Parks and Wildlife Department.

Predators

The coyote ranks first and the bobcat second as natural predators of white-tailed deer in Texas.

Cacti are an important, year-round food source for whitetails in the South Texas Plains. *Photo by Bob Allen; courtesy of the Caesar Kleberg Wildlife Research Institute.*

Typical antler and body development of mature whitetail buck (left) on good range in central Texas, and a mature doe in poor health on overpopulated range in the same region. *Photos courtesy of the Texas Parks and Wildlife Department.*

Coyotes have accounted for 50 percent of fawn mortality in the lower Post Oak Savannah (Carroll and Brown 1977), and deer has been found to be a dietary component of coyotes in the Rolling Plains (Meinzer et al. 1975).

Predators, mainly coyotes, have caused heavy fawn losses in the South Texas Plains (Cook et al. 1967, White 1973a, White 1973b, Knowlton 1964). In the same region, Beasom (1974) removed 188 coyotes and 120 bobcats from a 2,186-hectare (5,400-acre) enclosure in the early 1970s. In 1971 and 1972, the fawn/doe ratios were 0.47:1 and 0.82:1, respectively, compared with ratios of 0.12:1 and 0.32:1, respectively, in an adjacent uncontrolled area. Beasom concluded that the deer population could be increased by predator control, but such a program would be justified only if hunter harvest held the deer population below the density at which starvation, disease or other factors began to take a significant toll.

Except for the South Texas Plains, and portions of the Post Oak Savannah and Gulf prairies and marshes, predators do not significantly influence white-tailed deer populations. The Edwards Plateau supports relatively few natural predators, possibly because they are trapped and controlled to protect sheep and goats.

Coyote populations have flourished and spread despite predator control. In some cases they benefit certain whitetail populations by removing inferior animals and surplus fawns on overpopulated, underharvested range, as in the South Texas Plains.

Extensive predation by mountain lions on desert mule deer is believed to occur in the Big Bend area of the Trans-Pecos Region, although it has not been verified by field studies. However, the mountain lion has little effect on white-tailed deer populations in Texas.

Parasites and Diseases

Parasites and diseases have been factors in whitetail die-offs in Texas (Van Volkenberg and Nicholson 1943, Taylor and Hahn 1947, Marburger and Thomas 1965). Stomach worms caused significant mortality in the Edwards Plateau where deer were undernourished and ranges overgrazed (Taylor and Hahn 1947). Screwworm flies formerly caused extensive deer losses throughout the state, but they are no longer an important limiting factor (Teer et al. 1965).

At the Welder Wildlife Refuge in the South Texas Plains, the large American liver fluke, various nematodes, one blood sporozoan and nasal bots were reported in white-tailed deer (Glazener and Knowlton 1967). Almost 70 percent of 129 deer examined contained liver flukes, and deer were found to be the normal host for this parasite (*see also* Foreyt and Todd 1962, 1976). Infectious diseases were common among deer on the Welder Wildlife Area in 1963 (Cook et al. 1965). Seventy percent of the adult deer and 84 percent of the fawns reacted to tests for California encephalitis. Forty-one of 67 adult deer reacted to one or more of seven leptospirosis serotypes.

Theileriasis is a common disease of whitetails in Texas (Robinson et al. 1967), but its effect reportedly was insignificant when deer had a sufficiently high nutritional level. Various ticks, including the lone star tick, were found capable of transmitting theileriasis to whitetails (Kuttler et al. 1967).

Two species of *Eimeria* have been identified in white-tailed deer in Texas (Anderson and Samuel 1969). Infection of coccidia was highest for young deer, whitetails collected in the winter and those collected where vegetation was sparse (Samuel and Trainer 1971*b*). Bluetongue virus was reported in several areas (Stair et al. 1968, Thomas and Trainer 1970), including the South Texas Plains, where 89 percent of 484 whitetails were seropositive (Hoff et al. 1974).

In the Post Oak Savannah, the incidence of *Salmonella* in fawns ranged from 18 to 43 percent over the four-year period 1966–1969 (Robinson et al. 1970).

The effects of theileriasis, bluetongue and salmonellosis could be lessened significantly by proper deer harvest and improved habitat management (Marburger et al. 1971).

Malignant catarrhal fever has been reported as a continuing infection of deer in the South Texas Plains (Clark et al. 1970, 1972). There is no evidence, however, that this disease is a limiting factor in this region.

Several parasites have been reported on whitetails at the Welder Wildlife Refuge, including *Amblyomma inornatum* (Cook et al. 1969), javelina flea (Samuel and Trainer 1970*b*), three species of ticks (Samuel and Trainer 1970*a*), *Tricholipeurus parellelus* (Samuel and Trainer 1971*a*), pharyngeal botfly (Samuel et al. 1971), and the deer ked. In the South Texas Plains, it appeared that (1) keds were most numerous on deer living in areas of dense vegetation or sandy soils, (2) flooding reduced ked numbers, and (3) keds were transmitted from dam to offspring (Samuel and Trainer 1972).

Cattle fever ticks were found on white-tailed deer within a tick quarantine area in the South Texas Plains in 1972 (Marburger and Robinson 1973). Marshall et al. (1963) discussed the controversial issue of removing deer as a host for cattle fever ticks in Florida and along the Rio Grande in Texas. Cattle fever ticks apparently occur on wild and domestic mammal populations all along the Rio Grande River in southern Texas. Ranchers in the area regularly "dip" or externally treat cattle in an effort to control or eradicate these pests. The success of such treatment programs is questionable and the future is uncertain.

Kuttler et al. (1972) attempted to induce cattle *Babesia* infection into white-tailed deer and indicated that white-tailed deer in Texas are important or dead-end hosts for three California group arboviruses.

Throughout Texas, extensive whitetail losses to diseases and parasites usually indicate severe stress from malnutrition and overpopulation.

Competition

White-tailed deer in Texas compete heavily with sheep and goats for forbs, browse and mast. Continuous heavy grazing by cattle or by mixed classes of livestock eliminates preferred deer foods and adversely impacts other aspects of whitetail habitat (Reardon and Merrill 1976, Merrill et al. 1957, Merrill 1959). In areas of the Edwards Plateau, intensive competition between deer and livestock has almost destroyed the usefulness of native range for wildlife (Teer et al. 1965, Hahn 1945, Sanders 1941, Taylor and Hahn 1947, May 1959).

At least 51 species of exotic ungulates have been introduced into Texas, and they compete heavily with whitetails for food on nearly 2 million hectares (4.9 million acres) (Ramsey and Anderegg 1972, Sheffield et al. 1971, Cary 1976). The most common exotics are Axis deer, Mouflon-Barbados sheep, blackbuck antelope, fallow deer, Aoudad sheep, Sika deer and Nilgai antelope. The most serious competition between exotics and whitetails occurs on the Edwards Plateau, which already is overpopulated with native deer and overgrazed by livestock.

Several thousand hectares of white-tailed deer habitat in Texas are destroyed annually. Brushlands are converted to improved pasture

Whitetail deer (foreground) in proximity of axis deer. The climate and terrain of much of Texas is suitable for the introduction of exotic ungulates. However, where ranges already are overpopulated with whitetails and/or overgrazed by livestock, competition of these species is intense and serious, such as on parts of the Edwards Plateau. *Photo courtesy of the Texas Parks and Wildlife Department.*

and cropland, which often lack the variety of browse and forbs needed to sustain white-tailed deer throughout the year. The rate of conversion has become critical in the Cross Timbers and prairies, Post Oak Savannah, Rolling Plains, and the South Texas Plains. Industrial development, increased agricultural demands and water impoundments also contribute to this loss of deer habitat.

Regulation of Hunting

White-tailed deer hunting is regulated in Texas under the Uniform Wildlife Regulatory Act. The Texas Parks and Wildlife Department collects information annually on deer abundance, breeding success, sex ratios, predation, disease and the effects of hunting, as well as agricultural and other human population developments. The Parks and Wildlife Commission then establishes hunting season dates, bag limits, and the means and methods for harvesting deer. The proposed hunting regulations are presented annually at public meetings in every county. Citizens may testify for or against the proposals.

Although illegal hunting and violations of wildlife laws occur, they are not a limiting factor on the whitetail populations in Texas. The effects of illegal hunting in Texas are minimized by the extensive efforts of the Texas Parks and Wildlife Department's Law Enforcement Division, which had approximately 370 conservation law enforcement officers in 1982. In addition, Texas landowners strictly enforce the state's trespass law. And landowners are very protective of their property and "their" wildlife—even though, by law, wildlife belongs to the state. In most of Texas, potential wildlife-law violators are deterred by the prospect of expensive fines and court costs.

MANAGEMENT

Current Practices, Policies and Philosophies

White-tailed deer have been underharvested in much of Texas for several decades. Hunters have been able to focus attention on bucks and choose which deer to harvest, frequently to the detriment of deer population management. Landowners and hunters often have ignored the advice of wildlife biologists and managers to harvest antlerless deer and increase harvests. More recreational opportunities could be provided from existing deer populations. In many regions, deer quality and condition have declined seriously. Continued reduction in habitat and forage quality will compound the problem. Extensive efforts are being made by the Texas Parks and Wildlife Department, the Texas Agricultural Extension Service, the U.S. Department of Agriculture's Soil Conservation Service, and several state universities to inform and educate landowners and hunters about the need for improved deer population and habitat management.

Attempts to manage deer population levels are of little avail if the animals' habitat is ignored. For example, although a deer population may be reduced 50 percent by harvest, habitat still can be overpopulated because of grazing pressure and competition from domestic livestock. The need for improved habitat management is most critical in the Edwards Plateau, Cross Timbers, Post Oak Savannah, and Gulf prairie regions, where nutritional quality of forage is low.

Severe overgrazing reduces deer habitat to a fraction of its carrying capacity. In many cases, habitat could be improved considerably if landowners would reduce domestic livestock numbers, replace highly competitive sheep and goats with cows, and implement a deferred-rotation grazing system to rest pastures at periodic intervals. These changes are realistic and effective, but few landowners are willing to change "the old way" of ranching in Texas.

Conservation agencies and institutions should encourage Texas landowners to maintain and manage high-quality brush as food and cover for deer. Brush control operations should never eradicate or "control" more than about 40 percent of the woody cover and low brush in any given area. Preferably, about 75 percent of the range should be covered with desirable woody species. Although a complete canopy is not desirable, whitetails in Texas generally do best in dense brush and woods. Openings should not exceed 300 meters (985 feet) in width—less in flat terrain. Square or circular openings should not exceed 20 to 30 hectares (50–75 acres), and should be surrounded by dense escape cover. Canyon walls and all drainages should be left in native brush or woods.

Landowners should encourage the harvest of antlerless deer in addition to antlered bucks. The annual harvest rate for established deer populations should be approximately 20 per-cent of the total autumn population, including up to 50 percent of the population's antlered bucks. However, no more than 25 percent of the antlered bucks should be harvested if the landowner wants to maintain a considerable number of bucks four years of age and older.

Many landowners, sportsmen and wildlife managers do not agree about whether to manage for quality or quantity of deer. To produce trophy bucks, as in the South Texas Plains where there is strong interest in doing so (Williams et al. 1974, Brothers and Ray 1975, Zaiglin and DeYoung 1976), landowners must maintain habitat in good condition. Does must be harvested heavily to maintain the population at or below habitat carrying capacity, and overpopulation and undernourishment must be avoided. Spike bucks and inferior deer should be harvested when they are young.

The current "craze" among many deer managers in Texas involves extensive penned-deer "studies" to improve the genetics of whitetail populations on certain ranches. Such efforts take many forms, the most extravagant of which entails the construction of breeding pens and the breeding of captive does to bucks with trophy-class or otherwise outstanding antlers. The offspring are released into the wild in the hope that they are genetically superior to the rest of

Large-scale bulldozing and burning (left) of an area in the East Texas Pineywoods. The area was later planted in coastal bermuda grass for pasturage. This activity resulted in an almost complete loss of suitable deer habitat. Strip clearings (right) that retain 40 to 75 percent of woody cover and low brush and are in proximity to dense escape cover can be beneficial to whitetails, particularly if livestock are excluded from or not allowed to overgraze the site. *Right photo by John Suhrstedt; both photos courtesy of the Texas Parks and Wildlife Department.*

the wild population and, therefore, will improve the gene pool in the area in which they were released. The results and values of such penned-deer "studies" remain to be seen. However, if these investments of time and money were directed instead toward improving whitetail habitat—particularly by increasing the abundance of high-quality foods—the production of trophy or superior whitetails would be much more likely to succeed.

Besides the penned-deer "studies," many deer managers in Texas currently are practicing the art of trophy management by selectively harvesting inferior or "cull" bucks in a manner similar to the trophy management of red deer practiced for many decades in European forests. The success of these programs also will be difficult to evaluate. But when combined with more intensive habitat management, the selective culling of inferior bucks may prove to be worthwhile in some situations.

Supplemental feeding of white-tailed deer usually is unnecessary in areas where habitat and harvest management combine to keep deer populations (1) in balance with their habitats' year-round carrying capacity and (2) at levels tolerable to landowners. However, during periods of drought in summer and prolonged extreme cold in winter, artificial feeding operations can prevent massive die-offs in otherwise healthy whitetail populations. Such programs are quite expensive, but considerably less so than deer- and habitat-recovery programs, the elimination of disease and crop depredation, and other problems frequently associated with weather-induced die-offs of wild ungulates.

A wide variety of "deer blocks" are available from commercial feed companies. Pelleted deer feed ranging from 16 to 24 percent protein is perhaps the most economical and nutritious supplement, and it definitely is better than shelled corn.

A drop net is used to capture whitetails in a large pen, as part of a program of selective breeding to improve antler development. Such studies, with the aim of affecting genetic characteristics of whitetails, have become quite popular in Texas in recent years. The success of the efforts remains to be seen. *Photo courtesy of the Texas Parks and Wildlife Department.*

Quite a number of large ranches in Texas, ranging in size from 400 to 20,000 hectares (1,000–50,000 acres), are involved in trophy whitetail production. Deer-proof fences are constructed on many of these ranches to prevent movement of deer between properties. *Photo courtesy of the Texas Parks and Wildlife Department.*

Whitetails in central Texas feeding on corn and protein blocks set out to bring the deer through a dry winter. Artificial feeding also is used to attract deer to hunting areas. When judiciously and selectively done, the practice may reduce deer die-offs during winter in arid parts of the state. Where annual harvests maintain the deer populations in balance with forage supplies and within landowner tolerance levels, supplemental feeding invariably is harmful to the deer, their habitat and other land-management interests. *Photo by Robert E. Billingsley; courtesy of the U.S. Soil Conservation Service.*

In Texas, as well as many other areas, the artificial feeding of deer is a complex and controversial issue. In regions where whitetail abundance adversely impacts the deer population's health and productivity, damages habitat, is intolerable to landowners, or where the deer population is harvested adequately, supplemental feeding is ill-advised and invariably will perpetuate biological and economic problems. In such situations, biological considerations must supersede sociological ones.

On the other hand, where the provision of additional foods is desirable for maintaining a whitetail population at a tolerable density level with respect both to landowners and the animals' habitat, food plots are a reasonable alternative. During summer, whitetails in certain parts of Texas readily eat peas, beans and grains. In winter they will consume small grains that are green and succulent, such as oats, wheat and rye. Plantings of these preferred crops can supplement native plant foods in the whitetail diet during stress periods. In addition, they can attract deer away from or reduce competitive foraging situations with livestock. Such food plots should be fertilized and protected from livestock grazing. However, deer biologists and managers must recognize that there is no substitute for good management, including the production and maintenance of native habitat and forage.

OUTLOOK

Landowners are the key to healthy white-tailed deer populations in Texas. How they manage the vast amount of Texas landscape they control for other uses, such as livestock production, will continue to determine the amount and quality of habitat for whitetails. Simultaneously, the extent to which they permit access to hunters will determine the number and condition of whitetails on given ranges. In the absence of concerted habitat maintenance and improvement efforts and adequate harvests on private lands in Texas, the quality of white-tailed deer can be expected to continue to decline, and whitetail population sizes will fluctuate dramatically and continue to decrease as habitat deteriorates.

The role of wildlife biologists and managers must be to inform landowners of deer population dynamics under various circumstances, of the advantages of whitetail habitat and harvest management, and of deer management practices that are compatible with other land uses. This will require an improved data base with which to monitor deer populations and recommend harvest regulations, and better communication to assure public recognition that biological management of whitetails is in the best interest of landowners, the general public and the deer themselves.

Chapter 26

WESTERN CANADA

William D. Wishart
Wildlife Research Biologist
Alberta Fish and Wildlife Division
Edmonton, Alberta

ENVIRONMENT

Western Canada represents the northern limit of white-tailed deer. Two subspecies occur in vastly different physiographic regions separated by the continental divide (Figure 94). The Northwest white-tailed deer subspecies is found in mountain valleys of British Columbia between the western slope of the Rocky Mountains and the eastern slopes of the Cascades. The Dakota whitetail subspecies occurs in the interior plains of the prairie provinces, mainly in the aspen parkland region. It also is found extensively in bottomlands along major rivers and streams. In recent decades, the Dakota whitetail has become well-established in the Peace River Parklands of northern Alberta and northeastern British Columbia, and has extended its northern range to about 60 degrees latitude. A few whitetails have been recorded in the Northwest Territories (Kuyt 1966, Scotter 1974).

The climate of the whitetail range in western Canada, on the whole, is continental, with cold winters and short cool summers (Table 77). Agriculture is the primary land use of the prairies and aspen parklands of Alberta, while for-estry is the major industry of British Columbia. Both provinces own large tracts of forested lands that are leased for forestry, mining and grazing (Table 78).

Alberta

The aspen parkland region provides prime habitat for whitetails. This mosaic of prairie patches (dry sites) and aspen groves (moist, sheltered sites) extends from the southern foothills of Alberta northeastward across the southcentral part of Alberta into Saskatchewan (Figure 95). The dynamic parkland community forms a transition between the mixed boreal forest, foothills forest and prairies. Fire suppresses invasion of aspen into grassland, but allows aspen to expand into coniferous forests to the north and west. Isolated parkland areas occur in the Cypress Hills, Hand Hills and the Peace River region.

Aspen clones within the parkland are formed by parent trees sending out shoots or suckers that, in turn, grow into trees and put out their own suckers. Thus, the clone often has a rounded profile with the oldest and tallest trees

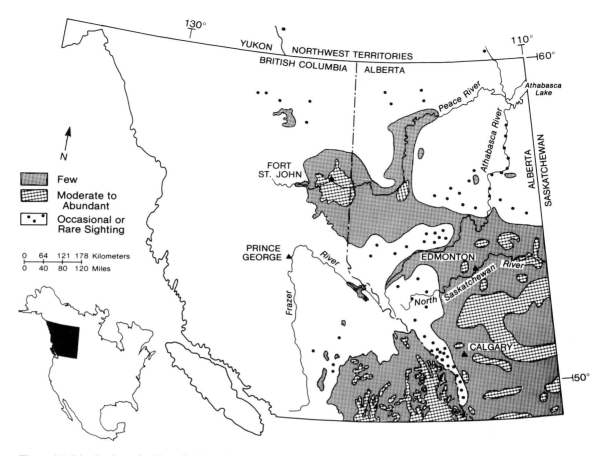

Figure 94. Distribution of white-tailed deer in western Canada.

in the center, and the youngest and shortest at the edge. Young clones occupy only a few square meters, while older ones cover several hectares or an entire hillside, providing an excellent diversity of edge.

Sucker growth at the edge of an aspen clone continually invades open grassland, trapping snow, filtering sunlight and retaining moisture in the soil. The borderline between aspen forest and grassland is marked by a dense growth of forbs and shrubs that provides prime food for deer. Wild peavine, woods rose and red-osier dogwood are common throughout the grove. Western snowberry, common choke-

Table 77. Climatic data for western Canada grassland and forest regions (Strong and Leggat 1981, Canada Year Book 1980–1981).

Habitat region	Average annual precipitation[a]	May-September temperature[b]			Extreme high (July) temperature[b]	Average number of frost-free days	December–February	
		Mean	Maximum	Minimum			Mean	Maximum
Grassland	40 (15.7)	14.5 (58.1)	15.0 (59.0)	13.5 (56.3)	42.2 (108.0)	110	−10.0 (14.0)	−6.0 (21.2)
Aspen parkland	45 (17.7)	13.0 (55.4)	15.0 (59.0)	10.0 (50.0)	34.4 (93.9)	95	−12.5 (9.5)	−7.0 (19.4)
Boreal forest	44 (17.3)	12.0 (53.6)	14.0 (57.2)	10.5 (50.9)	36.7 (98.1)	85	−15.5 (4.0)	−11.5 (11.3)
Montane	56 (22.0)	11.5 (52.7)	12.0 (53.6)	10.5 (50.9)	36.1 (97.0)	75	−7.5 (18.5)	−6.5 (20.4)

[a]In centimeters (inches).
[b]In degrees Celsius (Fahrenheit).

Table 78. Land ownership and jurisdiction in Alberta and British Columbia (Canada Year Book 1980–1981).

	Alberta			British Columbia		
	Square kilometers	Square miles	Percentage	Square kilometers	Square miles	Percentage
Privately owned land	183,521	70,858	27.7	55,040	21,251	5.8
Provincial parks	7,700	2,973	1.2	41,629	16,073	4.4
Provincial forests	343,098	132,471	51.9	303,663	117,245	32.1
Other provincial land	63,313	24,446	9.6	539,280	208,216	56.8
National parks	54,084	20,881	8.2	4,690	1,811	0.5
Indian reserves	6,566	2,535	1.0	3,390	1,309	0.3
Other federal land	2,903	1,121	0.4	904	349	0.1
Total area[a]	661,185	255,285		948,596	366,254	

[a]Including water-surface area.

A typical aspen parkland of western Canada. *Photo by William Wishart.*

Table 77. (continued)

temperature[b]	Extreme low (January) temperature[b]	Average number of days with snow cover	Average snow depth[a]
Minimum			
−15.0 (5.0)	−46.1 (−51.0)	105	35 (13.8)
−16.0 (3.2)	−48.3 (−54.9)	135	40 (15.7)
−23.0 (−9.5)	−47.8 (−54.0)	150	50 (19.7)
−9.5 (14.9)	−45.0 (−49.0)	145	50 (19.7)

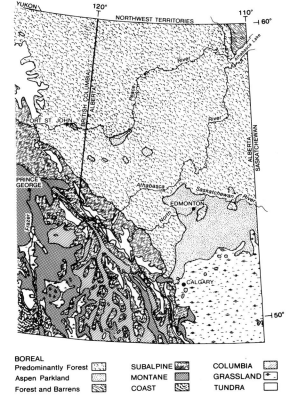

Figure 95. Forest regions of the white-tailed deer range in western Canada (after Rowe 1972).

cherry and prickly rose are found along the margins (Moss 1955).

The adjoining grassland harbors a large variety of forbs and shrubs. Asters, wild vetch, goldenrods and northern bedstraw are among the more conspicuous forbs. Shrubs such as western snowberry, rose, gooseberry, silverberry and saskatoon serviceberry add to its diversity. Most of these plants share common tolerance to drought, a short reproductive cycle and a need for direct sunlight. The grassland community of fescue, wheatgrass and needlegrass survives long dry periods. Wet weather benefits the aspen.

Variable topographic features within the parkland provide desirable interspersion of cover types for whitetails. Dense willow stands are found around the margins of marshes, potholes and lakes, and along the banks of streams and rivers. Pockets of white spruce and mixed forest are found in river valleys and on cool, moist, north-facing slopes. River "breaks" and bottoms, sandhills and precipitous glacial moraines provide both food and cover in the deep snow sections of the parkland and adjoining zones. Pockets and corridors of aspen and cottonwood contribute to the dispersal of deer from the aspen hubs.

British Columbia

Prime white-tailed deer habitat is found in the southeastern part of British Columbia in the Kootenay River system which forms part of the Rocky Mountain Trench. The several parallel mountain ranges extend in a general southeast-northwest direction. Prevailing westerly winds create a complex of wet regions on western slopes and dry regions on eastern slopes.

The dry Montane Forest extends northward from the U.S. border along the wind trench (8–24 kilometers:5–15 miles wide) for approximately 240 kilometers (150 miles) before merging with the humid Columbia Forest (*see* Figure 95). Ponderosa pine, the dominant tree on the benchlands, intermingles with Douglas-fir and western larch. Along lakes and in river bottoms, black cottonwood is predominant, often growing with dense thickets of willow, red-osier dogwood and rose. Scattered over open hillsides and in parklike areas are groves of aspen, paper birch and common chokecherry, with occasional stunted bushes of common juniper.

Since the early 1900s, the area has been virtually stripped of all merchantable timber. In

Floodplain habitat of white-tailed deer in the prairie region of Alberta. *Photo courtesy of the Alberta Department of Energy and Natural Resources.*

logged and burned areas, young pine and fir gradually are forming dense thickets. Ground cover in open areas consists mainly of bitterbrush, russet buffaloberry, Cascades mahonia, bearberry, and many native and introduced grasses such as cheatgrass.

Smith (1977) classified ten habitat types used by whitetails in the East Kootenay region. These were grassland, riparian brush, aspen, seral shrub, young fir, immature forest (open), immature forest (dense), mature forest (open), mixed-age fir and riparian mature spruce. Shrub utilization by whitetails was highest in riparian and young Douglas-fir habitats during winter. The young fir habitat is particularly valuable, since its trees provide both browse and cover in association with a productive shrub layer. Whitetail expansion into this region undoubtedly was a result of the flush of deciduous growth following logging and fires.

WHITETAIL POPULATIONS

History

White-tailed deer were first recorded in western Canada in the 1780s by E. Umfreville, a French-Canadian fur trader who spent each winter between 1784 and 1787 in a fort on the North Saskatchewan River near the Alberta/Saskatchewan boundary (Wallace 1954). It is quite evident that the region's Indians used fire to curtail forest encroachment on the prairies and to provide suitable habitat for deer and other ungulates (Bird and Bird 1967, Dawson 1880, Lewis 1977). Prior to 1880 however, whitetail deer numbers were not large in the parkland regions, probably because of intensive range competition with bison, moose and elk (Webb 1967). A catastrophic die-off of wild ungulates occurred in the 1880s, largely be-

A young whitetail doe (left) in winter pelage, using sagebrush as a screen for cover in British Columbia. Sagebrush is not a palatable browse species for the whitetails of western Canada. A prime buck (right) in summer coat, pausing in a bed of ponderosa pine cones in British Columbia. This is a "good" buck in western Canada, but not an exceptional animal. Note, too, the unusual branched tine on its left antler. *Photos by Tom W. Hall.*

cause of extremely cold winters and deep snow (Longley 1954). The cycle of cold weather persisted to the turn of the century, and deer numbers remained low.

Spectacular increases in white-tailed deer numbers occurred during the 1940s and 1950s. Their response in Alberta was mainly to habitat changes resulting from a series of wet years and an absence of prairie fires (Webb 1967). Aspen communities invaded prairie openings, improving old range and creating new range. Concurrently, whitetails expanded northward in response to the patchwork clearing of postwar homesteading, the planting of high protein crops such as clover and alfalfa, and the extirpation of predators. In British Columbia, whitetail increases were attributable largely to increased forage quantity and quality resulting from logging and extensive fires that occurred in low elevations during the mid-1930s (Langin

and Demarchi 1977). In general, whitetails in both Alberta and British Columbia responded to relatively mild weather, new habitat made available by human settlement, the absence of ungulate competition and scarcity of predators.

Condition and Productivity

The whitetail of western Canada is a large mobile deer with a high reproductive capacity. Table 79 shows average field-dressed weights of whitetails harvested in autumn (1968–1979) at the Wainwright Military Reserve in aspen parklands of Alberta. Antler diameters for yearling bucks averaged 2.4 centimeters (0.9 inch) and antler length averaged 28.7 centimeters (11.3 inches). The total number of points on both antlers averaged 6.2, with 66 percent of the yearling bucks having 6 to 8 points.

Table 79. Average field-dressed weights of white-tailed deer harvested from Camp Wainwright, Alberta, 1968–1979.

	Age class					
	Fawns		Yearlings		2.5 years and older	
Sex	Number	Kilograms (Pounds)	Number	Kilograms (Pounds)	Number	Kilograms (Pounds)
Male	195	31.7 (69.9)	179	53.9 (118.8)	249	77.6 (171.0)
Female	151	29.3 (64.6)	71	45.6 (100.5)	226	53.7 (118.5)

The reproductive potential of whitetails in western Canada is high. The fetal rate in does older than one year has been recorded at 2.08. *Photo by Tom W. Hall.*

In the same population, the pregnancy rate was 54 percent for female fawns and 100 percent for does more than one year of age (Hall 1973). The fetal rate in does more than one year old was 2.08. Its large body size and high reproductive potential have enabled the white-tailed deer to survive severe winter weather in this northwestern limit of the species' range.

Although the reproductive potential is high, postnatal survival of fawns in Alberta averages only 50 percent, and ranges from 35 to 60 percent in late autumn (Hall 1973). Thus, fawn/doe ratios vary from about 60:100 to 110:100. In Alberta, deer densities during winter range from 0.5 to 2.4 per square kilometer (1.3–6.2 per square mile), decreasing with increasing latitude. Densities are highest in the aspen parkland and adjoining grassland and boreal transition zones. Some isolated areas in the southern range sustain winter populations of 12 deer per square kilometer (31 per square mile).

Estimates of autumn whitetail populations in Alberta vary from about 100,000 following severe winters up to 200,000 after a series of mild winters (Rippin 1979). Long hunting seasons on bucks and short seasons on does have been the rule since the mid-1960s, with recent annual harvests of 8,000 to 14,000 deer. Doe-hunting seasons usually are closed after severe winters and, as a consequence, the annual harvest drops to about 6,000 bucks.

In British Columbia, whitetail densities are highest in the lower Kootenays. Populations have declined since the 1960s and, in 1980, were estimated at 25,000 deer (Petticrew and Jackson 1980). Either-sex seasons have been in effect since 1954, with occasional closures after severe winters. Approximately 2,500 deer are harvested annually, of which bucks comprise about 75 percent (Langin and Demarchi 1977).

Food Habits

The forage volume in 199 white-tailed deer rumens collected from November to May in Alberta during the period 1966–1975 averaged 60 percent browse, 26 percent forbs, 6 percent grasses and 8 percent unidentifiable material (Rhude and Hall 1977). Western snowberry, aspen and rose accounted for approximately two-thirds of the browse species consumed. Silverberry, common chokecherry, common juniper, willow, saskatoon serviceberry and bearberry comprised the balance. Important forbs were asters, peavine and scouringrush. Grasses and forbs were equal in volume to browse during April and May. Treichel and Hall (1975, 1976, 1977) examined rumens from 175 whitetails killed by collisions with vehicles on highways through farmlands of Alberta during winters of the period 1974–1977. They found

The relatively large body size of white-tailed deer in western Canada enables them to endure severe winter weather at the northernmost limit of the species' range. *Photo by Tom W. Hall.*

alfalfa in about equal volume to native legumes. Cereal grains (wheat and barley) were found in about the same proportion as western snowberry, aspen and rose.

Quality of forage varies considerably between seasons and plant species. Common chokeberry, silverberry and peavine were higher in protein than other species during winter and spring of 1969–1970 at the Wainwright Military Reserve, but grasses and forbs were highest during spring green-up (Table 80). Carotene content was highest in rose hips, common juniper, bearberry and scouringrush during winter, but emerging grasses were highest in April and May (Table 81). Fat content was highest throughout winter in common juniper (5.9 percent), bearberry (4.3 percent) and aspen (3.5 percent).

In southeastern British Columbia leaves of Douglas-fir and bearberry were the two most important winter food items for white-tailed deer (Demarchi and Demarchi 1967). Several years of forest succession and fire control drastically reduced the shrub habitat, and deer relied heavily on Douglas-fir as an emergency winter food. The most important forbs were pussytoes, hoods phlox and wild strawberry. Bitterbrush and other deciduous browse species comprised less than 10 percent of the winter diet. In spring, grasses, forbs and deciduous browse were the major components of the deer diet. Pussytoes, dryad, anemones, arrowleaf balsam root, wild strawberry, penstemons and buttercups were most prevalent. By late May, the leaves of saskatoon serviceberry, willow, common snowberry and birchleaf spirea comprised the bulk of the whitetail diet. Field observations of bitterbrush indicated that it may be utilized significantly more than shown by rumen samples (Langin and Demarchi 1977).

Table 80. Protein content of browse twigs and herbaceous leaves of preferred white-tailed deer forage from Camp Wainwright, November through May, 1969–1970 (Rhude and Hall 1977).

Plant part and forage species	Protein content[a]						
	November	December	January	February	March	April	May
Twigs							
Western snowberry	5.5	5.2	5.4	6.2	5.2		6.2
Aspen	8.5	8.0	8.1	8.9	7.9		7.8
Rose	6.4	6.0	5.8	5.5	6.3	6.2	6.4
Common chokecherry	12.3	7.2	8.4	12.3	11.4	12.9	17.0
Juniper spp.	7.1	7.2	5.9	7.2	7.1	7.3	6.7
Silverberry	14.5	14.6	12.3	13.4	15.5		15.4
Saskatoon serviceberry	6.9	6.3	7.3	7.1	9.1	8.8	9.0
Bearberry	5.5	5.0	5.2	5.3	5.2	4.9	5.3
Leaves							
Scouringrush	6.8	5.9	6.0	7.3	6.8	7.0	7.0
Peavine	11.8	12.1	12.0	11.8			30.7
Grasses						27.9	26.7
Crocus						14.5	17.1

[a]Percentage of dry weight.

A whitetail doe feeding on rosebushes in aspen parkland of Alberta. *Photo by W. M. Samuel.*

Table 81. Carotene content of preferred white-tailed deer foods from Camp Wainwright, November to May, 1969–1970 (Rhude and Hall 1977).

Plant part and forage species	Carotene content[a]						
	November	December	January	February	March	April	May
Twigs							
Western snowberry	2.1	1.6	0.7	1.5	0.4		0.7
Aspen	2.8	2.3	1.2	1.9	1.6		3.6
Rose (stems)	2.1	2.1	0.7	1.3	0.8	0.3	1.8
Common chokecherry	2.3	2.6	0.6	1.9	0.8	0.3	1.1
Juniper	14.2	12.6	6.5	9.0	7.2	0.7	19.4
Silverberry	5.2	4.5	3.8	3.1	2.3		4.1
Saskatoon serviceberry	2.7	1.9	1.2	2.4	1.2	0.3	1.9
Bearberry	11.0	8.0	6.5	6.1	4.8	0.3	14.6
Leaves							
Scouringrush	8.2	9.7	10.3	8.9	5.3	1.2	15.3
Peavine	0.0	0.0	0.0	0.4			3.7
Grasses						31.9	22.9
Crocus							10.0
Fruit							
Rose		18.3					7.3

[a]In milligrams per 454 grams (1 pound); for ruminants, 1 milligram of carotene is equivalent to 400 international units of vitamin A.

SPECIAL PROBLEMS

Weather

As a consequence of extreme winters, white-tailed deer in western Canada frequently are in a tenuous position. In Alberta, persistent low winter temperatures (less than 0 degrees Celsius [32 degrees Fahrenheit]) and prolonged snow cover adversely affected the physical condition of pregnant does at the time of fawning, as well as the size and development of their fawns (Hall 1973). The depth and duration of snow cover, particularly during November, March and April, were related inversely to femur marrow levels and fawn survival, and the physical condition of does. Where green forage was not available by mid-April, fawn survival declined. Hall (1973) concluded that the number of white-tailed deer in the northern fringe was regulated by low temperatures and the duration of snow cover rather than by condition of the range.

"Yarding" in the sense of large numbers of deer concentrating in restricted wooded areas during winter does not occur in the native habitats of Alberta, due in part to low densities. The whitetails disperse to a variety of microhabitats that minimize energy drain from travel through deep snow and from other heat-loss activities. The distance that deer move to favorable winter habitats varies inversely with the severity of winter weather. Chances of survival are best when deer have easy access in spring to south-facing, open exposures where forage green-up begins early.

In southeastern British Columbia, the major limiting factor for whitetails appears to be a loss of favorable winter habitat (Petticrew and Jackson 1980). In mild winters, deer occupied shrub zones of open-canopied or unforested habitats when available, and survival of young animals was high (Smith 1977). However, during winters when snow depths in the open exceeded 30 to 40 centimeters (12–16 inches), the deer moved into closed forest canopies and seriously depleted their forage. The net result was reduced survival and low production.

White-tailed deer populations in western Canada are limited more by depth and duration of snow than by range condition. *Photo by William Wishart.*

Whitetails of western Canada make extensive use of farm shelterbelts as travel lanes. *Photo courtesy of the Saskatchewan Department of Tourism and Natural Resources.*

Predation

With the extirpation of wolves and mountain lions during early settlement, predators no longer are a critical factor in deer survival. Currently, coyotes and dogs are the most serious predators, but they cause significant losses only under severe weather conditions and to unhealthy animals. Runge and Wobeser (1975) reported that during the severe winter of 1973–1974 in Saskatchewan, 81 percent of deer falling to predators (primarily coyotes and dogs) were predisposed by various disease conditions.

Diseases and Parasites

Probably the only viral disease of potential impact on white-tailed deer populations in western Canada is epizootic hemorrhagic disease. Die-offs of whitetails due to epizootic hemorrhagic disease have occurred in both Alberta and British Columbia (Trainer and Karstad 1970). During the outbreak in Alberta, carcasses of approximately 450 white-tailed deer, 20 mule deer and 15 pronghorn were found, principally along rivers and streams in the southeastern part of the province (Chalmers et al. 1964). Epizootic hemorrhagic disease outbreaks also have been reported among captive whitetails in Saskatchewan (Wobeser et al. 1973).

Several parasites complicate the health of deer in western Canada. Severe infections of lungworm have been reported in young mule deer of Saskatchewan (Runge and Wobeser 1975) and Alberta (W. H. Samuel personal communication:1982). Protozoan parasites, botfly larvae and lice have potential debilitating features in both white-tailed and mule deer (Koller et al. 1977, Runge and Wobeser 1975, Samuel et al. 1980).

The adult meningeal worm has not been recorded in Canada west of Manitoba. However, two close muscleworm relatives have been found in mule deer and white-tailed deer in western Canada (Platt and Samuel 1978, Pybus and Samuel 1981). Both muscleworms can severely damage muscles (adult stage) and lungs (eggs and larvae) of deer and, in some instances, other cervids such as moose (Pybus and Samuel 1980).

Competition

White-tailed deer may compete with other large ungulates for forage on the prairies and parklands of western Canada (Webb 1967). An example of deer in competition with elk, moose and bison exists in Elk Island National Park in central Alberta. In an area where elk and bison were excluded by fencing, deer densities in the enclosure were 2.4 per square kilometer (6.2 per square mile), whereas in the surrounding area there were only 0.5 deer per square kilometer (1.3 per square mile). The greatest range overlap was between elk and deer—97 percent in winter and 94 percent in summer. These species have remarkably similar food habits in Alberta (Cairns 1976).

Mule deer and whitetail food habits are similar, but the two species generally occupy different topographic features on the same landscape. Although the two species are known to hybridize (Wishart 1980), their continued and large-scale coexistence suggests that they occupy fairly divergent ecological niches with marginal overlap (Krämer 1973). Most documented shifts in species ratio have been caused by changes in habitat and differences in hunting mortality (Krämer 1972).

Competitive relationships between white-tailed deer and cattle in western Canada are contradictory. In Alberta, interference between deer and other ungulates was considered unimportant (Krämer 1973). On the other hand, cattle compete with deer where large

A whitetail/mule deer hybrid buck near Jasper, Alberta. Note the size and location of the metatarsal gland and the deer's dark tail. It has been suggested that such hybrids usually are sterile (Geist 1981), but recent evidence indicates that they usually are fertile. *Photo by L. Carbyn.*

MANAGEMENT

Hunting

Alberta and British Columbia regulate white-tailed deer hunting seasons and bag limits as a means of managing the deer populations. Antlerless deer seasons of varying lengths, interspersed with occasional closures, have been in effect since the 1950s. Extended buck seasons and short doe seasons have been the rule, and thus the buck harvest has significantly exceeded the doe harvest over the years, with little or no impact on the whitetail populations. In British Columbia, the licensed hunter can harvest mule deer and white-tailed deer. Bag limits from 1954 to 1968 were two bucks of either species, or one antlerless deer of either species and one antlered buck of either species. Since 1968, two antlerless deer have been

tracts of aspen forest are cleared annually for pasture. Deer habitat not only is destroyed, but surviving woodlots often are overstocked by cattle that systematically remove forbs and shrubs essential for whitetail food and cover (Weatherill and Keith 1969, Jaques 1980).

Forest management practices also may be competitive with deer. Clearcutting in large expansive blocks of 8 to 10 square kilometers (3–4 square miles) with no interspersion of residuals has created a sterile habitat for ungulates in western Alberta for years to come (Stelfox et al. 1976). In some areas, fire prevention has resulted in large stands of mature, even-aged coniferous forests that generally are unproductive for deer. For example, the potential big game winter range in southeastern British Columbia was reduced by 58 percent during 40 years of forest protection (Langin and Demarchi 1977).

White-tailed deer habitat in British Columbia is particularly vulnerable to land developments associated with transportation corridors. Railroads, highways and powerlines built along valley bottoms destroy valuable wildlife ranges. A series of hydroelectric impoundments on the Kootenay and Columbia rivers have flooded several hundred square kilometers of former riparian habitats of whitetails (Langin and Demarchi 1977).

Whitetails harvested in aspen parkland in eastcentral Alberta are recorded at check station. *Photo by William Wishart.*

permitted, one of each species. There are approximately 18,000 resident hunters in British Columbia who hunt both deer species in their overlapping range, with a harvest success rate of about 15 percent on whitetails (Langin and Demarchi 1977). In Alberta, whitetails have been on a separate license since 1960, with a bag limit of one buck or one of either sex during antlerless seasons. In recent years, resident whitetail hunters have numbered 45,000 to 65,000, with a harvest success rate of about 20 percent (Glasgow 1982).

Wildlife managers have a relatively free hand in setting deer hunting seasons in both Alberta and British Columbia. However, they tend to be cautious in liberalizing seasons, partly to avoid accusation of overharvest and partly to draw attention to the major factors that cause deer numbers to decline, that is, habitat losses due to major landscape changes by agriculture, forestry, mining, highway construction, hydroelectric projects and urban expansion.

Habitat

The overriding influence of climate precludes managing white-tailed deer in western Canada on the principle of carrying capacity. Winterkill of whitetails is an accepted fact in Alberta and British Columbia. Fortunately, when provided with favorable year-round habitat conditions, the whitetail has the reproductive capacity to recover quickly.

Continued success of the whitetail in western Canada depends on how grazing, logging, burning and cultivation are applied to the landscape. Grazing and fire prevention allow the encroachment of common snowberry and aspen onto the prairies, to the whitetail's advantage. Conversely, fire prevention in mixed wood and coniferous forest zones works against the whitetail. Small forest openings created by cultivation, logging, fires and clearcuts benefit the whitetail.

As a general guide, clearcuts in mixed forest habitat for moose, elk and deer should not exceed 40 hectares (approximately 100 acres), and residual blocks should have a minimum width of about 200 meters (655 feet) (Stelfox 1981). Rippin (1977) suggested that, in aspen forests and parkland, optimum white-tailed deer habitat consists of about 65-percent aspen cover, 20-percent grassland, and 15-percent mixed cropland and water, while areas leaving less than 35 percent tree cover provide unsuitable

Forest cutting blocks and residual stands of coniferous cover provide suitable habitat for whitetails in western Canada. Expansive clearcuts are virtually devoid of deer. *Photo courtesy of the Alberta Department of Energy and Natural Resources.*

overwinter habitat. Large-scale clearings of aspen and mixed forests involving several square kilometers without diversity are disastrous for whitetails.

OUTLOOK

Most whitetails occur on large tracts of leased provincial lands. Therefore, management decisions depend largely on intergovernmental agency cooperation and understanding. In this regard, British Columbia has developed a coordinated management plan of rest-rotation grazing and prescribed burning to enhance deer habitat. In Alberta, inventory and habitat teams continuously prepare and refine data to assist the wildlife manager at the negotiating table. For example, satellite imagery in conjunction with computers provide a continuous assessment of habitat conditions relative to grazing, logging, burning and flooding, and allow resource managers to apply the concept of multiple land use.

Ironically, the wildlife agencies do not have a well-defined mandate to purchase and manage land. Present acts and regulations are insufficient to prevent losses of wildlife habitat to other uses. As demand for wildlife resources continues to increase, it will be more important for the wildlife agencies to have the authority to select and direct efficient systems for biomass production. Telfer and Scotter (1975) predicted that, under intensive and coordinated management, aspen forests could produce a wide assemblage of ungulates, including white-tailed deer.

Chapter 27

PACIFIC NORTHWEST

Thomas A. Gavin
Assistant Professor of Wildlife Sciences
Department of Natural Resources
Cornell University
Ithaca, New York

HISTORY

In 1806, Lewis and Clark observed and recorded the presence of white-tailed deer along the Columbia River from the present location of The Dalles, Oregon, to Astoria on the coast (Thwaites 1905).

In 1829, David Douglas, Scottish naturalist and botanist, described a new subspecies of white-tailed deer based on two specimens collected in Oregon (Douglas 1829). The subspecies was variously referred to as "le Chevreuil," "Jumping Deer," "Long-tailed deer" and "Small deer." It eventually became known as the Columbian white-tailed deer. Douglas (1914) frequently encountered this deer along the Columbia River from 1823 to 1827. During August 1825, he shot or observed small deer along the Willamette River, but it is uncertain whether they were mule deer or whitetails. Douglas (1829:331) claimed that whitetails were common ". . . in the districts adjoining the river Columbia, more especially in the fertile prairies of the Cowalidske [Cowlitz] and Multnomah [Willamette] Rivers within one hundred miles of the Western Ocean."

Bailey (1936) and Jewett (1914) presented evidence that whitetails were present in the late 1800s in the Willamette Valley counties of Benton, Linn, Lane and Lincoln. Bailey and Jewett did not mention whitetails along the Columbia River, presumably because they believed the species had been eliminated from that area.

In 1940, the existence of whitetails along the lower Columbia River was verified by Scheffer (1940). This population—estimated to number 500 to 700 animals—was probably the densest concentration of white-tailed deer west of the Cascade Mountains. It included 150 deer on Puget Island, Washington, 100 to 200 deer on the Oregon side of the river near Westport, and 250 to 350 deer in the area now included in the Columbian White-tailed Deer National Wildlife Refuge.

In 1968, the Columbian white-tailed deer was designated an endangered species. The estimated population along the lower Columbia River was 300 to 400 deer.

Current Status

Today there are only two whitetail populations of any consequence west of the Cascade Mountains. One is located along the lower Columbia River on the Columbian White-tailed Deer National Wildlife Refuge. The other—known as the Roseburg herd—is located in Douglas County, Oregon (Figure 96). These two populations apparently are remnants of a population that once occurred continuously

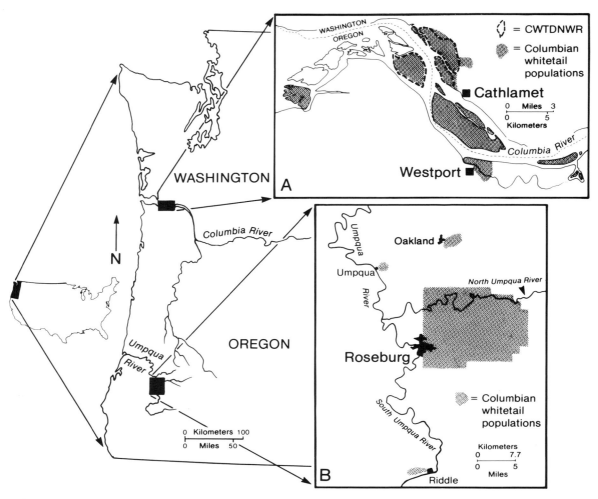

Figure 96. Distribution of white-tailed deer in western Washington and Oregon, 1983.

throughout the lower Columbia River in Washington and Oregon, the Cowlitz River in Washington, and the Willamette Valley in Oregon.

Under the Endangered Species Act of 1973, Columbian white-tailed deer cannot be harassed or killed, nor can any federal agency participate in activities that adversely affect this animal if its habitat has been documented as "critical" by the Secretary of the Interior. The safeguard against harassment has important implications for management of Columbian whitetails. It effectively precludes deer population control and habitat manipulation even when and where such activities would be in the animals' best interest. Permission to remove animals can be obtained with proper documentation, but because of the justifiably rigid nature of the law, the time, paperwork

and review required to get permission invariably are so complex and belabored as to prevent prompt action. Fortunately, the Columbian White-tailed Deer National Wildlife Refuge population has remained relatively stable and reduction has not been necessary, nor has there been any noticeable sign of habitat deterioration. On nonrefuge areas, the deer's endangered status prohibits their harassment even if they damage agricultural crops. Thus, wildlife officials are reluctant to attempt to establish new Columbian whitetail populations near existing agricultural areas.

In general, the endangered status of Columbian white-tailed deer has catalyzed public interest and support in its restoration, and has justified the creation of a refuge to protect the deer and their habitat.

COLUMBIA RIVER WHITETAIL POPULATION

Environment

The Columbian White-tailed Deer National Wildlife Refuge was established in 1972 to protect the Columbian white-tailed deer subspecies and a large portion of its remaining habitat. The refuge includes approximately 2,105 hectares (5,200 acres) of prime habitat on certain islands and bottomlands within a 15-kilometer (9.3-mile) stretch of the lower Columbia River (Figure 96). An additional 4,450 to 4,900 hectares (11,000–12,100 acres) of private land near the refuge are considered less suitable habitat, due mainly to intensive agriculture. Other lands provide potential habitat along the Columbia River, and there have been recent documented sightings of whitetails in several areas west of The Dalles (Davison 1979).

There is essentially no elevational relief to the lower Columbia River bottomlands, and whitetails are restricted to these flatlands. The elevation is about 3 meters (10 feet) above sea level. Most of the bottomlands have been diked and are crisscrossed with numerous sloughs and drainage ditches.

Native vegetation of the Columbia River "tidelands" consists of a dense, tall shrub or tree community containing Sitka spruce, red-osier dogwood, black cottonwood, red alder and willow (Franklin and Dyrness 1973). Most of the bottomlands have been cleared of trees and brush, and seeded to grasses and forbs that provide feed for beef and dairy cattle. Plants commonly found in the pastures include fescue, orchardgrass, clover, bluegrass, velvetgrass, creeping buttercup and ryegrass. Reed canary grass and water foxtail are common "invaders" on wet sites. Blackberries, rushes, sedges, roses, American elder and snowberries are common plants utilized as food or cover by deer.

On the Washington side of the river, the amount of woody cover has changed significantly (Suring 1974). In 1939, 70 percent of the land now contained in the mainland portion of the Columbian White-tailed Deer National Wildlife Refuge was classified as wooded. In 1972 however, only 17 percent was classified as wooded; the remainder had been converted to pasture. This reduction of year-round riparian cover is typical on Columbia River and Willamette Valley (Oregon) floodplains. Over most of the region, the acreage left in woodlots is far less than 17 percent.

Ocosta silty clay loam, the predominant soil type, is formed in deep silty and clayey depositions in coastal bays. It is located on low, poorly drained floodplains that are influenced by tides. Slopes range from 0 to 3 percent.

Climate of the lower Columbia River is moderate. The mean monthly maximum temperature is 17.7 degrees Celsius (63.9 degrees Fahrenheit) in August, and the mean monthly minimum is 4.0 degrees Celsius (39.2 degrees Fahrenheit) in January near the Columbian White-tailed Deer National Wildlife Refuge (R. B. Webb personal communication:1977). The 15-year mean annual rainfall is 270 centimeters (106 inches). An average of 211 centimeters (83 inches) falls from October to March. Snow cover is infrequent and of short duration.

The typical land-use pattern now used on private land near the refuge, as well as on refuge land when it was privately owned, involves pasturing cattle in March or April after the ground dries of winter rain. During May or June, cattle are taken off the pastures that then are cut for hay. Livestock grazing is resumed for the rest of the summer. In November, cattle are moved to feedlots, because the pastures usually become too wet to graze. Some farmers exclude a small portion of their land from grazing to grow hay or silage.

An adult doe during winter on the Columbian White-tailed Deer National Wildlife Refuge. Accumulations of snow are unusual at this elevation in southwestern Washington and, if snow persists, it could inhibit deer grazing on herbaceous vegetation. *Photo by Thomas A. Gavin.*

Cottonwood and spruce are cut commercially along the lower Columbia River. Douglas-fir, western redcedar and western hemlock are logged intensively in the uplands immediately adjacent to river bottomlands. These uplands apparently are not utilized by whitetails, but are densely populated with mule deer.

Deer Population

Observations of marked deer on the Columbian White-tailed Deer National Wildlife Refuge mainland indicated that individual whitetails had the same home ranges in successive years (Gavin 1979). The average home range was 158.5 hectares (391.5 acres) for does and 192.2 hectares (474.7 acres) for bucks. The area traveled by a deer in any 24-hour period, however, was considerably smaller than these averages. No movement by marked deer off the refuge was ever observed.

The population on the 790-hectare (1,952-acre) mainland portion of the Columbian White-tailed Deer National Wildlife Refuge was estimated at 200 to 230 during the winter of 1972–1973 (Suring 1974). This was an average density of 25.3 to 29.1 deer per square kilometer (65.6–75.4 per square mile). Gavin (1979) conservatively estimated the population in November of 1974, 1975, 1976 and 1977 to be 214, 180, 164 and 202, using a mark-recapture technique (Schnabel). The November–December population during 1978, 1979 and 1980 was estimated at 212, 191 and 159, respectively (Columbian White-tailed Deer Recovery Team 1982). During the past few years, the late autumn-early winter population has been relatively stable at 20 to 29 deer per square kilometer (52–75 per square mile). Recent population estimates for Columbian whitetails on off-refuge islands in the Columbia River near the refuge (Figure 96) include 50 to 75 for Puget Island, 70 to 80 for Wallace Island-Westport and 8 to 12 for Karlson Island (Columbian White-tailed Deer Recovery Team 1982).

Based on an age analysis of 121 yearling and adult whitetails found dead on the refuge between 1972 and 1977, the median age of death was three years for bucks and five years for does (fawns were not included in the analysis). The oldest male was 7.5 years of age at death, and the oldest female was 13 years old. The old-age structure was not too surprising, since there was no significant predation of adult deer and hunting has been prohibited since 1970. Causes of mortality included automobiles, dogs, drowning, malnutrition, poaching and necrobacillosis. Coyote predation on fawns was significant (Gavin 1979). From 1972 to 1976, yearling and adult does outnumbered bucks of the same age classes 3–4:1. This ratio is comparable to those of many populations subject to buck-only hunting.

An alert buck on the Columbian White-tailed Deer National Wildlife Refuge. Its antlers are typical for adult bucks on the Refuge. Note the piloerection on the animal's tail and on the tarsal glands inside its hind leg, signaling readiness to flee. *Photo by Thomas A. Gavin.*

Observations in May and June of 1975 indicated that 11 of 12 marked does two years of age or older were pregnant or observed with fawns later in the summer, but only 3 fawns (of at least 11) survived until November. In June 1976, 16 of 18 marked females were pregnant, and 10 fawns survived until November. Twins rarely were observed, and there were no indications of breeding by female fawns (Suring 1974, Gavin 1979).

Although nearly all adult does gave birth to one or more fawns, the low fawn survival and lack of production by one-year-old females resulted in a low annual recruitment rate. From 1972 through 1977, the number of fawns per 100 does in autumn ranged from 35 to 60 (Gavin 1979). Even lower fawn recruitment was reported for the period 1978–1980, due primarily to coyote predation on fawns (Columbian Whitetailed Deer Recovery Team 1982).

The large American fluke, cattle lungworm, sheep lungworms, stomach worms, whipworm, nodular worm, botfly and deer keds have been identified from autopsied deer that died from natural causes. Eight deer carcasses were examined from 1972 to 1974. Three were infested severely enough with stomach worms to cause death or be a major contributing factor (T. P. Kistner personal communications:1972, 1974). Of the 40 whitetails that were examined for parasites from 1974 to 1976, only a few were without some internal parasites, but severe parasite "loads" seldom were found. The liver and lungs were the most commonly infested organs (T. A. Gavin personal data).

Necrobacillosis was cited as the cause of death in four deer from the refuge (D. E. Olson personal communication:1975). Many other deer were observed or carcasses recovered with one or more feet swollen and ulcerous, indicating "foot rot." Although these carcasses were not searched for the bacterium-causing necrobacillosis, Rosen (1970) claimed that foot rot in deer was invariably caused by this disease. Bucks seemed to be afflicted more often by foot rot than were does, as evidenced by the number of limping deer of each sex observed (Gavin 1979). Deer with a chronic case of necrobacillosis may develop alveolitis or osteomyelitis of the bony tissue surrounding the buccal (mouth) cavity. In a sample of 108 sets of skulls with mandibles of Columbian whitetails at least one year old, accumulated between 1972 and 1977, 49 exhibited some indication of bony tissue disease. In addition, of

all mortalities located on the refuge from 1974 to 1977, 49 of 155 showed some symptom of the disease (Gavin 1979). It is probable that necrobacillosis plays an important role in the mortality patterns observed in this population.

The health of the refuge population was suggested by three adult bucks and two adult does killed by a poacher in late February 1975. All five animals had abundant body and kidney fat, no obvious parasite loads, and a femur marrow fat content that averaged 99 percent (Gavin 1979). Both does were pregnant with twins. Although two of the deer had feet slightly swollen in a condition resembling "foot rot," all five appeared to be in excellent physical condition at a time when deer usually experience nutritional stress. A conclusion, based on examination of deer found dead on the refuge, that the entire population is diseased and in poor condition is apparently risky and misleading.

Whitetails on the refuge were observed grazing on forbs and grasses almost exclusively during the early and mid-1970s. Suring (1974) and Suring and Vohs (1979) reported that grazing was detected in 99 percent of their nearly 18,000 observations of deer feeding. Stomach contents from 32 whitetails collected from all seasons in the period 1972 to 1977 consisted of grasses (59 percent), forbs (16 percent) and browse (25 percent) (B. B. Davitt personal communication:1981). Essentially all browse consumed was nonwoody (such as blackberry leaves). Dublin (1980) concluded that Columbian whitetails on the refuge selected for browse in every season except spring and selected for forbs in all seasons, but selected against grass (relative to its availability) in autumn, winter and spring. It is possible that at least part of this paradox in describing the food habits of these deer is due to a change in vegetation height, productivity and availability on the refuge between the early and late 1970s.

Refuge Managment

Prior to the establishment of the Columbian White-tailed Deer National Wildlife Refuge in 1972, there were 18 separate private holdings used primarily for grazing and hay production on the mainland portion of the area. The pastures were grazed heavily and supported 2,200 to 2,400 cattle for about seven months each year. After refuge establishment, grazing and haying were continued on a permit basis, but there was a general reduction in cattle numbers and acreage grazed. In 1975, for example, on 742 hectares (1,833 acres) under refuge management, 327 hectares (808 acres) were excluded from all agricultural use, 112 hectares (278 acres) were hayed or cut for silage, and 303 hectares (749 acres) were grazed from mid-April to November 1 by 475 cows, calves and yearling steers. Grazed and nongrazed pastures have been maintained in a checkerboard arrangement, and cattle excluded from most woodlots.

Although the level of pasture and livestock management practices that best meets the needs of the deer has not yet been determined, it appears that a combination of frequent mowing and heavy cattle grazing provides a desirable diversity of herbaceous plants, minimizes weed infestation and maintains the forage at a palatable stage (5–10 centimeters:2–4 inches) of growth.

The Tenas Illahee Island portion of the Columbian White-tailed Deer National Wildlife Refuge has a history of intensive grazing, but lower deer numbers than the mainland has. There were only 2 to 5 whitetails on this diked island in 1939 (Scheffer 1940), but a recent estimate puts the number at 30 to 40 (Columbian White-tailed Deer Recovery Team 1982). The island contains 830 hectares (2,050 acres) of habitat similar to the mainland portion of the refuge. About 27 percent of the vegetation is woody, but it is distributed in large stands on the perimeter outside of the dike. The distribution of woody cover may account, in part, for the marked difference in deer density between the island and the mainland. There obviously is potential, with proper habitat management, for deer population expansion on Tenas Illahee Island.

There is strong circumstantial evidence to suggest that Columbian whitetails along the Columbia River occasionally interbreed with

Cattle are used in some areas on the Columbian White-tailed Deer National Wildlife Refuge to keep grasses and forbs short, actively growing and nutritious. Deer are willing to enter pastures where cattle are present, but avoid approaching the livestock too closely. *Photo courtesy of the Oregon Department of Fish and Wildlife.*

A group of whitetail does during an evening feeding period in a field maintained by cattle grazing and/or hay cropping on the Columbian White-tailed Deer National Wildlife Refuge. *Photo courtesy of the Washington Department of Game.*

Columbian black-tailed deer. Suring (1974) observed interspecific mating behavior and T. A. Gavin (personal data) noted apparent hybrid deer on the mainland portion of the refuge. Coloration of the dorsal surface of the tail, length of tail and facial characteristics were used by Davison (1979) to classify 179 deer observed on the Columbian White-tailed Deer National Wildlife Refuge mainland. Nearly one-third (56) of the deer classified were thought to exhibit hybrid characteristics. None of the 48 deer classified on Puget Island or 37 deer observed on five other Columbia River islands was classified as hybrid; all exhibited typical whitetail characteristics (Davison 1979). There is other evidence to support the possibility of hybridization between these species. In a penned enclosure, blacktails from Oregon bred with whitetails from Tennessee to produce fertile offspring; all hybrids were indistinguishable from blacktails (Whitehead 1972). In contrast, whitetail characteristics prevailed when a Columbian whitetail buck from the lower Columbia River was bred to blacktail does and to his own female crossbred progeny (W. C. Lightfoot and F. F. Ives personal communication:1975).

ROSEBURG WHITETAIL POPULATION

Environment

White-tailed deer in Douglas County, Oregon, are found in an area roughly encompassed by the towns of Umpqua, Riddle and Oakland—an area that includes 1,199 square kilometers (463 square miles) (Smith 1982). The North Umpqua River and South Umpqua River bisect this region, and the densest concentration of whitetails is located along the south boundary of the former (Figure 96). Elevation ranges from 135 meters (443 feet) along the North Umpqua River to 505 meters (1,656 feet) at the ridge crest south of the river. Topography consists of numerous small mountains and rolling foothills scattered through the Umpqua Valley. Most of the whitetail range occurs on private sheep ranches of several hundred hectares each.

The natural vegetational community of the Umpqua Valley is oak woodland (Franklin and Dyrness 1973). Although whitetails are associated with the river bottom in Douglas County, which is dominated by Oregon white oak, Or-

Riparian scene along the North Umpqua River in Douglas County, Oregon, exhibiting more xeric habitat than is found along the Columbia River. *Photo by Thomas A. Gavin.*

egon ash, wild rose, viburnum, poison oak, rush and grass, they also occur on the drier uplands that are dominated by Oregon white oak, California black oak, madrone, poison oak and wild rose. Douglas-fir, ponderosa pine, red alder and big-leaf maple are additional tree species found in the area (Smith 1982).

Generally, the climate is hotter and drier in Roseburg than at the Columbian White-tailed Deer National Wildlife Refuge. The mean monthly minimum temperature was 4.9 degrees Celsius (40.8 degrees Fahrenheit) in January, and the mean monthly maximum was 20.2 degrees Celsius (68.2 degrees Fahrenheit) in August, for the period 1955–1980. Mean annual precipitation was 84.1 centimeters (33.1 inches), with an average of 67.8 centimeters (26.7 inches) falling from October to March (Smith 1982). The annual snowfall averages 17 centimeters (6.7 inches), but individual snow accumulations rarely persist on the ground more than a few days.

Deer Population

From 1928 to 1952, whitetails found northeast of Roseburg in an area containing approximately 79 square kilometers (30.5 square miles) were considered by the Oregon Department of Fish and Wildlife as part of the White-tailed Deer Refuge population. Hunting was prohibited. Crews (1939) estimated the number of whitetails in this high-density area at 200 to 300 deer in 1938. This refuge was dissolved in 1952, and hunting was resumed. In 1970, the Oregon Department of Fish and Wildlife, using spotlight counts, estimated that 450 to 500 whitetails existed in the "old refuge" area, at a density of 5.7 to 6.3 deer per square kilometer (14.8–16.3 per square mile) (Smith 1982). In a detailed study of Roseburg whitetails, Smith (1982) estimated the density in his 2,745-hectare (6,783-acre) study area along the North Umpqua River to be 22.9 to 27.0 deer per square kilometer (59–70 per square mile) in 1979–1980. He used a mark-recapture technique similar to that used by Gavin (1979) for the Columbia River population.

Composition of the Roseburg whitetail population in November-December 1979 was estimated to be 52 fawns per 100 does, and 30 bucks per 100 does (Smith 1982). Malnutrition and roadkills accounted for the largest proportion of known mortalities, with fence entanglement, predation and disease less common. A significant increase in fawn survival and recruitment in 1979 following a dramatic decrease in population density suggested an inverse relationship between these parameters (Smith 1982). Similar observation was made for the Columbia River population (Gavin 1979). Average home ranges were 44.5 hectares (109.9 acres) for does and 47.1 hectares (116.3 acres) for bucks in the Roseburg area (Smith 1982).

In 1975, the Oregon Department of Fish and Wildlife focused attention on the taxonomic status of the Roseburg whitetail in relation to the Columbia River whitetail (J. W. McKean personal communication to the Columbian White-tailed Deer Recovery Team:1975).

If both populations belonged to the same subspecies, *Odocoileus virginianus leucurus,* then the Roseburg population would have to be managed according to existing endangered-species legislation. State, federal and university personnel all agreed that a taxonomic evaluation was essential to determine the present

A Columbian white-tailed deer with a tail that appears normal in color tone and length for this subspecies. *Photo courtesy of the Oregon Department of Fish and Wildlife.*

status of the Columbian white-tailed deer. In summer 1978, Oregon wildlife officials decided, without a taxonomic study, to consider the Roseburg population as Columbian white-tailed deer, and change existing regulations to prohibit the hunting of whitetails in Douglas County. A taxonomic study of the entire subspecies, which probably will result in a new description of this taxon, currently is underway by T. A. Gavin and W. P. Smith.

MANAGEMENT

The goal in management of Columbian white-tailed deer is to remove the subspecies from "endangered" status. The Columbian White-tailed Deer Recovery Plan (Columbian White-tailed Deer Recovery Team 1982) has established separate criteria for the Columbia River and Roseburg populations before reclassification to "threatened" status. To warrant reclassification, the Columbia River whitetails must be restored to a minimum population of 400 and be distributed in at least three viable subpopulations, two of which must be located on habitat secure against adverse human impact. At present, only the refuge mainland has a subpopulation that is both viable and secure. Off-refuge remnants of the population have been identified along the Columbia River (Davison 1979). If protection of habitat in these areas can be obtained, their existence could form the nuclei for viable subpopulations and preclude the necessity of costly translocation operations. The Roseburg population will be reclassified if 1,000 deer can be maintained within the Umpqua Basin of Douglas County and if whitetail habitat in the area, most of which is on private land, remains relatively free from land clearing and residential development. To provide additional security for whitetail habitat in Douglas County and along the Columbia River, a variety of approaches will be employed: landowner incentives; local zoning ordinances; participation of private organizations, such as The Nature Conservancy, in acquiring habitat; and delineation of "essential habitat" as provided for by the Endangered Species Act of 1973.

Due to its size, public visibility and the amount of information collected, the Columbian White-tailed Deer National Wildlife Refuge population probably will remain the key deer population along the Columbia River. Thus, it should be monitored continuously for its age and sex characteristics, its size and dispersion in relation to habitat management on the refuge, and presence of epizootic diseases. Similar information should be obtained for key areas in Douglas County.

Columbian whitetails should be monitored periodically for evidence of hybridization with blacktails, which may be occurring on the Columbian White-tailed Deer National Wildlife Refuge mainland. A more rigorous and systematic method to detect hybrids needs to be employed; the use of electrophoretic techniques is appropriate in this regard. Competition between Roosevelt elk and whitetails on the refuge also requires better understanding, as does the long-term impact of coyote predation on fawns.

OUTLOOK

The prognosis for the recovery of Columbian whitetails along the Columbia River improved significantly with the acquisition of land and formation of the Columbian White-tailed Deer National Wildlife Refuge in 1972. A major environmental catastrophe could occur in this area—such as a flood caused by an eruption of Mount St. Helens—that would result in the wholesale elimination of whitetail habitat, but little can be done about this possibility. The recent study on whitetails near Roseburg documented the existence of many more whitetails west of the Cascade Mountains than was previously thought. If protection can be obtained for at least some of the habitat now on private land in Douglas County, the outlook for that population will improve also. It is noteworthy and important that questions traditionally regarded as only of theoretical interest—such as interspecific hybridization, taxonomy at the subspecific level, and a determination of the minimum population size required to remain viable—have all emerged in debate as appropriate topics in the recovery of this endangered taxon. The lesson may be that research at all levels of immediate application should be encouraged by wildlife management agencies.

Chapter 28

NORTHERN ROCKY MOUNTAINS

James M. Peek
Professor
College of Forestry, Wildlife
and Range Sciences
University of Idaho
Moscow, Idaho

White-tailed deer are native to the mountains of Idaho, Montana, Oregon, Washington and Wyoming. But being more secretive and selective of dense cover than are elk and mule deer, the whitetail often was overlooked in the past as an important part of the region's fauna and as a recreational resource. Now, however, hunters and other outdoor recreation and wildlife enthusiasts in the region have begun to appreciate the whitetail's unique characteristics and qualities, and the animal's popularity is on the upswing.

ENVIRONMENT

The habitat of white-tailed deer in the Northern Rocky Mountains region is characterized by dense coniferous forests, heavily to sparsely vegetated river bottoms, and croplands of grains, peas and hay. Elevations occupied by whitetails range from less than 300 meters (985 feet) to more than 2,000 meters (6,560 feet) above sea level. Annual precipitation varies from less than 37 centimeters (15 inches) to more than 100 centimeters (40 inches). Snow depths generally average less than 0.3 meter (1 foot) on low-elevation ranges of northeastern Idaho and eastern Washington, to more than 1 meter (3.3 feet) in interior mountains of northern Idaho. Temperatures are moderate in the western areas, where the mean temperature is −2 degrees Celsius (28 degrees Fahrenheit) in January and 19 degrees Celsius (66 degrees Fahrenheit) in July. Temperatures in the North Fork of the Flathead River area average 16.1 degrees Celsius (61 degrees Fahrenheit) in July and −9.3 degrees Celsius (15 degrees Fahrenheit) in January.

Cottonwood and willow communities typify riparian vegetation of the region. Sparse overstory of large cottonwoods occasionally dominates willow and herbaceous understory, forming ideal habitat for white-tailed deer on a year-round basis. Common shrubs along rivers include alders, red-osier dogwood, Saskatoon serviceberry, common chokecherry, rose and common snowberry (Kamps 1969). Douglas hawthorn, Saskatoon serviceberry and common snowberry provide important cover and forage in gullies and draws above the main rivers.

Whitetails range through ponderosa pine, Douglas-fir, cedar/hemlock, and spruce/fir forest types. Pine, Douglas-fir and juniper are important winter vegetation types. Hemlock and spruce/fir communities serve as vital habitat at other times of the year. Following logging or burning, seral successional stages of forest vegetation often provide preferred forage.

Croplands raise carrying capacity of whitetail winter habitat in the region. Croplands adjacent to forests often provide forage throughout winter (Tebaldi 1982). Where available, alfalfa and other hayfields are used extensively by whitetails.

WHITETAIL POPULATIONS

White-tailed deer were found in abundance in foothills and valleys of the Northwest by white explorers and trappers in the early 1800s (Pengelly 1961, Allen 1971).

The modern history of whitetails in the Coeur d'Alene region of northern Idaho probably is typical of the species in the Northern Rocky Mountains region. Whitetail populations were low in the early 1900s, due to over-exploitation, temporary habitat losses caused by forest fire, and severe winter weather. They increased to high levels in the late 1940s and early 1950s as a result of effective protection and improved habitat, and then decreased to low levels (although the deer still were common) as habitat again changed (Pengelly 1961). In recent decades, whitetails have extended their range in western Montana and eastern Washington to encompass an area greater than their range in 1940 (Allen 1971, L. D. Parsons personal communication:1976) (Figure 97).

In mountainous areas, most adult whitetail does conceive and carry 1.8 to 2.0 fetuses. Yearlings are slightly less productive—1.2 to 1.33 fetuses per doe—and fawns rarely breed (Pengelly 1961, Mundinger 1981*a*, Will 1973*a*). Mundinger (1981*a*) reported that alternate-year breeding by adult does in the Swan Valley of Montana was typical. Fawn loss in this area

In 1880, sheriff W. H. Bullard of Miles City, Montana bagged what then was referred to as ". . . the biggest whitetail buck ever" (Brown and Felton 1955:134). The deer's dressed weight was recorded as 96.2 kilograms (212 pounds). *Photo by L. A. Huffman; courtesy of Coffrin's Old West Gallery.*

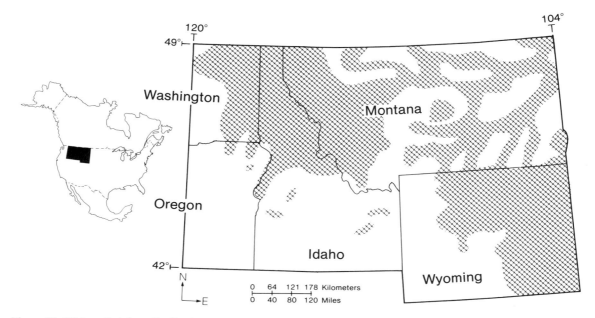

Figure 97. White-tailed deer distribution in the Northern Rocky Mountains region.

was estimated at 59 percent of the potential production. Deer along river bottoms and in agricultural areas may be slightly more productive.

Life tables constructed by Will (1973*a*) for Latah County, Idaho, showed a mean age of 4.2 years for whitetail does and 3.0 years for bucks. Approximately 16 percent of the does were 8.5 years of age or older, indicating a relatively old, stable population. Tebaldi (1982) reported similar age structures for whitetails in northeastern Wyoming. Mundinger (1981*b*) reported survival rates of 65.2 percent for adult whitetails in the Swan Valley of Montana, which, though lower than rates indicated in the Idaho and Wyoming studies, still are high.

Approximately 34,000 whitetails are harvested in the region annually: 8,000 in Idaho; 13,000 in Montana; 8,000 in Washington; 5,000 in Wyoming; and a small number in Oregon. The proportion of whitetails in the total deer harvest (including mule deer) has varied from a low of 3 percent in Wyoming to a high of 75 percent in northwestern Montana.

Hunting white-tailed deer in the Northern Rocky Mountains region is difficult, as illustrated by the hunter success average of 17 to 24 percent from 1975 to 1980 in the Swan Valley area of Montana (Mundinger 1981*b*). Will (1973*b*) reported that an average of 11 hours of hunting was required to see a deer in Idaho, and 92 hours were required to kill one of either sex. Only 27 percent of the hunters saw deer in an area where deer were "relatively abundant." Until it reaches depths that restrict hunter access and mobility, snow improves the hunter's chances of success. Still-hunting is the most popular method for hunting whitetails in the region, although drives are common.

Food Habits

Both evergreen and deciduous woody plants comprise more than half the midwinter diet of whitetails in the forests of Montana and Idaho. Douglas-fir and western redcedar are preferred conifers, while cottonwood and quaking aspen are preferred deciduous species (Singer 1979). In some areas, ponderosa pine is eaten readily and damaged by deer (Adams 1949). Creeping mahonia, Saskatoon serviceberry, common snowberry and redstem ceanothus are preferred nonconiferous species (Roberts 1956). Bearberry—a prostrate evergreen—and myrtle pachistima—a taller evergreen—are im-

A whitetail doe threatens another doe in competition for browse in a high-lined conifer stand. Conifers are especially important winter food and cover plants for white-tailed deer in the Northern Rocky Mountains region. *Photo courtesy of the Washington Department of Game.*

portant locally, and arboreal lichens are preferred when available (Keay and Peek 1980).

Spring diets are highly variable. Grasses and agricultural crops are important to whitetails in northcentral Montana (Kamps 1969, Martinka 1968), whereas forbs form a major share of the May diet in northwestern Montana (Hildebrand 1971). Alfalfa, clover and spreading pasqueflower are preferred forbs. Winter wheat also is highly palatable and, in local situations, may be severely damaged by deer. During late winter and early spring periods when green growth is initiated, forbs and grasses are sought (Keay and Peek 1980).

Forbs such as alfalfa and clover dominate summer diets in eastern portions of the region (Kamps 1969, Martinka 1968). In Latah County, Idaho, redstem ceanothus and common snowberry are important summer foods (Thilenius and Hungerford 1967), and forbs are common locally (Roberts 1956).

Autumn is a transition period when forbs of late summer give way to winter browse in the whitetail diet.

Agricultural crops are important to whitetails throughout the year and contribute to high deer populations along the forest/cropland ecotone. Browse is the major year-long diet along the western border of Glacier National Park (Singer 1979).

Habitat-use Patterns

Whitetails differ considerably in their winter habitat selection in the Northern Rocky Mountains region. During a mild winter in northern Idaho, deer concentrated in open areas, especially in shrub stages of the cedar/pachistima habitat type and in the Douglas-fir/ninebark type. Conversely, during a severe winter on the North Fork of the Flathead River, whitetails preferred dense, mature spruce stands and other areas where overstory was dense (Singer 1979). In the Snowy Mountains of central Montana, 85 percent of observed whitetails were in agricultural areas adjacent to ponderosa pine stands (Kamps 1969). Aspen and shrub types were used most heavily during the 1965–1966 winter in the Bear Paw Mountains of north-central Montana (Martinka 1968).

Closed-canopy mature forests are needed to provide cover during severe winters or where snow depths exceed 46 centimeters (18 inches).

During mild winters, whitetails in the Northern Rocky Mountains region seem to prefer to feed in open areas and on south-facing slopes. In severe winters they tend to congregate in forested riparian habitats and lowlands. *Top-left photo by W. E. Steuerwald; courtesy of the U. S. Forest Service. Top-right photo courtesy of the Wyoming Game and Fish Department. Bottom photo by K. D. Swan; courtesy of the U. S. Forest Service.*

Whitetails move about more easily beneath trees, where snow depths are less than in the open. They often develop trails that provide access to feeding areas adjacent to suitable winter cover. Closed canopies of mature forest along streams and lowlands are extremely important whitetail habitat.

Logging and fire significantly alter whitetail habitat in the region. While deer are able to exploit new habitats created by small crown fires or cuts that occur near suitable cover, large clearcuts and burns tend to be avoided (Keay and Peek 1980). Surface fires in ponderosa pine create highly preferred forage. Clearcut and large burned areas may provide important forage if there is sufficient cover nearby. When mature forests are burned or cut, white-tailed deer may shift to adjacent areas during the severest times of winter, but seral regrowth on the burned or cut areas will attract the deer by providing excellent forage in spring and autumn. In the Swan Valley of Montana, whitetails made only light use of clearcuts in winter (Mundinger 1981c). Cuts and prescribed burns should be restricted to less than 8 hectares (20 acres) in size, and selection cuts that do not reduce overstories to less than 70 percent crown closure should be used if important whitetail habitat must be logged (Mundinger 1981c, Owens 1981).

Cattle and white-tailed deer coexist part of the year in lower forests of northern Idaho and eastern Washington. Browse was a major part of the diet for both species (Thilenius and Hungerford 1967), but competition was relatively light on moderately stocked ranges. Heavy grazing that reduces dense shrub understories and decreases production of important forage can greatly reduce the value of an area for whitetails in this region.

Where rangeland in the region has not deteriorated due to livestock overgrazing and there is a variety of forbs and shrubs, little competition occurs between livestock and whitetails for forage. However, as grazing causes deterioration, and cover and food values inherent in shrubs and forbs deteriorate, whitetail use of an area will decline. *Photo courtesy of the Washington Department of Game.*

Whitetails of the region ordinarily bed in areas of heavy cover where they can minimize their visibility to potential predators and exposure to harsh elements, particularly wind. However, when undisturbed in winter, more open bedding areas may be used during daylight. *Photo by Larry L. Irwin.*

SPECIAL PROBLEMS AND MANAGEMENT

White-tailed deer habitat in the Northern Rocky Mountains region is constantly being modified by human activity. When encroachment of housing occurs, harassment of deer by dogs can become a serious problem. While whitetails frequently coexist with housing developments where sufficient cover has been retained, dogs that are allowed to run loose can virtually preclude the presence of deer. In the Coeur d'Alene River area of Idaho, dogs killed at least 12 deer during the winter of 1975 (Lowry and McArthur 1978). Some deer were killed outright, others were forced into the river and drowned. As many as nine dogs in a group were seen chasing deer. In addition to direct mortality, harassment of whitetails during the stresses of winter may predispose animals to other forms of mortality.

The other form of human activity that is of major concern involves logging. Whitetails in the forested area of the western portions of this region exist in the proximity of heavy cover (Owens 1981, Mundinger 1981c), even in summer, and the areas that receive high deer use often are among the most productive of timber as well. Recommendations to use either small clearcuts less than 8 hectares (20 acres) in size or selective logging systems in whitetail habitat are less efficient from the timber management standpoint than are larger cuts (Mundinger 1981c, Owens 1981). Until recently, very little concern was evident over the effects of timber harvest on cover values for whitetails. Investigations in the Swan Valley of Montana (Mundinger 1981c) and the Palouse Range in Idaho (Owens 1981) indicate that the need to coordinate logging with whitetail habitat requirements is very important in the region.

These problems illustrate a fundamental issue—human activity at some levels benefits habitat and, at other levels, it detracts. Certainly some human activity that has cleared dense forest for croplands and pasture has benefited whitetails in many of the more densely forested regions of the Northwest, where the scarcity of available forage previously was a limiting factor. And early logging activity that created openings and brushfields where forage was interspersed with high quality cover was a benefit as well, since forage supplies were enhanced. However, as logging has intensified and cover values of important whitetail habitats have been affected adversely, concern has increased that deer, in turn, will be similarly influenced.

Small clearcuts less than 8 hectares (20 acres) in size will provide forage used by whitetails in the Northern Rocky Mountains region. Deciduous browse species such as redstem ceanothus and mountain maple, which are benefitted by clearcutting and broadcast burning after logging, are preferred shrubs. In addition, the variety of herbaceous species that proliferate for a few years after cutting will provide forage. Forbs that produce milky, latex-like sap, such as prickly lettuce and dandelions, also are consumed. On both winter and summer range, small cuts surrounded by dense conifer cover more than 9.1 meters (30 feet) tall appear to be used most. *Photo by Kurt Jenkins.*

The Dworshak Reservoir on the North Fork of the Clearwater River and Libby Reservoir on the Kootenai River have eliminated a substantial amount of whitetail habitat. The Libby Reservoir flooded 4,800 hectares (11,860 acres) of winter habitat in 1972 (Firebaugh 1971). The Dworshak Reservoir flooded an estimated 4,000 hectares (9,885 acres) of big game winter range and displaced several thousand white-tailed deer (U.S. Fish and Wildlife Service 1960).

Dworshak Reservoir also caused considerable losses of deer to coyotes (Meske 1972). At least 95 whitetails were killed and/or eaten on the ice by coyotes in the winter of 1971–1972, and significant predation occurred again in 1975–1976. Deer tend to concentrate on the ice during severe winters and are particularly vulnerable when footing is insecure.

When Dworshak Reservoir was filling during the winter of 1971–1972, at least 110 deer drowned when marooned on small islands of ice and debris. Drownings also occur when whitetails try to cross thin ice. Fluctuating water levels in the reservoir and development of recreational areas on winter range will hamper mitigation further.

Loss of habitat as a result of the construction of Libby Reservoir was accentuated by relocation of a railroad grade through prime deer range. There also was an increased chance of deer mortality resulting from their collision with trains.

Winter ranges are critical to the welfare of whitetails in the Northern Rocky Mountains region. Because they usually are located along river bottoms and lakeshores, these ranges are especially vulnerable to encroachment by human activity, and their loss tends to be permanent. There is a pressing need for more definitive studies of such impacts and means to control them. As encroachment continues, the need to manage and maintain existing whitetailed deer habitats becomes increasingly critical.

One of the unpredicted consequences of creating large water impoundments in the Northern Rocky Mountains region has been additional mortality of deer. Besides eliminating habitat and blocking routes of seasonal movement or migration, dams and reservoirs have some direct effects on deer mortality in winter. Whitetails congregating on or crossing impoundment ice sometimes fall through and drown. Others slip and cannot regain their footing, thus becoming easy prey for coyotes. These whitetails fell through thin ice on the Dworshak Reservoir of northern Idaho and struggle futilely to escape. *Photo by Mike Harrop; courtesy of Ferris Weddle.*

If unmolested, whitetails in the Northern Rocky Mountains region are easily conditioned to the presence of people, as exemplified by this doe in Glacier National Park, which was photographed from less than 6 meters (20 feet) away. The deer's posture indicates alertness but not alarm. *Photo by James Peek.*

OUTLOOK

The outlook for whitetails in the Northern Rocky Mountains region can be tied directly to how human activity affects the deer. Whitetails in this region have not been given much attention because the region has a wide variety of big game species, most of which require more consideration in management, and the whitetail has always been relatively abundant.

Therefore, the greatest problems for conservation and management of whitetails are (1) lack of information and (2) lack of consideration for their welfare by humans. However, consideration for the needs of whitetails is increasing in the region. And with greater appreciation of the special needs for dense cover and awareness of how to coexist with the species, whitetails will continue to be a productive and important resource of the region.

Chapter 29

SOUTHERN ROCKY MOUNTAINS

Wain Evans
Assistant Director
New Mexico Department of Game and Fish
Santa Fe, New Mexico

The white-tailed deer in the Southern Rocky Mountains region is too common to be considered rare and too rare to be considered common. Its innocuous habits do not give it the aura of mystique associated with bears, mountain lions and exotic big game. Nonhunting interests tend to ignore the species because it is a game animal. Yet, as a game animal, the whitetail is overshadowed in this region by the larger and more numerous mule deer.

It is not surprising, therefore, that the white-tailed deer in the Southern Rocky Mountains region is a little studied and largely unknown species. In New Mexico, the available information is confined mainly to general surveys of distribution (Ligon 1927, Raught 1967) and to incidental observations reported in management documents by the Department of Game and Fish. In Arizona, the white-tailed deer has fared somewhat better—it is more numerous than in New Mexico and enjoys a degree of popularity among trophy hunters. Of the 117 trophy-record heads of the Coues white-tailed deer listed by the Boone and Crockett Club (Nesbitt and Wright 1981), 94 came from Arizona and only 2 from New Mexico.

ENVIRONMENT

Location

White-tailed deer range in the Southern Rocky Mountains region extends westward from a north-south line formed by mountain ranges at the westward extension of the southern Great Plains in New Mexico into the southwestern third of Arizona. The northern boundary in Arizona represents the northern range terminus of white-tailed deer in the Southwest (Figure 98).

Texas and Coues or Arizona white-tailed deer are the two recognized subspecies that occur within the region. The Rio Grande River in New Mexico generally is considered the dividing line between the two subspecies (Raught 1967, Ligon 1927).

The actual distribution of whitetails is pocketed and discontinuous. The largest block of continuous habitat extends from the Mogollon Plateau in central Arizona southeastward into New Mexico, terminating in the Black Range west of the Rio Grande.

In the southern portion of the range, occupied habitats have an island configuration represented by infrequent water courses and isolated mountain ranges rising from the desert floor.

To the east, where the southern Plains encounter the mountains in New Mexico, an almost continuous band of habitat exists from the Colorado line to the Texas border. However, within this band, the whitetail only occurs in scattered localities. In recent years, few white-tailed deer have been seen north of the Sacramento Mountains. Scattered and unverified reports suggest marginal populations may still exist in pockets in the Sangre De Cristo Mountains from Santa Fe northward. (W. Snyder personal communication:1979).

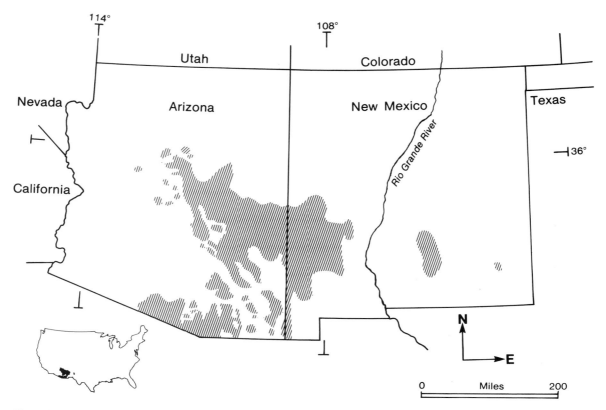

Figure 98. White-tailed deer range in the Southern Rocky Mountains region (from Southeastern Cooperative Wildlife Disease Study 1983).

A young Coues whitetail buck in Arizona. *Photo by Jerry Day; courtesy of the Arizona Game and Fish Department.*

Physiography

Whitetails occur in a wide range of habitat types, from elevations of 1,000 meters (3,280 feet) in Altar Valley, Arizona (Arizona Game and Fish Department 1977) to 4,200 meters (13,780 feet) in the Sangre De Cristo Mountains of northern New Mexico (Raught 1967). The animals generally are most abundant at elevations of 1,200 to 2,400 meters (3,940–7,875 feet).

White-tailed deer are observed most frequently in rough brushy country (Raught 1967). They seem to thrive on terrain too rugged for mule deer or livestock (with the exception of the domestic goat). Typical whitetail habitat consists of predominately steep mountains with an intricate network of deep, wide canyons interlaced with short and relatively shallow drainages (Arizona Game and Fish Department 1977).

Climate and Weather

Two periods of relatively high precipitation occur in summer and winter. Winter precipitation occurs from December through mid-March, falling as snow in New Mexico and in the higher elevations of Arizona. Spring and autumn normally are the driest times of the year. Occasionally, no precipitation will occur from April until summer rains begin in late June or early July. At higher elevations, summer rains may occur as afternoon showers almost daily through September or mid-October. At lower elevations, precipitation is reduced and occurs with less frequency.

Most of the region's white-tailed deer range receives 25 centimeters (10 inches) or more of precipitation annually. Some of the highest peaks within the whitetail range receive more than 63 centimeters (25 inches). Deer densities generally are highest where the annual precipitation averages about 38 centimeters (15 inches)—on island mountains in the southern portion of the region (Arizona Game and Fish Department 1977).

Temperatures within the best whitetail habitat generally range from about 38 degrees Celsius (100 degrees Fahrenheit) in early summer to 4.4 to 10 degrees Celsius (40–50 degrees Fahrenheit) in winter. In the northern mountains, summer temperatures seldom reach 27 degrees Celsius (80 degrees Fahrenheit), and below-zero temperatures (Fahrenheit) are common in the winter.

Vegetation

Detailed information on the vegetation of the region has been presented by G. Day (1964), Short et al. (1977), Wallmo (1951) and Barsch (1975).

In Arizona and extreme southwestern New Mexico, the principal habitats of white-tailed deer are within two major vegetative communities of Madrean evergreen woodland, as described by Brown and Lowe (1974). More than 75 percent of the whitetail harvest in Arizona comes from the oak woodland and the oak/pine woodland communities (Arizona Game and Fish Department 1977).

Riparian deciduous forests and desert grasslands are important to whitetails in both states. Upland desert communities of Sonoran desert scrub also are important in southwestern Arizona. The oak woodlands and pine woodlands of Arizona usually contain a mixture of oaks and juniper, varying from dense canopy to an open aspect where trees are intermixed with grass. At slightly higher elevations, the oak/pine woodlands are characterized in Arizona by Chihuahua and Apache pine and various species of oaks.

Riparian areas from 1,000 to 2,000 meters (3,280–6,560 feet) elevation historically were important whitetail habitat and, where free of human encroachment, still are. In many areas, human settlement, development, recreation, farming and ranching have destroyed or severely damaged the mixed broadleaf communities.

In northern portions of the region's whitetail range and in the higher mountains to the south, coniferous mountain forests form the major habitat type. Above 2,400 meters (7,875 feet), this type is characterized by stands of Douglas-fir and white fir, which become intermingled with ponderosa pine at lower elevations. Other species include Gambel and silverleaf oak, trembling aspen and New Mexican locust (Arizona Game and Fish Department 1977).

A Coues whitetail doe in southwestern New Mexico. Riparian habitat is important to whitetails throughout their range in the Southern Rocky Mountains region. *Photo by Starr Jenkins; courtesy of the U.S. Forest Service.*

WHITETAIL POPULATIONS

History and Status

Historical records suggest that white-tailed deer were more numerous and widely distributed when the white man arrived in the region than they are today. Guadalupe Hall, who was fatally shot in 1893, reported that, in the winter near the Animas, Chiricahua and San Luis mountains of New Mexico and Arizona, he saw large numbers of white-tailed deer congregating as they moved to lower country (Raught 1967:53). Hall claimed to have observed "hundreds of bucks" assembling for the move, and they appeared as a "forest of horns." Even allowing for exaggeration, any event remotely resembling Hall's report is unknown today.

During the Mexican boundary survey in 1855, naturalist C. B. R. Kennerly observed whitetails feeding on the hillsides near present-day Nogales, Arizona (Davis 1982:82). By mid-morning, the deer disappeared into dense shrubbery along the streams, at which time ". . . they could be killed as easily as rabbits by a hunter passing through the undergrowth with a gun charged with buckshot."

Mearns (1907) reported that white-tailed deer were abundant on both sides of the San Luis Mountains southeast of Cloverdale, where many deer were killed to furnish food for Mearns' biological survey party.

It seems likely that the islandlike distribution of the white-tailed deer in the Southern Rocky Mountains region began to take its present form during the settlement and development period following the Civil War. Prospecting and mining interests in the region in the latter half of the 1800s flourished and created further demand for beef and other agricultural products. Farming activities increased along the available water courses and the riparian vegetation began to disappear. Large numbers of cattle trailed westward from Texas and converted much of the area to overgrazed rangeland. The railroad brought homesteaders and squatters from the East and moved the fruits of settlement labor to market. Railroads needed fuel, ties and water. Timber was removed in large quantities from the higher mountains in the region to support the expanding economy. Water, in short supply and in great demand, was diverted from normal courses into irrigation ditches and pipelines. As free water became more difficult to find and

Late-1800s hunting party in the mountains of southern Arizona, with a displayed bag of 10 Coues white-tailed deer. *Photo by Ed Irwin; courtesy of the Irwin Brothers Collection, Arizona Historical Society.*

distribute, wells were drilled to tap the underground sources and water tables began to drop. Although poorly documented, the impact of these activities on wildlife, including white-tailed deer, must have been tremendous. In addition to the habitat destruction, the high cost of living, characteristic of a frontier economy, encouraged the human inhabitants to exploit the wildlife resource for food and profit. Market hunting was a common practice around southwestern population centers. Eliminated from its habitat along the major water courses and from other areas around population centers, the deer remained only in the least accessible mountains.

Even today, there is evidence that the range of whitetails in the Southwest is being restricted further, particularly in New Mexico. Raught (1967) compared the distribution of whitetails in the late 1960s to that reported in the late 1920s (Ligon 1927). Ligon identified a pocket of deer near Socorro, New Mexico, that since disappeared. One block of continuous whitetail distribution in the mountains of Catron and Grant counties declined in size and broke into two parts. Another continuous distribution of whitetails, from the headwaters of the Pecos River northward in the Sangre De Cristo Mountains to the Colorado border, dissolved into a pocket at the head of the Pecos River and another southwest of Raton. A small pocket of white-tailed deer east of Santa Fe disappeared.

In contrast to mule deer, whitetails have decreased in abundance in this century. In the late 1920s, white-tailed deer were more numerous than mule deer in southwestern New Mexico. In the 1930s, however, this relationship was reversed. Also during the early 1930s, whitetails were more abundant than mule deer in the Black Range. But in 1935, a heavy die-off occurred, and mule deer has been the predominant species since (Raught 1967). A whitetail die-off occurred in 1935 near Pueblo Park, New Mexico—the result of leptospirosis, a disease common among livestock (R. Snyder personal communication:1961), and the whitetail never recovered its predominant status over the mule deer (Raught 1967).

The white-tailed deer population in Arizona appears to be more stable than is the one in New Mexico. Little change has been indicated in the percentage of whitetails in the total hunter harvest during the last 25 years (Arizona Game and Fish Department 1977).

Population Size

The total deer population in New Mexico was estimated at 279,950 in 1977 (Ames 1978), of which whitetails comprised about 17,950, or approximately 7 percent. In Arizona, there were an estimated 24,000 whitetails in 1971, or approximately 17 percent of the state's total deer population (Arizona Game and Fish Department 1977).

Productivity

White-tailed deer productivity in the Southern Rocky Mountains region is difficult to assess. On surveys in New Mexico, observers see whitetails so rarely that meaningful information on sex ratios and fawn counts is not available. In Arizona, winter surveys indicate a buck/doe ratio of 1:1.34–2.27, excluding young of the year. If this ratio is representative of the fawning season, then 57 to 69 percent of the breeding population consists of potentially reproductive does.

In reconstructing the reproductive history of Coues whitetail does less than four years old in the Santa Rita Mountains of Arizona, Smith (1971) indicated that none of the observed yearlings fawned at one year of age. Two-year-old does had a ratio of 0.75 fawn per doe. Since a doe's first conception usually results in a single fawn, Smith's data suggest that approximately 25 percent of the two-year-old does did not give birth. In the three- and four-year-old age groups, the fawn-to-doe ratios were 1.33 and 1.50, respectively. The sex ratio among fawns was approximately 1:1 (Arizona Game and Fish Department 1977).

G. Day (1964) found an average conception rate of 87 percent for mature does in the Chiricahua Mountains of Arizona.

Food

In spring, or a few weeks after the rainy season begins, whitetails consume significant amounts of the new twig and leaf growth from numerous woody species. Many kinds of annual and perennial forbs and some grasses also are eaten during this time. At least 134 are known to be sources of food for deer (Arizona Game and Fish Department 1977). Vetch, fleabane, coralbells and falsetarragon sagebrush are a few of the more important species.

Forbs and grasses are important spring foods for whitetails in the Southern Rocky Mountains region. *Photo by Dave Daughtry; courtesy of the Arizona Game and Fish Department.*

At the end of the growing season in autumn, the whitetails' diet shifts toward browse. Deciduous leaves of woody species as well as the dried parts of some herbaceous perennials and annuals are consumed. After first frost, fallen leaves comprise a significant portion of the diet. The importance of browse in the diet continues to increase into the winter and spring. Mountain mahogany probably is the most important species (Arizona Game and Fish Department 1977). However, silktassel, desert ceanothus and skunkbush sumac also are eaten.

With the coming of warmer weather in early spring, filaree is one of the first species to green up. It is a choice forage of whitetails (Arizona Game and Fish Department 1977).

SPECIAL PROBLEMS

There is a decided lack of information concerning basic factors that control the whitetail populations in the Southern Rocky Mountains region. Most statements regarding limiting factors are largely speculative and based on findings from studies of mule deer. The relative emphasis on research and management is not likely to change since the whitetail is at the periphery of its range and approaching its limit

of tolerance in the region's harsh, arid climate. Realistically, then, the goal should be to stabilize the populations and prevent further habitat deterioration.

Competition

During dry years, particularly after a prolonged drought, the whitetail may compete with cattle and mule deer. Summer is the most critical season. If rains come, forage produced during the growing season will be sufficient to meet the needs of the whitetail and other ruminants through the dormant periods. If the rains fail, hard times are imminent and competitive relationships intensify. During summer, nutritional levels of common forage resources usually remain adequate, but the quality and quantity of forage required for winter invariably are reduced drastically. Animal species that normally have a degree of separation in food preferences and feeding zones during times of plenty tend to converge during drought years and enter into direct competition. Because of its small size and relatively limited home range, the whitetail is at a decided disadvantage in competition with the larger, more mobile mule deer and cattle.

Predation

In Arizona, predation was involved in 50 percent of the nonhunting causes of death identified in whitetail carcasses found from 1946 to 1960 (Arizona Game and Fish Department 1977). This estimate is conservative, since many dead deer—especially fawns—likely went undetected.

In Texas, predation appears in part to be tied to the weather cycle. Knowlton (1964) speculated that predation on fawns by coyotes was lowest during the spring rainy seasons when food supplies were most abundant.

Disease and Parasites

Disease usually has little impact on whitetails in the Southern Rocky Mountains region. Local problems may develop, however. In one study, disease was reported to have accounted for 29 percent of the nonhunting whitetail deaths (Arizona Game and Fish Department 1977). Incidental reports have been received of deaths caused by selenium poisoning and mucosal disease. Shipping fever is the suspected cause of some deaths.

Both fly larvae and winter ticks are common among whitetails of all age classes (Arizona Game and Fish Department 1977), but usually present little significant problem, except to whitetails weakened by malnutrition or old age, or when the infestations reach severe proportions.

Regulation of Hunting

In New Mexico, white-tailed deer are not distinguished from mule deer in hunting regulations. The hunting season is in November with an unlimited number of licenses. The bag limit generally is one buck per hunter. The annual harvest of white-tailed deer is not tabulated separately from that of mule deer and probably does not exceed 500 animals.

In Arizona, permits to hunt white-tailed deer are limited and allocated to hunters by random selection. Each hunter is assigned to a specific management unit so as to distribute hunting pressure. In recent years the bag limit in Arizona has been one buck per hunter. The annual whitetail buck harvest usually is 2,000 to 3,500 deer.

A startled trophy whitetail buck lunges from a grassy bed. About 80 percent of the documented record-class Coues whitetails have come from southeastern Arizona. *Photo by Kelly Neal; courtesy of the Arizona Game and Fish Department.*

MANAGEMENT

Current Practices

Occasionally, hunts are organized to reduce local overpopulations of deer. Otherwise there is little management directed specifically toward the whitetail in Arizona and New Mexico. Most whitetail habitats would not suffer overpopulations even if hunting in the region ceased entirely. The chronic problem throughout most of the region is too few deer rather than too many. Since only bucks are hunted, the harvest has little impact on the population.

Habitat manipulations such as selective burning may benefit whitetail habitat (Barsch 1975). However, such practices usually have livestock interests in mind rather than wildlife. In pinyon juniper habitats, which are common through the region's whitetail range, some of the management practices may harm rather than benefit the deer (Short et al. 1977).

Even when habitat manipulations benefit deer, they are costly. In 1975, it cost a minimum of $220 per hectare ($81 per acre) to treat the land (Arizona Game and Fish Department 1977). It is unlikely that whitetail numbers will increase enough to justify such cost.

Many biologists feel that livestock grazing is the most critical whitetail habitat management problem, especially during drought years. They recommend that livestock numbers be managed in response to range conditions, but this is not always possible and the costs usually are high.

OUTLOOK

White-tailed deer in the Southern Rocky Mountains region, because of marginal habitat conditions and livestock competition in many areas, probably will continue to be relatively scarce. Public interest will prevent the whitetail from decreasing to a "threatened" status. However, even under the most intensive management, the whitetail population cannot approach the productivity and abundance of eastern habitats. In Arizona and New Mexico, at least, the whitetail will continue to be sought by hunters who prize its novelty, beauty and other trophy qualities. In most cases it is and will remain a valued resource.

Chapter 30

MEXICO AND CENTRAL AMERICA

Eustorgio Méndez
Head
Department of Zoology
Gorgas Memorial Laboratory
Panama, Republic of Panama

ENVIRONMENT

Physiography and Ecoregions

The extensive landmass embracing Mexico and the Central America isthmus represents an assemblage of geographic elements influenced by diverse climatic conditions. Thousands of volcanoes and igneous extrusions form mountain chains, and numerous rivers empty their waters into the Pacific Ocean or the Caribbean Sea. Several volcanic lakes—such as Atitlan in Guatemala, and Managua and Nicaragua in the Republic of Nicaragua—are impressive bodies of water.

Alpine forests of fir, pine and oak give way to moist evergreen forests at lower altitudes (Figure 99). These in turn merge with the vegetation of the coastal lowlands. Tropical rain forests exist in some areas, particularly on the Atlantic slope. Arid sectors often predominate, notably in Mexico and Guatemala. Cultivated lands of excellent to poor productivity are found scattered throughout. Grazing lands and typical savannahs are concentrated on the Pacific slopes, particularly in Costa Rica and Panama, and within the tidal influence of both coasts. The intertidal zones support impenetrable mangrove swamps.

Climate and Weather

The four seasons characteristic of North America are clearly distinguishable over most of Mexico. In contrast, only dry and wet periods are identifiable for the Central American countries. Rainfall is abundant in the Atlantic lowlands and foothills, but is scant west of the mountain chains and in areas where the local climate has been influenced by burning, felling of trees and other activities.

Mexico. About 40 percent of the Mexican territory is tropical, with a mean annual temperature above 24 degrees Celsius (75 degrees Fahrenheit). The temperate zone has a mean temperature of 18 to 24 degrees Celsius (65–75 degrees Fahrenheit); and in the cool zone the mean temperature is 13 to 18 degrees Celsius (55–65 degrees Fahrenheit). There are areas of the country 3,000 meters (9,840 feet) above sea level, with a mean annual temperature below 10 degrees Celsius (50 degrees Fahrenheit). On volcanic peaks above 4,300 meters (14,100 feet), the mean annual temperature is less than 0 degree Celsius (32 degrees Fahrenheit).

On the Atlantic slope, annual precipitation may reach 400 centimeters (157 inches). The Pacific slope is much drier, and rainfall usually is less than 40 centimeters (16 inches) per year.

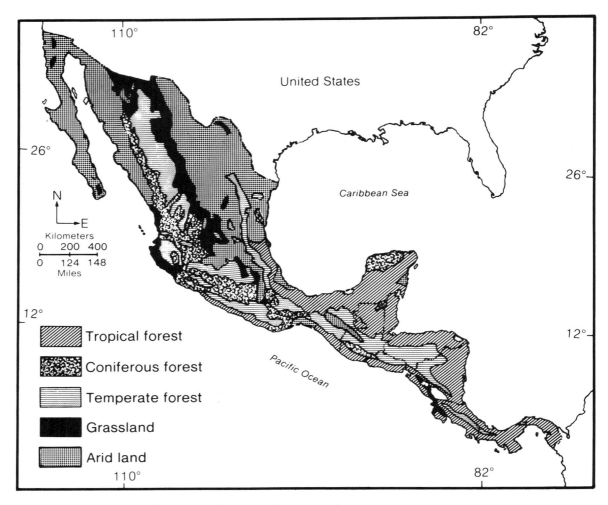

Figure 99. Major vegetational regions of Mexico and Central America.

Mean annual precipitation for Mexico is estimated at 58 centimeters (23 inches).

Guatemala. Guatemala has a complex climate. In the lowlands, from sea level to 600 meters (1,970 feet) elevation, the average annual temperature is about 32 degrees Celsius (90 degrees Fahrenheit). From 600 to 1,800 meters (1,970–5,900 feet) elevation, there is a temperate climate, with an average annual temperature of 22 degrees Celsius (72 degrees Fahrenheit). The higher basins of western Guatemala, between 1,800 and 3,250 meters (5,900 and 10,660 feet) above sea level, display an average temperature of 15 degrees Celsius (59 degrees Fahrenheit).

On the Caribbean slope, rainfall is heavy and exceeds 500 centimeters (197 inches) annually. In the much drier areas, mean annual precip-

itation is less than 100 centimeters (39 inches).
Belize. The tropical climate of Belize is influenced by the Caribbean waters. In the mountains, however, temperatures are slightly cooler. In northern and southeastern parts of the country, the mean annual temperature is about 28 degrees Celsius (82 degrees Fahrenheit), while in the uplands, it is approximately 22 degrees Celsius (72 degrees Fahrenheit). Average mean temperature for all of Belize is 25 degrees Celsius (77 degrees Fahrenheit).

Rainfall in Belize is more concentrated in the southern portion, where it reaches about 500 centimeters (197 inches) annually. In the North it is about 155 centimeters (61 inches). Average annual precipitation in Belize is 328 centimeters (129 inches).
Honduras. The climate of Honduras is hot and

humid in the coastal lowlands, and temperate in areas between 300 and 600 meters (985 and 1,970 feet) altitude, where the mean annual temperature is 26 to 28 degrees Celsius (79–82 degrees Fahrenheit). In valleys and mountain basins from 600 to 1,300 meters (1,970–4,265 feet) elevation, the mean annual temperature is 19 to 23 degrees Celsius (66–74 degrees Fahrenheit). Above 2,000 meters (6,560 feet), it drops to about 14 degrees Celsius (58 degrees Fahrenheit).

The northern and eastern coastal lands of Honduras get 170 to 300 centimeters (67–118 inches) of rain annually. The Pacific plains and mountain slopes receive 150 to 203 centimeters (59–80 inches) of annual precipitation, but some of the higher mountains are more humid and receive more than 300 centimeters (118 inches). Some valleys and mountain basins are relatively dry, with annual precipitation ranging from 102 to 170 centimeters (40–67 inches). The average annual precipitation for Honduras is 115 centimeters (45 inches).

El Salvador. Two seasons are characteristic of El Salvador. The wet or winter season extends from May to November, and the dry or summer season occurs from November to May. In Pacific lowlands and coastal areas of the country, the mean temperature is 29 degrees Celsius (85 degrees Fahrenheit). The higher regions are somewhat cooler, with the temperature fluctuating from 17 to 23 degrees Celsius (63–73 degrees Fahrenheit).

On El Salvador's coast and the Pacific inlands, annual precipitation averages about 173 centimeters (68 inches). The northern and southern mountain ranges have more than 200 centimeters (79 inches) of mean annual precipitation. On valleys and plateaulike areas, annual rainfall averages about 130 centimeters (51 inches). The average annual amount of precipitation known for the country as a whole is about 254 centimeters (100 inches).

Nicaragua. In the eastern lowlands of Nicaragua, the climate is hot and humid, with a mean annual temperature of 26 degrees Celsius (79 degrees Fahrenheit). The western lowlands are drier, and the mean annual temperature is 29 degrees Celsius (85 degrees Fahrenheit). Mountain ranges in the central part of the country have a humid, temperate climate, and the temperature ranges approximately from 9 to 22 degrees Celsius (48–72 degrees Fahrenheit) on the highest mountain peak.

On the country's Atlantic coast, the average annual rainfall is 634 centimeters (250 inches). The Pacific coast, which is much drier, has a mean annual precipitation of 191 centimeters (75 inches). In the central highlands, precipitation is moderate, averaging about 200 centimeters (79 inches) per year. Nicaragua's mean annual precipitation is about 191 centimeters (75 inches).

Costa Rica. Costa Rica has both tropical and subtropical climates. Regions less than 900 meters (2,950 feet) in altitude are more torrid and have mean annual temperatures of 22 to 27 degrees Celsius (72–80 degrees Fahrenheit). Between 900 and 2,300 meters (2,950 and 7,545 feet) elevation, the climate is temperate, and the mean annual temperature is about 16 degrees Celsius (61 degrees Fahrenheit). Above 2,300 meters (7,545 feet), the climate is cooler, with a mean annual temperature of about 10 degrees Celsius (50 degrees Fahrenheit).

East of the continental divide in Costa Rica, rainfall is heavy; in critical areas the mean annual precipitation is more than 600 centimeters (236 inches). On the Pacific slope, mean annual rainfall is about 250 centimeters (98 inches). In general, the country's annual precipitation averages about 185 centimeters (73 inches).

Panama. Panama has a tropical climate modified by ocean winds. In the lowlands, from sea level to 600 meters (1,970 feet), it is very hot and humid, the temperature ranging from 24 to 34 degrees Celsius (75–95 degrees Fahrenheit). At higher elevations the climate becomes moderate, with temperatures from 16 to 23 degrees Celsius (61–73 degrees Fahrenheit)—and about 9 degrees Celsius (48 degrees Fahrenheit) at Volcan Baru, in the western mountain range.

The Caribbean slope, with no distinct dry season, receives 495 to 627 centimeters (195–247 inches) of rain per year. On the Pacific slope, precipitation decreases to less than 100 centimeters (39 inches) on western lands. However, rainfall is high in evergreen forests of the eastern part of the country, with more than 500 centimeters (197 inches) of rain per year. Collectively, Panama has a mean annual precipitation of 300 centimeters (118 inches).

Human Dimensions

The size and human population characteristics of Mexico and the Central American countries are shown in Table 82.

Table 82. Area and human population size and density of Mexico and Central American countries, 1980.

Country	Area		Human population	Human population density	
	Square kilometers	Square miles		Square kilometer	Square mile
Mexico	1,972,546	761,600	62,944,000	34.1	88.3
Belize	22,965	8,866	158,000	5.8	15.0
Guatemala	108,889	42,042	7,006,000	64.3	166.5
Honduras	112,088	43,277	3,691,000	31.8	82.3
El Salvador	21,156	8,168	4,436,000	211.0	546.4
Nicaragua	127,664	49,291	2,732,500	22.0	56.9
Costa Rica	50,900	19,653	2,183,600	42.7	110.5
Panama	77,082	29,761	1,830,200	23.7	61.3
Total	2,493,290	962,658	88,981,300		
Average				54.4	140.9

WHITETAIL POPULATIONS

Since antiquity, the white-tailed deer has been an important game animal in Mexico and Central America. Archaeological searches in Mexico, Panama and other Latin American countries have revealed abundant remains of white-tailed deer and confirmed its important role in the development of pre-Columbian cultures (Bennett 1968, Linares 1976, Linares and White 1980, MacNeish 1964, MacNeish et al. 1967, Willey and McGimsey 1954, Willey et al. 1965). The deer extensively served as food and as a source of leather, sinew and other products such as awls, projectile points, tine flakers, bone scrapers, hammers and needles fashioned from the bones and antlers.

Over most of Middle America the whitetail is known by the Spanish names "venado" and "venado cola blanca." Mexican Indian groups have given to the whitetail such names as "Axuni" (the Tarascos), "Guej" (the Lacandones), "Macha" (the Huicholes), "Matzatl" (the Mexicas), "Muxati" (the Coras), and "Phatehe" (the Otomis). Central American Mayan names for whitetails are "Ceh" and "Uac Nac." In Panama, the deer is called "Beguí Torro" by Choco Indians and "Coée Pebenicat" by Cuna Indians.

There is a paucity of information on current populations, distribution and mortality of white-tailed deer (Figure 100). Only a minority of the local people regard deer hunting as recreation, but the whitetail still remains an important source of food and a primary source of animal protein.

Well-watered, natural pasturelands interspersed with wooded areas are the preferred whitetail habitat. However, the deer have spread into a variety of habitats, ranging from dense tropical rain forests to upland desert. Intensive agriculture, cattle ranching, lowland drainage, destruction of forests, pollution of water, indiscriminate hunting, and excessive use of insecticides and herbicides are responsible for a severe decline in deer numbers throughout Latin America since the 1950s.

The sucking louse *Solenopotes bipinolosus,* the biting louse *Tricholipeurus lipeuroides,* and the deer ked *Lipoptena (Lipoptenella) mazamae* are found throughout Mexico and Central America. In this region the whitetail also is an occasional host of the human bot fly *Dermatobia hominis.* Nasal bot flies (*Cephenemyia*) also have been detected in deer but have not been reported heretofore in the literature. *Amblyomma cajanense, A. oblongoguttatum, Anocentor nitens, Haemaphysalis juxtatochi, Ixodes affinis, I. boliviensis* and other species of ticks have been found on the whitetails of Middle America.

In Mexico and Central America, the whitetail is host to various helminths, including the serpentine trichostrongyle (*Trichostrongylus colubriformis*), the small intestinal roundworm *Cooperia pectinata,* the sheep wireworm *Haemonchus contortus,* the thread lungworm *Dictyocaulus filaria,* the nodular worm *Oesophagostomum venulosum* and the gullet worm *Gongylonema pulchrum* among the nematodes, the sheep tapeworm *Moniezia expansa* among the cestodes, and the large American fluke *Fascioloides magna,* the lancet fluke *Dicrocoelium dendriticum* and the "rumen fluke" *Paramphistomum cervi* among the trematodes.

In Middle America, brucellosis does not appear to be a real problem and, at present, foot-and-mouth disease does not exist. Such dis-

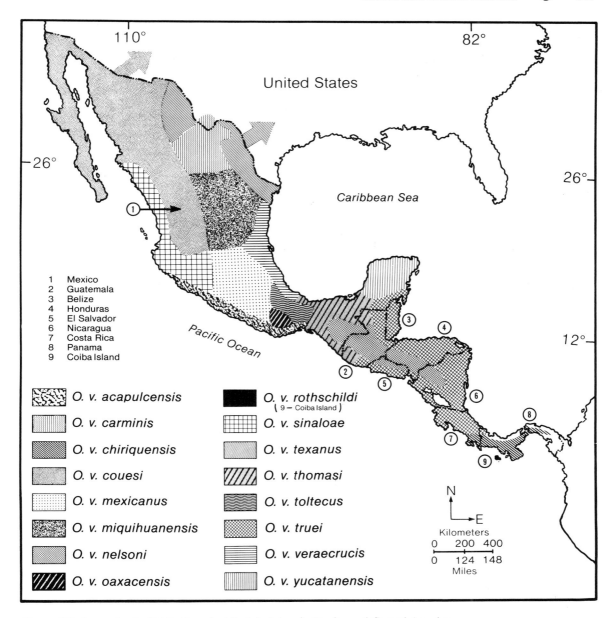

Figure 100. Approximate distribution of white-tailed deer in Mexico and Central America.

eases as rabies, Q fever, anaplasmosis, tuberculosis, necrotic stomatitis and others have not been evaluated.

The food preferred by deer, and their competition with other herbivores, are not well-known in certain areas of Latin America.

Whitetails are victims of various predators. The jaguar ranks first, followed by the mountain lion. These cats occur throughout Mexico and Central America, but are decreasing rapidly. The coyote ranges in Mexico and Central America as far south as Panama (Méndez et al. 1981). The gray wolf is restricted to isolated regions in the northern half of Mexico. Black and grizzly bear occasionally prey on deer, but are becoming rare; the grizzly has been almost extirpated.

Strategies of managing deer in Mexico and Central America should take into consideration the ways that various cultures perceive and utilize the natural resources available to them (Bennett 1976). A major concern in this connection should be with understanding the ecology and traditions of the Indian and non-Indian cultures that constitute the human population of this vast and diverse region. Among the major factors contributing to the loss of various important wildlife populations (including white-tailed deer) in some areas of Central America are (1) scant attention to conservation education and (2) lack of prudent land use.

Mexico

Most of Mexico consists of an elevated plateau transected by the Sierra Madre Occidental and the Sierra Madre Oriental mountain chains. These ranges come together to form the Sierra Madre del Sur, an extremely volcanic chain containing the country's highest peaks. The coastal plains generally are low, flat and sandy.

Mexico is undergoing profound change as a consequence of continuous human population growth and resulting pressure on natural resources. However, it has one of the leading systems of natural parks and wildlife reserves in America. At present there are more than 20 national parks, several of which support white-tailed deer.

The white-tailed deer is the most common animal in Mexican zoos. Although the whitetail probably is the most important game animal in Mexico (Leopold 1959), its population is scattered and unstable in some areas. According to Ezcurra and Gallina (1981), high population densities of whitetails are concentrated in mixed pine/oak forest, mainly in the Sierra Madre Occidental. Areas of El Gavilán in Chihuahua, of the mountains south of Durango, of the mesas of the Sierra de Tamaulipas and of the Sierra del Carmen, in the State of Coahuila, maintain the highest deer densities (12–16 whitetails per square kilometer: 31–41 per square mile). The whitetail is absent from Baja California. In northern Mexico, the whitetail population has declined steadily since 1900 due to continuous habitat destruction and overharvest, and its future there is problematical (Baker 1957). In areas such as Morelos and the Valley of Mexico, whitetails have been extirpated completely. In some regions of the State of Chiapas, deer have been killed on the primary premise that they feed on and destroy bean trees.

The Mexican Wildlife Conservation Department presently is introducing whitetails into previously occupied habitats. Also, the San Cayetano Experimental Station in the State of Mexico, a unit of the Wildlife Conservation Department, is raising white-tailed deer in captivity (Hernández 1964). And pilot management projects currently are underway in El Ocotal Recreational Park, of the State of Mexico, as well as in other research areas (Alcocer and Velásquez 1978). Also, since 1968 a few cooperative cynegetic farms have been established successfully in lands not suitable for agriculture, mainly in the State of Tamaulipas (B. Villa personal communication:1983).

White-tailed deer in Mexico eat a variety of grasses, ferns, weeds, algae, sedges, mosses, mushrooms, fruits and other plant material. Observations in 1976 on seasonal foods of whitetails at La Michilía Biosphere Reserve, State of Durango, revealed that during the dry season, bushes such as cypress mistletoe, pointleaf manzanita and others are preferred (*see* Alcocer and Velásquez 1978). Buds of oaks, pines and other trees are highly selected. During the rainy season, whitetail consumption of grasses is increased, but bushes still are preferred. After autumn, the fruits of *Arbutus glandulosa* are very esteemed.

At La Michilía Biosphere, the whitetail breeding season has been observed to begin in November and end in January.

Subsistence, commercial and recreational hunting are practiced in Mexico. Venison is consumed by natives and foreigners. The hide, antlers and other parts of white-tailed deer are used in the production of such by-products as wallets, travel bags, knife handles, key cases and ornamental objects.

Maya hunters lure deer with wooden whistles, imitating calls during the breeding season. According to Leopold (1959), 30 to 40 percent of the whitetail population could be harvested annually, but hunting pressure usually was not that intense. Recently more pressure is being placed on deer. Whitetails often are hunted illegally with dogs and by jacklighting at night.

A federal hunting law issued in 1952 allows only one adult buck per hunter per year. Throughout most of Mexico the open season extends from 1 October to 31 December. Hunting of whitetails is prohibited in the States of Mexico, Morelos, Quaretaro, Jalisco, Michoacan, Hidalgo, Tlaxcala and the Federal District. In the warmer areas of Mexico, the season is closed only from 1 August to 30 September.

A prayer stick used by a Huichol Indian of La Mesa in Nayarit, Mexico, to bring good luck in deer hunting. *Photo courtesy of the Museum of the American Indian, Heye Foundation.*

Belize

The terrain of Belize generally is low and flat, particularly in the northern half. The highest mountains reach an altitude of about 1,128 meters (3,700 feet) in the Cockscomb range of the southern half. Extensive savannahs occur south of these mountains. Coastal lands consist of mangrove swamps.

Cattle raising and exploitation of forests have eliminated much of the deer habitat. Even so, deer commonly are found in second-growth forests and thickets, forest edges, pine savannahs, and sometimes in milpas and other terrains near forests. Despite considerable clearing, deer have not increased in most areas, and in some areas sharp decreases have been noted, due mainly to overhunting for meat (Frost 1974, 1977).

The whitetail diet in Belize includes fruits, nuts, grasses and browse. Hunters set fire to savannahs in the lowlands to stimulate new shoots for deer to eat. During the flood season (June-July), whitetails go near rice fields and other high areas to obtain food.

In Belize, whitetails tend to be solitary, but occasionally two or three animals may be seen together. Groups of more than three deer are unusual.

In 1945, the Belize government approved a wildlife protection ordinance to control hunting of deer and other animals. This legislation established a closed season from 1 July to 30 September for bucks and to 31 December for does. Hunting is permitted by license. Jacklighting is prohibited. Enforcement of regulations is not effective, however, since there is no control on private lands.

The white-tailed deer is harvested actively by natives and foreign hunters. Venison is in great demand and often included in hotel menus. Frost (1974) reported that it was sold at the Belize City market for $0.23 to 0.27 per kilogram ($0.10–0.12 per pound) in British Honduras currency and for $0.34 per kilogram ($0.15 per pound) at Orange Walk Town.

Two areas of the country have been set aside as national parks. A 5-square-kilometer (2-square-mile) park in northern Belize is a typical rainforest and contains whitetails that probably are hunted by Indians. A 206-square-kilometer (80-square-mile) park in the south is administered by the Belize Audubon Society, but does not contain deer.

Guatemala

Guatemala is a land of contrasting topography. Highlands are prevalent on the central and the southern sectors. Vast and sparsely populated forests are found in the north. A strip of land between Belize and Honduras constitutes the Atlantic coastline. The Pacific slope, where human population is more concentrated, is characterized by marshes and grasslands.

Wild or semiwild conditions are prevalent in four areas: Peten; the Caribbean lowlands; the mountains of Alta Vera Paz and northern Quiche; and the Pacific lowlands, which is the most heavily hunted (Handley 1950).

The white-tailed deer is common except near human settlements, particularly on the Pacific and Atlantic slopes. It is found in lowland rainforests, brush lands, savannahs, semicleared farmlands, mountain cloud forest and dry oak woods (Handley 1950), but where the white-tailed deer is abundant, it is destructive to crops such as sugarcane, grasses, cucurbitas and legumes (Aguilar 1971).

The Tikal National Park, in the jungles of Peten (northern Guatemala), sustains more white-tailed deer than the area did in ancient times. Other national parks with deer are Río Dulce, Atitlán, Fraternidad or Trifinio, Cuchumatanes, La Pasión, Lachá, Bisis, Sierra de Las Minas, Sierra de Santa Cruz and Ixcán. Whitetails also are found in the Río Mopán and Poptún wildlife reserves.

White-tailed deer is the primary game animal (Handley 1950) and is sought persistently by sportsmen, commercial hunters and, to a lesser degree, Indians. Although Indians represent the major segment of the nation's population, they have limited access to firearms. The usual practices of deer hunting in the country are driving, following a hound and stalking (Handley 1950). Venison is very much esteemed in Guatemala, and deer antler, hooves and hides are prized highly, by all ethnic groups, as hunting trophies and for art crafts. Hides contribute to an important leather industry.

A whitetail mask worn by a Quiche (Mayan) Indian representing the species during the Deer Dance in Guatemala. *Photo courtesy of the Museum of the American Indian, Heye Foundation.*

Mayan Indians of Guatemala reportedly still perform an annual Deer Dance that has its origin in the pre-Spanish Conquest period. It is a serious and demanding ritual that symbolizes the struggle between mankind and animals. Participants (men only) must endure purification and physical training in advance of the event. The actual ceremony involves persons dressed and masked elaborately—as are the Zutugil Indians shown here—to represent various animals and mankind, who then dance around a centerpole almost continuously for up to 15 days. The objective is for the mankind representative to outlast the animal characters, thereby evincing domination (*see* Kelsey and Osborne 1939, Osborne 1965, Pettersen 1976). The Deer Dance is not to be confused with another Mayan ceremony described by Bancroft (1886), that featured a deer head and served as a devotional display to the gods of chase. *Photo courtesy of the Museum of the American Indian, Heye Foundation.*

A general hunting law, issued by the Guatemalan government in April 1970, helps protect the white-tailed deer and a number of vertebrates by regulation of hunting and the establishment of national parks, wildlife reserves and hunting districts. The hunting season is closed from November to March. Jacklighting is prohibited for hunting deer.

Honduras

The Republic of Honduras, the second largest country in Central America, essentially is a plateau with fertile plains interrupted by deep valleys and by mountains that reach altitudes of over 3,000 meters (9,840 feet). Because of the country's rapidly expanding human population, much of the natural wildlife habitat has been lost. However, white-tailed deer still are found in vast, sparsely inhabited tracts, forest edges, clearings and prairies. They are abundant in the thinly populated Departamentos of Gracias a Dios and Olancho.

A survey made by Varela (1980) in the Departamento de Olancho showed that the whitetail is predominately a night feeder and consumes common bean, sensitive-plant, jagua, wild fig, corn, nance, guacimo, encino and roseapple.

In 1974, a Wildlife Conservation Department was created. Since then it has been actively engaged in evaluating the utilization of deer. A law promoting the conservation, protection and management of wildlife has been prepared and awaits passage. Such legislation would prohibit hunting white-tailed deer from 15 October to 15 November for does and from 15 April to 15 November for bucks. At present, whitetails are overhunted without discrimination as to age, but there is a tendency to kill more bucks than does. During daytime, the deer are hunted from ambush and with the aid of dogs. Night hunting with spotlights is done on occasion.

The whitetail's mating season in Honduras is from August through November, and fawns are born from March through June. Antlers are renewed in February and March, and normally have a dichotomous branch.

In view of the intensive deforestation and an alarming decline of wildlife, there is a great need in Honduras for the creation of national parks and other types of wildlife refuges. Various projects have been initiated in order to set aside these conservation areas.

El Salvador

The Republic of El Salvador is the smallest but most densely populated country in Central America (*see* Table 82). Much of its rich and diversified flora has given way to agriculture and settlements. A few strips of lush and undisturbed land are found, primarily in the southwest. These natural areas represent about 20 percent of the country.

El Salvador is largely a plateau with a general elevation of about 610 meters (2,000 feet). High volcanic mountains are located on the north and central portions, and mangrove forests occur along the coasts.

The white-tailed deer ranges from coastal areas to second-growth forests up to 2,000 meters (6,560 feet), and is found chiefly in prairies and forest margins. Although its numbers have progressively declined, the whitetail has survived in El Salvador under tremendous pressure from man. Little protection is afforded the deer, and it is hunted indiscriminately year round for food and for its other by-products. It seems to be replaced in heavy forests by brocket deer.

In recent years, conservation has received a great deal of attention in El Salvador. Attempts are being made to establish several national parks and wildlife refuges in the hope that they will preserve the white-tailed deer and its habitat. The most important national park project concerns El Trifino, a mountainous area connecting Guatemala, Honduras and El Salvador. Unless strong efforts are made to stop the destruction of forest habitat, the future of white-tailed deer and other wildlife will be in jeopardy.

Nicaragua

Nicaragua's volcanic topography includes a great depression that extends diagonally across the country from northwest to southeast. This basin, in which most of the country's inhabitants live, contains Lake Managua and Lake Nicaragua near the Pacific coast. The rest of the country is primarily mountainous. The major portion of the Atlantic coast is bordered by mangroves and swamps. The climate is hot and humid along the coasts, but cool in the mountains.

White-tailed deer occur along the low plains and the gentler mountains of the Caribbean and Pacific slopes, and are quite common in

Twin female whitetail fawns in Nicaragua. *Photo by Arleen Mayorga-Law; courtesy of the Nicaragua National Parks and Wildlife Service.*

some of the pine forests. Deer are hunted heavily near populated areas, but their current population decrease is due mainly to habitat destruction as a result of excessive forest cutting and burning.

The Indians, particularly the Miskitos, are skillful hunters and place a high premium on white-tailed deer meat. The hide is used to make shoes, wallets, purses, drums, belts and other commercial leather goods.

The absence of effective law enforcement severely curtails proper management of deer and other wildlife in Nicaragua. Many areas that supported deer populations in the past now are used to raise cattle. The need for creation of wildlife refuges and national parks is urgent. The Cosigüina Peninsula wildlife reserve was established in the southwestern corner of the country in the 1970s, but several more reserves are needed.

Costa Rica

Costa Rica essentially is an elevated plateau. Most of the inhabitants live in the central part, called the Meseta Central. Many of the subtropical zones have been converted to coffee plantations, cornfields or grazing lands. The native vegetation has been extensively destroyed along both coasts, but most severely on the Atlantic slope. Despite human population pressures, some wild areas remain practically undisturbed, and the government is attempting to preserve them. Since the early 1970s, more than six national parks have been created, and Costa Rica probably is doing more to preserve its natural resources than any other Central American country.

The whitetail in Costa Rica is distributed widely and prefers second-growth forests, plantations of evergreen oaks and pastures. Peasants, recreational hunters and Indians hunt the deer in daytime and by night with the aid of battery lamps. Dogs commonly are used in deer hunts in which several persons frequently participate.

In Costa Rica, the whitetail breeding season is from September to October. Fawns are born in May or June. Hunting pressure and habitat destruction have reduced the deer population seriously along the western Pacific slope. Here, whitetails probably were common on large farms that had a combination of forest, pasture, chaparral and crops. Approximately 60,000 whitetail hides were exported to South America in 1944, and the majority of them were from the Province of Guanacaste (Mena 1978).

Venison is a highly favored food of the country's Indians, Hispano-Indians, Europeans and Asiatics, and is offered in some restaurants. Antlers are used as trophies and to adorn native huts. Whitetail hides are converted into a variety of leather goods and used as carpets to dry beans, rice, corn and coffee. The Bribris and Cabécare Indians use the hides to manufacture hatchet bindings, slingshots, drums and bed ornaments (R. A. Schlabach personal communication:1975).

In 1970, the National Assembly created a law protecting wild animals and regulating their use. Commercial hunting was prohibited, and recreational hunting was permitted during established seasons. In 1973, conservation authorities prohibited deer hunting for two years, but the results were unsatisfactory because of weak law enforcement. Currently, Costa Rica is divided into four hunting zones for big game (including whitetail and brocket deer). Killing of deer is limited to two animals per year per hunter in three of the zones. Hunting is prohibited completely in a major portion of the zone along the Atlantic slope.

Telemetric studies of whitetail home range and daily movements are being conducted by Dr. Miguel A. Rodriguez at the Palo Verde Wildlife Refuge, an area of 75 square kilometers (29 square miles) in the northeastern part of the country (C. Vaughan personal communication:1983).

Panama

The Republic of Panama has a diversified topography, including two major mountain chains, grasslands, valleys, mangrove forests and several rivers.

Once abundant in Panama, the white-tailed deer declined rapidly with destruction of the primeval forest habitat, development of the cattle industry and agriculture, and excessive hunting. It now is restricted to the zone from the central and western coastline to the mountains, primarily in open areas where the original forest has been disturbed (Méndez 1968). Whitetails sometimes make incursions into croplands and pastures. Their food consists of tender grasses, tree bark, tender branches, small mushrooms and fruits such as yellow mombin and purple mombin.

The whitetail is hunted in Panama for recreation, market and subsistence. Its meat is highly desired. Deer often are kept as pets, and some people raise them for profit. A fawn is worth about $50 in U.S. currency.

An insular race, *O. v. rothschildi*, inhabits Coiba Island—about 35 kilometers (22 miles) long and 21 kilometers (13 miles) wide and located near the Pacific Coast of Panama. This small subspecies stands about 0.7 meter (2.3 feet) tall at the shoulders, about the size of a domestic goat. Carnivores and other predators are absent on Coiba. The government maintains a penal settlement on the island, and agriculture and cattle raising are practiced. The deer frequently are hunted, but remain common in undisturbed and isolated areas.

In the early 1970s, white-tailed deer were introduced to Contadora Island, a tourist resort in the northern part of the Pearl Islands Archipelago. The island has an area of about 120 hectares (300 acres) and is partly covered with a dry, deciduous, broad-leaf forest and partly occupied by a human settlement. In less than 10 years, the deer population has grown from 2 bucks and 18 does originally introduced to more than 200, as estimated in 1981, showing the vigorous reproductive potential of the species when undisturbed.

The survival of the white-tailed deer on the Panama isthmus is uncertain, and an effective law for its protection should be passed as soon as possible. This action should be accompanied by the establishment of breeding areas, wildlife reserves, national parks and refuges, and through creation of conservation education programs.

Typical white-tailed deer habitat in Chiriqui Province, Panama. *Courtesy of the Panamanian Department of Renewable Natural Resources.*

OUTLOOK

The available information reveals that the whitetail is declining throughout most of its range in Mexico and Central America. The principal reasons for this situation are the destruction of habitat, illegal hunting, uncontrolled burning, and increasing use of land for lumbering, agriculture and livestock production. In addition, pollution of land, air and water also contributes to the degradation of the deer environment. It is obvious that the status of whitetails is more serious in some areas than in others. It is quite critical in El Salvador, for example, in view of the country's reduced forests and large human population. In addition, internal political conflict has increased ecological disturbances, with serious consequences for wildlife.

Unless more actions are taken soon throughout Mexico and Central America, the rapid rate of deer decline will lead to the loss, in certain areas, of a resource of inestimable economic, aesthetic and scientific value. It is urgent that more attention be placed on habitat protection and the enforced regulation of hunting. In this regard, closed seasons should be established and rigorously observed. Traditional hunting methods used by peasants and Indians should be encouraged, and the sophisticated and intensive methods used by other hunters should be prohibited.

Fires to clear areas must be strictly controlled, particularly during the dry season, and agriculture and other land exploitation should follow a scientific scheme in harmony with the environment. The use of cumulative pesticides, such as the chlorinated hydrocarbons, must be avoided. They can be replaced with less toxic, nonpersistent chemicals that are not as dangerous to wildlife and people.

The ever-growing food crisis facing the people of this region is promoting the search for sources of protein. Steps need to be taken to ensure the conservation of whitetails since, if properly managed, they can be a valuable resource in this regard, perhaps superior to any of the other native animals. In addition, conservation and management of deer as a vital food source could have favorable impact on pasturelands overgrazed by domestic livestock. The excellent adaptation of white-tailed deer to the region's environmental conditions heightens the prospect of "game-farming" this animal, even on small ranches, and increasing its reproductive capacity at the same time. Therefore, private landholders should be encouraged to allow production of deer, which can provide both personal and societal benefits.

More attention should be focused on utilization of deer by-products. At present, the hides and other usable parts of harvested whitetails are not always retained or utilized. This represents a substantial loss of potential income.

Inasmuch as there is little public understanding of the value of deer and deer management, educational and pilot programs are an important need, to make people aware of the significance of the whitetail resource and teach them how to utilize it wisely. This can be achieved through concerted media campaigns, literature dissemination and other mass communication means. In any case, the effort must emphasize the food value of conserved and managed whitetail populations.

Laws governing conservation programs need to be strengthened and enforced. And political decisions regarding white-tailed deer must be based on sound ecological principles that take social and cultural factors into consideration.

Research is needed on whitetail reproductive patterns, the species' actual range and density in every country of the region, and the carrying capacity of those habitats that can support whitetails on a sustained-yield basis. Examination should be made of the feasibility of reintroducing whitetails to areas from which they have been extirpated. More effort should be made to determine the rate of consumption by deer of the various nutrients utilized. These studies can be made by observation of food habits and analysis of stomach contents. It also is important to develop pilot projects to manage whitetail populations and habitats to enhance venison per deer and by unit of land.

The conservation and management of white-tailed deer require more and better cooperation among countries of the region, since they share the same problems. Improved communication among scientists and political authorities can result in a valuable and rewarding interchange of ideas and information. There also is need for technical and financial support of international organizations, such as the World Wildlife Fund, Agency for International Development, World Bank, International Union for Conservation of Nature and Natural Resources, and other conservation groups.

Chapter 31

SOUTH AMERICA

Peter A. Brokx
Project Manager
Ecology and Environment, Inc.
Buffalo, New York

ENVIRONMENT

White-tailed deer occur over a major part of northern South America and in each of its principal divisions—the Guiana Highlands, the Andes, and the Great Depression (Figure 101). The Brazilian/Guiana Highlands are geologically ancient, massive, rounded mountains and tabular uplands with an average elevation of about 1,000 meters (3,000 feet). The Andes are a complex system of more-or-less parallel mountain ranges, including peaks higher than 7,000 meters (22,000 feet), transverse ranges, ranges of volcanic origin, intermontane valleys, high plateaus and drainage basins with glacial lakes. The Great Depression is a sedimentary trough of which parts are known as the plains (llanos) of the Orinoco and Amazon rivers.

Whitetail distribution in South America is better defined as equatorial rather than as tropical. Representative climatic data for its range are assembled in Table 83. Northeast and southeast trade winds bring seasonal rains to much of the region, but wet and dry seasons vary greatly in duration and intensity depending on location. Most rain falls in the delta of the Amazon, in the upper Amazon River Basin and on the Pacific coast of Colombia, where annual precipitation is about 3 meters (10 feet) due to daily rains. The Guianas also are very humid, since two rainy seasons are separated by a brief dry spell. The northeast corner of Brazil and Caribbean coastal region of Colombia and Venezuela are very dry. The east slopes of the Andes are very humid while the west slopes are dry, due to the rainshadow effect. The cold Humboldt current contributes to a desert on the Pacific coast of Peru.

Diurnal temperature variations exceed seasonal differences. The variation is greatest at high elevations in the Andes, where freezing cold nights follow days heated by intense solar radiation. Since temperature decreases about 1 degree Celsius (1.8 degrees Fahrenheit) for each 150 meters (500 feet) increase in elevation, the tropical belt goes up to about 900 meters (3,000 feet) above sea level; temperate zones reach roughly 3,000 meters (10,000 feet); an alpine tundra is found above the treeline and perpetual snow occurs at approximately 4,600 meters (15,000 feet). White-tailed deer go up to at least 4,000 meters (13,000 feet) in the Andes from Bolivia north to Venezuela and Colombia, but these high plateau populations tend to be isolated from lowland deer by belts of montane rain, cloud or fog forest, as well as by barren xerophytic vegetation on steep slopes at intermediate elevations.

A major part of the whitetails' range is covered by broad-leafed evergreen and semideciduous forests, including tropical rainforests and humid montane forests (Figure 102). These "selvas" exclude the whitetails from large parts of the Amazon River Basin. Savannahs and deciduous forests provide woodland margins most characteristic of whitetail habitat. The demarcation is quite distinct in Venezuela for example, where white-tailed deer do not occur in cloud forest at Rancho Grande in the north, nor in humid foothill forests of the Sierra Períja on the Colombian border, although they are

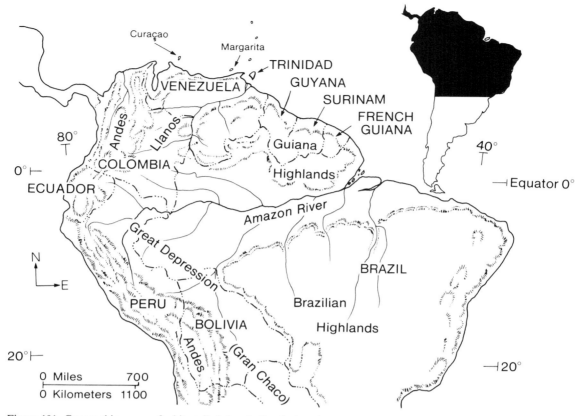

Figure 101. Geographic range of white-tailed deer in South America.

Table 83. Climatic conditions for selected cities within the range of white-tailed deer in South America.[a]

Country and location	Latitude/ longitude	Elevation in meters (feet)	Annual precipitation in centimeters (inches)	Average annual temperature in degrees Celsius (Fahrenheit)		Absolute temperature in degrees Celsius (Fahrenheit)	
				High	Low	High	Low
Brazil							
Natal	5.5S/35.1W	3(10)	137.7(54.2)	31.7(89)	18.3(65)	32.8(91)	15.0(59)
Manaus	3.1S/60.0W	60(197)	181.1(71.3)	36.1(97)	19.4(67)	38.3(101)	17.8(64)
Colombia							
Barranquilla	10.6N/74.5W	4.9(16)	74.4(29.3)	37.2(99)	18.3(65)	42.2(108)	12.8(55)
Bogota	4.4N/74.1W	2,644(8,675)	90.2(35.5)	23.9(75)	1.7(35)	25.0(77)	0.0(32)
Equador							
Quito	0.1S/78.3W	2,819(9,249)	122.7(48.3)	27.2(81)	1.7(35)	30.0(86)	0.0(32)
Guayaquil	2.1S/79.5W	3(10)	102.1(40.2)	35.6(96)	16.1(61)	36.7(98)	13.9(57)
Guyana							
Georgetown	6.5N/58.1W	2.1(7)	222.0(87.4)	32.2(90)	21.1(70)	33.9(93)	20.0(68)
Peru							
Lima	12.0S/77.0W	154(505)	3.0(1.2)	31.7(89)	10.6(51)	33.9(93)	9.4(49)
Cuzco	11.2S/71.6W	3,399(11,152)	81.3(32.0)	27.8(82)	−5.0(23)	28.9(84)	−8.9(16)
Surinam							
Paramaribo	5.5N/55.1W	3.7(12)	225.8(88.9)	35.6(96)	19.4(67)	37.2(99)	16.6(62)
Venezuela							
Maracaibo	10.4N/71.4W	6.1(20)	47.5(18.7)	37.2(99)	20.6(69)	38.9(102)	18.9(66)
Valencia	10.1N/68.0W	478(1,568)	115.1(45.3)			38.3(101)	17.2(63)

[a]From Showers (1973).

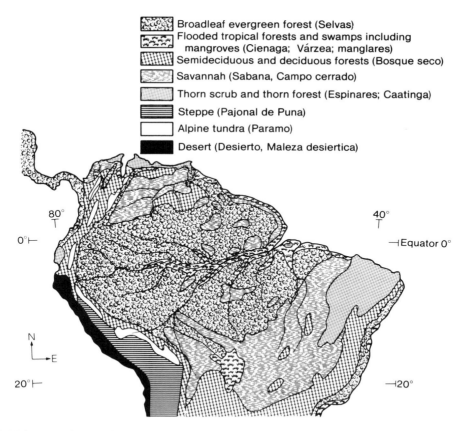

Broadleaf evergreen forest (Selvas)
Flooded tropical forests and swamps including mangroves (Cienaga; Várzea; manglares)
Semideciduous and deciduous forests (Bosque seco)
Savannah (Sabana, Campo cerrado)
Thorn scrub and thorn forest (Espinares; Caatinga)
Steppe (Pajonal de Puna)
Alpine tundra (Paramo)
Desert (Desierto, Maleza desiertica)

Figure 102. Major natural vegetational types of northern South America.

Table 83. (continued)

Mean temperature in degrees Celsius (Fahrenheit)[Month]	
Warmest	Coolest
27.2(81.0)[Jan]	24.4(75.9)[Jul]
27.8(82.2)[Sept]	26.3(79.3)[Jan]
14.9(58.8)[Apr]	13.8(56.8)[Aug]
13.4(56.1)[Sept]	13.1(55.6)[Jun]
26.6(79.9)[Apr]	24.0(75.2)[Jul]
27.8(82.0)[Sept]	26.3(79.3)[Jan]
22.4(72.3)[Feb]	15.2(59.3)[Aug]
14.4(58.0)[Nov]	10.3(50.5)[Jul]
28.6(83.5)[Oct]	26.4(79.5)[Jan]
29.1(84.3)[Aug]	26.9(80.5)[Jan]
25.6(78.1)[Apr]	24.0(75.2)[Jan]

found in adjacent regions of broken woodland and savannah at elevations that are lower only by a few hundred feet.

Savannahs have a more-or-less complete layer of grass. Few savannah regions are entirely open and devoid of trees, and extensive areas are characterized by scattered palms on wet sites or "palmares," by small, contorted, scleromorphic trees on dry sites or "chaparrales," and also by a type of mesquite, particularly on overgrazed secondary savannah or "cujízales." Streams are fringed by tall, semideciduous "gallery" forest on alluvium, and trees or groves of trees or "matas" occur as "islands," reflecting favorable hydrological conditions. The savannah grass layer can be dominated by a single species on lateritic soils and dry sands or "medanos," and by another on deeply flooded sites or "pantanales." In other sections, grasses and herbs occur in a diversity that defies attempts at systematic classification. These savannahs are distinguished as high ("banco") or low ("bajío, estero''), depending on small topographical differences.

The distribution of high and low savannah has an important bearing on wet and dry season carrying capacity for grazing animals. The dry season usually is the limiting factor, but wet season range can be a constraint in areas where inundations are deep and widespread. Savannahs of the Orinoco are a seasonal formation, subject to strong variation in available soil moisture (Sarmiento and Monastero 1975). Their counterpart in Brazil is the woodland savannah or ''campo cerrado.'' Nonseasonal savannah is found as a belt about 65 kilometers (40 miles) from the coast in the Guianas and on sterile sandy soils of elevated tablelands in the Guiana Highlands.

In northern Venezuela and northeastern Brazil, the savannah regions grade into areas of deciduous forest and very dry tropical forest types. Like the gallery forests and woodland groves in predominantly savannah areas, the deciduous forests include a variety of fruit-bearing trees and palms of importance to deer, especially during the dry season (Brokx and Andressen 1970). Very dry types (the ''espinares'' in Venezuela and ''Caatinga'' of Brazil) are rich in cactus and thorn scrub; ground cover is incomplete, and carrying capacity is very low.

Vegetation of the Andes region has a complex pattern and ranges from tropical valleys with palms to cold barren slopes. Rainforest is found as a belt on the Pacific coast of Colombia and on the east side of the Andes. The desert of the Pacific region of Peru grades at higher elevations into a steppe of grass and cactus. Xerophytic vegetation on dry slopes goes up to high elevations throughout the northern Andes. The zone above the treeline is covered by alpine meadows or ''paramos'' consisting of tussock grasses, wildflowers, herbaceous shrubs, and many species of ''frailejon'' or *Espeletia,* a rosette tree with wooly leaves up to 4–5 meters (12–15 feet) tall. The whitetail shares this range with sheep. In Peru and Bolivia, the deer are associated more closely with woody growth in the swales than are the taruca, alpaca and related animals also utilizing the high plateaus.

The low llanos of the Orinoco have an estuarine and lacustrine origin. Former drainages that filled with coarse sediment now appear as slightly elevated banks (''bancos'') next to low areas (''bajíos'' and ''esteros''). During the wet season, this ''bajío'' would be covered by a few feet of water and even the ''banco'' on the horizon would be wet and traversable only on horseback. Whitetails here are not migratory, but local movements to sectors including higher pasture have been reported. Capybara wallow in the only water that remains in March, but do not deter deer from drinking. In general, because of their dependence on water, capybara are less abundant than whitetails. The birds to the right of the doe include three plovers and two crested caracaras. *Photo by Peter A. Brokx.*

The area of distribution of white-tailed deer in South America covers approximately 5.5 million square kilometers (2.1 million square miles). The effective range, possibly less than 10 percent of the areas of Peru and Surinam, and more than 50 percent of Venezuela, totals approximately 1.7 million square kilometers (660,000 square miles) due to extensive humid forests and steppe. Only some of the remaining area is productive whitetail habitat, since parts are too steep, too arid or too intensively grazed by domestic animals, or because of other such limitations. Another important habitat factor is the human population, which lives concentrated in coastal areas and in the Andes where temperate zone crops have been grown for centuries. The savannah regions are less densely populated, but intensively used for livestock grazing, and stocking rates are high. Also, cutting followed by burning and grazing has established extensive secondary savannahs in adjacent forest zones. National goals, especially in Brazil, include development of the Amazon region. The present population of approximately 70 million people will be 90 million by 1990 and around 130 million by the year 2000 if Brazil realizes its projections for Amazonia.

WHITETAIL POPULATIONS

Taxonomy and Distribution

Early naturalists were aware of the close relationship between the North American white-tailed deer and "new" deer from tropical South America (Cuvier and St. Hilaire 1832). An illustration by Daubenton (*in* Buffon 1764) of a deer from Cayenne (French Guiana) showed the corneous metatarsal gland and white tuft typical of *Odocoileus virginianus,* but later investigators failed to discover the gland. For a time it was assumed that there were two distinct species—one with the gland and one without (Wiegmann 1833, Cabrera 1918). Brooke (1878) and Lydekker (1898) dismissed the taxonomic significance of the metatarsal gland and classed North and South America whitetails as a single species.

The classification of South American whitetails is out of date and based largely on descriptions of very few specimens rather than on series taking into account individual variation. The basis for distinction of at least several subspecies plainly is erroneous. For example, Wiegmann (1833) named *O. v. gymnotis* in an otherwise excellent account, because *O.*

White-tailed deer on South American savannahs are dwarfed by cattle but do not avoid them. In terms of weight, about 10 deer equal 1 cow, but the biomass tied up in deer is disproportionately small relative to that in cattle. Of 22 ranches included in a Venezuelan study, the smallest ranch included 1,948 hectares (4,814 acres) and 300 cattle, while the largest ranch was 78,200 hectares (193,232 acres) with 30,000 cattle. No whitetails were encountered on the smallest ranch. On the largest ranch there were 10 times more cattle than deer—an exceptionally high deer density. The norm is a ranch of about 10,000 hectares (24,700 acres) with about 2,500 head of livestock and perhaps 100 or fewer deer. *Photo by Peter A. Brokx.*

v. cariacou was supposed to have a metatarsal gland. The reason for retaining some of the subspecies in the nomenclature reflects Cabrera's (1918) concept that the whitetail is not represented by a single subspecies in different altitudinal and climatic zones or, for that matter, over a vast geographic area. Cabrera's (1961) list of seven South American subspecies included:

1. *O. v. cariacou* Boddaert, 1784
   Synonyms: *sylvaticus, campestris, suacuapara, spinosus.*
   Distribution: French Guiana and northeastern Brazil to lower río Negro.
   Type locality: Cayenne.

2. *O. v. goudotii* Gay and Gervais, 1846
   Synonyms: *columbicus, lasiotis.*
   Distribution: cordilleras of the Andes in Colombia to northeast in the Sierra de Merida in western Venezuela.
   Type locality: Nueva Granada region of Colombia.

3. *O. v. gymnotis* Wiegmann, 1833
   Synonyms: *savannarum, tumatumari, spinosus.*
   Distribution: the savannahs of Venezuela, Guyana and Surinam.
   Type locality: the region of the Orinoco River above San Tomás.

A typical, fully grown *Odocoileus virginianus gymnotis* buck in breeding condition during late March. It has an excellent set of antlers, which is characteristic of five-year-old and older bucks of this subspecies. This buck's estimated weight is 50 kilograms (110 pounds). *Photo by Peter A. Brokx.*

4. *O. v. margaritae* Osgood, 1910
   Synonyms: none.
   Distribution: restricted to Isla de Margarita, Venezuela.

5. *O. v. peruvianus* Gray, 1874
   Synonyms: *brachyceros, peruviana, philipii, peruanus.*
   Distribution: on the slopes of the Andes in Peru and Bolivia.
   Type locality: probably Cosmipata, Cuzco, Peru.

6. *O. v. tropicalis* Cabrera, 1918
   Synonyms: *columbicus, punensis.*
   Distribution: west of the Andes in Colombia and Ecuador
   Type locality: La María in the valley of río Dagua.

7. *O. v. ustus* Trouessart, 1910
   Synonyms: *peruvianus, abeli, gracilis, antonii, aequatorialis, consul.*
   Distribution: the Andes of Ecuador and perhaps southern Colombia.
   Type locality: near El Pelado, north of Quito.

In addition, Hummelinck (1940) identified the deer from Curaçao as *O. v. curassavicus*, but the animal may have been introduced from the mainland (Husson 1960). This deer is quite like the small deer from the Island of Margarita. The deer from the State (Edo.) of Apure in Venezuela and the llanos in eastern Colombia should be regarded as a distinct subspecies— *O. v. apurensis* (Brokx 1972*a*). Distribution of the South American white-tailed deer subspecies is shown in Figure 103.

Hershkovitz (1958) divided the white-tailed deer of South America into two "pelage phase groups" equivalent to subspecies. The tropical zone reddish or tawny "permanent summer pelage phase group," of which *O. v. cariacou* is the "type," includes the other lowland subspecies *O. v. gymnotis, O. v. tropicalis, O. v. margaritae* and *O. v. curassavicus.* The High Andes or temperate zone grayish "permanent winter pelage phase group," with *O. v. goudotii* as the "type," includes *O. v. ustus* and *O. v. peruvianus.* This classification stresses similarity apparent among highland subspecies and among lowland subspecies due to climatic adaptation, without giving consideration to genetic affinities. It also ignores that *O. v. gymnotis* has brown and red coats analogous to winter and summer coats of North American whitetails. The pelage characteristics of most subspecies still require detailed study. A definitive classification of the South American

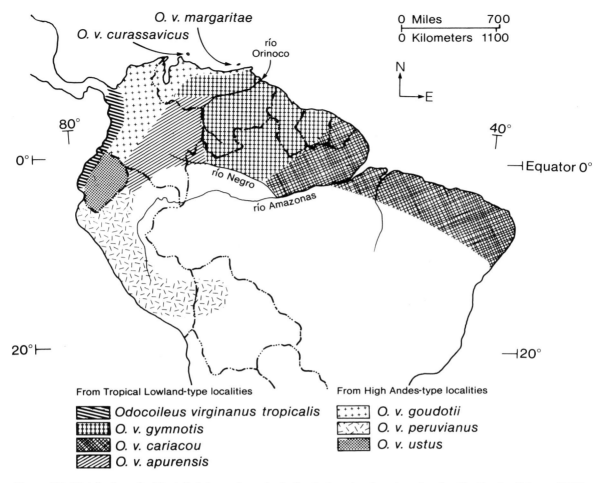

Figure 103. Distribution of white-tailed deer subspecies in South America, based on the classification by Cabrera (1961), with the addition of *Odocoileus virginianus curassavicus* and *O. v. apurensis*. The southern limit, occurrence and distribution of the species—especially in the upper Amazon River Basin—are unknown. Settlement and development now in progress in the Amazon region could cause a rapid southward expansion of whitetail distribution in Brazil, where other indigenous cervids (related to *Odocoileus*) have become endangered.

whitetails ultimately may take into consideration Tate's (1939) concept regarding the influences of Pleistocene glaciations. During the last glacial period, the temperature was many degrees cooler on the equator; in the Andes of Venezuela, glacial evidence is found 1,500 meters (5,000 feet) below the present snowline (Royo y Gomez 1959); and tropical rainforests were much more restricted by savannah (Sarmiento and Monastero 1975).

Only the winter coat of South American whitetails reveals subspecific differences. The red summer coat is very similar from one individual to another, even among representatives of distantly related species. Its hair has only two bands of pigment—that is, a red hair

with a black point. Winter hair has three zones of pigmentation which give the coat a less definite coloration and a "punctuated" or "speckled" pattern. *O. v. gymnotis* has a "reddish-yellow-speckled gray" pelage quite like that of the Virginia white-tailed deer (Wiegmann 1833). The winter pelage of this subspecies is short-haired and restricted to the head, back of the neck and back. Its coloration usually is brown or reddish-brown or fawn "speckled" or "punctuated" with black, gray and ochre. Adult bucks and old does tend to be brown or gray brown, while young deer and does are rufous brown. This coloration is much darker than that of subspecies in the High Andes group and it prevails over much of the llanos of Ven-

A typical *Odocoileus virginianus gymnotis* doe, gravid during late April, in central Venezuela. Her weight is approximately 35 kilograms (77 pounds). *Photo by Peter A. Brokx.*

ezuela and the Guiana Highlands as far east as the Rupununi Savannah on the Guyana/Brazilian border. All subspecies from the Andes are a gray blond or light yellowish-gray. The light color is emphasized by the length of the hair, which has a long colorless base. Cabrera (1918) described *O. v. goudotii* with a black semicircle in front of and below the eyes (Figure 104), but I did not find this feature on specimens from the Sierra de Merida. Whitetails from the Zulia llanos around Lake Maracaibo and northern coastal parts of Venezuela, including Edo. Lara, represent a lowland form of *O. v. goudotii*. These deer, as well as the small whitetails from the islands of Curaçao and Margarita, are sandy or ochre with a gray-speckled pattern on dorsal surfaces. The light coloration may be an adaptation to arid habitat. It more likely indicates a genetic tie to the Andes whitetails, which is explained by two low mountain ranges extending into coastal areas of northern Venezuela. Occasional light-colored specimens from range definitely belonging to *O. v. gymnotis* indicate a genetic factor and intergradation east of the Andes in northcentral Venezuela.

Figure 104. Profile and frontal views of *Odocoileus virginianus goudotii* from an unknown locality in Columbia (redrawn by Peter A. Brokx after Cabrera [1918], based on a specimen in the Museo Nacional de Ciencias Naturales). Cabrera (1918) described this deer—which he believed to have been collected in the High Andes because of such pelage characteristics as its long (35 millimeters: 1.4 inches) dorsal hair—as having a dark circle in front of and below the eye. This characteristic has not been verified or described by other authors, and is unique because South American whitetails have a light ring around the eyes. In fact, the light ring appears to be a generic feature common to all *Odocoileus* species as well as related South American genera (*Ozotocerus*, *Blastocerus* and *Hippocamelus*).

O. v. tropicalis from western Colombia also is likely to occur in the coastal region of Ecuador. This subspecies was described as rufous brown (Lydekker 1915, Cabrera 1918). Tate (1939) suspected it to be related closely to the whitetails of Panama. These deer are substantially smaller than *O. v. gymnotis*. Since the distribution of *O. v. tropicalis* is limited to the Pacific region, it is likely that the alpine subspecies (*O. v. goudotii, O. v. ustus* and *O. v. peruvianus*) are represented by lowland or intermediate forms in other parts of Colombia, Ecuador and Peru. If so, they have yet to be described in the literature.

O. v. apurensis also is smaller than *O. v. gymnotis,* and its tawny winter pelage is about the same color as its summer pelage, because hair of the winter coat is banded by only two zones of pigmentation instead of the usual three. Facial markings are less distinct, and even the fetus has a lighter tone than does the rufous brown fetus of *O. v. gymnotis*.

Whitetails from Surinam are rufous and rufous brown. Those from the coastal zone probably belong to *O. v. gymnotis,* while whitetails from the Sipaliwini and Paru savannahs on the Brazilian border may belong to *O. v. cariacou*. Cabrera and Yepes (1940) described the coloration of this subspecies in northeastern Brazil as bay (or yellowish) red. In coastal regions of Brazil, it may be slightly smaller than *O. v. gymnotis* from the río Branco savannah (C. T. de Carvalho personal communication:1977).

The southern limit of white-tailed deer in South America is vague. In places it may follow the Amazon River. Jungius (1974) confirmed the whitetail's presence in Bolivia and stated that whitetails might occur south of 15 degrees 15 minutes south latitude. Approximately the same latitude was reported for eastern Brazil (Miranda Ribeiro 1919). This was based on early reports that do not distinguish satisfactorily between white-tailed and pampas deer. However, with certainty, the sub-

Odocoileus virginianus apurensis doe and buck fawn (left) and adult buck (right). The fawn is about seven months old and has velvet-covered knobs. The doe displays a special color pattern in which the entire lower half of the head and neck is white and contiguous with the white on her abdomen; black labial spots on the lower jaw are absent. She weighs 25 to 27 kilograms (55–60 pounds). At about one year of age the fawn buck will develop small spikes not much larger than the velvet-covered knobs he now possesses. At that age he will no longer accompany his dam but will live in association with other bucks. The adult buck is losing antler velvet as he enters the rut in late January. He weighs approximately 40 kilograms (88 pounds), and his color is typically lighter (closer to ochre) than is the pelage of *O. v. gymnotis. Photos by Peter A. Brokx.*

species *O. v. cariacou* occurs as far south as the State of Pernambuco (8 degrees south latitude) (Cabrera 1943).

Physical Characteristics

The physical characteristics of South American whitetails as described here are based mainly on animals collected on the tropical savannahs of Venezuela. Specimens were part of the collection of the Estación Biológica de Rancho Grande, a zoological research station and museum maintained by the Ministerio de Agricultura y Cría, near Maracay, Venezuela. Age groups are differentiated on the basis of tooth development and wear (Brokx 1972*b*).

Weights and measurements.   South American deer are small in comparison with whitetails from North America but, with the exception of the small island forms from Margarita and Curaçao, substantially larger than those from Central America. Among the South American subspecies there appears to be a tendency toward larger body size at higher elevations (Tate 1939), but this was not confirmed by Cabrera and Yepes (1940).

The largest known *O. v. gymnotis* buck had a total length of 167 centimeters (67 inches), and weighed 65 kilograms (144 pounds). The largest Venezuelan whitetails come from wooded llanos at the foot of the Andes (Edo. Potuguesa). Mean total length increases from 130 centimeters (52 inches) for long-yearling bucks to 143 centimeters (57 inches) for the oldest buck group. Similar data for Venezuelan whitetail does are 124 centimeters (49.5 inches) and 133 centimeters (53 inches). Average body lengths (without tail) are 126 centimeters (49.6 inches) and 119 centimeters (46.9 inches) for adult *O. v. gymnotis* bucks and does, respectively, and 120 centimeters (47.2 inches) and 113 centimeters (44.5 inches), respectively, for the significantly smaller *O. v. apurensis* bucks and does. Other standard measurements for *O. v. gymnotis* and *O. v. apurensis,* respectively, are: height of ear—12.8 centimeters (5.0 inches) and 12.2 centimeters (4.8 inches) for bucks, and 12.1 centimeters (4.8 inches) and 11.7 centimeters (4.6 inches) for does; hindfoot—38.2 centimeters (15.0 inches) and 37.3 centimeters (14.7 inches) for bucks, and 35.7 centimeters (14.1 inches) and 35.0 centimeters (13.8 inches) for does; tail length—14.4 centimeters (5.7 inches) and 14.0 centimeters (5.5 inches) for

bucks, and 13.7 centimeters (5.4 inches) and 13.1 centimeters (5.2 inches) for does. Venezuelan whitetails have tails that are 13 to 14 percent of body length in contrast to tails that are 15 to 20 percent for North American whitetailed deer.

At birth, Venezuelan whitetail fawns weigh approximately 1.4 to 1.8 kilograms (3.1–4.0 pounds)—about 5 percent of the weight of the doe. At maturity, mean live weights are approximately 50 and 30 kilograms (110 and 66 pounds) for adult bucks and does, respectively. South American whitetails, on the average, are slightly heavier during the wet season than in the dry season. The hog-dressed weight (live weight less viscera) is approximately 77 percent of the whole weight. Hides of adult does and bucks average 2.3 to 3.7 kilograms (5–8 pounds). The heart, liver and lungs weigh approximately 1.1 to 1.6 kilograms (2.4–3.5 pounds) in the ratio of 2:5:3. And the mean weight of the kidneys is 101 to 118 grams (3.56–4.16 ounces). The carcass of a 50-kilogram (110-pound) buck will furnish approximately 18 kilograms (40 pounds) of good-quality meat. The mathematical equations for these relationships are quite similar to those described for North American whitetails.

Skulls of South American whitetails are larger than those of Central American and several Mexican subspecies. The largest *O. v. gymnotis* buck had a condylobasal length of 259 millimeters (10.2 inches), and the mean for adult bucks is 236 millimeters (9.3 inches). The condylobasal length of a small sample of *O. v. goudotii* and *ustus* from Colombia and Ecuador, respectively, was within the range of *O. v. gymnotis*. *O. v. apurensis* bucks have an average condylobasal length of 225.7 millimeters (8.9 inches), and the largest measured 235 millimeters (9.3 inches). Hummelinck (1940) listed a condylobasal length of 222 millimeters (8.7 inches) for *O. v. curassavicus*. Osgood's (1910) type specimen for *O. v. margaritae* is an immature deer, but its skull is very small in comparison with mainland whitetails of comparable age.

South American whitetails have relatively much larger molariform teeth and third molars than do North American whitetails. This significant difference is not explained by allometric growth, because small Central American whitetails have proportionately the same size molars as do the large forms from the United States.

Antlers. Typically, an antler of a mature South American whitetail buck consists of a main beam with a basal snag and two crown tines (Figure 105) similar in structure to those of North American whitetails (*see* Chapter 3). Occasionally the antlers branch dichotomously. Mean dimensions of 28 antler specimens at the Estación Biológica de Rancho Grande were: tip-to-tip spread, 17.5 centimeters (6.9 inches); greatest spread, 30.6 centimeters (12.0 inches); length of beams, 30.7 centimeters (12.1 inches); and circumference above burr, 8.8 centimeters (3.5 inches). Several specimens scored 85 to 100 points according to Boone and Crockett standards, as confirmed by Steve Gallizioli of the Arizona Fish and Game Department, who considered their presence in a museum collection indicative of the South American whitetails' capacity to grow trophy-size racks comparable to or approaching those of *O. v. couesi.*

O. v. gymnotis from the llanos generally have well-developed antlers, while those from the Guiana Highlands are considerably smaller though sturdy and with large burrs. Antlers of Brazilian whitetail bucks are comparable to

The almost fully developed antlers of this South American whitetail buck are quite remarkable for a deer weighing less than 40 kilograms (88 pounds). Antlers of this size on small cervids raise questions about theories regarding the spikes of brocket deer, and indicate the complex interrelationships of age, genetics, range condition, mineral availability, and dominance supported by endocrinological factors in determining antler morphology. *Photo by Peter A. Brokx.*

Two whitetail bucks—well-matched in size and antler development—running a doe on the savannah of La Trinidad, in río Arauco, Edo. Apure, during late January. The doe (located by arrow) is nearly hidden from view in a low area. The leading buck would halt from time to time to confront the second buck, which then would stop also. Theories regarding competition and dominance among cervids in northern regions are valid for South American whitetails as well. The concept that antlers have lost their value, or could not have evolved under tropical conditions because of asynchronous breeding and less intense competition, would appear to be erroneous. Since the rut for South American whitetails extends for a long period, fewer bucks compete for fewer females at any one time. They likely expend less energy on confrontations with subdominants and more on covering ground in search of receptive does. A level of competition is maintained by a degree of synchrony among bucks having the same status. It is not clear how this is attained; possibly bucks pitched against each other unavoidably synchronize their life processes. The trees on the horizon are moriche palms. *Photo by Peter A. Brokx.*

Figure 105. Antlers of South American white-tailed deer (drawn by Peter A. Brokx from a sample at the Estación Biológica de Rancho Grande in Venezuela, including the largest antlers in the collection). A, B, C and D show antlers of *Odocoileus virginianus apurensis* from Edo. Apure. D illustrates an inferior set, and was from the youngest buck—about 3.5 years old—represented in this series. The several small snags in place of tines on the main beams are a common feature of antlers from Apure. A, B and C are very well-developed antlers, especially because the live weight of the bearers likely was less than that of the largest *O. v. gymnotis* specimens shown in E, F, I and L. E, F, G, H, L, M and N represent antlers of *O. v. gymnotis* from the west-central llanos in Guarico and Cojedes. E and F are typical of fully grown bucks about 5–7 years of age; split basal snags and tines are a common feature. I, J and K are short but sturdy antlers of *O. v. gymnotis* from the Guiana Highlands in Edo. Bolivar; this antler form is characteristic eastward into Guyana and Surinam. I and J belong to the same age group as E and F. K—like G, H and L—shows antlers of an approximately 3.5-year-old deer, the short, stocky antlers being typical of the geographic locale. H is a dichotomous antler without basal snags (more characteristic of North American mule deer than whitetails). By adding a pair of short spikes to the L, M and N series, one can obtain a display of progressive antler development for South American white-tailed deer. M and N belonged to 2–2.5-year-old bucks. Specimens of antlers L, M and N were collected at the same site on the same day in October, and weighed in at 47.5 kilograms (105 pounds), 39.5 kilograms (87 pounds) and 40.0 kilograms (88 pounds), respectively. Whereas L antlers were new, M and N were old, worn and ready to be cast.

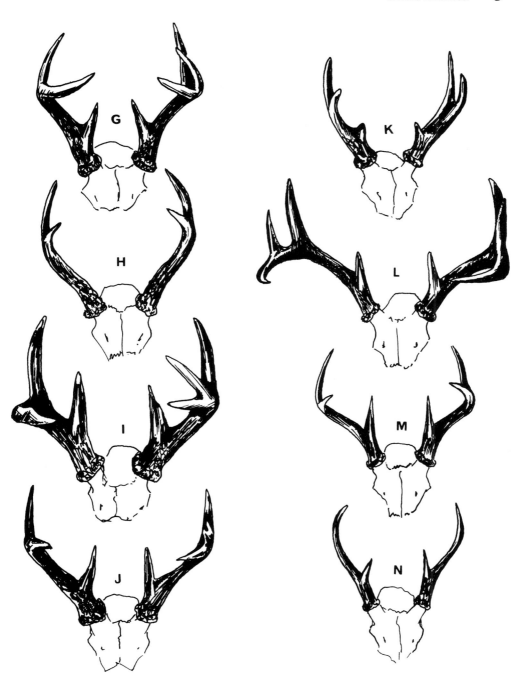

those of *O. v. gymnotis* on the llanos. *O. v. apurensis* antlers also can be large and well-developed, but frequently the anterior tines are not fully grown and are partially incorporated into the main beam from which they protrude as small snags. Antler rubbing of vegetation and antler clashing between bucks, including cases of locked antlers, have been observed on the savannah of Venezuela. This indicates that white-tailed deer antlers have not lost their ritual value in the equatorial region, as has been assumed by certain authors in connection with assumed asynchronous reproduction and rutting activity.

South American whitetails do well on overgrazed range covered by thornshrub as long as the vegetation is relatively diverse and not burned off to establish new pasture for domestic livestock. These two bucks are in the velvet stage of antler development during late January. The excellent set of antlers of the buck at left is practically fully grown and beginning to calcify. On the llanos, many local residents believe that whitetails are represented by two distinct species—those in velvet ("cacho peludo") and those with hard antlers ("venado caramerudo"). Surprisingly, even though deer in the cast-antler stage are referred to as "tocon" or "stump," few people seem to deduce an antler cycle. *Photo by Peter A. Brokx.*

Andes whitetails may have small antlers (based on a small sample and illustrations). Antlers illustrated in Figure 104 appear to be typical of complete development. At one time it was thought that neotropical whitetails shed antlers irregularly or not at all (*see* Hershkovitz 1958). This is not true for lowland deer. However, since the whitetail's periodicity for red coat and antler regeneration are correlated, it is a research priority to determine this physiological relationship for Andean whitetails. Since these deer do not appear to wear a red coat at any time, their velvet antler phase could be of short duration and cause reduced antler size.

Pelage. Fawns are born with a white-dappled coat that they begin to lose at about 2.5 months of age. Spots may remain visible on the hindquarters up to about seven months of age and occasionally are faintly visible along the spine on brown coats of old deer.

Basically, South American whitetails have two types of pelage that correspond to the winter and summer coats of the North American

An *Odocoileus virginianus apurensis* fawn hiding beneath a thornshrub or "guaica" in February. Fawns are distinctively spotted until the time of irruption of the first true molar, at about 2.5 months of age. The spots gradually are grown out of the pelage over the first seven months. A total of 210 spots were counted on a study skin. *Photo by Peter A. Brokx.*

subspecies. Lowland deer wear brown, thick-haired coats for about eight months, and a red thin-haired pelage is worn during the balance of the year. It is possible that deer living at high altitudes in the Andes molt gradually, from one brown coat into another, as an adaptation to low temperatures. *O. v. gymnotis* molts gradually from red to the brown pelage and rapidly from brown into red. The molt does not noticeably involve the flanks, legs and other inferior parts of the body, which remain tawny and short-haired, with the exception of such white parts as the abdominal region. The brown (winter) coat, as previously noted, is restricted to the head, back of the neck, shoulder region and back, and its hairs are considerably shorter than are those of winter coats of North American whitetails.

Although a few strands of underfur can be found in both their brown and red coats, tropical lowland deer do not have underfur at any time of the year. However, they have the capacity to grow thick underfur when translocated to higher elevations and cooler climatic conditions. Thin-haired red (summer) coats usually have a fawn or tawny coloration. This coat is worn, according to age, from June to October predominantly by deer *(O. v. gymnotis)* less than 1 year old, from December to June by deer 1 to 2.5 years old, and during the April-September period mainly by older deer. The red coat is a feature of bucks during the velvet phase of antler development.

Skin glands. South American white-tailed deer have preorbital, tarsal and interdigital glands. Metatarsal glands and surrounding tufts are not found on South American whitetails, though an occasional specimen will have a small rudimentary corneous glandular area on one or both of the hind legs. A dense tuft of hair always is present on the distal-posterior side of the metatarsals approximately 3 centimeters (1.2 inches) above the dewclaw. No glandular activity has been observed in relation to this tuft, of which the hair is about 10 millimeters (0.4 inch) long and lighter in color than the hair on the adjacent part of the hind foot. The tuft's position does not match that of the metatarsal gland of the North American white-tailed deer (*see* Chapter 3).

Other features. North American whitetails occasionally have small canine teeth in the maxillae (Severinghaus 1949*b*, Van Gelder and Hoffmeister 1953, Loveless and Harlow 1959, *see* Chapter 3). Such canines are much more common in South American whitetails. They occur with much greater frequency in does than in bucks, and geographical variation also is significant (Brokx 1972*c*). Other evidence of a degree of genetic isolation of whitetail populations in different parts of Venezuela are (1) dense fur on the back of the ears and (2) a lack of the normally rusty-brown color connection between black labial patches on the mandible. These characteristics are particularly associated with *O. v. apurensis,* but not constantly or exclusively.

Reproductive Cycle

Reproductive cycles of South American white-tailed deer are inadequately known. The description that follows is based on studies of *O. v. gymnotis* and *O. v. apurensis* in Venezuela.

Bucks. Reproduction is possible throughout the year, but the main rut of *O. v. gymnotis* occurs on the llanos from February through May (the dry season). For *O. v. apurensis,* the main rut is from May through August (first part of the wet season). For individuals of both subspecies, timing of the rut is a function of age; the oldest bucks tend to rut several months in advance of the others.

Antler growth is along the pattern displayed by North American whitetails; adult bucks grow antlers for approximately four months and wear them for the subsequent six or seven months. Buck fawns older than 2.5 months of age develop pedicles, and fawns 8 to 10 months of age typically have velvet-covered knobs. After fawn bucks are older than 10 months, the knobs calcify, and these yearlings carry very small spikes or knobs. On some of the young bucks, the knobs continue to grow into larger spikes or small weak forks that calcify at 15 or 16 months. These first spikes or forks are cast after a few months. Bucks in the 17–19-month age group will have cast their antlers at least once, and 75 percent of these animals will be growing or wearing a second set. The second pair of antlers is likely to consist of a well-developed spike or fork, and can be distinguished from the first pair by a corona on the burr. The cast-antler condition is common for animals about 19 months of age, and these bucks may have cast once or more usually twice, depending on the size of the first set of antlers. Older bucks will grow larger antlers at slightly less than 12-month intervals.

The synchrony of antler development and, hence, reproductive physiology among South American white-tailed deer of about the same age is well illustrated by these two bucks in velvet, probably about 2.5 years old. Bucks in velvet associate in fraternal groups. The birds near the water are black skimmers and terns. *Photo by Peter A. Brokx.*

Contrary to earlier reports (*see* Goss 1963), the antler cycle of tropical white-tailed deer is related to their reproductive cycle (as for northern whitetails), but age appears to be the major factor determining when individuals have polished antlers. In *O. v. gymnotis,* polished antlers occur as early as November and December for old (4.5 + years) bucks, from February to August for 2.5–4.5-year-olds and from June to October for bucks less than 2.5 years of age. In *O. v. apurensis,* the majority of bucks have polished antlers during the May-to-October period (significantly later in the year than *O. v. gymnotis,* when age is taken into consideration). Observations on this subspecies by R. I. Blouch (personal communication:1976) on the llanos of Colombia also indicate that deer with polished antlers can be collected throughout the year, but mostly during the period from March to September. Nothing has been published on the antler cycle of the Brazilian and Andean whitetails. Mean size of the testes of bucks with polished antlers and spikes is twice as large (28–35 cubic centimeters:1.7–2.1 cubic inches) as that of bucks during the velvet antler phase (11–22 cubic centimeters:0.7–1.3 cubic inches). The antler cycle is not governed by any obvious environmental periodicity.

Histological examination of young South American whitetail bucks, such as the one-year-old shown above, indicates the production of spermatozoa, but these deer are too small to do any breeding. If the young buck were bigger and sexually active, it would not be seen in association with bucks in velvet. *Photo by Peter A. Brokx.*

Females. On the Venezuelan llanos, does become sexually mature at an age having a wide latitude of individual variation. Only about 5 percent mature at 6 to 8 months of age; 35 percent of the young doe population is sexually mature at 10 to 12 months; 75 percent attain such maturity at 12 to 15 months; and all does are sexually mature when they are about 1.5 years old. Thus, some of the variation observed for the first antler cycle of young bucks reappears in the ovarian development of the Venezuelan does.

Since the does are polyestrus, ovulation is not restricted seasonally and fawning is possible throughout the year. The fawning period for *O. v. gymnotis* occurs mainly from July to November (rainy season), but a second peak occurs during February and March (dry season). The wet-season fawn crop is two to three times as large as that of the dry season. A fetus collection indicated that most young does (less than 2.5 years of age) are bred during the period from July to October, while older does are bred mainly during the dry season, from February through April. The coastal whitetails of Surinam also fawn throughout the year, with a peak during the months of July and August (J. P. Schulz personal communication:1977). The fawning peak of *O. v. apurensis* occurs mainly from November to February (the early part of the dry period), perhaps in adaptation to heavy rains and widespread flooding on the low llanos. In Peru, fawning varies regionally but generally occurs from January to March (A. Brack Egg personal communication:1977). I. Ceballos Bendezú (personal communication:1977) reported the fawning period for the Peruvian whitetails to be from November through January, with a peak during December. This is what would be expected south of the equator.

Ovarian cycles commence shortly after parturition, and does can be bred during the first cycle (Brokx 1972*d*). A high proportion of the three-year-olds will have given birth to three fawns as a result of brief intervals between successive gestation periods when does are simultaneously gravid and lactating. These intervals become considerably longer in older does. Indications are that hunting could have a significant influence on the timing of rutting and fawning peaks by determining the age structure of local populations. While a proportion of the young deer appear to defer the onset of their sexual maturity (as imposed by winter on deer in North America), most young does will be bred as soon as they first reach estrus. Older does seem to determine their ''periodicity'' by cycling, but they comprise a small percentage of the hunted population. The incidence of twin births is rare even for older does.

MANAGEMENT

The following information on the management of the white-tailed deer in South America is derived from observations made in Venezuela from 1965 to 1970 and complemented by questionnaires sent to wildlife experts in other countries during 1977. Information was not obtained for each country that has white-tailed deer, but the available information presents an overview of several deer management factors and concerns in South America.

Importance and Status

The white-tailed deer ranks as the most important game species in Venezuela because (1) it is the largest wild ungulate adapted to the savannah, (2) it is more abundant and has a more general distribution than peccaries and capybara, and (3) it occurs within relatively easy access of human population centers in coastal areas and cordilleras. The savannahs of the llanos of the Orinoco River constitute an extensive region of deer habitat both in Venezuela and in Colombia (the whitetail's relative importance also is high in Colombia and Guyana). Whitetail densities vary widely, from one deer per 500 hectares (one per 1,250 acres) to one deer per 8 to 25 hectares (one per 20–60 acres) on ranches where a degree of protection from hunting is given by the landowner. Local densities of one whitetail per 2 to 3 hectares (one per 5–7.5 acres) are encountered under exceptional conditions when no hunting at all is tolerated. Stocking rates for cattle are very high in comparison with rates in parts of the western United States. Less than 6 hectares (15 acres) per head is usual and less than 3 hectares (7.5 acres) per head is not uncommon on the southwestern llanos. Since water is provided for cattle, deer benefit from these sources (small reservoirs and ponds fed by mills) that, on the average, are about 2 to 3 kilometers (1.2–1.9 miles) apart. Much of the Venezuelan savannah could safely support 4 to 6 whitetails per square kilometer (10–15 per square mile) even under prevailing stocking levels for livestock.

Peccaries and brocket deer reduce the relative economic importance of the white-tailed deer in extensively and densely wooded regions. In Surinam, French Guiana, and in the Amazon parts of northern Brazil, the whitetail is much less important than other big game and is restricted in its distribution to coastal savannahs and specific savannah areas in the interior (J. P. Schulz personal communication:1977; F. Dias de Avila Pires personal communication:1977).

In the Andes countries, distribution of the whitetail is not limited by elevation but rather by steep arid habitat and by rainforest on the mountain slopes. In Peru, and probably in Ecuador, the white-tailed deer is the most important big game in the coastal zone, on the western slopes of the Andes and in intermontane valleys of the main Andean chain where forest growth is restricted by natural factors and human activities (A. Brack Egg personal communication:1977; I. Ceballos Bendezú personal communication:1977). It is less important on the high plains of southern Peru (the Puna or Altiplanos), where, at elevations of 3,800 meters (12,470 feet) or more, a southern relative of the whitetail, the taruca, is a more specialized competitor on steep terrain. White-tailed deer distribution in the Amazon River basin of these countries is poorly known, and curtailed by extensive rainforest. In this vast

An *Odocoileus virginianus gymnotis* buck, approximately three years old. This whitetail is somewhat emaciated, perhaps having worn itself out during the rut. In many areas, South American whitetails chose to drink water from tracks made by livestock at the edge of a water source. This may indicate fear of hazards, such as the alligators that inhabit most ponds, or relate to a need for the minerals in the sediments suspended in the water filling the hoofprints. In northcentral Venezuela, whitetails will trail on a daily basis—in some cases for considerable distances—to water sources in the more-or-less open savannah, in preference to drinking at nearby streams—generally fringed by steep banks and dense vegetation—where they may fall prey to the jaguar. They resort to streams only when other water sources are unavailable. South American whitetails enter water only when in mortal danger, for instance to elude hunters and dogs after having been wounded and when water is the only feasible escape avenue. *Photo by Peter A. Brokx.*

A buck group on ranchland on the savannah of Hato el Frío, grazing on grasses and flowers. For purposes of conservation and other policies, deer hunting on the ranch is not permitted. The whitetails are in poor condition because of overgrazing, and their incisors are worn early due to grazing, for lack of browse. This particular population would benefit from a well-managed hunter harvest. *Photo by Peter A. Brokx.*

territory, brocket deer, particularly *Mazama americana,* are of greatest economic significance in terms both of meat for local consumption and hides for the export (A. Brack Egg personal communication:1977). In all of Brazil, the brocket is also economically the most important game species, due to its extensive range and because tapir, pampas and swamp deer populations have diminished to the point of now having special protected status (F. Dias de Avila Pires personal communication:1977).

Unanimous professional opinion indicates white-tailed deer to be much less abundant now than they were prior to the mid-1940s in all of the region (Brazil, Venezuela, Peru and Surinam). The general decline appears to parallel a similar decrease in other wildlife and probably is a result of indiscriminate hunting, changes in land use and competition with domestic animals.

In the region from Merida north to Valera, Venezuela, the Andes subspecies *O. v. goudotii* was hunted to near extinction with the use of dogs during the 1950s. The island subspecies of *O. v. margaritae* is vulnerable to extirpation because of human population density and the aridity of the animal's habitat. Its actual status is probably that of rare. Whitetails of Curaçao have lived under special protection since the early 1930s in a population of about 100 deer (Husson 1960). No information was obtained on that population's present status. On the llanos, where *O. v. gymnotis* traditionally were abundant, deer generally are restricted to pockets rich in escape cover and under some degree of protection.

Based on the number of registered hunters and general hunting licenses issued, recreational hunters in the early 1970s numbered approximately 2,000 in Peru (A. Brack Egg personal communication:1977), 9,000 in Surinam (J. P. Schultz personal communication:1977) and 10,000 in Venezuela (Ministerio de Agricultura y Cría personal communications: 1966–1970). In most countries only a small proportion of the actual hunter numbers is registered, because there is little control over hunters from small urban and rural areas.

Parasites

South American whitetails generally are healthy, in good condition and appear to be more able than domestic animals to cope with external parasites. However, ticks (*Amblyoma* spp. and *Boophilus* spp.) and louseflies (*Lipoptena* sp.) occur on deer throughout the year—in much smaller numbers on does and young deer than on bucks. Investigation revealed that skin bots (*Dermatobia* sp.) and, less frequently, head bots (*Cephenemyia* sp.) were present on whitetails in small numbers (usually less than 10), particularly on deer from wooded localities and during the wet season. Only a few specimens suffered from screwworms (*Calliphora* sp.). In one of these deer, the infection was initiated by mange (*Demodex* sp.), and resulted in blood poisoning (*Micrococcus pyogenes),* causing the deer to be near death. A fawn had recovered from screwworm infection at the navel, which some ranchers believe to be a major cause of calf mortality. A few deer had several skin tumors.

Internal parasites of South American whitetails include an apparently harmless stomach fluke (*Cotylophoron* sp.), which is present in large numbers, especially on the low llanos. Wire worms (*Haemonchus contortus* and *Mecistocirrus* sp). occur in the abomasum and nodular worms *(Oesophagostomum asperum)* in the caecum of a large proportion of the deer, also without any indication of pathological effects. Bladderworm (*Taenia* sp.) infections are relatively common on the high llanos where the adult tapeworm may be harbored by fox and ocelot. Finds of a tapeworm (*Monieza* sp.), *Setaria* worms, larvae of unidentified lungworms and filarial worms encysted on the kidney and liver were so rare as to indicate chance infections. Blood smears once revealed microfilaria and large unidentified trypanosomes in three other specimens.

Foot-and-mouth disease, or "aftosa," occurs on the range of whitetails in South America, and ranchers reported that it last affected deer on the Venezuelan llanos during the 1950–1955 period. Both the presence of this disease and its potential impact on deer populations deserve consideration. Cases of anthrax are occasionally reported as rare outbreaks, but these are of less concern to deer management than is foot-and-mouth disease, which is endemic. Each year, when the savannah is drying in the western part of Edo. Apure, Venezuela, cattle and deer suffer from a disease apparently caused by an anaerobic organism thriving in stagnant water. It results in hoof rot and is accompanied by blisters in the mouth, because the animals lick their affected feet. It is said to be the cause of some mortality in both cattle and deer, and should be regarded as a serious condition because survivors require a long period of recovery and all deer collected at several ranches in the region were infected.

According to symptoms described by ranchers—strange, uncontrolled movements—equine encephalomyelitis caused large-scale deer mortality several times during this century. The last major outbreak was during the early 1940s.

Predators and Symbiotics

Man unquestionably is the most significant predator of South American whitetails. Other predators include the jaguar, which is extremely rare and endangered, and the ocelot, which is widely though illegally hunted for its fur. Mountain lions occasionally are encountered, and the small jaguarundi is capable of killing fawns. Ranchers pay an unoffical bounty to their employees for killing these cats. Local and not-so-reliable accounts tell of an occasional deer falling prey to the anaconda and boa. A fox *(Cerdocyon thous)* is very common, and rabies prevails during the dry season when these foxes and other wildlife assemble at waterholes. Foxes do not pose a direct threat to deer, but are a nuisance factor since they deter deer from drinking.

Whitetails enjoy a more amicable relationship with several bird species. The savannah hawk is called "pito venado" because its cry is believed to alert deer to impending danger. During the dry season, whitetails let themselves be deticked by flocks of grackles. And when tabanids are abundant during the wet season, a flycatcher *(Machefornis rixosa)* frequently hitches a ride on the deer's back. More remarkable is that this niche is also sought out by the yellow-headed caracara, an insectivorous and carrion feeder actually belonging to the birds of prey.

Hunting Regulations

A general hunting license is a basic requirement in all South American countries from which information was available. In addition to a license, the hunter in Peru has to buy a special permit to hunt white-tailed deer (A. Brack Egg personal communication:1977). In Venezuela, he needs both a gun license and a hunting license. The gun license is issued by the National Guard and belongs with the gun; the hunting license is free and must be renewed annually with the Division of Wildlife.

Hunting seasons generally are long. In Surinam, the season lasts from May through December, but this will be changed under a new game law (J. P. Schulz personal communication:1977). Both bucks and does can be harvested, and an estimated 250 deer were taken by about 100 hunters during 1976. Poaching is not considered to be severe. In Peru, the season lasts from April through December (I. Ceballos Bendezú personal communication: 1977). The aim is to establish seasons on a regional basis and to develop two large hunting preserves, each being approximately 60,000 hectares (148,260 acres) (A. Brack Egg personal communication:1977). A buck-only law exists but both sexes are hunted indiscriminately, and the illegal kill exceeds the legal kill. In Brazil, whitetail hunting seasons are established on a regional basis by the states, and tend to last from May or August through November. The hunter can legally take up to two bucks per day, but neither sex nor number is respected (F. Dias de Avila Pires personal communication:1977; C. T. de Carvalho personal communication:1977).

Since hunting traditions and socioeconomic levels of development are approximately similar in each of the countries under consideration (with the exception of Guyana and Surinam, which only recently became independent), the development of deer hunting regulations in Venezuela probably is typical. Hunting first was restricted in Venezuela in 1936. In 1941, licensing limited the deer harvest to bucks only without any limit on numbers. The law was revised in 1950 to prohibit definitively the hunting of does and a number of destructive hunting methods including commercial hunting. Periodic amendments were passed to reduce the hunters' take. Hunting of all wildlife was closed throughout the country during 1964 and 1965. It was opened again in 1966, from February through April, and provided for one buck per license. In 1967 and 1968, the hunter was not allowed to possess more than one buck at a time. In theory, a hunter was legally able to kill a buck every time he went hunting (Ministerio de Agricultura y Cría 1967). The season was closed again throughout the Republic during the early 1970s, at which time the law was revised completely.

In general, hunting laws are not respected in South America. This doe was killed illegally as she came to a lagoon with her yearling doe, which also was killed. The doe was about four years old and carried a 5.5-month-old fetus; the long-yearling also was gravid with a 4-month-old fetus. The photograph was taken in September, at the height of the wet season, indicating that deer on the dry high plains continue to visit watering places throughout the year and, therefore, are vulnerable during both seasons of the year. *Photo by Peter A. Brokx.*

The new law outlines both governmental responsibility and authority as well as the rules to be observed by hunters. Currently the hunting season usually lasts from February through April. It includes both the carnival and holy weeks, which traditionally have been reserved for hunting. The law now permits one buck per hunter per season, but is not respected, and illegal mortality exceeds the legal harvest.

Hunting Methods and Conditions

Until the mid-1940s, the Venezuelan hunting elite was a comparatively small group with a long tradition of unrestricted hunting, often with dogs. Little attention was given to production or harvest of trophy whitetails (Medina 1965). The hunters enjoyed strong ties with landowners and, hence, had easy access to game. The number of hunters multiplied with the development of a middle class that could afford to purchase a shotgun, the legal firearm for hunting, and also four-wheel-drive vehicles that make it possible to hook reflectors to car batteries for night hunting and to cover vast areas of savannah in a single weekend. Since the 1960s, recreational hunting pressure has in-

creased many times, but commercial (market) hunting is rare because it is against the law and whitetails have become scarce.

Management of wildlife (and other natural resources) is the responsibility of the Ministry of Agriculture. The regulation of firearms, and checking for infractions and permits, is done by the National Guard. This division of responsibility is not helpful. With exception of personnel in national parks, there is no equivalent of conservation law-enforcement officers. The burden of control rests with landowners, and hunting is subject to favoritism, compromises and mismanagement. Wildlife belongs to nobody until taken in possession, but the hunters should have permission from landowners to hunt. As a rule, landowners do not charge for hunting privileges nor do they want hunters on their land. However, efforts to exclude hunters generally are futile. According to law, deer cannot be hunted at night with the use of lights, nor when they come to drink at water holes. Nevertheless these are common methods of hunting. Many hunters are equipped with floodlights and headlights, and frequently with illegal .22-caliber rifles. Night hunting is widespread because of the behavior of the deer (they enter the open savannah after dark and again before dawn), the short range of the shotgun, landowner absenteeism, lack of public hunting areas and a general scarcity of deer.

Problems and Prognosis

Throughout the range of white-tailed deer in South America, wildlife laws and management plans usually fail because of a lack of wildlife protection and conservation law enforcement. With licensed recreational hunters in the minority, illegal kills vastly exceed the legal harvest, and neither the season length nor the buck-only law has had much of an effect. Season and bag limit restrictions remain extremely unpopular because they are thought to limit equal opportunity more than the hunter kill.

Attempts are being made in some countries to improve landowner/sportsmen relations. Venezuela has legislated an authoritative and democratic wildlife policy, but it is too early to assess its success. Peru plans to develop two large deer-hunting preserves (A. Brack Egg personal communication:1977). Brazil urgently needs to revise its wildlife conservation policy and to establish a wildlife management

The use of wildlife as a protein supplement is common in South America. These "llaneros" relish the opportunity of butchering a doe. They live and work at large estates and fetch their own meat to augment staple foods provided by the landowners. The notion of buck-only hunting probably is known, but likely is regarded as impractical and, if at all applicable, then only to sportsmen or "hunters from the city." *Photo by Peter A. Brokx.*

agency, with protection of wildlife populations and habitats receiving primary attention (C. T. de Carvalho personal communication:1977).

A shortage of trained wildlife professionals hampers management activities in all South American countries. Existing personnel usually are burdened by administrative responsibilities and multiple functions. The lack of professionals and field officers, as well as such factors as the shotgun being used for all game hunting and the preference for hunting (irrespective of species) during the dry period, leads to an opening and closing of seasons for all species on a national basis as most enforceable and administratively expedient. Hunting seasons are not based strictly on biological considerations, and wildlife laws and hunter registration are not enforced or only weakly so. Until such inadequacies are rectified, for instance through a system of deer tags and check stations, white-tailed deer management will remain largely superficial and ineffective.

A fundamental problem is that the whole field of wildlife ecology and management has gained little momentum because until recently the emphasis was on classical zoology for the continent, which has many wildlife species still to be identified and described. The conflict is compounded by the human population explosion (from about 20 million in 1930 to an an-

ticipated 100 million people by the year 2000 in the northern part of South America), with which the development of government services has difficulty keeping pace. Socioeconomic conditions put heavy pressure on renewable natural resources and especially on the whitetail as a source of protein.

Until recently, studies of deer were limited to the taxonomic nomenclature, with little practical management application. Further study of deer taxonomy is needed because regional variation is inadequately understood, but the question of periodicity in reproduction is far more important for management. Ecological studies on one subspecies or another are now in progress in several countries. For example, the white-tailed deer of the llanos in Venezuela are being studied by the Ministry of Agriculture. The National Science Foundation, Division of International Programs, has been funding a cooperative deer study in Surinam with the University of Georgia School of Forest Resources, but it is not restricted to white-tailed deer, and includes two species of brocket deer as well.

Also in Surinam, the Forest Service, in cooperation with the World Wildlife Fund and the International Union for the Conservation of Nature, is studying wildlife management procedures. These international agencies also are active in other South American countries. These programs, however, tend to be short-term and intermittent. In general there is a definite need for technical and financial support to conduct deer studies, but insofar as deer management is concerned, foreign technology should be a supplement to rather than a substitute for local and national conservation efforts. The establishment of a management infrastructure consisting of the use of field officers and checking stations in addition to hunter registration not only would greatly enhance the efficiency of biological baseline information collection, but also would serve to develop a rationale for integrating wildlife into multiple-use management, with economic incentives and benefits.

Note: A significant portion of the information in this chapter was gathered while the author was under contract as a biologist to Venezuela's Fondo Nacional de Investigaciones Agropecuaries, which largely funded the biological study, and the División de Fauna of the Ministerio de Agricultura y Cría, from February 1966 to June 1970.

Chapter 32

NEW ZEALAND

Lynn H. Harris
Department of Internal Affairs
New Zealand Wildlife Service
Wellington, New Zealand

The unique position of New Zealand in relation to exotic fauna was summarized by de Vos et al. (1956:181): "No other island group in the world provides such an interesting example of the havoc which introductions cause among native animals and plants as New Zealand. In no other area of comparable size has such a variety of mammals been introduced. Because of the long separation from other large land areas, a flora and fauna have evolved here which are very different from anything found elsewhere."

Prior to the arrival of Polynesian Maori immigrants about 1350 A.D., the only native land mammals on New Zealand were two species of bats. With the Maoris came the rat and the dog, species widely used for food. This ended the period during which the flora and avifauna of New Zealand evolved in the absence of browsing and predatory mammals.

A long period of importation and liberation of exotic species from around the globe began with the arrival of Captain Cook in 1773. More than 50 species of wild animals have since been introduced. Thirty-five of the exotic species—eight of them deer—have become acclimatized.

Five white-tailed deer (two bucks and three does) were introduced unsuccessfully into the Takaka Valley in the northern portion of the South Island in 1901. The whitetails were imported from Wichita, Kansas, by the Nelson Acclimatisation Society in an effort to establish a population for sporting purposes.

In 1905, New Zealander T. E. Donne, a government official, visited the United States and arranged for the purchase of whitetails from New Hampshire. Donne (1924) recalled that more than 100 deer were driven through 1 meter (3 feet) of snow into a large holding pen, and 24 healthy specimens were selected for shipment. Nineteen of these whitetails arrived in New Zealand in good condition.

Seven does and two bucks were released at Cook's Arm, Port Pegasus, Stewart Island, on 26 March 1905. Nine deer (sex ratio unknown) were liberated in the Rees Valley at the head of Lake Wakatipu in the South Island. One buck was turned out in the Takaka Valley in an attempt to supplement the five whitetails released there four years earlier. The Lake Wakatipu (Rees Valley) and the Stewart Island populations became well-established in two completely different habitat types. It is believed that they are the only populations of the *Odocoileus virginianus borealis* (Northern Woodland) subspecies in the southern hemisphere.

When white-tailed deer were introduced to New Zealand in the first decade of the 1900s, they quickly adapted to the seasonal changes and reversed the northern hemisphere pattern of antler shedding and regrowth, rutting, and parturition (Figure 106). Most antler rubbing and cleaning is in February, and by early March all bucks have fully hardened and cleaned antlers. Rutting commences about mid-April and peaks during May. Antlers are cast during October and November. The mature and older bucks cast first. Fawns normally are born from mid-December through January. Female fawns have been known to give birth as late as March. Multiple births are rare in the Wakatipu population and not known to occur on Stewart Island.

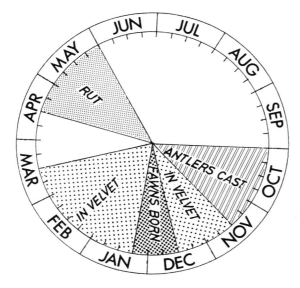

Figure 106. The seasonal pattern of antler shedding and regrowth, rutting, and parturition for white-tailed deer in New Zealand is almost a complete reversal of that shown in the northern hemisphere.

The whitetail is one of the few deer introduced into New Zealand that never equalled or exceeded the antler size of the originating stock in its native land. The top trophy head

from Lake Wakatipu measured 155 points, and the top trophy from Stewart Island measured 140 points (Boone and Crockett score). Trophy quality *per se* has improved in recent years. On Stewart Island, the biggest antlers have come from the east coast around Port Adventure and the poorest from the west coast around Doughboy Bay and Port Pegasus. Bucks from the Doughboy Bay region produce little more than spikes, probably because of a low plane of nutrition.

LAKE WAKATIPU WHITETAIL POPULATION

Environment

The 290-square-kilometer (112-square-mile) Lake Wakatipu lies across 45 degrees south latitude and is approximately the same distance from the equator as is northern New Hampshire (Figure 107). The lake is 309 meters (1,014 feet) above sea level.

Both the Dart and Rees catchments at the northern end of the 84-kilometer (52-mile) long lake are U-shaped glacial valleys with steep walls and extensive alluvial floors. The region

The lower Dart Valley, home of New Zealand's Lake Wakatipu white-tailed deer population. The steep slopes are unsuitable habitat. *Photo by J. H. G. Johns; courtesy of the New Zealand Forest Service.*

is subject to seasonal extremes between droughts and very wet periods (Bathgate 1976). Annual rainfall is approximately 102 centimeters (40 inches). Heavy snowfalls are common, and high elevations (up to 2,820 meters:9,250 feet) contain permanent snowfields and glaciers. Average annual temperature ranges from approximately 30 to −10 degrees Celsius (86–14 degrees Fahrenheit).

The principal forest type is southern false-beech. Mountain falsebeech is the dominant tree species. Halls totara and southern rata are associated in a band along midslope valley walls. The low altitude slopes below 600 meters (1,970

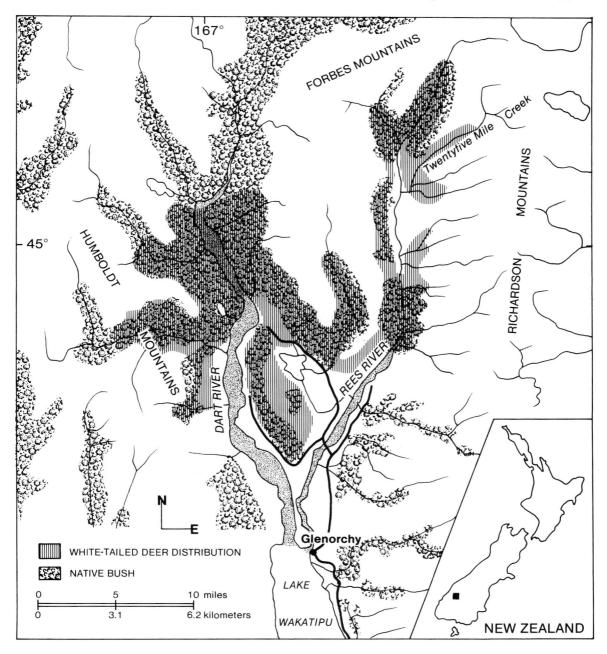

Figure 107. The 1982 range of New Zealand's Lake Wakatipu white-tailed deer population, along the Dart and Rees rivers. Map prepared by R. W. Fisher and Robert Pratt.

feet) and the river valley flats are preferred by white-tailed deer, particularly where the valleys contain a mixture of tussock and introduced grasses. Within the beech forest, species such as kupuka, karamu, hinahina and many other deer-preferred trees or shrubs are either absent or uncommon.

Vegetation has been modified substantially by other browsing animals, such as the brushtail opossum and red deer, the introductions of which pre-date the arrival of white-tailed deer. The river flats are grazed by domestic livestock, and cattle have had access to the beech forest on lower valley slopes. Hares are locally numerous on the river flats, and rabbits are scattered throughout the valley floor. Also, the area has been subjected to accidental fires.

Whitetail Population

The white-tailed deer population at Lake Wakatipu is limited to the northwestern end where the Dart and the Rees rivers combine to enter the lake (*see* Figure 107). The population has increased in its rate of dispersal in recent years, but its overall distribution still is quite restricted considering the period of occupation (Bathgate 1976). The present dispersal rate is 0.34 kilometer (0.21 mile) per year. The population received stringent protection from 1905 until 1919, when a limited number of hunting licenses were issued. All forms of protection were removed in 1926 and hunting became unrestricted.

In 1974, the combined population of red deer and white-tailed deer was 26.3 deer per square kilometer (68.2 per square mile) in the Earnslaw Burn, 21.7 deer per square kilometer (56.3 per square mile) in the Rees Valley and 16.7 deer per square kilometer (43.2 per square mile) in the Dart Valley. The estimated proportion of white-tailed deer in these catchments was 50, 40 and 40 percent, respectively (Bathgate 1976). The total white-tailed deer population within the survey area was approximately 840 animals, or 5.2 deer per square kilometer (13.6 per square mile).

A prime Lake Wakatipu whitetail buck in velvet hurdles a pasture fence to gain access to the shelter of an adjacent thicket. *Photo by J. H. G. Johns; courtesy of the New Zealand Forest Service.*

Whitetails prefer habitat on the valley floors and northeasterly slopes of less than 20 degrees within the first 300 meters (985 feet) of elevation. They rapidly diminish in number as elevation increases, and rarely are seen above 900 meters (2,950 feet). In contrast to red deer, whitetails do not utilize the subalpine zone of the montane grassland above 1,000 meters (3,280 feet).

For a number of years, white-tailed deer at Lake Wakatipu have been in poor condition and fawn mortality is high. Red deer, however, generally are in good physical condition. Competition between whitetails and red deer for available browse has been suggested as a cause for both the decline of the white-tailed deer population and its high fawn mortality (Harris 1970), but this was questioned by Bathgate (1976), whose survey showed very little range overlap.

Disease probably limits the whitetail population. For more than 20 years, emaciated deer have been noted and an occasional dead whitetail found with no visible signs of cause of death. Use of sheep and cattle pasture provides ample opportunity for the gregarious whitetail to become infected with a number of diseases and parasites. Christie and Andrews (1965) showed the presence in white-tailed deer of dog tapeworm cysts—a caecum nematode—and six species of trychostrongylid nematodes in the fourth stomach. In 1963, deaths of fawns and yearlings were attributed to pleuropneumonia (Daniel 1967). Bathgate (1976) reported the presence of strongyoids, nematodirus and dog-tapeworm eggs, lungworms, and oöcysts. Brucellosis and leptospira organisms have not been detected in the whitetail population at Lake Wakatipu.

Outlook

Continued existence of the Wakatipu whitetail population depends largely on the attitude of local farmers, since they own much of the favored habitat. Because the whitetails occur on terrain included in or bordering farmland and, for the past 30 years, farmers in the region have severely restricted hunting access in order to protect the remaining deer, the area has not been popular with hunters.

This small and unhealthy population of deer likely will never achieve prominence as a big game trophy population. By the same token, these deer are not likely to pose a serious threat to the soil and water retention value of the forests.

The Lake Wakatipu whitetails have been afforded unofficial protection by local farmers in recent years. As a result, the animals frequently are seen mixing with domestic livestock. *Photo by J. H. G. Johns; courtesy of the New Zealand Forest Service.*

STEWART ISLAND WHITETAIL POPULATION

Environment

Stewart Island, known to the Maori as Raki-ura (Land of Heavenly Glows), is the most southerly and smallest of the main islands of New Zealand (Figure 108), and lies between 40 degrees 40 minutes and 47 degrees 18 minutes south latitude. It is roughly triangular, with a coastline of about 756 kilometers (470 miles) and a total area of 1,721 square kilometers (664 square miles). Composed mostly of granite and gneiss, the interior—with the exception of the extensive swampland of the Freshwater River valley—is mountainous, with short precipitous gullies and steep ridges. In the northwest, the broken country rises rapidly in a series of ridges that culminate in Mt. Anglem (980 meters:3,215 feet), the highest point on the island. Winter snow lies on Mt. Anglem only for short periods.

The climate of the south, and other mountainous regions, is subantarctic and without extremes of heat and cold. Average annual temperature ranges from 27 to − 1 degrees Celsius (81–30 degrees Fahrenheit). The mean annual rainfall is about 150 centimeters (59 inches), fairly evenly distributed throughout the year.

The island is covered with forest and scrub, even though the soils are infertile, acid and poorly structured. Vegetation around the coastline consists mainly of wind-resistant scrub species. Puheretaiko is dominant. With increasing elevation, the narrow coastal scrub gives way to extensive podocarp-hardwood forest dominated by rimu and kamahi. At an altitude of about 300 meters (985 feet), this forest merges into a scrub belt dominated by manuka and bog pine. Between 500 and 700 meters (1,640–2,300 feet) elevation, the true subalpine scrub tupari dominates. Above 700 meters (2,300 feet), prostrate alpine species carpet the ground. There are no substantial tussock grasslands such as normally are found elsewhere in New Zealand above the bushline.

During their period of establishment in the early 1900s, white-tailed deer browsed the drier ridges of Stewart Island and destroyed much

White-tailed deer on Stewart Island prefer habitat at lower elevations along the coast and with a northern aspect and slopes of 10 to 20 degrees. *Photo by J. H. G. Johns; courtesy of the New Zealand Forest Service.*

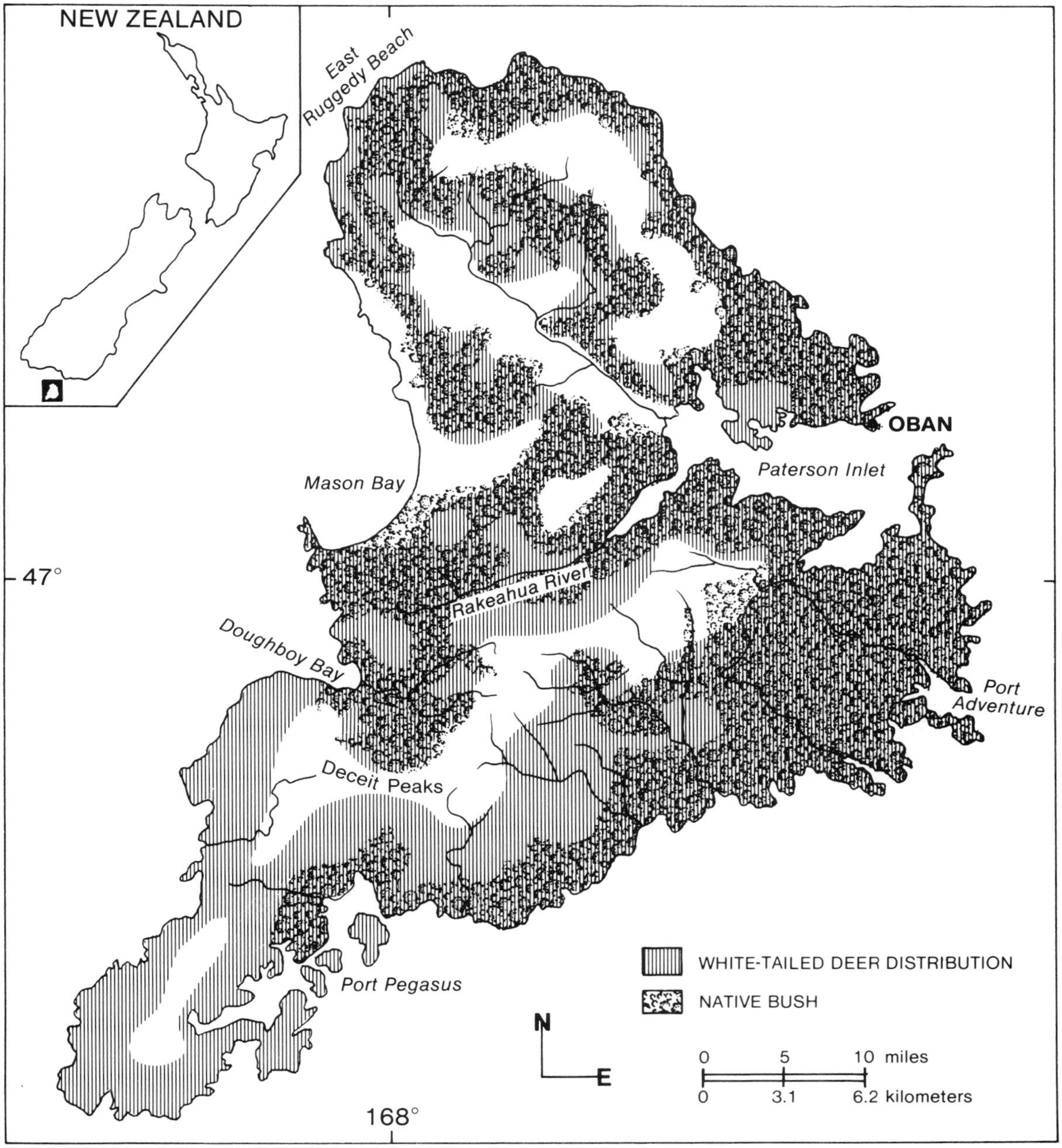

Figure 108. The 1982 range of New Zealand's Stewart Island white-tailed deer population. Map prepared by R. W. Fisher and Robert Pratt.

of the palatable vegetation. As the population increased, the deer moved to the moist gullies and small valleys that held an abundance of highly preferred food species. As a result of heavy browsing, this habitat was overused and now contains a dense mass of supplejack vines and unpalatable ferns. Elsewhere, the highly preferred species, such as five finger, karamu, wineberry, haumakaroa, pate and kupukatree, are heavily browsed and have been eliminated in some areas. Much of the diverse understory has been replaced with the prolific and unpalatable hard fern. Ground cover now favors red deer and brush-tail opossum (Williamson 1976).

Whitetail Population

Favored initially by strict protection, the Stewart Island population of whitetails spread northward soon after release in 1905 and increased rapidly (Harris 1970). They first were seen at the northern extremity of the island in 1926 (R. H. Traill personal communication:1976). The dispersal rate of 2.9 kilometers (1.8 miles) per year is approximately 8.5 times greater than that for white-tailed deer at Lake Wakatipu.

The first hunting season was opened in 1919, but only two licenses were issued for white-tailed deer. During the 1920s, the Department of Lands and Survey and the State Forest Service (now the New Zealand Forest Service) were asked by conservation organizations to initiate controls on the whitetail populations because of the animals' dramatic impact on the island's vegetation.

Protection was removed from all deer in 1926, and a bounty of $0.20 per recovered tail was instituted. During the next two years, a local hunter was engaged by government agencies to destroy deer for $0.50 per animal. These efforts were ineffective. The area was much too large and too rugged to be hunted with any degree of effectiveness by a single person. In addition, the bounty was insufficient to induce the few island residents to kill deer in numbers large enough to make a difference.

Between 1937 and 1952, teams of government professional hunters killed 6,380 deer, of which approximately 30 percent were whitetails. Between 1955 and 1958, a bounty was reintroduced and 791 red and 1,006 white-tailed deer were taken by sportsmen and local residents.

Between December 1975 and February 1976, a preliminary survey of whitetail distribution and density was made by the New Zealand Forest Service (Williamson 1976). A total of 6,300 pellet plots were established, and the density was assessed with 90-percent confidence limits, computed on the basis of a binomial distribution of pellet group frequencies. The percentage frequency of defecation group per plot was 1–5 light, 6–15 moderate and 16+ high.

A "skin line" with 13 white-tailed deer hides indicates a successful hunting expedition on Stewart Island. The trophies displayed on the table are typical of the poor-quality antlers of bucks on the island. *Photo by Brendan Coe.*

Currently, the highest densities of white-tailed deer occur along the western and northeastern coasts. The lowest population densities are within inland catchments of the Freshwater and Rakeahua rivers. Deer densities are highest at elevations below 30 meters (100 feet) (Williamson 1976). The whitetails on Stewart Island also favor a northerly aspect and slopes of 10 to 20 degrees or less. Above 30 meters (100 feet) elevation, habitat use by whitetails falls off markedly but continues up to about 250 meters (820 feet). While white-tailed deer favor the coastal scrub and rata-kamahi forest, there is little overlap with red deer that occupy elevations varying from 61 to 250 meters (200–820 feet).

White-tailed deer on Stewart Island are fond of water and swim long distances between islands in search of food or during the rut. They also take to water to escape dogs. Deer have been seen swimming in the open sea up to 4 kilometers (2.5 miles) from shore and for periods of up to 1.5 hours (M. Schofield personal communication:1976). The less frequented beaches and the shallows are used as playgrounds by deer. They eat certain seaweed, particularly common bull kelp, which is deposited on the beaches by falling tides.

During the 1940s and 1950s, two deer were shot that exhibited prominent characteristics of both red and white-tailed deer. The animals were recorded as hybrids but not subjected to scientific examination (M. C. Kershaw personal communication:1976).

The incidence of disease and parasites on Stewart Island is unknown.

Outlook

Because it is an island, Stewart Island is isolated, sparsely populated, relatively undeveloped and has much to offer the hunter, hiker or hardy tourist. The white-tailed deer is the island's main hunting attraction, and hunters spend considerable money for transportation, equipment and provisions. Hunting pressure likely will increase. Even now, all prime hunting areas are occupied for most of the year, and approximately 1,000 white-tailed deer are taken by sportsmen annually. However, even this substantial harvest—primarily from the narrow coastal forest belt—appears to be insufficient to ensure maintenance of a healthy forest.

A typical whitetail hunter's camp in the coastal forest of Stewart Island. *Photo by Brendan Coe.*

Vegetational surveys in 1977 showed that the vulnerable coastal forest favored by whitetails has been seriously affected by the combined feeding of opossums and deer. Such browsing pressure causes a lack of vigor, which then is compounded by harsh exposure to strong, salt-laden winds. As a result, much of the coastal forest belt on the north and northeast coasts of the island has been eliminated.

In 1980, the New Zealand Forest Service decided to embark on a trial deer poisoning program to determine if a significant impact on a peak white-tailed deer population could be made. The decision was made only after inquiries by conservation and other interested organizations had been satisfied. A substantial area of eastern Stewart Island was chosen and divided into three blocks, A, B and C, each containing strips of impoverished coastal forest from 0.4 to 1.0 kilometer (1,325–3,281 feet) wide. The technique involved application of a Carbopol-based gel containing 10 percent sodium monofluoroacetate (1080) from hand-applicator tubes to deer-preferred vegetation. Between 18 February and 15 March 1981, 2,600 baits were prepared by breaking down branches of favored browse species, mainly kupuka, and applying 1080 gel to about 15 to 20 leaves per bait. Block B between the two treated areas was used as a control block and not poisoned.

Systematic searches were made for dead deer during and immediately following the poison operation. A total of 217 carcasses were found, 60 and 157 respectively in or adjacent to blocks A and C. There were no obvious disparities in the age and sex composition of the deer found dead, suggesting that the poisoning was non-selective. There was no immediate evidence of birds or other nontarget species having been killed. Although complete data from subsequent searches and pellet counts are not yet available, it has been speculated that at least 75 percent of the white-tailed deer on both blocks were killed.

The experiment has shown that where recreational hunting is not of sufficient intensity to control deer numbers adequately the natural bait poisoning technique is an efficient method to reduce a whitetail population. However, because of hunter and general public opposition to any form of poisoning, especially of deer, any future use of the technique and its justification also would be subjected to the most searching scrutiny.

Chapter 33

CENTRAL EUROPE

Dušan Bojović
Chief
Department of Wildlife
Institute for Forestry and Wood Industry
Belgrade, Yugoslavia

Lowell K. Halls
Project Leader (Retired)
Southern Forest Experiment Station
U.S. Forest Service
Nacogdoches, Texas

White-tailed deer first were introduced into Central Europe near the Graffenegg Castle, Austria, in 1870. In 1875, the deer were transferred to an enclosure near Weidlingau and then to Vienna in 1910. The fate of these deer is uncertain. Possibly, they were moved from Austria to Czechoslovakia, or they may have disappeared by natural causes and poaching.

At present, there is a long-established population of whitetails in Czechoslovakia and a relatively new population in Yugoslavia.

CZECHOSLOVAKIA

The Dobris forest was the first home of white-tailed deer in Czechoslovakia. This 320-square-kilometer (124-square-mile) forest is located a few kilometers southwest of Prague, in rolling terrain between the Vltava and Beronka rivers. Originally, the forest types were mainly mixed beech/oak and beech/fir. But as a result of stand manipulations by foresters in the seventeenth and eighteenth centuries, the stands now are primarily spruce. The growing season in Czechoslovakia ranges from 130 to 165 days. Annual precipitation is about 55 centimeters (21.7 inches), 65 percent of which usually occurs in summer. The soil is relatively infertile and acid. Elevation is 350 to 660 meters (1,150–2,165 feet) above sea level.

In 1890, six white-tailed deer were imported from Canada and released into an enclosure within the Dobris forest. This nucleus was augmented by 6 additional whitetails from Canada

in 1896 and 16 more in 1906. Also, three deer from an unknown source were introduced from the Opočno forest near Prague in 1893. During World War I, the Dobris forest enclosure was destroyed. Most of the deer remained on the area, but a few dispersed 20 to 35 kilometers (12.4–21.7 miles) into adjacent forests.

Whitetails at the Dobris forest reproduced and acclimated well, and were harvested regularly from 1911 to 1915. Their numbers decreased during World War I. From then until 1928, no data are available on deer population and harvests. Thereafter, 12 deer were harvested annually from 1928 through 1932, 22 in 1933, 30 in 1934 and 24 in 1935. The whitetail population reached a high of 240 in 1936, but no harvest or population data are available from 1937 through 1956. From 1957 through 1970, 100 deer were harvested.

Because of a planned annual removal of 25 to 30 percent of the summer population, white-tailed deer have not increased the past few years, ranging in number from 66 to 155. To expand the population into new locations, eight deer were transported in 1965 to a 17-hectare (42-acre) enclosure in Holovous near Opočno, and two to a small enclosure near Košice in Slovakia. The deer at Holovous were released from the pen by accident in 1965 and that population remains unconfined.

Currently, the total whitetail population in Czechoslovakia is approximately 130 deer, with an age structure of 21 percent young males, 13 percent adult males, 44 percent mature females and 22 percent fawns.

The quality of harvested bucks, as reflected by antler size, generally has been good. At two international fairs in Brno and Česke Budjejovice in 1971 and 1976, respectively, the trophy points ranged from 246.1 to 317.8, according to Conseil International de la Chasse (CIC) formula.

An unfortunate aspect of the whitetail introduction into Czechoslovakia is that physical examinations of the translocated deer failed to detect the presence of big liver flukes. Thus, this internal parasite was introduced into Europe via the white-tailed deer and has infested other wildlife (mainly European red deer) and livestock. The fluke now is a major management problem in Czechoslovakia.

YUGOSLAVIA

White-tailed deer were introduced into Yugoslavia to fill a void of huntable big game species in small and discontinuous forested areas that previously had been occupied by European red deer. The whitetail was selected because of its ability to adapt to a wide variety of environmental conditions, its sedentary nature, its ability to produce trophy antlers at an

The release of white-tailed deer in Yugoslavia in 1970—part of a cooperative translocation project by the U.S. Department of Agriculture and the Yugoslavia Institute for Forestry and Wood Industry. *Photo courtesy of the Yugoslavia Institute for Forestry and Wood Industry, Department of Wildlife.*

early age, its high productive potential, and because it was less apt to conflict with forest management for timber production than were red deer. It was believed that if the whitetail could be introduced successfully, it would do much to revive hunting tourism and improve the economy in several depressed areas.

The introduction was a cooperative program of the U.S. Department of Agriculture and the Yugoslavia Institute for Forestry and Wood Industry. It began with the shipment of three does and two bucks from Virginia in October 1970. Additional shipments consisted of two does from Maryland in October 1971, one buck and three does from Pennsylvania in March 1973, and 4 does and 6 bucks from Louisiana in September 1973. In the 1970 and 1971 shipments, several deer died as a result of the long translocation, but losses were minimal in the 1973 shipments.

Since 1973, the whitetail production in Yugoslavia has increased steadily through reproduction. As a rule, does giving birth for the first time produce one fawn, and older females drop two fawns. There were 9 bucks and 16 does in March 1974, 16 bucks and 23 does in March 1975, 23 bucks and 29 does in March 1976, and 34 bucks and 36 does in February 1977. In 1977, fawns constituted 30 percent of the population, two-year-olds constituted 20 percent, three- and four-year-olds comprised 30 percent, and whitetails older than four years of age accounted for 20 percent. The oldest animal was an eight-year-old doe.

The first two shipments (1970 and 1971) of whitetails were kept in a 5-hectare (12.4-acre) enclosure 15 kilometers (9.3 miles) from Belgrade, where the deer were permitted to graze a wide variety of improved forage plants and were observed closely. These observations were the basis for selecting preferred forage species to be planted in large enclosures for expanding whitetail populations.

The 1973 shipments of white-tailed deer from the United States were confined to a 110-hectare (272-acre) enclosure in a bottomland hardwood forest along the Danube River at Karadjordjeve, 120 kilometers (75 miles) northwest of Belgrade. This area includes forest stands of black locust, willow and oaks mixed with maple, elm, hawthorn, dogwood and privet, natural and cultivated pastures, and feeding and salting areas. Cultivated pastures were planted to alfalfa, grasses, Jerusalem artichoke and turnip mustard. During winter, deer had limited access to a feed mixture of ground cereals plus vitamin additives and a silage made of molasses and branches from local woody species. In this enclosure, observations were made on the animals' daily behavior, including the kind and amount of plants eaten, as a basis for selecting habitats for population expansion. Examinations by veterinarians for incidence of big liver flukes were negative.

In spring 1975, small groups of deer were moved to two new locations. One buck and two does were situated at the Deliblato forest northeast of Belgrade in the foothills of the

White-tailed deer translocated to Yugoslavia from the United States in the early 1970s were confined in enclosures near Belgrade, so that scientists could observe the animals' health and feeding habits. *Photo courtesy of the Yugoslavia Institute for Forestry and Wood Industry, Department of Wildlife.*

Karpati Mountains. This sandy area is dominated by black locust and pine trees along with cottonwood, ash, juniper, alder and oak. Two bucks and three does were transported to Brac, one of the largest of a big group of islands in the Adriatic Sea. The Mediterranean climate there supports a mixture of evergreen shrubs including the holly oak. At both locations, the deer were confined in 5–10-hectare (12.4–24.7-acre) enclosures for acclimatization and observation for at least three years.

An additional transfer of six whitetails was scheduled for 1977 into the mountainous mixed forests of beech, fir and oaks in western Serbia.

In 1983, the white-tailed deer population at Karadjordjeve had increased to approximately 400 head and was spread over the region of forests about 200 kilometers (124 miles) along the Danube River. Regular hunting started in 1980. Obviously weak deer were removed as well as a few mature healthy bucks. Antlers on one buck scored 422.4 points on CIC scale.

Chapter 34

FINLAND

Kaarlo F.A. Nygrén
Game Biologist
Game and Fisheries Research Institute
Helsinki, Finland

In September 1934, eight white-tailed deer fawns arrived in Helsinki from the United States. Three of the deer had died enroute, and the remaining four does and one buck were transported to Laukko Estate, Vesilahti, in southwestern Finland. The five survivors were kept in captivity until May 1938, at which time the does were released from the enclosure. The buck had escaped previously, but remained nearby. This was the beginning of the free-ranging white-tailed deer population of Finland.

It is not known from precisely which areas of the United States the translocated deer were obtained. This can only be speculated on by studying the list of the Finnish emigrants willing to ". . . enrich the wildlife of the forests of Finland by sending over the sea the most beautiful and noblest animal of our new home areas, the Virginia- or White-Tailed Deer." The donation document, dated 18 August 1934, included the names of 72 private contributors and two public money-collection events in Virginia, Minnesota. The donors were from Duluth, Ely, Eveleth, Floodwood, Hibbing, Middle River, Iron Mountain, Nashwauk, New York Mills, Tower and Virginia, Minnesota. According to some personal communications, the shipment was completed by the addition of an unknown number of fawns from New York State.

Two more groups of whitetails were imported later, in 1937 and 1948. The history of the deer transported from New York State to Finland in 1937 is not known completely. However, four fawns were introduced into the Helsinki zoo for translocation purposes at that time. Also unknown is whether those four whitetails ever reached or established themsevles in open range. It is believed that they all died within several years of transport, and did not contribute to the existing population of Old World whitetails.

The last introduction took place in 1948, when three pairs of whitetails were transported to Laukko at the end of that year. Two or three of the deer died in captivity; the others were released in 1949. Local observers maintain that the animals did not survive the following winter.

The first five white-tailed deer stocked in Finland—from the United States—in 1934. *Photo taken on Laukko Estate, presumably by V. Nurminen.*

In 1948, there was a population of 90 to 100 whitetails in Finland. Single animals were seen moving to the southwest and west. In 1950, whitetails were seen on the southern coast of Finland and the population estimate reached 200. Reproduction obviously was quite high; does were seen with three and sometimes four fawns. Ten years later, the population was considered to be at least 1,000 (Brander 1962). The Finnish whitetail population at that time was booming. The increase was not halted even by the severest winters, such as that of 1965–1966, which culled at least 7 percent of the winter population (Koivisto et al. 1966).

Due to lack of adequate censusing methods, accurate figures describing the development of the Finnish deer population do not exist. Counting the number of deer visiting winter-feeding sites underestimates the actual size of the population, which uses narrow paths to and from feeding sites and is more or less nocturnal in its feeding and movements. The increase in population has shown some signs of slowing down in the last few years (1980–1982). It is not clear whether this is a lasting trend or merely the result of some severe winters combined with decreased winter-feeding activities in some areas.

In the 1960s, white-tailed deer were introduced at least to Oulujoki River Valley, situated about 450 kilometers (280 miles) north of the original 1938 release area, and to the town Mikkeli, about 200 kilometers (124 miles) east of Laukko. It appears that the Oulujoki introduction was not successful. The eastern group, however, became well established. Whitetails seen in the easternmost parts of Finland (Värtsilä, Kesälahti, Kitee) apparently are of that origin. According to some personal communications, the deer already may have crossed the border between Finland and the Soviet Union, where the mixed-wood forests of Ladoga Lake are potential deer biotopes.

Ten white-tailed deer also were sold to the Soviet Union in 1980. These were captured by the author in Honkola Estate, Urjala, where the highest deer densities in Finland now occur. The shipment was divided between Moscow and Leningrad, and the deer held in captivity. At least nine of the Russian whitetails were alive in 1981.

Ten deer (six does and four bucks) also were sold to Bulgaria in 1977 and introduced near Devin, less than 50 kilometers (31 miles) from the Bulgaria-Greece border. The population near Kozy Rog (Chamois Horn) Hunting Lodge

Trapping by drive net (left) and handling white-tailed deer (right) in Finland in 1980, for translocation to the Soviet Union. *Photos by Simo Ahlgren.*

was increasing in 1981. About 20 to 30 whitetails were seen in that area.

ENVIRONMENT

Laukko, the starting point of the Finnish white-tailed deer population, is situated in southwestern Finland (Figure 109). Most of the area is less than 100 meters (328 feet) above sea level. Private ownerships, in small land parcels, are scattered along rivers and lakeshores. The arable land is arranged in chains of narrow fields, leaving the forested area as big polygons split by forest roads, clearcut areas and marshes. There are few big lakes in this area. Instead, many rivers, creeks, small lakes and wetlands add to the variety of habitats. The soil includes the largest clay layers in Finland, shifting to the less fertile moraine formations in the north. Being part of the ancient bottom of the Baltic Sea, the areas closer to the coast still show cliffy islets with pine and rich bush and bottom-layer vegetation, typical of the Finnish archipelago.

The proportion of arable land increases to the west and southwest. Fields grow larger and forests smaller, which apparently discourages deer from establishing. Conditions are more favorable in the archipelago, where whitetails found their way in the late 1960s. The first of

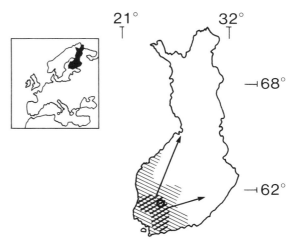

Figure 109. The geographical range (line screen) of the white-tailed deer in Finland. The most densely populated area is represented by the crosshatch screen and includes the original introduction site at Laukko Estate (circle). Arrows indicate sites to which whitetails have been introduced recently.

these were seen in 1972–1973 on some islands of Åland. To the east of the deer area, big lakes and waterways cut the whitetail's expansion routes. Snow depth seems to be another limiting factor—perhaps the most important.

The climate of the area occupied by deer is milder than the average at the same latitude elsewhere in Finland. Snow cover averages 20 to 30 centimeters (8–12 inches) and lasts about 135 days—as long as the mean growth period in summer. The sum of the effective temperatures (the sum of diurnal mean temperatures over 5 degrees Celsius: 41 degrees Fahrenheit) is between 1200 and 1300. The mean temperature in January is about −6 degrees Celsius (21 degrees Fahrenheit), and in July about 17 degrees Celsius (63 degrees Fahrenheit). Mean annual precipitation is 600 to 700 millimeters (23.6–27.6 inches), of which 275 to 300 millimeters (10.8–11.8 inches) occurs during the vegetative growth period.

Waterways freeze in December and become ice-free in April or May. The snow usually hardens in February or March. Crusty layers of icy snow often limit whitetail movements, confining the deer to well-trampled paths and "yards," preferably in the spruce thickets or close to winter feeding sites. In spring, snow melts first on the southern slopes of the hills, then on arable land. Large group of whitetails frequently are seen basking on hillsides and feeding in the first snow-free fields.

During the hottest and driest time of summer, the deer usually keep to moist riverbeds and marshy valleys, visiting young crops and gardens frequently.

It seems that, in general, the presence of cultivated land not too monotonous and extensive is essential to the welfare of whitetailed deer in Finland.

VEGETATION AND WHITETAIL FOOD HABITS

Southwestern Finland has the densest and fastest growing forests of the country. Being rather fertile and flat, most of the dry land has been cultivated. Forests cover 40 to 50 percent of its surface, representing some 80 to 100 cubic meters of wood per hectare (2,825–3,531 cubic feet per acre), which is well-above average in Finland. Scotch pine is the most common species of tree, closely followed by Norway spruce. Each species stands for about 40 percent of the total of tree-layer plants. A gradual shift toward the spruce in forestry is partially explained by browsing pressure of moose and deer, making it difficult for pine, silver birch and downy birch to regenerate. Spruce, on the other hand, is not favored by the large ungulates as a food source.

Birch seems to be more important for deer than is Scotch pine. Browsing and barking of spruce usually is considered to be a sign of critical range conditions. It often is seen in late winter, when snow cover is deep and deer are starving.

Common juniper is one of the most important winter food species due to its easy availability, good palatability and browse tolerance. This is seen in a study of whitetail winter food and activity (Andersson and Koivisto 1980), although the researchers did not give estimates of availability. Other studies of range use have shown that juniper is quite far from the top of the availability list in the whitetail area (K. F. A. Nygrén personal files). The area is frequently dominated by other conifers and many deciduous species, including quaking aspen, European mountain-ash, birches, mountain alder, willows, alder-buckthorn, bird cherry, red raspberry and currants.

Aspen and European mountain-ash frequently are high on the preference list. In fact, they are consumed very rapidly, even in summer, because their browse tolerance is limited. This is clearly seen in densely vegetated and canopied areas.

Among the shrubs, sourtop bilberry and cowberry are eaten even in winter and considered very important food plants for deer and moose. In winter, these shrubs are available only in mature spruce stands and other snow-sheltered places, where deer dig them out from snow 10 to 20 centimeters (4–8 inches) or more deep. Cowberry or lingonberry often grows in close proximity to heather, which is reached more easily on the windward slopes of typical deer-favored ridges and hills during winter.

Lichens—epiphytic and growing on the ground—also are consumed year round. They apparently are one of the factors attracting deer to timber-cutting areas.

The summer diet of whitetails in Finland is not well-known. It seems to consist of most of the herbs and shrubs available in the ecotones of mixed-wood forest openings, abandoned fields and natural meadows. The presence of ferns in the summer diet of deer is recognized. They are very abundant in the clay soil area, growing mostly in the dampest places. Their order of preference by whitetails is not known. The biggest of fern species include ladyfern, spiny woodfern and eagles wing. One of the most common species, common bracken fern, grows in a wide variety of habitats.

A typical 1.5-year-old Finnish whitetail buck and a doe at a feeding site. *Photo by I. Ala-ajos.*

Average winter food consumption by whitetails was estimated by Andersson and Koivisto (1980), using the methods of simulated browsing and cut-twig counting and measuring, and was calculated to be about 28 grams (1 ounce) fresh weight per kilogram per day of live deer weight.

Winter conditions in Finland are quite harsh for white-tailed deer. This is clearly demonstrated by Paatsama et al. (1973) in a study of the bone growth of deer. It seems that the growth of the whitetail skeleton is practically stopped in midwinter. This was especially evident with bucks that had too limited time to start a winter diet and gather essential nutrients for bone and antler growth. Paatsama et al. concluded that the white-tailed deer cannot reach optimal growth in Finland without intensive winter feeding.

MANAGEMENT

The translocation of whitetails to Finland was met with enthusiasm. It was a nice gesture from the Finnish emigrants in the United States. In addition, it was reasoned that the translocated deer fill an available ecological niche, as indeed they have. There were no other cervids smaller than the moose to use the available resources. Native wild reindeer were virtually

Without intensive supplemental feeding in winter, such as with the pellet-fodder feeder and salt lick shown above, Finnish whitetails would have difficulty surviving the harsh seasonal conditions, or at least be unable to achieve optimal growth. *Photo by I. Ala-ajos.*

extirminated and mixed with the more barren-ground types for domestication in northern parts of the country. Roe deer had been extirpated thousands of years ago by cooling climate change. They now have been reintroduced to Åland and the southwestern archipelago, and a free-ranging population is immigrating from Sweden and the Soviet Union.

At the time of the white-tailed deer introductions, attempts also were made to introduce fallow deer and red deer, but success was very limited with these species.

The booming population of whitetails in the 1950s and 1960s was quickly met with mixed feelings. The deer, dependent on the partially cultivated landscape, as previously noted, began to cause damage to agricultural crops. Such damage was and still is local. And although unimportant in terms of national economy, it frequently is excessive for a private landowner specializing in berry and vegetable production.

On the other hand, it was pointed out that the "Laukko deer" were not native to Europe. No one could predict the actual impact of the translocation on the Finnish landscape. It also was feared that the introduced whitetails could harbor larval stages of *Parelapostrongylus tenuis*, fatal to moose living in the same area. Studies showed, however, that the whitetails were free of that parasite (Andersson and Koivisto 1966). Furthermore, there was no evidence of competition between deer and moose, although many hunters have claimed that moose dislike areas inhabited by white-tailed deer.

Hunting of whitetails in Finland was started in 1958 in Urjala. The first deer shot were antlerless, and the first antlered buck was shot in 1961. The history of the white-tailed deer population growth and harvest in Finland is shown in Table 84 and Figure 110.

The dramatic increase in harvest for 1978 was due to a new statute that permitted shooting does that were with fawns at the beginning of the season. It also allowed the harvest of two fawns or one adult. In 1980, the statute was revised to permit the harvest of three fawns or one adult.

Toward the end of the 1970s, opposition to the general trends of the white-tailed deer population was sharpening. Agricultural producers and traffic safety organizations demanded strict control over deer and moose populations, although most damages caused by these animals were and are covered by a fund collected from hunting license sales. Special li-

Table 84. Hunting harvest of white-tailed deer in Finland, 1958 through 1981.

Year	Number of deer harvested	Percentage increase/decrease from previous year
1958–1962	Few	
1963	123	
1964	311	+ 153
1965	491	+ 58
1966	318	− 35
1967	536	+ 68
1968	538	0
1969	550	+ 2
1970	560	+ 2
1971	720	+ 29
1972	823	+ 14
1973	1,299	+ 58
1974	1,978	+ 52
1975	3,200	+ 62
1976	3,835	+ 17
1977	5,506	+ 44
1978	9,437	+ 71
1979	10,525	+ 12
1980	14,982	+ 42
1981	9,958	− 31

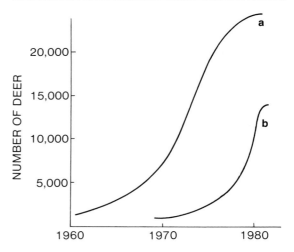

Figure 110. Development of (a) the white-tailed deer population in Finland and (b) its harvest.

censes were issued for shooting nuisance animals in the fields and gardens. In some instances, eliminating problem animals (by special license) succeeded in preventing damage, but in most cases the impact of shooting merely was a psychological boost for the persons affected by damages, with little measurable influence on the whitetail population.

Personnel of game management districts (Finland is divided into 14 such districts) situated around the original introduction area had to reconsider their attitude about whitetail

A team of Finnish white-tailed deer hunters in Urjala. *Photo by Simo Ahlgren.*

The antlers and skull of a trophy Finnish whitetail. *Photo by K. Nygrén; courtesy of the Finnish Game and Fisheries Research Institute.*

management. In many cases, a general recommendation was made to hunters not to feed or favor by any other means the deer migrating to those districts. Licenses were given out rather liberally in an attempt to control the whitetail population eruption and to gain time to set proper goals for the deer population in various management districts. This was considered necessary because of the crop and traffic damages, but even more because of reports of decreases in harvested whitetails' dressed weights and antler quality.

Trophy white-tailed deer and moose in Finland are evaluated annually in two or three major events. The best trophy whitetails no longer come from the heart of the deer range, but from the periphery. It is assumed that the reason for this is simply that bucks are overharvested. And this, in turn, is thought to be a result of a traditional doe-protection attitude, trophy hunting and the fact that Finnish hunters' families are not used to the taste of venison fat that is especially prevalent on does.

The deer hunting season opens October 15 and ends January 15. This is during the rut, which normally starts at the beginning of November. At this time, rutting bucks lose weight, and antlerless deer collect fat reserves for winter. Does frequently have subcutaneous fat

layers 40 to 50 millimeters (1.6–2.0 inches) thick on the back. Quite apparently, the disinclination of hunters' families toward the venison taste is caused at least in part by too-hasty or otherwise incompetent dressing (especially fat removal) and butchering.

Initial attempts already have been made to improve white-tailed deer management planning. They include:

1. More comprehensive and accurate censuses to ascertain whitetail population density, structure and recruitment.
2. Estimation of optimum density of the population, to avoid overuse of limited range resources and prevent crop damages.
3. Reduction of the whitetail population in selected management districts to a predetermined level or, if necessary, below it, to establish the sex ratio at 1:1. Usually this is done by increasing the antlerless-deer harvest.

4. Selective removal of physically inferior bucks to improve trophy quality. It is noteworthy that, by the norms of the Boone and Crocket Club, there are practically no atypical antlers in the Finnish white-tailed deer population. The abnormalities previously mentioned usually are odd tines protruding in unusual directions or a lack of tines, especially of the first ones. The most accurate selection is carried out with subadult bucks. Bucks three to five years of age generally are not removed if they have passed the first selection. Prime bucks are reduced to produce suitable "harem density." Such selective harvesting involves a voluntary but organized activity of hunters. In fact, this is nothing new in Finland, where moose hunting traditionally has been license-based and strictly organized. Whitetails mostly are hunted by the same clubs or groups that hunt moose.

THE FUTURE

White-tailed deer management in Finland is in a critical phase. Arguments for and against the presence of whitetails are ceasing. The result of the debate in recent decades seems to be that the deer are in Finland to stay and must be accepted and managed as part of the Finnish resources. However, the animals' range needs to be outlined, with all necessary management focused inside that area. Time and dollars should not be used outside areas suitable for whitetails.

Whitetail population densities must be kept reasonably low, and the quality of deer, whether economic or aesthetic, must be favored over quantity production in order to minimize habitat damages and landholder conflicts.

If winter feeding is to be continued, it should be oriented toward a carefully selected portion of the population, to help those animals through the hardest winters. This presumably will slow down natural selection of whitetails in Finland's extreme conditions—a situation that is not occurring outside the current whitetail management area.

Much of the whitetail's future success in Finland is dependent on its adaptability to the country's forested environments. Hunters often claim that this process is going on. Bucks frequently are seen staying in cover for some time before entering fields where antlerless deer have been feeding for hours. This may just be a response to the most common method of hunting—harvesting deer in a preferred feeding field.

Theoretically the chances for further adaptation of whitetails to Finland—particularly the northern parts—seem to be few, because the original gene pool (one buck, four does) was limited. Studies of the genetical variability of Finnish white-tailed deer have been started, to get a better basis for understanding the past and future of this remarkable animal.

IV. Whitetail Research and Management Practices

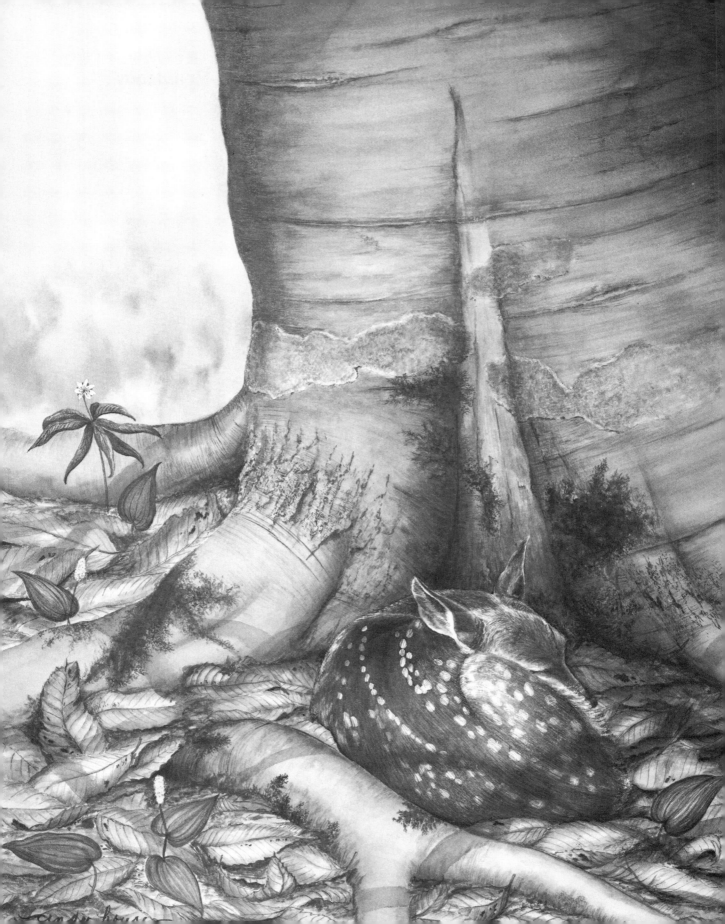

Chapter 35

BASIS AND ROLE OF MANAGEMENT

Robert L. Smith
Professor of Wildlife Biology
Division of Forestry and Wildlife
West Virginia University
Morgantown, West Virginia

Joe L. Coggin
Game Biologist Supervisor
Virginia Commission of Game
and Inland Fisheries
Eagle Rock, Virginia

The white-tailed deer is the most widely distributed, abundant, familiar and heavily hunted of all North American big game mammals. While other big game animals have "retreated" with the advance of human settlement and activity, the whitetail has thrived in close proximity to cities, suburban areas, farming country, extensive woodlands and remote wilderness. Its ability to persist in a diversity of habitats, subsist on a wide variety of foods and withstand extreme ranges in temperature has enabled white-tailed deer to recover from excessive, unregulated hunting and losses of native habitat. Today, it truly is the dominant big game species in North America.

ORIGIN OF MANAGEMENT

Historical Perspectives

In immediate pre-Columbian time, the distribution of white-tailed deer apparently was not too dissimilar to that occurring today. However, whitetail densities historically probably were considerably more patchy than are those of the present. Where locally abundant in the past, deer numbers may have exceeded those of today (*see* Chapter 2). But at the western and northern fringes of the historic range, whitetails were relatively few. Whitetails were most numerous about the marshes of the Atlantic and Gulf Coast, in the forest/grassland margins of the Midwest, on agricultural areas cleared and burned by Indians, and in openings created by such natural disturbances as lightning fires and hurricanes. Except for hunting by Indians and predation by wolves, mountain lions and other large carnivores, the white-tailed deer lived relatively undisturbed.

Coincident with settlement of North America, the fortunes of the white-tailed deer changed quickly. Equipped with more lethal weapons than their Indian predecessors had, colonists rapidly depleted local deer populations. Whitetails were virtually extirpated in most of eastern Massachusetts 18 years after the Pilgrims' landing at Plymouth Rock. They were hunted not only for meat but for other products as well: deer tallow was used in soap; hides were made into breeches, jackets, coats, gloves, stockings, snowshoe netting and "glass" for cabin windows; hair served as padding for saddles and furniture; and antlers were fashioned into knife handles, forks and ornaments. On the frontier, the hides also served as a medium of exchange (Young 1956).

Demand for deer meat and hides stimulated commercial hunting to accommodate local and foreign markets (*see* Chapter 2). Between 1763 and 1775, for example, 907,200 kilograms (2 million pounds) of deerskins and 600,000 deer carcasses were shipped to England from Savannah, Georgia. Whitetails in the prairie regions were killed to feed settlers and supply meat for the people of the growing urban communities. In the 1850s, extensive market hunting sent deer carcasses to Chicago, Milwaukee, Cleveland and Cincinnati. Wisconsin whitetails were shipped to Boston and New York (Dahlberg and Guettinger 1956). In Minnesota, market hunting peaked in the period 1870–1880, including the month of December 1872, when 5,445 kilograms (6 tons) of venison were loaded at Litchfield, Minnesota, for transport to Boston (Petraborg and Burcalow 1965). In 1878, 70,000 whitetail carcasses were shipped from the lower peninsula of Michigan; two years later, the number jumped to 100,000 (Jenkins and Bartlett 1959).

The time of the catastrophic decline of deer differed in various regions, but everywhere the pattern was similar. In New England, the low point occurred in the early 1800s. Other whitetail populations were depleted as miners, lumbermen, market hunters and settlers moved west and south, often following railroad lines. In many southeastern states, the declines extended into the 1950s because of constant poaching by rural residents and lack of law enforcement (Jenkins 1952).

Just as the near demise of bison and elk stimulated the conservation movement at federal levels in the United States (Trefethen 1975), the plight of white-tailed deer was the catalyst that initiated legislative action and management for terrestrial wildlife at the state level. Because the white-tailed deer was nonmigratory, responsibility for its management rested with states rather than with the federal government.

Current Perspectives

Although wildlife management practices and policies developed unevenly among the states, today all follow certain philosophical perspectives. The most persuasive of these was established rather early in the history of wildlife management in the case of *Geer versus Connecticut* in 1896. In that case, the courts ruled that states have the right to regulate and control the manner in which wild game is taken. The right was upheld on two grounds: (1) that wild animals were owned by the state; and (2) police powers of the state gave it the duty to maintain wildlife for the people. That and several other court cases established the fact that a state owns the wildlife within its borders, and holds it in trust for the people. And the state has an obligation to protect that trust.

Of all North American big game animals, none so closely impinges on the general public as does the white-tailed deer. It furnishes hunting recreation for millions of people and is considered an aesthetic resource by many millions more. Today, two groups—hunters and antihunters—are at odds on how deer should be managed. Deer are an economic asset, adding considerably to the seasonal income of sporting goods stores, gasoline dealers, hotels, motels, restaurants and other businesses, particularly in small towns. Whitetails also are a source of tons of meat and other by-products. On the other hand, whitetails can be an economic liability when they damage agricultural crops, gardens, orchards and tree plantations—and when they cause highway accidents. Deer are important ecologically, especially when abundant. By eliminating undergrowth, they destroy habitat for other forest wildlife, including small mammals and birds of the understory. By selective grazing on certain plants, deer can eliminate them from the forest community and alter the rate and/or direction of vegetational development.

Against that background, states have to make management decisions in the best interests of deer, the hunting and nonhunting public, and the landscape. Too often, optimal management decisions cannot be carried out because of political interference from many special interest groups. Some would have more deer, some want fewer deer, and others demand no deer hunting at all. It is no wonder that white-tailed deer management is a controversial and often political issue.

Throughout much of North America in the first decades of the twentieth century, the harvest of a white-tailed deer—much less a good-sized buck—was an uncommon and exciting event. In time, through concerted management efforts, whitetail populations and their harvests have increased substantially, yet there is no apparent decline in hunter satisfaction. *Photo courtesy of the Pennsylvania Game Commission.*

FRAMEWORK FOR MANAGEMENT

Protection of wildlife as a public trust by the state requires some form of administrative structure through which policy and management can be formulated and put into action. White-tailed deer management, like all aspects of wildlife management, requires a source of funding, qualified biologists and managers, acquisition of sound biological information on which policy and management alternatives can be based, and an enlightened and cooperative public.

Administrative Organization

United States.   Approaches to wildlife policy in the United States differ at the federal and state levels. Federal policies that reflect public needs and desires are established by the legislative and executive branches of the government, and occasionally are ruled on by the judicial branch. These policies then are administered by such agencies as the U.S. Forest Service, Fish and Wildlife Service, National Park Service and Bureau of Land Management.

At the state level, conservation or natural resource commissions or boards usually formulate wildlife policy. A governor ordinarily appoints the commissioners, the number of which varies from 1 in Alabama to 30 in Nevada. When formulating policy, commissioners consider advice from the state wildlife resource agency staff and input from the state legislature, private organizations and the public. Comissioners serve as links between the public and the wildlife agency and between the wildlife agency and state legislature. Most commissioners serve without pay, other than expenses. The commission appoints a director or wildlife agency head—ideally a professionally trained biologist—who is responsible for administering the work of the agency. The director, in turn, selects the personnel to work under him. Such an administrative structure usually helps prevent policy from being unduly influenced by political expediency.

Canada.   In contrast to the United States, Canada has no well-organized executive structure at the federal or provincial level to deal with wildlife resources. Also, neither the federal nor any of the provincial governments is formally committed to long-range objectives for wildlife. This situation arises from a different philosophy toward wildlife, and also from Canada's political organization.

Wildlife in Canada is considered government property rather than a public trust. As owners of wildlife, the federal and provincial governments may manage it according to existing values, goals, laws, customs and usage (Bossenmaier 1979). However, the governments' roles are not clearly established. In general these roles are viewed as flexible combinations of protection, control and allocation for providing social, cultural and economic benefits. That may involve such activities as research, monitoring wildlife populations, education and public communication.

There is no clearcut indication which government, federal or provincial, has jurisdiction over wildlife. Provinces claim proprietary rights to wildlife—a claim not challenged by the federal government. The federal government, however, takes a leading role in wildlife management activities, especially those mandated by the Migratory Bird Treaty Act of 1917 and the Canada Wildlife Act of 1973. It manages wildlife in national parks and national wildlife areas, negotiates international treaties, interacts with native peoples, agriculture, forestry, mining and rural development, and cooperates with provincial governments, with whom most Canadian wildlife management activity rests.

In the provincial governments, wildlife management is the responsibility of elected executive officials. They are inclined to be oriented more toward human interests than those of wildlife. Canadian legislatures prefer to leave wildlife administration as the responsibility of a line department within the executive branch, with little or no outside delegation of authority or legislative direction, requirements or restrictions.

Governmental organization at the provincial level follows no set pattern. Each administration organizes its affairs according to its objectives, perceptions and any applicable legislation. Basic wildlife legislation regulates the take of wildlife and protects certain critical habitats, but it does not demand or specify any action directed toward the protection and enhancement of wildlife or its habitat. Governmental resources, including wildlife, are managed at the pleasure of the current administration. The parliamentary system, with its party government and collective responsibility of the cabinet, together with a general

reluctance to earmark revenue for wildlife, do little to ensure long-range planning on the part of provincial governments or to provide stability for any wildlife program. Since the 1970s, both the provincial and federal governments have been integrating wildlife with management of other resources, viewing wildlife as a part of an ecological system rather than as individual species (Boyd 1979). Despite the organizational weaknesses and differences in approach, Canada, especially in the past two decades, has developed an extensive, modern, well-funded wildlife management program that places a high value on wildlife.

Mexico. According to the 1952 Federal Game Law, all wildlife in Mexico is the ". . . property of the nation, and the Ministry of Agriculture and Livestock is charged with authorizing the hunting of them and the appropriation of their products" (Leopold 1959:532). Individual states in Mexico have no jurisdiction over resident wildlife as do states in the United States and provinces in Canada. Administration of wildlife laws and other matters pertaining to wildlife are the charge of the Bureau of Wildlife, established in 1964 to replace the Bureau of Game. The Federal Game Law, which the Bureau administers, was passed in 1952—a revision of the 1940 Game Law. The Federal Game Law, among other things, eliminated commercial hunting and trade in wildlife. The wildlife laws of Mexico are well-intentioned, but lack adequate enforcement, administration and financing. Hunting for food is a year-round activity of the campesinos. Such subsistence hunting is a major drain on the country's wildlife resources, including white-tailed deer. Because of the remoteness of rural areas that support significant wildlife populations, and due to inadequate funding, enforcement of wildlife laws is minimal and virtually ineffective. Consequently, the campesinos largely are ignorant of game laws, have little regard for those they do know, and impose no form of restraint on harvests.

Funding for Wildlife

Wildlife management programs need money. In the early 1900s, when wildlife management in the United States was just getting started, legislatures of a few states appropriated small amounts of money from general revenues. Others authorized the use of fines from wildlife law violations to fund or subsidize wildlife administration, but such funding was small and unreliable.

To obtain the revenues necessary for adequate management of wildlife, a number of states began to license hunters and anglers under the philosophy that consumptive users of publicly owned resources should pay for the privilege. Some administrators, however, disliked the idea of a hunting license. They believed that money should come from general revenues because wildlife restoration provides benefits for the nongame as well as the game species.

By the late 1920s, many states had adopted a plan of resident hunting and fishing licenses, and earmarked the receipts for use by their respective wildlife agencies. Today, states have expanded licensing to include special licenses for archery and muzzleloader hunting of whitetails, and for doe deer and other big game. Some states require special stamps for hunting of bear, wild turkey and waterfowl. Currently, hunting license fees paid by sportsmen, who make up approximately 8 percent of the population, provide about 75 percent of the revenue used for state wildlife programs (Williamson 1981, L. L. Williamson personal communication to R. E. McCabe:1983).

Some states have other sources of revenue. For example, as of 1982, 23 states receive interest on invested funds accruing from the sale of hunting and fishing licenses and permits, and 36 states issue general obligation bonds. General funds are appropriated for regular operations or special projects in 30 states. Three agencies receive funds from state cigarette taxes. A 1976 referendum in Missouri imposed a one-eighth of 1-percent sales tax to help fund conservation programs, including those for white-tailed deer.

Each year, sportsmen in the United States invest more than $94 million in the Pittman-Robertson (Federal Aid in Wildlife Restoration Act) program. Since its inception in 1937, the program has provided more than $1 billion to restore and maintain the nation's wildlife (Wildlife Management Institute 1981). State and territorial agencies select wildlife projects that are subject to approval by the U.S. Fish and Wildlife Service. The cost of projects is borne one-fourth by the states (mainly from hunting license revenues) and three-fourths by Pittman-Robertson funds. States share in the Pittman-Robertson receipts based on the number of licensed hunters, land area and population of each state. Fifty percent of Pittman-Robertson expenditures are used to develop and improve habitat on acquired lands; 26 percent are devoted to wildlife research; 19 percent are used for land acquisition (through 1980, states had purchased more than 1,500,000 hectares [3,700,000 acres], and many additional millions of hectares have been added to state wildlife programs through cooperative agreements); and up to 8 percent of the funds (no general tax dollars) are used by the U.S. Fish and Wildlife Service to administer the program.

Problems arise when attempts are made to divert these funds from wildlife management to other uses such as enforcement of boating laws, maintenance of general recreational areas on state wildlife lands, and support for nongame and endangered species work. Because wildlife habitat management and restoration funds benefit many species other than game animals and support other programs outside of game management but within the framework of wildlife, state wildlife agencies need to secure additional revenues from the general public. A number of states have instituted volunteer programs, such as income tax checkoff, sale of decals and wildlife stamps. Such programs have provided some additional funds, but nothing near the volume of revenue expected or needed.

Private landowners, hunting clubs and conservation organizations in all states contribute to deer management projects. Some of the contributions are indirect, through backing of state agency programs. In other cases, the private sector directly contributes time and personnel to management and research projects. And many corporations that own extensive tracts of land employ their own wildlife biologists or obtain professional wildlife management expertise to assure accommodation of wildlife's welfare and citizen interests.

In Canada, as previously noted, wildlife programs are funded largely through general appropriations. Money from hunting-license sales is not earmarked for wildlife programs, but goes into the general revenues. However, some provinces impose special charges on recreational hunting to support wildlife damage control and habitat development programs. Some also have trust funds established through various governmental and private sources for the preservation and development of upland and wetland habitats.

Role of Professional Wildlife Biologists and Managers

An administrative framework for establishing wildlife policy and undertaking wildlife management is of little value unless a fund of biological information exists on which to base policy. Not until formal university training in wildlife management was instituted at a number of land grant colleges in the United States in the 1930s, stimulated by establishment of Cooperative Wildlife Research Units, did such information accumulate. Since then, the white-tailed deer has become the most studied big game animal of North America.

Acquiring knowledge about the life history of whitetails and their habitat relationships has involved study in innumerable scientific fields and disciplines. Nutritionists, for example, study the dietary requirements of deer for growth, reproduction and antler development. Behaviorists observe the social life of deer; and physiologists investigate the whitetails' morphological and phenotypical relationships. Other biologists examine population dynamics, range conditions, taxonomy, genetics, predation, parasites and diseases, and virtually all fields or conditions that influence whitetails individually, as populations and as a species. These are the areas of research that are the foundations of "on-the-ground" management—the actual regulating and monitoring of whitetail populations, their habitats and/or their users, usually by a different set of wildlife biologists—the administrators, planners and managers. Not to be excluded from the list of satellite activities that figure into professional management of white-tailed deer, as well as other wildlife, are law enforcement, communications and logistical support services. It is safe to say that wildlife management is a complex network of separate but intricately related specialties, with which all biologists and other resource managers must be familiar if not proficient.

Role of Landowners and the General Public

No matter how state or provincial wildlife agencies attempt to manage the size and well-being of their whitetail populations scientifically, their programs are contingent upon the understanding and cooperation of the general public, especially landowners. About 75 percent of white-tailed deer range in North America occurs on private lands. Private landowners, therefore, have the final say with regard to the two most critical ingredients of the deer management recipe—habitat and hunter harvest.

The extent and manner to which private landowners—from large corporations, such as timber and mining enterprises, to small-farm operators, to recreational property owners—willingly accommodate whitetails and other wildlife on their properties by selective manipulation of habitat features usually is a function of tolerance. Wildlife usually is perceived as a recreational and/or aesthetic amenity wherever it occurs, but only to an economic threshold (Yoho 1981). And this threshold differs from landowner to landowner, depending on a variety of static parameters—ranging from seasonal weather conditions to foreign trade.

White-tailed deer, as products of the landscape, are subject to the willingness of landowners to tolerate the damages they do or foster, at the expense of other resources on which the landowners depend for livelihood or hold in equal or greater favor.

With few exceptions, private landowners have no legal obligation to provide for wildlife. They do not need to adopt habitat management programs recommended by wildlife agencies, nor do they have to permit access to others to enjoy wildlife in any manner. Accordingly, besides economic considerations, the success or failure of nearly all white-tailed deer management programs in North America is predicated on landowner attitudes.

The attitudes that currently reflect landowner tolerance of and provision for whitetails principally relate to hunters and hunting. As discussed elsewhere in this book, hunting is the most practical, efficient and desirable means at present of regulating whitetail populations. Deer numbers, distributions and health are controlled by carefully planned harvests. In addition, whitetail hunting is of considerable economic, social and nutritional significance in North America. The key to managed harvests, however, is landowner willingness to permit hunting. Landowner tolerance of deer, therefore, not only concerns the existence of the animals on private property, but also their removal.

Access to white-tailed deer on private lands depends on landowner approval of hunters or hunting, or both. Some landowners disapprove of hunting and, for that reason, close their land to hunters. Others prohibit hunting because of the behavior of certain hunters. Illegal or unethical behavior committed intentionally or unintentionally even by a few hunters tends to heighten disenchantment with hunting not only among landowners but the general public as well. Landowners, even if amenable to hunting, are not likely to permit hunting on their land if their lives, property or ownership rights have been threatened or abused by careless or thoughtless hunters. One distasteful incident by an unthinking hunter can cause landowners to deny access to all other hunters indefinitely. The more land taken out of hunting by posting, the fewer the opportunities for hunters, the greater the competition among them, the fewer the satisfactions and the greater the probability of unethical behavior.

Each parcel of private land removed from deer hunting heightens the management problem of controlling the size and density of whitetail populations by altering hunter numbers and distribution. The growing number of such closures aggravates losses of deer habitat and hunting areas to such causes as urban sprawl, highways, industrialization and suburbanization.

Landowners also influence deer populations by leasing land for whitetail hunting. Although economic incentives are the motivation, landowners often fail to meet their objectives of increasing income and reducing deer damage. Nevertheless, large blocks of land with high deer populations all too often are restricted to a small number of hunters. The result is underharvest, followed by increased crop damage and deer habitat deterioration.

This problem could be alleviated, hunting improved, hunter/landowner relationships cultivated and deer populations controlled if landowners treated leasing as a business. Landowners could look after their own interest while providing a service for deer hunters. Rather than simply leasing land to a club or group of hunters, which in turn regulates hunting on its members' terms, landowners should dictate the conditions. For example, landowners could specify how many deer the hunters should remove and when the hunting should be conducted. To reduce crop damage in early autumn, landowners could require a certain level of bowhunting with the provision that only does and small bucks be taken. Trophy buck hunting could be restricted to the gun season. A

lessor also could require removal of a certain number of does during the antlerless-deer hunting season. Regulation of the number of hunters would be the responsibility of the lessees. If the latter failed to exert adequate hunting pressure, the landowner could open land to other fee hunters. In addition, he could require some means of hunter identification and registration of harvested deer to protect his lands from trespassers or abuses of the leasing privilege. In these ways, landowners could reduce property damage by hunters, crop damage by deer, aid in the control of deer population, and add to their income.

APPROACHES TO MANAGEMENT

Most white-tailed deer populations have a high rate of increase and require some form of removal to keep them in balance with year-round habitat resources. When natural predators are absent, some other form of population regulation, such as hunting, must be submitted. Otherwise, the deer population will exceed the capability of the range to support it, with the inevitable result of habitat deterioration, lowered deer reproduction and health, and frequent deer die-off. Two basic approaches to these management problems are population regulation and habitat manipulation.

Population Management

Whitetail populations can be managed by regulated harvests. Controls are exercised by varying the length of hunting seasons, season opening dates and times, numbers of hunters, weapons restrictions, and the age and sex of deer to be harvested from each management unit or area. Whitetail populations can be increased by establishing and enforcing a buck-only harvest regulation. They can be reduced by increasing the proportion of does in the harvest. Given these means of regulating the harvests, wildlife biologists and managers—in cooperation with the public and decision makers—can manage deer to desired population levels.

Management of white-tailed deer populations through harvest regulations is based on the premises that: (1) the more food available, the greater the rate of deer population increase; and (2) the further a deer population is reduced below habitat carrying capacity, the higher the rate of population increase. For each population density level, there is a potential rate of increase that will reflect the rate of harvest needed to maintain the population at a desired rate.

Rate of harvest depends on the management objective. If the objective is to hold the deer population at a current level, the annual harvest has to assure that total annual mortality equals the yearly population increase. For example, if a whitetail population is increasing 15 percent a year, its finite rate of increase is 1.16 and its exponential rate is 0.148. To hold the population stable, the rate of harvest per year also has to be 0.148. If a population is stable in the absence of hunting, then it cannot be harvested without reducing the population. Two options are available to the wildlife biologist or manager to increase such a deer population: (1) increase the deer's food supply through habitat management; or (2) reduce the deer population temporarily, thereby making more food available to each deer remaining in the population.

It is difficult to estimate the size of harvest needed to meet management objectives, and rarely is there sufficient information available on a deer population or its habitat to determine an absolute rate of harvest. However, important strides have been made in the past two decades in handling deer harvests on a sounder basis. Lacking any firm knowledge of deer population size or current harvest rates, wildlife agencies know only the yield they can regulate through hunting permits. Such a pragmatic approach seldom results in overharvesting.

Management units. White-tailed deer, like most other organisms, are not distributed uniformly across the landscape. Because of past land-use practices, such as the clearcutting of forests, land abandonment by agriculture, and suburbanization, the quality of deer habitat and the status of deer populations vary across a region and a state. In many states, each region has its own peculiar problems. In some, the whitetail populations may be low and in need of the opportunity to increase. In other parts of a state, deer may be too abundant for economic interests and current land uses, resulting in excessive deer damage to crops. And otherwise good deer habitat may be pockets of suburban developments, making adequate deer harvest difficult or impossible.

Whitetail populations in each of these areas require different approaches to management

and harvest. Some may need to be reduced or held at some level compatible with other land uses, so the harvest needs to be maintained or increased. Other areas can support no deer harvest. And in still other areas, weapon restrictions may be necessary for public safety. To adjust deer management and harvest to various conditions, some agencies have divided their states into management units or areas, each with its own set of regulations. As deer populations change within units, regulations can be changed to meet current needs of the deer and public demands. An example of this approach is that used in Wisconsin, and outlined in Chapter 11.

Justification of recreational hunting. As far as most sportsmen are concerned, the principal justification of deer hunting seasons is recreational—a chance to get outdoors to hunt a big game animal. As previously discussed, this viewpoint is not shared or accepted by a portion of the general public. Another segment of the public, including some foresters, orchardists, other agriculturalists and even some suburbanites, whose ornamental shrubbery is consumed by deer, demand deer population reduction. Because of economic losses, state wildlife agencies and other hunting groups have advanced the argument that recreational hunting should be a potent force in reducing whitetail populations—but until recently, it rarely worked out that way.

To reduce a whitetail population in a given area to a level at which it would not be an economic liability might require an extremely heavy initial harvest, followed by an adequate harvesting each subsequent year to hold the deer population at the lower level. Many forces work against such an approach. First, the vocal majority of the nonhunting public likely would protest the initial large harvest. Second, sportsmen who want the best odds possible to harvest a deer would object to heavy reduction of the deer population. Third, certain businesses would protest, because deer are an important tourist attraction or feature in many areas. Wildlife agencies, too, would be uneasy, because a smaller deer population would mean fewer dollars from hunting-license sales, especially from out-of-state hunters.

Increased harvest resulting from a more liberal hunting season aimed at reducing the deer population actually may stimulate the population's growth simply by cropping deer sufficiently to ensure increased recruitment because of improved nutrition. Although heavy hunting can reduce a deer population to a much lower level, there are few documented cases where recreational hunting has solved over-population problems in whitetail range.

Each wildlife agency has a different philosophy of deer population management. These philosophies tend to be predicated on environmental, socio-economic and biopolitical constraints. One end of the philosophical spectrum is maintenance of a large population of deer (regardless of the animals' qualitative characteristics), from which more hunters are assured of getting their deer. The opposite philosophical camp supports maintenance of a smaller population of trophy-quality whitetails. The latter seems to be of less interest to hunters than is the former, but is of greater merit in terms of managing a deer population.

The State of Louisiana has chosen a course in deer management closer to the latter philosophy, although the program has met with resistance from many hunters. Most of Louisiana's deer habitat is privately owned. Much of this habitat is leased to private hunting clubs

that restrict membership and numbers of hunters on an area. The hunting clubs and other hunters favor a buck-only season, and usually will not permit hunting of does on their leased lands. As a result, Louisiana is faced with too many deer for the available forage, and the result, contrary to the management philosophy, is low-quality deer.

To solve the dichotomy, Louisiana instituted in 1959 an either-sex hunting season of 1 to 10 days. The system is popular on state-owned lands but not on privately leased lands.

Using state wildlife areas as demonstration sites, the Louisiana Department of Wildlife and Fisheries showed that increased either-sex harvests resulted in increased individual deer size and buck antler development. On the Three Rivers Wildlife Area, for example, the average weight of a buck in 1971 was 54 kilograms (119 pounds), and 67 percent of 1.5-year-old bucks had spikes. By 1976, after five years of either-sex hunting seasons, the weight of 1.5-year-old deer had increased to 68 kilograms (149 pounds), and only 24 percent were spikes (Hughes 1982).

Production of trophy bucks may be the foremost public demand made on whitetail management in some areas. Implementation must be based on the potential of the deer population in question to produce bucks with trophy antlers, the ability to regulate hunter numbers and harvests, and the influence of such an objective on the deer population as a whole and on other public interests in the deer. Furthermore, what is a trophy whitetail? For the vast majority of hunters, it is any legal deer—harvested under the rules and ethics of fair chase—which tests the hunter's woodsmanship, shooting skills and tenacity. *Photos courtesy of the Tennessee Wildlife Resources Agency.*

The Louisiana Department of Wildlife and Fisheries in 1981 initiated a volunteer program with private landowners and hunting clubs having at least 202 hectares (500 acres) of land of which 101 hectares (250 acres) could be agricultural. In this program, wildlife biologists evaluate the whitetail population condition and habitat. Based on their evaluation, the biologists recommend an antlerless-deer harvest quota. Hunters tags are then issued that allow harvest of a predetermined number of antlerless deer. These tags are not issued until after the regular either-sex hunting season. The number of does harvested during the regular season is subtracted from the number recommended for removal (quota). The difference represents the number of tags to be issued during the last part of the hunting season. Once the whitetail population reaches a size compatible with its habitat, it is maintained at that level by removing only the annual surplus. Antlerless-deer tags are used to take yearling does, and bucks taken are spikes and trophy deer, leaving intermediate males as breeding stock and future trophies.

The one flaw in this type of management program is the potential for genetic deterioration of the deer population. While removal of spike bucks probably will eliminate deer with genes for small antlers, removal of large antlered bucks could result in the selective removal of the very males needed to sire superior deer (Ryman et al. 1981).

Conservation law enforcement. A common error within wildlife management agencies is to equate using laws to regulate the harvest with enforcement of the law. Restriction of the harvest too often is called wildlife law enforcement (*see* Sigler 1972). Regulation of the harvest through laws is one thing, enforcement of the law is another.

Successful achievement of legislatively mandated wildlife laws and associated regulations depends heavily on law enforcement carried out by conservation officers. Too often conservation officers in the United States are handicapped in performing their duties because they lack full police powers. Only 29 states grant conservation officers the status of peace officer (Morse 1980, in press).

Basis for law enforcement. The basic duty of conservation law enforcement officers is to enforce laws and regulations governing the use of wildlife resources. Wildlife law enforcement involves the criminal justice system, including magistrates, judges, district attorneys and others as well.

Early conservation law enforcement officers were known as game wardens. Frequently they were selected on their political acumen or their abilities to hunt and fish. Through time, however, professionalism has increased. Most modern day conservation law enforcement officers are given rigorous police training as well as some education in wildlife biology. More and more officers are college graduates in the wildlife field. The selection process has improved, political patronage has been deemphasized or eliminated, and advancement generally is based on merit and civil service examinations (Morse 1980).

While "game wardens" were concerned almost solely with apprehending law breakers, modern conservation law enforcement officers have greatly expanded responsibilities, perhaps to the detriment of good law enforcement in some cases. Maryland, for example, is phasing out the nonenforcement assignments of its conservation officers, enabling them to devote all their time to wildlife law enforcement. Elsewhere, conservation officers find themselves helping to gather research and management information, conducting wildlife surveys and censuses, controlling nuisance wildlife, investigating hunting accidents, running hunter safety courses, and speaking before school and other community groups (Bavin 1978). In effect they are the "front line" of the wildlife agency, the most visible representatives, and the impression they leave with the general public can reflect on the entire state wildlife program.

At best, enforcement of wildlife laws is beset with problems that do not seem to improve with time. A major problem is public apathy toward wildlife in general and toward wildlife law enforcement in particular. Violations of wildlife laws are taken less seriously than other types of illegal activity, and punishment frequently is meted out with less consistency and severity than necessary for it to serve as a deterrent. In some places, poachers are regarded as heroes rather than the criminals they are. Wildlife laws sometimes are written so poorly as to be confusing and not easily enforceable, and thus reduce public respect for wildlife laws. Restricted budgets in the face of an increasing human population, and a more urbanized user of the outdoors, mean expanding officers' workloads without commensurate compensation. What may be needed in some

Pennsylvania "game protectors" with the remains of 11 white-tailed deer confiscated in a raid on a poaching ring in 1966. Besides enforcing fish and wildlife laws in the public and resource interests, conservation officers in virtually all states and provinces participate in a variety of ground-level management activities, including wildlife population censusing, habitat maintenance and public relations. They are integral members of wildlife management teams. *Photo courtesy of Stanley E. Forbes.*

areas is a transformation of the strictly conservation law enforcement officer into a fully multiple-purpose field officer.

Curtailing illegal kills. The magnitude of the illegal deer kill is one of the unknowns of whitetail management, although Missouri estimates the number taken in that state to be around 10,000 annually (Witter 1980). What effect elimination of illegal deer kills would have on management and to what extent illegal kills affect deer populations are two questions that cannot be answered adequately because data are exceedingly difficult to obtain. Whitetails are abundant in so many areas that people living in those areas tend to be complacent about the poaching problem. Others accept it as a part of the social scene. Some illegal deer killing undoubtedly is the work of organized poaching rings, supplying an underground commercial market. Other illegal kills are made for subsistence purposes, especially in depressed rural areas. Considerable poaching is carried out simply for "the hell of it"—a type of recreation done with full knowledge and

perhaps in part because of its illegality (Sawhill and Winkel 1974). Such hunting usually is a group activity, spontaneous or planned, often involving consumption of alcohol.

Another form of illegal killing occurs during the legal deer hunting seasons and involves shooting protected deer or failure to report whitetails killed. By not reporting and tagging their kills, these deer hunters give themselves the opportunity to continue hunting. It was estimated that only 60 to 70 percent of hunters of antlered deer and only 50 to 60 percent of hunters of antlerless deer in Pennsylvania report their kill (Godshall 1981). A New Jersey study indicated that the actual number of deer taken during the bow season was double that of the reported kill (McDowell 1980).

Citizen cooperation. In 1980, there were approximately 6,000 conservation law-enforcement officers in the 50 states, in contrast to the millions of hunters and many more millions of people who use the woods and lakes for nonhunting recreation. Obviously, a small number of conservation law-enforcement officers cannot be expected to prevent widespread violations of wildlife laws. Like all laws and regulations, those pertaining to wildlife and other natural resources depend on voluntary compliance by the public and public willingness to report violations.

Public cooperation is a valuable tool in enforcing wildlife laws and reducing poaching and other illegal activities. In the case of 24 states responding to a survey, one-half of their successfully prosecuted closed-season conservation law violations resulted from citizen reports (Beattie 1975).

Because of recognition of the importance of public participation in conservation law enforcement, a number of states have undertaken programs to encourage sportsmen and others to aid in the apprehension of law violators, especially big game poachers. Michigan, for example, has a Report All Poaching program. New Mexico has Operation Game Thief, which provides a toll-free hotline number and a $250 reward for information leading to the arrest of wildlife law violators. The Colorado Division of Wildlife also has Operation Game Thief, which provides citizens who turn in poachers with rewards. The reward fund is administered by a citizen committee and maintained by private contributions. Maryland instituted Turn-In-A-Poacher, which awards $25 to anyone providing information leading to arrest and conviction of a wildlife law violator.

Poaching of whitetails is a serious threat to deer population management. Illegal killing not only is wasteful and can imbalance deer population numbers on which habitat- and harvest-management decisions are based, but it also places regulated recreational hunting in jeopardy by stimulating public antihunting and/or antihunter reactions. *Top photo by Russ Reagan; courtesy of the Missouri Department of Conservation. Bottom photo by Ed Bry; courtesy of the North Dakota Fish and Game Department.*

One of the more ambitious programs is Pennsylvania's Sportsmen Policing Our Ranks Together, begun in 1976. Aimed largely at hunters, the program was started to minimize conflicts between hunters and the general public. It has as its current objectives the promotion of higher sporting standards, ethics and conduct, and the elimination of hunter violations and conflicts with the nonhunting public. The program attempts to make hunters more aware of their public image and how their actions in the field reflect on all hunters and hunting in general. Rather than offering cash rewards for violation reports, the program focuses on improving hunter conduct and presents awards to individuals who make an outstanding contribution to the program's principles. The Pennsylvania Game Commission sells brassards for jackets to show involvement in the program and has provided hundreds of thousands of pieces of literature for distribution explaining the program. Because of its apparent success in reducing violations and improving hunter conduct, Sportsmen Policing Our Ranks Together has been adopted by a number of other states and Canadian provinces.

The Pennsylvania program and others are designed to reduce apathy toward conservation laws and their violations. Because of the importance of citizen participation, several studies have been undertaken to determine the motivations of those who report and those who do not report conservation law violations, especially deer poaching. In a survey involving 43 states, Beattie (1975) found that more than 70 percent of those who report violations do so to protect and preserve wildlife, as a reaction to criminal behavior, and/or because violators reduce the opportunity for success by legal hunters. Those who witnessed violations but did not report them did so because of an unwillingness to become involved as a "snitch," or later as a witness, and/or out of fear of violator revenge.

Predation and predator control. Before settlement of North America, predation by mountain lions, wolves and coyotes probably was a major cause of white-tailed deer mortality. The extermination of the mountain lion and the wolf over much of their historic ranges effectively eliminated predation as a significant cause of whitetail mortality, but predation by large carnivores still has an effect on some deer populations in certain regions within the range of the white-tailed deer (*see* Chapter 8).

In northern latitudes, where wolves still exist in relative abundance, whitetails reportedly constitute up to 80 percent of the wolf's diet in summer, and 90 percent in winter (Pimlott 1967). In southern latitudes, deer may comprise as much as 70 percent of the mountain lion's diet (Hornocker 1970). In the Southwest, deer may represent up to 70 percent of the coyote's seasonal diet (Cook et al. 1971).

Pimlott (1967) hypothesized that predation prevented whitetail populations from increasing beyond their food supply. If so, predation may work against the evolution of population regulatory mechanisms by obviating the need for them. And this could account in part for the rapid increase in deer populations when predatory pressures are removed.

An important modern-day whitetail predator is the feral dog. Feral dogs have always been considered a threat to local deer populations, especially in mountainous parts of the East, such as the southern Appalachians. In that region, where deer populations are low and feral and nonferal populations of dogs are high (Smith 1966, Allen and Cromer 1977), these predators may have a serious limiting effect, particularly on newly stocked areas or ones with an initially low deer population (Barick 1969). After a deer population reaches a high level, predation and harassment by feral dogs tends to become more an emotional issue than a biological one. In Pennsylvania, for example, there were 547 known dog kills of whitetails in 1981—a minimal number compared with a roadkill count of more than 24,699 for the same year (Pennsylvania Game Commission 1982).

Habitat Management

Like white-tailed deer population management, habitat management for whitetails has its problems (*see* chapters 36 and 37). One of these is the inability of wildlife biologists to have any great impact on habitat management on any sizable areas within the range of whitetails. Except for lands reserved specifically for wildlife management, much of whitetail habitat is beyond the control or direct influence of state or provincial wildlife agencies.

Whitetail habitat usually is gained or lost through land-use decisions made without deer or other wildlife in mind, such as silvicultural and agricultural practices, dam building, roadway construction, suburbanization and industrial developments. Wildlife professionals can make recommendations on land-use plans, but getting those recommendations implemented is another story. Even on wildlife areas, such as refuges and at state wildlife lands and public hunting areas, there may be difficulty initiating habitat improvement and management practices because the practices are too expensive or no market exists for the wood or other products removed in the process. However, a body of knowledge exists that relates the integration of other land-use practices with deer management. On selected areas and in various habitats across the range of white-tailed deer, these practices are being put into effect.

The white-tailed deer is a highly adaptable ungulate—an opportunist that can make use of a variety of foods, survive in a variety of habitat types, and thrive in areas where timber harvest, fire and land abandonment have created a diversity of vegetative types and conditions.

The continued growth and sprawl of human population into whitetail ranges are inevitable. Planned development of the landscape, through participation by professional wildlife managers, can help assure the space and other habitat ingredients necessary for healthy and productive whitetail populations. *Photo courtesy of the Illinois Department of Conservation.*

But whitetail habitat never is static, deteriorating with time as plant growth and vegetational community succession proceed. Providing and maintaining deer habitat involves the manipulation of vegetation, largely in forests. This involves the integration of silvicultural practices with habitat management for deer. Because silvicultural objectives can be at odds with whitetail management objectives, such integration may be difficult, especially on private lands where adjustments in tree harvesting patterns to favor wildlife may reduce returns from timber production, but overall yield greater financial returns than does single-purpose forest management.

Key to habitat management. The key to habitat management for deer is maintenance of certain vegetational types and age classes within a forest over time. Such management prevents the boom and bust cycles in whitetail food and cover resources so prevalent throughout the species' range. That objective can be met through a carefully planned forest harvest and regeneration.

Basically, there are two methods of forest regeneration—even-aged and uneven- or all-age management. A stand is even-aged if small age and size differences exist between individual trees. Even-aged stands can be established and maintained by clearcutting. An uneven-aged or all-age forest consists of trees that vary considerably both in age and size. Such a stand is maintained by selectively removing large mature trees and allowing all other age and size classes to remain until the next harvest (usually in 60 to 100 years) when the next generation or period of large mature trees will be removed.

With respect to whitetail management, both approaches have advantages and disadvantages. Extensive clearcut areas produce an abundance of foods for deer. The abundance, however, is short-lived, as vegetation soon grows out of reach of the deer and its canopy shades out food production on the forest floor. Such forest regeneration can result in a rapidly expanding whitetail population that ultimately is left with a scarcity of food and cover.

Selection cutting or uneven-aged management does not provide a maximum amount of food per given area, but because the high canopy usually is more open, herbaceous foods and low woody understory growth are relatively abundant. A more stable food supply is available over a longer period of time, because regeneration cuts are more frequent than are clearcuts. In a selection cut, vegetative regeneration will be stimulated every two to four years.

Ideally, most forests can be managed by utilizing both cutting practices, thereby optimizing timber harvest and maintaining a healthy and stable whitetail population or otherwise as dictated by deer management objectives for delineated management units and areas.

Because of the diversity of vegetational communities throughout the range of the white-tailed deer, and the different responses of vegetation to cutting, fire and other manipulations, applied management of both vegetation and deer varies widely across white-tailed deer country. For example, winter cover is critical in the northern part of deer range, while it is of only minor importance in the South. Maintenance of winter cover involves a different approach to forest management in northern whitetail habitat than it does in regions where such cover is less important.

Key to management of whitetails throughout their range are sound forestry practices that retain wildlife cover and provide suitable amounts of diverse and accessible forage. *Photo by Dean Tvedt; courtesy of the Wisconsin Department of Natural Resources.*

Northern deer yard management. In the northern parts of their range, white-tailed deer tend to "yard"—gathering in sheltered areas to escape the extremes of winter. While concentrated in winter yards, deer often are restricted in movement. They rarely travel more than 1.6 kilometers (1 mile) from cover, and frequently are limited to even shorter distances by snow exceeding 46 centimeters (18 inches) in depth, and so are unable to reach food.

A good deer yarding area is one that contains readily accessible food and thermal cover of large conifers, particularly on south-facing slopes or in lowland swamps. Prime deer yarding areas are those with pure stands of mature conifers with closed canopies, adjacent to a relatively open area with low woody growth. Such conifer stands are highly vulnerable to logging. To protect these critical and vulnerable deer yards, the State of Maine has included them in a comprehensive Land Use Plan for Plantations and Unorganized Townships for the State (Maine Department of Conservation 1969). The statute requires that protection subdistricts be established where development jeopardizes significant natural, recreational and historic resources, including but not limited to floodplains, precipitous slopes, wildlife habitat and other areas critical to the ecology of the region or state. These protection subdistricts do not prevent new development, but they do point out where protection is required and how the development will be regulated to protect the resource. Among the 11 protective subdistricts is a Fish and Wildlife Protection Subdistrict, the purpose of which is ". . . to conserve habitats essential to the citizens of Maine for the maintenance of fish and wildlife populations because of their economic, recreational, aesthetic, educational, and scientific value" (Maine Department of Conservation 1969:74). Among these habitats are deer wintering yards.

According to the standards, land uses in Maine that have significant detrimental effects will be regulated. Timber harvesting, agriculture, road construction and utility rights of way are permitted after review, if minimum standards are met and purposes of the subdistrict are upheld. Accordingly, the State Department of Inland Fisheries and Game identifies and maps critical deer yards, and delineates a special protective zone around them. Areas for consideration consist of at least 81 hectares (200 acres) of mature spruce and fir with a minimum of 70-percent canopy closure and cover and of which at least 61 hectares (150 acres) represent a deer yard. Landowners cannot cut timber within the deer yard without approval of the Land Use Commission, which reviews cutting plans to ensure protection of the biological integrity of deer yards and, at the same time, hopefully provide winter browse adjacent to them (*see* Gill 1957*b*). A similar management program is in operation in New Brunswick, Canada (Boer 1978).

Forest management in the Southeast. For forest lands of the Southeast, a great deal of controversy exists over the virtues of long-rotation management or selective harvesting of trees versus short-rotation management or clearcuttings for deer. Most foresters presently favor even-aged forest management. However, long-rotation selection cutting seems to provide the most stable whitetail habitat, even though the short-rotation cutting results in the most food for deer. Wildlife biologists have yet to agree on which approach is best for various forest types and site conditions, but there does seem to be agreement that if even-aged management is practiced, cutting should be in blocks small enough to assure that early successional plant communities always will be present on the forest management compartment (about 405 hectares: 1,000 acres).

Although a good deal of lip service is given to integrating timber harvest with deer management on forested lands, good examples of such integration are scarce. One such example is the management program on the Piedmont National Wildlife Refuge, a 13,355-hectare (33,000-acre) pine/hardwood forest located in central Georgia (U.S. Department of Interior 1969). It developed from 14,570 hectares (36,000 acres) of abandoned cotton land that had reverted mostly to pine. In areas of the refuge where cotton farming formerly was impracticable, forest growth has remained hardwood mixed with pine.

Acquired in the 1930s, the Piedmont National Wildlife Refuge was managed from 1940 to 1960 under the uneven-aged concept, but this type of management was incompatible with silvicultural practices advocated for southern pinelands, such as prescribed burning. Although selective cutting opened up stands enough to encourage growth of understory, heavy accumulations of litter and dense brushy growth resulted in deterioration of wildlife habitat and created serious fire hazards. In the 1960s, uneven-aged management was replaced

by a modified even-aged management, involving units of no more than 40 hectares (100 acres), no less than 4 hectares (10 acres) and averaging 20 hectares (50 acres). The forest management program was and is based on an 80-year rotation, a cutting cycle of 10 years, and a 4-year cycle of prescribed burning on pinelands. That cutting cycle, along with thinning operations, provides an even flow of timber products on a sustained-yield basis—approximately 250,000 board feet of lumber annually. It also ensures the stability of wildlife habitats and provides an array of successional stages at all times. The result is, in effect, uneven-aged management with even-aged units.

The objective of the refuge's management plan is to maintain 20 percent of the acreage in hardwoods (dictated by topographic sites), 75 percent in pineland, and 5 percent open. At the end of the 80-year rotation, 20 percent of the acreage will be in precommercial stands, 30 percent in pulpwood and 50 percent in sawtimber. That involves 10 major age groups of trees for each cutting cycle—2 in precommercial-age timber, 3 in pulpwood and 5 in sawtimber.

However, final regeneration cuts made annually on the refuge are restricted to 10 percent of the finest acreage. For example, the schedule for an annual harvest on a 40-hectare (100-acre) compartment would be 5 percent wildlife openings, 10 percent old timber replaced by young stands, and 85 percent commercially thinned stands. Maintaining a proper crown spacing in thinned stands allows sunlight to reach the forest floor, thereby encouraging low-growing woody shrubs and herbaceous vegetation. Prescribed burning in the thinned stands discourages forest regeneration.

Such forest management practices benefit all wildlife on the refuge, including deer. Whitetails were restocked on the area in the 1930s. Whitetail harvests over the past 10 years have amounted to 700 animals annually—about 1 deer per 20 hectares (50 acres), or 25 percent of the total population.

Forest management in the Midwest. Another example of integrating timber harvest with deer management on forested land is the program at the Mark Twain National Forest in Missouri. The hardwood and hardwood/pine forests on a variety of topographical situations on Mark Twain National Forest in the Missouri Ozarks is a strong contrast to the pineland forest of the Piedmont National Wildlife Refuge in Georgia. The wildlife/forest management objective on that national forest is a diversity of both habitats and wildlife, rather than accommodating just the needs of one species, such as deer. The program involves even-aged forest stands and is based on three components—forage-producing, mast-producing and old-growth timber. However simplistic the approach may seem, it effectively provides and maintains the range of wildlife habitat needs.

According to the Mark Twain National Forest's management guidelines (Anonymous 1973), 20 percent of the forest is to be maintained in forage production, including all herbaceous and woody material utilized as food by wildlife, such as fruits, grasses, forbs and woody browse. The guidelines provide for growth of young trees less than 10 years old, fruit-producing shrubs, perennial and annual forbs, old fields, and forest openings. Half of the forage production is to result from timber regeneration. The other half is permanent forage in old fields, pastures, abandoned homesteads and the like.

Mast includes the nuts and seeds of fruits of hardwood trees, dominated by acorns from oaks. Variety and stability in mast production require a balance of age-size classes from about 35 years old to old-growth timber. Forty percent of the forest is to be devoted to hard mast production. That requires a wide distribution of mast-bearing trees, especially oaks in the 40–80-year-old class. Some of these mast-bearing trees are in pine stands and on noncommercial timber sites.

Old-growth timber (100+ years) is essential habitat for wild turkeys, squirrels and cavity-nesting birds. Ten percent of the forest is to be maintained in old-growth forest.

Providing and maintaining the program's three component parts provide a variety of cover conditions, from permanent openings and recently logged stands to mature forests capable of producing a variety of mast to old-growth forests interspersed across forested landscape.

Achievement of such diversity requires some adjustments and flexibility in silvicultural practices. For example, even-aged management may not fit all situations. Timber harvest may be deferred on some compartments of the forest, and harvesting some immature stands may be accelerated to provide necessary amounts of early succession stage vegetation. To provide greater spacing of forage, production size of regeneration harvest cuts may be small and

dispersed. Oak stands are dispersed throughout the tract to achieve desired amounts of old-growth forest. Some stands may have to be retained well beyond their commercial age. The ultimate objective is to obtain a long-term interspersion of various cover types. In addition, other management practices are employed: one source of permanent water per 2.6 square kilometers (1 square mile); maintenance of pastures and improved grasslands; and manipulation of powerline rights of way, hollows, old homesteads and other areas that contribute to wildlife habitat diversity. Thus, the emphasis is not on management for white-tailed deer alone, but for the benefit of a diversity of wildlife.

Forest management on private lands. Integration of forest and wildlife management practices on private land, as previously discussed, usually is at the discretion of the landowner. Product-oriented private timber companies have few incentives, apart from public relations and dollar returns from hunting and other outdoor recreational opportunities, to integrate wildlife considerations with timber management. Even the American Forestry Institute provides no incentive for their cooperators to include wildlife in tree farm operations. And few federal agricultural programs provide financial assistance to encourage wildlife management practices. At least two surveys—one in Missouri (Kirby et al. 1981) and one in Vermont (Kelly 1981)—indicated that a slight majority of farmers have little interest in or incentive for wildlife management.

Such practices as clearcut regeneration, short rotations and planting genetically superior trees make forestry more agricultural and less natural, leaving little room for wildlife, including deer. To many private landowners, whitetails are considered a nuisance because of the damage they do to forest reproduction, nursery stock, Christmas tree plantations and agricultural crops. Wildlife agencies have the difficult task of convincing these landowners to incorporate deer management practices into their farming or forestry operations.

Controlling Damage by Deer

In many parts of North America, populations of white-tailed deer have reached densities that conflict directly with human economic interests (*see* Chapter 38). Such conflict does not necessarily mean that the deer have exceeded the carrying capacity of their habitat. In fact, whitetails have expanded their range and grown in number because, by the planting of crops, trees and other vegetation attractive to deer, human activity has increased the carrying capacity of many landscapes.

While whitetail populations have been increasing and hunting numbers continue to grow, deer harvests in some areas are not allowed to be sufficient enough to place and maintain the deer population at levels compatible with economic interests and landowner tolerance. As a result, deer damage complaints and deer/vehicle collisions are increasing.

Pennsylvania, for example, which supports one of North America's largest whitetail populations, reported 29,914 roadkilled deer in 1975 and 26,772 in 1980. In 1981, the number of reported roadkilled deer was 24,699, nearly 16.6 percent of the total hunter harvest of 148,530 whitetails for that year. Hansen (1978) estimated that the average deer/vehicle accident cost $730 in property damage alone, exclusive of any bodily injuries. The estimate was based on insurance claims. Using that criterion, it can be figured that deer/vehicle accidents in Pennsylvania in 1981 cost $18,030,270 worth of property damage or loss.

Because of the damage whitetails inflict on forestry and agricultural crops, and the damage they cause on roadways, considerable effort has been expended to determine ways of reducing such conflicts. The two most popular approaches are fencing and repellents. Deer repellents, however attractive and convenient they seem to the users, are not particularly effective. Odor, visual or sound repellents are of limited utility or practicality because they cannot be used on all crops, vary in effectiveness, and generally are too expensive for extensive use (Wingard et al. 1981).

To date, the best means of controlling deer damage, other than by harvesting, is with fencing. The most effective fencing is a 2.4-meter (8-foot) high or higher fence of woven wire, over which deer cannot jump. Such fencing will keep deer from crops and away from highways, but it is expensive to erect and maintain. Along the New York Thruway, fences 2.1 meters (7 feet) high reduced deer/vehicle collisions by 44.3 to 83.9 percent in fenced areas and by 12.9 to 24.7 percent beyond the ends of the fences (Free and Severinghaus no date). Fencing along a 27.8-kilometer (17.3-mile) section of highway in Colorado cost about $27,000 per kilometer ($43,450 per mile) in 1978 (Reed 1981).

An alternative means of fencing that appears promising is electrical fencing (Wingard et al. 1981). One form is the modified New Hampshire electrical deer fence; another is the Pennsylvania five-wire deer fence. Ordinary electrical fencing used to contain cattle in pastures is inadequate, because whitetails can easily clear it by jumping over or crawling underneath. To be effective, an electric fence first must jolt the deer and thereby discourage the animal from again approaching it close enough to jump over it.

The modified New Hampshire fence involves two electric fences on parallel rows 97 centimeters (38 inches) apart. One row has two strands of electric wire—the first 38 centimeters (15 inches) above the ground, low enough to stop a deer from crawling under, and a second strand 71 centimeters (28 inches) above the first. The other row is strung 76 centimeters (30 inches) above the ground. This arrangement prevents most deer from crawling under or jumping over the fence.

Simpler than the New Hampshire fence is the Pennsylvania five-wire fence. It consists of five wires strung on a single row of posts. The bottom wire is 25 centimeters (10 inches) above the ground, with the other four strung at 30-centimeter (12-inch) intervals. The wires are close enough to prevent crawling through and tall enough (147 centimeters: 58 inches) to deter deer from jumping over. Whitetails are quickly conditioned to electric shock, and once conditioned, will trail approximately 1 meter (3.3 feet) away from such a fence, a distance sufficient in most instances to discourage jumping.

Electric fencing using pressure-treated posts and high tensile wire that can absorb the impact of a deer has a life of 30 to 40 years and is relatively inexpensive to build and maintain.

Other approaches to whitetail damages involve forms of insurance or damage payment to landowners, underpass and overpass structures along highways, and improved planning of highway routes through deer range, including attention to plantings along new roads that may attract deer.

The ultimate solution to the deer damage problem, at least theoretically, is to maintain whitetails at a level compatible with human economic interests. This, of course, is easier

Roads and highways in the United States and Canada represent a multiple hazard for white-tailed deer and their management. Not only are deer/vehicle collisions costly and on the increase, but roadways dissect and eliminate vast amounts of deer habitat. In the United States alone, as of December 31, 1981, there were 6,200,147 kilometers (3,852,697 miles) of improved public roads and approximately 160,930 kilometers (100,000 miles) of primitive and unimproved roads (U.S. Federal Highway Administration, Highway Statistics Division personal communication to R. E. McCabe:1983). Of the improved public roads, 83.6 percent were in rural areas. And within the contiguous United States, paved roads and their rights-of-way account for about 1.1 percent of the country's land surface—equivalent to the areas of Rhode Island, New Hampshire, Vermont, Massachusetts and Connecticut combined. At present (1980–1983), new roadways in the U.S. are being constructed (graded and surfaced) at a rate of more than 18,000 kilometers (11,200 miles) per year. In addition to their interference with whitetail movements and the elimination of prime or critical deer habitat in many cases, roadways compound management difficulties by erosion-control, windrow and aesthetic plantings, and winter salting that attract deer. Fencing, overpass and underpass structures, and other means of preventing or reducing deer/vehicle accidents and accommodating deer movements are expensive, often prohibitively so. Increased attention to roadway site selection and construction planning is needed to alleviate current and future problems. *Photo by B. C. Venable; courtesy of the U.S. Soil Conservation Service.*

said than done, because of the diversity of social, political, economic and biological demands on and for the size of nearly all whitetail populations.

PUBLIC INFORMATION AND EDUCATION

State and provincial wildlife agencies have acquired a great amount of knowledge on whitetailed deer habitat, population dynamics and life history. However, they have not been especially successful in transmitting that information to the general public to generate understanding and support for deer management.

Most wildlife agencies are administered by persons who, more often than not, have little training and/or appreciation for information transfer (*see* Peek et al. 1982, Gilbert 1978). Although agencies communicate relatively easily with sportsmen, an information gap frequently exists between agencies and the general public, including nonhunters, antihunters, youngsters and politicians. Consequently the general public all too often senses some sort of "collusion" between agencies and sportsmen, or other special interest groups, to the detriment of the agencies' image and ability to conduct their programs in the best interest of the resources and all citizens.

Much of the problem rests with the wildlife agencies themselves. Some fail to keep a flow of information going to the press and other media concerning wildlife and its management. In such cases the released information tends to relate primarily to consumptive wildlife programs, is defensive, and is prepared and disseminated under the pressure of some crisis.

Many wildlife agencies publish magazines or newsletters for public distribution. Some of these serial publications are aimed at general audiences and cover a broad range of environmental, natural history and human interest topics and issues. Others are oriented primarily toward sportsmen. This latter type tends to reinforce the general public's attitude that wildlife agencies cater to special interests.

To "sell" their white-tailed deer management programs, wildlife agencies must be responsive to all their publics. They need to employ information exchanges that identify, explain and justify specific program investments and their overall missions. To generate and maintain public support, they must take the initiative in presenting information on their plans, activities and program results, and provide constructive mechanisms for public response. This will help to avoid "crisis reporting" that can damage an agency's image, credibility and effectiveness.

HUNTER EDUCATION

Since the late 1800s, the primary role of the white-tailed deer hunter has changed dramatically, from provisioner in years past to that of recreationist today. Technological advances in the production of domestic food and fiber, efficient transportation, refrigeration, urbanization and job specialization all have served to draw people away from self-sufficiency and dependence on raw products of the land. And with this social metamorphosis has come an attitudinal change about the purpose and values of hunting.

Since whitetail hunting for subsistence is no longer a fact in most areas, indulgence of it and participation in it primarily for recreation have been matters of personal decision. However, there are factions that loudly protest against hunting and/or hunters, for reasons ranging from moralism to humanism (Kellert 1978). Prohunting advocates have found it virtually impossible to argue with the so-called "antis," and vice versa, because the two camps

perceive the value of wildlife very differently (*see* Chapter 42). And it seems that, because the opposing viewpoints rarely attain a common cognitive denominator, mutual understanding or agreement is unlikely (*see* Poole 1971). On the other hand, antihunting proponents probably are not the most serious threat to future hunting—at least not to the degree perceived by hunters (Sitton 1976). Economic and ecological facts support *regulated* hunting and harvests of *designated* wildlife populations. Recreational hunters provide a valuable service in helping to manage deer and other wildlife populations. The real threat to recreational hunting is more insidious than are vocal groups of "antis." It is the hunters themselves and their behavior when afield.

In addition to the technological achievements of the past century, the human population has multiplied exponentially and expanded its area of occupation and sphere of influence on unoccupied landscape (Allen 1978). More hunters and fewer places to hunt each year have intensified competition for hunting and harvest opportunities. This, in turn, has spawned incidences of illegal or unethical hunter behavior. Just how extensive hunter misconduct is remains uncertain. But it is prevalent enough to have encouraged a growing number of private rural landowners to deny recreational access (Church 1979). Virtually hundreds of square miles of land are closed annually because of abuses by a small percentage of the total hunter population.

Besides the obvious impact of limiting recreational opportunities, hunter misconduct diminishes the ability of wildlife agencies and commissions to manage whitetail numbers and their habitats, by disallowing adequate harvests. It also provides emotional fodder for the antis, who may not sway the attitudes of biologists, other resource managers and sportsmen, but who do have the capability and willingness to stir sensitive biopolitical waters—waters in which the wildlife agencies must tread (Williamson and Teague 1971). Finally, illegal or unethical acts, even by a small minority of hunters, tend to cast an ill light on all hunters. For too long, concerns about the image of hunters and hunting have detracted from the real issue at hand—proper wildlife management in the best interest of society and the animals themselves.

As early as the late 1800s, there was concern about problems of sportsmanship as well as wildlife conservation (International Association of Fish and Wildlife Agencies 1981). Wildlife conservation gained its first real momentum in the 1930s, but a concerted effort to modify and improve hunter attitudes and behavior lagged by nearly two decades. Sportsmen's codes of ethics appeared early in the century, but programs to instill hunters with concepts of proper conduct afield did not begin in earnest until after World War II.

At that time, hunter safety programs were initiated in Kentucky (1945) and New York (1949). Other states and provinces gradually followed suit. For the most part, the early programs were directed at safe firearms handling—an admirable starting point, but not sufficient to help resolve the misconduct problems.

Within the past several decades and particularly since the early 1970s, hunter training has expanded to include principles of wildlife biology, ethics, legal and social responsibilities, wildlife identification, and landowner relationships, besides hunting techniques and weapons handling and safety. This was done because ". . . there exists agreement that State and Provincial hunter education and safety

programs can contribute significantly to greater awareness and enjoyment of the wildlife resource; and, further can contribute to an improved conservation ethic, lead to greater understanding of wildlife management issues, and assure that hunting will continue to provide outdoor recreation opportunities for millions of North Americans . . ." (International Association of Fish and Wildlife Agencies 1981:2). Not as specifically stated was the goal of improving public perception of hunting as a practical, efficient, economical and important management option, as well as a rewarding outdoor recreational activity.

To be sure, the objective of image enhancement may be considered a bit of propaganda (Reiger 1978), but the results of state and provincial hunter education programs speak for themselves. Thirty states and 7 provinces now have mandatory programs for first-time hunters, while the remainder—20 states and 5 provinces—have voluntary programs. As of 1981, more than 14 million students have successfully completed hunter education courses in the United States and Canada (tables 85 and 86).

Hunter education is a vitally important part of modern wildlife management programs. Youngsters and beginning hunters in North America are taught hunting ethics and basic principles of wildlife management as well as firearms handling and safety. Current programs have achieved considerable success in reducing hunting accidents and appear to be making progress in the improvement of hunter/landowner relations. In New York State, for example, the rate of landowner posting against recreational use (principally hunting) for the period 1972–1980 was less than half that of the 1963–1972 time span (Decker et al. 1982). And of the landowners who posted, 65 percent reportedly would allow hunting by permission. *Photo by Glen Mills; courtesy of the Texas Parks and Wildlife Department.*

Table 85. Profile of hunter education programs in the United States, 1981.[a]

State	Year program began	Sponsoring agency	Mandatory (M) or volunteer (V) participation	Legal requirement of participation	Number of active instructors	Required instructor training (in hours)	Average student age
Alabama	1973	Department of Conservation—Fish and Game Division	V		327	8	16
Alaska	1973	Fish and Game Department	V		400		15
Arizona	1955	Game and Fish Department	M	10–14 years of age for big game hunting	800	20	13
Arkansas	1971	Game and Fish Commission	V		630	11	11–18
California	1954	Fish and Game Department	M	First-time resident license buyers	1,500		18
Colorado	1969	Wildlife Division	M	Born after 1/1/49	550	28	12+
Connecticut	1957	Department of Environmental Protection	M	First-time license buyers and those who have not purchased new license in preceding five years	300	19	12–16
Delaware	1970	Fish and Wildlife Division	M	License buyers under 18 years of age	100	15	14
Florida	1971	Game and Fresh Water Fish Commission	V		565	12	20
Georgia	1964	Department of Natural Resources	M	Born after 1/1/61; exempt on own property, and for persons under 12 years of age	430	20	12–18
Hawaii	1978	Department of Land and Natural Resources	V		36	15	15
Idaho	1956	Fish and Game Department	M	12–14 years of age	887	12	12–13
Illinois	1959	Department of Conservation—Division of Law Enforcement	M	First-time license buyers under 16 years of age	2,300	12	15
Indiana	1975	Department of Natural Resources—Division of Law Enforcement	V		800	8	13–15
Iowa	1960	Conservation Commission	V		850	4	12–14
Kansas	1973	Fish and Game Commission	M	Born after 7/1/57	2,985	8	10–16
Kentucky	1945	Fish and Wildlife Department	V		300	12	12
Louisiana	1969	Wildlife and Fisheries Department	M		561	12	13
Maine	1958	Inland Fisheries and Wildlife Department	V		500	14	12

Table 85. (continued)

Minimum hours per course	Course part of school programs	Course content (mandatory [M] or optional [O])								Number of students certified in 1981	Number of students certified since program began
		Ethics	Conservation	Firearm handling	Bowhunting	Muzzleloading	Wildlife identification	Survival	First aid		
6	Yes	M	M	M	M	M	M	O	O	4,500	32,000
8	Yes	M	M	M	O	O	O	M	M	1,200	11,000
16	Yes	M	M	M	M	M	O	M	O	6,000	98,000
8	Yes	M	M	M	M	M	O	M	M	10,000	54,000
6	Yes	M	M	M	M	M	M	M	M	40,000	1,103,200
8	Yes	M	M	M	M	M	M	M	M	23,000	312,868
12	Yes	M	M	M	M	M	M	M	M	3,500	78,303
6	Yes	M	M	M	M	M	O	O	O	1,500	20,000
12	Yes	M	M	M	M	M	M	M	M	10,000	69,000
6	Yes	M	M	M	O	O	O	M	O	27,000	250,000
10	No	M	M	M	M	O	O	M	M	400	702
9	Yes	M	M	M	O	O	O	M	M	7,000	60,500
8	Yes	M	M	M	M	M	M	M	M	10,000	161,812
8	Yes	M	M	M	M	M	M	M	M	10,000	74,859
6	Yes	M	M	M	M	M	M	M	M	10,000	177,154
8	Yes	M	M	M	O	O	M	M	M	14,000	152,254
10	Yes	M	M	M	M	M	M	M	M	5,800	1,045,350
6	Yes	M	M	M	O	O	M	M	O	9,300	47,050
10	Yes	M	M	M	O	O	M	M	M	3,000	56,000

Table 85. (continued)

State	Year program began	Sponsoring agency	Mandatory (M) or volunteer (V) participation	Legal requirement of participation	Number of active instructors	Required instructor training (in hours)	Average student age
Maryland	1966	Department of Natural Resources	M	First-time hunters	288	21	10–14
Massachusetts	1954	Environmental Affairs—law enforcement officers	V	Persons 15–18 years of age must be accompanied by licensed adult or have passed hunter safety course	125	20	16
Michigan	1971	Natural Resources Department	M	First-time license buyers 12–16 years of age	1,800	4	11–16
Minnesota	1955	Natural Resources Department	M	Under 16 years of age	3,500	6	13
Mississippi	1971	Department of Wildlife Conservation	V		300	4	13
Missouri	1958	Conservation Department	V		1,061	8	15
Montana	1958	Department of Fish, Wildlife and Parks	M	License buyers under 18 years of age	640		11–18
Nebraska	1972	Game and Parks Commission	M	12–15 years of age	780	4	11–12
Nevada	1973	Wildlife Department	M	Persons under 21 years of age prior to first licensing	115	10	13
New Hampshire	1953	Fish and Game Department	M	First-time license buyers	675	8	14–16
New Jersey	1958	Department of Fish, Game and Wildlife	M	Persons without previous license	550	16	13–14
New Mexico	1965	Game and Fish Department	M	Hunters and license buyers under 18 years of age	594	15	12–13
New York	1949	Fish and Wildlife Division	M	First-time license buyers	6,721	12	14 +
North Carolina	1972	Wildlife Resources Commission	V		1,000	12	14–16
North Dakota	1972	Game and Fish Department	M	Born after 12/31/61	1,200	4	12–13
Ohio	1956	Wildlife Division	M	First-time license buyers	1,000	14–18	12–17
Oklahoma	1956	Wildlife Conservation Department	V		98	10	17
Oregon	1962	Fish and Wildlife Department	M	Under 18 years of age; parent's property exempt	1,383		12–13
Pennsylvania	1959	Game Commission	M	First-time hunters	4,200	6	12–16
Rhode Island	1956	Fish and Wildlife Department	M	First-time license buyers	129	10	14–17
South Carolina	1974	Wildlife and Marine Resources Department	V		300	15	12–15
South Dakota	1956	Department of Game, Fish and Parks	M	Less than 16 years of age; nonresidents exempt	400	8	11–13

Table 85. (continued)

Minimum hours per course	Course part of school programs	Course content (mandatory [M] or optional [O])								Number of students certified in 1981	Number of students certified since program began
		Ethics	Conservation	Firearm handling	Bowhunting	Muzzleloading	Wildlife identification	Survival	First aid		
7	Yes	M	M	M	M	M	O	O	O	10,000	125,000
10	Yes	M	M	M	M	O	M	M	O	4,000	77,698
9	Yes	M	M	M	M	M	M	M	M	40,000	661,000
12	No	M	M	M	M	M	M	M	M	22,000	553,800
6	Yes	M	M	M	O	O	O	O	O	8,000	64,000
6	Yes	M	M	M	M	M	M	M	M	12,500	290,000
10	No	M	M	M	M	M	M	M	M	5,600	171,950
6	Yes	M	M	M	O	M	O	O	O	7,100	74,000
10	Yes	M	M	M	M	M	M	M	M	4,500	33,000
12	Yes	M	M	M	M	M	M	M	M	4,500	50,000
10	No	M	M	M	O	O	M	M	M	15,000	319,420
8	Yes	M	M	M	M	O	O	M	M	7,500	106,000
6	Yes	M	M	M	M	O	M	O	O	95,000	2,200,000
6	Yes	M	M	M	M	M	O	M	M	23,316	191,854
12	Yes	M	M	M	O	O	O	M	M	5,000	37,990
6	Yes	M	M	M	M	O	M	M	M	25,000	367,411
6	Yes	M	M	M	M	M	M	M	M	6,000	91,266
8	Yes	M	M	M	M	M	O	M	O	10,000	280,000
6	Yes	M	M	M	M	M	M	O	O	50,000	900,000
10	Yes	M	M	M	M	M	M	M	M	1,300	19,500
12	Yes	M	M	M	M	M	M	M	M	11,000	38,000
12	No	M	M	M	M	M	M	M	M	4,500	139,000

Table 85. (continued)

State	Year program began	Sponsoring agency	Mandatory (M) or volunteer (V) participation	Legal requirement of participation	Number of active instructors	Required instructor training (in hours)	Average student age
Tennessee	1972	Wildlife Resources Agency	V		1,000	15	12–14
Texas	1972	Parks and Wildlife Department	V		1,200	6	11
Utah	1957	Wildlife Resources Division	M	License buyers under 16 years of age	285	20	12–14
Vermont	1959	Fish and Game Department	M	First-time license buyers	400	4	12
Virginia	1961	Commission of Game and Inland Fisheries	V		312	8	16
Washington	1957	Game Department	M	Under 18 years of age	650	8	12
West Virginia	1968	Department of	V		560	8	13–16
Wisconsin	1967	Department of Natural Resources	V		2,000	20	12–14
Wyoming	1961	Game and Fish Department	M	Persons born on or since 1/1/66	620	16	12
Totals				48,707			

[a]Compiled from Hunter Safety News (1982).

There is strong evidence that, besides improving safety aspects of the hunting experience, hunter education programs instill participants with an understanding of and appreciation for the role of scientific management in perpetuating wildlife and related natural resource and human benefits. *Photos reprinted with the permission of the National Shooting Sports Foundation.*

Table 85. (continued)

Minimum hours per course	Course part of school programs	Course content (mandatory [M] or optional [O])								Number of students certified in 1981	Number of students certified since program began
		Ethics	Conservation	Firearm handling	Bowhunting	Muzzleloading	Wildlife identification	Survival	First aid		
11	Yes	M	M	M	M	M	M	M	M	19,000	100,000
6	Yes	M	M	M	M	O	O	M	M	12,500	89,417
10	Yes	M	M	M	M	M	M	M	M	14,000	375,000
11	Yes	M	M	M	O	O	O	M	M	5,560	61,000
6	Yes	M	M	M	M	M	M	M	M	25,000	307,067
8	Yes	M	M	M	M	M	O	O	O	13,000	373,000
6	Yes	M	M	M	O	O	M	O	O	17,000	155,000
10	Yes	M	M	M	O	O	M	M	M	18,000	218,000
12	Yes	M	M	M	M	M	M	M	M	10,000	30,000
										702,076	12,303,425

The knowledge, aptitudes and attitudes gained by students in well-administered hunter education programs serve to diffuse at least some of the concerns about and objections to hunting by the antihunter public, thus preserving the important link between recreational hunting and effective management of white-tailed deer. *Photos reprinted with the permission of the National Shooting Sports Foundation.*

Table 86. Profile of hunter education programs in Canada, 1981.[a]

Province/ territory	Year program began	Sponsoring agency	Mandatory (M) or volunteer (V) participation	Legal requirement of participation	Number of active instructors	Required instructor training (in hours)	Average student age
Alberta	1964	Fish and Wildlife Division	V		1,500	40	16
British Columbia	1972	Ministry of Environment	M	First-time hunters over 14 years of age	360	8	14–16
Manitoba	1964	Department of Natural Resources	M	First-time hunters, including all under 19 years of age	528	12	15
New Brunswick	1972	Department of Natural Resources	M	Hunters 14–16 years of age	450	20	13–14
Newfoundland	1971	Department of Tourism— Wildlife Division	V	All big game hunters	150	24	16–18
Northwest Territories[b]	1980	Department of Renewable Resources	V				
Nova Scotia	1960	Department of Lands and Forests	M	All hunters who do not hold hunting certificate	350	8	18–20
Ontario	1957	Ministry of Natural Resources	M	First-time hunters— exam; under 20 years of age— course and exam	1,400	16	17
Prince Edward Island	1971	Fish and Wildlife Division	V		10	15–20	12–20
Quebec	1968	Department of Tourism— Fish and Game Division	M	All hunters	700	10	
Saskatchewan	1960	Department of Tourism and Renewable Resources	M	First-time hunters, including all under 17 years of age	950	8	14
Yukon Territory	1975	Department of Renewable Resources—Wildlife and Parks Branch	V		8	8	13–14
Totals					6,406		

[a]Compiled from Hunter Safety News (1982).
[b]Hunter education program currently under development.

Table 86. (continued)

Minimum hours per course	Course part of school programs	Course content (mandatory [M] or optional [O])								Number of students certified in 1981	Number of students certified since program began
		Ethics	Conservation	Firearm handling	Bowhunting	Muzzleloading	Wildlife identification	Survival	First aid		
30+	Yes	M	M	M	M	M	M	M	M	14,500	82,000
24	Yes	M	M	M	O	O	M	M	M	10,000	80,000
8	Yes	M	M	M	O	O	M	M	O	5,000	82,788
14	Yes	M	M	M	O	O	M	M	O	3,000	35,000
12	No	M	M	M	O	O	M	M	O	1,000	21,000
8–10	No	M	M	M	M	O	M	M	M	10,000	44,179
12	Yes	M	M	M	M	O	M	M	M	35,000	591,043
10	Yes	M	M	M	O	O	M	M	M	300	2,000
8	Yes	M	M	M			M	M		50,000	720,000
12	Yes	M	M	M	O	O	M	M	O	5,000	80,000
15–18	Yes	M	M	M	O	O	M	O	O	120	
										133,920	1,738,010

In addition to providing novices with the basics for proper hunter conduct, attitudes and skills, hunter education courses in a number of states have instituted programs encouraging citizen participation in reporting violations of conservation law. Also, sportsmen's organizations, such as the Izaak Walton League of America, have made major attempts to promote ethical conduct among their memberships, and invite a "policing of the ranks" to assure that hunting is done in a fair and judicious manner.

While difficult to quantify, it seems certain that these various actions to improve hunting have made substantial strides in making the recreation, particularly deer hunting, safer, more enjoyable, more successful and more socially acceptable than otherwise would have been the case. New York State, for example, had approximately 600,000 licensed hunters in the period 1937 through 1941. During that time there was an average of 30 fatal and 152 nonfatal hunting accidents per year—for rates of 5 and 25 accidents per 100,000 hunters, respectively. Since the early 1970s, New York has had more than 1 million licensed hunters.

The average annual number of hunting accidents has been 8.9 fatal and 88.8 nonfatal, for rates of 1 and 9 per 100,000 hunters, respectively. In sum, since the period 1937–1941, the fatal hunting accident rate in New York has decreased 400 percent, and the nonfatal accident rate has declined by about 180 percent. Elsewhere, in Virginia and West Virginia in 1981, where hunter education courses are not a prerequisite to obtain a hunting license, there were 9 and 7 hunters killed accidentally, respectively. In the adjacent states of Maryland and Pennsylvania, where hunter education courses are required, there were 0 and 2 hunting fatalities, respectively, in 1981. The figures are more impressive when one considers that Virginia and West Virginia have fewer hunters than do Maryland and Pennsylvania.

As impressive as the statistics are that show the effectiveness of hunter education programs, it remains the duty of each hunter to make a commitment to the sound tenets of safe and responsible hunting in order for it to continue to be an accepted and worthwhile individual privilege and a wildlife management option.

Chapter 36

HABITAT EVALUATION

Richard F. Harlow
Research Wildlife Biologist
U.S. Forest Service
Southeastern Forest Experiment Station
Clemson, South Carolina

White-tailed deer are considered to be browsers because they consume woody vegetation. In fact, they are compelled to do so in order to survive in winter yards. However, whitetails will eat almost any available form of plant life. Because of this adaptability, it is impossible to single out one habitat as greatly superior to others. Thus, to evaluate white-tailed deer habitat successfully, wildlife biologists and managers must recognize and measure many factors, including plant composition, vegetation condition and successional trends, and the structure and variability of forest stands. Interaction of deer and habitat then is analyzed by measuring food preference and utilization, quantity and quality of food, and availability of cover.

HABITAT CHARACTERISTICS

Plant Composition

Plant composition refers to the variety and arrangement of plants comprising a vegetative community. It is a qualitative expression and represents one or more plant species. Usually, the best whitetail habitat conditions occur where there is a wide variety and large quantity of palatable, nutritious food available to the deer (Figure 111, Table 87).

Vegetation Conditions and Successional Trend

Vegetation condition is the stage of development or growth of plants in a vegetative community at a specific time. Vegetation trend reflects changes of condition over time.

All vegetation and communities go through predictable stages of development before and including maturity (Figure 112). When mature trees in a forest are harvested, for example, and the canopy (or overstory) is reduced or eliminated, sunlight reaches the relatively bare forest floor. In response to this light, a great quantity and variety of plants emerge. At this early stage of plant succession, when vegetative growth is most rapid and annual changes are most noticeable, whitetails are able to find an abundance of forage. In time, however, fast-growing plants tend to dominate and frequently eliminate the low- and slow-growing species, some of which are attractive to deer. Accordingly, whitetail use of the habitat decreases. By the time that trees reach pole stage and canopy again reduces or prevents sunlight from reaching the ground, most understory is eliminated. Such loss of plant variety and quantity further diminishes the forest's food value to deer and its ability to support these animals.

In some forest types, such as in the southern Appalachian Mountains, shade-tolerant evergreen forbs and shrubs may be present in the understory. When within reach of deer, they can provide valuable winter foods. In all forest types, the degree of bare ground will depend to a large extent on the density of the tree stands.

Trees in a stand eventually reach harvestable size and are utilized or continue to age and die. When trees are felled, either in harvest or by natural forces, the canopy at that location opens up. Stands remaining unharvested and undisturbed may stay in a mature or climax stage for hundreds of years, depending on the forest type.

The rapidity with which successional stages occur is determined geographically by climate

Table 87. Forest types in various ecoregions in the United States within the range of white-tailed deer.[a]

Ecoregion	Forest type	Approximate growing season length (days) or conditions	Predominant vegetation
Warm continental (eastern)	Laurentian mixed forest	100–140	Four plant associations are recognized—spruce/fir forest, northern hardwoods, northern hardwoods/fir, and northern hardwoods/spruce
Hot continental	Eastern deciduous forest	140–200	Dominated by tall broad-leaved evergreen trees—mixed mesophytic forest, beech/maple forest, maple/basswood and oak savannah, Appalachian oak, and oak/hickory
Subtropical	Outer Coastal Plain and southern mixed forests	200–300	*Outer Coastal Plain*—evergreen oaks and members of the laurel and magnolia families; under-stories of tree ferns, small palms, shrubs and herbaceous plants *Southern mixed forest*—medium-tall to tall forests of broad-leaf deciduous and needleleaf evergreen trees (loblolly and shortleaf pines, hickory, sweetgum, black gum, red maple and winged elm)
Savannah	Everglades	Frost free	20 percent of area—tropical moist hardwood forests of cypress or mangrove; much of area is open marsh containing hydrophitic forbs and several areas are covered with sawgrass; within the grassland are mesic habitats (tree islands) that contain broad-leaved evergreen trees and shrubs
Prairie	Parkland	140–280	Intermingling of prairie, groves and strips of deciduous trees; upland forest dominated by oak and hickory; most prevalent grass is bluestem prairie
	Brushland	250–300	Arid grasslands in which shrubs and low trees grow singly or in bunches (bluestem, three awn, buffalo-grass, grama); also mesquite, oak and juniper
	Tallgrass	Annual precipitation ranges from 38 to 100 centimeters (15–40 inches) depending on area	Tallgrass and mixed grasslands; woody vegetation is rare except on the cottonwood floodplains
Steppe (lowland)	Great Plains shortgrass prairie	100–200	Formations of short grasses, usually bunched and sparsely distributed; scattered trees and shrubs occasionally appear

Table 87. (continued)

Ecoregion	Forest type	Approximate growing season length (days) or conditions	Predominant vegetation
Warm continental (western)	Columbia forest	100–140?	Mixed coniferous/deciduous forest predominates—Douglas-fir forest and cedar/hemlock/Douglas-fir forest are the two major types
Steppe (highland)	Rocky Mountain forest	Variable temperatures, cold winters; annual precipitation is less than 50 centimeters (20 inches)	Alpine zone—absence of trees; subalpine zone—spruce and fir; montane zone—pine and fir; foothill zone—mountain-mahogany and scrub oaks
Desert	American desert (Mojave, Colorado and Sonoran deserts)	High summer temperature, mild winters, very dry	Vegetation very sparse; cacti and thorny shrubs (cholla and mesquite) are conspicuous
Marine	Pacific forest	Mild temperature year round; rainfall heavy	Primarily montane; principal trees are Douglas-fir, western redcedar, grand fir, silver fir, Sitka spruce and Alaska cedar; numerous species of shrubs grow well

^aAdapted from Bailey (1980); *see* Figure 111.

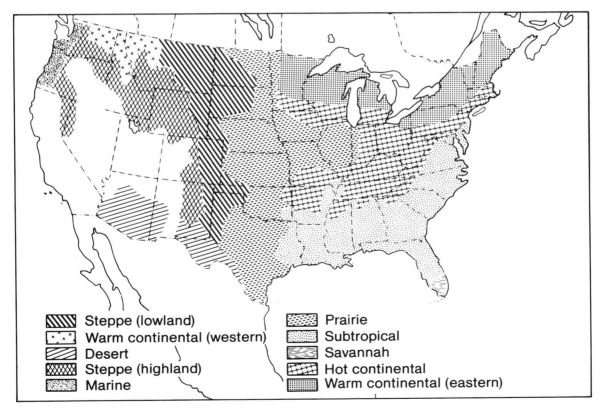

Figure 111. Ecoregions of the United States within the range of white-tailed deer (adapted from Bailey 1980).

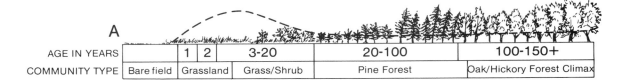

A						
AGE IN YEARS	1	2	3-20	20-100		100-150+
COMMUNITY TYPE	Bare field	Grassland	Grass/Shrub	Pine Forest		Oak/Hickory Forest Climax

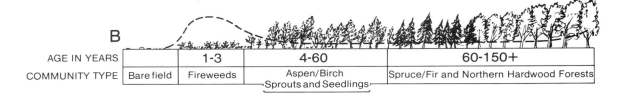

B				
AGE IN YEARS		1-3	4-60	60-150+
COMMUNITY TYPE	Bare field	Fireweeds	Aspen/Birch ⌐Sprouts and Seedlings⌐	Spruce/Fir and Northern Hardwood Forests

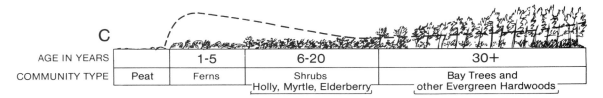

C			
AGE IN YEARS		1-5	6-20	30+
COMMUNITY TYPE	Peat	Ferns	Shrubs ⌐Holly, Myrtle, Elderberry⌐	Bay Trees and ⌐other Evergreen Hardwoods⌐

Figure 112. White-tailed deer forage supply in relation to secondary succession on (A) outer Coastal Plain and southern mixed-forest type on the Piedmont Plateau (Odum 1971), (B) burned habitat of Laurentian mixed-forest type on Isle Royale, Lake Superior (Oosting 1956), and (C) Everglades tree islands in southern Florida, after burning (Loveless 1959a).

The white-tailed deer diet includes a wide variety of plants, and the deer sometimes will go to unusual extremes to obtain preferred foods. This doe in eastern Texas is "bobbing" for moss. *Photo by James Kroll.*

(with vegetation growing more rapidly and for longer annual periods in the South), locally by the richness of the site (including factors of moisture, temperature and soil fertility), and by present and past land use.

Structure and Variability of Forest Stands

A "forest stand" is an aggregation of trees occupying a specific area and sufficiently uniform in composition, age, arrangement and condition to be distinguishable from other growth on adjoining areas. The most logical measure of tree stands is by individual tree size and spacing between trees. "Stand density" is the degree of stem crowding within an area. "Stocking" is a qualitative expression comparing the existing number of trees in a stand to the number desired. "Tree canopy" or "crown closure" represents the area occupied by the crown. A "closed-canopy stand," which sometimes occurs during the pole stage, is considered a fully stocked stand.

The greatest variability within tree stands occurs during the early successional phase and the least variability during the pole stage. Variability among stands depends on physiographic region, forest type, whether the stands are natural or planted, and past use of the land.

A camera-point study of plant succession over a period of 45 years in an upland corner of northern hardwoods in Cheboygan County, Michigan. Top photo taken in 1926 by P. S. Lovejoy shows the area shortly after logging and fire, at a time when whitetails were scarce in extensive stands of mature hardwoods. Center photo taken in 1952 by B. C. Jenkins, by which time the whitetail population had increased substantially (due to increased forage availability)—peaking in the mid-1940s. Bottom photo taken in 1977 by W. J. Montgomery shows the area having developed to dense pole-stage hardwood stands with limited understory, causing the deer population to decline gradually. *Photos courtesy of the Michigan Department of Natural Resources.*

Although white-tailed deer utilize forest stands in all stages of development, they obtain their greatest supplies of forage from stands in early stages of plant succession before the "tree canopy" is developed fully or, in old mature stands, where the trees have thinned out, permitting sunlight to flood the forest floor. Consequently, silvicultural practices that reduce canopy density generally benefit forested deer range.

Edge Cover and Forest Openings

The lack of available forage for white-tailed deer in unbroken forest stands containing dense overstories, and what happens to understory and ground cover when these overstories are thinned or removed and openings are created, have been well-documented. Three examples from different regions illustrate vegetative response to the creation of openings.

1. Blair and Brunett (1977) found that, in an all-aged loblolly/shortleaf pine and mixed hardwood forest in central Louisiana, herbage and browse yields peaked within two years after logging and progressively declined as overstory competition increased (Table 88).
2. Della-Bianca and Johnson (1965) studied the effects of an intensive cleaning on browse production in an 11-year-old hardwood sapling stand in the southern Appalachian Mountains of North Carolina. The stand contained an overstory in transition between the oak/hickory and cove hardwood types. More than 20 major timber species were present, as well as many shrubs and vines. A significant increase in browse occurred in both the upper and lower slopes—91 and 902 kilograms per hectare (81 and 805 pounds per acre), respectively—compared with unthinned stands that average only 3.4 kilograms per hectare (3 pounds per acre) on both slope positions (Table 89).
3. Portions of two mixed conifer swamps in Upper Michigan were subjected to the five different cutting methods—selection, shelterwood, diameter-limit, block and strip cutting (Krefting and Phillips 1970). Predominant overstory trees in both areas consisted of white cedar, black spruce, white spruce and balsam fir. All cutting methods resulted in increased browse production, with strip cutting (long, narrow strips cut adjacent to uncut strips) providing the most browse and providing good shelter (in the uncut strips) (Table 90). In these three studies, temporary openings were established through timber harvesting, and the whitetail foods that developed were from natural sources.

Table 88. White-tailed deer forage availability[a] following selective cutting in loblolly/shortleaf pine stands in central Louisiana (from Blair and Brunett 1977).

Vegetation class	Year after cutting[b]						
	1960	1961	1962	1964	1966	1968	1970
Herbaceous							
Grass and grasslike plants	80.7 (72)	99.8 (89)	74.0 (66)	37.0 (33)	23.5 (21)	21.3 (19)	15.7 (14)
Forbs	15.7 (14)	12.3 (11)	13.5 (12)	4.5 (4)	2.2 (2)	6.7 (6)	5.6 (5)
Total	96.4 (86)	112.1 (100)	87.4 (78)	41.5 (37)	25.8 (23)	28.0 (25)	21.3 (19)
Browse							
Leaves	225.3 (201)	238.7 (213)	233.1 (208)	182.7 (163)	143.5 (128)	125.5 (112)	90.8 (81)
Twigs	91.9 (82)	88.5 (79)	74.0 (66)	51.6 (46)	38.1 (34)	34.7 (31)	25.8 (23)
Total	317.2 (283)	327.3 (292)	307.1 (274)	234.3 (209)	181.6 (162)	160.3 (143)	116.6 (104)
Browse leaf-twig ratio	2.5:1	2.7:1	3.2:1	3.5:1	3.8:1	3.6:1	3.5:1

[a] In kilograms of dry matter per hectare (pounds per acre).
[b] Decline in forage productivity over time due to progressive closure of multitiered midstory.

Table 89. White-tailed deer forage availability[a] following thinning of a dense 11-year-old hardwood sapling stand in the Southern Appalachian Mountains of North Carolina (from Della-Bianca and Johnson 1965).

Browse species	Lower slope stand			Upper slope stand		
	Thinned	Dense	(control)	Thinned	Dense	(control)
White oaks	232.0 (207.0)	0.4	(0.3)	0.0 (0.0)	0.4	(0.3)
Red oaks	223.5 (199.4)	0.0	(0.0)	(0.0) (0.0)	1.0	(0.9)
Sourwood	214.5 (191.4)	0.0	(0.0)	0.0 (0.0)	0.4	(0.3)
Sassafras	119.9 (107.0)	0.0	(0.0)	1.0 (0.9)	0.0	(0.0)
Red maple	66.2 (59.1)	0.0	(0.0)	51.1 (45.6)	0.0	(0.0)
Eastern white pine	31.2 (27.8)	2.5	(2.2)	0.0 (0.0)	0.0	(0.0)
Black locust	12.1 (10.8)	0.0	(0.0)	34.5 (30.8)	0.0	(0.0)
Flowering dogwood	2.7 (2.4)	0.0	(0.0)	4.9 (4.4)	0.1	(0.1)
Black cherry	0.0 (0.0)	0.0	(0.0)	0.0 (0.0)	1.2	(1.1)
Yellow poplar	0.0 (0.0)	0.4	(0.3)	0.0 (0.0)	0.0	(0.0)
Total	902 ± 263 (805 ± 235)	4 ± 3	(3 ± 2)	91 ± 12 (81 ± 11)	4 ± 3	(3 ± 2)

[a]In kilograms per hectare (pounds per acre) oven-dry weight, and based on eighty 0.6-by-1.48-by-1.37-meter (2-by-4.85-by-4.5-foot) browse plots.

Permanent openings for white-tailed deer created in forested areas and purposely planted to some agricultural crop have been used by many state wildlife agencies and sportsman organizations. Larson (1969:47), looking for some positive aspects regarding such clearings in the southeastern United States, wrote that, "Diversity of habitat is necessary for successful management of deer populations and where this is lacking a system of clearings can provide openings, 'edge,' and diversity of food species." He found that, in large unbroken pine plantations, agricultural clearings produced lush green forage, often showing abundant use by deer in the form of droppings, tracks and grazing. One of the main values of such clearings was that they were tangible evidence to the public that "something was being done" for wildlife. On the other hand, Larson noted: "We have no sound evidence of the effect of clearings on wildlife production, movements, and harvest." He concluded that, "Where diversity of habitat is lacking, coordination with forest management will apply costs to several goals and keep single-purpose wildlife expenditures to a minimum."

Regarding the distribution and shape of forest cutting units in the Southeast, McGinnes (1969:70) noted that long, narrow clearcuts, by creating more edge, would benefit more deer than would large square or circular cuts. He also observed that, "Optimally, a clearcut should be no more than twice the distance which a deer will move from the forest edge; this appears to be 600 to 800 feet. Clearcuts up to one-quarter mile wide appear to be reasonable."

Table 90. White-tailed deer forage availability[a] after cutting in two areas of mixed conifer swamp in Upper Michigan (from Krefting and Phillips 1970).

Cutting method	Area 1[b]		Area 2[b]	
	1960	1966	1960	1966
Uncut	10.8 (9.6)	10.8 (9.6)	15.8 (14.1)	12.8 (11.4)
Selection	24.4 (21.8)	29.9 (26.7) [w]	32.7 (29.2) [z]	36.7 (32.7) [w]
Shelterwood	97.7 (87.2) [w]	32.4 (28.9) [w]	41.8 (37.3) [w,x]	47.5 (42.4)
Diameter-limit	81.5 (72.7)	38.4 (34.3)	40.7 (36.3) [x,y]	29.3 (26.1)
Block	71.1 (63.4)	44.9 (40.1)	33.3 (29.7) [y,z]	38.1 (34.0) [w]
Strip	92.2 (82.3) [w]	63.6 (56.7)	49.4 (44.1) [w]	51.4 (45.9)

[a]In kilograms of browse per hectare (pounds per acre) oven-dry weight.
[b]Within each column, values with the same bracketed letter(s) are not significantly different at the 0.5-percent level according to the Duncan Multiple Range Test.

Whitetails feed in an open area on a ranch near Tallahassee, Florida. The deer have been conditioned to feeding on corn that has been transported from a nearby silo onto feeding troughs. Once the deer have eaten their fill, they retreat into surrounding woodlands. As many as 100 whitetails have been observed feeding at the troughs at one time. *Photo by Lovett Williams; courtesy of the Florida Game and Fresh Water Fish Commission.*

FOOD PREFERENCE AND UTILIZATION

Basic to any appraisal of whitetail habitat is a knowledge of what foods the deer will consume, usually on a seasonal basis. After this has been determined, the biologist or manager can use the abundance or scarcity of these food plants as indices of habitat condition, and attempt to rehabilitate the habitat by increasing the more important plants. The degree to which certain plants are used by whitetails depends on the number of deer per unit of area, condition of the habitat, season, growth stage of available plants, age of stand and variety of plants within the area.

For example, when whitetails are forced to concentrate, as in winter yards, the most desired foods quickly become depleted from overuse, often resulting in starvation (Swift 1946, Latham 1950, Day 1964). However, this loss of life by overcrowding and starvation is not confined just to winter yards. In the Everglades of Florida, extended high-water levels force deer onto tree islands where they quickly deplete the life-sustaining plants (Loveless

1959*a*). In some habitats in the South, whitetails feed on twig growth primarily during the early spring period. The twig ends are most palatable and nutritionally beneficial at this time (Blair and Halls 1968, Harlow and Hooper 1972).

A standard technique in wildlife management is to determine the preferred browse plants within an area. As a matter of practicality, these plants then are singled out for intensive study (Shafer 1965). This approach has been particularly useful for categorizing winter deer yards (Maynard et al. 1935, Aldous 1944), although plant lists also have been developed for use in studying southern deer habitats (Moore 1967, Warren and Hurst 1981). These plant lists can be very misleading, however, if based only on field observation of utilization, since fruits, herbs, mushrooms and woody leaves can be consumed entirely, leaving no evidence of use (Harlow 1979).

The most common techniques used in studying the food preferences of white-tailed deer include rumen analysis, fecal analysis, lead deer studies and field observations of plants utilized. Each has advantages and disadvantages.

A vast expanse of sawgrass dotted by tree islands on Florida's Everglades Wildlife Management Area, which supports a large number of white-tailed deer. During periodic high-water levels, the deer are forced to remain on the islands until the food supply is exhausted (*see* Chapter 42). Side effects from the lack of nutritious forage at these times result in large deer die-offs. *Photo by Richard F. Harlow; courtesy of the Florida Game and Fresh Water Fish Commission.*

Grass is an important whitetail diet component in summer throughout the species' range. *Photo by Lynn L. Rogers.*

Rumen Analysis

Use of rumen contents to investigate the foods consumed by white-tailed deer was first reported in the Southeast by Ruff (1938). To identify and measure the foods taken, Ruff collected stomachs from whitetails on the Pisgah National Forest in North Carolina, and calculated the frequency of occurrence and percentage composition by volume of forages found in the stomachs. Harlow and Hooper (1972) obtained a good estimate both of frequency and composition of foods eaten by deer by sifting a composite sample collected from deer stomachs. A 9.51-millimeter (0.37-inch) sieve separated the largest food items immediately. A 5.66-millimeter (0.22-inch) sieve enabled recovery of any given food item that had reached its maximum frequency of occurrence.

Rumen analysis has several advantages. It will reveal deer consumption of forbs and the deciduous leaves of woody plants. Because whitetails consume such items entirely, utilization cannot always be detected by field inspection. Food preferences of deer can be investigated over an entire region or within a specific location in a relatively short time. For example, Puglisi et al. (1978) found that a five-man crew could process 80 to 100 one-quart rumen samples in eight hours. An obvious disadvantage is that animals have to be sacrificed in order for researchers to obtain an adequate sample. Also, differences in the digestibility of

Food matter is identified from the rumen contents of whitetails harvested in November from the Farmton Wildlife Management Area in Central Florida. Such analyses of food variety, percentage and volume weight are crucial to understanding the nutritional needs of whitetails in a given area and to planning habitat management accordingly. *Photo by Jim Reed; courtesy of the Florida Game and Fresh Water Fish Commission.*

plants make quantification of food items difficult and sometimes unreliable (Norris 1943).

Gray et al. (1980) described and compared three methods commonly used to analyze rumen contents—the point frame technique, the gross volumetric technique and the microhistologic technique.

The point frame method of analysis was much faster than gross volumetric and microhistological methods but sampled only 80 percent of the plant species or species groups identified by gross volumetric analysis. There was relatively close agreement between gross and microhistological techniques with the exception that fruits and fungi were estimated incorrectly or undetected microscopically, but were readily identified in gross analysis. Grasses and other herbaceous material, which were not detected or not identifiable with species by gross analysis, were identified more readily microscopically. Analyses of deer rumen contents were

found to be more complete if both gross and microhistological techniques were utilized.

Fecal Analysis

In the United States, Dusi (1949) was the first to study the food habits of herbivorous mammals by histological analysis of feces. Currently, however, the most widely used techniques for preparing reference slides and fecal samples are those of Baumgartner and Martin (1939). Sparks and Malechek (1968) used the Baumgartner/Martin method for preparing samples, and then developed the method commonly used today for estimating weight percentage of a plant in the diet from plant fragment density in feces.

When using the fecal analysis technique, Ward (1970) emphasized that only fresh droppings should be used, and that samples should be placed in plastic bags to prevent drying and then stored by refrigeration, or in any preservative. Also, a good plant reference collection is essential.

The principal advantages of fecal analysis over rumen analysis are that (1) animals do not have to be sacrificed, (2) adequate samples are relatively easy to obtain, and (3) a more extensive listing of plants can be obtained in the same amount of time it takes to analyze rumen samples (Anthony and Smith 1974, Mengak 1982). Disadvantages include the amount of time involved in the preparation of reference material, cost of equipment and difficulty of interpreting data quantitatively. This method has not been widely used on white-tailed deer probably because it requires a more sophisticated analysis than for rumen contents. However, it was used to determine the food habits of Key deer in Florida (Dickson 1955) and on whitetails in Mississippi (Mitchell 1980) and in the Coastal Plain of South Carolina (Mengak 1982).

Lead Deer Studies

Wallmo and Neff (1970) credited McMahan (1964) as first in the United States to observe specially trained wild ruminants to determine the kinds and amounts of forage taken on rangelands. Watts (1964) used specially raised whitetails to determine forage consumption in relation to seasonal availability of plant foods in hardwood forests in Pennsylvania. Healy (1967) also used tame whitetails to continue this work in other areas of Pennsylvania. Whelan et al. (1971) used three tame deer to determine food selectivity during early spring in western Virginia. They allowed the deer to feed for approximately one hour per day for the first week in order to familiarize them with the area. Then, during a 10-day data-gathering period, observers noted the number of times the deer selected a particular plant species and its parts.

Lead deer are domestically reared semitame animals. While being observed, the deer is kept under control by the scientist using a harness and a leash of about 6 meters (20 feet) in length (Healy 1967). Information is collected on the plant species and plant parts taken and the time it takes the deer to chew and swallow the item.

Lead deer studies enable researchers to collect data on feeding habits at close range during any time of the year. Also, rough quantification of foods taken can be made, since differential digestibility of foods will not be a factor

as in rumen analysis. Disadvantages include the time and expense involved in raising deer and trying to keep them tame. Furthermore, controlling deer in the field is difficult. Finally, the sample size with this method is comparatively small, and the researcher cannot be entirely certain that the diet of the tamed deer would be that of a free-roaming whitetail under similar time and space conditions and minus an observer.

"Lead deer studies of white-tailed deer enable researchers to collect data on the feeding habits and food preferences of these nervous herbivores at close range and year-round. There are drawbacks, however. *Photo courtesy of the Texas Parks and Wildlife Department.*"

Free-roaming whitetails sometimes can be tamed sufficiently to be observed closely without the use of a harness. This animal is nibbling on lichens under a fallen balsam. Information recorded by the observer will include the number of bites on each plant species, abundance of the species present in each habitat, and the size (weight) of the average bite taken of each plant species consumed. *Photo by Lynn L. Rogers.*

Field Observations of Plants

Possibly, the first studies of deer feeding habits were accomplished through observation of browsed plants. It probably is safe to say that deer utilize most the plants they like best, and in field observations, wildlife researchers are inclined to consider those plants utilized most as the ones most preferred. However, such observations may be misleading because of the effect of seasonal influence on plant abundance and palatability, and on the stage of succession of the habitat regarding availability of certain plants (Harlow 1979). For example, some of the less preferred plants may receive heavy utilization on overstocked range (Latham 1950, Goodrum and Reid 1962, Gill 1957b, Jenkins and Bartlett 1959). In other cases, preferred plants may have grown out of reach of deer or have been eliminated (Swift 1946).

Several investigators have used subjective methods to classify the extent of browse utilization by deer. Cole (1959) used three categories: (1) no browsing to light browsing (unaltered to slightly altered plants); (2) moderate (second-year growth somewhat lengthened and only moderately altered); and (3) severe (second-year growth relatively short and drastically altered from normal growth). Aldous (1944) used "H" to designate heavy browsing (50–100 percent of a plant showing evidence of utilization), "M" for moderate (10–50 percent of

plant utilized) and "L" for light (trace–10 percent of a plant utilized).

Subjective measurement data of whitetail utilization and food preference can be gathered rather quickly, so large areas often can be sampled in a relatively short time. One subjective habitat evaluation technique based on available forage, described by Williamson et al. (1978), provided a useful index to forage abundance and required about 20 percent of the time required for analogous vegetative sampling techniques. A big drawback is the potential degree of human error. Even experienced field workers find their estimates often vary widely.

Twig count and twig length are two direct methods of measuring whitetail utilization and preference in the field. In the twig-count method, browsed and unbrowsed twigs on each sampled plant are counted and their ratio expressed as a percentage (Bramble and Goddard 1953, Stiteler and Shaw 1966, Moore and Johnson 1967). The investigators used variable-sized plots (1–2 milacres to 0.0025 acre), some of which were shaped as transects, often permanently installed and systematically established to represent the important habitats. The twig-length method determines the average normal length of twigs and the average length after browsing. Deer use is expressed as a percentage of normal twig length. These lengths may be measured or estimated. Hormay (1943) used the twig-length method to estimate the amount of current twig growth grazed on bitterbrush. He established plots 50.8 centimeters (20 inches) wide and 40 or 60 meters (131–197 feet) long, which included 20 to 25 average-sized plants per plot. Hubbard and Dunaway (1958) found that a random sample of 19 to 39 leaders from each of five bitterbrush plants were required for estimating the true mean length within 10 percent of the actual value. Cole (1959) expressed plant leader use estimates as an average based on the percentage of total available leaders showing use. He recommended sampling about 25 browse plants within each sampling unit.

Exclosures have been used in many areas to study the effects of browsing on plants and to determine plant preference by white-tailed deer. In Pennsylvania, Grisez (1959) used a deer exclosure to demonstrate the effect of deer browsing on planted red pines and native woody plants. Shafer et al. (1961) used deer exclosures to demonstrate how deer browsing affects natural tree seedling and sprout reproduction in northeastern Pennsylvania. In the Southern Appalachian Mountains, Harlow and Downing (1970) used exclosures to determine the effect of deer browsing on the height growth of important timber species (Table 91).

For management purposes, it is important to know the extent to which preferred plants can sustain browsing. For example, Brown (1954) cited as an example the permissible use of antelope bitterbrush in California, which had been worked out to 60 percent of current twig growth. The remaining 40 percent must be left on the plant to maintain its vigor and ensure seed production. Krefting et al. (1966) found that mountain maple survived even though 100 percent of each year's current annual growth was clipped for nine consecutive years. Harlow and Halls (1972) found that dogwood seedlings in Texas were affected drastically when clipping intensities during summer reached 90 to 100 percent of annual growth. The investigators noticed that mortality of yellow poplar in North Carolina may be 40 percent or more if terminal twigs are removed, but losses were insignificant when only lateral twigs were

A deer exclosure on the Citrus Wildlife Management Area in central Florida. Note the abundance of ground cover and shrubs inside the exclosure, in contrast to the area outside. The scarcity outside was the result of heavy whitetail foraging—indication of a dense deer population. *Photo by Richard F. Harlow; courtesy of the Florida Game and Fresh Water Fish Commission.*

Table 91. White-tailed deer browsing influence on tree[a] seedling and sprout numbers and height in the Southern Appalachian Mountains (from Harlow and Downing 1970).

	Seedlings				Sprouts			
	Fenced plots		Unfenced plots		Fenced plots		Unfenced plots	
Year	Total number per 0.4 hectare (1 acre)	Percentage over 1.4 meters (4.5 feet) tall	Total number per 0.4 hectare (1 acre)	Percentage over 1.4 meters (4.5 feet) tall	Total number per 0.4 hectare (1 acre)	Percentage over 1.4 meters (4.5 feet) tall	Total number per 0.4 hectare (1 acre)	Percentage over 1.4 meters (4.5 feet) tall
1961	1,117	5.2	800	2.6	913	1.0	542	9.2
1963	3,875	3.2	3,771	3.3	1,154	20.2	963	18.2
1965	4,146	17.3	2,842	4.3	842	23.7	375	27.7
1967	2,734	51.3	2,375	12.9	621	61.1	350	46.4

[a]Includes all tree species of the region except black locust and American chestnut, which were being eliminated by disease.

browsed. In southeast Texas, Lay (1965a) found that species growing under a full stand of pine were highly variable in their resistance to clipping. He noted that the most tenacious species, when clipped, were greenbriers and large gallberry. Intermediate in survival and productivity were American beautyberry, yaupon, sweetbay and sassafras. The weakest plants were dogwood, supplejack, viburnum, water oak and farkleberry. Information on the tolerance of plants to utilization by deer is so limited as to be almost negligible when one considers the tremendous variety of plant species on which whitetails feed over their entire range.

QUANTITY OF FOOD

The method for measuring the quantity of food available in a habitat will depend on the objectives and scope of the survey, the season of the year and geographical location. In general, there are two approaches—one based on actual biomass and one on subjective estimate of the relative amount of key browse plants present from year to year.

Weight Survey Methods

Moore et al. (1960) used the U.S. Forest Service's Continuous Forest Inventory (CFI) to measure browse frequency and compute ratios for converting total length of new growth to weight. The forest inventory is a two-step method that includes land-use classification of points on aerial photographs followed by ground sampling of plots. The county is the basic work unit. Ground sample plots are at intervals, determined by the proportional acreage with each land-use class and by established limits of error. The method was used by the Georgia Forest Survey to index the amount and quality of browse in three important forest types—slash-pine, pine/hardwood and water oak/gum.

Shafer (1963) compared the usefulness of the twig-count, weight-estimation and clip-and-weigh methods employed in determining the weight of woody browse consumed by deer (Table 92). The twig-count method, which converts a count of twigs to weight of browse by use of an average weight per twig, was almost as fast as the weight-estimation method and just as accurate as the clip-and-weigh method. Shafer concluded that the twig-count method was desirable for extensive browse inventories

because it did not destroy the vegetation being surveyed, and its data could be analyzed statistically.

The clip-and-weigh method was used by Harlow (1959) in Florida, Blair (1960) in Louisiana, and Harlow and Downing (1969) in the Southern Appalachian Mountains (Table 93). The method consists of clipping and weighing all current annual growth of herbaceous and woody forage to a height of 1.52 meters (5 feet) in a plot 1 meter square (10.8 square feet). Blair (1960) considered the method costly, laborious and destructive of vegetation. Blair indicated that an impractical number of clipping plots would be necessary to achieve statistical reliability. On the other hand, Harlow (1977) considered the extra time worthwhile, because the method provided accurate and objective data on available forage if a sufficient number of plots were taken. This number can be calculated by determining total green weight and applying Snedecor's (1946) formula:

$$N = \frac{s^2 \pm t^2}{d^2}$$

where

N = number of plots required;
s^2 = variance of the initial 20 plots;
t = normal deviate—a value obtained from standard tables of "t" distribution when confidence level and degrees of freedom (df) are known (let df = number of plots in initial

Table 92. Number of plots and time required for different sampling methods to determine, at 95-percent probability level, the weight of woody browse consumed by white-tailed deer (from Shafer 1963).

Sampling method	Percentage of accuracy	Number of 9.3-square meter (100-square foot) circular plots	Total plot time (in hours)[a]
Weight-estimation			
	5	648	34
	10	162	8
	20	41	2
Twig-count			
	5	636	49
	10	159	12
	20	39	3
Clip-and-weigh			
	5	596	216
	10	149	54
	20	37	13

[a]Does not include plot establishment time or time between plots.

Table 93. White-tailed deer forage availability[a] during February inside and outside of clearcuttings after treatment on the Southern Appalachian Mountains in 1966, as determined by the clip-and-weigh sampling method (from Harlow and Downing 1969).

Forage plant or part	Outside clearcut	One 0.4-hectare (1.0-acre) clearcut	Four clearcuts (8.5–22.3 hectares: 21–55 acres)	Period of greatest use
Twig ends	4.5 (4)	60.5 (54)	169.2 (151)[b]	Spring
Evergreen foliage	39.2 (35)	88.5 (79)	179.3 (160)[b]	Winter
Forbs and grasses	6.7 (6)	28.0 (25)	39.2 (35)[c]	When available
Lichens, moss and mushrooms	12.3 (11)	6.7 (6)	20.2 (18)[d]	When available
Total	62.8 ± 6.7 (56 ± 6)	183.8 ± 87.2 (164 ± 78)	408.0 ± 59.4 (364 ± 53)	

[a]In kilograms per hectare (pounds per acre).
[b]Significantly different than for outside clearcuttings at the .01 level.
[c]Significantly different than for outside clearcuttings at the .05 level.
[d]Nonsignificant.

sample [20] minus 1); and

d = desired margin of error or the half-width of the desired confidence interval.

There are a number of ways that a value for d can be derived. Frequently, the investigator calculates this value by multiplying the arithmetic mean of the preliminary subsample by the desired accuracy. Harlow (1977) found that setting d equal to 20 percent of the sample mean from the 20 preliminary plots usually narrows the resulting confidence limits of the mean to an acceptable level.

Modifications of the clip-and-weigh method include the less precise weight-estimate technique developed by Pechanec and Pickford (1937), the ranked-set sampling method of Halls and Dell (1966), and the double-sampling technique introduced by Wilm et al. (1944) and modified for use in Florida by Hilmon (1959).

Halls and Dell (1966) found that ranked-set sampling was considerably more efficient than random sampling for estimating weights of browse and herbage in a pine/hardwood forest of eastern Texas. In this method, the investigator establishes sets of three closely grouped quadrats and ocularly ranks the quadrats within sets as highest, intermediate or lowest in biomass. Forage then is clipped and weighed from one quadrat of each set.

Hilmon (1959) considered double-sampling to be a compromise between clipping-and-weighing and estimating. With the double-sampling method, biomass is estimated on a larger number of plots, and forage is clipped and weighed on a small number of others. The ratio between actual and estimated forage weights is calculated and then used to correct the estimates obtained from the large sample (Table 94).

Table 94. Actual yield, standard errors, coefficients of variation and optimum ratio of clipped plots to total plots for species and groups double-sampled (from Hilmon 1959).

Species or group	Number of double-samples	Yield per plot[a]	Standard error[a]	Percentage coefficient of variation	Optimum clipped plot/ total plot ratio
Total herbage	80	196.3 (6.92)	5.3 (0.19)	2.7	1:11
Pineland threeawn	78	117.6 (4.15)	8.2 (0.29)	6.9	1:28
Delicate panicum	34	5.5 (0.19)	1.1 (0.04)	20.6	1:8
Other panicum	54	5.0 (0.18)	0.6 (0.02)	10.3	1:6
Rosemary	49	5.0 (0.18)	0.6 (0.02)	12.6	1:10
Blue maidencane	61	7.4 (0.26)	0.6 (0.02)	7.8	1:14
Other grasses	57	6.4 (0.23)	1.1 (0.04)	17.9	1:12
Beakrush	54	5.5 (0.19)	0.8 (0.03)	14.8	1:5
Other grasslikes	50	4.5 (0.16)	0.9 (0.03)	19.7	1:12
Forbs	57	3.7 (0.13)	0.8 (0.03)	22.7	1:15
Saw palmetto	32	31.7 (1.12)	4.1 (0.14)	13.0	1:26
Other shrubs	25	8.9 (0.31)	5.8 (0.20)	65.0	1:7

[a]In grams (ounces).

Ehrenreich and Murphy (1962) used a ratio of one clip-and-weigh quadrat to seven weight-estimate quadrats to measure forage production in forests of Missouri. Using this method, which was tied in with the Missouri Forest Survey, Ehrenreich and Murphy were able to inventory extensive areas and obtain information on forage yields as well as the frequency of herbaceous and woody vegetation in forest understory.

While conducting a whitetail browse-production survey in oak stands in central lower Michigan, Gysel and Stearns (1968) used four different kinds of plot sizes to measure plant characteristics. They felt that a single plot layout failed to measure all plant characteristics efficiently. All woody stems greater than 2.54 centimeters (1 inch) diameter at breast height were recorded by species and diameter at breast height on plots 6 by 15 meters (19.7 by 49.2 feet). Leaf and stem cover was recorded along 15-meter (49.2-foot) line transects placed through the center of the plots. Stems from 45.7 centimeters (18 inches) in height to 2.54 centimeters (1 inch) diameter at breast height were tallied in plots 0.31-meter (3.34-feet) square. And within these same plots, annual growth (stems and leaves) of all browse plants 0.46 to 1.8 meters (1.5–5.9 feet) in height were clipped and weighed. The amount of browse from woody plots and forbs below 45.7 centimeters (18 inches) in height was determined by clipping and weighing material from a plot 0.31 by 0.49 meter (1.0 by 1.6 feet) nested in a larger 0.31-square meter (3.34-square foot) plot.

Crawford et al. (1975*b*) used an electronic method to sample the weight of needles and small twigs of Virginia pine. A prediction model, expressing the relationship between weights of vegetation and microwave attenuation, overestimated oven-dry weight by 8.5 percent. With additional testing and calibration, the technique has potential for measuring vegetative production.

Stone and Crawford (1981) determined the relationship of twig and needle dry weight to tree height and diameter of root collar for spruce and fir. They found that the dry weight of twigs and needles was related (P < 0.05) to tree height times stem diameter at the root collar. After the initial regression equations have been established, an investigator needs only to measure tree heights and root collar diameters on additional plots to obtain available browse in-

stead of the more tedious and time-consuming job of clipping or twig counts.

Since fruits are major components of the white-tailed deer diet, information on their yield is essential to an evaluation of habitat. It is difficult to measure whitetail consumption of fruits because (1) they also are eaten by many other species of wildlife, (2) distribution is spotty, (3) yields fluctuate and differ greatly among fruit-producing plants of the same species, and (4) fruiting success is influenced by climate, heredity and stand conditions.

Production of oak mast usually is measured by placing one or more randomly located traps beneath a tree crown. Three popular types of traps and their sizes include: bushel baskets, 0.14 square meter (1.5 square feet) (Minckler and McDermott 1960); 250-liter (55-gallon) open-top barrels, 0.24 square meter (2.58 square feet) (Crawford and Leonard 1965, Segelquist and Green 1968); and hardware cloth on wooden framing with tops of 6.5-square-centimeter (1-square-inch) poultry netting, 1 square meter (10.8 square feet) (Downs and McQuillen 1944). Use of disposable oak seed traps, which are inexpensive and efficient, was described by Klawitter and Stubbs (1961) and Thompson and McGinnes (1963). Thompson (1962) demonstrated the necessity for using a large number of small traps to obtain statistical reliability. Using 18 traps, each 0.39 square meter (4.2 square feet) in size, he found that 53 to 1,228 traps were needed to obtain the required sampling intensity.

Some woody species, such as the scrub oaks, myrtle oak, sand live oak, Chapman oak and saw palmetto, have canopies low enough so that attached fruit can be counted accurately and conveniently, and the counts converted to weight. Under these conditions, traps are unnecessary.

Because of their ephemeral nature and wide dispersion, fleshy fungi are difficult to measure. Surveys can be facilitated by an examiner knowing when the fungi grow, their growth pattern, how long they remain available and their patterns of distribution. Survey plots should be at least 40.5 square meters (436 square feet) in size.

In evaluating the food resource of a whitetail habitat, the biologist or manager may modify or combine different methods of measurement. The choice of methods will depend on the type of information desired, the kind of habitat, personal preference, time, cost, desired precision

When weather and snow conditions permit, and where there is not a food shortage, whitetails will meander freely—as opposed to confining travel to well-worn trails—and taste a variety of foods. This healthy doe samples lichens from a tree stem in a stand of oak, birch and aspen. *Photo courtesy of the Michigan Department of Natural Resources.*

A hardwood shrub clipped by whitetails whose movements in a winter deer yard are constrained by snowfall accumulations. Such intense browsing may help to see deer through the winter, but loss of palatable shrubs or even those of secondary nutritional value may decrease the animals' survivability in subsequent winters of prolonged and deep snow. *Photo by Bill Cross; courtesy of the Maine Department of Inland Fisheries and Wildlife.*

and the main objective of the survey. If the objective is to determine carrying capacity, it will be necessary to employ an intensive sampling system to quantify the food resource on a weight basis. Such surveys are time consuming, but the results are more accurate than subjective methods and, consequently, more applicable for research studies. If the purpose is mainly to obtain information on how one habitat relates to another, then survey methods may include counts or subjective techniques that compare forage amounts by percentage estimates.

Subjective Survey Methods

Aldous's (1944) method of surveying deer browse originally was designed to estimate the percentage of browse occurrence and degree of browse utilization in winter deer yards. Aldous located 40.5-square meter (430.6-square foot) circular plots at predetermined intervals throughout the yard and, in these plots, estimated the occurrence and density of browse and its degree of deer use. Only plant species within reach of deer were included. Range of values for browsing on plants was considered heavy when 50 to 100 percent of the twigs on a plant were used. It was considered medium when 10 to 50 percent were used, and light when trace to 10 percent were used. For transposing these values, midpoint figures between the two extremes in each class were tallied by plots, and the average browsing percentage was obtained by dividing these midpoint figures by the number of plots in which the species occurred. Lay (1957c) used this method in eastern Texas, and considered it rapid and simple to use with little training. The method gives the relative percentages of foods available to deer, and enables biologists and managers to classify habitat types as good, fair or poor.

In the pine lands of southern Georgia, Buckner and Perkins (1975) used a systematic plot survey and a flexible field-scoring system to determine the quality of deer habitat. The sampler makes an ocular estimate of the abundance or scarcity of important deer foods, and each forest stand is classified as good, fair or poor deer habitat. The plot score for very poor habitat was 1, poor 2, fairly poor 3, fairly good 4, good 5 and excellent habitat 6. After all plot scores are recorded, the average habitat value can be calculated. To collect accurate information, the evaluator must be familiar with the habitat requirements of deer in the study area.

In the snowbelt region of the whitetail range in North America, deer confined too long in winter yards can eliminate available food supplies. They sometimes are forced to stand on their hind legs to reach life-sustaining evergreen leaves. Those unable to reach high enough invariably fall victim to malnutrition. *Photo courtesy of the Michigan Department of Natural Resources.*

Buckner and Perkins developed this method for use on International Paper Company lands in portions of Georgia, Florida and Alabama.

Patton and Hall (1966) evaluated wildlife habitat in New Mexico by browse age and form class. They considered the trend in condition to be upward when young plants were greater in number than decadent ones. Numerical values were assigned to express excellent (30), good (25), fair (20), poor (15) or very poor (10) range conditions.

Gates et al. (1956) used the line-point method and Canfield (1941) used the line-intercept method to evaluate present conditions and future trends of vegetation. In the line-point method, the dominant class of vegetation that occurs either directly under or over a 30.48-meter (100-foot) tape stretched between stakes is recorded at 0.3-meter (1-foot) intervals. The one-dimensional line-intercept method measures the linear intercept spread of ground cover along a stretched tape 15 or 30 meters (49.2 or 98.4 feet) in length. When vegetation covers 5 to 15 percent of the ground, a 15-meter (49.2-foot) line is recommended, and when ground cover vegetation is less than 5 percent, a 30-meter (98.4-foot) line is suggested (Canfield 1941). A record is made to the nearest centimeter (0.4 inch) of the spread of bare soil, rocks, litter, dead shrubs and living plants by species along the transect. The desired information can be expressed as percentage of cover. Although transects are used to relate changes in vegetation along a line or strip, they also may be treated as a sampling unit (Gregory 1957), in which case measurements are pooled and the transect is treated as a single observation or sample. Vegetation trends can be recorded over time by treating these transects as permanent plots, and periodically and seasonally remeasuring the vegetation.

Overstory

Overstory strongly influences the quantity and quality of food available to white-tailed deer. Usually, the greater the number and basal area of overstory stems, the less there is of the understory biomass. Because of its effect on ground cover (both herbaceous and woody plants less than 0.3 meter [1 foot] high) and also on midstory vegetation, canopy is as important to measure as understory levels or layers.

Many sampling techniques are available for measuring overstory cover (Oosting 1948, Greig-Smith 1964, Daubenmire 1968, Guilkey 1959). I have field tested and consider adequate the variable radius point-sampling technique (*see* Grosenbaugh 1952) in combination with a fixed plot at the same sampling point. I used a wedge prism with a basal area factor of 1 because it picked up a much larger number of stems at and over 13 centimeters (5.1 inches) diameter at breast height than did prisms with a higher basal area factor. A fixed plot of 0.02 hectare (0.05 acre:2,178 square feet) was located at each plot center to record 3–11-centimeter (1.2–4.3-inch) diameter breast-height class. The parameters measured included number of stems, basal area of trees per unit of land area, and stand age.

QUALITY OF FOOD

According to Dietz (1970), high quality deer forage possesses the following characteristics: high palatability; optimum levels of various nutrients in proper ratios; high digestibility of the nutrient components; volatile fatty acids in optimum proportions for efficient energy production; and efficient convertability into components necessary for the animal body over sustained periods.

The most important tests of forage quality include:
1. Proximate analysis. This is a measure of the chemical components in the vegetation, usually expressed as a percentage of dry matter. These components consist of crude protein (percentage nitrogen $\times$ 6.25), crude fat, crude fiber (an estimate of the less digestible portions of forage), nitrogen-free extract (an estimate of sugars, starch, cellulose, lignin and related substances in the diet) and ash (mineral components).
2. *In vitro* dry matter digestibility. This is an index of the percentage digestibility of the forage, and represents an estimate of the *in vivo* digestibility of the dry matter.
3. Phosphorus. This test separates phosphorus from ash.
4. Percentage of digestible energy. The gross energy figure is multiplied by the percentage of *in vitro* dry matter digestibility, and the value obtained from this is a close approximation of the digestible energy of the forage.

5. Percentage of soluble carbohydrate. This test estimates the quantity of the readily available energy component of the forage.

Table 95 shows results of nutritional analyses of some important winter foods of white-tailed deer, from various regions in the United States.

Wallmo et al. (1977) developed a model to show how information about the supply of available forage and deer protein and energy requirements could be used to estimate carrying capacity of seasonal ranges. Variables in the model were deer body weight (W), metabolic weight ($W^{0.75}$), activity metabolic rate (AMR), forage intake (INT), gross energy (GE) and dry matter digestibility of forage (DMD). The following provides an example of how the model can be applied to white-tailed deer in some areas of the southeastern United States, comparing summer and winter seasons and by using information from a variety of sources.

Sources of information used to construct daily energy supplies (Table 96) on the Savannah River Plant, Aiken, South Carolina, included:
1. The average weight (in kilograms) of whitetails from the Savannah River Plant—48.5 kilograms—is based on dead weights of 95 bucks and 85 does taken during November and December (Urbston 1976). For purposes of comparison, 4.99 kilograms (11.0 pounds) were added to the average summer weights of the Savannah River Plant deer.
2. Daily intake of white-tailed deer was derived from the results of experiments with penned southern deer fed a balanced ration by Fowler et al. (1968). Average food consumption was calculated in grams of food per kilogram of body weight.
3. The gross energy (summer) value of 4.7 kilocalories per gram was an average compiled from studies on forage collected in central Florida and southwestern Virginia by Crawford et al. (1975*b*) and Harlow et al. (1980). The winter values of 4.6 (without acorns) and 4.5 (with acorns) were taken from studies by Harlow et al. (1975*b*, 1980).
4. The dry matter digestibility values of 0.47 and 0.49 with acorns (summer) and 0.30 without acorns (winter) were derived from *in vitro* digestion tests on forages from southeastern Virginia and central Florida (Harlow et al. 1975*b*, 1980).
5. Metabolize energy (ME) is a constant 85 percent of the digestible energy (DE) (Wallmo et al. 1977).

Table 95. Nutritional analysis[a] on some important winter white-tailed deer foods in different habitats in North America.

Area	Plant species and parts	Percentage					
		Moisture loss	Crude protein	Ether extract	Crude fiber	Ash	Nitrogen-free extract
Florida Everglades	Water lily—entire plant including root stock	85	13.65	1.57	13.66	8.20	62.92
	Royal fern—frond	75	14.18	2.24	26.31	4.02	53.25
	Willow—leaves and twigs	71	15.05	3.08	24.14	6.31	51.42
South Carolina	Japanese honeysuckle—leaves and stems	78	17.50	4.10	14.80	7.00	50.70
	Greenbrier—leaves and stems	83	26.40	5.10	18.10	8.60	35.90
	Oak—fruit	32.3	5.00	9.70	33.50	2.00	46.40
New Hampshire	Eastern hemlock—foliage		7.5	8.7	26.7		54.10
	Hobblebush—twigs		6.9	6.9	30.0		52.30
	Mountain maple—twigs		9.9	3.6	38.5		44.90
Missouri	Sugar maple—twigs		5.7	2.6	31.6	4.2	44.8
	Red maple—twigs		4.6	4.7	31.2	3.1	48.3
	Sassafras—twigs		4.5	3.8	37.1	2.0	46.8
Western Virginia	Rhododendron—twigs	42.1	3.9	4.1	22.6	4.2	65.2
	Buffalo nut—twigs	47.2	9.2	3.6	25.8	5.4	56.1
	Dogwood—twigs	46.0	5.1	4.2	24.5	4.5	61.5
Michigan	Northern white cedar		2.9	3.1	16.7	2.2	21.0
	Jack pine—foliage, needles and twigs		3.8	4.2	15.1	1.2	22.2
	Large-toothed aspen		5.0	3.4	14.8	1.9	26.6

[a]Air-dry and oven-dry weights.
[b]In percentage of fresh weight.
[c]In kilocalories per gram.

Table 96. Forage evaluation model of daily energy supplies for white-tailed deer on the Savannah River Plant, Aiken, South Carolina (based on method by Wallmo et al. 1977).

Season	Body weight (kilograms)		Forage intake (grams per kilogram)		Gross energy (kilocalories per gram)		Dry matter digestibility		Metabolize energy (ratio)		Daily energy supply (kilocalories)
Summer	53.5	×	30	×	4.7	×	0.47	×	0.85	=	3,014
Winter											
Without acorns	48.5	×	28	×	4.6	×	0.30	×	0.85	=	1,593
With acorns	48.5	×	28	×	4.4	×	0.49	×	0.85	=	2,489

Table 97, on daily energy needs, was constructed from the following sources:
1. The activity metabolic rate factors of 1.98 (summer) and 1.23 (winter) were taken from Moen (1973), who estimated the activity metabolic rate of deer to range between these two figures times the basal metabolic rate (BMR)—AMR = (Factor)(BMR).
2. Basal metabolic rate is estimated at 70 kilocalories per kilogram per day times metabolic weight (Short 1975)—BMR = 70 kilocalories per day)$(W^{0.75})$.
3. Metabolic weight—$(W^{0.75})$—is from Wallmo et al. (1977).

Table 95. (continued)

Percentage				
Calcium	Phosphorus	Dry matter[b]	Gross energy[c]	Source
1.21	0.15			Loveless (1959*b*)
0.28	0.19			
1.23	0.30			
0.37	0.38			Thorsland (1967)
0.70	0.53			
0.04	0.08			
		44.6	5.13	Mautz et al. (1976)
		45.3	4.74	
		49.4	4.75	
1.31	0.13			Torgerson and Pfander (1971)
0.58	0.05			
0.47	0.08			
				Hundley (1959)
		45.9	2.36	Ullrey et al. (1964, 1967*b*)
		46.5	2.49	
		51.7	2.59	

Assuming that the extrapolated figures in Table 96 are realistic, then whitetails on the Savannah River Plant received sufficient energy to meet their daily needs during both the summer and winter periods. Since information used in the standard error calculations did not originate on the Savannah River Plant, these calculations only serve to illustrate the mechanics of the method.

After forage quality information has been obtained it then can be used in conjunction with forage quantity to ascertain carrying capacity of the habitat. Parameters to use in estimating carrying capacity include (1) supplies of forage, (2) intake limitations of deer, (3) requirements of deer for the primary nutrients—protein and digestible energy, and (4) availability of nutrients in forage. Using these parameters, a carrying capacity can be calculated based on forage quantity in terms of:

$$\text{carrying capacity} = \frac{A}{(B)(C)}$$

where

A = usable forage (one-half of total forage, expressed as kilograms per hectare),

B = daily deer intake, and

C = season (days of use).

These steps are used in Table 98 to compare winter carrying capacity estimates for deer habitat on the Savannah River Plant by Moore and Johnson (1967) and Wiggers et al. (1979).

Whelan et al. (1976) also developed a model for estimating seasonal forage supplies of a forest type and the energy conversion of food that is needed to meet seasonal energy needs of white-tailed deer. Data for this bioenergetics model (tables 99, 100 and 101) were based on nutrient determinations conducted in the ridge and valley forest types in southwestern Virginia and came from studies that determined dry matter production and digestible energy on composite diets of "key" deer food plants collected during four seasons in a mixed oak/pine forest type. The selection of food plants and their dietary importance were based on rumen analyses by Harlow et al. (1975*a*) and Harlow and Hooper (1972). Samples collected for nutritional analysis included at least 200 grams (7 ounces) fresh weight of each important forage species. They came from several areas within a forest stand and represented the actual portion of the plant that was consumed by deer. After collection, the plants or plant parts were dried to determine percentage of moisture, and then ground to pass through a 40-mesh screen and stored in airtight jars.

Table 97. Forage evaluation model of daily energy need of white-tailed deer on the Savannah River Plant, Aiken, South Carolina (based on method by Wallmo et al. 1977).

Season	Activity metabolic rate (factor)		Basal metabolic rate (kilocalories per kilogram)		Metabolic weight (kilograms)		Daily energy need (kilocalories)
Summer	1.98	×	70	×	19.8	=	2,744
Winter	1.23	×	70	×	18.4	=	1,584

Table 98. Estimation of winter range carrying capacity for white-tailed deer on the Savannah River Plant, Aiken, South Carolina, based on quantity and quality of available forage (based on method by Wallmo et al. 1977).

	Winter period	
Measurement	Moore (1967)	Wiggers (1979)
Based on forage quantity		
A. Usable forage (kilograms)	757,656[a]	1,457,579[b]
B. Daily deer intake (kilograms)	1.36	1.36
C. Season (days of use)	100	100
Carrying capacity $= \dfrac{A}{(B)(C)}$	5,571	10,717
Based on forage quality		
D. Ratio of protein intake to need	0.5[c]	0.5[c]
E. Ratio of energy intake to need	1	1
Carrying capacity	5,571	10,717

[a]Fifty percent of total browse in Table 96.
[b]Sixty-five percent of total browse in Table 97.
[c]Based on late-winter range of mule deer in Colorado (Wallmo et al. 1977).

Table 99. Seasonal dry matter production and digestible energy available in composite diets containing key forage plants from the mixed oak/pine cover type in the ridge and valley forest types of southwestern Virginia, 1973–1974 (Whelan et al. 1976).

Season	Date	Number of key species in composite diet[a]	*In vitro* dry matter digestibility (percentage)	Gross energy (kilocalories per kilogram)	Mean dry matter production (kilograms per hectare)[b]	Mean digestible energy (kilocalories per hectare per day)[c]
Spring flush[d]	4/1 – 4/30	7	26.0	4759	14.0 ± 5.1	577
Spring[d]	5/1 – 5/31	8	45.1	4693	21.6 ± 6.1	1474
Summer	6/1 – 9/15	6	44.0	4584	23.6 ± 6.5	444
Autumn[e]	9/16 – 11/30	6	31.3	4764	20.4 ± 4.8	400
Winter	12/1 – 3/31	8	44.4	4424	14.5 ± 5.2	235

[a]Species which comprised 75 percent by volume of rumen contents; composite diets were prepared by combining on a dry-weight basis each species represented in the seasonal diet.
[b]Eighty-percent confidence interval.
[c]Kilocalories per hectare per day = *in vitro* dry matter digestibility × gross energy × dry matter production ÷ length of season (days).
[d]Digestible-energy production for the two spring periods was calculated for each of the plant species that represented a "key" food plant and the mean value used, in lieu of a composite diet value.
[e]Acorns excluded from composite diet.

Table 100. Seasonal energy requirements for white-tailed deer population in the ridge and valley forest types of southwestern Virginia, 1973–1974 (Whelan et al. 1976).

Season and dates	Utilization of food energy	Energy requirement in kilocalories per day by age and sex class[a]						
		3 months to 1 year		1 year to 2 years		Over 2 years		
		Male (3)	Female (2)	Male (8)	Female (8)	Male (7)	Female (7)	Total
Spring flush	Basal metabolism	4,374	2,646	10,736	11,264	11,613	11,473	52,106
(4/1–4/30)	Voluntary activity	2,751	1,642	7,456	7,872	8,351	8,232	36,304
	Heat increment							9,549
	Growth	1,402	593		655	1,910	1,234	5,794
	Gestation				488		707	1,195
	Digestible energy[b]							223
Spring	Basal metabolism	4,533	2,754	11,088	11,600	12,040	12,677	54,692
(5/1–5/31)	Voluntary activity	2,868	1,720	10,936	11,760	8,715	8,638	44,637
	Heat increment							3,492
	Growth	920	886	2,560	2,618	1,864		8,848
	Gestation				1,824		2,632	4,456
	Digestible energy[b]							247

Table 100. (continued)

Season and dates	Utilization of food energy	3 months to 1 year		1 year to 2 years		Over 2 years		Total
		Male (3)	Female (2)	Male (8)	Female (8)	Male (7)	Female (7)	
Summer	Basal metabolism	5,166	3,332	12,064	10,888	13,146	11,711	56,307
(6/1–9/15)	Voluntary activity	2,523	1,644	7,968	7,072	9,016	7,875	36,098
	Heat increment							13,452
	Growth	449	237	1,089	1,260	1,727	409	5,171
	Digestible energy[c]							236
	Lactation[d]							
	June				16,167		23,341	39,508
	Digestible energy[e]							84
	July				17,050		24,618	41,668
	Digestible energy[e]							89
	August				10,746		15,518	26,264
	Digestible energy[d]							56
Autumn	Basal metabolism	3,633	2,134	11,768	10,912	13,013	10,892	52,352
(9/16–11/30)	Voluntary activity	2,223	1,284	8,288	7,584	9,548	7,742	36,669
	Heat increment							9,401
	Growth	449	237	1,125	1,318	1,736	387	5,142
	Digestible energy[c]							220
Winter	Basal metabolism	4,131	2,534	10,736	11,088	11,893	11,186	51,568
(12/1–3/31)	Voluntary activity	2,580	1,560	7,456	7,728	8,589	7,987	35,900
	Heat increment							9,480
	Growth	676	505		328		826	2,335
	Digestible energy[c]							211

Energy requirement in kilocalories per day by age and sex class[a]

[a]Estimated population of 35 whitetails on 573 hectares (1,416 acres): 15 percent less than one year of age; 46 percent one to two years of age; and 39 percent over two years old.

[b]Digestible energy (in kilocalories per hectare per day) = basal metabolism + voluntary activity + heat increment + growth + gestation ÷ 0.82 ÷ 573 hectares.

[c]Digestible energy (in kilocalories per hectare per day) = basal metabolism + voluntary activity + heat increment + growth ÷ 0.82 ÷ 573 hectares.

[d]Energy requirement (basal metabolism + voluntary activity + heat increment + growth) for fawns from June 1 to August 31 was met by consuming milk and forage; digestible energy derived from forage alone was 12, 17 and 33 kilocalories per hectare per day for June, July and August, respectively.

[e]Digestible energy (in kilocalories per hectare per day) = basal metabolism + voluntary activity + heat increment + growth + lactation ÷ 0.82 ÷ 573 hectares.

Table 101. Mean digestible energy in key forage species, digestible energy required by season for white-tailed deer population on the mixed oak/pine cover type in the ridge and valley forest types of southwestern Virginia, 1973–1974, and the capability of the oak/pine-forest type to meet daily population energy requirements at 100, 50 and 25 percent utilization of key forages (Whelan et al. 1976).

Season	Mean digestible energy (kilocalories per hectare per day)		Available-required ratio of mean digestible energy at percentages of utilization rates of key forages		
	Available	Required	100 percent	50 percent	25 percent
April	577	223	2.59	1.30	0.65
May	1,474	247	5.97	2.98	1.49
Summer					
June	444	248(332)[b]	1.79(1.34)	0.90(0.67)	0.45(0.34)
July[a]		253(342)[c]	1.75(1.30)	0.88(0.65)	0.44(0.33)
August[a]		269(325)[d]	1.65(1.37)	0.83(0.69)	0.42(0.35)
Autumn[e]	400	220	1.82	0.91	0.46
Winter	235	211	1.11	0.56	0.28

[a]Production data not available; June production data were used.

[b]248 + 84 (332): additional energy required for lactation.

[c]253 + 89 (342): additional energy required for lactation.

[d]269 + 56 (325): additional energy required for lactation.

[e]Acorns excluded.

White-tailed deer habitat succession in a mixed pine/hardwood community following prescribed burning or clearcutting and site preparation in the Southeast. During the first growing season (top left), the area supports an average herbaceous and browse forage yield of 1,120–1,680 kilograms per hectare (1,000–1,500 pounds per acre). With intensive mechanical preparation, herbaceous plants predominate. With no mechanical preparation, browse predominates. Three growing seasons after site modifications, preparation and pine regeneration (top center), forage yields peak at 2,240–3,360 kilograms per hectare (2,000–3,000 pounds per acre). Half or more of the total forage yield consists of browse, of which two-thirds is medium to high preference for whitetails. At 8 to 10 years of regrowth (top right), pine stands are apt to have a closed canopy, with forage yields of 112 kilograms per hectare (100 pounds per acre) or less. Stands approaching commercial pulpwood size (bottom left) provide good cover for whitetails, but very little forage. They remain unproductive until thinned or logged. Sawtimber stands (bottom center) with a tree basal area of 9.3 square meters (100 square feet) produce approximately 224 kilograms per hectare (200 pounds per acre) of forage. With thinning to a tree basal area of about 16.1 square meters per hectare (70 square feet per acre) and prescribed burning, forage yield may increase to 895 kilograms per hectare (800 pounds per acre), of which 20 to 25 percent is medium to high preference browse. When fertilized and seeded with winter grasses and clover (bottom right), small forest openings contribute to the nutritional level of deer. They also are excellent sites to locate hunting stands. *Photos courtesy of the U.S. Forest Service.*

SHELTER

Shelter is a vital component of white-tailed deer habitat. As previously discussed, canopy, midstory and ground cover are determinants of whitetail food resources and, therefore, deer population density in a given area. In addition, certain physiographic features, such as slope and terrain, are as important to deer as are thermal and escape cover. Surveys that measure forage yields also can show which stands of vegetation provide the best shelter and escape cover.

In the North, where shelter is a primary concern, biologists and managers must know how much of a winter yard provides shelter and how much provides food. During winter in northern Maine, whitetails preferred to stay in and near dense stands of fairly mature conifers (Gill 1957b). A study of many whitetail wintering areas in New York by Severinghaus (1953) indicated that deer seek areas where the topography of the land provides protection from cold winds and snow (Severinghaus 1953). These studies indicated that the safe ratio of food to shelter for deer yards changes by re-gion, depending on average annual snow depth and length of winter. Also, the pattern of food and shelter within a yard affects its value to deer. Gill (1957b:29) addressed the question of how much cover is needed, or more specifically, what proportion of a winter yard should consist of closed-canopy softwoods: "No rule of thumb answer can be given, partly because the problem has not received much study; partly because, as usual, 'it all depends.' Certainly, degree of interspersion of cover with food areas is as important as extent of cover area itself. Consequently, long, narrow strips of shelter are more efficient than blocks because strips have greater perimeter or 'edge.' Optimum spacing between strips depends on the distances deer commonly travel from cover to feed. A nearly ideal yard in northeastern Maine has alternate strips of dense cover and open brushy growth each about 100 feet wide. Further south, where deer travel longer distances to feed, cover strips spaced further apart would be preferable."

An evaluation of yarding areas requires a measurement of the amount and kind of shelter, as well as the quantity of available browse.

Dense conifer canopies benefit wintering whitetails in snowbelt regions by restricting wind penetration and limiting snowfall accumulations that otherwise would hinder deer movements to forage resources or at least cause their increased energy expenditure. *Photo by Tom Carbone; courtesy of the Maine Department of Inland Fisheries and Wildlife.*

In Maine, C. F. Banasiak (personal communication:1977) evaluated winter shelter by ocular estimation of the area involved and recording of tree characteristics. Aerial photographs were used to identify shelter boundaries. Banasiak considered the areas to be good shelter when conifers were 10.66 meters (35 feet) or higher and crown coverage averaged 70 percent or more. Banasiak also found that deer concentrated in these shelter areas during the severest part of the winter and fed on the low hardwoods and evergreen shrubs on the periphery.

Ruff (1938) observed that farther south, in the higher altitudes (Southern Appalachian Mountains), where low temperatures, snow and strong winds occur, exposed slopes and wind-swept ridgetops rarely were used by whitetails during the winter months. All coves and lower hillsides that contained a sufficient amount of laurel and rhododendron became points of mild concentration. The intensity of these deer concentrations varied as to location, density of shrubs and winter severity.

In those portions of the Southeast where inclement weather does not reach the harsh extremes found farther north, little information is available regarding the value of shelter. Studies in the southeastern Coastal Plain by Sweeney et al. (1971), using radio-collared whitetails, indicated they seek dense shelter to escape dogs. In some chases by dogs, the deer remained bedded in relatively dense shelter. In 34 of 46 chases, they responded by moving away from the disturbance created by hounds, to areas that offered more protection, such as dense cover or swamp. In another study conducted on the Savannah River Plant, Aiken, South Carolina, Sweeney (1970) observed a radio-monitored whitetail that moved into a very dense honeysuckle-thicketed area during freezing rain and sleet. The animal spent the greater part of a 24-hour period during this severe weather in or close to this shelter.

A measurement of shelter in terms of biomass by itself, in the Southeast, to my knowledge has not been attempted. The need for shelter by deer would be minimal compared to that of whitetails in the snow belt areas of the North. Surveys that equate biomass in terms of food also can provide wildlife biologists and other resource managers with information on areas possessing the greatest number of dense stands of vegetation that would provide shelter for whitetails.

SAMPLING CONSIDERATIONS

Seldom will a researcher have sufficient time and money to measure all vegetation, even in a small area. Instead he will have to measure a stand or vegetation type by sampling within certain prescribed statistical limits.

Stand Selection

Before sampling begins, boundaries of the stand or vegetation type in question must be delineated. The stand should represent closely the habitat type and condition one is attempting to evaluate. Also, vegetative variation within a sampling unit should be reduced as much as possible. Since variation in vegetation increases with sample area size, it is best to stratify the area into definable small units of homogenous character. Replicated sampling will provide data that can be extrapolated to describe areas beyond the sampling unit.

Plot Distribution

Within a sampling unit, plots can be distributed randomly, equally spaced in a grid pattern or distributed along transect lines at specified intervals from a randomly selected starting point. The last method gives greater accuracy from the same number of plots than does random distribution (Hummel 1952), and the plots are located easily. Simple random sampling implies that every spot in a vegetative type will have an equal chance of being selected. However, the random plots may fail to give adequate area coverage and, because many plant species occur in groups, some may be missed in the inventory. Also, considerable time can be spent trying to locate random plots.

Plot Size

Plot size depends on the number, distribution and size of the plants to be measured. For example, large plots are needed to inventory areas with widely spaced trees and other plants with a spotty distribution, such as mushrooms. Grasses, forbs and shrubs that are uniformly distributed can be measured conveniently on 1-square-meter (10.8-square-foot) plots. Circular plots approximately 40.5 square meters (436 square feet) in size are convenient for estimating percentage of plant coverage and for counting hard mast. A portable pole whose

On the Pisgah National Forest in North Carolina, exclosures of this type have been used to evaluate the degree of whitetail browsing of seedlings, sprouts and ground cover in clearcuttings. *Photo by Frank Johnson; courtesy of the U.S. Fish and Wildlife Service.*

length equals the radius of the circular plot simplifies the establishment of plot boundaries. In the case of a 40.5-square-meter (436-square-foot) plot, the radius would be 3.6 meters (11.8 feet). The precision of estimates increases as plots are made smaller and more numerous (Mesavage and Grosenbaugh 1956).

When clipping is involved and small-sized plots are used, square plots are more convenient than circular or rectangular plots. Collapsible frames, with one side that will open, are easy to transport and set up.

For measuring plant variation, elongated plots are superior to square plots of equal area (Daubenmire 1968). However, elongated plots have more margin in proportion to area, and inventories consequently are more subject to error than on square plots. Furthermore, elongated plots usually are more time-consuming to install.

Sample Size

The aim in planning a survey should be to take enough observations to obtain the desired precision (Freese 1967), and the number of observations needed will depend on the precision desired and the inherent variability of the plots' vegetation. It sometimes is advisable to obtain an estimate of this variation in the stand prior to the survey, to ascertain the approximate number of plots needed to obtain reliable information. In my surveys with the clip-and-weigh technique, I first sampled 20 plots in a stand of vegetation and then calculated the number of plots to sample from the formula $N = s^2 + t^2/d^2$ (*see* Weight Survey Methods). I placed the t^2 value at 0.05 and the d^2 value at 0.20. When N equalled 40, I took 20 more plots and computed confidence limits. When the confidence limits varied from the mean by no more than 20 percent, I considered the stand of vegetation sufficiently sampled. And I found this formula to work in all types of white-tailed deer habitat.

Area curves can be used to calculate the optimal number of plots for sampling individual stands. A characteristic curve is obtained when the number of plant species is plotted against the area sampled. The number of plant species tallied will increase sharply with the first increases in area sampled, but will level off soon. New species will increase only slightly with increase in the number of plots taken in the sampled area (Oosting 1948). Figure 113 illustrates the species area-curve concept based on two different-sized quadrats in an oak/hickory forest. Cain (1938) considered the sampling adequate when a 10-percent increase in sample area corresponded to a 10-percent increase in total plants present. Daubenmire (1968:90–91) suggested that, "Because sampling accuracy increased more easily by studying more plots rather than by increasing their size, the simplest way to evaluate sampling adequacy is to average the plot data from time to time as the stand is studied, and ascertain the point beyond which changes in the average become insignificant."

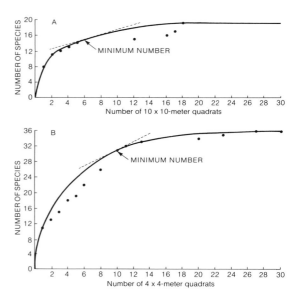

Figure 113. The species-curve concept for an oak/hickory forest in North Carolina, with (A) indicating a minimum of six 100-meter-square (1,076-foot-square) quadrats for sampling the arborescent strata, and (B) indicating a minimum of ten 16-meter-square (172-foot-square) quadrats for sampling the transgressive and shrub strata (from Oosting 1956). Note that the curves first rise abruptly then tend to level off as fewer species are added with increased sampling. The break in the curves represents the point beyond which increased sampling brings proportionately less information.

Chapter 37

HABITAT MANAGEMENT

Hewlette S. Crawford
Principal Research Wildlife Biologist
U.S. Forest Service
Northeastern Forest Experiment Station
Orono, Maine

Habitat is the sum of all environmental conditions of the place occupied by an animal population (Eabry 1970). Principal among the components of white-tailed deer habitat are food, water, shelter and escape cover, and space.

The goal of habitat management is to provide the essential components at the proper time and place. It is a dynamic process that includes the interaction of many factors, such as controlled burning, plantings, establishment and maintenance of openings, silvicultural practices, and land-use planning.

Habitat improvement, with respect to whitetails, implies that a biologist or manager is making habitat in a given area capable of supporting more deer. However, there is a point at which it is impossible or impractical to improve habitat further. Unfortunately, the increase of deer does not necessarily stop when habitat improvement stops. Instead, the whitetail population may continue to increase and, unless controlled, will damage the habitat and substantially reduce its capacity to support the population and degrade the physical characteristics of the animals themselves. Thus, habitat management and whitetail population management represent counterweights on opposite sides of an ecological scale. The biologist or manager must have the knowledge and tools to adjust the weights in accordance with management objectives and the best interest of the habitat and the deer it supports.

PRESCRIBED BURNING

Mineral ions bound in vegetation are released as ash when vegetation is burned. After burning, mineral ions retained in humus and soil are available on-site for subsequent plant growth, or may be transported elsewhere by water runoff. When fire removes overstory, allowing sunlight to reach the ground, vegetation fertilized by available mineral ions grows vigorously for a period of years and provides quality deer food. However, should fires burn so intensely that they destroy the protective humus layer and modify those structural characteristics of the soil that enhance retention of mineral ions, the site may lose its inherent fertility. Sites underlain with coarse, sandy soils and affected in this manner remain in early successional grass, sedge and fern stages and may produce poor quality deer foods. However, knowledgeable prescribed burning under conditions that do not degrade site attributes enhances on-site nutrient cycling and makes more nutrients available to animals. Hough (1981) found that little nitrogen was lost when the understory of slash pine stands was prescribed-burned at four- to six-year intervals, and that nitrogen and other elements may increase with repeated burning. The key is knowing when and how to burn.

Historically, fire played a major role in creating and maintaining white-tailed deer range.

Prescribed burning in logged areas reduces debris and stimulates new plant growth. Proper burning technique must be followed to assure that control of the fire is maintained. Ideally done in spring, the burn should allow regrowth within a few days and site coverage by the end of the growing season. *Photos by Hewlette S. Crawford.*

In precolonial times, extensive forest areas supplied consistent but limited food for deer. Early settlers only cut trees that were needed for their own use, and the shipbuilding trade cut only scattered prime pines. This light cutting produced small openings that grew up quickly and offered temporary food for deer. Banasiak (1964) described the increase in logging that started about 1820 in Maine, the fires following logging, and the resultant eruption in deer numbers. With growth and expansion of the continent's human population, the logging industry moved westward into the Great Lakes region, southern Canada and timberlands of the West. Cutting there generally was followed by major fires and increased whitetail populations. Substantial commercial cutting succeeded in setting back the successional stage.

Fire set it back even further, stimulating growth of desirable deer forage plants and giving whitetails ready access to these plants by reducing logging debris. Repeated intensive fires in some cases locked succession in an early stage that was unfavorable to deer habitat.

In forest and prairie border regions of the Midwest (Crawford 1970) and open pine forest of the South (Harlow and Jones 1965), where natural and Indian-caused fires commonly occurred, precolonial timber stands were more open and whitetails more plentiful than in moist forest types of more northern latitudes. Settlers kept these forests open by burning to provide forage for livestock. Initially, this practice continued to provide suitable habitat for deer. However, livestock overgrazing eventually reduced the fuel and fires became less intense.

Less volatile woody sprouts replaced the flammable herbaceous vegetation, road systems and fire-control efforts suppressed the occurrence of ecologically significant fires, and desirable interspersion of mature trees and open deer habitat was replaced with dense sapling and pole-sized hardwood trees. Intensive logging of mature trees and the demise of the chestnut further reduced the value of the habitat, and deer populations declined under increased hunting pressure.

Since unmanaged fire was an important causative factor affecting deer range, it was a logical assumption that managed fire could be an important tool in habitat management. This assumption was strongly challenged because of past problems associated with wildfire (Dahlberg and Guettinger 1956, Forbes et al. 1971). However, a number of wildlife agencies now use fire as a tool to manage deer habitat.

In the southern United States, prescribed burning in pine and pine/hardwood stands every three to five years is practiced or recommended by the Arkansas (R. G. Leonard personal communication:1976), Louisiana (J. W. Farrar personal communication:1983) and South Carolina (W. G. Moore personal communication:1983) wildlife agencies, and conducted by the U.S. Fish and Wildlife Service on refuges in Georgia (U.S. Department of the Interior 1969) and Mississippi (U.S. Department of the Interior no date). Old fields also are burned in Arkansas; the practice is considered effective in maintaining successional stages desirable for deer.

In the West, wildlife agencies in Idaho (E. G. de Reus personal communication:1976, T. A. Leege personal communication:1983) and Washington (J. R. Patterson personal communication:1976, R. L. Johnson personal communication:1983) have recognized the need for and value of controlled burning for deer range rejuvenation. They also have cooperative burning programs with the U.S. Forest Service (T. E. Burke personal communication:1976), and both agencies have expressed a need for expansion of controlled burning programs. Hickey and Leege (1970) showed the value of fire in rejuvenating growth of redstem ceanothus—a highly desirable deer and elk food plant in the Northwest.

Based on several studies, the Arizona Game and Fish Department (1977) recommended controlled burns as an economical and effective habitat manipulation tool in the Southwest.

Several studies have considered the relationship between prescribed burning and deer habitat response. Results varied widely because of the great number of factors—differences in study techniques, fuel characteristics, plant phenology and physiology, weather, and site characteristics. Dills (1970) reported no significant effects of burning on nutritive values of browse on the Cumberland Plateau in Tennessee. In Texas, Lay (1957*a*) noted that burning increased protein and phosphoric acid content up to 43 and 78 percent, respectively, but the increases lasted only for a year or two. Longer-term benefits to animals on burned range in Wisconsin were found by Vogl and Beck (1970). White-tailed deer tracks were 2.4 times more abundant on burned range than on unburned range eight years after burning. Most workers report that forage quantity is increased, but the amounts and durations of increase differ.

Prescribed fire now is recommended throughout most of the Midwest, where objections to burning once were strong. Rutske (1969) suggested five burning practices for Minnesota:

1. Burn logging slash to improve seedbeds and remove obstacles to deer, grouse and hunters.
2. Burn deteriorating aspen stands that will not be cut and otherwise will convert to balsam fir. This ensures a continuing aspen stand and provides for abundant browse for five years following burning.
3. Burn 4–8-hectare (10–20-acre) patches adjacent to deer yards during the dormant season, to encourage shrub and hardwood tree sprouting (*see* Buckman and Blankenship 1965).
4. Repeat burns in small areas to create and maintain forest openings.
5. Identify areas where accidental fires would not be extinguished.

The U.S. Forest Service and the Missouri Department of Conservation use prescribed burning to maintain habitat diversity on state and national forests. Prescribed burns are used for direct habitat improvement where the site index (height in feet to which codominant trees grow in 50 years) for commercial tree species is less than 45, and to maintain open conditions where the site index is greater than 45. Prescribed burning also is used to control invasion by eastern redcedar and encourage production of herbaceous forage (U.S. Forest Service 1973).

The Ohio Division of Wildlife burns about 600 hectares (1,500 acres) annually on state lands, to promote resprouting of woody growth and hold plant succession at an optimal level (R. W. Donohoe personal communication: 1983). The Oklahoma Department of Wildlife Conservation prescribe-burns approximately 2,000 hectares (5,000 acres) regularly, to maintain openings and arrest succession (J. Skeen personal communication:1983). Prescribed burning also is used by wildlife agencies in Kansas (J. A. Norman personal communication:1976) and Indiana (P. Meyer personal communication:1976).

The Tennessee Wildlife Resources Agency studied controlled burning and concluded that burning fields and burning in combination with fertilizing provides good results at low costs (Whitehead 1968). Controlled burning also has been studied as a habitat management tool in Pennsylvania (Forbes et al. 1971), and is being considered as a tool in Saskatchewan (E. Wiltse personal communication:1983).

I presently am evaluating the effects of controlled burning on white-tailed deer habitat in Maine, where the practice is being considered as a means of site preparation prior to reforestation. Preliminary results indicate changes in forage production and digestibility following burning. Controlled burning has not been used to any great extent in the Northeast, because of disastrous wildfires in the past and present heavy accumulations of fuel.

PLANTINGS

The objective of planting is to provide palatable, digestible and nutritious food for whitetails where needed—usually under prolonged abnormal conditions—to supplement natural forage and browse. Plantings also are used to concentrate deer for viewing or harvest. The need for supplemental planting is a subjective judgment to some extent, but must be based on habitat carrying capacity and seasonal (principally winter) food needs of the whitetail population in question.

Plant species chosen for planting should be adaptable to the site, easy to establish and maintainable at minimum cost. Since whitetail populations thrive in many agricultural areas (Nixon 1970) and because seed supplies and management experience usually are available, agricultural crops often are selected for plant-

ing. A number of wildlife agencies plant agricultural crops to provide food or cover for deer. In southern and mid-latitude habitats, where natural foods often are deficient in nutrients, several cool-season grass species that grow throughout much of the winter provide an important source of winter food rich in protein and phosphorous. Among these species are orchardgrass, the fescues, winter wheat, oats, rye, perennial ryegrasses, and forbs such as clover, alfalfa, and lespedezas. Stransky and Halls (1967) reported that oats, rye and legumes are planted for winter food in the southern pine/hardwood forest types. Fertilizing increases the quality, nutritive value, and palatability of the plants. In Arkansas and Missouri, plantings are made to supplement natural foods, primarily on public lands. In Arkansas, wildlife managers recommend four to six plots 0.4 to 0.8 hectare (1–2 acres) in size per each 2.6 square kilometers (1 square mile) (R. G. Leonard personal communication: 1976). In Missouri, one to four plots per section (2.6 square kilometers: 1 square mile) were recommended (U.S. Forest Service 1973). Plantings are made in North and South Carolina to concentrate deer and facilitate deer harvests (W. G. Moore personal communication:1983). In Nebraska, plantings serve to attract deer for harvest and to alleviate crop damage (K. Menzel personal communication:1976, K. L. Johnson personal communication:1983). Whitehead (1967), in Tennessee, reported heavier utilization of wheat than of orchardgrass and clover in mixture. Wheat grew faster than the grass/clover mixture, and the cost per pound of wheat consumed was considerably less than that of grass and clover.

Herbaceous plantings also were made farther north, where winter availability of deer food is determined by snowcover. Webb and Patric (1961) recommended planting and fertilizing clover in recently disturbed forest areas in New York where clover stands were heavily utilized by whitetails. Forbes et al. (1971) stated that plantings in Pennsylvania serve as a supplement to natural foods and that plots can be planted with a permanent pasture mix or with trees and shrubs, which should be cut periodically to encourage sprouting. A good planting of clover or trefoil produced four times more food than did the average clearcut.

Wildlife biologists in Nova Scotia recommended planting of skid roads, roadsides and yarding areas after logging to reduce erosion

A whitetail at the edge of a food plot in the Hiawatha National Forest in Michigan. Such plots can add to the diversity of forage resources for deer. *Photo by Freeman Heim; courtesy of the U.S. Forest Service.*

and increase plant diversity (A. Patton personal communication:1983). Planting of clover or alfalfa has been considered for habitat improvement in Saskatchewan (E. Wiltse personal communication:1983). Corn is planted in 0.1–0.4-hectare (0.25–1.0-acre) plots next to natural cover in Indiana (P. Meyer personal communication:1976).

Woody species are planted for food and cover. Honeysuckle is an important winter food of whitetails in the South (Sheldon and Causey 1974) and as far north as southern Ohio (Nixon et al. 1970). It is relatively shade tolerant and grows in forest understory. Honeysuckle is planted for habitat improvement in Arkansas (R. G. Leonard personal communication: 1976). Lay (1966) reported that yaupon seedlings planted on open sites in Texas would produce 1,770 kilograms of browse and 224 kilograms of fruit per hectare (1,580 pounds of browse and 200 pounds of fruit per acre) in the fourth year. Fruit-producing trees were planted at 15.25-meter (50-foot) spacing on abandoned agricultural land and along edges of immature woodlands in Kansas. Oaks, walnut, pecan, black cherry, persimmon, haw, and horticultural varieties of pear and apple were used (J. A. Norman personal communication:1976).

Browse plantings have been made in the West. In Washington, 123 browse species were tried and 18 selected for further trials (Brown and Martinsen 1959). These plants were equally palatable to white-tailed deer and mule deer (J. R. Patterson personal communication: 1976, R. L. Johnson personal communication:1983). Orme and Leege (1975) developed successful methods for seeding redstem ceanothus in Idaho. Scarification by boiling in water for one minute and planting 1.3-centimeter (0.5-inch) deep in mineral soil during October and November gave best seedling emergence and survival. Broadcast seeding in ashes was more successful than was seeding onto litter and duff.

Dense conifer plantations are recommended for winter cover on agricultural land in Indiana (P. Meyer personal communication:1976) and Delaware (T. W. Whittendale personal communication:1983), and in Minnesota where food is available and suitable cover is lacking (Rutske 1969).

Food plantings are costly. Creating openings in woodland and plowing and preparing a seedbed require considerable investment in heavy equipment. Expenses can be reduced if trees are killed with acceptable herbicides and seedbeds prepared with fire. Crawford and

Although wildlife food plantings generally are costly, grasses can be established relatively inexpensively in some habitats, such as the Ozark woodlands shown above. This was accomplished by aerial spraying of herbicides in early summer, burning in late summer, seeding grasses in the afterburn and fertilizing. *Photo by Hewlette S. Crawford.*

Figure 114. Regions of the United States' National Forest System.

Bjugstad (1967) economically established cool-season grasses on northern and eastern Ozark slopes by (1) applying phenoxy herbicide (2,4,5-Trichlorophenoxyacetic acid) to hardwoods in early summer, followed by (2) a late summer burn that removed the leaf litter but left the humus layers, (3) seeding grasses in the ashes, and (4) fertilizing to help ensure stand establishment. A considerable body of knowledge exists for the use of herbicides, fire, seeding and fertilizing by the most economical means. Lacking is the ability to put these technologies together for specific sites and situations and make them work. Success in this endeavor will make habitat management monies go much farther.

Larson (1967) and others questioned the biological and cost effectiveness of plantings. The question still is argued, even by biologists and managers who use plantings in their deer management programs. Proponents have not proven the value of plantings, nor have skeptics proven them worthless. Since plantings have been used as a management tool for years, unless objec-

tive evaluations are made, they may receive precedence over newer, possibly more effective techniques when management funds are limited. However, it must be emphasized that no management technique to enhance or improve habitat for white-tailed deer is sufficient by itself. Combinations of techniques must be planned and carried out in concert and on schedule if predictable, desired results are to be achieved.

FOREST OPENINGS

Whitetails make extensive use of forest openings, so management efforts often are made to retain these areas as a component of the animals' habitat. Classified as forest openings are areas where woody growth is the expected natural cover, uncultivated natural openings, unmaintained agricultural plots not yet reverted to closed tree stands (old fields), and places where tree cover has been reduced by means other than commercial cutting. In an ecological sense, these openings are not permanent but are held by some means or for some reason in an early seral stage for a longer period of time than would be the case with normal succession to a wooded condition. Openings created by silvicultural practices are more transient and will be considered separately.

Vegetation in overstory above the reach of deer intercepts the most photosynthetically efficient light waves. With no overstory, the zone of maximum photosynthetic efficiency lies within reach of deer, and quantity and quality of available food are improved. McCaffery and Creed (1969) found that whitetail activity in Wisconsin was significantly greater in northern hardwood stands with permanent grassy openings than in closed stands. The recommended maximum opening size was 2 hectares (5 acres), and maximum width was 100 meters (330 feet). Deer activity in openings was highest during spring and autumn, and appeared to be related to the abundance of forbs and grasses. In eastern Ohio, Nixon et al. (1970) found the fruiting of shrubs and vines to be three times greater in brush than in forest types, and recommended retaining 10 percent of woodland areas in old fields. On a per-area basis, these delayed-succession openings are more valuable for deer than are silviculturally created openings, because in the former, desirable vegetation is kept within the reach of deer many years longer than in silvicultural openings where the purpose is to regenerate and grow woody plants as quickly as possible.

In the southern and eastern regions of the U.S. Forest Service (Figure 114), natural forest openings are retained by use of chemical herbicides, burning, mowing or hand clearing, and temporary openings are created by slashing, chemical herbicide application or bulldozing. Creating and maintaining 8.1 hectares (20 acres) of temporary openings per 2.6 square kilometers (1 square mile) were recommended for each five years when no silvilcultural openings were made in the stand (U.S. Forest Service 1971). Clearing maintenance is recommended or practiced by many wildlife agencies. Arkansas (R. G. Leonard personal communication:1976), Missouri (U.S. Forest Service 1973), Minnesota (Rutske 1969), Indiana (P. Meyer personal communication:1983) and Delaware (T. W. Whittendale personal communication:1983) have such programs, as does the U.S. Fish and Wildlife Service on some of its refuges. The Columbian White-tailed Deer National Wildlife Refuge maintains openings by mechanical methods as well as by cattle grazing (J. R. Coykendall personal communication:1976, 1983).

Mechanical Means

Mechanical equipment often is used to maintain and improve forest openings for white-tailed deer. Cutting trees without follow-up treatment has only temporary value. Succession is not delayed, and the area reverts to a wooded condition at the same rate as natural succession on similar sites. A desirable browse species that is half-cut or hinge-cut, and the crowns bent within reach of deer, provides a direct source of food but does not effectively provide a substantial opening.

Mowing meadows helps maintain herbaceous plants at the expense of woody vegetation. A greater admixture of woody plants may be desirable, but when woody plants become too large, standard mowing bars cannot be used. Rotary blades such as a "bush-hog" are suitable for removal of larger woody stems. When areas of shrub growth are scarce, deer habitat can be improved if natural succession is allowed to proceed into the woody stage, then cut with a rotary blade. Many herbaceous plants—such as composites with evergreen basal rosettes and several species of legumes—will continue to grow under a light shrub overstory. Additionally, shrub stems and fruits are made available for food, and the shrubs also provide cover. Extensive mowed openings without interspersed woody or shrubby vegetation may be too cover-deficient to provide suitable deer habitat. Dispersed, irregularly shaped areas within meadows can be allowed to develop into shrub stage. The advantages of using a mower or bush-hog rather than a large drum chopper—commonly used for site preparation in forestry—are that they disturb the soil less than does the drum chopper and sod cover is not destroyed. On erosive or easily compacted soils this advantage is significant. The drum chopper may be preferred if greater mineral content of the soil is needed to establish desirable plants or if root sprouting is desired (Beckwith 1965).

Bulldozers also have been employed to create openings. Gysel (1961) concluded that bulldozing could be used for habitat management in sapling-pole stands of sugar maple and where staghorn sumac is a dominant plant species. In Tennessee, bulldozer blades are elevated 10 centimeters (4 inches) above the soil surface, and trees less than 10 centimeters (4 inches) in diameter are knocked down. These plants then sprout and produce five times more browse than in untreated areas over a five-year period (Lewis and Safley 1967*b*). Rutske (1969) indicated that in Minnesota, openings made by cuttings would maintain themselves longer and produce more herbaceous growth if stumps were bulldozed and the woody debris piled and burned.

Other mechanical methods used to create openings in brush or among small trees are roller chopping, root plowing and chaining (Hanson and Smith 1970, Box and Powell 1965). These practices are expensive, and it is difficult for wildlife agencies to justify their use exclusively for habitat management on extensive areas. However, machinery often is used to prepare sites for tree plantings or reseedings. Through proper coordination, such use of heavy equipment may benefit wildlife habitat as well.

Chemical Means

In the past 20 years, the greatest advances in maintaining clearings for deer habitat have been made through the use of chemicals. Large areas can be treated quickly and inexpensively. Krefting and Hansen (1969) evaluated the effectiveness of aerially applied 2,4-dichlorophenoxyacetic acid (2,4-D) to reduce low-preference browse such as hazel and increase desirable browse such as dogwood in Minnesota. Eight years after treatment, desirable browse had increased, and whitetail fecal pellet groups were more abundant on sprayed lots than on unsprayed areas. On an area in the Ozarks, Halls and Crawford (1965) found that preferred browse was less abundant the first two years after being aerially sprayed with 2,4,5-tricholorophenoxyacetic acid (2,4,5-T) than on an adjacent unsprayed area. However, the preferred browse grew in greater abundance on the sprayed area in succeeding years. Eight years after spraying, the production of preferred browse was six times greater on sprayed areas than on unsprayed sites. Mixtures of 2,4-D and 2,4,5-T have been effective in brush control (Crafts 1975).

Broadcast sprayings are nonselective in that all plants receive the chemical. Desirable plants can be retained by confining spray to trunks or root collars of undesirable plants or by stem injections. The foliage of shrubs and small trees can be sprayed with back-pack or tractor-mounted equipment. In national forest lands of Indiana and Ohio, Landes and Hamilton (1965) used herbicides to kill plants selectively to improve deer browse and cover.

Herbicides, like fire, can be dangerous if used unwisely. Directions on their containers must be read carefully *and* followed. However, both herbicides and fire offer potentially effective and economical means of habitat management and improvement.

SILVICULTURAL PRACTICES

The following description of understory response to cutting in eastern hardwood stands should apply in principle to forest stands in other regions (Crawford 1976:8–9): "Production of understory vegetation is related to forest type, stand structure, stand disturbance, and site. In stands that have not been disturbed by cutting for approximately 40 years, type, structure, and site operate together to influence the understory. Site influences forest type and—along with age—affects stand structure. The three factors to a large degree determine the amount and composition of the understory. . . . Woody growth increases as cutting intensity increases. On better sites, herbaceous growth is better able to compete initially with woody vegetation, although on the better sites the released woody growth soon forms a complete canopy and reduces the growth of herbaceous material, leaving only those species that are most shade-tolerant or capable of photosynthesizing when the overstory is leafless. Production of understory vegetation decreases as stands close after cutting and develop deeper canopies. When stands mature into sawtimber size, production of understory vegetation increases slightly as natural mortality thins the canopy, permitting increased light filtration to the understory. . . . Distribution and presence or absence of plant species also influence production of understory vegetation. Stands of similar forest type, structure, and site subjected to equal cutting are likely to have greater amounts of understory vegetation if there is an abundance of understory species that are more shade-tolerant. . . . Substantial disturbance of many stands results in a surge of new vegetation growth and may trigger an eruption in the deer herd. Generally, deer reach peak numbers after the stand has started to close and the peak of understory vegetation is past. An increasing herd on a decreasing range results in overuse and decline of many plant species. . . . Thus many interacting factors determine the volume and composition of understory vegetation. Light, water, nutrients, seed source, and plant and animal competition all interact."

For Food

With this mosaic of interacting factors it is difficult to determine if a given silvicultural practice is uniformly beneficial or detrimental to deer habitat. A given intensity of cutting in a mature stand on one site may cause renewed growth of deer forage that will remain available for as long as 10 years. On another site a similarly intense cutting may cause rapid growth of understory beyond reach of deer and shade out smaller plants in two or three years, resulting in habitat poorer in value than in an uncut stand. Habitat improvement by silvicultural means is affected strongly by site and, therefore, is dependent on the manager's knowledge of local conditions. Habitat improvement from silvicultural practices has occurred in the past; so too has habitat destruction. Coordination to improve deer habitat through silvicultural measures presently is being increasingly employed. Biologists and land managers coordinate silviculture in relation to wildlife habitat by using knowledge of local conditions, research findings, and trial and error. Improved knowledge of local conditions and additional research to predict responses on defined habitat sites will reduce reliance on trial and error.

Site preparation for tree planting can cause differential habitat response. The impact of roller chopping for site preparation prior to planting slash pine was considered detrimental to game food plants on sandhill sites in northwestern Florida (Hebb 1971) and beneficial in Piedmont loblolly pine stands in South Carolina (Cushwa and Jones 1969). Desirable wildlife plants did not grow as well on droughty sandhill sites as on Piedmont sites. Chopping increased the frequency of legumes and de-creased that of composites following preparation of longleaf pine sites in southwestern Gerogia (Buckner et al. 1979). On Alberta spruce sites scarified after clearcutting, the time that seral brush stages were available for deer depended on the availability of spruce seed. Abundant seeds hastened regeneration of dense spruce stands unsuitable for deer habitat (Stelfox 1962).

Thinning forest stands can have differing effects. Blair (1967) reported that loblolly pine plantations at 20 years of age were dense, with few understory plants. Heavy thinning of pine at 20 and 25 years released understory. After a third thinning at 30 years, this vegetation grew beyond reach of deer to form a dense midstory that inhibited understory growth. In comparison, light thinning gave less stimulus to the understory, but vegetation yields continued to increase after the third thinning. In the Ozarks, a light thinning of oaks increased the yields of desirable plant foods on sites where black oak site-index exceeded 70, but heavy thinning was necessary to increase desirable forage yield on poorer sites (Crawford 1971). In longleaf pine stands on the Ocala National Forest in Florida, reduction of oak trees had a greater negative impact on understory when oaks were scarce than when they were abundant (Strode 1957). In the southern Appalachians, browse production was 10 times greater on lower slopes than on upper slopes when all woody stems except selected crop trees were removed from a dense sapling stand of hardwoods (Della-Bianca and Johnson 1965).

Shaw (1971) recommended periodic thinning in oak stands to produce the quantity of acorns required by wildlife. Trees with large crowns should be left when oak stands are thinned, since they are more likely to produce seed (Christisen and Korschgen 1955).

Harvest cutting methods are another example of the need for local decisions to improve habitat. For years, foresters argued the merits of even-age versus uneven-age management. The debate was passed to wildlife biologists. After 30 years of light-diameter-limit cutting and other forms of high-grading timber stands, clearcutting looked like an important tool for managing deer habitat. In many cases it was, until too much was cut in too small an area. Large cuts produced much desirable deer food, but sometimes overlooked was the fact that when that food grew beyond the reach of deer and increasing canopies prevented understory growth, food was gone, and yet the area could not be commercially cut again for 50 to 100 or more years. Large areas were locked in a single age class of trees, and the situation—with respect to deer—was boom to bust. With the adoption of clearcutting in Louisiana, for example, excessive size and poor distribution of cuts plus destruction of upland and bottomland hardwoods soon changed the beneficial aspects of clearcutting (J. W. Farrar personal communication:1983).

Limitations on the size of clearcuts were suggested in an effort to provide diversity within the forest, and programs were developed employing this principle on national forest lands in the eastern United States. The program developed by the Missouri Department of Conservation and U.S. Forest Service adjusted the timber cutting practices on 404-hectare (1,000-acre) compartments to obtain a desirable balance of forage, mast, old-growth forest and water for wildlife (U.S. Forest Service 1973). Through the coordination of wildlife management with timber cutting, 10 to 15 percent of each compartment is scheduled to be in a productive forage class. This limitation prohibits large cuts and ensures a continuing supply of forage.

Other wildlife biologists and managers recommended clearcutting limitations to maintain forest diversity. Biologists in Nova Scotia recommended restricting clearcuts to a 12-hectare (30-acre) maximum, with adjacent cuts creating at least a 20-year difference in age class (A. Patton personal communication:1983). Their objective was to maintain variety in stand age classes and composition. They recommended that greenbelts 20 meters (66 feet) in minimum width on each side of streams be cut using only single-tree selection to a minimum 60 percent crown closure. Biologists in Arkansas planned evenly distributed clearcuts of 4 hectares (10 acres) on state lands (R. G. Leonard personal communication:1976). They also desired a component of mature and overmature timber for mast production. In Ohio, well-spaced clearcuts of 8 hectares (20 acres) or less were recommended for public forests (R. W. Donohoe personal communication:1983). Biologists in South Carolina desired clearcuts to be irregular in shape and small (2 hectares: 5 acres) where possible (W. G. Moore personal communication:1983). In North Carolina, habitat management on lands owned by the Wildlife Resources Commission was achieved primar-

ily through small pulpwood and sawtimber sales prepared by biologists with training in forestry (C. E. Hill personal communication:1976, G. L. Barnes personal communication:1983). The New York Department of Environmental Conservation recommended (1) cutting mature trees on coniferous forest winter ranges in a pattern that provides three different successional stages, and (2) a series of 25-year successional stages for mixed wood and hardwood areas. Their objective was to establish a continuous food supply (C. W. Severinghaus personal communication:1976, N. Dickinson personal communication:1983).

Because of depressed markets for the extensive stands of aspen, too little cutting in Minnesota resulted in declining habitat quality. Consequently, the Minnesota Department of Natural Resources initiated a forest wildlife program on 20,480 square kilometers (8,000 square miles) of state-owned land. Land inventories were made and mapped, and interdisciplinary teams scheduled commercial cuts designed to improve wildlife habitat. Where commercial sales were impractical because of access, temporary roads were built or improved to make logging economically feasible. Clearcuts "as small as practical" were recommended to avoid development of large even-aged stands; large blocks of even-aged stands were considered less desirable than a selectively cut block of the same size (Rutske 1969). Short rotations for pulp production were preferred over the longer sawlog rotations recommended in Missouri, since in Minnesota acorns are not as important as a wildlife food.

Forest stand diversity and whitetail habitat improvement can be achieved through small clearcuts or by using a selective system of cutting that opens the stand to a degree sufficient to initiate understory growth. Morriss (1954) reported that the number of stems per hectare of usable browse one to two years after cutting was approximately the same in a 28-hectare (70-acre) clearcut—all stems except 10 to 15 seed trees per hectare (4–6 per acre) removed—and a 34-hectare (84-acre) heavy selection cut—commercial sawlog cut followed by a sanitation and species improvement cut—in the southern Appalachians where hardwood growth is rapid on mesic sites. The clearcut was used heavily by deer the first year. Only edges and borders were used the second year. And by the third year, browse had grown beyond the reach of deer. Ripley and Campbell

(1960) studied the same area 10 years after treatment and found that tree composition and stocking density were more favorable on the clearcut area. They concluded that, while the clearcut had been heavily browsed, the cut area was large enough and produced enough suitable browse for the regenerating stand to escape excessive utilization by deer. The selectively cut area, in contrast, was severely browsed and tree regeneration inhibited.

Harlow and Downing (1969), also working in mesic, high-site-quality southern Appalachian stands, concluded that an 8-hectare (20-acre) clearcut was preferable to 0.4-hectare (1-acre) or 20-hectare (50-acre) clearcuts, because: (1) regeneration in the 0.4-hectare (1-acre) cut was eliminated quickly by deer and overstory competition; and (2) 20-hectare (50-acre) clearcuts grew too dense three years after cutting for deer to penetrate to the interior. By contrast, a 121-hectare (300-acre) selectively

cut area—all commercial stems removed except seedtrees—averaging 11.2 to 13.5 square meters per hectare (50–60 square feet per acre) of basal area in residual stand density remained accessible to deer and, therefore, had advantage for deer over clearcuts 20 hectares (50 acres) in size. Despite the accessibility for deer of the selectively cut cove, the area became adequately restocked, primarily with yellow poplar and yellow birch, both desirable browse species (Harlow and Downing 1970).

These studies indicate that, on high-quality Appalachian hardwood sites, selective cuts somewhere between 34 and 121 hectares (84–300 acres) in size can produce satisfactory tree reproduction when deer populations are high. An abundance of regeneration (and probably slash) from clearcutting soon limits deer penetration of clearcut stands making cut areas somewhat larger than 8 hectares (20 acres) inaccessible and of little value to deer.

Clearcuts of approximately 8 hectares (20 acres) provided whitetail food for a longer period of time than did larger cuts on high-quality sites in the southern Appalachians. *Photo by Jim Dean; courtesy of the North Carolina Wildlife Resources Commission.*

Crawford and Harrison (1971) reported that cutting all stems greater than 1.27 centimeter (0.5 inch) diameter breast height produced a 400-percent greater forage yield than did light selective cutting in Ozark black oak stands. The selective cutting was a large-diameter-limit or salvage cut, and did not open the stand (Murphy and Crawford 1970). Heavier cuts are needed to stimulate adequate growth of desirable vegetation on these xeric oak sites (Crawford 1971). Patton and McGinnes (1964) found that woody browse production increased with (1) the percentage basal area of stems greater than 7.6 centimeters (3 inches) diameter breast height removed, and (2) time since cutting in oak/pine stands in western Virginia. The lowest level of basal area removed by cutting was 30 percent, which gave browse yields three to five times greater than did yields in uncut stands. The greatest amount removed by cutting was 80 percent, which produced browse 15 to 25 times more abundant than in uncut stands.

The length of time required between regeneration cuts negated the initial advantage of clearcutting—all stems over 5.1 centimeters (2 inches) diameter at breast height—over selective cutting—approximately 20 percent of basal area in mature stems cut—for potential deer carrying capacity (summer) on xeric oak/pine sites in the mountains of western Virginia (Crawford et al. 1975*b*). Selectively cut stands had a dual advantage over clearcuts: (1) vegetation was rejuvenated by regeneration cutting that removes approximately 20 percent of the stand every 20 years over the crop tree rotation age of 100 years, whereas another regeneration cut could not take place for 100 years after clearcutting; and (2) with selective cutting, five times more area can be cut annually than can be clearcut to sustain regulated cutting.

The effects of regeneration cutting on deer habitat are related to intensity of cut, area cut, site quality—which influences the time the forage response lasts—and time before the area may be recut.

For Cover

In several northern states and Canadian provinces, there is a special need to maintain and improve certain areas of shelter for white-tailed deer during winter. In Maine, for example, whitetails find adequate winter shelter in coniferous forests where (1) a portion of the stand is composed of either spruce, fir, northern white cedar or hemlock, or (2) mixtures of these species predominate, and (3) the stands are at least 11 meters (36 feet) in height, with a crown closure of at least 70 percent (Gill 1957*b*). Periodic timber harvests at 5 to 15 year intervals were recommended to establish 6 or more (preferably 10) age classes of trees and simultaneously provide winter shelter and food (D. Marston personal communication:1983).

The cutting pattern of 2–5-hectare (5–12-acre) "patches" (foreground) retains important winter cover for whitetails in many northern forest habitats. *Photo courtesy of the New Brunswick Department of Natural Resources.*

Forest-cutting practices that allow retention of 70-percent crown closure in winter yards and 50–60 percent of spruce and fir trees taller than 12 meters (39 feet) and that leave scattered logging debris as browse are beneficial to whitetail populations in the Northeast. *Photo courtesy of the Maine Department of Inland Fisheries and Wildlife.*

Gill (1957a) also recommended a group selection cutting (several trees in a group, approximately 0.1 to 0.5 hectare: 0.25 to 1.25 acres) to intersperse the uncut stands with openings. Strip clearcuts no wider than 30 meters (98 feet) were recommended as a second option.

Telfer (1974) found large clearcuts harmful to deer range in boreal forests, and recommended logging to create a mosaic of small patches and strips less than 100 meters (328 feet) in width of different age classes. Before 1974, the New Brunswick Department of Natural Resources prohibited any cutting in deer wintering areas on Crown land in the province. After 1974, in coordination with commercial timber companies, department biologists attempted to maintain and improve food and shelter by creating 6 to 10 age classes within the deer yard and adjacent areas. They specified that 50 to 60 percent of the yard be retained in spruce and fir taller than 12 meters (39 feet), and have at least 70-percent crown closure (Moore and Boer 1977). Cutting in im-

portant deer wintering areas also may be prohibited on Crown lands in Quebec (Pichette 1977).

In eastern Ontario, white spruce and northern white cedar forests with an 80-year rotation were cut in patches 80.5 meters (264 feet) long and 20.1 to 40.2 meters (66–132 feet) wide to regenerate the white spruce for timber and the northern white cedar for deer food and shelter (Hepburn 1968). At least 80 percent of each wintering area had four even-aged classes of trees with a difference in age of 20 years between classes.

Where hardwood stands predominate in Vermont, a series of preliminary forest management guidelines was recommended to perpetuate winter ranges (Dickinson 1972):

A. Deer populations not controlled
    1. avoid heavy softwood cuts in hearts of existing deer wintering areas;
    2. maintain a continuous belt up to 61 meters (200 feet) in width of ade-

quate softwood shelter through the axis of the entire wintering area;

3. cut less than 50 percent of basal area of trees with diameters at breast height of 15 centimeters (6 inches) and over where there is heavy stocking of softwoods in wintering areas, and with lighter stocking, decrease the percentage of basal area removed;

4. spruce should be favored for retention over balsam fir and its regeneration encouraged;

5. when establishing shelter bands, the future should be considered by taking advantage of stands of immature softwoods;

6. mark all trees that are to be removed;

7. when partial cuts are not possible, consider exempting the area from any cutting;

8. when softwood stands are on steep south slopes, deficiencies in tree stocking are not as severe as they would be on north slopes or level ground;

9. apply silvicultural practices that perpetuate softwood stands and maintain cover;

10. remove hardwood from the hearts of wintering areas to prevent hardwood encroachment;

11. in cutting, favor softwood anywhere within or on the edge of the winter range to perpetuate its original size and shape;

12. minimize logging damage to residual softwoods; and

13. evelute all recommendations to determine their success.

B. Deer populations controlled

1. in addition to shelter maintenance, encourage and stimulate increased growth of existing softwood trees in wintering areas by removing overtopping hardwoods to improve the shelter quality of the stand;

2. release softwoods from hardwood competition to increase softwood cover and extend shelter away from the edges of existing wintering areas to increase their functional size and provide access for deer to additional feeding sites;

3. provide for a sustained forage sup-

ply rather than encouraging a boom and bust situation; and

4. protect softwood areas that have potential for future wintering areas.

Habitat management in New Hampshire has consisted of encouraging large landowners to retain softwood cover in known whitetail wintering areas (Laramie 1968).

In Michigan, Verme (1965b) recommended a management approach for conifer stands almost opposite to that recommended in the Northeast. For conifer stands that were primarily white cedar, he proposed clearcuts of 16 to 65 hectares (40–160 acres) to create five age classes, 15 to 20 years apart in a compartment. For deer yards smaller than 81 hectares (200 acres), Verme recommended clearcutting the entire area to force deer elsewhere during the timber restocking stage. He based his argument on the need to obtain enough white cedar regeneration to escape deer browsing yet form a satisfactorily stocked cedar stand. Wetzel et al. (1975) accepted Verme's recommendation for northeastern Minnesota. Krefting and Phillips (1970) recommended strip clearcuts over patch clearcuts, selection, diameter limit and shelterwood cuts in the same general area that Verme (1965b) studied, because suitable cover was provided next to an abundant supply of browse. They did not evaluate the quality of stands regenerated after strip clearcutting, but noted that browsing was light most winters and concentrated primarily on mountain maple.

In 1976, biologists in Washington and Montana recommended even-age units of approximately 4 hectares (10 acres) with varying age classes interspersed throughout winter range on national forests (T. E. Burke personal communication:1976, G. L. Halverson personal communication:1976, R. G. Hensler personal communication:1976). By 1983, research by the Montana Department of Fish, Wildlife and Parks indicated that white-tailed deer in northwestern Montana used mature, subclimax, coniferous forests in preference to cut areas for winter range (Mundinger 1985). These findings parallel those of Wallmo and Schoen (1980), which showed the dependence of Sitka black-tailed deer on mature coniferous forests in southeastern Alaska.

The ability of mature coniferous forests in Maine to provide autumn and winter habitat was indicated by the food preferences of tame whitetails (Crawford 1982). With equal access to open-canopy cut areas and closed-canopy mature stands, deer selected a highly digestible diet of mushrooms and dried leaves from the mature forest understory in autumn. In winter, primary foods were foliage and limbs that fell from the conifer canopy.

Evergreen canopy provides thermal protection for white-tailed deer in winter. However, of even greater benefit, it (1) functions to intercept and provide a substrate for sublimation of snow, and (2) drops a supply of protein-rich food that usually is unavailable in the understory. In heavy snowfall regions, whitetails often are able to move about and find fallen foods under dense, continuous conifer cover. Snow depths in nearby cut areas are deeper, and prevent access even when woody foods are available above the snow.

The management implication of the need for a continuous, mature conifer canopy in deep snow areas is clear. Uneven-age silvicultural systems are required instead of even-age systems that involve extensive cutting. Single-tree selection or group selection systems allow tim-

Deep, soft snow can severely limit whitetail access to suitable forage resources, increase the drain on energy reserves, and heighten competition among concentrated deer for available food in winter yards. *Photo by Tom Carbone; courtesy of the Maine Department of Inland Fisheries and Wildlife.*

ber harvest while maintaining adequate canopy cover. Unfortunately, many foresters and forest landowners dislike uneven-age management. It is costly because less volume can be harvested at one time from an area, and is more difficult to apply because allowable-cut determinations are more complicated. In short, uneven-age management requires more forestry skill and provides less short-term profit. However, if deer are to be considered a forest crop, as is timber, the justification for uneven-age management strengthens.

RANGE MANAGEMENT PRACTICES

Livestock grazing affects the vigor and composition of plants and the direction and rapidity of plant succession. Thus, it can significantly influence carrying capacity of white-tailed deer habitat.

Wildlife managers in Arkansas (R. G. Leonard personal communication:1976) and Louisiana (J. W. Farrar personal communication: 1983) object to cattle grazing in woodlands because cattle compete directly with deer and other wildlife for sparse woodland forage. Forage grown for deer on food plots also is eaten by cattle. Grazing exclusion has been recommended in Nebraska to protect suitable cover (K. Menzel personal communication:1976, K. L. Johnson personal communication:1983). Wildlife managers in Arizona recommend adjusting numbers of livestock to range conditions (Arizona Game and Fish Department 1977). When desirable range grasses are plentiful, competition between livestock and deer is minimal. But, when overgrazing or drought reduce range plant abundance and nutritive value, livestock—which commonly are fed supplements—have a substantial advantage over nutritionally stressed deer.

Rest-rotation or deferred-rotation grazing, where livestock grazing is suspended during a critical plant-growth phase, is recommended to improve deer habitat in Texas (R. L. Cook personal comunication:1977, C. K. Winkler personal communication:1983) and Montana (W. G. Freeman personal communication: 1976). Reardon et al. (1978) reported that frequent grazing deferment was beneficial to white-tailed deer. A seven-pasture, rapid-rotation grazing system supported more deer in Texas than did a four-pasture, deferred rotation system or a continuous grazing system. Contin-

Because they often have access to food supplements, cattle can graze overstocked ranges and have a distinct competitive advantage over whitetails for available forage on cohabited range. Where cattle and other livestock occupy woodland pastures, habitat qualities necessary for maintenance of deer can be damaged extensively. *Photo by Vernon Bostick; courtesy of the U.S. Forest Service.*

Rested pastures allow for rejuvenated growth of nutritious forbs and grasses, and are considerably more favorable for whitetails and livestock alike than are continuously grazed pastures. *Photo courtesy of the Washington Department of Game.*

uous grazing is considered detrimental even with light cattle stocking. Defoliation from continuous grazing reduces plant vigor and eventually the population of desirable plants. Deferred grazing allows plants to refoliate and recover vigor before being grazed again. The amount of rest a pasture needs depends on the type of livestock, site and plant species. Darr and Klebenow (1975) found that the effects of livestock competition with deer differed between cattle and sheep on different habitats.

Management practices in the Columbian White-tailed Deer National Wildlife Refuge in Washington are aimed at maintaining short-grass/forb pastures adjacent to woody cover. The desired successional stage is maintained by continuous evaluation of proper cattle grazing intensity and mechanical manipulation (J. R. Coykendall personal communication:1976, A. Clark personal communication:1983).

Many of the mechanical and chemical methods employed to maintain forest openings are used for rangeland manipulation as well. And plantings—primarily of shrubs suitable as deer food—and controlled burns also have been used. As in woodland conditions, these practices yield mixed results and depend on local conditions.

PLANT COMMUNITY PROTECTION

Wildlife biologists and managers in a number of states have taken steps to protect certain plant communities from land manipulation, to maintain and improve deer habitat. For example, in Texas, where most land is privately owned and operated, state wildlife biologists assist landowners in the development of ranch management plans that provide guidelines for deer habitat improvement, and identify those plant communities that are important to the welfare of the deer population (C. K. Winkler personal communication:1983). Despite a state "weed law," Montana wildlife authorities attempt to have all wildlife habitat produce natural vegetation through plant succession rather than through seedings, chemicals or other "unnatural" methods (W. G. Freeman personal communication:1977). In North Dakota, cropland retirement has benefited deer by an almost immediate response of two desirable browse species, prairie rose and wolfberry.

Wetland protection and enhancement also have benefited North Dakota deer (J. V. McKenzie personal communication:1983). Natural plant succession is allowed to prevail throughout the National Park System with as little influence from man as possible. Significant acreage of deer habitat is included in these lands.

WATER

The U.S. Forest Service develops water sources for wildlife on national forests in the eastern United States. It is not known if these sources are necessary for white-tailed deer. However, recommended for the Forest Service's southern region (Region 8) were permanent free water sources located 0.8 kilometer (0.5 mile) apart to distribute deer usage on dry ridges (U.S. Forest Service 1971). In Missouri, the objective was to provide one source of permanent water per 2.6 square kilometers (1 square mile) of habitat on federal and state lands (U.S. Forest Service 1973). In Ohio, small waterholes—less than 0.1 hectare (0.25 acre)—have been constructed on state forests and wildlife areas, and on the Wayne National Forest (R. W. Donohoe personal communication:1983). Waterholes also have been reconstructed on other national forests in the Midwest. Generally, these water sources should be designed to provide maximum storage with a minimum of surface area, to reduce evaporation and maintain water through drought periods (Yoakum et al. 1980).

LAND-USE PLANNING AND MANAGEMENT

Land-use planning and associated regulation carry strong implications for wildlife habitats and populations. Wildlife populations can be increased or decreased through the land use(s) specified in zoning for individual areas. To ensure that wildlife values are considered and used in decision-making, they should be identified initially in the planning process. Participation at the initial stage helps avoid debates at the end of the planning process when recommendations and conclusions are formulated. Many wildlife agencies have recognized this and added planners to their staffs.

Land-use regulation through zoning in the United States goes back half a century and is supported by a 1926 U.S. Supreme Court decision that upheld zoning as part of a community's authority to act for its general welfare. The fine line between the general welfare of a community and infringement of individual rights has been argued in and out of the courts ever since, with decisions going both ways. An April 1974 U.S. Supreme Court decision written by Justice Douglas favored zoning (Belle Terre, New York), and most authorities agree that its logical extension—land-use planning—is inevitable.

Several states and provinces have land-use laws. In Maine, for example, the Land Use Regulation Commission has jurisdiction over use of private land in unorganized townships that are too sparsely populated to have local governments. Critical wildlife lands, such as whitetail wintering areas and sea bird nesting sites, are designated as protected areas, and only uses compatible with the wildlife values on such lands are permitted. Vermont's Land Use and Development Law protects critical deer wintering areas (Dickinson 1977). Similar protection of wildlife resources is provided on Crown lands in New Brunswick and Quebec, through coordination among provincial wildlife managers and foresters. Canadian provinces have an advantage in land-use planning over states inasmuch as wild ungulate and waterfowl habitats were sampled in the Canada Land Inventory, which provided a base for land regulation in Canada.

In the United States, zoning—or land-use management—first came about through political measures, with planning often coming after zoning. Land and resource inventories seldom were conducted. As land-use management extends into rural and woodland areas, it is imperative that inventories precede planning and control. Land and resource inventories must be comprehensive and consider the potential of each unit of land to produce the optimal mix of goods and services. Wildlife managers must be able to compare the potential of the land to produce wildlife with its potential to produce other goods and services. Agriculturalists have learned to judge land potential for food and fiber production; the same can be done for deer and other wildlife.

Management practices applied successfully on one site may be unsuccessful on another site. If the results of each alternative land management practice are not correlated with definable characteristics of the site, the potential for managing units of landscape for wildlife in general and white-tailed deer in particular cannot be evaluated accurately. Counting deer numbers—even if it could be done accurately—does not necessarily give a reliable indication of site potential. There are many extraneous factors, such as poaching and some diseases, that prevent whitetail populations from existing in balance with the carrying capacity of their habitats. These factors do not operate uniformly from habitat to habitat. Whitetail movements would also bias site evaluations because the deer may range over a larger area including several habitat types. Ultimately, objective evaluation of habitat potential must be based on site characteristics and not on animal numbers.

The presence, size and well-being of deer populations are related to site or habitat characteristics, including the successional stage of vegetation. A given site in a given successional stage has a potential for each species of wildlife, for a mix of wildlife species, and for a mix of wildlife and other goods and services. Potential deer numbers can be estimated by recognizing sites of similar value for deer, measuring the site potential to produce deer under alternative land uses based on production of food and cover requisites, and comparing deer

opportunities with the capability of the site to produce other products (Crawford 1975). Comparisons of these potentials will provide an objective basis for integration of products in regional and local land-use evaluation and planning.

The responsibility for including and retaining wildlife values in land-use plans rests with those interested in the future of wildlife. Generally, land-use planners and commissions welcome input. However, such input must be factually supported if wildlife is to compete successfully with resource demands.

Newer methods of deer habitat management are compatible with multiple-product evaluation. They are based on a knowledge of food, water and cover requirements. These requirements are translated into plant components measurable by habitat inventory. Inventories such as those made on the Mark Twain National Forest in Missouri, using a wildlife management inventory system (WMIS) (U.S. Forest Service 1981), are being adapted to simulation models that incorporate data from several resource inventories. Such systems will enable land managers to evaluate the impacts of alternate land-use practices on several resources on differing sites.

Chapter 38

CROP DAMAGE AND CONTROL

George H. Matschke
Wildlife Biologist
U.S. Fish and Wildlife Service
Denver, Colorado

David S. deCalesta
Associate Professor
Department of Fisheries and Wildlife
Oregon State University
Corvallis, Oregon

John D. Harder
Associate Professor
Department of Zoology
Ohio State University
Columbus, Ohio

Colonial farmers in North America experienced crop depredations by white-tailed deer. Today, as whitetail populations increase and their habitats shrink, deer damage to agricultural and forest crops still is a significant problem in many areas, and its control is an important aspect of nearly all whitetail management programs.

THE PROBLEM

Field Crops

The seriousness of deer impact on agricultural crops varies widely. Heavy browsing pressure by whitetails may result in the loss of an entire crop (Flyger and Thoerig 1965, Hartman 1972, DeGarmo and Gill 1958, Barker 1972).

Heaviest crop damage occurs in fields bordered by woodlands. In Pennsylvania, more than 60 percent of deer-damaged field crops were adjacent to woodlands, whereas fields more than 670 meters (2,200 feet) from woodlands were undamaged (Thomas 1954). Farms in heavily wooded areas were damaged more frequently than were farms in lightly wooded areas. Hartman (1972), Flyger and Thoerig (1962), Thomas (1954), and deCalesta and Schwendeman (1978) noted that damage to crops was greatest on the edges of fields bordering woodlands and that damage declined as distance into the field increased. However, Flyger and Thoerig (1962) stated that, because tall corn affords protection similar to woodlands, damage is spread throughout cornfields rather than being concentrated near edges. These studies as well as investigation by Shope (1970) indicated that damage was most severe in fields less than 4 hectares (10 acres) in size. However, the relationship between field size and damage is inconsistent (deCalesta and Schwendeman 1978). Many variables affect damage and may have more influence on extent of damage than field size does.

Field crops commonly eaten by whitetails include broccoli, cauliflower, corn, hay, buckwheat, cabbage, soybeans and tomatoes. Damage is intensified on fertilized crops, and by dry weather, heavy snows and low quality of native forage.

This 2-hectare (5-acre) field of buckwheat was completely stripped of seed heads in three nights by white-tailed deer in northwestern Pennsylvania. Damage by white-tailed deer to most field crops occurs along field edges bordering woodlots. An exception is corn, where damage to fields often is spread throughout because the tall plants provide cover as well. *Photo by Stanley E. Forbes.*

A whitetail doe feeding at night on brussel sprouts in a family garden. Damage done by white-tailed deer to backyard gardens, fruit trees and ornamentals is a constant source of irritation and economic loss to landowners whose property abuts whitetail habitat. *Photo by George Shiras III; courtesy of the National Geographic Society.*

The season when damage is most severe depends largely on the kind of crop grown. For example, corn is most likely to be damaged in autumn, after ears have ripened; hay most often is damaged in spring and early summer; and most damage to potato crops occurs in autumn, after tubers are formed. Small grains such as wheat and oats may be grazed heavily when planted as winter pasture in the South.

There is unanimous support for the theory that intensity of crop damage is related directly to deer density (Carpenter 1967*b*, Barker 1972, Dahlberg and Guettinger 1956, Eadie 1954, Flyger and Thoerig 1962, Gerstell 1938, Hartman 1972, Shope 1970, Thomas 1954). More specifically, overpopulation of deer and subsequent degradation of native forage stocks are likely to result in high crop damage. However, Carpenter (1967*a*) noted that damage by just a few deer can exceed economically tolerable limits. DeGarmo and Gill (1958) observed that, where deer densities were light to moderate, crop damage usually was the work of a few deer that had habituated to the crop. Con-

versely, Shope (1970), observing deer behavior related to crop damage, argued that crop damage results from actions of local deer herds acting as a group rather than from actions of individual deer. Hartman (1972) stated that as long as even a few deer remain there will be crop damage, and its elimination requires that local deer be eradicated or effectively prevented access to crops.

Orchards

Whitetails most often damage orchard trees by browsing. Orchard fruits, such as apple and cherry, that are grown extensively within prime whitetail habitat receive heaviest use by deer. In mountains and forested regions of Pennsylvania, whitetails were the leading species in wildlife damage to orchards, having an index of detrimental importance of 126.8, compared with 80.3 for birds and 69.5 for small mammals. On a statewide basis, deer were second only to birds in detrimental importance (Anthony and Fisher 1977).

Browsing is most detrimental to trees less than three years old, when the terminal buds of major branches are within reach of deer. Browsing can kill trees (Boyce 1950, Beckwith and Stith 1968) and reduce their vitality and growth (Morse and Ledin 1958, Eadie 1961). Perhaps more importantly, browsing on young trees removes the terminal buds of leader branches, altering growth patterns and interfering with pruning and training systems aimed at developing well-formed scaffold branches. Thus, even though young trees often survive heavy browsing pressure, they are apt to be bushy, misshapen and of little value for fruit production (Harder 1970).

Deer also may reduce fruit production on small or dwarf trees where a large number of fruit buds are below the browse line (Boyce 1950, Morse and Ledin 1958), but very little quantitative information is available. Some reduction in fruit yield was recorded in 29 percent of the damaged citrus trees surveyed in Florida (Beckwith and Stith 1968). In an experiment involving simulated browsing, Katsma and Rusch (1980) found that removal of 40 percent of the buds and spurs on McIntosh apple trees led to a significant reduction of apples per blossom cluster.

Bark removal by antler-rubbing occurs far less frequently than terminal browsing (Bittner 1949), but the effects usually are more detrimental. Antler-rubbing damages trees by breaking small branches and removing bark and cambium along the vertical axis. Rubbing normally occurs in late autumn and early winter, thereby exposing xylem four to six months before the wound has a chance to heal. Harder (1970) found that about 12 percent of apple, cherry and peach trees died after being rubbed by deer. Of these, 84.6 percent had bark removed from their trunks. Nearly all small trees died, regardless of species, when bark was rubbed from more than 50 percent of their circumferences.

Harder (1970) also found that the fate of rubbed but unbroken limbs was a function of bark removal around the stem rather than along the longitudinal axis. When limbs had greater than 50-percent circumference bark removal, limb mortality was 90 percent, compared with only 46 percent mortality when less than 50 percent of the circumference bark was removed. The presence of shriveled terminals in winter was a reliable indicator of limb death during the dormant period.

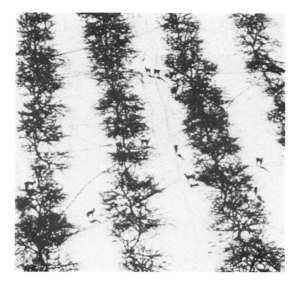

White-tailed deer are especially attracted to orchards, where fruit and woody browse are preferred foods. Even in areas where deer densities are not particularly high, damage to orchards can be severe. *Photo by Nick Drahos; courtesy of the New York Department of Environmental Conservation.*

Whitetail use of orchards in northern or mountainous states usually is greatest in winter (Eadie 1961), particularly when snow is deep and natural foods are scarce. However, Boyce (1950) reported browsing in Michigan orchards during both winter and summer.

Forest Plants

Deer may cause serious damage to young forests by browsing seedlings and small trees. Repeated browsing of terminal buds can kill seedlings or suppress their vertical growth. In Allegheny hardwood forests of Pennsylvania, bigtooth aspen, hawthorn, and the most valuable timber species—black cherry, white ash, and sugar maple—were almost nonexistent because of repeated browsing by whitetails (Grisez 1957, Shafer et al. 1961). On the northern shore of Lake Superior, natural regeneration of northern white cedar was eliminated by high populations of white-tailed deer, in combination with snowshoe rabbits and red-backed voles. Sometimes, whitetails pull seedlings out of ground that has heavy clay soil and is subject to frost heaving. Browsing damage usually is most severe in late winter and early spring. It is governed to some extent by the relative abundance of other more-preferred browse species.

In areas where whitetails traditionally are not hunted, such as parks, residential communities, golf courses, airports and other open spaces in urban/suburban settings, the deer can become a serious nuisance when unregulated population growth results in extensive feeding pressure on plantings as well as native vegetation. *Wildlife Management Institute photos.*

CONTROL MEASURES

Whitetail Population Control

The best solution to whitetail damage to forest and agricultural crops is to keep the deer population in balance with its natural habitat. To achieve this balance, deer harvest regulations must be liberal, and hunters must have access to areas where deer damage is a significant problem (Behrend et al. 1970, deCalesta in press). It is essential that antlerless deer be harvested in areas of intense crop damage (Baynes 1974, Eadie 1954, Shope 1970). In Pennsylvania, complaints about whitetail damage were reduced substantially by liberalized hunting laws that increased the deer harvest (Roberts 1964). Even with heavy deer harvests, damage to crops may persist in whitetail concentration areas. In these situations, some states have held special localized hunts (Turpin 1949).

Landowner cooperation is an essential element of deer population control (Behrend et al. 1970, Eadie 1954, Shope 1970). Population reduction is nearly impossible when property is posted against hunting (Baynes 1974, Carpenter 1967a, DeGarmo and Gill 1958). In

Pennsylvania, Shope (1970) reported a 20-percent higher harvest of whitetails from an unposted area than from an area where 26 percent of the land was posted.

Some states permit landowners to shoot depredating deer (McDowell and Pillsbury 1959), but the practice is time-consuming and rarely effective (Carpenter 1967a, Eadie 1954). DeGarmo and Gill (1958) cited an instance where a West Virginia farmer killed 19 whitetails over a two-month period and still lost most of his crop. In Pennsylvania, farmers may have killed whitetails simply because the deer were in crop fields, even though the deer were not damaging crops (Shope 1970). After 1923, Pennsylvania farmers were issued kill permits year after year, but reported crop damage did not decline. In some states, wildlife agency personnel shoot deer that are causing damage. Denney (1955) believed that spotlighting would be an efficient way to remove antler-rubbing bucks from orchards.

Trapping and Translocating

In the past, whitetails were trapped where high crop damage occurred and then released into areas with a low density (Eadie 1954).

Translocation programs are not popular because of high costs, trapping difficulty and lack of areas with low whitetail density (Baynes 1974, Carpenter 1967*a*, Floyd 1960, *see* Chapter 39).

Scare Devices

Many devices are available for scaring deer from croplands and orchards. Scare devices usually do not reduce or prevent deer depredations. Instead, they annoy neighbors and often are expensive to purchase and maintain, and deer normally habituate to them in a short time. Some of the devices depend on sound, such as fireworks, carbide or acetylene guns, rifle fire, human voices, electronic noise and clashing of large metal plates. Best results are obtained when sounds are spaced at irregular intervals (Howard 1967, Morse and Ledin 1958). For example, a "deer fly" device that emitted short blasts of sound at irregular intervals effectively reduced deer damage to orchards in New Hampshire (Lee 1954) and Colorado (Denney 1955). Flyger and Thoerig (1962) used a booby trap of strings and detonators to explode a firecracker each time a deer attempted to enter an orchard. The system was inexpensive and partially successful, but posed a threat to human safety. Tethering dogs in crop fields at night has been proposed, but deer quickly become accustomed to a dog and its barking (DeGarmo and Gill 1958). A mechanical scarecrow tested by White and Silver (1952) protected only those crops within a 1.2-hectare (4-acre) area. Scare devices work best where short-term protection is needed or when used in conjunction with other preventive measures.

Supplemental Planting

Special crops preferred by deer may be grown at strategic locations to draw deer away from high value crops (Eadie 1954). Thomas (1954) and Hartman (1972) suggested planting rows of low value crops between high value crops and native deer habitat. Campbell (1974) recommended planting preferred forbs to reduce damage to conifers.

In South Carolina, Walker (1965) found some evidence that Korean lespedeza was more effective as a cover crop than browntop panicum in preventing deer damage to apple trees. In Germany, the addition of mineral substances and trace elements attracted game animals to supplemental winter feed, thereby reducing forest vegetation damage to an economically acceptable level (Lindner et al. 1956). In Mississippi, buffer zones of fertilized native vegetation and winter pastures reduced whitetail browsing damage in cottonwood plantations, but the costs were excessive (Denton et al. 1969). Grisez (1960) proposed leaving hardwood slash from timber operations to protect tree species of high commercial value, particularly black cherry. In some cases, supplemental planting may cause deer to remain in close proximity to crops and, consequently, increase the damage.

Chemicals

The most effective nontoxic repellents contain putrefied egg products or are merely the stickers used to adhere repellents to plants. Known by the trade names BGR, Repel, Deer-away, and Hinder, these repellents exhibit varying degrees of success. The effectiveness of repellents depends on length of treatment period, species of tree, method and time of application, and amount of deer pressure (Besser and Welch 1959). The U.S. Forest Service goes by a rule of thumb which holds that, in areas where less than 20 percent of conifer seedlings are habitually damaged, the repellent will not pay for itself if applied, and if more than 80 percent of seedlings are damaged, the repellent will not deter browsing. Damage to conifer seedlings in plantings where deer damage falls within the 20 to 80 percent interval has been reduced by 60 to 90 percent for two to three months in the Pacific Northwest (U.S. Forest Service 1979). Palmer et al. (1983:165) reported that application of BGR to flowering dogwood shrubs in Pennsylvania reduced damage (22 percent of treated shrubs were browsed, 80 percent of untreated were browsed), but that the reduction was not cost effective. They concluded that repellents do ". . . not solve the economic problem of deer damage to agricultural crops in general."

At best, repellents give only short-term protection and most cannot be used on food crops (Palmer et al. 1983). Repellents generally are not effective in summer because they do not cover the new growth. However, they may be included with dormant-season fungicide sprays after growth has ceased in autumn or winter. Also, repellents will not deter starving deer

(Floyd 1960). Multiple applications may be required per season (Barker 1972, DeGarmo and Gill 1958, Eadie 1954), and treatment effects normally do not persist to subsequent years (Heidmann 1963). Complete coverage is necessary because untreated parts may be eaten (Barker 1972, DeGarmo and Gill 1958).

Copper carbonate effectively prevented deer browsing on loblolly pine seedlings, but proved to be toxic to the plants involved (Robinette and Causey 1977, Little and Mohr 1961).

Odor repellents have been used with varying degrees of success. Bone tar oil was ineffective when applied on the ground around the periphery of a cottonwood plantation and when applied aerially (Denton et al. 1969). However, when it was applied to a cotton rope surrounding the plantation, damage was reduced 41 percent. Tankage did not reduce whitetail damage to truck crops in Florida (Barker 1972) or to a large soybean field in Virginia (Carpenter 1967b), but it was effective on cornfields and orchards in Virginia. Tankage protected a northern white cedar windbreak in Minnesota (C. Sederits personal communication:1976), but reduced damage by only 10 percent in a cottonwood plantation (Denton et al. 1969). In California, napthalene flakes (mothballs) effectively reduced deer damage to orchards for one to two months (True 1932).

Preliminary screening of white-tailed deer repellents indicated that blood meal, Magic Circle and human hair ranked very low in repellency, whereas BGR ranked second of 14 materials tested (Harris et al. 1983).

Mechanical Devices

McNeel and Kennedy (1959) provided complete protection for young pines by wrapping the terminal buds with plastic in autumn. The plastic was removed the following spring to allow growth. In a similar study in Alabama, Robinette and Causey (1977) covered terminal buds of loblolly pine seedlings with plastic bags in February. Four months later only 8 percent of these buds were browsed. Failure to remove the plastic bags prior to spring growth probably caused a seedling mortality of 22 percent. Although effective in reducing deer damage, the technique was too costly for practical use.

Plastic tubes 0.91-meter (3-feet) tall and 5.1 to 7.6 centimeters (2–3 inches) in diameter and wire exclosures 0.91 or 0.30 meter (3 feet or 1 foot) in diameter were placed over natural black cherry seedlings in Pennsylvania (Flick 1976). Browsing occurred on seedlings protected by plastic tubing because the 0.91-meter (3-foot) and 7.6-centimeter (3-inch) tubes disintegrated, whereas the 5.1-centimeter (2-inch) tubes were too small in diameter. The wire exclosures effectively prevented browsing.

Vexar[R]—a product of E. I. DuPont de Nemours and Company, Incorporated—a polypropylene plastic netting formed into rigid tubes with a 5-centimeter (2-inch) inside diameter, has been used to protect Douglas-fir seedlings in the Pacific Northwest (Campbell and Evans 1975). On newly planted seedlings, deer browsing damage was reduced nearly 100 percent by placing 92-centimeter (36-inch) tubes over entire seedlings and 46-centimeter (18-inch) tubes over terminal branches of heavily browsed seedlings (Campbell 1969). Vexar tubing was evaluated as a browsing deterrent for southern hardwoods by Lasher and Hill (1977). They reported the tubes prevented deer browsing on oak seedlings and reduced seedling mortality on sweetgum seedlings.

Yawney and Johnson (1974) tested four kinds of wire devices designed to protect terminal buds of planted two-year-old sugar maple seedlings. Seedlings surrounded by a 1.52-meter (5-foot) wire fence were unbrowsed. Straight, single-strand, 11-gauge wire had no protective value. A spiked metal shield over the terminal bud and a 25.4-centimeter (10-inch) wire spine provided good protection for years 1 and 2, but was not as effective in years 3 and 4.

Fencing

Certain fences are nearly 100-percent effective in eliminating deer damage, but costs are justified only for the protection of high value crops over long periods of time (Barker 1972, Baynes 1974, Carpenter 1967a, 1967b, DeGarmo and Gill 1958, Eadie 1954, Floyd 1960, Hartman 1972, Messner et al. 1973). The conventional deer-proof fence is 2.1 to 2.4 meters (6.9 to 7.9 feet) high, with 1.2-meter (3.9-feet) widths of woven wire attached one above the other to poles or trees (Caslick 1980, Halls et al. 1965, Harlow and Jones 1965, Longhurst et al. 1962). In 1983, the cost of posts and wire was about $4,970 per kilometer ($8,000 per mile). Designs are available for constructing fences that straddle streams or ravines (Blair et al. 1963).

Slanting-type fences effectively exclude deer from crop fields (Blaisdell and Hubbard 1957, Longhurst et al. 1962, Messner et al. 1973). These fences are approximately 1.32 meters (4.33 feet) tall and slant away from the protected area at a 45-degree angle. White-tailed deer may try to crawl under the fence, but are thwarted from jumping over them by the overhanging wire (Barker 1972, Longhurst et al. 1962). A modified slanting fence can be built by placing the slanted portion atop a standard livestock fence.

Fences around individual trees may be warranted in special cases, such as replacement plantings in an orchard. Resner (1949) recommended 1.63-meter (5.34-foot) high poultry wire, 2.6 meters (15.1 feet) long, supported by three 0.79 by 0.79-centimeter (2.0 by 2.0-inch) posts. Other investigators have reduced or eliminated the need for supports by using heavy-gauge or welded wire. Wire cages are relatively inexpensive, require little maintenance and provide long-time protection.

Snowfences, usually spanning many miles, occasionally are used to prevent deer from moving into an agricultural area. Deer may be kept away from crop fields by fencing only the field edges that border woodland. However, such fencing must be long enough to discourage deer from walking around the ends (Barker 1972). An 8.0-kilometer (5-mile) fence, 2.13 meters (7 feet) tall, kept most whitetails out of an orchard in West Virginia (Johnson 1957).

A barrier constructed from debris piled up from clearing operations has effectively protected cottonwood plantations in Arkansas where deer populations exceeded one animal per 2 hectares (5 acres) (M. Rogers personal communication:1976).

Electric fences have been used since the late 1930s to exclude deer from orchards (McAtee 1939). They should be designed to contact parts of the deer that are least insulated against shock, such as ears, face, nose and forward portion of the legs. Smooth, triple-galvanized, high-tensile 13.5-gauge wire carrying a current of 35 milliamps and a 3,000 to 4,500 voltage is recommended. Barbed wire is undesirable because the barbs tend to rust, which insulates against shock. Vegetation must be kept away from live wires to avoid grounding.

Several designs of fencing energized with lower output (less than 1,000 volts) have provided some protection. However, deer were not sufficiently deterred by prior fence en-

Electrical fences can be an effective deterrent to whitetails, but must be high enough, sufficiently wired and of significant voltage to discourage deer from jumping over, crawling under or pushing through. Such fences are expensive to construct and maintain. *Photo by Ted Borg; courtesy of the South Carolina Wildlife and Marine Resources Department.*

counters and learned to jump over or run through the fences (Floyd 1960, Tierson 1969).

More recently, the advent of high-output fence chargers from New Zealand has led to a revitalization of electric fencing as an effective deterrent. A five-wire electrified fence, 1.5 meters (58 inches) tall, provided effective control of deer damage to orchards and gardens in Pennsylvania (George et al. 1983). The fence works on the principle that deer will attempt to go through the fence, receive a shock, and be strongly deterred from future fence crossings. The deterrent effect may break down under strong stimuli, such as starvation or fear. Twelve-strand wire electrified fences, 2.1 meters (84 inches) high prevent deer from jumping over or pushing through. Five-wire fences cost approximately $808 per linear kilometer ($1,300 per mile) in 1983. Electric fences may be used even in areas where snow accumulates on the ground. The high-tensile pressure on the wires (115 kilograms: 250 pounds per wire) eliminates sag, and the current is turned off in the lower wires when they are below the level of snow.

In Minnesota, C. Kinsey (personal communication:1976) tested aversion conditioning on deer with an electric fence. Aluminum foil strips backed with fabric tape were attached to an electric wire, and peanut oil was applied to the tape. As whitetails investigated the foil and touched the tape with their noses, they received an electric shock. After that, the deer usually avoided areas where the fence was present.

Compensation

According to a survey conducted by Hancock (1979), eight states (Colorado, Massachusetts, New Hampshire, Utah, Vermont, Washington, Wisconsin and Wyoming) paid landowners for damage by deer to orchards, crops under cultivation, fences, livestock forage and Christmas tree plantations. Monetary limit to compensation ranged from $1,000 per landowner in Washington to no limit in six states (in Wisconsin the obligation was to pay for 80 percent of damage). Funding for damage payments came from license revenues. To qualify for damage payments, landowners in all but Utah had to allow general public hunting on their land. Damage compensation does not prevent damage from occurring and can be a recurrent drain on limited budgets: damage payments nationwide ranged from $5,000 to $350,000 in 1979, with a median of $25,000 per state.

Potential Methods of Control

The natural resistance of plants to mammals also is being investigated (Radwan 1974). Dimock (1974) suggested that trees be bred selectively for low palatability to deer. Little and Trew (1976) developed a fast-growing loblolly/pitch pine hybrid, and recommended that it be planted in areas normally planted to Virginia pine. H. Yawney (personal communication:1976) recommended planting 1.83-meter (6-foot) tall sugar maple trees instead of two-year-old seedlings 0.46 to 0.61 meter (1.5–2.0

feet) tall. Likewise, in Mississippi, D. Arner (personal communication:1976) suggested that deer damage might be avoided by planting taller-than-normal cottonwoods at spacings of 7.32 by 7.32 meters (24 by 24 feet).

Researchers in Pennsylvania (Anonymous 1975) discouraged deer from crossing highways at traditional sites by using a plywood mock-up of a deer rump with the white tail held in a raised position. This may have application in damage situations as well.

SUMMARY

Deer damage to agricultural fields is heaviest where crops are adjacent to wooded cover. In orchards, young trees are damaged primarily by browsing or antler rubbing. In forests, most deer damage is by browsing on seedlings and young trees less than 1.8 meters (6 feet) tall. Crop damage by whitetails usually is related directly to deer density.

Reduction of deer populations by hunting currently is the best way to reduce the impact of whitetails on forest and agricultural crops, but complete relief in problem areas is rarely if ever achieved. In most instances, trapping and translocating whitetails is too expensive. Scare tactics work best where short-term protection is needed, but deer soon become accustomed to frightening agents. Preferred deer foods planted at strategic locations to draw deer away from high value crops has not proved economical. Taste or odor repellents give short-term protection and have the most utility on conifer or orchard seedlings. Exclusion devices, such as wire cylinders and plastic tubing placed over the terminal buds of seedlings, have proven successful. Barrier fences are effective but costly; electric fences are much cheaper and nearly as effective.

Future research and management initiatives should focus on: regulations designed to reduce local deer population numbers via innovative special damage-control hunts; altering deer behavior such that the animals do not enter areas with valued plants or are deterred from eating or otherwise damaging these plants; and plant engineering (selective breeding of plants for natural resistance to animal use, breeding of fast-growing hybrid seedlings, and planting other and taller seedlings).

Chapter 39

CAPTURE TECHNIQUES

Orrin J. Rongstad
Professor
Department of Wildlife Ecology
University of Wisconsin
Madison, Wisconsin

Robert A. McCabe
Professor
Department of Wildlife Ecology
University of Wisconsin
Madison, Wisconsin

Throughout history, man has, apart from outright killing with stones, spear or gun, captured ungulates for food, clothing, relocation, research and, on occasion, public display.

To capture and hold is one expression of man's superiority over beasts of the field. Thirty to forty thousand years ago, primitive man capitalized on natural pitfalls to capture and secure the large herbivores that were his main source of protein. Later, he drove these animals over ledges into deep and lethal canyons or ravines with the aid of fire and fences. And still later, he dug pits into which animals either fell or were driven. An animal helpless in a pit could be dispatched with great economy of time and effort, given the crude weapons of that era.

As recently as the mid-1900s, man attempted to trap deer alive in a concrete pit cushioned in the bottom with hay. This operation in Texas was discontinued because the construction cost was high, the number of deer captured was lower than expected, removal from the pit was difficult and, most importantly, there was high mortality among trapped deer. In short, ". . . deer losses from injuries alone made the method impractical" (Glazener 1949:17). A second attempt at pit trapping confirmed the results of the earlier effort, and the technique was abandoned.

Ultimately, with the evolution of man from a neolithic hunter in skins of the chase to the gadget-bedecked hunter of the civilized twentieth century, deer—a prime quarry—have become either too few or too many. To right these ecological situations, and to do so by capture without killing, taxes the skill and ingenuity of those responsible for natural resources. Live capture will allow managers of areas with an adequate deer population to supply areas with few deer or to remove deer where their excessive numbers challenge the integrity of the habitat. Traps in the form of a box, drop net, drive net, snare or even a corral (cul-de-sac) have been used to capture deer and to relocate them where desirable or away from habitats in need of protection.

These same devices used to capture deer for relocation often are refined to secure deer for research purposes. Coupled with capture, marking deer usually is done for future recognition. Such marking may be with tags or collars of various design, radio transmitters, branding, color paint or dye. The primary objective of most research is to amass data that will provide a scientific basis for population management that can ensure the welfare of deer and their habitats. Movement, home range, social behavior, physiology, fecundity and response to harvest pressures are some of the aspects of deer biology that have been investigated, predicated on the capture of deer to provide basic data.

Under special circumstances, taking deer alive is required by zoos and exhibits for public viewing. Fortunately, the "bring 'em back alive" effort is regulated by the agency in charge of wild animals, to assure that trapping method, holding and transport are in keeping with sound conservation and that the program is in the interest of the captured animal as well as the viewing public.

HISTORY OF TRAPPING DEVICES

Some trapping devices that were used to dispatch animals for food and associated by-products by neolithic man are today the research tools of modern investigators. Perhaps the first evidence of trapping of large herbivores can be found in the cave drawings of Europe (Figure 115). Bateman (1971:31) presented cave drawings from "... La Grande Roche de Naquane, Val Comonica Italy, showing ... animal trapped by its mouth ... the use of nets and ... enclosure traps." These petroglyphs are alleged to "carry over" from the Stone Age to the late Iron Age. Whether the interpretation of the illustration is correct is a matter of opinion.

The first object to be regarded as a catching device was a "treadle" trap, which according to Bateman (1971) was uncovered in 1921 in a Scotland bog. Similar mechanisms had been uncovered in Ireland in 1859, and in Germany in 1873, 1874 and 1877. Each of these appeared to be a trap on which an animal stepped, put its foot through an aperture and was held fast by a wooden spring-stick. On a stone cross at Clonmacnois (County Offaly), Ireland, there is carved a red deer caught in such a device (Figure 116). Bateman was vague in both conjecture and in bibliographic reference, so some important statements on early traps could not be checked. This foothold trap apparently was not unlike a steel trap later developed for catching deer. Gibson (1905:215) wrote: "The trap for taking [Virginia] deer should be large, strong and covered with spikes. The Newhouse (No. 4) is particularly adapted and is especially arranged for this purpose." Today, no such traps—however adapted—may be used to catch deer.

Figure 115. Stone Age petroglyphs in Italy detail paleolithic captures of large herbivores by net (lower left), "... by its mouth" (upper right) and "... enclosure trap" (lower right) (from Bateman 1971:31). It can be conjectured that the upper-right scene represents use of a snaring device, and the lower-right drawing shows a cliff drive.

Figure 116. An illustration on a cross slab (700–900 A.D.) at Clonmacnois, County Offaly, Ireland, shows a red deer with a forefoot held fast by a treadle trap—regarded as the earliest known catch device (from Bateman 1971).

a hanging device." However, he was uncertain whether deer actually were trapped that way. Ashcraft and Reese's (1957:193) double-loop foot snare was proposed in 1957 as "An improved device for capturing deer." Mossman et al. (1963) had success with a nonstrangle snare to live-capture African ungulates. The basic aspect of the snare, however, apparently has been unchanged in the last 5,000 years.

A major breakthrough in man's ability to trap animals was the development of the mesh net. The concept may have been borrowed from primitive fishermen. Bateman (1971:41), again without detailed references, described an early (circa 300 A.D.) illustration of horsemen in Africa ". . . driving beasts into nets camouflaged behind a prickly fig hedge. . . ." Torrey (1957) described an attempt to capture white-tailed deer on an island off the Georgia coast with the use of a drive net, but with limited success (two deer were caught). Silvy et al. (1975) discussed successful use of the same kind of net into which whitetails were driven and captured in Florida. Beasom et al. (1980) related similar success in New Mexico and Montana. Here

Figure 117. Snaring brocket and white-tailed deer apparently was common practice among pre-Columbian Indians of Central America. Snared Yucatan whitetails are hieroglyphically featured in several parts of the Mayan Codex, Tro-Cortesianus—original mid-fourteenth-century writings by Mayan Indians from the Petén region (presently in northern Guatemala) of the Yucatan Peninsula (Thomas 1882, Tozzer and Allen 1910). This 70-page primitive documentation was painted on paper manufactured from the leaves of the maguey plant. In addition to several glyphs depicting leghold snares, another symbolizes a deer in a spiked pitfall. Illustration by Robert Pratt; redrawn from Spinden (1917).

Perhaps the most universal technique for capturing animals, developed independently and used by primitive people the world over, has been the snare or sliding-loop that, when stepped in or through, pulls tight and holds the unsuspecting animal fast by leg, head or whole body (Figure 117). Snares have been recorded as having existed as early as 3500 B.C. in northern Sweden (Bateman 1971). Vereshchagin (1967:375), referring to the Upper Paleolithic in Siberia, reported that "Ungulates and even large predatory animals could be caught by means of strap loops [snares] with too, only the locations and accouterments were altered, but the net aspect has remained essentially the same for more than 1,500 years.

Mesh netting itself has been used more efficiently with the help of gravity in the "drop net" and the aid of explosives in the "rocket net" or "cannon net." The former is a net umbrella under which deer are lured with bait. At the most propitious moment, the net is dropped on the feeding animals. A small fall-net has been used for centuries to capture small mammals and birds by Cree and Chipewyan Indians in Canada, the Chukchee in Siberia, and other groups of native people (Cooper 1938). The deer net was patterned after this device. Bait also is used to entice deer in front of a battery of projectiles attached to a net that is drawn over the deer when the charges propelling the net are electrically set off. The end result is the same in all cases—deer are entangled in the netting and thus captured for whatever legal purpose.

The boxtrap or cage trap has taken on many forms, with diverse and complicated trigger mechanisms. Bird trappers of Thailand, for example, used a reed basket (box) with a cricket as bait (Van Tyne 1933), while some eskimos of Canada used meat bait and a line trigger releasing a door of ice to trap fox in an ice enclosure (Mason 1901). Bateman (1971:16), without reference, said of cage traps: "There is conclusive evidence of these traps having been in use as far back as the Middle Ages, and they come in a variety of sizes to deal with aquatic, terrestrial and aerial animals and to take creatures ranging from shrews to antelope and large cats."

Boxtraps for small mammals have taken on added sophistication in recent years (since 1920), which has carried over in the development of live traps for deer. The Stephenson and Pisgah live traps are prototypes of current deer live-capture traps.

RECENT CAPTURE DEVICES

Most deer-capturing during the 1930s and 1940s was done with wooden box traps. Since then, net-covered traps, rocket nets, drop nets, drive nets and tranquilizer guns have been used. Drugs and tranquilizer guns are described in Chapter 40. The best capture methods for any given project will depend on deer density, food availability, and the number of people available to help in handling deer. It often is beneficial to try several capture methods at the same time.

Corral Traps

Corral traps simply are a large box trap without a top, often operated manually instead of being triggered by the deer. Advantages of corral traps are: (1) they permit more than one animal to be caught at a time; (2) they are relatively open, so deer are not as reluctant to enter; and (3) they can be constructed around a natural salt lick or small feeding area. Disadvantages of corral traps are: (1) they are large and difficult to move; (2) deer are difficult to remove from them; and (3) because of the large open area within, deer may be injured or killed by running or jumping against the sides when trappers attempt to remove them. Problems can be minimized by using an immobilizing gun to sedate the deer before removing them from the corral.

Corral traps may be the most efficient of all devices for capturing whitetails, but they also cause the highest mortality because of the difficulty of removing deer from the trap. *Photo courtesy of the Wyoming Game and Fish Department.*

Rempel and Bertram (1975) described what they referred to as the Stewart modified corral trap. This trap was made of 2.4 by 2.4-meter (8 by 8-foot) panels constructed of 2.5 by 15.2-centimeter (1 by 6-inch) boards. Seven of these panels were put together in an octagon shape with a net drop as one of the sides. Small adjunct traps were placed in openings cut into two of the seven panels. When the main gate closed, deer would try to escape through the openings, thus entering the adjunct traps, where they would be confined in a smaller space and less likely to be injured.

Hawkins et al. (1967) found that corral traps were more efficient than box traps when man hours per deer were involved, but animal mortality in the corral trap was considerably higher.

Stephenson or Michigan Trap

J. H. Stephenson of the Michigan Game Division designed a trap 1.2 meters (4 feet) high, 1.2 meters (4 feet) wide and 3.7 meters (12 feet) long, made of wood with sliding drop doors at each end. He first used this trap in the winter of 1931 (McBeath 1941). The Stephenson or Michigan trap was used extensively throughout the United States in early restocking programs. It has undergone several modifications in size and materials, but essentially is unchanged. One version, described by Glazener

The Stephenson trap, also called the Michigan trap, probably was the most commonly used trap during the period (1930s–1960s) when extensive whitetail stocking programs were taking place. *Photo by Lovett Williams; courtesy of the Florida Game and Fresh Water Fish Commission.*

(1949), was made of aluminum and weighed 84 kilograms (185 pounds), half of a wooden model's weight.

Pisgah Trap

Another trap widely used in restocking operations was the Pisgah trap (Ruff 1938). This trap, developed at the Pisgah National Game Preserve (now Pisgah National Forest) in North Carolina, first was used in 1934. It was similar to the Stephenson trap, but had a screened

Frederick J. Ruff examines one of the first Pisgah deer traps in 1937 on the Pisgah National Game Preserve (National Forest), North Carolina, where the trap was devised and for which it is named. *Photo by B. W. Muir; courtesy of the U.S. Forest Service.*

approach—1.2 by 1.2 by 2.1 meters (4 by 4 by 7 feet)—added to the wooden double-door box trap. A deer entering the screened portion would trip the front door. The animal then would try to escape through the opening in the wooden part of the trap where it would trip double wooden doors. This portion of the trap was relatively dark, which would calm the deer.

Wisconsin Pole Trap

A modification of the Stephenson deer trap was used by Wallace Grange on his sandhill game farm in Wisconsin. This trap was 0.9 meter (3 feet) wide, 1.2 meters (4 feet) high and 2.4 meters (8 feet) long. The sides and top, instead of board construction, were made of hardwood poles about 2.5 centimeters (1 inch) in diameter placed lengthwise along the trap. It is not known if this material change improved the efficiency of the trap or was done simply as a matter of economics. The drop doors of this trap were similar to those of the Stephenson trap. The Wisconsin trap design was copied in some of the southern states' trapping operations (Findlay et al. 1946, Wood 1944).

Clover Trap

Wooden box traps were heavy and bulky, and the doors often swelled when wet, which prevented them from closing smoothly. Because of these problems, Clover (1954) developed a box trap of which the frame was made of pipe and covered with netting. This trap was 2.1 meters (7 feet) long, 1.1 meters (3.5 feet) high and 0.9 meter (3 feet) wide. It was collapsible, so that several could be hauled in a pickup truck and relatively easily carried to capture sites away from roads. Such a trap of 2-centimeter (0.8-inch) black pipe weighed 36.3 kilograms (80 pounds) or, when made of aluminum, only 15.9 kilograms (35 pounds). The first Clover trap had a drop gate at each end (Clover 1954). Clover (1956) later described a single-gate version of the same trap. The modified trap was 46 centimeters (18 inches) shorter than the previous model.

A problem that occurs with the use of Clover traps is that of rabbit damage to netting around the bottom. Rabbits go into the traps for the bait and often chew their way out through the closest side. During the course of a winter, the netting may be severed in this manner around

The Wisconsin pole trap was used by Wallace Grange at his Sandhill Game Farm near Babcock, Wisconsin. *Photo by Rex G. Schminr; courtesy of the Missouri Department of Conservation.*

The double-door (drop gate) Clover trap. Note the rat trap hung at the top center of the Clover trap; it is the gate-release mechanism. *Photo courtesy of the North Dakota Fish and Game Department.*

The single-gate version of the Clover trap is 46 centimeters (18 inches) shorter than the double-gate version. *Photo by Tom Larson; courtesy of the University of Wisconsin/Madison Department of Wildlife Ecology.*

the base of the entire trap. Roper et al. (1971) installed a horizontal rabbit bar on Clover traps, which allowed rabbits to come and go freely. Covering the bottom 30.5 centimeters (12 inches) of the trap with small mesh poultry wire also prevents rabbits from chewing, but makes folding the traps for transport or storage more difficult.

Oregon Panel Trap

The Oregon trap was designed for a mule deer project in Oregon (Lightfoot and Maw 1963), and has been successfully used to capture white-tailed deer at the Cedar Creek Natural History Area in Minnesota. It is triangular in shape with no top. Two of the sides are 2.1 by 2.4-meter (7 by 8-foot) panels made from 2.5 by 15.2-centimeter (1 by 6-inch) boards.

The Oregon panel trap is made of two 2.1-by-2.4-meter (7-by-8-foot) wooden panels and a drop-net gate front. *Photo by Orrin J. Rongstad; courtesy of the University of Wisconsin/Madison Department of Wildlife Ecology.*

The front consists of a 1.8-meter (6-foot) wide by 1.2-meter (4-foot) high net drop-gate similar to the drop gate of the Clover trap. Netting also covers the area above the drop gate. The two wooden panels are bolted to the 1.8-meter (6-foot) wide drop gate in the front and are wired together at the back to form a V-shaped, open-topped trap. This trap was found to be as efficient as the Clover trap and caused lower trapping mortality.

Drop Net

A 21.3 by 21.3-meter (70 by 70-foot) drop net with 17.8-centimeter (7-inch) mesh (stretch measure) was used to capture white-tailed deer in Texas (Ramsey 1968). The net was supported by four 3.0-meter (10-foot) corner posts and a 3.7-meter (12-foot) center post. It was pulled to the top of corner poles by a boat winch bolted to each post. The net was released by blasting caps attached to ropes holding up the corners and center of the net. The blasting caps, when fired electrically from a blind, broke the ropes and caused the net to drop on the deer. Ramsey (1968) averaged about 10 deer captured per drop, with 23 being the most caught at one time.

An aerial view of drop net. Note that the bait (corn) is distributed around the center pole. *Photo courtesy of the North Dakota Game and Fish Department.*

The drop net—shown here at the moment of release—has been used with success to trap whitetails in a number of states. Its costliness in terms of logistics and required personnel (to restrain trapped deer) is mitigated by the fact that 20 or more deer may be caught in a single drop. *Photo by Bill Duncan; courtesy of the Texas Parks and Wildlife Department.*

Rocket or Cannon Net

A 12.2 by 18.3-meter (40 by 60-foot) net of 20.3-centimeter (8-inch) mesh (stretch measure), propelled over deer by three rockets, was described by Hawkins et al. (1968). The rockets were fired from steel poles 1.4 meters (5 feet) above the ground, pulling the net that had been folded below the rocket poles. One side of the net was fastened to the ground below the poles and the other side of the net was fastened by ropes to the rockets. Some nets now in use are about the same size as the one described by Hawkins et al. (1968), but with 30.5-centimeter (12-inch) mesh (stretch measure) and pulled by four rockets.

The trapping location should be prebaited and, when deer have been attracted to the site regularly, the rockets can be armed and the net attended. Bait should be placed near the center of the net and within 0.9 to 1.8 meters (3–6 feet) of the folded net edge, so that when the rockets are fired, the deer cannot react quickly enough to run out from under the net before it settles down completely. When the rockets are fired, the net is propelled over the deer and extends the full 12.2 meters (40 feet) before it drops to the ground. Seven or more deer have been caught at one time with this method. Hawkins et al. (1968) also describes a switch mechanism that can be placed at the bait so that the deer will trigger the rockets during their feeding. Although this self-triggering may be time-saving, we feel that it would be a very dangerous practice to leave an armed net unattended, since a deer or person in front of the rockets could be severely injured. The rockets usually are fired from a distant blind by wires connected to the rockets. A 12-volt battery or blasting detonator usually is used to provide the charge. The rockets also can be fired by radio control if it is not convenient to use wires (Sharp and Lokemoen 1980, Grieb and Sheldon 1956).

Whitetails feeding (top) in front of a rocket net at the instant the rockets are fired electronically. Unless the deer are between the rockets and the center of the net when the rockets are fired, they may be able to react (bottom) quickly enough to run out from under the net before it drops over them. *Photos by R. J. Hayes; courtesy of the Tennessee Wildlife Resources Agency.*

Drive Net

Drive nets may be the best means of capturing whitetails in situations where deer will not come to baited traps or drop nets, when there is insufficient time to capture them with traps, or when there is some barrier (fence or canal) that deer may be driven against which will aid in routing them into a drive net.

A net 91 meters (300 feet) long and 2.1 meters (7 feet) high was used in Georgia in the early 1950s, but only two deer were captured and the method was discontinued (Torrey 1957). Silvy et al. (1975) used a 15.2 by 4.3-meter (50 by 14-foot) drive net to capture Key deer in housing subdivisions in Florida. This net was used in an area where there were canals that helped funnel deer to the net. When deer were observed, the drive net was set perpendicular to the canal and drivers moved the deer slowly to the net. This method worked best on dark nights when the deer could not easily see the net. Beasom et al. (1980) also used a drive net to capture mule deer, elk and bighorn sheep in the West. The animals were driven into the net by helicopter, where they were physically subdued. Beasom et al. recommended that two people be stationed for every 30.5 meters (100 feet) of net so that the animals can be subdued before they work free. The investigators used 40.6-centimeter (16-inch) mesh (stretch measure) net fabricated into 30.5 by 2.1-meter (100 by 7-foot) or 121.9 by 2.7-meter (400 by 9-foot) sections that were tied together to form the desired length.

Drive Trap

Stafford et al. (1966) caught more than nine whitetails per trap-day with a drive trap in Florida. They planted 0.4–1.2-hectare (1–3-acre) food patches of oats and ryegrass, and put the trap in a portion of the field. Wings made of either wire or netting extended outward from the trap. When deer entered the field to feed, drivers slowly moved them along the wings into the trap. The trap itself was similar to a corral trap and closed manually with a long trip wire.

Drive traps have been used at the edges of feeding fields to capture white-tailed deer in Florida. The wings of the traps are made either of fence wire (left) or netting (right). *Photos by Lovett Williams; courtesy of the Florida Game and Fresh Water Fish Commission.*

Net Gun

A gun that shoots a triangular (equilateral) net, similar to that described by Mechlin and Shaiffer (1980) for capturing waterfowl, has been used to capture red deer in New Zealand. The net (commercially available in the United States) is nylon, measuring 7.5 meters (25 feet) on a side and is shot by an operator from a helicopter after a deer is hazed into an open position. White-tailed deer usually are in cover too dense for this method to be successful, but under open range conditions, such as prairies and brushland, a net gun may be effective.

Snares

The foot snare, described by Ashcraft and Reese (1957), for capturing mule deer has not been used extensively to capture whitetails (Figure 118). Hawkins et al. (1967) tried foot snares in Illinois and caught only one deer in 132 snare nights. That animal broke its leg and

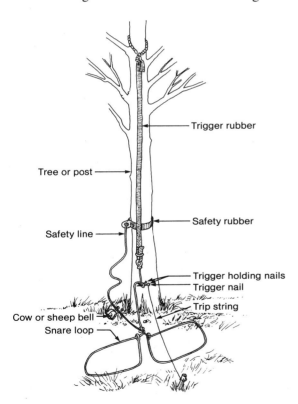

Figure 118. The foot snare has been employed successfully to capture mule deer, but has not been used extensively with whitetails (redrawn from Ashcraft and Reese 1957).

had to be killed. Neck snares similar to that used by Mossman et al. (1963) were tried in 1964 at the Cedar Creek Natural History Area in Minnesota. The first animal caught died in the snare, so further use was discontinued.

Trigger Mechanisms

Ruff (1938) described two types of trigger mechanisms for the Pisgah trap. One method used disengaging levers to hold up the door; the other used a rope and pulley. A wire stretched across the inside of the trap was tripped by feeding deer.

Webb (1943) developed a trigger device for the Stephenson trap that employed a trip wire to set off a number-1 steel trap that released the ropes holding up both doors.

Clover (1954) used a rat trap in a manner similar to the use of a steel trap by Webb (1943) for the release of drop gates on his trap.

In most cases, a trip wire or thin cord was stretched across the trap 15 to 30 centimeters (6–12 inches) above the trap floor. Findlay et al. (1946) had trouble with rabbits tripping the deer traps, so they raised the trip wire. They felt, however, that when the wire was much above 20 centimeters (8 inches), the deer were more reluctant to enter the trap. In double-door traps, the trip wire should be in the middle of the trap. And in single-door traps, this wire should be nearer the back, so that when tripped, the door can drop behind the deer. In some cases a large deer will stretch to reach the bait and back out of the trap, causing the gate to drop on the animal's back.

Clover (1956) described the trigger of his single-door trap as a trip wire connecting a rat trap on top of the trap and a piece of salt placed on a block of wood on the trap floor. The piece of salt was of sufficient weight to trip the rat trap. When a deer fed on the bait, it eventually would knock the salt off the block of wood, which then tripped the rat trap and released the door.

Roper et al. (1971) did not have adequate success with the rat-trap trigger for the Clover trap, and so developed a trip wire with a pin that fit into two parallel loops made of wire fastened to the bottom bar of the trap. A loop in the cord or wire that held up the door was held in place between the two loops of wire by the pin attached to the trip wire. The pin was held in place by the upward pressure of

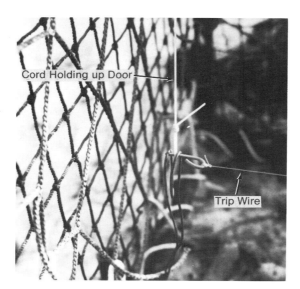

A simple triggering mechanism for a Clover trap is a double loop of stiff wire (fastened to the bottom bar of the trap), against which a pin on the trip wire can be held by the cord holding up the door. When a deer presses against the trip wire, the pin disengages from the double loop and cord, thus releasing the door or gate, which drops down. *Photo by Chris Wozencraft; courtesy of the University of Wisconsin/Madison Department of Wildlife Ecology.*

the cord holding up the door. When a deer hit the trip string it would pull the pin from between the two wire loops and release the loop on the cord holding the door. This mechanism was similar to what Ruff (1938) called the "metal-bar trigger." In our Wisconsin deer studies, we used the Roper technique with great success. The trip string across the trap was made of light monofilament line and the line holding the drop gate was string or a heavy monofilament. Monofilament was less affected by damp weather than was rope or cord, and less likely to be kinked than wire was.

CAPTURE AND HANDLING METHODS

Placement of Traps

Traps should be placed in areas where they will receive high exposure to deer. This can be along well-used trails or in feeding areas. Roper et al. (1971) felt the opening of a trap should face in the direction from which deer are likely to approach. Baiting an area around traps prior to trapping can increase catches greatly. McBeath (1941) described a man on snowshoes making a trail out 1.6 kilometers (1 mile) from the trapping area. Handfuls of hay were placed every 2.5 to 3 meters (8–10 feet) along this trail to lure deer to the trap site.

If trapping is done in an area where there are cattle, a double- or triple-strand fence may have to be built around the trap to keep cattle out but to allow deer to enter. The bottom strand should be high enough to allow deer to crawl under.

Traps should be placed out of sight of well-used roads so that passersby will not stop and disturb trapped animals or any deer about to enter the trap. It is natural for people to look at a deer in a trap if they happen to see one. A visit to a trap with a deer in it puts extra stress on the deer. There is no need to camouflage a trap, since deer will become accustomed to it no matter how conspicuous it is.

Traps should be on as level ground as possible so that the doors do not bind. They should be positioned so there are no obstructions in front of the door. When a deer is released from a trap, it often leaves at full speed. If there is any exit obstruction, the deer may run into it and be injured or killed.

Clover (1954) recommended cleaning the trap after every capture, and if the soil in the trap gets fouled with urine, the trap should be moved at least 1.8 meters (6 feet) from the original trapping site. Roper et al. (1971) advised moving traps when recaptures comprised 25 percent or more of the total catch.

Fawn Capture

Fawns are captured most easily during their first week of life. During this period they tend to stay motionless, because they cannot run fast enough to escape predators. Fawns can be captured rather easily either by hand or with a large fish net until they are about seven days old. After this age they usually will attempt to escape and are fast enough to elude capture by man. Trained dogs have been used to capture fawns up to three weeks of age (Diem 1954). Diem described a call that he would blow when a mule deer doe was observed. If the doe had a fawn, she was reluctant to leave the area; if no fawn was present, the doe would flee.

Downing and McGinnes (1969) observed that a whitetail doe with a very young fawn remained alone near her fawn and looked ner-

During their first week of life, fawns are not fast enough to escape predators, so remain motionless most of the time. Although this inactivity sometimes makes them difficult to locate, once found they are easily captured and handled for research and management purposes. There is no good evidence to indicate that the use of rubber gloves—or other methods to prevent human odor from getting on the fawn—helps prevent abandonment, although in the authors' experience, fawn abandonment by does has not been a serious problem anyway. *Top photo by H. L. Shantz; courtesy of the U. S. Forest Service. Bottom photo courtesy of the New Jersey Division of Fish, Game and Wildlife.*

After a week of age, whitetail fawns have the speed and agility to elude human captors. Until the animal is about one month old, the use of trained dogs or a fast and noisy approach by people may cause a fawn to "freeze" or drop into a hiding position, such that it can be caught with a net. Once captured fawns are relatively easy to restrain. *Top photo by John Pearce and B. C. Park; courtesy of the U. S. Forest Service. Bottom photo by Don Wooldridge; courtesy of the Missouri Department of Conservation.*

vously in its direction several times a minute. Because does nurse newborn fawns frequently, Downing and McGinnes recommended concentrating search efforts on single does and remaining in a vehicle until the fawn was sighted. Once a fawn was sighted the observer would make a noisy, fast approach. This usually caused the fawn to drop to the ground and hide.

In Wisconsin, we have captured more than 30 fawns during recent white-tailed deer studies. In one area, where spring deer densities probably were 23 to 29 per square kilometer (60–101 per square mile), a student captured eight fawns by hand between 27 May and 2 June by walking field edges adjacent to woods. In areas where spring deer densities were 4 to 6 per square kilometer (10.4–15.5 per square mile), we have achieved capture success by having groups of people systematically search what we considered good fawning areas. These were areas of dense grass or other herbaceous vegetation located within 46 meters (50 yards) of woody cover.

In areas where deer densities are less than 2 per square kilometer (5 per square mile), success in capturing fawns can be increased greatly if a number of does can be tagged with radio transmitters during winter, when they are concentrated and easier to catch. These does then can be observed daily during the fawning period in hopes of detecting a decrease in body size or a change in behavior indicating that fawns have been dropped. Such observations can provide clues to the type of fawning sites that can be expected to be used by other does (unmarked) in similar low-density habitat. An Iowa telemetry study found that pregnant does greatly reduce their movements about the time fawns are born (C. N. Huegel personal communication:1982). The area of reduced movement then can be searched intensively for the fawn or fawns. Our telemetry data indicate that a doe usually will be within 100 meters (330 feet) of her fawn. Twin or triplet fawns also may be separated by as much as 100 meters (330 feet).

Baits

Baits that are most successful for trapping deer vary with areas and times of year. Apples were found to be the best bait by Ruff (1938) in North Carolina. Corn (both ear and shelled) was used in Illinois (Montgomery and Hawkins 1967, Hawkins et al. 1967). Alfalfa and white cedar were most successful for Olson (1938) in Minnesota. During the summer in New York, salt was most productive for attracting whitetails (Mattfeld et al. 1972). In Florida, Stafford et al. (1966) tried corn, apples, hay, sweet potatoes and many vegetables with little success during winter trapping. The only green leafy native plant that attracted the Florida deer was mistletoe. But during this period deer had an affinity for well-fertilized oats, wheat, rye and summer legumes, especially peas. Hahn and Taylor (1950) used cottonseed cake and mistletoe as bait in Texas. Ear corn works well during the winter months in southern Wisconsin's agricultural areas, and white cedar or hemlock attracts best in northern Wisconsin's mixed forests, where deer pay little attention to ear corn.

Scarcity of natural foods caused by deep snow, drought or other factors will increase trapping success greatly. Consequently, a whitetail trapping program that fails in one year may be a huge success the next.

Shelled corn is set out to lure whitetails to a trapping site. *Photo by R. J. Hayes; courtesy of the Tennessee Wildlife Resources Agency.*

Removal of Deer from Traps

When a deer is in a trap, all equipment needed for removing or tagging the deer should be assembled and organized before the trap is approached. The approach should be made on foot and with as little noise as possible in order to minimize stress on the deer. The removal of a whitetail should be as fast as possible so the animal will not injure itself fighting the trap.

If a snowmobile or other noise-producing vehicle is used in deer-trapping, it should be parked about 40 to 50 meters (130–165 feet) from the trapping site, and the trap should be approached on foot. At the Cedar Creek Natural History Area in Minnesota, several injuries to trapped whitetails resulted when the animals were unduly alarmed as a snowmobile was driven alongside.

Removing deer from Stephenson or similar wooden box traps has been accomplished by ushering the deer into a smaller crate for tagging or transport. In some Stephenson traps, a sliding door the size of the crate opening was built into one of the drop gates. The tagging crate was moved against this door and the small door opened. Since the carrying crate usually is not as lightproof as the trap, the deer generally will move toward the light in the crate.

When releasing a whitetail from a Stephenson trap for handling purposes, the drop gate on the end where the net has been readied needs merely to be opened. The deer invariably will dash from the confines into the catch net. *Photo by Dean Tvedt; courtesy of the Wisconsin Department of Natural Resources.*

Whitetails sometimes are removed from Stephenson traps by running them into a carrying crate. The crate's small size and removable partition permit tagging and transporting of deer with relative ease and minimum potential of injury to the deer or handlers. *Photo courtesy of the Wisconsin Department of Natural Resources.*

Findlay et al. (1946) described a carrying crate 1.2 meters (4 feet) long, 46 centimeters (18 inches) wide and 91 centimeters (36 inches) high. This crate had a sliding door on each end, plus a sliding door 30 centimeters (12 inches) from one end to confine smaller deer. It had a hinged opening on the top of one end so that the head of the deer could be held for tagging purposes. Mikula (1955) also identified a handling crate of similar dimensions.

Removal from the Clover trap. Clover (1954) recommended a catch net for removing deer from the Clover trap. A rope woven around the edges of this net worked as a purse string to close the net around the deer. The catch net was hung on two hooks at the top of the trap and centered over the door; the purse string was attached to the trap, and the door opened. A person then could walk to the back of the trap, causing the deer to bolt to the other end, hitting the catch net, which closed around it. A similar net was used in Wisconsin to remove deer from Stephenson traps. Clover (1956) indicated that it should take no more than 10 seconds from the time the trappers get to the trap until the deer is in the net. If it takes longer than this, deer can be injured, because they constantly bolt against the side and ends of the trap when the handlers are trying to set up for removal.

A catch net is held in front of the single drop gate of a Clover trap. A person in the back of the trap scares the deer into the net. To assure that the procedure is accomplished quickly and the animal subdued immediately, this is a three-man operation, even for small whitetails. *Photo by Chris Wozencraft; courtesy of the University of Wisconsin/Madison Department of Wildlife Ecology.*

Sparrowe and Springer (1970) found that rather than using a catch net to remove deer from a Clover trap, it was easier to unfasten the cross wires that keep the trap from col-

lapsing and fold the trap side by side onto the deer. The deer then could be put on its side on the ground and tagged through the mesh netting. They also recommended using 15 by 15-centimeter (6 by 6-inch) mesh (stretch measured) rather than the 11.4 by 11.4-centimeter (4.5 by 4.5-inch) mesh recommended by Clover (1954), so that the deer could be tagged through the netting. In our Wisconsin studies, we had problems using a larger-mesh netting because fawns would stick their heads through the netting, and in one case a fawn got its head stuck by putting its head out through one opening in the mesh and back in another. We recommend using a smaller-size mesh, even though it requires removing the deer from the trap for tagging.

McCullough (1975) found that many deer escaped when he used the catch net recommended by Clover (1954). His success increased if he had two ends to the "purse strings," so the catch net would close more rapidly than it would if there were only one string. However, McCullough still lost some animals, so he modified the Clover traps so that they would fold top-to-bottom, rather than side-to-side as they were originally constructed. He then added snaps to the two front support cables so that when a deer was in the trap, he could unsnap the cables and fold the trap back on itself, with the deer underneath.

The use of catch nets with 12.7-by-12.7-centimeter (5-by-5-inch) mesh enables researchers to remove adult whitetails from Clover traps, restrain the deer adequately and tag through the netting. *Photo courtesy of the Illinois Department of Conservation.*

A number of researchers have advocated removing deer from box traps and crates (for subsequent handling, not release) by having one person grab—and hold extended—one or both of the animal's hind legs. Another person grasps the deer's antlers, neck or ears. The animal then is laid on the ground, with legs held extended. *Photo by Lovett Williams; courtesy of the Florida Game and Fresh Water Fish Commission.*

Attempts to remove deer—particularly adult bucks—from traps without the aid of a catch net or tranquilizing device may cause the animals undue stress and subject both animals and handlers to possible injury. Note that this mule deer buck's antlers have been roped—a reasonable precaution under the circumstances. *Photo courtesy of the Texas Parks and Wildlife Department.*

Roper et al. (1971) felt that the easiest way to remove deer from Clover traps was to raise the drop gate, grab a back leg, and flank the deer down. Bucks were subdued by having one man grab an antler through the net while another man reached into the trap and got hold of a back leg. With its leg held extended, the deer did not have a lot of power to kick and was less likely to get a back injury. Lightfoot and Maw (1963) also removed and handled deer from the Oregon panel trap by grabbing each animal's hind legs, wrestling it to the ground, and holding the hind legs extended while tags were attached.

Removal from drop nets or rocket nets. Deer caught in rocket nets and drop nets usually are tangled in the net mesh. If a tranquilizer is not used, a deer must be restrained physically or it may struggle and injure itself or work itself free. From our Wisconsin rocket-netting experience we found it best to have at least one person available to blindfold and hold each deer under the net. There should be two additional people to help tag and work them from under the net one at a time.

When caught in a drop net or rocket net, deer should be physically restrained until they can be worked out from under the net. Blindfolding animals captured in this manner will calm them, reduce their stress and ease handling. *Photo courtesy of the North Dakota Department of Game and Fish.*

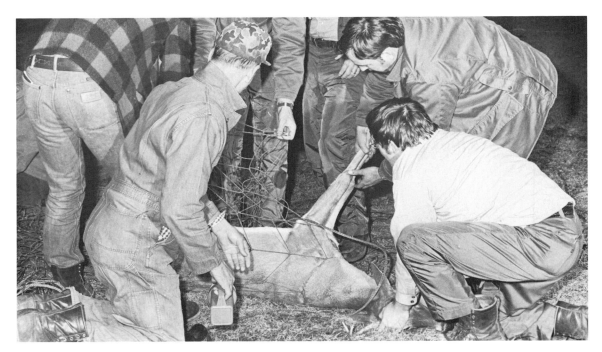

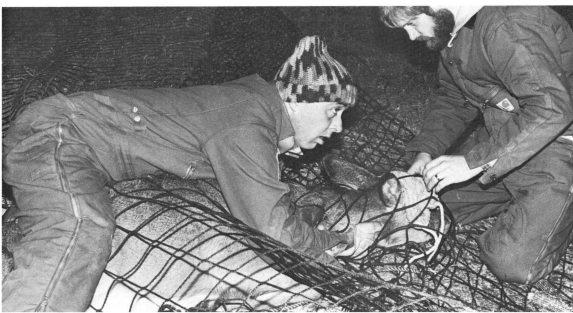

If more than one deer is caught in a rocket net, they should be untangled and processed one at a time unless a number of persons are available to assist. *Top photo courtesy of the South Carolina Wildlife and Marine Resources Department. Bottom photo courtesy of the North Dakota Department of Game and Fish.*

For moving deer to another location we put them in a carrying crate similar to those previously described. To get a deer in a crate, we place the crate on its side and then slide the deer in head first. When it is completely in, the door is closed and the crate uprighted.

In any deer-handling operation, whether a trap or net is used to capture deer, handlers should be as quiet as possible, since sudden noises will make the animal struggle.

When a whitetail is in a net or being held, it usually will struggle until exhausted or physically overpowered. Because they are larger and stronger than does, bucks are more difficult to subdue. Fawns are easiest to handle; one person can get on top of a fawn and hold it to the ground. When subduing or holding any whitetail, the handler(s) should make certain to stay away from the animal's legs. Most whitetails will bellow very loudly when being held for trapping, tagging or crating. *Photo courtesy of the North Dakota Department of Game and Fish.*

Transporting Captive Whitetails

Deer have been transported in the tagging or carrying crates used to remove deer from Stephenson box traps and also in larger crates of various sizes. Crates for individual deer make hauling cumbersome and not many deer can be hauled at one time in a pickup truck. Wood (1944) had hauling crates that were 1.8 meters (6 feet) long, 1.2 meters (4 feet) wide and 1.1 meters (3.5 feet) high, and transported 10 deer at a time in a pickup for long distances. Stafford et al. (1966) used a closed metal trailer in which he could haul 15 to 20 deer in crates, but could transport up to 30 deer in the trailer without crates. Findlay et al. (1946) carried six to seven deer in the closed back of a 0.5-ton pickup, and had a two-compartment box in the back of a 1.5-ton truck that could carry seven deer in each compartment. Deer could be held for up to four days before being transported in one of these compartments, and would readily take food and water.

Thomas et al. (1967*a*) described a rope truss for restraining a deer. We have tried this technique on two different occasions for transporting a deer, but could not restrain the animal adequately to prevent its struggling. A tranquilizer probably should be used with this technique, as suggested by Thomas et al. (1967*a*).

The antlers of large bucks may have to be sawed off in order to get these animals in crates. It also is safer to handle de-antlered bucks.

A rope truss has been used successfully to restrain captured deer, but it works most efficiently and safely in conjunction with a tranquilizer. *Photo by Tom Larson; courtesy of the University of Wisconsin/Madison Department of Wildlife Ecology.*

Whitetails can be transported in individual crates or otherwise secured, or they can be placed together in large hauling boxes. *Top photos courtesy of the Tennessee Wildlife Resources Agency. Bottom-left photo by Don Wooldridge; courtesy of the Missouri Department of Conservation. Bottom-right photo by Nancy Brower; courtesy of the North Carolina Wildlife Resources Commission.*

TRAPPING MORTALITY

Mortality of deer in traps or nets depends to great extent on the handlers' experience, the temperature, the condition of the animal, how long the deer is confined, and how rapidly it can be removed. Hawkins et al. (1967) reported mortalities for various methods of trapping deer. The corral trap had the highest mortality rate (14 percent). Other studies concur. Hawkins et al. (1967) had 42 deaths out of 302 captures in corral traps that varied from 30 to 76 meters (100–250 feet) in circumference. They had 47 captures with Stephenson traps and no mortalities. A mortality rate of 3 to 5 percent is not unusual in almost any type of trapping operation. In winter trapping in northern Wisconsin with Clover traps, we virtually eliminated mortality by checking the traps two times a day. Traps were checked between 8:00 and 9:00 in the morning and evening.

When traps were checked only in the morning, some deer entered the trap shortly thereafter and consequently were held in the confined space for almost 24 hours with only the bait for food. We believe that these were the animals found dead in our traps. Although necropsies were not performed on these deer, we suspected that death was due to exhaustion, lack of food or cold temperatures.

A technique that has been used to reduce the time an animal has to spend in a trap and also makes checking traps easier is to attach a radio transmitter to the trap door which shuts off when the door closes, thus alerting the trapper. This technique has been used with success on moose traps in Alberta and on deer traps in Wisconsin.

Another deer mortality factor that trappers should be aware of results from a disease called "capture myopathy." Mortality from this disease usually occurs 7 to 14 days after release and may occur as late as 30 days after release.

Chalmers and Barrett (1982) summarized the current information on capture myopathy. The disease is not fully understood, but seems to result from systemic acidosis caused by a build-up of lactic acid in the muscle. All of the causes of this disease are not known, but are believed to be associated with the vigorous use of all muscles by deer during their pursuit, capture, restraint and transport.

Chalmers and Barrett (1982:92) made the following recommendations with regard to trapping animals: ". . . every effort should be made to select trapping and translocation procedures that (1) do not exhaust animals, (2) reduce heat stress, (3) minimize direct contact with humans, and (4) shorten the period of captivity." They also pointed out that "The increased use of telemetry devices to monitor activities of animals following capture and release will, in all probability, provide new insights into capture-related mortalities."

During the 1972 and 1973 winters in southern Wisconsin, 11 of 42 radio-tagged does died from causes that could not be explained (O'Brien 1976). At the same time, only 1 of 39 radio-tagged does captured in northern Wisconsin died. The main difference between the captures of these two groups was that the southern Wisconsin whitetails were trapped in rocket nets while the northern Wisconsin deer were caught in Clover traps. It now appears that these mortalities were caused by capture myopathy.

Prolonged exertion against an immovable force, such as occurs when a deer is entangled in a net, probably is more likely to cause death due to capture myopathy than are trapping methods that confine animals but don't physically constrain them. Deer captured in rocket nets by C. Huegel (personal communication: 1983) in Iowa during 1981 and 1982 experienced such postcapture mortality, and J. Teer (personal communication:1983) reported similar mortality of whitetails captured with drop nets in Texas.

Reevaluation of old telemetry data may provide new insights into this cause of mortality. If our hypothesis is correct—that prolonged exertion against an immovable force is more damaging than the other confining methods—then tying a deer up as described by Thomas et al. (1967a) or any other form of tying a deer for transport may not be advisable.

Role in Management of Trapping and Translocating Whitetails

Whitetail capture during the 1930s and 1940s was primarily to reintroduce deer into ranges they formerly occupied, with some animals trapped and tagged to obtain movement data and other ecological information. Whitetails presently occur in most suitable areas of the United States and Canada, and few reintroductions need to be made. The main reason for capturing deer in recent years has been research.

Adequate attention seldom is given to the proper method of releasing transported whitetails. Deer usually will bolt to freedom through an opening and, because their eyes may not be adjusted to the sudden light when trap doors are opened, elevated releases can result in broken legs. If possible, hauling crates should be removed from the transport vehicle prior to the release, particularly if the ground conditions are slippery. When large crates cannot be removed, the vehicle should be backed against an embankment so that the released animal can run out on a fairly level surface. The top photos show potentially hazardous releases; the bottom scenes illustrate suitable techniques. *Top-left photo by Tom Taylor; courtesy of the North Carolina Wildlife Resources Commission. Top-right photo by Don Wooldridge; courtesy of the Missouri Department of Conservation. Bottom-left photo courtesy of the Wyoming Game and Fish Department. Bottom-right photo courtesy of the Florida Game and Fresh Water Fish Commission.*

Because densities of many whitetail populations are increasing, there sometimes is need for capturing deer for removal from overpopulated habitats and where hunter harvests cannot or do not remove a sufficient number of deer. Hunting may not be a suitable tool for whitetail population control in areas with dense human populations and where safety would be a problem. In other places, antihunting pressure may necessitate removal of animals alive in order to achieve management objectives. Although all whitetail trapping and translocation operations are expensive and require biological expertise, methods described in this chapter may help identify the most efficient and practical technique for a given situation.

Chapter 40

DRUG IMMOBILIZATION METHODS

Patrick F. Scanlon
Professor
Department of Fisheries
and Wildlife Sciences
Virginia Polytechnic Institute
and State University
Blacksburg, Virginia

Peggy Brunjak
Range Technician (Former)
Bureau of Land Management
Denver, Colorado

The use of immobilizing drugs in dealing with whitetails facilitates many aspects of deer management and research, ranging from live capture of free-ranging deer to safe handling of captive deer. From the standpoint of capturing free-ranging whitetails, injected drugs offer the distinct advantage of selectivity in that specific individual deer may be sought and captured, in contrast to such capture methods as trapping, netting or driving (*see* Chapter 39). This advantage is gained at the expense of effort expended in stalking subject animals and at the risk of accidental loss of valuable individuals by injury, overdose or drug reaction. Regarding captive deer, drugs accommodate a wide range of research procedures, including surgery, blood collection, physiological monitoring, health maintenance procedures, and such activities as implantation of catheters and radio transmission units. Here, too, there are risks to valuable subject deer in many of the procedures. Furthermore, immobilizing drugs may compromise physiological data and blood chemistries, or at least render interpretation of such data considerably more complex (Wesson et al. 1979a, 1979b).

Use of immobilizing drugs can be quite costly, particularly when the effort is to capture wild deer. Not only are the immobilizing equipment and many of the drugs expensive, but consid-erable time and logistical support must be invested. Such undertakings must conform to activity patterns of deer for best results.

While remotely injected immobilizing drugs have long been used by aboriginals, their modern development for use in wildlife management in North America occurred after World War II. Since then, significant improvements in the development of drugs have taken place, as have refinements of injection devices and projecting equipment. Further advances in the development of immobilizing drugs are likely; certainly, the ideal drug has yet to be developed, and progress still can be made with combinations of existing drugs. Additional improvements in injecting devices also are possible, particularly if lower-volume drugs are developed, and also in terms of greater accuracy of delivery.

The greatest need for continued development in drug immobilization methods and equipment seems to lie in delivery systems, and the problems here are formidable. The relatively large size of projectiles containing drugs necessarily limits the effective range of projection equipment. To an extent, this can be compensated for by increasing the projectile velocity and/or trajectory arc. Attempts to increase distances at which deer can be injected successfully must involve consideration of po-

Blood sampling is one procedure of biological and physiological data collection that can be facilitated by drug immobilization without sacrificing animals. The operator shown here is careful to avoid damaging the soft velvet antlers of the anesthetized standing buck. *Photo by Don Thompson; courtesy of the Wisconsin Department of Natural Resources.*

tential adverse aspects of projectile impact, since the target animal must absorb the momentum of the projectile while being injected. An additional risk is that long-distance shooting minimizes the prospect of accuracy—hitting appropriate areas on the animal. Advances in this area too are needed and possible, and may come about through the development of smaller and more ballistically reliable projectiles.

WHITETAILS AS IMMOBILIZATION SUBJECTS

An ideal subject animal for drug immobilization should:
1. be readily approachable;
2. be tolerant of a wide dose range of the drug of choice;
3. be of a species, population or cohort on which drugs have been used safely;
4. have no adverse reactions to the drug of choice;
5. have a short flight distance, if any, after an immobilization attempt;
6. be suitable for age and body-weight estimation and for sex identification prior to shooting;
7. have large muscle masses for injection sites;
8. have relatively predictable behavior; and
9. require minimal aftercare.

White-tailed deer possess most of these characteristics. Considerable work has been reported on immobilizing deer of both sexes and all ages. Accordingly, much information on dosages, reactions and, to some extent, aftercare of deer has been accumulated.

The major considerations in immobilizing whitetails are (1) the type of habitats they typically occupy and (2) the need to approach subject animals within effective range of immobilizing equipment. The range of most equipment is from less than 20 meters (66 feet) to no more than about 70 meters (230 feet), depending on site and sighting conditions.

Immobilizing semiwild or wild whitetails requires stalking within close range to assure an accurate shot. Generally, the easiest approach is with a vehicle—in areas where the deer are accustomed to automobile traffic. Actual shooting necessitates an open line of fire, to prevent projectile deflection. Note that the subject animal (on right) presents an excellent target. *Photo courtesy of Harold C. "Red" Palmer.*

Approaching wild whitetails is difficult under any circumstances, and is accomplished more frequently in vehicles rather than by stalking on foot or by other means. Such approaches usually dictate that roads be available and that the deer are accustomed to vehicular traffic in the proximity. Clear shots at the deer are imperative; projectiles must not be subject to deflection by brush. Once a whitetail is hit and injected, it must remain visible to the shooter (who preferably does not have to leave the vehicle before immobilization occurs) to allow judgement of the effects of the drug on the deer and also to allow for rapid retrieval and handling of the subject animal. Few habitats occupied by white-tailed deer are devoid of obstacles or logistical problems for the biologist or his immobilizing equipment. Overcoming environmental difficulties requires careful site selection, timing, patience, shooting skill and discretion, knowledge of the immobilizing equipment's limitations, and familiarity with the behavior of the subject animal or population.

Whitetails tend to be most active at dawn, dusk and during the night. Such behavioral periodicity necessarily limits the times when immobilizing success is likely to be maximal. Nighttime attempts minimize the biologist's ability to locate and get within adequate range of subject deer, to observe the deer once injected, and to retrieve them after immobilization and observe their recovery. Late evening and early morning generally are good times for efforts to immobilize whitetails in the wild.

White-tailed deer behavior varies with weather and season of the year, and these factors bear on judgements about immobilization procedures. In windy weather, whitetails tend to be difficult to locate, very nervous and poor subjects for immobilization, since they do not "hold" well for shooting attempts and are inclined to flee after shooting. Another consideration is that wind may deflect projectiles to quite an extent. Also, deer seem to "anticipate" forthcoming weather changes and modify their feeding and travel behavior, thereby frustrating some planned immobilization attempts.

Seasonality tends to be a factor in whitetail behavior in that it influences population size and/or concentration. Immobilization of a particular deer within a group is complicated by the fact that the group's alertness is elevated in proportion to the number of individuals it contains; the larger the group, the more difficult it is to approach *any* individual within it. Also, the difficulty of keeping watch on an immobilized deer is compounded by the group alarm and movement. Other effects of seasonality relate to changes in food-intake patterns, energy expenditures and consequent impact on physical condition. This has been shown to be a factor in whitetail immobilization attempts using succinylcholine chloride (Jacobsen et al. 1976). Hypothermia in cold weather is likely to be a major factor in aftercare of deer immobilized by xylazine hydrochloride (Gibson et al. 1982).

Whitetails possess large muscle masses suitable for injection, and the safest injection site is the hindquarter muscles. This is accomplished best by shooting the deer when it is standing at right angles (broadside) to the shooter's position. Shots at running deer should be avoided. Injection in the hindquarter muscles minimizes risk of bone breakage or puncture of vital organs. Because immobilization projectiles are of limited accuracy, risk of bone fracture or injection of drugs into body cavities exists with shots into other body areas, including lighter muscle masses. Thomas and Marburger (1964) reported relatively high rates of death and injury with injections into the thoracic region.

From the standpoint of aftercare, working with white-tailed deer has several advantages. They are less prone to ruminal tympany (bloat) than other ruminants. They are sufficiently small that simple resuscitation attempts are possible. Capture myopathy syndrome reported for other large animals appears to be rare (*see* Chapter 39). However, there are aspects of adverse intraspecific behavior (which presumably are antagonistic) that warrant further consideration relative to aftercare of immobilized deer (*see* Schurholtz 1974, Scanlon et al. 1977).

Equipment

Aside from drugs, the major pieces of immobilizing equipment consist of projecting devices and injecting devices.

Projecting devices. Projecting devices include longbows, crossbows, blowguns, and gas-powered and powder-charged guns. Pole syringes are included here, but other projecting devices of mainly historic significance will not be discussed.

Guns of whatever basic design generally have rifled barrels to improve accuracy. Gas-powered guns include both pistols and rifles. However, both have limited range. In addition, considerable inconsistency results from variations in gas pressure over the life of the CO_2 cartridges and especially in relation to air temperature and altitude (Rausch and Ritcey 1961, Jones 1976).

Powder-charged guns tend to give more consistent results, but because they generally are of the black powder variety, considerable maintenance of the guns is necessary. The variation in range is considerable, and is influenced by projectile weight and size of the powder charge. With heavy syringes, the effective range generally is 25 to 40 meters (82–130 feet). With the powder-injecting darts described by Liscinsky et al. (1969), the range can be about 60 meters (195 feet). Shooting at distances of more than 50 meters (165 feet) is discouraged because of difficulties in hitting whitetails in target muscle masses.

Longbows have been used to deliver specialized immobilization projectiles. Given the usual need to stalk subject whitetails and the value of stalking by vehicle, limitations on the use of longbows are apparent. Also, projectile weight (arrow plus injecting device) is considerable, and momentum is high at the time of impact. It is difficult to shoot such a projectile accurately with a longbow and control the impact so as not to injure the animal.

Crossbows may be somewhat more accurate than longbows, but otherwise have similar disadvantages, including difficulty of calibration, frayed strings and general awkwardness for use from a vehicle. Projectile deflection is an important constraint with any type of bow.

Blowguns are most useful in pen situations where "shooting" is not at long range. Long-range shooting with blowguns is possible, but excessively long blowguns are cumbersome and require considerable skill. At least one manufacturer has modified a blowpipe system to a type of rifle employing compressed air or CO_2 for propulsion. However, the effective range is likely to be 30 meters (100 feet) or less.

Pole syringes are useful for applying drugs to deer in pens or traps.

Injecting devices. Injecting devices have been undergoing considerable modification over time. They initially were designed to deliver dried drugs on pointed projectiles. The later, more sophisticated devices were intended to inject liquid drugs, and these have been the subject of much development. Essentially, devices to inject liquid drugs must be ballistically capable of reaching the subject deer, and must retain the drug until the deer is hit and inject the deer after impact.

Within many of the early syringes, drugs were retained in a chamber in front of some type of injecting device. In these types the hypodermic needle was "open" and could permit loss of the drug. On impact, the injecting device was activated by exerting centrifugal force or by pressure from gas generated by a chemical reaction or an explosion.

More recent designs employ a "closed" hypodermic needle with compressed gas or air in a separate chamber behind the one containing the drug (*see* Warren et al. 1979, Lochmiller and Grant 1983). Injection causes a slide to open a side-port in the needle, and the gas pressure causes the drug to inject. A dart described by Liscinsky et al. (1969) injects powdered succinylcholine chloride by centrifugal force, with the needle continuing its travel, thereby depositing the powder, and the dart housing being stopped by contact with the animal's skin.

Hypodermic needles at the end of projectile syringes vary. Some are a specially modified, exchangeable part of the syringe; others are modifications of disposable, detachable hypodermic needles. Many modern injecting devices have side-ports in the needle shaft, with the needle end being sealed. The side-port is closed by a movable sleeve that seals it when the syringe is pressurized, and which slides along the needle shaft during penetration of the skin. The port is thus opened and the liquid injected. Sections of liquid silicone rubber expressed from tubes and allowed to harden in long cylindrical shapes may be used as sleeves.

Overall length of needles is important (1) to minimize excessive penetration and (2) ensure satisfactory injection under all pelage conditions. Generally, 16 gauge, 3.8-centimeter (1.5-inch) needles have proved satisfactory for use with white-tailed deer. Positioning of the side-port should be well forward on such a needle and allow for injection at a depth of 2.5 centimeters (1 inch). Winter coats of white-tailed deer may interfere with depth of penetration, particularly with projectiles delivered with little force. Positioning of side-ports and the overall length of conventional needles warrant attention during such conditions.

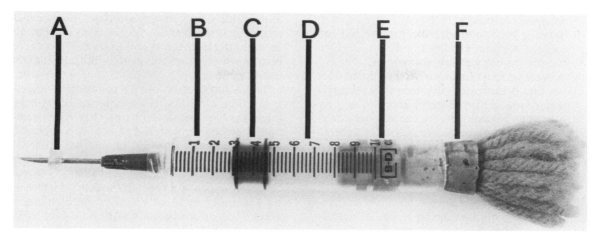

A syringe dart for immobilizing white-tailed deer, featuring (a) rubber needle-sleeve occluding side-port or lateral hole, (b) drug solution chamber, (c) mobile plunger, (d) pressurized chamber, (e) fixed rubber stopper, and (f) fletching cork (from Warren et al. 1979). *Photo courtesy of Roy L. Kirkpatrick.*

Barbs may be used on needles to cause the syringe unit to stay attached to the injected deer. This facilitates recovery of the syringe. However, if the deer fails to become immobilized or recovers before relocation, the barb-attached syringe may create a problem for the animal. Also, barbs may increase the amount of tissue damage at the injection site if removal is difficult. Typically, such barbs are attachments to or extrusions of the needle shaft metal. One variation is a beadlike swelling on the needle shaft. A possible value of using a barbed needle to keep the syringe attached to a deer involves the use of the radio-transmitter-equipped syringe described by Lovett and Hill (1977). Radio signals allow prompt recovery of immobilized deer, especially in densely vegetated areas.

Some form of fletching generally is used to improve the accuracy of syringe projectiles. A plug of fiber streamers often is added to the syringe unit. One manufacturer has fabricated a portion of the plastic unit such that it expands upon emerging from the gun barrel and provides a fletching effect.

Immobilizing Drugs

An ideal drug for immobilizing white-tailed deer should:
1. be chemically stable;
2. be readily soluble;
3. be effective in small doses;
4. be effective with intramuscular injections;

Dart syringes may remain attached after impact and injection. Barbs on the hypodermic needles promote their attachment. Although such barbs may result in some tissue damage, they usually enable the operator to identify the hit location readily and recover the syringe once the deer is immobilized. *Photo by Don Wooldridge; courtesy of the Missouri Department of Conservation.*

5. be quick acting;
6. have a wide tolerance limit (allow for overdose without fatality;
7. be reversible with an antagonist;
8. have a record of use with white-tailed deer so that doses/rates, reaction times, recovery times, etc., are known;
9. not present problems for future consumers (predators, man, scavengers) of treated deer;
10. have known effects on man;
11. cause no adverse reactions, pain or infection;
12. be relatively inexpensive;
13. be readily obtainable;
14. not be attractive for human abuse; and
15. not be restricted for the proposed use.

In addition, the pharmacological and physiological effects on white-tailed deer of the drug of choice should be well-known and documented through research prior to its use as a management aid.

Drugs possessing all the desirable features listed above do not exist. In fact, it is doubtful even if combinations of available drugs provide all of the ideal features. The choice of drug or drug combination for use with white-tailed deer should be dictated by the research or management objective(s). These may range from tranquilization—to facilitate handling of captive deer—to complete immobilization of wild or captive deer, to production of analgesia (such as relief from pain) or surgical anesthesia.

In the past, several drugs have been used extensively with white-tailed deer, including succinylcholine chloride, etorphine hydrochloride, xylazine hydrochloride, phencyclidine hydrochloride, and diazepan.

Succinylcholine chloride (Sucostrin, Anectine). This drug is a muscle-immobilizing agent without analgesic or anesthetic properties, and has been used quite extensively with white-tailed deer. It acts by inhibiting the action of acetylcholinesterase, with the result that acetylcholine accumulates at the myoneural junctions, causing their depolarization. Loss of control of the skeletal muscles results in an injected animal's inability to stand and in immobilization. Advantages of the drug include relatively fast action without excitation of the subject. Recovery also is rapid. Several disadvantages include a narrow tolerance range (that is, the margin of difference between effective and lethal doses), and considerable overlap between effective and ineffective dosage ranges and between effective and lethal doses. Further disadvantages are that dosage depends on age and on seasonal changes in condition of deer, there is no antidote, and the drug is not chemically stable in solution.

There is controversy as to whether succinylcholine chloride causes alarm and pain on injection. Speculative claims that pain is induced are unverified and of anthropomorphic origin, but have resulted in restricted use of the drug in some instances.

This drug is used as a liquid solution in syringes or in powder form in the darts described by Liscinsky et al. (1969). The latter method allows use at considerable distance—up to 70 meters (230 feet). In powder form, effective dosage ranges are 0.8 to 0.26 milligrams per kilogram (Wesson et al. 1974). Slightly lower dosages for solutions of succinylcholine chloride are effective, although fawns require slightly higher doses than do adult whitetails.

Mild overdosing with the drug results in paralysis of the diaphragm and inability to breathe. Resuscitation with air or oxygen is possible, as discussed later. Mortality of deer can be high—up to 10 percent (Wesson et al. 1974)—when using succinylcholine chloride in powder form under field conditions.

Etorphine hydrochloride (M-99). This drug is related chemically to morphine and is subject to strict legal control. It also is quite expensive. Use with white-tailed deer seems limited, possibly because of those constraints. The few reports in the literature dealing with its use on cervid species usually are concerned with combinations of etorphine plus tranquilizers. Tranquilizers are deemed necessary to overcome problems of excitation due to injection of etorphine. Etorphine hydrochloride has analgesic properties and a wide safety margin. It also has an antagonist—diphrenorphine (M50-50)—the use of which results in quick reversal. The use of diphrenorphine with white-tailed deer has not received extensive comment in the literature, particularly in cases where tranquilizers were given in addition to etorphine. Doses of 5 to 6 milligrams of etorphine per deer have been used successfully to immobilize white-tailed deer (Woolf 1970), as was etorphine in combination with xylazine hydrochloride (Presnell et al. 1973).

Xylazine hydrochloride (Rompun). This is a nonnarcotic drug with sedative, analgesic and muscle-relaxing properties, and has been used successfully for immobilization of white-tailed

Sedative drugs allow handlers to approach an injected deer. Sometimes the animal will continue to stand, so the immobilization effects must be gauged by symptoms other than collapse. Note the hit location in the muscle mass of the whitetail's hindquarter. *Photo by Don Thompson; courtesy of the Wisconsin Department of Natural Resources.*

deer (Roughton 1975, Mautz et al. 1980, Gibson et al. 1982). The degrees of sedation and analgesia, as well as induction and recovery times, seem dose-dependent in white-tailed deer (Gibson et al. 1982). Immobilization of deer typically occurs within 10 minutes of injection. Xylazine has a minimal effect on several important blood characteristics and is particularly well-suited for light sedation and restraint of captive deer. Its disadvantages are that heavy doses result in prolonged immobilization, potentially inducing hypothermia, and deer keep their eyes open during immobilization and, thereby, are exposed to injury (Gibson et al. 1982). Doses of 0.5 milligram per kilogram produce a sedative effect and allow easy restraint of captive deer. Immobilization is effective with doses of 1.0 to 2.0 milligrams per kilogram.

Phencyclidine hydrochloride (Sernylan). This drug has analgesic and anesthetic properties, depending on the dosage given, and its use on whitetails has been reported by Seal et al. (1972*a*) and Wesson et al. (1979*a*). Induction time is short (3 to 10 minutes), and the effects may be relatively long-lasting (*see* Wesson et al. 1979*a*).

A major problem with phencyclidine hydrochloride has been its involvement in human abuse and consequent restrictions on its use.

Tranquilizers facilitate safe handling of trapped or captive whitetails and reduce the potential of injury to the deer. Delivery (injection) of drugs may be accomplished by manually operated syringe in cases such as this net-trapping program. *Photo by Reagan Bradshaw; courtesy of the Texas Parks and Wildlife Department.*

This has limited its potential use with wildlife, even though phencyclidine has the important advantage of minimal effect on blood characteristics (Wesson et al. 1979*a*, 1979*b*). An analog of phencyclidine, ketamine hydrochloride (Vetelar), has been proposed as a substitute. However, it is of lower potency and requires relatively high-volume injections. Ketamine's potential for use with deer is limited accordingly, despite its value with other wild species.

Diazepan (Trunimul or Valium). Diazepan, as an oral tranquilizer mixed with grain, was used with some success in the capture of white-tailed deer (Murry and Dennett 1963, Murry 1965, Montgomery and Hawkins 1967, Thomas et al. 1967*b*). However, the drug is no longer available for immobilizing deer.

Other drugs. The development of drugs for immobilizing white-tailed deer has involved experimental use of many compounds, including gallemine triethiodide, nicotine and strychnine. All have major limitations.

AFTERCARE AND SAFETY

As powerful chemical agents, immobilizing drugs pose significant potential hazards to the deer on which they are used. Overdose is perhaps the greatest danger, followed closely by adverse side-effects. Safe immobilization requires careful planning and scheduling of the capture operation, precise coordination of participants, and familiarity with the subject animals' behavioral and physiological reactions and the treatment(s) thereof. In sum, immobilization should not be undertaken, even experimentally, by the inexperienced or without the logistical resources (including manpower) to perform the task efficiently and overcome unanticipated difficulties.

Immobilizing Procedure

The following are recommended steps or precautions for conducting drug immobilization of white-tailed deer safely.

1. The immobilization site should be fairly open, so that the deer can be approached within reasonable range, and, once shot, be kept in view for prompt recovery. Once the deer is immobilized the site should afford a quiet, comfortable and safe setting in which to perform the necessary handling or treatment expeditiously, and allow the animal to recover fully without undue disturbance.

2. Base the choice of drug(s) and dosage on the subject deer's scientific value (operation objective), its physiological condition and attendant risks. With orally active drugs, attention should be given to consumption amounts that can result in overdosing or underdosing. Solution of this problem is difficult, but judgement may be based most effectively on detailed observations of bait use by deer in the prebaiting period. A rapid-action drug may prevent overdosing and baiting dosages should be chosen accordingly.

3. Shoot deer only in large muscle masses to minimize injuries.

4. Avoid running shots and projectile-flight obstacles.

5. Know the interval for a second immobilization attempt after an unsuccessful first attempt (with many drugs this is not known—for succinylcholine chloride this interval is approximately 20 to 30 minutes).

6. If a barbed needle is used for injection, it should be removed carefully. The wound and/or injection site should be cleaned and dressed with antibiotic (and with fly repellent in the appropriate seasons). Administration of combiotic combats infections.

7. After use of xylazine hydrochloride, hypothermia may be a problem. This may be minimized by insulating deer from the ground and air in winter. Supplementary heat may be provided for captive whitetails.

8. Allow immobilized deer to lie in a comfortable position to prevent damage to eyes, legs and velvet antlers, and to minimize prospects for inhalation of saliva or ingesta if regurgitation results. Usually this will mean allowing the deer to lie in lateral recumbency (on its side), with protection for its eyes and free of obstructions to limb movement.

9. As recovery proceeds, the deer should be placed in sternal recumbency (on its brisket). Its head position should allow for drainage or swallowing of saliva. Secretion of saliva may be controlled by injection of atrophine.

10. As a drugged deer's eyes may remain open (such as with xylazine hydrochloride), its head should not be exposed to dust or grit;

Symptoms of immobilization prior to collapse of a drugged whitetail vary for different drugs. Operators' knowledge of these symptoms and their time intervals is essential to avoid injury to the handler or trauma for the deer. *Photo by Don Thompson; courtesy of the Wisconsin Department of Natural Resources.*

protection should be given by allowing the head to rest on a clean fabric surface or applying a clean blindfold or both. Such precautions will minimize facial injuries due to head movements during recovery, though blindfolds may be difficult to remove from a fully recovered deer.

11. Throughout recovery, vital signs should be monitored, particularly respiration when succinylcholine chloride is used. With xylazine hydrochloride, intermittent periods of apnea and hyperpnea may occur, but are not necessarily cause for alarm. In addition, check continually to assure that the deer is breathing freely.

12. Succinylcholine chloride may cause a deer to cease breathing through interruption of diaphragm function. Provision of artificial respiration sometimes is successful, provided the deer has not been overdosed. Oxygen or compressed air may be introduced gently by a tube into one nasal opening, while the mouth and other nasal openings are held closed. The effort should be directed at stimulating several deep inspirations and allowing normal expirations.

13. The subject animal should be protected during recumbency and recovery from potential attacks by predators or even conspecifics. Such attacks on cervids under the influence of xylazine hydrochloride and succinylcholine chloride have been reported by Schurholtz (1974) and Scanlon et al. (1977). The causes of these instances are not well-understood, although Schurholtz (1974) and others have speculated that immobilized animals may give off postural or pheromonal cues that elicit predator response or sexual aggression by conspecifics.

Effects of Immobilizing Drugs on Physiological Characteristics

As immobilizing drugs frequently are used in connection with physiological measurements or for collection of blood samples to determine blood chemistries, their impact on such characteristics is of particular importance. Handling and manual restraint of deer influence physiological characteristics in any event, and the drugs themselves may cause the characteristics to vary in different patterns.

After a whitetail has been immobilized and recovered and the syringe removed, the injection site should be cleaned and treated with antibiotics and, if necessary, fly repellent. Even though this deer is immobile, the operator maintains a precautionary position away from the animal's limbs. *Photo by Don Thompson, courtesy of the Wisconsin Department of Natural Resources.*

Wesson et al. (1979*a*) provided review material on the wide range of values published for some blood characteristics of white-tailed deer. Clearly, reports on such values have paid minimal attention to the effects of blood collection methods. Wesson et al. (1979*a*, 1979*b*) and others have provided abundant evidence that, in the evaluation of blood characteristics, consideration should be given to the time of sampling relative to drug application, as well as to the type of drug used. The choice of sampling time should depend on the drug involved and the blood characteristics of interest.

Safety of Operators

Because many factors influence the rate and degree of immobilization of drugged animals—including accuracy of the shot, type of drug, dosage, the animal's size and physical condition, and environmental circumstance—each situation must be approached and handled with caution. Operators have been injured by animals not fully immobilized or recovering. The best precaution against such injuries is experience—knowing danger signs and how to handle or treat the animal as expediently as possible. A team approach is best, with all participants knowing in advance what to do and anticipate, and one individual other than the operator assigned to check vital signs and watch for premature recovery and struggle.

In other cases, operators have been injected accidentally with immobilizing drugs. The weapons and projectile and injection devices can be awkward to handle, particularly in vehicles. Rifles, for example, are difficult to unload safely, and pressurized syringes may pose a loading problem. Accidental discharge can be prevented simply by not loading powder or other propellant charges before actual firing. Obviously, it is preferable to use drugs with antidotes.

Under all circumstances operators should have a contingency plan in the event of accident, including immediate transportation and radio communication capability.

Chapter 41

CARE OF CAPTIVE WHITETAILS

Roy L. Kirkpatrick
Professor of Wildlife Science
Department of Fisheries
and Wildlife Sciences
Virginia Polytechnic Institute
and State University
Blacksburg, Virginia

Patrick F. Scanlon
Professor of Wildlife Science
Department of Fisheries
and Wildlife Sciences
Virginia Polytechnic Institute
and State University
Blacksburg, Virginia

White-tailed deer often are kept in captivity for research purposes or for display to the public in zoological parks. Much of what is known about whitetails has been learned through the use and observation of captive animals.

Compared with other wild North American ungulates, white-tailed deer are fairly easy to maintain in captivity, provided that adequate facilities are available, the whitetails' nutritional requirements are recognized, and necessary precautions are taken to avoid disease, parasitism, injuries and digestive disorders. Before attempting to raise deer in captivity, one should be familiar with the federal regulations contained in the Animal Welfare Act of 1970 (PL 91-579), and relevant state and local restrictions.

HOLDING AND HANDLING FACILITIES

Facilities for keeping deer may range from small covered pens or stalls to large outdoor enclosures. In designing facilities, account should be taken of the whitetail's nervous disposition, agility and leaping ability. Pens should be constructed to minimize the possibility of injury. Sharp protrusions should be eliminated and corners avoided if possible. Alleyways should be narrow—approximately 1.1 meters

(3.6 feet). Spaces between boards and between gates and gateposts should be less than 2.5 centimeters (1 inch) to minimize the risk of broken legs. For small pens or stalls, a solid board construction is preferable to chain link or woven-wire fencing.

The deer pen facility at Virginia Polytechnic Institute and State University in Blacksburg illustrates many features desirable for an enclosure designed to segregate individual deer for research purposes. A pole-barn is covered with a galvanized roof and encloses 22 individual pens, a feed room and an office-laboratory area. Each pen is 3.7 by 7.3 meters (12 by 24 feet) in size and built on an asphalt slab that slopes to the outside. Asphalt was selected in preference to concrete because it is less slippery when wet. However, concrete is easier to clean. Individual pens are constructed of 5.1 by 15.3-centimeter (2 by 6-inch) boards to a height of 1.4 meters (4.6 feet), and topped with 1.7 meters (5.25 feet) of chain link fencing. Wooden doors, bolted on metal frames, are 1.22 meters (4 feet) wide and close the alleyway when open, thus facilitating movement of deer from pen to pen. Wooden platforms (1.4 meters by 1.4 meters by 10 centimeters: 4.6 feet by 4.6 feet by 4 inches) are provided so that the animals are not forced to lie on asphalt.

The pole-barn housing facility at Virginia Polytechnic Institute and State University is ideal for intensive research on captive whitetails. *Photo courtesy of the Virginia Polytechnic Institute and State University Department of Fisheries and Wildlife Sciences.*

A chain-link holding facility for whitetails in Texas. All building-type enclosures should have roofs that keep the stalls and deer dry and provide the animals with shade. Asphalt floors are less slippery but more difficult to clean than are concrete bases. When either surface is used, low wooden platforms should be provided, on which the deer can lie, for comfort and to prevent heat loss to the concrete or asphalt. *Photo by Jeffee Palmer; courtesy of the Texas Parks and Wildlife Department.*

Solid board is preferred over chain link or woven wire fencing for small pens or stalls used to house captive whitetails, since constructions of this material produce relatively fewer injuries when the deer are frightened and run into the sides of pens. *Photo by Roy L. Kirkpatrick.*

Woven wire with a snow fence backing also has been used for construction of small pens for holding captive whitetails. Snow fence backing provides some protection from wind and serves as a visual barrier that helps reduce incidence of frightened deer running into the walls of the facility. *Photo courtesy of Michigan Department of Natural Resources.*

Feeding and watering pails are located near doors of pens to minimize disturbance of deer by caretakers. Rubberized pails are used because they retain their form and are much more durable than metal or plastic pails. Clean water should be available to deer at all times. Water pails are provided with small inexpensive electrical heating units to prevent freezing during cold weather.

At the Houghton Lake Wildlife Research Station in Michigan, Verme and Ullrey (1972) used a 9 by 18-meter (29.5 by 59-foot) roofless pen to enclose four to six whitetails. The pens, located on natural soil, were built of woven wire with a backing of snow fence. Mud and feces were removed periodically from the soil surface and replaced with a mound of clean sand that also provided a dry area for the deer to lie down.

Where deer are confined to relatively small pens, a perimeter fence 1.5 meters (5 feet) high should be constructed at least 50 meters (165 feet) away to prevent approach by dogs and uninvited humans, as they may startle deer. Warning signs should be placed on the perimeter fence.

For enclosures 0.1 hectare (0.25 acre) or larger, woven wire or chain link fencing is adequate and should reach a height of approximately 3 meters (10 feet). Woven wire should be at least 11 gauge, otherwise it will rust and weaken within a few years. Halls et al. (1965) gave specific construction details and costs for a large enclosure.

A perimeter fence with warning signs should be constructed at least 50 meters (165 feet) from holding facilities to prevent disturbance of captive deer by unauthorized visitors and predators (principally dogs). *Photo by Roy L. Kirkpatrick.*

Larger outdoor pens for enclosing white-tailed deer can be built using woven wire fencing and should be at least 2.5 meters (8 feet) high, but preferably 3 meters (10 feet) in height. Shaded areas should be provided by leaving trees standing in the enclosure or by construction of artificial shade structures. *Photo by Roy L. Kirkpatrick.*

Special pens are needed to house newborn animals. They should be relatively small (3–6 square meters: 32.3–64.6 square feet) and have walls of plywood or be of similarly solid construction to prevent drafts. The floor and walls of these pens should be disinfected using a chlorinated or iodinated disinfectant (Wescodyne, a product of West Chemical Products, is used at Virginia Polytechnic Institute and State University). The floor should be bedded with good quality hay or straw to a depth of 7 to 10 centimeters (2.75–4 inches), and the bedding changed weekly or more often if it seems wet or soiled. If the pens are not completely enclosed, an infrared heat lamp should be suspended approximately 1 meter (3.3 feet) above the floor for use during cool (less than 15.5 degrees Celsius: 60 degrees Fahrenheit) nights and inclement weather to prevent chilling of newborn fawns.

When captive white-tailed deer are restrained and moved, great care must be taken to avoid injuries and fatalities. To restrain deer in Michigan, Verme and Ullrey (1972) drove them into a 0.6-meter (2-foot) wide chute, in front of which a nylon cargo net (10-centimeter [4-inch] mesh) was suspended. Deer entangled in the net were restrained readily by four or five handlers.

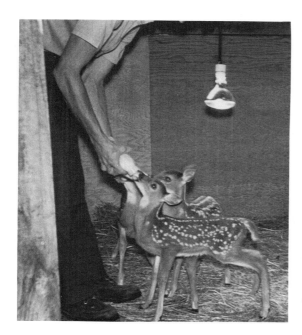

Small stalls constructed of plywood, containing a heat lamp and kept clean and disinfected are practical for housing newborn fawns that are being hand-reared. *Photo by W. A. Abler.*

At Virginia Polytechnic Institute and State University, manual pinning of deer against the wall of a pen (3.7 by 7.3 meters: 12 by 24 feet) completely enclosed with plywood has been the most satisfactory method of restraining deer with the least risk of injury. One handler enters the pen, pins the deer against the wall and, if possible, lifts the deer from the floor. Three or four other handlers secure the animal's front and rear feet and its head. The deer is then laid on its side and stretched to restrict the leverage in its legs. The head is laid on a folded burlap sack and held firmly to prevent injury. Thus restrained, the deer can be bled or treated readily for injury or illness. This method entails some risk to the handler, but it effectively restrains deer other than rutting bucks.

Immobilizing drugs are a safer restraint method for the handler, but of higher risk to the deer (Verme and Ullrey 1972, Presnell et al. 1973). Xylazine hydrochloride (0.5 milligram per kilogram) is used for immobilization at the Virginia Polytechnic Institute and State University deer pens. This makes possible the handling of deer by as few as two persons. The drug usually is administered by remote injection with a blowgun (Warren et al. 1979). Presnell et al. (1973) described the use of an etor-

phine hydrochloride/xylazine hydrochloride combination for use with deer. Succinylcholine chloride is a commonly used drug, especially in large enclosures. It usually is administered by remote injection with a dart gun, blowgun or pole-syringe. In small pens, the charges used to shoot dart guns should be minimal to avoid injury to deer. Harthoorn (1976) reviewed many aspects of the use of drugs for capture and restraint of wild animals (*see also* Chapter 40).

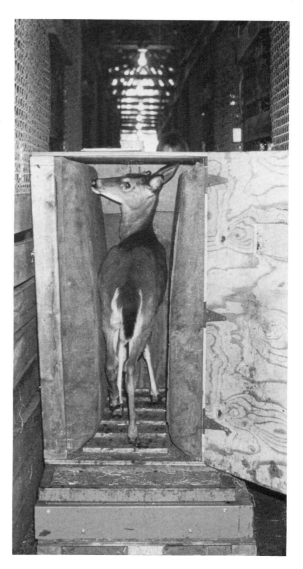

A solid box with a hinged door, placed on a platform scale in a narrow passageway, permits safe weighing of captive whitetails without any need for immobilizing drugs or more precarious physical restraint. *Photo by R. Warren.*

BREEDING, PREGNANCY AND PARTURITION IN CAPTIVITY

Almost all white-tailed deer are fertile and will reproduce in captivity. Bucks and does may be placed together in large enclosures during the breeding season, or does may be introduced to the male's pen for 10 to 15 minutes daily for estrus checking and breeding. As a rule, 1.5-year-old bucks are best for breeding in captivity because they are less aggressive, and thus less dangerous than older bucks (Severinghaus 1955*b,* Warren et al. 1978). Even when antlers are removed, an aggressive buck can severely injure a doe in a small pen by repeatedly butting her in the thoracic and abdominal areas.

Estrus in does usually is not readily apparent to humans. Some estrus does become extremely docile and exhibit an "immobility response" to humans similar to that seen in domestic swine when pressure is applied in the rump region (Warren et al. 1978). Ozoga and Verme (1975) found that pacing activity by penned does was 28 times greater one or two nights before estrus than at other stages of the estrus cycle. However, the only true criterion of estrus is a doe's acceptance of copulation with a buck.

Once pregnant, does do not require special care until two or three weeks prior to parturition. Care then should be taken to make certain that they have a clean dry area, preferably isolated from other deer, and are inspected daily for signs of illness or impending parturition. Normally, assistance at parturition is unnecessary. If delivery is restricted after the fetal membranes or feet are extruded, a veterinarian should be called to assist, unless the caretaker is experienced in assisting the parturition process in domestic animals.

FAWN REARING

If fawns are left with their captive mothers, little attention is needed from the caretaker. However, animals reared by their dams are less tractable, more excitable and more injury-prone when adults than are hand-reared fawns. Where deer are to be exposed continuously to humans in close quarters or used for intensive research (such as in physiology and nutrition studies), it is highly desirable, if not imperative, that they be hand-reared from a day or two after birth until weaning.

Successful rearing of fawns depends on regular feeding, good sanitation, prompt remedial attention to digestive disorders, and avoidance of drafts and other stressors (Murphy 1960, Long et al. 1961, Silver 1961, Trainer 1962, Reichert 1972, Verme and Ullrey 1972, Buckland et al. 1975).

Fawns may be fed nearly any type of milk, provided that feedings are regular and other management factors are adequate. Milk should be warmed to 38 degrees Celsius (100 degrees Fahrenheit) before feeding. During the first few days of a fawn's life, the addition of colostrum may increase its chance of survival. If not available from the mother, colostrum from Holstein cows may be substituted. Buckland et al. (1975) successfully fed pure Holstein colostrum to newborn fawns on their first day of life, a 50:50 mixture of colostrum and whole Holstein milk on the second day, and whole milk thereafter. Good results also have been obtained with a 50:50 mixture of whole cow's milk and water (Trainer 1962), condensed evaporated cow's milk (Murphy 1960, Silver 1961), raw milk from Jersey cows, homogenized milk, and commercially available milk replacer (Long et al. 1961). An appropriate feeding schedule is shown in Table 102.

Table 102. Feeding schedule of a captive hand-reared white-tailed deer fawn (adapted from Reichert 1972).

| Days after birth | Time of feedings | Amount per feeding | | Formula |
		Milliliters	Fluid ounces	
1–3	6 am, 10 am, 2 pm, 6 pm, 10 pm	60	2.029	Deer or Holstein colostrum
4–10	6 am, 10 am, 2 pm, 6 pm, 10 pm	120	4.058	Holstein milk
11–17	6 am, 10 am, 2 pm, 6 pm, 10 pm	180	6.087	Holstein milk
18–35	6 am, 10 am, 6 pm, 10 pm	240	8.115	Holstein milk
36–42	7 am, 1 pm, 7 pm	300	10.144	Holstein milk
43–56	7 am, 7 pm	300	10.144	Holstein milk
57–84	1 pm	300	10.144	Holstein milk
85	Weaned			

Sanitation is especially important during the first few weeks of a fawn's life. After each feeding, all bottles, nipples and accessory containers should be rinsed and placed in boiling water for at least 20 minutes, to minimize bacterial growth and contamination. During a fawn's first three to four weeks the caretaker should wipe the fawn's anal region with a moistened cloth or paper towel at least twice each day. This helps establish a normal pattern of urination and defecation, ensures the regular elimination of wastes, and provides a continual check for diarrhea. Animals infected with diarrhea should be isolated immediately in a disinfected and well-bedded pen with a heat lamp, and treated with medication. Kaopectate (The Upjohn Company) can be used alone in the same dosage recommended for human children or in the more complex mixture described by Buckland et al. (1975).

Fawns should be encouraged to eat solid food as soon as possible. At Virginia Polytechnic Institute and State University, captive fawns are moved to large pens (3.7 by 7.3 meters: 12 by 24 feet) at two to three weeks of age, and are provided with a commercial calf-developer feed (Southern States Cooperative), hay and water. Occasionally fawns must be force-fed to get them in the habit of taking solid food.

Wiping the anal region of whitetail fawns periodically with a damp cloth stimulates their defecation and urination, and calls attention to problems of diarrhea. *Photo by W. A. Abler.*

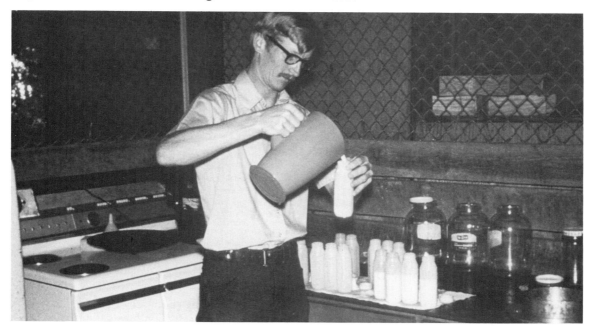

Equipment used in the feeding of hand-reared whitetail fawns should be thoroughly cleaned and sterilized, at least for the first two or three weeks, between feedings. *Photo courtesy of the Virginia Polytechnic Institute and State University Department of Fisheries and Wildlife Sciences.*

After a week on the pure calf developer, fawns are fed a 50:50 mixture of calf developer and a pelleted deer ration developed at Virginia Polytechnic Institute and State University (Table 103).

Fawns frequently eat soil if permitted to spend time in outside enclosures (Verme and Ullrey 1972, M. A. Ondik personal communication: 1977). The soil may be a source of iron. However, they seem to do well without it. For fawns kept on pavement, Verme and Ullrey (1972) suggest two 2.5 milliliters (0.0845 fluid ounce) intramuscular injections of Armidexan 100 (Bradley Products Incorporated, Chicago, Illinois) to prevent iron deficiency.

FEEDING CAPTIVE WHITETAILS

Deer can be fed commercially prepared rations that commonly are used in domestic animal feeding. For general purposes, rations containing 13 to 17 percent protein are suggested (Verme and Ullrey 1972). While 17 percent protein is in excess of requirements of nonlactating adult animals, it is sufficient for meeting requirements of young growing animals and lactating does. This protein level often is standard for feeding captive deer in research laboratories.

Deer will eat to satisfy energy requirements (Amman et al. 1973), and if they are given highly palatable and digestible feed, their energy needs are met easily by most commercially formulated rations. Commercially available vitamin and mineral supplements used in domestic ruminant nutrition seem adequate for use in deer rations. Salt can be included in the rations or made available in block or loose form. Since food consumption by whitetails varies widely throughout the year, it is imperative that rations be offered *ad libitum*. Sample rations used at Virginia Polytechnic Institute and State University and Michigan State University are shown in tables 103 and 104, respectively.

Deer also can be maintained on good-quality mixed grass/legume hay and oats or corn if simpler rations are desired. Supplements of dicalcium phosphate, trace mineralized salt and possibly a vitamin premix should be added.

HEALTH PROBLEMS

Captive whitetails are particularly vulnerable to injuries and digestive disorders. Injuries are difficult to treat, as restraint of the animal

Table 103. A sample ration for captive white-tailed deer fawns, used at Virginia Polytechnic Institute and State University, Blacksburg, Virginia.

Ingredient	Percentage	Kilocalories per kilogram
Alfalfa meal	17.0	
Soybean oil meal	10.0	
Corn	49.8	
Ground rice hulls	10.0	
Molasses	10.0	
Mineral salt	1.5	
Defluorinated rock phosphate	0.7	
Dairy Supplement Vitamin Package[a]	1.0	
Crude protein	13.0	
Digestible energy		3,043

[a]Sulphur = 1.4 percent, magnesium = 2.1 percent, manganese = 1.3 percent, copper = 0.2 percent, iodine = 0.02 percent, vitamin A = 1.1 × 10⁶ United States Pharmacopia (USP) units per kilogram, and vitamin E = 220 International Units (IU) per kilogram. Vitaway, Incorporated, Fort Worth, Texas.

Table 104. Composition of a complete diet for captive white-tailed deer, used at Michigan State University, East Lansing, Michigan (from Verme and Ullrey 1972).

Ingredient	Percentage	Kilocalories per kilogram
Corncob product, ground[a]	34.7	
Corn, ground yellow	29.5	
Soybean meal, dehulled solvent (49 percent)	18.0	
Linseed meal, solvent	10.0	
Alfalfa meal, dehydrated (17 percent crude protein)	3.0	
Cane molasses	3.0	
Corn oil	0.3	
Trace mineral salt, high zinc (0.8 percent)	0.5	
Limestone, ground	0.5	
Sodium sulfate, anhydrous	0.25	
Vitamins A, D and E premix[b]	0.25	
Crude protein	17.6	
Digestible energy		2,750

[a]Andersons No. 4 fines (The Andersons, Maumee, Ohio). Remainder of cob after hard cylinder has been removed for production of industrial abrasives. Consists of bracts and pith (soft parenchyma without vascular bundles). Cell wall constituents = 81 percent; acid detergent fiber = 37.5 percent; lignin = 6.5 percent.
[b]Supplied per kilogram of mixed diet: 3,300 International Units of Vitamin A; 220 International Units of vitamin D₂; and 44 International Units of vitamin E.

may exacerbate the injury or cause additional complications. Broken legs usually heal when left undisturbed, but with complex or compound fractures, a veterinarian should be consulted.

Irritation and infection between the hooves can be treated by cleaning and the application of iodine or a similar antibacterial solution. The pen floor should be kept clean and provided with clean bedding to prevent recontamination of the hooves. It usually helps to remove infected deer to larger pens after treatment.

The occurrence of digestive disorders can be minimized by (1) avoiding sudden changes in feed, (2) cleaning small pens and stalls at least every two weeks, and (3) supplying sufficient fresh bedding of straw, sawdust or wood shavings to keep the pen dry. Clean, dry pens are absolutely necessary in treating sick animals.

Commercially available livestock antidiarrheals, such as Kaopectate, usually are effective against diarrhea. Infected deer on a pel-leted-grain ration should be fed good-quality hay for a few days.

Hair eating and tail biting commonly are observed in captive nursing does, but the causes and remedies are unknown. Wounds caused by tail biting should be treated to minimize risk of infection.

BEHAVIOR IN CAPTIVITY

Variation in the behavior of captive whitetails is great, and this should be taken into account when penning animals together. In general, segregation of whitetails by age and sex is preferable, in order to prevent "bullying" by the larger dominant deer. Also, it is especially important to remove the antlers of older aggressive bucks prior to the rut. The

Antlers should be removed from captive whitetail bucks as soon as velvet atrophies and the antlers harden. *Photo by Don Wooldridge; courtesy of the Missouri Department of Conservation.*

Quite often adult whitetail bucks in captivity lose their fear of people and become very aggressive and dangerous. Handlers must be alert and cautious when around adult bucks to avoid personal injury. *Photo by Murray T. Walton; courtesy of the Wildlife Management Institute.*

antlers of captive bucks at Virginia Polytechnic Institute and State University routinely are sawed off immediately after velvet is shed. This minimizes the potential for injury not only to other deer but to caretakers as well. Adult bucks in captivity often have no fear of man and, in fact, may threaten and attack humans. Whereas antler removal does not ensure absence of injury, it significantly reduces the risk of serious harm to other animals and handlers.

V. Whitetail Benefits

Chapter 42

VALUES IN MANAGEMENT

Edward E. Langenau, Jr.
Wildlife Biologist
Department of Natural Resources
East Lansing, Michigan

Stephen R. Kellert
Associate Professor of Social Ecology
School of Forestry
and Environmental Studies
Yale University
New Haven, Connecticut

James E. Applegate
Professor of Wildlife Biology
Cook College, Department of Horticulture
and Forestry
Rutgers University
New Brunswick, New Jersey

The term "value" is used in a variety of ways. In each context, it has different denotations and individual or cultural interpretations. There is a great deal of confusion about what the term means and how it relates to wildlife species, populations and management. In this chapter, value is defined as the underlying standards and ideals used to guide preference, behavior and evaluation (Langenau and Peyton 1982). In its purest sense, it is an assigned unit of measurement along specified dimensions of worth.

When applied to whitetails, and other natural resources, there are two general classes of value—ascribed and intrinsic. Ascribed values, concerning the assigned units of measurement, are well-described by Bishop (1980:208), who argued that ". . . resources are not, they become." Thus, resources are assigned values based on a social consensus that certain attributes exist and have benefits to humans. Intrinsic values concern dimensions of worth beyond benefits to humans (Fox 1980). They have no ascribed unit of measurement, but can be translated into standards and ideals that guide resource management decisions and activities.

Values enter the process of scientific resource management at several places. "Management" is a process of deciding, doing and evaluating in order to maintain the best of "what is" and to change the remainder into "what ought to be." Every decision in this process involves two parts—beliefs and values (Simon 1945). Beliefs are propositions—either mythical or factual—about resources and resource relationships. A decision to improve whitetail habitat usually involves a wide range of beliefs, such as the relative number of deer supported by existing and potential habitats. Although the decision is based on certain beliefs, many of its factual propositions may not be true. Often, decisions are based more on myth than on fact.

Such a decision also may involve judgments about the good and bad effects of altered plant communities and the desirability of having more, the same or fewer deer in the area being considered. Quite often, only a few of many value components enter into scientific decision making. Values with little managerial or public visibility have a low political profile and may not be considered in the final decision. At times, ignoring certain value considerations may reflect the limited importance of these values to the general public. At other times, values that are common among the public may be ignored because they differ from administrative rules, executive attitudes or the basis of program funding. Due to this tendency, an intricate system of checks and balances has evolved in making public policy, which sometimes forces consideration of all important values.

Just as values enter the decision part of management, they also become involved in the implementation of action programs. Values considered in the planning process may or may not be relevant in the field. The planning process may or may not reflect problems and issues that are real at the local or site level of management. This tension between thinking and doing in deer management may help introduce new issues with new values. Field activities may become broadened if planning and implementing values coincide. The success of proposed change, therefore, is highly dependent on the relationship between values at the staff and field levels of deer management.

Evaluation, the last stage of management, needs a yardstick to measure the success or failure of deer management practices. This yardstick is a composite of values brought to the goal-setting process. There is a great deal of confusion as to the meaning of success or failure in management of white-tailed deer. This is due to conflicts over which values are in need of being maintained and which are in need of being changed.

VALUES RELATED TO WHITETAIL MANAGEMENT

Evolutionary Values

The earliest humans probably entered North America by crossing the Bering land bridge from the Old World about 11,000 to 24,000 years ago. In contrast, the white-tailed deer has been a native of North America for about 2.6 million years. Deer were here long before moose, caribou and elk (Figure 119). The mule deer, with certain fossil records dated to about 0.5 million years ago, also is much more recent than the whitetail. Deer were in North America well in advance of the mammoths and American mastodont, and at least 2 million years before the American bison (Kurten and Anderson 1980).

The white-tailed deer probably evolved from *Odocoileus brachyodontus,* which became extinct when *O. virginianus* appeared (*see also* Chapter 1). This ancestor of deer crossed the land bridge in a series of large migrations about 3.5 million years ago. The first white-tailed deer evolved at a time of relatively restricted seas and extensive building of mountains. Deer thrived in great numbers in regions where woodland met prairie and in river bottoms of the prairies. Fossil records have shown that the four Pleistocene glaciations had little effect on the morphology of deer. During lengthy periods of glacial advance and retreat, mature forests gave way to earlier seral stages of vegetation. Abundant deer remains have been found in brushy areas where fertile soil was deposited during interglacial periods. Humans appearing after the last continental glacial retreat were big game hunters and commonly killed white-tailed deer and other cervid species, several of which are now extinct (Kurten and Anderson 1980).

Whitetails played a significant part in the evolution of fauna and flora of North America. Like most herbivores, they coevolved with specific groups of plants. Changes in plant reproduction and dispersal probably occurred in response to herbivores. Similarly, several carnivore species coevolved with deer. It seems that the evolution of several plant and animal species might have been different if deer had not been present in geological history.

Evolution is a process that continues today. Aside from knowledge that humans have caused extinction of some forms of life, there are few ways to know if people will impact the development of current and future species. Humans have significantly impacted vegetation, air, water and soil. Thus, evolutionary concerns carry powerful value connotations, which may be expected to increase as the science of genetic engineering progresses.

Evolutionary values already have surfaced in a few deer management decisions. One such case involved the status of an endangered subspecies of white-tailed deer, *O. virginianus leucurus,* which inhabits the Columbia River Valley between Oregon and Washington (*see* Chapter 27). Research has shown that some factors relating to its decline have been conversion of habitat from woodlands to pasture and the lack of disturbance of closed canopy forests (Suring and Vohs 1979). The question in this case not only involved the biological

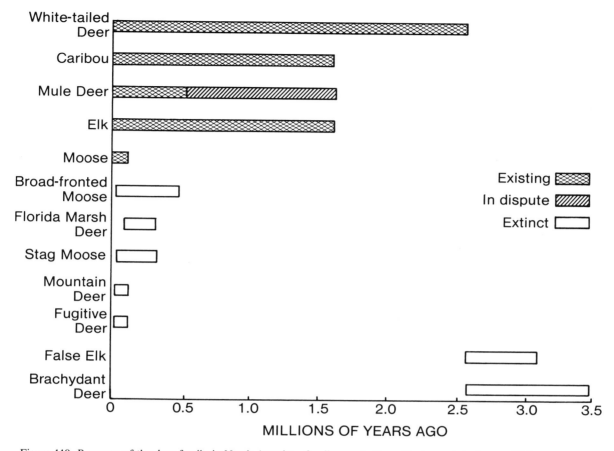

Figure 119. Presence of the deer family in North American fossil records (from Kurten and Anderson 1980).

basis of subspeciation, but also the variation in the total gene pool of white-tailed deer. Decisions about this subspecies required judgment as to whether its unique genetic character should be preserved and at what management, environmental and social costs. Review of the history of this endangered species controversy serves to identify the variety of public attitudes toward evolutionary values.

Intensive human harvest of whitetails also has focused attention on evolutionary values. Periodically, a proposition arises suggesting that hunting removes the most mature and genetically fit individuals because hunters select animals with large antlers. The result, it has been said, is that the smaller, younger, diseased, and less genetically fit deer survive to reproduce. The genotypes surviving presumably are better fit to avoid human predation, but less fit to survive winter hardships and further environmental change. Studies of deer proteins have shown differences within and between

discrete populations (Ramsey et al. 1979), but as yet there is no evidence that hunting produces changes in gene frequency. If so, there would be a wide assortment of opinions as to which genes should be favored. An alternative value judgment might advocate that white-tailed deer are one of the most adaptable species in current and prehistoric times. They have survived a number of selection pressures and outlasted many now-extinct predators. This value position might even support intense harvest by arguing that a succession of intense predation is precisely the mechanism maintaining genetic variability.

Cultural Values

Whitetails have important anthropological and cultural values. There is some dispute as to whether mankind immigrated to North America in advance of the last glacier. Some feel that early cultures survived the last ice age, but then were annihilated by other humans who invaded after the glacier receded (Bada and Helfman 1975). If so, deer and other prey may have encouraged the development of hunting cultures to the exclusion of food gatherers. In addition, deer may have influenced the social behavior and customs of early hunting cultures. The location and success of early human populations may have been influenced by deer distribution and abundance.

The importance of deer to early populations of American Indians is now legendary. As discussed elsewhere in this book, many tribes and nations were dependent on deer products for food, clothing, shelter, tools and implements (*see* Chapter 2). White-tailed deer also were of importance to the early development of European cultures in North America. Many colonists, explorers, trappers, market hunters, pioneers and others who built the early communities of this continent made extensive use of venison and buckskin (Langenau 1981).

Cultural values of deer have produced some serious issues in wildlife management. There are some tribes and rural communities that utilize deer products in excess of amounts allocated to licensed sportsmen. The controversy about hunting rights of American Indians deals specifically with this issue, as traditions (presumably assured by treaty) may not always coincide with regulations relating to scientific management. In addition, some wildlife management objectives have been designed specifically to consider the economic development of native communities. Value judgments on this issue involve defining which traditions of native cultures should be protected, and how this might affect the welfare of larger society. Cultural values also may restrict the improvement of deer habitat. Areas with significant historical value, such as Indian burial grounds and other archaeological sites, normally have severe land-use restrictions. There is no biological basis for these restrictions. Rather, a value judgment has been made that the archaeological sites are important to society.

Without question, whitetails have had an important cultural and historical influence on American society and prevailing attitudes toward wildlife. For example, free access to deer as a right of citizenship rather than as a privilege of rank or age has been an important aspect of the hunting tradition in this country, and this cultural value has been a significant element in the evolution of national wildlife law (Bean 1978). Not all of this effect is positive, as the presumed right of all Americans to hunt deer may have impeded development of a more selective hunting system based on standardized assessments of hunter abilities, knowledge and ethical standards.

The cultural value of white-tailed deer also has been identified as a key element in maintaining the American hunting tradition, primarily through family influence. Most hunters have fathers who hunt or hunted, and most began hunting at the earliest possible age (Schole 1973). For many, the process of deer hunting involves very traditional behaviors, locations and companions, and there is a symbolic passage into adulthood when a youngster joins in the sharing of such traditions. The hunting of deer thus provides a focus for the continuity of a cultural tradition that is of profound significance to many North American families.

Comradeship with peers represents another cultural value of deer derived from hunting. Applegate and Otto (1982) found that a majority of new hunters in New Jersey, age 15 and older, identified a friend of the same age as having had the most influence on their decision to take up hunting. In contrast, most hunters 14 years of age and younger identified their father as that influential person. Since the percentage of new hunters initiated by peers has been increasing over time (Applegate 1982), the comradeship dimension of hunting may be expected to increase in the future. This process has important ramifications in relation to formation of self-identity and peer-group identification during adolescence and early adulthood.

Ecological Values

White-tailed deer are very adaptable. They can exist in mature forests, cornfields, swamps and near airport runways. Two primary factors associated with abundant populations are "wetland corridors" and "brush." The number of deer per square kilometer seems to be highest when both factors are present. The brush component has received much attention in the habitat literature. Whitetail habitat management involves application of energy (such as crop plantings, water development and fertilizing) to push early successional stages forward or to revert late successional stages (by such activities as logging, prescribed burning,

Research has shown that, for many deer hunters, camaraderie is an important part of the hunting experience. Deer camps in particular are known for their traditions, fellowship and buck tales. *Photo courtesy of the Michigan Department of Natural Resources.*

marsh development and opening maintenance). This is done to get as close as possible to the brush stage of plant succession, thereby creating optimal deer range.

The belief components of managing plant stages are extremely complex, often employing sophisticated statistical methods. The value issues associated with the application of facts to alter plant communities are equally complex. Conflicting value positions have developed around issues involving species diversity, artificiality and effects of successional management on nongame species or populations.

"Species diversity" is a measurement that considers the total number of all plant and animal species that inhabit deer range, as well as the population size of each species. Values enter deer management decisions because there is no scientific solution to questions of whether or not habitat should be managed for species diversity, which species mix to favor, and which dimensions of diversity—species richness or species equitability—should be used to estab-

lish management goals. Value judgments need to be made to determine if deer management should be a dominant or subordinate use of specific sites. In recent years, wildlife biologists with the U.S. Forest Service have advocated a blend of management that can enhance species diversity and foster the well-being of featured species, such as important game species and threatened or endangered species (Thomas 1979).

Another basic question involving ecological values concerns the proportion of land that should be under management, and what forms of management should be employed. At one extreme are issues such as wilderness designation of public land, which restricts techniques designed to improve deer habitat. At the other extreme is completely artificial wildlife habitat with fencing to enclose or exclude deer.

Supplemental feeding of whitetails by sportsmen's groups, landowners and some wildlife management agencies is a good illustration of how value judgments can involve a choice between artificial management and natural management. The procedure has been used for some time in Europe, where big game is managed intensively. In North America, the practice of supplemental feeding of wild cervids usually is discouraged by wildlife agencies, using the argument that subsidized populations often have a detrimental effect on other components of the ecosystem. Recent research has shown that there may be ways to feed deer a nutritious diet, at the right time, to increase deer population size without inducing unbalanced browsing pressure on natural forage (Ozoga and Verme 1982). Since Ullrey et al. (1968) found that trace minerals can increase the digestibility of native browse, it may not be necessary to supply a total diet in order to generate increased productivity. Assuming that a scientifically correct way exists to feed deer artificially, there remains the value judgment of whether or not this artificiality is justified. One can ponder whether feeding deer agricultural crops in a hog-feeder really is any different, ecologically, from purposely planting crops for deer and leaving food patches unharvested.

Supplemental feeding of white-tailed deer poses a variety of value questions, including the extent to which artificiality should exist in wildlife management programs. *Photo by William B. Barbour; courtesy of the U.S. Forest Service.*

Several years ago, the U.S. Fish and Wildlife Service was sued for its failure to evaluate the effects of game habitat management on nongame species (Goodrich 1979). It was argued that projects carried out under the Federal Aid in Wildlife Restoration Act were remiss in not having made a full evaluation of each project's effects on nontarget species. This controversy concerned a value judgment—whether population management was more important than community management. Similar to judgments about species diversity, science was only part of the issue. The same questions about which species to favor, and at what expense to deer and other target species, could be resolved only through identification and discussion of differing value judgments.

Aside from these community concerns, the strategies used in whitetail population management also can make it difficult to separate fact from value. The white-tailed deer is a colonizing species that moves rapidly into disturbed habitats. It has a nutritionally sensitive reproductive pattern that permits immigration and emigration, exploitation of brushy sites, and rapid production of fawns. When the range of deer is expanded and environmental conditions are favorable, fawn mortality is adjusted. Population size is regulated further by territorial behavior of pregnant does (Ozoga et al. 1982), autumn dispersal of yearling bucks (Hawkins et al. 1971), and dispersal of 3.5-year-old females (Ozoga et al. 1982). In areas where whitetails are colonizing new brush stages, there is no deer population surplus. As the population expands to reach optimal size, there is a surplus of yearling bucks, fawns and dispersing females. There also is a seasonal surplus, if an area cannot support a given number of deer throughout the year. Surplus also can result from human activity, such as reducing predator populations, limiting hunter access by posting and changing agricultural crops planted. A large part of the whitetail biologist's or manager's daily work involves collection of data on deer population characteristics, to estimate the quantity of surplus deer for the purpose of recommending hunting season regulations.

Not everyone agrees with this management definition of surplus. Some individuals argue that deer that starve are not "surplus" *per se,* but are necessary to maintain carnivore populations and strengthen the genetic fitness of surviving deer.

Economic Values

Benefits from whitetails are allocated to people through political systems rather than by a competitive free-market economy. Governmental concern with the equitable distribution of public benefits from deer usually is of primary importance in management decisions. Costs of participating in deer-oriented recreation then are held at a lower level (P_1) than that (P_0) which would be determined in a competitive market (Figure 120). As a consequence, demand for deer exceeds supply, which is fixed by environmental factors in any given year. This process also creates an inefficient distribution of access to deer-related benefits. These benefits are distributed equally to all, rather than being allocated to citizens willing to pay the most. Some of the funds that could have been used to increase supply become required to operate this allocation system. Most importantly, it is impossible to estimate the size of demand or value of the resource by traditional methods when price is held below a free-market level (Bohm 1973).

Deer values also are difficult to define because externalities (economic side-effects of production or management programs) have not been considered in pricing decisions. The classic example of this process involves pollution (Kneese and Schultze 1975). A firm that re-leases waste products into a river may reduce the value of other commodities produced downstream, such as trout used for fishing recreation. If the external social and production costs are not included in the price of goods from the polluting firm, then the price will be understated. If external effects reduce the value of other commodities, then production levels that do not consider these side effects (Q_1) will be higher than the socially optimal level of production (Q_0). This means that failure to include social costs of hunting accidents, crop damage and deer/vehicle collisions will tend to justify higher levels of deer population (Q_1 minus Q_0) than are socially optimal (Figure 121).

These two distortions of pricing for deer-related benefits require that wildlife be evaluated differently than a box of cereal or other private goods. The economic literature on wildlife values is in a primitive state. Leitch and Scott (1977) have contributed a bibliography of 691 references and many of these references give seemingly conflicting results for dollar valuation of wildlife. Recent surveys by both the U.S. Fish and Wildlife Service and Canadian Wildlife Service compare several methods of describing the dollar value of deer and other wildlife (Lyons and Shaw 1982). The wildlife profession can expect some analytical comparisons from federal surveys in the United States and Canada and a further attempt to

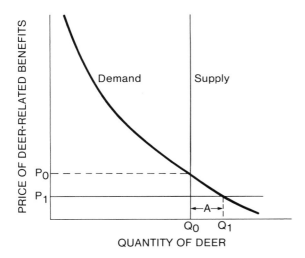

Figure 120. The optimal price (P_0) of deer-related benefits would occur at the intersection of demand and a fixed supply of deer (Q_0) in any given year. Political processes tend to lower the price of benefits to P_1. The quantity of deer demanded at price P_1 exceeds supply, thereby creating unsatisfied demand (A) (modification of Bohm 1973).

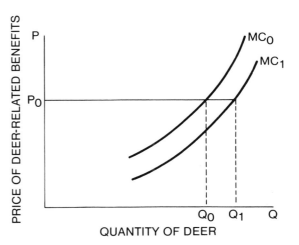

Figure 121. P_0 is the price that should be paid for the optimal number of deer (Q_0) demanded by society when externalities are included in calculating marginal costs (MC_0). If externalities are not considered, the marginal cost of production is lowered to MC_1. As a result, deer production is increased to Q_1, which is beyond the level demanded by society.

resolve the differences found in the results of other surveys.

The following is one example of economic valuation showing the magnitude of value involved with white-tailed deer in the United States. Williamson and Doster (1981) estimated that the total annual flow of values from whitetails in the United States was $8.22 billion during 1975. This figure included $1.01 billion in expenditures for food, lodging, transportation, equipment, licenses and fees for an estimated 8,227,856 white-tailed deer hunters. The value of 97,576,659 pounds of venison was estimated to be about $108 million. Another $1.80 billion was included as an estimate of the value of the 30 million days of hunting recreation that were devoted to white-tailed deer. Nonhunting activities related to white-tailed deer were estimated to be worth $5.40 billion. An average annual reproductive rate of 30 percent was then used to capitalize the $8.2 billion flow of values. The final estimate was that the whitetail population of the United States was worth $27.3 billion, or about $1,657 per deer. This total value was about three-fourths the farm value of cattle in the United States and about three times the value of swine, sheep and poultry combined. A larger value ($6,087 per deer) would result from using an 8-percent discount rate to capitalize annual interest.

White-tailed deer hunting in North America has a tremendous economic impact on restaurants, motels, sporting goods stores and other businesses. In many small communities in popular hunting areas, deer hunting—despite the season's relatively short duration—is a vital industry. *Photo courtesy of the Michigan Department of Natural Resources.*

Economic values consistently are mixed with scientific facts in white-tailed deer management decisions. There seems to be an underlying principle that a decision is right if it is economically justified and wrong if the balance is red. Fox (1980) argued against this value judgment in wildlife management, and proposed that moralistic and ecological values should be incorporated into decisions more frequently, even if this increases economic costs.

Social Values

Social definitions assign certain values to wildlife. For example, one species may have trophy value while another is considered a pest, worthy only of extermination in a given situation. The term "wildlife" also has had changing social value. In reviewing the history of wildlife legislation in the United States, Bean (1978) found that the meaning of wildlife has been broadening over time. Early definitions of wildlife reflected only a few social values, while recent definitions even include intangible benefits accruing from people just knowing that wildlife exists. Canadian and United States citizens place a very high social value on wildlife. Of all wild species, deer are the most preferred, and they are preceded in overall popularity only by the domestic horse and dog (Bart 1972).

The diversity of deer-related activity can be understood best by examining a classification system (Figure 122) designed by Lyons (1980). Three dimensions of human use of wildlife, according to this system, are interest level, activity form and location. Interest level can be primary, as when a person tries to view deer at dusk. Secondary uses occur when an individual engaged in some other activity, such as driving to work, incidentally encounters wildlife. Activity form can be direct, as when an individual sees or hears wildlife, or it can be indirect, as when a person watches a television program about deer. Location of wildlife use was divided into residential, nonresidential and artificial environments.

This classification system was used to design questions for the U.S. Fish and Wildlife Service's *1980 National Survey of Hunting, Fishing and Wildlife-associated Recreation* (Lyons and Shaw 1982). Preliminary estimates from this study, supplemented with information from

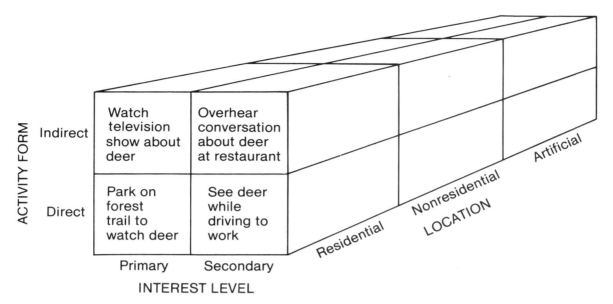

Figure 122. A taxonomy of human uses of deer, proposed by Lyons (1980).

the Canadian Wildlife Service, indicate that the combined hunting and nonhunting use of deer in North America exceeded 180 million person-days of recreation in 1980. Previous research has indicated that nonconsumptive uses, such as intentionally driving and hiking to view deer, have about three times more economic value than do consumptive uses (Horvath 1974). The 3:1 ratio also was found in a Michigan study (Langenau 1979a), where three citizens participated in nonconsumptive uses of deer for every deer hunter.

Whitetails represent an important aesthetic value to Americans. National surveys indicate that millions of hours are spent each year, year-round, by hunters and nonhunters alike in an attempt simply to view deer in natural settings. *Photo courtesy of the U.S. Forest Service.*

Whitetail management decisions are laden with judgments about hunting values. This is justified by intense public demand. White-tailed deer hunting was pursued by more than 10 million people in the U.S. and Canada in 1980. Williamson (1981) showed that participation in hunting has been stable for some time in the United States (Table 105). He argued that there is little evidence to indicate a long-range downward trend in the proportion of the United States population that hunts, and suggested that there is reason to expect increased hunting participation in the future. Individuals born during the post-World War II baby boom are approaching the age category of greatest participation in hunting (35 to 45 years old). The current shift of residence from urban to rural areas also may increase hunting participation, since this activity is more common among rural residents. In studies of 12–18-year-old hunters in Michigan, Langenau and Mellon (1980) came to a similar conclusion. They predicted an increase in hunting, especially in the late 1980s and early 1990s, when the "grandchildren" of the baby boom era become old enough to buy licenses.

In evaluating data on trends in hunting participation, it is important to note that aggregate data can mask variance in the separate states. Thus, while the overall picture of hunter populations is one of stability, it does not necessarily follow that this is the case in every state. The *1980 National Survey of Hunting, Fishing, and Wildlife-associated Recreation* shows rather large differences in participation rates (number of hunters compared to number of residents) among the standard census regions, with participation at 16 percent in the western northcentral and eastern southcentral regions

and only 6 percent in the New England and Pacific regions. Differences between individual states are even larger, ranging from 33 percent participation in Wyoming to 2 percent participation in Rhode Island. Since participation rates are probably related to hunting opportunity (game populations, accessible open space, etc.), hunting populations may be expected to decline in states with high human density and decreasing quantities of open space. As an example, firearm hunting-license sales in New Jersey have declined 30 percent between 1971 and 1981.

The kinds of experiences required for hunting satisfaction have been found to vary among individuals (Kennedy 1974, Potter et al. 1973, Hautaloma and Brown 1978). Some deer hunters, for example, place highest value on social components of the experience, while others are interested primarily in shooting skills or in the suspense and challenge of the hunt. Biologists and managers should be careful to avoid establishing management goals for the "average" hunter. It should not be assumed that everyone wants to hunt for the same reason, in the same manner and in the same kind of setting. Discussing this point, Bryan (1979) used an analogy of a carpenter who had been commissioned to design beds for a family of six. Nobody in the family was satisfied when the beds arrived, because they all were built to accommodate the average height of family members. The beds were too short for the adults and too long for the children. Managers can be guilty of this sort of miscalculation, by implementing uniform regulations throughout the entire area or series of management units under their jurisdiction. Where possible, regulation through such techniques as trophy areas, road closures and primitive-weapons hunts can diversify the opportunities available to hunters with differing definitions of "quality." In considering such regulations, biologists and managers need to remember that they themselves do not represent a random subset of the general population, and that their perception of "quality" may not be shared by all or even many hunters.

Kellert (1980*a*) analyzed the broad perceptions and behavioral relations to wildlife of Americans and described 10 separate values (Table 106) that were distributed differently among public groups. These basic value orientations can be used to explain many of the differences between "actors" in whitetail

Table 105. Number and percentage of licensed hunters in the United States population, 1955–1982.[a]

Year	United States population	Number of licensed hunters	Percentage of hunters in United States population
1955	164,588,000	14,088,608	8.56
1960	179,386,000	13,902,578	7.75
1965	193,223,000	14,330,549	7.42
1970	203,849,000	15,370,481	7.54
1975	212,748,000	16,597,807	7.80
1980	226,444,000	16,257,074	7.18
1982	231,009,000	16,748,541	7.25

[a]L. L. Williamson personal communication to R. E. McCabe:1983. *See also* Williamson (1981).

Table 106. Fundamental attitudes of Americans toward wildlife (Kellert 1980*a*).

Attitude	Definition
Naturalistic	Primary interest and affection are for wildlife and the outdoors.
Ecologistic	Primary concern is for the environment as a system, for wildlife species and for natural habitats.
Humanistic	Primary interest and strong affection are for individual animals, principally pets.
Moralistic	Primary concern is with the right and wrong treatment of animals, with strong opposition to exploitation and cruelty toward animals.
Scientistic	Primary curiosity is directed toward the physical attributes and functioning of animals.
Aesthetic	Primary interest is in the artistic and symbolic characteristics of animals.
Utilitarian	Primary concern is with the practical and material value of animals.
Dominionistic	Primary concern is with mastering and controlling animals.
Negativistic	Primary interest is in avoiding animals, due to fear, dislike or superstition.
Neutralistic	Primary orientation of indifference to and emotional detachment from animals.

management decisions. For example, three basic hunting values were reported by Kellert—naturalistic, utilitarian and dominionistic. Utilitarian (meat) hunters were most common, accounting for 44 percent of the persons who hunted during the previous five years. These individuals were concerned mostly with getting meat, and they viewed wildlife as a crop to be harvested. Dominionistic (sport or recreational) hunters were the next most numerous, comprising 38 percent of the hunting population. For dominionistic hunters, hunting represented a social and recreational activity, with competition, achievement and skill being predominant goals. Naturalistic (nature-oriented) hunters represented the smallest of the three basic hunter groups, and included 18 percent of the hunters. Desire for an active and participatory role in nature characterized these hunters, who viewed wildlife primarily with intellectual curiosity. Nature hunters were by far the most knowledgeable about animals.

In contrast to these hunting values, three types of antihunters were found in the United States—humanistic, moralistic and ecologistic (Kellert 1978). Humanistic antihunters per-

The naturalistic hunter considers predation to be a basic principle of nature and tends to view the outdoors with a sense of curiosity. *Photo by William E. Ruth.*

ceived wildlife to be kind and innocent. This group opposed hunting because of their perceptions of fear, terror and pain presumably inflicted on animals. Moralistic antihunters considered hunting for recreation and pleasure to be an immoral expression of violence, manifesting a lack of reverence for life. Ecologistic antihunters opposed hunting because they thought it was unsound to manipulate natural habitats for the sole purpose of providing selfish benefits to humans.

The actual extent of antihunting sentiment in American society is unclear. Most current national data on the subject (Kellert 1980*b*) suggest that it varies depending on the presumed reason for hunting (Table 107). The majority (59 to 62 percent) of Americans indicated their opposition to hunting if practiced solely for recreational pleasure. On the other hand, an overwhelming number (82 to 85 percent) supported hunting so long as it was linked to some practical benefit, such as using the meat or maintaining a subsistence-oriented life style. The implication is that the majority of Americans value hunting if some degree of practical or tangible benefit is involved—an attitude perhaps related to the cultural significance of hunting in American history.

Table 107. Public attitudes toward hunting in the United States (Kellert 1980*b*).

Reason for hunting	Percentage		
	Approve	No response	Disapprove
Traditional native hunting such as done by some Indians and Eskimos	82	3	15
Hunting game mammals such as deer for recreation and sport	37	1	62
Hunting waterfowl such as ducks for recreation and sport	40	1	59
Hunting for meat	85	1	14
Hunting for recreation and meat	64	2	34
Hunting for a trophy, such as horns or a mounted animal	18	2	80

Left column: the meat hunter tends to view huntable wildlife as a crop to be harvested and does not necessarily or primarily view his own hunting to be a form of recreation. *Photo by Russ Reagan; courtesy of the Missouri Department of Conservation.*

White-tailed deer biologists and managers periodically have been involved in controversies where conflicting values regarding hunting had to be evaluated carefully and considered in making or defending management decisions. For example, most of the Fund for Animals' opposition to white-tailed deer hunting during 1974 in the Great Swamp National Wildlife Refuge of New Jersey involved a conflict between humanistic values of antihunters and scientistic values of deer managers. On-site harassment of hunters by antihunters in Arizona, prompting new laws (HB 2291) in 1981, can be interpreted as a manifestation of conflicts between moralistic antihunter values and utilitarian hunter values.

Anti-deer-hunting protests in 1974 at the Great Swamp National Wildlife Refuge in New Jersey garnered considerable media attention. The beneficial effect has been expanded funding for scientific monitoring of whitetail populations at this and other national wildlife refuges. *Photo courtesy of the U. S. Fish and Wildlife Service.*

Such value-judgment conflicts between hunters and antihunters also were clearly shown in research done by the advertising firm of Batten, Barston, Durstine and Osborne for the National Shooting Sports Foundation (Rohlfing 1978). This research study showed that much of the public opposition to hunting was due to perceptions in the general population that hunters lacked hunting and shooting skill, needed no knowledge to purchase firearms or licenses, and showed a lack of respect for nature and for the rights of others. The conclusion of this research was that hunters need to become more responsible and knowledgeable in order to reduce public opposition to hunting. Jackson et al. (1979) discussed educational techniques that might be useful in expediting the movement of hunters through five hypothetical stages in the development of responsible hunting behavior: (1) the shooting stage, where individuals emphasize firearms and shooting skills; (2) the limiting-out stage, where success in killing game becomes important; (3) the trophy stage, where hunters specialize in difficult species or trophy individuals; (4) the methods stage, with an emphasis on techniques and expertise in specialized equipment; and (5) the mellowing-out stage, in which responsible sportsmanship is manifested. Jackson et al. (1981) felt that some irresponsible behavior of hunters was fostered by wildlife management agency programs, such as concentration of game for harvest. The researchers encouraged agencies and sportsmen to consider the effects of wildlife management programs on hunter behavior.

Unfortunately, there has been more discussion of differences in social values of wildlife than there has been about similarities. A notable exception was the work of Shaw (1975), who studied attitudes of deer hunters, National Audubon Society members and Fund for Animals supporters in Michigan. He found the biggest similarity between these groups was their concern for wildlife habitat. All three groups felt that the major threat to wildlife populations was the destruction of habitat through development, urban sprawl, overpopulation and pollution. Shaw concluded that wildlife management agencies should reduce some of the tensions between these groups by expanding their work on nongame, by considering appreciative uses in management plans and by involving nonhunters in land-acquisition programs.

In June 1982, floodwaters from two tropical storms forced about 5,500 white-tailed deer to high ground or "islands" in Florida's roughly 3,000-square kilometer (1,150-square mile) Everglades Wildlife Management Area, where the animals competed for scarce food resources. Within weeks, with little abatement of water level due to heavy July rains, the concentrated animals were suffering from stress and malnutrition. In an effort to avoid extensive habitat destruction and a massive die-off of deer due to starvation and parasitism, for which there was historic precedent, the Florida Game and Fresh Water Fish Commission authorized a two-day permit hunt in two sections of what is known as Conservation Area 3A. Alerted and spurred on by nationwide media coverge of the situation, antihunters—proposing to "rescue" and relocate 2,000 live deer in eight days—brought a temporary injunction that effectively halted the hunt in the northern section. (Eventually, their case was dismissed for lack of merit.) The southern-area hunt, however, proceeded. Estimates in October put total mortality of the "southern" deer population at 23 percent, including 17 percent to hunter harvest (723 of about 4,000 animals). Following the lowering of floodwaters and dispersal of the deer, the survivors were able to recover health and retain an adequate food supply. In the northern area, the rescue and relocation effort failed. At a cost of about $8,000, 18 deer were captured and relocated. As of mid-December, only six (all fawns) of those animals had survived. The remainder of the unharvested northern population fared little better. By October, roughly 66 percent of these animals (992 of 1,500) were lost to starvation or disease, and the "island" habitats were stripped to such an extent that recovery was expected to take a year or more (Lampton 1982, International Association of Fish and Wildlife Agencies 1982). *Top-left photo by John Walther; courtesy of The Miami Herald. Top-right photo by Vic Heller; courtesy of the Florida Game and Fresh Water Fish Commission. Bottom photo by Bob Ellis; courtesy of the Florida Game and Fresh Water Fish Commission.*

The 1982 Florida Everglades crisis points out the potential disruptive influence of persons who, though well-intentioned, do not have adequate understanding of wildlife population dynamics, management costs and biological implications. What began as concern for the well-being of the Everglades white-tailed deer population became an attack on hunting. In the end, the original management approach—removing deer by hunters—proved to be the most expedient, inexpensive and effective course of action. That it was stymied in part made the lesson a costly one. Hundreds of deer suffered and their habitat deteriorated—unnecessarily—because of the interference (*see* Florida Game and Fresh Water Fish Commission 1983). Also to be learned from the experience is the potency of the media. The peril of the deer made the situation newsworthy, and anti-hunting passions made it human-interest—a media event. Much of the coverage focused on the human emotions involved and, in so doing, tended to overstate or distort the management objectives and bring pressure to bear on the wildlife agency. Wildlife managers must recognize that biology alone rarely has news value. But because ". . . a wildlife management practice, no matter how well founded on biology and management principles, can become highly controversial if it is not understood and accepted by the general public" (Brantly 1982:18), the media must be treated with openness, sensitivity, and professional judgment. The information released to them must be sound. Prolonged debates, obfuscation, "stonewalling" or combatting emotionalism in kind only serve to fan media attention, public uncertainty and political intervention, none of which may be in the best interest of the resources in question. *Top-left photo by Vic Heller; courtesy of the Florida Game and Fresh Water Fish Commission. Top-right photo by John Walther; courtesy of The Miami Herald. Bottom photo by Charles Dennis; courtesy of the Florida Game and Fresh Water Fish Commission.*

Psychological Values

White-tailed deer can have a personal and unique meaning to an individual. They can be symbols of nature, wilderness, comradeship, stewardship, beauty, maternity and an array of other representative concepts. These symbolic values often are expressed in wildlife art, which is a growing commercial activity in North America. Waterfowl biologists and managers have capitalized on the aesthetic value of wildlife by involving artists and public groups in the production of hunting stamps. Many conservation groups, including Ducks Unlimited, the National Audubon Society and the Boone and Crockett Club, have promoted wildlife prints. Some wildlife agencies have sponsored wildlife art displays at fairs, museums and shopping centers. It is apparent that wildlife art represents an important psychological value and may be a good vehicle for wildlife management agencies to get closer to the public and become more involved in community affairs. The manager or biologist who is sensitive to aesthetic values of the public may secure additional support for ecological values needed to manage deer.

Commercial advertising of goods and services is another area in which the psychological value of wildlife and nature is particularly evident. Many products are promoted through media campaigns that subliminally or sensorially associate product attributes with characteristics of wild animals or places. It also has become good business to suggest that one's product bears a relationship to innate or perceived values of wildlife or nature by labeling (product name) or simply featuring the product in a natural setting, however unlikely such familiarity really is.

Symbolic reference to deer by individuals also can be expressed in an emotional manner. Powerful connotations of deer can be seen in word associations given by a sample of Michigan taxpayers (Langenau 1979*b*). The three most common associations to fawns were "cute," "beautiful" and "innocent." Common word associations to bucks were "majestic," "beautiful" and "strong." And does produced responses of "beautiful," "graceful" and "pretty." These psychological referents show that the symbolic value of deer can be highly personal and emotional. Although there is some dispute as to whether definitions of wildlife create or reflect psychological processes, it is clear that the youth of North America are exposed to numerous myths in children's literature (More 1977) and other forms of mass media.

Wildlife art has become big business in North America. Its popularity stems from increased public appreciation of wildlife's aesthetic dimensions, the relatively recent recognition of wildlife illustration, painting and sculpture as truly legitimate art forms, and perhaps an emerging desire to relate to the natural beauty, order and freedom of wild things and places as depicted by the growing number of talented artists who specialize in the genre. *Photo by Julie M. Wickham; courtesy of the Michigan Department of Natural Resources.*

Wildlife often is used in advertising to suggest product association with species traits. "Nothing runs like a Deere," for example, is the slogan and registered trademark of Deere and Company. *Photo courtesy of Deere and Company.*

Symbolic representations of deer and other wildlife may not be bad in all circumstances. People with little opportunity to encounter wildlife may become interested in nature initially through anthropomorphic presentations. Interest then may expand to the point where individuals seek outdoor experiences and then develop more realistic perceptions of wildlife. Also, anthropomorphic presentations may foster the development of larger conservation ethics that can impact management directly by generating public interest and support. Modern wildlife management requires a concerned and knowledgeable public and cannot exist with apathetic constituents.

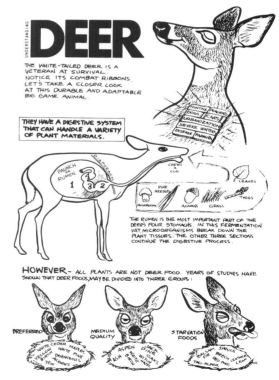

Children are generally taught at an early age to ascribe human traits, behavior and emotions to animals. Such anthropomorphising can be constructive by making youngsters more aware of animals, but not if it creates and perpetuates unrealistic beliefs, expectations and values. *Left photo by Bluford W. Muir; courtesy of the U. S. Forest Service. Bottom-right illustration by Ozz Warbach; courtesy of the Michigan Department of Natural Resources. Top-right scene courtesy of Walt Disney Productions, Inc. 1942.*

Public Service Values

White-tailed deer management in North America is a government function for the most part, rather than a private enterprise. Although individuals can modify deer range on private property or charge fees to hunters, the ultimate responsibility for whitetail populations resides with state and provincial governments. Hence, there are several public service values that relate to deer management decisions.

A public service value that has become superimposed on whitetail management is the judgment that all North American citizens should have an equal opportunity to derive benefits from this species. As a result, many management decisions involve allocation of deer to competing groups (such as bowhunters versus firearms hunters, landowners versus hunters, residents versus nonresidents). Often the factual aspects of management conflict with this goal of providing equal opportunity. A good example of this occurs in states that have a landowner preference system for the harvest of antlerless deer. Special privileges for landowners have developed to solve a problem caused by a perceived overharvest of deer on public land and an underharvest of deer on private land. The failure to remove enough antlerless deer on private land not only creates ecological and economic problems, but also tends to increase trespass of hunters on private lands. Landowners experiencing high rates of trespass may be reluctant to permit hunters on their land (Brown and Decker 1979), which further compounds the problem. To solve this problem, some wildlife agencies have two separate drawings for antlerless permits—one for landowners and another for general hunters. Other states give shooting permits to landowners or allow special hunts on agricultural lands. These procedures may be very efficient in providing a better harvest of deer on private land, but they compromise the spirit of equal opportunity.

Control of hunter densities also reflects certain public service values. Since consideration of equal opportunity keeps the price of hunting licenses below their true economic value, deer hunting often can become crowded. Some hunters like crowded conditions since this tends to keep deer in the locality on the move (Cue and Langenau 1979). In other cases, crowding reduces hunter satisfaction (Heberlein et al. 1982). Biologists and managers then become involved with value judgments about how crowded deer hunting should be, at what level hunter density should be controlled, and what regulations are desirable. Research has shown that Wisconsin deer hunters dislike controls, such as split season, hunting permits and assignment to specific hunting areas (Heberlein and Laybourne 1978). However, some wildlife agencies have found that the most successful method of controlling hunter numbers appears to be the creation of separate management units with different antlerless hunting quotas and various amounts of deer range improvement to affect whitetail population size.

Nearly all biologists and other natural resource managers are devoted to conservation principles, where conservation means the wise use of resources without waste. However, there is a tendency for these professionals to emphasize the resource for which they are responsible. As a result, whitetail biologists and managers may be dedicated to values of deer, and view other land-use products—such as timber, agricultural crops and livestock—as subordinate competitors for habitat. Since wildlife biologists and managers have values more ecological and less utilitarian than those of the general public, they are likely to view human benefits as outputs rather than inputs. It is easy for them to believe that the objective of management is to produce a maximum or optimum sustained yield, based on maximum or optimum carrying capacity of the land. Sometimes they want to produce more and more deer without knowing why. Human benefit, according to this view, comes after the maximum annual surplus has been produced. In this context, hunters come to be viewed collectively as a harvest machine, to keep whitetail populations at specified densities, rather than as the reason for maintaining a certain density.

The tendency of wildlife biologists and other natural resource managers to specialize on one product of the land also can cause a situation in which social costs of deer management become discounted. If this occurs, the costs of having too many deer may receive much less attention than do the benefits. As a result, a wildlife agency may become excessively concerned with treating symptoms of high whitetail populations rather than with addressing the cause and reducing deer populations through regulated removal of antlerless deer.

Differences in public service values between agencies also can impact decisions. An excellent example of this is the perception that species management is a state function and habitat management is a federal function (Thomas 1982). This view—common in western areas of the United States—has created numerous conflicts that compromise decisions. In actuality, wildlife habitat management is a function of land ownership. States with large acreages of fee-title land are involved actively in habitat improvement. Failure to view this more basic relationship correctly probably has arisen because of different value positions concerning states' rights, different revenue sources and different management objectives. The real issue underlying the conflict between agencies is not species management versus habitat management.

Due to great citizen interest in deer, this species has significant educational value. Deer are useful as a vehicle to teach basic principles of ecology. Government agencies have been actively involved in public education through organizational efforts to correct erroneous beliefs and to foster responsible use of resources. Field personnel frequently are requested to give talks to community groups and in schools.

Field contacts between people and deer can have significant educational impact. People may notice that deer prefer certain acorn species over others, for example, and gain insight into a wide assortment of other ecological relationships. Public agencies can assist in making these experiences more educational through appropriate news releases and public contact. Interpretive services, such as management demonstration areas, also can be provided to promote educational aspects of outdoor experiences.

People's interest in and curiosity about white-tailed deer can be a valuable stimulus in learning about ecological interrelationships in general and those of wildlife in particular. Using a deer population simulator in the form of a board game, these students learn principles of population dynamics and wildlife management. Developed at Rutgers University and produced by the Carolina Biological Supply Company, the game—"Oh My Deer!"—has proven to be an effective teaching aid in schools and hunter-education programs. *Photo by Guy Melter; courtesy of the New Jersey Agricultural Experiment Station.*

Political Values

Public interest in white-tailed deer gives management issues heightened media attention and great public visibility. Deer management issues often are surrounded by a significant amount of emotionalism and controversy. Because of this, deer have political value in uniting voters and political candidates. Campaign issues, especially in rural areas, can and have been developed around deer management controversy, and elections have been won and lost based on a candidate's position on a deer management question. Also, legislation concerning deer hunting regulations may involve the trading of support on several bills. Thus, a legislator may offer to take a position on a deer hunting regulation with the understanding that a colleague will support a bill in an unrelated area, such as welfare reform or unemployment compensation.

VALUE TRADE-OFFS

The direction of white-tailed deer management is clear when there is only one value to be considered. If a whitetail population was being managed to produce maximum possible hunter-days of recreation, then there would be little confusion in deciding between management alternatives, designing field programs, or measuring the success or failure of activities. The impact of management on production of other values from the deer population would not need to be considered.

As shown in the preceding section, management issues commonly involve several values of deer. Activities that produce the most of one value may reduce attainment of other values. For example, a whitetail management system designed to maximize legal harvest may increase crop damage and reduce values of deer to private landowners.

Social costs and/or trade-offs of whitetail management should be considered carefully, especially in areas where sufficient harvests cannot be achieved. *Photo courtesy of the Michigan Department of Natural Resources.*

Management first must be aware of conflicting values in order to determine trade-off relationships. This requires that values be separated from associated beliefs. In practice, this is not always accomplished. Individuals involved in decisions about deer often become committed prematurely to a value position. Challenging this value position creates stubbornness, screening of information and rejection of beliefs that vary from the value position. Only those facts that are aligned with the prematurely accepted value become recognized and incorporated in the process of resolving issues.

Whitetail biologists and managers are well-acquainted with this process of failing to separate values from facts. A good example involves the policy that local residents should have preference over nonresidents in hunting regulations. Information provided to show the relative harvest between resident and nonresident hunters rarely is perceived. Instead, an argument often develops over how the numbers were derived, and the wildlife management agency may be accused of distorting the numbers to sell more licenses. Continued presentation of biological facts on harvest rates will have little effect on changing opinion. This occurs because there is a conflict in values—specifically, how much the deer population should be managed for the benefit of nonresidents. Once a value conflict has been identified, it is necessary to determine the relative impacts of management on each dimension of worth. Although this sometimes is done through discussion, more commonly a management activity is implemented and the relative impact noticed. For example, wildlife management agencies tried to provide deer hunting closer to home after the energy shortage of 1973–1974. Many of these attempts did not succeed because of the hunters' appreciation for traditional sites. The agency value of reducing the energy costs of hunting had been identified and evaluated as less important than the hunters' concern for traditional sites. The value trade-off, in this case, was that traditional hunting sites be given the most attention, even if this failed to decrease the energy costs of hunting.

SETTING VALUE PRIORITIES

After trade-offs are determined, a final priority of values is established. There are many methods by which these values are given priority—agreement by consensus, acceptance as a trial, imposition by administrative rule, determination by funding systems, and compromise through legislation. In general, the mechanisms are political in nature and involve exchanges of influence and authority (Lindblom 1980). North Americans have decided that democracy is the most acceptable method of establishing priorities for values. Yet, only 11 percent of the sportsmen in the United States seek to have their values represented by joining an organized political group (Kellert 1980*a*). And scientists often become resentful of politics, especially when their advice about factual components is compromised to accommodate values. Just as Fox (1980) argued that humanism may have economic costs, compromises in rationality may be needed sometimes to maintain values.

At a minimum, articulation and setting priority of values promotes understanding as a basis for compromise. Too often, serious communication gaps are encountered between value positions in the management of white-tailed deer. Too often, setting priorities is based on a presumption that some value positions are foolish, misguided or based on ignorance. This is the point at which management has its greatest responsibility. It is the responsibility of the wildlife professional to act as an impartial and objective arbitrator of value positions. It is that individual's responsibility to encourage others to articulate their values and to establish an atmosphere in which cherished and fundamental values can be communicated, evaluated and accommodated.

The exercise of this responsibility necessitates a willingness to empathize with the values of others and to be a patient and intelligent interpreter of basic premises and bias. If the biologist or manager is particularly adept at understanding and expresses a desire to communicate in a variety of evaluative languages, then it may be possible to elevate the managerial discussion to some common ground where conflicting values may be reconciled. This effort need not involve trying to change the values of others, but rather should involve the assertion of values that may embrace the conflicting views of opposing interest groups. Historically, the evolution of an ecological value has provided the context for such a synthesis. The potential for ecological values to embrace those of lower priority probably is due to an alignment of intrinsic and ascribed values: the true values of the resource itself then are equivalent to values assigned by humans to that resource. This potential is perhaps no more dramatically suggested than by the fact that Joseph Wood Krutch—an eloquent spokesman for the antihunting position—eventually espoused the views of Aldo Leopold, perhaps the most articulate and poetic advocate of hunting's historical value.

Chapter 43

PHOTOGRAPHING THE WHITETAIL

Glenn D. Chambers
Regional Director
Ducks Unlimited
Columbia, Missouri

Leonard Lee Rue III
Leonard Rue Enterprises
Blairstown, New Jersey

The advent of the modern 35-mm single-lens reflex camera with its wide range of accessories, recent advances in film manufacturing and processing, and the ability of people to reach about any place where wild animals are found have made wildlife photography a fast-growing and popular nonconsumptive outdoor activity. The art of *good* photography has a prominent place in today's emphasis on outdoor recreation and scientific investigation.

In 1970, there were about 4.9 million wildlife photographers nine years of age or older in the United States—2.9 percent of the national population—whose photography accounted for more than 40 million recreation days (U.S. Fish and Wildlife Service 1972). Five years later, approximately 15 million wildlife photographers—8 percent of the population—spent 156.7 million recreation days (U.S. Fish and Wildlife Service 1977).

The latest national survey (U.S. Fish and Wildlife Service 1982) revealed that in 1980, nearly 128.7 million persons older than six years of age in the United States participated in nonconsumptive outdoor activities, including more than 34.1 million who made trips specifically to observe, photograph, listen to or otherwise enjoy wildlife. In addition, almost 89 million participated in at-home activities of which the primary nonconsumptive purposes were wildlife-related. For more than 104.6 million individuals who made trips away from home for a primary purpose *other than* enjoyment of wild-

life, 85.7 million reported that wildlife proved to be an important secondary nonconsumptive component of the event. And about 102.3 million Americans indicated enjoyment of unplanned opportunities to hear or see wildlife at home. There was, of course, overlap (94 percent) of numerical participants among the various primary and secondary categories. Nevertheless, it is quite obvious that, to a majority of the United States population, nonconsumptive appreciation for and use of wildlife are valuable recreational, aesthetic and/or educational experiences.

A total of 377.4 million days in 1980 were spent on trips to observe, feed or photograph wildlife, including 74.5 million days for wildlife photography alone. Approximately 5 billion days were spent by Americans observing and/or photographing wildlife around the home or neighborhood. The primary and secondary nonconsumptive users of wildlife spent about $14.7 billion in 1980, of which $10.7 billion was spent on equipment. Of the latter, $2.6 billion of the equipment expenditures was exclusively for nonconsumptive wildlife-related use. And $1.17 billion (45 percent) of the $2.6 billion was for binoculars and photo equipment. Wildlife photography, therefore, not only is a popular recreation, it is a big and growing business.

A study by Ducks Unlimited (1982) showed that, of that organization's 465,000 member/subscribers, 93.1 percent owned still-cameras and 26.1 percent owned movie cameras.

Both the viewing and the photographing of wildlife have gained tremendously in popularity in recent decades, and the trend is likely to continue. *Photograph courtesy of the Michigan Department of Natural Resources.*

Of all the camera owners, each had used on the average about 15 units of color film and 8 units of black and white film in the preceding 12-month period.

Wildlife photography is demanding, but it has special rewards. The photographer is afforded a unique opportunity to gain firsthand knowledge of and appreciation for the out-of-doors. Because of the very nature of some hard-to-reach subjects, wildlife photography also can provide physical exercise. But perhaps most importantly, there is freedom of expression in blending one's ecological savvy and artistic skills, which leads to a very real sense of enjoyment, accomplishment and satisfaction. Taking a "trophy" photo or building a collection of quality scenes involves challenges no less satisfying, no less enduring and certainly more vivid than one's fondest memories.

The scientific community often relies on the photographic "record" to document wildlife concentrations, behaviors and habitats. Photography in wildlife law enforcement is relatively new, but offers promise for effective monitoring of wildlife populations and their lawful use. In many such cases, a scientific record or documentation of a given situation at a given time really is all that the photographer provides. Nonetheless, any of those situations can demand a large amount of time, planning and expense to ensure that the subject is presented in a pleasing, educational and useful fashion.

Aerial photography—including infra-red imagery—is a valuable tool for the wildlife biologist and manager. It can provide an undisputable record of wildlife population numbers and distribution for inventory purposes, and is most useful when the subjects are contrasted against either water or snow.

Wildlife photography is a vital ingredient in progressive public information and educational programs. Sharp, well-composed, eye-catching photographs can be a considerable aid in drawing attention to important wildlife principles and conservation messages as well as explaining them to an uninformed but interested public. Likewise, cinematography is an impressive means of conservation education, and is used successfully by many wildlife agencies to convey ideas, plans, activities and program results to the public. The expense of making motion pictures on wildlife topics usually is justified by their appeal to large audiences.

For personal, commercial, scientific and educational purposes, wildlife photography truly proves the adage that "a picture is worth a thousand words."

EQUIPMENT

Today's photographer is not limited by the amount and kinds of equipment available for photography but rather by the expense. Camera bodies and lenses comprise the major costs of a photographic system. Usually, it is in the purchase of these components that people tend to cut costs and, in so doing, compromise quality in favor of "bargain" prices. One should keep in mind that, regardless of the photographer's expertise, inferior equipment results in inferior photographs. The serious wildlife photographer should set objectives concerning his desires, such as hobby versus profit, black-and-white work and/or color, scientific or popular publication, etc. Those objectives will help determine how elaborate a photographic system is needed.

Cost certainly must be a major consideration in selecting photo equipment, but we advise prospective wildlife photographers to stay with the top competitive lines. Choosing among them usually is a matter of personal preference. A suitable guideline is to examine captions for cover photographs shown on some of the major conservation, environmental and wildlife-oriented books and periodicals. It usually appears on the title page and may identify the kind of camera, lens, exposure and film type used to produce the cover scene. Armed with the information from *several sources,* it is possible to get an idea of the equipment used by persons whose work is publication quality.

Camera Bodies and Lenses

The very basic item of equipment is the camera body. Camera bodies come in all sizes, shapes, orders of sophistication and price ranges. The 35-mm single-lens reflex camera presently is the most popular of all modern still-cameras and is available in a wide price range (approximately $140 to $1,500 in 1983). Also, a wide variety of lenses and auxilliary equipment fit or can be adapted to most 35-mm camera bodies. The convenience and improved sophistication made possible by this interchangeability help justify the investment. All top competitive makes of camera bodies are reliable and can produce precision work.

The fully automatic cameras now available are a boon to professional wildlife photographers, particularly the programmed models. "Auto" systems are of great advantage when they operate properly, but all too often the user learns of a malfunction after the once-in-a-lifetime photo opportunity is gone. The more conventional, manual models may be more appropriate for beginning and "casual" wildlife photographers.

Some cameras have an interchangeable viewfinder screen. Special screens, such as ground glass, improve focusing, especially with long lenses at smaller apertures. Most split-image focusing screens partially black out when focusing, if the maximum aperture is smaller than f4.

Lenses are an equally important component of the photographic package. Once a camera body is selected, it generally is best to stay with that make for lenses. It sometimes is permissible and advisable to adapt a finer lens to a camera of a different make, but before that is done, the interchange should be checked out with the camera manufacturer or some other reliable source, because adapters are expensive.

The question of lens length depends a great deal on photography objectives as well as personal preference. Today's market has a wide range of good fixed focal-length lenses and zoom lenses. There are trade-offs to be made with either type, and the decision ultimately is up to the photographer.

Each type of lens has its advantages and disadvantages. For years, fixed focal-length lenses were considered to have finer quality, and this appears to have been the case, especially in the top-of-the-line lenses. But due to modern computer designing, optical quality of zoom lenses has improved considerably.

The fixed focal-length lens tends to be more compact, sharper at larger apertures and quite rugged. These are important considerations for wildlife photographers. Zoom lenses, on the other hand, have the important dimension of versatility—one lens can do the job of two or more fixed focal-length lenses. Perhaps the biggest advantage of the zoom lens is its ability to crop accurately and quickly in the viewfinder. This is especially important during a fast-breaking picture sequence when changing a lens could mean the loss of a good photo opportunity. In contrast, zoom lenses generally are heavier, bulkier and more expensive than fixed focal-length lenses, and generally produce poorer quality at larger apertures. Therefore, they are best suited to situations where light is bright and constant.

The photographer using fixed focal-length lenses to photograph white-tailed deer should have (1) a wide-angle lens not less than 35-mm (costing $150 to $975 at 1983 prices) (2) a 50-mm "normal" lens ($60–$480) (3) a 90- or 100-mm ($170–$1,020), (4) a 135-mm ($100–$975), (5) a 180- or 200-mm ($150–$1,585), (6) a 250- or 300-mm ($350–$1,900), (7) a 400-mm ($740–$2,070) and (8) a 500- or 560-mm. This array will give the serious photographer an op-

Cameras now made with automatic exposure settings are a definite asset to wildlife photography, and especially so for photographing whitetails in forested areas. With manual exposure-setting cameras, the serious photographer of deer must have a great deal of familiarity with his equipment regarding light sensitivity, since whitetail behavior rarely allows for experimentation. Overexposures (left) and underexposures (right) are not unusual. *Left photo courtesy of the New York Department of Environmental Conservation. Right photo courtesy of the Indiana Department of Natural Resources.*

portunity to photograph in almost any situation that will be encountered in whitetail country.

Zoom lenses come in several combinations. Because of price, the most popular zooms are 80–200-mm ($280–$2,695) or 70–210-mm ($280–$1,995). However, the 50–300-mm (about $1,925) zoom is most ideal for deer photography. Longer zoom lenses have smaller maximum apertures—a disadvantage for photographing deer under limited lighting conditions. Fixed focal-length lenses can be carried in addition, in order to cover subjects beyond the 300-mm range.

Good mirror lenses are offered in the 400–1000-mm range ($880–$1,050). They are compact and reasonable in price. They are fixed aperture and usually take sharp pictures, but will produce an unusual donut-shaped image when out of focus. Construction of mirror lenses is such that they are more fragile than zooms or fixed focal-length lenses.

Tele-extenders make long telephoto lenses out of shorter ones and can be adapted to most lenses in the high-quality makes. However, they drastically reduce light intake through the lens and, in the wooded settings where most whitetails are found, light already is at a premium. Top-of-the-line tele-extenders carry top-of-the-line prices.

Film

There is a wide range of photographic film available today. Most professional wildlife photographers use color because color work has greater market potential with most commercial serial publications than does black-and-white. However, quality black-and-whites are in demand for books, journals, tabloids, newsletters and some serials, and are not to be ignored by the photographer looking to sell his pictures. Experienced wildlife photographers often carry two camera bodies—one loaded with color film and the other with black-and-white film.

The person who photographs for scientific reasons has a mission different from that of the "artistic" photographer, and most likely will be using black-and-white film. That type of work generally involves documentation—photos that record an incident, behavior, a physiographic feature or habitat. It usually requires the same skills and effort as does artistic photography, but frequently necessitates a particularly discriminating eye for biological detail, as opposed to aesthetic composition of the entire scene as is the case in most color work.

The Kodak line of film is of proven quality in both color and black-and-white. Kodachrome and Ektachrome are very good basic color films. Each has strengths and weaknesses.

Kodachrome film is extremely fine-grained and gives excellent natural color rendition for outdoor use in both natural and artificial light. Setting up a Kodachrome processing laboratory is quite expensive, so the Kodak Company does a large portion of the Kodachrome processing. Consequently, the photographer usually will get consistent processing results. On the other hand, Kodachrome tends to be somewhat inconsistent in color balances as it ages. The serious photographer should consider buying larger lots of film, permitting it to age until the desirable color balance is achieved, and then freezing the film for future use. With proper use, Kodachrome film will provide good color quality for deer photographs even in shaded situations. Kodachrome 64 (ASA 64) is considered almost as fine-grained as Kodachrome 25 (ASA 25) and is the faster film.

Ektachrome film offers the widest ASA range in commercial color film, with speeds ranging from ASA 64 to ASA 400. For the photographer who must work in subdued light, Ektachrome is a film that can work in almost any setting. Ektachrome processing usually is available locally, but photographers should be aware that there is a considerable variance in quality control among Ektachrome processing laboratories. When satisfactory results are obtained from a certain processing laboratory, it is a good idea to have all processing done at that facility.

The wildlife photographer continually faces the dilemma of whether to use print or transparency film. Many prefer to shoot transparencies rather than use color negative film simply because it is more economical. And if color prints are needed, they can be made from the transparencies. Most publishers of color wildlife photographs prefer to work from original transparencies. Transparencies also are relatively easy to edit, file, store and mail.

It is possible to make black-and-white prints from transparencies or color prints. The process adds additional expense, and some quality of the original exposure always is sacrificed. Publishers discourage this conversion practice, and generally are inclined to use such prints only as a last resort. That color prints or transparencies cannot be made from black-and-white work is obvious. Yet it warrants mention because it may bear on film selection at the outset of a photography assignment or experience.

Persons who wish to sell their wildlife photography should keep in mind that quality black-and-white scenes are nearly as marketable as color work, though perhaps not as lucrative. They also should realize that competition for paying outlets is stiff. Color photographs certainly can be converted to black and white, but there inevitably is a loss of quality. The scenes above are superb photographs of whitetails in snow. The right scene, however, was taken with color film and converted to black and white. Much of the tone and dramatic quality was lost in the process. *Left photo by Leonard Lee Rue III. Right photo by Tom Gavin.*

As with color film, there is a wide range of black-and-white film available to the photographer. All black-and-white films available from the Kodak Company are good. Commercially, they range in film speeds from ASA 64 to ASA 400. The medium-range speed film, such as Kodak Plus X (ASA-125), is suitable for most situations. It is reasonably fine-grained and has good latitude. For poorer light conditions, the more-grainy Kodak Tri-X is sufficient to shoot about anything that the deer photographer would want.

Black-and-white film offers a wide latitude for special processing. By increasing development time, ASA speeds even greater than manufacturer recommendations can be realized. Special processing in the slower films can mean extremely fine-grain developing.

With black-and-white film, the photographer can set up his own rather inexpensive darkroom, to develop and print his own work, which will give a special sense of satisfaction as well as an economical break on prints.

There are other brands of film, both black-and-white and color, that are good products. Personal preference dictates which one best suits the situation; experimentation is encouraged.

Filters

In some instances, filters are useful. Most popular are the special-effect filters, but in wildlife photography, there seldom is a need for those types. Other filters with more specific applications often are desirable.

Color-balancing filters are effective for overcast and shady lighting conditions. The filter adjusts the film's response to changing color temperatures.

Polarizing filters deepen the color of blue sky and reduce reflections. There is no wide application for these in deer photography.

Filters most used in black-and-white photography are color-contrast filters. These filters block light from specific colors and alter the relationship between tones. A green filter lightens the appearance of vegetation and darkens any reds in the scene. A blue filter can be used to darken sky color. And a polarizing filter can be used with black-and-white film to reduce reflections.

One of wildlife photographers' most persistant problems is changing sunlight intensity, particularly as it relates to shutter speed. Shadowing is a corresponding problem. Proper camera positioning and exposure setting, plus experienced use of filters, will help prevent shadows that can render an otherwise attractive scene useless. *Left photo courtesy of the Missouri Department of Conservation. Right photo by John Hall; courtesy of the Vermont Fish and Game Department.*

Blinds

An important item of equipment for the whitetail photographer is a permanent or portable blind or "hide," in which the photographer can situate himself and his equipment and wait for deer to come nearby. The countless number of hours that the wildlife photographer spends in his blinds, waiting to get pictures of his subjects, is offset in part by the opportunity to learn by observing. From the photographic standpoint, not every day in the blind is productive. However, the opportunities that do occur invariably provide for spectacular results.

Blinds can be fabricated from objects or materials found at the photography site or constructed of wood and canvas and placed in position. Deer adjust to a blind rather rapidly. Once they have accepted it as a fixture of the landscape, they will ignore it and behave normally as long as there are no alarming disturbances. The longer a blind can be left in place, the more acceptable it will become to deer, so permanent blinds work especially well for deer photography. They should be placed in a natural setting that deer are known to frequent, be made to appear as much a part of the natural landscape as possible, and be positioned carefully to ensure optimum photographic vantages, especially with regard to preferred lighting positions at dawn and dusk when whitetails are most active.

Temporary, portable blinds are especially useful for seasonal photography and where there is a time restriction placed on use of the area. An acceptable portable blind that can be purchased is the pop tent from the Seely-Thermos Company. The 1.8-meter (6-foot) model is an ideal size because it is compact enough for storage and transport and has enough interior room to accommodate most photographers comfortably.

In addition to selecting a relatively flat but well-drained site to set up a blind, the photographer can make several adjustments to enhance his comfort and increase the chances that his subject animals will not be disturbed. First, assuming the site selection is strategic, there likely is no reason for a flooring, except in certain aquatic settings such as the Florida Everglades. Besides the noise factor, flooring can be messy and create moisture problems. Blinds should have openings on all sides and vary in height—from the ground—to permit a variety of camera angles. On a permanent blind,

canvas patches tacked on the inside will help keep out moisture when the blind is unattended. On canvas or other cloth blinds, a local auto upholsterer can sew 15-centimeter (6-inch), inverted, L-shaped, zippered openings (with double tabs in the zippers) at suitable places on all sides of the structure.

Within the blind, the photographer should have a camp stool where he can sit with relative comfort and stillness. Also, a towel or plastic garbage bag—on or in which to keep accessories—is a good item to have. Otherwise, it is advisable to have as few other objects as possible in the blind, as this will provide the photographer with freedom of movement from opening to opening and with a minimized chance of accidental noise.

Blinds should be camouflaged. The best material for this is vegetation from the surrounding area. In oak/hickory forest, oak limbs are good because most species of oaks retain their leaves during winter. Sugar maple limbs are good for the same reason. And red cedar is excellent because it covers well and is durable. Mixing species adds appreciably to the natural appearance.

By virtue of construction weight, most permanent blinds are heavy enough to be secure against wind problems. Portable blinds however must be securely fastened to trees, rocks or stakes driven into the ground at their base. In whitetail country, trees probably are the best source of a secure fastening for a portable blind. A blind sometimes can be placed next to a cedar or oak tree, tied in place and then camouflaged to make the setup look more natural. All loose canvas, burlap and covers should be tied down so that nothing flaps in the wind that might frighten deer away. Also, livestock are curious about blinds. They are also destructive, so it may be necessary to select a fenced site or set up a two-strand enclosure to keep the animals away.

Wind directions cannot be ignored when attempting to photograph whitetails from a blind. A deer's sense of smell is very acute, so the photographer should not waste time in a blind when the wind is blowing from behind, alerting the deer to his presence. Also, smoking, eating or drinking warm liquids, such as coffee, in a blind will discourage deer from approaching or remaining in the vicinity.

Bait should be scattered in close proximity to the blind. Shelled corn, sliced or whole apples and commercial feed pellets are excellent

Four types of blinds used to photograph white-tailed deer. *Photos by Leonard Lee Rue III.*

foods that are easy to obtain for use as bait. When bait is used, it is best not to photograph the deer feeding directly on the handout. The presence of shelled corn, sliced apples or commercial pellets in a deer photo tends to suggest or emphasize artificiality.

Some unusual exposures can be made of deer in different postures and exhibiting different behaviors if commercially prepared deer scent is applied to lower extremities of trees just outside the baited area. Deer will investigate those scents giving the photographer an opportunity to get some exciting pictures. This is especailly true just prior to and during the rut, when bucks are sexually active. By careful planning and maneuvering of blind, bait and commercial scent, it may often be possible to attract a whitetail buck to the exact picturesque spot that will make for remarkable photographs.

Assuming there are no state or local legal restrictions against it, baiting can be an effective way to attract whitetails to the vicinity of a photography blind. Normally, baiting should be started a number of days prior to the desired photo date, so that the deer locate and regularly visit the site, and become accustomed to the blind. When taking pictures it is important not to show the bait (top photo). The bottom scene is an excellent piece of photography, but the realism of the picture is diminished by the obvious presence of shelled corn. *Left photo by Leonard Lee Rue III. Right photo by Jimmie McDaniel; courtesy of the Florida Game and Fresh Water Fish Commission.*

Occasionally, a photographer will encounter a situation in which there just is not enough time to put up a blind and leave it to give the deer a two- or three-week adjustment period. In those cases, one can successfully photograph deer by arriving at mid-day, when the animals are inactive, and making a temporary setup using camouflage netting or shrubbery. Under such circumstances, the photographer must remember to keep the wind and light in proper perspective and not try to get in too close. At the longer distances, telephoto lenses should be used.

Sometimes a vehicle can be used as a blind. Deer seem to pay little attention to parked vehicles. A window pod or a sandbag cushion in the window is essential for photographing from an automobile.

When leaving a stationary blind, a good idea is to leave a make-believe lens secured in one or more of the blind's lens-openings so that the deer can see it when the photographer is not in the blind. This helps "condition the site." This mock lens can be made simply by painting a tin can with flat black paint.

Clothing

Camouflaged clothing should be worn while photographing deer, except during deer-hunting season. Even when the work is being done from a blind, camouflage tends to break the outlines of the photographer inside. Caution must be taken when moving the hands and fingers during change of lenses and aperture openings. Deer have extremely acute vision. Camouflaged gloves can be worn to help reduce the risk of frightening the animals away. All movements must be slow and deliberate, and noise held to an absolute minimum.

Tripod

A tripod is another very important piece of equipment for whitetail photography. Long telephoto lenses cannot be handheld with enough rigidity to give a sharp image on film, so a tripod can be set up and adjusted to hold the camera and lens in position. Metal tripods should be covered with camouflaged tape or spray-painted with a flat nongloss paint.

STALKING

Stalking or following whitetails to get photographs is time-consuming and difficult. The best places to undertake this type of photography are in parks or refuges where the deer are not hunted and are accustomed to the presence of human activity. Even so, it is not easy to get close to the subjects or capture on film all the behaviors that may be desired. On the other hand, stalking deer for "chance" photos has at least two major advantages. First, there can be a considerable degree of enjoyment in the "hunt"; moving about certainly is less monotonous than sitting in a blind. Second, by virture of movement, the photographer has a greater opportunity to shoot scenes of deer in different habitat settings.

Telephoto lenses are virtually mandatory for stalking whitetails. And the photographer must be very familiar with his equipment because he will constantly be exposed to varying light intensities and shooting distances that may require precise but efficient mechanical adjustments. As in a blind, quick and extraneous motions are to be avoided.

Soft-soled shoes and garments (camouflaged) that do not produce scratching sounds when brushed against vegetation are recommended. Chest-mount slings also are an important piece of equipment for this type of photography experience.

When stalking, the photographer's movements should be slow and deliberate. He should never approach the subject deer directly, but at a passing angle. And aside from coordinating movement in relation to wind direction (approach from downwind) and sunlight (approach with sunlight coming from behind), perhaps the most difficult aspect of photography by stalking is getting and staying close enough to deer to observe their behavior and be able to photograph them clearly. To a great extent, this depends on the animals' flightiness, the season, the amount of cover, and the photographer's woodsmanship and patience. As a rule, the photographer will get best results if he lets deer set the pace, and does not "push" them. Photo files are filled with scenes of deer leaving an area with their tails or "flag" waving.

White-tailed deer are very fleet, mobile animals. They are also easily alarmed. Photographers unprepared for a whitetail's sudden escape movements will shoot an underexposed and out-of-focus picture. However, when the photographer is alert for such behavior and has adjusted his camera accordingly, the resulting picture can be spectacular. *Left photo by Leonard Lee Rue III. Right photo by Irene Vandermolen.*

SPECIAL EFFECTS

Late afternoon gives the photographer an opportunity to capitalize on some unusual lighting situations. Kodachrome film will give true rendition of the browns, oranges and reds in the waning light conditions. Because of fading daylight, shutter speed may have to be slowed from the conventional 1/250-second speed used to capture deer movements.

On days when the skies are overcast, some attractive effects can be realized by using Ektachrome film that tends to emphasize blues, grays and greens. This is especailly true if foggy conditions develop. On those days, photographing in the early morning can give especially pleasing results if sunlight penetrates in shafts of light accented against the strong shadows of trees. In such cases, lighting from behind (the deer is between the photographer and the sun) can provide a backlit situation that highlights the animal's pelage and makes it look as though the deer is outlined in silver or gold. This effect is especially dramatic in color photos.

The use of long telephoto lenses can give interesting special effects, especially if some limbs or vegetation occur between the camera position and the deer. They can produce a mottled effect and break the monotony of the overall sharply-focused scenes for which most photographers strive. It is enjoyable to experiment with various combinations of the photographic components and the results sometimes are breathtaking.

Use of different focal-length lenses gives the photographer some variation in shooting a single subject, such as using two or more focal lengths from one position to photograph a whitetail buck. This can be done with either zoom or fixed focal-length lenses, though it is much easier with zoom. The shorter focal-length lenses will feature more of the habitat and surroundings whereas the short-to-long telephotos zero in on the subject more critically. It is wise to get several exposures with each focal length so that all possibilities have been covered.

Photographing at night opens some new horizons for the ambitious photographer of whitetails. Night photography is difficult because focus is critically important and requires lighting that usually frightens deer. Most night set-ups are dictated by the immediate setting and generally include more than one light source, which compounds the difficulty. Kodacolor VR, 1S0 1000 film, first released in 1983, provides a fast film with considerable potential for improving nighttime wildlife photography. The use of heat sensors and light beams to trigger present camera apparatus is acceptable. However, most professional wildlife photographers prefer to see exactly what is being photographed. Also, remote systems are costly, temperamental to say the least, and often yield marginal results. Photographers who are most successful with night effects usually are strongly electronics- and hobby-oriented or independently wealthy.

To photograph deer at night, a minimum of three strobe lights should be used to light the subject. Power sources generally are storage batteries with electronic short-cycle recharging times. The apparatus required for the work is more cumbersome and costly than most photographers want to deal with, especially for limited results. George Shiras III pioneered night photography of deer, and although his results were interesting, the scenes were more a reflection of his ingenuity and patience than they were actually artistic or of biological significance.

George Shiras III pioneered nighttime photography of wildlife in the 1890's. Since then, camera, film and flash equipment improvements have made night photography a popular art form—and of considerable advantage for scientific study, since whitetails are quite active at night. *Photo courtesy of the American Museum of Natural History.*

THE RIGHT PLACE AND TIME

As opposed to the behavior of the casual photography buff, who totes his camera about on the chance of capturing a unique scene on film, the actions of a wildlife photographer—amateur or professional—are considerably more premeditated. As previously discussed, the latter invariably has a mission—a particular subject or scene(s) he wants for a particular purpose. He has prepared himself and selected his equipment accordingly, and if unique photo opportunities avail themselves, he likely will be ready to take advantage. While the casual camera buff is forever hopeful of being in the right place at the right time for an outstanding scene, the serious wildlife photographer cannot afford *not* to be there. Outstanding wildlife photos, perhaps more so than in any other photography "specialty," rarely if ever are products of coincidence. They invariably are the result of training, experience, planning, logistical preparation, judgment and tenacity (Bauer 1983, Rue in press).

We emphasize that the key to getting a good collection of high-quality photographs of white-tailed deer is knowing when and where in a given area the animals will be and how they behave. Other chapters of this book, and in other books as well—such as Taylor (1956), Madson (1961), Rue (1979) and Wallmo (1981)—are excellent sources of information on seasonal deer population dynamics, including movements, habitats, feeding habits, and individual and group behavior. In fact, there may be more literature on whitetails than on any other North American wildlife species. The second essential element of knowing deer is field experience. Wildlife photographers, like biologists and managers, do not merely see deer in the wild; they observe them. And for both types of individuals, a critical eye is a trained eye. Such training is gained only by experience in the woods, *with and without camera*. Not surprisingly, a majority of the most accomplished wildlife photographers also are trained biologists, resource managers and/or hunters.

Where

The whitetail photographer's first job in the field is to select places where he will be likely to see deer rather than to try to locate the animals themselves. It *almost* goes without saying, therefore, that the photography site should be where deer are abundant. If the photographer is unfamiliar with the area, he is well-advised to speak with local wildlife agency officials (conservation officers especially), members of local sportsmen's organizations, county extension agents and rural landowners. This should be done in advance of the photography expedition, so there is time to scout as many potential sites as possible and obtain necessary permissions for access.

Public lands, such as national, state, provincial and county parks, forests and refuges, can be ideal photography locations because the deer may be unhunted and less sensitive to human presence. Particularly east of the Mississippi River such areas are quite common, and the photographer need not travel great distances nor spend long periods of time, and absorb associated expenses, when such "facilities" are close at hand. However, even public areas may have time or activity restrictions, and these constraints should be ascertained beforehand.

Private land, even with moderate hunting pressure, is a good bet for sites to photograph deer in natural settings. Although the deer may be "spookier," and photography planning and preparation accordingly more difficult, sites on private land can offer the desired degree of privacy, which is important to minimize unanticipated disturbances of the animals and for purposes of equipment security. Permission of the landowner and/or operator to scout and then use an area for photography is essential.

In any case, best success often is realized when the photographer can gain entry to an area of limited public access, preferably one behind lock and key. In that setting, a blind can be set up and left for future use. The longer a blind can be left in an attractive area, the more acclimated deer become to it.

When

Whitetails can be photographed year-round. Of course, it is easiest to get pictures in autumn, when the deer are congregated and foliage is sparse. Also, many of the commercial markets for whitetail photos are sporting magazines that emphasize trophy bucks in hunting season. Furthermore, autumn leaf coloration provides for spectacular backgrounds attractive to the variety of outlets that feature color work. A secondary reason for the popularity of whitetail photography in autumn is photographer comfort. In most areas, the relatively moderate temperatures of the season are an advantage to the photographer in a blind or stalking.

In many parts of North America, the whitetail rutting season occurs from about November 10 to December 15. It is during this period that whitetails are most active and their behaviors most pronounced. Courtship displays and competition usually are intense, and the prospect for dramatic photos is especially good.

For photographing whitetails in autumn, we offer three precautions. First, hunting seasons throughout North America coincide generally with the rut, from early autumn to winter. The cameraman in the field at this time should be very aware of the possibility of hunters, if not of their actual location in his area. And he must dress accordingly, in blaze orange or red, to assure his own visibility to others. Second, rutting bucks are aggressive, unpredictable and potentially dangerous. Since it is not always

possible to detect signs of aggression, the photographer is well-advised not to approach mature bucks during this season. Staying back and concealed and using a longer lens are the safest courses. Finally, the photographer's attention should focus on adult does, and caution should be exercised not to spook them, because their departure will draw away any bucks in the vicinity.

In seasons other than autumn, whitetail photography conditions may not be as good. The deer are relatively dispersed, less active and unusual in their behavior, and not necessarily in prime condition. Vegetational conditions may be less conducive to clear or open shots, and weather may involve photographer discomforts or equipment problems. Nevertheless, there are needs and uses for photographs in all seasons, as evidenced by the collection throughout this book. For scientific inquiry and technical and semitechnical publications, nonhunting-season photographs are particularly valuable. They record animal/habitat relationships and other interactions or conditions that are relevant to management and education.

A common mistake of inexperienced wildlife photographers is to ignore background. Background and foreground conditions are critical features of most wildlife photographs. They should be subdued or highlighted in relation to the animal(s), depending on the photographer's intent, but never ignored. *Left photo by Irene Vandermolen. Right photo* (note the flies on the whitetail buck's nose) *by Leonard Lee Rue III.*

By the same token, the serious wildlife photographer should not confine his shot selection to large antlered bucks. In most areas, trophy bucks represent only a small percentage of the whitetail population, and their behaviors and movements do not reflect interesting characteristics of the majority. For scientific purposes, all sex and age classes are equally important.

Usually, the most opportune time of day to photograph whitetails is late afternoon, since the deer seem to be more active feeders then, when natural lighting conditions for photography are best. Therefore, a blind should be positioned facing east, so that sunlight comes from behind the photographer's vantage. For optimal coverage of daily whitetail activity, the photographer might consider two blinds—one for early-morning sunlight conditions and one for dusk.

Wind and precipitation also are factors with which the whitetail photographer must reckon. The windier the weather, the more skittish whitetails will be. They are confronted with a variety of wind-generated sounds and smells that keep them even more alert and cautious than normally, and they are not likely to remain in one area for more than a few minutes, unless they bed down. Light precipitation (either rain or snow) has very little effect on deer behavior. It may help to attenuate human scent, to the photographer's benefit. Moist ground will aid photographers who stalk deer, by muffling footsteps, but it muffles movements of the deer as well and enhances the difficulty of their detection. Also, snow cover can highlight deer in most habitats and make them relatively easy to locate and observe. During precipitation, however, the difficulty of taking clear pictures and protecting camera equipment from moisture damage can offset any tactical advantage. And when precipitation and windy conditions occur together, whitetails often seek and remain in shelter, and are difficult to approach or photograph clearly.

TYPES OF WHITETAIL PHOTOGRAPHS

For all intents and purposes, there are four principal categories of white-tailed deer photographs: action; portrait; scenic; and illustration. In many if not most cases, a single photo can contain elements of and be represented in more than one category.

Action

Action photographs emphasize behavior. They freeze a particular event in a sequence of action and are meant to be characteristic of that action. The most important element usually is the subject animal's (or animals') posture(s). The entire deer (if it is just one) is best featured full-frame.

Portrait

Portrait shots also usually focus on individual animals. They are an attempt to capture a dramatic, typical, unmoving pose that highlights the entire deer or certain of its physiological characteristics. That the pose may be part of a special behavior or in a particular setting is of secondary importance.

Scenic

Scenic photos—the proverbial "pretty pictures"—are attempts to balance whitetails with features of their surroundings. Successful scenes can be considered a photographic collage, in that all elements of the scene are of equal or nearly equal clarity and visual impact, and the principal purpose is aesthetic.

Illustration

Illustration photos are those that primarily document a single habitat or physiological feature or relationship of the subject animal. The foremost purpose is educational, and other components of the scene are of nominal significance. Of the four categories, this one deals least with artistic merit (which is not to be confused with photo quality).

Composition

Important composition considerations for shooting photos in any of the aforementioned categories are framing (where the subject is in the entire image) and positioning (vertical versus horizontal images). These determinations are similar in nature to the selection of color or black-and-white.

Persons who regularly create or deal with two-dimensional art forms, such as paintings or photographs, recognize the critical importance of vertical and horizontal placement of subjects within the image area. The human eye

Action photos of white-tailed deer need to be very crisp, especially if they are to be reproduced in serial publications that use low-grade paper. In this translocation release scene, the shutter speed was too slow to catch the departing deer in detail. For such photo opportunities, the conventional speed is 1/250-second. *Photo courtesy of the Illinois Department of Conservation.*

is naturally attracted to key areas on a given format, and those areas optically occur on "the thirds" (Figure 123). This is a basic concept of artistic composition, known in some circles as the "golden mean." Fine art painters almost always situate principal or highlight objects in this manner for maximum visual impact. The wildlife photographer can and should use this same compositional practice for "framing" his photographic subjects (Figure 124).

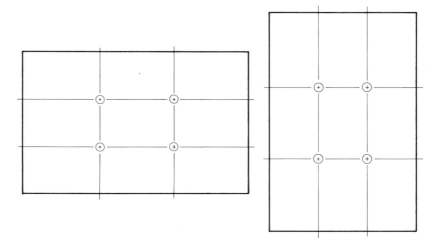

Figure 123. Horizontal and vertical image areas segmented "on the thirds" for optimal visual effect.

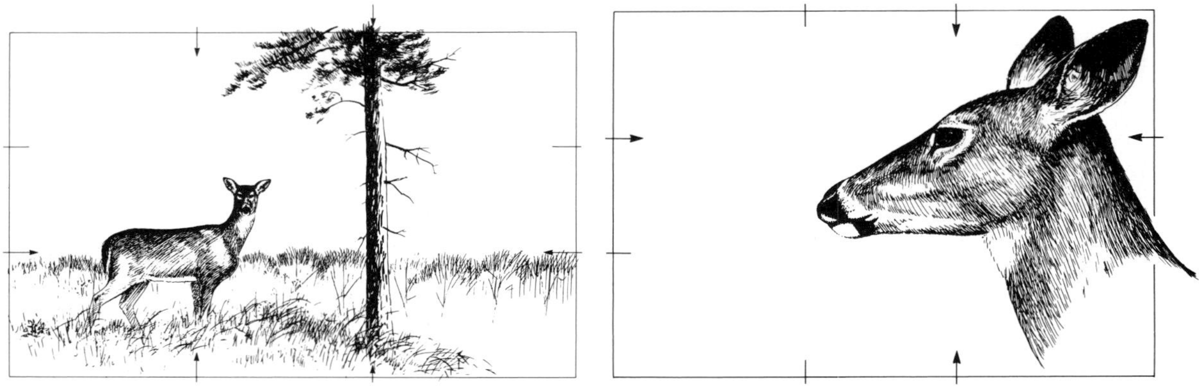

Figure 124. Examples of compositional placement of distant and close-up subjects according to the "golden mean," which applies to photography as well as fine art. Illustration by Robert Pratt.

For positioning, the photographer should consider his mission. For example, if he is shooting for a particular publication—such as a book like this one—with a two-column format, there may be a need for vertical photos. In many cases, horizontal images can be cropped to fit vertical formats, but not always. The reverse—vertical photographs for horizontal formats—rarely are possible, because of spatial limitations in the publication. Therefore, generally, horizontal photos are more useful than verticals. However, just as wildlife photographers are encouraged to use both black-and-white and color film, so too do we recommend that they shoot important scenes in both positions.

Since the photographer, no matter how experienced, never can be certain of the results of his work until the film is developed later, the best assurance of getting high-quality photos of desired scenes is to shoot plenty of film. Film is the least expensive part of photography, and when wildlife is the subject, a scene foregone because of hesitancy or conservation of film is likely a scene lost forever. Except for not having taken a photo when the opportunity was there, few things are worse to a wildlife photographer than having taken a single shot of an important subject or event only to have it be composed improperly.

HANDLING

Records

Whether done for fun or profit, wildlife photography involves paperwork. This means labeling or cataloguing photos in whatever form.

Also, prints and transparencies should carry at least (1) date photographed (time of day, if possible), (2) location, (3) photographer's name (address if possible and affiliation if any), (4) brief description and special note of detail, and (5) camera settings and film types. On slides, of course, there may not be room for all pertinent information. In such cases, the photographer's name and a code number should be written on the slide mounting. All information then should be written in a log book and keyed to the slide by its code number. For prints, the data can be placed on the back. We highly recommend writing or typing on press-on labels that then are put on the print backs. At the very least, writing on prints should be done only along the margin. Under no circumstances should the writing be done directly on the back of the image area. Oversized transparencies can be housed in clear plastic envelopes, with information on press-on labels placed on the envelopes—not on the transparencies.

Storage

Special precautions should be taken to safeguard camera equipment when not in use and to store prints, negatives and transparencies.

The first and most important form of protection that can be taken for cameras and lenses is insurance. A rider to a homeowner's policy is the most convenient and economical coverage. Annual premiums (1983) are roughly $2 per $100 of value. In any case, the photographer should maintain an itemized list of serial numbers on all equipment, plus other pertinent data (make, model, date and location of purchase, cost, etc.).

Proper composition of whitetail photographs requires a degree of "cooperation" from the subject(s). Note that the fawn and its dam in this award-winning photo are located on the thirds. The scene was photographed about 2 p.m. in mid-June under "soft light" conditions of a partially overcast sky, using a 35-mm Leicaflex camera and an SL/135-mm sumicron lens. It was exposed on Kodak Plus-X black-and-white film (ASA 125) at an aperture of f8 and a 1/250-second shutter speed. *Photo by Glenn D. Chambers.*

Cameras and lenses can be stored together, preferably in a cool, dry area, out of reach of children and pets. Ideal storage is in sheepskin-lined sacks or foam-cushioned cases.

When photographing whitetails in cool weather, it is recommended that the camera(s) and lenses to be used be kept securely in an unheated area for at least 24 hours prior to the session. This will prevent the lenses from fogging during the photography period.

Film should be kept in a dark, cool and dry place. In small lots, it can be placed effectively in a refrigerator or, in larger quantities, in a freezer, as previously mentioned. Such storage will retard oxidation and chemical reactions that age or destroy film. However, opened rolls of film should not be refrigerated.

Film taken from a refrigerator or freezer for use should be allowed to warm at room temperature for at least several hours to avoid condensation.

Prints, negatives and transparencies should be kept in an area as humidity- and dust-free as possible. Some photographers prefer to keep all photo materials resting on edge (upright), but horizontal stacking is acceptable if no extra or excess weight is placed on the items and if the humidity level is low and constant. Many of the polyvinylchloride (PVC) plastic or "vinyl" storage sheets are unsuitable. They usually contain plasticizers, solvents and residual catalysts that volatilize. Damage can occur when the sheets are in direct contact with photographs or when the volatile elements contaminate the interstitial air space. We recommend polypropylene products—such as Kimac and Franklin K-22 sleeves, and Safe-T-Stor and Vue-all pages—which contain no plasticizers and purportedly give archival storage quality. Special binders and file boxes also are available now that accommodate storage as well as organization.

Like all aspects of photography, storage and maintenance of equipment and materials involve considerations unique to each photographer. Beginners are encouraged to take heed of the basics, ask questions, read the *latest* literature and adapt the information and ideas to their individual circumstances and needs. This applies not only to the creative aspects of photography, but to the pragmatic matters as well, especially equipment care and handling.

Chapter 44

HUNTING THE WHITETAIL

John J. Stransky
Research Forester
Wildlife Habitat and Silviculture Laboratory
Southern Forest Experiment Station
U.S. Forest Service
Nacogdoches, Texas

In 1982, nearly 3 million white-tailed deer reportedly were bagged by about 12 million recreational hunters in the United States and Canada (Table 108). It is mathematically possible, given these base data, to calculate certain indirect economic benefits derived from whitetail hunting, such as income to sporting goods manufacturers, service stations, restaurants, hotels and motels, grocery stores, guide services, etc. It also is possible to compute the value of certain direct benefits, such as edible venison and leather products. However, there is no mathematical way to quantify the amount of satisfaction and enjoyment that people derive from the experience of whitetail hunting. For that matter, few persons can adequately express in any fashion the many values associated with the activity. Nevertheless, it is the intangible rewards of participation that make whitetail hunting one of the continent's most popular and celebrated outdoor recreations.

The purpose of this chapter is to prepare the individual for whitetail hunting, so that the satisfactions and enjoyments—regardless of harvest success—can be experienced and appreciated fully.

Table 108. Estimated legal harvest of white-tailed deer by hunters in the United States and Canada, 1982.[a]

State or province	Whitetail harvest	State or province	Whitetail harvest	State or province	Whitetail harvest
Alabama	Approx. 210,000	Manitoba	Approx. 25,000	Oklahoma	19,187
Alberta	Approx. 17,000	Maryland	15,060	Ontario	Approx. 11,000
Arizona	3,967	Massachusetts	4,002	Oregon	40
Arkansas	42,873	Michigan	Approx. 189,000	Pennsylvania	138,222
British Columbia	Approx. 3,400	Minnesota	109,443	Quebec	9,878
Colorado	Less than 200	Mississippi	210,684	Rhode Island	216
Connecticut	2,624	Missouri	60,393	Saskatchewan	36,216
Delaware	2,088	Montana	27,456	South Carolina	54,321
Florida	Approx. 65,000	Nebraska	15,085	South Dakota	Approx. 28,000
Georgia	Approx. 134,000	New Brunswick	Approx. 22,700	Tennessee	40,370
Idaho	43,634[b]	New Hampshire	4,674	Texas	337,621
Illinois	26,057	New Jersey	23,745	Vermont	9,946
Indiana	20,918	New Mexico	27,919	Virginia	88,872
Iowa	26,461	New York	185,455	Washington	Approx. 5,800
Kansas	13,078	North Carolina	37,902	West Virginia	88,096
Kentucky	25,311	North Dakota	32,208	Wisconsin	213,565
Louisiana	Approx. 143,000	Nova Scotia	42,784	Wyoming	7,608
Maine	28,834	Ohio	Approx. 51,000		
Subtotals	833,445		1,089,697		1,058,771
Total					2,981,913

[a]Information obtained from a 1983 mail and telephone survey by the Wildlife Management Institute.
[b]Includes mule deer and whitetails.

PREPARATION

Preparation is an integral part of any hunt and the best assurance of an enjoyable, safe and rewarding experience.

Hunting whitetails can be physically demanding, and even if the hunter considers himself to be in perfect health, it is wise for him to visit his physician well in advance of the hunting season to determine his physical condition. He should follow whatever conditioning program is prescribed. Ideally, conditioning is specific to the location, anticipated weather conditions and potential length of the planned hunt. A deer hunter must know his physical limitations *before* he goes afield.

All pertinent and current laws and regulations of the state or province in which a hunt is planned should be reviewed carefully to ascertain open season and bag limit requirements, personal responsibilities, and what constitutes a "legal" deer. A license is required in each state and province, and additional permits may be needed (Table 109). Before issuing a license, many states and provinces also require proof that the hunter has completed a hunter education course, with emphasis on safety (*see* Chapter 35).

Table 109. Resident and nonresident license costs and fees for hunting white-tailed deer in the United States and Canada, 1982.[a]

State or province	Resident							Nonresident
	Basic	Junior	Senior	Archery	Muzzle-loader	Deer tag	Other fees	Basic
Alabama	$10.25		$ 1.00				$ 5.25[b] 3.00[c]	$176.00
Alberta[e]	11.00		$ 5.00[f]			$10.00		11.00
Arizona	9.50					11.00		55.50
Arkansas	7.50			7.50[f]	$10.00[f]		350.00[j]	36.50
British Columbia[e]	17.00		1.00	6.00[f]		8.00		17.00[g] 93.00[h]
California	12.50	$2.50				3.75		43.50
Colorado	13.00						10.00[k]	90.00
Connecticut	5.00		5.00					27.00
Delaware	5.20							40.25
Florida	11.50	free	free	5.00[f]	5.00[f]		2.50[c] 10.00[c]	50.50
Georgia	6.50	free	free	4.50[f]		5.50	10.25[c]	36.00
Idaho	6.50	4.50		5.50[f]	5.50[f]	6.50		75.50
Illinois	7.50		free			15.00		m
Indiana	10.00			10.00	10.00			35.00
Iowa	6.00		1.25	15.00			15.00[o]	
Kansas	25.00						15.00[p]	
Kentucky	7.50	4.00	free			11.50		40.00
Louisiana	5.00	free	free	5.00		5.00		25.00
Maine	9.00	1.00	free		7.00		1.00[r] 5.00[s] 55.00[t]	65.00
Manitoba	3.00			15.00		15.00[u] 3.00[v]		80.00[g] 100.00[h]
Maryland	10.00	5.00	1.25			5.50		45.00
Massachusetts	12.50		6.25	5.10[f]	5.10[f]			48.50
Michigan	9.75	5.00[j]	4.00					75.25
Minnesota	14.00			14.00				75.00
Mississippi	13.00			7.00[f]	7.00[f]			60.00
Missouri	8.00			8.00[f]				50.50
Montana	8.00		4.00	3.00[f]			2.00[v] 5.00[w]	100.00
Nebraska						20.00	7.50[x]	100.00
Nevada	13.00	3.00	2.00			9.00	3.00[y]	75.00

For a deer hunt on private property, prior arrangement should be made and conditions clarified with the landowner(s) in question. Oral or written permission is needed to enter most private lands. Lease or fee arrangements are not uncommon. Whitetail hunters planning to hunt small tracts of land bordered by other private properties are well-advised to consult with the bordering landowners to secure permission to track wounded whitetails, in the event that such trailing is necessary.

If at all possible, before the season begins, a deer hunter should scout the area in which he will be hunting. There are many reasons for and advantages to this preliminary activity.

Table 109. (Continued)

	Nonresident (continued)		
Archery	Muzzle-loader	Deer tag	Other fees
			$ 3.25
			51.00[d]
$ 15.00		$ 75.00[g]	
		150.00[h]	
55.50	$55.00	75.50	
7.50[f]	10.00[f]	38.50	20.75[j]
6.00[f]		60.00	
		31.00	
		30.00	
5.00[f]	5.00[f]		15.50[l]
			2.50[c]
			10.00[c]
4.50[f]		36.00	21.00[l]
			10.25[c]
5.50[f]	5.50[f]	50.50	
		50.00[n]	
		or more	
35.00	35.00		
NOT ELIGIBLE TO HUNT DEER			
NOT ELIGIBLE TO HUNT DEER			
		11.50	
		20.00	10.00[q]
35.00	30.00		105.00[h]
			3.00[v]
		5.50	
5.10[f]	5.10[f]		
50.25			
35.00			
25.00[f]	25.00[f]		30.00[d]
			25.00[q]
25.50[f]			
			2.00[v]
			50.00[w]
			7.50[x]
		75.00	3.00[y]

Safety is paramount. Advance scouting of an area will give the hunter a feeling for the terrain he will be in. He should become familiar with landscape and property features that may affect shooting safety and distance. He can plan his movements and/or stand location relative to his hunting partners or other hunters in the proximity. If there is any possibility of his later having to enter or leave the area in limited daylight, he can orient himself to various landmarks. Advance knowledge of an area also can improve a whitetail hunter's chances of harvesting a deer. It will serve his objective of minimizing the amount of noise and movement he will make while hunting. The animals' travel routes and feeding, bedding and watering sites can be identified, and the hunter's movements and stand location(s) planned accordingly, taking into account concealing vegetation and terrain. Also, prehunt scouting should include visual review of property boundaries, so that trespassing can be avoided.

An aspect of white-tailed deer hunting preparation that too often is treated lightly is the selection of hunting companions. To begin with, it is a foregone conclusion that deer hunting usually is safer and more enjoyable in the company of friends or family, with whom the hunt's responsibilities, duties, hardships and rewards can be shared. Obviously, friendship is of primary consideration in selecting deer hunting partners. Other companion qualities to consider include hunting experience, physical health, shooting skill, maturity and reliability. If a companion is a novice or does not possess the aforementioned characteristics, the deer hunt must be tailored to ensure that hunter's safety and comfort. Accordingly, the hunting expectations of others in the group must be tempered. If a deer hunter is unfamiliar with the hunting area, at least one of his companions should be able to serve as a guide and assume primary responsibility for their (the pair's or the party's) whereabouts when in the field. From planning the location of a hunt to selecting logistical support to preparing meals to trailing a wounded deer to hauling a deer carcass out of the woods to cleaning up a campsite to rehashing the experiences of the day or season, hunting companions can and should be an integral part of the entire experience.

The whitetail hunter's clothes should suit the climate, weather and hunting method. For a trip of a week or more, it is advisable to have

Table 109. (Continued)

State or province	Resident							Nonresident
	Basic	Junior	Senior	Archery	Muzzle-loader	Deer tag	Other fees	Basic
New Brunswick[e]	10.00		5.00	10.00[f]		7.00[z] 7.00[aa]	7.00[z] 7.00[aa]	50.00
New Hampshire	11.25		free	11.00	10.00			59.00
New Jersey	14.00	7.50	7.50	15.00		10.00[w] 8.50[cc]	10.00[w] 8.50[cc]	40.50
New Mexico	12.50		10.50				5.00[dd] 3.25[ee] 2.25[ff]	121.00
New York	8.50	7.50[j]		5.25[f]	5.25[f]			55.50
North Carolina	9.50		10.00[gg]	6.00[hh,f]	6.00[hh,f]		4.50[b] 4.50[ii] 8.00[jj]	31.00
North Dakota	11.00			18.00		18.00		61.00
Nova Scotia[e]	15.00							75.00
Ohio	7.75					10.75		30.75
Oklahoma	7.50		11	10.75[f]	10.75[f]	10.75	5.00[w]	
Ontario[e]	15.00			1.00[f]			5.00[mm]	75.00
Oregon	8.00		free			4.00		75.00
Pennsylvania	8.25	5.25	5.25	2.20[f]	3.25[f]		3.35[nn]	60.50
Quebec[e]	10.00							50.00[g] 75.00[h]
Rhode Island	6.50					7.50[oo]		15.50
Saskatchewan	15.00							50.00[g] 100.00[h]
South Carolina	9.50		free			3.50[b,pp] 10.25[c]		46.50
South Dakota	2.00		free			15.00		2.00
Tennessee	10.50	5.50	free	10.50	10.50	15.00	10.50[c]	70.50
Texas	5.25	1.25	1.25	3.25[f]				100.75
Utah	10.00					10.00	10.00[qq]	120.00
Vermont	7.00	1.75		6.00[f]			10.00[qq]	55.00
Virginia	7.50	5.00				7.50	3.00[b] 2.00[w] 1.00[rr]	30.00
Washington	10.50			6.00[ss,f]	6.00[ss,f]	10.00		100.00
West Virginia	8.00						8.00[oo] 4.00[tt]	50.00
Wisconsin	11.00			9.50				80.50
Wyoming	15.00			10.00[f]				105.00

[a]In U.S. and Canadian currency accordingly. Information based on 1983 telephone survey by the Wildlife Management Institute. Note: these figures apply only to the 1982 white-tailed deer hunting seasons, and do not account for variations in costs and fees that occurred within the states and provinces.
[b]County license only.
[c]Wildlife management area permit.
[d]Seven-day license.
[e]Guide required for nonresidents.
[f]Fee in addition to basic license.
[g]Fee for nonresident Canadians.
[h]Fee for nonresident aliens.
[i]Pioneer license, free to residents over 75 years of age who have lived in Arizona for 25 or more consecutive years.
[j]Archery only license.
[k]Fee to hunt deer with rifle, shotgun or muzzleloading weapon.
[l]Ten-day trip license.
[m]Reciprocal with home state.
[n]Minimum nonresident deer tag fee is $50.00. If hunter's home state does not charge a deer tag fee, Illinois fee is $100.00.
[o]Shotgun permit.
[p]Farmer's license to hunt own property.

[q]Three-day trip license.
[r]License selling agent fee.
[s]In-state transport permit.
[t]Out-of-state/province transport permit.
[u]General firearm deer license.
[v]Conservation license or wildlife certificate; required of all hunters.
[w]Special season or district.
[x]Habitat stamp.
[y]Administrative fee.
[z]Bowhunting certificate.
[aa]Firearm hunting certificate.
[bb]Basic fee for nonresident juniors.
[cc]Junior/senior archery only.
[dd]Optional deer management permit to enable hunters to take a second deer on selected management areas only.
[ee]Special area tags.
[ff]Indian lands tag.
[gg]Covers both hunting and fishing for residents over 70.
[hh]Fee covers both archery and muzzleloaders.
[ii]Big game license.
[jj]Game land use permit.
[kk]Six-day nonresident license.

Table 109. (Continued)

| | Nonresident (continued) | | |
Archery	Muzzle-loader	Deer tag	Other fees
10.00[f]			
24.00	22.00		36.00[bb]
31.00			2.25[ff]
			6.50[ee]
5.25[f]	5.25[f]		
6.00[hh,f]	6.00[hh,f]		18.50[ii]
			25.00[kk]
100.00		100.00	
		10.75	
		100.75	
		50.00	
2.20[f]	3.25[f]		3.35[nn]
		20.00[oo]	
		25.50	25.25[c]
			12.50[q]
			22.00[l]
		75.00	
			10.50[c]
3.25[f]			
		10.00	
10.00[f]			15.00[qq]
		30.00	2.00[w]
			5.00[rr]
6.00[ss,f]	6.00[ss,f]	10.00	
15.00			4.00[tt]
60.50			
10.00[f]			

[ll]Residents over 65 can hunt deer with basic license only.
[mm]License per dog used in hunting.
[nn]Antlerless permit.
[oo]Applies to shotgun, archery, and primitive weapons.
[pp]No state license required in county of residence.
[qq]Antlerless bonus deer.
[rr]Damage stamp.
[ss]For special seasons.
[tt]Deer damage stamp.

clothing, including footgear, suitable for all potential weather. Also it is best to wear lightweight layered clothes that can be removed or added as needed. Safety colors—such as fluorescent orange, white or red—are required in most states and provinces (Table 110).

The white-tailed deer hunter's apparel should be selected on the basis of comfort and legal requirements for coloration. Deer-hunting comfort is relative to seasonal and daily weather conditions and the amount of exertion the hunter may undergo. The Virginia hunter, above, is not required to wear a distinctive color on or as part of his visible outerwear, but as in 36 of the 56 whitetail-hunting states and provinces in North America, the Wisconsin hunter, below, is so required. Despite the climatic and environmental differences to which these distant whitetail hunters are exposed, the clothing of both is layered, loose-fitting and textured to minimize sound when the hunters move. In warm climates, proper footwear is the most critical item of clothing; in the North, adequate headwear is most important. *Top photo by J. Steucke; courtesy of the U. S. Forest Service. Bottom photo by William E. Ruth and Richard E. McCabe.*

Table 110. Some general requirements for hunting white-tailed deer in the United States and Canada, 1982.[a]

State or province	Legal weapons/Minimum power[b]						Colored clothing required for gun hunting[c]
	Breechloading rifle/ caliber	Shotgun/ gauge	Muzzleloaders (rifled barrel)/ caliber	Handgun/ caliber	Bow/ pull weight	Crossbow/ draw weight	
Alabama	Yes/OR	Yes/NR	Yes/.40	Yes/OR	Yes/35	No	Yes
Alberta	Yes/.23	Yes/OR	Yes/.50	No	Yes/40	No	Yes
Arizona	Yes/NR	No/OR	Yes/NR	Yes/OR	Yes/40	No	No
Arkansas	Yes/OR	Yes/NR	Yes/.40	Yes/OR	Yes/40	Yes/120	Yes
British Columbia	Yes/NR	Yes/20	Yes/NR	No	Yes/40	Yes/120	No
California	Yes/OR	Yes/OR	Yes/.40	No	Yes/OR	No	No
Colorado	Yes/.24	No/NR	Yes/.40	Yes/.24	Yes/NR	No	Yes
Connecticut	Yes/OR	Yes/20	Yes/.45	No	Yes/OR	No	Yes
Delaware	No	Yes/20	Yes/.42	No	Yes/OR	No	Yes
Florida	Yes/OR	Yes/20	Yes/.40	Yes/OR	Yes/NR	Yes[f]/NR	No
Georgia	Yes/.22	Yes/OR	Yes/.44	Yes/OR	Yes/40	No	Yes
Idaho	Yes/OR	Yes/OR	Yes/.40	Yes/OR	Yes/40	Yes[f]/OR	No
Illinois	No	Yes/20	Yes/.45	No	Yes/45	No	Yes
Indiana	No	Yes/20	Yes/.44	No	Yes/35	No	Yes
Iowa	No	Yes/20	Yes/.44	No	Yes/NR	No	Yes
Kansas	Yes/.23	Yes/20	Yes/.40	No	Yes/45	No	Yes
Kentucky	Yes/.240	Yes/20	Yes/.38	Yes/OR	Yes/OR	Yes/100	Yes
Louisiana	Yes/OR	Yes/OR	Yes/.44	Yes/OR	Yes/30	Yes[e]/30	Yes
Maine	Yes/OR	Yes/NR	Yes/NR	Yes/OR	Yes/OR	No	Yes
Manitoba	Yes/OR	Yes/NR	Yes/.44	No	Yes/40	No	Yes
Maryland	Yes/OR	Yes/20	Yes/.40	Yes/OR	Yes/30	Yes[e]/NR	Yes
Massachusetts	No	Yes/NR	Yes/.44	No	Yes/40	No	Yes
Michigan	Yes/NR	Yes/NR	Yes/OR	Yes/NR	Yes/NR	No	Yes
Minnesota	Yes/.23	Yes/OR	Yes/.40	Yes/.23	Yes/40	No	Yes
Mississippi	Yes/.243	Yes/OR	Yes/.38	Yes/NR	Yes/NR	No	Yes
Missouri	Yes/OR	Yes/20	Yes/.40	Yes/OR	Yes/NR	Yes[f]/NR	Yes
Montana	Yes/NR	Yes/OR	No	Yes/NR	Yes/NR	Yes[f]/NR	Yes
Nebraska	Yes/OR	Yes/20	Yes/.40	Yes/.357	Yes/40	Yes[e]/NR	Yes
Nevada	Yes/.22	Yes/20	Yes/.44	Yes/.22	Yes/OR	No	No
New Brunswick	Yes/OR	Yes/NR	Yes/NR	No	Yes/45	No	Yes
New Hampshire	Yes/OR	Yes/NR	Yes/.40	Yes/OR	Yes/40	Yes[e]/NR	No
New Jersey	No	Yes/20	Yes/.44	No	Yes/35	No	Yes
New Mexico	Yes/OR	Yes/28	Yes/.40	Yes/OR	Yes/OR	No	No
New York	Yes/OR	Yes/20	Yes/.44	Yes/OR	Yes/OR	No	No
North Carolina[g]	Yes/OR	Yes/NR	Yes/NR	No	Yes/45	No	No
North Dakota	Yes/.22	Yes/20	Yes/.45	Yes/OR	Yes/OR	Yes[e]/NR	Yes
Nova Scotia	Yes/.23	Yes/OR	Yes/.23	No	Yes/40	No	No
Ohio	No	Yes/10	Yes/.38	No	Yes/NR	Yes/NR	No
Oklahoma	Yes/.24	Yes/20	Yes/.40	Yes/.24	Yes/40	Yes[e]/NR	Yes
Ontario	Yes/OR	Yes/OR	Yes/NR	No	Yes/40	Yes/100	No
Oregon	Yes/.23	Yes/12	Yes/.40	Yes/.284	Yes/40	No	No
Pennsylvania	Yes/OR	Yes/NR	Yes/.44	Yes/OR	Yes/NR	No	Yes
Quebec	Yes/OR	Yes/OR	Yes/OR	No	Yes/40	Yes/120	Yes
Rhode Island	No	Yes/OR	Yes[h]/NR	No	Yes/40	No	Yes
Saskatchewan	Yes/.23	Yes/OR	Yes/.23	No	Yes/40	No	Yes
South Carolina	Yes/OR	Yes/OR	Yes/.36	Yes/OR	Yes/NR	No	Yes
South Dakota	Yes/OR	Yes/OR	Yes/.44	Yes/OR	Yes/40	No	No
Tennessee	Yes/.24	Yes/OR	Yes/.40	Yes/.30	Yes/OR	No	Yes
Texas	Yes/OR	Yes/OR	Yes/NR	Yes/OR	Yes/OR	No	No

Table 110. (Continued)

Legal use of certain artificial devices and other hunting aids								
Dogs		Elevated stand or blind		Attractants and lures				
To hunt	To trail wounded deer	Gun	Archery	Commercial scents	Mineral blocks	Food bait	Electrical or mechanical sound	Harvest report and inventory procedure[d]
Yes	Yes	Yes	Yes	Yes	No	No	No	None
No	No	Yes	Yes	Yes	No	No	No	None
No	No	Yes	Yes	Yes	Yes	Yes	Yes	A,C
Yes	Yes	Yes	Yes	Yes	Yes	No	Yes	A
Yes	Yes	Yes	Yes	Yes	Yes	Yes	Yes	A
Yes	Yes	Yes	Yes	Yes	No	No	No	B
No	No	Yes	Yes	Yes	No	No	No	A,C
No	No	Yes	Yes	Yes	No	No	No	A
No	No	Yes	Yes	Yes	No	No	Yes	A,D
Yes	Yes	Yes	Yes	Yes	No	No	No	A,B,C
Yes	Yes	Yes	Yes	Yes	No	No	No	A,B
No	No	Yes	Yes	Yes	Yes	Yes	No	A,B
No	No	Yes	Yes	Yes	No	No	Yes	A,B
No	No	Yes	Yes	Yes	No	No	Yes	A,B
No	No	Yes	Yes	Yes	No	No	No	C
No	No	Yes	Yes	Yes	Yes	Yes	Yes	B
No	No	Yes	Yes	Yes	Yes	Yes	No	A
Yes	Yes	Yes	Yes	Yes	Yes	Yes	No	A,C
No	No	Yes	Yes	Yes	No	No	Yes	A
No	No	Yes	Yes	Yes	Yes	Yes	Yes	C
No	No	Yes	Yes	Yes	Yes	Yes	Yes	A
No	No	No	No	No	No	No	No	A
No	No	No	Yes	Yes	No	Yes	Yes	A,E
No	No	Yes	Yes	Yes	Yes	Yes	No	A
Yes	Yes	Yes	Yes	No	No	No	No	C
No	No	Yes	Yes	Yes	Yes	Yes	Yes	A,B,C,
No	No	Yes	Yes	No	No	No	Yes	A,B,C
Yes	Yes	Yes	Yes	Yes	Yes	Yes	Yes	A
No	No	Yes	Yes	Yes	Yes	Yes	Yes	B
No	No	Yes	Yes	Yes	Yes	Yes	Yes	A
No	No	Yes	Yes	Yes	No	Yes	No	A
No	No	Yes	Yes	Yes	Yes	Yes	Yes	A
No	No	Yes	Yes	Yes	No	No	No	A,C
No	No	Yes	Yes	Yes	No	No	Yes	A,B
Yes	Yes	Yes	Yes	Yes	Yes	Yes	No	A
No	No	Yes	Yes	Yes	Yes	Yes	Yes	C
No	No	Yes	Yes	Yes	Yes	Yes	Yes	B,C
No	No	Yes	Yes	Yes	Yes	Yes	No	A
No	No	Yes	Yes	Yes	Yes	Yes	Yes	A,C
Yes	Yes	Yes	Yes	Yes	Yes	Yes	Yes	A,C
No	No	Yes	Yes	Yes	Yes	Yes	Yes	C
No	No	Yes	Yes	Yes	No	No	Yes	B,F
No	No	Yes	Yes	Yes	Yes	Yes	Yes	A
No	No	Yes	Yes	Yes	No	No	No	A
No	No	Yes	Yes	Yes	Yes	Yes	Yes	A,C
Yes	Yes	Yes	Yes	Yes	Yes	Yes	Yes	A,G
No	No	Yes	Yes	Yes	No	Yes	No	B,C
No	No	Yes	Yes	Yes	Yes	No	Yes	A
Yes	Yes	Yes	Yes	Yes	Yes	Yes	No	C

Table 110. (Continued)

| State or province | Legal weapons/Minimum power[h] | | | | | | Colored clothing required for gun hunting[c] |
	Breechloading rifle/ caliber	Shotgun/ gauge	Muzzleloaders (rifled barrel)/ caliber	Handgun/ caliber	Bow/ pull weight	Crossbow/ draw weight	
Utah	Yes/OR	No	Yes/.40	Yes/OR	Yes/40	No	Yes
Vermont	Yes/NR	Yes/NR	No	Yes/NR	Yes/NR	Yes[e]/NR	No
Virginia	Yes/.23	Yes/NR	Yes/.45	Yes/OR	Yes/OR	No	No
Washington	Yes/.240	Yes/20	Yes/.40	Yes/OR	Yes/40	No	No
West Virginia	Yes/.23	Yes/OR	Yes/.44	No	Yes/NR	No	No
Wisconsin	Yes/OR	Yes/NR	Yes/.40	Yes/OR	Yes/30	Yes[e]/OR	Yes
Wyoming	Yes/.23	Yes/OR	Yes/.40	Yes/OR	Yes/40	Yes/90	Yes

[a]Telephone survey by Wildlife Management Institute, 1983. Readers are advised that data apply *only* to the 1982 deer hunting seasons and that, in each category, there usually were additional or conditional requirements. Also, affirmative answers indicate only that the category topic was legal in part of the state or province, but not necessarily state- or provincewide.
[b]OR = other or additional requirement(s); NR = no requirement.
[c]*See also* Missouri Department of Conservation (1983), Smith and Woolner (1983).
[d]A = check stations (not mandatory in all states and provinces in which this procedure is used); B = mail-in form (by hunters); C = random mail survey; D = hunters must report deer kills to conservation officer; E = spot traffic checks; F = spot locker-plant checks; G = hunting club surveys; H = spot field checks.
[e]For physically handicapped persons only.
[f]In firearms season only.
[g]Significant variance among counties in all respects.
[h]Smoothbore.

Among the auxiliary equipment needed by the well-equipped deer hunter are maps and a compass. Hunters should learn how to use a compass, carry it at all times and believe what it says (Reeves 1970). Aerial photographs or quadrangle maps are available for most sections of the country and can be obtained from U.S. Geological Survey's Distribution Section at the Federal Center in Denver, Colorado. A pocket-sized copy of a map of the hunt area should be carried by the hunter; the original map can be kept at the hunting base—be it tent, cabin, vehicle or other accommodation.

Other items that may seem insignificant but can make the difference between a pleasant and a disagreeable hunt are matches in a waterproof container, hand-wipe rag, sandwiches, jerky, candy bars, flashlight, knife, rope, raingear, cushion, handwarmer, hot beverage and plastic bags for transporting desirable internal parts (heart, liver, etc.) of a harvested deer. The hunter should be aware that equipment that produces an odor—such as a handwarmer or a hot beverage—can alert deer to his presence. Aftershave and tobacco smells also are "red flags" to deer in the hunter's vicinity. Preparing a detailed checklist of needed items prior to packing is a good procedure.

Field glasses often are needed to identify and appraise deer, especially in open country and where hunting is restricted to bucks or bucks with certain-sized antlers. Although many whitetail hunters carry scope-mounted rifles or shotguns, these should not be used for scanning, because it involves pointing a loaded gun at uncertain targets. Binoculars of 7 × 35- or 7 × 50-power magnification usually are sufficient under all conditions (Davis 1970). Many hunters prefer the increased field of vision available with wide-angle lenses. "Glasses" with a protective hard-rubber covering are increasingly popular with deer hunters because the covering protects against weather and bumping damage, and reduces the glare that some nonarmored binoculars can produce. For still-hunting, binoculars usually are carried most advantageously by a strap hung around the hunter's neck. Straps can be shortened so the binoculars will rest against the hunter's upper chest, clear of gun handling movements, immediately accessible with minimal motion, and clear of other objects, contact with which can produce noise that alerts the deer. For deer hunting afoot, binoculars can be carried in the aforementioned manner, but on horseback perhaps more practically in leather cases with

Table 110. (Continued)

| | | | | Legal use of certain artificial devices and other hunting aids | | | | |
| Dogs | | Elevated stand or blind | | Attractants and lures | | | | |
To hunt	To trail wounded deer	Gun	Archery	Commercial scents	Mineral blocks	Food bait	Electrical or mechanical sound	Harvest report and inventory procedure[d]
No	No	Yes	Yes	Yes	Yes	Yes	Yes	A,B,C
No	No	Yes	Yes	Yes	No	No	Yes	A
Yes	Yes	Yes	Yes	Yes	No	No	No	A
No	No	Yes	Yes	Yes	Yes	Yes	Yes	B,H
No	No	Yes	Yes	Yes	Yes	Yes	Yes	A
No	No	Yes	Yes	Yes	No	Yes	No	A
No	No	Yes	Yes	Yes	No	No	Yes	A,B,C

a shoulder strap or belt harness, hung on a short strap from the saddle horn, or placed in a saddlebag.

In many areas where hunting seasons are relatively short (9–21 days) and hunter numbers are high, overnight accommodations may be scarce. Campground or lodging reservations should be secured as far in advance of the season as possible.

Vehicles traveling to hunting sites should be packed carefully. Firearms in particular should be secured, to avoid damage or misalignment of sights. State and provincial regulations regarding the casing and loading of firearms differ greatly and should be reviewed annually, especially if interstate travel is involved. Using commercial travel with firearms, the hunter is advised to check on regulations, special luggage and insurance for the transport of firearms and ammunition. As a rule, hardcover, styrofoam-lined, locking cases are best for such transport. Some airlines require that firearms be clearly marked as such, that they be inspected before being loaded aboard and that ammunition be in a separate package item. Not all airlines provide special insurance for any or all firearms, so hunters should check their personal property coverages and obtain whatever policy riders may be necessary to insure against equipment loss, theft or damage.

From motel room to pup tent to cabin to mobile trailer, the hunting camp represents to many whitetail hunters a special place and time to enjoy the outdoors and to share in traditions and good fellowship. *Left photo by John Hall; courtesy of the Vermont Department of Fish and Game. Right photo by Don Wooldridge; courtesy of the Missouri Department of Conservation.*

CHOICE OF HUNTING ARMS

Selection of deer hunting weapons is conditioned by (1) the laws and regulations of the unit in which one plans to hunt (*see* Table 110), (2) personal experience and preference, (3) price, (4) the type of hunting to be done, and (5) compatibility with the landscape. In any case, the hunter should be familiar with his weapon—its size, ease of handling, recoil, accuracy, sound, safety catch, and loading, unloading, cocking and uncocking mechanisms—prior to the hunting season. Whether or not the hunting weapon has been used (for practicing, sighting-in or other hunting) immediately before commencement of the whitetail hunting season, it should be examined for cleanliness and barrel obstructions. Ideally the weapon is sighted-in to the hunter's satisfaction a week or two before the season, and is cleaned thereafter.

Rifles

The rifle is the most common and popular weapon for hunting white-tailed deer. In Missouri, 91 percent of the hunters used rifles and the rest used shotguns (Murphy 1969). In east Texas pine forests, 89 percent of successful deer hunters on a state game management area used rifles (Stransky 1967).

Rifles suitable for hunting white-tailed deer are available with lever, bolt, pump and semiautomatic actions, and in double-barreled, single-shot and rifle/shotgun combinations. The choice should be governed by type of habitat to be hunted, length of shots anticipated, the gun-action type with which the shooter is familiar and comfortable, and local regulations governing the use of rifles for deer hunting (*see* Table 110). Table 111 gives ballistics of some center-fire rifle cartridges popular for whitetail hunting.

Lever-action rifles are popular in the East. These rifles tend to be relatively inexpensive, light, short and advantageous for shooting in thick cover where shooting range seldom exceeds 40 to 50 meters (44–55 yards). The most popular calibers are .30-30 Winchester, .300 Savage and .35 Remington, because they use relatively heavy, round- or flat-nosed bullets that are not deflected easily by brush.

Table 111. Ballistics for center-fire rifle cartridges commonly used to hunt white-tailed deer in parts of North America, 1982.

	Bullet		Velocity[c]				Energy[d]		
Cartridge	Weight[a]	Type[b]	Muzzle	91 meters (100 yards)	183 meters (200 yards)	274 meters (300 yards)	Muzzle	91 meters (100 yards)	183 meters (200 yards)
.243 Winchester	6.5 (100)	PSPCL	902 (2,960)	822 (2,697)	746 (2,449)	675 (2,215)	269 (1,945)	223 (1,615)	184 (1,332)
6mm Remington	6.5 (100)	PSPCL	954 (3,130)	871 (2,857)	792 (2,600)	718 (2,357)	301 (2,175)	250 (1,812)	207 (1,501)
.250 Savage	6.5 (100)	PSP	859 (2,820)	763 (2,504)	674 (2,210)	590 (1,936)	244 (1,765)	192 (1,392)	150 (1,084)
.25-'06 Remington	7.8 (120)	PSPCL	917 (3,010)	838 (2,749)	763 (2,502)	692 (2,269)	334 (2,414)	278 (2,013)	231 (1,668)
.270 Winchester	8.4 (130)	PSPCL	948 (3,110)	860 (2,823)	778 (2,554)	701 (2,300)	386 (2,791)	318 (2,300)	260 (1,883)
.280 Remington	10.7 (165)	SPCL	859 (2,820)	765 (2,510)	677 (2,220)	594 (1,950)	403 (2,913)	319 (2,308)	249 (1,805)
.30-'06 Springfield	9.7 (150)	PSPCL	887 (2,910)	798 (2,617)	714 (2,342)	635 (2,083)	390 (2,820)	315 (2,281)	252 (1,827)
.308 Winchester	9.7 (150)	PSPCL	859 (2,820)	772 (2,533)	690 (2,263)	612 (2,009)	366 (2,648)	295 (2,137)	236 (1,705)
.30-30 Winchester	11.0 (170)	SPCL	670 (2,200)	577 (1,895)	493 (1,619)	421 (1,381)	252 (1,827)	187 (1,355)	137 (989)
.35 Remington	12.9 (200)	SPCL	634 (2,080)	517 (1,698)	419 (1,376)	347 (1,140)	265 (1,921)	177 (1,280)	116 (841)

[a]In grams (grains).
[b]PSPCL = pointed soft-point core-lokt; SPCL = soft-point core-lokt; and PSP = pointed soft-point.
[c]In meters (feet) per second.
[d]In meter-kilograms (foot-pounds).
[e]In centimeters (inches).

Popular in the East, but also suitable for shooting in open country, are pump and semi-automatic rifles in the .270 Winchester, .280 Remington, .308 Winchester and .30-06 Springfield calibers. For open country, lighter weight and pointed projectiles may be preferred.

Bolt-action rifles have the long-range accuracy needed for open country shooting. In addition to the .270 Winchester, .280 Remington, .308 Winchester and .30-06 Springfield calibers, bolt-action rifles with relatively light recoil include the .243 Winchester, 6mm Remington, .250 Savage and .257 Roberts.

Surplus military rifles have become available in recent years. Most of these rifles are in 7×57mm, 8×57mm and .303 British calibers. Most are well-suited for hunting deer.

Double-barreled rifles are imported by several dealers. If well-balanced, these rifles will handle as easily as the double-barreled shotgun, and may be found in such calibers as 7×57R, 7×65R, .303 British, .308 Winchester and .30-06 Springfield. They are most effective in drive hunts and where two quick shots may be needed.

Rifle/shotgun combinations are useful when other game, such as turkey or grouse, can be hunted at the same time as deer. The most common combinations have one rifle and one shotgun barrel, but some have two shotgun barrels with a rifle barrel underneath (drilling), chambered for the 7×57R, 7×65R, 8×57R, .308 Winchester or .30-06 Springfield cartridges.

Personal preference must determine what is the best all-round rifle. As Taylor (1956:261) stated: "If hunters could not argue ballistics and discuss the relative merits of their favorite firearms, some of them would give up deer hunting."

Open sights are satisfactory for a person who has good vision and hunts in forests or understory where sunlight is reduced and quick shooting may be at close range. Because they can be aligned quite accurately, peep sights are preferred by some hunters (Figure 125).

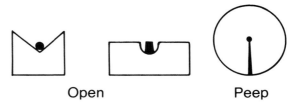

Open   Peep

Figure 125. Typical open and peep rifle-sights for white-tailed deer hunting.

The rifle is the most popular weapon for hunting white-tailed deer in North America. All modern rifles of legal caliber and projectile type can be used effectively to harvest deer. The model and make of rifle and sighting-apparatus selected are matters of hunters preference, for the most part, but predicated on physical characteristics of the hunting site (primarily topography and vegetative cover) and the method(s) of hunting. *Photo courtesy of the North Dakota Game and Fish Deparment.*

Table 111. (Continued)

Energy[d]	Trajectory[e]		
274 meters (300 yards)	91 meters (100 yards)	183 meters (200 yards)	274 meters (300 yards)
150	4.8	0.0	−19.8
(1,089)	(1.9)	(0.0)	(−7.8)
170	4.3	0.0	−17.3
(1,233)	(1.7)	(0.0)	(−6.8)
115	5.8	0.0	−24.1
(832)	(2.3)	(0.0)	(−9.5)
189	4.8	0.0	−18.8
(1,372)	(1.9)	(0.0)	(−7.4)
211	4.3	0.0	−18.0
(1,527)	(1.7)	(0.0)	(−7.1)
192	5.8	0.0	−23.9
(1,393)	(2.3)	(0.0)	(−9.4)
200	5.3	0.0	−21.6
(1,445)	(2.1)	(0.0)	(−8.5)
186	5.8	0.0	−23.1
(1,344)	(2.3)	(0.0)	(−9.1)
99	5.1	−12.2	−63.7
(720)	(2.0)	(−4.8)	(−25.1)
80	6.3	−16.0	−85.3
(577)	(2.5)	(−6.3)	(−33.6)

These sights should be used with large-diameter openings or with the disc removed to let in more light at dawn or dusk. Removing the disc also increases the field of vision, permitting quicker sighting, especially on moving animals.

Telescope sights are most suitable for deer hunting in relatively open country during good weather and when long-range shots are anticipated (Figure 126). A 2- or 2.5-power magnification is adequate for ranges of 200 meters (219 yards) or less and for moving targets. A 4-power telescope is good for most conditions, as are most scopes of variable magnification, ranging from 2 to 7 or 3 to 9 power.

The scope should be sturdy, with bases firmly attached to the rifle and rings tightly clamped on the scope's tube. Lens fogging can be prevented by using lens covers with plastic see-through caps.

Swing-aside or pivot mounts can be used if the hunter wants or needs to use the iron sights, as conditions permit. European "claw-mounts" will allow expedient removal and replacement of the telescope without altering the line of sight (Stransky 1970).

Rifles—especially those mounted with telescopes—are sensitive, precision instruments and should be protected from dirt, moisture and impact. Plastic, canvas or leather cases also provide good protection. In damp climates, rifles should not be stored in cases for long periods because moisture can condense inside the case and cause rusting.

Shotguns

In some areas, shotguns are the only shoulder arms allowed for hunting white-tailed deer

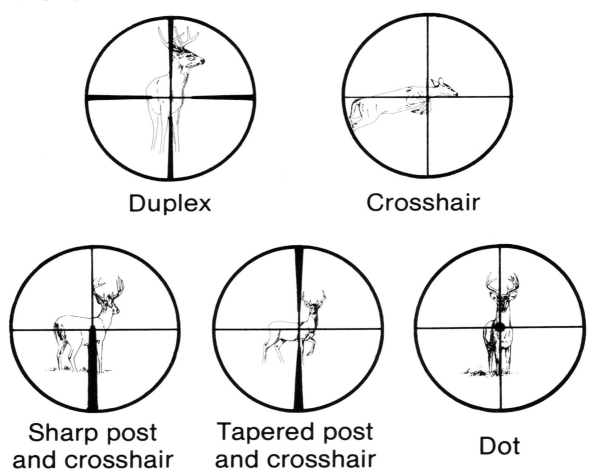

Duplex **Crosshair**

Sharp post and crosshair **Tapered post and crosshair** **Dot**

Figure 126. A variety of telescopic reticles for white-tailed deer hunting. Illustrations by Robert Pratt.

More than 11.4 million persons hunted deer in the United States in 1980 and spent approximately 102.5 million days doing so. Nearly 60 percent (7 million) of the deer hunters used either rifles or shotguns and accounted for about 78 percent (79.5 million) of the deer hunter-days. *Photo by Bill Reaves; courtesy of the Texas Parks and Wildlife Department.*

(*see* Table 110). They are available in a variety of action systems—break-open single- and double-barreled, bolt, pump, and semiautomatic. Buckshot or slugs can be shot from these guns, depending on local regulations.

The most effective buckshot patterns generally are produced by full-choke barrels. At 35 to 40 meters (38–44 yards), the pattern is tight and pellets have sufficient energy for penetration (Ormond 1970). A variety of pellet sizes are available in each gauge (Table 112).

Shotgun slugs are most accurate from cyl-

inder or improved-cylinder barrels. For pump and autoloading shotguns, several firms make special slug barrels, 51 or 56 centimeters (20 or 22 inches) long and equipped with open iron or peep sights that improve accuracy. Although slugs used to hunt whitetails have an effective killing range of approximately 100 meters (110 yards), their accuracy diminishes significantly beyond about 45 meters (50 yards). Consequently, most ballistics data for this projectile type give figures only to the latter range (Table 113).

Table 112. Buckshot loads commonly used to hunt white-tailed deer in parts of North America, 1982.

Gauge	Shell length		Powder charge	Pellet	
	Millimeters	Inches	Dram equivalent	Size	Number per load
12 Magnum	76	3.00	4.50	000	10
12 Magnum	76	3.00	4.50	00	15
12 Magnum	76	3.00	Maximum	1	24
12 Magnum	76	3.00	4.50	4	41
12 Magnum	70	2.75	4.00	00	12
12 Magnum	70	2.75	4.00	1	20
12	70	2.75	3.75	000	8
12	70	2.75	3.75	00	9
12	70	2.75	3.75	0	12
12	70	2.75	3.75	1	16
12	70	2.75	3.75	4	27
16	70	2.75	3.00	1	12
20	70	2.75	2.75	3	20

Table 113. Ballistics of rifled slugs commonly used to hunt white-tailed deer in parts of North America, 1982.

| | Shell length | | Powder charge | Rifled slug weight | | Velocity[a] | | Energy[b] | |
| | Millimeters | Inches | Dram equivalent | Grams | Ounces | Muzzle | 45 meters (50 yards) | Muzzle | 45 meters (50 yards) |
Gauge									
12	70	2.75	3.75	28	1.0	475 (1,560)	358 (1,175)	327 (2,364)	185 (1,342)
16	70	2.75	3.00	23	0.80	488 (1,600)	358 (1,175)	275 (1,990)	149 (1,075)
20	70	2.75	2.75	18	0.625	488 (1,600)	358 (1,175)	215 (1,555)	116 (840)
.410	64	2.50	Maximum	6	0.20	558 (1,830)	407 (1,335)	90 (650)	48 (345)

[a]In meters (feet) per second.
[b]In meter-kilograms (foot-pounds).

Shotguns, like rifles, can be equipped with telescopes. Scopes of 2- or 3-power usually are preferred because of their wide field of vision. However, scopes with no magnification, but allowing a clear sight image, also are used.

Muzzle-loaders

Muzzle-loading shotguns and rifles are legal for hunting deer in a number of states and some provinces, and are the only guns allowed in "primitive weapon" hunting areas. Minimum muzzle-loading rifle caliber, barrel length and projectile type regulations vary across North America (*see* Table 110). Shotguns and rifles may be flintlock or percussion types and either single or double barreled. Some jurisdictions require that only one barrel of a double-barreled piece be loaded and that only blackpowder be used. Recommended charges have been published by many blackpowder enthusiasts and manufacturers of loading components and blackpowder guns (Table 114). Estimating distances correctly is important when shooting muzzle-loaders because the projectile trajectory curve is more pronounced than with a modern cartridge. The effective range for whitetail hunting with a .45-caliber muzzle-loader—using round-ball projectiles and open sights—usually is below 91 meters (100 yards), and the practical range normally is less than half of that distance (J. Crockford personal communication:1982). Muzzle-loader hunters also are advised to be highly selective of shots.

Handguns

Where hunting whitetails with handguns is permissible (*see* Table 110), they should not

In 1980, roughly 833,000 persons hunted with primitive firearms in the United States, and accounted for 5.6 million days afield. Persons new in whitetail hunting with muzzle-loading rifles must be particularly selective of shots taken because of the weapon's limitations. Projectiles fired from muzzle-loaders do not have the velocity, range or energy that bullets fired from modern firearms do. By the same token, these limitations are part of the attraction for a growing legion of latter-day Nimrods. *Photo by Leroy Williamson; courtesy of the Texas Parks and Wildlife Department.*

be fired at deer farther away than 50 meters (55 yards), not because modern cartridges lack sufficient energy beyond that range, but because few handgunners can shoot accurately enough to hit vital areas. Fitting telescopes to handguns and shooting from a rest can improve bullet placement greatly.

Table 114. Ballistics of selected muzzle-loading rifle charges commonly used to hunt white-tailed deer in parts of North America, 1982.[a]

| Caliber | Bullet weight | | Bullet type | Powder weight | | Muzzle velocity | | Muzzle energy | |
	Grams	Grains		Grams	Grains	Meters per second	Feet per second	Meter-kilograms	Foot-pounds
.45	8	127	Round ball	5.8	90	610	2,003	157	1,140
				6.5	100	634	2,081	170	1,231
				7.1	110	658	2,158	183	1,324
.45	14	220	Maxi ball	5.8	90	506	1,659	186	1,345
				6.5	100	531	1,743	205	1,485
.50	11	175	Round ball	5.8	90	594	1,950	171	1,571
				6.5	100	625	2,052	240	1,739
				7.1	110	651	2,135	260	1,883
.50	24	370	Maxi ball	5.8	90	409	1,344	205	1,484
				6.5	100	432	1,418	228	1,652
.54	15	230	Round ball	5.8	90	537	1,761	219	1,584
				6.5	100	565	1,855	243	1,758
				7.1	110	588	1,931	263	1,905
				7.8	120	604	1,983	278	2,009
.54	28	430	Maxi ball	5.8	90	385	1,263	210	1,523
				6.5	100	410	1,345	239	1,728
				7.1	110	435	1,428	269	1,948
				7.8	120	457	1,499	297	2,146

[a]Data from Thompson/Center Arms Company; test figures obtained with DuPont FFG black powder.

In fact, most modern handguns in .357, .41 and .44 magnum and other potent calibers have sufficient energy and accuracy to kill cleanly under 100 meters (110 yards) (Table 115). Heaviest bullets usually are best—preferably the flat-nosed or hollow-point projectile with a short, copper jacket. Use of full-jacketed bullets is illegal.

In 1980, more than 1.3 million people in the United States hunted with handguns, and tallied 10.7 million days of hunting. In 1982, handgun hunting for whitetails was permitted in 35 of the 48 states that have huntable whitetail populations. Its rate-of-popularity-increase in the past two decades appears to exceed that of all other deer hunting modes. *Photo courtesy of the National Rifle Association.*

Table 115. Ballistics for centerfire handgun cartridges commonly used to hunt white-tailed deer in parts of North America, 1982.

| Cartridge | Bullet | | Velocity[b] | | | Energy[c] | | | Trajectory elevation[d] | |
	Weight[a]	Type	Muzzle	45 meters (50 yards)	91 meters (100 yards)	Muzzle	45 meters (50 yards)	91 meters (100 yards)	45 meters (50 yards)	91 meters (100 yards)
.357 Smith and Wesson Magnum	10.2 (158)	Soft point	376 (1,235)	336 (1,104)	309 (1,105)	74 (535)	59 (428)	50 (361)	2.0 (0.8)	8.9 (3.5)
.41 Remington Magnum	13.6 (210)	Soft point	396 (1,300)	354 (1,162)	324 (1,062)	109 (788)	87 (630)	73 (526)	1.8 (0.7)	8.1 (3.2)
.44 Remington Magnum	15.5 (240)	Soft point	259 (1,180)	329 (1,081)	308 (1,010)	102 (741)	86 (623)	75 (543)	2.3 (0.9)	9.4 (3.7)

[a]In grams (grains).
[b]In meters (feet) per second.
[c]In meter-kilograms (foot-pounds).
[d]In centimeters (inches).

Archery

Whereas the first Americans hunted white-tails with bow and arrow as a matter of subsistence, today's archery hunters—of which there are more than 2 million (U.S. Fish and Wildlife Service 1982)—first and foremost are recreationists. Most contemporary archers are also considerably better equipped than their bow hunting predecessors (Conatser 1977).

Modern fiber bowstrings do not stretch when moist, and laminated recurved fiberglass bows have greater strength than the wooden longbows used historically. The compound bow, a recent innovation, has a set of pulleys to ease drawing and holding the string. Aiming devices, arrow racks and other accessories also aid the whitetail-hunting archer. Arrowshafts—principally of aluminum (Table 116) or fiberglass—fletching and points have improved dramatically in recent decades.

Most states and provinces offer a special whitetail hunting season for archers, before, during or after the gun season(s). Most also dictate the minimum pull (draw) required for bows (*see* Table 110), and the type and width of broadhead arrowpoints. Poisoned arrowheads or projectiles with narcotics, however, are specifically outlawed in nearly all jurisdictions.

Table 116. Ballistics for aluminum-shaft broadhead arrows shot from 200 compound bows used for hunting white-tailed deer in Wisconsin (from Helgeland 1982).

Bow draw weight		Number of bows in sample	Ballistics (average)					
			Weight		Velocity		Initial kinetic energy	
Kilograms	Pounds		Grams	Grains	Meters per second	Feet per second	Meter-kilograms	Foot-pounds
22.7–24.5	50–54	19	35.64	550	54.25	178	5.35	38.70
24.9–26.8	55–59	56	34.41	531	57.61	189	5.82	42.13
27.2–29.0	60–64	53	36.03	556	58.83	193	6.36	46.00
29.5–31.3	65–69	35	36.20	560	61.26	201	6.95	50.25
31.7–33.6	70–74	20	36.55	564	64.01	210	7.64	55.24
34.0–35.8	75–79	9	36.81	568	65.84	216	8.14	58.86
36.3–38.1	80–84	6	36.94	570	67.06	220	8.47	61.27
38.6+	85+	2	37.91	585	68.58	225	9.09	65.78

More than 2 million persons in the United States hunted with bow-and-arrow in 1980, for a total of 17.5 million days afield. Bowhunting for whitetails is legal in all states and provinces where the species occurs. Archers tend to consider bowhunting for whitetails as more than recreation and meat gathering; rather, they think of this resurrected primitive hunting method as an art—and there are few other hunters who will argue. *Photo by Irene Vandermolen.*

The bowhunter, by choice, faces challenges spared those who use firearms. The quarry must be at close range and unobscured by vegetation for a safe and effective shot—usually within 30 meters (33 yards) (Bear 1980). However, at this range, any movement, noise or scent is easily detected by a whitetail. For this reason and to improve visibility, many bowhunters prefer to build blinds in trees, usually on a platform that gives safe footing and sufficient room to draw the bow. Although an elevated stand reduces the bowhunter's chance of being detected by whitetails, the position optically distorts the arrow's flight path. According to Bear (1979), downward shooting requires no correction, and adjustment may lead to a low shot or a miss.

Hunting white-tailed deer with a crossbow is illegal in most states and provinces, allegedly because it is an efficient poaching weapon (*see* Haugen and Metcalf 1963). Where permitted, crossbow hunting for whitetails usually is restricted to primitive weapon areas or to hunting by handicapped persons (*see* Table 110). Crossbows, especially the powerful ratchet-drawn types, are slower to operate than longbows, but once drawn, they simply are shouldered and aimed in the manner of a rifle. The modern crossbow produces virtually the same projectile velocity and energy as does the longbow of equivalent draw weight (Bear 1979).

IN FOREST AND FIELD

Hunting Methods

Stalking. Stalking refers to hunter movement on foot. The hunter may follow a random course, hoping to chance upon a whitetail, or actually pursue deer by following a trail, spoor, hoofprints or other sign. Successful stalkers of white-tailed deer tend to be those who move quietly and slowly. A slow pace will minimize noise that could alert deer and also enable the hunter to detect a whitetail's subtle movements, such as a head turn or flicking ear, that otherwise might go unnoticed. Many hunters who stalk whitetails find that a movement pattern of walking for a few minutes and remaining still for a few minutes produces favorable results. When a deer is spotted, the hunter should remain still and wait for the deer to resume normal activity and reach a point where a clear, safe shot is possible (W. H. Holsworth personal communication:1977).

Stalking is done to greatest advantage in hilly, forested areas and when there is soft snow cover sufficient in depth to show tracks and to muffle the hunter's footsteps. It is not a particularly effective hunting method when done in windy conditions that tend to make whitetails more alert and skittish. It also is not recommended for beginning hunters since the degree of success depends largely on the hunter's ability to "read the landscape" along with his knowing the behavior patterns and mannerisms of deer. Using this method also is not advisable for persons not intimately familiar with the area in which they are hunting.

The whitetail stalker must be particularly well-conditioned and wear clothing that not only permits quiet movement but also prevents overheating and perspiring, which can cause chilling when the stalker stops for any length of time.

Stalking is the most difficult of techniques for hunting white-tailed deer. It is particularly difficult when done on flat terrain with limited cover and without benefit of snow on the ground. It also requires the hunter be intimately familiar with the landscape and knowledgeable about whitetail habits. However, whether or not a deer is harvested, stalking can be the most satisfying of whitetail hunting experiences. *Photo by J. E. Osman; courtesy of the Pennsylvania Game Commission.*

Advantages of stalking include being able to cover a relatively wide area, maintaining warmth in cold weather and generally gaining greater fulfillment from the hunting experience by forced use of more sensory capabilities than are involved in most other whitetail hunting methods. Its principal disadvantage is that of increased detection by deer. In essence, the whitetail relies on sight, sound and smell to detect hunters, while the stalker depends almost exclusively on sight. Furthermore, the whitetail's senses are much more acute than those of people. Stalking also is fatiguing, and it is less safe than some other methods since, by virtue of movement and usually being alone, the stalker exposes himself to changing conditions and situations (such as walking into areas occupied by other hunters) and is with limited recourse in the event of disabling injury.

Still-hunting. Still-hunting requires the hunter to maintain a location (or "stand") in order to intercept deer in the course of the animal's movement in or through an area. A stand can take almost any form, but usually employs a measure of concealment, enabling the hunter to "blend in" with the surroundings. Blinds and elevated platforms frequently benefit the still-hunter, although some states and provinces regulate their use.

Still-hunters usually try to select a stand in proximity to well-used deer trails, bedding and feeding sites, watering areas and scrapes. They select a position that offers "corridors" or alleys of visibility that will allow for clear shooting yet conceal their own movements in preparation to shoot. Such positions invariably are downwind from the anticipated direction from which whitetails will approach.

Even when a hunter is in a comfortable and spacious blind, whitetails may be able to see him silhouetted against the light background of the portholes. The hunter either can close the porthole on one side of the blind or sit in a corner. The blind should be checked ahead of time to see that it is safe, noiseless and well-camouflaged. Most importantly, hunters should not climb to or descend from an elevated stand with a loaded weapon.

Still-hunting for whitetails requires the hunter to remain as motionless and soundless as possible, often for several hours at a time. The hunter should select a site or stand upwind from a trail or location deer are likely to visit, and position himself as unobtrusively and comfortably as possible and with a maximum range of visibility. The hunter above-left may have a suitable vantage, but he likely will not remain comfortable and immobile for the length of time it would take an unsuspecting deer to come within reasonable range. Also, his position does not allow much range of movement for his weapon, should a harvestable deer approach from any direction except those within the primary sighting planes (forward and left for the right-handed shooter)—or for follow-up shots. Permanent or stationary platforms, as permitted by local regulations, allow deer hunters better and safer shooting positions and greater freedom of movement when necessary. However, weapons should be unloaded and secured (especially arrows) when the hunter climbs up to or down from an elevated station. *Left photo courtesy of the Illinois Department of Conservation. Right photo by P.F. Heim; courtesy of the U.S. Forest Service.*

Hunting whitetails from elevated blinds is a common practice in Texas, where dense vegetation limits shooting opportunity by other techniques. Frequently the area around such blinds is baited. Such methods somewhat lessen the sporting aspect of the hunt, but they may be essential to ensure a biologically adequate harvest. *Photo by G. McKinney; courtesy of the Texas Parks and Wildlife Department.*

Driving. The driving method of hunting whitetailed deer amounts to canvassing a fairly large area, by means of hunters, unarmed "drivers" or dogs, and chasing deer in the direction of hunters on stands. Stationary hunters should be concealed on the ground or in stands, have good visibility, and be aware of the location of other occupied stands. Standers may be stationed in flanking positions in the event that the deer move away from the line of the drive.

Drivers should be close enough to see the closest driver on both sides and move in a straight line in the designated direction. Usually, a drive will take less than two hours. Depending on cover conditions, whitetails frequently maintain a distance of as much as 200 meters (220 yards) from drivers. But they have been observed in some areas (Maine, Texas, Arkansas and elsewhere) to break cover at approximately 50 meters (55 yards). Weller (1970) successfully used the drive-hunting method for many years in eastern Pennsylvania. It also is common in the Midwest.

Another form of driving is for two partners to walk slowly and parallel to each other about 250 meters (273 yards) apart; one hunter may get a shot at a deer that has been spooked by the other hunter. In still another method, one hunter takes cover while the other walks around him in a large circle at least 0.8-kilometer (0.5-

Standers on a drive hunt for white-tailed deer should know what shooting angles are permissible—away from other standers and on-coming drivers. A clear field of vision and unobstructed aiming "corridors" or "alleys" are necessary because the deer will be moving, sometime very quickly. This stander would be better off at either edge of the woods, so approaching or passing deer will not see him first. *Photo by W. H. Morin; courtesy of the U.S. Forest Service.*

mile) in radius and tries to move deer toward or past his partner. These procedures have been used successfully in forested southern Maine, eastern Texas and elsewhere.

Driving white-tailed deer with hounds is prohibited or restricted by many states and provinces (*see* Table 110). It remains a controversial hunting method. Proponents argue that it is the only way to move deer in large bottomland forests of the South. They also point out that deer wounded by hunters seldom are lost when hounds are used in the chase. Opponents claim that pregnant does abort when chased, fawns sometimes are killed by hounds and, when deer are driven by dogs, stalkers or still-hunters in the area have reduced chances of a successful hunt.

Drive hunting for whitetails, in the literal sense, is illegal in nearly all states. However, it is allowed in some brush country of the Southwest, where movement afoot is impractical or observance of deer at ground level impossible. Such hunting cannot be done on or along public roads, but is popular on ranches and along certain utility rights-of-way. *Photo by Ed Dutch; courtesy of the Texas Parks and Wildlife Department.*

Rattling up bucks—clashing and twisting two antlers together to simulate the sound of antler engagement by two rutting bucks—can be a successful luring technique in areas where the buck percentage of the deer population is relatively high (intense socialization) and hunter density is low (so the deer are not distracted). Although successful results have been achieved in other parts of North America, rattling is not widely practiced outside of Texas. *Photo by Bill Reaves; courtesy of the Texas Parks and Wildlife Department.*

Luring. In central and south Texas, an effective method of attracting white-tailed deer is by imitating the sound of antler clashes between fighting bucks in the rut. The hunter rams a pair of antlers together and then pushes and pulls them apart for about a half minute. After a minute, the process is repeated.

Calls that imitate a deer's bleating sound are available commercially, but they are illegal in some states. A whistle or hissing sound may cause walking or running deer to stop. The chances of attracting a buck by calls are improved by sitting near rubs, scrapes or trails.

Commercially available buck scents are advertised as successful attractants of deer or, at least, suppressants of human odor. Food plots, mineral blocks and feeders probably are the most widely used means of luring deer, but are not legal in all states and provinces (*see* Table 110).

Shooting

The shooting objective of the white-tailed deer hunter is to make a clean, quick kill with a single shot in a vital organ. Before making a shot, the deer hunter has four primary considerations: (1) distance; (2) angles; (3) clearest vantage; and (4) background.

The distance consideration is very important. As previously noted, every legal weapon can produce a clean kill if the whitetail is hit in a vital spot and within the weapon's killing range. Beyond that range, the deer may be hit, but not with enough force to kill it quickly or drop it after a short run. Also, accuracy of shots decreases with distance. If a hunter is unable to judge distance in the area he is hunting—and this is quite common in open landscapes—he ought to confine his hunting to methods that permit prehunt checking, by stepping off or otherwise measuring distance. This, of course, presumes the hunter prerequisite of knowing the capability (maximum kill range) of his weapon. Nearly every hunter has heard stories of deer killed at distances exceeding several hundred meters. Kills at such distances are the exception; crippling is the rule.

To make a clean kill, the whitetail hunter must recognize two sets of angles: (1) the facing position of the deer (Figure 127); and (2) the hunter's vertical relationship to the deer.

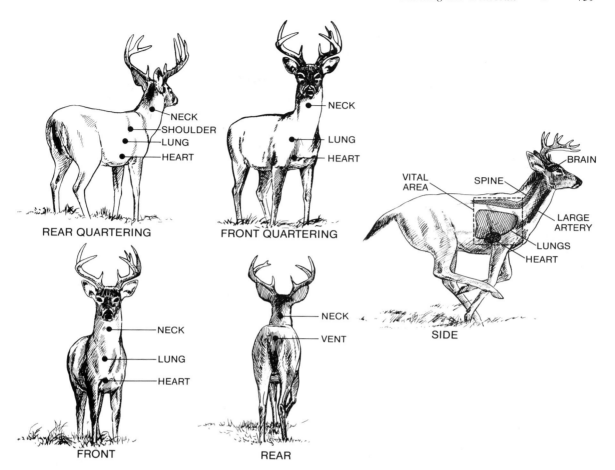

Figure 127. Vital shot placements in white-tailed deer. Illustrations by Robert Pratt.

Neck and chest shots are possible when the deer is facing the hunter, and a neckshot is possible when the animal is facing away from the hunter. The commonly used shot is at the animal's side, in the chest region in front of the diaphragm.

Few hunters can hit running whitetails with a well-placed shot, even at short distances. Simulation of a shotgunner's follow-through is perhaps the best way of hitting a running deer.

Reports and stories of long killing shots at bounding whitetails are legendary among the hunting fraternity. They also are recognized by sportsmen for what most really are— puffery. Not only are such successful shots rare, but they probably are unnecessary and certainly dangerous. The whitetail hunter who makes a close, clean kill of a deer, without ruining meat with a poorly placed shot, has exhibited more hunting skill and sensitivity than has the person who "pot-shoots" at a distant or fast-moving form of a deer—and likely into an uncertain background. *Photo by J. E. Osman; courtesy of the Pennsylvania Game Commission.*

An aiming lead varies with distance, speed of the animal and kind of weapon used. Shooting at a running whitetail as it passes between an opening among trees may result in a hit behind the lung/heart region.

Shooting uphill or downhill requires a low aiming point when relatively slow-traveling lead bullets are used. Modern deer hunting rifles at distances not exceeding 150 meters (164 yards) and angles of less than 40 degrees rarely need aiming adjustment. At greater distances and more acute angles up or down, it is advisable to aim slightly low. Preseason shooting practice and sighting-in under such conditions can pay off during the season.

Visibility also is a critical consideration. Even when a hunter is certain of his quarry and all other considerations permit a shot, he must examine the flight path of the projectile. A perfectly aimed shot at a vital organ with any hunting weapon can be deflected by brush, leaves or woody material. The shot may be missed altogether or result in a wounded and lost deer. The corridor concept of shooting, as mentioned earlier (*see* Still-hunting), can help overcome such obstacles.

The hunter who takes aim at a deer must be aware of the background. This is particularly true for follow-up shots and those at running whitetails. The distance and velocity of missed shots, including those that could ricochet, are cause for concern with respect to human injury and property damage. The best precautions against mishaps of this nature are (1) proper orientation to surroundings, (2) knowing weapon and projectile capabilities, and (3) restraint when in doubt.

Bowhunters may use elevated stands to hunt whitetails in most areas. Downward shooting with bow and arrow at deer at a reasonable distance requires little or no aiming adjustment, as opposed to the adjustments required for certain firearms. *Photo by Richard Simms; courtesy of the Tennessee Wildlife Resources Agency.*

The "corridor concept" of hunting white-tailed deer or other big game involves the selection of stands affording corridors or lanes of unobstructed vision. These corridors ideally radiate out from the stand and afford the hunter space in which to make clear identification and open shots. The hunter who recognizes such corridors and positions himself accordingly will increase his chances for accurate shooting, particularly if his quarry is running. *Photo courtesy of the Michigan Department of Natural Resources.*

"Buck fever" is a state of extreme excitement when a hunter confronts a deer. It is characterized usually by nearly uncontrollable trembling or "freezing," and invariably adversely affects the primary considerations as well as the ability to shoot accurately. Though not a usual response, it is not uncommon either. And while it is more prevalent among first-timers, buck fever can occur among experienced deer hunters.

Much of the information on shooting seems so obvious as to preclude mention, but statistics on crippling losses of white-tailed deer indicate otherwise. Perfecting the mechanical act of shooting accurately, and at reasonable distances and angles, is a matter of practice. When hunting whitetails, however, with the excitement of anticipation of shooting a deer, the shooting itself involves much more than mechanics—safety and success depend on proper judgment and concentration.

Signs of hit. Whitetails often give little or no immediate sign of being hit. The ears or tail may flap slightly. If a deer keeps its tail down, it likely has sustained a fatal wound. Running toward water or downhill may indicate a serious wound. And when deer stagger and run into trees, they will not go far.

Instantaneous kills usually occur if the brain or spinal cord is hit. Some spine shots, however, may ruin much good meat. Neck shots that only cut through fleshy tissue of the gullet or windpipe may result in a slow death, often after the deer has run a long distance. If only the large vessels of the neck are severed, a deer may run up to 300 meters (328 yards), but will leave a clear blood trail.

If shot in the jaw or muzzle, the whitetail frequently stops and rocks its head; blood is sparse and mixed with mucous saliva.

Shots that hit antler likely will cause a deer to collapse, but the animal soon will get to its feet and run off. If the hunter is aware of such a hit, it is wise for him to be prepared to shoot again when the deer rises.

Heart shots either drop a whitetail instantly or cause it to lurch forward and run. The length of the run seldom exceeds 30 to 70 meters (33–77 yards). Blood from such a wound is dark red, sparse at first, then increasing on the trail.

Lung shots usually are indicated by a great leap, followed by a run of about 50 to 80 meters (55–87 yards). Lung fragments often are found at the onshot (where the animal was standing when hit). Bright red, foamy blood is abundant and frequently is smeared on trees, shrubbery and weeds along the whitetail's departure path. Lung shots tend to kill quickly and cleanly, and spoil little meat.

If its leg is hit, a whitetail will stumble or fall, but regain balance and run. Blood from muscle tissue is dark, and its flow may be abundant at first but decreases with distance. Leg shots often leave tubular bone fragments and chips of meat at the onshot.

A gutshot deer will kick out with one or both hind legs, and walk or run off with its back humped. If not disturbed, it beds down not far from the onshot. The blood trail usually is sparse and mixed with digested or undigested food remnants. A whitetail rarely recovers from such a shot.

Trailing Wounded Whitetails

Unless a clean kill is registered, deer nearly always make a startled jump and bound or run off at the report of the shot. And as previously noted, it is not always immediately evident whether or not the animal has been hit. Even when a shot has been taken and the whitetail has run off—apparently not hit—the hunter should make a concerted search of the onshot site and the animal's flight line for blood or other sign of wounding. Following the flight line to the point of the deer's disappearance from view or at least several hundred meters is advised. All too often hunters *assume* their shots were misses and, thinking it imprudent to move and potentially start up other deer in the vicinity, fail to make a check. They should keep in mind that, after a gunshot, it is very unlikely that other deer will remain nearby. Also, there is little so debasing to the hunting experience and values as leaving a wounded or dead deer in the field.

When a whitetail has been hit, there are several appropriate courses of action. First and foremost is reloading, as smoothly and noiselessly as possible and certainly before any movement toward the onshot or downed deer. If the deer is visible, the hunter should remain quietly on his stand, with weapon at the ready, for at least 10 to 20 minutes before making an approach. Assuming the initial shot was not immediately fatal, waiting will give the animal time to expire or weaken considerably, lessening the chances of potential loss of the deer—or having to shoot it again. If the hunter is on an elevated stand (*see* Table 110), and can observe a deer he has downed, after waiting an appropriate interval he should unload before descending. The weapon should be reloaded when the hunter reaches the ground and before approaching the animal.

If a deer may be hit but runs out of sight, the hunter again should remain in place and still for not less than 30 minutes. After that, he should approach the onshot site rather than going directly to animal's point of vanish. Examination of the blood trail will give some indication of where the deer was hit. This will key the hunter as to the type and speed of pursuit. Generally, whitetails shot in the heart or lungs will not go far. Deer wounded in the legs, muscle or abdominal cavity may be able to travel 1.6 kilometers (1 mile) or more, so trailing should be delayed for two or three hours. In any case, the trail should be followed as cautiously as possible until the animal is seen.

If the trail is lost, the hunter should return to the last clear blood sign and mark its location with plastic flagging, a handkerchief or other conspicuous material. He then proceeds again, in an expanding loop or spiral pattern in the direction of the flight path. The hunter may be inclined to move hurriedly and directly along the flight path, but patient and methodical searches as indicated usually are most productive. The mark-and-search procedure should be followed until the deer is found.

When a trail is lost after a thorough and patterned search, the hunter should seek assistance, after marking the final trail sign and orienting himself to that locality. In some areas, it is legal to use dogs to search for wounded deer (*see* Table 110).

Although there are innumerable circumstances that influence the pace and pattern of searching for a wounded deer, a few deserve discussion here. First, deer shot at or trailed until dusk without being recovered present a particular problem. Invariably, the hunter should abandon the search until daylight, when it can be resumed at the last marking point. Second, trailing hunters should make certain that, when on the move, they are as conspicuously visible as possible, as a safety precaution. This is done most easily by adjusting colored clothing to maximize its exposure both front and back. Third, trailing wounded deer to property on which the hunter does not have permission to enter invites an ethical and legal dilemma. As a rule, and despite the inconven-

Finding, following and marking a blood trail is the surest way to locate a wounded whitetail. Hunters on such a trail invariably feel an urge to rush forward in the direction in which the wounded deer departed, but such haste can cost valuable time if the trail is spotty. *Photo by Julie Wickham; courtesy of the Michigan Department of Natural Resources.*

ience, it is best to interrupt the search and obtain the necessary permission. This difficulty can be eliminated in advance if the hunter contacts proximity landowners and reaches an understanding in this regard. Fourth, once a trailing hunter enters unfamiliar landscape, he should mark his own trail, especially in forested areas.

Once the downed deer is sighted after a search, regardless of the amount of time that has passed since its wounding, the hunter ought to wait up to 20 minutes before making his final approach. When the hunter comes within 1.5 to 2.5 meters (5–8 feet) of the deer, it should be prodded with a stick or by tossing a stone or some other object to determine whether the animal is dead. The weapon should be readied for use if the deer should rise. If still alive, the deer should be killed quickly with a head or upper neck shot through the spine.

Downed deer should be approached slowly from the rear and the side away from the animal's legs; flailing hooves and antlers are powerful and dangerous. The hunter's weapon should be at the ready. Once reached, the deer should be prodded from a distance of 1.5–2.5 meters (5–8 feet), which will allow the hunter time and room to react should the deer rise. The hunter above-left has made a safe approach. The hunter above-right has made a dangerous mistake if he has grasped the antlers to determine if the deer is dead. *Left photo courtesy of the Virginia Commission of Game and Inland Fisheries. Right photo courtesy of the Illinois Department of Conservation.*

AFTER THE KILL

Carcass Care in the Field

When a white-tailed deer is shot and recovered, the hunter's first task, after unloading his weapon, is to affix a tag as required and in the manner prescribed by individual state and provincial regulations, to show legal possession. The carcass then should be field dressed immediately.

It should be kept in mind that, by at least one estimate (Fishing and Hunting News 1978), half of all deer taken from the field have not been properly or completely gutted or cleaned. This translates to a 25 to 50 percent loss of otherwise edible meat from an average-sized deer carcass (Warner 1977).

Since field dressing a whitetail can be somewhat messy and strenuous, the hunter may be inclined to remove his outer garment. If this article of clothing contains or carries required special coloration, it can be hung close by so as to be plainly visible and serve as an alert to other hunters in the vicinity. In any case, the hunter should make certain that his presence and activity are signalled.

In the past, it was widely believed that a deer should be bled immediately after bagging, by severing the carotid artery, jugular vein or other veins around the heart. This was practiced regularly in frontier days, before enforced season regulations, when deer frequently were killed in warm or hot weather. Bleeding also was a conventional aspect of butchering livestock and poultry. The objective was to reduce the animal's body temperature quickly.

Today, it is generally recognized that bleeding of deer usually is unnecessary (Craven and Buege 1979, Nelson 1977, cf. Warner 1977). Prompt field dressing and hanging will remove blood sufficiently, even in warm weather. A dead deer does not bleed, but the body cavity should be drained soon after field dressing. Bleeding live, wounded deer is difficult and dangerous.

With carcasses of bucks that were in the rut, some hunters cut off the tarsal glands that are on the inside surface of the hind legs (point "Y" in Figure 128A). This is not recommended, but for those who insist, it should be done carefully so that neither hand nor knife touches the glands, otherwise contacted meat will be contaminated with the scent (glandular secretion). If these glands are considered a problem, they can be cut off together with the lower leg. Bardwell et al. (1964) stressed that tarsal glands need not be removed prior to skinning.

For field dressing a whitetail, the following steps were recommended by Simpson (1963):
1. Prop the deer on its back using two large rocks or logs under the shoulders and two under the hips. Keep the animal's head uphill, if possible. If the deer is a buck,

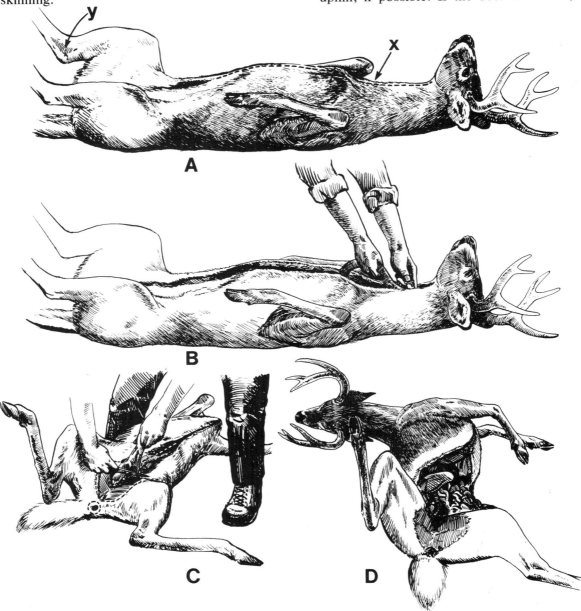

Figure 128. The general procedure for field dressing a white-tailed deer carcass: A = suitable starting position in which to prop the carcass—dotted line represents placement of initial skin cut, X is the approximate forward endpoint for the initial cut if the animal's head is to be mounted, and Y shows the location of the tarsal gland (on both hind legs) which the hunter should avoid; B = removal of the windpipe, if the hunter so chooses; C = removal of genitals and urinary tract—dotted lines show cuts around anus and split to the pelvic girdle; D = repositioning of carcass to remove internal organs. Illustration by Robert Pratt.

remove the genitalia. If it is a doe, remove the bag.

2. Begin cutting between the legs; do not cut deep enough to reach the intestines (Figure 129). Cut up middle, through the breastbone and all the way to the jaw, unless the head is to be mounted. If it is to be mounted, cut only to point ''X'' in Figure 128A, just below the top of the animal's brisket.

3. Remove the windpipe by reaching into the throat cut (point depending on whether specimen is to be mounted) and pull it out by jerking toward the tail (Figure 128A); intestines will come free to the middle section.

4. Move the bracing rocks and turn the deer on its side. Slide a knife into the midsection and slice through (Figure 128D), freeing the intestines held by membrane at that point. Roll the deer on its other side and repeat the process. Then grip the intestines and pull out.

5. Prop the deer as before, putting a large rock or log under its rump. Feel for the seam of the pelvis and cut through it. Hammer the knife with a rock if necessary (Figure 130),

Figure 129. The positioning of hands and a knife for making the abdominal incision when field dressing a harvested whitetail. The initial cut is a shallow incision only through the hide and a thin layer of muscle tissue for a length of 2.5–5.1 centimeters (1–2 inches) between the hind legs and ahead of the crotch. Two fingers of the free hand are formed into a V and slipped inside the cut (palm up) to press down the paunch and intestines. The knife held in the other hand is placed blade up—between the two fingers, and both hands are moved forward in the illustrated manner to make a shallow cut toward the brisket (sternum). Illustration by Charles W. Schwartz.

and then clean out the anal cavity. Special care should be given to removing the bladder intact; spillage of urine from this pear-shaped, translucent sac located low in the abdomen can taint meat, affecting its taste.

Field dressing a whitetail can be messy and awkward, but haste invariably results in a loss of edible meat. Note the proper positioning of the buck carcass. *Photo by William E. Ruth.*

Figure 130. The position for splitting the rib cage or pelvic bridge of a harvested white-tailed deer. In both cases it may be safer, faster and easier to make these difficult cuts after the carcass has been hauled to camp and a saw or axe is available. Illustration by Robert Pratt, after Charles W. Schwartz *in* Geissman and Murphy (1982).

R. A. McCabe (personal communication:1983) recommended that the hunter pinch off the tube from the deer's kidneys at the point of connection with the bladder. The tube or top of the bladder then can be severed above the pinch, and the sac and its contents discarded.

The latter step is not always accomplished with ease. Splitting the pelvic bridge (girdle) with a knife—even a strong knife pounded with a rock—is difficult. If neither an axe or a saw is at hand, the hunter may just as well *not* attempt this cut until the deer carcass has been hauled to a camp or other place where proper cutting tools are available. In addition, split-

ting the bridge in the woods invariably further exposes the carcass cavity and meat to dirt and debris, and makes the carcass floppy and that much more difficult to drag. Also, such a split is not essential for removal of remaining organs and the hind gut. O. J. Rongstad (personal communication:1983) recommended an initial cut around the anus of a buck and the vaginal opening of a doe. Once this circular cut is completed, the anus can be pulled out slightly and cuts can be made around the large intestine and vagina to free them from surrounding tissue. When freed, this section can be pulled forward into the body cavity and removed with the rest of the viscera.

After the belly cut is made from the chest (sternum) of a whitetail carcass to the vent (anus), and if an axe or saw is available, the hunter can split the pelvic bone and expose the gut. Then cutting around the vent and genitals and freeing them from connective tissue and muscle will enable the entrails, including the gut, to be removed intact (*see* Figure 128C). If cuts through the large intestine are necessary during the evisceration process, fecal matter in the gut can be worked forward or backward by hand as necessary so the cut is only through intestinal wall. The cut end then is pinched off while the entire entrails are removed. *Photo by Leonard Lee Rue III.*

Once the deer's cavity is empty, a dry cloth, moss or dry leaves can be used to wipe away any remaining blood. In doing this the hunter should avoid using water or snow, which can wash away taste, discolor the meat and promote bacterial growth (National Meat Institute 1979, cf. Giessman and Murphy 1982). Nelson (1977) noted that using water to clean out an eviscerated carcass can accelerate spoilage in mild, moist weather, but in arid "quick-dry" climates, such flushing is not a problem.

Many hunters regard the heart and liver as delicacies. The tongue and testicles also are edible. These parts can be put in plastic bags or placed inside the carcass for transporting from the field.

Safety should be the foremost consideration in hauling harvested deer from the woods. Under no circumstances should the hunter sling the carcass over his shoulder, as he might be mistaken by others for a live deer. Nor should the hunter exert himself needlessly by trying to drag the carcass over long distances in rough terrain. It is best to get the assistance of at least one other person. The carcass can then best be dragged (by a rope fastened to the antlers) to a road, trail or lake accessible by vehicle, packhorse or boat.

Carrying a whitetail carcass is *not* a good idea. At a distance or in thick cover other hunters may be able to detect the coloration, antlers or other parts of the deer but not distinguish the carrier. Furthermore, it is a very strenuous and messy procedure, and it is difficult to safeguard the weapon and other equipment. *Left photo by Martin Lufler; courtesy of the Texas Parks and Wildlife Department. Right photo by D. O. Todd; courtesy of the U.S. Forest Service.*

There are innumerable ways to haul a whitetail carcass from the field safely and with relative ease. The most common method is dragging, but lengthy hauls over rough or wet ground can be harmful to venison. The assistance of another person and immediate care of the carcass after reaching camp can help to eliminate difficulties. *Left photos courtesy of the Virginia Commission of Game and Inland Fisheries. Top-right photo courtesy of the North Dakota Game and Fish Department. Bottom-right photo courtesy of the Michigan Department of Natural Resources.*

In many states and provinces, the carcass of a harvested white-tailed deer must be taken to a check station where the animal's age, sex and weight are recorded along with other data pertinent to deer population management (*see* Table 110). The hunter who plans to mount the head of his harvested whitetail should ask the check station operator not to slit the animal's cheek to expose its molars when examining for age determination.

Storage in Camp

Once the harvested whitetail carcass is hauled to the campsite, it should be hung (preferably by the antlers or neck) right away in a cool, shaded place. Under no circumstances should the carcass be laid flat or on the ground. When the carcass is hung, the cavity should be propped open with a stick to promote rapid cooling and facilitate blood drainage. However, there is re-cent evidence that quick freezing of the car-cass of a freshly killed deer makes the meat tough (O. J. Rongstad personal communica-tion:1983). This would apply in northern areas where temperatures are −18 to −34 degrees Celsius (0 to −30 degrees Fahrenheit). In such cases the hunter ought to keep the carcass cool, but prevent its freezing in under 24 hours.

After the carcass is hung, a dry or slightly moist (vinegar water) cloth can be used to re-move any dirt, hair, clotted blood or other mat-ter from exposed parts of the cavity. Venison will pick up taint from nearly everything it touches. Warner (1977) recommended wash-ing out the body cavity and flushing out all bullet holes or blood bubbles from other wounds, and noted that failure to treat dam-aged tissue and blood bubbles can result in a loss of from 2.3 to 9.1 kilograms (5–20 pounds) of meat. He also stressed that, after such treat-ment, the carcass be dried thoroughly.

In most states and provinces (40 of 53 in 1982) that permit whitetail hunting, harvested deer must be recorded at designated official check stations by wildlife agency personnel or representatives, before the carcass is transported for meat processing. *Left photo by J. L. Herring; courtesy of the Louisiana Department of Wildlife and Fisheries. Right photo by John Hall; courtesy of the Vermont Fish and Game Department.*

As soon as possible after a whitetail carcass has been field dressed it should be hung and propped open to allow for additional draining, cleaning of exposed meat if necessary, and cooling. *Photo by L. G. Kesteloo; courtesy of the Virginia Commission of Game and Inland Fisheries.*

In warm weather—above 7 degrees Celsius (45 degrees Fahrenheit)—the carcass should be placed in cold storage, at a temperature of 4 to 5 degrees Celsius (39–41 degrees Fahrenheit), to prevent spoilage, intensify meat flavor and increase tenderness (Hosch 1976). The hunter also must decide, under such circumstances, whether to skin his deer, since a key to meat quality is rapid and reasonably uniform cooling of the carcass. In areas where daytime temperature exceeds 10 degrees Celsius (50 degrees Fahrenheit) and nighttime temperature remains above freezing, and/or the carcass is exposed to moisture, skinning may be advisable. Under most other circumstances, the carcass is suitably left with the hide on, as a protection against moisture, dirt and insects. Freezing, thawing and refreezing of the carcass is to be avoided.

If skinned in camp, the carcass should be loosely wrapped in clean burlap or a cheesecloth stockinette (commercially available), to keep off insects. The same can be done, if necessary, with carcasses "in the hide." In any event, the deer should be checked periodically to make sure insects have not invaded; liberal sprinkling of black pepper on exposed meat also will discourage flies. And if a carcass—skinned or not—may be subjected to rain, and assuming it cannot be placed in a dry shelter, it should be covered umbrella-like to keep it dry—without restricting air circulation.

Whether or not the carcass is skinned, identification tags must not be removed until the deer has been taken to a check station or otherwise recorded, as variously required by state and provincial regulations. Tags may not be removed, as required by law, if the carcass is to be transported, even after check station recording.

Also upon arrival at camp, the hunter should promptly refrigerate the deer's heart, liver or other internal organs, since these organs tend to spoil quickly.

Transporting

When preparing to leave camp, the hunter should firmly secure the carcass away from the vehicle engine's heat. The carcass ought to be covered with a tarpaulin or plastic sheet to protect against precipitation. Some states and provinces require that, while the carcass is being transported, part of the animal (usually the head) and/or an affixed tag remain visible. Hunters are advised to check unit, state or provincial regulations on this requirement.

Finally, before the hunter departs, his camp or campsite should be cleaned up, and trash removed to an appropriate disposal location or facility. This is important, to maintain positive landowner/hunter relationships. Also, the owner(s) and/or operator(s) of the land hunted should be notified of the hunter's or hunting party's departure.

Processing the Carcass

Aging of white-tailed deer carcasses is a common practice, and, if done properly, it can increase the tenderness and palatability of venison. When a deer or any living organism is

Transported whitetail carcasses should be kept away from the heat of the vehicle's engine. In many parts of North America the carcass must remain tagged or identifiable while in transit. A covering of plastic or canvas will protect the carcass from moisture or dirt. Hunters also should recognize that a deer carcass secured on a vehicle for transport may be viewed by a good number of people, and may provoke adverse sensitivities among nonhunters. The hunter need not apologize for the necessary procedure, but at the same time should not make an intentional display of the carcass or delay in its delivery. *Photo courtesy of the Minnesota Department of Natural Resources.*

killed or dies, it begins to decay. Aging, in fact, is simply the process of allowing limited decay to tenderize the meat.

Alexander (1982) recommended aging with the skin on (to prevent dehydration and discoloration of the outside lean) for three to five days at 1 to 3 degrees Celsius (34–38 degrees Fahrenheit). Field et al. (1973) also advised not skinning deer before aging—at 4 degrees Celsius (40 degrees Fahrenheit) for seven days— was completed because the hide helped moisture retention and cleanliness. McCabe and Bray (1955) proposed aging for up to three weeks at a temperature just above freezing. Craven and Buege (1979) approved aging for up to two weeks at just above freezing, but below 4 degrees Celsius (40 degrees Fahrenheit). The National Meat Institute (1979:5) indicated that proper aging time—"about a week from the time the animal was shot, is usually sufficient"—depends on the weight, age and fatness of the deer, and concluded that, ideally, a whitetail carcass should be hung in a well-ventilated (but no direct drafts) area with a temperature between 0 and 1 degree Celsius (32–34 degrees Fahrenheit) and a humidity of

88 percent. Marshall (1978) recommended a minimum of four days for aging. Bardwell et al. (1964) suggested that venison aged in controlled temperatures of 1 to 2 degrees Celsius (34–36 degrees Fahrenheit) for at least seven days develops better-flavored and more tender meat. Schmidt (1978b) observed that temperatures above 4 degrees Celsius (40 degrees Fahrenheit) will shorten recommended aging periods, and that once a carcass has been exposed to daytime temperatures above 16 to 21 degrees Celsius (60–70 degrees Fahrenheit), it should be butchered and frozen within a few days.

The hunter may skin and process his deer carcass himself or have it done commercially. Skinning and butchering a carcass require knowledge of deer anatomy, special meatcutting tools, time, and a cool area in which to work. The advantages of commercial processing include better cuts of meat, less wastage and proper packaging. Some commercial processors also will grind the meat and make ground venison or a wide variety of sausages (at additional cost of $0.40–$1.00 per pound [Craven and Buege 1979]). The hunter needs to designate the type of cuts, number of cuts (steaks, roasts, chops, stew meat, etc.) per package, the approximate percentage and type (venisonburger, sausage, salami, bratwurst, etc.) of ground meat, the percentage of pork or beef fat to be added—if any—to ground meat (usually 25 to 50 percent), whether to save the hide, antlers or other inedible parts, and whether to freeze packaged meat. The cost for skinning is about $5 to $10 (1982). For butchering and packaging, the price can vary depending on the hunter's special requests. In 1978, the average cost of cutting and wrapping venison was $0.40 to $0.55 per kilogram ($0.18–$0.25 per pound) (Fishing and Hunting News 1978). The cost for this service in 1983 is estimated at $0.57 to $0.88 per kilogram ($0.26–$0.40 per pound). The principal advantage of a hunter doing his own processing is the monetary savings. He also is assured of receiving meat only from the deer he harvested—and all the meat on the carcass. Excellent directions and diagrams for deer carcass butchering were presented by McCabe and Bray (1955), National Meat Institute (1979), Fischl and Rue (1981), Fagan (1982) and Caslick (1982). The person who has little or no experience with butchering or does not have the time, equipment and work-

area to process the carcass thoroughly probably should not attempt it (*see* Schmidt 1978*b*).

For skinning, the carcass can be hung either by the neck or the hind legs (figures 131 and 132). Skinning a deer hung by its hindlegs (Figure 133) actually is quicker than skinning a deer hung by its antlers or neck. Also, the former method ("hog dressing") is preferable because there is little danger of cutting into the meat or hide (a piece of cheesecloth wrapped around the hand will aid in removing skin from the carcass rump and back). It also will leave a thin layer of fat on the carcass, which will help prevent dehydration and make the meat tastier. By cutting the skin around the neck, knees, and the insides of the forelegs and hindlegs, the hunter can pull off the hide with very little use of a knife. For fast skinning and when the skin is not to be saved, the same cuts can be made and the hide attached to a vehicle by means of a rope. Moving the vehicle away from the stationary carcass will strip the hide off in less than a minute. However, this is not a procedure to be undertaken by the inexperienced, nor is wastage of the hide recommended.

Skinning the whitetail carcass is a fairly uncomplicated task. Whether the carcass is hung head-up or head-down, the procedure simply involves detachment cuts and stripping the hide downward. Care should be taken around wounding sites, so that additional meat is not pulled away and the hide does not tear. After the hide is removed, loose hairs adhering to fat or muscle tissue on the carcass should be brushed off. *Photo by Irene Vandermolen.*

Figure 131. The recommended tail-up position for hanging a field-dressed white-tailed deer carcass, for aging and skinning. Illustration by Charles W. Schwartz.

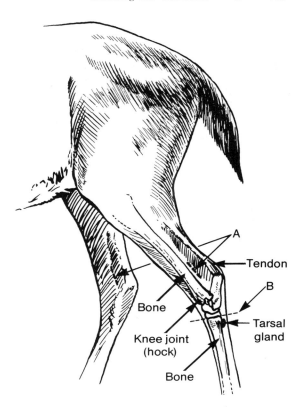

Figure 133. Cutting diagram for (A) insertion of stick or rod with which to hang a deer for hog-dressing, and (B) removal of lower hind legs in the butchering process. Redrawn by Robert Pratt from McCabe and Bray (1955).

To preserve a hide for tanning, flesh and fat remnants should be scraped off and the flesh side salted before folding the edges and rolling into a bundle (hair side out). The hide can be kept in a freezer or other refrigerated space until it can be taken or shipped to a tannery (*see also* Kick 1982).

Generally, northern whitetails have thicker hides than do southern deer, and bucks' hides are thicker than those of does. Also, deer hides are thicker on the back than on the belly side. These considerations could be of importance when selecting hides for clothing or leather goods.

The subsequent butchering process should take the following steps to produce select cuts of meat (Ruhl 1956, *see also* McCabe and Bray 1955, National Meat Institute 1979, Alexander 1982) (Figure 134):

1. Forelegs cut off at the knee joints with a saw or hatchet, or ligaments cut and the legs twisted off;

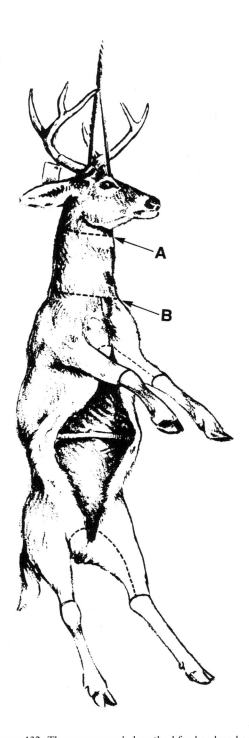

Figure 132. The recommended method for head-up hanging of a white-tailed deer carcass. A stick suffices to keep the body cavity open to air circulation and cooling. The broken lines indicate the locations of cuts for skinning: line A is the neck cut for a deer that will not be shoulder mounted; line B is the uppermost hide cut for a shoulder mount (*see* Figure 131). Illustration by Charles W. Schwartz.

Processing or butchering a whitetail carcass most assuredly ought to be done under the direction of—or by—a person who is familiar with deer anatomy and meat cuts and has the proper equipment and facility. By observing or assisting in the activity, a hunter can gain insight into deer physiology, the experience necessary to perform the work himself, and a fuller appreciation for total hunting experience, including the qualities of venison. *Photo by Leonard Lee Rue III.*

2. Shoulders separated by pulling the legs outward and cutting through connecting tissue;
3. Hams cut off;
4. Ribs sawed off about a hand's width from and parallel to the backbone;
5. Meat from the neck, pelvis and sometimes the shoulders is removed (for ground meat).

Nelson (1977) wrote that the fundamental rule is to take meat cuts across the grain of muscle structure, not with the grain.

Estimating meat yield from live whitetails or whitetail carcasses is not easy. Hunters invariably are too liberal in their estimations and expectations. Figure 135 charts approximate conversions of live weight to field- or hog-dressed weight to edible weight for white-tailed deer.

Palatability of venison is influenced by a number of factors, including animal age, sex and diet, immediacy of death, wound location, immediacy and skill of field dressing, aging (time/temperature), method of packaging, length of storage (frozen), and cooking method (National Meat Institute 1979, Bardwell et al. 1964). Hosch (1976) reported that venison from animals that ran some distance under wounding stress was relatively tough and scored consistently low in consumer satisfaction tests.

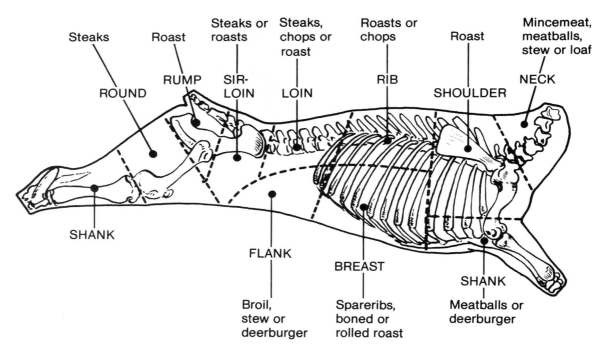

Figure 134. Meat cuts from various parts of the white-tailed deer carcass. Redrawn by Robert Pratt from National Meat Institute (1979).

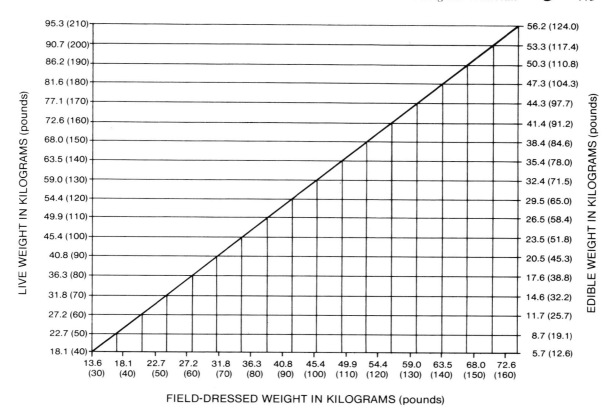

Figure 135. A conversion chart for ascertaining approximate field-dressed and edible weights from live weights of white-tailed deer (from Severinghaus 1949c).

Wounding or even the threat of danger will instantaneously trigger the release of adrenalin, which accelerates the animal's heartbeat and constricts visceral blood vessels. This chemical-physiological chain reaction then "floods" the deer's muscles with blood—the fuel for defense or flight. The sudden and exaggerated metabolism of extra blood in muscle tissue produces a build-up of lactic and pyruvic acids, both metabolic waste products. Adrenalin in blood-engorged muscles, in combination with uneliminated metabolic wastes, is the principal cause of strong- or gamy-tasting cooked venison.

Freezing venison is best done commercially by "blast freezing"—a rapid process at −29 degrees Celsius (−20 degrees Fahrenheit) that prevents formation of ice crystals in the meat fibers. Favorable results are possible in a home freezer, assuming there is air space between each piece and the quantity of fresh meat to be frozen does not exceed 15.9 kilograms (35 pounds) for a 0.4-cubic-meter (15-cubic-foot) freezer, 24.9 kilograms (55 pounds) for a 0.5-cubic-meter (18-cubic-foot) freezer, 31.8 kilograms (70 pounds) for a 0.6-cubic-meter (22-cubic-foot) freezer, and 38.6 kilograms (85 pounds) for a 0.7-cubic-meter (26-cubic-foot) freezer (National Meat Institute 1979).

In any case, prior to packaging for freezing, meat should be cleaned of all hair, clotted blood and fatty tissue (which are major contributors to the so-called "gamy" or wild taste) and dried (absorbent towels are suitable). The meat then should be well-chilled, wrapped in air-tight moisture/vapor-proof freezer paper (*see* Davis 1980), marked (date, cut and amount), placed in a freezer—away from its walls, and frozen completely at the freezer's lowest possible setting.

Frozen venison maintained at −18 degrees Celsius (0 degrees Fahrenheit) can retain its quality for up to one year. At 20 degrees colder for any length of time, there is a possibility of freezer burn (dehydration that can discolor meat and change its consistency, but does not ruin it). If the temperature is kept higher than −18 degrees Celsius (0 degrees Fahrenheit), the meat's storage life is reduced considerably. For example, venison quality will begin to deteriorate after six months if maintained at −15 degrees Celsius (5 degrees Fahrenheit), after two months at −12 degrees Celsius (10 degrees Fahrenheit), after 3 weeks at −10 degrees Celsius (15 degrees Fahrenheit), after 10 days at −7 degrees Celsius (20 degrees Fahrenheit) and after 5 days at −4 degrees Celsius (25 degrees Fahrenheit). Caslick (1982) recommended that, for best quality, venison be eaten within six to nine months. Craven and Buege (1979) noted that ground venison stored in a freezer for more than four months may develop an "off taste."

Prior to cooking, frozen venison should be thawed slowly—8 to 12 hours in a refrigerator or 4.5 to 6.5 hours per kilogram (2–3 hours per pound) at room temperature. Thawing in a sink or on a countertop can cause external parts of meat to warm up and become susceptible to bacteria long before the inside defrosts.

A number of cookbooks provide delicious recipes, including Klussman et al. (no date), Dunn (1979), Steindler (1965), Angier (1975), Cone (1974), Michigan United Conservation Clubs (1981) and Gorton (1957). As a rule, venison—being drier and less tender than domestic meats—should not be overcooked; juicy preparations frequently produce better-tasting meat than do dry recipes, and are best cooked at low to moderate heat. Dry-heat cooking methods—roasting, broiling, pan broiling and frying—generally are preferred for cuts of meat that are naturally tender (steaks and chops), whereas moist-heat cooking—braising, stewing or pressure cooking—usually is favored for the less tender cuts (shoulder, neck, breast, rump, round, shank and flank), as it helps soften tough or stringy connective tissue (Dunn 1979).

Quality of deer meat—in terms of protein and vitamins—is equal to or exceeds that of domestic sources. Venison also has considerably higher calcium, phosphorus and iron contents, and less fat and fewer calories than equivalent portions of beef or pork (Table 117) (Pennington and Church 1980). Moreover, venison contains no artificial growth hormones, dye or flavor.

Another measure of the quality of deer meat is market value. Where available, from sources that are licensed to sell game meat, venison commands a relatively high price (Table 118). *Game animals sold have been domestically raised; the selling of wild game is expressly forbidden in virtually all states.*

Table 117. Comparative food values of venison and some domestic raw meats (extrapolated from Pennington and Church 1980).

Food	Quantity			Protein		Fat				
	Grams	Ounces	Calories	Grams	Ounces	Grams	Ounces	Calcium[a]	Phosphorus[a]	Iron[a]
Beef										
Hamburger, fried	99.25	3.5	197	19.2	0.67	12.8	0.45	5.3	165	[b]
T-bone steak, broiled	99.25	3.5	247	25.2	0.88	15.4	0.54	10.5	181	3.8
Rib roast, cooked	99.25	3.5	132	12.4	0.43	2.9	0.10	3.5	95	1.5
Veal, loin chop, cooked	99.25	3.5	226	12.1	0.42	19.3	0.68	3.1	100	1.5
Lamb, loin chop, cooked	99.25	3.5	90	10.9	0.38	4.8	0.17	3.5	86	1.2
Pork										
Bacon, fried	99.25	3.5	172	6.3	0.22	15.7	0.55	4.7	77	0.7
Ham, fresh, cooked	99.25	3.5	111	17.3	0.61	4.1	0.14	3.1	129	1.1
Loin chop, cooked	99.25	3.5	183	15.1	0.53	13.1	0.46	5.8	118	2.3
Poultry (domestic)										
Chicken, broiled	99.25	3.5	151	20.2	0.71	7.2	0.25	14.0	200	1.5
Duck	99.25	3.5	326	16.0	0.56	28.6	1.01	15.0	188	1.8
Goose	99.25	3.5	322	28.1	0.99	22.4	0.79	10.0	265	4.6
Turkey, roasted	99.25	3.5	200	30.9	1.09	7.6[b]	0.27	30.0	400	5.1
Venison										
Roast, cooked	99.25	3.5	146	29.5	1.04	2.2	0.07	20.0	264	3.5
Steak, broiled	99.25	3.5	201	33.5	1.18	6.4	0.23	29.0	286	7.8

[a]In milligrams.
[b]Reliable data are sparse.

Table 118. Comparative prices of meat from domestically raised game animals, December 1982.[a]

Meat source	Price	
	Per kilogram	Per pound
Pheasant	$8.27–13.21	$3.75–5.99
Partridge	$15.41–17.64	$6.99–8.00
Quail	$5.51–42.99	$2.50–19.50
Squab	$8.82–19.91	$4.00–9.03
Ducks (mallard)	$4.17–12.32	$1.89–5.59
Guinea hens	$3.53–18.94	$1.60–8.59
Goose	$4.39–5.93	$1.99–2.69
Rabbit	$3.28–8.80	$1.49–3.99
Bison	$5.18–24.23	$2.35–10.99
Bear (ground)	$15.32	$6.95
Moose (ground)	$12.54	$5.69
Pronghorn (ground)	$12.90	$5.85
Venison		
Leg	$19.82–20.94	$8.99–9.50
Loin	$17.86–24.03	$8.10–10.90
Ground	$12.01	$5.45
Roast	$14.77	$6.70
Bone-in	$15.39	$6.98
Boneless	$38.84	$13.99

[a]From McNees' (1983) survey of wholesalers and retailers in the Washington, D.C. metropolitan area.

Trophy Care

Neck mounts. To prepare a trophy whitetail for a neck or shoulder mount, the hunter should begin skinning just behind the forelegs on top of the withers. The cut should progress along the back of the neck to the top of the head, and then fork to the antler bases (Figure 136).

The head then can be skinned, with care taken not to cut into the skin of the eyelids, lips and ears. Antlers are cut off with a portion of the skull large enough to fit the artificial head form used by a taxidermist. It is better to have a larger portion of the skull than a part that is too small. Since shoulder or cape mounting is a rather exact art, it usually is prudent to skin only the shoulders and neck, and leave skinning of the head to a taxidermist. Taxidermy costs for such services range from about $125 to $250 (1982–1983 prices).

Antler mounts. Antler mounts are more easily prepared, less costly and take up less wall space than neck mounts. To remove antlers intact and suitable for mounting, the following steps should be followed:
1. The forehead with antlers is cut from the skull with a bonesaw or hacksaw. Cutting is easier if the skin is removed to behind the antlers and ears. The saw cut begins

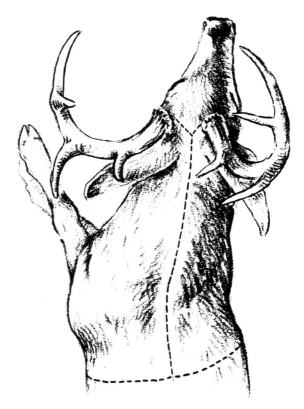

Figure 136. The skinning pattern for a shoulder or cape mount of a white-tailed deer. Illustration by Charles W. Schwartz.

behind the antlers and proceeds in a line toward the middle of the nose (Figure 137). If done correctly, about one-third of the eye-socket will remain on the forehead.
2. When the forehead and antlers are removed intact, the brain matter and as much muscle and connective tissue as possible are removed without scratching the skull bone.

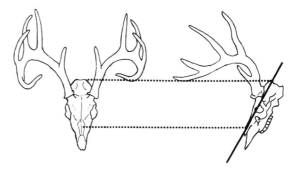

Figure 137. The cut line (right) for removal of white-tailed deer antlers for mounting.

3. The bone is soaked in cold water for one day, with the water changed two to three times, to rinse blood from the bone.

4. With only the skull bone submerged, cold water is brought to a boil slowly; the antlers will discolor if submerged. When all remaining tissue separates, the bone is cleaned off with a knife and by rubbing with clean cloth or paper towels. After a few more minutes of boiling, the cleaning process is repeated.

5. The skull is boiled again for about 20 minutes, beginning with clean cold water. When removed for final cleaning, the skull should be submerged immediately in cold water. This submersion will prevent grease from setting in the tissue and later causing yellowing of the bone.

6. The skull then can be dried, and will retain its natural white coloration. Bleaching the skull in the sun for a few hours or more will produce an even purer white. When thoroughly dry, the skull and attached antlers are ready to be fastened to a plaque or other display by means of wood screws. Costs for antler mounts range from $25 to $45 (1982–1983 prices).

Other Useful Items

Deerhide can be prepared by professional tanners. In preparation for shipment, the skin side of the hide should be rubbed with salt—2.3 kilograms (5.1 pounds) (Rockwell 1971)—and then folded. With the hair on, a hide makes a handsome though not very durable rug. Tanned without hair, the skin can be made into attractive jackets, gloves, purses and other useful articles. Costs for tanning range from about $20 to $50 per hide (1982–1983 prices).

Forelegs (with hooves attached) can be made into gun racks, hat racks or lamp stands. While still flexible, the hooves should be bent at the ankle joint into the desired shape. Stored in a safe place, they will dry and harden in a few weeks.

Hair from the tail of a white-tailed deer furnishes the "bucktail" coveted by many anglers who tie artificial lures.

Trophy Scoring

In the East, scoring of trophy white-tailed deer is determined by the total number of points on the right and left beam. In the West, only the points on one beam are counted—usually the beam with the most points.

Antler spread, symmetry, diameter and length of beams, and number and length of tines are criteria for evaluating antlers by the Boone and Crockett Club's copyrighted scoring system (Nesbitt and Wright 1981). All correspondence concerning trophy recordkeeping, scoring materials, trophy entry and related matters for past and present programs should be directed to the Boone and Crockett Club, 205 S. Patrick Street, Alexandria, Virginia 22314.

The same scoring system is used by the Conseil International de la Chasse. European sources also use this scoring system, with measurements in centimeters rather than inches (Haltenorth and Trense 1956, Bieger and Nüsslein 1977). Antler weight was included, for the first time, among the supplementary data by Bieger and Nüsslein (1977).

The Pope and Young scoring system, named for renowned bowhunters Dr. Saxton Pope and Arthur Young (Bear 1980), is used to evaluate and rank archery trophies. It considers essentially the same measurements as those taken for Boone and Crockett scoring, but minimum entry levels to trophy classes are somewhat lower. Inquiries about this system should be directed to the Pope and Young Club, Route 1, Box 147, Salmon, Idaho 83467.

TILL NEXT SEASON

Once the whitetail hunt has concluded, arms and equipment need to be cleaned and stored properly until preparations for the next season. Such maintenance could save the hunter much headache and money in replacement and repair bills. It also could be the key to a rewarding hunting experience the next time out.

Sporting Arms

Rules of safety and maintenance care apply to putting up all firearms. The first order of business is to double-check the gun's chamber(s) and magazine to make certain they are empty.

For all guns, but particularly those that were subject to moisture during the hunt, it is well to remove the action from the stock, in order to clean, dry and oil the metal parts thoroughly, especially the trigger mechanism. Cleaning the bore of a modern firearm is not a problem because the noncorrosive ammunition produced today leaves little if any rust-causing residue in the barrel. Cleaning with a well-fitting oily patch on the end of a cleaning rod should be followed by swabbing with several dry patches, until they come out clean. Finally, a lightly oiled patch should be used to leave a fine film of oil in the bore to prevent rusting. Likewise, the actions should be cleaned and lightly oiled. With semiautomatic, pump, tip-open or falling-block systems, the cleaning of the action is very important. Lint, breadcrumbs, feathers, tobacco, leaves and other particles from the hunter's pockets can cling to cartridges that, when loaded, can easily foul up sensitive action mechanisms, leading to malfunction. If the hunter is not familiar with the internal components of his firearm, he can have a gunsmith do the cleaning and explain the weapon's workings.

Muzzleloaders, of course, should be cleaned as soon as possible after firing. Before putting such a gun away, it should be thoroughly cleaned again. The bore should be swabbed with hot water and soap, then dried completely and lightly oiled.

Handgun barrels and cylinders (on revolvers) should be cleaned, with particular attention paid to any lead or lubricant residues. The slide, magazine and magazine well of semiautomatics must be kept free of dirt. And the popular single-shot pistols should receive the same care as rifle actions.

Releasing the tension on the firing-pin spring of a gun also is recommended. Guns often are stored, with their springs under tension, for many months during the off-season. This could lead to weakening of the spring or even breakage, necessitating expensive repairs. Also, it is not advisable to plug or tape the muzzles of guns to be stored because these materials absorb moisture that can cause rusting.

Most bows (except the compound types) should be unstrung and hung vertically or placed horizontally across two pegs—never stood on end in a corner. A light coat of furniture or automobile wax will help to protect a bow from scratches and keep out moisture.

Ideally, weapons are stored under lock and key, and they certainly should be inaccessible to children and others who should not handle them. Special trigger-guard locks are available for most firearms. The storage area itself should

be a cool, dry place. In regions where high humidity is frequent, the hunter should check his weapons periodically for signs of rusting. Basements and attics generally are too hot, cold or damp to be suitable storage areas. Guns should not be stored in their carrying cases or holders, which also tend to absorb moisture. For the same reason, slings should be removed prior to storage. And when a gun is placed in storage, the hunter should handle it with a cloth, to avoid leaving oily or moist fingerprints on the weapon's metal parts.

Finally, as every gun owner ought to do, the hunter should make certain he has a separate record of the identification number of each of his weapons, plus a complete description of make, model, size and other distinguishing features, in case of loss or theft.

Ammunition

It is imperative that ammunition be kept separate from the weapons, and preferably in an entirely different part of the residence. Cartridges and shells should be returned to their original boxes or in clearly marked individual holders.

Stored in a cool, dry place, modern cartridges will keep for several years. If there is doubt about the length of time certain ammunition can be stored safely and without loss of shootability, the manufacturer should be consulted.

Gunpowder is best kept in tightly sealed containers, also in a cool, dry place. Primers and percussion caps can absorb moisture in storage and should be placed in air-tight containers. Improper storage may result in misfires or hangfires.

Arrows should be kept in their shipping box or loosely in a quiver so as not to damage fletchings. Broadheads can be given a light coat of oil or vaseline to prevent rusting.

Clothing

After the hunting season, wool garments should be cleaned and moth-proofed or stored in bags inaccessible to moths. If space permits, all garments exclusively for hunting—shirts, jackets, raingear, insulated underwear, socks, caps, etc.—should be placed together in a locker, ready for use the next year.

Shoes and boots should be dried, brushed clean, and oiled or greased. Well-fitting shoe-trees will help to keep boots in shape or, if such are not available, stuffing with newspaper also will do a good job. Other leather goods, such as rifle scabbards, handgun holsters, rifle slings, cartridge belts and knife sheaths, can be treated with a light coat of neatsfoot or mink oil to keep them pliable. A repeated application of oil four to six months later will safeguard against drying and cracking that reduces the durability and longevity of leather products.

Other Equipment

Unless in use year-round, knives, axes, saws, hacksaws and bone saws should be washed, dried and coated with vaseline. Miscellaneous items on the whitetail hunter's checklist, including compass, maps, ropes, cheesecloth, honing stones or steel, sleeping bags, knapsack, etc., preferably are kept together for the sake of convenience when preparations begin anew for the next white-tailed deer hunting season.

VI. Whitetail Management Needs and Opportunities

Chapter 45

RESEARCH PROBLEMS AND NEEDS

Lowell K. Halls
Project Leader (Retired)
Southern Forest Experiment Station
U.S. Forest Service
Nacogdoches, Texas

The quest for information about the white-tailed deer—its requirements for food and cover, and its response to management practices—has been a major undertaking of state, provincial and federal wildlife agencies and by private organizations and individuals for more than 50 years. The phenomenal increase in whitetail populations throughout most of the species' range during these years is concrete evidence that many of the major problems have been solved to the extent that management practices can be formulated and implemented with a reasonable degree of success. The wildlife managers are keenly aware, however, that current prescriptions often are broad and inexact, that techniques and methods constantly need refining, and that the solving of current problems often brings to light unforeseen complexities.

The challenges of white-tailed deer management and the ability of individual biologists or other resource managers or, in fact, entire wildlife agencies to meet them will become increasingly complex with the inevitable growth in human populations and changes of deer habitat, and because of continually shifting political, economic and ecological interrelationships. On the bright side, the availability of modern scientific equipment and facilities—particularly in the areas of electronics, communications and computers—enables researchers to collect, analyze and process data, and implement their findings in a manner unheard of in the past.

For the most part, the research needs and problems described here are considered to be of the highest priority by agencies, biologists and managers currently involved in white-tailed deer management and research. Many of the problems, such as deer census, are common throughout the whitetail range, although the priority may vary regionally. Other problems, such as the maintenance and management of winter deer yards, are pretty much local, although collectively, they can be critically important in northern latitudes. And some factors, such as politics, do not involve the deer *per se,* but indirectly have a marked effect on the whitetail's well-being.

WHITETAIL POPULATIONS

Population Appraisal

The difficulty of censusing whitetail populations continually plagues wildlife biologists and managers. The statistics are used by wildlife administrators to evaluate the quantity and quality of deer and to provide readily understood indices of population trends. The data are especially important in developing policy, establishing hunting quotas and communicating with the public.

If administrators are to use deer census data in management decisions, and they do, then there should be reasonable assurance that the data are within prescribed limits of error. Currently, much of the white-tailed deer population data presented in annual reports are the best information available, and frequently contain no reference to confidence limits. In some cases, the population figures may be educated guesses. Such unrefined estimates can lead to erroneous assumptions that take years to rectify.

Although there has been much improvement in census methodology during the past decade, there is a definite need to refine and test existing systems further, particularly in such difficult-to-census areas as southern and eastern forest habitats. In these areas, census by sightings is unlikely to be satisfactory because of the dense cover. Infrared photography, although currently expensive and difficult to evaluate, deserves additional attention, including investigation of how it is affected by time of year, timber overstory and the presence of other warm-blooded animals. Also needed is a simple, reliable census technique for the private landowner who wants to know how many and what kind of deer his property supports, but who does not have the time or facilities to conduct an intensive survey.

Some wildlife administrators consider precise deer census data to be relatively unimportant in a population appraisal of white-tailed deer. They are convinced that the most meaningful and practical information that can be generated yearly is available through statistics that indicate whether the whitetail population in question is increasing or decreasing and whether it is above, below or in balance with carrying capacity of its habitat. In this case, a combination of measurable factors—such as body weight, antler size, age, sex ratio, and reproduction and mortality rates—are combined to assess the population's well-being. This is a workable approach, but it requires a firm understanding of the functional relationships involved. It also requires a management strategy that remains consistent and contains elements that will indicate maximum sustainable yield, since it is easy to exceed maximum sustainable yield using the aforementioned criteria.

Systems are needed, and some already are available, whereby objective data concerning these variables can be collected efficiently and analyzed and presented in an understandable fashion. Herein lies a wide-open opportunity

for the use of computer simulations. It must be realized, however, that the reliability of the simulation output is a reflection of the accuracy of input data; a program only produces a predictive value, which must then be tempered with common sense and experience. Also, a system should be tested, refined and field-verified under actual conditions before it is recommended for widespread application.

Reproduction

Reproductive rate—the life blood of any wildlife population—must equal or exceed mortality rate for a population to persist. Much research has been accomplished in this general area of whitetail fact-finding and management, yet many questions merit further investigation:

1. What are the total effects of overpopulation on reproduction? Overpopulation with a resultant reduction in food supply causes reduced ovulation and low reproduction rates. These facts need to be demonstrated satisfactorily on a regional basis.
2. Is it possible to have too few bucks in a population to breed all receptive does?
3. Is there a decrease in the vigor and survival of fawns conceived during a late estrus cycle?
4. How can available information on regional stress factors best be formulated into a practical management scheme and implemented to ensure a high reproductive rate?

Mortality

Legal hunting.   Through the years, and mostly by trial and error, workable systems have been developed to account for the number and sex of legally harvested whitetails. The greatest need now is to reduce costs and improve the efficiency of systems that have proved the most practical under specific situations. Here again, the availability of computer and new statistical innovations offers unlimited opportunities.

Since, in most parts of North America, legal hunting is the major cause of white-tailed deer mortality, it is the prime factor in population management. The wildlife biologist or manager always has been and always will be faced with the problem of the number, age and sex of deer to be removed legally each year in order to keep the population productive and in balance with its seasonal habitats. Even though biological data and systems are available to make adequate determinations in most cases, they need to be tested and refined locally. Hunter harvest of whitetails perhaps is the most efficient and economically practical means of controlling populations, but the number of deer that needs to be taken in a given area to achieve a specific population management objective will vary annually, according to habitat and other environmental conditions. Some harvest management systems already have been developed but are in need of further testing and refinement. In all cases, the systems need to be based on biologically sound data that can be gathered and analyzed objectively, yet are simple and flexible enough to be applied so as to maximize potential for attaining predetermined objectives at minimum cost.

Nonhunting. Nonhunting mortality may be the most significant unknown parameter in population modeling and monitoring.When unaccounted for, it can seriously inhibit the setting of hunting regulations to optimize a legal whitetail harvest. Unreported kills or deaths of whitetails are likely to exploit the deer population at a higher rate than desired. Information is needed on the functional relationship of hunting and nonhunting mortalities, but also on how to separate and identify the components of each of these mortality types. In particular, it is important to know if and to what extent compensatory mortality exists. Does natural mortality decrease under heavy hunting pressure? And if so, to what extent?

1. Nutrition. The relationship between whitetail nutritional level and availability of winter food to winter mortality has received considerable attention in some areas. In general, it has been shown that fawns succumb first and the older deer next, particularly bucks. Pregnant does of prime age are least susceptible to winterkill, although their unborn fawns may be aborted. And in some cases, these does may bear young that are too small to survive. Seemingly, a reduction in population size to bring whitetail numbers in balance with winter food supply would alleviate this situation. However, solution of the problem is not that simple. For example, in extreme northern ranges, winter mortality of whitetails is not always density-dependent and, therefore, cannot be reduced by increasing the number of deer harvested in autumn. This is in contrast to the theory that winter death losses decrease as deer populations get smaller in southern ranges. Thus, since the relationship is not constant among different environments, further research is warranted in specific critical habitats.

2. Poaching. Poaching perhaps is the most elusive factor in assessing nonhunter mortality, and may be one of the biggest problems in management, because it cannot be assumed that poaching occurs in a density-dependent manner. It also varies with technology and effort, which is influenced by a variety of external forces, such as the economy. Because of the manner in which poaching occurs, and because of legal and moral complications, precise deer mortality figures are impossible to obtain. However, biologists definitely agree that a reasonably accurate account is needed to establish legal hunting quotas. The data are important in order to incorporate computer-assisted population models effectively into a management program. Even if direct assessment cannot be made, some indices or formulas should be established for each local area or management unit. To what extent is poaching related to economic trends, deer population density, and land ownership and social factors? Knowledge of what types of poaching cause the greatest deer population loss would make it easier to structure laws and develop more effective law enforcement procedures to reduce the incidence of poaching and apprehend offenders.

3. Roadkills. Unlike with poaching, the number, age and sex of white-tailed deer killed on highways is a relatively simple statistic to obtain. Deer/vehicle accidents not only result in deer mortality but also cause destruction of property and sometimes a loss of human life. The main problem is in how to keep whitetails off the highways. Even though noise-making contraptions, visual reflectors, caution signs and fences have been used with some degree of success, roadkills continue to increase and are likely to do so with expanded populations of humans and deer. Presently, the easiest way to avoid heavy losses is by proper fencing, but in many cases, the cost is prohibitive. Obviously, more practical ways of averting roadkill losses are needed. Strategic location of improved food plots and other attractants away from roadways, establishment or accommodation of deer travel

corridors, and design of highway rights-of-way to increase visibility in areas of high deer density offer promise for lessening deer/vehicle accidents. Research can focus on the height, spacing and type of plantings used to control erosion and provide aesthetics along new roadways and which currently attract deer or impair driver vision. Also to be considered in this regard is the legally complicated question of how to dispose of the carcasses of vehicle-killed deer.

4. Diseases and parasites. These factors by themselves seldom are a major cause of death, but when attended by other stresses, such as starvation and weather extremes, they may trigger heavy white-tailed deer mortality. They are usually density-dependent population influencing factors.

Epizootic hemorrhagic disease is potentially devastating to whitetails, and frequently causes a heavy death loss locally, particularly in the southeastern United States. It commonly occurs in late summer and early autumn, and ceases after the first frost. Its mode of transmission is unknown and there is no known effective treatment or control.

The meningeal worm is widespread among deer, but rarely is serious except where deer may be carriers to other highly susceptible wild ungulates, such as elk, moose, mule deer and pronghorn. The transmission problem becomes more acute as the white-tailed deer expands its range, particularly in the West, into areas occupied by other wild ungulates.

A number of other parasites are found in whitetails. The incidence of parasites in deer stomachs (abomasum parasite count) has been used as an index of deer health and should be tested further as a condition indicator.

Perhaps the greatest needs in disease and parasite research are to develop detection and monitoring systems, to prevent epidemics, and to curtail transmission from whitetails to other wild and domestic animals and to man. Research should be organized regionally. Some of the more pertinent questions to be addressed are: what is the incidence and distribution of the meningeal worm? what are the interrelations between livestock and wildlife-borne diseases? what is the relative vulnerability of each age and sex class of deer to epizootic hemorrhagic disease prior to the hunting season? what are the economic and public-health complications of deer disease? how can the impacts of disease and parasites be alleviated or re-duced to an acceptable level? and what are the factors that determine interspecific and intraspecific transmission of disease and parasites? Perhaps above all, it is important to know the effect of diseases and parasites on deer population density, and their relationship to other mortality factors.

5. Weather. Except in extreme northern habitats of whitetails, weather alone seldom is a debilitating factor to the deer. But when associated with poor nutrition, it can cause a decrease in productivity and moderate-to-heavy mortality. In some areas, winter weather keeps maximum density of deer at a level below that which the range can support. Indices have been developed locally to predict the impact of severity of weather in terms of snow depth and characteristics, temperatures, and length of winter, but they need to be refined and tested over a broader area. It is important to know, by region, what percentage of the total deer population is lost to weather-related phenomena during winter, and also how to prevent such losses. Again, it is very important to examine the influence of weather on whitetail density, and particularly in relation to other factors limiting deer population density.

6. Predators. Whitetail losses to predators—primarily coyotes and free-running dogs—for the most part are local problems and often quite controversial. In some areas where dog harassment and predation are particularly heavy, the whitetail populations do not reach their potential levels. In other areas, the dog chasing apparently has little or no effect on deer productivity. The problem presents a real challenge to establish relationships that can be used to predict mortality and damage to deer under varying habitat and population conditions.

Population Control Without Hunting

In areas such as national parks, it is necessary to regulate deer populations without hunter harvests. Whether to let nature take its course or impose some management regime is an emotional issue yet to be resolved. Trapping and moving excess whitetails to other more suitable areas is only a temporary solution—with severe economic and spatial limitations. The possibility of sterilizing deer to limit reproduction has been tested but found to be impractical to date. The problem becomes increasingly serious as white-tailed deer populations expand; it now is being faced in critical urban areas and near airports.

A problem of a similar nature is how to manage whitetail populations in refuges. Should excess deer be moved to other areas or allowed to disperse naturally to surrounding areas where they would be subject to a legal harvest? Would it be feasible to maintain a refuge in heavily populated regions or in midwestern farmland areas? What size should the refuges be? Would food plots be necessary in refuges to reduce depredation on surrounding private lands? Where would the money come from to establish and maintain the refuges?

Refuge questions are particularly pertinent with respect to whitetail populations in Central and South America, where there is a critical need to identify and set aside suitable habitat to prevent local whitetail extirpations.

Genetics

Little is known about the manner in which white-tailed deer relate to their habitat in a genetic sense. The degree to which genetic changes within whitetail populations correspond to changes in habitat might suggest that at a specific locus, genetic changes could be adaptive to the particular environments in which the deer occur. What is the relationship between whitetail population genetic make-up and its habitat? Are ecotones areas of rapid genetic changes? And do certain types of habitats within an area have higher levels of genetic variability than do other habitat types? If so, then the numerous hypotheses concerning the importance of genetics would take on considerably more importance.

Further research is needed to determine the relative contribution of genetics to whitetail antler development, body weight and reproductive capacity under different environmental conditions. For example, what are the specific relationships between nutritional level and the phenotypic potential of each whitetail subspecies?

WHITETAIL RANGE AND HABITAT

Habitat Loss

With a species as adaptable, widespread and abundant as the white-tailed deer, it is almost inconceivable that its existence eventually may be threatened by loss of habitat. Yet, roughly a century ago, whitetail numbers were decimated or severely reduced throughout the species' range. That too, prior to the fact, had been inconceivable. But it happened. And it could happen again. Troublesome spots already exist.

In Mexico and Central America several whitetail subspecies have been perilously close to extinction for some time, mainly due to reduction and degradation of habitat. In Maine, severe outbreaks of spruce budworm have defoliated spruce and fir stands that comprise much of the deer yards essential to winter survival of whitetails. Also, many deer wintering areas are jeopardized by commercial logging. And with relentless competition for various wildland uses, the availability of suitable whitetail habitat assuredly will diminish.

Currently, the habitat availability problem may not seem critical over most of the whitetail's range, but it will have to be reckoned with eventually. Simultaneously, it is a problem of local, regional, national and international scope, and involves numerous other wildlife species. And it will be extremely difficult to resolve because of the many social, economic, political and ecological interactions that cause it to be ignored or postponed.

A necessary ingredient to resolution of the habitat loss/degradation problem is the creation of a realistic, uniform habitat-classification system incorporating whitetail food and cover requirements and the needs of other wildlife. Although some efforts currently are underway to classify and map wildlands, they are concerned mostly with the needs of threatened and endangered species. Few if any efforts in this regard are concerned directly with whitetailed deer and other widely spread and abundant species. Certainly the attention being paid to the "sensitive" wildlife species and populations is warranted and commendable only so long as it does not exclude whitetails and other healthy and productive populations. These latter species, given actual and potential rates of habitat attrition, are not so secure and resilient as to be able to continue to thrive if neglected.

After land classification and mapping have been accomplished, the problem becomes one of developing and implementing programs to preserve whitetail habitats before they are overwhelmed, displaced or eradicated by human activity and sprawl. In some cases, this may require zoning, with definite restrictions on land use, and perhaps a like-for-like replacement mitigation where drainage, clearing, overgrazing and impoundments have preempted wildlife use. In critical areas, outright purchase of land by wildlife agencies may be the only feasible assurance of the whitetail's continued existence.

Carrying Capacity

Provided they are familiar with the vegetation, and whitetail food habits, wildlife biologists and other resource managers generally can determine, by observation and general surveys, whether a site is suitable deer habitat. However, since there are no standard guides for predicting carrying capacity, such estimates are subjective and open to potential wide margins of error. Furthermore, the term "carrying capacity" is poorly understood and loosely interpreted by many biologists and other resource managers. For example, the term may have a different connotation for a whitetail population managed for "quantity" in contrast to a population managed for "quality." Does it imply that the food supply is seasonally or annually adequate for a specified number of deer? What criteria should be used to determine whether deer populations are in balance with their habitats? What is the relationship of deer carrying capacity to other resources? Should decisions be based on condition of deer or is it best to rely on a survey of range vegetational conditions? How is carrying capacity affected by changes in food availability? For instance, to what extent is deer carrying capacity changed when forage yields increase from 1,121 to 2,242 kilograms per hectare (1,000–2,000 pounds per acre)? And what is the time lag?

There is a definite need for better definition of habitat factors that contribute most to whitetail productivity potential. What are the minimizing factors? And why do some areas that appear to be good deer ranges support only a few deer?

Once the most meaningful habitat factors have been isolated, the problem arises of how to inventory them on a statistically sound basis and within economic limitations. To date, there has been no satisfactory method devised to sample objectively the seasonal availability of deer food despite numerous seminars and extensive methodology research and experience.

Satellite imagery offers new possibilities for defining and mapping the major deer habitat types and periodically documenting their trends in condition and extent.

In forested areas, carrying capacity for whitetailed deer is related closely to stand conditions, and it continually changes regardless of the degree of animal pressure. Many data are available to show how the forage complex is related to forest stand density and to thinning and cutting practices, but the big question is, to what extent do these practices influence whitetail productivity and well-being? Formulas are needed to help predict what will happen to the deer population in 1, 3, 5 or 10 years as a result of forest management practices that include a combination of silvicultural and cutting treatments. As forestry practices intensify, the need to integrate forest/wildlife management becomes more acute. The forest landowner needs a series of options he can consider in making management decisions to fit his particular site and situation. Resolution of public or private forest land management problems involves not only biological considerations, but economic, social and recreational aspects as well.

Considerable research has been conducted to show that the quantity and quality of whitetail food can be increased by creating forest openings and planting special food plants to compensate for nutritional deficiencies during critical periods. However, the most economical and practical size, shape, distribution and management of food plots in the variety of habitats throughout the whitetail's range in North America are poorly defined. Also, very little has been done to show how these improvement practices influence the distribution and productivity of the deer population and the extent to which hunter use is affected as a result. Another need in this respect is the matter of selecting and testing fast-growing palatable forage plants that can survive competition in forests, and not compete severely with trees important as timber crops.

The cost effectiveness of habitat improvement practices needs to be evaluated. Actual costs of land preparation, seeding and fertilizing are determined readily, but overall dollar benefits to the landowner are obscure. It is important to understand the impacts of habitat management practices on whitetail conditions and productivity, but converting the advantages into dollar values is equally urgent.

As whitetail numbers approach or exceed range carrying capacity, the deer are apt to damage other resources. Frequently they seriously damage or destroy tree seedlings and, in some cases, may even destroy their own choice food sources. Too often in the past, the damage is well-advanced before it becomes obvious to the wildlife biologist or manager. Body condition of the deer is not a good meter because of the time lag involved, and signs of overbrowsing are unlikely to be detected until after the browse plant becomes deformed and loses its vigor. Indices are needed to foretell potential trouble and suggest remedial alternatives.

Whitetails damage agricultural crops and orchards in many areas. Although most farmers have a favorable attitude toward deer, they react quickly when crops are eaten or trampled. Deer population reduction is a partial solution, but in many areas damage occurs even at low deer densities—particularly when the deer concentrate in a local area. In some cases, landowners take it upon themselves to control the population and this, of course, creates legal and moral complications unless carried out under appropriate permits. Land posting and inadequate deer harvests further complicate the situation. Many repellents now on the market are fairly effective and practical for small-area application. The particular need now is for a chemical or physical repellent that is economically feasible for a one-time large field application.

PUBLIC RELATIONS

Every state and provincial wildlife management agency continually faces the question of how to establish and enforce hunting regulations that will effectively utilize the deer resource without adversely compromising biological and political principles. In many cases, application of hunting regulations is hampered by conflicting attitudes of landowners. For example, several states authorize and encourage harvest of does as a whitetail population control measure, but some landowners in those states disagree and limit hunters on their land to harvesting bucks only. And often these landowners receive strong political support from local commissioners or other public officials. Ways must be found to provide sound management information and improve troubled areas if the white-tailed deer resource is to be man-

aged in the best interest of the deer, their habitat and all persons who use the animals, consumptively or otherwise.

Somewhere along the line, wildlife and other resource managers must define deer hunters and their characteristics. What are the hunter's attitudes, expectations and satisfactions? What proportion are meat hunters or trophy hunters? Attitudes and demographics of Texas whitetail deer hunters are quite apt to differ from those of whitetail hunters in New York. Therefore, the ways and means of satisfying hunter desires and expectations have to be approached differently and on a local management unit or area (combination of units) basis. Also, desires of deer hunters often have been ignored in setting hunting seasons and establishing other regulations. Procedures should be developed to ensure public participation in rule making.

There is a need to evaluate more clearly the economic importance of white-tailed deer resources. Knowledge of both negative and positive values is necessary to justify management effort and direction. Deer compete with other resources that are identified more easily in dollar values. To date, arguments based largely on aesthetics, quality of life and moral responsibility have not carried sufficient weight in management and political decisions. Better information is required to demonstrate the importance of deer as an economic as well as an aesthetic resource and stimulus to local communities, counties, regions, states and provinces.

Education is the answer to most public relations problems. The public generally is uninformed or misinformed about concepts, goals, objectives and practices of deer management. Much can be done to alleviate the information gap by greater investment in education and communication. The problem to be faced is not whether the public should be informed, but how the informational process should be organized, implemented and financed. Workshops, seminars, television and radio programs are used to some extent in every state and province, but such programs often are funded poorly and staffed inadequately. All too often, educational programs are instituted too late to be effective. The hunter education program for beginning hunters is an excellent example of how efforts can be organized to save lives, to teach future hunters the moral and ethical responsibilities of sportsmanship, and to inform the next generation of the basic premises and values of scientific wildlife resource management.

In final analysis, much information is available to improve management of white-tailed deer and their habitats. But this technical knowledge does not serve its intended biological purpose until it is transferred to the wildlife biologist or manager and properly implemented in the field. And it is not likely to serve its ecological mission unless the program intent, methodologies and results are conveyed to the public—whose confidence and support are needed by every wildlife and other resource management agency—in a timely, accurate and convincing manner. These transactions, although seemingly incidental to the science of white-tailed deer management, may be the greatest challenge currently faced by resource managers.

Chapter 46

THE OUTLOOK

E. L. Cheatum
Director (Retired)
Institute of Natural Resources
University of Georgia
Athens, Georgia

This book is a compendium of data, ideas, techniques and policies pertaining to white-tailed deer biology and management. The careful reader cannot help but be amazed, if not somewhat concerned, about the differences from region to region in each of the compendium aspects. Such disparity reflects not only the dynamic status of virtually all whitetail populations and their habitats, but also the temporal nature of human social and economic conditions. It also belies the momentum and flexibility of wildlife management, a blend of art and science still in its infancy.

The preceding chapters of the book present the whitetail in its many subspecies and radically diverse environments. The existence of these subspecies is testimony to a fundamental characteristic of the whitetail—its genetic plasticity. In its varied forms, the white-tailed deer has evolved over thousands of years, for the most part during the time when environmental change was gradual. The fact that it produced forms that successfully occupied environments ranging from hot arid desert communities to frigid wet forests to sea-buffeted, subtropical islands to northern aspen parklands is reason enough to view the deer's future with optimism.

But what about the whitetail's future environments? We are witnessing rapid change in many areas, and it results directly and indirectly from man's quest to improve or simply maintain his social and economic life. It would seem to lead eventually to a confrontation in which people eliminate the essentials that are needed to sustain wild populations of whitetails. This is less a forecast than a projection, and its inevitability is predicated on continued human population expansion and attendant increased demand on the earth's limited resources.

The whitetail has adapted remarkably well to environmental changes wrought by people. It is a resourceful animal, having the capacity to take advantage of changed opportunities for the necessities of life. It is an opportunist, but it also is vulnerable. The whitetail has proven unable to survive in areas where it is subject to uncontrolled human predation, even in an apparent abundance of food and shelter, and conversely, in areas where its food and shelter have been destroyed, even though the animals were fully protected.

We are now armed with an impressive fund of knowledge and experience about the whitetail in general and specifically about intensively studied subspecies in the United States and Canada. There is growing confidence that many, if not most, whitetail populations can be managed to achieve a defined objective. The objective may range from the single purpose of preserving an endangered subspecies, such as the Key deer, to the multiple purposes of providing recreation, hunting and food from whitetail populations in designated management units. In some cases, management may include the controlling of self-destructive damage deer do to overpopulated home range. In other cases it may involve prevention of economic damage from deer foraging on valued forest trees, cultivated crops and ornamentals.

All too often there is a wide gap between what is theoretically possible and what is actually achievable. In a society where management objectives and regulatory authority are subject to the sway of public opinion, the agency charged with wildlife management may find its authority limited or constrained, whether by law or by self-imposition as the result of political pressure. The lack or inflexibility of authority is cited by several authors in this book as inhibiting sound deer management. It is a legitimate complaint, but I see little hope of it changing soon, unless much greater confidence in management expertise and responsiveness can be engendered in the minds of the citizens the agencies serve. This will require demonstrated results and great persistence, as well as continuing education and debate from one generation of white-tailed deer enthusiasts to the next.

I used to proceed on the simple assumption that if my audience shared the same facts available to me about the biology and habits of deer, they would arrive at similar if not identical conclusions on how deer should be managed. It took a long time for me to be disabused of this notion. I have learned and am still learning that, given the same set of data, even the experts may differ on the lessons to be drawn. In fact, data may support a variety of conclusions, some of which can be diametrically opposed to each other. In such cases, re-examination of objectives, methodologies and personal biases relative to the research or management mission not only is advisable, but usually most productive.

When well-informed, most people eventually support wildlife management objectives based on fact. This is especially true when there is an understanding of the positive values of deer to be maintained and the negative values to be mitigated.

None of the authors in this volume predicts the total demise of the whitetail in any of its forms. This reflects either a general confidence in the ability of deer to survive in the face of change or an unwillingness of authors to speculate. Some authors, however, concede that where and when the majority of people perceive deer to be in direct competition for the resources that people think they need, then the whitetail's welfare fades from serious consideration. This is likely to continue only as a local phenomenon, but the cumulative effect in any given region may be very discouraging to wildlife biologists and managers, hunters, and others who wish only to have the opportunity to observe or be near deer.

It is no more difficult to sustain optimism regarding the survival of whitetails than regarding the survival of mankind. Both species are remarkably adaptive and capable of changing their life styles in response to environmental change. If we reflect on what is happening to man's own concept of his place in the universe, we find encouragement. There is a growing realization that man's own future, indeed his very survival, depends on how well he husbands the living resources around him. It may be no mere coincidence that the celebration of Earth Day in the United States in 1970 followed on the heels of flight to the moon, when a new perspective was gained on the beauty, finiteness and fragility of our planet.

The discovery of our dependence on plant and animal associates is not new by any means. What is new is the breadth with which the concept of interdependence is being applied to our behavior toward these associates, including white-tailed deer. In the United States, this is manifested in national legislation such as the National Environmental Policy Act, the Endangered Species Act, and the setting of standards for cleaner air and cleaner water.

Dwindling supplies of nonrenewable resources, such as fossil fuels and metals, are forcing another trend. More attention is focusing on the substitution of renewable resources for nonrenewable ones in such areas as energy, fibers, construction materials and synthetics. As a consequence, increased values are being attached to forest lands. Depending on how these forests are managed, deer populations associated with them may either benefit or be disadvantaged.

As we grow in our understanding of the long-range and short-term values of maintaining an ecological balance in our environment, we will tend to encourage diversity in plant and animal communities, and to maintain an adequate ratio between cleared, developed tracts and lands in native vegetation set aside more or less permanently. The national parks, forests, wilderness areas and even the smaller "natural areas" are manifestations of this trend. The general white-tailed deer population has and will continue to be affected by these changes in land use—gaining in some areas, losing in others.

We have the technical ability to determine where and how deer survive, and what roles they play in our cultures, now and in the future. Engineering a consensus on the human roles to be played and acquiring flexibility in applying the management techniques to achieve the agreed objectives are basic requirements and the ultimate challenge.

What is the outlook for the deer hunter? Some would classify him as a "threatened species" in this period of rising antihunting sentiment. It is evident that the reckless, selfish and sometimes criminal acts of some while hunting have generated antipathy to all hunters. Isolating and disciplining those who commit irresponsible or unethical acts probably can be handled most effectively by other hunters in their own self-interest.

Some groups opposed to hunting are avid supporters of wildlife restoration and preservation projects—providing the objectives are not to supply more and better hunting. In the case of white-tailed deer, there is a strange contradiction when public deer hunting is opposed despite the presence of a burgeoning deer population destroying its range. That public hunting is the most economically effective means of reducing the deer population matters not. If indeed it is necessary to reduce the population, other means must be found—so it is argued. It is doubtful that this faulty logic can prevail in any significant number of instances, yet the emotional fervor of its unenlightened champions is not to be taken lightly.

Hunters themselves are having to adapt to change, and the outlook for them signals more discipline, not less. As hunting regulations become more complex in certain areas to achieve more precise deer population management objectives, compliance will require a high level of cooperation and understanding. Hunters must never forget that hunting is a privilege that can be lost; it is not a right and cannot be taken for granted.

In sum, there are undeniable inconsistencies in the data concerning white-tailed deer, as well as differing interpretations of the data. Questions remain unsolved, not only about deer *per se,* but also about people for and by whom deer ultimately are managed. Thus, more volumes will and should be written about the outlooks for both whitetails and humankind itself. The link between the two is real.

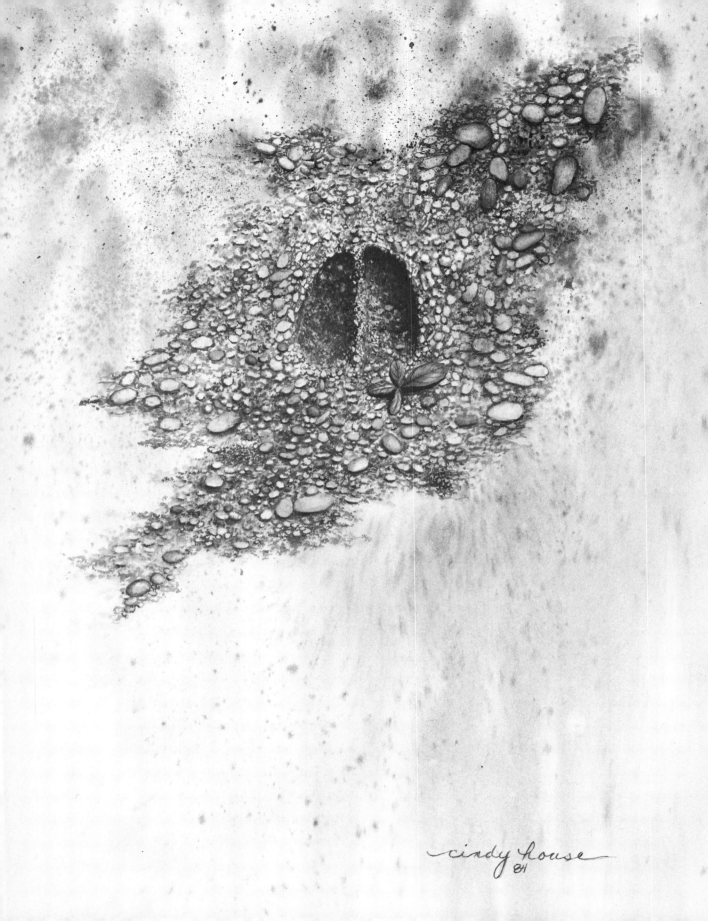

ALPHABETICAL LIST OF PLANTS CITED IN THE TEXT

Acacia, catclaw: *Acacia greggii*
Agaricus, or common mushroom: *Campestris agaricus*
Alder, mountain: *Alnus incana*
Alder, red: *Alnus rubra*
Alder, speckled: *Alnus rugosa*
Alder-buckthorn: *Rhamnus frangula*
Alfalfa: *Medicago sativa*
Algae: *Alaria*
Alligatorweed: *Alternanthera philoxeroides*
Andromeda, downy: *Andromeda glaucophylla*
Anemone: *Anemone*
Apes-earring: *Pithecellobium keyense*
Apple: *Pyrus malus*
Arrowhead, bulltongue: *Sagittaria lancifolia*
Ash, black: *Fraxinus nigra*
Ash, green: *Fraxinus pennsylvanica*
Ash, Oregon: *Fraxinus latifolia*
Ash, white: *Fraxinus americana*
Aspen, big-tooth: *Populus grandidentata*
Aspen, trembling or quaking: *Populus tremuloides*
Aster, acuminate: *Aster acuminatus*
Baldcypress, common: *Taxodium distichum*
Balsamroot, arrowleaf: *Balsamorhiza sagittata*
Barley: *Hordeum vulgare*
Basswood: *Tilia americana*
Beakrush: *Rhynchospora*
Bean, common: *Phaseolus vulgaris*
Bearberry: *Arctostaphylos uva-ursi*
Beautyberry, American: *Callicarpa americana*
Bedstraw, northern: *Galium boreale*
Beech, American: *Fagus grandifolia*
Bilberry, sourtop: *Vaccinium myrtilloides*
Birch, bog: *Betula pumila*
Birch, downy: *Betula pubescens*
Birch, gray: *Betula populifolia*
Birch, paper: *Betula papyrifera*
Birch, river: *Betula nigra*
Birch, silver: *Betula verrugosa*
Birch, yellow: *Betula alleghaniensis*
Bitterbrush, antelope: *Purshia tridentata*
Blackberry: *Rubus*
Black-mangrove: *Avicennia germinans*
Bladdernut: *Staphylea trifolia*
Blueberry, highbush: *Vaccinium corymbosum*
Bluegrass: *Poa*
Bluestem, big: *Andropogon gerardi*
Bluestem, broomsedge: *Andropogon virginicus*
Bluestem, little: *Andropogon scoparius*
Bogrosemary: *Andromeda*
Boxelder: *Acer negundo*
Brome, cheatgrass: *Bromus tectorum*

Broomweed: *Gutierrezia dracunculoides*
Buckeye: *Aesculus*
Buckthorn, Carolina: *Rhamnus caroliniana*
Buckthorn, southern: *Bumelia lycoides*
Buffaloberry, russett: *Shepherdia canadensis*
Buffaloberry, silver: *Shepherdia argentea*
Buffalograss: *Buchloe dactyloides*
Buffalo-nut, or Allegheny oilnut: *Pyrularia pubera*
Bull kelp, common: *Durvillia antarctica*
Bulrush, California: *Scirpus californicus*
Bulrush, Olney: *Scirpus olneyi*
Bulrush, saltmarsh: *Scirpus robustus*
Buttercup, creeping: *Ranunculus repens*
Buttonbush, common: *Cephalanthus occidentalis*
Button-mangrove: *Conocarpus*
Canarygrass, reed: *Phalaris arundinacea*
Cane: *Arundinaria*
Cattail, common: *Typha latifolia*
Ceanothus, buckbrush: *Ceanothus cuneatus*
Ceanothus, desert: *Ceanothus greggii*
Ceanothus, redstem: *Ceanothus sanguineus*
Ceanothus, snowbrush: *Ceanothus velvitnus*
Cedar, Alaska or yellow: *Chamaecyparis nootkatensis*
Cedar, northern white, or eastern arborvitae: *Thuja occidentalis*
Cherry, bird: *Prunus padus*
Cherry, black: *Prunus serotina*
Cherry, pin: *Prunus pensylvanica*
Chestnut, American: *Castanea dentata*
Chinaberry: *Melia*
Chokeberry, red: *Aronia arbutifolia*
Chokecherry, common: *Prunus virginiana*
Cholla: *Opuntia*
Cinquefoil: *Potentilla*
Clover, red: *Trifolium pratense*
Compassplant: *Silphium laciniatum*
Condalia: *Condalia*
Coralbells: *Heuchera sanguinea*
Coralberry, Indiancurrant: *Symphoricarpos orbiculatus*
Cordgrass, marshhay: *Spartina patens*
Cordgrass, smooth: *Spartina alterniflora*
Corn, Indian: *Zea mays*
Cottonwood, black: *Populus trichocarpa*
Cottonwood, eastern: *Populus deltoides*
Cowberry: *Vaccinium vitis-idaea*
Cowpea, hairypod: *Vigna repens* var. *luteola*
Crabgrass: *Digitaria*
Creosotebush: *Larrea tridentata*
Crocus, prairie: *Anemone patens*
Cucurbitas: *Cucurbita*
Curly-mesquite: *Hilaria belangeri*

Currant: *Ribes*
Cypress: *Cupressus*
Cyrilla, swamp: *Cyrilla racemiflora*
Dacrydium, Bidwill: *Dacrydium bidwillii*
Dacrydium, rimu: *Dacrydium cuppressinum*
Dahoon: *Ilex cassine*
Dandelion: *Taraxacum*
Devil's walking stick: *Aralia spinosa*
Dewberry: *Rubus*
Dogwood, alternate-leaf: *Cornus alternifolia*
Dogwood, bunchberry: *Cornus canadensis*
Dogwood, flowering: *Cornus florida*
Dogwood, gray: *Cornus racemosa*
Dogwood, red-osier: *Cornus stolonifera*
Dogwood, roughleaf: *Cornus drummondii*
Douglas-fir: *Pseudotsuga menziesii*
Dryad: *Dryas*
Eagles wing: *Mattecuccia struthiopterus*
Elder, American, or elderberry: *Sambucus canadensis*
Elm, American: *Ulmus americana*
Elm, winged: *Ulmus alata*
Encino: *Quercus*
Euonymus, brook, or strawberrybush: *Euonymus americanus*
Falsebeech, mountain: *Nothofagus solandri* var. *cliffortioides*
Falsecypress, whitecedar: *Chamaecyparis thyoides*
Farkleberry: *Vaccinium arboreum*
Fern, common bracken, or eagleswing: *Pteridium aquilinum*
Fern, hard: *Blechnum discolor*
Fern, royal: *Osmunda regalis*
Fescue: *Festuca*
Fetterbush, swamp: *Leucothoe racemosa*
Fig, wild: *Ficus*
Filaree: *Erodium cicutarium*
Fir, balsam: *Abies balsamea*
Fir, grand: *Abies grandis*
Fir, silver: *Abies amabalis*
Fir, white: *Abies concolor*
Five-finger: *Neopanax arboreum*
Flax: *Linum*
Fleabane: *Erigeron*
Floweringspurge: *Euphorbia corollata*
Foxtail, water: *Alopecurus geniculatus*
Frailejon: *Espeletia*
Fringetree, white: *Chionanthus virginicus*
Galax: *Galax*
Gallberry, tall or large: *Ilex coriacea*
Gayfeather, dotted: *Liatris punctata*
Goldenrod, *Solidago*
Gooseberry: *Ribes*
Grama, sideoats: *Bouteloua curtipendula*
Grape, panhandle: *Vitis acerifolia*
Grape, summer: *Vitis aestivalis*
Grass, Bermuda: *Cynodon*
Greasewood: *Sarcobatus*
Greenbrier, cat: *Smilax glauca*
Greenbrier, common: *Smilax rotundifolia*
Greenbrier, lanceleaf: *Smilax smallii*
Greenbrier, laurel, or bamboo-vine: *Smilax laurifolia*
Greenbrier, saw: *Smilax bona-nox*
Guacimo: *Gauzuma ulmifolia*
Hackberry, common: *Celtis occidentalis*
Hackberry, dwarf: *Celtis tenuifolia*
Hackberry, netleaf: *Celtis reticulata*
Haumakaroa: *Neopanax simplex*

Haw: *Viburnum*
Hawthorn, Douglas: *Crataegus douglasii*
Hawthorn, parsley: *Crataegus marshallii*
Hazel, American: *Corylus americana*
Hazel, beaked: *Corylus cornuta*
Hemlock, eastern: *Tsuga canadensis*
Hemlock, ground or Canada: *Tsuga canadensis*
Hemlock, western: *Tsuga heterophylla*
Hickory, black: *Carya texana*
Hickory, pecan: *Carya illinoensis*
Hickory, pignut: *Carya glabra*
Hickory, shagbark: *Carya ovata*
Hickory, swamp: *Carya leidodermus*
Hickory, water: *Carya aquatica*
Hinahina: *Melicytus ramiflorus*
Holly, American or deciduous: *Ilex decidua*
Holly, inkberry: *Ilex glabra*
Holly, yaupon: *Ilex vomitoria*
Honeylocust, common: *Gleditsia triacanthos*
Honeysuckle, Japanese: *Lonicera japonica*
Hophornbeam, eastern: *Ostrya virginiana*
Hornbeam, American, or blue beech: *Carpinus caroliniana*
Hornwort, common: *Ceratophyllum demersum*
Horsetail, scouring-rush: *Equisetum hyemale*
Horseweed, Canada: *Erigeron canadensis*
Huckleberry: *Gaylussacia*
Hydrangea, smooth: *Hydrangea arborescens*
Indiangrass, yellow: *Sorghastrum nutans*
Indianmulberry: *Morinda royoc*
Indigoberry, white: *Randia*
Jagua: *Genipa americana*
Jerusalemartichoke: *Helianthus tuberosus*
Jessamine, Carolina or yellow: *Gelsemium sempervirens*
Juniper, Ashe: *Juniperus ashei*
Juniper, common: *Juniperus communis*
Juniper, redberry: *Juniperus pinchotii*
Juniper, Rocky Mountain: *Juniperus scopulorum*
Kalmia, mountain-laurel: *Kalmia latifolia*
Kamahi: *Weinmannia racemosa*
Karamu: *Coprosma robusta*
Kupukatree: *Griselinia littoralis*
Ladyfern: *Athyrium*
Larch, tamarack: *Larix laricina*
Larch, western: *Larix occidentalis*
Laurel, mountain: *Kalmia latifolia*
Leadplant: *Amorpha canescens*
Leatherleaf, Cassandra: *Chamaedaphne calyculata*
Lechuguilla: *Agave lechuguilla*
Ledum, labrador-tea: *Ledum groenlandicum*
Lespedeza, common: *Lespedeza striata*
Lespedeza, Korean: *Lespedeza stipulacea*
Lettuce, prickly: *Lactuca serriola*
Locust, black: *Robinia pseudoacacia*
Locust, New Mexico: *Robinia neomexicana*
Madrone, Pacific: *Arbutus menziezii*
Madrone, Texas: *Arbutus menziezii*
Magnolia, cucumber-tree: *Magnolia acuminata*
Magnolia, sweetbay: *Magnolia virginiana*
Mahonia, Cascades: *Mahonia nervosa*
Mahonia, creeping: *Mahonia repens*
Maidencane, blue: *Amphicarpum muhlenbergianum*
Mangrove, red or American: *Rhizophora mangle*
Manuka: *Leptospermum scoparium*
Manzanita, pointleaf: *Arctostaphylos pungens*
Maple, bigleaf: *Acer macrophyllum*
Maple, mountain: *Acer spicatum*

Maple, red: *Acer rubrum*
Maple, silver: *Acer saccharinum*
Maple, striped: *Acer pensylvanicum*
Maple, sugar: *Acer saccharum*
Mayflower, Canada, or Canada beadruby:
    Maianthemum canadense
Mesquite, common: *Prosopis juliflora*
Mesquite, honey: *Prosopis glandulosa*
Millet, Walter's, or coast barnyardgrass: *Echinochloa*
    walterii
Mistletoe, cypress: *Phoradendron bolleanum*
Mistletoe, oak: *Phoradendron villosum*
Mombin, purple: *Spondias purpurea*
Mombin, yellow: *Spondias mombin*
Moss: *Cetraria*
Mountain-ash, American: *Sorbus americana*
Mountain-ash, European: *Sorbus aucuparia*
Mountainmahogany, true: *Cercocarpus breviflorus* var.
    montanus
Mulberry, red: *Morus rubra*
Mustard: *Brassica*
Nailwort: *Paronychia*
Nance: *Birsonima crassifolia*
Needlegrass, Texas: *Stipa leucotricha*
Ninebark, common: *Physocarpos opulifolius*
Ninebark, mallow: *Physocarpos malvaceus*
Oak, black: *Quercus velutina*
Oak, blackjack: *Quercus marilandica*
Oak, bur: *Quercus macrocarpa*
Oak, California black: *Quercus kelloggii*
Oak, Chapman: *Quercus chapmanii*
Oak, cherrybark: *Quercus falcata* var. *pagodaefolia*
Oak, chestnut: *Quercus prinus*
Oak, chinkapin: *Quercus muehlenbergii*
Oak, Gambel: *Quercus gambelii*
Oak, holly: *Quercus ilex*
Oak, Lacy: *Quercus laceyi*
Oak, laurel: *Quercus laurifolia*
Oak, live: *Quercus virginiana*
Oak, myrtle: *Quercus myrtifolia*
Oak, northern pin or jack: *Quercus ellipsoidalis*
Oak, northern red: *Quercus rubra*
Oak, Nuttall: *Quercus nuttallii*
Oak, Oregon white: *Quercus garryana*
Oak, overcup: *Quercus lyrata*
Oak, pin: *Quercus palustris*
Oak, post: *Quercus stellata*
Oak, scarlet: *Quercus coccinea*
Oak, scrub: *Quercus ilicifolia*
Oak, shin: *Quercus havardii*
Oak, silverleaf: *Quercus hypoleucoides*
Oak, southern red: *Quercus falcata*
Oak, Spanish or Texas: *Quercus texana*
Oak, swamp chestnut: *Quercus michauxii*
Oak, water: *Quercus nigra*
Oak, white: *Quercus alba*
Oak, willow: *Quercus phellos*
Oat: *Avena*
Orchardgrass: *Dactylis glomerata*
Pachistima, myrtle: *Pachistima myrsinites*
Palm, moriche: *Mauritia minor*
Palma, Ilanera: *Copernicia tectorum*
Palmetto, cabbage: *Sabal palmetto*
Palmetto, dwarf: *Sabal minor*
Palmetto, saw: *Serenoa repens*
Panicum, browntop: *Panicum fasciculatum*
Panicum, deertongue: *Panicum clandestinum*

Panicum, delicate: *Panicum chamaelonche*
Panicum, maidencane: *Panicum hemitomon*
Panicum, switchgrass: *Panicum virgatum*
Pasqueflower, spreading: *Anemone patens*
Pate: *Schefflera digitata*
Pawpaw, common: *Asimina triloba*
Pea, garden: *Pisum sativum*
Peanut, cultivated: *Arachis hypogaea*
Pear: *Pyrus*
Peashrub, Siberian: *Caragana arborescens*
Peavine, wild: *Lathyrus ochroleucus*
Pecan, bitter: *Carya lecontei*
Pencilflower: *Stylosanthes*
Pennywort: *Hydrocotyle*
Penstemon, beard-tongue: *Penstemon*
Peppervine: *Ampelopsis arborea*
Persea, redbay: *Persea borbonia*
Persimmon, common: *Diospyros virginiana*
Phlox, Hood: *Phlox hoodii*
Pickerelweed, common: *Pontederia cordata*
Pine, Apache: *Pinus engelmannii*
Pine, Chihuahua: *Pinus leiophylla*
Pine, eastern white: *Pinus strobus*
Pine, jack: *Pinus banksiana*
Pine, loblolly: *Pinus taeda*
Pine, longleaf: *Pinus palustris*
Pine, pinyon: *Pinus edulis*
Pine, pitch: *Pinus rigida*
Pine, ponderosa: *Pinus ponderosa*
Pine, red: *Pinus resinosa*
Pine, sand: *Pinus clausa*
Pine, scotch: *Pinus sylvestris*
Pine, shortleaf or yellow: *Pinus echinata*
Pine, slash: *Pinus elliotti*
Pine, Virginia: *Pinus virginiana*
Plum, American: *Prunus americana*
Plum, Chickasaw or sand: *Prunus angustifolia*
Podocarpus, Halls tutara: *Podocarpus hallii*
Poison-ivy, common: *Toxicodendron radicans*
Poison-oak: *Toxicodendron quercifolium*
Pokeberry, common: *Phytolacca americana*
Polypody: *Polydium*
Poplar, balsam: *Populus balsamifera*
Poplar, tulip or yellow: *Liriodendron tulipifera*
Potato: *Solanum purpureum*
Pricklypear, common: *Opuntia humifusa*
Pricklypear, plains: *Opuntia macrorhiza*
Privet: *Ligustrum*
Puheretaiko: *Senecio rotundifolius*
Pussytoes: *Antennaria*
Rabbitbrush, rubber: *Chrysothamnus nauseosus*
Ragwort, tansy: *Senecio jacobaea*
Raspberry: *Rubus*
Rata, southern: *Metrosideros umbellatta*
Redbud, eastern: *Cercis canadensis*
Redcedar, eastern, or eastern juniper: *Juniperus*
    virginiana
Redcedar, western, or giant arborvitae: *Thuja placata*
Reed, common: *Phragmites communis*
Rhododendron, rosebay: *Rhododendron maximum*
Rice: *Oryza*
Rose, Japanese multiflora: *Rosa multiflora*
Rose, prairie: *Rosa setigera*
Rose, prickly: *Rosa acicularis*
Rose, woods: *Rosa woodsii*
Rose-apple: *Eugenia jamboa*
Rosemary: *Ceratiola ericoides*

Rush, needlegrass: *Juncus roemerianus*
Rye, common: *Secale cereale*
Ryegrass, Italian: *Lolium multiflorum*
Ryegrass, perennial: *Lolium perenne*
Saffronplum: *Bumelia angustifolia*
Sagebrush, falsetarragon, or tarragon sagewort: *Artemisia dracunculoides*
Sagebrush, sand: *Artemisia filifolia*
Saltbush, fourwing: *Atriplex canescens*
Saltgrass, seashore: *Distichlis spicata*
Saltwort, maritima: *Batis maritima*
Sassafras, white: *Sassafras albidum*
Sawgrass, Jamaica: *Cladium jamaicense*
Sedge: *Carex*
Sensitive-plant: *Mimosa albida*
Serviceberry, Saskatoon: *Amelanchier alnifolia*
Silktassel, Wright: *Garrya wrightii*
Silverberry: *Elaeagnus commutata*
Silverpalm, Florida: *Coccothrinax argentata*
Snowberry, common: *Symphoricarpos albus*
Snowberry, western: *Symphoricarpos occidentalis*
Soapberry, western: *Sapindus drummondii*
Sorghum, common: *Sorghum vulgare*
Sorrel, sheep: *Rumex acetosella*
Sotol: *Dasylirion leiophyllum*
Sourwood: *Oxydendrum arboreum*
Soybean: *Glycine*
Spicebush, common: *Lindera benzoin*
Spikerush, dwarf: *Eleocharis parvula*
Spirea, birchleaf: *Spireae betulifolia*
Spruce, black: *Picea mariana*
Spruce, Norway: *Picea abies*
Spruce, red: *Picea rubens*
Spruce, Sitka: *Picea sitchensis*
Spruce, white or Alberta: *Picea glauca*
Strawberry, Virginia: *Fragaria virginiana*
Strawberry, wild: *Fragaria ovalis*
Sugarberry: *Celtis laevigata*
Sugarcane: *Saccharum officinarum*
Sumac, aromatic: *Rhus aromatica*
Sumac, dwarf or flameleaf: *Rhus copallina*
Sumac, skunkbush: *Rhus trilobata*
Sumac, staghorn: *Rhus typhina*
Sunflower: *Helianthus*

Supplejack, Alabama: *Berchemia scandens*
Swamp privet: *Foresteria acuminata*
Sweetfern, alien: *Comptonia peregrina*
Sweetgum, American: *Liquidambar styraciflua*
Sweet-potato: *Osmorhiza*
Sweetspire, Virginia: *Itea virginica*
Sycamore, American: *Platanus occidentalis*
Tamarisk, French: *Tamarix gallica*
Tarbush: *Flourensia*
Tasajillo: *Opuntia leptocaulis*
Thatchpalm, brittle or Key: *Thrinax microcarpa*
Thornshrub, or guaica: *Rochefortia spinosa*
Threeawn, pineland: *Aristida stricta*
Trefoil or deervetch: *Lotus*
Trumpetcreeper, common: *Campsis radicans*
Tuliptree: *Liriodendron*
Tupari: *Olearia colensoi*
Tupelo, blackgum, or black gum: *Nyssa sylvatica*
Tupelo, water: *Nyssa aquatica*
Velvetgrass, common: *Holcus lanatus*
Vetch, American: *Vicia americana*
Viburnum, arrowwood: *Viburnum dentatum*
Viburnum, hobblebush, or witch-hobble: *Vibrunum alnifolium*
Viburnum, mapleleaf: *Viburnum acerifolium*
Viburnum, rusty blackhaw: *Viburnum rufidulum*
Walnut, black: *Juglans nigra*
Waterhyacinth, common: *Eichhornia crassipes*
Waterlily: *Nymphaea*
Watermelon: *Citrullus vulgaris*
Waxmyrtle, southern: *Myrica cerifera*
Wheat, winter or bread: *Triticum aestivum*
Wheatgrass, western: *Agropyron smithii*
Whitebrush: *Lippia wrighti*
Widgeongrass, common: *Ruppia maritima*
Willow, black: *Salix nigra*
Willow, sandbar: *Salix interior*
Wineberry: *Aristotelia serrata*
Wintergreen, checkerberry: *Gaultheria procumbens*
Witchhazel, common: *Hamamelis virginiana*
Wolfberry: *Lycium*
Woodfern, spiny: *Dryopteris austriaca*
Yew, Canada: *Taxus canadensis*
Yucca: *Yucca*

ALPHABETICAL LIST OF ANIMALS CITED IN THE TEXT

Alligator, American: *Alligator mississipiensis*
Antelope, Blackbuck: *Antilope cervicapra*
Antelope, Nilgai: *Boselaphus tragocamelus*
Badger: *Taxidea taxus*
Bear, black: *Ursus americanus*
Bear, grizzly: *Ursus arctos*
Beaver: *Castor canadensis*
Bison, American: *Bison bison*
Bobcat: *Felis rufus*
Caracara, crested: *Caracara plancus*
Caracara, yellow-headed: *Milvago chimachima*
Caribou: *Rangifer tarandus*
Cat, domestic: *Felis catus*
Catfish, bullhead: *Ictalurus*
Cattle, domestic: *Bos taurus*
Coyote: *Canis latrans*
Deer, Acapulco white-tailed: *Odocoileus virginianus acapulcensis*
Deer, Andean: *Hippocamelus*
Deer, Avery Island white-tailed: *Odocoileus virginianus mcilhennyi*
Deer, axis: *Axis axis*
Deer, Blackbeard Island white-tailed: *Odocoileus virginianus nigribarbis*
Deer, Bulls Island white-tailed: *Odocoileus virginianus taurinsulae*
Deer, burro mule: *Odocoileus hemionus eremicus*
Deer, California mule: *Odocoileus hemionus californicus*
Deer, Carmen Mountains white-tailed: *Odocoileus virginianus carminis*
Deer, Cedros Island mule: *Odocoileus hemionus cerrosensis*
Deer, Chiapas white-tailed: *Odocoileus virginianus nelsoni*
Deer, Chinese water: *Hydroptes inermis*
Deer, Chiriqui white-tailed: *Odocoileus virginianus chiriquensis*
Deer, Coiba Island white-tailed: *Odocoileus virginianus rothschildi*
Deer, Columbian black-tailed: *Odocoileus hemionus columbianus*
Deer, Columbian white-tailed: *Odocoileus virginianus leucurus*
Deer, Coues or Arizona white-tailed: *Odocoileus virginianus couesi*
Deer, Dakota white-tailed: *Odocoileus virginianus dacotensis*
Deer, desert mule: *Odocoileus hemionus crooki*
Deer, Eurasian red: *Cervus elaphus*
Deer, fallow: *Dama dama*

Deer, Florida white-tailed: *Odocoileus virginianus seminolus*
Deer, Florida coastal white-tailed: *Odocoileus virginianus osceola*
Deer, Florida Key white-tailed: *Odocoileus virginianus clavium*
Deer, Hilton Head Island white-tailed: *Odocoileus virginianus hiltonensis*
Deer, Hunting Island white-tailed: *Odocoileus virginianus venatorius*
Deer, Inyo mule: *Odocoileus hemionus inyoensis*
Deer, Kansas white-tailed: *Odocoileus virginianus macrourus*
Deer, Mexican lowland white-tailed: *Odocoileus virginianus thomasi*
Deer, Mexican tableland white-tailed: *Odocoileus virginianus mexicanus*
Deer, Miquihana white-tailed: *Odocoileus virginianus miquihuanensis*
Deer, musk: *Moschus moschiferus*
Deer, Nicaragua white-tailed: *Odocoileus virginianus truei*
Deer, northern Veracruz white-tailed: *Odocoileus virginianus veraecrucis*
Deer, northern woodland white-tailed: *Odocoileus virginianus borealis*
Deer, Northwest white-tailed: *Odocoileus virginianus ochrourus*
Deer, Oaxaca white-tailed: *Odocoileus virginianus oaxacensis*
Deer, pampas: *Ozotoceros campestris*
Deer, peninsula mule: *Odocoileus hemionus peninsulae*
Deer, Père David's: *Elaphurus davidianus*
Deer, rainforest white-tailed: *Odocoileus virginianus toltecus*
Deer, red brocket: *Mazama americana*
Deer, Rocky Mountain mule: *Odocoileus hemionus hemionus*
Deer, roe: *Capreolus capreolus*
Deer, Sambar: *Cervus unicolor*
Deer, sika: *Cervus nippon*
Deer, Sinaloa white-tailed: *Odocoileus virginianus sinaloae*
Deer, Sitka black-tailed: *Odocoileus hemionus sitkensis*
Deer, southern mule: *Odocoileus hemionus fuliginatus*
Deer, swamp: *Blastocerus dichotomus*
Deer, Texas white-tailed: *Odocoileus virginianus texanus*
Deer, Tiburon Island mule: *Odocoileus hemionus sheldoni*
Deer, tufted: *Elaphodus cephalophus*

Deer, Virginia white-tailed: *Odocoileus virginianus virginianus*
Deer, Yucatan white-tailed: *Odocoileus virginianus yucatanensis*
Dog, domestic: *Canis familiaris*
Drumfish: *Aplodinotus grunniens*
Eagle, bald: *Haliaeetus leucocephalus*
Eagle, golden: *Aquila chrysaetos*
Elk, eastern: *Cervus elaphus canadensis*
Elk, Manitoba: *Cervus elaphus manitobensis*
Elk, Merriam: *Cervus elaphus merriami*
Elk, Rocky Mountain: *Cervus elaphus nelsoni*
Elk, Roosevelt: *Cervus elaphus roosevelti*
Elk, Tule: *Cervus elaphus nannodes*
Fisher: *Martes pennanti*
Fox, gray: *Urocyon cinereoargenteus*
Fox, red: *Vulpes vulpes*
Goat, domestic: *Capra hircus*
Grackle, carib: *Quiscalis lugubris*
Grouse, ruffed: *Bonasa umbellus*
Hare, snowshoe: *Lepus americanus*
Hawk, savannah: *Heterospizias meridionalis*
Heron, Cocoi: *Ardea cocoi*
Hog, feral: *Sus scrofa*
Horse, domestic: *Equus*
Jaguar: *Felis onca*
Jay: *Cyanocitta*
Lion, mountain: *Felis concolor*
Lynx: *Felis lynx*
Mammoth: *Mammothus*
Mastodon: *Mammut*
Moose, American: *Alces alces*
Mouse, Oldfield: *Peromyscus polionotus*

Muntjac: *Muntiacus*
Ocelot: *Felis pardalis*
Opossum, brush-tail: *Trichosurus vulpecula*
Opossum, Virginia: *Didelphis virginiana*
Pronghorn: *Antilocapra americana*
Pudu: *Pudu*
Quail, bobwhite: *Colinus virginianus*
Rabbit, cottontail: *Sylvilagus*
Raccoon: *Procyon lotor*
Rattlesnake: Crotalidae
Raven, American: *Corvus corax*
Reindeer: *Rangifer tarandus*
Sheep, Aoudad: *Ammotragus leruia*
Sheep, Barbary, or auodad: *Ammotragus lervia*
Sheep, domestic: *Ovis aries*
Sheep, Mouflon: *Ovis musimon*
Sheep, mountain or bighorn: *Ovis canadensis*
Skimmer, black: *Rynchops nigra*
Squirrel, eastern gray: *Sciurus carolinensis*
Squirrel, eastern fox: *Sciurus niger*
Stork, jabiru: *Jabiru mycteria*
Swan: *Cygnus*
Tapir, Baird's: *Tapirus bairdii*
Taruca: *Hippocamelus antisensis*
Turkey, wild: *Meleagris gallopavo*
Turtle, eastern box: *Terrapine carolina*
Vole, Gapper's red-backed: *Clethrionomys gapperi*
Vole, northern red-backed: *Clethrionomys rutilus*
Vulture, black: *Coragyps atratus*
Vulture, turkey: *Cathartes aura*
Wolf, gray or timber: *Canis lupus*
Wolf, red: *Canis rufus*
Wolverine: *Gulo gulo*

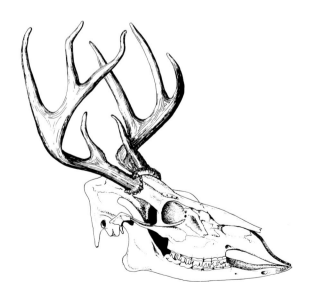

REFERENCES CITED

Abbott, C. C. 1893. A pre-Columbian dinner. Archaeologist 1(1):30–33.

Abler, W. A., D. E. Buckland, R. L. Kirkpatrick, and P. F. Scanlon. 1976. Plasma progestins and puberty in fawns as influenced by energy and protein. J. Wildl. Manage. 40(3):442–446.

Adair, J. 1775. The history of the American Indians. London: printed for E. and C. Dilly. 464 pp.

Adams, L. 1949. The effects of deer on conifer reproduction in northwestern Montana. J. For. 47(11):909–913.

Adams, W. H., Jr. 1960. Population ecology of white-tailed deer in northeastern Alabama. Ecology 41(4):706–715.

Agassiz, L. 1850. Lake Superior: its physical character, vegetation and animals compared with those of other similar regions. Boston: Gould, Kendall and Lincoln. 428 pp.

Aguilar, C. A. 1971. Venados de Guatemala. Guatemala City: Direccion de Recursos Naturales Renovables. 13 pp.

Alcocer, F., J. M. Velázquez, and N. Velázquez. 1978. Parque recreativo "El Ocotal." Atractivos faunisticos productivos. Publicación de la Direccion General de Fauna Silvestre. Mexico City. 57 pp.

Aldous, S. E. 1944. A deer browse survey method. J. Mammal. 25(2):130–136.

Alexander, B. G. 1968. Movements of deer in northeast Texas. J. Wildl. Manage. 32(3):618–620.

Alexander, M. A. 1982. Processing the venison carcass. In Missouri deer hunting, ed. N. Giessman and D. A. Murphy, pp. 15–20. Jefferson City: Missouri Conservation Commission. 20 pp.

Alldredge, A. W., J. F. Lipscomb, and F. W. Whicker. 1974. Forage intake rates of mule deer estimated with fallout cesium-137. J. Wildl. Manage. 38(3):508–516.

Allen, D. A. 1978. The enjoyment of hunting. In Wildlife and America, ed. H. P. Brokaw, pp. 28–41. Washington, D. C.: Council on Environmental Quality. 532 pp.

Allen, D. L. 1954. Our wildlife legacy. New York: Funk and Wagnalls. 422 pp.

———. 1956. We're wasting our deer. Sports Afield 135(2):64–65, 129.

———. 1970. Historical perspective. In Land use and wildlife resources, pp. 1–28. Compiled by Committee on Agricultural Land Use and Wildlife Resources, Division of Biology and Agriculture, National Research Council. Washington, D.C.: National Academy of Science. 262 pp.

Allen, E. O. 1971. White-tailed deer. In Game management in Montana, ed. T. W. Mussehl and F. W. Howell, pp. 69–79. Helena: Montana Fish and Game Department. 250 pp.

Allen, G. M. 1929. History of the Virginia deer in New England. The Game Breeder:203–256.

Allen, R. E., and D. R. McCullough. 1976. Deer-car accidents in southern Michigan. J. Wildl. Manage. 40(2):317–325.

Allen, R. H., Jr. 1965. History and results of deer restocking in Alabama. Bull. 6. Montgomery: Alabama Department of Conservation. 50 pp.

Allen, T. J., and J. I. Cromer. 1977. White-tailed deer in West Virginia. Wildl. Resour. Div. Bull. No. 7. Charleston: West Virginia Department of Natural Resources. 66 pp.

Allman, R. C. 1976. Canaan Valley and the black bear. Parsons, W. Va.: McClain Printing Company. 120 pp.

Allouez, C. J. 1858. Relation of 1669–70. De la mission de saint Francois Xavier dans la Baye de Puans, ou plûtôt des Eaux Puantes. Lettre du P. Allouex, qui a en charge de cette mission, au R. P. Superieur. *In* Relations des Jesuits dans la Nouvelle France 3:92–102. Quebec.

Alvord, C. W., and L. Bidgood. 1912. The first explorations of the trans-Allegheny region by the Virginians, 1650-1674. Cleveland: Arthur H. Clark. 275 pp.

Ames, N., ed. 1978. New Mexico Department of Game and Fish comprehensive plan, part 1: strategic section. Santa Fe: New Mexico Department of Game and Fish. 76 pp.

Ammann, A. P., R. L. Cowan, C. L. Mothershead, and B. R. Baumgardt. 1973. Dry matter and energy intake in relation to digestibility in white-tailed deer. J. Wildl. Manage. 37(2):195–201.

Anderson, A. E. 1981. Morphological and physiological characteristics. *In* Mule and black-tailed deer of North America, ed. O. C. Wallmo, pp. 27–97. Lincoln: Univ. of Nebraska Press. 624 pp.

Anderson, A. E., D. E. Medin, and D. C. Bowden. 1971. Adrenal weight in a Colorado mule deer population. J. Wildl. Manage. 35(4):689–697.

Anderson, A. E., D. E. Medin, and D. C. Bowden. 1972. Indices of carcass fat in a Colorado mule deer population. J. Wildl. Manage. 36(2):579–594.

Anderson, A. E., D. E. Medin, and D. C. Bowden. 1974. Growth and morphometry of the carcass, selected bones, organs, and glands of mule deer. Wildl. Monogr. 39. Washington, D. C.: The Wildlife Society. 122 pp.

Anderson, D. D. 1964. The status of deer in Kansas. Misc. Publ. No. 39. Lawrence: University of Kansas, Museum of Natural History. 36 pp.

Anderson, D. R., and W. M. Samuel. 1969. *Eimeria* (Protozoa: Eimeriidae) from white-tailed deer, *Odocoileus virginianus*, in Pennsylvania, Texas, and Wisconsin, with descriptions of two new species. Bull. Wildl. Dis. Assoc. 5(3):351–356.

Anderson, D. T. 1979. The effect of dog harassment on translocated white-tail deer (*Odocoileus virginianus virginianus*) on the Cumberland Plateau in Tennessee. Tech. Rep. No. 79-8. Nashville: Tennessee Wildlife Resources Agency. 78 pp.

Anderson, F. M., G. E. Connolly, A. N. Halter, and W. M. Longhurst. 1974. A computer simulation study of deer in Mendocino County, California. Agr. Exp. Stn. Tech. Bull. 130. Corvallis: Oregon State University. 72 pp.

Anderson, R. C. 1972. The ecological relationships of meningeal worm and native cervids in North America. J. Wildl. Dis. 8(4):304–310.

Anderson, R. C., and U. R. Strelive. 1966. Experimental cerebrospinal nematodiasis (*Pneumostrongylus tenuis*) in sheep. Can. J. Zool. 44(5):889–894.

Anderson, S., and J. K. Jones, Jr., eds. 1967. Recent mammals of the world, a synopsis of families. New York: Ronald Press Co. 453 pp.

Andersson, E., and I. Koivisto. 1980. Valkohäntäpeuran talviravinto ja vuorokausirytmi [Summary: White-tailed deer's winter food and diurnal rhythm]. Suomen Riista: 27:84–92.

Angier, B. 1975. Home book of cooking venison and other natural meats. Harrisburg, Pa.: Stackpole Books. 192 pp.

Anonymous. 1856–1865. Records of the colony of Rhode Island and Providence plantation in Northeast. 10 vols. Providence: A. C. Green and Bros.

———. 1906. Wild animals of Indiana. Ind. Mag. Hist. 2:13–16.

———. 1973. Wildlife habitat on the Mark Twain National Forest. Program evaluation and economic analysis. Jefferson City: U. S. Forest Service and Missouri Department of Conservation. 61 pp.

———. 1975. Deer response on highways measured. Penn. State Univ. Instit. Res., Land, Water Res. Newsletter 6(3):1.

Anthony, R. G., and A. B. Fisher. 1977. Wildlife damage in orchards—a need for better management. Wildl. Soc. Bull. 5(3):107–112.

Anthony, R. G., and N. S. Smith. 1974. Comparison of rumen and fecal analysis to describe deer diets. J. Wildl. Mange. 38(3):535–540.

Anthony, R. G., and N. S. Smith. 1977. Ecological relationships between mule deer and white-tailed deer in southeastern Arizona. Ecol. Monogr. 47(3):255–277.

Applegate, J. E. 1973. Some factors associated with attitudes toward deer hunting in New Jersey residents. Trans. N. Amer. Wildl. and Natur. Resour. Conf. 38:267–273.

———. 1975. Attitudes toward deer hunting in New Jersey: a second look. Wildl. Soc. Bull. 3(1):3–6.

———. 1982. A change in the age structure of new hunters in New Jersey. J. Wildl. Manage. 46(2):490–492.

Applegate, J. E., and R. A. Otto. 1982. Characteristics of first-year hunters in New Jersey. Pub. No. R-12381-(1)-82. New Brunswick: New Jersey Agric. Exp. Stn. 27 pp.

Arizona Game and Fish Department. 1977. The Arizona whitetail deer. Spec. Rep. 6. Phoenix: Arizona Game and Fish Department. 108 pp.

Armstrong, D. N. 1972. Distribution of mammals in Colorado. Lawrence: University of Kansas, Museum of Natural History. 415 pp.

Armstrong, R. A. 1950. Fetal development of the northern white-tailed deer (*Odocoileus virginianus borealis* Miller). Amer. Midl. Nat. 43(3):650–666.

Arnold, G. W. 1966a. The special senses in grazing animals. I. Sight and dietary habits in sheep. Aust. J. Agric. Res. 17(4):521–529.

———. 1966b. The special senses in grazing animals. II. Smell, taste, and touch and dietary habits in sheep. Aust. J. Agric. Res. 17(4):531–542.

Arnold, L. A., Jr. 1976. Seasonal food habits of white-tailed deer (*Odocoileus virginianus texanus*) on the Zachry Ranch in South Texas. M. S. Thesis. Texas A & I University, Kingsville. 59 pp.

Ashcraft, G., and D. Reese. 1957. An improved device for capturing deer. Calif. Fish and Game 43(2):193–199.

Atkeson, T. D. 1983. Aspects of social communication in white-tailed deer. Ph. D. Thesis. University of Georgia, Athens. 163 pp.

Atkeson, T. D., and R. L. Marchinton. 1982a. Scent communication in white-tailed deer. (Abstract.) Southeast Deer Study Group. 58–9.

Atkeson, T. D., and R. L. Marchinton. 1982b. Forehead glands in white-tailed deer. J. Mammal. 63(4):613–617.

Atkeson, T. D., V. F. Nettles, Jr., R. L. Marchinton, and W. V. Branan. Unpublished. Nasal glands in the cervidae. Submitted to J. Mammal.

Austin, D. D., P. J. Urness, and M. L. Wolfe. 1977. The influence of predator control on two adjacent wintering deer herds. Great Basin Nat. 37(1):101–102.

Austin, M. E. 1965. Land resource regions and major land resource areas of the United States, exclusive of Alaska and Hawaii. Handbook 296. Washington D. C.: U. S. Department of Agriculture. 82 pp.

Avila-Pirés, F. D. de. 1975. Cervidos neotropicales: estado actual y futuro. Inst. Invest. Cien., Univ. Autón. Nuevo León Monterrey, N. L., México. Publ. Biol. 1(7):155–167.

Axtell, J. 1981. The Indian peoples of eastern America. New York: Oxford Univ. Press. 233 pp.

Baccus, R., H. O. Hillestad, P. E. Johns, M. N. Manlove, R. L. Marchinton, and M. H. Smith. 1977. Prenatal selection in white-tailed deer. Proc. Ann. Conf. Southeast. Assoc. of Fish and Wildl. Agencies 31:173–179.

Baccus, R., N. Ryman, M. H. Smith, C. Reuterwall, and D. Cameron. 1983. Genetic variability and differentiation of large grazing mammals. J. Mammal. 64(1):109–120.

Bada, J. L. and P. M. Helfman. 1975. Aminoacid racemization dating of fossil bone. World Archaeol. 7:160–173.

Bahnak, B. R., J. C. Holland, L. J. Verme, and J. J. Ozoga. 1979. Seasonal and nutritional effects on serum nitrogen constituents in white-tailed deer. J. Wildl. Manage. 43(2):454–460.

Bahnak, B. R., J. C. Holland, L. J. Verme, and J. J. Ozoga. 1981. Seasonal and nutritional effects on growth hormone and thyroid activity in white-tailed deer. J. Wildl. Manage. 45(1):140–147.

Baile, C. A., and J. Mayer. 1969. Depression of feed intake of goats by metabolites injected during meals. Amer. J. Physiol. 217(6):1830–1836.

Bailey, A. G. 1937. The conflict of European and eastern Algonkian cultures, 1504–1700: a study in Canadian civilization. Toronto: Univ. Toronto Press. 218 pp.

Bailey, R. G. 1980. Description of the ecoregions of the United States. USDA Misc. Publ. No. 1391. Ogden, Utah: USDA Forest Service, Intermountain Region. 77 pp.

Bailey, V. 1907. Destruction of deer by the northern timber wolf. USDA Bur. Biol. Surv. Circ. 55:1–6.

———. 1936. The mammals and life zones of Oregon. North American Fauna 55. Washington, D. C.: USDA Bureau of Biological Survey. 416 pp.

Baird, E. 1900. Reminiscences of life in territorial Wisconsin. Wis. Hist. Colls. 15:205–263.

Bakeless, J. 1965. Daniel Boone. Harrisburg, Pa.: The Stackpole Co. 492 pp.

Baker, P. E. 1955. The forgotten Kutenai. Boise, Idaho: Mountain States Press. 64 pp.

Baker, R. H. 1957. El futuro de la fauna sylvestre en el norte de Mexico. [The future of the forest fauna in northern Mexico.] Anales del Instituto de Biologia [Mexico] 28(1/2):349–357.

Baldwin, H. A. 1971. Long range immobilization method. *In* Statewide invest., pp. 53–86. P-R Job Prog. Rep., Arizona Proj. W-7815/WP-1/J-9. Tucson: Arizona Game and Fish Department.

Ballard, W. B., T. H. Spraker, and K. P. Taylor. 1981. Causes of neonatal moose calf mortality in south central Alaska. J. Wildl. Manage. 45(2):335–342.

Banasiak, C. F. 1964. Deer in Maine. Game Div. Bull. No. 6. Augusta: Maine Department of Inland Fisheries and Game. 159 pp.

———. 1976. Big game project report. Augusta: Maine Department of Inland Fisheries and Wildlife. Wildl. Leaflet Ser. 9(2):1–24.

———. 1977. Analysis of deer biological data. Annual Performance Report, P-R Proj. W-67-R-8, Job I-162. Augusta: Maine Department of Inland Fisheries and Wildlife. 13 pp. mimeo.

———. 1981. Big game project report. Augusta: Maine Department of Inland Fisheries and Wildlife. Wildl. Leaflet Ser. 15(2). 36 pp.

Bancroft, H. H. 1886. The works of Hubert Howe Bancroft. Vol. II. The native races: Vol. II. Civilized nations. San Francisco: The History Company. 805 pp.

Bandelier, A. F., ed. 1905. The journey of Alvar Nunez Cabeza de Vaca and his companions from Florida to the Pacific. N. Y.: A. S. Barnes and Co. 231 pp.

Banville, D. 1981. Le controle des prédateurs du gros gibier au Québec de 1905 à 1980. Rapp. Spec. no 15. Québec: Ministère du Loisir de la Chasse et de la Pêche, Direction Generale de la Faune. 54 pp.

Barber, H. L. 1962. "Browse" study shows food availability for herds. Kentucky Happy Hunting Ground 18(5):4–6.

———. 1971. A report on the status of the Fort Knox deer population. Frankfort: Kentucky Department of Fish and Wildlife. 15 pp.

Barber, T. A., and J. G. Nagy. 1971. Effects of pesticides on mule deer rumen bacteria. Trans. N. Amer. Wildl. and Natur. Resour. Conf. 36:153–162.

Barbour, T., and G. M. Allen. 1922. The white-tailed deer of eastern United States. J. Mammal. 3(2):65–78.

Bardwell, F. H., E. B. Wilcox, and J. B. Low. 1964. Factors influencing the quality and palatability of venison in Utah. Salt Lake City: Utah Department of Fish and Game. 57 pp.

Barick, F. B. 1952. Deer trapping coordinated with weather. Wildl. in N. C. 16(10):10–11, 20.

———. 1969. Deer predation in North Carolina and other southeastern states. *In* White-tailed deer in the southern forest habitat, pp. 25–31. Proc. Symp. Nacogdoches, Tex. New Orleans: USDA Forest Service, South. For. Exp. Stn. 130 pp.

Barkalow, F. S., Jr., and W. E. Keller. 1950. Escape behavior of the white-tailed deer. J. Wildl. Manage. 14(2):246–247.

Barker, R. L. 1972. Prevention of deer damage to truck crops in north central Florida. M. S. Thesis. University of Florida, Gainesville. 64 pp.

Barlowe, A. 1589. Arthur Barlowe's discourse on the first voyage. *In* The principall navigations, voiages and discoveries of the English nation, by R. Hakluyt, pp. 728–733. Reprinted *in* The Roanoke Voyages, 1584–1590, ed. D. B. Quinn, 1955, Vol. I:91–116. London: Cambridge Univ. Press. 496 pp.

Barnes, W. B. 1945. The white-tailed deer in Indiana. Outdoor Indiana 12(2):4–5, 16.

Barnwell, J., ed. 1908. The Tuscarora expedition: letters of Colonel John Barnwell. S. C. Hist. and Geneal. Mag. 9(1):28–54.

Barrett, J. W., ed. 1962. Regional silviculture of the United States. New York: Ronald Press Co. 610 pp.

Barrett, S. W., and S. F. Arno. 1982. Indian fires as an ecological influence in the northern Rockies. J. For. 80(10):647–651.

Barrier, M. J., J. K. Reed, and L. G. Webb. 1970. Pesticide residues in selected tissues of the white-tailed deer, *Odocoileus virginianus*, in Calhoun County, South Carolina. Proc. Ann. Conf. Southeast. Assoc. Game and Fish Comm. 24:31–45.

Barron, J. C., and W. F. Harwell. 1973. Fertilization rates of south Texas deer. J. Wildl. Manage. 37(2):179–182.

Barsch, R. 1975. Browse, water and cover as determinants of the distribution of deer (*Odocoileus virginianus cousii*) in burned and unburned stands of pinyon pine. Q. Rep. Arizona Coop. Wildl. Res. Unit 25(4):8–9.

Bart, W. M. 1972. A hierarchy among attitudes towards animals. J. Env. Educ. 3:4–6.

Bartholow, J. 1981. POP50 system documentation. Unpubl. rep. available from author, 328 Overland Trail, Ft. Collins, Colorado 80521. 19 pp.

Bartlett, C.O. 1955. Starvation of deer on Navy Island. Tech. Bull. Wildl. Series 5. Toronto: Ontario Department of Lands and Forests. 18 pp.

———. 1958. A study of some deer and forest relationships in Rondeau Provincial Park. Wildl. Series No. 7. Toronto: Ontario Department of Lands and Forests. 172 pp.

Bartlett, I. H. 1939. Those controversial deer population figures. Mich. Conserv. 9(2):7–10.

———. 1949. Whitetail deer—United States and Canada. Trans. N. Amer. Wildl. Conf. 14:543–553.

———. 1950. Michigan deer. Lansing: Michigan Department of Conservation, Game Division. 50 pp.

Bartlett, W. W. 1929. History, tradition and adventure in the Chippewa Valley. Chippewa Falls, Wis.: The Chippewa Printery. 244 pp.

Bartram, W. 1794. Travels through North and South Carolina, Georgia, East and West Florida, the Cherokee country, the extensive territories of the Muscogulges or Creek Confederacy and the country of the Choctaws. London: J. Johnson. 526 pp.

———. 1928. The travels of William Bartram. M. Van Doren, ed. Facsimile of 1791 edition. New York: Dover Publications, Inc. 414 pp.

Bassett, J. S. 1901. The writings of "Colonel William Byrd of Westover in Virginia Esq." New York: Doubleday, Page and Co. 461 pp.

Basso, K. H. 1983. Western Apache. *In* Southwest, ed. A. Ortiz, pp. 462–488. Handbook of North American Indians, Vol. 10. Washington, D. C.: Smithsonian Institution. 868 pp.

Batcheler, C. L., and C. M. H. Clarke. 1970. Note on kidney weights and the kidney fat index. New Zealand J. Sci. 13(4):663–668.

Bateman, J. A. 1971. Animal traps and trapping. Harrisburg, Pa.: Stackpole Books. 286 pp.

Bathgate, J. 1976. Wakatipu white-tail—a population census. Unpubl. New Zealand For. Serv. Rep. 12 pp.

Bauer, E. A. 1983. Deer in their world. New York: Outdoor Life Books. 242 pp.

Bauer, W. A. 1977. Forage preferences of tame deer in the aspen type of northern Michigan. M. S. Thesis. Michigan Technological University, Houghton. 85 pp.

Baumgartner, L. L., and A. C. Martin. 1939. Plant histology as an aid in squirrel food habits studies. J. Wildl. Manage. 3(2):266–268.

Bavin, C. R. 1978. Wildlife law enforcement. *In* Wildlife and America, ed. H. P. Brokaw, pp. 350–364. Wash-

ington, D. C.: Council on Environmental Quality. 532 pp.

Baynes, A. S. 1974. Measures for controlling deer depredation. Wildl. in N. C. 38(5):18–19.

Beach, F. C., ed. 1911. The Americana. 20 vols. New York: The Scientific American.

Beaglehole, E. 1936. Hopi hunting and hunting ritual. Yale University Publ. in Anthrop. 4. New Haven, Conn.: Yale Univ. Press. 26 pp.

Bean, M. J. 1978. Federal wildlife law. *In* Wildlife and America, ed. H. P. Brokaw, pp. 279–289. Washington, D. C.: Council on Environmental Quality. 532 pp.

Bear, F. 1979. World of archery. Garden City, N. Y.: Doubleday & Co., Inc. 402 pp.

———. 1980. The archer's bible. Revised edition. Garden City, N. Y.: Doubleday & Co., Inc. 173 pp.

Beasom, S. L. 1974. Relationships between predator removal and white-tailed deer net productivity. J. Wildl. Manage. 38(4):854–859.

Beasom, S. L., W. Evans, and L. Temple. 1980. The drive net for capturing western big game. J. Wildl. Manage. 44(2):478–480.

Beattie, K. H. 1975. Antipoaching campaigns—a tool of wildlife law enforcement? Proc. Ann. Conf. Southeast. Assoc. Game and Fish Comm. 29:728–743.

Beatty, J. 1964. Other cultures. New York: The Free Press. 283 pp.

Beatty, K. H., C. J. Cowles, and R. H. Giles, Jr. 1980. Estimating illegal kill of deer. *In* White-tailed deer population management in north central states, ed. R. L. Hines and S. Nehls, pp. 65–71. Proc. 1979 Symp. N. Cent. Sect. Wildl. Soc. 116 pp.

Beauchamp, W. M. 1902. Horn and bone implements of the New York Indians. N. Y. State Mus. Bull. 50:244–350.

Beckwith, S. L. 1965. Management. *In* The white-tailed deer in Florida, ed. R. F. Harlow and F. K. Jones, pp. 140–162. Tech. Bull. 9. Tallahassee: Florida Game and Fresh Water Fish Commission. 240 pp.

Beckwith, S. L., and L. G. Stith. 1968. Deer damage to citrus groves in south Florida. Proc. Ann. Conf. Southeast. Assoc. Game and Fish Comm. 21:32–38.

Behrend, D. F. 1966. Behavior of white-tailed deer in an Adirondack forest. New York Job Compl. Rep. Proj. W-105-R-7, Job No. V-A. Albany: Department of Environmental Conservation. 143 pp.

———. 1970. The nematode, *Pneumostrongylus tenuis*, in white-tailed deer in the Adirondacks. N. Y. Fish and Game J. 17(1):45–49.

Behrend, D. F., and R. A. Lubeck. 1968. Summer flight behavior of white-tailed deer in two Adirondack forests. J. Wildl. Manage. 32(3):615–618.

Behrend, D. F., and J. F. Witter. 1968. *Pneumostrongylus tenuis* in white-tailed deer in Maine. J. Wildl. Manage. 32(4):963–966.

Behrend, D. F., G. F. Mattfeld, W. C. Tierson, and F. E. Wiley, III. 1970. Deer density control for comprehensive forest management. J. For. 68(11):695–700.

Behrend, D. F., G. F. Mattfeld, and J. E. Wiley III. 1973. Incidence of liver flukes in a sample of white-tailed deer from the Adirondacks. N.Y. Fish and Game J. 20(2):158–161.

Behrendt, G. 1960. Estudio sobre la creación de formas del *Odocoileus peruanus* Gray. Min. Agric., Lima, Peru. Pesca y Caza 10:149–166.

Bell, R. L., and T. J. Peterle. 1975. Hormone implants control reproduction in white-tailed deer. Wildl. Soc. Bull. 3(4):152–156.

Bellis, E. D., and H. B. Graves. 1971. Deer mortality on a Pennsylvania interstate highway. J. Wildl. Manage. 35(2):232–237.

Bennett, C. F. 1968. Human influence on the zoogeography of Panama. Berkeley: University of California Press. 112 pp.

———. 1976. Cultural diversity in Central America and Panama: its relationship to conservation and planning. Rev. Biol. Trop. 24 (Suppl. 1):5–12.

Bennett, L. J., P. F. English, and R. McCain. 1940. A study of deer populations by use of pellet-group counts. J. Wildl. Manage. 4(4):398–403.

Bennitt, R., and W. O. Nagel. 1937. A survey of the resident game and furbearers of Missouri. Univ. Missouri Studies 12(2):77–85.

Benson, A. B. 1937. The America of 1750: Peter Kalm's travel in North America. 2 vols. New York: Wilson-Erickson, Inc. 797 pp.

Benson, D. A., and D. G. Dodds. 1977. The deer of Nova Scotia. Halifax: Nova Scotia Department of Lands and Forests. 92 pp.

Berger, M. E. 1974. Texas hunters: characteristics, opinions, and facility preferences. Ph. D. Thesis. Texas A & M University, College Station. 131 pp.

Berry, R. J. 1971. The scientific management of animal and plant communities for conservation. In The 11th Symp. Brit. Ecol. Soc., Univ. England Angilia, Norwich, ed. E. Duffey and A. S. Watt, pp. 177–206. Oxford: Blackwell Scientific Publ. 652 pp.

Bersing, O. S. 1966. A century of Wisconsin deer. Madison: Wisconsin Conservation Department. 272 pp.

Besser, J. F. 1957. Effectiveness of repellent treatments for protection of trees from animal damage (1956–57). Spec. Rep., Wildl. Res. Lab. Denver: U.S. Fish and Wildlife Service, 19 pp.

Besser, J. F., and J. F. Welch. 1959. Chemical repellents for the control of mammal damage to plants. Trans. N. Amer. Wildl. Conf. 24:166–173.

Beverley, R. 1705. The history and present state of Virginia, in four parts . . . by a native and inhabitant of the place. London: printed for R. Parker. 83 pp.

Beverton, R. J. H., and S. J. Holt. 1957. On the dynamics of exploited fish populations. United Kingdom Min. Agric. and Fish, Fisheries Invest. (Series 2)19:533.

Bieger, J. F., and F. Nüsslein. 1977. Die Bewertung der europäischen Jagdtrophäen. 6th ed. Berlin and Hamburg: Paul Parey Verlag. 80 pp.

Biehn, E. R. 1951. Crop damage by wildlife in California with special emphasis on deer and waterfowl. Game Bull. 5. Sacramento: California Department of Fish and Game. 71 pp.

Biggar, H. P. 1929. The works of Samuel de Champlain. Vol. 3. Toronto: The Champlain Society. 433 pp.

Bigler, W. J., and R. G. McLean. 1973. Wildlife as sentinels for Venezuelan equine encephalomyelitis. J. Amer. Vet. Med. Assoc. 163(6):657–661.

Bindernagle, J. A., and R. C. Anderson. 1972. Distribution of the meningeal worm in white-tailed deer in Canada. J. Wildl. Manage. 36(4):1349–1353.

Bird, C. D., and R. D. Bird. 1967. The aspen parkland. In Alberta—a natural history, ed. W. G. Hardy, pp. 135–149. Vancouver, B. C.: Evergreen Press. 343 pp.

Bishop, C. A. 1981. Northeastern Indian concepts of conservation and the fur trade: a critique of Calvin Martin's thesis. In Indians, animals and the fur trade, ed. S. Krech, pp. 41–58. Athens: Univ. Georgia Press. 207 pp.

Bishop, R. C. 1980. Endangered species: an economic perspective. Trans. N. Am. Wildl. and Nat. Resour. Conf. 45:208–218.

Bittner, C. S. 1949. Protecting Pennsylvania orchards against mice, deer and rabbits. Circ. 342. University Park: Pennsylvania State Coll. Agric. Ext. Serv. 8 pp.

Blackard, J. J. 1971. Restoration of the white-tailed deer in the southeastern United States. M. S. Thesis. Louisiana State University, Baton Rouge. 171 pp.

Blair, R. M. 1960. Deer forage increased by thinnings in a Louisiana loblolly pine plantation. J. Wildl. Manage. 24(4):401–405.

———. 1967. Deer forage in a loblolly pine plantation. J. Wildl. Manage. 31(3):432–437.

———. 1969. Timber stand density influences food and cover. In White-tailed deer in the southern forest habitat. Proc. Symp. Nacogdoches, Texas. New Orleans: USDA Forest Service, South. For. Exp. Stn. 130 pp.

Blair, R. M., and L. E. Brunett. 1977. Deer habitat potential of pine-hardwood forests in Louisiana. Res. Pap. SO-136. New Orleans: USDA Forest Service, South. For. Exp. Stn. 11 pp.

Blair, R. M., and L. K. Halls. 1968. Growth and forage quality of four southern browse species. Proc. Ann. Conf. Southeast Assoc. Game and Fish Comm. 21:57–62.

Blair, R. M., J. A. Hays, and L. E. Brunett. 1963. Stream-crossing structure for deer fence. J. Wildl. Manage. 27(1):129–132.

Blaisdell, J. A., and R. L. Hubbard. 1957. An outrigger type deer fence. Calif. Fish and Game 43(1):100–102.

Blouch, R. I. 1961. Winter deer mortality on two private hunting clubs. Pap. Michigan Acad. Sci., Arts and Lett. 46:277–287.

Boer, A. 1978. Management of deer wintering areas in New Brunswick. Wildl. Soc. Bull. 6:200–205.

Bogardus, A. H. 1874. Field, cover and trap shooting. New York: J. B. Ford and Co. 343 pp.

Bohley, L. 1964. The great Hinkley hunt. Ohio Conserv. Bull. 18(10):11, 31–32.

Bohm, P. 1973. Social efficiency: a concise introduction to welfare economics. New York: John Wiley and Sons. 150 pp.

Bollinger, J. G., O. J. Rongstad, A. Soom, and R. G. Eckstein. 1973. Snowmobile noise effects on wildlife. 1972–1973 Report. Madison: University of Wisconsin. 85 pp.

Book, S. A., G. E. Connolly, and W. M. Longhurst. 1972. Fallout 137Cs accumulation in two adjacent populations of northern California deer. Health Phys. 22:379–385.

Bookhout, T. A. 1965. Feeding coactions between snowshoe hares and white-tailed deer in northern Michigan. Trans. N. Amer. Wildl. and Natur. Resour. Conf. 30:321–335.

Borland, H. 1975. The history of wildlife in America. Washington, D.C.: National Wildlife Federation. 208 pp.

Borrero, J. I. 1967. Mamiferos neotropicales. Dep. Biol., Univ. Valle, Colombia. 110 pp.

Bossenmaier, E. F. 1979. Wildlife management in Canada—a perspective. Trans. N. Amer. Wildl. and Natur. Resour. Conf. 44:81–89.

Boucher, P. 1663. Histoire véritable et naturelle des moeurs et productions du pays de la Nouvelle-France. Reédition de G. Coffin, 1882. Montréal: Bastien et Cie. 164 pp.

Bourne, E. G., ed. 1904. Narratives of the career of Hernando de Soto. New York: A. S. Barnes and Co. 2 vols.

Bowers, A. W. 1950. Mandan social and ceremonial organization. Chicago: Univ. Chicago Press. 407 pp.

Bowers, R. R. 1953. The free-running dog menace. Va. Wildl. 14(10):5–7.

Bowns, J. E. 1976. Field criteria for predator damage assessment. Utah Sci. 37(1):26–30.

Box, T. W., and J. Powell. 1965. Brush management techniques for improved forage values in south Texas. Trans. N. Amer. Wildl. and Natur. Resour. Conf. 30:285–296.

Boyce, A. P. 1950. Orchard damage. Mich. Conserv. 19(6):9–10, 26.

Boyce, D. W. 1978. Iroquoian tribes of the Virginia-North Carolina coastal plain. *In* Northeast, ed. B. G. Trigger, pp. 282–289. Handbook of North American Indians, Vol. 15. Washington, D.C.: Smithsonian Institution. 924 pp.

Boyd, H. 1979. Federal roles in wildlife management in Canada. Trans. N. Amer. Wildl. and Natur. Resour. Conf. 44:90–96.

Boyd, R. J. 1978. American elk. *In* Big game of North America, eds. J. L. Schmidt and D. L. Gilbert, pp. 11–29. Harrisburg, Pa.: Stackpole Books. 494 pp.

Boydston, G., and F. Harwell. 1982. Texas big game investigations. Performance report, Fed. Aid Proj. W-109-R-5. Job No. 4: Big game harvest regulations. Austin: Texas Parks and Wildlife Department. 135 pp.

Brady, P. S., L. J. Brady, P. A. Whetter, D. E. Ullrey, and L. D. Fay. 1978. The effect of dietary selenium and vitamin E on biochemical parameters and survival of young among white-tailed deer (*Odocoileus virginianus*). J. Nutr. 108(9):1439–1448.

Bramble, W. C., and M. K. Goddard. 1953. Seasonal browsing of woody plants by white-tailed deer in the Ridge and Valley section of central Pennsylvania. J. For. 51(11):815–819.

Branan, W. V., and R. L. Marchinton. In press. Reproductive ecology of white-tailed and red brocket deer in Suriname. Proceedings of symposium on the biology and management of the Cervidae. Front Royal, Virginia: Smithsonian Institution.

Brander, T. 1962. Valkohäntäpeurasta Suomessa, etenkin Lounais-Hämeessä. Lounais-Hämeen Luonto 12.

Brannian, R. E., N. Giessman, W. Porath, and G. L. Hoff. 1983. First documentation of epizootic hemorrhagic disease virus in Missouri. J. Wildl. Dis. 19(4):357–358.

Brantly, R. M. 1982. A look at the hot summer of '82. Fla. Wildl. 36(4):18–19.

Brasser, T. J. 1978. Early Indian-European contacts. *In* Northeast, ed. B. G. Trigger, pp. 78–88. Handbook of North American Indians, Vol. 15. Washington, D.C.: Smithsonian Institution. 924 pp.

Braun, E. L. 1950. Deciduous forests of eastern North America. Philadelphia: The Blakiston Co. 596 pp.

———. 1964. Deciduous forests of eastern North America. New York and London: Hafner Publishing Co. 596 pp.

Brazda, A. R. 1957. Dogs vs. deer. N. D. Outdoors 19(7):17.

Bridges, R. J. 1968. Individual white-tailed deer movement and related behavior during the winter and spring in northwestern Florida. M. S. Thesis. University of Georgia, Athens. 86 pp.

Brinkman, K. A., and E. I. Roe. 1975. Quaking aspen: silvics and management in the Lake States. Agric. Handb. 486. Washington, D.C.: USDA Forest Service. 52 pp.

Brokx, P. A. J. 1972a. A study of the biology of the Venezuelan white-tailed deer (*Odocoileus virginianus gymnotis* Wiegmann, 1833), with a hypothesis on the origin of South American cervids. Ph. D. Thesis. University of Waterloo, Waterloo, Ontario. 355 pp.

———. 1972b. Age determination of Venezuelan white-tailed deer. J. Wildl. Manage. 36(4):1060–1067.

———. 1972c. Ovarian composition and aspects of the reproductive physiology of Venezuelan white-tailed deer (*Odocoileus virginianus gymnotis*). J. Mammal. 53(4):760–773.

———. 1972d. The superior canines of *Odocoileus* and other deer. J. Mammal. 53(2):359–366.

Brokx, P. A. J., and F. M. Andressen. 1970. Analisis estomacales del venado caramerudo de los llanos venezolanos. Boletin de la Sociedad Venezolana de Ciencias Naturales 27(117–118):330–353.

Brooke, V. 1878. On the classification of the cervidae, with a synopsis of existing species. Proc. Zool. Soc. London 1878:883–928.

Brothers, A., and M. E. Ray, Jr. 1975. Producing quality whitetails. Laredo, Tex.: Fiesta Publishing Co. 246 pp.

Browman, L. G., and H. S. Sears. 1956. Cyclic variation in the mule deer thymus. Proc. Soc. Exp. Biol. Med. 93(1):161–162.

Brown, B. A., and D. H. Hirth. 1979. Breeding behavior in white-tailed deer. Proc. First Welder Wildl. Foundation Symp. 1:83–95.

Brown, B. A., Jr. 1974. Social organization in male groups of white-tailed deer. *In* The behaviour of ungulates and its relation to management, ed. V. Geist and F. Walther, pp. 436–446. 2 vol. New Series Publ. 24. Morges, Switzerland: IUCN. 940 pp.

Brown, D. 1954. Methods of surveying and measuring vegetation. Commonwealth Bur. Pastures and Field Crops Bull. 42. Farnham Royal, England: Commonwealth Agricultural Bureaux. 223 pp.

Brown, D. E., and C. H. Lowe. 1974. A digitized computer-compatible classification for natural and potential vegetation in the Southwest with particular reference to Arizona. J. Ariz. Acad. Sci. 9(2):1–11.

Brown, E. R. 1961. The black-tailed deer of western Washington. Biol. Bull. 13. Olympia: Washington Department of Game. 124 pp.

Brown, E. R., and C. F. Martinsen. 1959. Browse planting for big game in the state of Washington. Biol. Bull. No. 12. Olympia: Washington Department of Game. 63 pp.

Brown, M. H., and W. R. Felton. 1955. The frontier years. New York: Bramhall House. 272 pp.

Brown, T. L., and D. J. Decker. 1979. Incorporating farmers' attitudes into management of white-tailed deer in New York. J. Wildl. Manage. 43(1):236–239.

Brown, T. L., D. J. Decker, and C. P. Dawson. 1978. Willingness of New York farmers to incur white-tailed deer damage. Wildl. Soc. Bull. 6(4):235–239.

Browning, M. 1972. Forty-four years of the life of a hunter. Ed., E. Stabler. Port Washington, N.Y.: Kennikat Press. 400 pp.

Brownlee, S. 1975. The effects of hunting pressure on population dynamics of desert mule deer. Unpublished manuscript on file at Texas Parks and Wildlife Department, Alpine. 10 pp.

Brunett, L. E. 1959. The Tensas deer herd. Proc. Ann. Conf. Southeast. Assoc. Game Fish Comm. 12(1958):213–224.

Brunetti, O. A. 1969. Redescription of *Parelaphostrongylus* (Boer and Schuls, 1950) in California deer, with studies on its life history and pathology. Calif. Fish and Game 55:307–316.

Bry, T. de. 1590. Admiranda narratio, fida tamen, de commodis et incolarum ritibus Virginiae [America. pt. 1. Latin] . . . Anglico scripta sermone à Thomas Hariot . . . Nunc autem primum Latio donata à C. C. A. Francoforti ad Moenum, Typis I. Wecheli, sumtibus T. de Bry, venales reperiùtur in officina S. Feierabendii. 91 pp.

———. 1591. Brevis narratio eorum quae in Florida Americae porvicia Callis acciderunt, secunda in illam nauigatione, duce Renato de Laundoñiere . . . anno MDLXIII [America. pt. 2. Latin]. Quae est secunda pars Americae . . . Auctore Iacobo Le Moyne, cui cognomen de Morgues . . . Nunc primum Gallico sermone à Theodoro de Bry Leodiense in lucem edita: Latio verò donata à C. C. A. Francoforti ad Moenum, Typis I. Wecheli, sumtibus vero T. de Bry, venales reperiùtur in officina S. Feierabendii. 32 pp.

Bryan, H. 1979. Conflict in the great outdoors. Sociological Studies. No. 4. Tuscaloosa: University of Alabama. 99 pp.

Bryan, D. A. 1980. White-tailed deer fawn mortality, home range, and habitat utilization in east central Missouri. M.S. thesis. Columbia, Mo.: Univ. of Missouri. 45 pp.

Bryant, E. H. 1974. On the adaptive significance of enzyme polymorphisms in relation to environmental variability. Amer. Natur. 108(1959):1–19.

Bryant, L. D., and C. Maser. 1982. Classification and distribution. *In* Elk of North America: ecology and management, ed. J. W. Thomas and D. E. Toweill, pp. 1–59. Harrisburg, Pa.: Stackpole Books. 698 pp.

Bubenik, A. B. 1971. Social well-being as a special aspect of animal sociology. Presented at the 1st Internat. Conf. on the behavior of ungulates and its relation to management, Nov. 2–5, 1971, University of Calgary, Calgary, Alberta.

———. 1982. Physiology. *In* Elk of North America: ecology and management, ed. J. W. Thomas and D. E. Toweill, pp. 125–179. Harrisburg, Pa.: Stackpole Books. 698 pp.

Buckland, D. E., W. A. Abler, R. L. Kirkpatrick and J. B. Whelan. 1975. Improved husbandry system for rearing fawns in captivity. J. Wildl. Manage. 39(1):211–214.

Buckman, H. O., and N. C. Brady. 1960. The nature and properties of soils. 6th rev. ed. New York: Macmillan Co. 567 pp.

Buckman, R. E., and L. H. Blankenship. 1965. Abundance and vigor of aspen root suckering. J. For. 63(1):23–25.

Buckner, J. L., J. L. Landers, J. A. Barker, and C. J. Perkins. 1979. Wildlife food plants following preparation of long-leaf pine sites in southwest Georgia. South. J. Appl. For. 3(2):56–59.

Buckner, J. L., and C. J. Perkins. 1973. A plan of forest wildlife habitat evaluation. Southlands Exp. Stn. Res. Letter No. 18. Bainbridge, Ga.: International Paper Co. 11 pp.

Buckner, J. L., and C. J. Perkins. 1975. A plan of forest wildlife habitat evaluation and its use by International Paper Company. Proc. Ann. Conf. Southeast. Assoc. Game and Fish Comm. 28:675–682.

Buechner, H. K. 1944. The range vegetation of Kerr County, Texas, in relation to livestock and white-tailed deer. Amer. Midl. Nat. 31(3):697–743.

Buffon, G. L. L. 1764. Histoire naturelle, générale et particulière; avec la description du Cabinet du Roy. Vol. 12. Paris: De l' Imprimeric royale.

Burgin, B. E. 1964. Second deadliest deerslayer—the automobile. N.Y. State Conserv. 19(2):2–3.

Burgoyne, G. E., Jr. 1976. Deer checking station data—1975. Surveys and Stat. Serv. Rep. 151. Lansing: Michigan Department of Natural Resources. 16 pp.

Burke, D., A. Deatly, R. E. Eriksen, R. C. Lund, P. A. McConnell, and R. P. Winkel. 1973. An assessment of deer hunting in New Jersey. Prepared by the Deer Research Project. Trenton: New Jersey Division of Fish, Game and Shellfisheries. 173 pp.

Burlend, R. 1848. A true picture of emigration: or fourteen years in the interior of North America; being a full and impartial account of the various difficulties and ultimate success of an English family who emigrated from Barwick-in-Elmet, near Leeds, in the year 1831. London: G. Berger. 62 pp.

Burt, J., and R. B. Ferguson. 1973. Indians of the Southeast: then and now. Nashville, Tenn.: Abingdon Press. 304 pp.

Burt, W. H. 1943. Territoriality and home range concepts as applied to mammals. J. Mammal. 24(3):346–352.

Bushong, C. 1960. Deer capture and release. *In* White-tailed deer investigation, pp. 22–27. P-R Q. Prog. Rep., Proj. W-2-R-21/WP-3/J-A/Qu2. Indianapolis: Indiana Division of Fish and Wildlife.

Buttrey, G. W. 1974. Food habits and distribution of the bobcat, *Lynx rufus rufus* (Schreber), on the Catoosa Wildlife Management Area. M. S. Thesis. Tennessee Technological University, Cookeville. 64 pp.

Byelich, J. D., J. L. Cook, and R. I. Blouch. 1972. Management for deer. *In* Aspen: symposium proceedings, pp. 120–125, Gen. Tech. Rep. NC-1. St. Paul, Minn.: USDA Forest Service, N. Cent. For. Exp. Stn. 154 pp.

Byford, J. L. 1970*a*. Movement responses of white-tailed deer to changing food supplies. Proc. Ann. Conf. Southeast Assoc. Game and Fish Comm. 23:63–78.

———. 1970*b*. Movements and ecology of white-tailed deer in a logged floodplain habitat. Ph. D. Thesis. Auburn University, Auburn, Ala. 157 pp.

———. 1971. Telemetrically determined movements of two white-tailed deer fawns in southwestern Alabama. Proc. Ann. Conf. Southeast. Assoc. Game and Fish Comm. 24:57–63.

Byrd, E. E., A. K. Prestwood, and W. P. Maples. 1967. A new host and two new locality records for the blood fluke, *Heterobilharzia americana* Price, 1929. J. Parasitol. 53(5):1115–1116.

Byrd, W. 1928. Histories of the dividing lines betwixt Virginia and North Carolina. Ed. W. K. Boyd. Raleigh: North Carolina Historical Commission. 341 pp.

———. 1966. Prose works of William Byrd of Westover: narratives of a colonial Virginian. Ed. L. B. Wright. Cambridge, Mass.: Belknap Press of Harvard Univ. Press 438 pp.

Cabrera, A. 1918. Sobre los Odocoileus de Colombia. Bol. Real Soc. Esp. Hist. Nat. 18:300–307.

———. 1943. Sobre la sistemática del vanado y su variación individual y geográfica. Rev. Museo de la Plata, Zool. 3(18):5–41.

———. 1961. Catalogo de los mamíferos de America del Sur. Rev. Mus. Argent. Cienc. Nat. ''Bernardino Rivadavia,'' Buenos Aires, Cienc. Zool. 4(2):309–732.

Cabrera, A., and J. Yepes. 1940. Historia natural Ediar; mamíferos sud-americanos (vida costumbres y descripción). Buenos Aires: Compan. Argentina de Editores. 370 pp.

Cain, S. A. 1938. The species-area curve. Amer. Midl. Natur. 19(1):573–581.

Cairns, A. L. 1976. Distribution and food habits of moose, wapiti, deer, bison and snowshoe hare in Elk Island National Park, Alberta. M. S. Thesis. University of Calgary, Alberta. 169 pp.

Calhoun, J., and F. Loomis. 1974. Prairie whitetails. Springfield: Illinois Department of Conservation. 50 pp.

Callendar, C. 1978a. Fox. *In* Northeast, ed. B. G. Trigger, pp. 636–647. Handbook of North American Indians, Vol. 15. Washington, D.C.: Smithsonian Institution. 924 pp.

———. 1978b. Illinois. *In* Northeast, ed. B. G. Trigger, pp. 673–680. Handbook of North American Indians, Vol. 15. Washington, D.C.: Smithsonian Institution. 924 pp.

———. 1978c. Miami. *In* Northeast, ed. B. G. Trigger, pp. 681–689. Handbook of North American Indians, Vol. 15. Washington, D.C.: Smithsonian Institution. 924 pp.

Camp, R. R., ed. 1957. The hunter's encyclopedia. Harrisburg, Pa.: The Stackpole Co. 1,172 pp.

Campbell, D. L. 1969. Plastic fabric to protect seedlings from animal damage. *In* Wildlife and reforestation in the Pacific Northwest, Symp. Proc., ed. H. C. Black, pp. 87–88. Corvallis: Oregon State University. 92 pp.

———. 1974. Establishing preferred browse to reduce damage to Douglas-fir seedlings by deer and elk. *In* Wildlife and forest management in the Pacific Northwest, ed. H. C. Black, pp. 187–192. Corvallis: Oregon State University. 236 pp.

Campbell, D. L., and J. Evans. 1975. Improving wildlife habitat in young Douglas-fir plantations. Trans. N. Amer. Wildl. and Natur. Resour. Conf. 40:202–208.

Campbell, T. N. 1983. Coahuiltecans and their neighbors. *In* Southwest, ed. A. Ortiz. pp. 343–358.Handbook of North American Indians, Vol. 10. Washington, D. C.: Smithsonian Institution. 868 pp.

Canada Year Book. 1981. Ottawa: Statistics Canada. 1,004 pp.

Canfield, R. H. 1939. Effect of intensity and frequency of clipping on density and yield of black grama and tobosa grass. USDA Tech. Bull. 681. Washington, D. C.: U.S. Department of Agriculture. 32 pp.

———. 1941. Application of the line interceptional method in sampling range vegetation. J. For. 39:388–394.

Carbaugh, B., J. P. Vaughan, E. D. Bellis, and H. B. Graves. 1975. Distribution and activity of white-tailed deer along an interstate highway. J. Wildl. Manage. 39(3):570–581.

Carlile, F., and F. C. Lowry. 1975. Big game report 1975. Oklahoma City: Oklahoma Department of Wildlife Conservation. 30 pp.

Carlsen, J. C., and R. E. Farmes. 1957. Movements of white-tailed deer tagged in Minnesota. J. Wildl. Manage. 21(4):397–401.

Carpenter, M. 1967a. Control of deer damage. Va. Wildl. 28(5):8–9.

———. 1967b. Methods of repelling deer in gardens, orchards, and fields in Virginia. Proc. Ann. Conf. Southeast. Assoc. Game and Fish Comm. 20:233–235.

Carr, L. 1897. The food of certain American Indians and their method of preparing it. Antiquarian 1(3):69–76.

Carroll, B. K., and D. L. Brown. 1977. Factors affecting neonatal fawn survival in southern-central Texas, 1971–1973. J. Wildl. Manage. 41(1):63–69.

Carroll, B. R. 1836. Historical collections of South Carolina. 2 vols. New York: Harper and Bros. 576 pp.

Carroll, T. D. 1957. Antlerless deer harvest (the first three years). Bull. 37. Austin: Texas Game and Fish Commission. 26 pp.

Carroll, W. M. 1961. Deer economics and public policy. *In* Deer management in Pennsylvania, pp. 3–4. University Park: Pennsylvania State University, College of Agric., Ex. Serv. 20 pp.

Carter, W. T. 1931. The soils of Texas. Bull. No. 431. College Station: Texas Agric. Exp. Stn. 192 pp.

Cartwright, D. W. 1875. Natural history of western wild animals. Toledo: Blade Printing and Paper Co. 280 pp.

Cartwright, M. E. 1975. An ecological study of white-tailed deer in northwestern Arkansas: home range, activity and habitat utilization. M. S. Thesis. University of Arkansas, Fayetteville. 147 pp.

Caruso, J. A. 1959. The Appalachian frontier. New York: Bobbs-Merrill Co., Inc. 408 pp.

Carver, J. 1778. Travels through the interior parts of North America in the years 1766, 1767 and 1768. London: Printed for author. 543 pp.

Cary, E. R. 1976. Blackbuck menu. Tex. Parks and Wildl. 34(4):16–18.

Caslick, J. 1980. Deer-proof fences for orchards: a new look at economic feasibility. Proc. Ninth Vert. Pest Conf. 161–162.

———. 1982. Venison: boning, freezing and cooking. Misc. Bull. 99. Ithaca, N. Y.: Cornell University Coop. Ext. 16 pp.

Catesby, M. 1754. The natural history of Carolina, Florida and Bahama Islands. . . . 2 vols. London: Printed by author for C. Marsh.

Caton, J. D. 1877. The antelope and deer of America. New York: Hurd and Houghton. 426 pp.

Caughley, G. 1976. Wildlife management and the dynamics of ungulate populations. Appl. Biol. 1:183–246. London: Academic Press.

———. 1977. Analysis of vertebrate populations. New York: John Wiley and Sons, Inc. 234 pp.

Chabreck, R. H. 1970. Marsh zones and vegetative types in the Louisiana coastal marshes. Ph. D. Thesis. Louisiana State University, Baton Rouge. 113 pp.

Chalmers, G. A., and M. W. Barrett. 1982. Capture myopathy. *In* Noninfectious diseases of wildlife, eds. G. L. Hoff and J. W. Davis, pp. 84–94. Ames: Iowa State Univ. Press. 174 pp.

Chalmers, G. A., H. N. Vance, and G. J. Mitchell. 1964. An outbreak of epizootic hemorrhagic disease in wild ungulates in Alberta. Wildl. Dis. 42:1–6.

Chamberlain, A. F. 1906. Indians of the eastern provinces of Canada. *In* Annual Archaeological Report 1905, pp. 122–136. Report of the Minister of Education. Toronto: L. K. Cameron. 294 pp.

Champlain, S. de. 1922–1936. The works of Samuel de Champlain. Ed. H. P. Biggar. 6 vols. Toronto: The Champlain Society.

Chamrad, A. D., and T. W. Box. 1968. Food habits of white-tailed deer in south Texas. J. Range Manage. 21(3):158–164.

Charlevoix, P. F. X. de. 1763. Letters to the Duchess of Lesdiguerre; giving an account of a voyage to Canada . . . 1761. London: Printed for R. Goodby and sold by R. Baldwin in Pater-Noster-Row. 400 pp.

Chase, W. W., and D. H. Jenkins. 1962. Productivity of the George Reserve deer herd. Proc. Nat. White-tailed Deer Disease Symp. 1:78–88.

Chatillon, G. 1976. L'histoire de l'agriculture au Québec. Montréal: Editions l'Etincelle. 125 pp.

Cheatum, E. L. 1949*a*. Bone marrow as an index of malnutrition in deer. N. Y. State Conserv. 3(5):19–22.

———. 1949*b*. The use of corpora lutea for determining ovulation incidence and variations in fertility of the white-tailed deer. Cornell Vet. 39(3):282–291.

Cheatum, E. L., and C. W. Severinghaus. 1950. Variations in fertility of white-tailed deer related to range conditions. Trans. N. Amer. Wildl. Conf. 15:170–190.

Cheatum, E. L., L. L. Williamson, and A. S. Johnson. 1969. Sociological and economic considerations in management of white-tailed deer. *In* White-tailed deer in the southern forest habitat, pp. 123–126. Proc. Symp. Nacogdoches, Texas. New Orleans: USDA Forest Service, South. For. Exp. Stn. 130 pp.

Chesser, R. K., M. H. Smith, and I. L. Brisbin, Jr. 1980. Management and maintenance of genetic variability in endangered species. Int. Zool. Yearb. 20:146–154.

Chesser, R. K., M. H. Smith, P. E. Johns, M. N. Manlove, D. O. Straney, and R. Baccus. 1982. Spatial, temporal, and age-dependent heterozygosity of beta-hemoglobin in white-tailed deer. J. Wildl Manage. 46(4):983–990.

Chittenden, H. R. 1935. The American fur trade of the far West. 2 vols. New York: Press of the Pioneers, Inc. 1,014 pp.

Choquette, L. P. E. 1970. Anthrax. *In* Infectious diseases of wild mammals, ed. J. W. Davis, L. H. Karstad, and D. O. Trainer, pp. 256–266. Ames: Iowa State Univ. Press. 421 pp.

Choquette, L. P. E., and E. Broughton. 1981. Anthrax. *In* Infectious diseases of wild mammals, ed. J. W. Davis, L. H. Karstad, and D. O. Trainer, pp. 288–296. Ames: Iowa State Univ. Press. 421 pp.

Christian, J. J., V. Flyger, and D. E. Davis. 1960. Factors in mass mortality of a herd of Sika Deer (*Cervus nippon*). Chesapeake Sci. 1(2):79–95.

Christiansen, F. B., and O. Frydenberg. 1973. Selection component analysis of natural polymorphisms using population samples including mother-offspring combinations. Theor. Popul. Biol. 4(4):425–445.

Christie, A. H. C., and J. R. H. Andrews. 1965. Introduced ungulates in New Zealand. B. Virginia deer. Tuatara 13(1):1–8.

Christisen, D. M., and L. J. Korschgen. 1955. Acorn yields and wildlife usage in Missouri. Trans. N. Amer. Wildl. Conf. 20:337–357.

Church, W. L. 1979. Private lands and public recreation. Washington, D. C.: National Association of Conservation Districts. 33 pp.

Clark, K. A., R. M. Robinson, R. G. Marburger, L. P. Jones and J. H. Orchard. 1970. Malignant catarrhal fever in Texas cervids. J. Wildl. Dis. 6(4):376–383.

Clark, K. A., R. M. Robinson, L. L. Weishuhn, and S. McConnell. 1972. Further observations on malignant catarrhal fever in Texas deer. J. Wildl. Dis. 8(1):72–74.

Clarke, S. H., and C. W. Severinghaus. 1979. Sex ratios among fawn white-tailed deer. N. Y. Fish and Game J. 26(2):193–195.

Clawson, M. 1950. The western range livestock industry. New York: McGraw-Hill Book Co. 401 pp.

Clayton, J. 1965. The Reverend John Clayton, a parson with a scientific mind: his scientific writings and other related papers. Ed. E. Berkeley and D. S. Berkeley. Charlottesville: Univ. Virginia Press. 170 pp.

Cline, M. G. 1961. Soils and soil associations of New York. Cornell Ext. Bull. 930. Ithaca: N. Y. State College of Agriculture. 64 pp.

Clover, M. R. 1954. A portable deer trap and catch-net. Calif. Fish and Game 40(4):367–373.

———. 1956. Single-gate deer trap. Calif. Fish and Game 42(3):199–201.

Coblentz, B. E. 1970. Food habits of George Reserve deer. J. Wildl. Manage. 34(39:535–540.

———. 1975. Serum cholesterol level changes in George Reserve deer. J. Wildl. Manage. 39(2):342–345.

———. 1977. Comments on deer sociobiology. Wildl. Soc. Bull. 5(2):67.

Cochran, W. 1978. Twice-fooled hunter bags elusive buck. Roanoke (Va.) Times and World-News, Nov. 12, p. C–13.

Coffman, C. C. 1968. Three physical measurements of male white-tailed deer in West Virginia correlated with soil fertility and population density. M. S. Thesis. Marshall University, Huntington, W. Va. 74 pp.

Cole, G. F. 1959. Key browse survey method. Paper presented at the Western Assoc. Fish and Game Comm., Portland, Ore. Helena: Montana Department of Fish and Game. 10 pp.

Columbian White-tailed Deer Recovery Team. 1982. Columbian white-tailed deer recovery plan. Revision of 1976 Plan. Portland: Oregon Department of Fish and Wildlife. 88 pp.

Comar, C. L. 1965. Movement of fallout radionuclides through the biosphere and man. Ann. Rev. Nucl. Sci. 15:175–206.

Conatser, D. 1977. Bowhunting the whitetail deer. New York: Winchester Press. 171 pp.

Cone, J. 1974. Easy game cooking. McLean, Va.: EPM Publications. 144 pp.

Connolly, G. E. 1970. A population model for deer on the Hopland Field Station, Mendocino County, California. M. A. Thesis. Sonoma State College, Rohnert Park, Calif. 54 pp.

———. 1978. Predators and predator control. *In* Big game of North America: ecology and management, ed. J. L. Schmidt and D. L. Gilbert, pp. 369–394. Harrisburg, Pa.: Stackpole Books. 494 pp.

———. 1981. Limiting factors and population regulation. *In* Mule and black-tailed deer of North America, ed. O. C. Wallmo, pp. 245–285. Lincoln: University of Nebraska Press. 605 pp.

Connolly, G. E., and W. M. Longhurst. 1975. Deer production at Hopland Field Station. Calif. Agric. 29(6):8–9.

Conrad, H. R., A. D. Pratt, and J. W. Hibbs. 1964. Regulation of feed intake in dairy cows. I. Change in importance of physical and physiological factors with increasing digestibility. J. Dairy Sci. 47(1):54–62.

Cook, D. B., and W. J. Hamilton, Jr. 1942. Winter habits of white-tailed deer in central New York. J. Wildl. Manage. 6(4):287–291.

Cook, F. W. 1945. White-tailed deer in the Great Plains region. J. Wildl. Manage. 9(3):237–242.

Cook, J. H. 1923. Fifty years on the old frontier. New Haven, Conn.: Yale Univ. Press. 291 pp.

Cook, R. L. 1974. Management implications of heavy hunting pressure on Texas white-tailed deer on the Kerr Wildlife Management Area. Proc. Ann. Conf. Southeast. Assoc. Game and Fish Comm. 27:114–119.

Cook, R. S., W. C. Glazener, and D. O. Trainer. 1969. White-tailed deer, a new host for *Amblyoma inoratum*. Bull. Wildl. Dis. Assoc. 5(2)108–109.

Cook, R. S., D. O. Trainer, W. C. Glazener, and B. D. Nassif. 1965. A serological study of infectious diseases of wild populations in south Texas. Trans. N. Amer. Wildl. and Natur. Resour. Conf. 30:142–155.

Cook, R. S., M. White, D. O. Trainer, and W. C. Glazener. 1967. Radiotelemetry for fawn mortality studies. Bull. Wildl. Dis. Assoc. 3(4):160–165.

Cook, R. S., M. White, D. O. Trainer, and W. C. Glazener. 1971. Mortality of young white-tailed deer fawns in south Texas. J. Wildl. Manage. 35(1):47–56.

Cooper, J. M. 1938. Snares, deadfalls, and other traps of the Northern Algonquians and northern Athapaskans. Anthropological Series No. 5. Washington, D. C.: The Catholic University of America. 144 pp.

Cooperrider, A. Y. 1974. Computer simulation of the interaction of a deer population with northern forest vegetation. Ph.D. Thesis. SUNY College of Environmental Science and Forestry, Syracuse. 220 pp.

Cooperrider, A. Y., and D. F. Behrend. 1980. Simulation of forest dynamics and deer browse production. J. For. 78(2):85–88.

Copway, G. 1850. The traditional history and characteristic sketches of the Ojibway nation. London: C. Gilpin. 298 pp.

Corbett, R. L., R. L. Marchinton, and C. E. Hill. 1972. Preliminary study of the effects of dogs on radio-equipped deer in a mountainous habitat. Proc. Ann. Conf. Southeast. Assoc. Game and Fish Comm. 25:69–77.

Core, W. L. 1966. Vegetation of West Virginia. Parsons, W. Va.: McLain Printing Co. 217 pp.

Corty, F. L., and A. C. Main. 1974. Louisiana forest industry; its economical importance and growth. Agribusiness Res. Rep. 462. Baton Rouge: Louisiana State University, Department of Agricultural Economics. 47 pp.

Cosgrove, G. E., L. C. Satterfield, and V. S. Nettles. 1981. Neoplasia. *In* Diseases and parasites of white-tailed deer, ed. W. R. Davidson, F. A. Hayes, V. F. Nettles, and F. E. Kellogg, pp. 62–71. Tallahassee, Fla.: Tall Timbers Research Station. 458 pp.

Costley, R. J. 1948. Crippling losses among mule deer in Utah. Trans. N. Amer. Wildl. Conf. 13:451–458.

Cothran, E. G., R. K. Chesser, M. H. Smith, and P. E. Johns. 1983. Influences of genetic variability and maternal factors on fetal growth in white-tailed deer. Evolution 37(2):282–291.

Coues, E., ed. 1965. The manuscript journals of Alexander Henry and David Thompson, 1799–1814. 2 vols. Minneapolis: Ross and Haines, Inc. 1,027 pp.

Cowan, I. M. 1956. What and where are the mule and black-tailed deer? *In* The deer of North America, ed. W. P. Taylor, pp. 335–359. Harrisburg, Pa.: The Stackpole Company. 668 pp.

Cowan, I. M., and C. W. Holloway. 1973. Threatened deer of the world: conservation status. Biol. Conserv. 5(4):243–250.

Cowan, R. L., and T. A. Long. 1962. Studies on antler growth and nutrition of white-tailed deer. Proc. Nat. White-tailed Deer Dis. Symp. 1:54–60.

Cowey, A. 1981. *In* The Oxford companion to animal behavior, ed. D. McFarland, pp. 581–593. New York: Oxford University Press. 657 pp.

Craddock, G. W., and C. L. Forsling. 1938. The influence of climate and grazing on spring-fall sheep in southern Idaho. Tech. Bull. 600. Washington, D. C.: U.S. Department of Agriculture. 42 pp.

Crafts, A. S. 1975. Weed control in forest and range. *In* Modern weed control, ed. A. S. Crafts, pp. 319–340. Berkeley and Los Angeles: Univ. California Press. 440 pp.

Crane, P. P. 1878. Article in *Beloit* (Wis.) *Free Press*, Jan. 24.

Crane, V. W. 1928. The southern frontier, 1670–1732. Durham, N. C.: Duke Univ. Press. 391 pp.

Craven, S., and D. Buege. 1979. So you got a deer. Ext. Publ. G1598. Madison: University of Wisconsin. 5 pp.

Crawford, G. J. 1962. A preliminary investigation of the white-tailed deer on Crab Orchard National Wildlife Refuge. M. A. Thesis. Southern Illinois University, Carbondale. 42 pp.

Crawford, H. S., Jr. 1970. Midwestern deer habitat. *In* White-tailed deer in the Midwest, a symp., pp. 19–22. Res. Pap. NC-39. St. Paul, Minn.: USDA Forest Service, N. Cent. For. Exp. Stn. 34 pp.

———. 1971. Wildlife habitat changes after intermediate cutting for even-aged oak management. J. Wildl. Manage. 35(2):275–286.

———. 1975. Soil-site and forest land management decisions in relation to wildlife. *In* Forest soils and forest land management, pp. 571–581. Proc. 4th N. Amer. For. Soils. Laval University, Quebec: Les Presses. 675 pp.

———. 1976. Relationships between forest cutting and understory vegetation: an overview of eastern hardwood stands. Res. Pap. NE-349. Upper Darby, Pa.: USDA Forest Service, Northeast For. Exp. Stn. 9 pp.

———. 1982. Seasonal food selection and digestibility by tame white-tailed deer in central Maine. J Wildl. Manage. 46(4):974–982.

Crawford, H. S., and A. J. Bjugstad. 1967. Establishing grass range in the southwest Missouri Ozarks. Res. Note NC-22. St. Paul, Minn.: USDA Forest Service, N. Cent. For. Exp. Stn. 4 pp.

Crawford, H. S., and W. M. Harrison. 1971. Wildlife food on three Ozark hardwood sites after regeneration cutting. J. Wildl. Manage. 35(3):533–537.

Crawford, H. S., and R. G. Leonard. 1965. The Sylamore deer study. Proc. Ann. Conf. Southeast. Assoc. Game and Fish Comm. 17:9–13.

Crawford, H. S., W. L. Stutzman, and R. E. Marshall. 1975*a*. Sampling weight of pine foliage and twigs by microwave signal attenuation. Res. Note SE-225. Asheville, N. C.: USDA Forest Service, Southeast For. Exp. Stn. 7 pp.

Crawford, H. S., J. B. Whelan, R. F. Harlow, and J. E. Skeen. 1975*b*. Deer range potential in selective and clearcut oak-pine stands in southwestern Virginia. Res. Pap. SE-134. Asheville, N.C.: USDA Forest Service, Southeast For. Exp. Stn. 12 pp.

Crawford, J. C., and D. C. Church. 1971. Response of black-tailed deer to various chemical taste stimuli. J. Wildl. Manage. 35(2):210–215.

Creed, W.A. 1964. Calculating deer populations by the sex-age-kill method. Report filed with Wisconsin Department of Natural Resources, Bureau of Research, Rhinelander. 2 pp.

Creed, W. A., and F. P. Haberland. 1980. Deer herd management—putting it all together. *In* White-tailed deer population management in the north central states, ed. R. L. Hines and S. Nehls, pp. 83–88. Proc. 1979 Symp. N. Cent. Sect. Wildl. Soc. 116 pp.

Creed, W. A., B. E. Kohn, and K. R. McCaffery. 1979. Deer populations measurements in management units. Prog. Rep. P-R Proj. W-141-R-11. Madison: Wisconsin Department of Natural Resources. 17 pp.

Creed, W. A., and J. F. Kubisiak. 1973. Experimental deer hunt at Sandhill. Wisconsin Conserv. Bull. 38(4)24–26.

Crete, M. 1976. Importance of winter climate in the decline of deer harvest in Quebec. Can. Field-Natur. 90(4):404–409.

Crews, A. K. 1939. A study of the Oregon white-tailed deer, *Odocoileus virginianus leucurus* (Douglas). M. S. Thesis. Oregon State College, Corvallis. 46 pp.

Crichton, R. 1956. We must shoot more deer. Saturday Evening Post 229(18):49, 126–129.

Crockford, J. A., F. A. Hayes, J. H. Jenkins, and S. D. Feurt. 1957. Nicotine salicylate for capturing deer. J. Wildl. Manage. 21(2):213–220.

Crockford, J. A., F. A. Hayes, J. H. Jenkins, and S. D. Feurt. 1958. An automatic projectile type syringe. Vet. Med. 53(3):115–119.

Cromer, J. I. 1967. Southern West Virginia deer study. Charleston: West Virginia Department of Natural Resources. 19 pp.

Croyle, R. C. 1969. Nutrient requirements of young white-tailed deer for growth and antler development. M. S. Thesis. Pennsylvania State University, University Park. 103 pp.

Cue, D. C., and E. E. Langenau, Jr. 1979. Satisfaction and deer hunter density. Wildl. Div. Rep. No. 2848. Lansing: Michigan Department of Natural Resources. 15 pp.

Culin, S. 1975. Games of the North American Indians. New York: Dover Publ. Inc. 846 pp.

Cumming, W. P., ed. 1958. The discoveries of John Lederer. Charlottesville: Univ. Virginia Press. 148 pp.

Cumming, W. P., S. E. Hillier, D. B. Quinn, and G. Williams. 1974. The exploration of North America 1630–1776. New York: G. P. Putnam's Sons. 272 pp.

Curtis, E. S. 1970. The North American Indian: being a series of volumes picturing and describing the Indians of the United States, and Alaska. 20 vol. New York: Johnson Reprint.

Cushing, F. H. 1896. Exploration of ancient key dwellers' remains on the Gulf Coast of Florida. Philadelphia: Amer. Philos. Soc. Proceedings 35:329–432.

Cushman, H. B. 1899. History of the Choctaw, Chickasaw, and Natchez Indians. Greenville, Texas: Headlight Printing House. 607 pp.

Cushwa, C. T., and E. V. Brender. 1966. The response of herbaceous vegetation to prescribed burning. Res. Note SE-53. Asheville, N.C.: USDA Forest Service, Southeast For. Exp. Stn. 2 pp.

Cushwa, C. T., and M. B. Jones. 1969. Wildlife food plants on chopped areas in the Piedmont of South Carolina. Res. Note SE-11. Asheville, N.C.: USDA Forest Service, Southeast For. Exp. Stn. 4 pp.

Cuvier, F., and G. St. Hilaire. 1832. Histoire naturelle des mammifères (1824–1847). Livre LXV. Paris: A. Belin.

Dagg, A. I., and A. Taub. 1970. Flehman. Mammalia 34(4):686–695.

Dahl, A. H., F. W. Whicker, G. C. Farris, and T. E. Hakonson. 1967. A study of the food chain pattern of strontium-90, cesium-137, and iodine-131 in a wild deer population. Fifth Tech. Prog. Rep. Contract AT (11-1)-1156. Fort Collins: Colorado State University Research Foundation. 71 pp.

Dahlberg, B. L., and R. C. Guettinger. 1956. The white-tailed deer in Wisconsin. Tech. Wildl. Bull. 14. Madison: Wisconsin Conservation Department. 282 pp.

Dailey, R. C. 1968. The role of alcohol among North American Indians as reported in the Jesuit relations. Anthropologia 9:45–59.

Dalton, C. J. 1984. Fawn mortality in the Missouri Ozarks. Univ. of Missouri, Columbia. M. S. Thesis in preparation.

Daniel, M. J. 1967. A survey of diseases in fallow Virginia and Japanese deer, chamois, tahr, and feral goats and pigs in New Zealand. New Zealand J. Sci. 10:949–963.

Daniel, W. S. 1976. Investigation of factors contributing to sub-normal fawn production and herd growth patterns. Final Rep. Fed. Aid Proj. No. W-82-R-18, Job No. 10. Austin: Texas Parks and Wildlife Department. 45 pp.

Darlington, W. M., ed. 1893. Christopher Gist's journals. Pittsburgh: J. R. Weldin and Co. 296 pp.

Darr, G. W., and D. K. Klebenow. 1975. Deer, brush control, and livestock on the Texas Rolling Plains. J. Range Manage. 28(2):115–119.

Dasmann, R. F. 1964. Wildlife biology. New York: John Wiley and Sons, Inc. 231 pp.

Dasmann, W. 1971. If deer are to survive. Harrisburg, Pa.: Stackpole Books. 128 pp.

Daubenmire, R. F. 1968. Plant communities; a textbook of plant synecology. New York: Harper and Row. 300 pp.

Davidson, W. R., F. A. Hayes, V. F. Nettles, and F. E. Kellogg, eds. 1981. Diseases and parasites of white-tailed deer. Misc. Publ. No. 7. Tallahassee, Fla.: Tall Timbers Research Station. 458 pp.

Davidson, W. R., M. B. McGhee, V. F. Nettles, and L. C. Chappell. 1980. Haemonchosis in white-tailed deer in the southeastern United States. J. Wildl. Dis. 16(4):499–508.

Davies, W. E. 1968. Physiography. *In* Mineral resources of the Appalachian region, pp. 37–45. U. S. Geological Survey Prof. Pap. 580. Washington, D. C.: U. S. Geological Survey and U. S. Bureau of Mines. 492 pp.

Davis, F. 1980. Wild game—from field to freezer. Louisiana Conservationist 32(1):30.

Davis, G. P., Jr. 1982. Man and wildlife in Arizona: the American exploration period 1824–1865. Scottsdale: Arizona Game and Fish Department. 232 pp.

Davis, J. R. 1979. The white-tailed deer in Alabama. Spec. Rep. 8. Montgomery: Alabama Department of Conservation and Natural Resources. 60 pp.

Davis, J. W., L. H. Karstad, and D. O. Trainer, eds., 1970. Infectious diseases of wild mammals. Ames: Iowa State Univ. Press. 421 pp.

Davis, M. R. 1970. Which binocular for the hunter. *In* The NRA guidebook for hunters, pp. 40–43. Washington, D. C.: National Rifle Association of America. 264 pp.

Davis, R. B. 1951. The food habits of white-tailed deer on the cattle stocked, live oak-mesquite ranges of the King Ranch, as determined by analysis of deer rumen contents. M. S. Thesis. Texas A & M College, College Station. 97 pp.

———. 1952. The use of rumen contents data in a study of deer-cattle competition and "animal equivalence." Trans. N. Amer. Wildl. Conf. 17:448–458.

Davis, R. B., and C. K. Winkler. 1968. Brush versus cleared range as deer habitat in southern Texas. J. Wildl. Manage. 32(2):321–329.

Davison, M. A. 1979. Columbian white-tailed deer status and potential on off-refuge habitat. Compl. Rep. E-1, Study 2. Olympia: Washington Game Department. 71 pp.

Dawson, G. M. 1880. Report on the climate and agricultural value, general geological features and minerals of economic importance of part of the northern portion of British Columbia, and of the Peace River country. Canada Geological Survey. *In* Report to the Canadian Pacific Railway, 1880, ed. S. Fleming, pp. 107–131. Ottawa: Maclean, Roger & Co. 373 pp.

Dawson, M. R. 1967. Fossil history of the families of recent mammals. *In* Recent mammals of the world: a synopsis of families, ed. S. Anderson and J. K. Jones, Jr., pp. 12–53. New York: The Ronald Press Co. 453 pp.

Day, B. W., Jr. 1964. The white-tailed deer in Vermont. Wildl. Bull. 64-1. Montpelier: Vermont Fish and Game Department. 25 pp.

———. 1968. Vermont's 1967 big game seasons in review. Montpelier: Vermont Fish and Game Department. 38 pp.

Day, G. I. 1964. Carrying capacity of various vegetative types for white-tailed deer. Job Comp. Rep. Fed. Aid Proj. WO78-R-7/8, WPS, J6. Phoenix: Arizona Game and Fish Department. 73 pp.

———. 1968. Capturing and marking techniques. *In* Statewide investigation project, pp. 13–25. P-R Job Prog. Rep. Proj. W-78-R-12/WP-1/J-8. Phoenix: Arizona Game and Fish Department.

———. 1969. Cap-Chur problems and remedies. Abstract 2. Phoenix: Arizona Game and Fish Department. 4 pp.

Day, G. I., R. P. Dyson, and F. H. Landeen. 1965. A portable resuscitator for use on large game animals. J. Wildl. Manage. 29(3):511–515.

Day, G. M. 1953. The Indian as an ecological factor in the northeastern forest. Ecology 34(2)329–346.

———. 1978. Western Abenaki. *In* Northeast, ed. B. G. Trigger, pp. 148–159. Handbook of North American Indians, Vol. 15. Washington, D. C.: Smithsonian Institution. 924 pp.

Dean, R. E., M. D. Strickland, J. L. Newman, E. T. Thorne, and W. G. Hepworth. 1975. Reticulo-rumen characteristics of malnourished mule deer. J. Wildl. Manage. 39(3):601–604.

Dean, R. E., and A. H. Winward. 1974. An investigation into the possibility of tansy ragwort poisoning of black-tailed deer. J. Wildl. Dis. 10(2):166–169.

DeBoer, S. G. 1957. Waste in the woods. Wis. Conserv. Bull. 22(10):10–15.

———. 1958. Less waste in the woods. Wisconsin Conserv. Bull. 23(10):13–17.

deCalesta, D. S. In press. Influence of regulations on deer harvest. *In* Symposium on game harvest management (1983), S. L. Beasom, ed. Kingsville: Texas A&I University.

deCalesta, D. S., J. G. Nagy, and J. A. Bailey. 1974. Some effects of starvation on mule deer rumen bacteria. J. Wildl. Manage. 38(4):815–822.

deCalesta, D. S., and D. B. Schwenderman. 1978. Characterization of deer damage to soybean plants. In prep.

Dechert, J. A. 1968. The effects of overpopulation and hunting on the Fort Knox deer herd. Proc. Ann. Conf. Southeast. Assoc. Game and Fish Comm. 21:15–23.

Decker, D. O., T. L. Brown, D. L. Hustin. 1981. Farmers' preferences for white-tailed deer densities in New York: comparison of 2 regions with different agricultural and deer population characteristics. N. Y. Fish and Game J. 28(2):202–207.

Decker, D. O., T. L. Brown, S. O. Tuttle, and O. W. Kelley. 1982. Posting of private lands in New York: a continuing problem. N. Y. State College of Agric. and Life Sciences, Conserv. Circ. 20[7]:1–6.

DeGarmo, W. R., and J. Gill. 1958. West Virginia whitetails. Conserv. Comm. Bull. 4. Charlestown: West Virginia Division of Game Management. 87 pp.

Deliette, L. 1934. Memoirs of DeGannes concerning the Illinois country [1702]. Ed. T. C. Pease and R. C. Werner. Coll. Ill. St. Hist. Lib. 23:302–395.

DeLignery, C. M. 1868. Renewal of the Fox war. Wis. Hist. Coll. 5:86–91.

Della-Bianca, L., and F. M. Johnson. 1965. Effect of an intensive cleaning on deer-browse production in the southern Appalachians. J. Wildl. Manage. 29(4):729–733.

Deloria, V., Jr. 1970. We talk, you listen: new tribes, new turf. New York: The Macmillan Co. 227 pp.

Demarchi, R. A., and D. A. Demarchi. 1967. Winter and spring food habits of white-tailed deer in the East Kootenays. Unpublished report on file at the British Columbia Fish and Wildlife Branch, Kamloops. 10 pp.

de Miranda Ribeiro, A. 1919. Os veados de Brasil segundo as collecoes Rondon e de varios museus nacionaes e estrangeiros. Rev. Mus. Paulista 11:213–307.

Dengler, H. 1923. American Indians. New York: Albert and Chas. Boni. 80 pp.

Denig, E. T. 1930. Indian tribes of the Upper Missouri. *In* 46th Ann. Rep. Bur. Amer. Ethnol. to the Secretary of the Interior, 1928–1929, ed. J. N. B. Hewitt, pp. 375–628. Washington, D. C.: Government Printing Office. 628 pp.

Denney, R. N. 1955. Deer damage problems in Colorado. Proc. Western Assoc. State Game and Fish Comm. 35:131–134.

Densmore, F. 1929. Chippewa customs. Bur. Amer. Ethnol., Bull. 86. Washington, D. C.: Government Printing Office. 204 pp.

Denton, D. C., E. H. Hodil, and D. H. Arner. 1969. Prevention and control of damage to trees. *In* White-tailed deer in the southern forest habitat, pp. 93–97. Proc. Symp. Nacogdoches, Texas. New Orleans: USDA Forest Service, South. For. Exp. Stn. 130 pp.

Den Uyl, D. 1962. The central region. *In* Regional silviculture of the United States, ed. J. W. Barnett, pp. 137–177. New York: The Ronald Press. 610 pp.

de Pourtales, L. F. 1877. Hints on the origin of the flora and fauna of the Florida keys. Amer. Natur. 11:137–144.

d'Escalante Fontaneda, H. 1575. Memoir of D d'Escalante [sic] Fontaneda respecting Florida, written in Spain, about the year 1575. Translated from the Spanish with notes by Buckingham Smith, Washington, 1854. Reprinted, with revisions, Miami, Florida, 1944, ed. D. O. True. Misc. Publ. 1. Miami: University of Miami and the Historical Association of Southern Florida. 77 pp.

De Voe, T. F. 1862. The market book. 2 vols. New York: Printed for author.

de Vos, A., R. H. Manville, and R. G. Van Gelder. 1956. Introduced mammals and their influence on native biota. Zoologica (N. Y.) 41(4):163–194.

DeVoto, B. 1947. Across the wide Missouri. Boston: Houghton, Mifflin Co. 454 pp.

De Vries, D. P. 1857. Voyages from Holland to America, A. D. 1632 to 1644. Translated from Dutch by H. C. Murphy. Coll. N. Y. Hist. Soc., Ser. 2, 3(1):1–136.

———. 1912. From the "Korte Historiael ende journaels aenteyckeninge," 1630–1633, 1634 [1655]. *In* Narratives of early Pennsylvania, west New Jersey and Delaware, 1630–1707, ed. A. C. Myers, pp 1–29. New York: Barnes and Noble. 476 pp.

Dick, E. 1941. The story of the frontier. New York: Tudor Publ. Co. 590 pp.

Dickinson, N. R. 1972. Deer management considerations in forest management. Bull. D1. Montpelier: Vermont Fish and Game Department. 13 pp.

———. 1976. Observations on steep-slope deer wintering areas in New York and Vermont. N. Y. Fish and Game J. 23(1):51–57.

———. 1977. Vermont's winter deer habitat protection program. Trans. N. E. Fish and Wildl. Conf., Boston, Mass. 159 pp.

———. 1978. Evidence of browsing as a guide to mapping winter deer range. N. Y. Fish and Game J. 25(2):170–174.

———. 1982. Basis for using selected sex ratios in the harvest for deriving quotas for harvesting antlerless deer. N. Y. Fish and Game J. 29(1):75–89.

Dickinson, N. R., and L. E. Garland. 1974. The white-tailed deer resource of Vermont. Montpelier: Vermont Fish and Game Department. Mimeo. 63 pp.

Dickson, J. D., III. 1955. An ecological study of the Key deer. Tech. Bull. 3. Gainesville: Florida Game and Fresh Water Fish Commission. 104 pp.

Diem, K. L. 1954. Use of a deer call as a means of locating deer fawns. J. Wildl. Manage. 18(4):537–538.

Dietz, D. R. 1970. Definition and components of forage quality. *In* Range and wildlife habitat evaluation—a research symposium, pp. 1–9. Misc. Publ. 1147. Washington, D. C.: USDA Forest Service. 220 pp.

Dietz, D. R., and J. R. Tigner. 1968. Evaluation of two mammal repellents applied to browse species in the Black Hills. J. Wildl. Manage. 32(1):109–114.

Dijkstra, R. G. 1981. Listeriosis. *In* Infectious diseases of wild mammals, ed. J. W. Davis, L. H. Karstad, and D. O. Trainer, pp. 306–316. Ames: Iowa State Univ. Press. 421 pp.

Dikmans, G., and J. T. Lucker. 1935. New records of nematode parasites from deer in the United States. Proc. Helminthol. Soc., Washington, D. C. 2:83.

Dill, H. H. 1947. Bobcat preys on deer. J. Mammal. 28(1):63.

Dills, G. G. 1970. Effects of prescribed burning on deer browse. J. Wildl. Manage. 34(3):540–545.

Dimock, E. J., II. 1974. Animal resistant Douglas-fir: how likely and how soon. *In* Wildlife and forest management in the Pacific Northwest, ed. H. C. Black, pp. 95–101. Corvallis: Oregon State University. 236 pp.

Doan, K. H. 1970. Effects of snowmobiles on fish and wildlife resources. Proc. Int. Assoc. Game, Fish and Conserv. Comm. 60:97–103.

Dodds, D. G. 1963. The white-tail in Nova Scotia. Halifax, N. S.: Department of Lands and Forests. 30 pp.

Dodge, R. I. 1877. The plains of the great west and their inhabitants. New York: G. P. Putnam's Sons. 448 pp.

Doherty, P. 1971. Effects on fish and game management. *In* Conference on snowmobiles and all-terrain vehicles, ed. R. W. Butler, P. S. Elder, H. N. Janish, and B. M. Petrie, pp. E28–E30. London, Ont.: University of Western Ontario. 237 pp.

Doig, H. E. 1968. Index plants of a deer herd and the condition of the range. Conservationist 22(3):22–27.

Donaldson, D., C. Hunter, and T. H. Holder. 1951. Arkansas' deer herd. Fed. Aid Publ., Proj. 17-D & 20-R. Little Rock: Arkansas Game and Fish Commission. 72 pp.

Donne, T. E. 1924. The game animals of New Zealand. London: John Murray Ltd. 322 pp.

Dooley, A. L. 1974. Foods of the Key deer (*Odocoileus virginianus clavium*). M. A. Thesis. Southern Illinois University, Carbondale. 80 pp.

Dorn, R. D. 1971. White-tailed deer in southeastern Minnesota: winter observations. J. Minn. Acad. Sci. 37(1):16–18.

Dorrance, M. J., P. J. Savage, and D. E. Huff. 1975. Effects of snowmobiles on white-tailed deer. J. Wildl. Manage. 39(3):563–569.

Dorsey, J. O. 1891. Games of the Teton Dakota children. Amer. Anthrop. 4:329–343.

Douglas, D. 1829. Observations on two undescribed species of North American mammalia (*Cervus leucurus et Ovis californianus*). Zool. J. 4:330–332.

———. 1914. Journal kept by David Douglas during his travels in North America 1823–27. London: W. Wesley and Son. 364 pp.

Douglas, F. H. and R. d'Harnoncourt. 1941. Indian art of the United States. New York: The Museum of Modern Art. 210 pp.

Douglass, D. W. 1970. History and status of the wolf in Michigan. *In* Proc. Symp. on wolf management in selected areas of North America, eds. S. E. Jorgensen, C. E. Faulkner, and L. D. Mech, pp. 6–8. Twin Cities, Minn.: U. S. Fish and Wildlife Service. 50 pp.

Downing, R. L. 1972. Comparison of crippling losses of white-tailed deer caused by archery, buckshot and shotgun slugs. Proc. Ann. Conf. Southeast. Assoc. Game and Fish Comm. 25:77–82.

———. 1980. Vital statistics of animal populations. *In* Wildlife management techniques manual, ed. S. D. Schemnitz, pp. 257–262. 4th ed. Washington, D. C.: The Wildlife Society. 686 pp.

Downing, R. L., and B. S. McGinnes. 1969. Capturing and marking white-tailed deer fawns. J. Wildl. Manage. 33(3):711–714.

Downing, R. L., and B. S. McGinnes. 1976. Movement patterns of white-tailed deer in a Virginia enclosure. Proc. Ann. Conf. Southeast. Assoc. Game and Fish Comm. 29:454–459.

Downing, R. L., B. S. McGinnes, R. P. Petcher, and J. L. Sandt. 1969. Seasonal changes in movements of white-tailed deer. *In* White-tailed deer in the southern forest habitat, pp. 19–24. Proc. Symp. Nacogdoches, Texas. New Orleans: USDA Forest Service, South. For. Exp. Stn. 130 pp.

Downs, A. A., and W. E. McQuillan. 1944. Seed production of southern Appalachian oaks. J. For. 42(12):912–920.

Dozer, D. M. 1976. Portrait of the free state. Cambridge, Md.: Tidewater Publ. 652 pp.

Drake, W. E., and S. E. Forbes. 1971. An evaluation of tolerance to deer browsing and selected species of trees and/or shrubs. Final Job Rep. Harrisburg: Pennsylvania Game Commission. 8 pp.

Drake, W. E., J. Kritz, S. Liscinsky, and M. Puglisi. 1978. The overwintering deer carrying capacity of a pole-timber size, northern hardwood stand. Final Job Rep. Harrisburg: Pennsylvania Game Commission. 22 pp.

Drawe, D. L. 1968. Mid-summer diet of deer on the Welder Wildlife Refuge. J. Range Manage. 21(3):164–166.

Driver, H. E. 1968. On the population nadir of Indians in the United States. Current Anthrop. 9:330.

———. 1969. Indians of North America. Chicago: Univ. Chicago Press. 632 pp.

Driver, H. E., and W. C. Massey. 1957. Comparative studies of North American Indians. Philadelphia: Trans. Amer. Philos. Soc. XLVII:165–456.

Drolet, C. A. 1976. Distribution and movements of white-tailed deer in southern New Brunswick in relation to environmental factors. Can. Field-Natur. 90(2):123–136.

Dublin, H. T. 1980. Relating deer diets to forage quality and quantity: the Columbian white-tailed deer (*Odocoileus virginianus leucurus*). M. S. Thesis. University of Washington, Seattle. 135 pp.

Duck, L. G., and J. B. Fletcher. 1945. A survey of the game and furbearing animals of Oklahoma. Bull. 3. Oklahoma City: Oklahoma Game and Fish Commission. 144 pp.

Ducks Unlimited. 1982. Profile study of the 1981 Ducks Unlimited member/subscribers. Chicago: Ducks Unlimited, Inc. 5 pp.

Duguay, J. 1949. La situation du chevreuil dans la province de Québec. *In* Rapport Général du Ministère de la Chasse et des Pêcheries concernant les activités de la chasse et de la pêche pour l'année finissant le 31 mars 1948, pp. 190–199. Québec: Ministère de la Chasse et des Pêcheries. 249 pp.

Dunkeson, R. L. 1955. Deer range appraisal for the Missouri Ozarks. J. Wildl. Manage. 19(3):358–364.

Dunkeson, R. L., and D. A. Murphy. 1953. Missouri's deer herd: reproduction and checking station data. Jefferson City: Missouri Conservation Commission. 7 pp.

Dunn, C. M. 1979. Now it's venison. Ext. Publ. B2095. Madison: University of Wisconsin. 9 pp.

Dusi, J. L. 1949. Methods for the determination of food habits by microtechniques and histology and their application to cottontail rabbit food habits. J. Wildl. Manage. 13(3):295–298.

Eabry, S., ed. 1970. A glossary of deer terminology. Prepared by the terminology committee, northeastern deer study group. New York: Wildlife Research Laboratory. 31 pp.

Eadie, W. R. 1954. Animal control in field, farm, and forest. New York: The Macmillan Co. 257 pp.

———. 1961. Control of wildlife damage in orchards. Bull. 1055. Ithaca: New York State Agric. Ext. Stn. 15 pp.

East, B. 1963. The deer war. Outdoor Life 132(6):17–19, 111–114.

Eastman, C. 1911. Soul of the Indian. New York: Houghton Mifflin Co. 170 pp.

Eberhardt, L. L. 1960. Estimation of vital characteristics of Michigan deer herds. Game Div. Rep. No. 2282. Lansing: Michigan Department of Conservation. 192 pp.

———. 1969. Population analysis. *In* Wildlife management techniques, ed. R. H. Giles, Jr., pp. 457–495. Washington, D. C.: The Wildlife Society. 623 pp.

Eberhardt, L. L., and R. C. Van Etten. 1956. Evaluations of the pellet group count as a deer census method. J. Wildl. Manage. 20(1):70–74.

Ebert, P. N. 1976. Recent changes in Oregon's mule deer population and management. Proc. West. Assoc. Fish and Game Comm. 56:408–414.

Edson, O., and G. D. Merrill. 1894. History of Chautauqua County, New York. Vol. 1. Boston: W. A. Ferguson and Co. 975 pp.

Ehrenreich, J. H., and D. A. Murphy. 1962. A method of evaluating habitat for forest wildlife. Trans. N. Amer. Wildl. and Natur. Resour. Conf. 27:376–384.

Elder, W. H. 1965. Primeval deer hunting pressures revealed by remains from American Indian middens. J. Wildl. Manage 29(2):366–370.

Ellerman, J. R., and T. C. S. Morrison-Scott. 1951. Checklist of Palaearctic and Indian mammals, 1758 to 1946. London: British Museum (Natur. Hist.). 810 pp.

Ellis, G. E. 1882. The red man and white man in North America. Boston: Little, Brown and Co. 642 pp.

Ellisor, J. E. 1969. Mobility of white-tailed deer in south Texas. J. Wildl. Manage. 33(1):220–222.

Emory, W. H. 1867. Report on the United States and Mexican boundary survey. Wasington, D. C.: U. S. Geological Survey. 2(11):50.

Erickson, A. B., V. E. Gunvalson, M. H. Stenlund, D. W. Burcalow, and L. W. Blankenship. 1961. The white-tailed deer of Minnesota. Tech. Bull. 5. St. Paul: Minnesota Department of Conservation. 64 pp.

Errington, P. L. 1967. Of predation and life. Ames: Iowa State Univ. Press. 277 pp.

Estes, R. D. 1974. Social organization of the African bovidae. *In* The behaviour of ungulates and its relation to management, ed. V. Geist and F. Walther, pp. 166–205. 2 vol. New Series Publ. 24. Morges, Switzerland: IUCN. 940 pp.

Evans, J. H. 1910. Reminiscences of Grant County. Proc. Wis. Hist. Soc. 57:232–245.

Evans, J. V., and J. H. Whitlock. 1964. Genetic relationship between maximum hematocrit values and hemoglobin type in sheep. Science 145(3638):1318.

Evans, R. D. 1974. Wildlife habitat management program: a concept of diversity for the public forests of Missouri. *In* Timber-wildlife management symp., pp. 78–83. Occas. Pap. 3. Columbia: Missouri Acad. Sci. 131 pp.

Eve, J. H. 1975. A study of two Oklahoma deer herds. Outdoor Okla. 21(8):6–9.

Eve, J. H., and F. E. Kellogg. 1977. Management implications of abomasal parasites in southeastern white-tailed deer. J. Wildl. Manage. 41(2):169–177.

Eveland, W. C. 1970. Listeriosis. *In* Infectious diseases of wild mammals, ed. J. W. Davis, L. H. Karstad, and D. O. Trainer, pp. 273–282. Ames: Iowa State Univ. Press. 421 pp.

Everitt, J. H., and D. L. Drawe. 1974. Spring food habits of white-tailed deer in the south Texas plains. J. Range Manage. 27(1):15–20.

Ewan, J., and N. Ewan. 1970. John Banister and his natural history of Virginia, 1678–1692. Urbana: Univ. Illinois Press. 485 pp.

Ewers, J. C. 1980. The horse in Blackfoot Indian culture. Washington, D. C.: Smithsonian Institution. 374 pp.

Ezcurra, E., and S. Gallina. 1981. Biology and population dynamics of white-tailed deer in northwestern Mexico. *In* Deer biology, habitat requirements and management in western North America, ed. P. F. Ffolliott and S. Galina, pp. 79–108. Mexico: Instituto de Ecologia. 238 pp.

Faatz, W. C. 1976. Mother-offspring relations and ontogeny of behavior in white-tailed deer. Ph. D. Thesis. Texas A & M University, College Station. 109 pp.

Fagan, R. 1982. Butchering your deer. Outdoor Life 170(4):86–87.

Farb, P. 1968. Man's rise to civilization as shown by the Indians of North America from primeval times to the coming of the industrial state. New York: E. P. Dutton and Co. 332 pp.

Farrand, E. P. 1961. Deer and forestry. *In* Deer management in Pennsylvania, pp. 5–7. University Park: Pennsylvania State University College of Agric. Ext. Serv. 20 pp.

Favre, D. S., and G. Olsen. 1982. Surplus population: a fallacious basis for sport hunting. Clark's Summit, Pa.: Society for Animal Rights, Inc. 12 pp.

Fay, L. D. 1970. Skin tumors of the Cervidae. *In* Infectious diseases of wild mammals, ed. J. W. Davis, L. H. Karstad, and D. O. Trainer, pp. 385–392. Ames: Iowa State Univ. Press. 421 pp.

Fay, L. D., A. P. Boyce, and W. G. Youatt. 1956. An epizootic in deer in Michigan. Trans. N. Amer. Wildl. Conf. 21:173–184.

Feest, C. F. 1978. Virginia Algonquians. *In* Northeast, ed. B. G. Trigger, pp. 253–270. Handbook of North American Indians, Vol. 15. Washington, D. C.: Smithsonian Institution. 924 pp.

Feest, J. E., and C. F. Feest. 1978. Ottawa. *In* Northeast, ed. B. G. Trigger, pp. 772–786. Handbook of North American Indians, Vol. 15. Washington, D. C.: Smithsonian Institution. 924 pp.

Fenneman, N. M. 1931. Physiography of western United States. New York: McGraw-Hill Book Co. 534 pp.

———. 1938. Physiography of eastern United States. New York: McGraw-Hill Book Co., Inc. 714 pp.

Fenton, W. N. 1965. The journal of James Emlen kept on a trip to Canandaigua, N. Y., September 15 to October 30, 1794 to attend the treaty between the United States and the six Nations. Ethnohistory 12(4):279–342.

———. 1978. Northern Iroquoian culture patterns. *In* Northeast, ed. B. G. Trigger, pp. 296–321. Handbook of North American Indians. Vol. 15. Washington, D. C.: Smithsonian Institution. 924 pp.

Fenton, W. N., and E. Tooker. 1978. Mohawk. *In* Northeast, ed. B. G. Trigger, pp. 466–480. Handbook of North American Indians, Vol. 15. Washington, D. C.: Smithsonian Institution. 924 pp.

Fernald, M. L. 1950. Gray's manual of botany. New York: American Book Co. 1,632 pp.

Ferris, D. H., and B. J. Verts. 1964. Leptospiral reactor rates among white-tailed deer and livestock in Carroll County, Illinois. J. Wildl. Manage. 28(1):35–41.

Field, R. A., F. C. Smith, and W. G. Hepworth. 1973. The mule deer carcass. Bull. 589. Laramie: University of Wyoming Agric. Exp. Stn. 6 pp.

Findlay, J. D., F. W. Eatman, and L. DeBerry. 1946. The Uwharrie deer project. N. C. State Bull. Series Vol. 1, No. 1. Raleigh: North Carolina Department of Conservation and Development. 19 pp.

Findley, J. S., A. H. Harris, D. E. Wilson, and C. Jones. 1975. Mammals of New Mexico. Albuquerque: University of New Mexico Press. 360 pp.

Finley, R. B., Jr., and R. E. Pillmore. 1963. Conversion of DDT to DDD in animal tissue. AIBS Bull. 13(3):41–42.

Firebaugh, J. E. 1971. Deer on the tracks. Montana Outdoors 2(2):9–11.

Fischl, J., and L. L. Rue, III. 1981. After your deer is down. Tulsa, Okla.: Winchester Press. 137 pp.

Fishing and Hunting News. 1978. Game meat deserves extra special care. Fishing and Hunting News 34(41):12.

Fleming, G. 1789. Survey of Township 17, Chenango 20 townships. New York Department of Public Works, Field Book 4.

Fletch, A. L. 1970. Foot-and-mouth disease. *In* Infectious diseases of wild mammals, ed. J. W. Davis, L. H. Karstad, and D. O. Trainer, pp. 68–75. Ames: Iowa State Univ. Press. 421 pp.

Fletcher, A. C., and F. La Flesche. 1972. The Omaha tribe. 2 vols. Lincoln: Univ. Nebraska Press. 660 pp.

Flick, V. C. 1976. Final report for evaluation of six devices to protect individual seedlings from deer browsing. Upper Darby, Pa.: USDA Forest Service, Northeast. For. Exp. Stn. 25 pp.

Florida Game and Fresh Water Fish Commission. 1983. Everglades emergency deer hunt controversy. Tallahassee: State of Florida. 35 pp.

Flower, S. S. 1931. Contributions to our knowledge of the duration of life in vertebrate animals. Vol. V. Mammals. Proc. Zool. Soc. Lond.: 145–234.

Floyd, J. 1960. Crop damage by deer and bear: suggestions for control. Fla. Wildl. 14(5):18–21.

Flyger, V. F. and T. Thoerig. 1962. Preliminary report on a new principal for prevention of crop damage by deer. Proc. Ann. Conf. Southeast. Assoc. Game and Fish Comm. 15:119–122.

Flyger, V. F., and T. Thoerig. 1965. Crop damage caused by Maryland deer. Proc. Ann. Conf. Southeast. Assoc. Game and Fish Comm. 16:45–52.

Foote, L. E. 1945. The Vermont deer herds, a study in productivity. State Bull., P-R Series 13. Montpelier: Vermont Fish and Game Service. 125 pp.

Forbes, S. E., L. M. Lang, S. A. Liscinsky, and H. A. Roberts. 1971. The white-tailed deer in Pennsylvania. Res. Bull. 170. Harrisburg: Pennsylvania Game Commission. 41 pp.

Foreyt, W. J., and A. C. Todd. 1972. The occurrence of *Fascioloides magna* and *Fasciola hepatica* together in the livers of naturally infected cattle in south Texas, and the incidence of the flukes in cattle, white-tailed deer and feral hogs. J. Parasitol. 58(5):1010–1011.

Foreyt, W. J., and A. C. Todd. 1976. Development of the large American liver fluke, *Fascioloides magna*, in white-tailed deer, cattle, and sheep. J. Parasitol. 62(1):26–32.

Foromozov, A. N. 1946. The snow cover as an environment factor and its importance in the life of mammals and birds. Otdel. Zool. n. 5 (xx). Translation from Russian published by Boreal Institute, University of Alberta, Edmonton. 176 pp.

Forsyth, T. 1911. An account of the manners and customs of the Sauk and Fox nations of Indian traditions [1827]. *In* The Indian tribes of the upper Mississippi Valley and region of the Great Lakes, ed. E. H. Blair, 183–245. Vol. 2. Cleveland: Arthur H. Clark. 357 pp.

Fosberg, S. A. 1975. Isolation and characterization of epizootic hemorrhagic disease virus (EHDV) from white-tailed deer (*Odocoileus virginianus*) in eastern Washington. M. S. Thesis. University of Idaho, Moscow. 41 pp.

Fosburgh, P. 1946. New York's record heads. New York State Conservationist 1(2): 16–17, 30.

Foster, J. W., and J. D. Whitney. 1850. Report on the geology and topography of a portion of the Lake Superior land district. Part 1. Copper Lands. Washington, D. C.: Printed for the U. S. House of Representatives. 224 pp.

Fowler, J. F., J. D. Newsom, and H. L. Short. 1968. Seasonal variation in food consumption and weight gain in male and female white-tailed deer. Proc. Ann. Conf. Southeast. Assoc. Game and Fish Comm. 21:24–31.

Fowler, M. E. 1974. Restraint and anesthesia in zoo animal practice. J. Amer. Vet. Med. Assoc. 164 (7):706–711.

Fox, J. R., and M. R. Pelton. 1974. Observation of a white-tailed deer die-off in the Great Smoky Mountain National Park. Proc. Ann. Conf. Southeast. Assoc. Game and Fish Comm. 27:297–301.

Fox, M. W. 1980. Returning to eden: animal rights and human responsibility. New York: The Viking Press. 281 pp.

Franklin, J. F., and C. T. Dyrness. 1973. Natural vegetation of Oregon and Washington. Gen. Tech. Rep. PNW-8. Portland, Ore.: USDA Forest Service, Pacific Northwest For. and Range Exp. Stn. 417 pp.

Franklin, W. V. 1932. Virginia and the Cherokee Indian trade, 1673–1754. E. Tenn. Hist. Soc. Publ. 4:3–21.

Franzmann, A. W., and R. E. LeResche. 1978. Alaska moose blood studies with emphasis on condition evaluation. J. Wildl. Manage. 42(2):334–351.

Franzmann, A. W., C. C. Schwartz, and R. O. Peterson. 1980. Moose calf mortality in summer on the Kenai Peninsula, Alaska. J. Wildl. Manage. 44(3):764–768.

Fraser, A. F. 1968. Reproductive behaviour in ungulates. New York: Academic Press. 202 pp.

Fred Bear Sports Club. 1978. The American bowhunter. Big Sky 6(4):1–6.

Freddy, D. J. 1982. Predicting mule deer harvest in Middle Park, Colorado. J. Wildl. Manage. 46(3):801–806.

Free, S. L., and C. W. Severinghaus. n. d. Report on the effectiveness of a "deer proof" fence on the New York State thruway. Special P-R Proj. Rep. W-89-R-3. Albany: New York Department of Environmental Conservation. 22 pp.

Free, S. L., W. T. Hesselton, and C. W. Severinghaus. 1964. The gains and losses in a deer population for five sections of New York State. Albany: New York Department of Environmental Conservation. 34 pp. mimeo.

Freese, F. 1967. Elementary statistical methods for foresters. Agric. Handbook 317. Washington, D. C.: USDA Forest Service. 87 pp.

French, B. F. 1869. Historical collections of Louisiana, embracing many rare and valuable documents relating to the natural, civil and political history of that state. 5 parts. New York: Wiley and Putnam.

French, C. E., L. C. McEwen, N. D. Magruder, R. H. Ingram, and R. W. Swift. 1955. Nutritional requirements of white-tailed deer for growth and antler development. Bull. 600. University Park: Pennsylvania Agric. Exp. Stn. 50 pp.

French, C. E., L. C. McEwen, N. D. Magruder, R. H. Ingram, and R. W. Swift. 1956. Nutrient requirements for growth and antler development in the white-tailed deer. J. Wildl. Manage. 20(2):221–232.

Friedrich, P. D., and G. Burgoyne. 1981. Deer productivity and condition: 1981 spring survey results. Wildl. Div. Rep. 2903. Lansing: Michigan Department of Natural Resources. 11 pp.

Friedrich, P. D., and H. R. Hill. 1982. Doe productivity and physical condition: 1982 spring survey results. East Lansing: Michigan Dept. Nat. Res., Wildl. Div. Rep. 2926. 12 pp.

Frijlink, J. H. 1977. Patterns of wolf pack movements prior to kills as read from tracks in Algonquin Provincial Park, Ont., Canada. Bijdrafen tot de dierkunde 47(1):131–137.

Frison, G. C. 1978. Prehistoric hunters of the high Plains. New York: Academic Press. 457 pp.

Fritts, S. H., and L. D. Mech. 1981. Dynamics, movements, and feeding ecology of a newly protected wolf population in northwestern Minnesota. Wildl. Monogr. 80. Washington, D. C.: The Wildlife Society. 79 pp.

Fritts, S. H., and J. A. Sealander. 1978. Diets of bobcats in Arkansas with special reference to age and sex differences. J. Wildl. Manage. 42(3):533–539.

Froiland, S. G. 1962. The genus *Salis* (willows) in the Black Hills of South Dakota. Tech. Bull. 1269. Ft. Collins, Colo.: USDA Forest Service. 75 pp.

Frost, M. 1974. A biogeographical analysis of some relationships between man, land, and wildlife in Belize (British Honduras). Ph. D. Thesis. Oregon State University, Corvallis. 361 pp.

———. 1977. Wildlife management in Belize: program status and problems. Wildl. Soc. Bull. 5(2):48–51.

Fundaburk, E. L., ed. 1958. Southeastern Indians life portraits: a catalogue of pictures 1564–1860. Birmingham, Ala.: Birmingham Printing Co. 136 pp.

Garcilaso de la Vega. 1723. La Florida del Inca. Historia del adelontado, Hernando de Soto, governador, y capitan general del reino de la Florida y de otros heroicos Caballeros, Espanoles, e Indios. 2nd ed. Madrid: N. Rodriquez Franco. 268 pp.

Garland, L. E. 1972. Bow hunting for deer in Vermont. Some characteristics of the hunter, the hunt and the harvest. Montpelier: Vermont Fish and Game Department. 19 pp.

———. 1976. Summary of female deer reproductive rate studies. Vermont separate report, Pittman-Robertson W-34-R-14, Job I-3. Montpelier: Vermont Fish and Game Department. 125 pp.

———. 1977. White-tailed deer study. Annual performance report, Pittman-Robertson Project W-34-R-14, Study I–IV. Montpelier: Vermont Fish and Game Department.

Garner, G. W., J. A. Morrison, and J. C. Lewis. 1978. Mortality of white-tailed deer fawns in the Wichita Mountains, Oklahoma. Proc. Ann. Conf. Southeast. Assoc. Fish and Wildl. Agencies 30:493–506.

Gasaway, W. C., R. O. Stephenson, J. L. Davis, P. E. K. Shepherd, and O. E. Burris. 1984. Interrelationships of wolves, prey, and man in interior Alaska. Wildl. Monogr. 84. 50 pp.

Gates, D. H., L. A. Stoddart, and C. W. Cook. 1956. Soil as a factor influencing plant distribution on salt deserts of Utah. Ecol. Manage. 26:155–174.

Gavin, T. A. 1979. Population ecology of the Columbian white-tailed deer. Ph. D. Thesis. Oregon State University, Corvallis. 149 pp.

Gavitt, J. D. 1973. Disturbance effect of free-running dogs on deer reproduction. M. S. Thesis. Virginia Polytechnic Institute, Blacksburg. 53 pp.

Gavitt, J. D., R. L. Downing, and B. S. McGinnes. 1975. Effect of dogs on deer reproduction in Virginia. Proc. Ann. Conf. Southeast. Assoc. Game and Fish Comm. 28:532–539.

Gazin, C. L. 1955. A review of the Upper Eocene Artiodactyla of North America. Smithsonian Misc. Coll. 128. Washington, D. C.: Smithsonian Institution. 96 pp.

Geist, V. 1966. The evolution of horn-like organs. Behaviour 27:175–214.

———. 1971. Mountain sheep: a study in behavior and evolution. Chicago: Univ. Chicago Press. 383 pp.

———. 1981. Behavior: adaptive strategies in mule deer. *In* Mule and black-tailed deer of North America, ed. O. C. Wallmo, pp. 157–223. Lincoln: Univ. Nebraska Press. 624 pp.

George, J. L., R. G. Wingard, and W. L. Palmer. 1983. Penn State's 5-alive deer fence. Amer. For. 89:30–32, 59–63.

Gerstell, R. 1938. Electric fencing as a deer control agency. Pa. Game News 8(12):8–9, 32.

Gibson, D. F., P. F. Scanlon, and R. J. Warren. 1982. Xylazine hydrochloride for immobilizing captive white-tailed deer (*Odocoileus virginianus*). Zool. Biol. 1:311–322.

Gibson, W. H. 1905. Camp life in the woods and the tricks of trapping and trap making. New York and London: Harper and Bros. 300 pp.

Giessman, N. 1982. White-tailed deer population measurement, harvest analysis, and season recommendations. P-R Proj. Rep. No. W-13-R-35. Columbia: Missouri Department of Conservation. 51 pp.

Giessman, N., and D. A. Murphy, eds. 1982. Missouri deer hunting. Jefferson City: Missouri Conservation Commission. 20 pp.

Gifford, E. W. 1936. Northeastern and western Yavapai. Berkeley: Univ. of California Publications in Amer. Archaeol. and Ethnol. 34(4):247–354.

Gilbert, A. H. 1973. Expenditure patterns of Vermont sportsmen. Trans. Northeast Sec. Wildl. Soc. 30:171–190.

———. 1977. Influence of hunter attitudes and characteristics on wildlife management. Trans. N. Amer. Wildl. and Natur. Resour. Conf. 42:226–236.

Gilbert, D. L. 1978. Sociological considerations in management. *In* Big game of North America: ecology and management, ed. J. L. Schmidt and D. L. Gilbert,

pp. 409–416. Harrisburg, Pa.: Stackpole Books. 512 pp.

Gilbert, F. F. 1966. Aging white-tailed deer by annuli in the cementum of the first incisor. J. Wildl. Manage. 30(1):200–202.

Gilbert, W. H., Jr. 1943. The eastern Cherokee. Bur. Amer. Ethnol. 133:177–413.

Giles, R. H., Jr. 1960. The free-running dog. Va. Wildl. 21(6):6–7.

Gilfillan, J. A. 1896. Report. *In* First annual report of the chief fire warden of Minnesota for the year 1895, by C. C. Andrews, pp. 99–100. St. Paul: Pioneer Press Co. 192 pp.

Gill, J. D. 1956. Regional differences in size and productivity of deer in West Virginia. J. Wildl. Manage. 20(3):286–292.

———. 1957a. Effects of pulpwood cutting practices on deer. Proc. Soc. Amer. For. 1957:137–146.

———. 1957b. Review of deer yard management 1956. Game Div. Bull. 5. Augusta: Maine Department of Inland Fish and Game. 61 pp.

Gill, R. B., and O. C. Wallmo. 1973. Middle Park deer study—physical characteristics and food habits. *In* Game Res. Rep. July, 1973, Part Two, pp. 81–103. Fort Collins: Colorado Division of Wildlife. 275 pp.

Gipson, P. S., and J. A. Sealander. 1974. Dog: deer friend or foe. Ark. Game and Fish 6(3):10–13.

Gipson, P. S., and J. A. Sealander. 1977. Ecological relationships of white-tailed deer and dogs in Arkansas. *In* Proc. 1975 Predator Symp., ed. R. L. Phillips and C. Jonkel, pp. 3–16. Missoula: Montana For. Conserv. Exp. Stn., University of Montana. 268 pp.

Gladfelter, L. 1980. Deer population estimates in the Midwest farmland. *In* White-tailed deer population management in north central states, ed. R. L. Hines and S. Nehls, pp. 5–11. Proc. 1979 Symp. N. Cent. Sect. Wildl. Soc. 116 pp.

Glasgow, W. M. 1982. Fisheries and wildlife resources and the agricultural land base in Alberta. Edmonton: Environment Council of Alberta. 65 pp.

Glazener, W. C. 1949. Operation deer traps. Texas Game and Fish 7(10):6–7, 17, 26.

Glazener, W. C., and F. F. Knowlton. 1967. Some endoparasites found in Welder Refuge deer. J. Wildl. Manage. 31(3):595–597.

Glover, R. L. 1982. Characteristics of deer poachers and poaching in Missouri. M. S. Thesis. University of Missouri, Columbia. 161 pp.

Goddard, I. 1978. Delaware. *In* Northeast, ed. B. G. Trigger, pp. 213–239. Handbook of North American Indians, Vol. 15. Washington, D. C.: Smithsonian Institution. 924 pp.

Godshall, T. Conservation news. Pa. Game News 52(5):39.

———. 1978. Over 26,000 roadkills. Pa. Game News 45(5):50.

Goldman, E. A., and R. Kellogg. 1940. Ten new white-tailed deer from North and Middle America. Proc. Biol. Soc. Washington 53:81–90.

Goodrich, J. W. 1979. Political assault on wildlife management: is there a defense? Trans. N. Amer. Wildl. and Natur. Resour. Conf. 44:326–336.

Goodrum, P. D. 1969. Short and long rotations in relation to deer management in southern forests. *In* White-tailed deer in the southern forest habitat, pp. 71–73. Proc. symp., Nacogdoches, Texas. New Orleans: USDA Forest Service, South. For. Exp. Stn. 130 pp.

Goodrum, P. D., and V. H. Reid. 1962. Browsing habits of white-tailed deer in the western Gulf region. Proc. National White-tailed Deer Dis. Symp. 1:9–14.

Goodwin, H. C. 1859. Pioneer history of Cortland County and the border wars of New York. New York: A. B. Burdick. 456 pp.

Gorton, A. A. 1957. The venison book: how to dress up, cut up and cook your deer. Brattleboro, Vt.: Stephen Greene Press. 78 pp.

Goss, R. J. 1963. The deciduous nature of deer antlers. *In* Mechanisms of hard tissue destruction, pp. 339–369. Publ. No. 75. Washington, D. C.: American Association for the Advancement of Science. 6 pp.

———. 1969*a*. Photoperiodic control of antler cycles in deer: I. Phase shift and frequency changes. J. Exp. Zool. 170(3):311–324.

———. 1969*b*. Photoperiodic control of antler cycles in deer: II. Alterations in amplitude. J. Exp. Zool. 171(2):223–234.

Gosse, P. H. 1859. Natural history of America. London: Morgan and Chase. 306 pp.

Gould, F. W. 1962. Texas plants—a checklist and ecological summary. MP-585. College Station: Texas Agric. Exp. Stn. 112 pp.

Gould, S. J. 1974. The origin and function of "bizarre" structures: antler size and skull size in the "Irish elk," *Megaloceros giganteus*. Evolution 28(2):191–220.

Graham, F., Jr. 1971. Man's dominion. New York: M. Evans and Co., Inc. 339 pp.

Graham, S. A. 1954. Changes in northern Michigan forest from browsing by deer. Trans. N. Amer. Wildl. Conf. 19:526–533.

Graham, S. A., R. P. Harrison, Jr., and C. E. Westell, Jr. 1963. Aspens: phoenix trees of the Great Lakes region. Ann Arbor: Univ. Michigan Press. 272 pp.

Gramly, R. M. 1977. Deerskins and hunting territories: competition for a scarce resource of the northeastern woodlands. Amer. Antiq. 42(4):601–605.

Gray, J. A. 1959. Texas angora goat production. B-926. College Station: Texas Agric. Exp. Stn. 15 pp.

Gray, M. H., G. K. Yarrow, and H. A. Jacobson. 1980. Comparison of three deer rumen content identification techniques. Presented at the Third Annual Southeast Deer Study Group Meeting, Nacogdoches, Texas. 19 pp.

Green, H. 1963. New technique for using the Cap-Chur gun. J. Wildl. Manage. 27(2):292–296.

Greenwood, R. J., Y. A. Greichus, and E. J. Hugghins. 1967. Insecticide residues in big game mammals of South Dakota. J. Wildl. Manage. 31(2):288–292.

Gregory, R. A. 1957. Some silvical characteristics of western redcedar in southeast Alaska. Ecology 38:646–649.

Gregory, W. K. 1951. Evolution emerging. A survey of changing patterns from primeval life to man. Vol. II. New York: The Macmillan Co. 1,013 pp.

Greig-Smith, P. 1964. Quantitative plant ecology. 2nd ed. London: Butterworth and Co. 256 pp.

Grieb, J. R., and M. G. Sheldon. 1956. Radio-controlled firing device for the cannon-net trap. J. Wildl. Manage. 20(2):203–205.

Griffin, P. F., R. L. Chatham, and R. N. Young. 1968. Anglo-America: a systematic and regional geography. 2nd ed. Palo Alto, Calif.: Fearon Publ. 456 pp.

Grignon, A. 1857. Seventy-two years' recollection of Wisconsin. Wis. Hist. Colls. 3:194–296.

Grimwood, I. R. 1969. Notes on the distribution and status of some Peruvian mammals 1968. Sp. Publ. No. 21.

New York: Amer. Comm. Internatl. Wild Life Protection and New York Zool. Soc. 86 pp.

Grinnell, G. B. 1972. The Cheyenne Indians. 2 vols. Lincoln: Univ. Nebraska Press. 788 pp.

Grinnell, G. B., and C. B. Reynolds. 1894. A plank. Forest and Stream XLII:89.

Grisez, T. J. 1957. Deer-browsing in the Poconos. Pa. Game News 28(2):7–10.

———. 1959. The Hickory Run deer exclosure. Res. Note 87. Upper Darby, Pa.: USDA Forest Service. 4 pp.

———. 1960. Slash helps protect seedlings from deer browsing. J. For. 58(5):385–387.

Grosenbaugh, L. R. 1952. Plotless timber estimates—new, fast, easy. J. For. 50(1):32–37.

Gross, J. E., J. E. Roelle, and G. L. Williams. 1973. Program ONEPOP and information processor: a system modeling and communications project. Prog. Rep. Fort Collins: Colorado Coop. Wildl. Res. Unit, Colorado State University. 327 pp.

Grzimek, h. c. B. 1972. Grzimek's animal life encyclopedia. Vol. 13: Mammals IV. New York: Van Nostrand Reinhold Co. 566 pp.

Gue, B. F. 1903. History of Iowa. 4 vols. New York: Century History Co.

Guilday, J. E. 1971. Biological and archeological analysis of bones from a 17th century Indian village (46 PU 31), Putnam County, West Virginia. Rep. Archeol. Investig. No. 4. Morgantown: West Virginia Geological and Economic Survey. 64 pp.

Guilday, J. E., P. W. Parmalee, and D. P. Tanner. 1962. Aboriginal butchering techniques at the Eschelman Site (36 La 12), Lancaster County, Pa.: Pa. Archeol. 32(2):59–83.

Guilday, J. E., and D. P. Tanner. 1965*a*. Vertebrate remains from the Kipp Island Site. *In* The archeology of New York State, ed. W. A. Ritchie, pp. 241–242. Garden City, N. Y.: Natural History Press. 357 pp.

Guilday, J. E., and D. P. Tanner. 1965*b*. Vertebrate remains from the Mount Carbon Site (46 Fa 7), Fayette County, West Virginia. W. Vir. Archeol. 18:1–14.

Guilkey, P. C. 1959. The influence of vegetational layers on cover measurements. *In* Techniques and methods of measuring understory vegetation, pp. 101–104. New Orleans: USDA Forest Service, South. and Southeast. For. Exp. Stns. 174 pp.

Guthrie, D. A. 1968. The tarsus of early Eocene artiodactyls. Amer. Mus. Novit. 128. New York: American Museum of Natural History. 96 pp.

Guynn, D. C., Jr., S. P. Mott, W. D. Cotton, and H. A. Jacobson. 1983. Cooperative management of white-tailed deer on private lands in Mississippi. Wildl. Soc. Bull. 11(3):211–214.

Gwynn, J. V. 1965. Sustained yield deer herd management. Va. Wildl. 25(11):4–6.

———. 1976. The Virginia deer management program. Proc. Northeast Deer Study Group 12:14.

Gysel, L. W. 1961. Bulldozing to produce browse for deer. Michigan Agric. Exp. Stn. Q. Bull. 43(4):722–731.

Gysel, L. W., and F. Stearns. 1968. Deer browse production of oak stands in central lower Michigan. Res. Note NC-48. St. Paul, Minn.: USDA Forest Service, N. Cent. For. Exp. Stn. 4 pp.

Hafez, E. S. E., ed. 1968. Reproduction in farm animals. 2nd ed. Philadelphia: Lea and Febiger. 440 pp.

Hagan, W. T. 1961. American Indians. Chicago: Univ. Chicago Press. 190 pp.

Hahn, H. C., Jr. 1945. The white-tailed deer in the Edwards Plateau region of Texas. Austin: Texas Game, Fish and Oyster Commission. 52 pp.

——. 1949. A method of censusing deer and its application in the Edwards Plateau of Texas. Austin: Texas Game, Fish and Oyster Commission. 24 pp.

Hahn, H. C., Jr., and W. P. Taylor. 1950. Deer movements in the Edwards Plateau. Texas Game and Fish 8(12)4–9, 31.

Haigh, J. C. 1976. Some mechanical faults associated with dart immobilization. J. Zoo Anim. Med. 7(2):12–14.

Haigh, J. C., and H. C. Hopf. 1976. The blowgun in veterinary practice: its uses and preparation. J. Amer. Vet. Med. Assoc. 169(9):881–883.

Haines, F. 1938. The northward spread of horses among the Plains Indians. Amer. Anthrop. 40:429–437.

Hakluyt, R. 1589. The principall voiages and discoveries of the English nation. 3 vols. London: G. Bishop and R. Newberrie.

Halford, D. K., and A. W. Alldredge. 1975. Behavior associated with parturition in captive Rocky Mountain mule deer. J. Mammal. 56(2):520–522.

Hall, C. C., ed. 1910. Narratives of early Maryland, 1633–1684. New York: Chas. Scribner's Sons. 460 pp.

Hall, D. I., and J. D. Newsom. 1978. The coyote in Louisiana. La. Agric. 21(4):4–5.

Hall, E. R. 1981. The mammals of North America. 2nd ed. New York: John Wiley & Sons. Vol. II:601–1180 + 90 pp.

Hall, E. R., and K. R. Kelson. 1959. The mammals of North America. New York: The Ronald Press Co. Vol. II:547–1083.

Hall, T. C., E. B. Taft, W. H. Baker, and J. C. Aub. 1953. A preliminary report of the use of Flaxedil to produce paralysis in the white-tailed deer. J. Wildl. Manage 17(4):516–520.

Hall, W. K. 1973. Natality and mortality of white-tailed deer in Camp Wainwright, Alberta. M. S. Thesis. University of Calgary, Calgary, Alberta. 117 pp.

Halloran, A. F. 1943. Management of deer and cattle on the Aransas National Wildlife Refuge, Texas. J. Wildl. Manage. 7(2):203–216.

Halls, L. K. 1970. Relative browsing of 16 species by white-tailed deer. J. Range Manage. 23(2):146–147.

——. 1978. White-tailed deer. *In* Big game of North America: ecology and management, ed. J. L. Schmidt and D. L. Gilbert, pp. 43–65. Harrisburg, Pa.: Stackpole Books. 494 pp.

Halls, L. K., C. E. Boyd, D. W. Lay, and P. D. Goodrum. 1965. Deer fence construction and costs. J. Wildl. Manage. 29(4):885–888.

Halls, L. K. and H. S. Crawford. 1965. Vegetation response to an Ozark woodland spraying. J. Range Manage. 18(6):338–340.

Halls, L. K., and T. R. Dell. 1966. Trial of ranked-set sampling for forage yields. For. Sci. 12(1):22–26.

Halls, L. K., and T. H. Ripley. 1961. Deer browse plants of southern forests. New Orleans: USDA Forest Service, South. and Southeast. For. Exp. Stns. 78 pp.

Haltenorth, T., and W. Trense. 1956. Das Grosswild der Erde und seine Trophäen. Bonn: Bayerischer Landwirtschaftsverlag. 436 pp.

Hamilton W. D. 1971. Geometry for the selfish herd. J. Theor. Biol. 31(2):295–311.

Hammond, Incorporated. 1973. Atlas of United States history. Maplewood, N. J.: Hammond, Inc. 64 pp.

Hancock, N. V. 1979. Survey of game and nongame wildlife damage questionnaire sent to all states in July 1979. Salt Lake City: Utah Division of Wildlife Resources. 66 pp. Mimeo.

Handley, C. O., Jr. 1950. Game mammals of Guatemala. *In* A Fish and wildlife survey of Guatemala, ed. G. B. Saunders, A. D. Holloway, and C. O. Handley, Jr., pp. 141–162. Spec. Scient. Rep. Wildl. 5. Washington, D. C.: USDI Fish and Wildlife Service. 162 pp.

——. 1966. Checklist of the mammals of Panama. *In* Ectoparasites of Panama, ed. R. L. Wenzel and V. J. Tipton, pp. 753–795. Chicago: Field Museum of Natural History. 861 pp.

Hanna, C. A. 1911. The wilderness trail; or, venturers and adventures of the Pennsylvania traders on the Allegheny path, with some new annals of the old West, and the records of some strong men and some bad ones. 2 vols. New York: G. P. Putnam and Sons.

Hansen, C. S. 1977. Social costs of Michigan's deer habitat improvement program. Ph. D. Thesis. University of Michigan, Ann Arbor. 188 pp.

——. 1978. Social costs of Michigan's deer habitat improvement program. Wildl. Div. Rep. No. 2808. Lansing: Michigan Department of Natural Resources. 61 pp.

Hanson, W. C., A. H. Dahl, F. W. Whicker, W. M. Longhurst, V. Flyger, S. P. Davey, and K. R. Gree. 1963. Thyroidal radioiodine concentrations in North American deer following 1961–1963 nuclear weapons tests. Health Phys. 9:1235–1239.

Hanson, W. C., and J. G. Smith. 1970. Significance of forage quality as a tool in wildlife management. *In* Range and wildlife habitat evaluation—a research symposium, pp. 25–31. Misc. Publ. 1147. Washington, D.C.: USDA Forest Service. 220 pp.

Harder, J. D. 1969. A photoelectric cell system for recording nocturnal activity of mule deer. J. Wildl. Manage. 33(3):704–709.

——. 1970. Evaluating winter deer use of orchards in western Colorado. Trans. N. Amer. Wildl. and Natur. Resour. Conf. 35:35–47.

——. 1975. Physical and reproductive characteristics of a deer population at record-high density. Paper presented at 37th Midwest Fish and Wildl. Conf., Toronto, Ontario.

——. 1980. Reproduction of white-tailed deer in the northcentral United States. *In* White-tailed deer population management in the north central states, R. L. Hine and S. Nehls, eds., pp. 23–25. Proc. 1979 Symp. North Central Section, The Wildlife Society, 116 pp.

Harder, J. D., and T. J. Peterle. 1974. Effect of diethylstilbestrol on reproductive performance of white-tailed deer. J. Wildl. Manage. 38(2):183–196.

Hardin, J. W. 1974. Behavior, socio-biology, and reproductive life history of the Florida Key deer, *Odocoileus virginianus clavium*. Ph. D. Thesis. Southern Illinois University, Carbondale. 243 pp.

Hardin, J. W., and J. L. Roseberry. 1975. Estimates of unreported loss resulting from a special deer hunt on Crab Orchard National Wildlife Refuge. Proc. Ann. Conf. Southeast. Assoc. Game and Fish Comm. 29:460–466.

Hardister, J. P. 1965. Dog: man's best friend. Wildl. in N.C. 29(2):20–21.

Hare, F. K., and M. K. Thomas. 1974. Climate Canada. Toronto: Wiley Publishers of Canada, Ltd. 256 pp.

Hariot, T. 1893. Narrative of the first English plantation of Virginia. First printed at London in 1588, now reproduced after de Bry's illustrated edition printed at Frankfort in 1590. London: B. Quaritch. 111 pp.

Harlow, R. F. 1959. An evaluation of white-tailed deer habitat in Florida. Tech. Bull. 5. Tallahassee: Florida Game and Fresh Water Fish Commission. 64 pp.

———. 1961. Fall and winter foods of Florida white-tailed deer. Q. J. Fla. Acad. Sci. 24(1):19–38.

———.1977. A technique for surveying deer forage in the Southeast. Wildl. Soc. Bull. 5(4):185–191.

———. 1979. In defense of inkberry—dangers of ranking deer forage. Wildl. Soc. Bull. 7(1):21–24.

Harlow, R. F., H. S. Crawford, and D. F. Urbston. 1975a. Rumen contents of white-tailed deer: comparing local with regional samples. Proc. Ann. Conf. Southeast. Assoc. Game and Fish Comm. 28:562–567.

Harlow, R. F., J. B. Whelan, H. S. Crawford, and J. E. Skeen. 1975b. Deer foods during years of oak mast abundance and scarcity. J. Wildl. Manage. 39(2):330–336.

Harlow, R. F., and R. L. Downing. 1969. The effects of size and intensity of cut on production and utilization of some deer foods in the southern Appalachians. Trans. Northeast Fish and Wildl. Conf. Northeast Sect., The Wildl. Soc. 26:45–55.

Harlow, R. F., and R. L. Downing. 1970. Deer browsing and hardwood regeneration in the southern Appalachians. J. For. 68(5):298–300.

Harlow, R. F., and L. K. Halls. 1972. Response of yellowpoplar and dogwood seedlings to clipping. J. Wild. Manage. 36(4):1076–1080.

Harlow, R. F., and R. G. Hooper. 1972. Forages eaten by deer in the Southeast. Proc. Ann. Conf. Southeast. Assoc. Game and Fish Comm. 25:18–46.

Harlow, R. F., and F. K. Jones, Jr., eds. 1965. The white-tailed deer in Florida. Tech.Bull. 9. Tallahassee: Florida Game and Fresh Water Fish Commission. 240 pp.

Harlow, R. F., and W. F. Oliver, Jr. 1967. Natural factors affecting deer movement. Q. J. Fla. Acad. Sci. 30(3):221–226.

Harlow, R. F., B. A. Sanders, J. B. Whelan, and L. C. Chappel. 1980. Deer habitat on the Ocala National Forest: improvement through forest management. South. J. of Appl. For. 4:98–102.

Harlow, R. F., D. D. Strode, and L. M. Oliphant. 1966. Timber and deer thrive under even-aged hardwood management. South. Lumberman 213(2656):118–120.

Harmel, D. E. 1980. Antler formation in white-tailed deer. Texas Fed. Aid Proj. W-109-R-3, Job 16. Austin: Texas Parks and Wildlife Department. 29 pp.

Harris, L. H. 1970. Hunting whitetail deer. Wellington: New Zealand Forest Service. 19 pp.

Harris, M. J., T. H. J. Huisman, and F. A. Hayes. 1973. Geographic distribution of hemoglobin variants in the white-tailed deer. J. Mammal. 54(1):270–274.

Harris, M. T., W.L. Palmer, and J. L. George. 1983. Preliminary screening of white-tailed deer repellents. J. Wildl. Manage. 47(2):516–519.

Harthoorn, A. M. 1976. The chemical capture of animals. London: Baillier Tindall. 416 pp.

Hartman, D. C. 1972. Behavioral characteristics of the white-tailed deer (*Odocoileus virginianus*) in relation to agricultural damage in Columbia County, Pennsylvania. M. S. Thesis. Pennsylvania State University, University Park. 128 pp.

Hartsook, E. W., J. B. Whelan, and M. A. Ondik. 1975. Changes in blood proteins of deer during gestation and suckling. J. Wildl. Manage. 39(2):346–354.

Hartwell, H. D. 1973. Putrefied fish—a promising repellent for reducing spring deer browsing on Douglas-fir trees. Note 4. Olympia: Washington Department of Natural Resources. 10 pp.

Harwell, W. F., and J. C. Barron. 1975. The breeding season of the white-tailed deer in southern Texas. Tex. J. Sci. 26(3–4):417–420.

Haugen, A. O. 1959. Breeding records of captive white-tailed deer in Alabama. J. Mammal. 40(1):108–113.

———. 1975. Reproductive performance of white-tailed deer in Iowa. J. Mammal. 56(1):151–159.

Haugen, A. O., and L. A. Davenport. 1950. Breeding records of white-tailed deer in the Upper Peninsula of Michigan. J. Wildl. Manage. 14(3):290–295.

Haugen, A. O., and H. G. Metcalf. 1963. Field archery and bowhunting. New York: The Ronald Press Co. 213 pp.

Haugen, A. O., and D. W. Speake. 1957. Parturition and early reactions of white-tailed deer fawns. J. Mammal. 38(3):420–421.

Hautaloma, J., and P. J. Brown. 1978. Attributes of the deer hunting experience: a cluster-analytic study. J. Leisure Res. 10:271–287.

Hawkins, R. E. 1973. The involvement of big game animals in the event of foot-and-mouth disease introduction into the United States. *In* Proc. industry advisory group foot and mouth disease, pp. 34–41. Washington, D. C.: USDA Animal and Plant Health Inspection Service. 47 pp.

———. 1974. Wildlife considerations as a prerequisite to combating foreign diseases. *In* Animal disease monitoring, ed. D. G. Ingram, W. R. Mitchell, and S. W. Martin, pp. 68–71. Springfield, Ill.: Charles C. Thomas, Publ. 215 pp.

———. 1976. Role of wildlife in exotic diseases. *In* Proc. Foreign Anim. Dis. Seminar, pp. 99-105. Athens, Ga.: Wildlife Disease Foundation. 106 pp.

Hawkins, R. E., D. C. Autry, and W. D. Klimstra. 1967. Comparison of methods used to capture white-tailed deer. J. Wildl. Manage. 31(3):460-464.

Hawkins, R. E., and W. D. Klimstra. 1970a. A preliminary study of the social organization of the white-tailed deer. J. Wildl. Manage. 34(2):407–419.

Hawkins R. E., and W. D. Klimstra. 1970b. Deer trapping correlated with weather factors. Trans. Ill. State Acad. Sci. 63(2):198–201.

Hawkins, R. E., W. D. Klimstra, and D. C. Autry. 1970. Significant mortality factors of deer on Crab Orchard National Wildlife Refuge. Trans. Ill. State Acad. Sci. 63(2):202–206.

Hawkins, R. E., W. D. Klimstra, and D. C. Autry. 1971. Dispersal of deer from Crab Orchard National Wildlife Refuge. J. Wildl. Manage. 35(2):216–220.

Hawkins, R. E., L. D. Martoglio, and G. G. Montgomery. 1968 Cannon-netting deer. J. Wildl. Manage. 32(1):191–195.

Hawkins, R. E., and A. K. Prestwood. 1977. Helminth parasite relations between white-tailed deer and domestic livestock. Abstract. J. Amer. Vet. Med. Assoc. 17(10):1088.

Hayes, F. A. 1981. Preface. *In* Diseases and parasites of white-tailed deer, ed. W. R. Davidson, F. A. Hayes,

V. F. Nettles, and F. E. Kellogg, pp. VII–XII. Tallahassee, Fla.: Tall Timbers Research Station. 458 pp.

Hayes, F. A., and A. K. Prestwood. 1969. Some considerations for diseases and parasites of white-tailed deer in the southeastern United States. *In* White-tailed deer in the southern forest habitat, pp. 32–36. Proc. Symp. Nacogdoches, Tex. New Orleans: USDA Forest Service, South. For. Exp. Stn. 130 pp.

Hayne, D. W., and J. V. Gwynn. 1976. Percentage does in total kill as a harvest strategy. Proc. Joint NE-SE Deer Study Group Meeting, Blackstone, Va. 1:117–123.

Heady, H. F. 1964. Palatability of herbage and animal preference. J. Range Manage. 17(2):76–82.

Healy, W. M. 1967. Forage preferences of captive deer while free ranging in the Allegheny National Forest. M. S. Thesis. Pennsylvania State University, University Park. 93 pp.

———. 1971. Forage preferences of tame deer in a northwest Pennsylvania clear-cutting. J. Wildl. Manage. 35(4):717–723.

Hearne, S. 1958. A journey from Prince of Wales Port in Hudson's Bay to the Northern Ocean . . . in the years 1769, 1770, 1771, and 1772. Ed. R. Glover. Toronto: The Macmillan Co. 301 pp.

Heath, R. 1974. A look at snowmobile damage. ORV Monitor. Berkeley, Calif.: Environmental Defense Fund. 8 pp.

Hebb, E. A. 1971. Site preparation decreases game food plants in Florida sandhills. J. Wildl. Manage. 35(1):155–162.

Heberlein, T. A., and B. Laybourne. 1978. The Wisconsin deer hunter: social characteristics, attitudes, and preferences for proposed hunting season changes. Working Paper 10, School of Natural Resources. Madison: University of Wisconsin College of Agriculture and Life Sciences. 96 pp.

Heberlein, T. A., J. N. Trent, and R. N. Baumgartner. 1982. The influence of hunter density on firearm deer hunters' satisfaction: a field experiment. Trans. N. Amer. Wildl. and Natur. Resour. Conf. 47:665–676.

Hedger, R. S. 1981. Foot-and-mouth disease. *In* Infectious diseases of wild mammals, ed. J. W. Davis, L. H. Karstad, and D. O. Trainer, pp. 87–96. Ames: Iowa State Univ. Press. 421 pp.

Heezen, K. L., and J. R. Tester. 1967. Evaluation of radiotracking by triangulation with special reference to deer movements. J Wildl. Manage. 31(1):124–141.

Hegsted, D. M. 1964. Protein requirements. *In* Mammalian protein metabolism, ed. H. N. Munro and J. B. Allisons, pp. 135–171. Vol. 2. New York: Academic Press. 642 pp.

Heidenreich, C. E. 1971. Huronia: a history and geography of the Huron Indians, 1600–1650. Toronto: McClelland and Stewart. 337 pp.

———. 1978. Huron. *In* Northeast, ed. B. G. Trigger, pp. 368–388. Handbook of North American Indians, Vol. 15. Washington, D. C.: Smithsonian Institution. 924 pp.

Heidmann, L. J. 1963. Deer repellents are effective on ponderosa pine in the Southwest. J. For. 61(1):53–54.

Heizer, R. F. 1955. Primitive man as an ecologic factor. Kroeber Anthro. Soc. Papers 13:1–31.

Helgeland, G. 1981. Bowhunting big game records of North America. Ripon Wis.: Ripon Community Printers. 253 pp.

———. 1982. Arrow speed isn't everything. American Hunter 10(7):10–11.

Hendee, J. C. 1969. Appreciative versus consumptive uses of wildlife refuges: studies of who gets what and trends in use. Trans. N. Amer. Wildl. and Natur. Resour. Conf. 34:352–264.

———. 1972. Management of wildlife for human benefits. Proc. West. Assoc. Game and Fish Comm. 52:175–181.

———. 1974. A multiple-satisfaction approach to game management. Wildl. Soc. Bull. 2:104–113.

Hendee, J. C., and C. Schoenfeld, eds. 1973. Human dimensions in wildlife programs. Washington, D. C.: Wildlife Managment Institute. 193 pp.

Hendee, J. C., G. H. Stankey, and R. C. Lucas. 1978. Wilderness management. Misc. Publ. No. 1365. Washington, D. C.: USDA Forest Service. 381 pp.

Henderson, J., and E. L. Craig. 1932. Economic mammology. Springfield, Ill.: Thomas Books. 397 pp.

Henderson, J., and J. P. Harrington. 1914. Ethnozoology of the Tewa Indians. Bull. 56. Washington, D. C.: Bureau of American Ethnology. 76 pp.

Hendry, L.C., T. M. Goodwin, and R. F. Labisky. 1982. Florida's vanishing wildlife. Circ. 485 (Revised). Gainesville: University of Florida Coop. Ext. Serv. 69 pp.

Henry, A. 1901. Travels and adventures in Canada and the Indian territories between the years 1760–1776. Ed. J. Bain. Boston: Little, Brown. 347 pp.

Henson, J., F. Sprague, and G. Valentine. 1977. Soil Conservation Service assistance in managing wildlife on private lands in Texas. Trans. N. Amer. Wildl. and Natur. Resour. Conf. 42:264–270.

Hepburn, N. W. 1959. Effects of snow cover on mobility and local distribution of deer in Alonquin Park. M. S. Thesis. University of Toronto, Toronto, Ontario. 55 pp.

Hepburn, R. L. 1968. Experimental management of mixed conifer swamps for deer and timber in eastern Ontario. Sect. Rep. (Wildl.) 69. Toronto: Ontario Department of Lands and Forests. 44 pp.

Hergenrader, T., and C. Wooten. 1978. North Carolina deer roundup. Raleigh: North Carolina Wildlife Resources Commission. 24 pp.

Hernández Corzo, R. 1964. Los mamiferos de Chiapas. A. C. No. 21. Mexico City: Ediciones del Inst. Mex. Rec. Nat. Ren. 63 pp.

Hershkovitz, P. 1948. The technical name of the Virginia deer with a list of the South American forms. Proc. Biol. Soc. Wash. 61:41–48.

———. 1958. The metatarsal glands in white-tailed deer and related forms of the neotropical region. Mammalia 22(4):537–546.

———. 1982. Neotropical deer (Cervidae). Part 1. Pudus, genus *Pudu* Gray. Fieldiana Zool., N. S. No. 11. 86 pp.

Hesselton, W. T., and L. W. Jackson. 1971. Some reproductive anomalies in female white-tailed deer from New York. N. Y. Fish and Game J. 18(1):42–51.

Hesselton, W. T., and L. W. Jackson. 1973. Breeding and parturition dates of white-tailed deer in New York. N. Y. Fish and Game J. 20(1):40–47.

Hesselton, W. T., and L. W. Jackson. 1974. Reproductive rates of white-tailed deer in New York State. N. Y. Fish and Game J. 21(2):135–152.

Hesselton, W. T., and P. R. Sauer. 1973. Comparative physical condition of four deer herds in New York according to several indices. N. Y. Fish and Game J. 20(2):77–107.

Hesselton, W. T., C. W. Severinghaus, and J. E. Tanck. 1965. Population dynamics of deer at the Seneca Army Depot. N. Y. Fish and Game J. 12(1):17–30.

Hibler, C. P. 1981. Diseases. *In* Mule and black-tailed deer of North America, ed. O. C. Wallmo, pp. 129–155. Lincoln: Univ. Nebraska Press. 624 pp.

Hickerson, H. 1965. The Virginia deer and intertribal buffer zones in the upper Mississippi Valley. *In* Man, culture and animals: the role of animals in human ecological adjustments, ed. A. Leeds and A. Vayda, pp. 43–65. Washington, D. C.: American Association for the Advancement of Science. 304 pp.

———. 1973. Fur trade colonialism and the North American Indian. J. Ethnic Studies 1:15–44.

Hickey, W.O., and T. A. Leege. 1970. Ecology and management of redstem ceanothus, a review. Wildl. Bull. 4. Boise: Idaho Fish and Game Department. 18 pp.

Hickie, P. 1937. Four deer produce 160 in six seasons. Mich. Conserv. 7:6–7, 11.

Hildebrand, P. R. 1971. Biology of white-tailed deer on winter ranges in the Swan Valley, Montana. M. S. Thesis. University of Montana, Missoula. 91 pp.

Hill, R. R., and D. Harris. 1943. Food preference of Black Hills deer. J. Wildl. Manage. 7(2):233–236.

Hilmon, J.B. 1959. Determination of herbage weight by double-sampling: weight estimate and actual weight. *In* Technique and methods of measuring understory vegetation, pp. 20–25. New Orleans: USDA Forest Service, South, and Southeast. For. Exp. Stns. 174 pp.

Hipschman, D. 1959. Department history. *In* Looking back past 50 years, pp. 13–73. Pierre: South Dakota Department of Game, Fish and Parks. 154 pp.

Hirth, D. H. 1973. Social behavior of white-tailed deer in relation to habitat. Ph. D. Thesis. University of Michigan, Ann Arbor. 255 pp.

———. 1977*a*. Social behavior of white-tailed deer in relation to habitat. Wildl. Monogr. 53. Washington, D. C.: The Wildlife Society. 55 pp.

———. 1977*b*. Observations of loss of antler velvet in white-tailed deer. Southwest Natur. 22(2):278–280.

Hirth, D. H., and D. R. McCullough. 1977. Evolution of alarm signals in ungulates with special reference to white-tailed deer. Amer. Natur. 111:31–42.

Hodge, F. W. 1907. Handbook of American Indians north of Mexico. Bur. Amer. Ethnol., Bull. 30. Part 1. Washington, D.C.: Government Printing Office. 972 pp.

———, ed. 1910. Handbook of American Indians north of Mexico. Bur. Amer. Ethnol., Bull. 30. Part 2. Washington, D. C.: Government Printing Office. 1,221 pp.

Hoebel, E. A. 1960. The Cheyennes. New York: Holt, Rinehart and Winston. 103 pp.

Hoekstra, T. W. 1968. Cap-Chur syringes modified for easier locating. J. Wildl. Manage. 32(3):626–628.

Hoff, G. L., and D. O. Trainer. 1978. Bluetongue and epizootic hemorrhagic disease viruses: their relationship to wildlife species. Adv. Vet. Sci. Comp. Med. 22:111–132.

Hoff, G. L., and D. O. Trainer. 1981. Hemorrhagic diseases of wild ruminants. *In* Infectious diseases of wild mammals, ed. J. W. Davis, L. H. Karstad, and D. O. Trainer, pp. 45–53. Ames: Iowa State Univ. Press. 421 pp.

Hoff, G. L., D. O. Trainer, and M. M. Jochim. 1974. Bluetongue virus and white-tailed deer in an enzootic area of Texas. J. Wildl. Dis. 10(2):158–163.

Hoffman, R. A., and P. F. Robinson. 1966. Changes in some endocrine glands of white-tailed deer as affected by season, sex and age. J. Mammal. 47(2):266–280.

Hoffman, W. J. 1896. The Menomini Indians. Ann. Rep. Bur. Amer. Ethnol. 14(1):5–328.

Hoffmeister, J. F., and H. G. Multer. 1968. Geology and origin of the Florida Keys. Geol. Soc. Amer. Bull. 79:1487–1502.

Holsworth, W. N. 1973. Hunting efficiency and white-tailed deer density. J. Wildl. Manage. 37(3):336–342.

Holter, J. B., H. H. Hayes, and S. H. Smith. 1979. Protein requirement of yearling white-tailed deer. J. Wildl. Manage. 43(4):872–879.

Holter, J. B., W. E. Urban, Jr., and H. H. Hayes. 1977. Nutrition of northern white-tailed deer throughout the year. J. Anim. Sci. 45(2):365–376.

Hood, R. E. 1971. Seasonal variations in home range, diel movement and activity patterns of white-tailed deer on the Rob and Bessie Welder Wildlife Refuge (San Patricio County, Texas). M. S. Thesis. Texas A & M University, College Station. 173 pp.

Hood, R. E., and J. M. Inglis. 1974. Behavioral responses of white-tailed deer to intensive ranching operations. J. Wildl. Manage 38(3):488–498.

Horejsi, R. G. 1973. Influence of brushlands on white-tailed deer diets in north-central Texas. M. S. Thesis. Texas Technical University, Lubbock. 69 pp.

Hormay, A. L. 1943. A method of estimating grazing use of bitterbrush. Res. Note 45. Berkeley: USDA Forest Service, California For. and Range Exp. Stn. 4 pp.

Hornaday, W. T. 1914. Wild life conservation in theory and practice. New Haven, Conn.: Yale Univ. Press. 240 pp.

———. 1931. Thirty years war for wildlife. Stamford, Conn.: Permanent Wildlife Protection Fund. 292 pp.

———. 1935. Hornaday's American natural history. New York: Chas. Scribner's Sons. 449 pp.

Hornocker, M. G. 1970. An analysis of mountain lion predation upon mule deer and elk in the Idaho primitive area. Wildl. Monogr. 21. Washington, D. C.: The Wildlife Society. 39 pp.

Horsley, S. B. 1977*a*. Allelopathic inhibition of black cherry by fern, grass, goldenrod, and aster. Can. J. For. Res. 7:205–216.

———. 1977*b*. Allelopathic inhibition of black cherry. II. Inhibition by woodland grass, fern, and club moss. Can. J. For. Res. 7:515–519.

Horvath, J. C. 1974. Southeastern executive summary: economic survey of wildlife recreation. Env. Research Group. Atlanta: Georgia State University. 68 pp.

Hosch, J. A. 1976. The quality of white-tailed deer meat (*Odocoileus virginianus*) as influenced by slaughtering and handling practices. M. S. Thesis. Texas A & M University, College Station. 47 pp.

Hoskinson, R. L., and L. D. Mech. 1976. White-tailed deer migration and its role in wolf predation. J. Wildl. Manage. 40(3):429–441.

Hosley, N. W. 1937. Some interrelations of wildlife management and forestry management. J. For. 35(7):674–678.

———. 1956. Management of the white-tailed deer in its environment. *In* The deer of North America, ed. W. P. Taylor, pp. 187–260. Harrisburg, Pa.: The Stackpole Co. 668 pp.

Hough, F. B. 1883. Journals of Major Robert Rogers. Albany, N. Y.: Joel Munsell's Sons. 297 pp.

Hough, W. A. 1981. Phytomass and nutrients in the understory and forest floor of slash/longleaf pine stands. For. Sci. 28:359–372.

Houghton Lake *Resorter*. 1952. Front page editorial, Dec. 4, 1952. The Heights, Mich.

Houston, T. E. 1977. The structure of sickling deer hemoglobins. Ph. D. Thesis. University of South Carolina, Columbia. 100 pp.

Howard, V. W., Jr. 1969. Behavior of white-tailed deer within three northern Idaho plant associations. Ph. D. Thesis. University of Idaho, Moscow. 71 pp.

Howard, W. E. 1967. Biocontrol and chemosterilants. *In* Pest control, ed. W. W. Kilgore and R. L. Doutt, pp. 343–386. New York: Academic Press. 477 pp.

Howe, D. L. 1970. Anaplasmosis. *In* Infectious diseases of wild animals, ed. J. W. Davis, L. H. Karstad, and D. O. Trainer, pp 363–371. Ames: Iowa State Univ. Press. 421 pp.

Howley, J. P. 1915. The Beothuks, or Red Indians: the aboriginal inhabitants of Newfoundland. Cambridge, England: Cambridge Univ. Press. 348 pp.

Hubbard, R. L., and D. Dunaway. 1958. Variation in leader growth of bitterbrush. Res. Note 145. Berkeley: USDA Forest Service, California For. and Range Exp. Stn. 4 pp.

Hudkins, G., and T. P. Kistner, 1977. *Sarcocystis hemionilatrantis* (Sp. N.) life cycle in mule deer and coyotes. J. Wildl. Dis. 13(1):80–84.

Hudson, C. M., Jr. 1981. Why southeastern Indians slaughtered deer. *In* Indians, animals and the fur trade, ed. S. Krech, pp. 155–176. Athens: Univ. Georgia Press. 207 pp.

Huemoeller, W. A., K. J. Nicol, E. O. Heady, and B. W. Spaulding. 1976. Land use: ongoing developments in the north central region. Ames: Iowa State University, Center for Agricultural and Rural Development. 294 pp.

Hughes, J. 1982. Louisiana's new intensive deer management program. Louisiana Conservationist 2:10–14.

Huisman, T. H. J., A. M. Dozy, M. H. Blunt, and F. A. Hayes. 1968. The hemoglobin heterogeneity of the Virginia white-tailed deer: a possible genetic explanation. Arch. Biochem. Biophys. 127:711–717.

Humelinck, P. W. 1940. Mammals of the genera Odocoileus and Sylvilagus. Studies Fauna Curacao 2(6):83–108.

Hummel, F. C. 1952. An experiment on the sampling of early thinning. Forestry 25(1):19–31.

Hundley, L. R. 1959. Available nutrients in related deer-browse species growing on different soils. J. Wildl. Manage. 23(1):81–90.

Hunter, G. N., and L. E. Yeager. 1956. Management of the mule deer. *In* The deer of North America, ed. W. P. Taylor, pp. 449–482. Harrisburg, Pa.: Stackpole Company. 668 pp.

Hunter Safety News. 1982. Hunter safety program profile. Hunter Safety News 10(2):2, 4–5, 7.

Huntington, D. W. 1904. Our big game. New York: Chas. Scribner's Sons. 347 pp.

Huot, J. 1972. Winter habitat preferences and management of white-tailed deer (*Odocoileus virginianus borealis*) in the area of Thirty-One Mile Lake area (Gatineau and Labelle counties, Quebec). M. S. Thesis, University of Toronto, Toronto, Ontario. 163 pp.

———. 1973. Le cerf de Virginie au Québec. [The white-tailed deer in Quebec.] Service de la Faune, Bull. 17. Québec: Ministère du Tourisme, de la Chasse et de la Pêche. 49 pp.

———. 1977. The status of white-tailed deer in Quebec. Trans. Northeast Deer Study Group Meeting 11:9–24.

———. 1982. Body condition and food resources of white-tailed deer on Anticosti Island, Québec. Ph.D. Thesis. University of Alaska, Fairbanks. 240 pp.

Huot, J., D. Banville, and H. Jolicoeur. 1978. Etude de la prédation par le loup sur le cerf de Virginie dans la région de l'Outaouais. Québec: Ministère du Tourisme, de la Chasse et de la Pêche. 77 pp.

Husson, A. M. 1960. De Zoogdieren van de Nederlandse Antillen. Fauna Ned. Ant. 2:1–70.

Hutchinson, W. H. 1972. The remaking of the Amerind: a dissenting voice raised against the resurrection of the myth of the noble savage. Westways 64(10):18.

Hymen, L. H. 1957. Comparative vertebrate anatomy. Chicago, Ill.: Univ. of Chicago Press. 544 pp.

Illige, D. 1951. An analysis of the reproductive pattern of white-tailed deer in south Texas. J. Mammal. 32(4):411–421.

Inglis, J. M., R. E. Hood, B. A. Brown, and C. A. DeYoung. 1979. Home range of white-tailed deer in Texas coastal prairie brushland. J. Mammal. 60(2):377–389.

International Association of Fish and Wildlife Agencies. 1981. Hunter education in the United States and Canada, with recommendations for improvement. Washington, D. C.: International Association of Fish and Wildlife Agencies. 125+ pp.

———. 1982. South Florida study planned. IAFWA Newsletter 8(15):7.

Irwin, L. L. 1975. Deer-moose relationships on a burn in northeastern Minnesota. J. Wildl. Manage. 39(4):653–662.

Ivey, T. L., and M. K. Causey. In press. Movements and activity patterns of female white-tailed deer during rut. Proc. Ann. Conf. Southeast. Assoc. Fish and Wildl. Agencies.

Jackson, A. S. 1961. Panhandle game management survey. Fed. Aid Proj. W-15-R-10. Austin: Texas Game and Fish Commission. 23 pp.

Jackson, H. H. T. 1961. Mammals of Wisconsin. Madison: Univ. Wisconsin Press. 504 pp.

Jackson, R. M., M. White, and F. F. Knowlton. 1972. Activity patterns of young white-tailed deer fawns in south Texas. Ecology 53(2):262–270.

Jackson, R. R., R. Norton, and R. Anderson. 1979. Improving ethical behavior in hunters. Trans. N. Amer. Wildl. and Natur. Resour. Conf. 44:306–318.

Jackson, R. R., R. Norton, and R. Anderson. 1981. The resource manager and the public: an evaluation of historical and current concepts and practices. Trans. N. Amer. Wildl. and Natur. Resour. Conf. 46:208–221.

Jacobs, W. R. 1972. Dispossessing the American Indian: Indians and whites on the colonial frontier. New York: Charles Scribner's Sons. 240 pp.

Jacobsen, N. K. 1979. Alarm bradycardia in white-tailed deer fawns (*Odocoileus virginianus*). J. Mammal. 60(2):343–349.

———. 1973. Physiology, behavior and thermal transactions of white-tailed deer. Ph. D. Thesis. Cornell University, Ithaca, N. Y. 364 pp.

Jacobsen, N. K., W. P. Armstrong, and A. N. Moen. 1976. Seasonal variation in succinylcholine immobilization of captive white-tailed deer. J. Wildl. Manage. 40(1):44–53.

James, G. A., F. M. Johnson, and F. B. Barick. 1964. Relations between hunter access and deer kill in North Carolina. Trans. N. Amer. Wildl. and Natur. Resour. Conf. 29:454–463.

Jaques, D. 1980. Ecological analysis of wildlife habitat in Red Deer County, Alberta. Calgary, Alberta: Kananaskis Centre for Environmental Research, University of Calgary. 55 pp.

Jenkins, D. H. 1970. Harvest regulations and population control for midwestern deer. *In* White-tailed deer in the Midwest, a symp., pp. 23–27. Res. Pap. NC-39. St. Paul, Minn.: USDA Forest Service, N. Cent. For. Exp. Stn. 34 pp.

Jenkins, D. H., and I. H. Bartlett. 1959. Michigan whitetails. Lansing: Michigan Department of Conservation, Game Division. 8 pp.

Jenkins, D. H., and T. T. Fendley. 1971. Radionuclide biomagnification in coastal-plain deer. Nat. Symp. Radioecol. 3:116–122.

Jenkins, J. H. 1952. The extirpation and restoration of north Georgia deer—a sixty year history. Trans. N. Amer. Wildl Conf. 17:472–476.

———. 1953. The game resources of Georgia. Atlanta: Georgia Game and Fish Commission. 114 pp.

Jenkins, J. H., and T. T. Fendley. 1968. The extent of contamination, detections, and health significance of high accumulations of radioactivity in southeastern game populations. Proc. Ann. Conf. Southeast. Game and Fish Comm. 22:89–95.

Jenkins, J. H., and E. E. Provost. 1964. The population status of the larger vertebrates on the Atomic Energy Commission's Savannah River Plant site. TID-19562. Washington, D.C.: U. S. Atomic Energy Comm., Div. Biol. and Med. 44 pp.

Jennings, F. 1978. Susquehannock. *In* Northeast, ed. B. G. Trigger, pp. 362–367. Handbook of North American Indians, Vol. 15. Washington, D. C.: Smithsonian Institution. 924 pp.

Jeter, L. K., and R. L. Marchinton. 1967. Preliminary report of telemetric study of deer movements and behavior on the Eglin Field reservation in northwestern Florida. Proc. Ann. Conf. Southeast. Assoc. Game and Fish Comm. 18:140–152.

Jewell, S. R. 1966. Pesticide residue concentrations in mule deer. Colorado Coop. Wildl. Res. Unit, Tech. Pap. 8. Presented at annual meeting Central Mountains and Plains Section of The Wildlife Society, Pingree Park, Colorado, August 15, 1966. 11 pp.

Jewett, S. G. 1914. The white-tailed deer and other deer in Oregon. The Oregon Sportsman 2(8):5–9.

Johns, P. E., R. Baccus, M. N. Manlove, J. E. Pinder, III, and M. H. Smith. 1977. Reproductive patterns, productivity and genetic variability in adjacent white-tailed deer populations. Proc. Ann. Conf. Southeast. Assoc. Fish and Wildl. Agencies 31:167–172.

Johnson, O. W. 1969. Flathead and Kootenay. Glendale, Calif.: The Arthur H. Clark Co. 392 pp.

Johnson, S. 1957. Too many deer and a five mile fence. W. Va. Conserv. 21(4):19–20.

Johnson, W., and C. L. Nayfield. 1970. Elevated levels of cesium-137 in common mushrooms (Agaricaceae) with possible relationship to high levels of cesium-137 in white-tailed deer, 1968–1969. Radiol. Health Data Rep. 11(10):527–531.

Jones, A. D. 1838. Illinois and the West. Philadelphia: W. Marshall and Co. 255 pp.

Jones, C. C. 1883. The history of Georgia. 2 vols. New York: Houghton, Mifflin and Co.

Jones, D. M. 1976. An assessment of weapons and projectile syringes used for capturing mammals. Vet. Rec. 99(13):250–253.

Jones, J. R., Jr. 1964. Distribution and taxonomy of mammals of Nebraska. Vol. 16. Lawrence: University of Kansas, Museum of Natural History. 356 pp.

Jones, R. L., R. I. Tamayo, W. Porath, N. Giessman, L. S. Selby, and G. M. Buening. 1983. A serologic evaluation and survey of white-tailed deer (*Odocoileus virginianus*) responses to *Brucella abortus*. J. Wildl. Dis. 19(4):321–323.

Jones, W. 1906. Central Algonkin. *In* Annual Archaeological Report 1905, pp. 136–146. Rep. Minister of Educ. Toronto: L. K. Cameron. 294 pp.

Jordan, J. S. 1967. Deer browsing in northern hardwoods after clearcutting. Effect of height, density and stocking of regeneration of commercial species. Res. Pap. NE-57. Upper Darby, Pa.: USDA Forest Service, Northeast. For. Exp. Stn. 15 pp.

Julander, O., and W. L. Robinette. 1950. Deer and cattle range relationships in Oak Creek in Utah. J. For. 48(6):410–415.

Julander, O., W. L. Robinette, and D. A. Jones. 1961. Relation of summer range condition to mule deer herd productivity. J. Wildl. Manage. 25(1):54–60.

Jungius, H. 1974. Beobachtungen am weifswedelhirsch und anderen Cerviden in Bolivien. Zeit. fur Saugetierkunde 39:373–383.

Kammermeyer, K. E. 1975. Movement-ecology of white-tailed deer in relation to a refuge and hunted area. M. S. Thesis. University of Georgia, Athens. 114 pp.

Kammermeyer, K. E., and R. L. Marchinton. 1976*a*. The dynamic aspects of deer populations utilizing a refuge. Proc. Ann. Conf. Southeast. Assoc. Game and Fish Comm. 29:466–475.

Kammermeyer, K. E., and R. L. Marchinton. 1976*b*. Notes on dispersal of male white-tailed deer. J. Mammal. 57(4):776–778.

Kammermeyer, K. E., and R. L. Marchinton. 1977. Seasonal change in circadian activity of radio-monitored deer. J. Wildl. Manage. 41(2):315–317.

Kamps, G. F. 1969. Whitetail and mule deer relationships in the Snowy Mountains of central Montana. M. S. Thesis. Montana State University, Bozeman. 59 pp.

Karstad, L. 1962. Viral and rickettsial diseases of deer: a review. Proc. National White-tailed Deer Disease Symposium 1:138–144.

———. 1964. Diseases of the Cervidae: a partly annotated bibliography. Wildl. Dis. 43. 233 pp.

———. 1969. Diseases of the Cervidae: bibliography supplement I. Wildl. Dis. 52. 114 pp.

———. 1970. Arboviruses. *In* Infectious diseases of wild mammals, ed. J. W. Davis, L. H. Karstad, and D. O. Trainer, pp. 60–67. Ames: Iowa State Univ. Press. 421 pp.

Katsma, D. E. 1976. Effects of simulated deer browsing on branches of apple trees. Unpublished paper presented at 38th Midwest Fish and Wildl. Conf., Dearborn, Michigan. December 7, 1976.

Katsma, D. E., and D. H. Rusch. 1980. Effects of simulated deer browsing on branches of apple trees. J. Wildl. Manage. 44(3):603–612.

Keating, W. H. 1824. Narrative of an expedition to the source of St. Peter's River . . . 1823. Vol. 1. Philadelphia: Carey and Lea. 439 pp.

Keay, J. A., and J. M. Peek. 1980. Relationship between fires and winter habitat of deer in Idaho. J. Wildl. Manage. 44(2):372–380.

Keener, J. M. 1970. History of the wolf in Wisconsin. *In* Proc. symp. on wolf management in selected areas of North America, eds. S. E. Jorgensen, C. E. Faulkner, and L. D. Mech, pp. 4–5. Twin Cities, Minn.: U. S. Fish and Wildlife Service. 50 pp.

Keith, L. B. 1983. Population dynamics of wolves. *In* Wolves in Canada and Alaska: their status, biology and management, ed. L. N Carbyn. Proc. Canadian/Alaskan Wolf Symp. Canadian Wildlife Service Rep. 45.

Kellert, S. R. 1978. Attitudes and characteristics of hunters and antihunters. Trans. N. Amer. Wildl. and Natur. Resour. Conf. 43:412–423.

———. 1980*a*. Public attitudes towards critical wildlife and natural habitat issues. Phase I. Doc. No. 024-010-00-623-4. Washington, D. C.: Government Printing Office. 138 pp.

———. 1980*b*. Activities of the American public relating to animals. Phase II. Doc. No. 024-010-00-624-2. Washington, D.C.: Government Printing Office. 178 pp.

Kellogg, F. E., A. K. Prestwood, and R. E. Noble. 1970. Anthrax epizootic in white-tailed deer. J. Wildl. Dis. 6(4):226–228.

Kellogg, R. 1937. Annotated list of West Virginia mammals. U. S. Nat. Mus. Proc. 84(3022):443–479.

———. 1956. What and where are the whitetails? *In* The deer of North America, ed. W. P. Taylor, pp. 31–35. Harrisburg, Pa.: The Stackpole Co. 688 pp.

Kelly, R. G. 1981. Forest, farms, and wildlife in Vermont: a study of landowner values. *In* Wildlife management on private lands, ed. R. T. Dumke, G. V. Burger, and J. R. March, pp. 102–111. Madison: Wisconsin Chapter, The Wildlife Society. 569 pp.

Kelsall, J. P. 1969. Structural adaptation of moose and deer for snow. J. Mammal. 50(2):302–310.

Kelsey, V., and L. d. J. Osborne. 1939. Four keys to Guatemala. New York: Funk & Wagnalls Company. 332 pp.

Kennedy, J. J. 1974. Attitudes and behaviors of deer hunters in a Maryland forest. J. Wildl. Manage. 38(1):1–8.

Kennedy, M. S., ed. 1961. The Assiniboines. Norman: Univ. Oklahoma Press. 209 pp.

Kennedy, P. C., J. H. Whitlock, and S. J. Roberts. 1952. Neurofilariosis, a paralytic disease of sheep. I. Introduction, symptomatology and pathology. Cornell Vet. 42(1):118–124.

Kick, T. J. 1982. Home tanning technique. *In* Missouri deer hunting, ed. N. Giessman and D. A. Murphy, pp. 13–14. Jefferson City: Missouri Conservation Commission. 20 pp.

Kile, T. L., and R. L. Marchinton. 1977. White-tailed deer rubs and scrapes: spatial, temporal and physical characteristics and social role. Amer. Midl. Natur. 97(2):257–266.

Kimball, D., and J. W. Kimball. 1969. The market hunter. Minneapolis: Dillon Press, Inc. 132 pp.

Kimber, E. 1744. A relation or journal of a late expedition to the gates of St. Augustine, on Florida; conducted by the Hon. General James Oglethorpe with a detachment of his regiment, etc., from Georgia. In a letter to Mr. Isaac Kimber in London. By a gentleman volunteer in the said expedition. London: T. Astley. 36 pp.

Kimura, M., and T. Ohta. 1971. Theoretical aspects of population genetics. Monographs in population biology, v. 4. Princeton: Princeton Univ. Press. 219 pp.

Kincer, J. S. 1941. Climate and weather data for the United States. *In* Climate and man, pp. 685–1169. USDA Yearbook. Washington, D. C.: Government Printing Office. 1,248 pp.

Kingston, N. 1981. Protozoan parasites. *In* Diseases and parasites of white-tailed deer, ed. W. R. Davidson, F. A. Hayes, V. F. Nettles, and F. E. Kellogg, pp. 193–214. Tallahassee, Fla.: Tall Timbers Research Station. 458 pp.

Kirby, S. B., K. M. Babcock, S. C. Sheriff, and D. J. Witter. 1981. Private land and wildlife in Missouri: a study of farm operator values. *In* Wildlife management on private lands, ed. R. T. Dumke, G. V. Burger, and J. R March, pp. 88–97. Madison: Wisconsin Chapter, The Wildlife Society. 569 pp.

Kirkpatrick, R. L., D. E. Burkland, W. A. Abler, P. F. Scanlon, J. B. Whelan, and H. E. Burkart. 1975. Energy and protein influences on blood urea nitrogen of white-tailed deer fawns. J. Wildl. Manage. 39(4):692–698.

Kirkpatrick, R. L., J. P. Fontenot, and R. F. Harlow. 1969. Seasonal changes in rumen chemical components as related to forages consumed by white-tailed deer of the southeast. Trans. N. Amer. Wildl. and Natur. Resour. Conf. 34:229–238.

Kistner, T. P. 1982. Diseases and parasites. *In* Elk of North America: ecology and management, ed. J. W. Thomas and D. E. Toweill, pp. 181–218. Harrisburg, Pa.: Stackpole Books, Inc. 736 pp.

Kitchen, H. 1969. Heterogeneity of animal hemoglobins. *In* Advances in veterinary science and comparative medicine, ed. C. A. Brandly and C. E. Cornelius, pp. 247–308. New York: Academic Press. 418 pp.

Kitchen, H., F. W. Putnam, and W. J. Taylor. 1964. Hemoglobin polymorphism: its relation to sickling of erythrocytes in white-tailed deer. Science 144(3623):1237–1239.

Kitchen, H., F. W. Putnam, and W. J. Taylor. 1966. The structural basis for the polymorphic hemoglobins of white-tailed deer (*Odocoileus virginianus*). A comparison of the hemoglobins associated with sickled and non-sickled erythrocytes. *In* International Symposium on Comparative Hemoglobin Structure, ed. D. J. Polychronakos, pp. 73–82. Thessaloniki, Greece. 166 pp.

Kitchen, H., F. W. Putnam, and W. J. Taylor. 1967. Hemoglobin polymorphism in white-tailed deer: subunit basis. Blood 29:867–877.

Kitts, W. D., I. M. Cowan, J. Bandy, and A. J. Wood. 1956. The immediate post-natal growth in Columbian black-tailed deer in relation to the composition of the milk of the doe. J. Wildl. Manage. 20(2):212–214.

Klawitter, R. A., and J. Stubbs. 1961. A reliable oak seed trap. J. For. 59(4):291–292.

Klein, D. R. 1968. The introduction, increase, and crash of reindeer on St. Matthew Island. J. Wildl. Manage. 32(2):350–367.

Klimstra, W. D., J. W. Hardin, M. D. Carpenter, and S. Jenkusky. 1980. Florida Key deer recovery plan.

Washington, D. C.: U. S. Fish and Wildlife Service. 52 pp.

Klimstra, W. D., J. W. Hardin, N. J. Silvy, B. N. Jacobson, and V. A. Terpening. 1974. Key deer investigations final report. Period of study: December 1967–June 1973. Carbondale: Southern Illinois University. 184 pp.

Klimstra, W. D., and K. Thomas. 1964. Effects of deer browsing on soybean plants, Crab Orchard National Wildlife Refuge. Trans. Illinois State Acad. Sci. 57(3):179–181.

Kline, P. D. 1965. Status and management of the white-tailed deer in Iowa, 1954–1962. Iowa Acad. Sci. Proc. 72:207–217.

Klussman, W., C. Ramsey, and F. Reasonover. n. d. Wild game care and cooking. B-987. College Station: Texas Agric. Ext. Serv. 15 pp.

Kneese, A. V., and C. L. Schultze. 1975. Pollution, prices and public policy. Washington, D. C.: The Brookings Institution. 125 pp.

Knowles, C. J. 1976. Observations of coyote predation on mule deer and white-tailed deer in the Missouri River breaks, 1975–1976. *In* Montana deer studies, pp. 117–138. Prog. Rep., PR Proj. W-120-R-7. Helena: Montana Fish and Game Department. 170 pp.

Knowlton, F. F. 1964. Aspects of coyote predation in south Texas with special reference to white-tailed deer. Ph. D. Thesis. Purdue University, Lafayette, Ind. 147 pp.

———. 1976. Potential influence of coyotes on mule deer populations. *In* Mule deer decline in the west—a symposium, ed. G. W. Workman and J. B. Low, pp. 111–118. Logan: Utah State University. 134 pp.

Kohn, B. E. 1975. Winter severity measurements. Final Rep. P-R Proj. W-141-R-10. Madison: Wisconsin Department of Natural Resources. 11 pp.

Koivisto, I. 1966. Yhteenveto valkohäntäpeuralaskennasta vuonna 1966. [Census of white-tailed deer (*Odocoileus virginianus*) in Finland in 1966.] Suomen Riista 19:100–104.

Koivisto, I., P. Andersson, and A. Jukkara. 1966. Valkohäntäpeurojen joukkokuolema talvessa 1965–1966 [Summary: Mass death of white-tailed deer (*Odocoileus virginianus*) in the winter of 1965–1966 in Finland.] Suomen Riista 19:20–29.

Kolenosky, G. B. 1972. Wolf predation on wintering deer in east-central Ontario. J. Wildl. Manage. 36(2):357–369.

Koller, L. D., T. P. Kistner, and G. G. Hudkins. 1977. Histopathologic study of experimental *Sarcocystis hemionilatrantis* infection in fawns. Amer. J. Vet. Res. 38(8):1205–1209.

Koopman, K. F. 1967. Artiodactyls. *In* Recent mammals of the world; a synopsis of families, ed. S. Anderson and J. K. Jones, Jr., pp. 385–406. New York: The Ronald Press Co. 453 pp.

Kopischke, E. D. 1972. Effects of snowmobile activity on the distribution of white-tailed deer in south-central Minnesota, 1971–72. Minnesota Dep. Natur. Resour. Game Res. Proj. Q. Prog. Rep. 32(3):139–146.

Korschgen, L. J. 1957a. Food habits of coyotes, foxes, house cats and bobcats in Missouri. P-R Publ. 15. Jefferson City: Missouri Conservation Commission. 64 pp.

———. 1957b. Food habits of the coyote in Missouri. J. Wildl. Manage. 21(4):424–435.

———. 1962. Foods of Missouri deer, with some management implications. J. Wildl. Manage. 26(2):164–172.

Korschgen, L. J., and D. A. Murphy. 1967. Pesticide-wildlife relationships: reproduction, growth, and physiology of deer fed dieldrin contaminated diets. Missouri Fed. Aid Proj. 13-R-21 (1967). Work Plan 8, Job 1. Prog. Rep. Jefferson City: Missouri Conservation Commission. 24 pp.

Korschgen, L. J., W. R. Porath, and O. Torgerson. 1980. Spring and summer foods of deer in the Missouri Ozarks. J. Wildl. Manage. 44(1):89–97.

Krämer, A. 1972. A review of the ecological relationships between mule and white-tailed deer. Occas. Pap. 3. Edmonton: Alberta Fish and Wildl. Div. 54 pp.

———. 1973. Interspecific behavior and dispersion of two sympatric deer species. J. Wildl. Manage. 37(3):288–300.

Krausman, P. R. 1976. Ecology of the Carmen Mountains white-tailed deer. Ph. D. Thesis. University of Idaho, Moscow. 220 pp.

Krech, S., III. 1981a. "Throwing bad medicine": sorcery, disease and the fur trade among the Kutchin and other northern Athapaskans. *In* Indians, animals and the fur trade, ed. S. Krech, pp. 75–108. Athens: Univ. Georgia Press. 207 pp.

———. 1981b. Indians, animals and the fur trade. Athens: Univ. Georgia Press. 207 pp.

Krefting, L. W., and J. B. Fletcher. 1941. Notes on the cruising method of censusing white-tailed deer in Oklahoma. J. Wildl. Manage. 5(4):412–415.

Krefting, L. W., A. B. Erickson, and V. E. Gunvalson. 1955. Results of controlled deer hunts on the Tamarac National Wildlife Refuge. J. Wildl. Manage. 19(3):346–352.

Krefting, L. W., and H. L. Hansen. 1969. Increasing browse for deer by aerial applications of 2,4-D. J. Wildl. Manage. 33(4):784–790.

Krefting, L. W., and R. S. Phillips. 1970. Improving deer habitat in upper Michigan by cutting mixed-conifer swamps. J. For. 68(11):701–704.

Krefting, L. W., M. H. Stenlund, and R. K. Seemel. 1966. Effect of simulated and natural deer browsing on mountain maple. J. Wildl. Manage. 30(3):481–488.

Krull, J. N. 1964. Deer use of a commercial clear-cut area. N.Y. Fish and Game J. 11(2):115–118.

Kubisiak, J. F. 1982. Deer population and range changes following herd removal at the Sandhill Wildlife Area. Perf. Rep. P-R Proj. W-141-R-17. Madison: Wisconsin Department of Natural Resources.

Kubota, J., and G. A. Swanson. 1958. Wildlife and soils in New York. N. Y. State Conserv. 13(1):16–18.

Küchler, A. W. 1964. The potential natural vegetation of the conterminous United States. Special Res. Publ. No. 36. New York: American Geographical Society. 116 pp.

———. 1966. Potential natural vegetation. *In* The national atlas of the United States of America, p. 90. 1970. Washington, D. C.: USDI Geological Survey. 417 pp.

Kulp, J. L. 1961. The geologic time scale. Science 133(3459): 1105–1114.

Kurten, B., and E. Anderson. 1980. Pleistocene mammals of North America. New York: Columbia Univ. Press. 442 pp.

Kuttler, K. L. 1981. Anaplasmosis. *In* Diseases and parasites of white-tailed deer, ed. W. R. Davidson, F. A. Hayes, V. F. Nettles, and F. E. Kellogg, pp. 126–137. Tallahassee Fla.: Tall Timbers Research Station. 458 pp.

Kuttler, K. L., O. H. Graham, S. R. Johnson, and J. L. Trevino. 1972. Unsuccessful attempts to establish cattle

Babesia infections in white-tailed deer. J. Wildl. Dis. 8(1):63–66.

Kuttler, K. L., R. M. Robinson, and R. R. Bell. 1967. Tick transmission of Theileriasis in a white-tailed deer. Bull. Wildl. Dis. Assoc. 3(4):182–183.

Kuyt, E. 1966. White-tailed deer near Fort Smith, N.W.T. Blue Jay 24(4):1974.

Lack, D. 1954. The natural regulation of animal numbers. Oxford, England: Clarendon Press. 343 pp.

Lahontan, Louis Armand de Lom d'Arce, baron de. 1703. New voyages to North America. 2 vols. London: Printed for H. Bonwicke, T. Goodwin, M. Wotton, B. Tooke, and S. Manship.

Lambiase, J. T., Jr., R. P. Amann, and J. S. Lindzey. 1972. Aspects of reproductive physiology of male white-tailed deer. J. Wildl. Manage. 36(3):868–875.

Lampton, B. 1982. Controversy in the 'Glades. Fla. Wildl. 36(4):12–18.

Landes, R. K., and R. Hamilton. 1965. Selected maintenance of edge forest areas of national forest lands in Indiana and Ohio. Unpublished paper presented at 27th Midwest Fish and Wildl. Conf., Lansing, Michigan. Mimeo.

Lang, L. M. 1968. Statement of policy. Transactions Northeast Deer Study Group 4:3–4.

———. 1971. Antlerless deer license allocations. Pa. Game News 37(10):9–13.

Lang, L. M., and G. W. Wood. 1976. Manipulation of the Pennsylvania deer herd. Wildl. Soc. Bull. 4(4):159–166.

Langenau, E. E., Jr. 1979a. Nonconsumptive uses of the Michigan deer herd. J. Wildl. Manage. 43(3):620–625.

———. 1979b. Human dimensions in the management of white-tailed deer: a review of concepts and literature. Wildl. Div. Rep. No. 2846. Lansing: Michigan Department of Natural Resources. 68 pp.

———. 1981. Bureaucracy and wildlife: a historical overview. Int. J. Stud. Anim. Prob. 32:140–157.

Langenau, E. E., Jr., and G. C. Jamsen. 1975. A preliminary report on the attitudes of firearm deer hunters towards experimental clearcutting. Wildlife Div. Rep. 2744. Lansing: Michigan Department of Natural Resources. 29 pp.

Langenau, E. E., Jr., G. C. Jamsen, R. L. Levine, and P. M. Lange. 1975. Attitudes of forest recreationists, other than firearm deer hunters, using experimental clearcuttings: a preliminary report. Wildl. Div. Rep. 2748. Lansing: Michigan Department of Natural Resources. 22 pp.

Langenau, E. E., Jr., and J. M. Lerg. 1976. The effects of winter nutritional stress on maternal and neonatal behavior in penned white-tailed deer. Appl. Anim. Ethology 2:207–223.

Langenau, E. E., Jr., and P. M. Mellon. 1980. Characteristics and behaviors of Michigan 12- to 18-year-old hunters. J. Wildl. Manage. 44(1):69–78.

Langenau, E. E., Jr., R. J. Moran, and J. R. Terry. 1981. Relationship between deer kill and ratings of the hunt. J. Wildl. Manage. 45(4):959–964.

Langenau, E. E., Jr., and R. B. Peyton. 1982. Policy implications of human dimensions research for wildlife information and education programs. Trans. Northeast Fish and Wildlife Conf. 39:119–135.

Langin, H. D., and R. A. Demarchi. 1977. Deer management in the Kootenays. Unpublished report on file at the British Columbia Fish and Wildlife Branch, Cranbrook. 115+ pp.

Laramie, H. A. 1968. Deer management and recommendations in New Hampshire. In The white-tailed deer of New Hampshire, ed. H. R. Siegler, pp. 204–216. Survey Rep. 10. Concord: New Hampshire Fish and Game Department. 256 pp.

Laroque, F. 1910. Journal of Laroque from the Assiniboine to the Yellowstone, 1805. Publ. No. 3. Ottawa: Canada Archives. 82 pp.

Larson, J. S. 1967. Forests, wildlife and habitat management—a critical examination of practice and need. Res. pap. SE-30. Asheville, N. C.: USDA Forest Service, Southeast. For. Exp. Stn. 28 pp.

———. 1969. Agricultural clearings as sources of supplemental food and habitat diversity for white-tailed deer. In White-tailed deer in the Southern forest habitat, pp. 46–50. Proc. Symp. Nacogdoches, Tex. New Orleans: USDA Forest Service, South. For. Exp. Stn. 130 pp.

Larson, T. J., O. J. Rongstad, and F. W. Terbilcox. 1978. Movement and habitat use of white-tailed deer in southcentral Wisconsin. J. Wildl. Manage. 42(1):113–117.

Lasher, D. N., and E. P. Hill. 1977. An evaluation of polypropylene mesh tubing as a deer browse deterrent for southern hardwood seedlings. Proc. Ann. Conf. Southeast. Assoc. Game Fish Comm. 31:239–245.

Latham, R. M. 1943. Our deer—past, present and future. Pa. Game News 14(9):4–5, 26–27.

———. 1950. Pennsylvania's deer problem. Pa. Game News Spec. Issue 1. (Sept.). Harrisburg: Pennsylvania Game Division. 48 pp.

Laudonnière, R. G. 1586. L'histoire notable de la Floride située ès Indes Occidentales, contenant les trois voyages faits en icelle par certains Cápitaines et Pilotes français, descrits par le Cápitaine Laudonniere qui y a commande l'espace d'un an trois moys: a laquelle a esté adiousté un quatriesme voyage fait par le Cápitaine Gourgues. Mise en lumière par M. Basanier. Paris: G. Annray. 123 pp.

Lavigne, G. R. 1976. Winter response of deer to snowmobiles and selected natural factors. M. S. Thesis. University of Maine, Orono. 67 pp.

Lawson, J. 1860. History of Carolina, containing the exact description and natural history of that country. Raleigh, N. C.: Strother and Marcom. 390 pp.

———. 1967. A new voyage to Carolina [1709]. Ed. H. T. Lefler. Chapel Hill: Univ. North Carolina Press. 305 pp.

Lay, D. W. 1957a. Browse quality and the effects of prescribed burning in southern pine forests. J. For. 55(5):342–347.

———. 1957b. Some nutrition problems of deer in the southern pine type. Proc. Ann. Conf. Southeast. Assoc. Game and Fish Comm. 10:53–58.

———. 1957c. Extensive deer range survey. Job Compl. Rep. P-R Proj. W-63-R-4 Job 6. Austin: Texas Game, Fish and Oyster Commission. 17 pp.

———. 1965a. Effects of periodic clipping on yield of some common browse species. J. Range Manage. 18(4):181–184.

———. 1965b. Fruit utilization by deer in southern forests. J. Wildl. Manage. 29(2):370–375.

———. 1966. Forest clearings for browse and fruit plantings. J. For. 64(10):680–683.

———. 1969. Foods and feeding habits of white-tailed deer. In White-tailed deer in the southern forest habitat, pp. 8–13. Proc. Symp. Nacogdoches, Tex. New Orleans: USDA Forest Service, South. For. Exp. Stn. 130 pp.

Lechleitner, R. R. 1969. Wild mammals of Colorado: their appearance, habits, distribution, and abundance. Boulder, Colo.: Pruett Publ. Co. 254 pp.

Lee, J. 1954. The deer fly. N. Y. State Conserv. 8(3):32.

Leitch, J. A., and D. F. Scott. 1977. A selected annotated bibliography of economic values of fish and wildlife and their habitats. Rep. No. 27. Fargo: North Dakota Agric. Exp. Stn. 132 pp.

Le Moyne de Morgues, J. 1875. Narrative of Le Moyne, an artist who accompanied the French expedition to Florida under Laudonnière, 1564. Trans. Fred B. Perkins. Boston: James R. Osgood and Co. 15+ pp.

Lendt, D. L. 1979. Ding: the life of Jay Norwood Darling. Ames: Iowa State Univ. Press. 202 pp.

Leopold, A. 1918. The popular wilderness fallacy. Outer's Book-Recreation 58:1, 46.

———. 1933. Game management. New York: Charles Scribner's Sons. 481 pp.

———. 1943. Wisconsin's deer problem. Wis. Conserv. Bull. 8(8):1–11.

———. 1949. A Sand County almanac. New York: Oxford Univ. Press. 226 pp.

Leopold, A., L. K. Sowls, and D. L. Spencer. 1947. A survey of overpopulated deer ranges in the United States. J. Wildl. Manage. 11(2):162–177.

Leopold, A. S. 1959. Wildlife of Mexico: the game birds and mammals. Berkeley: Univ. California Press. 568 pp.

Leopold, A. S., S. A. Cain, C. M. Cottam, I. N. Gabrielson, and T. L. Kimball. 1963. Study of wildlife problems in national parks. Trans. N. Amer. Wildl. and Natur. Resour. Conf. 28:29–45.

Leopold, A. S., S. A. Cain, C. M. Cottam, I. N. Gabrielson, and T. L. Kimball. 1964. Predator and rodent control in the United States. Trans. N. Amer. Wildl. and Natur. Resour. Conf. 29:27–49.

Le Page du Pratz, A. S. 1758. Histoire de la Louisiane. 3 vols. Paris: De Bure.

———. 1975. The history of Louisiana. Ed. J. G. Tregle, Jr. Transl. from French; facsimile of 1774 edition. Baton Rouge: Louisiana State Univ. Press. 405 pp.

Leresche, R. E., U. S. Seal, P. D. Karns, and A. W. Franzmann. 1974. A review of blood chemistry of moose and other cervidae with emphasis on nutritional assessment. Nat. Can. (Que.) 101(1/2):263–290.

Lescarbot, M. 1907. Histoire de la Nouvelle France (1609). Vol. I. Translated by W. L. Grant. 3 vols. Toronto: The Champlain Society.

Lett, W. P. 1884. The deer of the Ottawa Valley. Ottawa Field Natur. Club Trans. 5, 2(1):101–117.

Levy, G. F. 1970. The phytosociology of northern Wisconsin upland openings. Amer. Midl. Natur. 83(1):213–237.

Levy-Bruhl, L. 1966. How natives think. L. A. Clare, trans. New York: Washington Square Press. 392 pp.

Lewis, D. M. 1968. Telemetry studies of white-tailed deer on Red Dirt Game Management Area, Louisiana. M. S. Thesis. Louisiana State University and A & M College, Baton Rouge. 65 pp.

Lewis, H. T. 1977. Maskuta: the ecology of Indian fires in northern Alberta. West. Can. J. Anthropol. 7(1):15–48.

Lewis, J. B. 1967. Management of the eastern turkey in the Ozarks and bottomland hardwoods. *In* The wild turkey and its management, ed. O. H. Hewitt, pp. 371–407. Washington, D. C.: The Wildlife Society. 589 pp.

Lewis, J. C., and L. E. Safley. 1967a. A comparison of some deer census methods in Tennessee. Proc. Ann. Conf. Southeast. Assoc. Game and Fish Comm. 20:56–63.

Lewis, J. C., and L. E. Safley. 1967b. The central peninsula deer herd, 1950–1966: some population characteristics. Nashville: Tennessee Game and Fish Comm. 19 pp.

Lightfoot, W. C., and V. Maw. 1963. Trapping and marking mule deer. Proc. West. Assoc. Fish and Game Comm. 43:138–142.

Ligon, J. S. 1927. Wildlife of New Mexico: its conservation and management. Albuquerque: New Mexico Department of Game and Fish. 212 pp.

Linares, O. F. 1976. "Garden hunting" in the American tropics. Human Ecol. 4(4):331–349.

Linares, O. F., and R. S. White. 1980. Terrestrial fauna from Cerro Brujo (CA-3) in Bocas del Toro and La Pitahaya (IS-3) in Chiriqui. Peabody Mus. Monogr. No. 5:181–193.

Lindblom, C. E. 1980. The policy-making process. Englewood Cliffs, N. J.: Prentice-Hall, Inc. 131 pp.

Lindner, A., M. Brandt, and E. Wyler. 1956. New methods to prevent game damage. Allg. Forsztzg. 67:233–237.

Lindzey, J. S. 1950. The white-tailed deer in Oklahoma. P-R Rep. 37R. Oklahoma City: Oklahoma Game and Fish Department. 105 pp.

Linsdale, J. M., and P. Q. Tomich. 1953. A herd of mule deer. Berkeley: Univ. California Press. 567 pp.

Liscinsky, S. A., G. P. Howard, and R. B. Waldeisen. 1969. A new device for injecting powdered drugs. J. Wildl. Manage. 33(4):1037–1038.

Little, S., and J. J. Mohr. 1961. Tests of deer and rabbit repellents on planted loblolly pines in eastern Maryland. Tree Plant. Notes 48:17–19.

Little, S., and I. F. Trew. 1976. Breeding and testing pitch × loblolly pine hybrids for the northeast. Proc. Northeast. For. Tree Improvement Conf. 23:71–85.

Lochmiller, R. L., and W. E. Grant. 1983. A sodium bicarbonate-acid powered blow-gun syringe for remote injection of wildlife. J. Wildl. Dis. 19:48–51.

Logan, T. 1973. Study of white-tailed deer fawn mortality on Cookson Hills Deer Refuge, eastern Oklahoma. Proc. Ann. Conf. Southeast. Assoc. Game and Fish Comm. 26:27–39.

Long, J. 1922. Voyages and travels in the years 1768–1788. Chicago: R. R. Donnelley and Sons Co. 238 pp.

Long, T. A., R. L. Cowan, G. D. Strawn, R. S. Wetzel, and R. C. Miller. 1965. Seasonal fluctuations in feed consumption of the white-tailed deer. Prog. Rep. 262. University Park: Pennsylvania State Univ. Agric Exp. Stn. 5 pp.

Long, T. A., R. W. Cowan, C. W. Wolfe, T. Rader, and R. W. Swift. 1959. Effect of seasonal feed restriction on antler development of white-tailed deer. Prog. Rep. 209. University Park: Pennsylvania State Univ. Agric. Exp. Stn. 11 pp.

Long, T. A., R. L. Cowan, C. W. Wolfe, and R. W. Swift. 1961. Feeding the white-tailed deer fawn. J. Wildl. Manage. 25(1):94–95.

Longhurst, W. M., H. K. Oh, M. B. Jones, and R. E. Kepner. 1968. A basis for the palatability of deer forage plants. Trans. N. Amer. Wildl. and Natur. Resour. Conf. 33:181–192.

Longhurst, W. M., M. B. Jones, R. R. Parks, L. W. Newbauer, and M. W. Cummings. 1962. Fences for controlling deer damage. Circ. 514. Berkeley: Univ. California Agric. Exp. Stn. 15 pp.

Longley, R. W. 1954. Temperature trends in Canada. *In* Proc. Toronto Meteorological Conf., pp. 206–211. London: Royal Met. Soc. 294 pp.

Lorant, S., ed. 1965. The new world: the first pictures of America. Rev. ed. New York: Duell, Sloan and Pearce. 292 pp.

Lord, W. 1958. The historical development of an instrument for live capture of animals. Southeast. Vet. 9(4):147–148, 155.

Loveless, C. M. 1959*a*. A study of the vegetation of the Florida Everglades. Ecology 40:1–9.

———. 1959*b*. The Everglades deer herd: life history and management. Tech. Bull. 6. Tallahassee: Florida Game and Fresh Water Fish Commission. 104 pp.

Loveless, C. M., and R. F. Harlow. 1959. Canine teeth in Florida white-tailed deer (*Odocoileus virginianus seminolus* Goldman and Kellogg). Q. J. Florida Acad. Sci. 22:76–77.

Loveless, C. M., and F. J. Ligas. 1959. Range conditions, life history, and food habits of the Everglades deer herd. Trans. N. Amer. Wildl. Conf. 24:201–215.

Lovett, J. W., and E. P. Hill. 1977. A transmitter syringe for recovery of immobilized deer. J. Wildl. Manage. 41(2):313–315.

Lowery, G. H., Jr. 1974. The mammals of Louisiana and its adjacent waters. Baton Rouge: Louisiana State Univ. Press. 565 pp.

Lowie, R. H. 1956. The Crow Indians. New York: Holt, Rinehart and Winston. 350 pp.

Lowry, D. A., and K. L. McArthur. 1978. Domestic dogs as predators on deer. Wildl. Soc. Bull. 6(1):38–39.

Lull, H. W. 1968. A forest atlas of the Northeast. Upper Darby, Pa.: U. S. For. Serv. Northeast. For. Exp. Stn. 44 pp.

Lull, R. S. 1924. Organic evolution. New York: The Macmillan Co. 729 pp.

Lund, T. A. 1980. American wildlife law. Berkeley: Univ. California Press. 179 pp.

Lussier, J. L. 1970. La prospérité rurale par une meilleure utilisation de la forêt. Forêt Conservation 36(2):10–13.

Lydekker, R. 1898. The deer of all lands; a history of the family *Cervidae* living and extinct. London: Rowland Ward, Ltd. 353 pp.

———. 1915. Catalogue of the ungulate mammals in the British Museum (Natural History). Vol. 4 Artiodactyla. London: British Museum. 438 pp.

Lyons, J. R. 1980. A conceptual framework for the identification of recreational users of wildlife resources: who is the clientele of wildlife management? Paper presented at the Nat. Symp. on Leisure Research, Phoenix, Arizona. 25 pp.

Lyons, J. R., and W. W. Shaw. 1982. The 1980 national survey of fishing, hunting and wildlife associated recreation: a plan for data analysis. Div. Program Plans. Washington, D. C.: U. S. Fish and Wildlife Service. 77 pp.

Maas, J., G. M. Buening, and W. Porath. 1981. Serologic evidence of *Anaplasma marginale* infection in white-tailed deer (*Odocoileus virginianus*) in Missouri. J. Wildl. Dis. 17(1):45–47.

MacLeod, W. C. 1936. Conservation among primitive hunting peoples. Sci. Monthly 43:562–566.

MacNeish, R. S. 1964. The food-gathering and incipient agriculture stage of prehistoric Middle America. *In* Handbook of Middle American Indians, Vol. 1, ed. R. C. West, pp. 413–426. Austin: Univ. Texas Press. 570 pp.

MacNeish, R. S., A. Nelken-Terner, and I. W. Johnson. 1967. Bone, antler, shell, and copper artifacts. *In* The prehistory of the Tehuacan Valley, Vol. 2, pp. 141–149. Austin: Univ. Texas Press. 258 pp.

Madson, J. 1953. Iowa's early deer story. Iowa Conservationist 12(1):101.

———. 1961. The white-tailed deer. East Alton, Ill.: Olin Mathieson Chemical Corp. 108 pp.

Magee, A. C. 1957. Goats pay for clearing Grand Prairie rangelands. MP-206. College Station: Texas Agric. Exp. Stn. 8 pp.

Maguire, H. F., and C. W. Severinghaus. 1954. Wariness as an influence on age composition of white-tailed deer killed by hunters. N. Y. Fish and Game J. 1(1):98–109.

Maine Department of Conservation. 1977. Land use districts and standards for plantations and unorganized townships of the state of Maine. *In* Commission rules and regulations, pp. 52–56. Augusta: Maine Department of Conservation. 99 pp.

Manlove, M. N., J. C. Avise, H. O. Hillestad, P. R. Ramsey, M. H. Smith, and D. O. Straney. 1976. Starch-gel electrophoresis for the study of population genetics in white-tailed deer. Proc. Ann. Conf. Southeast. Assoc. Game and Fish Comm. 29:392–403.

Manlove, M. N., R. Baccus, M. R. Pelton, M. H. Smith, and D. Graber. 1980. Biochemical variation in the black bear. *In* Bears—their biology and management, ed. C. J. Martinka and K. L. McArthur, pp. 37–41. Washington, D. C.: Government Printing Office. 375 pp.

Manlove, M. N., M. H. Smith, H. O. Hillestad, S. E. Fuller, P. E. Johns, and D. O. Straney. 1978. Genetic subdivision in a herd of white-tailed deer as demonstrated by spatial shifts in gene frequencies. Proc. Ann. Conf. Southeast. Assoc. Fish and Wildl. Agencies 30:487–492.

Mansell, W. D. 1974. Productivity of white-tailed deer on the Bruce Peninsula, Ontario. J. Wildl. Manage. 38(4):808–814.

Mapes, C. R., and D. W. Baker. 1950. The white-tailed deer, a new host of *Dicrocoelium dendriticum* (Rudolphi, 1819) Looss, 1899 (Trematoda: Dicrocoeliidae). Cornell Vet. 40:211–212.

Marburger, R. G., and R. M. Robinson. 1973. Diagnosis of wildlife diseases. P-R Job Prog. Rep., Proj. W-93-R-8, Job 10. Austin: Texas Parks and Wildlife Department. 6 pp.

Marburger, R. G., R. M. Robinson, J. W. Thomas, and K. A. Clark. 1971. Management implications of disease of big game animals in Texas. Proc. Ann. Conf. Southeast. Assoc. Game and Fish Comm. 24:46–50.

Marburger, R. G., and J. W. Thomas. 1965. A die-off in white-tailed deer of the Central Mineral Region of Texas. J. Wildl. Manage. 29(4):706–716.

Marchinton, R. L. 1964. Activity cycles and mobility of central Florida deer based on telemetric and observational data. M.S. Thesis. University of Florida, Gainesville. 100 pp.

———. 1968. Telemetric study of white-tailed deer movement—ecology and ethology in the Southeast. Ph. D. Thesis. Auburn University, Auburn, Ala. 138 pp.

———. 1969. Portable radios in determination of ecological parameters of large vertebrates with reference to deer. *In* Remote sensing in ecology, ed. P. L. Johnson, pp. 148–163. Athens: Univ. Georgia Press. 244 pp.

Marchinton, R. L., and T. D. Atkeson. In press. Plasticity of sociospatial behavior of white-tailed deer and the concept of facultative territoriality. Internat. conf. biology of deer production. Dunedin, New Zealand.

Marchinton, R. L., and L. K. Jeter. 1967. Telemetric study of deer movement-ecology in the Southeast. Proc. Ann. Conf. Southeast. Assoc. Game and Fish Comm. 20:189–206.

Marchinton, R. L., and W. G. Moore. 1971. Auto-erotic behavior in male white-tailed deer. J. Mammal. 52(3):616–617.

Marchinton, R. L., A. S. Johnson, J. R. Sweeney, and J. M. Sweeney. 1971. Legal hunting of white-tailed deer with dogs: biology, sociology and management. Proc. Ann. Conf. Southeast. Assoc. Game and Fish Comm. 24:74–89.

Marcy, R. B. 1859. The prairie traveller. New York: Harper and Brothers, Publ. 354 pp.

Mare, C. J. 1976. African trypanosomiasis. *In* Proc. Foreign Anim. Dis. Seminar, pp. 68–72. Athens, Ga.: Wildlife Disease Foundation. 106 pp.

Margry, P. 1886. Découvertes et établissements des Français dans l'ouest et dans le sud de l'Amerique septentrionale, 1614–1754. 6 vols. Paris: D. Jouaust.

Marks, S., and L. K. Bustad. 1963. Thyroid neoplasms in sheep fed radioiodine. J. Nat. Cancer Inst. 30:661–673.

Marquette, J. 1900. First voyage, 1673. Jesuit Relations, 59:86–163.

Marquis, D. A. 1975. The Allegheny hardwood forests of Pennsylvania. Gen. Tech. Rep. NE-15. Broomall, Pa.: USDA Forest Service, Northeast. For. Exp. Stn. 32 pp.

———. 1981. Effect of deer browsing on timber production in Allegheny hardwood forests of northwestern Pennsylvania. Res. Pap. NE 475. Broomall, Pa.: USDA Forest Service, Northeast. For. Exp. Stn. 10 pp.

Marquis, D. A., and T. J. Grisez. 1978. The effect of deer exclosures on the recovery of vegetation in failed clearcuts on the Allegheny Plateau. Re. Note NE-270. Broomall, Pa.: USDA Forest Service, Northeast. For. Exp. Stn. 5 pp.

Marsh, P. 1976. Are there too many wild deer in Vermont? Yankee 40(11):132–145.

Marshall, A. D., and R. W. Whittington. 1969. A telemetric study of deer home ranges and behavior of deer during managed hunts. Proc. Ann. Conf. Southeast. Assoc. Game and Fish Comm. 22:30–46.

Marshall, C. L. 1975. The Mayflower destiny. Harrisburg, Pa.: Stackpole Books. 191 pp.

Marshall, C. M., G. A. Seaman, and F. A. Hayes. 1963. A critique on the tropical cattle fever tick controversy and its relationship to white-tailed deer. Trans. N. Amer. Wildl. and Natur. Resour. Conf. 28:225–232.

Marshall, F. H. A. 1937. On the change over in the oestrus cycle in animals after transference across the equator, with further observations on the incidence of the

breeding season and the factor controlling sexual periodicity. Proc. Royal Soc. London, Ser. B. 122:413–428.

Marshall, J. 1978. Venison: care before cooking. BC Outdoors 34(8):16–17.

Marshall, R. 1936. Address of Mr. Robert Marshall of the United States Indian Service. Trans. N. Amer. Wildl. Conf. 1:224–229.

Marston, D. L. 1977. Deer wintering area management in Maine—a progress report. Trans. Northeast Deer Study Group 11:103–110.

Marston, M. 1912. Letter to Reverend Dr. Jedidiah Morse from Major Marston, U. S. A., commanding at Fort Armstrong, Illinois, November 1820. *In* The Indian Tribes of the Upper Mississippi Valley and the Region of the Great Lakes, ed. E. H. Blair, pp. 137–182. Vol. 2. Cleveland: Arthur H. Clark. 857 pp.

Marston, M. A. 1942. Winter relations of bobcats to white-tailed deer in Maine. J. Wildl. Manage. 6(4):328–337.

Martin, C. 1978. Keepers of the game. Berkeley: Univ. California Press. 226 pp.

Martin, P. P., and G. P. Rasmussen. 1981. An investigation into the mode of inheritance of white coat color in white-tailed deer. A separate report in partial fulfillment of Fed. Aid in Wildl. Res. Proj. W-89-R, Job IX-2. Albany: New York State Dept. Envir. Conser. 21 pp. Mimeo.

Martin, P. S., and H. E. Wright, Jr., eds. 1967. Pleistocene extinctions. The search for a cause. New Haven: Yale Univ. Press. 453 pp.

Martinka, C. J. 1968. Habitat relationships of white-tailed deer and mule deer in northern Montana. J. Wildl. Manage. 32(3):558–565.

Mason, O. T. 1901. The annual report of the Board of Regents of the Smithsonian Institution, showing the operations, expenditures, and condition of the Institution for the year ending June 30, 1901. Washington, D. C.: Smithsonian Institution. 782 pp.

Mathews, C. v. C. 1908. Andrew Ellicott, his life and letters. New York: The Grafton Press. 256 pp.

Matschke, G. H. 1976. Diethylstilbestrol effects on antler and reproductive gland morphology in male deer. Proc. Ann. Conf. Southeast. Assoc. Game and Fish Comm. 30:649–655.

———. 1977*a*. Microencapsulated diethylstilbestrol as an oral contraceptive in white-tailed deer. J. Wildl. Manage. 41(1):87–91.

———. 1977*b*. Antifertility action of two synthetic progestins in female white-tailed deer. J. Wildl. Manage. 41(2):194–196.

———. 1977*c*. Fertility control in white-tailed deer by steroid implants. J. Wildl. Manage. 41(4):731–735.

———. 1978. Diethylstilbestrol effects on antler and reproductive gland morphology in male deer. Proc. Ann. Conf. Southeast. Assoc. Game and Fish Comm. 30:649–655.

———. 1980. Efficacy of steroid implants in preventing pregnancy in white-tailed deer. J. Wildl. Manage. 44(3):756–758.

Mattfeld, G. F. 1974. The energetics of winter foraging by white-tailed deer. A perspective on winter concentration. Ph. D. Thesis. State University of New York, Syracuse. 306 pp.

Mattfeld, G. F., R. W. Sage, R. D. Masters, and M. J. Tracy. 1977. Deer movement patterns in the Adirondacks—a progress report. Trans. Northeast Deer Study Group 11:157–167.

Mattfeld, G. F., J. E. Wiley III, and D. R. Behrend. 1972. Salt versus browse-seasonal baits for deer trapping. J. Wildl. Manage. 36(3):996–998.

Matthew, W. D. 1908. Osteology of *Blastomeryx* and phylogeny of the American Cervidae. Bull. Amer. Mus. Natur Hist. 24:535–562.

———. 1915. Climate and evolution. Ann. New York Acad. Sci. 24:171–318.

Matthiessen, P. 1959. Wildlife in America. New York: The Viking Press. 304 pp.

Mautz, W. W. 1978. Nutrition and carrying capacity. *In* Big game of North America: ecology and management, ed. J. L. Schmidt and D. L. Gilbert, pp. 321–348. Harrisburg, Pa.: Stackpole Books. 494 pp.

Mautz, W. W., U. S. Seal, and C. B. Boardman. 1980. Blood serum analyses of chemically and physically restrained white-tailed deer. J. Wildl. Manage. 44(2):343–351.

Mautz, W. W., H. Silver, J. B. Holter, H. H. Hayes, and W. E. Urban, Jr. 1976. Digestibility and related nutritional data for seven northern deer browse species. J. Wildl. Manage. 40(4):630–638.

Maxwell, H. 1910. The use and abuse of forest by Virginia Indians. William and Mary Coll. Quart. Hist. Mag. 10:73–103.

Maxwell, J. A., ed. 1978. America's fascinating Indian heritage. Pleasantville, N. Y.: The Reader's Digest Assoc., Inc. 416 pp.

May, M. 1959. A study of the plant composition and utilization by mixed classes of livestock and white-tailed deer on the Kerr Wildlife Management Area. Ph. D. Thesis. Texas A & M University, College Station. 131 pp.

Mayhall, M. P. 1939. The Indians of Texas: the Atakapa, the Karankawa, the Tonkawa. Ph. D. Thesis. University of Texas, Austin. 712 pp.

Maynard, C. J. 1872. Catalogue of the mammals of Florida, with notes on their habits, distribution, etc. Bull. Essex Inst. 4(10):135–150.

Maynard, L. A., G. Bump, R. Darrow, and J. C. Woodward. 1935. Food preferences and requirements of the white-tailed deer in New York State. Joint Bull. 1. Albany: New York State Conservation Department and New York State College of Agriculture. 35 pp.

McAtee, W. L. 1918. A sketch of the natural history of the District of Columbia together with an indexed edition of the U. S. Geological Survey's 1917 map of Washington and vicinity. Washington, D. C.: Press of H. L. and J. B. McQueen, Inc. 142 pp.

———. 1939. The electric fence in wildlife management. J. Wildl. Manage. 3(1):1–13.

McBeath, D. Y. 1941. Whitetail traps and tags. Mich. Conserv. 10(11):6–7, 11.

McCabe, R. A. 1964. Some aspects of wildlife and hunting in northern Wisconsin. Trans. Wis. Acad. Sci., Arts and Letters 53(A):57–65.

McCabe, R. A., and R. Bray. 1955. Did you get that deer? Ext. Spec. Circ. 41. Madison: University of Wisconsin. 4 pp.

McCabe, R. E. 1976. Our growing trespass problem. Fins and Feathers 5(9):8, 57–59.

———. 1982. Elk and Indians: historical values and perspectives. *In* Elk of North America: ecology and management, ed. J. W. Thomas and D. E. Toweill, pp. 61–164. Harrisburg, Pa.: Stackpole Books. 736 pp.

McCaffery, K. R. 1973a. Road-kills show trends in Wisconsin deer populations. J. Wildl. Manage. 37(2):212–216.

———. 1973b. Reinventory of statewide deer range. Final Rep. P-R Proj. W-141-R-8. Madison: Wisconsin Department of Natural Resources. 31 pp.

———. 1976a. Pellet survey review. Final Rep. P-R Proj. W-141-R-11. Madison: Wisconsin Department of Natural Resources. 19 pp.

———. 1976b. Deer trail counts as an index to populations and habitat use. J. Wildl. Manage. 40(2):308–316.

———. 1978. Development of winter loss survey. Final Rep. P-R Proj. W-141-R-13. Madison: Wisconsin Department of Natural Resources. 8 pp.

———. 1979. Deer trail survey improvement. Final Rep. P-R Proj. W-141-12-14. Madison: Wisconsin Department of Natural Resources. 9 pp.

McCaffery, K. R., and W. A. Creed. 1969. Significance of forest openings to deer in northern Wisconsin. Tech. Bull. 44. Madison: Wisconsin Department of Natural Resources. 104 pp.

McCaffery, K. R., L. D. Martoglio, and F. L. Johnson. 1974a. Maintaining wildlife openings with picloram pellets. Wildl. Soc. Bull. 2(2):40–45.

McCaffery, K. R., J. Tranetzki, and J. Piechura, Jr. 1974b. Summer foods of deer in northern Wisconsin. J. Wildl. Manage. 38(2):215–219.

McCauley, C. 1887. The Seminole Indians of Florida. Washington, D. C.: Ann. Rep. Bur. Ethnol. 5:475–531.

McConnell, P. A., R. C. Lund, and N. R. Boss. 1976. The 1975 outbreak of hemorrhagic disease among white-tailed deer in northwestern New Jersey. Trans. Northeast Sec. Wildl. Soc. 33:35–44.

McCullough, D. R. 1975. Modification of the Clover deer trap. Calif. Fish and Game 61(4):242–244.

———. 1978. Essential data required on population structure and dynamics in field studies of threatened herbivores. *In* Threatened deer, pp. 302–317. Morges, Switzerland: IUCN. 434 pp.

———. 1979. The George Reserve deer herd: population ecology of a K-selected species. Ann Arbor: Univ. Michigan Press. 271 pp.

———. 1982a. Evaluation of night spotlighting as a deer study technique. J. Wildl. Manage. 46(4):963–973.

———. 1982b. Population growth rate of the George Reserve deer herd. J. Wildl. Manage. 46(4):1079–1083.

———. 1982c. Antler characteristics of George Reserve white-tailed deer. J. Wildl. Manage. 46(3):821–826.

———. 1983. Rate of increase of white-tailed deer on the George Reserve: a response. J. Wildl. Manage. 47(4):1248–1250.

———. In press. The theory and management of *Odocoileus* populations. *In* Biology and management of cervids, ed. C. Wemmer.

McCullough, D. R., and W. J. Carmen. 1982. Management goals for deer hunter satisfaction. Wildl. Soc. Bull. 10:49–52.

McDonough, J. 1968. Policy statement, Massachusetts. Trans. Northeast Deer Study Group 4:21–30.

McDowell, R. 1980. Rate of nonreporting legal bow and arrow deer kills in New Jersey. Trans. Northeast Wildl. Conf. 57:129–133.

McDowell, R. D., and H. W. Pillsbury. 1959. Wildlife damage to crops in the United States. J. Wildl. Manage. 23(2):240–241.

McEwen, L. C., C. E. French, N. D. Magruder, R. W. Swift, and R. H. Ingram. 1957. Nutrient requirements of the white-tailed deer. Trans. N. Amer. Wildl. Conf. 22:119–132.

McGinnes, B. S. 1969. How size and distribution of cutting units affect food and cover of deer. *In* White-tailed deer in the southern forest habitat, pp. 66–70. Proc. Symp. Nacogdoches, Tex. New Orleans: USDA Forest Service, South. For. Exp. Stn. 130 pp.

McGinnes, B. S., and R. L. Downing. 1970. Fawn mortality in a confined Virginia deer herd. Proc. Ann. Conf. Southeast. Assoc. Game and Fish Comm. 23:188–191.

McGinnes, B. S., and R. L. Downing. 1977. Factors affecting the peak of white-tailed deer fawning in Virginia. J. Wildl. Manage. 41(4):715–719.

McGinnes, B. S., and J. H. Reeves, Jr. 1958. Deer jaws from excavated Indian sites let us compare Indian-killed deer with modern deer. Vir. Wildl. 19(12):8–9.

McHugh, T. 1972. The time of the buffalo. Lincoln: Univ. Nebraska Press. 350 pp.

———. 1979. The time of the buffalo. Lincoln: Univ. Nebraska Press. 374 pp.

McKeever, S. 1954. Ecology and distribution of the mammals of West Virginia. Unpubl. manuscript on file at North Carolina State University, Raleigh. 5 pp.

McKenney, T. L. 1827. Sketches of a tour to the lakes. Baltimore: F. Lucas, Jr. 493 pp.

McKinley, D. 1960. A chronology and bibliography of wildlife in Missouri. Columbia: University of Missouri Bull. 61(13):1–128.

McLeod, D. 1846. History of Wiskonsan. Buffalo, N. Y.: Steele's Press. 310 pp.

McMahan, C. A. 1961. Food habit study of livestock and deer. Job Comp. Rep., Fed. Aid Proj. No. W-76-R. Austin: Texas Game and Fish Commission. 156 pp.

———. 1964. Comparative food habits of deer and three classes of livestock. J. Wildl. Manage. 28(4):798–808.

———. 1966. Suitability of grazing enclosures for deer and livestock research on the Kerr Wildlife Management Area, Texas. J. Wildl. Manage. 30(1):151–162.

McMahan, C. A., and J. M. Inglis. 1974. Use of Rio Grande Plain brush types by white-tailed deer. J. Range Manage. 27(5):369–374.

McMahan, C. A., and C. W. Ramsey. 1965. Response of deer and livestock to controlled grazing in central Texas. J. Range Manage. 18(1):1–7.

McMichael, E. V. 1963. 1963 excavations at the Buffalo Site, 46 PU 31. W. Vir. Archeol. 16:12–23.

McMichael, T. J. 1970. Rate of predation on deer fawn mortality. *In* Wildlife research in Arizona, 1969–70, pp. 77–83. P-R Rep. Proj. W-78-14, Job No. 6. Phoenix: Arizona Game and Fish Department. 207 pp.

McMillin, J. M., U. S. Seal, K. D. Keenlyne, A. W. Erickson, and J. E. Jones. 1974. Annual testosterone rhythm in the adult white-tailed deer (*Odocoileus virginianus borealis*). Endocrinology 94:1034–1040.

McNeel, W., Jr., and J. Kennedy. 1959. Prevention of browsing by deer in a pine plantation. J. Wildl. Manage 23(4):450–451.

McNees, P. 1983. Here's where the wild things are—and how much they cost. Washington Post, Jan. 5, 1983:E19.

McNeil, R. J. 1974. Deer in New York State. Extension Bulletin 1189. Ithaca, N.Y.: New York State College of Agriculture and Life Sciences, Cornell Univ. 24 pp.

McNeill, R. E., Jr. 1971. Interactions of deer and vegetation on the Mid-Forest Lodge and Gladwin Game

Refuge. Ph. D. Thesis. University of Michigan, Ann Arbor. 214 pp.

Mearns, E. A. 1907. Mammals of the Mexican boundary. Smithsonian Inst. U. S. Nat. Mus. Bull. 56. Washington, D. C.: Government Printing Office. 530 pp.

Mech, L. D. 1966. The wolves of Isle Royale. Nat. Parks Fauna Series No. 7. Washington, D. C.: Government Printing Office. 210 pp.

———. 1970. The wolf; the ecology and behavior of an endangered species. Garden City, N. Y.: Natural History Press. 384 pp.

———. 1971. Wolves, dogs, coyotes. *In* Proc. white-tailed deer in Minnesota symp., ed. H. M. Nelson, pp. 19–22. St. Paul: Minnesota Department Natural Resources. 88 pp.

———. 1973. Wolf numbers in the Superior National Forest of Minnesota. Res. Pap. NC-97; St. Paul, Minn.: USDA Forest Service, N. Cent. For. Exp. Stn. 10 pp.

———. 1977*a*. Productivity, mortality and population trend in wolves from northeastern Minnesota. J. Mammal. 58(4):559–574.

———. 1977*b*. Wolf pack buffer zones as prey reservoirs. Science 198:320–321.

Mech, L. D., and L. D. Frenzel, Jr. 1971*a*. An analysis of the age, sex, and condition of deer killed by wolves in northeastern Minnesota. *In* Ecological studies of the timber wolf in northeastern Minnesota, ed. L. D. Mech and L. D. Frenzel, Jr., pp. 35–51. Res. Pap. NC-52. St. Paul: USDA Forest Service, N. Cent. For. Exp. Stn. 62 pp.

Mech, L. D., and L. D. Frenzel, Jr., eds. 1971*b*. Ecological studies of the timber wolf in northeastern Minnesota. Res. Pap. NC-52. St. Paul: USDA Forest Service, N. Cent. For. Exp. Stn. 62 pp.

Mech, L. D., and P. D. Karns. 1977. Role of the wolf in a deer decline in the Superior National Forest. Res. Pap. NC-148. St. Paul: USDA Forest Service, N. Cent. For. Exp. Stn. 23 pp.

Mech, L. D., and M. Korb. 1978. An unusually long pursuit of a deer by a wolf. J. Mammal. 59(4):860–861.

Mechlin, L. M. and C. W. Shaiffer. 1980. Net-firing gun for capturing breeding waterfowl. J. Wildl. Manage. 44(4):895–896.

Medin, D. E., and A. E. Anderson. 1979. Modeling the dynamics of a Colorado mule deer population. Wildl. Monogr. 68. Washington, D. C.: The Wildlife Society. 77 pp.

Medina, A. R. 1965. Differentes aspectos de la caza en Venezuela. Caracas: Litofotos Prieto. 11 pp.

Meinzer, W. P., D. N. Ueckert, and J. T. Flinders. 1975. Food-niche of coyotes in the Rolling Plains of Texas. J. Range Manage. 28(1):22–27.

Mena, R. A. 1978. Fauna y caza en Costa Rica. San José, Costa Rica: Imprenta Lehmann. 256 pp.

Méndez, E. 1968. Las especies Panameñas de venados. Rev. Panameña Biol. 1(1):1–14.

———. 1970. Los principales mamiferos silvestres de Panamá. Panamá: Edition Privada. 238 pp.

Méndéz, E., F. Delgado, and D. Miranda. 1981. The coyote (*Canis latrans*) in Panama. Int. J. Stud. Anim. Prob. 2(5):252–255.

Mengak, M. T. 1982. A comparison of two diet analysis techniques applied to white-tailed deer in coastal South Carolina. M. S. Thesis. Clemson University, Clemson, S. C. 73 pp.

Menzel, K., and R. Havel. 1974. Surveys and management of deer. Nebraska Game and Parks Commission, Work Plan A-76, Pittman-Robertson Proj. Rep. W-15-R-33. 33 pp.

Merrill, L. B. 1957. Livestock and deer ratios for Texas range lands. MP-22. College Station: Texas Agric. Exp. Stn. 9 pp.

———. 1959 Heavy grazing lowers range carrying capacity. Tex. Agric. Prog. 5(2):18.

Merrill, L. B., and J. E. Miller. 1961. Economic analysis of year-long grazing rate studies on Substation No. 14, near Sonora. MP-484. College Station: Texas Agric. Exp. Stn. 8 pp.

Merrill, L. B., J. G. Teer, and O. C. Wallmo. 1957. Reaction of deer populations to grazing practices. Tex. Agric. Prog. 3(5):10–12.

Merrill, L. B., and V. A. Young. 1954. Results of grazing single classes of livestock in combination with several classes when stocking rates are constant. Prog. Rep. 1726. College Station: Texas Agric. Exp. Stn. 7 pp.

Merritt, H. C. 1904. The shadow of a gun. Chicago: F. T. Peterson and Co. 450 pp.

Mershon, W. B. 1923. Recollections of my fifty years hunting and fishing. Boston: The Stratford Co. 259 pp.

Mesavage, C., and L. R. Grosenbaugh. 1956. Efficiency of several cruising designs on small tracts in north Arkansas. J. For. 54(9):569–576.

Meserole, H. T., ed. 1968. Seventeenth century American poetry. New York: W. W. Norton and Co., Inc. 541 pp.

Meske, T. A. 1972. Big game habitat improvement studies in the Dworshak Reservoir area. Comp. Rep. Boise: Idaho Fish and Game Dep. 31 pp.

Messner, H. E., D. R. Dietz, and E. C. Garrett. 1973. A modification of the slanting deer fence. J. Range Manage. 26(3):233–235.

Meyer, R. W. 1977. The village Indians of the Upper Missouri. Lincoln: Univ. Nebraska Press. 368 pp.

Michael, E. D. 1964. Birth of white-tailed deer fawns. J. Wildl. Manage. 28(1):171–173.

———. 1965. Movements of white-tailed deer on the Welder Wildlife Refuge. J. Wildl. Manage. 29(1):44–52.

———. 1966. Daily and seasonal activity patterns of white-tailed deer on the Welder Wildlife Refuge. Ph. D. Thesis. Texas A & M University, College Station. 216 pp.

———. 1967. Behavioral interactions of deer and some other mammals. Southwest Natur. 12(2):156–162.

———. 1968a. Drinking habits of white-tailed deer in south Texas. Proc. Ann. Conf. Southeast. Assoc. Game and Fish Comm. 21:51–57.

———. 1968b. Aggressive behavior of white-tailed deer. Southwest Natur. 13(4):411–420.

———. 1970. Activity patterns of white-tailed deer in south Texas. Tex. J. Sci. XXI(4):417–428.

Michelson. T. 1927. Contributions to Fox ethnology. Bulletin 85. Washington, D. C.: Bur. Amer. Ethnol. 168 pp.

Michigan United Conservation Clubs. 1981. Wildlife chef. Appleton, Wis.: Banta. 112 pp.

Mikula, E. J. 1955. An efficient handling crate for whitetail deer. J. Wildl. Manage. 19(4):501–502.

Miller, F. L. 1974. Four types of territoriality observed in a herd of black-tailed deer. *In* The behavior of ungulates and its relation to management, ed. V. Geist and F. R. Walther, 2:644–60. IUCN New Series Publ. 24. Morges, Switzerland: IUCN.

Miller, R., A. A. Prado, and R. A. Young. 1977. Congestion, success and the value of Colorado deer hunting experiences. Trans. N. Amer. Wildl. and Natur. Resour. Conf. 42:129–136.

Miller, W. J., A. O. Haugen, and D. J. Roslien. 1965. Natural variation in the blood proteins of white-tailed deer. J. Wildl. Manage. 29(4):717–723.

Milne, L. J., and M. Milne. 1962. The mountains. New York: Time Inc. 192 pp.

Milo Smith and Associates, Inc., and Hale and Kullgren, Inc. 1970. Environment and identity: a plan for development in the Florida Keys. Proj. P-116. Ser. 1-1. Washington, D.C.: Department of Housing and Urban Development. 201 pp.

Minckler, L. S., and R. E. McDermott. 1960. Pin oak acorn production and regeneration as affected by stand density, structure, and flooding. Res. Bull. 750. Columbia: Missouri Agric. Exp. Stn. 24 pp.

Ministerio de Agricultura y Cria. 1967. Aspectos legales y technicos de la caza en 1967. Caracas, Venezuela: Ministerio de Agricultura y Cria. 11 pp.

Miranda Ribeiro, A. de. 1919. Os veados de Brasil segundo as colleccoes Rondon e de varios museus nacionaes e estrangeiros. Rev. Mus. Paulista II: 213–307.

Mirarchi, R. E., B. E. Howland, P. F. Scanlon, R. L. Kirkpatrick, and L. M. Sanford. 1978. Seasonal variation in plasma LH, FSH, Prolactin, and testosterone concentrations in adult male white-tailed deer. Can. J. Zool. 56:121–127.

Mirarchi, R. E., P. F. Scanlon, and R. L. Kirkpatrick. 1977a. Annual changes in spermatozoan production and associated organs of white-tailed deer. J. Wildl. Manage 41(1):92–99.

Mirarchi, R. E., P. F. Scanlon, R. L. Kirkpatrick, and C. B. Schreck. 1977b. Androgen levels and antler development in captive and wild white-tailed deer. J. Wildl. Manage. 41(2):178–183.

Mississippi Game and Fish Commission. 1972. Unpublished mimeo report. Jackson, Mississippi.

Missouri Department of Conservation. 1983. Hunter orange update. Hunter Safety News 10(6):4–5.

Mitchell, W. A. 1980. Evaluation of white-tailed deer and cattle diets in two southeastern pine forests. Vol. I and II. Ph. D. Thesis. Mississippi State University, Mississippi State. 368 pp.

Moen, A. N. 1968a. Energy balance of white-tailed deer in the winter. Trans. N. Amer. Wildl. and Natur. Resour. Conf. 33:224–236.

———. 1968b. Energy exchange of white-tailed deer, western Minnesota. Ecology 49(4):676–682.

———. 1973. Wildlife ecology. San Francisco: W. H. Freeman and Co. 458 pp.

———. 1976. Energy conservation by white-tailed deer in the winter. Ecology 57(1):192–198.

———. 1978. Seasonal changes in heart rates, activity, metabolism, and forage intake of white-tailed deer. J. Wildl. Manage. 42(4):715–738.

———. 1980. The biology and management of wild ruminants. Part I. Physical, Chemical and Genetic Characteristics of Wild Ruminants. Ithaca, N.Y.: Cornell Univ. Mimeo.

———. 1982. The biology and management of wild ruminants. Part II. Behavior of Wild Ruminants. Ithaca, N.Y.: Cornell Univ. Mimeo.

Moen, A. N., and C. W. Severinghaus. 1981. The annual weight cycle and survival of white-tailed deer in New York. N. Y. Fish and Game J. 28(2):162–177.

Mohler, L. L., J. H. Wampole, and E. Fichter. 1951. Mule deer in Nebraska National Forest. J. Wildl. Manage. 15(2):129–157.

Momaday, N. S. 1970. An American land ethic. *In* Ecotactics: the Sierra Club Handbook for Environmental Activists, ed. J. G. Mitchell and C. L. Stallings, pp. 97–105. New York: Simon and Schuster. 288 pp.

Moncrief, L. W. 1970. An analysis of hunter attitudes toward the state of Michigan's antlerless deer hunting policy. Ph. D. Thesis. Michigan State University, East Lansing. 283 pp.

Monson, R. A., W. B. Stone, B. L. Weber, and F. J. Spadaro. 1974. Comparison of Riney and total kidney fat techniques for evaluating the physical condition of white-tailed deer. N. Y. Fish and Game J. 21(1):67–72.

Montgomery, G. G. 1963. Nocturnal movements and activity rhythms of white-tailed deer. J. Wildl. Manage. 27(3):422–427.

Montgomery, G. G., and R. E. Hawkins. 1967. Diazepam bait for capture of white-tailed deer. J. Wildl. Manage. 31(3):464–468.

Montgomery, M. J., and B. R. Baumgardt. 1965. Regulation of food intake in ruminants. 1. Pelleted rations varying in energy concentration. J. Dairy Sci. 48(5):569–574.

Moore, G., and V. Bevill. 1978. Game on your land. Part 2, Turkey and deer. Columbia: South Carolina Wildlife and Marine Resources Department. 59 pp.

Moore, G. C., and A. H. Boer. 1977. Forestry practices and deer habitat management. Deer Manage. Rep. 4. Fish and Wildl. Branch. Fredericton: New Brunswick Department of Natural Resources. 52 pp.

Moore, W. G. 1971. An investigation into the existence of sign posts and their relationship to social structure and communication in white-tailed deer. M. S. Thesis. University of Georgia, Athens. 46 pp.

Moore, W. G., and R. L. Marchinton. 1974. Marking behavior and its social function in white-tailed deer. *In* The behaviour of ungulates and its relation to management, ed. V. Geist and F. R. Walther, pp. 447–456. IUCN Publ. 24. Morges, Switzerland: IUCN.

Moore, W. H., and F. M. Johnson. 1967. Nature of deer browsing on hardwood seedlings and sprouts. J. Wildl. Manage. 31(2):351–353.

Moore, W. H., and R. B. Manney. 1962. Deer browse plants in loblolly and water oak-gum types of Piedmont Georgia. Resour. Bull. SE-4. Asheville, N.C.: USDA Forest Service, Southeast. For. Exp. Stn. 20 pp.

Moore, W. H., T. H. Ripley, and J. L. Clutter. 1960. Trials to determine relative deer range carrying capacity values in connection with the Georgia forest survey. Proc. Ann. Conf. Southeast. Assoc. Game and Fish Comm. 14:98–104.

Moran, R. J. 1973. The Rocky Mountain elk in Michigan. Res. and Dev. Rep. No. 267. Lansing: Michigan Department of Natural Resources. 93 pp.

More, T. A. 1977. An analysis of wildlife in children's stories. *In* Children, nature, and the urban environment, ed. D. Linton, pp. 84–92. Tech. Rep. NE-30. Broomall, Pa.: USDA Forest Service, Northeast For. Exp. Stn. 261 pp.

Morgan, L. H. 1851. League of the Iroquois. Rochester, N. Y.: Sage and Bro. 477 pp.

Morgan, R. P., II, J. A. Chapman, L. A. Noe, and C. J. Henry. 1974. Electrophoresis as a management tool. Trans. Northeast. Fish and Wildl. Conf. 31:63–71.

Morrison, C. C. 1878. Appendix F. Executive and descriptive report of Lieutenant Charles C. Morrison, Sixth Cavalry, on the operations of party no. 2, Colorado section, field season 1877. *In* Annual Report of the Geographical Surveys of the U. S. West of the 100th Meridian, by G. M. Wheeler, pp. 131–139. Washington, D. C.: Government Printing Office. 234 pp.

Morrison, J. 1967. Dog versus deer: a losing contrast. Ga. Game and Fish 2(1):14–16.

———. 1968. Hounds of hell. Ga. Game and Fish 3(12):13–19.

Morriss, D. J. 1954. Correlation of wildlife management with other uses on the Pisgah National Forest. J. For. 52(6):419–422.

Morse, E. W. 1962. Canoe routes of the voyageurs. Toronto: The Quetico Found. 41 pp.

Morse, J. 1822. A report to the Secretary of War of the United States on Indian affairs, comprising a narrative of a tour performed in the summer of 1820, under a commission of the President of the United States, for the purpose of ascertaining, for the use of the government, the actual state of the Indian tribes in our country. New Haven, Conn.: S. Converse. 400 pp.

Morse, M. A. 1942. Wildlife restoration and management planning project, Minnesota. Pittman-Robertson Q. 2(1):24–25.

Morse, M., and D. Ledin. 1958. Deer, apples and exploders. Conserv. Volunteer (Minn.) 21(121):29–31.

Morse, W. B. 1980. Wildlife law enforcement, 1980. Proc. West. Assoc. State Fish and Wildl. Agencies 1980:162–180.

———. In press. Sidearm policy and assaults on wildlife law enforcement officers. Proc. West. Assoc. State Fish and Wildl. Agencies 1982.

Morton, G. H., and E. L. Cheatum. 1946. Regional differences in breeding potential of white-tailed deer in New York. J. Wildl. Manage. 10(3):242–248.

Morton, T. 1883. New English Canaan, with introductory matter and notes by C. F. Adams, Jr. Vol. 14. Boston: The Prince Society. 381 pp.

Moss, E. H. 1955. The vegetation of Alberta. Bot. Rev. 21(9):493–567.

Mossman, A. S., P. A. Johnstone, C. A. R. Savory, and R. F. Dasmann. 1963. Neck snare for live capture of African ungulates. J. Wildl. Manage. 27(1):132–135.

Mourt, G. 1963. A journal of the pilgrims at Plymouth: Mourt's relation. Ed. Dwight Heath. New York: Corinth Books. 176 pp.

Moyle, J. B., ed. 1965. Big game in Minnesota. Div. Game and Fish Tech. Bull. 9. St. Paul: Minnesota Department of Conservation. 231 pp.

Mueller, C. C., and R. M. F. S. Sadleir. 1979. Age at first conception in black-tailed deer. Biol. Reprod. 21:1099–1104.

Muir, J. 1965. The story of my boyhood and youth. Madison: Univ. Wisconsin Press. 246 pp.

Mullan, J. 1861. Report . . . military road from Fort Benton to Fort Walla Walla. 36th Cong., 2nd Sess., H. R. Exec. Doc. 44. Washington, D. C.

Müller-Schwarze, D. 1971. Pheromones in black-tailed deer (*Odocoileus hemionus columbianus*). Anim. Behav. 19(1):141–152.

Mundinger, J. G. 1981*a*. White-tailed deer reproductive biology in the Swan Valley, Montana. J. Wildl. Manage. 45(1):132–139.

———. 1981*b*. Population ecology and habitat relationships of white-tailed deer in coniferous forest habitat of northwestern Montana. *In* Study N. BG-2.0, Job No. 1., pp. 53–72. Helena: Montana Department of Fish, Wildlife and Parks.

———. 1981*c*. Impacts of timber harvest on white-tailed deer in the coniferous forests of northwestern Montana. Paper presented at Northwest Section, The Wildlife Society, Coeur d'Alene, Idaho, April 22, 1981.

———. 1985. Biology of the white-tailed deer in coniferous forests of northwestern Montana. *In* Fish and Wildlife Relationships in Old Growth Forests: Proceedings of a Symposium. (Juneau, Alaska, 12–15 Apr. 1982), ed. W. R. Meehan, T. R. Merrell, Jr., and T. A. Hanley, Ashland, Oh.: Bookmasters.

Munson, P. J., P. W. Parmalee, and R. A. Yarnell. 1971. Subsistence ecology of Scovill, a terminal middle woodland village. Amer. Antiquity 36(4):410–431.

Murphy, D. A. 1959. Cause of death—accidental. Mo. Conserv. 20(9):1–3.

———. 1960. Rearing and breeding white-tailed fawns in captivity. J. Wildl. Manage. 24(4):439–441.

———. 1962. Deer harvests from refuge areas in Missouri. Proc. Ann. Conf. Southeast. Assoc. Game and Fish Comm. 15:37–42.

———. 1969. Hunting methods, limits, and regulations. *In* White-tailed deer in the southern forest habitat, pp. 54–58. Proc. Symp. Nacogdoches, Texas. New Orleans: USDA Forest Service, South. For. Exp. Stn. 130 pp.

———. 1970*a*. Deer range appraisal in the Midwest. *In* White-tailed deer in the Midwest, a symp., pp. 2–10. Res. Pap. NC-39. St. Paul: USDA Forest Service, N. Cent. For. Exp. Stn. 34 pp.

———. 1970*b*. White-tailed deer. *In* Conservation contrasts, ed. W. O. Nagel, pp. 129–138. Jefferson City: Missouri Department of Conservation. 453 pp.

Murphy, D. A., and J. A. Coates. 1966. Effects of dietary protein on deer. Trans. N. Amer. Wildl. and Natur. Resour. Conf. 31:129–139.

Murphy, D. A., and H. S. Crawford. 1970. Wildlife foods and understory vegetation in Missouri's national forests. Tech. Bull. 4. Jefferson City: Missouri Department of Conservation. 47 pp.

Murphy, J. M. 1879. Sporting adventures in the far West. London: Sampson Low, Marston, Searle and Rivington. 404 pp.

Murphy, P. K., and R. E. Noble. 1973. The monthly availability and use of browse plants by deer on a bottomland hardwood area in Tensas Parish, Louisiana. Proc. Ann. Conf. Southeast. Assoc. Game and Fish Comm. 26:39–57.

Murry, R. E. 1965. Tranquilizing techniques for capturing deer. Proc. Ann. Conf. Southeast, Assoc. Game and Fish Comm. 19:4–5.

Murry, R. E., and D. Dennett. 1963. A preliminary report on the use of tranquilizing compounds in capturing wildlife. Proc. Ann. Conf. Southeast. Assoc. Game and Fish Comm. 17:134–139.

Mussehl, T. W., and F. W. Howell, eds. 1971. Game management in Montana. Helena: Montana Fish and Game Department. 238 pp.

Mustard, E. W., and V. Wright. 1964. Food habits of Iowa deer. P-R Proj. W-99-R-3. Des Moines: Iowa Conservation Commission. 35 pp.

Myers, A. C., ed. 1912. Narratives of early Pennsylvania, West New Jersey and Delaware, 1630–1707. New York: Barnes and Noble. 476 pp.

Nagy, J. G., H. W. Steinhoff, and G. M. Ward. 1964. Effects of essential oils of sagebrush on deer rumen microbial function. J. Wildl. Manage. 28(4):785–790.

Nagy, J. G., G. Vidacs, and G. M. Ward. 1967. Previous diet of deer, cattle, and sheep and ability to digest alfalfa hay. J. Wildl. Manage. 31(3):443–447.

Nagy, J. G., and W. L. Regelin. 1975. Comparison of digestive organ size of three deer species. J. Wildl. Manage. 39(3):621–624.

Nash, C. H., and R. Gates, Jr. 1962. Chucalissa Indian town. Tenn. Hist. Quart. 21:103–121.

National Meat Institute. 1979. The whitetail deer . . . from field to table. Montreal: National Meat Institute, Inc. 64 pp.

Nebraska Game and Parks. 1979. The market place. Nebraskaland 57(7):17.

Neil, P. H., R. W. Hoffman, and R. B. Gill. 1975. Effects of harassment on wild animals—an annotated bibliography of selected references. Spec. Rep. 37. Denver: Colorado Division of Wildlife. 21 pp.

Neiland, K. A. 1970. Weight of dried marrow as indicator of fat in caribou femurs. J. Wildl. Manage. 34(4):904–907.

Nelson, E. W. 1934. The influence of precipitation and grazing upon black grama grass range. Tech. Bull. 409. Washington, D. C.: U. S. Department of Agriculture. 32 pp.

Nelson, F. P. 1969. The goals of state conservation agencies in deerherd management. *In* White-tailed deer in the southern forest habitat, ed. L. K. Halls, pp. 88–89. Proc. Symp. Nacogdoches, Tex. New Orleans: USDA Forest Service, South. For. Exp. Stn. 130 pp.

Nelson, M. E., and L. D. Mech. 1981. Deer social organization and wolf predation in northeastern Minnesota. Wild. Monogr. 77. Washington, D. C.: The Wildlife Society. 53 pp.

Nelson, M. E., and L. D. Mech. 1984. Observation of a swimming wolf killing a swimming deer. On file at U. S. Fish and Wildlife Service, N. Central For. Exp. Stn., St. Paul, Minn. 5 pp.

Nelson, M. M. 1971. Predator management with emphasis on the timber wolf. *In* The white-tailed deer in Minnesota, ed. M. M. Nelson, pp. 68–77. St. Paul: Minnesota Department of Natural Resources. 88 pp.

Nelson, N. 1977. Game meat: handle it with care. Fishing and Hunting News 33(41):10–12.

Nesbitt, W. H., and P. L. Wright, eds. 1981. Records of North American big game. Alexandria, Virginia: The Boone and Crockett Club. 421 pp.

Nettles, V. F., F. A. Hayes, and W. M. Martin. 1977. Observation on injuries in white-tailed deer. Proc. Ann. Conf. Southeast. Assoc. Game and Fish Comm. 30:474–480.

Nevo, E. 1978. Genetic variation in natural populations: Patterns and theory. Theor. Popul. Biol. 13:121–177.

Newcomb, W. W., Jr. 1983. Karankawa. *In* Southwest, ed. A. Ortiz, pp. 359–367. Handbook of North American Indians, Vol. 10. Washington, D. C.: Smithsonian Institution. 868 pp.

Newhouse, S. 1869. The trapper's guide. New York: Oakley, Mason and Co. 216 pp.

Newhouse, S. J. 1973. Effects of weather on behavior of white-tailed deer of the George Reserve, Michigan. M.S. Thesis. University of Michigan, Ann Arbor. 154 pp.

Newsom, J. D. 1969. History of deer and their habitat in the South. *In* White-tailed deer in the southern forest habitat, ed. L. K. Halls, pp. 1–4. Proc. Symp. Nacogdoches, Tex. New Orleans: USDA Forest Service, South. For. Exp. Stn. 130 pp.

Newsom, W. M. 1930. The common bobcat a deer killer. Amer. Game 19(2):42, 50.

Nichol, A. A. 1936. The experimental feeding of deer. Trans. N.Amer. Wildl. Conf. 1:403–410.

———. 1938. Experimental feeding of deer. Tech. Bull. 75. Tucson: University of Arizona. 30 pp.

Nichols, E. A., V. M. Chapman, and F. H. Ruddle. 1973. Polymorphism and linkage for mannosephosphate isomerase in *Mus musculus*. Biochem. Genet. 8(1):47–53.

Nichols, E. C. 1923. A sketch of the Nichols deer hunting camps. *In* Recollections of my fifty years hunting and fishing, ed. W. B. Mershon, pp. 89–97. Boston: The Stratford Co. 259 pp.

Nichols, R. G., and C. J. Whitehead, Jr. 1978. The effects of dog harassment on relocated white-tailed deer. Proc. Ann. Conf. Southeast. Assoc. Fish and Wildl. Agencies 32:195–201.

Niebauer, T. J., and O. J. Rongstad. 1977. Coyote food habits in northwestern Wisconsin. *In* Proc. 1975 Predator Symp., ed. R. L. Phillips and C. Jonkel, pp. 237–251. Montana For. Conserv. Exp. Stn. Missoula: University of Montana. 268 pp.

Nielsen, D. B. 1975. Coyotes and deer. Utah Sci. 36(3):807–890.

Nielsen, D. G., M. J. Dunlap, and K. V. Miller. 1982. Pre-rut rubbing by white-tailed bucks: nursery damage, social role, and management options. Wildl. Soc. Bull. 10(4):341–348.

Nielsen, S. W., and J. A. Aftosmis. 1964. Spinal nematodiasis in two sheep. J. Amer. Vet. Med. Assoc. 144(2):155–158.

Nielson, A. E. 1974. Hunter report card analysis. Job Prog. Rep., Proj. W-138-R-6, Job 1. Boise: Idaho Fish and Game Department. 13 pp.

Nixon, C. M. 1965a. The relationship between the annual accidental deer kill and the legal harvest in Ohio. Game Res. in Ohio 3:137–152.

———. 1965b. White-tailed growth and productivity in eastern Ohio. Game Res. in Ohio 3:123–136.

———. 1970. Deer populations in the Midwest. *In* White-tailed deer in the Midwest, a symp., pp. 11–18. Res. Pap. NC-39. St. Paul: USDA Forest Service, N. Cent. For. Exp. Stn. 34 pp.

———. 1971. Productivity of white-tailed deer in Ohio. Ohio J. Sci. 71(4):217–225.

Nixon, C. M., M. W. McClain, and K. R. Russell. 1970. Deer food habits and range characteristics in Ohio. J. Wildl. Manage. 34(4):870–886.

Noble, R. E. 1974. Reproductive characteristics of Mississippi white-tailed deer. Jackson: Mississippi Game and Fish Commission, Game Division. 58 pp.

Norberg, E. R. 1957. White-tailed deer movements and foraging on the Cedar Creek Forest, Minnesota. M. S. Thesis. University of Minnesota, St. Paul. 77 pp.

Nordan, H. C., I. M. Cowan, and A. J. Wood. 1968. Nutritional requirements and growth of black-tailed deer, *Odocoileus hemionus columbianus*, in captivity. *In* Comparative nutrition of wild animals, ed. M. A. Crawford, pp. 89–96. New York: Academic Press. 429 pp.

Norris, J. J. 1943. Botanical analysis of stomach contents as a method of determining forage consumption of range sheep. Ecology 24(2):244–251.

Noy-Meir, I. 1975. Stability of grazing: an application of predator-prey graphs. J. Ecol. 63:459–481.

Nuttall, T. 1821. A journal of travels into Arkansas territory during the year 1819. Philadelphia: Thomas N. Palmer. 196 pp.

O'Brien, R. D. 1967. Insecticides: action and metabolism. New York: Academic Press. 332 pp.

O'Brien, T. F. 1976. Seasonal movement and mortality of white-tailed deer in Wisconsin. M. S. Thesis. University of Wisconsin, Madison. 18 pp.

O'Callaghan, E. B. 1849–1851. The documentary history of the State of New York. 5 vols. Albany, N. Y.: Weed, Parsons and Co.

O'Callaghan, E. B., and B. Fernow, eds. 1856–1887. Documents relative to the colonial history of the State of New York. 12 vols. Albany, N. Y.: Weed, Parsons and Co.

Odum, E. P. 1971. Fundamentals of ecology. 3rd ed. Philadelphia: W. B. Saunders Co. 574 pp.

Oh, H, K., M. B. Jones, and W. M. Longhurst. 1968. Comparison of rumen microbial inhibition resulting from various essential oils isolated from relatively unpalatable plant species. Appl. Microbiol. 16(1):39–44.

Oldys, H. 1911. The game market to-day. *In* U. S. Department of Agriculture Yearbook 1910, pp. 243–254. Washington, D. C.: U. S. Department of Agriculture.

Olson, H. F. 1938. Deer tagging and population studies in Minnesota. Trans. N. Amer. Wildl. Conf. 3:280–286.

Olson, H. F., J. M. Keener, and D. R. Thompson. 1955. Evaluation of the deer pellet count as a census method. Rep. filed Wisconsin Dep. Natur. Resour., Bus. Res., Madison, Wisconsin. 12 pp.

Oosting, H. J. 1948. The study of plant communities, an introduction to plant ecology. San Francisco: W. H. Freeman and Co. 389 pp.

———. 1956. The study of plant communities; an introduction to plant ecology. 2d ed. San Francisco: W. H. Freeman and Co. 440 pp.

O'Pezio, J. P. 1978. Mortality among white-tailed deer fawns on the Seneca Army Depot. N. Y. Fish and Game J. 25(1):1–15.

O'Pezio, J. P., and P. R. Sauer. 1974. Evaluating deer life equation data from the Seneca Army Depot. Job Progress Report for Fed. Aid in Wildl. Res., Report W-89-R. Albany: New York State Dept. Envir. Conser. Mimeo.

Opler, M. E. 1969. Apache odyssey: a journey between two worlds. New York: Holt, Rinehart and Winston. 301 pp.

———. 1983. Chiracahua Apache. *In* Southwest, ed. A. Ortiz, pp. 401–418. Handbook of North American Indians, Vol. 10. Washington, D. C.: Smithsonian Institution. 868 pp.

Orme, M. L., and T. A. Leege. 1975. The reproduction ecology of redstem (*Ceanothus sanguineus*). Job Compl. Rep. Job 6, Proj. W-160-R-2. Boise: Idaho Fish and Game Department. 95 pp.

Ormond, C. 1970. Shotguns for deer. *In* The NRA guidebook for hunters, pp. 263–264. Washington, D. C.: National Rifle Association of America. 264 pp.

O'Roke, E. C., and F. N. Hamerstrom, Jr. 1948. Productivity and yield of the George Reserve deer herd. J. Wildl. Manage. 12(1):78–86.

Osborne, L. d. J. 1965. Indian crafts of Guatemala and El Salvador. Norman: Univ. Oklahoma Press. 278 pp.

Osgood, W. H. 1910. Mammals from the coast and islands of northern South America. Field Mus. Natur. Hist. Zool. Ser. 10:23–32.

———. 1912. Mammals from western Venezuela and eastern Colombia. Field Mus. Natur. Hist., Publ. 155, Zool. Ser. 10(5):33–66.

———. 1914. Four new mammals from Venezuela. Field Mus. Natur. Hist., Publ. 175, Zool. Ser. 10(11):135–141.

Oswalt, W. H. 1966. This land was theirs: a study of the North American Indians. New York: John Wiley and Sons, Inc. 560 pp.

Otis, D. L., K. P. Burnham, G. C. White, and D. R. Anderson. 1978. Statistical inference from capture data on closed animal populations. Wildl. Monogr. 62. Washington, D. C.: The Wildlife Society. 135 pp.

Overton, W. S., and D. E. Davis. 1969. Estimating the numbers of animals in wildlife populations. *In* Wildlife management techniques, ed. R. H. Giles, pp. 403–455. 3rd ed. Washington, D. C.: The Wildlife Society. 623 pp.

Owens, T. F. 1981. Movement patterns and determinants of habitat use of white-tailed deer in northwestern Idaho. M. S. Thesis. University of Idaho. Moscow. 48 pp.

Ozoga, J. J. 1968. Variations in microclimate in a conifer swamp deeryard in northern Michigan. J. Wildl. Manage. 32(3):574–585.

———. 1969. Longevity records for female white-tailed deer in northern Michigan. J. Wildl. Manage. 33(4):1027–1028.

———. 1972. Aggressive behavior of white-tailed deer at winter cuttings. J. Wildl. Manage. 36(3):861–868.

Ozoga, J. J., and L. W. Gysel. 1972. Response of white-tailed deer to winter weather. J. Wildl. Manage. 36(3):892–896.

Ozoga, J. J., and E. M. Harger. 1966. Winter activities and feeding habits of northern Michigan coyotes. J. Wildl. Manage. 30(4):809–818.

Ozoga, J. J., and L. J. Verme. 1970. Winter feeding patterns of penned white-tailed deer. J. Wildl. Manage. 34(2):431–439.

Ozoga, J. J., and L. J. Verme. 1975. Activity patterns of white-tailed deer during estrus. J. Wildl. Manage. 39(4):679–683.

Ozoga, J. J., and L. J. Verme. 1978. The thymus gland as a nutritional indicator status in deer. J. Wildl. Manage. 42(4):791–798.

Ozoga, J. J., and L. J. Verme. 1982*a*. Physical and reproductive characteristics of a supplementally-fed white-tailed deer herd. J. Wildl. Manage. 46(2):281–301.

Ozoga, J. J., and L. J. Verme. 1982*b*. Predation by black bears on newborn white-tailed deer. J. Mammal. 63(4):695–696.

Ozoga, J. J., L. J. Verme, and C. S. Bienz. 1982*a*. Parturition behavior and territoriality in white-tailed deer; impact on neonatal mortality. J. Wildl. Manage. 46(1):1–11.

Ozoga, J. J., C. S. Bienz, and L. J. Verme. 1982*b*. Red fox feeding habits in relation to fawn mortality. J. Wildl. Manage. 46(1):242–243.

Paatsama, S., H. Suomus, and E. Tanhuanpää. 1973. Valkohäntäpeura tutkimuksen valokeilassa. Metsästäjä 1973:4, 6–7.

Paige, S. 1912. Geologic atlas of the United States. Llano-Burnet folio, No. 183. Washington, D.C.: USDI Geological Survey. 16 pp.

Palmer, R. S. 1951. The whitetail deer of Tomhegan Camps, Maine, with added notes on fecundity. J. Mammal. 32(3):267–280.

Palmer, W. L., G. M. Kelley, and J. L. George. 1982. Alfalfa losses to white-tailed deer. Wildl. Soc. Bull. 10(3):259–261.

Palmer, W. L., R. G. Wingerd, and J. L. George. 1983. Evaluation of white-tailed deer repellants. Wildl. Soc. Bull. 11(2):164–165.

Palmer, Z., and D. D. Devet. 1966. Prescribed burning techniques on the national forests in South Carolina. Proc. Ann. Conf. Southeast. Assoc. Game and Fish Comm. 19:23–25.

Park, W. J. 1877. Madison, Dane County and surrounding towns. Madison: W. J. Park Co. 664 pp.

Parker, K. W. 1942. A method for estimating grazing use in mixed grass types. Res. Note 105. USDA Forest Service, Southwest For. and Range Exp. Stn. 5 pp.

Parmalee, P. W. 1965. The food economy of Archaic and Woodland peoples at the Tick Creek Cave Site, Missouri. Missouri Archeologist 27(1):1–34.

Partain, L. E. 1952. Exploitation of resources. Trans. N. Amer. Wildl. Conf. 17:71–81.

Patterson, G. D. P. 1949. Boxing the deer. Md. Conserv. 26(1):20–21.

Patton, A. 1982. 1981 deer harvest. Conservationist 6:3–4.

Patton, D. R., and J. M. Hall. 1966. Evaluating key areas by browse age and form class. J. Wildl. Manage. 30(3):476–480.

Patton, D. R., and B. S. McGinnes. 1964. Deer browse relative to age and intensity of timber harvest. J. Wildl. Manage. 28(3):458–463.

Paulin, C. O. 1932. Atlas of the historical geography of the United States. Baltimore: Carnegie Institute of Washington and American Geographic Society of N. Y. 162 + pp.

Payne, R. L. 1970. White-tailed deer physiological indices. *In* Deer population dynamics and census methods: a review, pp. 29–35. Deer Population Dynamics Subcommittee, Forest Game Committee, Southeast. Assoc. Game and Fish Comm. 59 pp.

Pearson, R. 1964. Animals and plants of the Cenozoic Era. London: Butterworth & Co. Ltd. 236 pp.

Pearson, R. W., and L. E. Ensminger. 1957. Southeastern uplands. *In* Soil, ed. A. Stefferud, pp. 579–594. USDA Yearbook. Washington, D. C.: Government Printing Office. 784 pp.

Pechanec, J. F., and G. D. Pickford. 1937. A weight estimate method for the determination of range or pasture production. J. Amer. Soc. Agron. 29:894–904.

Peek, J. M., R. J. Pedersen, and J. W. Thomas. 1982. The future of elk and elk hunting. *In* Elk of North America: ecology and management, ed. J. W. Thomas and D. E. Toweill, pp. 599–625. Harrisburg, Pa.: Stackpole Books. 698 pp.

Peery, C. H., and J. Coggin. 1978. Virginia white-tailed deer. Richmond: Virginia Commission of Game and Inland Fisheries. 159 pp.

Pekins, P. J. 1981. Summer and fall food habits of lead deer in southern New Hampshire. Trans. Northeast Deer Study Group 17:9–10.

Pengelly, W. L. 1961. Factors influencing production of white-tailed deer on the Coeur d'Alene National Forest, Idaho. Missoula, Mont.: U. S. Forest Service, Northern Region. 190 pp.

Pennington, J., and H. N. Church, eds. 1980. Food values of portions. 13th ed. New York: Harper and Row. 186 pp.

Pennsylvania Game Commission. 1982. Road-killed deer. Pa. Game News 53(6):66.

Perry, M. C., and R. H. Giles, Jr. 1971. Studies of deer-related dog activity in Virginia. Proc. Ann. Conf. Southeast. Assoc. Game and Fish Comm. 24:64–73.

Peterle, T. J. 1967. Characteristics of some Ohio hunters. J. Wildl. Manage. 31(2):375–389.

Peterson, E. T. 1979. Hunter's heritage. A history of hunting in Michigan. Lansing: Michigan United Conservation Clubs. 54 pp.

Peterson, H. A. 1940. Are bears predators? U. S. For. Serv. North. Reg. News 12:14.

Peterson, R. L. 1966. The mammals of eastern Canada. Toronto: Oxford Univ. Press. 465 pp.

Peterson, R. O. and R. E. Page. 1983. Wolf-moose fluctuations in Isle Royale National Park, Michigan, U. S. A. Acta Zoologica Fennica.

Peterson, W. J. 1969. A literature review on deer harvest. Spec. Rep. 22. Fort Collins: Colorado Division of Game, Fish and Parks, and Cooperative Wildlife Research Unit. 15 pp.

Petraborg, W. H., and D. W. Burcalow. 1965. The white-tailed deer in Minnesota. *In* Big game in Minnesota, ed. J. B. Moyle, pp. 11–56. St. Paul: Minnesota Department of Conservation, Division of Fish and Game. 227 pp.

Petraborg, W. H., and V. E. Gunvalson. 1962. Observations on bobcat mortality and bobcat predation on deer. J. Mammal. 43(3):430–431.

Pettersen, C. L. 1976. The Maya of Guatemala, their life and dress. Guatemala City: Ixchel Museum. 274 pp.

Petticrew, P. S., and L. Jackson. 1980. Preliminary deer management plan for British Columbia. Unpublished report on file at British Columbia Fish and Wildlife Branch, Cranbrook. 32 pp.

Phillips, P. C. 1961. The fur trade. 2 vols. Norman: Univ. Oklahoma Press. 1,355 pp.

Pichette, C. 1977. Research and mechanism of deer management in Quebec. Trans. Northeast Deer Study Group 11:3–7.

Pierce, A. W. 1957. Studies on salt tolerance of sheep. I. The tolerance of sheep for sodium chloride in the drinking water. Aust. J. Agric. Res. 8(6):711–722.

———. 1959. Studies on salt tolerance of sheep. II. The tolerance of sheep for mixtures of sodium chloride and magnesium chloride in the drinking water. Aust. J. Agric. Res. 10(5):725–735.

Pietsch, L. R. 1954. White-tailed deer populations in Illinois. Biol. Notes 34. Champaign: Illinois Natural History Survey Division. 22 pp.

Pilgrim, G. E. 1941*a*. The dispersal of the Artiodactyla. Biol. Rev., Cambridge Phil. Soc. 16(2):134–163.

———. 1941*b*. The relationship of certain variant fossil types of "horn" to those of the living Pecora. Ann. Mag. Natur. Hist. 7:172–184.

Pillmore, R. E. 1961. Insecticide residues in big game animals. Denver: U. S. Fish and Wildlife Service, Denver Wildlife Research Center. 9 pp.

Pillmore, R. E., and R. B. Finley, Jr. 1963. Residues in game animals resulting from forest and range insecticide applications. Trans. N. Amer. Wildl. and Natur. Resour. Conf. 28:409–422.

Pimlott, D. H. 1959. Reproduction and productivity of Newfoundland moose. J. Wildl. Manage. 23(4):381–401.

———. 1967. Wolf predation and ungulate populations. Amer. Zool. 7(2):267–278.

Pimlott, D. H., J. R. Bider, and R. C. Passmore. 1968. Investigation into the decline of deer in the counties north of Montreal. Québec: Ministère du Tourisme, de la Chasse et de la Pêche. 53 pp.

Pimlott, D. H., J. H. Shannon, and G. B. Kolenosky. 1969. The ecology of the timber wolf in Algonquin Provincial Park. Wildl. Res. Rep. No. 87. Ottawa: Ontario Department of Lands and Forests. 92 pp.

Pistey, W. R., and J. F. Wright. 1961. The immobilization of captive wild animals with succinylcholine. II. Can. J. Comp. Med. Vet. Sci. 25(3):59–68.

Platt, T. R., and W. M. Samuel. 1978. A redescription and neotype designation for *Parelaphostrongylus odocoilei* (Nematoda: METASTRONGYLOIDEA). J. Parasitol. 64(2):226–232.

Pledger, J. M. 1975. Activity, home range, and habitat utilization of white-tailed deer (*Odocoileus virginianus*) in southeastern Arkansas. M. S. Thesis. University of Arkansas, Fayetteville. 75 pp.

———. 1977. Deer disease runs its course. Ark. Game and Fish 9(2):12–14.

Plotka, E. D., U. S. Seal, M. A. Latellier, L. J. Verme, and J. J. Ozoga. 1979. Endocrine and morphologic effects of pinealectomy in white-tailed deer. *In* Animal models for research on contraception and fertility, ed. N. J. Alexander, pp. 452–466. Hagerstown, Md.: Harper and Row. 607 pp.

Plotka, E. D., U S. Seal, G. C. Schmoller, P. D. Karns, and K. D. Keenlyne. 1977*a*. Reproductive steroids in the white-tailed deer (*Odocoileus virginianus borealis*). I. Seasonal changes in the female. Biol. Reprod. 16(3):340–343.

Plotka, E. D., U. S. Seal, L. J. Verme, and J. J. Ozoga. 1977*b*. Reproductive steroids in the white-tailed deer (*Odocoileus virginianus borealis*). II. Progesterone and estrogen levels in peripheral plasma during pregnancy. Biol. Reprod. 17(1):78–83.

Plotka, E. D., U. S. Seal, L. J. Verme, and J. J. Ozoga. 1980. Reproductive steroids in deer. III. Luteinizing hormone, estradiol and progesterone around estrus. Biol. Reprod. 22(3):576–581.

Plotka, E. D., U. S. Seal, L. J. Verme, and J. J. Ozoga. 1982. Reproductive steroids in white-tailed deer. IV. Origin of progesterone during pregnancy. Biol. Reprod. 26:258–262.

Plummer, F. B. 1943. The carboniferous rocks of the Llano region of central Texas. Bull. No. 4329. Austin: University of Texas. 170 pp.

Pojar, T. M. 1977. Use of a population model in big game management. Proc. West. Assoc. Game and Fish Comm. 57:82–92.

Poole, D. A. 1971. Insuring the future of hunting and fishing. Wildl. Soc. News 136:45–46.

Poole, R. W. 1974. An introduction to quantitative ecology. New York: McGraw Hill Book Co. 532 pp.

Porath, W. R. 1980. Fawn mortality estimates in farmland deer range. *In* White-tailed deer population management in the north central states, ed. R. L. Hines and S. Nehls, pp. 55–63. Proc. 1979 Symp. N. Cent. Sect. Wildl. Soc. 116 pp.

Porath, W. R., S. L. Sheriff, D. J. Witter, and O. Torgerson. 1980. Deer hunters: a traditional constituency in a time of change. Proc. Internat. Assoc. Fish and Wildl. Agencies 70:41–53.

Porath, W. R., and O. Torgerson. 1975. Deer population trend measurements. P-R Rep. W-13-R-29. Columbia: Missouri Department of Conservation. 19 pp.

Porath, W. R., and O. Torgerson. 1976. Deer harvest analysis and season recommendations. P-R Rep. W-13-R-30. Columbia: Missouri Department of Conservation. 74 pp.

Pospahala, R. S. 1969. A literature review on computers in wildlife biology. Spec. Rep. 23. Denver: Colorado Division of Game, Fish and Parks. 15 pp.

Post, G. 1952*a*. Investigation of anesthetic materials to determine the safest drug for animal anesthesia. *In* Big game survey, pp. 110–115. P-R Job Comp. Rep., Proj. W-27-R-5/WP-13/J-2. Cheyenne: Wyoming Game and Fish Department.

———. 1952*b*. Development of an anesthesia projectile. *In* Big game survey, pp. 104–109. P-R Job Comp. Rep., Proj. W-27-R-5/WP-13/J-1. Cheyenne: Wyoming Game and Fish Department.

Potter, D. R., J. C. Hendee, and R. N. Clark. 1973. Hunting satisfaction: game, guns or nature. Trans. N. Amer. Wildl. and Natur. Resour. Conf. 38:220–229.

Potvin, F., and J. Huot. 1975. Mortalité de cerf de Virginie dans le ravage de Pohénegamook, 1971–75. Québec: Ministère du Tourisme, de la Chasse et de la Pêche, Service de la Recherche Biologique. 21 pp.

Potvin, F., J. Huot, and F. Duchesneau. 1981. Deer mortality in the Pohénégamook wintering area, Québec. Can. Field Nat. 95:80–84.

Potvin, F., R. Joly, M. Bélanger, J. M. Brassard, S. Georges, and P. Lessard. 1977. Problématique de la chasse du cerf au Québec. Rapport Spécial 8. Quebec: Ministère du Tourisme, de la Chasse et de la Pêche, Direction Générale de la Faune. 150 pp.

Powell, H. M. T. 1931. The Santa Fe trail to California, 1849–1852. Ed. D. S. Watson. San Francisco: The Book Club of California. 272 pp.

Presnall, C. C. 1942. Original game conservation in present wartime economy. Trans. N. Amer. Wildl. Conf. 7:62–67.

———. 1943. Wildlife conservation as affected by American Indian and caucasian concepts. J. Mammal. 24(4):458–464.

Presnell, K. R., P. J. A. Presidente, and W. A. Rapley. 1973. Combination of etorphine and xylazine in captive white-tailed deer. I: sedative and immobilization properties. J. Wildl. Dis. 9(4):336–341.

Prestwood, A. K. 1970. Neurologic disease in a white-tailed deer massively infected with meningeal worm. J. Wildl. Dis. 6(1):84–86.

———. 1972. *Parelaphostrongylus andersoni* sp. N. (Metastrongyloidea: Protostrongylidae) from the musculature of white-tailed deer (*Odocoileus virginianus*). J. Parasitol. 58(5):897–902.

Prestwood, A. K., F. A. Hayes, J. H. Eve, and J. F. Smith. 1973. Abomasal helminths of white-tailed deer in southeastern United States, Texas and the Virgin Islands. J. Amer. Vet. Med. Assoc. 163(5):556–561.

Prestwood, A. K., and F. E. Kellogg. 1971. Naturally occurring haemonchosis in a white-tailed deer. J. Wildl. Dis. 7(2):133–134.

Prestwood, A. K., F. E. Kellogg, S. R. Pursglove, and F. A. Hayes. 1975. Helminth parasitisms among intermingling insular populations of white-tailed deer, feral cattle, and feral swine. J. Amer. Vet. Med. Assoc. 166(8):787–789.

Prestwood, A. K., T. P. Kistner, F. E. Kellogg, and F. A. Hayes. 1974. The 1971 outbreak of hemorrhagic diseases among white-tailed deer of the southeastern United States. J. Wildl. Dis. 10(3):217–224.

Prestwood, A. K., and S. R. Pursglove, Jr. 1981. Gastrointestinal nematodes. *In* Diseases and parasites of white-tailed deer, ed. W. R. Davidson, pp. 318–350. Athens, Ga.: Southeastern Cooperative Wildlife Disease Study. 458 pp.

Prestwood, A. K., S. R. Pursglove, and F. A. Hayes. 1976. Parasitism among white-tailed deer and domestic sheep on common range. J. Wildl. Dis. 12(3):380–385.

Prestwood, A. K., J. F. Smith, and J. Brown. 1971. Lungworms in white-tailed deer of the southeastern United States. J. Wildl. Dis. 7(3):149–154.

Progulske, D. R., and T. S. Baskett. 1958. Mobility of Missouri deer and their harassment by dogs. J. Wildl. Manage. 22(2):184–192.

Progulske, D. R., and D. C. Duerre. 1964. Factors influencing spotlighting counts of deer. J. Wildl. Manage. 28(1):27–34.

Prunty, M. C. 1965. Some geographic views of the role of fire in settlement processes in the South. Proc. Tall Timbers Fire Ecol. Conf. 4:161–167.

Puglisi, M. J., J. S. Lindzey, and E. D. Bellis. 1974. Factors associated with highway mortality of white-tailed deer. J. Wildl. Manage. 38(4):799–807.

Puglisi, M. J., S. A. Liscinsky, and R. F. Harlow. 1978. An improved methodology of rumen content analysis for white-tailed deer. J. Wildl. Manage. 42(2):397–403.

Pursglove, S. R., A. K. Prestwood, V. F. Nettles, and F. A. Hayes. 1976. Intestinal nematodes of white-tailed deer in southeastern United States. J. Amer. Vet. Med. Assoc. 169(9):896–900.

Pursglove, S. R., A. K. Prestwood, T. R. Ridgeway, and F. A. Hayes. 1977. *Fascioloides magna* infection in white-tailed deer of southeastern United States. J. Amer. Vet. Med. Assoc. 171(9):936–938.

Putnam, D. F., and R. G. Putnam. 1970. Canada: a regional analysis. Don Mills, Ont.: J. M. Dent and Sons (Canada) Ltd. 390 pp.

Pybus, M. J., and W. M. Samuel. 1980. Pathology of the muscleworm, *Parelaphostrongylus odocoilei* (Nematoda: Metastrongyloidea), in moose. Proc. N. Amer. Moose Conf. Workshop 16:152–170.

Pybus, M. J., and W. M. Samuel. 1981. Nematode muscleworm from white-tailed deer of southeastern British Columbia. J. Wildl. Manage. 45(2):537–542.

Queal, L. M. 1962. Behavior of white-tailed deer and factors affecting social organization of the species. M.S. Thesis. University of Michigan, Ann Arbor. 140 pp.

———. 1968. Attitudes of landowners toward deer in southern Michigan, 1960 and 1965. Pap. Michigan Acad. Sci., Arts and Letters 53:51–72.

Quick, H. J. 1963. Animal population analysis. *In* Wildlife investigational techniques, ed. H. S. Mosby, pp. 190–228. 2nd ed. Rev. Washington, D. C.: The Wildlife Society. 419 pp.

Rabon, E. W. 1968. Some seasonal and physiological effects on 137Cs and 89, 90Sr content of the white-tailed deer, *Odocoileus virginianus*. Health Phys. 15:37–42.

Radisson, P. 1882. Fourth voyage. Wis. Hist. Coll. 11:71–96.

Radwan, M. A. 1972. Differences between Douglas-fir genotypes in relation to browsing preference by black-tailed deer. Can. J. For. Res. 2(3):250–255.

———. 1974. Natural resistance of plants to mammals. *In* Wildlife and forest management in the Pacific Northwest, ed. H. C. Black, pp. 85–94. Corvallis: Oregon State University. 236 pp.

Rahn, M. 1983. A history of wildlife and hunting on the Upper Missouri River. Rock Island, Ill.: Upper Missouri River Conservation Committee. 105 pp.

Ramsey, C. W. 1968. A drop-net deer trap. J. Wildl. Manage. 32(1):187–190.

Ramsey, C. W., and M. J. Anderegg. 1972. Food habits of an Aoudad sheep, *Ammotragus lervia* (Bovidae), in the Edwards Plateau of Texas. Southwest. Natur. 16(3–4):267–280.

Ramsey, P. R., J. C. Avise, M. H. Smith, and D. F. Urbston. 1979. Biochemical variation and genetic heterogeneity in South Carolina deer populations. J. Wildl. Manage. 43(1):136–142.

Ransom, A. B. 1965. Kidney and marrow fat as indicators of white-tailed deer conditions. J. Wildl. Manage. 29(2):397–398.

———. 1966a. Breeding seasons of white-tailed deer in Manitoba. Can. J. Zool. 44(1):59–62.

———. 1966b. Determining age of white-tailed deer from layers in cementum of molars. J. Wildl. Manage. 30(1):197–199.

———. 1967. Reproductive biology of white-tailed deer in Manitoba. J. Wildl. Manage. 31(1):114–123.

Raught, R. W. 1967. White-tailed deer in New Mexico: in wildlife management. Santa Fe: New Mexico Department of Game and Fish. 250 pp.

Rausch, R. A., and R. W. Ritcey. 1961. Narcosis of moose with nicotine. J. Wildl. Manage. 25(3):326–328.

Reardon, P. O., and L. B. Merrill. 1976. Vegetative response under various grazing management systems in the Edwards Plateau of Texas. J. Range Manage. 29(3):195–198.

Reardon, P. O., L. B. Merrill, and C. A. Taylor, Jr. 1978. White-tailed deer preferences and hunter success under various grazing systems. J. Range Manage. 31:40–42.

Reed, D. F. 1981. Conflicts with civilization. *In* Mule and black-tailed deer of North America, ed. O. C. Wallmo, pp. 509–535. Lincoln: Univ. Nebraska Press. 624 pp.

Reeves, C. C., Jr. 1970. The hunter and his compass. *In* The NRA guidebook for hunters, pp. 62–64. Washington, D. C.: National Rifle Association of America. 264 pp.

Reichert, D. W. 1972. Rearing and training deer for food habits studies. USDA Forest Service Res. Note RM-208. Fort Collins, Colo.: USDA Forest Service, Rocky Mountain For. and Range Exp. Stn. 7 pp.

Reid, V. H., and P. D. Goodrum. 1958. The effect of hardwood removal on wildlife. Proc. Soc. Amer. For. Meeting 1957:141–147.

Reiger, G. 1978. Hunting and trapping in the new world. *In* Wildlife and America, ed. H. P. Brokaw, pp. 42–52. Washington, D. C.: Council on Environmental Quality. 532 pp.

Reiger, J. F. 1975. American sportsmen and the origins of conservation. New York: Winchester Press. 316 pp.

Rempel, R. D., and R. C. Bertram. 1975. The Stewart modified corral trap. Calif. Fish and Game 61(4):237–239.

Resner, O. L. 1949. Control of big game depredation on agriculture. Proc. Ann. Conf. West. Assoc. State Game and Fish Comm. 29:96–97.

Rhoads, S. N. 1903. The mammals of Pennsylvania and New Jersey. Philadelphia: privately published. 266 pp.

Rhodes, R. R. 1952. Timber and forage production in pine-hardwood stands in Texas. J. For. 59(6):456–469.

Rhude, P., and W. K. Hall. 1977. Food habits of white-tailed deer and mule deer in Camp Wainwright, Alberta. Unpublished report on file at the Alberta Fish and Wildlife Division, Edmonton. 84+ pp.

Ribinski, R. F., G. W. Wood, and J. L. George. 1969. The effects of wildfire on quantity and quality of deer browse production in central Pennsylvania. Pennsylvania State Univ. Sch. For. Resour., Agric. Exp. Stn. Res. Briefs 4(3):27–29.

Rich, E. E. 1960. Trade habits and economic motivation among the Indians of North America. Can. J. Econ. Pol. Sci. 26:35–53.

Rich, E. E., and A. M. Johnson, eds. 1949. James Isham's observations on Hudson's Bay, 1743. . . . Toronto: The Champlain Soc. 352 pp.

Richards, T. 1949. A history of the white-tailed deer in New Hampshire. Proc. N. H. Acad. Sci. 1(9):46–52.

Richardson, A. H., and L. E. Petersen. 1974. History and management of South Dakota deer. Bull. 5. Pierre: South Dakota Department of Game, Fish and Parks. 113 pp.

Richardson, L. W. 1981. The acoustic behavior of white-tailed deer. M. S. Thesis. Mississippi State University, Starkville. 68 pp.

Richens, V. B., and G. R. Lavigne. 1978. Response of white-tailed deer to snowmobiles and snowmobile trails in Maine. Can. Field-Natur. 92:334–344.

Ricker, W. E. 1954. Stock and recruitment. J. Fish. Res. Board of Canada 11:559–623.

———. 1975. Computation and interpretation of biological statistics of fish populations. Bull. 191. Ottawa: Fisheries Research Board of Canada. 382 pp.

Riggs, S. R. 1890. A Dakota-English dictionary. Contributions to North American Ethnology, vol. VII. U.S. Govt. Print. Off.: Washington, D.C. 665 pp.

Riney, T. 1955. Evaluating condition of free-ranging red deer (*Cervus elaphus*), with special reference to New Zealand. New Zealand J. Sci. Technol. Sect. B. 36(5):429–463.

Ripley, T. H., and R. A. Campbell. 1960. Browsing and stand regeneration in clear- and selectively-cut hardwoods. Trans. N. Amer. Wildl. and Natur. Resour. Conf. 25:407–415.

Rippin, B. 1977. W.M.U. P238 white-tailed deer survey. Unpublished report on file at the Alberta Fish and Wildlife Division, Edmonton. 16 pp.

———. 1979. A review of Alberta white-tailed deer status and proposal for future management. Unpublished report on file at the Alberta Fish and Wildlife Division, Edmonton. 51 pp.

Ritchie, W. A. 1932. The Lakoma Lake site: the type station of the Archaic Algonkin period in New York. Researches and Trans. of the NYS Archeol. Assoc. 7(4):79–134.

———. 1955. The Indian and his environment. Conservationist (Dec.–Jan.):23–26.

———, ed. 1965. The archaeology of New York State. Garden City, N.Y.: Natural History Press. 358 pp.

———. 1969. The archaeology of New York State. Garden City, N. Y.: Natural History Press. 358 pp.

Ritzenthaler, R. E. 1978. Southwestern Chippewa. *In* Northeast, ed. B. G. Trigger, pp. 743–759. Handbook of North American Indians, Vol. 15. Washington, D. C.: Smithsonian Inst. 924 pp.

Robb, D. 1951. Missouri's deer herd. Jefferson City: Missouri Conservation Commission. Unpaged.

———. 1959. Missouri's deer herd. Jefferson City: Missouri Conservation Commission. 44 pp.

Robbins, C. T., and A. N. Moen. 1975*a*. Milk composition and weight gain of white-tailed deer. J. Wildl. Manage. 39(2):355–360.

Robbins, C. T., and A. N. Moen. 1975*b*. Uterine composition and growth in pregnant white-tailed deer. J. Wildl. Manage. 39(4):684–691.

Robbins, C. T., and A. N. Moen. 1975*c*. Composition and digestibility of several deciduous browses in the Northeast. J. Wildl. Manage. 39(2):337–341.

Robbins, C. T., A. N. Moen, and J. T. Reid. 1974*a*. Body composition of white-tailed deer. J. Anim. Sci. 38:871–876.

Robbins, C. T., A. N. Moen, and W. J. Visek. 1974*b*. Nitrogen metabolism of white-tailed deer. J. Anim. Sci. 38:186–191.

Robbins, C. T., P. J. Van Soest, W. W. Mautz, and A. N. Moen. 1975. Feed analyses and digestion with reference to white-tailed deer. J. Wildl. Manage. 39(1):67–79.

Roberts, H. A. 1964. Pennsylvania's 45 years of deer damage control . . . Decades of deer damage. Pa. Game News 35(4):12–15.

Roberts, H. B. 1956. Food habits and productivity of white-tailed deer in the Hatter Creek enclosure. M. S. Thesis. University of Idaho, Moscow. 57 pp.

Robinette, D. L. 1973. A study of white-tailed deer associated with even-aged management of southern pine. Ph. D. Thesis. Auburn University, Auburn, Alabama. 183 pp.

Robinette, D. L., and M. K. Causey. 1977. Tests of repellents to loblolly seedlings from browsing by white-tailed deer. Proc. Ann. Conf. Southeast. Assoc. Game and Fish Comm. 30:481–486.

Robinette, W. L. 1947. Deer mortality from gunshot wounds. Wildl. Leaflet 295. Washington, D. C.: USDI Fish and Wildlife Service. 8 pp.

———. 1966. Mule deer home range and dispersal in Utah. J. Wildl. Manage. 30(2):335–349.

Robinette, W. L., C. H. Baer, R. E. Pillmore, and C. E. Knittle. 1973. Effects of nutritional change on captive mule deer. J. Wildl. Manage. 37(3):312–326.

Robinette, W. L., and J. S. Gashwiler. 1950. Breeding season, productivity, and fawning period of the mule deer in Utah. J. Wildl. Manage. 14(4):457–469.

Robinette, W. L., J. S. Gashwiler, D. A. Jones, and H. S. Crane. 1955. Fertility of mule deer in Utah. J. Wildl. Manage. 19(1):115–136.

Robinette, W. L., J. S. Gashwiler, J. B. Low, and D. A. Jones. 1957. Differential mortality by sex and age among mule deer. J. Wildl. Manage. 21(1):1–16.

Robinette, W. L., J. S. Gashwiler, and O. W. Morris. 1959. Food habits of the cougar in Utah and Nevada. J. Wildl. Manage. 23(3):261–273.

Robinette, W. L., N. V. Hancock, and D. A. Jones. 1977. The Oak Creek mule deer herd in Utah. Publ. No. 77-15. Salt Lake City: Utah Division of Wildlife. 148 pp.

Robinson, R. M. 1981. Salmonellosis. *In* Diseases and parasites of white-tailed deer, ed. W. R. Davidson, F. A. Hayes, V. F. Nettles, and F. E. Kellogg, pp.

155–160. Tallahassee, Fla.: Tall Timbers Research Station. 458 pp.

Robinson, R. M., R. J. Hildago, W. S. Daniel, D. W. Rideout, and R. G. Marburger. 1970. Salmonellosis in white-tailed deer fawns. J. Wildl. Dis. 6(4):389–394.

Robinson, R. M., K. L. Kuttler, J. W. Thomas, and R. G. Marburger. 1967. Theileriasis in Texas white-tailed deer. J. Wildl. Manage. 31(3):455–459.

Robinson, R. M., J. W. Thomas, and R. G. Marburger. 1965. The reproductive cycle of male white-tailed deer in central Texas. J. Wildl. Manage. 29(1):53–59.

Robinson, W. B. 1952. Some observations on coyote predation in Yellowstone National Park. J. Mammal. 33:470–476.

Robison, W. C. 1960. Cultural plant geography of the middle Appalachians. Ph. D. Thesis. Boston University, Boston. 329 pp.

Rochelle, J. A., I. Gauditz, O. Katashi, and J. H. K. Oh. 1974. New developments in big game repellents. *In* Wildlife and forest management in the Pacific Northwest, ed. H. C. Black, pp. 103–112. Corvallis: Oregon State University. 236 pp.

Rockwell, R. H. 1971. Field notes on the preservation of big game trophies. *In* North American big game, ed. R. C. Alberts, pp. 37–45. Pittsburgh, Pa.: Boone and Crockett Club. 403 pp.

Rogers, E. S. 1970. Algonkians of the eastern woodlands. Toronto: Royal Toronto Museum. 16 pp.

———. 1978. Southeastern Ojibwa. *In* Northeast, ed. B. G. Trigger, pp. 760–771. Handbook of North American Indians, Vol. 15. Washington, D. C.: Smithsonian Institution. 924 pp.

Rogers, M. H., and M. Cartwright. 1977. Sylamore deer and forest game management study. P-R Rep. W-53-18. Little Rock: Arkansas Game and Fish Commission. 29 pp.

Rohlfing, A. H. 1978. Hunter conduct and public attitudes. Trans. N. Amer. Wildl. and Natur. Resour. Conf. 43:404–411.

Rokeach, M. 1968. Beliefs, attitudes and values, a theory of organization and change. San Francisco: Jossey and Bass. 214 pp.

Roller, N. E. G. 1974. Airphoto mapping of ecosystem development on the Edwin S. George Reserve. M. S. Thesis. University of Michigan, Ann Arbor. 70 pp.

Romans, B. 1775. A concise natural history of East and West Florida. Vol. 1. New York: Printed for author. 342 pp.

Romer, A. S. 1966. Vertebrate paleontology. 3rd. ed. Chicago: Univ. Chicago Press. 468 pp.

Rongstad, O. J., and J. R. Tester. 1969. Movements and habitat use of white-tailed deer in Minnesota. J. Wildl. Manage. 33(2):366–379.

Roosevelt, T., T. S. Van Dyke, D. G. Elliot, and A. J. Stone. 1902. The deer family. New York: The MacMillan Co. 334 pp.

Roper, L. A., R. L. Schmidt, and R. B. Gill. 1971. Techniques of trapping and handling mule deer in northern Colorado with notes on using automatic data processing for data analysis. Proc. West. Assoc. Game and Fish Comm. 51:471–477.

Rose, K. D. 1982. Skeleton of *Diacodexis*, oldest known artiodactyl. Science 216(4546):621–623.

Roseberry, J. L. 1980. Age determination of white-tailed deer in the Midwest—methods and problems. *In* White-tailed deer population management in the northcentral states, ed. R. L. Hines and S. Nehls, pp. 73–82. Proc. 1979 Symp. N. Cent. Sect. Wildl. Soc. 116 pp.

Roseberry, J. L., D. C. Autry, W. D. Klimstra, and L. A. Mehrhoff. 1969. A controlled deer hunt on Crab Orchard National Wildlife Refuge. J. Wildl. Manage. 33(4):791–795.

Roseberry, J. L., and W. D. Klimstra. 1970. Productivity of white-tailed deer on Crab Orchard National Wildlife Refuge. J. Wildl. Manage. 34(1):23–28.

Roseberry, J. L., and W. D. Klimstra. 1974. Differential vulnerability during a controlled deer harvest. J. Wildl. Manage. 38(3):499–507.

Rosen, M. N. 1970. Necrobacillosis. *In* Infectious diseases of wild mammals, ed. J. W. Davis, L. H. Karstad, and D. O. Trainer, pp. 286–292. Ames: Iowa State Univ. Press. 421 pp.

Roth, E. E. 1962. Bacterial diseases of white-tailed deer. Proc. Natl. White-tailed Deer Dis. Symp. 1:145–150.

Roughton, R. D. 1975. Xylazine as an immobilizing agent for captive white-tailed deer. J. Amer. Vet. Med. Assoc. 167(7):574–576.

———. 1979. Effects of oral melengestrol acetate on reproduction in captive white-tailed deer. J. Wildl. Manage. 42(2):428–436.

Rowe, J. S. 1972. Forest regions of Canada. Dep. Env., Can. Forest Service Publ. 1300. Ottawa: Information Canada. 1972 pp.

Royo y Gomez, J. 1959. El glaciarismo Pleistoceno en Venezuela. Asociacion Venezolana de Geologia, Mineralogia y Petrologia, Boletín Informativo 2(11):333–357.

Ruch, L. C. 1965. Rifle River Area deer season, 1965. Wildl. Div. Rep. 2486. Lansing: Michigan Department of Natural Resources. 14 pp.

Rue, L. L., III. 1962. The world of the white-tailed deer. Philadelphia and New York: J. B. Lippincott Co. 134 pp.

———. 1978. The deer of North America. New York: Crown Publ., Inc. 463 pp.

———. In press. How I do wildlife photography. New York: World Almanac.

Ruedi, D., and J. Voellm. 1976. The blow gun—an anaesthetizing instrument for the immobilization of wild animals. Vet. Med. Rev. 1/76:85–90.

Ruff, F. J. 1938. Trapping deer on the Pisgah National Game Preserve, North Carolina. J. Wildl. Manage. 2(3):151–161.

Ruhl, H. D. 1956. Hunting the whitetail. *In* The deer of North America, ed. W. P. Taylor, pp. 261–331. Harrisburg, Pa.: The Stackpole Co. 668 pp.

Runge, W., and G. Wobeser. 1975. A survey of deer winter mortality in Saskatchewan. Wildl. Rep. 4. Regina: Saskatchewan Department of Tourism and Renewable Resources. 22 pp.

Russo, J. P. 1964. The Kaibab north deer herd—its history, problems and management/a research and management study. Wildl. Bull. 7. Phoenix: Arizona Game and Fish Department. 195 pp.

Rutske, L. H. 1969. A Minnesota guide to forest game habitat improvement. Tech. Bull. 10. St. Paul: Minnesota Department of Conservation, Division of Game and Fish. 68 pp.

Rutter, R. J., and D. H. Pimlott. 1968. The world of the wolf. Philadelphia: J. B. Lippincott Co. 202 pp.

Ryel, L. A. 1976. Deer hunters' opinion survey, 1975. Surveys and Stat. Serv. Div. Rep. 153. Lansing: Michigan Department of Natural Resources. 19 pp.

———. 1980. Deer hunters' opinion survey, 1979. Wildl. Div. Rep. 2864. Lansing: Michigan Department of Natural Resources. 7 pp.

Ryel, L. A., and C. L. Bennett, Jr. 1971. Technical report on the spring 1971 dead deer searches. Res. Dev. Rep. 247. Lansing: Michigan Department of Natural Resources. 32 pp.

Ryel, L. A., and W. G. Youatt. 1972. Deer biological data 1971–72. Res. Dev. Rep. 271. Lansing: Michigan Department of Natural Resources. 30 pp.

Ryman, N., R. Baccus, C. Reuterwall, and M. H. Smith. 1981. Effective population size, generation interval, and potential loss of genetic variability in game species under different hunting regimes. Oikos 36:257–266.

Sachdeva, K. K., O. P. S. Sengar, S. N. Singh, and I. L. Lindahl. 1973. Studies on goats: I. Effect of plane of nutrition on the reproductive performance of does. J. Agric. Sci. (Camb.) 80:375–379.

Sadleir, R. M. F. S. 1979. Energy and protein intake in relation to growth of suckling black-tailed deer fawns. Can. J. Zool. 58(7):1347–1354.

———. 1980. Milk yield of black-tailed deer. J. Wildl. Manage. 44(2):472–478.

Sage, R. W., Jr., W. C. Tierson, G. F. Mattfeld, and D. F. Behrend. 1983. White-tailed deer visibility and behavior along forest roads. J. Wildl. Manage. 47(4):940–953.

Sahlins, M. 1976. The use and abuse of biology: an anthropological critique of sociobiology. Ann Arbor: Univ. Michigan Press. 120 pp.

Salwen, B. 1970. Cultural references from faunal remains: examples from three Northeast coastal sites. Pa. Archeol. 40(1–2):1–8.

———. 1978. Indians of southern New England and Long Island: early period. *In* Northeast, ed. B. G. Trigger, pp. 160–176. Handbook of North American Indians, Vol. 15. Washington, D. C.: Smithsonian Institution. 924 pp.

Samuel, W. M., and W. C. Glazener. 1970. Movement of white-tailed deer fawns in south Texas. J. Wildl. Manage. 34(4):959–961.

Samuel, W. M., E. R. Grinnell, and A. J. Kennedy. 1980. Ectoparasites (mallophaga, anoplura, acari) on mule deer, *Odocoileus hemionus*, and white-tailed deer, *Odocoileus virginianus*, of Alberta. Can. J. Med. Entomol. 17(1):15–17.

Samuel, W. M., and J. C. Holmes. 1974. Search for elaphostrongyline parasites in cervidae from Alberta. Can. J. Zool. 52(3):401–403.

Samuel, W. M., and D. O. Trainer. 1970a. *Amblyomma* (Acarina: Ixodidae) on white-tailed deer, *Odocoileus virginianus* (Zimmerman), from south Texas with implications for Theileriasis. J. Med. Entomol. 7(5):567–574.

Samuel, W. M., and D. O. Trainer. 1970b. *Pulex porcinus*, Jordan and Rothschild, 1923 (Siphonaptera: Pulicidae), an occasional parasite of white-tailed deer from the Welder Refuge in southern Texas. J. Wildl. Dis. 6(3):182–183.

Samuel, W. M., and D. O. Trainer. 1971a. Seasonal fluctuations of *Tricholipeurus parallelus* (Osborn, 1896) (Mallophaga: Trichodectidae) on white-tailed deer, *Odocoileus virginianus* (Zimmerman, 1978) from south Texas. Amer. Midl. Natur. 85(2):507–513.

Samuel, W. M., and D. O. Trainer. 1971b. Some ecological factors influencing *Eimeria mccordocki*, Honess, 1941, in white-tailed deer, *Odocoileus virginianus* (Zimmerman). J. Protozool. 18(2):306–308.

Samuel, W. M., and D. O. Trainer. 1972. *Lipoptena mazamae* Rodani, 1878 (Diptera: Hippoboscidae) on white-tailed deer in southern Texas. J. Med. Entomol. 9(1):104–106.

Samuel, W. M., D. O. Trainer, and W. C. Glazener. 1971. Pharyngeal botfly larvae in white-tailed deer. J. Wildl. Dis. 7:142–146.

Sandburg, C. 1926. Abraham Lincoln. 2 vol. New York: Harcourt, Brace and Co.

Sander, I. L. 1977. Manager's handbook for oaks in the north central states. Gen. Tech. Rep. NC-37. St. Paul: USDA Forest Service, N. Cent. For. Exp. Stn. 35 pp.

Sanders, E. 1941. A preliminary report on the study of white-tailed deer in the Edwards Plateau of Texas. J. Wildl. Manage. 5(2):182–190.

Sanders, R. D. 1939. Results of a study of the harvesting of whitetail deer in the Chequamegon National Forest. Trans. N. Amer. Wildl. Conf. 4:549–553.

Sanderson, G. C. 1966. The study of mammal movements—a review. J. Wildl. Manage. 30(1):215–235.

Sarmiento, G., and M. Monastero. 1975. A critical consideration of the environmental conditions associated with the occurrence of savanna ecosystems in tropical America. *In* Tropical ecological systems, trends in terrestrial and aquatic research, ed. F. B. Golley and E. Medino, pp. 223–250. Ecological Studies 11. Berlin: Springer Verlag. 398 pp.

Sauer, P. R. 1973. Seasonal variation in physiology of white-tailed deer in relation to cementum annulus formation. Ph. D. Thesis. State University of New York, Albany. 85 pp.

———. 1978. Measuring overwinter deer losses. Pittman-Robertson Project W-89-R. N. Y. Final Report, Job IV-5. Albany: New York Department of Environmental Conservation. Mimeo. 16 pp.

Sauer, P. R., J. E. Tanck, and C. W. Severinghaus. 1969. Herbaceous food preferences of white-tailed deer. N. Y. Fish and Game J. 16(2):145–157.

Sawhill, G. S., and R. Winkel. 1974. Methodology and behavioral aspects of the illegal deer hunter. Proc. Ann. Conf. Southeast. Assoc. Game and Fish Comm. 28:715–719.

Sawyer, T. G. 1981. Behavior of female white-tailed deer with emphasis on pheromonal communication. M. S. Thesis. University of Georgia, Athens. 149 pp.

Sawyer, T. G., R. L. Marchinton, and C. W. Berisford. 1982. Scraping behavior in female white-tailed deer. J. Mammal. 63(4):696–697.

Scanlon, P. F., and R. E. Mirarchi. 1974. Variation in reaction of white-tailed deer to immobilization attempts using darts containing succinylcholine chloride. Proc. Ann. Conf. Southeast. Assoc. Game and Fish Comm. 27:296.

Scanlon, P. F., R. E. Mirarchi, and J. A. Wesson III. 1977. Aggression toward immobilized white-tailed deer by other deer and elk. Wildl. Soc. Bull. 5(4):193–194.

Schaeffer, B. 1947. Notes on the origin and function of the artiodactyl tarsus. Amer. Mus. Novit. 1356. New York: American Museum of Natural History. 24 pp.

Scheffer, V. B. 1940. A newly located herd of Pacific white-tailed deer. J. Mammal. 21(3):271–282.

Schemnitz, S. D. 1975. Marine island-mainland movements of white-tailed deer. J. Mammal. 56(2):535–537.

Schenck, T. E., III, R. L. Linder, and A. H. Richardson. 1972. Southern Black Hills. *In* Food habits of deer in the Black Hills, pp. 19–35. Bull. 606. Brookings: South Dakota State University. Agric. Exp. Stn. 35 pp.

Schilling, E. A. 1938. Management of the whitetail deer on the Pisgah National Game Preserve (summary of a five-year study). Trans. N. Amer. Wildl. Conf. 3:248–255.

Schlegel, M. 1976. Factors affecting calf elk survival in north central Idaho. Proc. Ann. Conf. West. Assoc. Fish and Game Comm. 56:342–355.

Schmautz, J. E. 1949. Seasonal migration of white-tailed deer in the Fisher River drainage. P-R Proj. 36-R, Q. Rep. Oct.–Dec. Helena: Montana Department of Fish, Wildlife and Parks. 5 pp.

Schmidt, J. L. 1978a. Early management: intentional and otherwise. *In* Big game of North America: ecology and management, ed. J. L. Schmidt and D. L. Gilbert, pp. 257–270. Harrisburg, Pa.: Stackpole Books. 512 pp.

———. 1978b. Care and use of the harvested animal. *In* Big game of North America: ecology and management, ed. J. L. Schmidt and D. L. Gilbert, pp. 437–451. Harrisburg, Pa.: Stackpole Books. 512 pp.

Schneeweis, J. C., K. E. Severson, and L. E. Petersen. 1972. Northern Black Hills. *In* Food habits of deer in the Black Hills, pp. 3–18. Bull. 606. Brookings: South Dakota State University. Agric. Exp. Stn. 35 pp.

Schoepf, J. D. 1911. Travels in the confederation, 1783–1784. 2 vols. Philadelphia: J. W. Campbell.

Schole, B. J. 1973. A literature review on characteristics of hunters. Publ. GFP-R-S-33. Ft. Collins: Colorado Division of Wildlife. 15 pp.

Schoolcraft, H. R. 1855. Summary of an exploratory expedition to the sources of the Mississippi River in 1820: resumed and completed by the discovery of its origin in Itasca Lake in 1832. Philadelphia: Lippincott, Grambo and Co. 596 pp.

Schoonveld, G. G., J. G. Nagy, and J. A. Bailey. 1974. Capability of mule deer to utilize fibrous alfalfa diets. J. Wildl. Manage. 38(4):823–829.

Schorger, A. W. 1953. The white-tailed deer in early Wisconsin. Trans. Wis. Acad. Sci., Arts and Letters 42:197–247.

Schulte, B. A., U. S. Seal, E. D. Plotka, M. A. Latellier, L. J. Verme, and J. J. Ozoga. 1981. The effect of pinealectomy on seasonal changes in prolactin secretion in white-tailed deer (*Odocoileus virginianus borealis*). Endocrinology 108:173–178.

Schulte, J. W., W. D. Klimstra, and W. G. Dyer. 1976. Protozoan and helminth parasites of Key deer. J. Wildl. Manage. 40(3):579–581.

Schultz, V. 1965. Comparison of strontium-90 levels between antler and mandible of white-tailed deer. J. Wildl. Manage. 29(1):3–38.

Schurholz, G. 1974. Experience with immobilized deer and aggression. Unasylva 26:35–38.

Schwartz, C. C., and J. G. Nagy. 1974. Pesticide effects on in vitro dry matter digestion in deer. J. Wildl. Manage. 38:531–534.

Schwartz, C. W., and E. R. Schwartz. 1981. The wild mammals of Missouri. Rev. ed. Columbia: Univ. Missouri Press and Missouri Department of Conservation. 356 pp.

Scott, M. D., and K. Causey. 1973. Ecology of feral dogs in Alabama. J. Wildl. Manage. 37(3):253–265.

Scott, T. G. 1937. Mammals of Iowa. Iowa St. Col. J. Sci. 12(1):43–97.

Scott, W. B. 1962. A history of land mammals in the western hemisphere. Rev. ed. New York: Hafner Publ. Co. 786 pp.

Scotter, G. W. 1974. White-tailed deer and mule deer observations in southwestern district of Mackenzie, Northwest Territories. Can. Field-Natur. 88:487–489.

Seal, U. S., M. E. Nelson, L. D. Mech, and R. L. Hoskinson. 1978a. Metabolic indicators of habitat differences in four Minnesota deer populations. J. Wildl. Manage. 42(4):746–754.

Seal, U. S., L. J. Verme, and J. J. Ozoga. 1978b. Dietary protein and energy effects on deer fawn metabolic patterns. J. Wildl. Manage. 42(4):776–790.

Seal, U. S., L. J. Verme, and J. J. Ozoga. 1981. Physiologic values. In Diseases and parasites of white-tailed deer, ed. W. R. Davidson, pp. 17–34. Misc. Publ. No. 7. Tallahassee, Fla.: Tall Timbers Research Station. 458 pp.

Seal, U. S., J. J. Ozoga, A. W. Erickson, and L. J. Verme. 1972a. Effects of immobilization on blood analyses of white-tailed deer. J. Wildl. Manage. 36(4):1034–1040.

Seal, U. S., L. J. Verme, J. J. Ozoga, and A. W. Erickson. 1972b. Nutritional effects on thyroid activity and blood of white-tailed deer. J. Wildl. Manage. 36(4):1041–1052.

Seal, U. S., L. J. Verme, J. J. Ozoga, and E. D. Plotka. 1983. Metabolic and endocrine responses of white-tailed deer to increasing population density. J. Wildl. Manage. 47(1):38–44.

Seamans, R. A. 1946. The time is now. P-R 1-R. Montpelier: Vermont Fish and Game Service. 48 pp.

Segelquist, C. A., and W. E. Green. 1968. Deer food yields in four Ozark forest types. J. Wildl. Manage. 32(2):330–337.

Segelquist, C. A., M. Rogers, F. D. Ward, and R. G. Leonard. 1973. Forest habitat and deer populations in an Arkansas Ozark enclosure. Proc. Ann. Conf. Southeast. Assoc. Game and Fish Comm. 26:15–22.

Segelquist, C. A., H. L. Short, F. D. Ward, and R. G. Leonard. 1972. Quality of some winter deer forage in the Arkansas Ozarks. J. Wildl. Manage. 36(1):174–177.

Segelquist, C. A., F. D. Ward, and R. G. Leonard. 1969. Habitat-deer relations in two Ozark enclosures. J. Wildl. Manage. 33(3):511–520.

Selander, R. K. 1976. Genic variations in natural populations. In Molecular evolution, ed. F. J. Ayala, pp. 21–45. Sunderland, Mass.: Sinauer Assoc., Inc. 277 pp.

Selander, R. K., and D. W. Kaufman. 1973. Genic variability and strategies of adaption in animals. Proc. Nat. Acad. Sci. 70(6):1875–1877.

Selander, R. K., M. H. Smith, S. Y. Yang, W. E. Johnson, and J. B. Gentry. 1971. Biochemical polymorphism and systematics in the genus *Peromyscus*. I. Variation in the old-field mouse (*Peromyscus polionotus*). Studies in Genetics VI. Univ. Texas Publ. 7103:49–90.

Sellards, E. H., W. S. Adkins, and F. B. Plummer. 1932. The geology of Texas. Vol. 1: Stratigraphy. Bull. No. 3232. Austin: University of Texas. 1,007 pp.

Semeyn, R. D. 1963. An investigation of the influence of weather on the movements of white-tailed deer in winter. M. S. Thesis. Michigan State University, East Lansing. 72 pp.

Seton, E. T. 1909. Life histories of northern mammals. Vol. I. New York: Chas. Scribner's Sons. 673 pp.

———. 1929. Lives of game animals. Vol. III, Part I. Garden City, N. Y.: Doubleday, Doran and Co., Inc. 409 pp.

Severinghaus, C. A. 1949a. The willingness of nursing deer to adopt strange fawns. J. Mammal. 30(1):75–76.

———. 1949b. Tooth development and wear as criteria of age in white-tailed deer. J. Wildl. Manage. 13(2):195–216.

———. 1949c. The liveweight-dressed weight and liveweight-edible meat relationships (in deer). N. Y. State Conserv. 4(2):26.

———. 1953. Springtime in New York—another angle. What goes on in our Adirondack deer yards. N. Y. State Conserv. 7(5):2–5.

———. 1955a. Deer weight as an index of range conditions on two wilderness areas in the Adirondack region. N. Y. Fish and Game J. 2(2):154–160.

———. 1955b. Some observations on the breeding behavior of deer. N. Y. Fish and Game J. 2(2):239–241.

———. 1956. History, management, and ecology of white-tailed deer in Allegheny State Park. N. Y. Fish and Game J. 3(1):80–87.

———. 1969. Minimum deer populations on the Moose River Recreation Area. N. Y. Fish and Game J. 16(1):19–26.

———. 1974. Deer population—a wildlife roller coaster. Conservationist 28(5):36–38.

Severinghaus, C. W. 1947. Relationship of weather to winter mortality and population levels among deer in the Adirondack region of New York. Trans. N. Amer. Wildl. Conf. 12:212–223.

———. 1972. Weather and the deer population. Conservationist 27(2):28–31.

———. 1980. Over winter weight loss in white-tailed deer in New York. N. Y. Fish and Game J. 28(1):61–67.

Severinghaus, C. W., and C. P. Brown. 1956. History of the white-tailed deer in New York. N. Y. Fish and Game J. 3(2):129–167.

Severinghaus, C. W., and E. L. Cheatum. 1956. Life and times of the white-tailed deer. In The deer of North America, ed. W. P. Taylor, pp. 57–186. Harrisburg, Pa.: The Stackpole Co. 668 pp.

Severinghaus, C. W., and R. W. Darrow. 1976. The philosophy of deer management. Conservationist. Reprint. 2 pp.

Severinghaus, C. W., and S. Eabry. 1973. Deer losses in the peripheral Adirondacks. N. Y. Fish and Game J. 20(1):32–39.

Severinghaus, C. W., and L. W. Jackson. 1970. Feasibility of stocking moose in the Adirondacks. N. Y. Fish and Game J. 17(1):18–32.

Severinghaus, C. W., and H. F. Maguire. 1955. Use of age composition data for determining sex ratios among adult deer. N. Y. Fish and Game J. 2(2):242–246.

Severinghaus, C. W., H. F. Maguire, R. A. Cookingham, and J. E. Tanck. 1950. Variations by age class in the antler beam diameters of white-tailed deer related to range condition. Trans. N. Amer. Wildl. Conf. 15:551–568.

Severinghaus, C. W., and A. N. Moen. 1983. Prediction of weight and reproductive rates of a white-tailed deer population from records of antler beam diameter among yearling males. N. Y. Fish and Game J. 30(1):30–38.

Severinghaus, C. W., and P. R. Sauer. 1969. Estimated area of deer habitat in New York State. N. Y. Fish and Game J. 16(2):129–135.

Seymour, C., and T. M. Yuill. 1981. Arboviruses. In Infectious diseases of wild mammals, ed. J. W. Davis, L. H. Karstad, and D. O. Trainer, pp. 54–86. Ames: Iowa State Univ. Press. 421 pp.

Shafer, E. L., Jr. 1963. The twig-count method for measuring hardwood deer browse. J. Wildl. Manage. 27(3):428–437.

———. 1965. Deer browsing of hardwoods in the northeast: a review and analysis of the situation and the research needed. Res. Pap. NE-33. Upper Darby, Pa.: USDA Forest Service, Northeast. For. Exp. Stn. 37 pp.

Shafer, E. L., Jr., T. J. Grisez, and E. Sowa. 1961. Results of deer exclosure studies in northeastern Pennsylvania. Res. Note 121. Upper Darby, Pa.: USDA Forest Service, Northeast. For. Exp. Stn. 7 pp.

Sharp, D. E., and J. T. Lokemoen. 1980. A remote-controlled firing device for cannon net traps. J. Wildl. Manage. 44(4):896–898.

Shasby, M., and N. E. Jennings. 1977. Nebraska's forest resource and industries—1977. Dep. For., Fish., and Wildl. NSF-1-77. Lincoln: University of Nebraska. 18 pp.

Shaw, C. R., and R. Prasad. 1970. Starch gel electrophoresis of enzymes—a compilation of recipes. Biochem. Genet. 4:297–320.

Shaw, S. P. 1971. Wildlife and oak management. *In* Oak Symposium Proceedings, pp. 84–89. Broomall, Pa.: USDA Forest Service, Northeast. For. Exp. Stn. 161 pp.

Shaw, S. P., and C. L. McLaughlin. 1951. The management of white-tailed deer in Massachusetts. Pittman-Robertson Res. Bull. 13. Boston: Massachusetts Division of Fisheries and Game. 59 pp.

Shaw, S. P., and T. H. Ripley. 1965. Managing the forest for sustained yield of woody browse for deer. Proc. Soc. Amer. For. 1965:229–233.

Shaw, W. M. 1977. A survey of hunting opponents. Wildl. Soc. Bull. 5(1):19–24.

Shaw, W. W. 1975. Attitudes towards hunting: social and psychological determinants. Wildl. Div. Rep. 2740. Lansing: Michigan Department of Natural Resources. 84 pp.

Sheffield, W. J., Jr., E. D. Ables, and B. A. Fall. 1971. Geographic and ecologic distribution of Nilgai antelope in Texas. J. Wildl. Manage. 35(2):250–257.

Sheldon, J. J., and K. Causey. 1974. Deer habitat management: use of Japanese honeysuckle by white-tailed deer. J. For. 72(5):286–287.

Shelford, V. E. 1963. The ecology of North America. Urbana: Univ. Illinois Press. 610 pp.

Shiras, G., III. 1921. The wild life of Lake Superior, past and present. Nat. Geogr. 40(2):113–204.

———. 1935. Hunting wildlife with camera and flashlight. Vol. I. Washington, D. C.: National Geographic Society. 450 pp.

Shoesmith, M. W., and W. H. Koonz. 1977. The maintenance of an urban deer herd in Winnipeg, Manitoba. Trans. N. Amer. Wildl. and Natur. Resour. Conf. 42:278–285.

Shope, R. E., L. G. MacNamara, and R. Mangold. 1955. Report on the deer mortality: epizootic hemorrhagic disease of deer. N. J. Outdoors 6:15–21.

Shope, W. K. 1970. Behavioral characteristics of the white-tailed deer (*Odocoileus virginianus*) in relation to crop damage in Centre County, Pennsylvania. M. S. Thesis. Pennsylvania State University, State College. 84 pp.

Short, C. 1970. Morphological development and aging of mule and white-tailed deer fetuses. J. Wildl. Manage. 34(2):383–388.

Short, H. L. 1964. Postnatal stomach development of white-tailed deer. J. Wildl. Manage. 28(3):445–458.

———. 1971. Forage digestibility and diet of deer on southern upland range. J. Wildl. Manage. 35(4):698–706.

———. 1972. Ecological framework for deer management. J. For. 70(4):200–203.

———. 1975. Nutrition of southern deer in different seasons. J. Wildl. Manage. 39(2):321–329.

———. 1981. Nutrition and metabolism. *In* Mule and black-tailed deer of North America, ed. O. C. Wallmo, pp. 99–127. Lincoln: Univ. Nebraska Press. 624 pp.

Short, H. L., and J. C. Reagor. 1970. Cell wall digestibility affects forage value of woody twigs. J. Wildl. Manage. 34(4):964–967.

Short, H. L., and E. E. Remmenga. 1965. Use of fecal cellulose to estimate plant tissue eaten by deer. J. Range Manage. 18(3):139–144.

Short, H. L., R. M. Blair, and C. A. Segelquist. 1974. Fiber composition and forage digestibility by small ruminants. J. Wildl. Manage. 38(2):197–209.

Short, H. L., W. Evans, and E. L. Boeker. 1977. The use of natural and modified pinyon pine-juniper woodlands by deer and elk. J. Wildl. Manage. 41(3):543–559.

Short, H. L., J. D. Newsom, G. L. McCoy, and J. F. Fowler. 1969*a*. Effects of nutrition and climate on southern deer. Trans. N. Amer. Wildl. and Natur. Resour. Conf. 34:137–146.

Short, H. L., E. E. Remmenga, and C. E. Boyd. 1969*b*. Variations in ruminoreticular contents of white-tailed deer. J. Wildl. Manage. 33(1):187–191.

Short, R. V. 1963. A syringe projectile for use with a bow and arrow. Vet. Rec. 75(35):883–885.

Short, R. V., and J. M. King. 1964. The design of a cross-bow and dart for the immobilization of wild animals. Vet. Rec. 76(23):628–630.

Shult, M. J. 1975. Range fertilization as related to deer management. 1975 Prog. Rep. College Station: Texas Agric. Ext. Serv. 9 pp.

Siegler, H. R., ed. 1968. The white-tailed deer of New Hampshire. Concord: New Hampshire Fish and Game Department. 156 pp.

Sigler, W. F. 1972. Wildlife law enforcement. 2nd ed. Dubuque, Iowa: Wm. C. Brown. 360 pp.

Siglin, R. J. 1965. Movements and capture techniques/a literature review of mule deer. Game Res. Div. and Coop. Wildl. Res. Unit Spec. Rep. 4. Denver: Colorado Department of Game, Fish and Parks. 38 pp.

Silver, H. 1957. A history of New Hampshire game and furbearers. Surv. Rep. No. 6. Concord: New Hampshire Fish and Game Department. 466 pp.

———. 1961. Deer milk compared with substitute milk for fawns. J. Wildl. Manage. 25(1):66–70.

———. 1968*a*. Environmental conditions and history. *In* The white-tailed deer of New Hampshire, ed. H. R. Siegler, pp. 3–28. Concord: New Hampshire Fish and Game Department. 256 pp.

———. 1968*b*. Mortality factors other than legal kill. *In* The white-tailed deer of New Hampshire, ed. H. R. Siegler, pp. 65–68. Concord: New Hampshire Fish and Game Department. 256 pp.

Silver, H., N. F. Colovos, J. B. Holter, and H. H. Hayes. 1969. Fasting metabolism of white-tailed deer. J. Wildl. Manage. 33(3):490–498.

Silvy, N. J. 1975. Population density, movements, and habitat utilization of Key deer, *Odocoileus virgini-*

anus clavium. Ph. D. Thesis. Southern Illinois University, Carbondale. 168 pp.

Silvy, N. J., J. W. Hardin, and W. D. Klimstra. 1975. Use of a portable net to capture free-ranging deer. Wildl. Soc. Bull. 3(1):27–29.

Simon, H. A. 1945. Administrative behavior. New York: The Macmillan Company. 364 pp.

Simpson, G. 1963. Now that you've killed it. Texas Game and Fish 21(10):16–17.

Simpson, G. G. 1945. The principles of classification and a classification of mammals. Bull. Amer. Mus. Natur. Hist. Vol. 85. New York: American Museum of Natural History. 350 pp.

———. 1951. The meaning of evolution. New York: Mentor Books. 192 pp.

Simpson, R. D. 1953. The Hopi Indians. Leaflet 25. Los Angeles: Southwest Museum. 91 pp.

Singer, F. J. 1975. Wildfire and ungulates in the Glacier National Park area, northwestern Montana. M. S. Thesis. University of Idaho, Moscow. 53 pp.

———. 1979. Habitat partitioning and wildlife relationships of cervids in Glacier National Park, Montana. J. Wildl. Manage. 43(2):437–444.

Sitton, G. D. 1976. The hunter: reality, myth and public opinion. Riverside, Ct.: National Shooting Sports Foundation. 9 pp. Mimeo.

Skinner, A. B. 1913. Notes on the Florida Seminoles. Amer. Anthrop. 15:63–77.

———. 1921. Material culture of the Menomini. Indian Notes and Monographs, Misc. Ser. 20, New York: Museum of the American Indian, Heye Foundation. 478 pp.

Skinner, M. P. 1929. White-tailed deer formerly in Yellowstone Park. J. Mammal. 10(2):101–115.

Skinner, M. R., and O. C. Kaiser. 1947. The fossil *Bison* of Alaska and preliminary revision of the genus. Bull. Amer. Mus. Natur. Hist. 89:127–256.

Skinner, W. R., and E. S. Telfer. 1974. Spring, summer, and fall foods of deer in New Brunswick. J. Wildl. Manage. 38(2):210–214.

Slobodkin, L. B. 1961. Growth and regulation of animal populations. New York: Holt, Rinehart, and Winston. 184 pp.

Smith, A. D., and D. D. Doell. 1968. Guides to allocating forage between cattle and big game in big game winter range. Publ. 68-11. Salt Lake City: Utah Division of Fish and Game. 32 pp.

Smith, B. 1871. Relation of Alvar Núñez Cabeza de Vaca. New York: Printed by J. Munsell for H. C. Murphy. 300+ pp.

Smith, B. D. 1974. Middle Mississippi exploitation of animal populations: a predictive model. Amer. Antiquity 39(2 pt. 1):274–291.

———. 1975. Middle Mississippi exploitation of animal populations. Mus. Anthro. Pap. 57. Ann Arbor: University of Michigan. 233 pp.

Smith, B. E. 1945. Wildcat predation on deer. J. Mammal. 26(4):439–440.

Smith, C. A. 1976. Deer sociobiology—some second thoughts. Wildl. Soc. Bull. 4(4):181–182.

———. 1977. The habitat use patterns and associated movements of white-tailed deer in southeastern British Columbia. M. S. Thesis. University of British Columbia, Vancouver. 139 pp.

Smith, C. M. 1974. Regional size differences in West Virginia white-tailed deer. M. S. Thesis. West Virginia University, Morgantown. 81 pp.

Smith, F. H., Jr. 1970. Daily and seasonal variation in movements of white-tailed deer on Eglin Air Force Base, Florida. M. S. Thesis. University of Georgia, Athens. 99 pp.

Smith, G. E., and R. W. Woolner. 1983. Hunter orange regulations. Hunter Safety News 10(6):4–5.

Smith, J. G., and O. Julander. 1953. Deer and sheep competition in Utah. J. Wildl. Manage. 17(2):101–112.

Smith, M. 1974. Some straight talk about deer. Kentucky Happy Hunting Ground 30(6):7–10.

Smith, M. H. 1981. Review of the George Reserve deer herd: population ecology of a K-selected species. J. Mammal. 62:218–219.

Smith, M. H., C. T. Garten, and P. R. Ramsey. 1975. Genic heterozygosity and population dynamics in small mammals. *In* Isozymes IV, genetics and evolution, ed. C. L. Markert, pp. 85–102. New York: Academic Press. 965 pp.

Smith, M. H., H. O. Hillestad, M. N. Manlove, and R. L. Marchinton. 1976. Use of population genetics data for the management of fish and wildlife populations. Trans. N. Amer. Wildl. and Natur. Resour. Conf. 41:119–133.

Smith, M. H., M. N. Manlove, and J. Joule. 1978. Spatial and temporal dynamics of the genetic organization of small mammal populations. *In* Populations of small mammals under natural conditions, ed. D. P. Snyder, pp. 99–113. The Pymatuning Symp. in Ecol. Pennsylvania Spec. Publ. Series 5. Pittsburgh: Univ. Pittsburgh Press. 237 pp.

Smith, M. H., R. K. Selander, and W. E. Johnson. 1973. Biochemical polymorphism and systematics in the genus *Peromyscus*. III. Variation in the Florida deermouse (*Peromyscus floridanus*), a pleistocene relict. J. Mammal. 54(1):1–13.

Smith, N. S. 1971. Reproduction in the Coues white-tailed deer of the Santa Rita Mountains, Arizona. Arizona Coop. Wildl. Res. Unit Q. Rep. 21(2):5–6.

Smith, R. L. 1966. Wildlife and forest problems in Appalachia. Trans. N. Amer. Wildl. and Natur. Resour. Conf. 31:212–226.

Smith, R. P. 1978. Deer hunting. Harrisburg, Pa.: Stackpole Books. 256 pp.

Smith, S. E., R. W. Gardner, and G. A. Swanson. 1963. A study of the adequacy of cobalt nutrition in New York deer. N. Y. Fish and Game J. 10:225–227.

Smith, S. H., J. B. Holter, H. H. Hayes, and H. Silver. 1975. Protein requirements of white-tailed deer fawns. J. Wildl. Manage. 39(3):582–589.

Smith, W. P. 1982. Status and habitat use of Columbian white-tailed deer in Douglas County, Oregon. Ph. D. Thesis. Oregon State University, Corvallis. 273 pp.

Smythe, R. H. 1975. Vision in the animal world. New York: St. Martins Press. 165 pp.

Snedecor, G. W. 1946. Statistical methods applied to experiments in agriculture and biology. 4th ed. Ames, Iowa: The Collegiate Press, Inc. 485 pp.

Snider, C. C., and J. M. Asplund. 1974. *In vitro* digestibility of deer foods from the Missouri Ozarks. J. Wildl. Manage. 38(1):20–31.

Snow, D. R. 1978*a*. Eastern Abenaki. *In* Northeast, ed. B. G. Trigger, pp. 137–147. Handbook of North American Indians, Vol. 15. Washington, D. C.: Smithsonian Institution. 924 pp.

———. 1978*b*. Late prehistory of the east coast. *In* Northeast, ed. B. G. Trigger, pp. 58–69. Handbook of North

American Indians. Vol. 15. Washington, D. C.: Smithsonian Institution. 924 pp.

———. 1981. "Keepers of the game" and the nature of exploration. *In* Indians, animals and the fur trade, ed. S. Krech, pp. 61–71. Athens: Univ. Georgia Press. 207 pp.

Society of American Foresters. 1967. Forest cover types of North America (exclusive of Mexico); report. Washington, D.C.: Society of American Foresters. 67 pp.

Soper, J. D. 1964. The mammals of Alberta. Edmonton, Alberta: The Hamly Press, Ltd. 402 pp.

Soulsby, E. J. L. 1968. Helminths, arthropods, and protozoa of domesticated animals. 6th ed. of Monnig's veterinary helminthology and enthomology, rev. by Soulsby. Baltimore: Williams and Wilkins Co. 824 pp.

Southeastern Cooperative Wildlife Disease Study. 1980. Disease surveillance among white-tailed deer in the Southeast. Athens: University of Georgia College of Veterinary Medicine. 21 pp.

———. 1981. APHIS/SCWDS hemorrhagic disease surveillance among white-tailed deer in the southeast in 1981. Athens: University of Georgia College of Veterinary Medicine. 23 pp.

———. 1983. White-tailed deer populations 1982. A map prepared in cooperation with the Emergency Programs, Veterinary Services, Animal and Plant Health Inspection Service, U. S. Department of Agriculture, through cooperative agreement 12-16-5-2230. Athens: University of Georgia. 1 p.

Sparks, D. R., and J. C. Malechek. 1968. Estimating percentages dry weight in diets using a microscopic technique. J. Range Manage. 21:264–265.

Sparrowe, R. D., and P. F. Springer. 1970. Seasonal activity patterns of white-tailed deer in eastern South Dakota. J. Wildl. Manage. 34(2):420–431.

Speck. F. G. 1909. Ethnology of the Yuchi Indians. Anthro. Publ. Univ. Mus. Vol. 1, No. 1. Philadelphia: University of Pennsylvania Museum. 154 pp.

———. 1938. Aboriginal conservators. Audubon, July:258–261.

———. 1949. Midwinter rites of the Cayuga long house. In collaboration with A. General. Philadelphia: Univ. Pennsylvania Press. 192+ pp.

Spelman, H. 1884. Relation of Virginia, 1609. *In* Captain John Smith, Works, 1608–1631, ed. E. Arber, pp. ci–cxiv. London: Chiswick Press. 984 pp.

Spinden, H. J. 1917. Ancient civilization of Mexico and Central America. Handbook Series No. 3. New York: American Museum of Natural History. 238 pp.

———. 1928. The population of ancient America. Geogr. Rev. 18:641–660.

Stafford, S., C. T. Lee, and L. E. Williams, Jr. 1966. Drive-trapping white-tailed deer. Proc. Ann. Conf. Southeast. Assoc. Game and Fish Comm. 20:63–69.

Staines, B. W. 1974. A review of factors affecting deer dispersion and their relevance to management. Mammal. Rev. 4(3):79–91.

Stair, E. L., R. M. Robinson, and L. P. Jones. 1968. Spontaneous bluetongue in Texas white-tailed deer. Pathol. Vet. 5(2):164–173.

Stankey, G. H., R. C. Lucas, and R. R. Ream. 1973. Relationships between hunting success and satisfaction. Trans. N. Amer. Wildl. and Natur. Resour. Conf. 38:234–242.

Stanton, D. C. 1963. A history of the white-tailed deer in Maine. Bull. No. 8. Augusta: Maine Game Division. 75 pp.

Stauber, E. 1968. Epizootic hemorrhagic disease of deer (EHD). Washington State Univ. Anim. Health Notes 7(1):3–6.

Steel, R. G. D., and J. H. Torrie. 1960. Principles and procedures of statistics with special references to biological sciences. New York: McGraw-Hill Book Co. 481 pp.

Steer, H. B. 1948. Lumber production in the United States, 1799–1946. Misc. Publ. 669. Washington, D.C.: U.S. Department of Agriculture. 233 pp.

Steindler, G. 1965. The Shooter's Bible cookbook. South Hackensack, N. J.: Shooter's Bible, Inc. 208 pp.

Stelfox, J. G. 1962. Effects on big game of harvesting coniferous forests in western Alberta. For. Chron. 38(1):94–107.

———. 1981. Effects on ungulates of clearcutting in western Alberta. The first 25 years. Unpublished report on file at the Canadian Wildlife Service, Edmonton. 42+ pp.

Stelfox, J. G., G. M. Lynch, and J. R. McGillis. 1976. Effects of clearcut logging on wild ungulates in the central Albertan foothills. For. Chron. 52(2):1–6.

Stenlund, M. H. 1955. A field study of the timber wolf (*Canis lupus*) on the Superior National Forest, Minnesota. Tech. Bull. 4. St. Paul: Minnesota Department of Conservation. 55 pp.

Stephenson, B. 1973. Deer management in the North-Montreal region. Québec: Ministère de l'Agriculture et de la Colonisation. 126 pp.

Stern, W. L., and G. K. Brizicky. 1957. The woods and flora of the Florida Keys. Introduction. Tropical Woods 107:36–55.

Sternitzke, H. S., and J. E. Christopher. 1972. Southern timber supply, trends and outlooks. For. Prod. J. 22(7):13–16.

Stewart, O. C. 1951. Burning and natural vegetation in the United States. Geogr. Rev. 41:317–320.

———. 1954. Forest fires with a purpose. Southwestern Lore 20(4):59–64.

Stickel, L. F. 1968. Organochlorine pesticides in the environment. Spec. Sci. Rep. Wildl. 119. Washington, D.C.: U.S. Bureau of Sport Fisheries and Wildlife. 32 pp.

Stiteler, W. M., Jr., and S. P. Shaw. 1966. Use of woody browse by whitetail deer in heavily forested areas of the northeastern United States. Trans. N. Amer. Wildl. and Natur. Resour. Conf. 31:205–212.

Stoddart, L. A., and D. I. Rasmussen. 1945. Deer management and range livestock production. Circ. 121. Logan: Utah Agric. Exp. Stn. 77 pp.

Stone, T. L., and H. S. Crawford, Jr. 1981. Estimating foliage and twig weight of spruce and fir. J. Wildl. Manage. 45(1):280–281.

Stormer, F. A. 1972. Population ecology and management of white-tailed deer of Crane Naval Ammunition Depot. Ph.D. thesis. West Lafayette, Ind.: Purdue Univ. 294 pp.

Strachey, W. 1849. The historic and travaile into Virginia Britannia, expressing the cosmographie and commodities of the country, together with the manners and customs of the people. Vol. 6. London: Hakluyt Soc. 203 pp.

————. 1953. The historic travell into Virginia Britania [1612]. L. B. Wright and V. Freund, eds. London: Printed for the Hakluyt Soc. 221 pp.

Stransky, J. J. 1967. East Texas deer guns. Amer. Rifleman 115(2):69–70.

————. 1970. Claw mount accuracy. Amer. Rifleman 118(9):105–107.

Stransky, J. J., and L. K. Halls. 1967. Timber and game food relations in pine-hardwood forests of the southern United States. Munich, Germany. Proc. Internat. Union For. Res. Org. Congress 14:208–217.

Strecker, J. K. 1927. The trade in deer skins in early Texas. J. Mammal. 8(2):106–110.

Strode, D. D. 1954. The Ocala deer herd. Game Publ. 1. Tallahassee: Florida Game and Fresh Water Fish Commission. 42 pp.

————. 1957. A preliminary report of the effects of the T. S. I. program on the wildlife habitat in the Ocala National Forest. Proc. Ann. Conf. Southeast. Assoc. Game and Fish Comm. 10:59–68.

Strode, D. D., and W. J. Cloward. 1969. The goals of the southern national forests in white-tailed deer management. *In* White-tailed deer in the southern forest habitat, pp. 85–87. Proc. symp., Nacogdoches, Texas. New Orleans: USDA Forest Service, South. For. Exp. Stn. 130 pp.

Strong, T. N. 1906. Cathlamet of the Columbia. Portland: Holly Press. 24 pp.

Strong, W. L., and K. R. Leggat. 1981. Ecoregions of Alberta. Edmonton: Alberta Department of Energy and Natural Resources. 64 pp.

Stumpf, W. A., and C. O. Mohr. 1962. Linearity of home ranges of California mice and other animals. J. Wildl. Manage. 26(2):149–154.

Suring, L. H. 1974. Habitat use and activity patterns of the Columbian white-tailed deer along the lower Columbia River. M. S. Thesis. Oregon State University, Corvallis. 59 pp.

Suring, L. H., and P. A. Vohs, Jr. 1979. Habitat use by Columbian white-tailed deer. J. Wildl. Manage. 43(3):610–619.

Swank, W. G. 1958. The mule deer in Arizona chaparral and an analysis of other important deer herds. Wildl. Bull. 3. Phoenix: Arizona Game and Fish Department. 109 pp.

Swanson, E. B. 1940. The history of Minnesota game 1850–1900. Ph. D. Thesis. University of Minnesota, St. Paul. 294 pp.

Swanton, J. R. 1911. Indian tribes of the lower Mississippi Valley and adjacent coast of the Gulf of Mexico. Bull. 43. Washington, D. C.: Bureau of American Ethnology. 387 pp.

————. 1922. Early history of the Creek Indians and their neighbors. Bull. 68. Washington, D. C.: Bur. of Amer. Ethnology. 492 pp.

————. 1931. The Caddo social organization and its possible historical significance. J. Wash. Acad. Sci. 21(9):203–206.

————. 1946. The Indians of the southwestern United States. Bull. 137. Washington, D. C.: Bureau of American Ethnology. 943+ pp.

Sweeney, J. R. 1970. The effects of harassment by hunting dogs on the movement patterns of white-tailed deer on the Savannah River Plant, South Carolina. M. S. Thesis. University of Georgia, Athens. 103 pp.

Sweeney, J. R., R. L. Marchinton, and J. M. Sweeney. 1971. Responses of radio-monitored white-tailed deer chased by hunting dogs. J. Wildl. Manage. 35(4):707–716.

Swenson, J. E. 1982. Effects of hunting on habitat use by mule deer on mixed-grass prairie in Montana. Wildl. Soc. Bull. 10:115–120.

Swift, E. 1946. A history of Wisconsin deer. Publ. 323. Madison: Wisconsin Conservation Department. 96 pp.

Symington, D. F., and W. A. Benson. 1957. White-tailed deer in Saskatchewan. Conserv. Bull. No. 2. Regina: Saskatchewan Department of Natural Resources. 17 pp.

Taber, R. D. 1953. Studies of black-tailed deer reproduction on three chaparral cover types. California Fish and Game 39(2):177–186.

————. 1958. Development of the cervid antler as an index of late winter physical condition. Proc. Montana Acad. Sci. 18:27–28.

Tate, G. H. H. 1939. The mammals of the Guiana region. Bull. Amer. Mus. Natur. Hist. 76:151–229.

Tax, S. 1955. The social organization of the Fox Indians. *In* Social anthropology of North American Indian tribes, ed. F. Eggan, pp 243–282. Chicago: Univ. Chicago Press. 456 pp.

Taylor, C. 1975. The warriors of the Plains. London: The Hamlyn Publishing Group Ltd. 144 pp.

Taylor, W. J., and C. W. Easley. 1977. Multiple hemoglobin α-chains in the sika deer (*Cervus nippon*). Biochem. Ciophy. Acta 492:126–135.

Taylor, W. J., C. W. Easley, and H. Kitchen. 1972. Structural evidence for heterogeneity of two hemoglobin α-chain gene loci in white-tailed deer. J. Biol. Chem. 247(22):7320–7324.

Taylor, W. P., ed. 1956. The deer of North America. Harrisburg, Pa.: The Stackpole Co. 668 pp.

Taylor, W. P., and H. C. Hahn. 1947. Die-offs among the white-tailed deer in the Edwards Plateau of Texas. J. Wildl. Manage. 11(4):317–323.

Tebaldi, Q. 1982. Importance of private croplands to production of white-tailed deer. Job Final Rep. FW-3-R-27. Cheyenne:Wyoming Game and Fish Department. 49 pp.

Teer, J. G. 1963. Texas deer herd management. Bull. 44. Austin: Texas Parks and Wildlife Department. 69 pp.

Teer, J. G., and N. K. Forrest. 1968. Bionomic and ethical implications of commercial game harvest programs. Trans. N. Amer. Wildl. and Natur. Resour. Conf. 33:192–204.

Teer, J. G., J. W. Thomas, and E. A. Walker. 1965. Ecology and management of white-tailed deer in the Llano Basin of Texas. Wildl. Monogr. 15. Washington, D. C.: The Wildlife Society. 62 pp.

Telfer, E. S. 1967a. Comparison of a deer yard and a moose yard in Nova Scotia. Can. J. Zool. 45(4):485–490.

————. 1967b. Comparison of moose and deer winter range in Nova Scotia. J. Wildl. Manage. 31(3):418–425.

————. 1974. Logging as a factor in wildlife ecology in the boreal forest. For. Chron. 50(5):186–190.

Telfer, E. S., and G. W. Scotter. 1975. Potential for game ranching in boreal aspen forests of western Canada. J. Range Manage. 28(3):172–180.

Tester, J. R., and K. L. Heezen. 1965. Deer response to a drive census determined by radio tracking. BioScience 15(2):100–104.

Texas Game, Fish and Oyster Commission. 1945. Principal game birds and mammals of Texas. Austin, Tex.: Von Boeckmann-Jones Co. 149 pp.

Texas Parks and Wildlife Department. 1972. Conservation chronicle. Tex. Parks and Wildl. 30(2):28–31.

Thilenius, J. F., and K. E. Hungerford. 1967. Browse use by cattle and deer in northern Idaho. J. Wildl. Manage. 31(1):141–145.

Thomas, C. 1882. A study of the manuscript Troano. Washington, D. C.: Government Printing Office. 37 + 237 pp.

Thomas, D. W. 1954. An economic analysis of deer damage to farm crops, and income from deer hunters, Potter and Monroe counties, Pennsylvania 1951. Ph. D. Thesis. Pennsylvania State University, State College. 396 pp.

Thomas, F. C. 1981. Hemorrhagic disease. *In* Diseases and parasites of white-tailed deer, ed. W. R. Davidson, F. A. Hayes, V. F. Nettles, and F. E. Kellogg, pp. 87–96. Tallahassee, Fla.: Tall Timbers Research Station. 458 pp.

Thomas, F. C., and D. O. Trainer. 1970. Bluetongue virus in white-tailed deer. Amer. J. Vet. Res. 31(2):271–278.

Thomas, G. W., and R. J. Hildreth. 1957. Farming and ranching risk as influenced by rainfall. II. Edwards Plateau and Trans-Pecos. MP-216. College Station: Texas Agric. Exp. Stn. 39 pp.

Thomas, G. W., and V. A. Young. 1954. Relation of soils, rainfall, and grazing management to vegetation. Bull. 786. College Station: Texas Agric. Exp. Stn. 22 pp.

Thomas, J. W., ed. 1979. Wildlife habitats in managed forests: the Blue Mountains of Oregon and Washington. Agric. Handbook No. 553. Washington, D. C.: USDA Forest Service. 512 pp.

———. 1982. Needs for and approaches to wildlife habitat assessment. Trans. N. Amer. Wildl. and Natur. Resourc. Conf. 47:35–46.

Thomas, J. W., and R. G. Marburger. 1964. Mortality in deer shot in thoracic area with the Cap-Chur gun. J. Wildl. Manage. 28(1):173–175.

Thomas, J. W., and R. G. Marburger. 1965. Quantity vs. quality. Reprint. Austin: Texas Parks and Wildlife Department. 8 pp.

Thomas, J. W., R. M. Robinson, and R. G. Marburger. 1965. Social behavior in a white-tailed deer herd containing hypogonadal males. J. Mammal 46(2):314–327.

Thomas, J. W., R. M. Robinson, and R. G. Marburger, 1967a. A rope truss for restraining deer. J. Wildl. Manage. 31(2):359–361.

Thomas, J. W., R. M. Robinson, and R. G. Marburger. 1967b. Use of diazepam in the capture and handling of cervids. J. Wildl. Manage. 31(4):686–692.

Thomas, J. W., J. G. Teer, and E. A. Walker. 1964. Mobility and home range of white-tailed deer on the Edwards Plateau in Texas. J. Wildl. Manage 28(3):463–472.

Thomas, K. P. 1966. Nocturnal activities of the white-tailed deer on Crab Orchard National Wildlife Refuge. M. S. Thesis. Southern Illinois University, Carbondale. 37 pp.

Thompson, C. B., J. B. Holter, H. H. Hayes, H. Silver, and W. E. Urban, Jr. 1973. Nutrition of white-tailed deer. I. Energy requirements of fawns. J. Wildl. Manage 37(3):301–311.

Thompson. D. 1961. David Thompson's narrative of his explorations in western America, 1784–1812. Publ. No. 12. Toronto: The Champlain Society. 582 pp.

Thompson, D. Q. 1952. Travel, range and food habits of timber wolves in Wisconsin. J. Mammal. 33(4):429–442.

Thompson, D. R. 1978. 1978 deer management unit surveys of deer and snowshoe hare populations. Surv. Rep. Madison: Wisconsin Department of Natural Resources. 3 pp.

———. 1979. Survey of dead deer in northern Wisconsin, spring 1979. Surv. Rep. Madison: Wisconsin Department of Natural Resources. 3 pp.

Thompson. J. G. 1922. *In* Neenah (Wis.) *News*, April 11.

Thompson, R. L. 1962. An investigation of some techniques for measuring availability of oak mast and deer browse. M. S. Thesis. Virginia Polytechnic Institute and State University, Blacksburg. 65 pp.

Thompson, R. L., and B. S. McGinnes. 1963. A comparison of eight types of mast traps. J. For. 61(9):679–680.

Thompson, W. H. 1963. The increase of depredation. *In* Deer in California—1963. Outdoor California 24(10):24–25.

Thompson, Z. 1853. The natural history of Vermont. Rutland, Vt.: Chas. E. Tuttle Co. 286 pp.

Thorsland, O. A. 1967. Nutritional analysis of selected deer foods in South Carolina. Proc. Ann. Conf. Southeast. Assoc. Game and Fish Comm. 20:84–104.

Thwaites, R. G., ed. 1896–1901. The Jesuit relations and allied documents: travel and explorations of the Jesuit missionaries in New France, 1610–1791; the original French, Latin, and Italian texts, with English translations and notes. 73 vols. Cleveland: Burrows Bros.

———, ed. 1905. Original journals of the Lewis and Clark expedition, 1804–1806. Vol. 4. New York: Dodd, Mead and Co. 372 pp.

———. 1959. The Jesuit relations and allied documents: travel and exploration of the Jesuit missionaries in New France, 1610–1791; the original French, Latin, and Italian texts, with English translation and notes. 73 vols. New York: Pageant.

———, ed. 1966. Early western travels—1748–1846. 38 vols. New York: AMS Press, Inc.

———, ed. 1969. Original journals of the Lewis and Clark expedition, 1804–1806. 8 vols. New York: Arno Press.

Tibbs, A. L. 1967. Summer behavior of white-tailed deer and the effects of weather. M. S. Thesis. Pennsylvania State University, University Park. 93 pp.

Tierson. W. C. 1969. Controlling deer use of forest vegetation with electric fences. J. Wildl. Manage. 33(4):922–926.

Tierson, W. C., E. F. Patric, and D. F. Behrend. 1966. Influence of white-tailed deer on the logged northern hardwood forest. J. For. 64(12):801–805.

Torgerson, O., and W. H. Pfander. 1971. Cellulose digestibility and chemical composition of Missouri deer foods. J. Wildl. Manage. 35(2):221–231.

Torgerson, O., and W. R. Porath. 1976. Nutritional value of Missouri deer foods. P-R Rep. W-13-R-29. Jefferson City: Missouri Department of Conservation. 34 pp.

Torgerson, O., and W. Porath. 1977. Impact of river-bottom habitat, refuges, and hunting deer populations in the Lower Grand River Valley. P-R Proj. W-13-R-30. Jefferson City: Missouri Department of Conservation. 32 pp.

Torrey, H. B. 1957. They catch wild deer with their hands. Saturday Evening Post 229:34–35, 160, 162, 165.

Towar, D. R., R. M. Scott, and L. S. Goyengs. 1965. Tuberculosis in a captive deer herd. Amer. J. Vet. Res. 26(111):339–346.

Townsend, M. T., and M. W. Smith. 1933. The white-tailed deer of the Adirondacks. Roosevelt Wildl. Bull. 6(2):161–325.

Townsend, T. W. 1973. Factors affecting individual rank in the social hierarchy of penned white-tailed deer (*Odocoileus virginianus borealis*). Ph. D. Thesis. University of Guelph, Guelph, Ontario. 149 pp.

Townsend, T. W., and E. D. Bailey. 1975. Parturitional, early maternal, and neonatal behavior in penned white-tailed deer. J. Mammal. 56(2):347–362.

Tozzer, A. M., and G. M. Allen. 1910. Animal figures in the Maya codices. Papers of the Peabody Museum of American Archaeology and Ethnology, Harvard Univ. 9(3):279–372.   .

Trainer, C. E. 1975. Direct causes of mortality in mule deer fawns during summer and winter periods on Steens Mountain, Oregon. Proc. Ann. Conf. West. Assoc. Fish and Game Comm. 55:163–170.

Trainer, D. O. 1962. The rearing of white-tailed deer fawns in captivity. J. Wildl. Manage. 26(3):340–341.

———. 1964. Epizootic hemorrhagic disease in deer. J. Wildl. Manage. 28(2):377–381.

Trainer, D. O., and R. P. Hanson. 1969. Serologic evidence of arbovirus infections in wild ruminants. Amer. J. Epidemiol. 90(4):354–358.

Trainer, D. O., and L. H. Karstad. 1970. Epizootic hemorrhagic disease. *In* Infectious diseases of wild mammals, ed. J. W. Davis, L. H. Karstad, and D. O. Trainer, pp. 50–54. Ames: Iowa State Univ. Press. 421 pp.

Trefethen, J. B. 1970. The return of the white-tailed deer. Amer. Her. 21(2):97–103.

———. 1975. An American crusade for wildlife. New York: Winchester Press. 409 pp.

Treichel, B. H., and W. K. Hall. 1975. Deer necropsy progress report 1974–75. Unpublished report on file at Alberta Fish and Wildlife Division, Edmonton. 14 + pp.

Treichel, B. H., and W. K. Hall. 1976. Deer necropsy progress report 1975–76. Unpublished report on file at Alberta Fish and Wildlife Division, Edmonton. 21 + pp.

Treichel, B. H., and W. K. Hall. 1977. Deer necropsy progress report 1976–77. Unpublished report on file at Alberta Fish and Wildlife Division, Edmonton. 34 + pp.

Trelease, A. W. 1960. Indian affairs in colonial New York: the seventeenth century. Ithaca, N. Y.: Cornell Univ. Press. 379 pp.

Trigger, B. G. 1969. The Huron, farmers of the North. New York: Holt, Rinehart, and Winston. 130 pp.

———. 1976. The children of Aataentsic: a history of the Huron people to 1660. 2 vols. Montreal: McGill-Queen's Univ. Press.

———. 1978. Early Iroquoian contacts with Europeans. *In* Northeast, ed. B. G. Trigger, pp. 344–356. Handbook of North American Indians, Vol. 15. Washington, D. C.: Smithsonian Institution. 924 pp.

———. 1981. Ontario native people and the epidemics of 1634–1640. *In* Indians, animals, and the fur trade, ed. S. Krech, pp. 21–38. Athens: Univ. Georgia Press. 207 pp.

Trippensee, R. E. 1948. Wildlife management. Upland game and general principles. Vol. 1. New York: McGraw-Hill Book Company. 479 pp.

———. Unpublished. Game Division handbook. On file at Virginia Commission of Game and Inland Fisheries, Richmond. pp. 1–5.

True, G. H., Jr. 1932. Repellents and deer damage control. California Fish and Game 18(2):156–165.

Tuck, J. A. 1978. Regional cultural development, 3000 to 300 B. C. *In* Northeast, ed. B. G. Trigger, pp. 28–43. Handbook of North American Indians, Vol. 15. Washington, D. C.: Smithsonian Institution. 924 pp.

Turner, L. M. 1894. Ethnology of the Ungava district. Washington, D. C.: Bur. Amer. Ethnol. Ann. Rep. 11:167–350.

Turner, L. W., and S. A. Caron. 1973. Review of *Time to Cry Wolf*. J. Wildl. Manage. 37(4):594–595.

Turner, O. 1850. Pioneer history of the Holland Purchase of western New York. Buffalo, N. Y.: G. H. Derby and Co. 670 pp.

Turner, R. W. 1974. Mammals of the Black Hills of South Dakota and Wyoming. Misc. Publ. No. 60. Lawrence: University of Kansas, Museum of Natural History. 178 pp.

Turpin, R. L. 1949. Agricultural damages. Proc. Internat. Assoc. Game, Fish and Conserv. Comm. 39:87–91.

Tyler, H. A. 1975. Pueblo animals and myths. Norman: Univ. Oklahoma Press. 274 pp.

Tyler, L. G., ed. 1907. Narratives of early Virginia, 1606–1625. New York: Barnes and Noble. 478 pp.

Tyson, E. L. 1952. Estimating deer populations from tracks: a preliminary report. Presented at 6th Ann. Conf. Southeast. Assoc. Game and Fish Comm., Savannah, Ga. 15 pp.

Ullrey, D. E., W. G. Youatt, H. E. Johnson, A. B. Cowan, R. L. Covert, and W. T. Magee. 1972. Digestibility and estimated metabolizability of aspen browse for white-tailed deer. J. Wildl. Manage. 36(3):885–891.

Ullrey, D. E., W. G. Youatt, H. E. Johnson, A. B. Cowan, L. D. Fay, R. L. Covert, W. T. Magee, and K. K. Keahey. 1975a. Phosphorus requirements of weaned white-tailed deer fawns. J. Wildl. Manage. 39(3):590–595.

Ullrey, D. E., W. G. Youatt, H. E. Johnson, L. D. Fay, R. L. Covert, and W. T. Magee. 1975b. Consumption of artificial browse supplements by penned white-tailed deer. J. Wildl. Manage. 39(4):699–704.

Ullrey, D. E., W. G. Youatt, H. E. Johnson, L. D. Fay, and B. E. Brent. 1967a. Digestibility of cedar and jack pine browse for the white-tailed deer. J. Wildl. Manage. 31(3):448–454.

Ullrey, D. E., W. G. Youatt, H. E. Johnson, L. E. Fay, and B. L. Bradley. 1967b. Protein requirement of white-tailed deer fawns. J. Wildl. Manage. 31(4):679–685.

Ullrey, D. E., W. G. Youatt, H. E. Johnson, L. D. Fay, B. E. Brent, and K. E. Kemp. 1968. Digestibility of cedar and balsam fir browse for the white-tailed deer. J. Wildl. Manage. 32(1):162–171.

Ullrey, D. E., W. G. Youatt, H. E. Johnson, L. D. Fay, D. B. Purser, B. L. Schoepke, and W. T. Magee. 1971. Limitations of winter aspen browse for the white-tailed deer. J. Wildl. Manage. 35(4):732–743.

Ullrey, D. E., W. G. Youatt, H. E. Johnson, L. D. Fay, B. L. Schoepke, and W. T. Magee. 1969. Digestible energy requirements for winter maintenance of Michigan white-tailed does. J. Wildl. Manage. 33(3):482–490.

Ullrey, D. E., W. G. Youatt, H. E. Johnson, L. D. Fay, B. L. Schoepke, and W. T. Magee. 1970. Digestible and metabolizable energy requirements for winter maintenance of Michigan white-tailed does. J. Wildl. Manage. 34(4):863–869.

Ullrey, D. E., W. G. Youatt, H. E. Johnson, L. D. Fay, B. L. Schoepke, W. T. Magee, and K. K. Keahey. 1973. Calcium requirements of weaned white-tailed deer fawns. J. Wildl. Manage. 27(3):187–194.

Ullrey, D. E., W. G. Youatt, H. E. Johnson, P. K. Ku, and L. D. Fay. 1964. Digestibility of cedar and aspen browse for the white-tailed deer. J. Wildl. Manage. 28(4):791–797.

Ullrey, D. E., W. G. Youatt, and P. A. Whetter. 1981. Muscle selenium concentrations in Michigan deer. J. Wildl. Manage. 45(2):534–536.

U. S. Bureau of the Census. 1961. U. S. census of agriculture: 1959. Vol. 1., Counties, Part 37, Texas. Washington, D.C.: Government Printing Office. 567 pp.

U. S. Department of Agriculture. 1941. Climate and man. Washington, D.C.: Government Printing Office. 1,248 pp.

———. 1957. Soil: the 1957 yearbook of agriculture. Washington, D. C.: Government Printing Office. 784 pp.

———. 1975. Agricultural statistics 1975. Washington, D.C.: Government Printing Office. 621 pp.

U.S. Department of the Interior. 1969. Piedmont National Wildlife Refuge, wildlife and timber. RL-417-R. Washington, D.C.: U. S. Fish and Wildlife Service. 11 pp.

———. 1970. Big game inventory for 1969. Wildlife Leaflet 492. U. S. Fish and Wildl. Serv. Washington, D.C.: U. S. Department of the Interior. 4 pp.

———. n.d. Noxubee wildlife and timber management. Noxubee National Wildlife Refuge, Miss.: U. S. Fish and Wildlife Service.

U. S. Energy Research and Development Administration. 1976. Environmental monitoring report. Idaho Falls, Idaho: U. S. Department of Energy. 41 pp.

U. S. Fish and Wildlife Service. 1960. A report on the fish and wildlife resources affected by the Bruces Eddy Dam and Reservoir Project, North Fork Clearwater River, Idaho. Washington, D. C.: U. S. Department of the Interior. 40 pp.

———. 1970. Unpublished report. On file at U. S. Fish and Wildlife Service, Atlanta, Ga.

———. 1972. National survey of fishing and hunting. Resource Publication 95. Washington, D. C.: Government Printing Office. 108 pp.

———. 1977. National survey of hunting, fishing and wildlife-associated recreation. Washington, D. C.: U. S. Department of the Interior. 100 pp.

———. 1982. 1980 national survey of fishing, hunting and wildlife-associated recreation. Washington, D.C.: U. S. Government Printing Office. 164 pp.

U. S. Forest Service. 1970. 50 year history of the Monongahela National Forest. Elkins, W. Va.: Monongahela National Forest, Supervisor's Office. 66 pp.

———. 1971. Wildlife habitat management handbook. FSH 2609.23R. Atlanta: USDA Forest Service Southern Region. 189 pp.

———. 1973. Wildlife habitat management guide for the national forests in Missouri. Rolla, Mo.: USDA Forest Service. 42 pp.

———. 1979. Animal damage control handbook. Portland: USDA Forest Service. (Pagination by chapters).

———. 1981. Compartment prescription handbook, wildlife habitat system. Chapter 300. U. S. Forest Service Handbook, 2409.21d-R-9. Washington, D. C.: U. S. Forest Service.

U. S. Soil Conservation Service. 1968. Report for development of water resources in Appalachia. *In* Appendix A—agriculture, forestry and conservation, pp. A-27-A-28. Morgantown, W. Va.: U. S. Department of Agriculture.

U. S. Weather Bureau. 1960. Climates of the states— Texas. Washington, D. C.: Government Printing Office. 28 pp.

———. 1961. The climate of central and coastal Texas watersheds. Asheville, N. C.: U. S. Weather Bureau. 14 pp.

Unonius, G. 1936. New Upsala. Wis. Mag. Hist. 19(3):294–318.

Urbston, D. F. 1968. Herd dynamics of a pioneer-like deer population. Proc. Ann. Conf. Southeast. Assoc. Game and Fish Comm. 21:42–57.

———. 1976. Descriptive aspects of two fawn populations as delineated by reproductive differences. Ph. D. Thesis. Virginia Polytechnic Institute, Blacksburg. 104 pp.

Utter, F. M., F. W. Allendorf, and H. O. Hodgins. 1973. Genetic variability and relationships in Pacific salmon and related trout based on protein variation. Syst. Zool. 22(2):257–270.

Uvacek, E. 1961. Preliminary livestock numbers of counties. Memo to County Agricultural Agents, dated 14 August. College Station: Texas Agric. Exp. Stn.

Van Ballenberge, V. 1983. Rate of increase of white-tailed deer on the George Reserve: a re-evaluation. J. Wildl. Manage. 47(4):1245–1247.

Van der Donck, A. 1841. A description of the New Netherlands . . . together with remarks on the character and peculiar customs of the savages or natives of the land. Coll. N. Y. Hist. Soc., 2nd ser. 1(5):125–242.

Van der Leeden, F., and F. L. Troise. 1974. Climates of the states. Vol. 1, Eastern states plus Puerto Rico and the U. S. Virgin Islands. Port Washington, N. Y.: National Oceanic and Atmosphere Administration and U. S. Department of Commerce Water Information Center. 480 pp.

Van Etten, R. C., D. F. Switzenberg, and L. L. Eberhardt. 1965. Controlled deer hunting in a square-mile enclosure. J. Wildl. Manage. 29(1):59–73.

Van Gelder, R. G., and D. F. Hoffmeister. 1953. Canine teeth in white-tailed deer. J. Wildl. Manage. 17(1):100.

Vangilder, L. D., O. Torgerson, and W. R. Porath. 1982. Factors influencing diet selection by white-tailed deer. J. Wildl. Manage. 46(3):711–718.

Van Ness, G. B. 1981. Anthrax. *In* Diseases and parasites of white-tailed deer, ed. W. R. Davidson, F. A. Hayes, V. F. Nettles, and F. E. Kellogg, pp. 161–167. Tallahassee, Fla.: Tall Timbers Research Station. 458 pp.

Van Soest, P. J. 1967. Development of a comprehensive system of feed analyses and its application to forages. J. Anim. Sci. 26(1):119–128.

Van Tets, P., and I. M. Cowan. 1966. Some sources of variation in the blood sera of deer (*Odocoileus*) as revealed by starch-gel electrophoresis. Can. J. Zool. 44(4):631–647.

Van Tyne, J. 1933. Native bird traps of French Indo-China. Scientific Monthly 37:562–565.

Van Volkenberg, H. L., and A. J. Nicholson. 1943. Parasitism and malnutrition of deer in Texas. J. Wildl. Manage. 7(2):220–223.

Varela Márquez, J. 1980. Estudio preliminar sobre la ecología del venado cola blanca en el Departamento de

Olancho, Honduras, C. A. Informe de la Secretaría de Recursos Naturales, Direccion General de Recursos Naturales Renovables. 20 pp.

Vereshchagin, N. K. 1967. Primitive hunters and Pleistocene extinction in the Soviet Union. *In* Pleistocene extinctions, ed. P. S. Martin and H. E. Wright, Jr., pp. 365–398. New Haven: Yale Univ. Press. 453 pp.

Verme, L. J. 1962. Mortality of white-tailed deer fawns in relation to nutrition. Proc. Nat. White-tailed Deer Dis. Symp. 1:15–38.

———. 1963. Effect of nutrition on growth of white-tailed deer fawns. Trans. N. Amer. Wildl. and Natur. Resour. Conf. 28:431–443.

———. 1965*a*. Reproduction studies on penned white-tailed deer. J. Wildl. Manage. 29(1):74–79.

———. 1965*b*. Swamp conifer deeryards in northern Michigan, their ecology and management. J. For. 63(7):523–529.

———. 1967. Influence of experimental diets on white-tailed deer reproduction. Trans. N. Amer. Wildl. and Natur. Resour. Conf. 32:405–420.

———. 1968. An index of winter severity for northern deer. J. Wildl. Manage. 32(3):566–574.

———. 1969. Reproductive patterns of white-tailed deer related to nutritional plane. J. Wildl. Manage. 33(4):881–887.

———. 1973. Movements of white-tailed deer in upper Michigan. J. Wildl. Manage. 37(4):545–552.

———. 1974. Reproductive biology of the white-tailed deer in northern Michigan. Wildl. Div. Inform. Circ. 175. Lansing: Michigan Department of Natural Resources. 4 pp.

———. 1977. Assessment of natal mortality in Upper Michigan. J. Wildl. Manage. 41(4):700–708.

———. 1979. Influence of nutrition on fetal organ development in deer. J. Wildl. Manage. 43(3):791–796.

———. 1983. Sex ratio variation in *Odocoileus*: a critical review. J. Wildl. Manage. 47(3):573–582.

Verme, L. J., and J. C. Holland. 1973. Reagent-dry assay of marrow fat in white-tailed deer. J. Wildl. Manage. 37(1):103–105.

Verme, L. J., and J. J. Ozoga. 1971. Influence of winter weather on white-tailed deer in Upper Michigan. *In* Proc. snow and ice in relation to wildlife and recreation symp., ed. A. O. Haugen, pp. 16–28. Ames: Iowa Cooperative Wildlife Research Unit, Iowa State University. 280 pp.

Verme, L. J., and J. J. Ozoga. 1980*a*. Influence of protein-energy intake on deer fawns in autumn. J. Wildl. Manage. 44(2):305–314.

Verme, L. J., and J. J. Ozoga. 1980*b*. Effect of diet on growth and lipogenesis in deer fawns. J. Wildl. Manage. 44(2):315–324.

Verme, L. J., and J. J. Ozoga. 1981. Sex ratio of white-tailed deer and the estrus cycle. J. Wildl. Manage. 45(3):710–715.

Verme, L. J., and D. E. Ullrey. 1972. Feeding and nutrition of deer. *In* Digestive physiology and nutrition of ruminants. Vol. 3, Practical nutrition of ruminants, ed. D. C. Church, pp. 275–291. Corvallis: Oregon State University. 350 pp.

Vermont Fish and Game Department. 1951. Electric fences for the control of deer damage. State Bull. P-R Ser. 16. Montpelier: Vermont Fish and Game Service. 77 pp.

Veteto, G., R. Hart, Jr., and E. Davis. 1971. Browsers or grazers. Texas Parks and Wildl. 29(3):12–15.

Vilkitis, J. R. 1971. The violation simulation formula proves as reliable as field research in estimating closed-season illegal big game kill in Maine. Trans. Northeast. Sec. Wildl. Soc. 28:141–144.

Villa, R. B. 1950. Los Venados en Mexico. Boletín de Divulgación No. 1. Mexico City: Secretaria de Agricultura y Ganadería, Departamento de Caza, Mexico. 132 pp.

Viret, J. 1961. Artiodactyla. *In* Traité de Paléontologie, ed. J. Piveteau, pp. 887–1,021. Paris: Masson. 1,138 pp.

Vogl, R. J., and A. M. Beck. 1970. Response of white-tailed deer to a Wisconsin wildfire. Amer. Midl. Natur. 84(1):270–273.

Volk, A. A., and V. E. Montgomery. 1974. Hunting in South Dakota, 1973. Bull. 112. Vermillion: University of South Dakota. 41 pp.

Volkman, N. J. 1981. Some aspects of olfactory communication of black-tailed and white-tailed deer: responses to forehead, orbital and metatarsal secretions. M. S. Thesis. State University of New York, Syracuse. 85 pp.

Walker, D. E., Jr. 1978. The Indians of Idaho. Moscow: Univ. Press of Idaho. 207 pp.

Walker, E. A., R. R. Ramsey, F. R. Rogers, Jr., and J. G. Teer. 1955. To determine game harvest. Job Compl. Rep. Fed. Aid Proj. No. W-62-R-2. Austin: Texas Game and Fish Commission. 6 pp.

Walker, E. P., F. Warnick, S. E. Hamlet, K. I. Lange, M. A. Davis, H. E. Uible, and P. F. Wright. 1975. Mammals of the world. 3rd ed., vol. 2, pp. 647–1,500. Baltimore: Johns Hopkins Univ. Press.

Walker, J. R. 1905. Sioux games. J. Amer. Folk-Lore 18(71):277–290.

Walker, K. C., D. A. George, and J. C. Maitlen. 1965. Residues of DDT in fatty tissues of big game animals in the states of Idaho and Washington in 1962. ARS 33-105. Washington, D. C.: U. S. Department of Agriculture. 21 pp.

Walker, M. L., and W. W. Becklund. 1970. Checklist of the internal and external parasites of deer, *Odocoileus hemionus* and *O. virginianus*, in the United States and Canada. Spec. Publ. 1, Index-Catalogue of Medical and Veterinary Zoology. Washington, D. C.: Government Printing Office. 45 pp.

Walker, M. W. 1965. The effects of selected chemical repellents on deer browse of young apple trees. Job Comp. Rep. W-38-R-1. Work Plan 3, Job A. Columbia: South Carolina Division of Game and Boating. 45 pp.

Wallace, W. S., ed. 1954. The present state of Hudson's Bay, by Edward Umfreville, containing a full description of that settlement, and the adjacent country, and likewise of the fur trade with hints of its improvement, 1829. Toronto: Ryerson Press. 122 pp.

Wallmo, O. C. 1951. White-tailed deer populations and habitat study. Job. Compl. Rep. Fed. Aid Prog. W-46-R-2, J5. Phoenix: Arizona Game and Fish Commission. 7 pp.

———. 1981. Distribution and habitats. *In* Mule and black-tailed deer of North America, ed. O. C. Wallmo, pp. 1–25. Lincoln: Univ. Nebraska Press. 624 pp.

Wallmo O. C., L. H. Carpenter, W. L. Regelin, R. B. Gill, and D. L. Baker. 1977. Evaluation of deer habitat on a nutritional basis. J. Range Manage. 30(2):122–127.

Wallmo, O. C., and R. B. Gill. 1971. Snow, winter distribution, and population dynamics of mule deer in the central Rocky Mountains. *In* Proc. snow and ice in relation to wildlife and recreation symp., ed. A. O. Haugen, pp. 1–15. Ames: Cooperative Wildlife Research Unit. Iowa State University. 280 pp.

Wallmo, O. C., and D. J. Neff. 1970. Direct observations of tamed deer to measure their consumption of natural forage. *In* Range and wildlife habitat evaluation—a research symposium, pp. 105–110. Misc. Publ. 1147. Washington, D.C.: USDA Forest Service. 220 pp.

Wallmo. O.C., and J. W. Schoen. 1980. Response of deer to secondary forest succession in southeast Alaska. For. Sci. 26(3):448–462.

Walters, C. J., and J. E. Gross. 1972. Development of big game management plans through simulation modeling. J. Wildl. Manage. 36(1):119–128.

Ward, A. L. 1970. Stomach content and fecal analysis: methods of forage identification. *In* Range and wildlife habitat evaluation—a research symposium, pp. 146–158. Misc. Publ. 1147. Washington, D. C.: USDA Forest Service. 220 pp.

Ward, L. W. 1948. Decline in deer mortalities. W. Va. Conserv. 12(7):9–10.

———. 1954. What's it going to be, deer or dogs in southern West Virginia. W. Va. Conserv. 18(6):3–5.

Warner, H. C. 1977. Game meat: a butcher's view. Fishing and Hunting News 33(46):12–13.

Warren, R. C., and G. A. Hurst. 1981. Ratings of plants in pine plantations as white-tailed deer food. Infor. Bull. 18. Mississippi State: Mississippi Agric. and For. Exp. Stn. 14 pp.

Warren, R. J., N. L. Schauer, J. T. Jones. P. F. Scanlon, and R. L. Kirkpatrick. 1979. A modified blowgun syringe for remote injection of captive wildlife. J. Wildl. Dis. 15(4):537–541.

Warren, R. J., R. W. Vogelsang, R. L. Kirkpatrick, and P. F. Scanlon. 1978. Reproductive behaviour of captive white-tailed deer. Anim. Behav. 26(1):179–183.

Watkins, B. E. 1980. Iodine status and thyroid activity of white-tailed deer (*Odocoileus virginianus borealis*). Ph. D. Thesis. Michigan State University, East Lansing. 119 pp.

Watt, P. G., G. L. Miller, and R. J. Robel. 1967. Food habits of white-tailed deer in northeastern Kansas. Trans. Kansas Acad. Sci. 70(2):223–240.

Watts, C. R. 1964. Forage preferences of captive deer while free ranging in a mixed oak forest. M. S. Thesis. Pennsylvania State University, University Park. 65 pp.

Weatherill, R. G., and L. B. Keith. 1969. The effect of livestock grazing on an aspen forest community. Tech. Bull. 1. Edmonton: Alberta Fish and Wildlife Division. 31 pp.

Webb, R. 1959. Alberta's big game resources. Edmonton: Queens Printer. 31 pp.

———. 1967. The range of white-tailed deer in Alberta: Unpublished report on file at Alberta Fish and Wildlife Division, Edmonton. 16 pp.

Webb, R., A. Johnston, and J. D. Soper. 1967. The prairie world. *In* Alberta, a natural history, ed. W. G. Hardy, pp. 93–115. Edmonton, Alberta: The Patrons, Distributed by M. G. Hurtig. 115 pp.

Webb, S. D., and B. E. Taylor. 1980. The phylogeny of hornless ruminants and a description of the cranium of *Archaeomeryx*. Bull. Amer. Mus. Natur. Hist. 167(3):117–158.

Webb, W. L. 1943. Trapping and marking white-tailed deer. J. Wildl. Manage. 7(3):346–348.

———. 1948. Environmental analysis of a winter deer range. Trans. N. Amer. Wildl. Conf. 13:442–450.

Webb, W. L., R. T. King, and E. F. Patric. 1956. Effect of white-tailed deer on a mature northern hardwood forest. J. For. 54(6):391–398.

Webb, W. L., and E. F. Patric. 1961. Seeding herbaceous perennials in forest areas for game food and erosion control. N. Y. Fish and Game J. 8(1):19–30.

Weber, S. J., W. W. Mautz, J. W. Lanier, and J. E. Wiley III. 1981. Discriminant deer yard analysis in northern New Hampshire. Trans. Northeast Deer Study Group 17:11–12.

Wedel, W. R. 1957. The central North American grassland: manmade or natural? *In* Studies in human ecology, pp. 39–69. Soc. Sci. Sect., Dep. Cultural Affairs. Washington, D. C.: Pan American Union. 138 pp.

Weeks, H. P., Jr., and C. M. Kirkpatrick. 1976. Adaptations of white-tailed deer to naturally occurring sodium deficiencies. J. Wildl. Manage. 40(4):610–625.

Weeks, R. A., R. D. Zahnizer, and G. L. Chute. 1968. Geography. *In* Mineral resources of the Appalachian Region, pp. 27–37. U.S. Geol. Surv. Prof. Pap. 580. Washington, D. C.: U.S. Geological Survey and U.S. Bureau of Mines. 492 pp.

Weeth, H. J., and L. H. Haverland. 1961. Tolerance of growing cattle for drinking water containing sodium chloride. J. Anim. Sci. 20(3):518–521.

Wegge, P. 1975. Reproduction and early calf mortality in Norwegian red deer. J. Wildl. Manage. 39(1):92–100.

Weishuhn, L. L., R. M. Robinson, and R. G. Marburger. 1972. Nutritional status of white-tailed deer in selected areas of Texas. College Station: Report to Texas Agric. Exp. Stn. 4 pp.

Welch, B. L. 1962. Adrenals of deer as indicators of population conditions for purposes of management. *In* Proc. Nat. White-tailed Deer Disease Symp. 1:94–108.

Welch, J. F. 1954. Rodent control: a review of chemical repellents for rodents. J. Agric. Food Chem. 2(3):142–149.

Welch, J. M. 1960. A study of seasonal movements of white-tailed deer (*Odocoileus virginianus couesi*) in the Cave Creek Basin of the Chiricahua Mountains. M. S. Thesis. University of Arizona, Tucson. 79 pp.

Weld, I., Jr. 1799. Travels through the states of North America and the provinces of upper and lower Canada during the years 1795, 1796 and 1797. London: J. Stockdale. 464 pp.

Weller, J. 1970. Drive-hunting. Pts. 1 and 2. *In* The NRA guidebook for hunters, pp. 108–115. Washington, D. C.: National Rifle Association of America. 264 pp.

Weltfish, G. 1977. The lost universe. Lincoln: Univ. Nebraska Press. 526 pp.

Wenhold, L. L. 1936. A 17th century letter of Gabriel Diaz Vara Calderon, bishop of Cuba, describing the Indians and Indian missions of Florida. Misc. Coll. Vol. 95, No. 16. Washington, D. C.: Smithsonian Institution. 14 pp.

Wentges, H. 1975. Medicine administration by blowpipe. Vet. Rec. 97(15):281.

Wesson, J. A., III, P. F. Scanlon, R. L. Kirkpatrick, and H. S. Mosby. 1979a. Influence of chemical immobilization and physical restraint on packed cell volume, total protein, glucose, and blood urea nitrogen in blood of white-tailed deer. Can. J. Zool. 57:756–767.

Wesson, J. A., III, P. F. Scanlon, R. L. Kirkpatrick, H. S. Mosby, and R. L. Butcher. 1979b. Influence of chemical immobilization and physical restraint on steroid hormone levels in blood of white-tailed deer. Can. J. Zool. 57:768–776.

Wesson, J. A., III, P. F. Scanlon, and R. E. Mirarchi. 1974. Immobilization of white-tailed deer with succinylcholine chloride: success rate, reactions of deer and some physiological effects. Proc. Ann. Conf. Southeast. Assoc. Game and Fish Comm. 28:500–506.

Wetmore, R. Y. 1975. First on the land. Winston-Salem, N. C.: John F. Blair, Publ. 196 pp.

Wettersten, R. 1971. Environmental impact of snowmobiling. *In* Conference on snowmobiles and all-terrain vehicles, ed. R. W. Butler, P. S. Elder, H. N. Janich, and B. M. Petrie, pp. E10–E13. London, Ont.: University of Western Ontario. 237 pp.

Wetzel, J. F., J. R. Wambaugh, and J. M. Peek. 1975. Appraisal of white-tailed deer winter habitats in northern Minnesota. J. Wildl. Manage. 39(1):59–66.

Whelan, J. B. 1975. Managing primary production in deer wintering areas to meet secondary production requirements of the herd. Trans. Northeast Deer Study Group 11:111–118.

Whelan, J. B., R. F. Harlow, and H. S. Crawford. 1971. Selectivity, quality, and *in vitro* digestibility of deer foods: a tentative model. Trans. Northeast Fish and Wildl. Conf., Northeast. Sect., Wildl. Soc. 28:67–81.

Whelan, J. B., K. I. Morris, R. F. Harlow, and H. S. Crawford. 1976. The bioenergetic approach to forest management. Trans. Northeast Deer Study Group 10:28–43.

Whicker, F. W., G. C. Harris, and A. H. Dahl. 1966. Radioiodine in Colorado deer and elk thyroids during 1964–65. J. Wildl. Manage. 30(4):781–785.

Whicker, F. W., G. C. Harris, and A. H. Dahl. 1968. Wild deer as a source of radionuclide intake by humans and as indicators of fallout hazards. *In* Proc. First Int. Congr. Radiat. Prot., pp. 1,105–1,110. New York: Pergamon Press. 1,623 pp.

Whicker, F. W., G. C. Harris, E. E. Remmenga, and A. H. Dahl. 1965. Factors influencing the accumulation of fallout 137Cs in Colorado mule deer. Health Phys. 11:1407–1414.

Whisenhunt, M. H., Jr. 1949. The flora of two experimental plots in Mason County, Texas, with special reference to its utilization by white-tailed deer. M. S. Thesis. Texas A&M University, College Station. 88 pp.

White, D. L. 1968a. Condition and productivity of New Hampshire deer. *In* The white-tailed deer of New Hampshire, ed. H. R. Siegler, pp. 69–113. Surv. Rep. 10. Concord: New Hampshire Fish and Game Department. 256 pp.

———. 1968b. The New Hampshire hunter and his harvest. *In* The white-tailed deer of New Hampshire, ed. H. R. Siegler, pp. 114–173. Surv. Rep. 10. Concord: New Hampshire Fish and Game Department. 256 pp.

White, D. L., and W. T. Silver. 1952. Determination and prevention of damage to haylands. Job Compl. Rep. Invest. Proj W-13-R-5. Concord: New Hampshire Fish and Game Department. 2 pp.

White, M. 1973a. Description of remains of deer fawns killed by coyotes. J. Mammal. 54(1):291–293.

———. 1973b. The whitetail deer of the Aransas National Wildlife Refuge. Tex. J. Sci. 24(4):457–489.

White, M., F. F. Knowlton, and W. C. Glazener. 1972. Effects of dam-newborn fawn behavior on capture and mortality. J. Wildl. Manage. 36(3):897–906.

White, R. W. 1957. An evaluation of the white-tailed deer (*Odocoileus virginianus couesi*) habitats and foods in southern Arizona. M. S. Thesis. University of Arizona, Tucson. 60 pp.

Whitehead, C. J. 1965. Catoosa wildlife management research. For Investigations Project, pp. 36–40. Ann. Prog. Rep. W-35-R-5. Nashville: Tennessee Wildlife Resources Agency.

———. 1967. Catoosa wildlife management research. *In* Big game surveys, Tennessee, pp. 17–18. Ann. Prog. Rep. W-35-R-7-R-1. Nashville: Tennessee Wildlife Resources Agency.

———. 1968. Catoosa wildlife management research. *In* Big game surveys, Tennessee, pp. 14–15. Ann. Prog. Rep. W-35-8-B-1. Nashville: Tennessee Wildlife Resources Agency.

———. 1972. A preliminary report on white-tailed and black-tailed deer crossbreeding studies in Tennessee. Proc. Ann. Conf. Southeast. Assoc. Game and Fish Comm. 25:65–69.

Whitehead, G. K. 1972. Deer of the world. London: Constable. 194 pp.

Whitehead, P. E., and E. H. McEwan. 1973. Seasonal variation in the plasma testosterone concentration of reindeer and caribou. Can. J. Zool. 51(6):651–658.

Whitlock, S. C., and L. Eberhardt. 1956. Large-scale dead deer surveys: methods, results and management implications. Trans. N. Amer. Wildl. Conf. 21:555–566.

Whittington, D. [R. W.] 1970. How many deer? Georgia Game and Fish 5(12):10–12.

Wied, Maximilian, Prince of. 1843. Travels in the interior of North America. Translated by H. Evans Lloyd. London: Ackermann and Company. 520 pp.

Wiegmann, A. F. A. 1833. Über eine neue Art des Hirschgeschlechts. Isis von Oken 1833:952–970.

Wiersma, G. B. 1968. Seasonal deer browsing in an Adirondack forest. Ph. D. Thesis. SUNY College of Forestry, Syracuse. 194 pp.

Wiggers, E. P., D. L. Robinette, J. R. Sweeney, R. F. Harlow, and H. S. Hill, Jr. 1979. Predicability of deer forages using overstory measurements. Proc. Ann. Conf. S. E. Assoc. Fish and Wildl. Agencies 32:187–194.

Wilcox, S. W. 1974. Deer production in the United States. Tempe: Arizona State University. Privately published. 10 pp.

———. 1975. Deer production in the United States. Tempe: Arizona State University. Privately published. 4 pp.

———. 1976. Deer production in the United States. Tempe: Arizona State University. Privately published. 4 pp.

Wilde, S. A. 1958. Forest soils, their properties and relation to silviculture. New York: The Ronald Press Co. 537 pp.

Wildlife Management Institute. 1978. The future. *In* Big game of North America: ecology and management, ed. J. L. Schmidt and D. L. Gilbert, pp. 417–424. Harrisburg, Pa.: Stackpole Books. 524 pp.

———. 1981. Dollars for wildlife. Washington, D. C.: Wildlife Management Institute. 2 pp.

Wiley, J. E. III, K. F. Strong, J. W. Lanier, and B. J. Hill. 1978. Winter habitat management for white-tailed deer in New Hampshire—a case history. Trans. Northeast Deer Study Group 14:63–72.

Wilhelm, A. R., and D. O. Trainer. 1966. A serological study of epizootic hemorrhagic disease of deer. J. Wildl. Manage. 30(4):777–780.

Will, G. C. 1973*a*. Population characteristics of northern Idaho white-tailed deer, 1969–1971. Northwest Sci. 47(2):114–122.

———. 1973*b*. Hunting success of northern Idaho white-tailed deer, 1969–1971. Northwest Sci. 47(4):250–255.

Willey, G. R., and C. R. McGimsey. 1954. The Montagrillo culture of Panama. Papers of the Peabody Museum of Arch. and Eth. Vol. 49, No. 2. Boston: Harvard University. 158 pp.

Willey, G. R., W. R. Bullard, Jr., J. B. Glass, and J. C. Gifford. 1965. Prehistoric Maya settlements in the Belize Valley. Papers of the Peabody Museum of Arch. and Eth. Vol. 54. Boston: Harvard University. 589 pp.

Williams, G. L. 1981. An example of simulation models as decision tools in wildlife management. Wildl. Soc. Bull. 9:101–107.

Williams, L. E. 1972. Fort Shantok and Fort Corchang: a comparative study of seventeenth century culture contact in the Long Island Sound area. Ph.D. Thesis. New York University, New York. 455 pp.

Williams, R. 1936. A key into the language of America [1643]. 5th ed. Providence: R. I. and Providence Plantation Tercentennial Committee. 205 pp.

Williams, S. C. 1928. Early travels in the Tennessee country, 1540–1800. Johnson City, Tenn.: Watanga Press. 551 pp.

Williams, W. J., S. C. Kierce, and W. F. Harwell. 1974. Producing trophy bucks. Texas Parks and Wildl. 32(11):6–8.

Williamson, J. F., D. G. Guynn, and C. J. Perkins. 1978. The feasibility of a subjective habitat evaluation technique. Proc. Ann. Conf. Southeast. Assoc. Game and Fish Comm. 32:154–159.

Williamson, L. L. 1981. Hunting—an American tradition. Amer. Hunter 10(3):12–13.

Williamson, L. L., and G. L. Doster. 1981. Socio-economic aspects of white-tailed deer disease. *In* Diseases and parasites of white-tailed deer, ed. W. R. Davidson, pp. 434–439. Tallahassee, Fla.: Tall Timbers Research Station. 472 pp.

Williamson, L. L., and R. D. Teague. 1971. The role of social sciences in wildlife management. *In* A manual of wildlife conservation, ed. R. D. Teague, pp. 34–37. Washington, D. C.: The Wildlife Society. 206 pp.

Williamson, M. 1976. Unpublished report on noxious animal survey of Northern Stewart Island. New Zealand Forest Service. 17 pp.

Willoughby, C. C. 1935. Antiquities of the New England Indians with notes on ancient cultures of the adjacent territory. Cambridge, Mass.: Harvard University, Peabody Museum of Archeology and Ethnology. 314 pp.

Wilm, H. G., D. F. Costello, and G. E. Klipple. 1944. Estimating forage yield by the double-sampling method. J. Amer. Soc. Agron. 36(3):194–203.

Wilson, S. N., and R. R. McMaster. 1974. Ten years of deer management on White River National Wildlife Refuge. Proc. Ann. Conf. Southeast. Assoc. Game and Fish Comm. 27:143–152.

Wingard, R. G., J. L. George, and W. L. Palmer. 1981. Alleviating deer damage to Pennsylvania agriculture. Final Rep. School of For. Resour., College of Agric. University Park: Pennsylvania State University. 42 pp.

Winship, G. P. 1896. The Coronado expedition, 1540–1542. Fourteenth Annual Report of the Bureau of American Ethnology for the Years 1892–1893. Part 1:329–613.

Wintemberg, W. J. 1906. Bone and horn harpoon heads of the Ontario Indians. *In* Annual Archaeological Report 1905, pp. 33–56. Rep. Ont. Minister of Educ. Toronto: L. K. Cameron. 249 pp.

Winter, K., and W. Higby. 1950. Anesthesia projectile for use in capturing game animals. *In* P-R Job Compl. Rep., pp. 74–76. Proj. 33-R-3/WP-5/J-1. Cheyenne: Wyoming Game and Fish Department.

Winters, E. 1957. The east-central uplands. *In* Soil, ed. A. Stefferud, pp. 553–578. USDA Yearbook. Washington, D. C.: U. S. Government Printing Office. 784 pp.

Winters, H. D. 1969. The Riverton culture: a second millenium occupation in the Central Wabash Valley. Rep. Invest. 10. Springfield: Illinois State Museum. 164 pp.

Wishart, W. D. 1980. Hybrids of white-tailed and mule deer in Alberta. J. Mammal. 61:716–720.

Wislocki, G. B., J. C. Aub, and C. M. Waldo. 1947. The effects of gonadectomy and the administration of testosterone propionate on the growth of antlers in male and female deer. Endocrinology 40(3):202–224.

Wissler, C. 1966. Indians of the United States. New York: Doubleday and Co. 336 pp.

Witter, D. J. 1980. Wildlife values: applications and information needs in state wildlife management agencies. *In* Wildlife values, ed. W. W. Shaw and E. H. Zube, pp. 83–98. Inst. Rep. No. 1. Tucson: Center for Assessment of Noncommodity Natural Resource Values. 117 pp.

Witter, J. F. 1981. Brucellosis. *In* Infectious disease of wild mammals, ed. W. R. Davis, L. H. Karstad, and D. O. Trainer, pp. 280–287. Ames: Iowa State Univ. Press. 458 pp.

Witter, J. F., and D. C. O'Meara. 1970. Brucellosis. *In* Infectious diseases of wild mammals, ed. J. W. Davis, L. H. Karstad, and D. O. Trainer, pp. 249–255. Ames: Iowa State Univ. Press. 421 pp.

Witthoft, J. 1953*a*. The American Indian—hunter. Part 1, The white man and the Indian. Pa. Game News 24(2):12–16.

———. 1953*b*. The American Indian—hunter. Part 2, The world view of the Indian hunter. Pa. Game News 24(3):16–22.

———. 1953*c*. The American Indian—hunter. Part 3, Indian hunting and trapping. Pa. Game News 24(4):8–13.

———. 1967. The American Indian as hunter. Harrisburg: Pennsylvania Historical Museum Commission. 23 pp.

Wobeser, G., J. A. Majka, and J. H. L. Mills. 1973. A disease resembling malignant catarrhal fever in captive white-tailed deer in Saskatchewan. Can. Vet. J. 14(5):106–109.

Wobeser, G., and W. Runge. 1975*a*. Rumen overload and rumenitis in white-tailed deer. J. Wildl. Manage. 39(3):596–600.

Wobeser, G., and W. Runge. 1975*b*. Anthropathy in white-tailed deer and a moose. J. Wildl. Dis. 11:116–121.

Wobeser, G., W. Runge, and D. Noble. 1975. Necrobacillosis in deer and pronghorn antelope in Saskatchewan. Can. Vet. J. 16(1):3–9.

Wolfe, W. M. 1890. The Virginia deer. *In* The big game of North America, ed. G. O. Shields, pp. 185–200. Chicago: Rand, McNally and Co. 581 pp.

Wood, F. E. 1910. A study of the mammals of Champaign County, Illinois. Ill. Lab. Nat. Hist. Bull. 8(5):501–613.

Wood, R. 1944. Arkansas' deer transplanting program. Trans. N. Amer. Wildl. Conf. 9:162–167.

Wood, W. 1865. Wood's New England prospect [1634]. Boston: Publications of the Prince Society. 131 pp.

Woodbury, P. P., T. Savage, and W. Patten. 1851. History of Bedford, New Hampshire. Boston: A. Mudge. 364 pp.

Woods, J. 1822. Two years residence in the settlement on the English prairie in the Illinois country, United States, with an account of its animal and vegetable productions, agriculture, etc., etc. A description of the principal towns, villages, etc., etc., with the habits and customs of the backwoodsmen. London: Longman, Hurst, Rees, Orme, and Brown. 310 pp.

Woodson, D. L., E. T. Reed, R. L. Downing, and B. S. McGinnes. 1980. Effect of fall orphaning of white-tailed deer fawns and yearlings. J. Wildl. Manage. 44(1):249–252.

Woodward, A. 1965. Indian trade goods. Portland: Metropolitan Press for Oregon Archaeological Society.

Woolf, A. 1970. Immobilization of captive and free ranging white-tailed deer (*Odocoileus virginianus*) with etorphine hydrochloride. J. Amer. Vet. Med. Assoc. 157:636–640.

Woolf, A., and J. D. Harder. 1979. Population dynamics of a captive white-tailed deer herd with emphasis on reproduction and mortality. Wildl. Monogr. 67. 53 pp.

Wozencraft, W. C. In press. Melanistic deer in southern Wisconsin. J. Mammal.

Wright, S. 1951. The genetic structure of populations. Ann. Eugen. 15(4):323–354.

Wrong, G. M., ed. 1939. The long journey to the country of the Hurons, by Father Gabriel Sagard. Trans. H. H. Langton. Toronto: The Champlain Society. 411 pp.

Wynne-Edwards, V. C. 1962. Animal dispersion in relation to social behavior. New York: Hafner. 653 pp.

Wyoming Game and Fish Department. 1976. Annual report on big game harvest, 1975. Cheyenne: Wyoming Game and Fish Department. 191 pp.

———. n. d. A strategic plan for the comprehensive management of wildlife in Wyoming, 1975–1980. Vol. 1. Cheyenne: Wyoming Game and Fish Department. 110 pp.

Yaw, E. 1966. Key deer investigations progress report. Key Deer National Wildlife Refuge. 1956–1966. Washington, D. C.: U. S. Bureau of Sport Fisheries and Wildlife. 12 pp.

Yawney, H. W., and E. P. Johnson. 1974. Protecting planted sugar maple seedlings from deer browsing. Hardwood Res. Coun. Ann. Hardwood Symp. 2:97–108.

Yoakum, J., W. P. Dasmann, H. R. Sanderson, C. M. Nixon, and J. S. Crawford. 1980. Habitat improvement techniques. *In* Wildlife techniques manual, ed. S. D. Schemnitz, pp. 329–403. 4th ed. Washington, D. C.: The Wildlife Society. 686 pp.

Yoho, N. S. 1981. Private forest industry program and potentials for wildlife management. *In* Wildlife management on private lands, ed. R. T. Dumke, G. V. Burger, and J. R. March, pp. 218–226. Madison: Wisconsin Chapter, The Wildlife Society. 569 pp.

Youatt, W. G., L. D. Fay, and H. D. Harte. 1975. 1975 spring deer survey, doe productivity and femur fat analysis, April 1–June 1. Wildl. Div. Rep. 2743. Lansing: Michigan Department of Natural Resources. 11 pp.

Youatt, W. G., D. E. Ullrey, and W. T. Magee. 1976. Vitamin A concentration in livers of white-tailed deer. J. Wildl. Manage. 40(1):172–173.

Youatt, W. G., L. J. Verme, and D. E. Ullrey. 1965. Composition of milk and blood in nursing white-tailed deer does and blood composition of their fawns. J. Wildl. Manage. 29(1):79–84.

Young, J., and A. Boyce. 1971. Recreational uses of snow and ice in Michigan and some of its effects on wildlife and people. *In* Proc. snow and ice in relation to wildlife and recreation symposium, ed. A. O. Haugen, pp. 193–196. Ames: Iowa State University.

Young, S. P. 1956. The deer, the Indians and the American pioneers. *In* The deer of North America, ed. W. P. Taylor, pp. 1–27. Harrisburg, Pa.: The Stackpole Co. 668 pp.

Young, S. P., and E. A. Goldman. 1944. The wolves of North America. Washington, D. C.: American Wildlife Institute. 660 pp.

Zagata, M. D. 1972. Range and movement of Iowa deer in relation to Pilot Knob State Park, Iowa. Ph. D. Thesis. Iowa State University, Ames. 249 pp.

Zagata, M. D., and A. O. Haugen. 1973*a*. Winter movement and home range of white-tailed deer at Pilot Knob State Park, Iowa. Iowa Acad. Sci. Proc. 79(2):74–78.

Zagata, M. D., and A. O. Haugen. 1973*b*. Pilot Knob State Park: a winter deer haven. Iowa St. J. Res. 47(3):199–217.

Zagata, M. D., and A. O. Haugen. 1974. Influence of light and weather on observability of Iowa deer. J. Wildl. Manage. 38(2):220–228.

Zagata, M. D., and A. N. Moen. 1974. Antler shedding by white-tailed deer in the Midwest. J. Mammal. 55(3):656–659.

Zaiglin, R., and C. DeYoung. 1976. Protein for trophies. Tex. Hunters Hotline 2(2):24–25.

Zeedyk, W. D. 1969. Critical factors in habitat appraisal. *In* White-tailed deer in the southern forest habitat, pp. 37–41. Proc. symp. Nacogdoches, Tex. New Or-leans: USDA Forest Service, South. For. Exp. Stn. 130 pp.

Zeisberger, D. 1910. History of the North American Indians. Ed. A. B. Hulbert and W. N. Schwarze. Ohio St. Arch. and Hist. Quart. 19:1–189.

INDEX

Intestines, 88, 115
Iodine-131, 181

Jaguars, 517, 544

Key deer
food habits of, 386–387
history of, 383–384
management of, 388–389
mortality factors of, 386–387
outlook for, 389–390
physical stature of, 385
Kidneys, 88

Land-use planning, 645–646
Law enforcement
basis for, 580–581
importance of citizen cooperation in, 581–583
problems in, 580
Lead deer studies, 611
Leaping, 78
Lens filters, 726
License fees, 740–743
Life tables, 204–205
Lipogenesis, 106–107
Listeriosis, 178
Liver, 88
Livestock, 455, 470, 501, 512, 643–644
Llano Basin, Texas
censusing deer on, 263–267
deer population density of, 266, 269
deer productivity on, 272–274
described, 261–263
factors affecting deer density on, 267–272
harvests on, 283–286
management recommendations for, 289–290
mortality factors on, 280–282
rate of deer population increase on, 278–280
shooting preserves on, 286
socioeconomics of harvests on, 286–288
Lungs, 87
Luring, 53–54, 758

M-99, 682
Maine
harvests in, 321, 322
management of deer yards in, 585–586
Management
administrative organization for, in Canada, 573–574
administrative organization for, in Mexico, 574
administrative organization for, in U.S., 573
basis for decisions in, 572
bias of managers in, 716
buck-only vs. any-age-or-sex harvest, 230–232
captive deer, 687–696
current practices in Appalachian Mountains region, 343–344
drug immobilization methods in, 677–686
efforts in South America, 545–546
estimating populations for, 318–319
for crop damage control, 587–589, 650–654
for hunter satisfaction, 237–239
for nonhunter satisfaction, 240–241
for trophy buck production, 232–235, 377, 473, 568
funding of, 574–576
habitat, in eastern mixed forests, 353–354
habitat, on Piedmont Plateau, 364, 365
harvest, 320–321, 437, 454
harvest, in Midwest oak/hickory forests, 423–426
harvest, in northern Great Lakes states and Ontario forests, 405–406, 407
harvest, in southeastern Canada, 302–303

harvest, on Piedmont Plateau, 365–366
harvest report and inventory procedures for, in U.S. and Canada, 745, 747
harvestable surplus concept in, 222–223
history of, 571–572
hunter education programs in, 590–600
hunting regulations and harvest in, 235–236
importance of private landowners to, 576–577
in Central and Southern Plains region, 453–456
in Finland, 565–568
in Midwest agricultural region, 436–439
in northern Great Lakes states and Ontario forests, 407–409
in Northern Plains region, 448
in Pacific Northwest, 491–493, 495–496
in Southern Rocky Mountains, 511–512
in Texas, 471–474
in western Canada, 485–486
information and education programs in, 589–590
inhibition of reproduction to control deer populations, 184–185
law enforcement programs in, 580
manipulating doe harvests in, 236–237
models for, 214–216
of Columbian white-tailed deer, 491–493, 495–496
of habitats, 583–587
of populations, 577–583
of wintering habitats, 329–330
on Florida keys, 388–389
population censusing techniques in, 263–266
population inventories in, 253–257
predator control programs in, 200, 302, 583
prioritizing values in, 719–720
professionalism and, 241–242
programs of Coastal Plain states, 376–380
programs to encourage citizen cooperation, 582–583
quota permit systems in, 173
recommendations for Llano Basin, Texas 288–290
recommendations for Midwest agricultural region, 439–440
registration of harvested deer in, 251–252
setting goals for, 228–230
significance of predation in, 226–227
socioeconomic considerations in, 327–328
surveys, 436–437
techniques for measuring mortality, 204
techniques for measuring population size, 206–208
techniques for measuring population trends, 208–210
techniques for measuring reproduction, 205–206
to reduce deer/vehicle collisions, 588, 589
translocating captive deer in, 673
trapping and translocation techniques for, 675–676
units of, 247, 426, 578
value considerations in, 699–700, 700–718
value trade-offs in, 718–719
Wisconsin's harvest, 243–246
Wisconsin's harvest recommendations, 258–259
Wisconsin's policy and goals for, 246–250
Mark and recapture technique, 207
Mark Twain National Forest, 586–587
Market hunting, 66–69, 572
Massachusetts
harvests in, 322, 323
Masturbation, whitetail buck, 150
Maximum sustained yield, 219–220
Mean body weights, 114
Meat
cost of commercial, 777
cuts of, 774
food values of, 777
freezing, 775–776
see also Carcass care, Venison
Melanism, 74
Metatarsal gland
geographic variation in, 16, 18

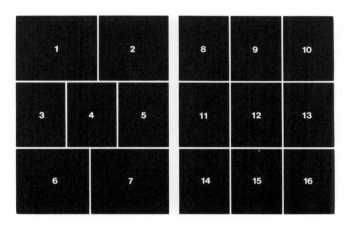

PHOTO CREDITS FOR BACK ENDSHEETS

1 North Carolina Wildlife Resources Commission; photo by Curtis Wooten
2 Missouri Department of Conservation; photo by Don Wooldridge
3 North Carolina Wildlife Resources Commission; photo by Jim Lee
4 South Carolina Wildlife and Marine Resources Department
5 Tennessee Wildlife Resources Agency
6 Florida Game and Fresh Water Fish Commission
7 North Dakota Game and Fish Department
8 U.S. Fish and Wildlife Service
9 Texas Parks and Wildlife Department
10 Photo by Donna Rogers
11 Louisiana Department of Wildlife and Fisheries; photo by Joe L. Herring
12 Florida Game and Fresh Water Fish Commission; photo by Stan Kirkland
13 Photo by Donna Rogers
14 Florida Game and Fresh Water Fish Commission; photo by Jim Reed
15 South Carolina Wildlife and Marine Resources Department
16 New Brunswick Department of Natural Resources